THE *Chicago* CUBS ENCYCLOPEDIA

In the series

Baseball Encyclopedias of North America

edited by Rich Westcott

Also in the series:

The New Phillies Encyclopedia, by Rich Westcott
and Frank Bilovsky, 1993

The Braves Encyclopedia, by Gary Caruso,
1995

The Cleveland Indians Encyclopedia, by Russell Schneider,
1996

The White Sox Encyclopedia, by Richard C. Lindberg,
1997

The Red Sox Encyclopedia, by George Sullivan,
forthcoming

Jerome Holtzman and George Vass

THE Chicago CUBS ENCYCLOPEDIA

Temple University Press | Philadelphia

Temple University Press, Philadelphia 19122
Copyright © 1997 by Temple University
All rights reserved
Published 1997
Printed in the United States of America

⊛ The paper used in this publication meets the requirements
of the American National Standard for Information Sciences—
Permanence of Paper for Printed Library Materials,
ANSI Z39.48–1984

Library of Congress Cataloging-in-Publication Data

Holtzman, Jerome.
     The Chicago Cubs encyclopedia / Jerome Holtzman and George Vass.
          p.   cm.—(Baseball encyclopedias of North America)
     ISBN 1-56639-547-X (alk. paper)
     1. Chicago Cubs (Baseball team)—History.   I. Vass, George.
II. Title.   III. Series.
GV875.C6H65   1997
796.357′64′0977311—dc21   97–5284

Contents

Introduction

For the last half century, since 1945 when they won their last pennant, the Chicago Cubs often have been characterized as "lovable losers." Even Dallas Green, when he took over the club following the 1981 season, was unaware of the Cubs' glorious history and launched a promotional campaign titled "Building a New Tradition."

It was an understandable mistake. The Cubs have been without a pennant longer than any other major league club and set a record for consecutive second-division finishes, 20. Still, all that was needed was one or two championship teams, certainly not a new tradition. The Cubs have won 16 pennants, set the one-season major league record for victories, 116 in 1906, and are the only charter member of the National League to play in the same city, 121 years, without interruption.

They were baseball's first major league dynasty—six pennants in the National League's first 11 seasons. Twice they won three consecutive pennants and four in a five-year sequence. Beginning in 1929 they won every third year for the next nine seasons. A platoon of Hall of Famers have paraded across the Chicago scene:

Adrian Constantine Anson, the original Mr. Cub, the most dominant player-manager of the 19th century; Frank Chance, the Peerless Leader; Tinker to Evers to Chance, an ordinary double-play combination converted into a legend because of a sportswriter's poem; Three-Finger Mordecai Brown; Gabby Hartnett; Hack Wilson, who in 1930 hit 56 home runs and drove in 190 runs, league records that still stand; and more recently, Ernie Banks, Billy Williams, Ron Santo, Ferguson Jenkins, and Ryne Sandberg.

Originally known as the White Stockings, the Cubs and the National League were born in rebellion, the direct descendant of the National Association of Professional Base Ball Players, organized in a New York saloon, which had lasted five years. The new league, anchored by Chicago, was formed with the purpose of correcting Association abuses: bribery, dishonest play, intemperance, and contract jumping. Money had been bet openly while games were in progress.

The *Chicago Tribune,* on April 2, 1876, reported:

"The Chicago Club management have secured the base of a fine mansion, No. 1030 Wabash Avenue, for their club-house. This is perhaps the most eligible location in the city for the purpose, scarcely more than a block from the grounds. The house is very fine. The basement will be fitted up for a billiard room and the parlors elegantly furnished. The day of opening has not been fixed but will be shortly announced, together with the arrangements."

Eight teams were admitted to the new league. The entrance fee was $100 per club (it had been $10 in the Association), with the provision that no city with fewer than 75,000 population could become a member. Each city could be represented by only one club, eliminating the danger of local competition. A standard player contract was designed to prevent the best players from being lured away by rival organizations.

William A. Hulbert was the founding father. A Chicago businessman, Hulbert in 1875 had agreed to assume the presidency of the weak Chicago entry in the Association. In secret negotiations during that season, he persuaded Albert Goodwill Spalding, the leading baseball figure of the time, to join him and start a new league. Spalding was then the star pitcher of the Boston club, which had dominated the Association.

Three other Boston stars also pledged allegiance to the fledgling White Sox—second baseman Ross Barnes, first baseman Cal McVey, and catcher Jim "Deacon" White. Another recruit, who had signed with reluctance—his wife had urged him to remain in Philadelphia—was Cap Anson, the star third baseman of the Philadelphia Athletics.

When the Chicago players began their preseason practice, Anson showed up but explained he had come there to obtain release from his contract. It was a chilly day. According to historian Lee Allen, Anson was wearing a buttoned ulster. During batting practice Anson asked manager Spalding to pitch to him. Spalding refused to accommodate him unless he took off his overcoat and began to honor his contract. Anson agreed, grabbed a bat, and remained for 22 years.

Ernie Banks, the most celebrated Cub player of the second half of the 20th century, rode a wave of popularity throughout his 19-year career.

Hulbert was ready when the other teams in the Association threatened the jumpers with expulsion. He and Spalding had drawn a constitution for their new league which, in effect, was the seed and foundation of what was to become known as organized baseball.

Each club was scheduled to play 70 regular-season games, 10 with each of the other seven teams. Three games a week were carded from April 22 until October 21. Play began in late afternoon, and games were frequently called because of darkness. Admission was 50 cents. Latecomers were admitted for 10 cents and were penned, like bulls, behind ropes in foul territory beyond first and third base, a custom that gave rise to the term "bullpen" for the area where relief pitchers warm up.

The White Stockings won the first pennant. Only 11 players were on the roster: Spalding, pitcher-manager; White, catcher; McVey, first base and substitute pitcher; Barnes, second base; John Peters, shortstop; Anson, third base; John Glenn, left field; Paul Hines, center field; Bob Addy and Oscar Bielaski, right field; and Fred Andrus, utility. Peters, Glenn, Hines, and Addy—who 10 years earlier was the first player to slide into a base—were holdovers from the Chicago entry in the Association. Only Spalding was born and raised in Illinois.

Pitchers threw underhand, with little strain, able to work three times a week and more, if necessary. The ball had to be delivered with the arm swinging parallel to the side of the body, in the manner of a bowler; the arm, in being swung forward, could not be raised above the hip.

Foul balls were not counted as strikes, but a foul caught on the first bounce was an out. Nine balls constituted a walk. The batter had to be accommodated; he had the option of requesting a high or low ball. The pitching distance was 45 feet. There was no mound, and the pitcher was confined to a four-by-six-foot box. Substitutions were not allowed after the fourth inning.

In midseason, in the July 30 edition of the *Chicago Tribune,* Hulbert's new league and the White Stockings were hailed, prematurely, and with considerable exaggeration, for the cleansing of professional baseball:

"There is a great truth about base-ball which lies back of all the stories that have been made public, and that is that it is not from its nature a game to bet on; it is undoubtedly the finest athletic exhibition in the world, and the most enjoyable. It should be played by gentlemen of as much honor and honesty as are found in any other pursuit of life. It has absolutely nothing in common with dissipation, with the low life of the gambler, or with the bummers who hang about the pool box.

"Its very life and essence are freedom from these things, and it can only hope to live as the national sport by keeping clear of them. The Chicago team for 1876 has effectually disposed of the idea that a player must be a bummer and associate with bummers, gamblers, and thieves. Not one of the present Club can be pointed out as the friend or companion of any member of the gambling or pool-selling class."

The first stars were Spalding, who retired after the 1878 season and became a multimillionaire, founding what was to become a worldwide sporting goods empire that still bears his name; and Anson, a place hitter, who 19 times batted over .300, was the first player to amass 3,000 hits, and retired with a .329 lifetime average. Anson also managed the club for 18 full seasons. Five pennants were won during his reign.

But it was Spalding who was in command. He was the manager and pitching hero of the first championship season with 47 wins in 60 decisions. Spalding was 1–0 in four games in 1877 when he played most of the season at first base. He appeared in only one game the following season, and though he then withdrew as an active player, he was an administrative power in the Cub and National League boardrooms for many years to come.

Spalding took over the club presidency in 1882, after the death of Hulbert, and held that position for 10 years. In 1890 he was chairman of a well-financed National League War Committee, which prompted a rebel players' league, the Brotherhood, to sue for peace. To promote the game and the sale of equipment, he twice took teams on world tours. He was also responsible for the myth that Abner Doubleday, a Civil War general, had invented baseball in 1839 in Cooperstown, New York, a fiction that for many years successfully subdued the truth that it had evolved from earlier English games.

Anson's influence was limited to the playing field. As he grew older and his players younger, the Cubs were known as Anson's Colts because of their youth and inexperience; when many of the front-line players departed, they became Anson's Orphans. The nickname Cubs was adopted in 1902 and has been in use ever since.

Anson departed that same year, released when Spalding, previously his benefactor, refused to support him in a front-office dispute.

The Cubs were involved in the most controversial game in the 20th century, a playoff for the 1908 National League pennant, necessary because of "Merkle's Boner." Rookie Fred Merkle of the New York Giants, on first base, ran directly to the clubhouse without touching second as a runner on third scored on what the hated Giants assumed was a game-winning single to center field. When the ball was retrieved, it was relayed to second base for a side-retiring force-out. The umpires nullified the run; the game was ruled a tie.

After the Cubs and Giants had finished the regular schedule with identical 98–55 records, a one-game playoff was necessary to determine the National League champion. It was played on October 8 at the Polo Grounds, the Giants' home field, and drew "the biggest crowd that had ever seen a baseball game." The bluffs overhanging the Polo Grounds were filled with fans, some of whom climbed rooftops and telegraph poles. The elevated trains couldn't run because people were sitting on the tracks.

Three-Finger Brown, in an interview 36 years later, recaptured the scene:

"I can still see Christy Mathewson making his lordly entrance. He'd always wait until about ten minutes before game-time, then he'd come from the Giants' clubhouse across the field in a long linen duster like auto drivers wore in those days, and at every step the crowd would yell louder and louder. This day they split the air. I watched him enter as I went out to the bullpen, where I was to keep ready. Frank Chance insisted on starting Jack Pfiester."

Pfiester, known as Jack the Giant Killer, was knocked out in the first inning. Brown, who had started or relieved in 11 of the previous 14 games, was summoned. He finished the inning without further cost, went the rest of the way, and outdueled the great Matty, 4–2. Player-manager Husk Chance was the offensive star. He drove in two runs and had three of the eight Chicago hits, including a decisive fourth-inning double.

"We made it to the dressing room and barricaded the door," Brown recalled. "Outside, wild men were yelling for our blood—really. As the mob got bigger, the police came up and formed a line across the door. We read the next day that the cops had to pull their revolvers to hold them back. I couldn't say as to that. We weren't sticking our heads out to see.

"When it was safe we rode to our hotel in a patrol wagon, with two cops on the inside and four riding the running boards and the rear step. That night when we left for Detroit and the World Series we slipped out the back door and were escorted down the alley in back of our hotel by a swarm of policemen."

It was the third consecutive Chicago pennant. The Cubs finished second to Pittsburgh the following season but won again the next year, their fourth championship in five seasons. They won again in 1918 when the schedule was curtailed because of World War I. The return to glory began in 1929. From '29 through '38 they won the pennant every third year.

The most dramatic moment in Cub history, Gabby Hartnett's "Homer in the Gloaming," occurred at Wrigley Field on September 28, 1938, against the Pirates. The score was tied 5–5 after Pittsburgh batted in the ninth. Darkness had descended. The umpires decided to allow the Cubs to finish the inning and announced the game would be called because of darkness.

Hartnett, then the Cubs' player-manager, stepped in with two outs in the bottom of the ninth, the bases empty, and homered into the left-field stand off reliever Mace Brown on an 0–2 pitch. "A lot of people told me they didn't see the ball," Hartnett said years later. "I did. I knew it the minute I hit it." It was the Cubs' ninth successive victory and lifted them into first place, .002 percentage points ahead of the Pirates. They clinched the pennant three days later.

For the next six seasons the Cubs finished fourth or lower, usually more than 30 games out. The next and last flag came in 1945. Like 1918, it was a war year. First baseman Phil Cavarretta, a Chicago native who grew up a mile from Wrigley Field, was the batting star. He led the league with a .355 average and won the Most Valuable Player award, the Cubs' first MVP since Hartnett in 1935.

They finished third the next season. A severe drought followed—20 consecutive years in the second division. The fiery Leo Durocher, who had managed pennant-winning teams in Brooklyn and New York, arrived in 1966 and immediately announced, "This isn't an eighth-place club." He was right. The Cubs finished tenth. They were second in '69, '70, and '72 and won divisional titles in '84 and '89.

Down Through the Seasons

Note: Parentheses around items in statistical tables indicate the player led the league in the category for the year.

1876

Record: 52–14
Finish: First
Games Ahead: 6
Manager: Al Spalding

Strengthened by the addition of Boston's "Big Four"—pitcher Al Spalding, catcher Jim "Deacon" White, first sacker Cal McVey, and second baseman Ross Barnes—the White Stockings won the first National League pennant. They opened the season on April 25, 1876, in Louisville with a 4–0 victory behind Spalding, achieved against James Devlin, an outstanding pitcher considered to be almost in a class with Spalding.

It was the first major league shutout and gave rise to the term "Chicagoed." There were 15 hits, mostly singles, eight by Chicago, seven by Louisville. Spalding had three of the Chicago hits. Two days later he pitched the second major league shutout.

Here is the account of the opener, in part, as reported in the *Chicago Tribune:*

"The ball was the deadest possible to be found. The ground was not in good shape and was moist, sticky, and soft in the outfield, and very soggy all over. The credit for the victory belongs to Spalding more than to anyone else, and it is safe to say that better pitching was hardly ever seen.

"Third baseman [Cap] Anson and shortstop [Johnny] Peters faced some stiff hits and fielded them in beautiful style, the throwing of both men being as accurate as rifle shooting. Taken as a whole, the first game of the Chicagos of 1876 was a creditable one and promises well for the score at the end of the season."

The most heated were the Chicago-Boston games. Anson, in his memoir *A Ball Player's Career,* tells of the first of these 10 matches, played in Boston:

"The advent of the Big Four in a new uniform was the big attraction and long before the hour set for the game people were wending their way in steady streams toward the action. Every kind of conveyance that could be used was pressed into service, from the lumbering stage coach that had been retired from active service, to the coach-and-four of the millionaire. Street cars were jammed to suffocation. Seats in express wagons were sold at a premium.

"It was Decoration Day, a holiday, and it seemed as if all Boston had determined to be present. When the gates were closed the crowd began to swarm over the fences and the special policemen employed had their hands full of trouble. The Big Four was given a great ovation. As might have been expected, the game was played under difficulties but thanks to the excellent pitching of Spalding and the fine support

given to him by the entire team we won 5–1 and the Hubbites were sorer than ever over the Big Four's defection."

The White Stockings won the next eight matches: 9–3, 8–4, 18–7, 11–3, 15–0, 9–3, 7–2, and 12–0. Boston prevented a sweep with a 10–9 victory in the tenth and final game. Boston, which had won the four previous pennants in the National Association, finished fourth, 15 games out.

Spalding was 47–13 on the season, credited with all but five of the Chicago victories. Despite his defection, the *Boston Times* rated Spalding "second to none," except for his belligerent disposition "to crowd the umpire."

Second baseman Ross Barnes, another of the Boston defectors, won the batting championship with a .429 average, more than 60 points ahead of his nearest rival, and led in runs, 126; hits, 138; doubles, 21; and triples, 14. Barnes hit the National League's first home run, connecting against Cincinnati's William "Cherokee" Fisher on May 2, and was also the first player with six hits in six at bats. Cap Anson batted .309.

	W	L	ERA	G	GS	CG	IP	H	BB	K
Al Spalding	(47)	13	1.75	61	60	53	528⅔	542	26	39
Cal McVey	5	1	1.52	11	6	5	59⅓	57	2	9
Deacon White	0	0	0.00	1	0	0	2	1	0	3
Ross Barnes	0	0	20.25	1	0	0	1⅓	7	0	0
Johnny Peters	0	0	0.00	1	0	0	1	1	1	0
	52	14	1.76	75	66	58	592⅓	608	29	51

Shutouts: Spalding 8.

	G	AB	H	2B	3B	HR	R	RBI	AVG
Regulars									
1B Cal McVey	63	308	107	15	0	1	62	53	.347
2B Ross Barnes	66	322	(138)	(21)	(14)	1	(126)	59	(.429)
SS Johnny Peters	66	316	111	14	2	1	70	47	.351
3B Cap Anson	66	309	110	13	7	1	63	59	.356
RF Bob Addy	32	142	40	4	1	0	36	16	.282
CF Paul Hines	64	305	101	(21)	3	2	62	59	.331
LF John Glenn	66	276	84	9	2	0	55	32	.304
C Deacon White	66	303	104	18	1	1	66	(60)	.343
Substitutes									
Oscar Bielaski	32	139	29	3	0	0	24	10	.209
Fred Andrus	8	36	11	3	0	0	6	2	.306
Pitchers									
Al Spalding	66	292	91	14	2	0	54	44	.312
		2,748	926	135	32	7	624	441	.337

1877

Record: 26–33
Finish: Fifth
Games Behind: 15½
Manager: Al Spalding

The White Stockings of 1877 not only were unable to repeat, but plunged to last place, finishing fifth, 15½ games out of first place. Al Spalding continued as the manager, his

Cap Anson, the original "Mr. Cub," had a 22-year career as a player and player-manager. He was the first major leaguer with 3,000 hits.

5

last season at the helm, but in effect retired as a pitcher; he won his only start. He played the full season as a infielder, mostly at first base, and hit a disappointing .256.

The fair-foul hit was disallowed, to the dismay of the diminutive Ross Barnes (5 feet 8 inches and 145 pounds) whose specialty was the bunt that bounced foul. Once the rule was changed, Barnes was deprived of his edge. Hereafter the ball had to be in fair territory when it cleared first or third base.

Henry Chadwick of the *New York Clipper,* universally regarded as the "Father of Baseball," rated him "the model second baseman, superior in judgement, range, and speed." Barnes was sidelined by illness from mid-May to early September. With diminished strength, he appeared in only 22 games and batted .272, a drop of .132 points.

Barnes was traded to Cincinnati after the season ended and sued the club for the one-third of his $2,500 salary withheld during his sickness. The case was dismissed. The White Stockings also suffered from the loss of catcher Deacon White, who returned to Boston and took the championship back with him.

Spalding was only 26 but was beginning to detect signs of increasing ineffectiveness. He was determined to leave the box while still at his peak. Also, he wanted to focus more of his attention on his mushrooming sporting goods firm, A. G. Spalding & Bros., which the year before began supplying the National League with the "official" Spalding ball.

Spalding was replaced on the mound by George Bradley. The season before, Bradley had pitched all 64 games for St. Louis and had won only two fewer games than Spalding. Bradley was unable to match this success and finished with an 18–23 record. The 1887 White Stockings won only 26 of their 59 games, 21 fewer victories than Spalding, alone, had won the previous season.

The league was reduced from eight to six teams. Philadelphia and Brooklyn were dropped. The Hartford club played all of its home games in Brooklyn. Cincinnati played 72 games but was not listed in the final standings because of the failure to pay the $100 membership fee. Had Cincinnati's 19–53 record been allowed, the White Stockings would have finished fifth, not last.

Prior to the 1877 season, Chadwick offered the first of an endless series on the dangers of the escalating player salaries:

"Say what you will, gentlemen of the league, you must come down in your price; you must come down to the 25 cent admission fee; and you must proportionately lower your salaries; $1,000 for seven months of such services as a professional ball-player is called on to perform, even when he is not indisposed, is amply sufficient. Catchers and pitchers deserve more than players at other positions, but $1,000 is good pay for them, and $100 a month (for six months) is sufficient for the other positions."

	G	AB	H	2B	3B	HR	R	RBI	AVG
Regulars									
1B Al Spalding	60	254	65	7	6	0	29	35	.256
2B Ross Barnes	22	92	25	1	0	0	16	5	.272
SS Johnny Peters	60	265	84	10	3	0	45	41	.317
3B Cap Anson	59	255	86	19	1	0	52	32	.337
RF Paul Hines	60	261	73	11	7	0	44	23	.280
CF Dave Eggler	33	136	36	3	0	0	20	20	.265
LF John Glenn	50	202	46	6	1	0	31	20	.228
C Cal McVey	60	266	98	9	7	0	58	36	.368
Substitutes									
George Bradley	55	214	52	7	3	0	31	12	.243
Harry Smith	24	94	19	1	0	0	7	3	.202
Cherokee Fisher	1	4	0	0	0	0	0	0	.000
Jimmy Hallinan	19	89	25	4	1	0	17	11	.281
Charlie Eden	15	55	12	0	1	0	9	5	.218
Charlie Waitt	10	41	4	0	0	0	2	2	.098
Joe Quinn	4	14	1	0	0	0	1	0	.071
Charley Jones	2	8	3	1	0	0	1	2	.375
Dave Rowe	2	7	2	0	0	0	0	0	.286
Pitchers									
Laurie Reis	4	16	2	0	0	0	3	1	.125
		2,273	633	79	30	0	366	248	.278

1878

Record: 30–30
Finish: Fourth
Games Behind: 11
Manager: Bob Ferguson

It was the year of Chicago's first managerial change. William Hulbert, now president of both the White Stockings and the National League, appointed Robert Ferguson to succeed Spalding. There was only minimal improvement in 1878: a 30–30 won-loss record and a fourth-place finish.

"The trouble with Ferguson," Spalding later wrote, "was not a lack of intelligence, courage or integrity; but, rather, a want of diplomacy. He was no master of the arts of finesse. He had no tact and knew nothing of the subtle science of handling men by strategy rather than by force."

Fifty years later, in the 1928 *Spalding Guide,* a roll call of all the previous National League managers was published. Ferguson was listed but with the following notation: "Spalding was the real manager."

Ferguson, a shortstop, had been the last president of the old National Association of Professional Base Ball Players, and in 1876 had been accused of "selling" games. Described as "an awfully good player when he had a mind to be," Ferguson hit .351, tied for the club lead with first baseman Joe Start, who led the league in hits with 100. Cap Anson batted .341 and was the only other .300 hitter.

Spalding played in only one game, at second base on September 6 against Boston, which won its second successive pennant. Spalding had two singles in four trips and was charged with four errors on seven chances. Terry Larkin, a right-hander, won 29 games, all but one of the club's 30 victories, but also lost 26.

Two new rules were adopted, both unpopular and soon discarded: If rain continued for 30 minutes after play had been stopped, the game was terminated; and after the completion of the second inning, spectators were not given refunds.

	W	L	ERA	G	GS	CG	IP	H	BB	K
George Bradley	18	23	3.31	50	44	35	394	452	39	59
Cal McVey	4	8	4.50	17	10	6	92	129	11	20
Laurie Reis	3	1	0.75	4	4	4	36	29	6	11
Al Spalding	1	0	3.27	4	1	0	11	17	0	2
Dave Rowe	0	1	18.00	1	1	0	1	3	2	0
	26	33	3.37	76	60	45	534	630	58	92

Shutouts: Bradley 2, Reis 1.

	W	L	ERA	G	GS	CG	IP	H	BB	K
Terry Larkin	29	26	2.24	56	56	56	506	511	31	163
Laurie Reis	1	3	3.25	4	4	4	36	55	4	8
Frank Hankinson	0	1	6.00	1	1	1	9	11	0	4
	30	30	2.37	61	61	61	551	577	35	175

Shutouts: Larkin 1.

	G	AB	H	2B	3B	HR	R	RBI	AVG
Regulars									
1B Joe Start	61	(285)	100	12	5	1	58	27	.351
2B Bill McClellan	48	205	46	6	1	0	26	29	.224
SS Bob Ferguson	61	259	91	10	2	0	44	39	.351
3B Frank Hankinson	58	240	64	8	3	1	38	27	.267
RF John Cassidy	60	256	68	7	1	0	33	29	.266
CF Jack Remsen	56	224	52	11	1	1	32	19	.232
LF Cap Anson	60	261	89	12	2	0	55	40	.341
C Bill Harbidge	54	240	71	12	0	0	32	37	.296
Substitutes									
Al Spalding	1	4	2	0	0	0	0	0	.500
Jimmy Hallinan	16	67	19	3	0	0	14	2	.284
Bill Sullivan	2	6	1	0	0	0	1	0	.167
Phil Powers	8	31	5	1	1	0	2	2	.161
Bill Traffley	2	9	1	0	0	0	1	1	.111
Pitchers									
Terry Larkin	58	226	65	9	4	0	33	32	.288
Laurie Reis	5	20	3	0	0	0	2	0	.150
		2,333	677	91	20	3	371	284	.290

1879

Record: 46–33
Finish: Fourth
Games Behind: 10½
Managers: Cap Anson, Silver Flint

Adrian Constantine (Cap) Anson took the reins from Ferguson in 1879, the beginning of a remarkable 19-year managerial reign. During the early years of his command, the White Stockings were the National League's first dynasty. In a seven-year sequence they won five pennants, including three in a row, an accomplishment only twice surpassed.

The 1879 club was bolstered by the acquisition of outfielder Abner Dalrymple, a strong left-handed hitter, also outstanding on defense; and third baseman Ned Williamson, who was to become the 19th-century home run champion. They were plucked off the rosters of the abandoned Milwaukee and Indianapolis franchises. The White Sox paid a reported $2,500 to Milwaukee for Dalrymple, who later claimed his $300 monthly salary was the highest on the '79 club.

Dalrymple, who was from Warren, Illinois, knew all the tricks of the game. For example, against Boston, he robbed Ezra Sutton of a two-out, ninth-inning grand-slam home run. "A smoky haze had settled over the field," Dalrymple recalled. "It was a furious wallop. The ball soared over the left field fence. I had in the blouse of my uniform an extra ball that I kept there for an emergency. I seized the concealed ball, stretched my hand upward, leaped, and came down with the ball in my hand. The umpire called Sutton out."

Perhaps inspired by Anson, the White Stockings set the early pace. They won eight of their first nine games, 14 of 15, and 23 of 27, and were still in front on August 4 with a 35–12 record. But they collapsed in the stretch, losing 21 of their last 32 games, and finished in fourth place with a 46–33 record, 10½ games behind first-place Providence. Anson led the league with a .396 average.

It was the first season every pitch had to be called either a ball, strike, or foul. Three strikes were required for an out, nine balls for a walk. Another rule change, of considerably more importance, was the introduction of the reserve clause. To prevent the big-name stars from jumping to another club, each team was permitted to reserve five players, a disputed practice designed to reduce wages. Subsequently, the entire roster came under the reserve clause. Despite repeated player litigation, it remained in force for 97 years.

	W	L	ERA	G	GS	CG	IP	H	BB	K
Terry Larkin	31	23	2.44	58	58	57	513⅓	514	30	142
Frank Hankinson	15	10	2.50	26	25	25	230⅔	248	27	69
	46	33	2.46	84	83	82	744	762	57	211

Shutouts: Larkin 3, Hankinson 2.

	G	AB	H	2B	3B	HR	R	RBI	AVG
Regulars									
1B Cap Anson	51	227	90	20	1	0	40	34	(.396)
2B Joe Quest	83	334	69	16	1	0	38	22	.207
SS Johnny Peters	83	379	93	13	2	1	45	31	.245
3B Ned Williamson	80	320	94	20	13	1	66	36	.294
RF Orator Shaffer	73	316	96	13	0	0	53	35	.304
CF George Gore	63	266	70	17	4	0	43	32	.263
LF Abner Dalrymple	71	333	97	25	1	0	47	23	.291
C Silver Flint	79	324	92	22	6	1	46	41	.284
Substitutes									
Lew Brown	6	21	6	1	0	0	2	1	.286
John Stedronsky	4	12	1	0	0	0	0	0	.083
Herm Doscher	3	11	2	0	0	0	1	1	.182
Frank Hankinson	44	171	31	4	0	0	14	8	.181
Jack Remsen	42	152	33	4	2	0	14	8	.217
Bill Harbidge	4	18	2	0	0	0	2	1	.111
Tom Dolan	1	4	0	0	0	0	0	0	.000
Pitchers									
Terry Larkin	60	228	50	12	2	0	26	18	.219
		3,116	826	167	32	3	437	291	.265

1880

Record: 67–17
Finish: First
Games Ahead: 15
Manager: Cap Anson

The Anson dynasty began in 1880. The White Stockings won 21 of their first 22 games and cruised to the pennant, without challenge, after putting together a 21-game winning streak—undefeated from June 2 through July 8. They finished with 67 wins and only 17 losses, a .798 winning percentage. It was, and still is, the National League record, since approached only once, by the descendant 1906 Cubs, who set the modern mark with 116 victories against 36 losses, a .763 percentage.

A superior judge of talent, Cap Anson prevailed on owner William Hulbert to sign Mike Kelly, a young outfielder and "change" catcher who had played the previous two seasons with Cincinnati. The grandstands were soon ringing with a chant that was to become part of American folklore: "Slide, Kelly, Slide."

Kelly was a solid hitter, was often spectacular in the field, had a strong arm, and was among the leading base stealers of the time. He also bent the rules, usually without penalty. On hits to right field, for example, when Kelly was on first or second base, he seldom touched third. According to a contemporary account, "The bleacherites would howl in glee when he cut the base by ten or 15 feet and made home with a fancy slide."

Anson broke from tradition and began alternating two pitchers, though most clubs still had only one regular pitcher and depended on other members of the team for occasional relief. Anson's starters were Larry Corcoran and Fred Goldsmith. They divided the work so evenly and were so equally effective that each season their winning percentages were almost identical.

In 1880, for example, Corcoran was 43–14, .754 percent, Goldsmith 21–3, .875 percent, a club record for more than a century, surpassed in 1984 when Rick Sutcliffe was 16–1. Corcoran authored the first Chicago no-hitter, against Boston on August 19, and is also believed to be the first pitcher to work out a system of signals with his catcher.

He invariably carried a mammoth chew of tobacco in his mouth. He shifted the chew from one cheek to the other. Noticing this habit, Silver Flint, one of his catchers, suggested he make shifting the chew to the left side his signal for the curve. It worked like a charm, and the opposition was consistently fooled.

Center fielder George Gore led the league in batting with a .360 average. Anson hit .337, Abner Dalrymple .330, and Tom Burns, a rookie shortstop, .309. There were two rule changes: A walk was reduced from nine to eight balls; and the catchers were required to catch the ball on the third strike for a strikeout. Previously they could catch the ball on the first bounce for the out. As a result, the catchers moved closer to the plate.

	W	L	ERA	G	GS	CG	IP	H	BB	K
Larry Corcoran	43	14	1.95	63	60	57	536⅓	404	99	268
Fred Goldsmith	21	3	1.75	26	24	22	210⅓	189	18	90
Tom Poorman	2	0	2.40	2	1	0	15	12	8	0
Charlie Guth	1	0	5.00	1	1	1	9	12	1	7
King Kelly	0	0	0.00	1	0	0	3	3	1	1
Tom Burns	0	0	0.00	1	0	0	1⅓	2	2	1
	67	17	1.93	94	86	80	775	622	129	367

Shutouts: Corcoran 5, Goldsmith 4.

	G	AB	H	2B	3B	HR	R	RBI	AVG
Regulars									
1B Cap Anson	86	356	120	24	1	1	54	74	.337
2B Joe Quest	82	300	71	12	1	0	37	27	.237
SS Tom Burns	85	333	103	17	3	0	47	43	.309
3B Ned Williamson	75	311	78	20	2	0	65	31	.251
RF King Kelly	84	344	100	17	9	1	72	60	.291
CF George Gore	77	322	116	23	2	2	70	47	(.360)
LF Abner Dalrymple	86	(382)	(126)	25	12	0	91	36	.330
C Silver Flint	74	284	46	10	4	0	30	17	.162
Substitutes									
Larry Corcoran	72	286	66	11	1	0	41	25	.231
Fred Goldsmith	35	142	37	4	2	0	24	15	.261
Tommy Beals	13	46	7	0	0	0	4	3	.152
Tom Poorman	7	25	5	1	2	0	3	0	.200
Pitchers									
Charlie Guth	1	4	1	0	0	0	0	0	.250
		3,135	876	164	39	4	538	378	.279

1881

Record: 56–28
Finish: First
Games Ahead: 9
Manager: Cap Anson

It was more of the same in 1881. With the same lineup the White Stockings won their second consecutive flag. Cap Anson led the league in batting with a .399 average, and Larry Corcoran won 31 games, also the league high. The only difference was that it was a closer race. Providence, second in 1880, 15 games back, was again the runner-up but only nine games back.

Anson had two new players, Andy Piercy and "Little Hughey" Nicol, reserve infielders. Both were used sparingly. The regulars were intact: The batting order was Abner Dalrymple, lf; George Gore, cf; Mike Kelly, rf; Anson, 1b; Ned Williamson, 3b; Tom Burns, ss; Silver Flint, catching; Joe Quest, 2b; and Corcoran and Fred Goldsmith, pitchers.

Chicago took its home opener in wintry weather. Worcester won its first eight games and was the early leader. The White Stockings broke the Worcester streak on May 14 with a 4–3 victory when Burns "sent the ball to the clubhouse" for a home run. A big black dog owned by William Hulbert was sleeping on the clubhouse platform. As the ball rolled to the dog, Worcester left fielder Buttercup Dickerson was afraid of the animal or pretended to be. The dog paid no attention to Dickerson but Worcester claimed interference, "a silly protest" that was overruled.

Six days later, when Cincinnati came to Chicago, before the game began, the Reds demanded the removal of the animal from the clubhouse platform, also that the clubhouse doors be closed lest some Chicago player hit the ball through the opening. "There's no rule covering dogs and doors," team owner Hulbert barked. "But if it will make you any happier the dog shall be bounced and the door closed."

The Chicago attendance soared as the White Stockings drew away from the field. The Fourth of July gate exceeded 10,000. The final home game of the season, on August 25, was a festive occasion. Hulbert brought his dog out of retirement, but he was "carefully conducted to his lair before the game started."

The concluding championship game on September 27, Chicago at Troy, New York, was played in a heavy rainstorm. The White Stockings won 10–8, but the ball was so slippery and the field so muddy that the game was a farce. The paid attendance was 12, lowest in major league history.

Among the records set were seven stolen bases in one game by center fielder Gore. To help the hitters, the pitcher's box was moved back, from 45 to 50 feet. In a companion legislation, the pitchers, then restricted to an underhand delivery, were compelled to face the batter. The visiting club had to submit a batting order by 9 A.M. on the day of the game, and no substitutions were allowed except in cases of injury or illness.

	W	L	ERA	G	GS	CG	IP	H	BB	K
Larry Corcoran	(31)	14	2.31	45	44	43	396⅔	380	78	150
Fred Goldsmith	24	13	2.59	39	39	37	330	328	44	76
Ned Williamson	1	1	2.00	3	1	1	18	14	0	2
	56	28	2.43	87	84	81	744⅔	722	122	228

Shutouts: Goldsmith 5, Corcoran 4.

	G	AB	H	2B	3B	HR	R	RBI	AVG
Regulars									
1B Cap Anson	84	343	(137)	21	7	1	67	(82)	(.399)
2B Joe Quest	78	293	72	6	0	1	35	26	.246
SS Tom Burns	84	342	95	20	3	4	41	42	.278
3B Ned Williamson	82	343	92	12	6	1	56	48	.268
RF King Kelly	82	353	114	(27)	3	2	84	55	.323
CF George Gore	73	309	92	18	9	1	(86)	44	.298
LF Abner Dalrymple	82	362	117	22	4	1	72	37	.323
C Silver Flint	80	306	95	18	0	1	46	34	.310
Substitutes									
Andy Piercy	2	8	2	0	0	0	1	0	.250
Hugh Nicol	26	108	22	2	0	0	13	7	.204
Pitchers									
Larry Corcoran	47	189	42	8	0	0	25	9	.222
Fred Goldsmith	42	158	38	3	4	0	24	16	.241
		3,114	918	157	36	12	550	400	.295

1882

Record: 55–29
Finish: First
Games Ahead: 3
Manager: Cap Anson

Larry Corcoran pitched his second no-hitter and crashed the first grand-slam home run in Chicago history. Cap Anson led the club with a .362 average, and seven players—Mike Kelly, Abner Dalrymple, George Gore, Ned Williamson, Tom Burns, Silver Flint, and Hugh Nicol—in an unprecedented offensive display, each produced four hits in a 35–4 romp over Cleveland.

These achievements were among the highlights of the 1882 season as the White Stockings continued their domination with a record third consecutive National League pennant. The Providence Grays, also for the third year in a row, finished second but were gaining, only three games out.

Chicago had a losing record in August but clinched on September 29 with an 11–5 romp over Buffalo. The root of the Chicago success was eight victories in 12 games against Providence. Had the Grays won half of these games, they would have taken the flag.

According to the *Spalding Guide,* "It was the most noteworthy season ever known in the annals of the game. The general character of play in the four departments of the game—pitching, batting, fielding, and base running—was in advance of any previous season's work and another step forward toward the eventual point of perfect play."

Dan Brouthers, the Buffalo first baseman, led the league in batting, but three White Stockings were among the top nine hitters: Anson, Gore, and Kelly. Corcoran won 27 games, one less than Fred Goldsmith, but had the smallest percentage of earned runs charged against him. Corcoran was 27–13 for a .675 winning percentage, Goldsmith 28–16, .636.

Anson rested the day after the clinching and was replaced at first base by 16-year-old Milton Scott, the youngest player in Chicago history. Scott responded with two hits in five trips but never again appeared in Chicago flannels. Anson played 15 more years.

William Hulbert, truly the father of the National League and also the chief executive officer of the White Stockings and the most influential baseball figure of the 19th century, died of heart disease on April 10 at the age of 49. Spalding assumed command of the club. Arthur H. Soden, the Boston owner, finished Hulbert's term as the National League president and at the season's end was succeeded by A. G. Mills.

The reserve clause, drawn by Soden and Hulbert, which initially allowed the clubs to reserve five players, was expanded to cover the services of 11 players, virtually a complete roster. A walk was reduced to seven balls, and the players no longer were assessed 50 cents a day for board while the team was on the road. No player except the captain was permitted to address an umpire.

	W	L	ERA	G	GS	CG	IP	H	BB	K
Fred Goldsmith	28	16	2.42	44	44	44	405	377	38	109
Larry Corcoran	27	13	(1.95)	40	40	39	355⅔	281	63	170
Ned Williamson	0	0	6.00	1	0	0	3	9	1	0
	55	29	2.22	85	84	83	763⅔	667	102	279

Shutouts: Goldsmith 4, Corcoran 3.

	G	AB	H	2B	3B	HR	R	RBI	AVG
Regulars									
1B Cap Anson	82	348	126	29	8	1	69	83	.362
2B Tom Burns	84	355	88	23	6	0	55	48	.248
SS King Kelly	84	377	115	(37)	4	1	81	55	.305
3B Ned Williamson	83	348	98	27	4	3	66	60	.282
RF Hugh Nicol	47	186	37	9	1	1	19	16	.199
CF George Gore	84	367	117	15	7	3	(99)	51	.319
LF Abner Dalrymple	84	(397)	117	25	11	1	96	36	.295
C Silver Flint	81	331	83	18	8	4	48	44	.251
Substitutes									
Joe Quest	42	159	32	5	2	0	24	15	.201
Milt Scott	1	5	2	0	0	0	1	0	.400
Pitchers									
Fred Goldsmith	45	183	42	11	1	0	23	19	.230
Larry Corcoran	40	169	35	10	2	1	23	24	.207
		3,225	892	209	54	15	604	451	.277

1883

Record: 59–39
Finish: Second
Games Behind: 4
Manager: Cap Anson

The Chicago reign came to an end in 1883. A local sportswriter who covered all 98 games offered the following explanation:

"Now that the White Stockings have been beaten there are plenty of grumblers who fault management for attempting to go through the season with 10 players, for Billy Sunday, the 11th man, a pet of Anson's, is rated a cipher.

"The club management is accused of stinginess in not having secured three or four serviceable substitutes to guard against accident and disability. The cry is that the club, for the most part, had but one pitcher this year. Goldsmith has grown fat and lazy, and has pitched very few good games.

"Next year, in all probability, President Spalding will try the auxiliary plan of developing players. The eleven men reserved will be kept, and nearly as many semi-professionals and amateurs will probably be engaged on small salaries."

Despite this tale of woe, the White Stockings had a 59–39 record, 20 games over .500, and finished second, only four games behind Boston. Chicago won 15 of its first 21 games and held the lead through May. This success was followed by what, years later, was to become a traditional June swoon, eight victories and 11 losses. Still, the team was in contention in early September—until Boston swept a four-game series.

Larry Corcoran again led the club with 34–20 record. Fred Goldsmith was 25–19. There were only two .300 hitters—George Gore at .334 and Cap Anson at .308. Second baseman Fred Pfeffer, among the best defensive players of his time, was the only newcomer and gave the club what was referred to as the Stonewall Infield, the first time that term was used in baseball to denote an impregnable defense.

There were several outstanding moments, including a 31–7, July 3 romp over Buffalo that included 14 doubles, four each by Anson and Abner Dalrymple; and a record 18 seventh-inning runs on September 6 in a 26–6 victory over Detroit. Tommy Burns led the rally with eight total bases—two doubles and a home run—a one-inning record for the most long hits.

As for Billy Sunday, Anson first saw him in a footrace at a firemen's picnic in Anson's hometown, Marshalltown, Iowa, where Sunday drove an undertaker's wagon. Sunday appeared in 14 games in 1883, his rookie season, and batted .241. An outstanding base runner and an excellent player defensively, he had a eight-year major league career. After he retired from baseball he became a nationally known evangelist.

	W	L	ERA	G	GS	CG	IP	H	BB	K
Larry Corcoran	34	20	2.49	56	53	51	473⅔	483	82	216
Fred Goldsmith	25	19	3.15	46	45	40	383⅓	456	39	82
Cap Anson	0	0	0.00	2	0	0	3	1	1	0
King Kelly	0	0	0.00	1	0	0	1	1	0	0
Ned Williamson	0	0	9.00	1	0	0	1	1	1	1
	59	39	2.78	106	98	91	862	942	123	299

Shutouts: Corcoran 3, Goldsmith 2.

	G	AB	H	2B	3B	HR	R	AVG
Regulars								
1B Cap Anson	98	413	127	36	5	0	70	.308
2B Fred Pfeffer	96	371	87	22	7	1	41	.235
SS Tom Burns	97	405	119	37	7	2	69	.294
3B Ned Williamson	98	402	111	(49)	5	2	83	.276
RF King Kelly	98	428	109	28	10	3	92	.255
CF George Gore	92	392	131	30	9	2	105	.334
LF Abner Dalrymple	80	363	108	24	4	2	78	.298
C Silver Flint	85	332	88	23	4	0	57	.265
Substitutes								
Larry Corcoran	68	263	55	12	7	0	40	.209
Fred Goldsmith	60	235	52	12	3	1	38	.221
Billy Sunday	14	54	13	4	0	0	6	.241
		3,658	1,000	277	61	13	679	.273

RBI statistics not available.

1884

Record: 62–50
Finish: Fourth (tie)
Games Behind: 22
Manager: Cap Anson

In Chicago—but not elsewhere—1884 was the Year of the Home Run. The White Stockings finished in a fourth-place tie, 22 games behind the pennant-winning Providence Grays, but had the National League's top four home run hitters: Ned Williamson, 27; Fred Pfeffer, 25; Abner Dalrymple, 22; and Cap Anson, 21.

The previous season this "mighty" foursome, combined, had five home runs: Williamson and Dalrymple two each, Pfeffer one, and Anson none. A quick assumption might be that they went to the gym during the off-season and engaged in weight-training programs. Wrong. A rule was changed. What previously had been a ground-rule double was now declared a home run.

According to the late John Tattersall of Philadelphia, a pioneer statistician who exhumed the box scores and charted every major league home run, no precise measurement was available of the distance from the plate to the right-field fence in Lake Park, Chicago's home grounds. Tattersall estimated it as 230 feet, not merely in the corner but also in the gap—or as he described it, "across the field."

Because the dimensions were so short, balls driven into this sector previously were ground-rule doubles. But prior to the '84 season "some brilliant strategist in the Chicago camp somehow legalized that any ball that cleared the fence was a home run."

The National League one-season record had been nine. Williamson's 27, 25 at Lake Park, was listed without an asterisk and was not surpassed for 35 years—until Babe Ruth hit 29 in 1919. Williamson was not the equal of Ruth, either as a

player or a personality, but he was an idol in his day and excelled in the field until a bulging waistline forced him to the sideline and an early death.

Five home runs were hit in the Chicago home opener. Williamson connected three times in the morning game of a Memorial Day doubleheader, an accomplishment matched by Anson on August 6. Since Anson had hit two in the previous game, he had five home runs in two consecutive games, a mark first equaled by Ty Cobb in 1925.

According to Tattersall, there were 197 home runs in Lake Park, 130 by the White Stockings, a team record that stood until the New York Giants hit 221 in 1947. The Chicago average of 2.32 home runs a game at home has not been equaled.

The ambidextrous Larry Corcoran, a natural right-hander suffering with a painful right index finger and the only pitcher available, worked four innings throwing both right- and left-handed on June 16 in a 20–9 loss to Buffalo. He finished the game at shortstop and had two triples and a single.

His finger healed, Corcoran pitched his third no-hit game against Providence 11 days later as baseball was inching into the modern age. The National League amended its rules and supplied a players' bench for both teams; up to then the team at bat had sat on the one bench provided. Six called balls now entitled a batter to take first base.

	W	L	ERA	G	GS	CG	IP	H	BB	K
Larry Corcoran	35	23	2.40	60	59	57	516⅔	473	116	272
Fred Goldsmith	9	11	4.26	21	21	20	188	245	29	34
John Clarkson	10	3	2.14	14	13	12	118	94	25	102
Joe Brown	4	2	4.68	7	6	5	50	56	7	27
Tom Lee	1	4	3.77	5	5	5	45⅓	55	15	14
George Crosby	1	2	3.54	3	3	3	28	27	12	11
John Hibbard	1	1	2.65	2	2	2	17	18	9	4
Fred Andrus	1	0	2.00	1	1	1	9	11	2	2
Mike Corcoran	0	1	4.00	1	1	1	9	16	7	2
Thomas Lynch	0	0	2.57	1	1	0	7	7	3	2
King Kelly	0	1	8.44	2	0	0	5⅓	12	2	1
Ned Williamson	0	0	18.00	2	0	0	2	8	2	0
Cap Anson	0	1	18.00	1	0	0	1	3	1	1
Fred Pfeffer	0	0	9.00	1	0	0	1	3	1	0
	62	49	3.03	121	112	106	997⅓	1,028	231	472

Shutouts: Corcoran 7, Goldsmith 1, Hibbard 1.

	G	AB	H	2B	3B	HR	R	AVG
Regulars								
1B Cap Anson	112	475	159	30	3	21	108	.335
2B Fred Pfeffer	112	467	135	10	10	25	105	.289
SS Tom Burns	83	343	84	14	2	7	54	.245
3B Ned Williamson	107	417	116	18	8	(27)	84	.278
RF King Kelly	108	452	160	28	5	13	(120)	(.354)
CF George Gore	103	422	134	18	4	5	104	.318
LF Abner Dalrymple	111	521	161	18	9	22	111	.309
C Silver Flint	73	279	57	5	2	9	35	.204
Substitutes								
Walt Kinzie	19	82	13	3	0	2	4	.159
Thomas Lynch	1	4	0	0	0	0	0	.000
Billy Sunday	43	176	39	4	1	4	25	.222
John Clarkson	21	84	22	6	2	3	16	.262
Joe Brown	15	61	13	1	0	0	6	.213
Sy Sutcliffe	4	15	3	1	0	0	4	.200
Pitchers								
Larry Corcoran	64	251	61	3	4	1	43	.243
Fred Goldsmith	22	81	11	2	0	2	11	.136
Tom Lee	6	24	3	1	0	0	0	.125
George Crosby	3	13	4	0	0	1	1	.308
John Hibbard	2	7	0	0	0	0	0	.000
Fred Andrus	1	5	1	0	0	0	3	.200
Mike Corcoran	1	3	0	0	0	0	0	.000
		4,182	1,176	162	50	142	834	.281

RBI statistics not available.

1885

Record: 87–25
Finish: First
Games Ahead: 2
Manager: Cap Anson

Cap Anson rallied his troops to another flag in 1885. The White Stockings moved into a new stadium, West Side Park, at Congress and Loomis streets. Without the short right-field fence, home run production returned to normal, 55, twice as many as any other club and almost one-third of the league total. Abner Dalrymple led the league with 11. Ned Williamson had three, 24 fewer than the previous season.

The park was a 15-minute ride from downtown. The club didn't use the conventional omnibus. The players were transported in open carriages, four players to a carriage. Their white-stockinged legs were always in evidence. Above these stretches of white, they wore short but wide Dutch pants of a dark hue, sometimes changing to black tights. They also introduced bathrobes of streaky and checkered colored patterns.

The only regulars to hit over .300 were George Gore, .313, and Anson, .310. Nonetheless, they outscored their opponents by an enormous margin, 834–470. John Clarkson, a durable right-hander who joined the club late in the 1884 season, was the new pitching star and led the league in six categories: victories, 53; starts, 70; complete games, 68; innings, 623; strikeouts, 318; and shutouts, 10.

Fred Goldsmith was gone, tending bar, and Larry Corcoran was fading. Corcoran, who had won 170 games during the previous five seasons, appeared in only seven games, winning five and losing two. Corcoran went to an early grave. Wasted away with dissipation and Bright's disease, he died six years later, in 1891, at the age of 32.

To bolster the staff, Spalding picked up Jim McCormick, a veteran campaigner, from the Providence Grays. McCormick won 21 games, 20 with the White Stockings, 14 in succession. After July it was a two-team race between Chicago and the New York Giants. The clincher came on the last day of September in the midst of a three-game sweep over the stunned Giants; going into this series, New York had defeated the White Stockings nine times in 12 games. The Giants finished second, two games out.

In mid-October, two weeks after the season ended, the National League owners signed a joint agreement with the rival American Association. The legislation included a salary ceiling of $2,000, with a $1,000 minimum. Nine New York players, led by shortstop John Montgomery Ward, were so angered they formed the Brotherhood of Professional Base Ball Players. Ward was elected president. Four years later the Brotherhood formed a rival league that had no salary limits.

	W	L	ERA	G	GS	CG	IP	H	BB	K
John Clarkson	(53)	16	1.85	(70)	(70)	(68)	(623)	497	97	(318)
Jim McCormick	20	4	2.43	24	24	24	215	187	40	88
Ted Kennedy	7	2	3.43	9	9	8	78⅔	91	28	36
Larry Corcoran	5	2	3.64	7	7	6	59⅓	63	24	10
Fred Pfeffer	2	1	2.56	5	2	2	31¾	26	8	13
Ned Williamson	0	0	0.00	2	0	0	6	2	0	3
Wash Williams	0	0	13.50	1	1	0	2	2	5	0
	87	25	2.23	118	113	108	1,015⅔	868	202	468

Shutouts: Clarkson (10), McCormick 3, Corcoran 1.

	G	AB	H	2B	3B	HR	R	RBI	AVG
Regulars									
1B Cap Anson	112	464	144	35	7	7	100	114	.310
2B Fred Pfeffer	112	469	113	12	6	6	90	71	.241
SS Tom Burns	111	445	121	23	9	7	82	70	.272
3B Ned Williamson	113	407	97	16	5	3	87	64	.238
RF King Kelly	107	438	126	24	7	9	(124)	74	.288
CF George Gore	109	441	138	21	13	5	115	51	.313
LF Abner Dalrymple	113	(492)	135	27	12	11	109	58	.274
C Silver Flint	68	249	52	8	2	1	27	19	.209
Substitutes									
Jimmy Ryan	3	13	6	1	0	0	2	2	.462
Billy Sunday	46	172	44	3	3	2	36	20	.256
Wash Williams	1	4	1	0	0	0	0	0	.250
Bill Krieg	1	3	0	0	0	0	0	0	.000
Sy Sutcliffe	11	43	8	1	1	0	5	4	.186
Jim McCauley	3	6	1	0	0	0	1	0	.167
Ed Gastfield	1	3	0	0	0	0	0	0	.000
Pitchers									
John Clarkson	72	283	61	11	5	4	34	31	.216
Jim McCormick	25	103	23	1	4	0	13	16	.223
Ted Kennedy	9	36	3	0	0	0	3	0	.083
Larry Corcoran	7	22	6	1	0	0	6	4	.273
		4,093	1,079	184	74	55	834	598	.264

1886

Record: 90–34
Finish: First
Games Ahead: 2½
Manager: Cap Anson

Chicago repeated as champion in 1886, their fifth and last championship under Anson's leadership. It was their sixth pennant in the 11-year existence of the National League and was achieved with two significant adjustments. Cap Anson used a three-man pitching rotation and often benched some, but not all, of his four left-handed hitters against left-handed pitchers, a strategy which has since become common. Today it is known as platooning.

The overwhelming majority of pitchers in the league were right-handed; only three lefties started more than 10 games. Convinced the lefty-lefty advantage favored the pitcher, Anson presented a different lineup in the 16 games when his club was confronted by a left-handed starter. Against right-handers there was comparatively little change.

The lefty-swinging Abner Dalrymple, who had been among the league's leading hitters in the first half of the 1880s, was the principal victim of Anson's platooning. He appeared in only 82 of the expanded 124-game schedule and was replaced in left field by either Jimmy Ryan, a rookie sensation, or Jocko Flynn, a pitcher-outfielder, both right-handed batters. There was another new wrinkle: catcher Steven "Silver" Flint, a right-handed hitter, led off or batted third against lefties; against righties he generally batted ninth.

In addition to the left-right adjustments, Anson also alternated catchers. Mike "King" Kelly, his best hitter—who led the league with a .388 average—was a premier catcher in an era when it was physically difficult to catch every day. Kelly was too valuable to sit on the bench, and so Anson shuttled him back and forth to right field.

The White Stockings, as a result, had not only a potent offense but also an exceptionally deep bench. Still, they didn't take the lead until August and finished with a 90–34 won-loss record, two and a half games ahead of Detroit. They achieved this success principally because they "beat the brains out of the bums." They were 47–6 against the last three clubs: 13–4 against St. Louis and 17–1 against Kansas City and Washington.

Clarkson and McCormick combined for 66 victories, Clarkson winning 35, McCormick 31. Rookie Jocko Flynn was not far behind and, at 24–6, had the league's best winning percentage, .800. Anson was the runner-up, behind Kelly, for the batting title with a .371 average. George Gore batted .304, scored 150 runs, and drew a league-high 102 walks. It would be 20 years before Chicago won another pennant.

	W	L	ERA	G	GS	CG	IP	H	BB	K
John Clarkson	35	17	2.41	55	55	50	466⅔	419	86	(340)
Jim McCormick	31	11	2.82	42	42	38	347⅔	341	100	172
Jocko Flynn	24	6	2.24	32	29	28	257	207	63	146
Jimmy Ryan	0	0	4.63	5	0	0	23⅓	19	13	15
Ned Williamson	0	0	0.00	2	0	0	3	2	0	1
	90	34	2.54	136	126	116	1,097⅔	988	262	674

Shutouts: Clarkson 3, McCormick 2, Flynn 2.

	G	AB	H	2B	3B	HR	R	RBI	SB	AVG
Regulars										
1B Cap Anson	125	504	187	35	11	10	117	(147)	29	.371
2B Fred Pfeffer	118	474	125	17	8	7	88	95	—	.264
SS Ned Williamson	121	430	93	17	8	6	69	58	—	.216
3B Tom Burns	112	445	123	18	10	3	64	65	—	.276
RF Jimmy Ryan	84	327	100	17	6	4	58	53	—	.306
CF George Gore	118	444	135	20	12	6	150	63	—	.304
LF Abner Dalrymple	82	331	77	7	12	3	62	26	—	.233
C Silver Flint	54	173	35	6	2	1	30	13	—	.202
Substitutes										
King Kelly	118	451	175	32	11	4	(155)	79	—	(.388)
Jocko Flynn	57	205	41	6	2	4	40	19	—	.200
Billy Sunday	28	103	25	2	2	0	16	6	—	.243
George Moolic	16	56	8	3	0	0	9	2	—	.143
Lew Hardie	16	51	9	0	0	0	4	3	—	.176
Pitchers										
John Clarkson	55	210	49	9	1	3	21	23	—	.233
Jim McCormick	42	174	41	9	2	2	17	21	—	.236
		4,378	1,223	198	87	53	900	673	—	.279

Stolen base statistics not available for most players.

1887

Record: 71–50
Finish: Third
Games Behind: 6½
Manager: Cap Anson

The White Stockings finished third in 1887 but provided the baseball world with one of the biggest stories of the decade: the sale of King Kelly to Boston for $10,000, a princely and unprecedented sum. To convince an unbelieving public, the Boston management supplied newspapers with the sales agreement.

It was more than twice as much as the previous high of $4,700 for Fred "Sure-Shot" Dunlap, purchased by Detroit from St. Louis in midseason the year before. Initially, Boston offered $5,000 for Kelly. In a typical ownership response, Spalding replied by letter: "We wouldn't think of letting Kelly go at the figure you offer, but for double that amount we would consider it."

Kelly was the most popular player of the time. A 25-cent book, *Play Ball,* ghostwritten for Kelly, published after the '87 season, may have been baseball's first player autobiography. "Slide, Kelly, Slide" was America's first pop hit recording.

A heavy drinker, but with a pleasant and hearty nature, Kelly had tested Cap Anson's patience. A disciplinarian, Anson had no regrets. Said Anson: "In minutes he could throw in enough whiskey that would put an ordinary man under the table." But near the end of his life it was the King who was under the table. He died at the age of 36.

Aware of the value of publicity, good or bad, Spalding happily weathered the storm. The more the newspapers attacked him, the better the gate. "Harmony" White of the *Chicago Daily News* was especially vitriolic. When the criticism began to subside, Spalding asked White why he was letting up. White said he was running out of ammunition. Spalding then began sending White weekly dispatches with inside information that allowed him to fill his quiver and sustain the assault. Attendance soared. So did Spalding's bankroll. The club showed a larger profit than ever before.

Spalding backed up the truck. The slumping Abner Dalrymple was traded to Pittsburgh. Reliable George Gore, after eight strong seasons with Chicago, also departed. Jocko Flynn, the 1886 pitching sensation, developed arm trouble and appeared in only one more game. John Clarkson led the league with 38 victories, but this total was counterbalanced by 21 losses.

The established stars were replaced by younger players, "Anson's Colts." Despite a weakened lineup, the Colts were competitive. They never fully recovered from a poor start—only 11 wins in their first 26 games—but by the end of July were in second place. They finished third, 6½ games behind Detroit and three behind Philadelphia.

Walks were counted as base hits. Anson batted .421 to lead the league. Years later, with walks eliminated, his average was dropped to .347, second in the league behind Detroit's Sam Thompson's .372. King Kelly, the "Ten Thousand Dollar Beauty," didn't come through as expected. He batted .322, a 66-point decline from the previous season. Boston finished in the second division, 10 games behind Chicago.

	W	L	ERA	G	GS	CG	IP	H	BB	K
John Clarkson	(38)	21	3.08	(60)	(59)	(56)	(523)	(513)	92	(237)
Mark Baldwin	18	17	3.40	40	39	35	334	329	122	164
George Van Haltren	11	7	3.86	20	18	18	161	177	66	76
Jimmy Ryan	2	1	4.20	8	3	2	45	53	17	14
Shadow Pyle	1	3	4.73	4	4	3	26⅔	32	21	5
Charlie Sprague	1	0	4.91	3	3	2	22	24	13	9
Emil Geis	0	1	8.00	1	1	1	9	17	3	4
Marty Sullivan	0	0	7.71	1	0	0	2⅓	6	1	1
Ned Williamson	0	0	9.00	1	0	0	2	2	1	0
Bob Pettit	0	0	0.00	1	0	0	1	3	2	0
	71	50	3.46	139	127	117	1,126	1,156	338	510

Shutouts: Clarkson 2, Baldwin 1, Van Haltren 1.

	G	AB	H	2B	3B	HR	R	RBI	SB	AVG
Regulars										
1B Cap Anson	122	472	164	33	13	7	107	102	27	.347
2B Fred Pfeffer	123	479	133	21	6	16	95	89	57	.278
SS Ned Williamson	127	439	117	20	14	9	77	78	45	.267
3B Tom Burns	115	424	112	20	10	3	57	60	32	.264
RF Billy Sunday	50	199	58	6	6	3	41	32	34	.291
CF Jimmy Ryan	126	508	145	23	10	11	117	74	50	.285
LF Marty Sullivan	115	472	134	13	16	7	98	77	35	.284
C Tom Daly	74	256	53	10	4	2	45	17	29	.207
Substitutes										
Patsy Tebeau	20	68	11	3	0	0	8	10	8	.162
Emil Geis	3	12	1	0	0	0	0	0	0	.083
George Van Haltren	45	172	35	4	0	3	30	17	12	.203
Bob Pettit	32	138	36	3	3	2	29	12	16	.261
Charlie Sprague	3	13	2	0	0	0	0	0	0	.154
Jocko Flynn	1	0	0	0	0	0	0	0	0	—
Silver Flint	49	187	50	8	6	3	22	21	7	.267
Dell Darling	38	141	45	7	4	3	28	20	19	.319
Pitchers										
John Clarkson	63	215	52	5	5	6	40	25	6	.242
Mark Baldwin	41	139	26	1	1	4	18	17	4	.187
Shadow Pyle	4	16	3	1	0	1	1	4	1	.188
		4,350	1,177	178	98	80	813	655	382	.271

1888

Record: 77–58
Finish: Second
Games Behind: 9
Manager: Cap Anson

Having extracted $10,000 from Boston for King Kelly, Al Spalding tried again and pocketed another $10,000 from the Beaneaters for pitcher John Clarkson, who had given Cap Anson yeoman service—136 wins in four seasons. Clarkson held up his end of Boston's $20,000 battery with 33 wins, three fewer victories than his Chicago average. Kelly batted only .318. Boston climbed only one notch, to fourth place.

The White Stockings finished second in 1888, nine games behind New York, and led the league in scoring and home runs but had an inadequate pitching staff: only one 20-game winner, rookie Gus Krock, the first left-hander in Chicago history, who was 24–14. Searching for a stopper, Anson used 11 pitchers. His other two starters, Mark Baldwin and George Van Haltren, combined for 26 wins but lost 28. Rookie John Tener was 7–5 and had a brighter future as a politician. He became the governor of Pennsylvania and later the president of the National League.

Anson's .344 led the league. Outfielder Jim Ryan, developing into a star, also led in home runs, 16; hits, 182; and doubles, 33. On July 28, Ryan had a single, double, triple, and home run against Detroit, the first Chicago player to hit for the cycle. The famed Hugh Duffy, another of the Chicago rookies, batted .282. Six seasons later, when he was with Boston, Duffy hit .438, still the major league record.

Billy Sunday was gone, traded to Pittsburgh. For Anson it was both a professional and personal loss. Sunday, who subsequently gained fame as an evangelist, was an Anson discovery. A disciplinarian who walked the straight and narrow, Anson told his fellow Iowan, "May luck be with you." Never a reliable hitter, Sunday, according to Anson, was "the fastest man in the profession, and one who could run the bases like a scared deer . . . a good fielder and a strong and accurate thrower."

Anson's Colts set the pace early and were in the lead continuously from May 5 to July 23 but then dropped to third behind New York and Detroit. New York pulled away in September. Chicago finished second, nine games back, and was shut out nine times compared to only three calciminings suffered by the Giants.

"The lesson that was learned," wrote the editor of the *Spalding Guide*, "is that the pennant cannot be won by any costly outlay in securing the services of this, that, or the other 'greatest player in the country.' It is well-managed and harmonious teams, not picked nines led by special stars, which win in the long run." Boston finished 15½ games out.

	W	L	ERA	G	GS	CG	IP	H	BB	K
Gus Krock	24	14	2.44	39	39	39	339⅔	295	45	161
Mark Baldwin	13	15	2.76	30	30	27	251	241	99	157
George Van Haltren	13	13	3.52	30	24	24	245¾	263	60	139
John Tener	7	5	2.74	12	12	11	102	90	25	39
George Borchers	4	4	3.49	10	10	7	67	67	29	26
Ad Gumbert	3	3	3.14	6	6	5	48⅔	44	10	16
Frank Dwyer	4	1	1.07	5	5	5	42	32	9	17
Jimmy Ryan	4	0	3.05	8	2	1	38⅓	47	12	11
Charlie Brynan	2	1	6.48	3	3	2	25	29	7	11
Dad Clarke	1	0	5.06	2	2	1	16	23	6	6
Willard Mains	1	1	4.91	2	2	1	11	8	6	5
	76	57	2.96	147	135	123	1,186⅓	1,139	308	588

Shutouts: Krock 4, Van Haltren 4, Baldwin 2, Tener 1, Borchers 1, Dwyer 1.

	G	AB	H	2B	3B	HR	R	RBI	SB	AVG
Regulars										
1B Cap Anson	134	515	177	20	12	12	101	(84)	28	(.344)
2B Fred Pfeffer	135	517	129	22	10	8	90	57	64	.250
SS Ned Williamson	132	452	113	9	14	8	75	73	25	.250
3B Tom Burns	134	483	115	12	6	3	60	70	34	.238
RF Hugh Duffy	71	298	84	10	4	7	60	41	13	.282
CF Jimmy Ryan	129	549	(182)	(33)	10	(16)	115	64	60	.332
LF Marty Sullivan	75	314	74	12	6	7	40	39	9	.236
C Tom Daly	65	219	42	2	6	0	34	29	10	.192
Substitutes										
George Van Haltren	81	318	90	9	14	4	46	34	21	.283
Bob Pettit	43	169	43	1	4	4	23	23	7	.254
George Borchers	10	33	2	2	0	0	3	2	1	.061
Ad Gumbert	7	24	8	0	1	0	3	2	0	.333
Charlie Brynan	3	11	2	0	1	0	1	1	0	.182
Dad Clarke	2	7	2	0	1	1	4	2	0	.286
Willard Mains	2	7	1	0	0	0	1	0	0	.143
Duke Farrell	64	241	56	6	3	3	34	19	8	.232
Silver Flint	22	77	14	3	0	0	6	3	1	.182
Dell Darling	20	75	16	3	1	2	12	7	0	.213
Pitchers										
Gus Krock	39	134	22	0	0	1	9	11	1	.164
Mark Baldwin	30	106	16	1	2	1	11	5	4	.151
John Tener	12	46	9	1	0	0	4	1	1	.196
Frank Dwyer	5	21	4	1	0	0	2	2	0	.190
		4,616	1,201	147	95	77	734	569	287	.260

1889

Record: 67–65
Finish: Third
Games Behind: 19
Manager: Cap Anson

The White Stockings finished a distant third behind New York and Boston in 1889 and, had it not been for the hitting of Cap Anson and Jimmy Ryan, would have tumbled into the second division. Anson batted .311, and Ryan hit .307 with 17 home runs, including six leading off a game, a National League record that remained in the books until late into the next century, when it was broken by Bobby Bonds of the San Francisco Giants in 1973.

Ryan, who was to have a brilliant 18-year big league career, 15 in Chicago, was among the first players to bat right-handed and throw left-handed. He was difficult to handle. Anson fined him repeatedly for his failure to run out a base hit. More often than not, he walked to first base.

The club was never in contention. The pitching was erratic, forcing Anson into a four-man rotation. There were three 16-game winners, rookie Bill Hutchison, Frank Dwyer, and Addison "Ad" Gumbert. John Tener was 15–15. Gus Krock, the pitching sensation of the previous year, had arm trouble, was 3–3, and was traded to Indianapolis early in the season. The White Stockings led the league in home runs and in one-run victories, winning 20 of these close encounters and losing 22.

Ned Williamson, an Anson stalwart, suffered a severe knee injury during a lengthy off-season "around the world tour," arranged by Al Spalding. The mishap occurred in Paris when he slid into a sharp stone on a sand and gravel playing surface. Popular with his teammates and an avid card player, Williamson appeared in only 47 games in 1889, his average dropping to .237, with only one home run. He played only one more season.

The National League had now been in existence for 14 years. Anson was among the five players who played every season. At this point, he led the league in total hits with 1,928 and had never batted below .308. There was only one significant rule change in 1889. Four called balls constituted a walk, same as today.

	W	L	ERA	G	GS	CG	IP	H	BB	K
Bill Hutchison	16	17	3.54	37	36	33	318	306	117	136
John Tener	15	15	3.64	35	30	28	287	302	105	105
Frank Dwyer	16	13	3.59	32	30	27	276	307	72	63
Ad Gumbert	16	13	3.62	31	28	25	246⅓	258	76	91
Gus Krock	3	3	4.90	7	7	5	60⅔	86	14	16
Egyptian Healy	1	4	4.50	5	5	5	46	48	18	22
Bill Bishop	0	0	18.00	2	0	0	3	6	6	1
	67	65	3.73	149	136	123	1,237	1,313	408	434

Shutouts: Hutchison 3, Gumbert 2, Tener 1.

	G	AB	H	2B	3B	HR	R	RBI	SB	AVG
Regulars										
1B Cap Anson	134	518	177	32	7	7	100	117	27	.342
2B Fred Pfeffer	134	531	121	15	7	7	85	77	45	.228
SS Ned Williamson	47	173	41	3	1	1	16	30	2	.237
3B Tom Burns	136	525	127	27	6	4	64	66	18	.242
RF Hugh Duffy	136	584	182	21	7	12	144	89	52	.312
CF Jimmy Ryan	135	576	187	31	14	17	140	72	45	.325
LF George Van Haltren	134	543	168	20	10	9	126	81	28	.309
C Duke Farrell	101	407	101	19	7	11	66	75	13	.248
Substitutes										
Charlie Bastian	46	155	21	0	0	0	19	10	1	.135
Ad Gumbert	41	153	44	3	2	7	30	29	2	.288
Dell Darling	36	120	23	1	1	0	14	7	5	.192
Silver Flint	15	56	13	1	0	0	6	9	1	.232
Pete Sommers	12	45	10	5	0	0	5	8	0	.222
Pitchers										
John Tener	42	150	41	4	2	1	18	19	2	.273
Frank Dwyer	36	135	27	1	1	1	14	6	0	.200
Bill Hutchison	37	133	21	1	1	1	14	7	2	.158
Gus Krock	7	24	4	0	0	0	4	2	0	.167
Egyptian Healy	5	20	2	0	0	0	2	1	0	.100
Bill Bishop	2	1	0	0	0	0	0	0	0	.000
		4,849	1,310	184	66	79	867	705	243	.270

1890

Record: 84–53
Finish: Second
Games Behind: 6
Manager: Cap Anson

The players revolted in 1890, the climax of a long-festering resentment against the policies of the owners. The reserve clause, which bound a player to a club for life—unless traded or sold—was the centerpiece of the dispute, which was fueled prior to the start of the season when management implemented a maximum salary scale according to grade: A—$2,500; B—$2,250; C—$2,000; D—$1,750; and E—$1,500.

Cap Anson lost a dozen players to the rival Players League,

among them front-liners Fred Pfeffer, Jimmy Ryan, Ned Williamson, Hugh Duffy, Charley Farrell, Frank Dwyer, John Tener, and George Van Haltren. The only established players who didn't jump were third baseman Tommy Burns and pitcher Bill Hutchison. Burns was rewarded for his loyalty. Eight years later he replaced Anson as the Chicago manager.

Confronted with the massive defection, Anson recruited younger players who were styled Cubs, Colts, and Babies. Eventually, the name Cubs stuck and became a term of endearment, quickly surpassing the original cognomen of White Stockings in popularity with the fans.

Never lower than fifth, the Cubs finished well, six games behind the Brooklyn Bridegrooms. As he had done so many times in the past, Anson led his team with a .312 average and 107 runs batted in, a number reconstructed after the RBI became an official statistic in 1920. Bill Hutchison, 42–25, anchored the pitching and won complete-game victories in both games of a Memorial Day doubleheader. Rookie Pat Luby won 20 games, including 17 in succession, a club record.

Anson, in his biography *A Ball Player's Career*, recalled the second-place finish with pride:

"It was an achievement to be proud of. The defections left me with a comparatively green team but long before the season came to a close constant practice had made it one of the best teams in the league. Few people, however, appreciate the amount of work that was necessary. I myself worked as hard as they did. I have never asked the men under my control to do anything that I was not willing to do myself. If we took a three-mile run, I was at their head setting the pace."

	W	L	ERA	G	GS	CG	IP	H	BB	K
Bill Hutchison	(42)	25	2.70	(71)	(66)	(65)	(603)	505	199	289
Pat Luby	20	9	3.19	34	31	26	267⅔	226	95	85
Ed Stein	12	6	3.81	20	18	14	160⅔	147	83	65
Mike Sullivan	5	6	4.59	12	12	10	96	108	58	33
Roscoe Coughlin	4	4	4.26	11	10	10	95	102	40	29
Bob Gibson	1	0	0.00	1	1	1	9	6	2	1
Fred Demarris	0	0	0.00	1	0	0	2	1	1	1
Ed Eiteljorg	0	1	22.50	1	1	0	2	5	1	1
Ossie France	0	0	13.50	1	0	0	2	3	2	0
	84	51	3.24	152	139	126	1,237⅓	1,103	481	504

Shutouts: Hutchison 5, Stein 1.

	G	AB	H	2B	3B	HR	R	RBI	SB	AVG
Regulars										
1B Cap Anson	139	504	157	14	5	7	95	107	29	.312
2B Bob Glenalvin	66	250	67	10	3	4	43	26	30	.268
SS Jimmy Cooney	135	574	156	19	10	4	114	52	45	.272
3B Tom Burns	139	538	149	16	6	6	86	86	44	.277
RF Jim Andrews	53	202	38	4	2	3	32	17	11	.188
CF Walt Wilmot	139	571	159	15	12	(14)	114	99	76	.278
LF Cliff Carroll	136	(582)	166	16	6	7	134	65	34	.285
C Malachi Kittredge	96	333	67	8	3	3	46	35	7	.201
Substitutes										
Pete O'Brien	27	106	30	7	0	3	15	16	4	.283
Ed Hutchinson	4	17	1	1	0	0	0	0	0	.059
Pat Wright	1	2	0	0	0	0	0	0	0	.000
Howard Earl	92	384	95	10	3	6	57	51	17	.247
Elmer Foster	27	105	26	4	2	5	20	23	18	.248
Pop Lytle	1	4	0	0	0	0	1	0	0	.000
Tom Nagle	38	144	39	5	1	1	21	11	4	.271
Jake Stenzel	11	41	11	1	0	0	3	3	0	.268
Chuck Lauer	2	8	2	1	0	0	1	2	0	.250
Marty Honan	1	3	0	0	0	0	0	1	0	.000
Pitchers										
Bill Hutchison	71	261	53	7	2	2	28	27	6	.203
Pat Luby	36	116	31	5	3	3	27	17	3	.267
Ed Stein	20	59	9	1	0	0	4	7	1	.153
Mike Sullivan	12	40	5	1	0	0	1	7	0	.125
Roscoe Coughlin	11	39	10	1	1	0	5	1	0	.256
Bob Gibson	1	4	0	0	0	0	0	0	0	.000
Fred Demarris	1	2	0	0	0	0	0	0	0	.000
Ed Eiteljorg	1	1	0	0	0	0	0	0	0	.000
Ossie France	1	1	0	0	0	0	0	0	0	.000
		4,891	1,271	146	59	68	847	653	329	.260

1891

Record: 82–53

Finish: Second

Games Behind: 3½

Manager: Cap Anson

The Players League, also known as the Brotherhood, collapsed after one season. Outfielder Jimmy Ryan, second baseman Fred Pfeffer, and pitcher Ad Gumbert rejoined Anson in 1891. Unlike Pfeffer, who remained a staunch unionist, Ryan was disillusioned by the experience and said in an interview:

"Let the men who put up the capital manage the game, and let the men who do the playing get paid for it and keep still. This is all any ballplayer should ask. There is one thing certain and that is that I will not play again under the same conditions."

Ryan's average dropped to .287, but on July 1, in a 9–3 victory over Detroit, he became the only Cub player to twice hit for the cycle. A career .253 hitter, Pfeffer batted .247 and continued his outstanding work in the field; he was generally considered the best defensive second baseman of his time. Gumbert was 17–11. For the second consecutive season, Bill Hutchison led the league in wins with 43; appearances, 66; starts, 58; complete games, 56; and innings, 561.

Third baseman Bill Dahlen, another Anson find who was born in Nellistown, New York, not far from Cooperstown, was among the newcomers. Dahlen hit .263 and had a strong and accurate arm but was unsure in the field. He was high-strung and stubborn, repeatedly ejected by the umpires, and seemed to enjoy agitating Anson. He was a heavy bettor, on the horses, and constantly sought salary advances. Despite these faults, "Bad Bill" had an eight-year Chicago career.

Anson, 40 in April, was showing signs of his age. He batted .291, his first season under .300. Some sportwriters began calling him Pop and the Old Man, suggesting it was time for a younger player to take over first base.

Irritated, Anson mocked his critics by playing an entire game in masquerade, wearing a shaggy gray wig and a long gray false beard. "The Captain knows he is not a youngster," one of his admirers wrote "but he also knows his years do not weigh on him. He is well able to run, bat, and play ball generally as well as any of his Colts."

His team, more experienced than Anson publicly acknowledged, held first place during 15 weeks of the 24-week season. Going into the final week the Colts had the pennant in their grasp, but they were unable to hang on. They lost two out of three to Cleveland and three more to last-place Cincinnati. Boston finished first, 3½ games ahead.

It was a crushing blow to Anson—his nine previously had beaten the Cleveland and Cincinnati clubs with ease. But Anson had suffered a much more significant and distressing defeat seven months earlier, in April, when Al Spalding resigned as the club president and chose James A. Hart to succeed him.

	W	L	ERA	G	GS	CG	IP	H	BB	K
Bill Hutchison	(43)	19	2.81	(66)	(58)	(56)	(561)	(508)	178	261
Ad Gumbert	17	11	3.58	32	31	24	256⅓	282	90	73
Pat Luby	8	11	4.76	30	24	18	206	221	94	52
Ed Stein	7	6	3.74	14	10	9	101	99	57	38
Tom Vickery	5	5	4.07	14	12	7	79⅔	72	44	39
George Nicol	0	1	4.91	3	2	0	11	14	10	12
Jimmy Ryan	0	0	1.59	2	0	0	5⅔	11	2	2
	80	53	3.47	161	137	114	1,220⅔	1,207	475	477

Shutouts: Hutchison 4, Gumbert 1, Stein 1.

	G	AB	H	2B	3B	HR	R	RBI	SB	AVG
Regulars										
1B Cap Anson	136	540	157	24	8	8	81	(120)	17	.291
2B Fred Pfeffer	137	498	123	12	9	7	93	77	40	.247
SS Jimmy Cooney	118	465	114	15	3	0	84	42	21	.245
3B Bill Dahlen	135	551	145	20	13	9	116	76	29	.263
RF Cliff Carroll	130	515	132	20	8	7	87	80	31	.256
CF Jimmy Ryan	118	505	145	22	15	9	110	66	27	.287
LF Walt Wilmot	121	498	139	14	10	11	102	71	42	.279
C Malachi Kittredge	79	296	62	8	5	2	26	27	4	.209
Substitutes										
Tom Burns	59	243	55	8	1	1	36	17	18	.226
Elmer Foster	4	16	3	0	0	1	3	1	1	.188
Pop Schriver	27	90	30	1	4	1	15	21	1	.333
Bill Bowman	15	45	4	1	0	0	2	5	0	.089
Bill Merritt	11	42	9	1	0	0	4	4	0	.214
Tom Nagle	8	25	3	0	0	0	3	1	0	.120
Marty Honan	5	12	2	0	0	1	1	3	0	.167
Pitchers										
Bill Hutchison	67	243	45	4	2	2	27	25	5	.185
Ad Gumbert	34	105	32	7	4	0	18	16	4	.305
Pat Luby	32	98	24	2	4	2	19	24	3	.245
Ed Stein	14	43	7	1	0	0	4	4	0	.163
Tom Vickery	14	39	7	1	0	0	3	1	3	.179
George Nicol	3	6	2	0	1	0	0	3	0	.333
		4,875	1,240	161	87	61	834	684	246	.254

1892

Record: 70–76

Finish: Seventh

Games Behind: 30

Manager: Cap Anson

New club president James Hart, who had been the field manager of the Louisville and Boston clubs, was Cap Anson's principal rival and had been the business manager of the American phase of Al Spalding's world tour. When Spalding suggested that everyone chip in to purchase a gift for

Hart, specifically a pair of diamond buttons, Anson refused to participate and, with characteristic bluntness, said, "He was paid a salary and expenses. I see no reason for such a valuable gift."

Spalding was aware Anson would be astonished when he named Hart his successor and wrote Anson a conciliatory letter insisting Hart was a figurehead. But Anson realized his position had been weakened. He was no longer second in command. The disastrous 1892 season contributed to Anson's insecurity.

Because of the addition of four new clubs, absorbed from the defunct American Association, the National League expanded to 12 teams and played a split season for the first and only time (except for the strike-interrupted 1981 campaign). The Colts finished eighth in the first half and seventh in the second, with a combined 70–76 won-loss record. It was Anson's first experience with a club unable to win half its games.

Bill Hutchison, for the third year in a row, led the league in victories, 37; starts, 71; complete games, 67; and innings, 627. He also lost 34 games and was only three games better than a .500 pitcher. Anson's secondary starters, Ad Gumbert and Pat Luby, combined, were 32–36. There were no .300 hitters. Bill Dahlen's .295 led the club. Anson was fourth at .272.

The season apparently was marred by destructive behavior. The editor of the *Spalding Guide* was moved to write:

"Drunkenness and bummerism are atrocious evils among players who are paid three and four times the money they could possibly earn in ordinary avocations. When a man is paid $300 to $500 per month for five months of enjoyable sport—say, 60 games in all—or an average of $30 per game—with his traveling expenses borne by the club, and himself carted about the country in palace cars and fed at first-class hotels, the least he can do is present himself on the field in fit condition to render something near an equivalent for such extravagant compensation."

The *Guide* was also critical of the focus on batting averages, which, same as today, are not always an accurate measure of a player's value. Also deplored was the increased emphasis on the home run, which was described as a "showy" hit:

"The poorest batsman, in doing team work, seldom gets the best position in the record of batting averages. But the most valuable men are those instrumental in sending runners around the diamond. The batsman who goes through the ordeal of making a 120-yard spurt secures that one run at the loss and cost of considerable strength, while the batsmen, who, by a single safe hit, sends a runner home from third benefits the side just as much as the batsman did with the showy hit, but at one-fourth the cost of the fatigue sustained in the home run hit."

	W	L	ERA	G	GS	CG	IP	H	BB	K
Bill Hutchison	(37)	34	2.74	(75)	(71)	(67)	(627)	572	187	316
Ad Gumbert	22	19	3.41	46	45	39	382⅔	399	107	118
Pat Luby	10	17	3.13	31	26	24	247⅓	247	106	64
Harry DeMiller	1	1	6.38	4	2	2	24	29	16	15
George Meakim	0	1	11.00	1	1	1	9	18	2	0
Frank Griffith	0	1	11.25	1	1	0	4	3	6	3
John Hollison	0	0	2.25	1	0	0	4	1	0	2

Shutouts: Hutchison 5, Luby 1.

	G	AB	H	2B	3B	HR	R	RBI	SB	AVG
Regulars										
1B Cap Anson	146	559	152	25	9	1	62	74	13	.272
2B Jimmy Canavan	118	439	73	10	11	0	48	32	33	.166
SS Bill Dahlen	143	587	173	23	19	5	116	58	60	.295
3B Jiggs Parrott	78	335	72	9	5	2	40	22	7	.215
RF Sam Dungan	113	433	123	19	7	0	46	53	15	.284
CF Jimmy Ryan	128	505	148	21	11	10	105	65	27	.293
LF Walt Wilmot	92	380	82	7	7	2	47	35	31	.216
C Pop Schriver	92	326	73	10	6	1	40	34	4	.224
Substitutes										
Jimmy Cooney	65	238	41	1	0	0	18	20	10	.172
Jim Connor	9	34	2	0	0	0	0	0	0	.059
Fred Roat	8	31	6	0	1	0	4	2	2	.194
George Decker	78	291	66	6	7	1	32	28	9	.227
Pat Luby	45	163	31	3	2	2	14	20	3	.190
Charlie Newman	16	61	10	0	0	0	4	2	2	.164
Malachi Kittredge	69	229	41	5	0	0	19	10	2	.179
Pitchers										
Bill Hutchison	77	263	57	10	5	1	23	22	8	.217
Ad Gumbert	52	178	42	1	2	1	18	8	5	.236
Harry DeMiller	4	10	3	0	0	0	2	5	2	.300
George Meakim	1	5	2	0	0	0	1	2	0	.400
John Hollison	1	3	0	0	0	0	0	0	0	.000
Frank Griffith	1	1	0	0	0	0	0	0	0	.000
	5,071	1,197	150	92	26	639	492	233	.236

1893

Record: 56–71
Finish: Ninth
Games Behind: 29
Manager: Cap Anson

The split season was abandoned in 1893. The Colts never challenged and dropped to ninth, their lowest finish. They didn't stir until September, their only winning month, when they won 14 of 22 decisions. Otherwise there wasn't much for the Chicago cranks to cheer about—except the debut of Wild Bill Lange, who led the club in stolen bases with 47 and in home runs with eight. Lange hit .281 and drove in 88 runs, three fewer than Anson

Lange was powerfully built, 6 feet, 2 inches and 195 pounds, huge for his time, and was among the most popular players of the 19th century. A center fielder, Lange made several catches that have since entered the realm of folklore. Fleet of foot, he stole bases so freely that nearly every single seemed as good as a double.

Some of his success on the base paths could be laid to his size. Few were the second basemen who held their ground when Big Bill came whirling into the bag. Al Spink, founding editor of *The Sporting News*, remembered Lange as "Ty Cobb enlarged, fully as great in speed, batting skill, and base running."

The Colts had another noteworthy rookie, Clark Griffith, who later jumped to Charles A. Comiskey's crosstown White Sox and for many years after that was the owner of the Washington Senators. A right-hander, Griffith started two games and worked only 19⅔ innings. The next season he won 21, the first in a run of six consecutive 20-win seasons.

It was a landmark year in baseball history. In a successful effort to fuel the offense and blunt the effect of the "cyclone" pitchers—now known as power pitchers—the mound was set back from 55 feet to 60 feet, 6 inches, a distance that remains to this day. The change-up, designed to upset the batter's timing, began to flourish, but it was now necessary for the pitchers to make adjustments on their curveballs so they crossed the plate in the strike zone. The increased distance was a boon for the catchers and reduced the number of passed balls.

Groping for an effective rotation, Cap Anson was constantly experimenting and used 12 starters. His top three pitchers—Bill Hutchison, Willie McGill, and Hal Mauck—were unable to win half their decisions. Hutchison, previously the star of the staff, was 16–23. The Colts finished 29 games behind first-place Boston.

	W	L	ERA	G	GS	CG	IP	H	BB	K
Bill Hutchison	16	23	4.75	44	40	38	348⅓	420	156	80
Willie McGill	17	18	4.61	39	34	26	302⅔	311	181	91
Hal Mauck	8	10	4.41	23	18	12	143	168	60	23
Fritz Clausen	6	2	3.08	10	9	8	76	71	39	31
Gus McGinnis	2	5	5.35	13	5	3	67⅓	85	31	13
Bert Abbey	2	4	5.46	7	7	5	56	74	20	6
Frank Donnelly	3	1	5.36	7	5	3	42	51	17	6
Tom Parrott	0	3	6.67	4	3	2	27	35	17	7
Clark Griffith	1	1	5.03	4	2	2	19⅔	24	5	9
Sam Shaw	1	0	5.63	2	2	1	16	12	13	1
Jim Hughey	0	1	11.00	2	2	1	9	14	3	4
Jimmy Ryan	0	0	0.00	1	0	0	4⅔	3	0	1
Gus Yost	0	1	13.50	1	1	0	2⅔	3	8	1
Doc Parker	0	0	13.50	1	0	0	2	5	1	0
Abe Johnson	0	0	36.00	1	0	0	1	2	2	0
	56	69	4.81	159	128	101	1,117⅓	1,278	553	273

Shutouts: Hutchison 2, McGill 1, Mauck 1.

	G	AB	H	2B	3B	HR	R	RBI	SB	AVG
Regulars										
1B Cap Anson	103	398	125	24	2	0	70	91	13	.314
2B Bill Lange	117	469	132	8	7	8	92	88	47	.281
SS Bill Dahlen	116	485	146	28	15	5	113	64	31	.301
3B Jiggs Parrott	110	455	111	10	9	1	54	65	25	.244
RF Sam Dungan	107	465	138	23	7	2	86	64	11	.297
CF Jimmy Ryan	83	341	102	21	7	3	82	30	8	.299
LF Walt Wilmot	94	392	118	14	14	3	69	61	39	.301
C Malachi Kittredge	70	255	59	9	5	2	32	30	3	.231
Substitutes										
Llewellan Camp	38	156	41	7	7	2	37	17	30	.263
Charlie Irwin	21	82	25	6	2	0	14	13	4	.305
Bob Glenalvin	16	61	21	3	1	0	11	12	7	.344
Tom Parrott	7	27	7	1	0	0	4	3	0	.259
Bad Bill Eagan	6	19	5	0	0	0	3	2	4	.263
John O'Brien	4	14	5	0	1	0	3	1	0	.357
George Decker	81	328	89	9	8	2	57	48	22	.271
Henry Lynch	4	14	3	2	0	0	0	2	0	.214
Bob Caruthers	1	3	0	0	0	0	0	0	0	.000
Pop Schriver	64	229	65	8	3	4	49	34	4	.284
Pitchers										
Bill Hutchison	46	162	41	7	3	0	14	25	2	.253
Willie McGill	40	124	29	4	0	0	18	13	5	.234
Hal Mauck	23	61	9	0	0	0	2	4	0	.148
Fritz Clausen	10	33	4	0	0	0	2	0	0	.121
Bert Abbey	7	26	6	1	0	0	2	2	0	.231
Gus McGinnis	13	25	6	0	0	0	8	7	0	.240
Frank Donnelly	7	18	8	1	2	0	4	3	0	.444
Clark Griffith	4	11	2	0	0	0	1	2	0	.182
Sam Shaw	2	7	2	0	0	0	1	1	0	.286
Jim Hughey	2	2	0	0	0	0	1	0	0	.000
Doc Parker	1	1	0	0	0	0	0	0	0	.000
Gus Yost	1	1	0	0	0	0	0	0	0	.000
Abe Johnson	1	0	0	0	0	0	0	0	0	—
		4,664	1,299	186	93	32	829	682	255	.279

1894

Record: 57–75
Finish: Eighth
Games Behind: 34
Manager: Cap Anson

It was another dreary season in 1894, an eighth-place finish, 34 games behind Baltimore, which won its first National League pennant. Of the 12 clubs, only Cap Anson's Colts never set foot in the first division. They lost eight of their first nine games, a dismal .111 percentage, revived somewhat in July and August when they were 31–22, but had a 9–17 record in September.

It was a spectacular season for shortstop Bill Dahlen, an aggressive fielder whose career total of 972 errors remains a major league record. Dahlen batted safely in 42 consecutive games, from June 20 to August 7. After being held hitless on August 7—when the Cincinnati duo of Chauncey Fisher and Tom Parrott silenced him in six at bats—Dahlen immediately began another streak of 28 games, broken by Brooklyn's Connie Lucid on September 15.

A lifetime .274 hitter, the son of a masonry contractor, Dahlen batted .398 in the first streak, .415 in the second. His overall records for the 71-game sequence included a .397 batting average, 96 runs scored, and 56 runs driven in. His 42-game streak, then a record, was topped three years later by Willie Keeler, who hit safely in 44 consecutive games.

Dahlen hit .362 for the season, high on the Colts but ranked only 17th among players with more than 300 at bats. The effect of the extended pitching distance had more than the desired effect. The cumulative league average, .245 in 1892, soared to an unparalleled .309. Philadelphia had a team average of .349, never since approached. Four players hit .400 or better. Hugh Duffy of Boston was the leader at .438, still the all-time one-season major league record.

The new pitching distance diminished the effectiveness of the "cyclone" pitchers and helped give birth to what was described as the scientific style. The pitchers who had relied on "dangerous" speed for their success were forced to add a variety of breaking balls to their repertoire.

A notable feat was achieved by William "Pop" Schriver, the Chicago catcher, who caught a ball thrown from the top of the Washington Monument. Colt pitchers Hutchison and Griffith went to the top of the shaft. After allowing a practice ball to bounce on the ground, Schriver caught the second ball. It was an unprecedented exploit, equaled 14 years later by Charles "Gabby" Street of the Washington club.

	W	L	ERA	G	GS	CG	IP	H	BB	K
Bill Hutchison	14	15	6.06	36	34	28	277⅔	373	140	59
Clark Griffith	21	11	4.92	36	30	28	261⅓	328	85	71
Willie McGill	7	19	5.84	27	23	22	208	272	117	58
Adonis Terry	5	11	5.84	23	21	16	163⅓	232	123	39
Scott Stratton	8	5	6.03	15	12	11	119⅓	198	40	23
Bert Abbey	2	7	5.18	11	11	10	92	119	37	24
Kid Camp	0	1	6.55	3	2	2	22	34	12	6
Fritz Clausen	0	1	10.38	1	1	0	4⅓	5	3	1
	57	70	5.68	152	134	117	1,148	1,561	557	281

Shutouts: None.

	G	AB	H	2B	3B	HR	R	RBI	SB	AVG
Regulars										
1B Cap Anson	83	347	137	28	4	5	82	99	17	.395
2B Jiggs Parrott	127	532	139	17	9	3	83	64	30	.261
SS Bill Dahlen	121	508	184	32	14	15	150	107	42	.362
3B Charlie Irwin	128	498	144	24	9	8	84	95	35	.289
RF Jimmy Ryan	108	481	173	37	7	3	133	62	11	.360
CF Bill Lange	111	442	145	16	9	6	84	90	65	.328
LF Walt Wilmot	133	597	197	45	12	5	134	130	74	.330
C Pop Schriver	96	349	96	12	3	3	55	47	9	.275
Substitutes										
George Decker	91	384	120	17	6	8	74	92	23	.313
Llewellan Camp	8	33	6	2	0	0	1	1	0	.182
John Houseman	4	15	6	3	1	0	5	4	2	.400
Scott Stratton	23	96	36	5	4	3	29	23	3	.375
Adonis Terry	30	95	33	4	2	0	19	17	3	.347
Sam Dungan	10	39	9	2	0	0	5	3	1	.231
Malachi Kittredge	51	168	53	8	2	0	36	23	2	.315
Pitchers										
Clark Griffith	46	142	33	5	4	0	27	15	6	.232
Bill Hutchison	39	136	42	3	0	6	30	16	2	.309
Willie McGill	27	82	20	5	0	0	10	3	1	.244
Bert Abbey	11	39	5	0	0	0	3	4	1	.128
Kid Camp	3	11	0	0	0	0	0	0	0	.000
Fritz Clausen	1	1	0	0	0	0	0	0	0	.000
		4,995	1,578	265	86	65	1,044	895	327	.316

1895

Record: 72–58
Finish: Fourth
Games Behind: 15
Manager: Cap Anson

Instead of being arrested for another season of erratic play in 1895, the Colts drew the wrath of the Sunday Observance League and were almost jailed for violating the Sabbath. Play was stopped in the third inning of a June 23 game against Cleveland, and a court order was issued for "aiding and abetting the forming of a noisy crowd on a Sunday." Club president James Hart posted bail, and the Colts were allowed to finish the game. They won 13–4.

Bill Lange had his best season. He led the league in fewest strikeouts, four; batted .389, still the club record; and stole 67 bases. The darling of the Chicago fans, Lange also led in feminine companions. He was the idol of ladies of every age and according to published reports had enough correspondence to form a lonely hearts club. Every day in the clubhouse scented letters, usually on pink paper, awaited his arrival.

Chicago had three other .300 hitters: Rookie third baseman Bill Everitt hit .358, the first of his five consecutive .300 seasons. Anson batted .335, Jimmy Ryan .323. The offense, nonetheless, was inadequate. The Colts scored 867 runs, seventh lowest production in the league. Shortstop Dahlen, last year's hero, struggled throughout. His average dropped 89 points to .273. He was also charged with a league-leading 86 errors.

Clark Griffith led the pitchers with a 25–13 record. Bill "Adonis" Terry was 21–14. Bill Hutchison, fading badly and soon to retire, was 13–21; worse, he was 1–8 against the bottom four clubs. Five pitchers divided the other 12 victories. In a rare rule change that helped the pitchers, a foul tip was now classified as a strike.

The Colts finished fourth, snapping a string of five second-division finishes. They were 72–58 overall, 14 games above .500, but were never in serious contention despite a good showing in the September stretch, 15 wins and only eight losses, and had a record home gate of 382,299 which in-

cluded 22,913 paid admissions in the afternoon game of a July 4 doubleheader against Cincinnati. It was the first Chicago crowd in excess of 20,000.

The annual lament continued against batting averages as the primary index of offensive excellence. "The only true test of effective batting," wrote the editor of the *Spalding Guide*, "is that which yields the highest percentage of runners forwarded by base hits. A 'slugging' batsman may have three three-baggers in a game yet not forward a single runner but another batsman may forward three base runners by a single base hit and would only have the slightest credit."

	W	L	ERA	G	GS	CG	IP	H	BB	K
Clark Griffith	25	13	3.93	42	41	39	353	434	91	79
Adonis Terry	21	14	4.80	38	34	31	311⅓	346	131	88
Bill Hutchison	13	21	4.73	38	35	30	291	371	129	85
Doc Parker	4	2	3.68	7	6	5	51⅓	65	9	9
Danny Friend	2	2	5.27	5	5	5	41	50	14	10
Walter Thornton	2	0	6.08	7	2	2	40	58	31	13
Scott Stratton	2	3	9.60	5	5	3	30	51	14	4
Monte McFarland	2	0	5.14	2	2	2	14	21	5	5
John Dolan	0	1	6.55	2	2	1	11	16	6	1
Bert Abbey	0	1	4.50	1	1	1	8	10	2	3
	71	57	4.67	147	133	119	1,150⅔	1,422	432	297

Shutouts: Hutchison 2, Parker 1.

	G	AB	H	2B	3B	HR	R	RBI	SB	AVG
Regulars										
1B Cap Anson	122	474	159	23	6	2	87	91	12	.335
2B Ace Stewart	97	365	88	8	10	8	52	76	14	.241
SS Bill Dahlen	129	509	139	19	10	7	107	62	38	.273
3B Bill Everitt	133	550	197	16	10	3	129	88	47	.358
RF Jimmy Ryan	108	443	143	22	8	6	83	49	18	.323
CF Bill Lange	123	478	186	27	16	10	120	98	67	.389
LF Walt Wilmot	108	466	132	16	6	8	86	72	28	.283
C Tim Donahue	63	219	59	9	1	2	29	36	5	.269
Substitutes										
Harry Truby	33	119	40	3	0	0	17	16	7	.336
Charlie Irwin	3	10	2	0	0	0	4	0	0	.200
George Decker	73	297	82	9	7	2	51	41	11	.276
Scott Stratton	10	24	7	1	1	0	3	2	1	.292
Jiggs Parrott	3	4	1	0	0	0	0	0	0	.250
Malachi Kittredge	60	212	48	6	3	3	30	29	6	.226
Bill Moran	15	55	9	2	1	1	8	9	2	.164
Pitchers										
Clark Griffith	43	144	46	3	0	1	20	27	2	.319
Adonis Terry	40	137	30	3	2	1	18	10	1	.219
Bill Hutchison	38	126	25	3	3	0	12	11	1	.198
Doc Parker	7	22	7	0	1	0	3	2	0	.318
Walter Thornton	8	22	7	1	0	1	4	7	0	.318
Danny Friend	5	17	4	0	0	0	4	1	0	.235
Monte McFarland	2	7	1	0	0	0	0	0	0	.143
Bert Abbey	1	3	1	0	0	0	0	0	0	.333
John Dolan	2	3	0	0	0	0	0	0	0	.000
		4,706	1,413	171	85	55	867	727	260	.300

1896

Record: 71–57
Finish: Fifth
Games Behind: 18½
Manager: Cap Anson

At the finish of the 1895 season, Cap Anson predicted, "We'll win next year." Aware his managerial tenure was coming to a close and in the belief braggadocio was now a necessity, or simply the victim of wishful thinking, Anson insisted better days were ahead. He was wrong. The Colts dropped one notch in 1896, into fifth place, 18½ games behind the Baltimore Orioles, who won their third successive flag, an achievement previously accomplished only by Anson's White Stockings and the Boston Beaneaters.

It was farewell to Bill Hutchison who went to St. Louis, won one game, and retired. Clark Griffith was now Anson's established pitching star and had a 22–13 record. Unlike his fellow moundsmen, Griffith had excellent success against the first-division clubs, winning 10 of 15 of these encounters. Rookie Danny Friend, Anson's number-two starter, was 18–14 but was 5–6 in head-to-head competition against the tailenders.

The Colts batted a robust .288, but it was still two points below the league average. They had five .300 hitters—Dahlen led at .361, followed by Anson, .331; Lange, .326; Everitt, .320; and Ryan, .312. In the original stats, Lange had 100 stolen bases, but researchers have since insisted he had only 84 steals. Whatever, Lange and Dahlen, who hit nine home runs, were the only Chicago players among the league leaders in any of the offensive categories.

Chicago fattened up against the weaker teams, a combined 18–6 over St. Louis and Louisville, the bottom two clubs, and were 11–1 against sixth-place Pittsburgh. But Cleveland, which finished second to Baltimore, was 9–2 against Anson's men. The Colts were 6–5 in April, for them a good start, but were under .500 going into June.

They played their best ball in July when they won 20 of 27 games. Among these 20 victories was a 9–8 July 13 triumph over Philadelphia in which Ed Delahanty, "The King of Swat," drove in all but one of the Phillies' runs with four home runs and a single—17 total bases. Two of the home runs cleared the fence, one soaring over the scoreboard in right center, which according to the *Chicago Tribune,* was the longest blow of the year at the Chicago grounds. The fans stood on their chairs and cheered the visiting slugger. The roar of the crowd didn't subside until Delahanty boarded the Philadelphia omnibus.

	W	L	ERA	G	GS	CG	IP	H	BB	K
Clark Griffith	22	13	3.54	36	35	35	317⅔	370	70	81
Danny Friend	18	14	4.74	36	33	28	290⅔	298	139	86
Adonis Terry	15	13	4.28	30	28	25	235⅓	268	88	74
Buttons Briggs	12	8	4.31	26	21	19	194	202	108	84
Doc Parker	1	5	6.16	9	7	7	73	100	27	15
Monte McFarland	0	4	7.20	4	3	2	25	32	21	3
Walter Thornton	2	1	5.70	5	5	2	23⅔	30	13	10
Malachi Kittredge	0	0	5.40	1	0	0	1⅔	2	1	0
	70	58	4.41	147	132	118	1,161	1,302	467	353

Shutouts: Friend 1, Terry 1.

	G	AB	H	2B	3B	HR	R	RBI	SB	AVG
Regulars										
1B Cap Anson	108	402	133	18	2	2	72	90	24	.331
2B Fred Pfeffer	94	360	88	16	7	2	45	52	22	.244
SS Bill Dahlen	125	476	172	30	19	9	153	74	51	.361
3B Bill Everitt	132	575	184	16	13	2	130	46	46	.320
RF Jimmy Ryan	128	490	153	24	10	3	83	86	29	.312
CF Bill Lange	122	469	153	21	16	4	114	92	84	.326
LF George Decker	107	421	118	23	11	5	68	61	20	.280
C Malachi Kittredge	65	215	48	4	1	1	17	19	6	.223
Substitutes										
Barry McCormick	45	168	37	3	1	1	22	23	9	.220
Harry Truby	29	109	28	2	2	2	13	31	4	.257
Josh Reilly	9	42	9	1	0	0	6	2	2	.214
George Flynn	29	106	27	1	2	0	15	4	12	.255
Algie McBride	9	29	7	1	1	1	2	7	0	.241
Walter Thornton	9	22	8	0	1	0	6	1	2	.364
Tim Donahue	57	188	41	10	1	0	27	20	11	.218
Con Daily	9	27	2	0	0	0	1	1	1	.074
Pitchers										
Clark Griffith	38	135	36	5	2	1	22	16	3	.267
Danny Friend	37	126	30	3	3	1	12	10	2	.238
Adonis Terry	30	99	26	4	2	0	14	15	4	.263
Buttons Briggs	26	78	10	0	2	0	5	6	0	.128
Doc Parker	10	36	10	0	1	0	4	4	0	.278
Monte McFarland	4	12	0	0	0	0	0	0	0	.000
	4,585	1,320	182	97	34	831	660	332	.288

1897

Record: 59–73
Finish: Ninth
Games Behind: 34
Manager: Cap Anson

The Colts finished ninth, 34 games out of first place. Cap Anson, in his autobiography, reflects on the 1897 season and his dismissal, a tale of woe:

"The team with which I started out was certainly good enough to win the pennant, or finish in the front rank. That it failed to do so can only be explained by the underhanded work by some of the players looking toward my downfall. They were aided and abetted by President Hart who refused to enforce the fines levied by myself as manager and in that way belittling my authority and making it impossible to enforce the discipline necessary to making the team a success.

"Lack of discipline and insubordination began to show from the start. Fines were remitted in spite of all the protests that I could make, several members of the club being allowed to do about as they pleased. There could be but one result: poor ball playing. The ringleader in this business was Jimmy Ryan, between whom and the Club's President the most perfect understanding seemed to exist, and for this underhanded work Ryan was rewarded by being made the team captain.

"Late that fall the newspapers published articles that I was to be released but as no official notice to that effect had been served on me, and as I was conscious of always having done my duty by the organization of which I was a stockholder, I for some time paid no attention to the matter. From mere rumors, these newspaper articles took a more definite form, coupled with references to my management of the team that were, to say the least, both uncalled for and venomous."

Anson was with the Chicago club for 22 years, all as a player, 19 as a player-manager. Until Babe Ruth he was the most widely known player in the game. His clubs won five pennants and finished second four times. Twice he hit over .400 and only twice under .300. Using a heavy bat, never over-swinging, and content to meet the ball, he was the first player with 3,000 hits. He had a .337 lifetime average; a century later it was adjusted to .300. He was succeeded by Tommy Burns, his one-time infielder.

	W	L	ERA	G	GS	CG	IP	H	BB	K
Clark Griffith	21	19	3.72	41	38	(38)	343⅔	410	86	102
Danny Friend	12	11	4.52	24	24	23	203	244	86	58
Nixey Callahan	12	9	4.03	23	22	21	189⅔	221	55	52
Buttons Briggs	4	17	5.26	22	22	21	186⅔	246	85	60
Walter Thornton	6	7	4.70	16	16	15	130⅓	164	51	55
Roger Denzer	2	8	5.13	12	10	8	94⅔	125	34	17
Jim Korwan	1	2	5.82	5	4	3	34	47	28	12
Adonis Terry	0	1	10.13	1	1	1	8	11	6	1
Dave Wright	1	0	15.43	1	1	1	7	17	2	4
	59	74	4.53	145	138	131	1,197	1,485	433	361

Shutouts: Callahan 1, Griffith 1.

	G	AB	H	2B	3B	HR	R	RBI	SB	AVG
Regulars										
1B Cap Anson	114	424	128	17	3	3	67	75	11	.302
2B Jim Connor	77	285	83	10	5	3	40	38	10	.291
SS Bill Dahlen	75	277	82	18	8	6	67	40	15	.296
3B Bill Everitt	92	379	119	14	7	5	63	39	26	.314
RF Jimmy Ryan	136	520	160	33	17	5	103	85	27	.308
CF Bill Lange	118	479	163	24	14	5	119	83	(73)	.340
LF George Decker	111	428	124	12	7	5	72	63	11	.290
C Malachi Kittredge	79	262	53	5	5	1	25	30	9	.202
Substitutes										
Barry McCormick	101	419	112	8	10	2	87	55	44	.267
Nixey Callahan	94	360	105	18	6	3	60	47	12	.292
Fred Pfeffer	32	114	26	0	1	0	10	11	5	.228
Walter Thornton	75	265	85	9	6	0	39	55	13	.321
Tom Hernon	4	16	1	0	0	0	2	2	1	.063
Tim Donahue	58	188	45	7	3	0	28	21	3	.239
Pitchers										
Clark Griffith	46	162	38	8	4	0	27	21	2	.235
Danny Friend	25	88	25	5	0	0	12	9	1	.284
Buttons Briggs	22	81	13	0	1	0	5	5	1	.160
Roger Denzer	12	39	6	1	0	0	4	1	0	.154
Jim Korwan	5	12	0	0	0	0	0	0	0	.000
Adonis Terry	1	3	0	0	0	0	1	0	0	.000
Dave Wright	1	3	1	0	0	0	1	1	0	.333
		4,804	1,369	189	97	38	832	681	264	.285

1898

Record: 85–64
Finish: Fourth
Games Behind: 17⅓
Manager: Tom Burns

The left-handed-hitting Bill Everitt, who had been playing third, replaced Anson at first base and batted .319. Lange also hit .319. Jimmy Ryan, the new team captain, was the only other .300 hitter; his .323 led the club. Ryan also led in runs, 122; triples, 13; and stolen bases, 29.

Because they had lost their Pop the club had a new nickname, Anson's Orphans. They also had a much improved pitching staff that was responsible for a surprisingly successful 1898 season: fourth place, 20 games over .500 with an 85–65 record, 17½ games behind the pennant-winning Boston nine. It was Chicago's best showing in eight years.

It is not clear whether Al Spalding bought Cap Anson's small block of stock in the club—130 shares, all available for purchase. If he did, the indications are that he paid little, if anything. "My confidence in A. G. Spalding has dwindled away to nothing," Anson wrote three years later. When Spalding, still posing as a pal, began planning a fund-raising testi-

monial dinner, Anson refused to cooperate. "I am not a pauper," he said. "The public owes me nothing."

Just as Spalding's sporting goods empire was expanding, so were his baseball profits. For the first time the club had a home gate in excess of 400,000. Attendance was rising. The *Spalding Guide* reported that at the games played in Chicago, Cleveland, and St. Louis on June 19, "there was an aggregate of 40,000 paid admissions . . . 22,000 alone being present at the Chicago-Cincinnati game."

The Orphans led the league in earned run average, 2.83, and had the league's individual ERA leader in Clark Griffith, 1.88. A control pitcher, Griffith had four of the club's league-high 13 shutouts and a ratio of less than two walks for every nine innings of toil. He was 26–10 on the season; 17–3 in 20 decisions against the second-division clubs.

Nixey Callahan was 20–10. Like Griffith, Callahan fattened up against the bottom clubs. Walter Thornton, a "cunny-thumb" (a soft-throwing, cunning left-hander), was 13–10, including a 2–0 August 21 no-hitter against Brooklyn. Rookie Jack Taylor, who joined the club late in the season, won all five of his starts.

Frank Chance also made his big league debut, the beginning of his spectacular 15-year career in Chicago flannels. A wealthy young Californian who insisted he played not for money but for the love of the game, Chance broke in as a catcher-outfielder, and in the next century was known as the Cubs' Peerless Leader. He appeared in 53 games and batted .286. The Orphans had only two months of better than .500 ball: 19–8 in June; 7–1 in October.

	W	L	ERA	G	GS	CG	IP	H	BB	K
Clark Griffith	24	10	(1.88)	38	38	36	325⅔	305	64	97
Nixey Callahan	20	10	2.46	31	31	30	274⅓	267	71	73
Walter Thornton	13	10	3.34	28	25	21	215⅓	226	56	56
Walt Woods	9	13	3.14	27	22	18	215	224	59	26
Matt Kilroy	6	7	4.31	13	11	10	100⅓	119	30	18
Frank Isbell	4	7	3.56	13	9	7	81	86	42	16
Jack Taylor	5	0	2.20	5	5	5	41	32	10	11
Buttons Briggs	1	3	5.70	4	4	3	30	38	10	14
Bill Phyle	2	1	0.78	3	3	3	23	24	6	4
Danny Friend	0	2	5.29	2	2	2	17	20	10	4
John Katoll	0	1	0.82	2	1	1	11	8	1	3
Henry Clarke	1	0	2.00	1	1	1	9	8	5	1
	85	64	(2.83)	167	152	137	1,342⅔	1,357	364	323

Shutouts: Griffith 4, Woods 3, Callahan 2, Phyle 2, Thornton 2.

	G	AB	H	2B	3B	HR	R	RBI	SB	AVG
Regulars										
1B Bill Everitt	149	596	190	15	6	0	102	69	28	.319
2B Jim Connor	138	505	114	9	9	0	51	67	11	.226
SS Bill Dahlen	142	524	152	35	8	1	96	79	27	.290
3B Barry McCormick	137	530	131	15	9	2	76	78	15	.247
RF Sam Mertes	83	269	80	4	8	1	45	47	27	.297
CF Bill Lange	113	442	141	16	10	6	79	69	22	.319
LF Jimmy Ryan	144	572	185	32	13	4	122	79	29	.323
C Tim Donahue	122	396	87	12	3	0	52	39	17	.220
Substitutes										
Harry Wolverton	13	49	16	1	0	0	4	2	1	.327
Frank Martin	1	4	0	0	0	0	0	0	0	.000
Walter Thornton	62	210	62	5	2	0	34	14	8	.295
Danny Green	47	188	59	4	3	4	26	27	12	.314
Nixey Callahan	43	164	43	7	5	0	27	22	3	.262
Frank Isbell	45	159	37	4	0	0	17	8	3	.233
Walt Woods	48	154	27	1	0	0	16	8	3	.175
Matt Kilroy	26	96	22	4	1	0	20	10	0	.229
Henry Clarke	2	4	1	0	0	0	0	0	0	.250
Frank Chance	53	147	42	4	3	1	32	14	7	.286
Art Nichols	14	42	12	1	0	0	7	6	6	.286
Pitchers										
Clark Griffith	38	122	20	2	3	0	15	15	1	.164
Jack Taylor	5	15	3	2	0	0	4	2	0	.200
Buttons Briggs	4	14	6	1	0	0	2	1	0	.429
Bill Phyle	4	9	1	0	0	0	1	0	0	.111
Danny Friend	2	7	2	1	0	0	0	0	0	.286
John Katoll	2	4	0	0	0	0	0	0	0	.000
		5,222	1,433	175	83	19	828	656	220	.274

1899

Record: 75–73
Finish: Eighth
Games Behind: 26
Manager: Tom Burns

Tommy Burns, who had hoped to become a Chicago fixture, went the way of all managerial flesh after the Colts tumbled back into the second division. Encouraged by their fourth-place finish the season before, the team and its supporters expected continued improvement in 1899. Instead the Colts limped home eighth, 24 games behind first-place Brooklyn.

Bill Lange led the club with a .325 average. Then at the top of his career, Lange shocked the baseball world and announced his retirement. The father of Lange's newest sweetheart, a California real estate mogul, refused to approve his daughter's marriage to a professional ballplayer. So Lange, at the age of 28, hung it up. Despite huge salary offers from clubs in the newly formed American League, he never returned to professional play. The marriage ended in divorce.

The Colts started well. On April 29 they drew a crowd of 27,489, largest in the league to that point. They were 9–6 in April, 15–9 in May, and 13–9 in June but were unable to maintain the pace and were 10 games under .500 thereafter. They were 13–1 against the last-place Cleveland Spiders, who won only 20 games and lost 134 for a .130 percentage, the worst record in big league history.

The Spiders were so badly outclassed that on the last day of the season, in Cincinnati, a cigar stand clerk at the Gibson Hotel, Eddie Kolb, pitched for Cleveland and was defeated 19–3. After the game, the Cleveland players presented a diamond locket to George Muir, their traveling secretary. "We're doing this for you because you deserve it," a club spokesman said. "You are the only person who had to watch us in all our games."

Chicago used 10 pitchers, none of them amateurs such as Kolb, but only two of the four rotation starters had winning

records. Griffith was 22–13, his sixth successive 20-win season, Nixey Callahan also pitched well, 21–12, and had the best record, 12–8, against first-division opponents. Jack Taylor, undefeated in five games the previous season, had a disappointing 18–21 record. Taylor, alias "The Brakeman," sometimes was confused with "Brewery Jack" Taylor, a contemporary who pitched for four National League clubs.

	W	L	ERA	G	GS	CG	IP	H	BB	K
Jack Taylor	18	21	3.76	41	39	39	354⅔	380	84	67
Clark Griffith	22	13	2.79	38	38	35	319⅔	329	65	73
Nixey Callahan	21	12	3.06	35	34	33	294⅓	327	76	77
Ned Garvin	9	13	2.85	24	23	22	199	202	42	69
Bill Phyle	1	8	4.20	10	9	9	83⅔	92	29	10
Dick Cogan	2	3	4.30	5	5	5	44	54	24	9
John Katoll	1	1	6.00	2	2	2	18	17	4	1
John Malarkey	0	1	13.00	1	1	1	9	19	5	7
Skel Roach	1	0	3.00	1	1	1	9	13	1	0
	75	72	3.37	157	152	147	1,331⅓	1,433	330	313

Shutouts: Garvin 4, Callahan 3, Taylor 1.

	G	AB	H	2B	3B	HR	R	RBI	SB	AVG
Regulars										
1B Bill Everitt	136	536	166	17	5	1	87	74	30	.310
2B Barry McCormick	102	376	97	15	2	2	48	52	14	.258
SS Gene DeMontreville	82	310	87	6	3	0	43	40	26	.281
3B Harry Wolverton	99	389	111	14	11	1	50	49	14	.285
RF Danny Green	117	475	140	12	11	6	90	56	18	.295
CF Bill Lange	107	416	135	21	7	1	81	58	41	.325
LF Jimmy Ryan	125	525	158	20	10	3	91	68	9	.301
C Tim Donahue	92	278	69	9	3	0	39	29	10	.248
Substitutes										
Jim Connor	69	234	48	7	1	0	26	24	6	.205
George Magoon	59	189	43	5	1	0	24	21	5	.228
Bill Bradley	35	129	40	6	1	2	26	18	4	.310
Doc Curley	10	37	4	0	1	0	7	2	0	.108
Sam Mertes	117	426	127	13	16	9	83	81	45	.298
Nixey Callahan	47	150	39	4	3	0	21	18	9	.260
Frank Quinn	12	34	6	0	1	0	6	1	1	.176
Dick Cogan	8	25	5	1	2	0	4	4	0	.200
Frank Chance	64	192	55	6	2	1	37	22	10	.286
Art Nichols	17	47	12	2	0	1	5	11	3	.255
Pitchers										
Jack Taylor	42	139	37	9	2	0	25	17	0	.266
Clark Griffith	39	120	31	5	0	0	15	14	2	.258
Ned Garvin	24	71	11	0	0	0	1	1	0	.155
Bill Phyle	10	34	6	0	0	0	2	1	0	.176
John Katoll	2	7	0	0	0	0	1	0	0	.000
John Malarkey	1	5	1	1	0	0	0	0	0	.200
Skel Roach	1	4	0	0	0	0	0	0	0	.000
		5,148	1,428	173	82	27	812	661	247	.277

1900

Record: 65–75
Finish: Fifth (tie)
Games Behind: 19
Manager: Tom Loftus

It was the dawn of a new century, and the National League reduced its membership from 12 to eight teams for the 1900 season. The Louisville, Baltimore, Cleveland, and Washington franchises were abandoned. The newly formed American League put a team in Chicago that was owned by Charles A. Comiskey, who immediately named his nine the White Stockings. President James Hart submitted to the invasion after Comiskey, the cofounder of the new league, agreed to build his ballpark on what was then the far South Side where Hart was convinced it would have minimum patronage.

The Orphans had a new manager. Tom Loftus, who had a two-year reign, replaced Tommy Burns at the helm. Despite a porous defense and a weakened pitching staff, the Orphans showed some improvement and scrambled into a fifth-place tie with St. Louis, both clubs finishing with 65–75 won-lost records, 19 games behind the runaway Brooklyn Superbas.

Chicago's four-man pitching rotation was without a big winner. Clark Griffith, who led the league in shutouts with four, was 14–13, the only regular starter above .500. Nixey Callahan was 13–16, Jack Taylor 10–17. Ned Garvin, who had a 2.41 earned run average, second lowest in the league to Rube Waddell, was 10–18. None of Loftus's other six starters won in double figures.

The club's one-time outstanding defense and its "Stonewall Infield" were faint memories. The Orphans were charged with 418 errors; only the last-place New York Giants committed more. Third baseman Bill Bradley, then in his first full big league season, drew 61 errors. Clarence "Cupid" Childs, a veteran second baseman approaching the end of his career, was next with 52 errors. Shortstops Barry McCormick and Billy Clingman had 48 and 34 errors, respectively.

Bill Everitt, who had succeeded Cap Anson at first base, appeared in only 23 games and departed in an early-season trade in exchange for John Ganzel, also a first baseman. Jimmy Ryan was released in October. Ryan was the only holdover from the championship teams of the 1880s, batted over .300 in 11 of his 14 full Chicago seasons, twice hit for the cycle, and had five five-hit games. Johnny Kling, a catcher who later helped in the winning of four pennants, joined the club and batted .294 in 15 games. The five-sided home plate was adopted.

	W	L	ERA	G	GS	CG	IP	H	BB	K
Nixey Callahan	13	16	3.82	32	32	32	285⅓	347	74	77
Clark Griffith	14	13	3.05	30	30	27	248	245	51	61
Ned Garvin	10	18	2.41	30	28	25	246⅓	225	63	107
Jack Taylor	10	17	2.55	28	26	25	222⅓	226	58	57
Jock Menefee	9	4	3.85	16	13	11	117	140	35	30
Bert Cunningham	4	3	4.36	8	7	7	64	84	21	7
Frank Killen	3	3	4.67	6	6	6	54	65	11	4
Long Tom Hughes	1	1	5.14	3	3	3	21	31	7	12
Mal Eason	1	0	1.00	1	1	1	9	9	3	2
Ervin Harvey	0	0	0.00	1	0	0	4	3	1	0
	65	75	3.23	155	146	137	1,271	1,375	324	357

Shutouts: Griffith (4), Callahan 2, Taylor 2, Garvin 1.

	G	AB	H	2B	3B	HR	R	RBI	SB	AVG
Regulars										
1B John Ganzel	78	284	78	14	4	4	29	32	5	.275
2B Cupid Childs	138	538	131	14	5	0	70	44	15	.243
SS Barry McCormick	110	379	83	13	5	3	35	48	8	.219
3B Bill Bradley	122	444	125	21	8	5	63	49	14	.282
RF Jimmy Ryan	105	415	115	25	4	5	66	59	19	.277
CF Danny Green	103	389	116	21	5	5	63	49	28	.298
LF Jack McCarthy	124	503	148	16	7	0	68	48	22	.294
C Tim Donahue	67	216	51	10	1	0	21	17	8	.236
Substitutes										
Billy Clingman	47	159	33	6	0	0	15	11	6	.208
Sammy Strang	27	102	29	3	0	0	15	9	1	.284
Bill Everitt	23	91	24	4	0	0	10	17	2	.264
Harry Wolverton	3	11	2	0	0	0	2	0	1	.182
Sam Mertes	127	481	142	25	4	7	72	60	38	.295
Cozy Dolan	13	48	13	1	0	0	5	2	2	.271
Sam Dungan	6	15	4	0	0	0	1	1	0	.267
Frank Chance	56	151	46	8	4	0	26	13	8	.305
Charlie Dexter	40	125	25	5	0	2	7	20	2	.200
Johnny Kling	15	51	15	3	1	0	8	7	0	.294
Art Nichols	8	25	5	0	0	0	1	0	1	.200
Roger Bresnahan	2	2	0	0	0	0	0	0	0	.000
Pitchers										
Nixey Callahan	32	115	27	3	2	0	16	9	5	.235
Clark Griffith	30	95	24	4	1	1	16	7	2	.253
Ned Garvin	30	91	14	1	0	0	12	4	0	.154
Jack Taylor	28	81	19	3	1	1	7	6	1	.235
Jock Menefee	17	46	5	0	0	0	5	4	0	.109
Bert Cunningham	8	27	4	1	0	0	5	1	1	.148
Frank Killen	6	20	3	0	0	0	0	2	0	.150
Long Tom Hughes	3	6	0	0	0	0	0	0	0	.000
Mal Eason	1	3	0	0	0	0	0	0	0	.000
Ervin Harvey	2	3	0	0	0	0	0	0	0	.000
		4,916	1,281	201	52	33	638	519	189	.261

1901

Record: 53–86
Finish: Sixth
Games Behind: 37
Manager: Tom Loftus

There was little cheering at the West Side Grounds in 1901. The upstart American League, in its second season, declared major league status and, offering higher salaries, succeeded in acquiring many of the National League's top players. Of the 185 players employed in 1901 by the Americans, who also had an eight-team league, 111 had previously played in the National.

But as the late Lee Allen, a ranking diamond historian, explained, not all had violated the reserve clause. Some had merely played in the National League at one time during their career. According to the 1902 *Spalding Guide*, 74 players went over to the American League in the first two years of the war.

The Colts were among the clubs hardest hit in the initial "raid" and lost seven players from their 1900 roster. Worse, three of their stars, Clark Griffith and Nixey Callahan, their two best pitchers, and outfielder Sam Mertes jumped to Comiskey's crosstown White Sox.

The Americans assigned the persuasive Griffith to induce Honus Wagner, the great Pittsburgh shortstop, to join the exodus. Wagner refused and said, "If I let Griff talk to me I won't be able to turn him down. So I just won't see him."

Because of the mass defections, the Chicago sportswriters renamed the team the Remnants. They were never in contention and finished sixth, 33 games below .500 and 37 games out of the lead. More embarrassing was that the pennant-winning White Stockings easily won the Chicago attendance battle with a home gate of 354,350 paid admissions, 50,000 more than their established city rivals.

The Remnants finished only one game ahead of last-place Cincinnati. Their leading hitters were outfielders Tully "Topsy" Hartsel, .335, and Danny Green, .313. Pitcher Rube Waddell, a future Hall of Famer who was purchased from Pittsburgh in May, was 13–15, a .464 winning percentage, tops on the club. Prior to the next season, all jumped to the American League.

	W	L	ERA	G	GS	CG	IP	H	BB	K
Long Tom Hughes	11	21	3.24	37	35	32	308⅓	309	115	225
Jack Taylor	13	19	3.36	33	31	30	275⅔	341	44	68
Rube Waddell	13	15	2.81	29	28	26	243⅔	239	66	168
Mal Eason	8	17	3.59	27	25	23	220⅔	246	60	68
Jock Menefee	8	13	3.80	21	20	19	182⅓	201	34	55
Bert Cunningham	0	1	5.00	1	1	1	9	11	3	2
Charlie Ferguson	0	0	0.00	1	0	0	2	1	2	0
	53	86	3.33	149	140	131	1,241⅔	1,348	324	586

Shutouts: Hughes 1, Eason 1.

	G	AB	H	2B	3B	HR	R	RBI	SB	AVG
Regulars										
1B Jack Doyle	75	285	66	9	2	0	21	39	8	.232
2B Cupid Childs	63	237	61	9	0	0	24	21	3	.257
SS Barry McCormick	115	427	100	15	6	1	45	32	12	.234
3B Fred Raymer	120	463	108	14	2	0	41	43	18	.233
RF Frank Chance	69	241	67	12	4	0	38	36	30	.278
CF Danny Green	133	537	168	16	12	6	82	60	31	.313
LF Tops Hartsel	140	558	187	25	16	7	111	54	41	.335
C Johnny Kling	74	253	70	6	3	0	26	21	7	.277
Substitutes										
Charlie Dexter	116	460	123	9	5	1	46	66	22	.267
Pete Childs	61	213	48	5	1	0	23	14	4	.225
Jim Delahanty	17	63	12	2	0	0	4	4	5	.190
Mike Hickey	10	37	6	0	0	0	4	3	1	.162
Larry Hoffman	6	22	7	1	0	0	2	6	1	.318
Germany Schaefer	2	5	3	1	0	0	0	0	0	.600
Cozy Dolan	43	171	45	1	2	0	29	16	3	.263
Jock Menefee	48	152	39	5	3	0	19	13	4	.257
Bill Gannon	15	61	9	0	0	0	2	0	5	.148
Harry Croft	3	12	4	0	0	0	1	4	0	.333
Mike Kahoe	67	237	53	12	2	1	21	21	5	.224
Pitchers										
Long Tom Hughes	38	118	14	1	0	0	7	5	0	.119
Jack Taylor	35	106	23	6	0	0	12	2	0	.217
Rube Waddell	30	98	25	3	3	2	16	14	2	.255
Mal Eason	27	87	12	1	0	0	4	6	1	.138
Bert Cunningham	1	1	0	0	0	0	0	0	0	.000
Charlie Ferguson	1	1	0	0	0	0	0	0	0	.000
		4,845	1,250	153	61	18	578	480	203	.258

1902

Record: 68–69
Finish: Fifth
Games Behind: 34
Manager: Frank Selee

Frank Selee, who during the 1880s had guided Boston to five National League pennants, was the new Chicago manager. Taciturn and publicity shy, Selee had almost no playing background but was an undisputed master of inside baseball. He favored the hit-and-run, understood the value of the strategically stolen base, and used signals to deploy his team defensively.

Like Pop Anson, Selee had great success in player selection and development. His eye for talent was so keen that he supposedly could "tell a ballplayer in his street clothes." He also had remarkable success in converting players from one position to another. Upon his arrival in Chicago he shifted Frank Chance, a catcher-outfielder, to first base; moved Joe Tinker from third to short; and anchored Johnny Evers at second base.

On September 15, 1902, in a 6–3 victory over Cincinnati, Tinker-to-Evers-to-Chance combined for their first double play. They were to become a legendary trio. Because double plays were not part of the game's statistics until 1919, it is not precisely known how many twin killings they manufactured, but their teamwork was to provide a keystone for the club's future success. Newspaperman Franklin P. Adams memorialized them with eight lines of doggerel in the old *New York Mail:*

> *These are the saddest of possible words—*
> *Tinker to Evers to Chance.*
> *Trio of Bear Cubs and fleeter than birds—*
> *Tinker to Evers to Chance.*
> *Thoughtlessly pricking our gonfalon bubble,*
> *Making a Giant hit into a double,*
> *Words that are weighty with nothing but trouble—*
> *Tinker to Evers to Chance.*

Selee emphasized youth to such an extent the club was now being called the Cubs. Jimmy Slagle, the new center fielder, led in batting with a .315 average and was among the league leaders in stolen bases with 40. The only other .300 hitters were outfielders Davy Jones, .305, and John Dobbs, .302. Selee was without a power hitter. The club had an aggregate of six home runs, Tinker and utility man Charles Dexter leading with two each. Johnny Kling, now the regular catcher, led in runs batted in with 57.

"Brakeman" Jack Taylor, so-called presumably because of his ability to stop losing streaks, had one of his best seasons, 22–11, with eight shutouts and a league-leading 1.33 earned run average. An iron man, Taylor's victories included a dis-

Charlie Dexter

tance-going 19-inning triumph over Pittsburgh. No other pitcher won more than 12 games. The Cubs finished fifth. There was little doubt that pennants would follow.

	W	L	ERA	G	GS	CG	IP	H	BB	K
Jack Taylor	22	11	(1.33)	36	33	33	324⅔	271	43	83
Pop Williams	12	16	2.51	31	31	26	254⅓	259	93	94
Jock Menefee	12	10	2.42	22	21	20	197⅓	202	26	60
Carl Lundgren	9	9	1.97	18	18	17	160	158	45	68
Bob Rhoads	4	8	3.20	16	12	12	118	131	42	43
Jim St. Vrain	4	6	2.08	12	11	10	95	88	25	51
Deacon Morrissey	1	3	2.25	5	5	5	40	40	8	13
Alex Hardy	2	2	3.60	4	4	4	35	29	12	12
Jim Gardner	1	2	2.88	3	3	2	25	23	10	6
Mal Eason	1	1	1.00	2	2	2	18	21	2	4
Fred Glade	0	1	9.00	1	1	1	8	13	3	3
	68	69	2.21	150	141	132	1,275⅓	1,235	279	437

Shutouts: Taylor 8, Menefee 5, Hardy 1, Rhoads 1, Lundgren 1, St. Vrain 1, Williams 1.

	G	AB	H	2B	3B	HR	R	RBI	SB	AVG
Regulars										
1B Frank Chance	75	236	67	9	4	1	40	31	28	.284
2B Bobby Lowe	121	472	116	13	3	0	41	31	16	.246
SS Joe Tinker	133	501	137	19	5	2	54	54	27	.273
3B Germany Schaefer	81	291	57	2	3	0	32	14	12	.196
RF Davy Jones	64	243	74	12	3	0	41	14	12	.305
CF John Dobbs	59	235	71	8	2	0	31	35	3	.302
LF Jimmy Slagle	115	454	143	11	4	0	64	28	40	.315
C Johnny Kling	114	434	124	19	3	0	50	57	23	.286
Substitutes										
Charlie Dexter	69	266	60	12	0	2	30	26	13	.226
Jack Taylor	55	186	44	6	1	0	18	17	6	.237
Hal O'Hagan	31	108	21	1	3	0	10	10	8	.194
Johnny Evers	26	89	20	0	0	0	7	2	1	.225
Fred Clark	12	43	8	1	0	0	1	2	1	.186
Deacon Morrissey	7	22	2	0	0	0	1	0	0	.091
Mike Jacobs	5	19	4	0	0	0	1	2	0	.211
Sammy Strang	3	11	4	0	0	0	1	0	1	.364
Ed Glenn	2	7	0	0	0	0	0	0	0	.000
Jock Menefee	65	216	50	4	1	0	24	15	4	.231
Dakin Miller	51	187	46	4	1	0	17	13	10	.246
Bunk Congalton	45	179	40	3	0	1	14	24	3	.223
Art Williams	47	160	37	3	0	0	17	14	9	.231
Jim Murray	12	47	8	0	0	0	3	1	0	.170
Larry Schlafly	10	31	10	0	3	0	5	5	2	.323
Mike Lynch	7	28	4	0	0	0	4	0	0	.143
Jack Hendricks	2	7	4	0	1	0	0	0	0	.571
Chick Pedroes	2	6	0	0	0	0	0	0	0	.000
Snapper Kennedy	1	5	0	0	0	0	0	0	0	.000
R. E. Hildebrand	1	4	0	0	0	0	1	0	0	.000
Ed Hughes	1	3	0	0	0	0	0	0	0	.000
Mike Kahoe	7	18	4	1	0	0	0	2	0	.222
Pete Lamer	2	9	2	0	0	0	2	0	0	.222
Pitchers										
Pop Williams	38	116	23	1	2	0	14	13	0	.198
Carl Lundgren	20	66	7	1	0	0	2	5	2	.106
Bob Rhoads	16	45	10	0	0	0	0	2	1	.222
Jim St. Vrain	12	31	3	0	0	0	2	0	0	.097
Alex Hardy	4	14	3	1	0	0	3	4	0	.214
Jim Gardner	3	10	2	0	0	0	0	2	0	.200
Mal Eason	2	5	1	0	0	0	0	0	0	.200
Fred Glade	1	3	1	0	1	0	0	0	0	.333
		4,807	1,207	131	40	6	530	423	222	.251

1903

Record: 82–56
Finish: Third
Games Behind: 8
Manager: Frank Selee

Now playing a running game, the Cubs leaped into contention, hung in, and finished third in 1903, the best showing in 12 years. They were only a game and a half out of

second place and eight games behind Pittsburgh, which won its third consecutive championship. Manager Selee's emphasis on inside baseball was evident throughout: 16 victories in the final inning.

The Cubs had only one .300 hitter, Frank Chance, who batted .327 and led the league with 67 stolen bases. The club also led in walks and averaged almost two steals a game. Baserunning and sharp defensive work, especially in the infield, were their strengths. The .275 team batting average was the third highest in the league. Constantly scrambling, they probably led in base runners.

The pitching was also improved. Two starters, the veteran Jack Taylor and Jake Weimer, each won 21 games. Combined, they were 19 games over .500: Taylor 21–14, Weimer 21–9. Bob Wicker was next at 19–10. Weimer led the league in fewest hits allowed per nine innings, 7.69.

Taylor was then in the midst of his remarkable complete-game record. He finished all 33 of his starts. In a five-season sequence, from June 20, 1901, to August 9, 1906, Brakeman Jack pitched 188 consecutive complete games. He finished an additional 15 games out of the bullpen for a total of 1,727 innings without relief.

Taylor won the 1903 opener 11–0 but was ineffective in his next three starts, all of which he lost. Rumors immediately circulated that he had thrown these games. The allegations were never substantiated, but when the season ended Selee sent him to St. Louis in a deal for "Three-Finger" Mordecai Brown, who was coming off a 9–13 rookie season.

It was another example of Selee's eye for talent. In 1906, Brown began a string of six successive 20-win seasons and helped in the winning of four Chicago pennants. He had a 14-year big league career and a lifetime record of 239 victories against only 129 losses for a .649 winning percentage, 17th highest in modern baseball history.

For the second successive season the Cubs failed to reach double figures in home runs. They had only nine, one-fourth as many as the champion Pirates. Still, they were the only club with a series edge over Pittsburgh, 12–8. Johnny Kling, who batted .297, led the team in home runs with three and had 13 triples, a National League record for catchers still not surpassed but equaled 63 years later by Tim McCarver of the St. Louis Cardinals.

	W	L	ERA	G	GS	CG	IP	H	BB	K
Jack Taylor	21	14	2.45	37	33	33	312⅓	277	57	83
Jake Weimer	21	9	2.30	35	33	27	282	241	104	128
Bob Wicker	19	10	3.02	32	27	24	247	236	74	110
Carl Lundgren	10	9	2.94	27	20	16	193	191	60	67
Jock Menefee	8	8	3.00	20	17	13	147	157	38	39
Clarence Currie	1	2	2.97	6	3	2	33⅓	35	9	9
Alex Hardy	2	1	6.39	3	3	1	12⅔	21	7	4
Peaches Graham	0	1	5.40	1	1	0	5	9	3	4
Pop Williams	0	1	5.40	1	1	1	5	9	0	2
John Doscher	0	1	12.00	1	1	0	3	6	2	5
	82	56	2.77	163	139	117	1,240⅓	1,182	354	451

Shutouts: Weimer 3, Menefee 1, Taylor 1, Wicker 1.

	G	AB	H	2B	3B	HR	R	RBI	SB	AVG
Regulars										
1B Frank Chance	125	441	144	24	10	2	83	81	(67)	.327
2B Johnny Evers	124	464	136	27	7	0	70	52	25	.293
SS Joe Tinker	124	460	134	21	7	2	67	70	27	.291
3B Doc Casey	112	435	126	8	3	1	56	40	11	.290
RF Dick Harley	104	386	89	9	1	0	72	33	27	.231
CF Davy Jones	130	497	140	18	3	1	64	62	15	.282
LF Jimmy Slagle	139	543	162	20	6	0	104	44	33	.298
C Johnny Kling	132	491	146	29	13	3	67	68	23	.297
Substitutes										
Otto Williams	38	130	29	5	0	0	14	13	8	.223
Bobby Lowe	32	105	28	5	3	0	14	15	5	.267
Bill Hanlon	8	21	2	0	0	0	4	2	1	.095
George Moriarty	1	5	0	0	0	0	1	0	0	.000
Jack McCarthy	24	101	28	5	0	0	11	14	8	.277
John Dobbs	16	61	14	1	1	0	8	4	0	.230
Jim Cook	8	26	4	1	0	0	3	2	1	.154
Tommy Raub	36	84	19	3	2	0	6	7	3	.226
Larry McLean	1	4	0	0	0	0	0	1	0	.000
Pitchers										
Jack Taylor	40	126	28	3	4	0	13	17	3	.222
Jake Weimer	35	107	21	4	0	0	10	6	0	.196
Bob Wicker	32	98	24	5	2	0	18	8	1	.245
Jock Menefee	22	64	13	3	0	0	3	2	0	.203
Carl Lundgren	27	61	7	0	0	0	6	3	1	.115
Clarence Currie	6	12	5	0	0	0	1	3	0	.417
Alex Hardy	3	6	1	0	0	0	0	1	0	.167
Peaches Graham	1	2	0	0	0	0	0	0	0	.000
Pop Williams	2	2	0	0	0	0	0	0	0	.000
John Doscher	1	1	0	0	0	0	0	0	0	.000
		4,733	1,300	191	62	9	695	548	259	.275

1904

Record: 93–60
Finish: Second
Games Behind: 13
Manager: Frank Selee

It was the third and last full season under Frank Selee's command, and, as in the previous two seasons, the club improved in 1904 and finished second to John McGraw's New York Giants, who won 106 games, including a record 18-game winning streak. The Cubs were 93–60, 13 games out, but were the only club to hold the Giants even on the season, splitting 22 games.

The Colts were in the lead in early June. The Giants went ahead to stay on June 13, two days after Bob Wicker, Selee's number-three pitcher, held them hitless for nine innings in a Polo Grounds duel with Joe McGinnity, the New York ace. Wicker was nicked for a harmless hit in the tenth and won, 1–0, on Johnny Evers' single in the 11th.

Selee had five pitchers with 15 or more victories: Jake Weimer, 20–14; Buttons Briggs, 19–11; Wicker, 17–8; Carl Lundgren, 17–10; and Three-Finger Brown, 15–10. They had a 2.30 team earned run average, second lowest in the league, but were handicapped by a light-hitting outfield. None of the regular outfielders hit higher than .264.

Frank Chance, with a .310 average, was the only .300 hitter for the second year in a row. Chance also led in home runs with six and in stolen bases with 42, one more than shortstop Joe Tinker. Outfielder George Schulte, a late-season arrival, appeared in 20 games and batted .286.

Schulte had a 13-year Chicago career and was among the club's most colorful players. He was a great admirer of Lillian Russell, the heroine of the theatrical world, who reciprocated with her affection and often attended the Colt games, home and away.

One spring when the curvaceous Miss Russell was touring in the play *Wildfire,* she hosted a big soiree for the Chicago

players. Schulte, who owned trotting horses, was smitten, responded by naming his favorite steed Wildfire, and thereafter was known as Wildfire Schulte. In 1911, the romance wilting, Schulte devoted all of his energies to the game and became the first player with 20 or more doubles, triples, home runs, and stolen bases in the same season.

	W	L	ERA	G	GS	CG	IP	H	BB	K
Jake Weimer	20	14	1.91	37	37	31	307	229	97	177
Buttons Briggs	19	11	2.05	34	30	28	277	252	77	112
Carl Lundgren	17	10	2.60	31	27	25	242	203	77	106
Bob Wicker	17	8	2.67	30	27	23	229	201	58	99
Three-Finger Brown	15	10	1.86	26	23	21	212⅓	155	50	81
Frank Corridon	5	5	3.05	12	10	9	100⅓	88	37	34
Ed Groth	0	2	5.63	3	2	2	16	22	6	9
	93	60	2.30	173	156	139	1,383⅔	1,150	402	618

Shutouts: Weimer 5, Brown 4, Wicker 4, Briggs 3, Lundgren 2.

	G	AB	H	2B	3B	HR	R	RBI	SB	AVG
Regulars										
1B Frank Chance	124	451	140	16	10	6	89	49	42	.310
2B Johnny Evers	152	532	141	14	7	0	49	47	26	.265
SS Joe Tinker	141	488	108	12	13	3	55	41	41	.221
3B Doc Casey	136	548	147	20	4	1	71	43	21	.268
RF Davy Jones	98	336	82	11	5	3	44	39	14	.244
CF Jack McCarthy	115	432	114	14	2	0	36	51	14	.264
LF Jimmy Slagle	120	481	125	12	10	1	73	31	28	.260
C Johnny Kling	123	452	110	18	0	2	41	46	7	.243
Substitutes										
Frank Corridon	19	58	13	1	0	0	3	1	0	.224
Shad Barry	73	263	69	7	2	1	29	26	12	.262
Otto Williams	57	185	37	4	1	0	21	8	9	.200
Bob Wicker	50	155	34	1	0	0	17	9	4	.219
Harry McChesney	22	88	23	6	2	0	9	11	2	.261
Wildfire Schulte	20	84	24	4	3	2	16	13	1	.286
Broadway Aleck Smith	10	29	6	1	0	0	2	1	1	.207
Solly Hofman	7	26	7	0	0	1	7	4	2	.269
George Moriarty	4	13	0	0	0	0	0	0	0	.000
Ike Van Zandt	3	11	0	0	0	0	0	0	0	.000
Bill Carney	2	7	0	0	0	0	0	0	0	.000
Dutch Rudolph	2	3	1	0	0	0	0	0	0	.333
Jack O'Neill	51	168	36	5	0	1	8	19	1	.214
Fred Holmes	1	3	1	1	0	0	1	0	0	.333
Tom Stanton	1	3	0	0	0	0	0	0	0	.000
Pitchers										
Jake Weimer	37	115	21	3	0	0	5	11	1	.183
Buttons Briggs	34	94	16	1	0	1	6	4	0	.170
Carl Lundgren	31	90	20	3	2	0	7	8	1	.222
Three-Finger Brown	31	89	19	3	1	0	8	8	0	.213
Ed Groth	3	6	0	0	0	0	0	0	0	.000
		5,210	1,294	157	62	22	597	470	227	.248

1905

Record: 92–61
Finish: Third
Games Behind: 13
Managers: Franke Selee, Frank Chance

Manager Frank Selee retired 90 games into the 1905 season and passed the baton to Frank "Husk" Chance, soon to be known as the Peerless Leader. Selee, the son of a New England clergyman, had never been robust. When he departed he was gravely ill with tuberculosis and was given an indefinite leave of absence. He moved to Denver and died five years later. In his 16 years as a major league manager his teams never finished lower than fifth.

A disciple, Chance followed Selee's preference for inside baseball. In the beginning it was a necessity. The 1905 Cubs, like their immediate predecessors, couldn't deliver the long ball and were unable to play for the big inning. They hit only

12 home runs, low in the league, and were next-to-last in batting with a collective .245 average.

The pitching and defense kept them alive. Outfielder Jack McCarthy threw three runners out at the plate in a 2–1 win over Pittsburgh. According to a leading Boswell of the day, "The Cubs had the best pitching and team play and inside work." Their 2.04 earned run average, best in the league, was made possible by a league-high 23 shutouts. They also led in fielding and were second in stolen bases. Outfielder Billy Maloney, in his only Chicago season, tied for the league lead in steals with 59.

The burden of the managerial assignment did not affect Chance's play. Now officially named the Cubs, which Chance preferred over the Colts, they once again had only one .300 hitter. Chance batted .316 and was the lone Cub among the league's top 29 hitters. He also led the club in runs batted in with 70. Shortstop Joe Tinker, who never hit for much of an average but was tough in the clutch, was second in RBIs with 66.

Five pitchers, all of whom had excellent winning percentages, won in double figures. Three-Finger Brown and Jake Weimer had identical 18–12 records. Ed Reulbach, a brainy rookie with an excellent curveball, won 18, nine consecutively. He went the distance in 28 of his 29 starts, had a 1.42 ERA, and twice won marathon games, an 18-inning 1–0 victory on June 24 against the Cardinals, and two months later 1–0 against Philadelphia in 20 innings.

The Cubs started slowly but were in contention in August and September. They were 7–0 in October but were unable to pass New York and Pittsburgh. The Giants, 105–48, won the pennant. The Cubs, 52–38 under Selee and 40–23 after Chance took over, finished third, 13 games out. On June 13, Christy Mathewson, the Giant great, stopped the Cubs with his second no-hitter. Three-Finger Brown was the loser.

	W	L	ERA	G	GS	CG	IP	H	BB	K
Ed Reulbach	18	13	1.42	34	29	28	292	208	73	152
Jake Weimer	18	12	2.27	33	30	26	250	212	80	107
Three-Finger Brown	18	12	2.17	30	24	24	249	219	44	89
Bob Wicker	13	7	2.02	22	22	17	178	139	47	86
Carl Lundgren	13	4	2.24	23	19	16	169	132	53	69
Buttons Briggs	8	8	2.14	20	20	13	168	141	52	68
Big Jeff Pfeffer	4	5	2.50	15	11	9	101	84	36	56
	92	61	(2.04)	177	155	133	1,407	1,135	385	627

Shutouts: Reulbach 5, Briggs 5, Brown 4, Wicker 4, Lundgren 3, Weimer 2.

	G	AB	H	2B	3B	HR	R	RBI	SB	AVG
Regulars										
1B Frank Chance	118	392	124	16	12	2	92	70	38	.316
2B Johnny Evers	99	340	94	11	2	1	44	37	19	.276
SS Joe Tinker	149	547	135	18	8	2	70	66	31	.247
3B Doc Casey	144	526	122	21	10	1	66	56	22	.232
RF Billy Maloney	145	558	145	17	14	2	78	54	(59)	.260
CF Jimmy Slagle	155	568	153	19	4	0	96	37	27	.269
LF Wildfire Schulte	123	493	135	15	14	1	67	47	16	.274
C Johnny Kling	111	380	83	8	6	1	26	52	13	.218
Substitutes										
Solly Hofman	86	287	68	14	4	1	43	38	15	.237
Shad Barry	27	104	22	2	0	0	10	10	5	.212
Hans Lobert	14	46	9	2	0	0	7	1	4	.196
Jack McCarthy	59	170	47	4	3	0	16	14	8	.276
Jack O'Neill	53	172	34	4	2	0	16	12	6	.198
Pitchers										
Ed Reulbach	35	110	14	0	0	0	6	7	0	.127
Three-Finger Brown	31	93	13	1	1	1	6	3	1	.140
Jake Weimer	33	92	19	1	1	0	8	6	0	.207
Bob Wicker	25	72	10	0	0	0	5	3	1	.139
Carl Lundgren	24	61	11	1	1	0	6	3	0	.180
Buttons Briggs	20	57	3	0	0	0	1	1	0	.053
Big Jeff Pfeffer	15	40	8	3	0	0	4	3	2	.200
		5,108	1,249	157	82	12	667	522	267	.245

1906

Record: 116–36
Finish: First
Games Ahead: 20
Manager: Frank Chance

The 1906 Cubs, during the regular National League season, were the most dominant team in major league history. They led the league in the three principal departments—batting, pitching, and fielding. They also led in shutouts and were second in stolen bases; six more steals and they would have been first in that category.

They breezed to the pennant with a remarkable record of 116 wins and only 36 losses: most wins in one season, and the highest winning percentage, .763. The defending champion New York Giants were second, 20 games out; John McGraw, the Giants' manager, conceded in late August. Fourth-place Philadelphia was 45½ games behind the Cubs. Last-place Boston was 66½ out.

Still, the Cubs started slowly. Their monthly record follows: 10–6 in April; 19–9 in May; 17–5 June; 20–8 July; 26–3 August; 21–5 September; and 3–0 in October. They won 50 of their final 58 games, an .862 ratio. They scored almost twice as many runs as their opponents, 704 to 381; batted .262; and had a 1.76 team earned run average.

Steady as ever, Chance hit .319 and scored a league-leading 103 runs. But Chance wasn't alone. Two newcomers, third baseman Harry Steinfeldt and outfielder Jimmy Sheckard, veterans in their late 20s acquired in trades, helped lead the assault. Steinfeldt (who was to become a trivia question—he was the fourth man in the celebrated Tinker-to-Evers-to-Chance infield) batted .327, third best in the league, and drove in 83 runs. Sheckard, a superb all-around player, scored 90 runs and hit .262.

Mordecai Brown, 26–6 with a 1.04 ERA and 10 shutouts, headed what, in effect, was an invincible pitching staff. Jack Pfiester, a 28-year-old left-hander rescued from the minors, was 20–8. Ed Reulbach was 19–4, led the league in winning percentage, .826, and had an incredible average of allowing five hits per nine innings, the equivalent of a five-hitter for each of his 33 starts.

His team hurt by injuries and frantic in pursuit, McGraw purchased outfielder Cy Seymour from Cincinnati, an established .300 hitter then in midcareer, and sent aging outfielder Sam Mertes and $10,000 to St. Louis for two younger players. These deals came in the wake of what may have been the most embarrassing day in Giant history, June 7, when they lost 19–0 to the Cubs, who pounded Mathewson and McGinnity for 11 first-inning runs.

Pfiester presided in the 19–0 rout and thereafter was known as Jack the Giant Killer. Pfiester also blanked the Pirates, 4–0, in the 116th and final victory. Carl Lundgren, the number-four starter, was 17–6. Orval Overall and the returning Brakeman Jack Taylor, whose consecutive complete-game streak was broken on August 13, were each 12–3.

But the biggest winner was Charles W. Murphy, a former Cincinnati sportswriter who bought the Cubs prior to the 1906 season for $125,000 from the financially depressed James Hart. Murphy was financed by Charles P. Taft, a Cincinnati newspaper publisher and the half brother of William Howard Taft. Eight years later, after considerable annual

The 1906 Cubs won a record 116 games.

profit taking, Murphy sold his 53 percent holdings to Taft for $397,500.

	W	L	ERA	G	GS	CG	IP	H	BB	K
Three-Finger Brown	26	6	(1.04)	36	32	27	277⅓	198	61	144
Jack Pfiester	20	8	1.56	31	29	20	241⅔	173	63	153
Ed Reulbach	19	4	1.65	33	24	20	218	129	92	94
Carl Lundgren	17	6	2.21	27	24	21	207⅔	160	89	103
Jack Taylor	12	3	1.83	17	16	15	147⅓	116	39	34
Orval Overall	12	3	1.88	18	14	13	144	116	51	94
Bob Wicker	3	5	2.99	10	8	5	72⅓	70	19	25
Fred Beebe	7	1	2.70	14	6	4	70	56	32	55
Jack Harper	0	0	0.00	1	1	0	1	0	0	0
	116	36	(1.76)	187	154	125	1,379⅓	1,018	446	702

Shutouts: Brown 10, Reulbach 6, Lundgren 5, Pfiester 4, Taylor 2, Overall 2.

	G	AB	H	2B	3B	HR	R	RBI	SB	AVG
Regulars										
1B Frank Chance	136	474	151	24	10	3	(103)	71	(57)	.319
2B Johnny Evers	154	533	136	17	6	1	65	51	49	.255
SS Joe Tinker	148	523	122	18	4	1	75	64	30	.233
3B Harry Steinfeldt	151	539	(176)	27	10	3	81	(83)	29	.327
RF Wildfire Schulte	146	563	158	18	(13)	7	77	60	25	.281
CF Jimmy Slagle	127	498	119	8	6	0	71	33	25	.239
LF Jimmy Sheckard	149	549	144	27	10	1	90	45	30	.262
C Johnny Kling	107	343	107	15	8	2	45	46	14	.312
Substitutes										
Pete Noonan	5	3	1	0	0	0	0	0	0	.333
Solly Hofman	64	195	50	2	3	2	30	20	13	.256
Doc Gessler	34	83	21	3	0	0	8	10	4	.253
Pat Moran	70	226	57	13	1	0	22	35	6	.252
Tom Walsh	2	1	0	0	0	0	0	0	0	.000
Bull Smith	1	1	0	0	0	0	0	0	0	.000
Pitchers										
Three-Finger Brown	36	98	20	1	0	0	11	4	0	.204
Jack Pfiester	31	84	4	0	0	0	5	1	0	.048
Ed Reulbach	34	83	13	0	0	0	4	4	0	.157
Carl Lundgren	28	67	12	3	0	0	4	2	0	.179
Orval Overall	18	53	9	1	0	0	6	3	1	.170
Jack Taylor	17	53	11	3	0	0	5	3	0	.208
Fred Beebe	14	29	3	1	0	0	1	3	0	.103
Bob Wicker	10	20	2	0	0	0	1	1	0	.100
Jack Harper	1	0	0	0	0	0	0	0	0	—
		5,018	1,316	181	71	20	704	539	283	(.262)

1907

Record: 107–45
Finish: First
Games Ahead: 17
Manager: Frank Chance

Immediately after the record 116-victory season, the Cubs were upset in the 1906 World Series by the White Sox, their crosstown rivals, and so when the next season began there was an urgency to demonstrate anew that they were base-ball's best team. There was only one avenue for redemption: to capture another National League pennant and win the World Series.

The 1907 Cubs did both. They repeated as the league champions with a record of 107 wins against 45 losses, not as impressive as the previous season but more than adequate for the cause. They had won the 1906 flag by 20 games, and the degree of domination in '07 was almost identical: 17 games ahead of the second-place Pittsburgh Pirates, 55½ ahead of last-place St. Louis.

The Cub pitching was still the most effective in the league, but the offense no longer was terrorizing. There were no .300 hitters. The home run total dropped to 13. Only Philadelphia, with 12, hit fewer. Also, for the first time a pennant-winning club didn't have a slugger with 80 or more runs batted in. Harry Steinfeldt was the RBI leader with 70. Johnny Evers was next with 51.

The unflappable Frank Chance, who missed one-third of the season because of injuries, led the hitters with a .293 average, the first time in five seasons he was under .300. Shortstop Joe Tinker and outfielder Wildfire Schulte were also disabled. Tinker appeared in only 117 games, Schulte in 97. Utility man "Circus Solly" Hofman, who played the outfield and all four infield positions, got into 134 games and came to the rescue, batting .268, with 67 runs scored, third high on the club.

Three-Finger Brown and Ed Reulbach were also on the casualty list but effective, nonetheless. Brown was 20–6 with a 1.39 earned run average. For the second successive year, Reulbach, 17–4, led the league in winning percentage. Pfiester was 15–9. The pitching star was Orval Overall, who picked up the slack with a 23–8 mark and a league-high eight shutouts.

After the usual early skirmishing, the Cubs went into first place to stay on May 30. They fattened up against the bottom three clubs and were 35 games over .500 with an aggregate 50–15 record against Cincinnati, Boston, and St. Louis. The Pittsburgh Pirates were the only troublesome foe, winning 10 of the 22 matches. At the finish, Chance told reporters, "Had we lost I would have had to retire to the Sierra Madre mountains to escape hearing from the anvil chorus."

In December, after their World Series triumph against Detroit, the Cub brass hosted a "victory celebration" during the annual league meeting. The banquet, the first of its kind, was held at the Waldorf Astoria.

According to the *Reach Guide,* "Over one hundred guests enjoyed the hospitality of the World Champion Chicago club. The menu was first class, the wine the best, and the decorations beautiful. The souvenir for each guest was a base-ball, cut open in the center, in which ice was served."

	W	L	ERA	G	GS	CG	IP	H	BB	K
Orval Overall	23	8	1.70	35	29	26	265⅓	199	69	139
Three-Finger Brown	20	6	1.39	34	27	20	233	180	40	107
Carl Lundgren	18	7	1.17	28	25	21	207	130	92	84
Jack Pfiester	15	9	(1.15)	30	22	13	195	143	48	90
Ed Reulbach	17	4	1.69	27	22	16	192	147	64	96
Chick Fraser	8	5	2.28	22	15	9	138⅓	112	46	41
Jack Taylor	6	5	3.29	18	13	8	123	127	33	22
Kid Durbin	0	1	5.40	5	1	1	16⅔	14	10	5
	107	45	1.73	199	154	114	1,370⅓	1,052	402	584

Shutouts: Overall 8, Lundgren 7, Brown 6, Reulbach 4, Pfiester 3, Fraser 2.

	G	AB	H	2B	3B	HR	R	RBI	SB	AVG
Regulars										
1B Frank Chance	111	382	112	19	2	1	58	49	35	.293
2B Johnny Evers	151	508	127	18	4	2	66	51	46	.250
SS Joe Tinker	117	402	89	11	3	1	36	36	20	.221
3B Harry Steinfeldt	152	542	144	25	5	1	52	70	19	.266
RF Wildfire Schulte	97	342	98	14	7	2	44	32	7	.287
CF Jimmy Slagle	136	489	126	6	6	0	71	32	28	.258
LF Jimmy Sheckard	142	484	129	23	1	1	76	36	31	.267
C Johnny Kling	104	334	95	15	8	1	44	43	9	.284
Substitutes										
Del Howard	51	148	34	2	2	0	10	13	3	.230
Bill Sweeney	3	10	1	0	0	0	1	1	1	.100
Heinie Zimmerman	5	9	2	1	0	0	0	1	0	.222
Solly Hofman	134	470	126	11	3	1	67	36	29	.268
Newt Randall	22	78	16	4	2	0	6	4	2	.205
Kid Durbin	11	18	6	0	0	0	2	0	0	.333
Pat Moran	65	198	45	5	1	1	8	19	5	.227
Mike Kahoe	5	10	4	0	0	0	0	1	0	.400
Jack Hardy	1	4	1	0	0	0	0	0	0	.250
Pitchers										
Orval Overall	36	94	20	4	2	0	6	9	0	.213
Three-Finger Brown	36	85	13	0	2	1	6	7	0	.153
Carl Lundgren	28	66	7	0	0	0	4	3	0	.106
Jack Pfiester	30	64	6	1	0	0	4	1	0	.094
Ed Reulbach	27	63	11	1	0	1	4	3	0	.175
Jack Taylor	18	47	9	2	0	0	2	1	0	.191
Chick Fraser	22	45	3	0	0	0	4	2	0	.067
		4,892	1,224	162	48	13	571	450	235	.250

1908

Record: 99–55
Finish: First
Games Ahead: 1
Manager: Frank Chance

The Cubs won their third consecutive pennant in 1908 with the help of "Merkle's Boner," probably the most famous and controversial play of the 20th century. On a simple force-out, Fred Merkle, a rookie first baseman for the New York Giants, killed a ninth-inning rally when he failed to touch second base on what should have been a game-winning hit.

The game was played on September 23 at the Polo Grounds. Thousands of fans, joyous in the belief the Giants had won 2–1, flooded the field. Further play was impossible. Three days later the game was officially ruled a 1–1 tie. It was also decided that the game would be replayed the day after the season ended, if necessary. It was necessary: The Cubs and Giants finished in a first-place tie.

The "Merkle Boner," in brief:

Moose McCormick reached on a fielder's choice. Subbing for Tenney, young Merkle, who had played in only 33 games, also singled, sending McCormick to third. With two outs, McCormick seemingly scored on Al Bridwell's single to center. Seeing McCormick cross the plate, Merkle ran directly to the clubhouse without touching second, a common practice at the time.

Second baseman Johnny Evers, on the alert for such a possibility, called for the ball. When it was retrieved Evers stepped on second for the force. The rule, then as now, is that a third-out force play nullifies both a run and a hit. Umpire Hank O'Day ruled the run didn't count. O'Day had also worked a Cub-Pittsburgh game three weeks earlier when Evers attempted a similar force at second. On that occasion, O'Day didn't call it; he said he didn't see it. But he advised Evers such a play was legal.

The playoff game, first in league history, was played two weeks later, on October 8, also in the Polo Grounds. The interest was so high that the fans broke down the ticket gates and the outfield fence. Hundreds of spectators climbed onto the grandstand roof. Jack Pfiester made the pitching start for the Cubs and was knocked out in the first inning. "Three-Finger" Brown was summoned and outdueled the great Mathewson, 4–2. The victory broke the tie and gave the Cubs their third consecutive flag. The Giants and Pirates finished in a second-place tie, one game out.

It had been a hectic three-club race from the beginning between Chicago, Pittsburgh, and New York. No other club was ever in first or second place except the Phillies, who held second place during the last two weeks of May. On May 31 the Phillies were 3½ games behind the Cubs, who set the early pace and led, continuously, from April through mid-July, when Pittsburgh took over.

The Giants led through all of September, despite a doubleheader loss to the Cubs on September 22, the day before "Merkle's Boner." Three-Finger Brown relieved in the opener and went the distance in the second game. The Pirates led on October 2 but were eliminated on the final day of the regular season, losing to the Cubs 5–2. Had the Cubs lost, Merkle would have been forgotten in the fog of time. Either the Pirates or the Giants would have won the flag.

The Cubs tied for fifth in league batting with a .249 team average. Johnny Evers was their leading hitter at .300. Brown and Reulbach had their best years. Brown was 29–9 with a 1.47 ERA. Reulbach, who had four two-hitters, was 24–7, the third consecutive season he led the league in winning percentage. The Cubs finished with a 99–55 record, the first time in five years the pennant winner failed to win 100 games.

	W	L	ERA	G	GS	CG	IP	H	BB	K
Three-Finger Brown	29	9	1.47	44	31	27	312⅓	214	49	123
Ed Reulbach	24	7	2.03	46	35	25	297⅔	227	106	133
Jack Pfiester	12	10	2.00	33	29	18	252	204	70	117
Orval Overall	15	11	1.92	37	27	16	225	165	78	167
Chick Fraser	11	9	2.27	26	17	11	162⅔	141	61	66
Carl Lundgren	6	9	4.22	23	15	9	138⅔	149	56	38
Andy Coakley	2	0	0.89	4	3	2	20⅓	14	6	7
Rube Kroh	0	0	1.50	2	1	0	12	9	4	11
Carl Spongburg	0	0	9.00	1	0	0	7	9	6	4
Bill Mack	0	0	2.84	2	0	0	6⅓	5	1	2
	99	55	2.14	218	158	108	1,434	1,137	437	668

Shutouts: Brown 9, Reulbach 7, Overall 4, Pfiester 3, Fraser 2, Lundgren 1, Coakley 1.

	G	AB	H	2B	3B	HR	R	RBI	SB	AVG
Regulars										
1B Frank Chance	129	452	123	27	4	2	65	55	27	.272
2B Johnny Evers	126	416	125	19	6	0	83	37	36	.300
SS Joe Tinker	157	548	146	23	14	6	67	68	30	.266
3B Harry Steinfeldt	150	539	130	20	6	1	63	62	12	.241
RF Wildfire Schulte	102	386	91	20	2	1	42	43	15	.236
CF Jimmy Slagle	104	352	78	4	1	0	38	26	17	.222
LF Jimmy Sheckard	115	403	93	18	3	2	54	22	18	.231
C Johnny Kling	126	424	117	23	5	4	51	59	16	.276
Substitutes										
Heinie Zimmerman	46	113	33	4	1	0	17	9	2	.292
Solly Hofman	120	411	100	15	5	2	55	42	15	.243
Del Howard	96	315	88	7	3	1	42	26	11	.279
Jack Hayden	11	45	9	2	0	0	3	2	1	.200
Kid Durbin	14	28	7	1	0	0	3	0	0	.250
Pat Moran	50	150	39	5	1	0	12	12	6	.260
Doc Marshall	12	20	6	0	1	0	4	3	0	.300
Vin Campbell	1	1	0	0	0	0	0	0	0	.000
Pitchers										
Three-Finger Brown	46	121	25	0	0	0	5	4	2	.207
Ed Reulbach	46	99	23	6	2	0	10	9	1	.232
Jack Pfiester	33	79	8	1	0	0	2	2	1	.101
Orval Overall	38	70	9	1	1	0	3	9	1	.129
Chick Fraser	26	50	6	1	0	0	3	1	1	.120
Carl Lundgren	23	47	7	0	0	0	2	1	0	.149
Andy Coakley	4	6	0	0	0	0	0	0	0	.000
Rube Kroh	2	4	0	0	0	0	0	0	0	.000
Bill Mack	2	3	2	0	1	0	1	0	0	.667
Carl Spongburg	1	3	2	0	0	0	0	0	0	.667
		5,085	1,267	197	56	19	625	492	212	.249

1909

Record: 104–49
Finish: Second
Games Behind: 6½
Manager: Frank Chance

According to an account of the day, the Cubs suffered "a trifling diminution of athletic force" in 1909. More plainly, after three successive pennants they had an understandable letdown. Still, it couldn't have been severe. They won 104 games, five more than the previous season, but were unable to catch Pittsburgh and finished a secure second, 6½ games out, and 12½ ahead of third-place New York.

It was the year Tinker and Evers stopped talking. They continued to excel on the field, but otherwise there was no communication. Many years later Joe Tinker told the story:

"We were playing an exhibition game in Bedford, Indiana. We dressed in the hotel and went to the ballpark in hacks. Evers got in a hack all by himself and drove off, leaving me and several others to wait until the hack returned. As soon as we got to the ballpark I went up to him and said, 'Who the hell are you that you've got to have a hack all to yourself?'

"One word led to another and we had a fight. After we were pulled apart, I told Evers, 'If you and I talk to each other we're only going to be fighting. So don't talk to me and I won't talk to you. You play your position and I'll play mine and let it go at that.'"

Johnny Evers, known as "The Crab," had a breakdown during the season and was granted a rare leave of absence "to recover from the strain of active service on the field." It was a brief absence. He played in 127 of the Cubs' 153 games, led the team in runs with 88; stole 28 bases, one short of the club lead, and batted his usual .263.

The man who was missed most was catcher Johnny Kling, among the few players of the time of Jewish heritage. Kling had begun his professional career at the age of 18 with the Kansas City Schmeltzers, then joined the Cubs in 1900. In 1909 he refused to report after a contract dispute and sat out most of the season, remaining at his home in Kansas City, where he operated a billiard parlor.

Jimmy Slagle retired prior to the 1909 season and was replaced in center field by Solly Hofman, who led the club in hitting with a .285 average. Husk Chance, often injured and in decline at the plate, appeared in only 93 games and batted .272. But once again the Cubs had the best pitching. The pitching staff had the lowest ERA, 1.75, and led the league in fewest runs allowed.

The heroic Three-Finger Brown had a 1.31 ERA, with eight shutouts, and led the league in wins, 27; complete games, 32; and innings pitched, 342⅔. Overall was next at 20–11, followed by Reulbach at 19–10, including a 14-game winning streak. The Cubs were in the lead only once, in early April. They were 9–13 against Pittsburgh and came within one victory of sweeping their 22-game schedule with last-place Boston.

	W	L	ERA	G	GS	CG	IP	H	BB	K
Three-Finger Brown	(27)	9	1.31	(50)	34	(32)	(342⅔)	246	53	172
Orval Overall	20	11	1.42	38	32	23	285	204	80	(205)
Ed Reulbach	19	10	1.78	35	32	23	262⅔	194	82	105
Jack Pfiester	17	6	2.43	29	25	13	196⅔	179	49	73
Rube Kroh	9	4	1.65	17	13	10	120⅓	97	30	51
Rip Hagerman	4	4	1.82	13	7	4	79	64	28	32
Irv Higginbotham	5	2	2.19	19	6	4	78	64	20	32
Ray Brown	1	0	2.00	1	1	1	9	5	4	2
King Cole	1	0	0.00	1	1	1	9	6	3	1
Carl Lundgren	0	1	4.15	2	1	0	4⅓	6	4	0
Rudy Schwenck	1	1	13.50	3	2	0	4	16	3	3
Pat Ragan	0	0	2.45	2	0	0	3⅔	4	1	2
Chick Fraser	0	0	0.00	1	0	0	3	2	4	1
Andy Coakley	0	1	18.00	1	1	0	2	7	3	1
	104	49	(1.75)	212	155	111	1,399½	1,094	364	680

Shutouts: Overall 9, Brown 8, Reulbach 6, Pfiester 5, Kroh 2, Hagerman 1, Cole 1.

	G	AB	H	2B	3B	HR	R	RBI	SB	AVG
Regulars										
1B Frank Chance	93	324	88	16	4	0	53	46	29	.272
2B Johnny Evers	127	463	122	19	6	1	88	24	28	.263
SS Joe Tinker	143	516	132	26	11	4	56	57	23	.256
3B Harry Steinfeldt	151	528	133	27	6	2	73	59	22	.252
RF Wildfire Schulte	140	538	142	16	11	4	57	60	23	.264
CF Solly Hofman	153	527	150	21	4	2	60	58	20	.285
LF Jimmy Sheckard	148	525	134	29	5	1	81	43	15	.255
C Jimmy Archer	80	261	60	9	2	1	31	30	5	.230
Substitutes										
Del Howard	69	203	40	4	2	1	25	24	6	.197
Heinie Zimmerman	65	183	50	9	2	0	23	21	7	.273
Fred Luderus	11	37	11	1	1	1	8	9	0	.297
Joe Stanley	22	52	7	1	0	0	4	2	0	.135
John Kane	20	45	4	1	0	0	6	5	1	.089
George Browne	12	39	8	0	1	0	7	1	3	.205
Bill Davidson	2	7	1	0	0	0	2	0	1	.143
Pat Moran	77	246	54	11	1	1	18	23	2	.220
Tom Needham	13	28	4	0	0	0	3	0	0	.143
Pitchers										
Three-Finger Brown	50	125	22	3	1	0	13	9	0	.176
Orval Overall	38	96	22	6	1	2	7	11	0	.229
Ed Reulbach	35	86	12	2	1	0	3	7	0	.140
Jack Pfiester	29	65	11	1	0	0	5	4	1	.169
Rube Kroh	17	40	6	0	0	0	4	0	1	.150
Irv Higginbotham	19	26	6	0	0	0	1	0	0	.231
Rip Hagerman	13	23	3	1	0	0	2	1	0	.130
King Cole	1	4	3	0	1	0	1	0	0	.750
Rudy Schwenck	3	4	1	0	0	0	0	0	0	.250
Ray Brown	1	3	0	0	0	0	0	1	0	.000
Carl Lundgren	2	2	1	0	0	0	1	1	0	.500
Pat Ragan	2	2	0	0	0	0	0	0	0	.000
Chick Fraser	1	1	0	0	0	0	0	0	0	.000
Andy Coakley	1	0	0	0	0	0	0	0	0	—
		4,999	1,227	203	60	20	632	496	187	.245

1910

Record: 104–50
Finish: First
Games Ahead: 13
Manager: Frank Chance

The cork-center ball was introduced in an effort to increase the hitting, and the 1910 Cubs, among others, obliged with 34 home runs, at that time a long-ball blizzard. It was the most home runs by a Cub team since 1897, Cap Anson's last year at the helm. They also led the league in triples and stolen bases, were second in batting with a robust .268, and averaged 4.6 runs a game.

Offense alone doesn't win a flag, but the Cubs continued to benefit from a superior pitching staff, with a 2.51 ERA, and romped home with the pennant, 13 games ahead of the second-place Giants. The Cubs started slowly and were in fifth place in mid-May, but they had a commanding lead in July and led the rest of the way.

It was Chicago's fourth championship in five seasons and the first time a major league club, after winning three times in a row, then losing, regained the title within a year. It was the end of Chicago's greatest dynasty. Seven long years, including two in the second division, passed before the Cubs won another pennant.

Catcher Johnny Kling returned from his pool hall sabbatical but was slow getting into shape. For the first time since he became a regular in 1902, Kling had fewer than 300 at bats and stole only three bases, five to six times below his previous average. Jimmy Archer, when he wasn't subbing for the injured Frank Chance at first base, alternated with Kling behind the plate.

Born in Dublin, Ireland, Archer had a golden arm but a brass bat. He was acknowledged as the best-throwing catcher in the league. He batted .259, nine points above his career average, and drove in 41 runs. Outfielder Solly Hofman led the club with a .325 average, fifth high in the league. Wildfire Schulte hit 10 home runs, 15 triples, and 29 doubles. His 10 home runs tied him for the league lead with Boston's Fred Beck.

Three-Finger Brown was the workhorse on a deep pitching staff, which included six winners in double figures. As usual, Brown led the club in victories with a 25–13 record, two wins fewer than Mathewson. Brown went into the season with an 11–6 career edge over Mathewson in head-to-head starts. He beat Matty again on June 10 but this time in relief of Lew Richie.

It was the fifth successive 20-victory season for Brown; in this five-year span he won 127 games. Brown went the distance in 27 of his 31 starts, made 15 relief appearances, and had a new and wonderful pitching companion in rookie Len "King" Cole, who the previous season was at Bay City, Michigan, a postage-stamp stop on the baseball map. Cole was 20–4, including a no-hitter against St. Louis, aborted after seven innings when both teams had to catch a train.

	W	L	ERA	G	GS	CG	IP	H	BB	K
Three-Finger Brown	25	13	1.86	46	31	27	295⅓	256	64	143
King Cole	20	4	1.80	33	29	21	239⅔	174	130	114
Harry McIntyre	13	9	3.07	28	19	10	176	152	50	65
Ed Reulbach	12	8	3.12	24	23	13	173⅓	161	49	55
Orval Overall	12	6	2.68	23	21	11	144⅔	106	54	92
Lew Richie	11	4	2.70	30	11	8	130	117	51	53
Jack Pfiester	6	3	1.79	14	13	5	100⅓	82	26	34
Big Jeff Pfeffer	1	0	3.27	13	1	1	41⅓	43	16	11
Rube Kroh	3	1	4.46	6	4	1	34⅓	33	15	16
Orlie Weaver	1	2	3.66	7	2	2	32	34	15	22
Alex Carson	0	0	4.05	2	0	0	6⅔	6	1	2
Bill Foxen	0	0	9.00	2	0	0	5	7	3	2
	104	50	2.51	228	154	99	1,378⅔	1,171	474	609

Shutouts: Brown 7, Cole 4, Overall 4, Richie 3, McIntyre 2, Pfiester 2, Reulbach 1.

	G	AB	H	2B	3B	HR	R	RBI	SB	AVG
Regulars										
1B Frank Chance	88	295	88	12	8	0	54	36	16	.298
2B Johnny Evers	125	433	114	11	7	0	87	28	28	.263
SS Joe Tinker	133	473	136	25	9	3	48	69	20	.288
3B Harry Steinfeldt	129	448	113	21	1	2	70	58	10	.252
RF Wildfire Schulte	151	559	168	29	15	(10)	93	68	22	.301
CF Solly Hofman	136	477	155	24	16	3	83	86	29	.325
LF Jimmy Sheckard	144	507	130	27	6	5	82	51	22	.256
C Johnny Kling	91	297	80	17	2	2	31	32	3	.269
Substitutes										
Heinie Zimmerman	99	335	95	16	6	3	35	38	7	.284
Fred Luderus	24	54	11	1	1	0	5	3	0	.204
Ginger Beaumont	56	172	46	5	1	2	30	22	4	.267
John Kane	32	62	15	0	0	1	11	12	2	.242
Jimmy Archer	98	313	81	17	6	2	36	41	6	.259
Tom Needham	31	76	14	3	1	0	9	10	1	.184
Doc Miller	1	1	0	0	0	0	0	0	0	.000
Pitchers										
Three-Finger Brown	46	103	18	1	2	0	9	6	1	.175
King Cole	34	91	21	2	1	0	7	9	1	.231
Harry McIntyre	30	66	17	2	0	1	3	8	0	.258
Ed Reulbach	24	56	6	0	0	0	4	2	1	.107
Orval Overall	25	41	5	1	0	0	4	1	0	.122
Lew Richie	30	40	9	4	1	0	6	1	0	.225
Jack Pfiester	14	33	3	0	0	0	1	2	0	.091
Big Jeff Pfeffer	14	17	3	1	1	0	1	2	0	.176
Orlie Weaver	7	13	2	0	0	0	1	0	0	.154
Rube Kroh	6	12	3	0	0	0	1	1	0	.250
Bill Foxen	2	2	0	0	0	0	0	0	0	.000
Alex Carson	2	1	0	0	0	0	0	0	0	.000
		4,977	1,333	219	(84)	(34)	711	586	(173)	.268

1911

Record: 92–62
Finish: Second
Games Behind: 7½
Manager: Frank Chance

Home run production in the big leagues rose 50 percent in 1911, and the Cubs kept pace with 54. Wildfire Schulte led the league with 21 and added 21 triples, a remarkable achievement for a long-ball hitter. But Frank Chance's pitchers were no longer dominant—their earned run average was 2.90, and the Cubs were unable to repeat. They finished second behind New York, 7½ games out.

It was a difficult season throughout. Three-Finger Brown had a poor start, and Ed Reulbach, who had his usual good control warming up, was "hopelessly wild" during the first two months. King Cole was stricken with malaria. Johnny Evers, still troubled with headaches, was replaced at second base by Heinie Zimmerman. Evers appeared in 46 games, with only 155 at bats.

Worse, Chance required constant medical care. He had a habit of leaning over the plate and had been hit in the head so many times by pitched balls that his vision was impaired. He missed 123 of the club's 154 games and gave way at first base to Vic Saier, who didn't live up to promise.

On July 6, a frustrated Chance told reporters, "I am going into the game at some personal risk. The doctors tell me my head is not right and I don't know how long I can stick. But if I have to come out again I'm going to quit, that's all."

Chance also seemed to be losing his grip. On August 10 he fined shortstop Joe Tinker $150 and suspended him for the rest of the season for insubordination and indifferent play. Tinker had allowed two routine pop flies to drop behind him. He was reinstated within 72 hours. Two weeks later Zimmerman was slapped with a $100 plaster, also for lackadaisical play. Chance lifted the fine the next day.

Still, the Cubs played well through August. Five teams moved in and out of the lead, Chicago among them. The Cubs twice led in July, dropped back, regained the lead on August 3 and held it through August 23. The Giants moved in front the next day and led thereafter. The Cubs won 92 games, seven fewer than the Giants. The *Reach Guide* saluted Chance for a "wonderful race under adverse conditions."

Perhaps one of the most exciting events of the season occurred on May 28 when the Cubs had to catch a train from St. Louis to Pittsburgh for a makeup game. The train was 90 minutes late getting into Columbus, Ohio. Because of the delay the original schedule had to be adjusted.

Here is a fanciful account from the *Reach Guide*:

"A dining car was shanghaied and tacked on behind the two Cub sleepers, and with a heavy baggage car for ballast, away they went with Casey Jones at the throttle. It was like walking the quarterdeck of a lake steamer in a cyclone to go the length of a car. Once the dining car tilted so far that Doc Semens, who was trying to inhale some cold roast beef, was thrown out of his chair into the aisle, with a bunch of crockery on top of him.

"Before the wild ride ended the merriest of the care-free players was sobered by the thought of what a misplaced or a split switch meant at 90 miles an hour, and every switchyard looked like a straightaway to Casey Jones. The run of 191 miles was covered in 215 minutes, five minutes faster than the previous record."

	W	L	ERA	G	GS	CG	IP	H	BB	K	R	ER
Three-Finger Brown	21	11	2.80	(53)	27	21	270	267	55	129	110	84
Lew Richie	15	11	2.31	36	28	18	253	213	103	78	88	65
Ed Reulbach	16	9	2.96	33	29	15	221⅓	191	103	79	97	73
King Cole	18	7	3.13	32	27	13	221⅓	188	99	101	87	77
Harry McIntyre	11	7	4.11	25	17	9	149	147	33	56	81	68
Fred Toney	1	1	2.42	18	4	1	67	55	35	27	36	18
Reggie Richter	1	3	3.13	22	5	0	54⅔	62	20	34	30	19
Orlie Weaver	3	2	2.06	6	4	1	43⅓	29	17	20	12	10
Charlie Smith	3	2	1.42	7	5	3	38	31	7	11	11	6
Jack Pfiester	0	4	4.01	6	5	3	33⅓	34	18	15	25	15
Cy Slapnicka	0	2	3.38	3	2	1	24	21	7	10	12	9
Bill Foxen	1	1	2.08	3	1	0	13	12	12	6	6	3
Larry Cheney	1	0	0.00	3	1	0	10	8	3	11	0	0
Cliff Curtis	1	2	3.86	4	1	0	7	7	5	4	4	3
Ernie Ovitz	0	0	4.50	1	0	0	2	3	3	0	2	1
Jack Rowan	0	0	4.50	1	0	0	2	1	2	0	4	1
Hank Griffin	0	0	18.00	1	1	0	1	1	3	1	2	2
	92	62	2.90	254	157	85	1,411	1,270	525	582	607	454

Shutouts: Richie 4, Cole 2, Reulbach 2, McIntyre 1, Smith 1, Weaver 1.

	G	AB	H	2B	3B	HR	R	RBI	SB	AVG
Regulars										
1B Vic Saier	86	259	67	15	1	1	42	37	11	.259
2B Heinie Zimmerman	143	535	164	22	17	9	80	85	23	.307
SS Joe Tinker	144	536	149	24	12	4	61	69	30	.278
3B Jim Doyle	130	472	133	23	12	5	69	62	19	.282
RF Wildfire Schulte	154	577	173	30	21	(21)	105	(121)	23	.300
CF Solly Hofman	143	512	129	17	2	6	66	70	30	.252
LF Jimmy Sheckard	156	539	149	26	11	4	(121)	50	32	.276
C Jimmy Archer	116	387	98	18	5	4	41	41	5	.253
Substitutes										
Johnny Evers	46	155	35	4	3	0	29	7	6	.226
Dave Shean	54	145	28	4	0	0	17	15	4	.193
Frank Chance	31	88	21	6	3	1	23	17	9	.239
Kitty Bransfield	3	10	4	2	0	0	0	0	0	.400
Wilbur Good	58	145	39	5	4	2	27	21	10	.269
Al Kaiser	27	84	21	0	5	0	16	7	6	.250
Bill Collins	7	5	1	1	0	0	2	0	0	.200
Johnny Kling	27	80	14	3	2	1	8	5	1	.175
Peaches Graham	36	71	17	3	0	0	6	8	2	.239
Tom Needham	27	62	12	2	0	0	4	5	2	.194
Pitchers										
Three-Finger Brown	53	91	23	4	1	0	8	6	0	.253
Lew Richie	36	91	14	0	1	0	7	4	0	.154
King Cole	32	79	12	1	1	0	7	0	1	.152
Ed Reulbach	33	67	6	3	0	0	6	3	0	.090
Harry McIntyre	26	53	14	4	0	0	9	2	0	.264
Fred Toney	18	18	2	0	0	0	1	0	0	.111
Orlie Weaver	6	17	1	0	0	0	0	0	0	.059
Charlie Smith	7	13	1	0	0	0	0	1	0	.077
Jack Pfiester	6	11	2	0	0	0	0	2	0	.182
Reggie Richter	22	10	1	0	0	0	1	1	0	.100
Cy Slapnicka	3	9	2	0	0	0	0	1	0	.222
Larry Cheney	3	4	1	0	0	0	0	0	0	.250
Bill Foxen	3	4	1	1	0	0	0	0	0	.250
Cliff Curtis	4	2	1	0	0	0	1	0	0	.500
Jack Rowan	1	1	0	0	0	0	0	0	0	.000
Hank Griffin	1	0	0	0	0	0	0	0	0	—
Ernie Ovitz	1	0	0	0	0	0	0	0	0	—
		5,132	1,335	218	101	54	757	640	214	.260

1912

Record: 91–59
Finish: Third
Games Behind: 11½
Manager: Frank Chance

It was a great year for Heinie Zimmerman, who won the Triple Crown, but not so good for the Peerless Leader. Frank Chance was dismissed on September 28, 1912, when he was in the hospital recovering from surgery, closing his glorious Chicago managerial reign that included four pennants and two second-place finishes. Second baseman Johnny Evers succeeded him.

The financially independent son of a bank president, Chance had a 10 percent stake in the club. Charles Murphy, president and majority owner who had wielded the ax, offered $20,000 for Chance's holdings, twice the original cost. Dissatisfied, Chance entered into an agreement with Harry Ackerland of Pittsburgh, who was willing to pay $35,000. Murphy's attempt to block the sale failed.

Chance had been in almost constant dispute with Murphy, beginning after the 1906 season when Chance asked for a salary increase; Chance, who was paid $5,500, discovered that McGraw's compensation was $18,000. After Chance threatened to quit, Murphy gave him a $5,000 raise. The battle never abated. Prior to his dismissal, Chance insisted that Murphy, despite annual profits that had made him a millionaire, had repeatedly "refused to sign quality players."

Still suffering from severe headaches, Chance collapsed during an April game against Cincinnati. He appeared in only two games: one hit in five at bats. He underwent surgery late in the season. In announcing that he was retiring as a player, Chance said, "Another blow on the head or another collapse would finish me. I owe Chicago a great deal, but I don't feel that I owe baseball or the Chicago public my life."

The Cubs finished third, 11½ games behind the victorious Giants (McGraw's fourth pennant) but only a game and a half out of second place. There was a hollow consolation: a 13–9 season edge over the Giants, who finished with 103 wins. The Giants were 50–11 on July 1, an .820 winning percentage; if it had been maintained they would have broken the Cubs' 1906 record of 116 victories.

Chicago's two long-time mound horses, Three-Finger Brown and Ed Reulbach, broke down. Combined, they were 15–12. His arm ailing, wounded, Brown appeared in 15 games and accounted for only five of the victories. Rookies Larry Cheney and Jimmy Lavender picked up the slack. Cheney, 26–10, tied for the league lead in wins with Rube Marquard and was second in complete games, 28. Lavender was 16–13 and the winner of a July matchup against the Giants when Marquard's 19-game winning streak was broken.

Evers, restored to full health, was back at second base and had a big season—.341, a career high. But the big hitter was Zimmerman, who became the first 20th-century National Leaguer to win the Triple Crown. Zimmerman hit .372 with 14 home runs and 103 runs batted in. He also led the league in hits, doubles, slugging percentage, and total bases and had a 23-game batting streak.

George Yantz, a reserve catcher, became a footnote in diamond history: one of the 60 players to retire with a 1.000 batting average. Yantz singled in his only at bat. Joe Tinker

was traded to Cincinnati after the season ended, leaving Evers the only holdover from the famed Tinker-to-Evers-to-Chance trio.

	W	L	ERA	G	GS	CG	IP	H	BB	K
Larry Cheney	(26)	10	2.85	42	37	(28)	303⅓	262	111	140
Jimmy Lavender	16	13	3.04	42	31	15	251⅓	240	89	109
Lew Richie	16	8	2.95	39	27	15	238	222	74	69
Ed Reulbach	10	6	3.78	39	19	8	169	161	60	75
Charlie Smith	7	4	4.21	21	5	1	94	92	31	47
Three-Finger Brown	5	6	2.64	15	8	5	88⅔	92	20	34
Lefty Leifield	7	2	2.42	13	9	4	70⅔	68	21	23
Fred Toney	1	2	5.25	9	2	0	24	21	11	9
Jim Maroney	1	1	4.56	10	3	1	23⅔	25	17	5
Harry McIntyre	1	2	3.80	4	3	2	23⅔	22	6	8
King Cole	1	2	10.89	8	3	0	19	36	8	9
George Pearce	0	0	5.52	3	2	0	14⅔	15	12	9
Grover Lowdermilk	0	1	9.69	2	1	1	13	17	14	8
Len Madden	0	1	2.92	6	2	0	12⅓	16	9	5
Ensign Cottrell	0	0	9.00	1	0	0	4	8	1	1
Joe Vernon	0	0	11.25	1	0	0	4	4	6	1
Rudy Sommers	0	1	3.00	1	0	0	3	4	2	2
Bill Powell	0	0	9.00	1	0	0	2	2	1	0
	91	59	3.42	257	152	80	1,358⅔	1,307	493	554

Shutouts: Cheney 4, Richie 4, Lavender 3, Brown 2, Leifield 1.

	G	AB	H	2B	3B	HR	R	RBI	SB	AVG
Regulars										
1B Vic Saier	122	451	130	25	14	2	74	61	11	.288
2B Johnny Evers	143	478	163	23	11	1	73	63	16	.341
SS Joe Tinker	142	550	155	24	7	0	80	75	25	.282
3B Heinie Zimmerman	145	557	(207)	(41)	14	(14)	95	(103)	23	(.372)
RF Wildfire Schulte	139	553	146	27	11	13	90	70	17	.264
CF Tommy Leach	82	265	64	10	3	2	50	32	14	.242
LF Jimmy Sheckard	146	523	128	22	10	3	85	47	15	.245
C Jimmy Archer	120	385	109	20	2	5	35	58	7	.283
Substitutes										
Red Downs	43	95	25	4	3	1	9	14	5	.263
Ed Lennox	27	81	19	4	1	1	13	16	1	.235
Tom Downey	13	22	4	0	2	0	4	4	0	.182
Charley Moore	5	9	2	0	1	0	2	2	0	.222
Frank Chance	2	5	1	0	0	0	2	0	1	.200
Ward Miller	86	241	74	11	4	0	45	22	11	.307
Solly Hofman	36	125	34	11	0	0	28	18	5	.272
Cy Williams	28	62	15	1	1	0	3	1	2	.242
Wilbur Good	39	35	5	0	0	0	7	1	3	.143
Tom Needham	33	90	16	5	0	0	12	10	3	.178
Dick Cotter	26	54	15	0	2	0	6	10	1	.278
Harry Chapman	1	4	1	0	1	0	1	1	1	.250
Mike Hechinger	2	3	0	0	0	0	0	0	0	.000
George Yantz	1	1	1	0	0	0	0	0	0	1.000
Pitchers										
Larry Cheney	42	106	24	5	2	1	13	12	0	.226
Jimmy Lavender	42	87	13	3	0	0	6	5	0	.149
Lew Richie	39	76	10	1	0	0	7	4	2	.132
Ed Reulbach	39	55	6	2	0	0	3	4	0	.109
Charlie Smith	21	35	9	1	0	0	4	2	0	.257
Three-Finger Brown	16	31	9	1	0	0	3	5	1	.290
Lefty Leifield	13	26	3	1	1	0	3	1	0	.115
Harry McIntyre	8	10	3	0	1	0	1	5	0	.300
Jim Maroney	10	6	3	1	0	0	1	1	0	.500
George Pearce	3	6	1	1	0	0	1	0	0	.167
King Cole	8	5	2	1	0	0	0	1	0	.400
Fred Toney	9	5	0	0	0	0	0	0	0	.000
Grover Lowdermilk	2	4	0	0	0	0	0	0	0	.000
Len Madden	6	4	1	0	0	0	0	0	0	.250
Joe Vernon	1	2	0	0	0	0	0	0	0	.000
Ensign Cottrell	1	1	0	0	0	0	0	0	0	.000
Bill Powell	1	0	0	0	0	0	0	0	0	—
Rudy Sommers	1	0	0	0	0	0	0	1	0	—
		5,048	1,398	245	91	43	756	649	164	.277

1913

Record: 88–65
Finish: Third
Games Behind: 13½
Manager: Johnny Evers

Johnny Evers was the new manager in 1913. He was given a five-year contract and presented with a chest of silverware during the opening-day ceremonies, but it was a brief honeymoon. He rallied the Cubs at the start and had them in first place from April 24 to May 4. It was downhill thereafter. They never regained the lead and finished third with an 88–65 record, 13½ laps behind the New York Giants.

Alias "The Crab," for his sour disposition, Evers fought with the umpires, and though there is no accurate count of his ejections, he probably was given the thumb in as many as 20 games. Contemporary reports mention that if Evers hadn't been kicked out of so many games the Cubs might have made a better showing.

Like Chance, Evers was a player-manager. He batted .284 in 135 games. He repeatedly enraged McGraw and Fred Clarke of Pittsburgh with statements that he had a considerable advantage over bench managers. "I would sooner play in a doubleheader," Evers said. "Watching a game from the bench is tiresome. I don't know how some of them do it, sitting and pulling for others."

Evers was not easy to play for. Al Bridwell, the new shortstop, almost came to blows with the apprentice manager. Tommy Leach had several disputes with "The Crab," and on one occasion ran in from center field for a face-to-face confrontation. Heinie Zimmerman was fined for insubordination. Evers was dismissed at the end of season but returned as the Cub manager eight years later, only to be fired during the season.

Zimmerman, ejected three times in a five-day sequence, led the club in batting with a .313 average and in runs batted in with 95, second highest in the league. First baseman Vic Saier, previously a disappointment, had a career year: .288, with 21 triples, which tied the club record. He was also third in the league in RBIs and home runs and fifth in slugging percentage.

Three-Finger Brown, who had been with the club since 1904 and had six consecutive 20-win seasons, was gone—traded to Cincinnati. Larry Cheney was now the horse, leading the league with 54 appearances. He started 36 games, had a 21–14 record, and worked 305 innings, 101 innings more than anyone else on the staff. Included in Cheney's victories was a 14-hit, 7–0 win against the Giants.

Bert Humphries, acquired from Cincinnati in the Tinker deal, was a pleasant surprise. Humphries, who had 16–15 records in his two previous big league seasons, was 16–4 and led the league in winning percentage. A control pitcher, he allowed 1.19 walks for every nine innings, second only to Christy Mathewson's 0.62. George Pearce, a rookie left-hander out of Aurora, Illinois, was the only other pitcher with more than 10 wins; he was 13–5 with a 2.31 earned run average.

	W	L	ERA	G	GS	CG	IP	H	BB	K
Larry Cheney	21	14	2.57	(54)	36	25	305	271	98	136
Jimmy Lavender	10	14	3.66	40	20	10	204	206	98	91
Bert Humphries	16	4	2.69	28	20	13	181	169	24	61
George Pearce	13	5	2.31	25	21	14	163⅓	137	59	73
Charlie Smith	7	9	2.55	20	17	8	137⅔	138	34	47
Orval Overall	4	5	3.31	11	9	6	68	73	26	30
Lew Richie	2	4	5.82	16	6	1	65	77	30	15
Hippo Vaughn	5	1	1.45	7	6	5	56	37	27	36
Eddie Stack	4	2	4.24	11	7	3	51	56	15	28
Fred Toney	2	2	6.00	7	5	2	39	52	22	12
Ed Reulbach	1	3	4.42	9	2	1	38⅔	41	21	10
Earl Moore	1	1	4.45	7	2	0	28⅓	34	12	12
Lefty Leifield	0	1	5.48	6	1	0	21⅓	28	5	4
Doc Watson	1	0	1.00	1	1	1	9	8	6	1
Zip Zabel	1	0	0.00	1	1	0	5	3	1	0
	88	65	3.13	243	154	89	1,372⅓	1,330	478	556

Shutouts: Pearce 3, Cheney 2, Humphries 2, Vaughn 2, Overall 1, Smith 1, Stack 1.

	G	AB	H	2B	3B	HR	R	RBI	SB	AVG
Regulars										
1B Vic Saier	148	518	149	14	(21)	14	93	92	26	.288
2B Johnny Evers	135	444	126	20	5	3	81	49	11	.284
SS Al Bridwell	135	405	97	6	6	1	35	37	12	.240
3B Heinie Zimmerman	127	447	140	28	12	9	69	95	18	.313
RF Wildfire Schulte	132	495	138	28	6	9	85	72	21	.279
CF Tommy Leach	130	454	131	23	10	6	(99)	32	21	.289
LF Mike Mitchell	81	278	72	11	6	4	37	35	15	.259
C Jimmy Archer	110	367	98	14	7	2	38	44	4	.267
Substitutes										
Art Phelan	90	259	65	11	6	2	41	35	8	.251
Red Corriden	45	97	17	3	0	2	13	9	4	.175
Fritz Mollwitz	2	7	3	0	0	0	1	0	0	.429
Chick Keating	2	5	1	1	0	0	1	0	0	.200
Ward Miller	80	203	48	5	7	1	23	16	13	.236
Cy Williams	49	156	35	3	3	4	17	32	5	.224
Otis Clymer	30	105	24	5	1	0	16	7	9	.229
Wilbur Good	49	91	23	3	2	1	11	12	5	.253
Tuffy Stewart	9	8	1	1	0	0	1	2	1	.125
Milo Allison	2	6	2	0	0	0	1	0	1	.333
Roger Bresnahan	68	161	37	5	2	1	20	21	7	.230
Tom Needham	20	42	10	4	1	0	5	11	0	.238
Bubbles Hargrave	3	3	1	0	0	0	0	1	0	.333
Mike Hechinger	2	2	0	0	0	0	0	0	0	.000
Pete Knisely	2	2	0	0	0	0	0	0	0	.000
Ed McDonald	1	0	0	0	0	0	0	0	0	—
Pitchers										
Larry Cheney	56	104	20	3	0	0	6	7	0	.192
Jimmy Lavender	40	68	8	1	0	0	2	1	0	.118
Bert Humphries	28	62	12	1	0	0	8	3	0	.194
George Pearce	25	55	4	1	0	0	5	1	0	.073
Charlie Smith	20	45	4	0	0	0	1	0	0	.089
Orval Overall	11	24	6	2	0	0	1	2	0	.250
Hippo Vaughn	7	21	4	0	0	0	3	1	0	.190
Lew Richie	16	17	2	1	0	0	2	0	0	.118
Eddie Stack	11	16	1	0	0	0	0	2	0	.063
Ed Reulbach	9	12	3	0	0	0	1	0	0	.250
Fred Toney	7	12	3	0	1	0	0	2	0	.250
Earl Moore	7	8	1	0	0	0	2	0	0	.125
Lefty Leifield	7	7	0	0	0	0	1	0	0	.000
Doc Watson	1	2	0	0	0	0	1	0	0	.000
Zip Zabel	1	2	0	0	0	0	0	0	0	.000
		5,010	1,286	194	96	59	720	621	181	.257

1914

Record: 78–76
Finish: Fourth
Games Behind: 16½
Manager: Hank O'Day

Hank O'Day, the umpire who had called Fred Merkle of the Giants out at second base, a decision that helped the Cubs win the 1908 pennant, was the new Chicago manager in 1914 and, like Evers, said farewell after one season. The Cubs were never in the lead, and according to I. E. Sanborn, the *Tribune* Boswell, the club played "without spirit."

Still, the Cubs held second place, without interruption, for more than a month, from June 29 to August 9, and never fell into the second division. They finished fourth, two games above .500 and 16½ games behind the Miracle Boston Braves, who won their first flag with an exciting finish beyond compare.

In last place on the morning of July 16, fifteen games behind the pace-setting Giants, the Braves stampeded into the lead 37 days later, on September 7, with an 8–3 win over the Giants, and breezed home, 10½ games in front. They won 61 of their last 77 games, led by pitchers Bill James and Dick Rudolph, who were, combined, 35–2 during the surge.

Miracles were a stranger to manager O'Day, but he did have a pair of 20-game winners, Larry Cheney, a reigning spitballer, and James "Hippo" Vaughn, an American League castoff who was to become the winningest left-hander in Cub history. Cheney was 20–18 and, as usual, among the league leaders in appearances, complete games, and innings; he also gave up a league-high 140 walks. Vaughn was 21–13 and led the club with a 2.05 earned run average.

The Cubs' excellent defense was long gone, forgotten in the fog of time. They committed 310 errors, 200 in the infield. Heinie Zimmerman, never a star with the glove, continued to lead all third basemen in errors with 39. Bill Sweeney, who replaced Evers at second base, was charged with 35, shortstop Red Corriden with 46. The double play was seldom turned—85, seventh in the league.

A breach developed between outfielders Wildfire Schulte and O'Day. Schulte was unaware he had been benched in favor of Pete Kniseley until the starting lineup was announced. Zimmerman was fined $100 when he made a wild throw to first on what should have been a routine double play.

There was a simmering feud between Zimmerman and Roger Bresnahan, who replaced the injured Jimmy Archer behind the plate. Zimmerman and Bresnahan exchanged blows, in Brooklyn, during the club's final eastern trip. Bresnahan's refusal to confirm or deny reports that he was about to jump to the St. Louis Cardinals as a player-manager was also unsettling. O'Day was fired at the end of the season and returned to umpiring.

	W	L	ERA	G	GS	CG	IP	H	BB	K
Larry Cheney	20	18	2.54	(50)	(40)	21	311⅓	239	(140)	157
Hippo Vaughn	21	13	2.05	42	35	23	293⅔	236	109	165
Jimmy Lavender	11	11	3.07	37	28	11	214⅓	191	87	87
Bert Humphries	10	11	2.68	34	22	8	171	162	37	62
George Pearce	8	12	3.51	30	16	4	141	122	65	78
Zip Zabel	4	4	2.18	29	7	2	128	104	45	50
Charlie Smith	2	4	3.86	16	5	1	53⅔	49	15	17
Casey Hageman	2	1	3.47	16	1	0	46⅔	44	12	17
Eddie Stack	0	1	4.96	7	1	0	16⅓	13	11	9
George McConnell	0	1	1.29	1	1	0	7	3	3	3
Elmer Koestner	0	0	2.84	4	0	0	6⅓	6	4	6
	78	76	2.71	266	156	70	1,389⅓	1,169	528	651

Shutouts: Cheney 6, Vaughn 4, Humphries 2, Lavender 2.

	G	AB	H	2B	3B	HR	R	RBI	SB	AVG
Regulars										
1B Vic Saier	153	537	129	24	8	18	87	72	19	.240
2B Bill Sweeney	134	463	101	14	5	1	45	38	18	.218
SS Red Corriden	107	318	73	9	5	3	42	29	13	.230
3B Heinie Zimmerman	146	564	167	36	12	4	75	87	17	.296
RF Wilbur Good	154	580	158	24	7	2	70	43	31	.272
CF Tommy Leach	153	577	152	24	9	7	80	46	16	.263
LF Wildfire Schulte	137	465	112	22	7	5	54	61	16	.241
C Roger Bresnahan	86	248	69	10	4	0	42	24	14	.278
Substitutes										
Claud Derrick	28	96	21	3	1	0	5	13	2	.219
Bob Fisher	15	50	15	2	2	0	5	5	2	.300
Art Phelan	25	46	13	2	1	0	5	3	0	.283
Art Bues	14	45	10	1	1	0	3	4	1	.222
Chick Keating	20	30	3	0	1	0	3	0	0	.100
Fritz Mollwitz	13	20	3	0	0	0	0	1	1	.150
Herman Bronkie	1	1	1	1	0	0	1	1	0	1.000
Jimmy Johnston	50	101	23	3	2	1	9	8	3	.228
Cy Williams	55	94	19	2	2	0	12	5	2	.202
Pete Knisely	37	69	9	0	1	0	5	5	0	.130
Johnny Bates	9	8	1	0	0	0	2	1	0	.125
Jimmy Archer	79	248	64	9	2	0	17	19	1	.258
Bubbles Hargrave	23	36	8	2	0	0	3	2	2	.222
Tom Needham	9	17	2	1	0	0	3	3	1	.118
Earl Tyree	1	4	0	0	0	0	1	0	0	.000
Milo Allison	1	1	1	0	0	0	0	0	0	1.000
Tuffy Stewart	2	1	0	0	0	0	0	0	0	.000
Pitchers										
Larry Cheney	50	100	18	2	2	0	8	10	1	.180
Hippo Vaughn	42	97	14	3	1	1	10	3	2	.144
Jimmy Lavender	37	63	11	3	1	0	8	5	2	.175
Bert Humphries	35	55	13	0	0	0	4	6	0	.236
George Pearce	30	45	4	1	0	0	2	3	0	.089
Zip Zabel	29	38	7	0	0	0	2	4	0	.184
Casey Hageman	16	15	7	1	0	0	2	1	0	.467
Charlie Smith	16	11	1	0	0	0	0	0	0	.091
Eddie Stack	7	4	0	0	0	0	0	0	0	.000
George McConnell	1	2	0	0	0	0	0	0	0	.000
Elmer Koestner	5	1	0	0	0	0	0	0	0	.000
	5,050	1,229	199	74	42	605	502	164	.243

1915

Record: 73–80
Finish: Fourth
Games Behind: 17½
Manager: Roger Bresnahan

Catcher Roger Bresnahan succeeded Hank O'Day at the helm in 1915, the Cubs' third manager in three years. In an effort to motivate his players, Bresnahan told them he would reward them with hats when they were in first place. Bresnahan bought the "Kelleys" in early June. The Cubs relinquished the lead on June 9, were back on top on June 17, and led until July 12, but the team played poorly thereafter and finished fourth with a 73–80 record. It was the first time in 13 years the Cubs finished below .500.

Hippo Vaughn led an ineffective pitching staff with 20 wins. Larry Cheney, who had won 67 games in the previous three seasons, was a major disappointment. Cheney was 8–9 when he was traded to Brooklyn in a late-season deal. Jimmy Lavender pitched a no-hitter against the Giants on August 31 but was 10–16 overall. The only other pitcher to win in double figures was left-hander George Pearce, 13–9.

It was also a bad year for infielder Heinie Zimmerman, who gave Bresnahan nothing but woe. The burly Zimmerman, who had averaged .322 during the previous three seasons, dropped to .265 with only three home runs and 62 runs batted in, and he played with such indifference that his teammates "read the riot act to him" during a train trip from Cincinnati to Chicago.

Correspondent George Robbins, in the July 8 issue of the *Sporting News,* told the sad tale:

"Zimmerman was surrounded and besieged by his irate teammates. Peeved with Zim's behavior in kicking himself out of a game [being ejected by an umpire] which the Cubs lost, leading members of the team told the big fellow what they thought of his actions.

"In the attacking force that swept down on him were such orators as Saier, Archer, Cheney, and Schulte. The party was reinforced by such handy word painters as Good, Phelan, and Vaughn. They formed a flying wedge and assaulted the big fellow so viciously and with such unanimity that it is said Heinie came near to weeping.

"The players told Heinie his services were needed and that he would have to brace up and work for the good interests of the team. They said they meant business and that they would not tolerate a repetition of his foolishness. Zim capitulated and told his teammates, 'If I get kicked out again I'll make a present of $5 to each member of the club.' This means the next time Zim willfully kicks himself out of game he will hand over $105 in good money to his irate teammates."

Despite their erratic play the Cubs held first place a total of 41 days, approximately one-fourth of the season. George "Zip" Zabel set a major league relief record that still stands. On June 8 against Brooklyn, Zabel was summoned from the bullpen with two outs in the first inning, when starter Bert Humphries suffered a hand injury, and worked 18⅓ innings in a 4–3, 19–inning victory. Bresnahan was relieved of his command after the season.

	W	L	ERA	G	GS	CG	IP	H	BB	K
Hippo Vaughn	20	12	2.87	41	34	18	269⅔	240	77	148
Jimmy Lavender	10	16	2.58	41	24	13	220	178	67	117
George Pearce	13	9	3.32	36	20	8	176	158	77	96
Bert Humphries	8	13	2.31	31	22	10	171⅓	183	23	45
Zip Zabel	7	10	3.20	36	17	8	163	124	84	60
Larry Cheney	8	9	3.56	25	18	6	131⅓	120	55	68
Pete Standridge	4	1	3.61	29	3	2	112⅓	120	36	42
Karl Adams	1	9	4.71	26	12	3	107	105	43	57
Phil Douglas	1	1	2.16	4	4	2	25	17	7	18
Brad Hogg	1	0	2.08	2	2	1	13	12	6	0
Ed Schorr	0	0	7.50	2	0	0	6	9	5	3
Bob Wright	0	0	2.25	2	0	0	4	6	0	3
	73	80	3.11	275	156	71	1,399	1,272	480	657

Shutouts: Humphries 4, Vaughn 4, Zabel 3, Cheney 2, Pearce 2, Lavender 1, Douglas 1, Hogg 1.

	G	AB	H	2B	3B	HR	R	RBI	SB	AVG
Regulars										
1B Vic Saier	144	497	131	35	11	11	74	64	29	.264
2B Heinie Zimmerman	139	520	138	28	11	3	65	62	19	.265
SS Bob Fisher	147	568	163	22	5	5	70	53	9	.287
3B Art Phelan	133	448	98	16	7	3	41	35	12	.219
RF Wilbur Good	128	498	126	18	9	2	66	27	19	.253
CF Cy Williams	151	518	133	22	6	13	59	64	15	.257
LF Wildfire Schulte	151	550	137	20	6	12	66	69	19	.249
C Jimmy Archer	97	309	75	11	5	1	21	27	5	.243
Substitutes										
Polly McLarry	68	127	25	3	0	1	16	12	2	.197
Alex McCarthy	23	72	19	3	0	1	4	6	2	.264
Eddie Mulligan	11	22	8	1	0	0	5	2	2	.364
Chick Keating	4	8	0	0	0	0	1	0	1	.000
Joe Schultz	7	8	2	0	0	0	1	3	0	.250
Red Murray	51	144	43	6	1	0	20	11	6	.299
Pete Knisely	64	134	33	9	0	0	12	17	1	.246
John Fluhrer	6	6	2	0	0	0	0	0	1	.333
Red Corriden	6	3	0	0	0	0	1	0	0	.000
Roger Bresnahan	77	221	45	8	1	1	19	19	19	.204
Bubbles Hargrave	15	19	3	0	1	0	2	2	0	.158
Jack Wallace	2	7	2	0	0	0	1	1	0	.286
Bob O'Farrell	2	3	1	0	0	0	0	0	0	.333
Pitchers										
Hippo Vaughn	43	86	14	3	0	0	8	9	3	.163
Jimmy Lavender	46	67	9	3	0	0	1	0	0	.134
George Pearce	36	56	11	2	1	0	4	2	0	.196
Zip Zabel	37	54	4	0	0	0	2	0	2	.074
Bert Humphries	31	46	8	0	1	0	3	1	0	.174
Larry Cheney	25	40	6	0	0	0	2	2	0	.150
Pete Standridge	30	40	9	2	1	0	5	4	0	.225
Karl Adams	26	30	0	0	0	0	0	0	0	.000
Phil Douglas	4	8	0	0	0	0	0	0	0	.000
Brad Hogg	2	3	0	0	0	0	0	0	0	.000
Ed Schorr	2	2	1	0	0	0	1	0	0	.500
Bob Wright	2	0	0	0	0	0	0	0	0	—
	5,114	1,246	212	66	53	570	492	166	.244	

1916

Record: 67–86
Finish: Fifth
Games Behind: 26½
Manager: Joe Tinker

William A. Weeghman, an energetic Chicago restaurateur who had been the principal owner of the Chicago Whales in the outlaw Federal League, formed a purchase group that bought 100 percent of the Cubs for $500,000. The deal was completed on January 20, 1916. Charles P. Taft of Cincinnati had owned 90 percent of the stock, Harry Ackerland of Pittsburgh, 10 percent.

William Wrigley, Jr., a local chewing gum magnate, was among Weeghman's associates and invested $100,000. Three years later, after Weeghman had suffered severe financial losses, Wrigley had majority control. The Cubs remained a Wrigley possession for 62 years. The inheritors were William Jr.'s son Philip and his grandson William, who sold the club to the Tribune Company in 1981.

Weeghman's Whales had been the anchor and the most successful of the Federal League clubs; for the previous two seasons the Whales had challenged the Cubs and the White Sox for the Chicago baseball dollar. As part of the peace settlement, negotiated when the Federals folded after the 1915 season, the National League owners, anxious to welcome Weeghman and have him on their side, paid $50,000 of Charles Taft's purchase price.

Joe Tinker, who had managed the Whales to the 1915 Federal flag, was Weeghman's choice to pilot the Cubs. Initially, Weeghman and Tinker believed an amalgamation of the

Whales and the Cubs would strengthen the club, but the only player from the Whales to play a major role was Cy Williams, a slugging center fielder who batted .279 and led the Cubs in home runs with 12.

The club moved from its West Side Grounds to the North Side, to Weeghman Park, later renamed Wrigley Field. The enterprising Weeghman, who had a pleasant personality, was well received by the Chicago fans. He was the first owner to hire a press agent, John O. Seys, a former Chicago baseball writer who visited newspaper offices in advance of the club. Weeghman also pioneered the giveaway promotion. Fans who purchased "meal tickets" at Weeghman's chain of cafeterias were admitted to Cub games without charge.

Like his three managerial predecessors, Tinker was limited to one year. Heinie Zimmerman was as cantankerous as ever. In mid-August, after "The Baron" had thrown to the wrong base, Tinker confronted him.

"Aw, shut up!" Zimmerman shouted.

"You're fined ten dollars for that," Tinker said.

"Better make it fifty," Zimmerman replied. Snapping his fingers, Zimmerman said, "Ten means that much to me."

Tinker did as advised and, after consulting with Weeghman, suspended Zimmerman. On August 28, Zimmerman was gone—traded to McGraw's Giants for second baseman Larry Doyle and two undistinguished outfielders. Wildfire Schulte, never guilty of insubordination, had been dealt to Pittsburgh a month earlier. The Cubs finished fifth with a 67–86 record, 26½ games out of first place.

	W	L	ERA	G	GS	CG	IP	H	BB	K
Hippo Vaughn	17	14	2.20	44	35	21	294	269	67	144
Claude Hendrix	8	16	2.68	36	24	15	218	193	67	117
Jimmy Lavender	10	14	2.82	36	25	9	188	163	62	91
George McConnell	4	12	2.57	28	20	8	171⅓	137	35	82
Gene Packard	10	6	2.78	37	15	5	155⅔	154	38	36
Mike Prendergast	6	11	2.31	35	10	4	152	127	23	56
Tom Seaton	6	6	3.27	31	14	4	121	108	43	45
Three-Finger Brown	2	3	3.91	12	4	2	48⅓	52	9	21
Paul Carter	2	2	2.75	8	5	2	36	26	17	14
Scott Perry	2	1	2.54	4	3	2	28⅓	30	3	10
George Pearce	0	0	2.08	4	1	0	4⅓	6	1	0
	67	85	2.65	275	156	72	1,416⅔	1,265	365	616

Shutouts: Lavender 4, Vaughn 4, Hendrix 3, Packard 2, Prendergast 2, McConnell 1, Perry 1.

	G	AB	H	2B	3B	HR	R	RBI	SB	AVG
Regulars										
1B Vic Saier	147	498	126	25	3	7	60	50	20	.253
2B Otto Knabe	57	145	40	8	0	0	17	7	3	.276
SS Chuck Wortman	69	234	47	4	2	2	17	16	4	.201
3B Heinie Zimmerman	107	398	116	25	5	6	54	64	15	.291
RF Max Flack	141	465	120	14	3	3	65	20	24	.258
CF Cy Williams	118	405	113	19	9	12	55	66	6	.279
LF Les Mann	127	415	113	13	9	2	46	29	11	.272
C Jimmy Archer	77	205	45	6	2	1	11	30	3	.220
Substitutes										
Rollie Zeider	98	345	81	11	2	1	29	22	9	.235
Eddie Mulligan	58	189	29	3	4	0	13	9	1	.153
Steve Yerkes	44	137	36	6	2	1	12	10	1	.263
Alex McCarthy	37	107	26	2	3	0	10	6	1	.243
Fritz Mollwitz	33	71	19	2	0	0	1	11	4	.268
Mickey Doolan	28	70	15	2	1	0	4	5	0	.214
Charlie Pechous	22	69	10	1	1	0	5	4	1	.145
Larry Doyle	9	38	15	5	1	1	6	7	2	.395
Joe Tinker	7	10	1	0	0	0	0	1	0	.100
Charlie Deal	2	8	2	1	0	0	2	3	0	.250
Marty Shay	2	7	2	0	0	0	0	0	0	.286
Herb Hunter	2	4	0	0	0	0	0	0	0	.000
Wildfire Schulte	72	230	68	11	1	5	31	27	9	.296
Joe Kelly	54	169	43	7	1	2	18	15	10	.254
Dutch Zwilling	35	53	6	1	0	1	4	8	0	.113
Earl Smith	14	27	7	1	1	0	2	4	1	.259
Solly Hofman	5	16	5	2	1	0	2	2	0	.313
Merwin Jacobson	4	13	3	0	0	0	2	0	2	.231
Bill Fischer	65	179	35	9	2	1	15	14	2	.196
Art Wilson	36	114	22	3	1	0	5	5	1	.193
Rowdy Elliott	23	55	14	3	0	0	5	3	1	.255
Nick Allen	5	16	1	0	0	0	0	1	0	.063
Clem Clemens	10	15	0	0	0	0	0	0	0	.000
John O'Connor	1	0	0	0	0	0	0	0	0	—
Bob O'Farrell	1	0	0	0	0	0	0	0	0	—
Eddie Sicking	1	1	0	0	0	0	0	0	0	.000
Pitchers										
Hippo Vaughn	44	104	14	1	1	0	4	7	0	.135
Claude Hendrix	45	80	16	3	0	1	4	5	0	.200
George McConnell	48	57	9	0	0	0	2	0	0	.158
Gene Packard	44	54	7	3	0	0	9	1	0	.130
Jimmy Lavender	36	53	8	1	0	0	1	0	0	.151
Mike Prendergast	35	46	7	0	0	0	1	1	0	.152
Tom Seaton	35	38	7	1	1	0	4	2	2	.184
Three-Finger Brown	12	16	4	0	0	0	2	0	0	.250
Paul Carter	8	12	2	0	0	0	1	0	0	.167
Scott Perry	4	11	3	1	0	0	0	1	0	.273
George Pearce	4	0	0	0	0	0	0	0	0	—
	5,179	1,237	194	56	46	520	456	133		.239

1917

Record: 74–80
Finish: Fifth
Games Behind: 24
Manager: Fred Mitchell

Two notable Chicago debuts occurred in 1917: Cap Anson made his first appearance at the Majestic Theater reciting a sketch prepared by *Tribune* baseball writer Ring Lardner; and Fred Mitchell made his bow as the Cub manager. Mitchell, who played all nine positions during an undistinguished 13-year big league career, was born Frederick Yapp in Cambridge, Massachusetts; he took his mother's maiden name at the suggestion of a Boston sportswriter.

The season began with great expectations. The Cubs had a good early run and were in first place after reeling off 10 consecutive victories in mid-May but dropped out of the lead when the Phillies swept them in a controversial four-game "beanball" series. Grover Cleveland Alexander, who had one of the best fastballs in the National League, threw a half dozen knockdown pitches in the opener.

Mitchell raged and ordered pitcher Phil Douglas to retaliate, "to do the dusting," but the Phillies beat him 4–3 on May 21 and took over first place. The Cubs hung on and were in the first division until July 7 but never threatened thereafter. They finished fifth, six games under .500 and 24 games out of the lead.

It was the year America entered World War I, and the Cubs, like the other big league clubs, showed their patriotism. They dug foxholes and marched under the direction of an army sergeant during daily one-hour drills at their Pasadena, California, training camp. A recruiting station was installed at Weeghman Park on opening day, ready to enlist "any fan with the martial spirit."

Vic Saier, who had developed into the league's best first baseman, broke a leg sliding into the plate on April 15, in the sixth game of the new season. Fred Merkle, whose "boner" had helped the Cubs win the 1908 pennant, was purchased from Brooklyn in a cash sale six days later and finished the season at first base.

Second baseman Larry Doyle suffered a succession of injuries. Catcher Art Wilson was also sidelined with a series of hand injuries and was behind the plate in only 75 games. Chuck Wortman, installed at shortstop, didn't hit as expected and in midseason was replaced by Pete Kilduff. Wortman, who hit .174, had 190 at bats, Kilduff 202.

It was the year of the famous Hippo Vaughn–Fred Toney double no-hitter, the ultimate pitchers' duel. Neither allowed a hit for the first nine innings. Toney, a right-hander with the Cincinnati Reds, won the game 1–0 on an unearned run in the tenth when Vaughn, who faced the minimum 27 batters in the first nine innings, was nicked for two hits. Jim Thorpe drove in the winning run with a two-out high bouncer to the left of the mound.

The Cubs were seventh in the league in hitting with a .239 team average and in home runs with 17. Their leading hitter was outfielder Les Mann, .273. The only pitcher, among the starters, who was over .500 was Hippo Vaughn, 23–13. Phil Douglas was next in victories with 14. Paddy Driscoll, who played professional football and along with Thorpe was among the first to perform in both sports, batted .107 in 13 games.

	W	L	ERA	G	GS	CG	IP	H	BB	K
Hippo Vaughn	23	13	2.01	41	39	27	295⅔	255	91	195
Phil Douglas	14	20	2.55	(51)	37	20	293⅓	269	50	151
Claude Hendrix	10	12	2.60	40	21	13	215	202	72	81
Al Demaree	5	9	2.55	24	18	6	141⅓	125	37	43
Paul Carter	5	8	3.26	23	13	6	113¾	115	19	34
Vic Aldridge	6	6	3.12	30	6	1	106⅔	100	37	44
Mike Prendergast	3	6	3.35	35	8	1	99½	112	21	43
Tom Seaton	5	4	2.53	16	9	3	74½	60	23	27
Dutch Ruether	2	0	2.48	10	4	1	36⅓	37	12	23
Harry Weaver	1	1	2.75	4	2	1	19⅔	17	7	8
Roy Walker	0	1	3.86	2	1	0	7	8	5	4
Gene Packard	0	0	10.80	2	0	0	1⅔	3	0	1
	74	80	2.62	278	158	79	1,404	1,303	374	654

Shutouts: Douglas 5, Vaughn 5, Aldridge 1, Demaree 1, Hendrix 1, Seaton 1.

	G	AB	H	2B	3B	HR	R	RBI	SB	AVG
Regulars										
1B Fred Merkle	146	549	146	30	9	3	65	57	13	.266
2B Larry Doyle	135	476	121	19	5	6	48	61	5	.254
SS Chuck Wortman	75	190	33	4	1	0	24	9	6	.174
3B Charlie Deal	135	449	114	11	3	0	46	47	10	.254
RF Max Flack	131	447	111	18	7	0	65	21	17	.248
CF Cy Williams	138	468	113	22	4	5	53	42	8	.241
LF Les Mann	117	444	121	19	10	1	63	44	14	.273
C Art Wilson	81	211	45	9	2	2	17	25	6	.213
Substitutes										
Rollie Zeider	108	354	86	14	2	0	36	27	17	.243
Pete Kilduff	56	202	56	9	5	0	23	15	11	.277
Dutch Ruether	31	44	12	1	3	0	3	11	0	.273
Charlie Pechous	13	41	10	0	0	0	2	1	1	.244
Paddy Driscoll	13	28	3	1	0	0	2	3	2	.107
Vic Saier	6	21	5	1	0	0	5	2	0	.238
Roy Leslie	7	19	4	0	0	0	1	1	1	.211
Herb Hunter	3	3	0	0	0	0	0	0	0	.000
Harry Wolter	117	353	88	15	7	0	44	28	7	.249
Morrie Schick	14	34	5	0	0	0	3	3	0	.147
Turner Barber	7	28	6	1	0	0	2	2	1	.214
Bill Marriott	2	6	0	0	0	0	0	0	0	.000
Harry Wolfe	9	5	2	0	0	0	1	1	0	.400
Rowdy Elliott	85	223	56	8	5	0	18	28	4	.251
Pickles Dillhoefer	42	95	12	1	1	0	3	8	1	.126
Bob O'Farrell	3	8	3	2	0	0	1	1	1	.375
Jimmy Archer	2	2	0	0	0	0	0	0	0	.000
Earl Blackburn	2	2	0	0	0	0	0	0	0	.000
Pitchers										
Hippo Vaughn	41	100	16	2	1	0	7	6	1	.160
Phil Douglas	51	89	11	0	1	0	3	3	0	.124
Claude Hendrix	48	86	22	3	1	0	7	7	1	.256
Al Demaree	24	41	5	0	0	0	0	1	0	.122
Paul Carter	23	33	6	1	0	0	4	2	0	.182
Vic Aldridge	30	29	4	0	0	0	3	1	0	.138
Mike Prendergast	35	28	7	2	0	0	1	0	0	.250
Tom Seaton	16	21	5	1	0	0	2	1	0	.238
Harry Weaver	4	5	1	0	0	0	0	0	0	.200
Roy Walker	2	1	0	0	0	0	0	0	0	.000
Gene Packard	2	0	0	0	0	0	0	0	0	—
	5,135	1,229	194	67	17	552	458	127	.239

1918

Record: 84–45
Finish: First
Games Ahead: 10½
Manager: Fred Mitchell

Owner Charles Weeghman, now known as Spendthrift Charlie, opened his purse in an unsuccessful effort to acquire Rogers Hornsby from the Cardinals. "I went as far as I could," Weeghman said after offering two front-liners and $50,000. "We will try to get some other strong batter, but if we have to go into the pennant race with what we have I still think we will be in the fight for the flag."

Weeghman's prophecy came true. Not only were the Cubs in contention in 1918, but they also lapped the field. They won almost twice as many games as they lost, 84–45, and breezed to their first pennant since 1910, ten and a half games ahead of the second-place Giants. Because of the "work or fight" order, the season was shortened. Play was terminated after Labor Day.

Before the season Fred Mitchell, in his second year at the helm, insisted it was necessary to improve the defense and starting pitching. Dode Paskert, a fleet-footed outfielder who was beyond the draft age, arrived from Philadelphia in exchange for Cy Williams, who could hit but couldn't throw.

A much more publicized deal with the Phillies brought the battery of Grover Cleveland Alexander—"Alexander the Great"—and Bill Killefer. Alexander was among the best pitchers in diamond history and was coming off three successive 30-victory seasons. To swing the deal, the Cubs paid $60,000 and parted with pitcher Mike Prendergast and catcher Pickles Dillhoefer.

But the most significant newcomer was rookie shortstop Charlie Hollocher. Previously with Portland of the Pacific Coast League, Hollocher was a defensive wizard beyond a doubt. The question was, Could he hit? Hollocher answered with a .316 average, fourth high in the league. He led in total bases, was third in steals, and was fourth in runs.

Hollocher was the Pete Rose of his time. He played with unusual intensity and often slid into first base on ground balls. By midseason he was acclaimed as a better fielder than the Giants' Dave Bancroft, previously the league's reigning defensive shortstop. A half century later reserve catcher Bob O'Farrell, the last survivor of the 1918 champions, said the pennant could not have been won without Hollocher: "He was the spark plug of the team."

"Alexander the Great" wasn't a contributor. Signed for the princely salary of $12,000, plus a $5,000 bonus, he was called by the army after he had made his third start. He worked only 26 innings and departed with a 2–1 record. Catcher Killefer, the other player in the deal, was the "steal." Killefer was an outstanding handler of pitchers and led all catchers in fielding percentage.

The outfield defense of Paskert in center, Les Mann in left, and Max Flack in right was first-rate, and along with a strong inner defense, helped the pitchers. The Cubs led the league in fewest runs allowed, as well as in scoring. Third baseman Charlie Deal and first baseman Fred Merkle were also outstanding. Merkle hit .297 and led the club in RBIs with 65.

Mitchell's "Big Three" of Hippo Vaughn, Claude Hendrix, and Lefty George Tyler, combined, were 53–20 on August 21, a .726 winning percentage. At the finish they were 60–26 for .698 and were 1-2-3 in the league in victories: Vaughn had 22; Hendrix and Tyler, 19 each. Tyler and Vaughn tied for first in shutouts with eight apiece. Mitchell was hailed as a managerial "genius."

	W	L	ERA	G	GS	CG	IP	H	BB	K
Hippo Vaughn	(22)	10	(1.74)	35	(33)	27	(290⅓)	216	76	(148)
Lefty Tyler	19	9	2.00	33	30	22	269⅓	218	67	102
Claude Hendrix	19	7	2.78	32	27	21	233	229	54	86
Phil Douglas	9	9	2.13	25	19	11	156⅔	145	31	51
Paul Carter	4	1	2.71	21	4	1	73	78	19	13
Speed Martin	6	2	1.84	9	5	4	53⅔	47	14	16
Roy Walker	1	3	2.70	13	7	2	43⅓	50	15	20
Harry Weaver	2	2	2.20	8	3	1	32⅔	27	7	9
Grover Alexander	2	1	1.73	3	3	3	26	19	3	15
Vic Aldridge	0	1	1.46	3	0	0	12⅓	11	6	10
Buddy Napier	0	0	5.40	1	0	0	6⅔	10	4	2
	84	45	2.18	183	131	92	1,197	1,050	296	472

Shutouts: Tyler (8), Vaughn (8), Carter 4, Hendrix 3, Douglas 2, Martin 1, Weaver 1.

	G	AB	H	2B	3B	HR	R	RBI	SB	AVG
Regulars										
1B Fred Merkle	129	482	143	25	5	3	55	65	21	.297
2B Rollie Zeider	82	251	56	3	2	0	31	26	16	.223
SS Charlie Hollocher	131	(509)	(161)	23	6	2	72	38	26	.316
3B Charlie Deal	119	414	99	9	3	2	43	34	11	.239
RF Max Flack	123	478	123	17	10	4	74	41	17	.257
CF Dode Paskert	127	461	132	24	3	3	69	59	20	.286
LF Les Mann	129	489	141	27	7	2	69	55	21	.288
C Bill Killefer	104	331	77	10	3	0	30	22	5	.233
Substitutes										
Pete Kilduff	30	93	19	2	2	0	7	13	1	.204
Charlie Pick	29	89	29	4	1	0	13	12	7	.326
Bill McCabe	29	45	8	0	1	0	9	5	2	.178
Chuck Wortman	17	17	2	0	0	1	4	3	3	.118
Turner Barber	55	123	29	3	2	0	11	10	3	.236
Bob O'Farrell	52	113	32	7	3	1	9	14	0	.283
Rowdy Elliott	5	10	0	0	0	0	0	0	0	.000
Tom Daly	1	1	0	0	0	0	0	0	0	.000
Tommy Clarke	1	0	0	0	0	0	0	0	0	—
Fred Lear	2	1	0	0	0	0	0	0	0	.000
Pitchers										
Lefty Tyler	38	100	21	1	0	0	9	8	0	.210
Hippo Vaughn	35	96	23	3	2	0	13	8	4	.240
Claude Hendrix	35	91	24	3	3	3	14	17	1	.264
Phil Douglas	25	55	14	1	0	0	2	5	0	.255
Paul Carter	21	25	6	0	0	0	2	2	0	.240
Speed Martin	9	16	3	1	0	0	0	0	0	.188
Roy Walker	13	11	0	0	0	0	0	0	0	.000
Grover Alexander	3	10	1	0	0	0	1	0	0	.100
Harry Weaver	8	8	2	0	0	0	0	0	1	.250
Vic Aldridge	3	3	1	1	0	0	1	1	0	.333
Buddy Napier	1	3	1	0	0	0	0	0	0	.333
	4,325	1,147	164	53	21	538	438	159		.265

1919

Record: 75–65
Finish: Third
Games Behind: 21
Manager: Fred Mitchell

"Alexander the Great" returned from France, a war hero, and was welcomed by a huge crowd at the LaSalle Street Station. "One would have thought the President of the United States was arriving," wrote George Robbins in *The Sporting News,* also predicting, "This gives the Cubs the best pitching staff in baseball."

Alexander, reportedly "muscle-bound by his experiences in the war," had a poor start and didn't win his first game in 1919 until June 2. Nonetheless, he led the league with a 1.72 earned run average and won 16 games, nine of them shutouts to equal the club record. Among Alexander's calciminings was a 58-minute 3–0 victory over Boston on September 21, the fastest game in Cub history.

Otherwise, it was a slow and dismal season for the defending champions. The schedule was reduced from 154 to 140 games. As early as mid-May, when the Giants swept them in a four-game series—beating Alexander, Hippo Vaughn, Phil Douglas, and Lefty George Tyler in that order—it was apparent that a second successive Cub pennant was not likely.

The pennant race was a duel between Cincinnati and New York, with the Reds capturing their first flag. The Cubs limped home a distant third, 21 games out, and won only three season series—against Boston, St. Louis, and Philadelphia, the three bottom clubs.

Fred Mitchell, who had the dual title of president-manager, turned in his president's badge in midseason. He was succeeded in that capacity by William L. Veeck, a former traveling Chicago baseball writer who wrote under the name Bill Bailey and had been the inspiration for the popular song "Won't You Come Home, Bill Bailey?" He was also the father of Bill Veeck, Jr., a baseball maverick who would operate three American League franchises.

In an attempt to rouse the club, Mitchell and Veeck were constantly changing personnel. Outfielder Les Mann and infielder Charlie Pick were traded for Buck Herzog, a pepper-pot second baseman. "Shufflin' " Phil Douglas, an alcoholic pitcher, was sent to New York, and Pete Kilduff was traded for veteran infielder Lee Magee, who appeared in 79 games. At the end of the season Magee was suspended for life for "selling games" in 1918 when he was with Cincinnati, the first public exposure of dishonesty since the Louisville Crooks in 1877.

Expected to have a strong hitting team, the Cubs had a marshmallow offense. They were last in the league in scoring and had only one .300 hitter, Turner Barber, .313 in 76 games. The pitchers caught up with the suddenly injury-prone Charles Hollocher, the rookie sensation of the previous season. Hollocher's average dropped 46 points to .270. Merkle, an aging reliable, led the club in runs batted in with 62.

Shufflin' Phil Douglas, who was implicated in a gambling scandal

Vaughn was the star of the pitching staff with a 21–14 record, followed by Alexander, 16–11. Lefty Tyler, 19–9 the previous season, was mostly on the shelf, appearing in only six games, and finished with a 2–2 record. Tyler was in pain from the moment he reported to spring training; in November he was sent to the Mayo Institute, where doctors announced he was "a perfect physical specimen" except for his teeth. Tyler returned to Chicago and had all his teeth extracted.

	W	L	ERA	G	GS	CG	IP	H	BB	K
Hippo Vaughn	21	14	1.79	38	(37)	25	(306⅔)	264	62	(141)
Grover Alexander	16	11	(1.72)	30	27	20	235	180	38	121
Claude Hendrix	10	14	2.62	33	25	15	206⅓	208	42	69
Speed Martin	8	8	2.47	35	14	7	163⅓	158	52	54
Phil Douglas	10	6	2.00	25	19	8	161⅔	133	34	63
Paul Carter	5	4	2.65	28	7	2	85	81	28	17
Sweetbreads Bailey	3	5	3.15	21	5	0	71⅓	75	20	19
Lefty Tyler	2	2	2.10	6	5	3	30	20	13	9
Harry Weaver	0	1	10.80	2	1	0	3⅓	6	2	1
Joel Newkirk	0	0	13.50	1	0	0	2	2	3	1
	75	65	2.21	219	140	80	1,265	1,127	294	495

Shutouts: Alexander 9, Douglas 4, Vaughn 4, Hendrix 2, Martin 2.

	G	AB	H	2B	3B	HR	R	RBI	SB	AVG
Regulars										
1B Fred Merkle	133	498	133	20	6	3	52	62	20	.267
2B Charlie Pick	75	269	65	8	6	0	27	18	17	.242
SS Charlie Hollocher	115	430	116	14	5	3	51	26	16	.270
3B Charlie Deal	116	405	117	23	5	2	37	52	11	.289
RF Max Flack	116	469	138	20	4	6	71	35	18	.294
CF Dode Paskert	87	270	53	11	3	2	21	29	7	.196
LF Les Mann	80	299	68	8	8	1	31	22	12	.227
C Bill Killefer	103	315	90	10	2	0	17	22	5	.286
Substitutes										
Buck Herzog	52	193	53	4	4	0	15	17	12	.275
Pete Kilduff	31	88	24	4	2	0	5	8	1	.273
Fred Lear	40	76	17	3	1	1	8	11	2	.224
Lee Magee	79	267	78	12	4	1	36	17	14	.292
Turner Barber	76	230	72	9	4	0	26	21	7	.313
Dave Robertson	27	96	20	2	0	1	8	10	3	.208
Bill McCabe	33	84	13	3	1	0	8	5	3	.155
Barney Friberg	8	20	4	1	0	0	0	1	0	.200
Hal Reilly	1	3	0	0	0	0	0	0	0	.000
Bob O'Farrell	49	125	27	4	2	0	11	9	2	.216
Tom Daly	25	50	11	0	1	0	4	1	0	.220
Pitchers										
Hippo Vaughn	38	98	17	4	0	0	5	2	0	.173
Claude Hendrix	36	78	15	1	0	1	6	6	0	.192
Grover Alexander	30	70	12	1	0	0	6	4	0	.171
Phil Douglas	25	51	8	2	0	0	3	3	0	.157
Speed Martin	35	44	8	1	0	0	3	2	0	.182
Paul Carter	29	26	7	0	0	0	2	2	0	.269
Sweetbreads Bailey	21	18	7	1	0	0	1	1	0	.389
Lefty Tyler	6	7	1	0	0	0	0	1	0	.143
Joel Newkirk	1	1	0	0	0	0	0	0	0	.000
Harry Weaver	2	1	0	0	0	0	0	0	0	.000
		4,581	1,174	166	58	21	454	387	150	.256

1920

Record: 75–79
Finish: Fifth (tie)
Games Behind: 18
Manager: Fred Mitchell

Grover Alexander, who had totaled only 18 wins for the Cubs in the previous two seasons, was once again "Alexander the Great." In 1920 he led the league in six categories: wins, 27; earned run average, 1.91; starts, 40; complete games, 33; innings, 363⅓; and strikeouts, 173. He was second in shutouts, 7, and had an 11-game winning streak, broken on June 4 in St. Louis when Rogers Hornsby tagged him for a pair of triples to deep center. Alexander insisted Hornsby was a better hitter than Babe Ruth.

The 154-game schedule was restored, and Alexander was without sufficient assistance. The temperamental Hippo Vaughn won 19 games but lost 16, a career high. Lefty Tyler, fitted with a new set of choppers, was ineffective in the early going. "I'll win when the weather warms up," he said. He did, but it was too late; he was 11–12 on the season. Spitballer Claude Hendrix, 9–12, was the only other slabman to win more than four games.

The Cubs had their usual cheerful and optimistic press corps. A strong showing, possibly a pennant, was predicted. The Cubs started well enough and were tied for the lead on May 31, dropped to third the next day, and were unable to recover from a June swoon, a 10-game losing streak, triggered by Hornsby's destruction of Alexander. They finished in a fifth-place tie with a disappointing 75–79 record, 18 games behind first-place Brooklyn.

Shortstop Charlie Hollocher led the offense with a .319 average and, from mid-June to early July, batted safely in 23 of 24 games. According to a contemporary account, Hollocher would have had a 24-game streak if not for a bad call in Brooklyn by official scorer Abe Yaeger. Instead of crediting Hollocher with a hit, Yaeger charged Zack Wheat with an error on Hollocher's fly down the left field line. With a runner on third base, Wheat allowed the ball to drop, convinced it would fall foul.

Hollocher was in and out of the lineup with a bad boiler and appeared in only 80 games. He underwent surgery for appendicitis in early August and didn't return. Catcher Bill Killefer was twice disabled with broken fingers. The only regulars to escape injury and bat .300 were outfielders Max Flack and Dave Robertston. The sturdy Robertson led the club in RBIs and in extra-base hits.

Second baseman Buck Herzog, in his 13th and final big league season, hit a dreary .193 and was suspended on June 14 by manager Mitchell for violating training rules and for indifferent play—after he had failed to get under an easy fly ball. Trade talks for Herzog were immediately initiated but not consummated. According to one of the Chicago Boswells, Herzog had "a peculiar contract" that gave him a voice in a trade. Mitchell was fired on November 1.

	W	L	ERA	G	GS	CG	IP	H	BB	K
Grover Alexander	(27)	14	(1.91)	46	(40)	(33)	(363⅓)	(335)	69	(173)
Hippo Vaughn	19	16	2.54	40	38	24	301	301	81	131
Claude Hendrix	9	12	3.58	27	23	12	203⅔	216	54	72
Lefty Tyler	11	12	3.31	27	27	18	193	193	57	57
Speed Martin	4	15	4.83	35	13	6	136	165	50	44
Paul Carter	3	6	4.67	31	8	2	106	131	36	14
Sweetbreads Bailey	1	2	7.12	21	1	0	36⅔	38	11	8
Virgil Cheeves	0	0	3.50	5	2	0	18	16	7	3
Chippy Gaw	1	1	4.85	6	1	0	13	16	3	4
Percy Jones	0	0	11.57	4	0	0	7	15	3	0
Joel Newkirk	0	1	5.40	2	1	0	6⅔	8	6	2
Joe Jaeger	0	0	12.00	2	0	0	3	6	4	0
Ted Turner	0	0	13.50	1	0	0	1⅓	2	1	0
	75	79	3.27	247	154	95	1,388⅔	1,442	382	508

Shutouts: Alexander 7, Vaughn 4, Tyler 2.

	G	AB	H	2B	3B	HR	R	RBI	SB	AVG
Regulars										
1B Fred Merkle	92	330	94	20	4	3	33	38	3	.285
2B Zeb Terry	133	496	139	26	9	0	56	52	12	.280
SS Charlie Hollocher	80	301	96	17	2	0	53	22	20	.319
3B Charlie Deal	129	450	108	10	5	3	48	39	5	.240
RF Max Flack	135	520	157	30	6	4	85	49	13	.302
CF Dode Paskert	139	487	136	22	10	5	57	71	16	.279
LF Dave Robertson	134	500	150	29	11	10	68	75	17	.300
C Bob O'Farrell	94	270	67	11	4	3	29	19	1	.248
Substitutes										
Turner Barber	94	340	90	10	5	0	27	50	5	.265
Buck Herzog	91	305	59	9	2	0	39	19	8	.193
Bill Marriott	14	43	12	4	2	0	7	5	1	.279
Hal Leathers	9	23	7	1	0	1	3	1	1	.304
Sumpter Clarke	1	3	1	0	0	0	0	0	0	.333
Babe Twombly	78	183	43	1	1	2	25	14	5	.235
Barney Friberg	50	114	24	5	1	0	11	7	2	.211
Bill Killefer	62	191	42	7	1	0	16	16	2	.220
Tom Daly	44	90	28	6	0	0	12	13	1	.311
Bill McCabe	3	2	1	0	0	0	1	0	0	.500
Pitchers										
Grover Alexander	46	118	27	4	1	1	9	14	0	.229
Hippo Vaughn	40	102	22	3	1	1	14	12	0	.216
Claude Hendrix	34	83	15	3	0	0	10	6	2	.181
Lefty Tyler	29	65	17	3	1	0	6	6	0	.262
Speed Martin	35	44	7	1	0	1	5	4	1	.159
Paul Carter	31	35	6	1	1	0	3	4	0	.171
Sweetbreads Bailey	21	7	1	0	0	0	0	0	0	.143
Virgil Cheeves	5	4	0	0	0	0	0	0	0	.000
Chippy Gaw	6	4	1	0	0	0	1	0	0	.250
Joel Newkirk	2	3	0	0	0	0	1	0	0	.000
Percy Jones	4	2	0	0	0	0	0	0	0	.000
Joe Jaeger	2	1	0	0	0	0	0	0	0	.000
Ted Turner	1	1	0	0	0	0	0	0	0	.000
	5,117	1,350	223	67	34	619	536	115	.264

1921

Record: 64–89
Finish: Seventh
Games Behind: 30
Managers: Johnny Evers, Bill Killefer

Johnny Evers, "The Crab," was summoned for his second term as the Cub manager. Evers had less success in 1921 than he had had in 1913, when the club finished third. Some of the players were openly hostile, particularly the aging Hippo Vaughn, who hung it up after 17 appearances, explaining he was weary of Evers' constant "nagging." Vaughn pitched his last game on July 9; a month later Evers also was gone, replaced by Bill Killefer, a one-time Cub star but now a reserve catcher.

A five-time 20-game winner, Vaughn departed with a 3–11 record, and according to one report, "looked like an old washerwoman fielding his position." Of all the pitchers with more than five decisions, only Alexander, 15–13, finished above .500 and with an earned run average under 4.00.

The only other pitchers to win in double figures were Speed Martin, 11–15, and Virgil Cheeves, 11–12. Cheeves, 20, didn't smoke, drink, or use profanity. Alexander took him under his wing, predicting he would develop into a big winner. Alexander was a better pitcher than prophet. Cheeves won only 26 games in a six-year big league stay.

For the first time, the club trained on Catalina Island, a luxurious setting off the California coast, property of owner William Wrigley, Jr. Wrigley's $100,000 steamer was used for recreation and transport. Still, the regimen was strict. Eager to whip his players into shape, Evers limited them to two meals a day, with the exception of Alexander, Vaughn, Martin, and Lefty Tyler, who were allowed to enter the dining room at will.

It was the first year of the lively ball. National League home run production soared, from 261 in 1920 to 460. The last-place Phillies led the league with 88 home runs. But the Cubs apparently were still whaling away at a dead sphere and hit 37 home runs, only three more than in the previous season. To help the hitters, trick deliveries, including the spitball, had been outlawed.

The pitchers now had to hold the ball continuously in sight of the batter. Also, at the first sign of roughness, the umpires were instructed to throw in shiny new balls; the gloss made them difficult to grip. League presidents John Heydler of the National and Ban Johnson of the American, for reasons of economy and to ease the pitchers' burden, reversed themselves in midseason and told the umpires to keep a bruised ball in play as long as possible.

The Cubs were afflicted by the usual injuries. Alexander was troubled with a sore arm and in early June was sent to Youngstown, Ohio, to see James "Bonesetter" Reese, an unschooled former Welsh coal miner so skillful and renowned at skeletal manipulation that the Ohio legislature gave him a special medical certificate. At a cost of $10, a ligament in Alexander's elbow was snapped back into place. Outfielder Max Flack suffered a neck injury but didn't have the luxury of the "Bonesetter's" attention. He recovered with the help of the team trainer.

The only pleasant surprise was the all-around play of first baseman Oscar Ray Grimes, who replaced George Maisel in the cleanup spot. Grimes, who had only one game of previous major league experience, led the club with a .321 average and 79 runs batted in. The Cubs were 41–55 under Evers' command, 23–34 with Killefer. They finished seventh, 15 games out of fourth place.

	W	L	ERA	G	GS	CG	IP	H	BB	K
Grover Alexander	15	13	3.39	31	29	21	252	286	33	77
Speed Martin	11	15	4.35	37	28	13	217⅓	245	68	86
Buck Freeman	9	10	4.11	38	20	6	177⅓	189	70	42
Virgil Cheeves	11	12	4.64	37	22	9	163	192	47	39
Lefty York	5	9	4.73	40	10	4	139	170	63	57
Hippo Vaughn	3	11	6.01	17	14	7	109⅓	153	31	30
Percy Jones	3	5	4.56	32	5	1	98⅔	116	39	46
Elmer Ponder	3	6	4.74	16	11	5	89½	117	17	31
Lefty Tyler	3	2	3.24	10	6	4	50	59	14	8
Vic Keen	0	3	4.68	5	4	1	25	29	9	9
Tony Kaufmann	1	0	4.15	2	1	1	13	12	3	6
George Stueland	0	1	5.73	2	1	0	11	11	7	4
Ollie Hanson	0	2	7.00	2	2	1	9	9	6	2
Sweetbreads Bailey	0	0	3.60	3	0	0	5	6	2	2
Oscar Fuhr	0	0	9.00	1	0	0	4	11	0	2
	64	89	4.39	273	153	73	1,363	1,605	409	441

Shutouts: Alexander 3, Martin 1, Cheeves 1, York 1.

	G	AB	H	2B	3B	HR	R	RBI	SB	AVG
Regulars										
1B Ray Grimes	147	530	170	38	6	6	91	79	5	.321
2B Zeb Terry	123	488	134	18	1	2	59	45	1	.275
SS Charlie Hollocher	140	558	161	28	8	3	71	37	5	.289
3B Charlie Deal	115	422	122	19	8	3	52	66	3	.289
RF Max Flack	133	572	172	31	4	6	80	37	17	.301
CF George Maisel	111	393	122	7	2	0	54	43	17	.310
LF Turner Barber	127	452	142	14	4	1	73	54	5	.314
C Bob O'Farrell	96	260	65	12	7	4	32	32	2	.250
Substitutes										
John Kelleher	95	301	93	11	7	4	31	47	2	.309
Bill Marriott	30	38	12	1	1	0	3	7	0	.316
Hooks Warner	14	38	8	1	0	0	4	3	1	.211
Carter Elliott	12	28	7	2	0	0	5	0	0	.250
Joe Klugman	6	21	6	0	0	0	3	2	0	.286
John Sullivan	76	240	79	14	4	4	28	41	3	.329
Babe Twombly	87	175	66	8	1	1	22	18	4	.377
Dave Robertson	22	36	8	3	0	0	7	14	0	.222
Red Thomas	8	30	8	3	0	1	5	5	0	.267
Tom Daly	51	143	34	7	1	0	12	22	1	.238
Bill Killefer	45	133	43	1	0	0	11	16	3	.323
Kettle Wirtz	7	11	2	0	0	0	0	1	0	.182
Pitchers										
Grover Alexander	31	95	29	3	1	1	8	14	0	.305
Speed Martin	37	73	17	4	1	0	2	6	1	.233
Buck Freeman	38	53	11	1	0	0	3	2	0	.208
Virgil Cheeves	37	48	8	1	0	0	3	0	0	.167
Hippo Vaughn	17	41	10	2	0	1	2	5	0	.244
Lefty York	40	39	5	1	0	0	2	5	0	.128
Elmer Ponder	16	33	4	1	0	0	0	2	0	.121
Percy Jones	32	27	6	0	0	0	1	3	0	.222
Lefty Tyler	19	26	6	2	0	0	4	2	0	.231
Tony Kaufmann	2	5	2	1	0	0	0	0	0	.400
Vic Keen	5	5	0	0	0	0	0	0	0	.000
Ollie Hanson	2	3	0	0	0	0	0	0	0	.000
George Stueland	2	3	1	0	0	0	0	1	0	.333
Oscar Fuhr	1	1	0	0	0	0	0	0	0	.000
Sweetbreads Bailey	3	0	0	0	0	0	0	0	0	—
		5,321	1,553	234	56	37	668	609	70	.292

1922

Record: 80–74
Finish: Fifth
Games Behind: 13
Manager: Bill Killefer

The 1922 campaign was Bill Killefer's first full season at the helm, and the players who had smarted under the abrasive Johnny Evers responded to his comparatively light touch. Often described as the "boy manager"—he was 35, youngest manager in the league—Killefer rallied the troops to a fifth-place finish. It was the third successive year in the second division but nonetheless an improvement: 16 more victories than the previous season.

Lawrence "Hack" Miller, acquired from Portland of the Pacific Coast League in an off-season deal, was the new leader. The colorful Miller was an immediate sensation, on and off the field. He grew up on the North Side of Chicago within walking distance of the ballpark and, as one newsman reported, came from "a family of power."

Miller's father, a German immigrant, had been a circus strongman and after arriving in Chicago won several weight-lifting championships. Miller's sister was also a lifter and, according to a contemporary account, could "swing the weights around like a bag of peanuts." To entertain his teammates, Miller "drove nails through a two-inch board with his fists." He could also twist an iron bar and, like Samson, uproot young trees.

Stumpy—5 feet, 9 inches tall and weighing 200 pounds— "Hercules" Miller batted .352 in his rookie season, fifth in the league, with 12 home runs and 78 runs batted in, power totals exceeded on the club only by first baseman Ray Grimes, who had a career year: .354, 14 home runs, and 99 RBIs. Shortstop Charlie Hollocher, who had three triples in one game, August 13 against St. Louis, also had his best year and was among the league leaders with a .340 average.

The Cubs hit .293 as a team but didn't lead the league; three other clubs batted over .300, further evidence of the lively ball. Outfielder Arnold "Jigger" Statz, after abandoning his attempt to switch-hit, swung only from the right side and had a 19-game hitting streak. On August 25, the Cubs beat the Phillies 26–23; the record of 49 runs in one game still stands. Miller led the assault with two home runs and six RBIs.

Outfielder Max Flack, who had fallen from favor when he jumped the club in April and "no longer had his heart in his work," was traded to St. Louis for outfielder Cliff Heathcote between games of a May 30 doubleheader. The deal became a footnote in baseball history: perhaps the first time two players played for two teams on the same day.

The Cubs were in the chase most of the way but held the undisputed lead for only one day, April 22. They were in second place as late as August but were not a factor in the September stretch and for the second year in a row didn't have a 20-game winner. Cap Anson, who had guided the Cubs to five 19th-century pennants, died on April 14 at the age of 70. The league paid the burial expenses.

	W	L	ERA	G	GS	CG	IP	H	BB	K
Vic Aldridge	16	15	3.52	36	34	20	258⅓	287	56	66
Grover Alexander	16	13	3.63	33	31	20	245⅔	283	34	48
Tiny Osborne	9	5	4.50	41	14	7	184	183	95	81
Virgil Cheeves	12	11	4.09	39	23	9	182⅔	195	76	40
Percy Jones	8	9	4.72	44	26	7	164	197	69	46
Tony Kaufmann	7	13	4.06	37	9	4	153	161	57	45
George Stueland	9	4	5.92	34	12	4	111	129	48	43
Vic Keen	1	2	3.89	7	3	2	34⅔	36	10	11
Buck Freeman	0	1	8.77	11	1	0	25⅔	47	10	10
Fred Fussell	1	1	4.74	3	2	1	19	24	8	4
Ed Morris	0	0	8.25	5	0	0	12	22	6	5
Speed Martin	1	0	7.50	1	1	0	6	10	2	2
Uel Eubanks	0	0	27.00	2	0	0	1⅔	5	4	1
	80	74	4.34	293	156	74	1,397⅓	1,579	475	402

Shutouts: Aldridge 2, Jones 2, Alexander 1, Cheeves 1, Kaufmann 1, Osborne 1.

	G	AB	H	2B	3B	HR	R	RBI	SB	AVG
Regulars										
1B Ray Grimes	138	509	180	45	12	14	99	99	7	.354
2B Zeb Terry	131	496	142	24	2	0	56	67	2	.286
SS Charlie Hollocher	152	592	201	37	8	3	90	69	19	.340
3B Marty Krug	127	450	124	23	4	4	67	60	7	.276
RF Barney Friberg	97	296	92	8	2	0	51	23	8	.311
CF Jigger Statz	110	462	137	19	5	1	77	34	16	.297
LF Hack Miller	122	466	164	28	5	12	61	78	3	.352
C Bob O'Farrell	128	392	127	18	8	4	68	60	5	.324
Substitutes										
John Kelleher	63	193	50	7	1	0	23	20	5	.259
Sparky Adams	11	44	11	0	1	0	5	3	1	.250
George Grantham	7	23	4	1	1	0	3	3	2	.174
Walt Golvin	2	2	0	0	0	0	0	1	0	.000
Joe Klugman	2	2	0	0	0	0	0	0	0	.000
Cliff Heathcote	76	243	68	8	7	1	37	34	5	.280
Turner Barber	84	226	70	7	4	0	35	29	7	.310
Marty Callaghan	74	175	45	7	4	0	31	20	2	.257
George Maisel	38	84	16	1	1	0	9	6	1	.190
Max Flack	17	54	12	1	0	0	7	6	2	.222
Howie Fitzgerald	10	24	8	1	0	0	3	4	1	.333
Gabby Hartnett	31	72	14	1	1	0	4	4	1	.194
Kettle Wirtz	31	58	10	2	0	1	7	6	0	172
Butch Weis	2	2	1	0	0	0	2	0	0	.500
Harvey Cotter	1	1	1	1	0	0	0	0	0	1.000
Pitchers										
Vic Aldridge	36	100	26	1	3	0	8	13	1	.260
Grover Alexander	33	85	15	1	0	0	4	11	0	.176
Tiny Osborne	41	67	9	2	0	0	6	4	1	.134
Virgil Cheeves	39	62	13	1	1	1	6	3	0	.210
Percy Jones	44	47	4	0	0	0	2	3	0	.085
Tony Kaufmann	38	45	9	2	1	1	4	4	0	.200
George Stueland	35	31	4	0	0	0	2	2	0	.129
Vic Keen	7	12	4	0	0	0	1	0	1	.333
Buck Freeman	11	8	1	1	0	0	1	0	0	.125
Fred Fussell	3	6	0	0	0	0	1	0	0	.000
Ed Morris	5	4	1	0	0	0	0	1	0	.250
Uel Eubanks	2	1	1	1	0	0	1	0	0	1.000
Speed Martin	1	1	0	0	0	0	0	0	0	.000
		5,335	1,564	248	71	42	771	667	97	.293

1923

Record: 83–71
Finish: Fourth
Games Behind: 12½
Manager: Bill Killefer

First baseman Ray Grimes was disabled in May when he wrenched his back sliding into second; two months later he was sidelined again for surgery to repair a hernia. But the biggest blow of 1923—and it became a season-long mystery—was the constant stomach ailments suffered by Charlie Hollocher, the brilliant shortstop.

Bedridden with the flu in February, Hollocher reported to spring training on March 1, underweight and without color. He was in camp only for a few days before he returned to his home in St. Louis without leaving notice. He was hospitalized in May, rejoined the club in June, and was in and out of the lineup for the next three months. On September 3 he jumped the club again, this time with a "goodbye" note for manager Bill Killefer.

According to the *Spalding Guide,* "Physicians who examined him seemed to think it was more a matter of nerves than actual physical distress." But Hollocher could not be persuaded to return. There was also the belief he was looking to be traded to the Cardinals. Club president William Veeck apparently tried to oblige. According to several accounts, Hollocher and two or three other front-liners were offered in exchange for Rogers Hornsby.

Whether Veeck entered into serious negotiations is not

known. What is known is that Hollocher missed more than half the 1923 season. He appeared in 66 games and batted .342. Earl "Runt" Adams, at 5 feet, 5½ inches, among the smallest players in diamond history, and also known as Sparky Adams, was Hollocher's principal replacement and batted a creditable .289.

Grimes appeared in 64 games, two fewer than Hollocher, and led the club with a .329 average, but was usually unable to take a full swing with his customary power. Considering these losses, the Cubs played remarkably well and climbed to fourth in the standings, principally because of a combined 29–15 record against Boston and Philadelphia, the bottom two clubs.

The Cubs led the league in stolen bases with 181 and set a club record with 90 home runs, 20 by Hack Miller. Third baseman Barney Friberg and Miller, both of whom hit over .300, led the team in RBIs, each with 88. Bob O'Farrell, tough in the clutch and now the full-time catcher—Killefer had retired as a player—also had a strong year: .319, 84 RBIs, and 12 home runs. Gabby Hartnett, a future Hall of Famer, was the number-two receiver, and had eight home runs. Jigger Statz hit .319.

Alexander led the pitchers with 22 wins and set a league record, 51 consecutive innings without a walk. Alexander worked 305 innings and was among the first pitchers to yield less than one pass a game. He also tied for the league lead with teammate Tiny Osborne, who worked 128 fewer innings, for the most gopher balls, 17.

In mid-September, outfielder Cliff Heathcote was sent home because of his "prolonged kicking" against umpire Pat Moran. Pitcher Tony Kaufmann also made an early departure when he smashed his thumb while tinkering with his automobile. A monument was erected, with the help of league funds, and dedicated on September 16 over Cap Anson's grave in Chicago's Oakwood Cemetery.

	W	L	ERA	G	GS	CG	IP	H	BB	K
Grover Alexander	22	12	3.19	39	36	26	305	308	30	72
Vic Aldridge	16	9	3.48	30	30	15	217	209	67	64
Tony Kaufmann	14	10	3.10	33	24	18	206⅓	209	67	72
Tiny Osborne	8	15	4.56	37	25	8	179⅔	174	89	69
Vic Keen	12	8	3.00	35	17	10	177	169	57	46
Nick Dumovich	3	5	4.60	28	8	1	94	118	45	23
Fred Fussell	3	5	5.54	28	2	1	76⅓	90	31	38
Virgil Cheeves	3	4	6.18	19	8	0	71½	89	37	13
Rip Wheeler	1	2	4.88	3	3	1	24	28	5	5
George Stueland	0	1	5.63	6	0	0	8	11	5	2
Phil Collins	1	0	3.60	1	1	0	5	8	1	2
Ed Stauffer	0	0	13.50	1	0	0	2	5	1	0
Guy Bush	0	0	0.00	1	0	0	1	1	0	2
	83	71	3.82	261	154	80	1,366⅔	1,419	435	408

Shutouts: Alexander 3, Aldridge 2, Kaufmann 2, Osborne 1.

	G	AB	H	2B	3B	HR	R	RBI	SB	AVG
Regulars										
1B Ray Grimes	64	216	71	7	2	2	32	36	5	.329
2B George Grantham	152	570	160	36	8	8	81	70	43	.281
SS Sparky Adams	95	311	90	12	0	4	40	35	20	.289
3B Barney Friberg	146	547	174	27	11	12	91	88	13	.318
RF Cliff Heathcote	117	393	98	14	3	1	48	27	32	.249
CF Jigger Statz	154	655	209	33	8	10	110	70	29	.319
LF Hack Miller	135	485	146	24	4	20	74	88	6	.301
C Bob O'Farrell	131	452	144	25	4	12	73	84	10	.319
Substitutes										
Charlie Hollocher	66	260	89	14	2	1	46	28	9	.342
John Kelleher	66	193	59	10	0	6	27	21	2	.306
Allen Elliott	53	168	42	8	2	2	21	29	3	.250
Pete Turgeon	3	6	1	0	0	0	1	0	0	.167
Marty Callaghan	61	129	29	1	3	0	18	14	2	.225
Otto Vogel	41	81	17	0	1	1	10	6	2	.210
Denver Grigsby	24	72	21	5	2	0	8	5	1	.292
Butch Weis	22	26	6	1	0	0	2	2	0	.231
Tony Murray	2	4	1	0	0	0	0	0	0	.250
Gabby Hartnett	85	231	62	12	2	8	28	39	4	.268
Kettle Wirtz	5	5	1	0	0	0	2	1	0	.200
Bob Barrett	3	3	1	0	0	0	0	0	0	.333
Pitchers										
Grover Alexander	39	111	24	3	1	1	10	10	0	.216
Tony Kaufmann	33	74	16	2	0	2	10	10	0	.216
Vic Aldridge	30	71	19	3	0	0	5	4	0	.268
Tiny Osborne	37	60	12	2	0	0	3	3	0	.200
Vic Keen	35	53	8	2	0	0	9	2	0	.151
Nick Dumovich	28	29	7	0	1	0	4	0	0	.241
Virgil Cheeves	19	23	4	1	0	0	1	1	0	.174
Fred Fussell	28	20	4	1	0	0	2	0	0	.200
Rip Wheeler	3	9	1	0	0	0	0	2	0	.111
Phil Collins	1	2	0	0	0	0	0	0	0	.000
Guy Bush	1	0	0	0	0	0	0	0	0	—
Ed Stauffer	1	0	0	0	0	0	0	0	0	—
George Stueland	6	0	0	0	0	0	0	0	0	—
		5,259	1,516	243	52	90	756	675	(181)	.288

1924

Record: 81–72
Finish: Fifth
Games Behind: 12
Manager: Bill Killefer

Charlie Hollocher rejoined the club in mid-May of 1924. In the first inning of his first game, against the Giants' "Handsome Hugh" McQuillan, he lined a ball over first base, a double under ordinary circumstances. But when the ball landed in right field it veered toward foul territory and rolled through a hole under the grandstand. Outfielder Ross Young, in pursuit, was unable to "extract the pill from its hiding place," and Hollocher had an inside-the-park home run.

Hollocher also had two singles in this game, and in the second game of the series he handled 10 chances, some of them difficult, without flaw. He missed the third game to have stomach X rays, returned for the fourth and final game of the series, and again had three hits.

It was a wonderful beginning for the talented Hollocher, who sometimes was compared with the great Honus Wagner, generally acknowledged as the best shortstop in league history. But Sparky Adams was now the Cubs' starting shortstop. Hollocher's stomach problems continued. He appeared in only 76 games and batted .245, 50 points below his lifetime. It was his last season. He retired at the age of 28, when he should have been in midcareer. He died in 1940 by his own hand.

But the sun continued to shine on the Cubs. The hulking Charles Leo "Gabby" Hartnett, a reserve receiver during the previous two seasons, came forward. Hartnett replaced Bob

O'Farrell as the everyday catcher and had the first of his many extraordinary seasons: a club-leading 16 home runs, 67 runs batted in, and a .299 average.

There were other changes. Hack Miller, after two strong seasons, was in decline, supplanted in left field by Denver Grigsby, who batted .299. Ray Grimes was also going the way of all baseball flesh. Replaced by Harvey Cotter at first base, Grimes appeared in 51 games, had 177 at bats, and drove in only 34 runs. A subdued Cliff Heathcote, no longer badgering umpire Moran, played the full season without incident, also without distinction.

Tony Kaufmann, his thumb healed, led the pitchers with 16 victories, followed by Vic Aldridge and Vic Keen, 15 each. Alexander worked 169⅓ innings, half his usual portion. After losing his first start, he won eight in a row, hurt his wrist, and won only four games thereafter, including number 300 on September 30 against the Giants. The Cubs were in the lead in April and again in mid-June, were second during the entire month of July, and finished fifth, two games out of the first division.

	W	L	ERA	G	GS	CG	IP	H	BB	K
Vic Aldridge	15	12	3.50	32	32	20	244⅓	261	80	74
Vic Keen	15	14	3.80	40	28	15	234⅔	242	80	75
Tony Kaufmann	16	11	4.02	34	26	16	208⅓	218	66	79
Elmer Jacobs	11	12	3.74	38	22	13	190⅓	181	72	50
Grover Alexander	12	5	3.03	21	20	12	169⅓	183	25	33
Sheriff Blake	6	6	4.57	29	11	4	106⅓	123	44	42
Rip Wheeler	3	6	3.91	29	4	0	101⅓	103	21	16
Guy Bush	2	5	4.02	16	8	4	80⅔	91	24	36
George Milstead	1	1	6.07	13	2	1	29⅔	41	13	6
Ray Pierce	0	0	7.36	6	0	0	7⅓	7	4	2
Herb Brett	0	0	5.06	1	1	0	5⅓	6	7	1
Tiny Osborne	0	0	3.00	2	0	0	3	3	2	2
	81	72	3.83	261	154	85	1,380⅔	1,459	438	416

Shutouts: Kaufmann 3, Jacobs 1.

	G	AB	H	2B	3B	HR	R	RBI	SB	AVG
Regulars										
1B Harvey Cotter	98	310	81	16	4	4	39	33	3	.261
2B George Grantham	127	469	148	19	6	12	85	60	21	.316
SS Sparky Adams	117	418	117	11	5	1	66	27	15	.280
3B Barney Friberg	142	495	138	19	3	5	82	82	19	.279
RF Cliff Heathcote	113	392	121	19	7	0	66	30	26	.309
CF Jigger Statz	135	549	152	22	5	3	69	49	13	.277
LF Denver Grigsby	124	411	123	18	2	3	58	48	10	.299
C Gabby Hartnett	111	354	106	17	7	16	56	67	10	.299
Substitutes										
Charlie Hollocher	76	286	70	12	4	2	28	21	4	.245
Ray Grimes	51	177	53	6	5	5	33	34	4	.299
Bob Barrett	54	133	32	2	3	5	12	21	1	.241
Ted Kearns	4	16	4	0	1	0	0	1	0	.250
Allen Elliott	10	14	2	0	0	0	0	0	0	.143
Ralph Michaels	8	11	4	0	0	0	0	2	0	.364
Otto Vogel	70	172	46	11	2	1	28	24	4	.267
Butch Weis	39	133	37	8	1	0	19	23	4	.278
Hack Miller	53	131	44	8	1	4	17	25	1	.336
Howie Fitzgerald	7	19	3	0	0	0	1	2	0	.158
Bob O'Farrell	71	183	44	6	2	3	25	28	2	.240
John Churry	6	7	1	1	0	0	0	0	0	.143
Pitchers										
Vic Aldridge	32	85	15	3	0	0	6	11	0	.176
Vic Keen	40	77	12	1	0	0	2	8	0	.156
Tony Kaufmann	35	76	24	5	0	1	6	14	0	.316
Grover Alexander	21	65	15	2	0	1	3	10	0	.231
Elmer Jacobs	38	54	6	0	0	0	3	5	0	.111
Rip Wheeler	29	32	7	0	0	0	3	2	0	.219
Sheriff Blake	29	31	9	0	1	0	5	3	0	.290
Guy Bush	16	26	4	1	0	0	1	4	0	.154
George Milstead	13	6	1	0	0	0	0	0	0	.167
Herb Brett	1	2	0	0	0	0	0	0	0	.000
Tiny Osborne	2	0	0	0	0	0	0	0	0	—
Ray Pierce	6	0	0	0	0	0	0	0	0	—
		5,134	1,419	207	59	66	698	634	137	.276

1925

Record: 68–86
Finish: Eighth
Games Behind: 27½
Managers: Bill Killefer, Rabbit Maranville, George Gibson

The general belief is that Philip K. Wrigley, in 1961, pioneered the system of rotating managers. But P.K.'s father, William, did much the same in 1925. The Cubs had three managers—Bill Killefer, Walter "Rabbit" Maranville, and George Gibson. And for the first time in the 20th century they finished last, 27½ games behind the pennant-winning Pittsburgh Pirates, who prevented McGraw's Giants from capturing a fifth consecutive flag.

Killefer was dismissed in midseason and replaced by Maranville, who said, "This club is better than it has shown." Maranville was wrong. The Cubs were worse under his command. Gibson, who had previously managed in Pittsburgh, took over with three weeks remaining. They were 33–42 with Killefer, a .440 winning percentage; 23–30 under Maranville, .434; and 12–14 under Gibson, .462.

They were last in hitting, next to last in runs. Still, there was something to cheer about. First baseman Charlie Grimm, acquired in a deal with Pittsburgh and later to be a three-term Cub manager, was superb in the field and led the club with a .306 average. It was also the first full season for catcher Gabby Hartnett, who hit five home runs in the first five games. Only July 3, Hartnett had 20 home runs and according to an enthusiastic account, was likely to "eclipse Babe Ruth." It was Hartnett who went into eclipse. He hit only four more.

Maranville, who also came in the Grimm deal, was a 13-year National League veteran—a light-hitting, prankster shortstop known mostly for his "fun-loving" approach. Because of an ankle injury and a weakened arm, the Pirates had moved him to second base the previous season. He reinjured the ankle during the exhibition season. Nonetheless, he was considered a valuable addition, "instilled spirit" in the club, and was appointed the team captain.

With Charlie Hollocher gone but not forgotten—Veeck made several trips to St. Louis, inquiring about his health—shortstop was still a problem. The Cubs used seven players at this position in 1925, all of whom played without distinction. Maranville appeared in the most games, 75, batted a characteristic .233 with 23 RBIs, and was the only "regular" with more than 250 at bats who failed to hit a home run.

The Rabbit had no previous managerial experience. The day after he succeeded Killefer he got into a fight with a New York cab driver. When Veeck asked for an explanation, Maranville said the beef began when the cabby "mumbled something about the tip." Gibson, who spent most of the season scouting the minor leagues, searching for players, got the ax when the season ended.

Grover Alexander led the club with a 15–11 record and was the only pitcher above .500. Tony Kaufmann was 13–13, Wilbur Cooper 12–14, and Sheriff Blake 10–18. The Cubs were never higher than second, occupying this position during the first week in May. Two weeks later they were in the second division to stay. They were bunched with Brooklyn and Philadelphia at the bottom, all with 68 victories. If the Cubs hadn't lost to St. Louis on the final day, they would have finished sixth.

	W	L	ERA	G	GS	CG	IP	H	BB	K
Grover Alexander	15	11	3.39	32	30	20	236	270	29	63
Sheriff Blake	10	18	4.86	36	31	14	231⅓	260	114	93
Wilbur Cooper	12	14	4.28	32	26	13	212⅓	249	61	41
Tony Kaufmann	13	13	4.50	31	23	14	196	221	77	49
Guy Bush	6	13	4.30	42	15	5	182	213	52	76
Percy Jones	6	6	4.65	28	13	6	124	123	71	60
Vic Keen	2	6	6.26	30	8	1	83⅓	125	41	19
Elmer Jacobs	2	3	5.17	18	4	1	55⅔	63	22	19
George Milstead	1	1	3.00	5	3	1	21	26	8	7
Herb Brett	1	1	3.63	10	1	0	17⅓	12	3	6
Jumbo Brown	0	0	3.00	2	0	0	6	5	4	0
George Stueland	0	0	3.00	2	0	0	3	2	3	2
Bob Osborn	0	0	0.00	1	0	0	2	6	0	0
Barney Friberg	0	0	0.00	0	0	0	0	0	0	0
	68	86	4.41	269	154	75	1,370	1,575	485	435

Shutouts: Kaufmann 2, Alexander 1, Jacobs 1, Jones 1.

	G	AB	H	2B	3B	HR	R	RBI	SB	AVG
Regulars										
1B Charlie Grimm	141	519	159	29	5	10	73	76	4	.306
2B Sparky Adams	149	(627)	180	29	8	2	95	48	26	.287
SS Rabbit Maranville	75	266	62	10	3	0	37	23	6	.233
3B Howard Freigau	117	476	146	22	10	8	77	71	10	.307
RF Cliff Heathcote	109	380	100	14	5	5	57	39	15	.263
CF Mandy Brooks	90	349	98	25	7	13	55	72	10	.281
LF Art Jahn	58	226	68	10	8	0	30	37	2	.301
C Gabby Hartnett	117	398	115	28	3	24	61	67	1	.289
Substitutes										
Pinky Pittenger	59	173	54	7	2	0	21	15	5	.312
Barney Friberg	44	152	39	5	3	1	12	16	0	.257
Ike McAuley	37	125	35	7	2	0	10	11	1	.280
Ralph Michaels	22	50	14	1	0	0	10	6	1	.280
Bob Barrett	14	32	10	1	0	0	1	7	1	.313
Gale Staley	7	26	11	2	0	0	2	3	0	.423
Ted Kearns	3	2	1	0	0	0	0	0	0	.500
Tommy Griffith	76	235	67	12	1	7	38	27	2	.285
Butch Weis	67	180	48	5	3	2	16	25	2	.267
Jigger Statz	38	148	38	6	3	2	21	14	4	.257
Denver Grigsby	51	137	35	5	0	0	20	20	1	.255
Hack Miller	24	86	24	3	2	2	10	9	0	.279
Alex Metzler	9	38	7	2	0	0	2	2	0	.184
Joe Munson	9	35	13	3	1	0	5	3	1	.371
Chink Taylor	8	6	0	0	0	0	2	0	0	.000
Mike Gonzalez	70	197	52	13	1	3	26	18	2	.264
Bob O'Farrell	17	22	4	0	1	0	2	3	0	.182
John Churry	3	6	3	0	0	0	1	1	0	.500
Mel Kerr	1	0	0	0	0	0	1	0	0	—
Pitchers										
Wilbur Cooper	32	82	17	2	1	2	12	10	0	.207
Grover Alexander	32	79	19	4	1	2	7	12	0	.241
Sheriff Blake	36	79	12	1	0	0	4	7	0	.152
Tony Kaufmann	31	78	15	7	0	2	8	13	0	.192
Guy Bush	42	57	11	0	0	0	3	2	0	.193
Percy Jones	28	39	6	0	0	0	2	2	0	.154
Vic Keen	30	25	6	1	0	0	2	1	0	.240
Elmer Jacobs	18	13	3	0	0	0	0	0	0	.231
George Milstead	5	7	0	0	0	0	0	0	0	.000
Herb Brett	10	1	0	0	0	0	0	0	0	.000
Jumbo Brown	2	1	0	0	0	0	0	0	0	.000
George Stueland	2	1	1	0	0	0	0	0	0	1.000
Bob Osborn	1	0	0	0	0	0	0	0	0	—
		5,353	1,473	254	70	85	723	660	94	.275

1926

Record: 82–72
Finish: Fourth
Games Behind: 7
Manager: Joe McCarthy

Joe McCarthy, the new manager in 1926, represented a compromise between the managers who raged at their players and those who jollied them. A failed infielder, McCarthy never played in a big league, but he was not unknown. He had an impressive apprenticeship: six seasons in the

American Association as the manager of the Louisville club, which thrived under his direction.

He knew what he wanted: a balanced and, above all, a disciplined club. He found himself in command of a curious collection of callow and castoff players. His first significant move, which he didn't make until June 22, virtually in mid-season, was to dump "Alexander the Great" who was sold for the $4,000 waiver price to the Cardinals; four months later Grover Alexander was a World Series hero.

Now 39, Alexander had been pitching poorly—seven starts and a 3–3 record. If he had been performing to his capabilities, McCarthy might have kept him. What enraged the new boss was Alexander's alcoholism, gently described in the press as his "off the field habits."

In mid-June, after a month on the shelf, Alexander, inebriated, was unable to make a scheduled start in Philadelphia. Not only did McCarthy deny him entrance to the clubhouse, but he also suspended him and ordered him to return to Chicago. Said McCarthy: "I absolutely refuse to allow him to disrupt our team and will not have him around in that condition."

With Alexander gone, along with veteran left-hander Wilbur Cooper, traded to Detroit, McCarthy inserted Charlie Root and Guy Bush into the rotation; both took advantage of the opportunity. Root, 18–17, led the club in victories. Bush was 13–9 and had an eight-game winning streak, which he might have extended if he hadn't attempted to go against the Phillies with only two days of rest.

McCarthy's desire for team balance was achieved. He had five winning pitchers. The staff earned run average of 3.26 was the lowest in the league, an improvement of more than one run a game over the previous season. Root and Bush were among the league's ERA leaders, Root second with 2.82, Bush fourth with 2.86.

Shortstop Jimmy Cooney and third baseman Howard Freigau led the league in fielding at their positions. The second base combination of Cooney and Sparky Adams, with Charlie Grimm, a fielding wizard at first base, may have been the best Cub trio since Tinker-to-Evers-to-Chance. It is not known how many 6–4–3 or 4–6–3 double plays were converted, but the Cubs set a league record with 174 twin killings.

McCarthy also had the league's second most productive offense and the league's most powerful hitter in Hack Wilson, a McGraw castoff plucked off the Toronto roster in the winter draft. Wilson, built like a fireplug—5 feet, 6 inches, 210 pounds—led the league in home runs with 21 and was second in RBIs with 109. Outfielder Riggs Stephenson made his Chicago bow and batted .338. The Cubs finished fourth, seven games out. McCarthy was hailed as a genius.

	W	L	ERA	G	GS	CG	IP	H	BB	K
Charlie Root	18	(17)	2.82	42	32	21	271⅓	267	62	127
Sheriff Blake	11	12	3.60	39	27	11	197⅔	204	(92)	95
Tony Kaufmann	9	7	3.02	26	21	14	169⅔	169	44	52
Percy Jones	12	7	3.09	30	20	10	160⅓	151	90	80
Guy Bush	13	9	2.86	35	16	7	157⅓	149	42	32
Bob Osborn	6	5	3.63	31	15	6	136⅓	157	58	43
Bill Piercy	6	5	4.48	19	5	1	90⅓	96	37	31
George Milstead	1	5	3.58	18	4	0	55⅓	63	24	14
Wilbur Cooper	2	1	4.42	8	8	3	55	65	21	18
Grover Alexander	3	3	3.46	7	7	4	52	55	7	12
Walter Huntzinger	1	1	0.94	11	0	0	28⅔	26	8	4
Johnny Welch	0	0	2.08	3	0	0	4⅓	5	1	0
	82	72	3.26	269	155	77	1,378⅓	1,407	486	508

Shutouts: Blake 4, Bush 2, Cooper 2, Jones 2, Root 2, Kaufmann 1.

	G	AB	H	2B	3B	HR	R	RBI	SB	AVG
Regulars										
1B Charlie Grimm	147	524	145	30	6	8	58	82	3	.277
2B Sparky Adams	154	624	193	35	3	0	95	39	27	.309
SS Jimmy Cooney	141	513	129	18	5	1	52	47	11	.251
3B Howard Freigau	140	508	137	27	7	3	51	51	6	.270
RF Cliff Heathcote	139	510	141	33	3	10	98	53	18	.276
CF Hack Wilson	142	529	170	36	8	(21)	97	109	10	.321
LF Riggs Stephenson	82	281	95	18	3	3	40	44	2	.338
C Gabby Hartnett	93	284	78	25	3	8	35	41	0	.275
Substitutes										
Clyde Beck	30	81	16	0	0	1	10	4	0	.198
Chick Tolson	57	80	25	6	1	1	4	8	0	.313
Red Shannon	19	51	17	5	0	0	9	4	0	.333
Hank Schreiber	10	18	1	1	0	0	2	0	0	.056
Joe Graves	2	5	0	0	0	0	0	0	0	.000
Pete Scott	77	189	54	13	1	3	34	34	3	.286
Joe Kelly	65	176	59	15	3	0	16	32	0	.335
Joe Munson	33	101	26	2	2	3	17	15	0	.257
Mandy Brooks	26	48	9	1	0	1	7	6	0	.188
Mike Gonzalez	80	253	63	13	3	1	24	23	3	.249
John Churry	2	4	0	0	0	0	0	0	0	.000
Ralph Michaels	2	0	0	0	0	0	1	0	0	—
Pitchers										
Charlie Root	42	91	13	1	0	1	8	7	0	.143
Sheriff Blake	39	65	14	0	0	0	2	4	0	.215
Tony Kaufmann	30	60	15	2	0	1	9	7	1	.250
Percy Jones	30	50	13	4	0	0	4	6	0	.260
Guy Bush	35	48	8	0	0	0	1	2	0	.167
Bob Osborn	31	41	6	1	0	0	1	4	0	.146
Bill Piercy	19	35	9	3	0	0	2	3	0	.257
George Milstead	18	19	1	0	0	0	1	0	0	.053
Wilbur Cooper	8	18	7	0	1	0	2	2	1	.389
Grover Alexander	7	15	7	2	0	0	1	3	0	.467
Walter Huntzinger	11	7	1	0	0	0	1	0	0	.143
Johnny Welch	3	1	1	0	0	0	0	0	0	1.000
		5,229	1,453	291	49	66	682	630	85	.278

1927

Record: 85–68
Finish: Fourth
Games Behind: 8½
Manager: Joe McCarthy

The Cubs had power to burn in 1927. Beginning on April 26, the third week of the season, after Gabby Hartnett connected in Pittsburgh, they hit one or more home runs in 11 consecutive games, a National League record; the previous mark was seven. The barrage included 14 home runs, three each by Hartnett, Hack Wilson, and Earl Webb.

There were other notable achievements. On May 14 and 16, the Cubs won consecutive marathon struggles against Boston: 7–2 in 18 innings behind Guy Bush, who went the distance; and 4–3 in 22 innings, with Bob Osborn working 14 scoreless innings in relief. Two weeks later, in the morning game of a Memorial Day doubleheader, shortstop Jimmy Cooney completed an unassisted triple play.

Right-hander Charlie Root, an American League castoff—he was sent to the minors after the 1923 season when he was 0–4 with the St. Louis Browns—allowed less than one hit an inning and led the Cubs and the league in victories with 26 and in innings with 309. Irving Vaughan wrote in the *Chicago Tribune:* "He has blinding speed and his curve cracks like amplified static on a sultry night."

McCarthy was constantly patching. On June 7 he made the first of several deals with the Phillies—veteran pitcher Hal Carlson for shortstop Cooney and pitcher Tony Kaufmann. Carlson was 4–1 in his first month with the Cubs; after two months he was 8–2. But he won only four more games and lost four consecutive September starts.

The departure of Cooney forced McCarthy to revamp his infield. Sparky Adams, who had been at third, replaced Cooney at short, and the switch-hitting Eddie Pick, who also came in a deal with the Phillies, was installed at third base. First baseman Charlie Grimm, .311, was the only infielder who played the full season at the same position.

Pick didn't hit—.171 in 54 games—and was benched in favor of Woody English, 19, who had impressed McCarthy two years earlier when McCarthy was managing at Louisville. English was acquired from Toledo for $50,000 and was to become an infield fixture at third base. As a schoolboy, he was so embarrassed by the size of his hands that he hid them in class by sitting on them. One writer believed English's hands were the largest of any player in the big leagues.

Wayland Dean, who had refused to pitch for the Phillies, also came aboard. In mid-July, after he had worked only one inning for the Cubs, Dean revealed he had a sore arm. Like Alexander six years earlier, he was sent to Youngstown to see "Bonesetter" Reese. A psychiatrist might have been more beneficial. Dean pitched only one more inning and was suspended when he accompanied the club on the second eastern trip but failed to appear at the Polo Grounds.

The Cubs had three long winning streaks: the first, 12 games, longest in the league since 1915; the others, nine games. They were in contention until the final month, in first place during all of August, and six games in front when they embarked on their final eastern swing. They might have won the flag if they had played .500 ball the rest of the way.

"McCarthy doesn't appear concerned," reported the *Sporting News,* "and the players share his attitude." It was a classic case of overconfidence. The Cubs were 12–18 in September, which included seven successive losses, and finished fourth, 8½ games behind the first-place Pirates, Hack Wilson tied for the league lead in home runs with 30 and was second in RBIs with 129. Outfielder Riggs Stephenson was fourth in batting with a .344 average.

	W	L	ERA	G	GS	CG	IP	H	BB	K
Charlie Root	(26)	15	3.76	(48)	36	21	(309)	296	(117)	145
Sheriff Blake	13	14	3.29	32	27	13	224⅓	238	82	64
Guy Bush	10	10	3.03	36	22	9	193⅓	177	79	62
Hal Carlson	12	8	3.17	27	22	15	184⅓	201	27	27
Jim Brillheart	4	2	4.13	32	12	4	128⅔	140	38	36
Percy Jones	7	8	4.07	30	11	5	112⅔	123	72	37
Bob Osborn	5	5	4.18	24	12	2	107⅓	125	48	45
Tony Kaufmann	3	3	6.41	9	6	3	53⅓	75	19	21
Art Nehf	1	1	1.37	8	2	2	26⅓	25	9	12
Luther Roy	3	1	2.29	11	0	0	19⅔	14	11	5
Lefty Weinert	1	1	4.58	5	3	1	19⅔	21	6	5
Henry Grampp	0	0	9.00	2	0	0	3	4	1	3
Wayland Dean	0	0	0.00	2	0	0	2	0	2	2
Johnny Welch	0	0	9.00	1	0	0	1	0	3	1
	85	68	3.65	267	153	75	1,385	1,439	514	465

Shutouts: Root 4, Blake 2, Carlson 2, Bush 1, Jones 1, Nehf 1.

	G	AB	H	2B	3B	HR	R	RBI	SB	AVG
Regulars										
1B Charlie Grimm	147	543	169	29	6	2	68	74	3	.311
2B Clyde Beck	117	391	101	20	5	2	44	44	0	.258
SS Woody English	87	334	97	14	4	1	46	28	1	.290
3B Sparky Adams	146	(647)	189	17	7	0	100	49	26	.292
RF Earl Webb	102	332	100	18	4	14	58	52	3	.301
CF Hack Wilson	146	551	175	30	12	(30)	119	129	13	.318
LF Riggs Stephenson	152	579	199	(46)	9	7	101	82	8	.344
C Gabby Hartnett	127	449	132	32	5	10	56	80	2	.294
Substitutes										
Eddie Pick	54	181	31	5	2	2	23	15	0	.171
Jimmy Cooney	33	132	32	2	0	0	16	6	1	.242
Howard Freigau	30	86	20	5	0	0	12	10	0	.233
Chick Tolson	39	54	16	4	0	2	6	17	0	.296
Elmer Yoter	13	27	6	1	1	0	2	5	0	.222
Harry Wilke	3	9	0	0	0	0	0	0	0	.000
Cliff Heathcote	83	228	67	12	4	2	28	25	6	.294
Pete Scott	71	156	49	18	1	0	28	21	1	.314
Mike Gonzalez	39	108	26	4	1	1	15	15	1	.241
John Churry	1	1	1	0	0	0	0	0	0	1.000
Fred Haney	4	3	0	0	0	0	0	0	0	.000
Tommy Sewell	1	1	0	0	0	0	0	0	0	.000
Pitchers										
Charlie Root	48	122	27	6	1	0	15	8	0	.221
Sheriff Blake	32	83	16	0	0	0	2	3	0	.193
Hal Carlson	27	67	11	0	0	0	1	9	0	.164
Guy Bush	36	65	8	1	0	0	2	1	0	.123
Jim Brillheart	32	44	1	0	0	0	1	1	0	.023
Percy Jones	30	40	14	1	0	0	3	4	0	.350
Bob Osborn	24	39	8	0	1	0	1	4	0	.205
Tony Kaufmann	9	16	5	0	0	1	2	6	0	.313
Art Nehf	8	7	3	1	0	0	0	3	0	.429
Lefty Weinert	5	5	1	0	0	0	1	0	0	.200
Luther Roy	11	3	1	0	0	0	0	1	0	.333
Wayland Dean	2	0	0	0	0	0	0	0	0	—
Henry Grampp	0	0	0	0	0	0	0	0	0	—
Johnny Welch	1	0	0	0	0	0	0	0	0	—
		5,303	1,505	266	63	74	750	692	65	.284

1928

Record: 91–63
Finish: Third
Games Behind: 4
Manager: Joe McCarthy

In anticipation of a pennant, a new press box was erected in 1928. It was glass enclosed and electrically heated, seated 100, and was suspended beneath the second deck like the gondola of a dirigible. The construction was premature. The Cubs were in almost constant contention, never too far off the pace but in first place for only seven days in May, altogether a disappointing season considering that the acquisition of Hazen "Kiki" Cuyler had been expected to give them the best hitting outfield in league history.

This trio, eventually, was as good as advertised. But not in 1928. Cuyler was constantly troubled with a hand injury and batted .285 with 17 home runs, far below expectations; he had hit for a .338 cumulative average the previous four seasons with the Pirates. The two other Cub gardeners, Hack Wilson and Riggs Stephenson, were on target.

Wilson led the league with 31 home runs and drove in 120 runs. But unlike the streak-hitting Wilson, who was often in slumps, Stephenson was consistent throughout. Though he possessed only occasional power—eight home runs—opponents considered Stephenson the best hitter. He led the club with a .324 average and 36 doubles, and struck out only 29 times in 512 at bats.

The year before, the Cubs had been the first franchise in league history with a home gate in excess of a million. Attendance was also in seven figures in 1928. But in retrospect, there were only two reasons for joy: On May 14, John McGraw, the hated manager of the New York Giants, was knocked down by a taxi as he was leaving Wrigley Field; and the Cubs, with a 14–8 series edge, prevented the Giants from winning the pennant. The Giants finished second, two games behind St. Louis. The Cubs were third, four out.

The Cubs were coming off a surprising successful season. Charlie Root had led the league with 26 victories in 1927. An even better season, possibly 30 wins, was predicted for 1928. But Root, who had been holding out, was 27 pounds overweight when he reported for spring training at Catalina Island, the million-dollar playground of owner William Wrigley, Jr. It was an ominous beginning.

Root never shaped up. He was unable to win in his first three starts, lost seven in a row in late June and early July, and was 14–18 on the season. Pat Malone and Sheriff Blake, both of whom lost no-hitters in the eighth inning, picked up some of the slack. Malone was 18–13, Blake 17–11. Hal Carlson, a pitching hero from the previous year, was disabled most of the season and won only three games.

Still, the Cubs played well enough to provide sugarplum visions of the flag. They were fourth during the entire month of June, held second place for a week in mid-July, and, after defeating the front-running Cardinals on September 13, were only two games out of the lead. The middle of the lineup, which should have been the club's strength, was inconsistent and, along with weak pitching, kept them anchored in third place.

Cuyler came from the Pirates in a major off-season deal for infielder Sparky Adams and outfielder Pete Scott. He was hitting .203 in May and .250 in July, and he didn't get to .300 until late August. Hack Wilson was so frustrated that he jumped the rail and assaulted a heckler at a cost of $100 and a five-day suspension. The only players who performed better than expected were catcher Gabby Hartnett, .302, and Fred Maguire, who led all second basemen in chances and batted .279.

	W	L	ERA	G	GS	CG	IP	H	BB	K
Pat Malone	18	13	2.84	42	25	16	250⅔	218	99	155
Sheriff Blake	17	11	2.47	34	29	16	240⅔	209	101	78
Charlie Root	14	18	3.57	40	30	13	237	214	73	122
Guy Bush	15	6	3.83	42	24	9	204⅓	229	86	61
Art Nehf	13	7	2.65	31	21	10	176⅔	190	52	40
Percy Jones	10	6	4.03	39	18	9	154	164	56	41
Hal Carlson	3	2	5.91	20	5	2	56⅓	74	15	11
Ed Holley	0	0	3.77	13	1	0	31	31	16	10
Lefty Weinert	1	0	5.29	10	1	0	17	24	9	8
Ben Tincup	0	0	7.00	2	0	0	9	14	1	3
Johnny Welch	0	0	15.75	3	0	0	4	13	0	2
	91	63	3.40	276	154	75	1,380⅔	1,380	508	531

Shutouts: Blake 4, Bush 2, Malone 2, Nehf 2, Jones 1.

	G	AB	H	2B	3B	HR	R	RBI	SB	AVG
Regulars										
1B Charlie Grimm	147	547	161	25	5	5	67	62	7	.294
2B Freddie Maguire	140	574	160	24	7	1	67	41	6	.279
SS Woody English	116	475	142	22	4	2	68	34	4	.299
3B Clyde Beck	131	483	124	18	4	3	72	52	3	.257
RF Kiki Cuyler	133	499	142	25	9	17	92	79	(37)	.285
CF Hack Wilson	145	520	163	32	9	(31)	89	120	4	.313
LF Riggs Stephenson	137	512	166	36	9	8	75	90	8	.324
C Gabby Hartnett	120	388	117	26	9	14	61	57	3	.302
Substitutes										
Johnny Butler	62	174	47	7	0	0	17	16	2	.270
Norm McMillan	49	123	27	2	2	1	11	12	0	.220
Joe Kelly	32	52	11	1	0	1	3	7	0	.212
Elmer Yoter	1	0	0	0	0	0	0	0	0	—
Earl Webb	62	140	35	7	3	3	22	23	0	.250
Cliff Heathcote	67	137	39	8	0	3	26	18	6	.285
Mike Gonzalez	49	158	43	9	2	1	12	21	2	.272
Johnny Moore	4	4	0	0	0	0	0	0	0	.000
Ray Jacobs	2	2	0	0	0	0	0	0	0	.000
Pitchers										
Pat Malone	42	95	18	3	0	1	8	11	0	.189
Sheriff Blake	35	88	19	1	0	0	10	5	0	.216
Guy Bush	42	73	6	0	0	0	3	2	0	.082
Charlie Root	40	73	13	5	0	0	5	5	0	.178
Art Nehf	31	58	11	0	1	1	4	3	0	.190
Percy Jones	39	56	11	0	0	0	1	5	1	.196
Hal Carlson	20	19	5	0	0	0	1	1	0	.263
Ed Holley	13	5	0	0	0	0	0	1	0	.000
Ben Tincup	2	3	0	0	0	0	0	0	0	.000
Lefty Weinert	10	2	0	0	0	0	0	0	0	.000
Johnny Welch	3	0	0	0	0	0	0	0	0	—
		5,260	1,460	251	64	92	714	665	83	.278

1929

Record: 98–54
Finish: First
Games Ahead: 10½
Manager: Joe McCarthy

It was the year of the great Wall Street crash, but stock in the Cubs soared in 1929. A $200,000 investment in Rogers Hornsby, acquired in a deal with Boston, helped the Cubs win their first pennant in 11 years. It was the highest price paid for a player and provided the Cubs with a window-breaking offense that included the best hitting outfield in National League history.

The outfield of Stephenson in left, Wilson in center, and Cuyler in right, combined, hit for a record .355 average. Second baseman Hornsby, the possessor of a .361 lifetime average who had won seven league batting crowns, checked in at .380. He finished so strongly it seemed likely, had play continued for another week or two, that he would have had his fourth .400-plus season.

Hornsby had been the player-manager of the Braves and was available because Judge Emil Fuchs, who held the Boston franchise, was in financial peril. The deal quieted the judge's creditors and relieved him of Hornsby's $40,000 salary. To compound the saving, Fuchs, who had been a minor magistrate in New York City, succeeded Hornsby as the team manager. The Cubs also sent Boston five players: pitchers Percy Jones, Bruce Cunningham, and Socks Seibold, infielder Fred Maguire, and catcher Lou Legett.

The Cub assault had the force of a sledgehammer. Wilson set a league record with 159 RBIs. Hornsby broke the mark for runs scored with 156 and led in total bases and slugging percentage, was second in doubles, third in batting and hits, and tied with Wilson for third in home runs, 39. Stephenson was fifth in batting. Cuyler led in stolen bases.

Stephenson hit .362, Cuyler .360, and Wilson .345. The Cubs had a .303 average and scored a record 982 runs; they would easily have exceeded 1,000 if Hartnett hadn't missed half the season, afflicted with a severe tonsil infection and an arm injury. They had ten consecutive hits in one inning and three times scored 16 runs. In mid-July, aroused after a bench-clearing fight with Cincinnati, they came from behind for six consecutive victories, two against the Giants, four against the Phillies.

The Cincinnati brawl occurred on July 4 and began on the field. Pitcher Ray Kolp, from the dugout, showered Wilson with insults after he had reached with a single. Wilson leaped into the dugout and delivered two rights to the jaw. That night, when both teams were at Union Station, Cincinnati pitcher Pete Donahue overheard Wilson say he was going into the Reds' car to extract an apology from Kolp. Donahue warned him, "You won't come out alive," whereupon Wilson split Donahue's lip with a right uppercut. Wilson was suspended for three days and fined $100.

Remarkably, the Cubs' longest winning streak was only nine games. They finished 10½ games ahead of the runner-up Pirates and were alone in first place 97 days but didn't shake off the Cardinals and Pirates until July 28, when they went into the lead to stay. They pulled away gradually, were 24–8 with one tie in July, and were 58–35 after August 1. They clinched on September 18, with two weeks of the season remaining, and finished with a 98–54 record, 44 games over .500.

Victory seldom is achieved on hitting alone, and the Cubs had good enough pitching. Perce "Pat" Malone, 22–10, had a career year. Root returned to form and was 19–6, the league's best winning percentage. Guy Bush was 18–7. His wins included a 10-game winning streak, and he was second in percentage. Sheriff Blake was 14–13. Hal Carlson, seemingly recovered from injuries, was 11–5.

	W	L	ERA	G	GS	CG	IP	H	BB	K
Charlie Root	19	6	3.47	43	31	19	272	286	83	124
Guy Bush	18	7	3.66	(50)	29	18	270⅔	277	107	82
Pat Malone	(22)	10	3.57	40	30	19	267	283	102	(166)
Sheriff Blake	14	13	4.29	35	30	13	218⅓	244	103	70
Art Nehf	8	5	5.59	32	15	4	120⅔	148	39	27
Hal Carlson	11	5	5.16	31	14	6	111⅔	131	31	35
Mike Cvengros	5	4	4.64	32	2	0	64	82	29	23
Claude Jonnard	0	1	7.48	12	2	0	27⅓	41	11	11
Trader Horne	1	1	5.09	11	1	0	23	24	21	6
Ken Penner	0	1	2.84	5	0	0	12⅔	14	6	3
Bob Osborn	0	0	3.00	3	1	0	9	8	2	1
Henry Grampp	0	1	27.00	1	1	0	2	4	3	0
	98	54	4.16	295	156	79	1,398⅔	1,542	537	548

Shutouts: Malone 5, Root 4, Bush 2, Carlson 2, Blake 1.

	G	AB	H	2B	3B	HR	R	RBI	SB	AVG
Regulars										
1B Charlie Grimm	120	463	138	28	3	10	66	91	3	.298
2B Rogers Hornsby	156	602	229	47	8	39	(156)	149	2	.380
SS Woody English	144	608	168	29	3	1	131	52	13	.276
3B Norm McMillan	124	495	134	35	5	5	77	55	13	.271
RF Kiki Cuyler	139	509	183	29	7	15	111	102	(43)	.360
CF Hack Wilson	150	574	198	30	5	39	135	(159)	3	.345
LF Riggs Stephenson	136	495	179	36	6	17	91	110	10	.362
C Zack Taylor	64	215	59	16	3	1	29	31	0	.274
Substitutes										
Clyde Beck	54	190	40	7	0	0	28	9	3	.211
Chick Tolson	32	109	28	5	0	1	13	19	0	.257
Footsie Blair	26	72	23	5	0	1	10	8	1	.319
Cliff Heathcote	82	224	70	17	0	2	45	31	9	.313
Johnny Moore	37	63	18	1	0	2	13	8	0	.286
Danny Taylor	2	3	0	0	0	0	0	0	0	.000
Mike Gonzalez	60	167	40	3	0	0	15	18	1	.240
Earl Grace	27	80	20	1	0	2	7	17	0	.250
Johnny Schulte	31	69	18	3	0	0	6	9	0	.261
Gabby Hartnett	25	22	6	2	1	1	2	9	1	.273
Tom Angley	5	16	4	1	0	0	1	6	0	.250
Pitchers										
Pat Malone	40	105	22	3	0	2	8	11	0	.210
Charlie Root	43	96	15	3	4	1	8	15	0	.156
Guy Bush	50	91	15	0	0	0	5	3	1	.165
Sheriff Blake	38	81	14	2	0	0	11	4	0	.173
Art Nehf	32	45	13	3	0	0	3	5	0	.289
Hal Carlson	31	39	9	2	0	0	4	8	0	.231
Mike Cvengros	33	15	6	1	0	0	5	1	0	.400
Claude Jonnard	12	10	2	1	1	0	1	2	0	.200
Trader Horne	11	5	2	0	0	0	1	0	0	.400
Bob Osborn	3	4	1	0	0	0	0	0	0	.250
Ken Penner	5	4	1	0	0	0	0	1	0	.250
Henry Grampp	1	0	0	0	0	0	0	0	0	—
		5,471	1,655	(310)	46	139	(982)	933	103	.303

1930

Record: 90–64
Finish: Second
Games Behind: 2
Managers: Joe McCarthy, Rogers Hornsby

Hack Wilson drove in 190 runs in 1930, setting a major league record that has been approached twice but never equaled. He also hit 56 home runs, a National League record that still stands. Riggs Stephenson batted .367, Kiki Cuyler .355. Catcher Gabby Hartnett, recovered from injuries, had his best year, a .339 average alone with 122 runs batted in and 37 home runs.

These numbers may seem indicative of a second consecutive pennant. But the Cubs finished second because second baseman Rogers Hornsby sat out most of the season with multiple leg injuries. He talked his way into the lineup on several occasions, but the Rajah was without his accustomed offensive skills; in 42 games and 104 at bats, he hit .308 with only two home runs and 18 RBIs.

It was the worst of times for Hornsby but the best of times for Wilson and his fellow sluggers. The ball was livelier than ever. Six of the eight teams hit .303 or higher; 71 players who appeared in more than 10 games hit .300. The Phillies led the league with 194 home runs and finished last, 40 games out.

As for Wilson, none of his 56 home runs came with the bases filled; 23 were with the bases empty; the remaining 33 home runs drove in 97 runs. He batted in 48 runs with singles, 26 with doubles, five with triples, eight on sacrifice flies, four on fielder's choices, and two on bases-loaded walks.

Wilson didn't connect until the seventh game. On June 23 he hit for the cycle, with six RBIs. He was seventh in the majors with 25 home runs on July 18. Three days later he hit

three against the Phillies. August was his best month: 13 homers and 53 RBIs, the latter believed to be a major league record. He drove in 34 more in September—87 RBIs in two months. Home runs number 55 and 56 and his 190th RBI were delivered in the final game of the season.

For Hornsby it was a season of constant woe. He underwent off-season surgery for bone spurs in his right heel and was unable to perform for an extended period. Footsie Blair had to take over for him at second base. Against doctor's orders, Hornsby put himself in the lineup in early May. Two weeks later he fractured his left ankle, sliding. Compounding his travail were several September newspaper reports, none confirmed, that he and manager Joe McCarthy were feuding.

The Cubs were in first place for 40 days and 40 nights. They took the lead for the first time on June 28—after winning 24 of 31 games, their best extended showing. Brooklyn led during the first week of July. There were many lead changes, prompting Irving Vaughan of the *Chicago Tribune* to observe: "Our Cubs had a noon meal in first place, but when the supper bell rang they were right back in second." The Cubs were in command the last three weeks of August and the first week in September, once by as much as six games. St. Louis led thereafter.

The team batting average, a record .309, was balanced by a 4.80 earned run average, highest in club history. Pat Malone led the league with 20 wins, but only one other pitcher, Guy Bush, 15–10, was five games over .500. Hal Carlson, who had won four of six decisions, was found dead in his room at the Carlos hotel on May 28. The cause of death was stomach hemorrhaging, a condition he had developed after he was gassed in World War I. McCarthy resigned on September 25 with four games to play and was succeeded by Hornsby.

	W	L	ERA	G	GS	CG	IP	H	BB	K
Pat Malone	(20)	9	3.94	45	35	(22)	271⅓	290	96	142
Guy Bush	15	10	6.20	46	25	11	225	291	86	75
Charlie Root	16	14	4.33	37	30	15	220⅓	247	63	124
Sheriff Blake	10	14	4.82	34	24	7	186⅔	213	99	80
Bud Teachout	11	4	4.06	40	16	6	153	178	48	59
Bob Osborn	10	6	4.97	35	13	3	126⅔	147	53	42
Lynn Nelson	3	2	5.09	37	3	0	81⅓	97	28	29
Hal Carlson	4	2	5.05	8	6	3	51⅓	68	14	14
Jesse Petty	1	3	2.97	9	3	0	39⅓	51	6	18
Al Shealy	0	0	8.00	24	0	0	27	37	14	14
Mal Moss	0	0	6.27	12	1	0	18⅔	18	14	4
Lon Warneke	0	0	33.75	1	0	0	1⅓	2	5	0
Bill McAfee	0	0	0.00	2	0	0	1	3	2	0
	90	64	4.80	330	156	67	1,403⅔	1,642	528	601

Shutouts: Root 4, Malone 2.

	G	AB	H	2B	3B	HR	R	RBI	SB	AVG
Regulars										
1B Charlie Grimm	114	429	124	27	2	6	58	66	1	.289
2B Footsie Blair	134	578	158	24	12	6	97	59	9	.273
SS Woody English	156	638	214	36	17	14	152	59	3	.335
3B Clyde Beck	83	244	52	7	0	6	32	34	2	.213
RF Kiki Cuyler	156	642	228	50	17	13	155	134	(37)	.355
CF Hack Wilson	155	585	208	35	6	(56)	146	(190)	3	.356
LF Riggs Stephenson	109	341	125	21	1	5	56	68	2	.367
C Gabby Hartnett	141	508	172	31	3	37	84	122	0	.339
Substitutes										
Les Bell	74	248	69	15	4	5	35	47	1	.278
George Kelly	39	166	55	6	1	3	22	19	0	.331
Doc Farrell	46	113	33	6	0	1	21	16	0	.292
Rogers Hornsby	42	104	32	5	1	2	15	18	0	.308
Chick Tolson	13	20	6	1	0	0	0	1	0	.300
Danny Taylor	74	219	62	14	3	2	43	37	6	.283
Cliff Heathcote	70	150	39	10	1	9	30	18	4	.260
Zack Taylor	32	95	22	2	1	1	12	11	0	.232
Pitchers										
Pat Malone	45	105	26	0	0	4	12	10	0	.248
Charlie Root	37	80	21	8	0	1	4	6	1	.263
Guy Bush	46	78	22	0	1	0	7	7	0	.282
Sheriff Blake	36	66	15	0	0	0	5	2	0	.227
Bud Teachout	42	63	17	4	1	0	8	5	0	.270
Bob Osborn	35	42	4	0	0	0	0	3	0	.095
Hal Carlson	8	20	5	0	0	0	1	3	0	.250
Lynn Nelson	37	18	4	1	1	0	0	2	0	.222
Jesse Petty	9	13	3	1	0	0	1	1	0	.231
Mal Moss	12	11	3	0	0	0	0	2	0	.273
Al Shealy	24	5	3	1	0	0	2	0	0	.600
Bill McAfee	2	0	0	0	0	0	0	0	0	—
Lon Warneke	1	0	0	0	0	0	0	0	0	—
		5,581	1,722	305	72	(171)	998	940	70	.309

1931

Record: 84–70
Finish: Third
Games Behind: 17
Manager: Rogers Hornsby

Club President William Veeck tossed Hack Wilson one of the National League's new baseballs. This was in late February 1931 as the Cubs were assembling at their Catalina Island spring training camp. Wilson inspected the ball, twisted it in his hand, and told Veeck, "It looks the same to me."

As Wilson and other sluggers discovered, to their dismay, it wasn't the same ball. It had been deadened with the introduction of the cushion cork center and a thicker cover. Also, to allow the pitchers a stronger grip, crucial in the delivery of breaking pitches, particularly the curveball, the seams were raised.

Home run production diminished, and nobody was more affected than Wilson, whose salary had been increased from $22,500 to $35,000. Wilson's average fell to .261. Worse, he hit only 13 home runs, 43 fewer than in the previous season; the drop in his RBIs was equally dramatic, from a record 190 to 61.

Wilson was also engaged in season-long disputes with Hornsby, who was in his first full season as the Cub manager. Wilson was repeatedly benched for failure to produce—also for violating the midnight curfew. Twice he was suspended: for one day in July, after a caper in Boston, and again on September 6, when Hornsby set him down for the remainder of the season. Two months later he was traded to Brooklyn.

Several of his teammates offered the theory that Wilson not merely was the victim of the deadened ball but also suffered from an inflated ego that "got out of control" during vaudeville engagements that followed his record-breaking season: "Hack got the notion that he had a sweet voice, was a nifty dancer . . . a personality boy who could triumph on the stage."

For the 1931 Cubs there was no triumph. They never held the lead by themselves, and they finished third, 17 games out. The only consolation was the arrival of two new infielders, Billy Jurges and Billy Herman. A natural shortstop, Jurges joined the club in spring training. He appeared in 54 games at third base and batted .201. Herman arrived later. He was acquired from Louisville for $50,000 and two players. In his Cub debut, on September 6, he was hit in the head with a pitch and carried off the field.

The Rajah batted .331, tied for the club lead with first baseman Charlie Grimm, and led in home runs with 16 and in RBIs with 90. Hornsby started well. He hit a game-winning home run in the second game and a three-run home run two days later, and on April 24 in Pittsburgh he was a one-man wrecking crew in a 10–6 victory: three home runs in succession and eight RBIs. It was the first three-home-run game of his career.

Even then, he was in pain, slow running the bases, and unable to slide. Off the field, he walked with a limp. He played only 69 games at second base and then, conceding his handicap, moved to third base. He benched himself in late July and thereafter seldom appeared in more than two games in a row.

The pitchers profited from the deadened ball. The team ERA dropped almost a full point to 3.97. Charlie Root led with 17 wins, followed by Pat Malone and Guy Bush, 16 each, and Bob Smith, 15. Malone "brutally assaulted" two Chicago baseball writers, shattering the teeth of one. Veeck reimbursed the scribe with $1,000 for a new set of dentures. The writer used the money to purchase a new car. Malone apologized in November when Veeck threatened to trade him.

	W	L	ERA	G	GS	CG	IP	H	BB	K
Charlie Root	17	14	3.48	39	31	19	251	240	71	131
Bob Smith	15	12	3.22	36	29	18	240⅓	239	62	63
Pat Malone	16	9	3.90	36	30	12	228⅓	229	88	112
Guy Bush	16	8	4.49	39	24	14	180⅓	190	66	54
Les Sweetland	8	7	5.04	26	14	9	130⅓	156	61	32
Jakie May	5	5	3.87	31	4	1	79	81	43	38
Ed Baecht	2	4	3.76	22	6	2	67	64	32	34
Lon Warneke	2	4	3.22	20	7	3	64⅓	67	37	27
Bud Teachout	1	2	5.72	27	3	1	61⅓	79	28	14
Sheriff Blake	0	4	5.22	16	5	0	50	64	26	29
Johnny Welch	2	1	3.74	8	3	1	33⅔	39	10	7
	84	70	3.97	300	156	80	1,385⅔	1,448	524	541

Shutouts: Root 3, Malone 2, Smith 2, Bush 1.

	G	AB	H	2B	3B	HR	R	RBI	SB	AVG
Regulars										
1B Charlie Grimm	146	531	176	33	11	4	65	66	1	.331
2B Rogers Hornsby	100	357	118	37	1	16	64	90	1	.331
SS Woody English	156	634	202	38	8	2	117	53	12	.319
3B Les Bell	75	252	71	17	1	4	30	32	0	.282
RF Kiki Cuyler	154	613	202	37	12	9	110	88	13	.330
CF Hack Wilson	112	395	103	22	4	13	66	61	1	.261
LF Riggs Stephenson	80	263	84	14	4	1	34	52	1	.319
C Gabby Hartnett	116	380	107	32	1	8	53	70	3	.282
Substitutes										
Bill Jurges	88	293	59	15	5	0	34	23	2	.201
Footsie Blair	86	240	62	19	5	2	31	29	1	.258
Billy Herman	25	98	32	7	0	0	14	16	2	.327
Jimmy Adair	18	76	21	3	1	0	9	3	1	.276
Danny Taylor	88	270	81	13	6	5	48	41	4	.300
Vince Barton	66	239	57	10	1	13	45	50	1	.238
Johnny Moore	39	104	25	3	1	2	19	16	1	.240
Mike Kreevich	5	12	2	0	0	0	0	0	1	.167
Rollie Hemsley	66	204	63	17	4	3	28	31	4	.309
Earl Grace	7	9	1	0	0	0	2	1	0	.111
Zack Taylor	8	4	1	0	0	0	0	0	0	.250
Pitchers										
Charlie Root	39	90	20	8	0	0	7	8	0	.222
Bob Smith	36	87	19	2	0	0	7	4	0	.218
Pat Malone	36	79	17	2	0	1	12	4	0	.215
Guy Bush	39	57	7	1	0	0	6	9	0	.123
Les Sweetland	29	56	15	4	2	0	8	9	0	.268
Jakie May	31	22	5	2	0	0	3	2	0	.227
Bud Teachout	37	21	5	0	0	0	4	0	0	.238
Lon Warneke	20	19	5	2	0	0	3	2	0	.263
Ed Baecht	22	18	5	0	0	0	3	2	0	.278
Sheriff Blake	16	16	8	0	0	0	4	1	0	.500
Johnny Welch	8	12	5	2	0	0	2	2	0	.417
		5,451	1,578	340	67	83	828	765	49	.289

1932

Record: 90–64
Finish: First
Game Ahead: 4
Managers: Rogers Hornsby, Charlie Grimm

In 1932 the Cubs won their 13th flag, the sixth since 1906, but William Wrigley, a benevolent owner who had an open purse and enjoyed the companionship of his players, wasn't at the pennant party. He had died of a stroke on January 26, at the age of 70, in his Phoenix home, one of his four palatial mansions. His estate was in excess of $50 million, including holdings of $30 million in Illinois. The value of the Cubs was estimated at $5 million.

Wrigley was among Hornsby's admirers. Had Wrigley lived, Hornsby more than likely would have finished the season as the Cub manager. Wrigley's son Philip inherited the club but deferred baseball decisions to President William Veeck. Never a Hornsby booster, Veeck released Hornsby on August 2 and appointed veteran first baseman Charlie Grimm to succeed him.

After the first two weeks, the Cubs were never lower than second. When Hornsby was relieved, they trailed Pittsburgh by five games. The players immediately responded to Grimm's comparatively gentle and loose manner. They took three of their next four. Three weeks later they broke the race open. Beginning on August 16, they had their best streak: 20 of 21.

The full depth of the players' hostility toward Hornsby was revealed when they refused to award him a World Series share. Hornsby appealed to the commissioner, Judge Kenesaw Mountain Landis, asserting that he had been with the club two-thirds of the season and had helped in the development of pitcher Lon Warneke and infielders Billy Jurges and Billy Herman, all of whom succeeded beyond expectations. The complaint was dismissed.

There was constant turmoil. On the morning of July 7, Jurges was shot by his girlfriend, Violet Popovich Valli, a young divorcée who danced and modeled under the name Violet Valli. She came to Jurges's room at the Carlos Hotel packing a .25 caliber revolver. Jurges tried to get the pistol away. In the struggle, one bullet caromed off Jurges's ribs and exited near his right shoulder; another slug grazed the little finger of his left hand.

When she departed, she left several empty gin bottles and a note that read: "To me, life without Billy isn't worth living, but why should I leave this earth alone? I'm going to take Billy with me."

There was also a horse betting scandal. When Hornsby was dismissed, he told Veeck he wanted the remaining money due on his contract in a lump sum. An inveterate horse player, Hornsby was in debt to six or seven of his players and wanted to repay them. The Chicago papers ran banner front-page headlines. The caption under a photograph of Guy Bush contended the Cub players owed $38,000 to bookmakers. Landis probed but made no charges.

The Cub pitching staff was the most effective in the league. Lon Warneke, in his first full season with the Cubs, led the league with 22 victories and had winning streaks of five and nine games. Guy Bush was 19–11, Charlie Root 15–10. Pat Malone also won 15 games but was out for two weeks with a toothache, retribution for knocking out the teeth of a Chicago baseball writer.

Jurges and Herman had remarkable range and gave the Cubs a brilliant second base combination. Free of injuries, Riggs Stephenson led the offense with a .324 average. Hornsby batted .224 with one home run and seven RBIs; he appeared in 19 games, ten in right field, six at third base, and three as a pinch hitter.

	W	L	ERA	G	GS	CG	IP	H	BB	K
Lon Warneke	(22)	6	(2.37)	35	32	25	277	247	64	106
Guy Bush	19	11	3.21	40	30	15	238⅔	262	70	73
Pat Malone	15	17	3.38	37	33	17	237	222	78	120
Charlie Root	15	10	3.58	39	23	11	216⅓	211	55	96
Burleigh Grimes	6	11	4.78	30	18	5	141⅓	174	50	36
Bob Smith	4	3	4.61	34	11	4	119	148	36	35
Bud Tinning	5	3	2.80	24	7	2	93⅓	93	24	30
Jakie May	2	2	4.36	35	0	0	53⅓	61	19	20
LeRoy Herrmann	2	1	6.39	7	0	0	12⅔	18	9	5
Carroll Yerkes	0	0	3.00	2	0	0	9	5	3	4
Ed Baecht	0	0	0.00	1	0	0	1	1	1	0
Marv Gudat	0	0	0.00	1	0	0	1	1	0	2
Bobo Newsom	0	0	0.00	1	0	0	1	1	0	0
	90	64	3.44	286	154	79	1,401	1,444	409	527

Shutouts: Warneke 4, Malone 2, Bush 1, Grimes 1, Smith 1.

Lon Warneke, alias the Arkansas Hummingbird, one of the star Cub pitchers of the '30s

	G	AB	H	2B	3B	HR	R	RBI	SB	AVG
Regulars										
1B Charlie Grimm	149	570	175	42	2	7	66	80	2	.307
2B Billy Herman	154	656	206	42	7	1	102	51	14	.314
SS Bill Jurges	115	396	100	24	4	2	40	52	1	.253
3B Woody English	127	522	142	23	7	3	70	47	5	.272
RF Kiki Cuyler	110	446	130	19	9	10	58	77	9	.291
CF Johnny Moore	119	443	135	24	5	13	59	64	4	.305
LF Riggs Stephenson	147	583	189	49	4	4	86	85	3	.324
C Gabby Hartnett	121	406	110	25	3	12	52	52	0	.271
Substitutes										
Stan Hack	72	178	42	5	6	2	32	19	5	.236
Mark Koenig	33	102	36	5	1	3	15	11	0	.353
Harry Taylor	10	8	1	0	0	0	1	0	0	.125
Lance Richbourg	44	148	38	2	2	1	22	21	0	.257
Vince Barton	36	134	30	2	3	3	19	15	0	.224
Marv Gudat	60	94	24	4	1	1	15	15	0	.255
Rogers Hornsby	19	58	13	2	0	1	10	7	0	.224
Frank Demaree	23	56	14	3	0	0	4	6	0	.250
Danny Taylor	6	22	5	2	0	0	3	3	1	.227
Rollie Hemsley	60	151	36	10	3	4	27	20	2	.238
Zack Taylor	21	30	6	1	0	0	2	3	0	.200
Pitchers										
Lon Warneke	35	99	19	1	1	0	8	9	0	.192
Guy Bush	40	84	15	2	1	0	6	1	0	.179
Pat Malone	37	78	14	2	0	1	7	7	0	.179
Charlie Root	39	76	13	1	0	1	4	10	0	.171
Burleigh Grimes	30	44	11	1	0	0	4	5	1	.250
Bob Smith	36	42	10	4	1	0	5	4	1	.238
Bud Tinning	24	23	2	1	0	0	3	1	0	.087
Jakie May	35	8	1	0	0	0	0	0	0	.125
Carroll Yerkes	2	3	1	0	0	0	0	0	0	.333
LeRoy Herrmann	7	2	1	0	0	0	0	0	0	.500
Ed Baecht	1	0	0	0	0	0	0	0	0	—
Bobo Newsom	1	0	0	0	0	0	0	0	0	—
		5,462	1,519	296	60	69	720	665	48	.278

1933

Record: 86–68
Finish: Third
Games Behind: 6
Manager: Charlie Grimm

Hoping to win another pennant, the Cubs opened their pocketbook again in 1933. At a cost of $75,000 and four players, the contract of Floyd Caves "Babe" Herman was purchased from the Cincinnati Reds. According to a contemporary ac-

count, Cincinnati owner Sidney Weil, when he discovered the check didn't bounce, was so delighted "he almost swooned."

A 6-foot, 4-inch left-handed hitter, Herman was a right fielder who was known as "the other Babe"; his career paralleled that of Babe Ruth. Herman had little of Ruth's power but was a high-average spray hitter. He batted .381 in 1929 and .393 the next year but didn't win the batting title in either year. Lefty O'Doul hit .398 in '29, Bill Terry .401 in '30.

For seven long seasons Herman was the spirit of Brooklyn's "Daffiness Boys" and had a penchant for being involved in the unusual. His principal contribution to baseball lore occurred when he doubled into a double play. He was also hit on the head with a fly ball but always insisted the ball bounced off his shoulder, not his dome.

With the Cubs he was none of the above. But he did have one big day: three home runs and eight RBIs in a 10–1 rout on July 1. His stats were fairly impressive—16 home runs and 93 runs batted in—but he hit only .289 on the season, and the traveling Chicago writers considered him "the flop of the year." Even Veeck concurred.

It was the first full season of Grimm's managerial reign. Early on, he announced he would be a bench manager; he would carry neither a bat nor a glove. In an effort to inspire the sagging troops, Grimm returned to the lineup, but he withdrew in mid-June when, according to Irving Vaughan of the *Tribune,* "His average was shrinking faster than a flannel shirt in its first washing."

Kiki Cuyler fractured his leg sliding into second base on March 30, during the final week of spring training, and missed the first half of the season. It wasn't until late July that Grimm was able to present a lineup that included both of his outfield stars, Riggs Stephenson and Cuyler. Stephenson had a succession of minor injuries and was out for two weeks with malaria. He hit .329 but appeared in only 97 games.

The Cubs led only during the first week. They were in seventh place during the entire month of May and were strongest in September, 16–10, which lifted them to a third-place finish, six games behind the Giants. The stretch kick also saved Grimm's job which, Veeck conceded, had been in jeopardy.

William L. Veeck, the former Chicago baseball writer who had been the club president since 1919, died on October 5 at the age of 52. Several months earlier Veeck had begun promoting interleague play, to begin on July 4 and continue for one month, the results counting in the standings. Veeck's proposal did not win acceptance. It was on the agenda for the winter meetings but was dismissed, presumably for lack of a sponsor.

	W	L	ERA	G	GS	CG	IP	H	BB	K
Lon Warneke	18	13	2.00	36	34	(26)	287⅓	262	75	133
Guy Bush	20	12	2.75	41	32	20	258⅔	261	68	84
Charlie Root	15	10	2.60	35	30	20	242⅓	232	61	86
Pat Malone	10	14	3.91	31	26	13	186⅓	186	59	72
Bud Tinning	13	6	3.18	32	21	10	175⅓	169	60	59
Lynn Nelson	5	5	3.21	24	3	3	75⅔	65	30	20
Burleigh Grimes	3	6	3.49	17	7	3	69⅔	71	29	12
Roy Henshaw	2	1	4.19	21	0	0	38⅔	32	20	16
LeRoy Herrmann	0	1	5.57	9	1	0	21	26	8	4
Beryl Richmond	0	0	1.93	4	0	0	4⅔	10	2	2
Carroll Yerkes	0	0	4.50	1	0	0	2	2	1	0
	86	68	2.93	251	154	95	1,361⅓	1,316	413	488

Shutouts: Bush 4, Warneke 4, Tinning 3, Malone 2, Root 2, Grimes 1.

	G	AB	H	2B	3B	HR	R	RBI	SB	AVG
Regulars										
1B Charlie Grimm	107	384	95	15	2	3	38	37	1	.247
2B Billy Herman	153	619	173	35	2	0	82	44	5	.279
SS Bill Jurges	143	487	131	17	6	5	49	50	3	.269
3B Woody English	105	398	104	19	2	3	54	41	5	.261
RF Babe Herman	137	508	147	36	12	16	77	93	6	.289
CF Frank Demaree	134	515	140	24	6	6	68	51	4	.272
LF Riggs Stephenson	97	346	114	17	4	4	45	51	5	.329
C Gabby Hartnett	140	490	135	21	4	16	55	88	1	.276
Substitutes										
Mark Koenig	80	218	62	12	1	3	32	25	5	.284
Harvey Hendrick	69	189	55	13	4	4	30	23	4	.291
Stan Hack	20	60	21	3	1	1	10	2	4	.350
Dolf Camilli	16	58	13	2	1	2	8	7	3	.224
Kiki Cuyler	70	262	83	13	3	5	37	35	4	.317
Jim Mosolf	31	82	22	5	1	1	13	9	0	.268
Taylor Douthit	27	71	16	5	0	0	8	5	2	.225
Gilly Campbell	46	89	25	3	1	1	11	10	0	.281
Zack Taylor	16	11	0	0	0	0	0	0	0	.000
Babe Phelps	3	7	2	0	0	0	0	2	0	.286
Pitchers										
Lon Warneke	39	100	30	6	1	2	9	13	0	.300
Guy Bush	41	88	11	4	0	0	4	3	0	.125
Charlie Root	35	85	8	3	0	0	1	0	0	.094
Bud Tinning	32	67	14	2	0	0	3	10	0	.209
Pat Malone	31	63	10	0	0	0	5	4	0	.159
Lynn Nelson	29	21	5	1	1	0	5	1	0	.238
Burleigh Grimes	17	20	3	0	0	0	1	4	0	.150
Roy Henshaw	21	10	2	0	0	0	1	0	0	.200
LeRoy Herrmann	9	6	1	0	0	0	0	0	0	.167
Beryl Richmond	4	1	0	0	0	0	0	0	0	.000
Carroll Yerkes	1	0	0	0	0	0	0	0	0	—
		5,255	1,422	256	51	72	646	608	52	.271

1934

Record: 86–65
Finish: Third
Games Behind: 8
Manager: Charlie Grimm

Lon Warneke opened the '34 season with consecutive one-hitters, both on the road: April 17 in Cincinnati's home opener and five days later in St. Louis. The Cubs won their first seven games and ten of the first 12, encouraging sugarplum visions of another pennant, particularly since the hard-hitting Chuck Klein was aboard. Klein had been ac-

quired in a major off-season deal with the Phillies—for $65,000 and three players.

Warneke didn't falter. He finished with a 22–10 record and more remarkable, never lost successive starts. Slugger Klein was a colossal bust, just as Babe Herman, another costly import, had been the year before. After averaging 34 home runs and 138 runs batted in during the previous four seasons with the Phillies, Klein's power numbers plunged to 20 homers and 80 RBIs. His average also dropped, from a league-leading .368 in 1933 to .301.

What went wrong? The Cub brass didn't take into account the significant change of scenery. At the bandbox Baker Bowl, Klein had an easy home run target—280 feet down the right-field line. Wrigley Field wasn't as friendly; the distance was 321 feet. Although Klein hadn't hit below .337 in any of his six previous big league seasons, he never had much success against left-handed pitching.

This weakness wasn't as apparent in the Baker Bowl, where a routine fly ball, an out elsewhere, cleared the tin right-field fence or rattled off it. To further frustrate Klein and Babe Herman, who also batted left-handed, rival managers adjusted their rotations and whenever possible threw their left-handed pitchers against the Cubs. Herman was also affected: 14 home runs and 84 RBIs. The right-handed-hitting Gabby Hartnett led the club with 22 homers and 90 RBIs.

The Cubs were afflicted with their usual injuries. Klein, who had 14 home runs on June 9 but only six thereafter, was in 115 games and missed all of August. Shortstop Billy Jurges underwent an appendectomy in mid-June. Kiki Cuyler sat with an infected hand, inflicted while he was giving himself a clubhouse manicure. Guy Bush had ear trouble. Warneke, suffering from a severe cold, lost weight and was put on a beer and raw egg diet.

The pitching was erratic. Through action of June 16, after 55 games, manager Charlie Grimm needed two or more relievers in 28 of these games. Warneke completed 23 of his 35 starts, tied for second in completions with Carl Hubbell. Pat Malone and the 6-foot, 6-inch Jim Weaver, the tallest player of that time, required constant help. Malone was knocked out in 13 of his 21 starts, Weaver in 12 of 20.

After setting the early pace, the Cubs were 15–14 in May. They were in second place through August and finished third, eight games behind the Cardinals' "Gashouse Gang." Confronted with continual reports that Grimm wouldn't last the season, William L. Walker, who had succeeded Veeck as president, gave Grimm the ultimate vote of confidence. On August 25, Grimm was extended for another season. Phil Cavarretta, an 18-year-old Chicago schoolboy, appeared in seven games and on September 25 hit his first major league home run to give the Cubs a 1–0 win over Cincinnati.

	W	L	ERA	G	GS	CG	IP	H	BB	K
Lon Warneke	22	10	3.21	43	35	23	291⅓	273	66	143
Bill Lee	13	14	3.40	35	29	16	214½	218	74	104
Guy Bush	18	10	3.83	40	27	15	209½	213	54	75
Pat Malone	14	7	3.53	34	21	8	191	200	55	111
Jim Weaver	11	9	3.91	27	20	8	159	163	54	98
Bud Tinning	4	6	3.34	39	7	1	129½	134	46	44
Charlie Root	4	7	4.28	34	9	2	117⅔	141	53	46
Roy Joiner	0	1	8.21	20	2	0	34	61	8	9
Charlie Wiedemeyer	0	0	9.72	4	1	0	8⅓	16	4	2
Dick Ward	0	0	3.18	3	0	0	5⅔	9	2	1
Lynn Nelson	0	1	36.00	2	1	0	1	4	1	0
	86	65	3.76	281	152	73	1,361	1,432	417	633

Shutouts: Lee 4, Warneke 3, Bush 1, Malone 1, Tinning 1, Weaver 1.

According to team tradition, after their first victory in September, the Cub players destroyed their straw hats and replaced them, courtesy of the club, with felt fedoras. This picture was taken on a shopping expedition in 1934 at Herberts Men's Store in Chicago. Left to right: coach Mike Kelley, Woody English, Chuck Klein, Riggs Stephenson, Gabby Hartnett, Kiki Cuyler, Lon Warneke, Charlie Root, and Babe Herman. (George Brace photo)

	G	AB	H	2B	3B	HR	R	RBI	SB	AVG
Regulars										
1B Charlie Grimm	75	267	79	8	1	5	24	47	1	.296
2B Billy Herman	113	456	138	21	6	3	79	42	6	.303
SS Bill Jurges	100	358	88	15	2	8	43	33	1	.246
3B Stan Hack	111	402	116	16	6	1	54	21	11	.289
RF Babe Herman	125	467	142	34	5	14	65	84	1	.304
CF Kiki Cuyler	142	559	189	(42)	8	6	80	69	15	.338
LF Chuck Klein	115	435	131	27	2	20	78	80	3	.301
C Gabby Hartnett	130	438	131	21	1	22	58	90	0	.299
Substitutes										
Woody English	109	421	117	26	5	3	65	31	6	.278
Augie Galan	66	192	50	6	2	5	31	22	4	.260
Don Hurst	51	151	30	5	0	3	13	12	0	.199
Dolf Camilli	32	120	33	8	0	4	17	19	1	.275
Phil Cavarretta	7	21	8	0	1	1	5	6	1	.381
Tuck Stainback	104	359	110	14	3	2	47	46	7	.306
Riggs Stephenson	38	74	16	0	0	0	5	7	0	.216
Babe Phelps	44	70	20	5	2	2	7	12	0	.286
Bob O'Farrell	22	67	15	3	0	0	3	5	0	.224
Bennie Tate	11	24	3	0	0	0	1	0	0	.125
Pitchers										
Lon Warneke	52	113	22	3	0	0	12	8	0	.195
Bill Lee	40	76	10	3	0	0	6	7	0	.132
Guy Bush	41	70	16	1	0	0	4	10	2	.229
Pat Malone	34	64	11	0	0	0	2	6	0	.172
Jim Weaver	27	52	3	0	0	0	1	0	0	.058
Charlie Root	34	40	7	3	0	2	3	4	0	.175
Bud Tinning	39	39	7	2	0	0	2	3	0	.179
Roy Joiner	20	10	2	0	0	0	0	0	0	.200
Dick Ward	3	1	0	0	0	0	0	0	0	.000
Charlie Wiedemeyer	4	1	0	0	0	0	0	0	0	.000
Lynn Nelson	2	0	0	0	0	0	0	0	0	—
	5,347	1,494	263	44	101	705	664	59		.279

1935

Record: 100–54
Finish: First
Games Ahead: 4
Manager: Charlie Grimm

John McGraw's 1916 New York Giants set the major league record for the most consecutive victories, 26, but it was a hollow triumph; the Giants were not in contention and finished fourth. The Cubs of 1935 hold a more significant record: the longest winning streak that culminated in the winning of a pennant, 21 in a row.

According to a contemporary account, manager Grimm assembled his players for a clubhouse meeting after the Cubs had returned from a long August road trip. The date was September 2, Labor Day, prior to a doubleheader with Cincinnati. "We're home for the next 20 games," Grimm advised the troops. "And we either do or we don't. But we *are* going to be loose."

The Cubs split the doubleheader with the Reds. The next day was an open date. The winning streak began on September 4 with an 8–2 victory over the Phillies. Twenty-three days later, on September 27, in the opener of a doubleheader at St. Louis, Bill Lee pitched the clincher and singled in the winning run in a 6–2 win over Dizzy Dean and the second-

The great Cub infield of the 1930s: Phil Cavarretta, Billy Herman, Bill Jurges, and Stan Hack

place Cardinals. It was the Cubs' 20th successive victory. Number 21 came in the second game, 5–3.

The Cubs scored 18 runs in one game, 15 runs twice, and 13 in another. More stats: They averaged 6.5 runs, four more than their opponents. They won 11 games after trailing going into the seventh inning. Augie Galan batted .360 with 21 runs batted in and hit five of the club's nine home runs, four in the first nine games. Frank Demaree, who replaced Kiki Cuyler in center field, batted .408 with 13 RBIs; Billy Herman .383 with 15 RBIs.

Only seven pitchers participated. Bill Lee and Larry French each won five games, all complete. Charlie Root and Lon Warneke won four games. Roy Henshaw won two games, including one in relief. Tex Carleton went the distance in his only appearance. The opposition was held to two runs or less in 12 games. Lee, Root, and Warneke each pitched a shutout. It was an unprecedented blitz, under pressure, the equivalent of the finish staged by the 1914 Miracle Braves.

The Cubs outscored their opponents by 250 runs, a remarkable differential. They were 40–32 at the All-Star break (July 8), in third place behind the Giants and the Cardinals. "Owner Wrigley denies Grimm is in trouble," wrote Ed Burns of the *Chicago Tribune*. "Yet, there is every symptom that Grimm is carrying a bomb in the seat of his bloomers, just waiting for someone to touch off the fuse."

Grimm managed the Cubs for the next two and a half sea-

sons, but 1935 was his next-to-last year as a player. A .290 career hitter, he was 0-for-35 in spring training and appeared in only two regular-season games, hitless in eight at bats. Phil Cavarretta, a native Chicagoan in his first full big league season who was to have a glorious Cub career, replaced him at first base.

Cavarretta hit .275 and was third on the club in RBIs with 82. The Cubs had five .300 hitters: Gabby Hartnett, who won the MVP award, .344; Herman, .341; Demaree, .325; Galan, .314; and Stan Hack, .311. Herman led the league in hits, 227, and in doubles 57; Galan in runs, 133, and in stolen bases, 22. Galan did not ground into a double play in 646 at bats, still the NL record. Lee was 20–6 and led the league in winning percentage.

	W	L	ERA	G	GS	CG	IP	H	BB	K
Lon Warneke	20	13	3.06	42	30	20	261⅓	257	50	120
Bill Lee	20	6	2.96	39	32	18	252	241	84	100
Larry French	17	10	2.96	42	30	16	246¼	279	44	90
Charlie Root	15	8	3.08	38	18	11	201⅓	193	47	94
Tex Carleton	11	8	3.89	31	22	8	171	169	60	84
Roy Henshaw	13	5	3.28	31	18	7	142⅔	135	68	53
Fabian Kowalik	2	2	4.42	20	2	1	55	60	19	20
Hugh Casey	0	0	3.86	13	0	0	25⅔	29	14	10
Clay Bryant	1	2	5.16	9	1	0	22⅔	34	7	13
Clyde Shoun	1	0	2.84	5	1	0	12⅔	14	5	5
Roy Joiner	0	0	5.40	2	0	0	3⅓	6	2	0
	100	54	3.26	272	154	81	1,394⅓	1,417	400	589

Shutouts: French 4, Henshaw 3, Lee 3, Root 1, Warneke 1.

	G	AB	H	2B	3B	HR	R	RBI	SB	AVG
Regulars										
1B Phil Cavarretta	146	589	162	28	12	8	85	82	4	.275
2B Billy Herman	154	666	(227)	(57)	6	7	113	83	6	.341
SS Bill Jurges	146	519	125	33	1	1	69	59	3	.241
3B Stan Hack	124	427	133	23	9	4	75	64	14	.311
RF Chuck Klein	119	434	127	14	4	21	71	73	4	.293
CF Frank Demaree	107	385	125	19	4	2	60	66	6	.325
LF Augie Galan	154	646	203	41	11	12	(133)	79	(22)	.314
C Gabby Hartnett	116	413	142	32	6	13	67	91	1	.344
Substitutes										
Woody English	34	84	17	2	0	2	11	8	1	.202
Charlie Grimm	2	8	0	0	0	0	0	0	0	.000
Freddie Lindstrom	90	342	94	22	4	3	49	62	1	.275
Kiki Cuyler	45	157	42	5	1	4	22	18	3	.268
Tuck Stainback	47	94	24	4	0	3	16	11	1	.255
Ken O'Dea	76	202	52	13	2	6	30	38	0	.257
Walter Stephenson	16	26	10	1	1	0	2	2	0	.385
Johnny Gill	3	3	1	1	0	0	2	1	0	.333
Pitchers										
Bill Lee	39	102	24	3	0	0	8	11	0	.235
Lon Warneke	44	91	20	1	0	0	9	15	0	.220
Larry French	42	85	12	1	0	0	4	5	0	.141
Charlie Root	38	69	14	2	1	1	8	7	0	.203
Tex Carleton	31	62	8	0	0	0	4	2	0	.129
Roy Henshaw	31	51	13	1	0	0	5	2	0	.255
Fabian Kowalik	20	15	3	0	0	0	1	1	0	.200
Clay Bryant	12	6	2	0	0	1	2	2	0	.333
Hugh Casey	13	6	1	0	0	0	1	0	0	.167
Clyde Shoun	5	3	0	0	0	0	0	0	0	.000
Roy Joiner	2	1	0	0	0	0	0	0	0	.000
		5,486	1,581	303	62	88	847	782	66	.288

1936

Record: 87–67
Finish: Second (tie)
Games Behind: 5
Manager: Charlie Grimm

Grateful to the troops for their heroic 1935 finish, manager Charlie Grimm announced that all of his front-line players would be given salary boosts and that there would be no changes in the uniformed personnel. This was in early January 1936. Two days later, in a dueling press conference, vice president Charley Drake, who outranked Grimm and sometimes was described as owner Wrigley's "valet," revealed that Fred Lindstrom was being given his unconditional release.

It was an ominous beginning. Grimm, who had returned to his Missouri farm, expressed surprise. A heady veteran, career .311 hitter, and future Hall of Famer, the 30-year-old Lindstrom had been acquired in a trade with Pittsburgh the previous winter. Alternating between third base and the outfield, he hit a solid .275 and scored or drove in the winning run seven times during the Cubs' 21-game winning streak.

Chicago-born, Lindstrom had a reputation for speaking his mind. Giants manager Bill Terry, it was said, traded him to Pittsburgh because he "coveted" Terry's job. Two seasons later, Pie Traynor, the Pittsburgh manager, dealt him to the Cubs with the charge that Lindstrom was a "clubhouse lawyer." But there was never any indication of a similar rupture with Grimm, who had repeatedly lauded Lindstrom for his excellent play.

Whatever, Lindstrom was the first casualty. Chuck Klein, the sometime slugger who was a bust in Chicago, was returned to the Phillies on May 21. In 29 games with the Cubs, Klein had batted .294, with five home runs. Seven weeks later, on July 10 in Pittsburgh, Klein became the fourth big league player to hit four home runs in one game.

Still, it was a good deal. Outfielder Ethan Allen and pitcher Curt Davis came in the exchange. A bald-headed graduate of the University of Cincinnati, Allen, who hit .295, replaced Klein in left field and along with Augie Galan in center and Frank Demaree in right gave the Cubs a superior outer defense. Davis won 11 games and had a 3.00 earned run average, lowest on the staff.

The Cubs were in contention throughout. They were in first place in early May, fell to sixth later in the month, and after a 15-game winning streak, reclaimed the lead on June 28. They held it without interruption from July 13 through August 3 and finished with an 87–67 record, 13 fewer victories than the previous season, tied for second place with St. Louis, five games behind the Giants.

For the second consecutive season, Bill Lee and Larry French led the pitchers, each with 18 victories. French won seven of eight in midseason with a companion sequence of 30 successive scoreless innings. Ailing early, Lon Warneke was unable to finish his first four starts but came around in June and won three games during the 15-game winning streak. Warneke led the club in strikeouts and fanned Walter Alston on September 27, a footnote in diamond history: it was the first and last major league at bat for Alston, who later became a successful manager with the Brooklyn and Los Angeles Dodgers.

Demaree and Billy Herman were among the league's top batters. Demaree was fourth with a .350 average. Herman was sixth with .334 and for the second successive year knocked out 57 doubles. In a rare show of anger, Grimm called a clubhouse meeting in early August and accused Herman, Jurges, and Galan of indifferent play. When the season ended there were several published reports that Gabby Hartnett would succeed Grimm as the Cub manager.

	W	L	ERA	G	GS	CG	IP	H	BB	K
Bill Lee	18	11	3.31	43	33	20	258⅔	238	93	102
Larry French	18	9	3.39	43	28	16	252⅓	262	54	104
Lon Warneke	16	13	3.44	40	29	13	240⅔	246	76	113
Tex Carleton	14	10	3.65	35	26	12	197⅓	204	67	88
Curt Davis	11	9	3.00	24	20	10	153	146	31	52
Roy Henshaw	6	5	3.97	39	14	6	129⅓	152	56	69
Charlie Root	3	6	4.15	33	4	0	73⅔	81	20	32
Clay Bryant	1	2	3.30	26	0	0	57⅓	57	24	35
Fabian Kowalik	0	2	6.75	6	0	0	16	24	7	1
Clyde Shoun	0	0	12.46	4	0	0	4⅓	3	6	1
	87	67	3.53	293	154	77	1,382⅔	1,413	434	597

Shutouts: Carleton 4, French 4, Lee 4, Warneke 4, Henshaw 2.

	G	AB	H	2B	3B	HR	R	RBI	SB	AVG
Regulars										
1B Phil Cavarretta	124	458	125	18	1	9	55	56	8	.273
2B Billy Herman	153	632	211	57	7	5	101	93	5	.334
SS Bill Jurges	118	429	120	25	1	1	51	42	4	.280
3B Stan Hack	149	561	167	27	4	6	102	78	17	.298
RF Frank Demaree	154	605	212	34	3	16	93	96	4	.350
CF Augie Galan	145	575	152	26	4	8	74	81	16	.264
LF Ethan Allen	91	373	110	18	6	3	47	39	12	.295
C Gabby Hartnett	121	424	130	25	6	7	49	64	0	.307
Substitutes										
Woody English	64	182	45	9	0	0	33	20	1	.247
Charlie Grimm	39	132	33	4	0	1	13	16	0	.250
Gene Lillard	19	34	7	1	0	0	6	2	0	.206
Johnny Gill	71	174	44	8	0	7	20	28	0	.253
Chuck Klein	29	109	32	5	0	5	19	18	0	.294
Tuck Stainback	44	75	13	3	0	1	13	5	1	.173
Ken O'Dea	80	189	58	10	3	2	36	38	0	.307
Walter Stephenson	6	12	1	0	0	0	0	1	0	.083
Pitchers										
Bill Lee	43	87	12	0	1	1	5	3	0	.138
Larry French	43	85	18	2	0	0	5	5	0	.212
Lon Warneke	40	84	17	1	0	1	9	5	0	.202
Tex Carleton	35	60	14	0	0	3	9	11	0	.233
Curt Davis	24	53	8	1	0	0	6	3	0	.151
Roy Henshaw	39	44	6	1	0	0	3	1	0	.136
Charlie Root	33	15	5	0	0	0	1	0	0	.333
Clay Bryant	32	12	5	0	0	0	4	2	0	.417
Fabian Kowalik	6	5	0	0	0	0	1	0	0	.000
Clyde Shoun	4	0	0	0	0	0	0	0	0	—
		5,409	1,545	275	36	76	755	707	68	.286

1937

Record: 93–61
Finish: Second
Games Behind: 3
Manager: Charlie Grimm

Gabby Hartnett, the All-Star catcher who had been fluttering in the wings, replaced Charlie Grimm as the Cub manager in 1937. But Hartnett reigned for only 11 days, from July 15 to 26, an interim appointment when Grimm was hospitalized with a sore back, a sciatic nerve affliction originally suffered in a 1925 collision at first base with Jack Scott of the Giants.

Grimm was stricken in Boston during an eastern trip. He was pushed in a wheelchair to a railroad station, several blocks distant, and boosted onto a St. Louis–bound train for examination by Dr. Robert Hyland, the Cardinals' team physician. The Cubs had begun to fade but were only a half game out of first place.

Hartnett, in his managerial debut, was rewarded with a 5–1 win over Boston that returned the Cubs to the lead. They lost the next day, then swept a four-game series in Brooklyn and a doubleheader in Philadelphia—seven wins in Hartnett's first eight games at the helm; overall they were 9–3.

The Cubs had expanded their lead to two games when Grimm returned on July 27. According to one account, "Grimm was feeling better but forbidden by his doctors to

Coach Roy Johnson (center), who later managed the Cubs, with outfielders Augie Galan (left) and Tuck Stainback

leave the dugout. He sat on a cushion and had his feet encased in carpet slippers."

Except for July 14, when Grimm went down, the Cubs were in first place continuously from June 15 through August 29. Their biggest lead was seven games on August 3. They were six ahead after an August 8 doubleheader sweep over Boston, Tex Carleton winning the opener with a one-hitter. The Giants overtook them in the September stretch. The Cubs were never lower than second thereafter and finished three games out. The Giants were now supreme. It was their 15th National League pennant, one more than the Cubs.

The Chicago attack was sporadic. Their only consistent hitters were Hartnett, third in the league with a .354 average; Billy Herman, .335; Frank Demaree, .324; and Bill Jurges, .298. Hartnett increased his iron-man record, the 12th season he caught more than 100 games. He also had a 26-game hitting streak, from June 29 through August 25—39 for 90, a .433 pace.

Galan was erratic at the plate and was repeatedly benched. He batted .252 and during one midseason stretch had only a bunt single in 45 at bats. Neither Joe Marty nor Phil Cavarretta, platooned in center field, made a significant contribution. Tucker Stainback, the fourth outfielder, was under .150 most of the season.

Still, the Cubs led the league with a .287 team batting average, as well as in scoring. The pitching was terribly ineffective, a 3.97 earned run average, sixth in the league. Roy Parmelee was the biggest disappointment. Acquired from the Cardinals along with first baseman James (Rip) Collins for Lon Warneke, Parmelee won only seven games; Warneke won 18, two more than any Cub starter. Collins batted a respectable .274 but missed the last seven weeks of the season with a broken ankle.

On September 3, when the flag was slipping away—7–9 on a disastrous eastern trip—owner Wrigley dispelled published reports that Grimm was to be dismissed. Wrigley flew to New York where he boarded the Cubs' homeward-bound train. Wrigley summoned Grimm to his compartment and extended his contract through the 1938 season.

	W	L	ERA	G	GS	CG	IP	H	BB	K
Bill Lee	14	15	3.54	42	33	17	272⅓	289	73	108
Tex Carleton	16	8	3.15	32	27	18	208⅓	183	94	105
Larry French	16	10	3.98	42	28	11	208	229	65	100
Charlie Root	13	5	3.38	43	15	5	178⅔	173	32	74
Roy Parmelee	7	8	5.13	33	18	8	145⅔	165	79	55
Clay Bryant	9	3	4.26	38	10	4	135⅓	117	78	75
Curt Davis	10	5	4.08	28	14	8	123⅔	138	30	32
Clyde Shoun	7	7	5.61	37	9	2	93	118	45	43
Bob Logan	0	0	1.42	4	0	0	6⅓	6	4	2
Kirby Higbe	1	0	5.40	1	0	0	5	4	1	2
Newt Kimball	0	0	10.80	2	0	0	5	12	1	0
	93	61	3.97	302	154	73	1,381⅓	1,434	502	596

Shutouts: Carleton 4, French 4, Lee 2, Bryant 1.

	G	AB	H	2B	3B	HR	R	RBI	SB	AVG
Regulars										
1B Ripper Collins	115	456	125	16	5	16	77	71	2	.274
2B Billy Herman	138	564	189	35	11	8	106	65	2	.335
SS Bill Jurges	129	450	134	18	10	1	53	65	2	.298
3B Stan Hack	154	582	173	27	6	2	106	63	16	.297
RF Frank Demaree	154	615	199	36	6	17	104	115	6	.324
CF Joe Marty	88	290	84	17	2	5	41	44	3	.290
LF Augie Galan	147	611	154	24	10	18	104	78	(23)	.252
C Gabby Hartnett	110	356	126	21	6	12	47	82	0	.354
Substitutes										
Lonny Frey	78	198	55	9	3	1	33	22	6	.278
Phil Cavarretta	106	329	94	18	7	5	43	56	7	.286
Tuck Stainback	72	160	37	7	1	0	18	14	3	.231
Carl Reynolds	7	11	3	1	0	0	0	1	0	.273
Ken O'Dea	83	219	66	7	5	4	31	32	1	.301
John Bottarini	26	40	11	3	0	1	3	7	0	.275
Bob Garbark	1	1	0	0	0	0	0	0	0	.000
Dutch Meyer	1	0	0	0	0	0	0	0	0	—
Pitchers										
Bill Lee	42	87	15	2	0	1	4	4	0	.172
Tex Carleton	34	71	12	3	1	0	4	9	0	.169
Larry French	42	71	9	1	0	0	1	0	0	.127
Charlie Root	43	67	12	2	0	1	7	9	0	.179
Roy Parmelee	37	52	9	0	0	2	7	8	0	.173
Clay Bryant	47	45	14	2	1	1	13	7	0	.311
Curt Davis	28	40	12	2	0	1	6	9	0	.300
Clyde Shoun	37	29	4	2	0	0	3	1	0	.138
Kirby Higbe	1	3	0	0	0	0	0	0	0	.000
Newt Kimball	2	1	0	0	0	0	0	0	0	.000
Bob Logan	4	1	0	0	0	0	0	0	0	.000
	5,349	1,537	253	74	96	811	762	71		(.287)

1938

Record: 89–63
Finish: First
Games Ahead: 2
Managers: Charlie Grimm, Gabby Hartnett

The Cubs won another pennant in 1938, their 15th, in a season-long drama without compare. Included was the most famous hit in Cub history—Gabby Hartnett's "Homer in the Gloamin' "; the comeback of the sore-armed Dizzy Dean; and the heroics of Bill Lee, who won six games in 20 days early in the season and later, in the September stretch, when the pressure was greatest, became the first National League pitcher in 27 years to record shutouts in four consecutive starts.

Often described as "the perfect catcher," the son of a Massachusetts streetcar conductor and the oldest of 14 children, Hartnett was elevated to the manager's role on July 21, succeeding Charlie Grimm. Hartnett batted only .274 on the season, 80 points below his 1937 average, but on September 28 came through with what has become a legendary ninth-inning home run off Pittsburgh reliever Mace Brown.

The score was tied at 5–5. Darkness had descended on Wrigley Field. The umpires had announced the game would be called after the Cubs had batted in the ninth; a doubleheader would be played the next day. The Pirates had held the lead since July 12 and were a half game ahead of the Cubs.

Hartnett connected with two outs and the bases empty, on an 0–2 curveball. "I swung with everything I had," Hartnett said later, "and then I got that feeling when the blood rushes out of your head and you get dizzy. A lot of people told me they didn't know the ball was in the bleachers. I did. I knew it the minute I hit it."

When he reached second base, he couldn't see third; his teammates and dozens of fans had run out on the field. "I don't think I walked a step to the plate," Hartnett recalled. "I was carried in." The home run extended the Cubs' winning streak to nine games and lifted them into first place, a half game ahead of the Pirates. They beat the Pirates 10–1 the next day, behind Lee, and clinched two days later.

Dean, who pitched only 74⅔ innings, was also a heroic figure in the decisive Pittsburgh series, winning the September 27 opener. His fastball gone, Dean held the Pirates to seven hits in a courageous 8⅔-inning stint. Hartnett then went to the bullpen and summoned Lee, who fanned Al Todd for the final out.

Dean, the league's last 30-game winner, had been acquired on April 13, three days before the season opener, in a highly publicized transaction with the Cardinals for three second-line players and $185,000. It was the third biggest cash deal for a player, ranking behind the $250,000 the Boston Red Sox paid Washington for Joe Cronin in '35 and the Cubs' $200,000 purchase of Rogers Hornsby in '29.

Dean had hurt his arm the previous August and was in obvious decline. Still, he won his first two Cub starts, the second on April 24, a distance-going four-hitter in St. Louis before 34,520. He injured his arm in his next start and had to be taken out in the fourth, but he remained in the rotation and on May 3 responded with seven strong innings in a 5–2 win over the Phillies.

Insisting his arm was dead, Dean was on the shelf for the next two and a half months. Grimm accused him of malingering. Reporters began describing him as the "$185,000 problem." Grimm met with owner Wrigley on July 11 and told him Dean should be made to pitch or be retired for the rest of the season. Dean pitched again on July 17, won four more games, and finished with a 7–1 record.

Prior to Hartnett's Homer in the Gloamin', the Cubs were in first place only once, June 6–8. Bill Lee led the league in the three most important pitching categories: wins, 22; ERA, 2.66; and winning percentage, .710. He tied for the lead in starts, 37, and tied for second in innings pitched, 291. The Cubs were 45–36 under Grimm, 44–27 thereafter. They won 21 of their last 25 games.

	W	L	ERA	G	GS	CG	IP	H	BB	K
Bill Lee	(22)	9	(2.66)	44	(37)	19	291	281	74	121
Clay Bryant	19	11	3.10	44	30	17	270⅓	235	(125)	(135)
Larry French	10	19	3.80	43	27	10	201⅓	210	62	83
Tex Carleton	10	9	5.42	33	24	9	167⅔	213	74	80
Charlie Root	8	7	2.86	44	11	5	160⅔	163	30	70
Jack Russell	6	1	3.34	42	0	0	102⅓	100	30	29
Dizzy Dean	7	1	1.81	13	10	3	74⅔	63	8	22
Vance Page	5	4	3.84	13	9	3	68	90	13	18
Al Epperly	2	0	3.67	9	4	1	27	28	15	10
Bob Logan	0	2	2.78	14	0	0	22⅔	18	17	10
Kirby Higbe	0	0	5.40	2	2	0	10	10	6	4
Newt Kimball	0	0	9.00	1	0	0	1	3	0	1
	89	63	3.37	302	154	67	1,396⅔	1,414	454	583

Shutouts: Lee 9, Bryant 3, French 3, Dean 1.

	G	AB	H	2B	3B	HR	R	RBI	SB	AVG
Regulars										
1B Ripper Collins	143	490	131	22	8	13	78	61	1	.267
2B Billy Herman	152	624	173	34	7	1	86	56	3	.277
SS Bill Jurges	137	465	114	18	3	1	53	47	3	.245
3B Stan Hack	152	609	195	34	11	4	109	67	(16)	.320
RF Frank Demaree	129	476	130	15	7	8	63	62	1	.273
CF Carl Reynolds	125	497	150	28	10	3	59	67	9	.302
LF Augie Galan	110	395	113	16	9	6	52	69	8	.286
C Gabby Hartnett	88	299	82	19	1	10	40	59	1	.274
Substitutes										
Tony Lazzeri	54	120	32	5	0	5	21	23	0	.267
Steve Mesner	2	4	1	0	0	0	2	0	0	.250
Bobby Mattick	1	1	1	0	0	0	0	1	0	1.000
Phil Cavarretta	92	268	64	11	4	1	29	28	4	.239
Joe Marty	76	235	57	8	3	7	32	35	4	.243
Coaker Triplett	12	36	9	2	1	0	4	2	0	.250
Jim Asbell	17	33	6	2	0	0	6	3	0	.182
Ken O'Dea	86	247	65	12	1	3	22	33	1	.263
Bob Garbark	23	54	14	0	0	0	2	5	0	.259
Pitchers										
Clay Bryant	50	106	24	2	1	3	16	15	0	.226
Bill Lee	44	101	20	3	1	0	10	13	1	.198
Tex Carleton	33	65	15	4	1	0	9	7	1	.231
Larry French	43	62	13	3	1	0	7	7	0	.210
Charlie Root	44	48	8	1	0	0	2	3	0	.167
Jack Russell	42	32	7	1	1	0	4	3	0	.219
Dizzy Dean	13	26	5	1	0	0	3	1	0	.192
Vance Page	13	26	4	0	0	0	2	1	0	.154
Al Epperly	9	8	2	1	0	0	2	5	0	.250
Kirby Higbe	2	3	0	0	0	0	0	0	0	.000
Bob Logan	14	3	0	0	0	0	0	0	0	.000
Newt Kimball	1	0	0	0	0	0	0	0	0	—
		5,333	1,435	242	70	65	713	673	49	.269

1939

Record: 84–70
Finish: Fourth
Games Behind: 13
Manager: Gabby Hartnett

There wasn't much for Cub fans to cheer about in 1939, and so they had to be content with the occasional cry "Error Bartell!" a mock tribute to Dick Bartell, an aging shortstop acquired in a six-player off-season trade with the Giants. The principals were shortstop Bill Jurges and outfielder Frank Demaree, both long-time Chicago favorites, for Bartell and outfielder Hank Leiber.

Leiber batted .310 with 24 home runs and had one particularly big day: three home runs in the opener of a July 4 doubleheader against the Cardinals. For Bartell it was a year of agony. In his 12th big league season, Bartell, previously a consistent .300 hitter, hit .238, a career low. He also floundered in the field.

Bartell's woes began in spring training. He was walking the path to the ballpark with teammates Dizzy Dean and Woody English. Ahead of them was a heavyset fellow who had to twist sideways to get through the gate. Bartell called out, "Hey, what time does the balloon go up?"

Dean said, "Do you know who that is? That's Ed Burns, the writer for the *Chicago Tribune*."

Burns turned, pointed a finger at Bartell, and shouted, "You'll hear from me all summer!"

Burns was among the official scorers and, according to Bartell, "He charged me with errors on plays where there was no error, like a double play we didn't finish. And the headline in the *Tribune* would read: 'Cubs Win! Bartell Makes Error No. 14.' The other writers in the press box heard 'Error, Bartell!' so often they'd sing out 'Error, Bartell!' Then the

Dick Bartell, Hank Leiber, and Gus Mancuso in 1939, celebrating baseball's 100th anniversary

fans picked it up. They booed me plenty but I never got mad because they were right. I had a lousy year."

So did the Cubs. For the first time in 12 years they finished lower than third—in fourth place, 13 games behind the pennant-winning Cincinnati Reds. The Cubs were in the lead for only six days, all in early and mid-April, and were in third place continuously from August 1 through September 23.

Bill Lee and Clay Bryant, who had combined for 41 wins in 1938, were unable to maintain the pace. Lee had one shutout, eight fewer than the previous season, and made six unsuccessful starts in pursuit of his sixth victory. He finished with a respectable 19–15 record but, on an average, allowed 12 base runners for every nine innings of toil. Bryant was ailing, on the shelf for three months, and of no help: four starts, two wins, and one loss.

Larry French, the veteran left-hander, was 15–8. The only other pitcher to win in double figures was Claude Passeau, 13–9, who arrived from the Phillies in a favorable May 29 exchange for three players. Dizzy Dean was 6–4 and had a comparatively silent season, on and off the field.

Player-manager Hartnett batted .278 and shared the catching duties with Gus Mancuso. Hartnett caught 86 games, Mancuso 76. Aware a second successive pennant was a fantasy, the usually flamboyant and jovial Hartnett began growling at his players. In midseason a Chicago newspaper ran a photographic "Drizzlepuss Derby" to determine the league's grumpiest manager. Hartnett won the contest. Bill Terry of the Giants was the runner-up.

Pitchers Clay Bryant (left) and Bill Lee

	W	L	ERA	G	GS	CG	IP	H	BB	K
Bill Lee	19	15	3.44	37	(36)	20	282⅓	295	85	105
Claude Passeau	13	9	3.05	34	27	13	221	215	48	108
Larry French	15	8	3.29	36	21	10	194	205	50	98
Charlie Root	8	8	4.03	35	16	8	167⅓	189	34	65
Vance Page	7	7	3.88	27	17	8	139⅓	169	37	73
Dizzy Dean	6	4	3.36	19	13	7	96⅓	98	17	27
Earl Whitehill	4	7	5.14	24	11	2	89⅓	102	50	42
Jack Russell	4	3	3.67	39	0	0	68⅔	78	24	32
Gene Lillard	3	5	6.55	20	7	2	55	68	36	31
Clay Bryant	2	1	5.74	4	4	2	31⅓	42	14	9
Kirby Higbe	2	1	3.18	9	2	0	22⅔	12	22	16
Ray Harrell	0	2	8.31	4	2	0	17⅓	26	6	5
Vern Olsen	1	0	0.00	4	0	0	7⅔	2	7	3
Joe Marty	0	0	0.00	0	0	0	0	0	0	0
	84	70	3.80	292	156	72	1,392⅓	1,501	430	584

Shutouts: Dean 2, French 2, Lee 1, Page 1, Passeau 1, Whitehill 1.

	G	AB	H	2B	3B	HR	R	RBI	SB	AVG
Regulars										
1B Rip Russell	143	542	148	24	5	9	55	79	2	.273
2B Billy Herman	156	623	191	34	(18)	7	111	70	9	.307
SS Dick Bartell	105	336	80	24	2	3	37	34	6	.238
3B Stan Hack	156	641	191	28	6	8	112	56	(17)	.298
RF Jim Gleeson	111	332	74	19	6	4	43	45	7	.223
CF Hank Leiber	112	365	113	16	1	24	65	88	1	.310
LF Augie Galan	148	549	167	36	8	6	104	71	8	.304
C Gabby Hartnett	97	306	85	18	2	12	36	59	0	.278
Substitutes										
Bobby Mattick	51	178	51	12	1	0	16	23	1	.287
Phil Cavarretta	22	55	15	3	1	0	4	0	2	.273
Steve Mesner	17	43	12	4	0	0	7	6	0	.279
Carl Reynolds	88	281	69	10	6	4	33	44	5	.246
Bill Nicholson	58	220	65	12	5	5	37	38	0	.295
Joe Marty	23	76	10	1	0	2	6	10	2	.132
Gus Mancuso	80	251	58	10	0	2	17	17	0	.231
Bob Garbark	24	21	3	0	0	0	1	0	0	.143
Pitchers										
Bill Lee	37	103	13	0	0	1	3	3	0	.126
Claude Passeau	35	77	12	2	0	1	6	6	0	.156
Larry French	36	73	14	2	0	1	6	7	0	.192
Charlie Root	35	57	10	2	1	2	4	6	0	.175
Vance Page	27	47	12	3	0	0	2	6	0	.255
Dizzy Dean	19	34	5	1	0	0	4	1	1	.147
Earl Whitehill	24	29	3	0	0	0	1	0	0	.103
Jack Russell	43	17	0	0	0	0	1	0	0	.000
Clay Bryant	28	14	3	1	0	0	9	1	0	.214
Gene Lillard	23	10	1	0	0	0	3	0	0	.100
Kirby Higbe	9	7	2	1	0	0	0	1	0	.286
Ray Harrell	4	5	0	0	0	0	0	0	0	.000
Vern Olsen	4	1	0	0	0	0	1	0	0	.000
		5,293	1,407	263	62	91	724	671	61	.266

1940

Record: 75–79
Finish: Fifth
Games Behind: 25½
Manager: Gabby Hartnett

Philip K. Wrigley, who had become an absentee owner—he rarely saw the Cubs play—descended into the trenches. On April 20, 1940, he announced he was taking a six-month leave of absence from his gum company and moving his office from Michigan Avenue to Wrigley Field for a closer view of the day-by-day operations. "We have a darned good team," Wrigley said.

The Cubs didn't have "a darned good team" and plunged to fifth place, their first second-division finish in 15 years. They lost a league high of 31 one-run games and were never in contention. They occupied third place for 12 days in May, their best run, and finished four games under .500, 25½ games behind the triumphant Cincinnati Reds.

Early on, in mid-January, Wrigley and Dizzy Dean had become pen pals. Dean wrote him a long letter, explaining how he had been constantly confused by the varying medical diagnoses and recommended cures for his ailing arm. Wrigley described it as "a swell letter" and responded in kind. Pleased, Dean called Wrigley long-distance. "We had a nice talk," Dean told reporters. Dean also agreed to sign for $10,000, a 50 percent pay cut.

But Dean was unable to conform. He jumped the club during the final week of spring training after a ferocious argument with Gabby Hartnett, who fined him $100 for insubordination. Four days later, Dean's wife, Pat, located him in Topeka, Kansas. Dean returned to Chicago, "meek as a lamb," and denied he had called Hartnett Tomato Face or Picklepuss. He left the club, he said, because Hartnett had re-

fused to allow him to visit his mother's grave in Lucas, Arkansas.

Forgiving, Hartnett used him in the rotation. After five starts and one relief appearance—46 base runners in 28 innings—it was apparent he couldn't help the club. The Cubs put him on waivers; when there were no claims he was optioned to Tulsa of the Texas League. Dean departed on June 3 without complaint. The warmer climate would be beneficial; also, against lesser competition he would have the opportunity to work on a new sidearm delivery.

Clay Bryant was also a problem. Bryant said he couldn't pitch because he had weakened his arm during the 1938 pennant season when he won 19 games and often worked out of turn. Wrigley suspended him indefinitely—without pay. After several turbulent days, Wrigley relented and agreed to pay $50 a week for the next month, not to Bryant, but to Mrs. Bryant.

Bryant requested his release. It would allow him to seek a new connection. Wrigley refused. It raised an interesting legal question: How long could a club keep a player on reserve while not paying his salary? Bryant appealed to the commissioner, Judge Kenesaw Mountain Landis, who listened but offered no relief. Bryant made his first appearance on August 21, his salary restored. He was 0–1 on the season. Dean returned on September 11 and was 3–3.

Claude Passeau emerged as the club's new pitching star. Passeau was 20–13 and among the league leaders in wins, innings, ERA, appearances, strikeouts, and complete games. He also led all rotation starters in fewest home runs allowed—nine in 280⅔ innings, one every 36⅔ innings. Bill Lee, the Cubs' one-time hero, was 9–17.

Stan Hack led the hitters with a .317 average and for the fifth consecutive season scored 100 or more runs, a record. Bill Nicholson, discarded by the Philadelphia A's in 1936 when he was 0-for-12, was the most pleasant surprise: 25 home runs and 98 RBIs in his first full season with the Cubs. Hartnett was dismissed on November 13 and succeeded by Jimmie Wilson, who in five seasons as the Phillies' manager never had a club finish higher than seventh.

	W	L	ERA	G	GS	CG	IP	H	BB	K
Claude Passeau	20	13	2.50	46	31	20	280⅔	259	59	124
Larry French	14	14	3.29	40	33	18	246	240	64	107
Bill Lee	9	17	5.03	37	30	9	211⅓	246	70	70
Vern Olsen	13	9	2.97	34	20	9	172⅔	172	62	71
Ken Raffensberger	7	9	3.38	43	10	3	114⅔	120	29	55
Jake Mooty	6	6	2.92	20	12	6	114	101	49	42
Charlie Root	2	4	3.82	36	8	1	113	118	33	50
Vance Page	1	3	4.42	30	1	0	59	65	26	22
Dizzy Dean	3	3	5.17	10	9	3	54	68	20	18
Clay Bryant	0	1	4.78	8	0	0	26⅓	26	14	5
Julio Bonetti	0	0	20.25	1	0	0	1⅓	3	4	0
	75	79	3.54	305	154	69	1,393	1,418	430	564

Shutouts: Olsen 4, Passeau 4, French 3, Lee 1.

	G	AB	H	2B	3B	HR	R	RBI	SB	AVG
Regulars										
1B Phil Cavarretta	65	193	54	11	4	2	34	22	3	.280
2B Billy Herman	135	558	163	24	4	5	77	57	1	.292
SS Bobby Mattick	128	441	96	15	0	0	30	33	5	.218
3B Stan Hack	149	603	191	38	6	8	101	40	21	.317
RF Bill Nicholson	135	491	146	27	7	25	78	98	2	.297
CF Hank Leiber	117	440	133	24	2	17	68	86	1	.302
LF Jim Gleeson	129	485	152	39	11	5	76	61	4	.313
C Al Todd	104	381	97	13	2	6	31	42	1	.255
Substitutes										
Rip Russell	68	215	53	7	2	5	15	33	1	.247
Zeke Bonura	49	182	48	14	0	4	20	20	1	.264
Rabbit Warstler	45	159	36	4	1	1	19	18	1	.226
Billy Rogell	33	59	8	0	0	1	7	3	1	.136
Bobby Sturgeon	7	21	4	1	0	0	1	2	0	.190
Dom Dallessandro	107	287	77	19	6	1	33	36	4	.268
Augie Galan	68	209	48	14	2	3	33	22	9	.230
Bob Collins	47	120	25	3	0	1	11	14	4	.208
Gabby Hartnett	37	64	17	3	0	1	3	12	0	.266
Clyde McCullough	9	26	4	1	0	0	4	1	0	.154
Pitchers										
Claude Passeau	46	98	20	5	1	1	12	6	2	.204
Larry French	40	85	14	3	0	0	5	9	0	.165
Bill Lee	37	76	10	2	0	0	4	3	0	.132
Vern Olsen	35	57	15	3	0	0	4	5	2	.263
Jake Mooty	24	38	10	0	0	0	2	2	0	.263
Charlie Root	36	31	4	0	0	0	4	1	0	.129
Ken Raffensberger	43	30	5	0	0	0	2	0	0	.167
Dizzy Dean	10	18	4	0	0	0	2	0	0	.222
Vance Page	31	13	4	2	0	0	1	0	0	.308
Clay Bryant	16	9	3	0	0	0	4	1	0	.333
Julio Bonetti	1	0	0	0	0	0	0	0	0	—
		5,389	1,441	272	48	86	681	627	63	.267

1941

Record: 70–84
Finish: Sixth
Games Behind: 30
Manager: Jimmie Wilson

The '41 season was the beginning of the downward plunge. Except for opening day when they were tied for the lead, the Cubs were never in first place and continued to sink as the season progressed: 12 games out on May 31; 17 out at the All-Star break; 27½ on Labor Day. They limped home sixth, their worst showing since 1925. It was an indication of what was to come: 24 second-division finishes in the next 26 years.

Gabby Hartnett, after 19 years of service, went the way of all baseball flesh. He was sold to the Giants. Jimmie Wilson, Hartnett's replacement, traded veteran second baseman Billy Herman to Brooklyn on May 6 for two obscure players and about $50,000. It strengthened Wilson's managerial grip but weakened the club. Herman had been a fan favorite. Had owner Wrigley promoted from within, Herman more than likely would have been Hartnett's successor.

Bill Nicholson—alias Swish, for the mighty air currents generated when he swung and missed—led the club in RBIs with 98, same as the previous season, and increased his home run total to 26, one shy of the league lead and the most by a Cub since Hack Wilson's heroic 56 in 1930. Nicholson also struck out 97 times.

Third baseman Stan Hack, one of the few survivors from the glory years, batted .317, the only .300 hitter. Lou Stringer and Bobby Sturgeon, the new second base combination, were adequate but not nearly the equal of Herman and Jurges. Babe Dahlgren, famous for having succeeded Lou Gehrig at first base after Gehrig had played in a record 2,130

successive games, was acquired in a midseason deal. He responded with 59 RBIs and 16 home runs.

Louis Alexander Novikoff, the "Mad Russian," made his big league bow. Purchased for $100,000 from the Los Angeles Angels of the Pacific Coast League, Novikoff was a spring training holdout. Instead of reporting to the Cubs' Catalina Island camp, he risked employment in the oil fields. Wirephoto pictures printed in the Chicago newspapers showed him working in greasy raiment. Ed Burns of the *Tribune* was impressed: "The pictures appear to be genuine, nothing like those shipyard photos of [the draft-dodging] Jack Dempsey and similar phonus bolognus poses of sports figures at hard labor."

Lou Novikoff was a press agent's delight. Born in Glendale, Arizona, he was one of 12 children and spoke only Russian until he was 10. He was a harmonica virtuoso, had a booming baritone, and had been a "strongman" and striptease performer. The previous season, with the Angels, he had batted .363 with 171 RBIs and 41 home runs. But he didn't hit in Chicago and was optioned to Milwaukee on June 23 when he was batting .237. Recalled in September, he finished the season at .241 with five home runs and 24 RBIs.

James Timothy Gallagher, formerly a crusty Chicago baseball writer, was the new general manager. After the 1941 season, Gallagher was advised to purchase material for the installation of lights for night baseball. Gallagher accumulated 165 tons of steel, 35,000 feet of copper wire, stanchions, and aluminum reflectors, all of which were hidden under the stands. On December 8, the day after Pearl Harbor was attacked, Wrigley donated the material to the War Department. It wasn't until 1988—47 years later—that lights were installed in Wrigley Field.

Outfielder Lou Novikoff, the "Mad Russian," with infielder Lou Stringer

	W	L	ERA	G	GS	CG	IP	H	BB	K
Claude Passeau	14	14	3.35	34	30	20	231	262	52	80
Vern Olsen	10	8	3.15	37	23	10	185⅔	202	59	73
Bill Lee	8	14	3.76	28	22	12	167⅓	179	43	62
Jake Mooty	8	9	3.35	33	14	7	153⅓	143	56	45
Paul Erickson	5	7	3.70	32	15	7	141	126	64	85
Larry French	5	14	4.63	26	18	6	138	161	43	60
Charlie Root	8	7	5.40	19	15	6	106⅔	133	37	46
Tot Pressnell	5	3	3.09	29	1	0	70	69	23	27
Vallie Eaves	3	3	3.53	12	7	4	58⅔	56	21	24
Vance Page	2	2	4.28	25	3	1	48⅓	48	30	17
Johnny Schmitz	2	0	1.31	5	3	1	20⅔	12	9	11
Ken Raffensberger	0	1	4.50	10	1	0	18	17	7	5
Russ Meers	0	1	1.13	1	1	0	8	5	0	5
Walt Lanfranconi	0	1	3.00	2	1	0	6	7	2	1
Wimpy Quinn	0	0	7.20	3	0	0	5	3	3	2
Emil Kush	0	0	2.25	2	0	0	4	2	0	2
Hank Gornicki	0	0	4.50	1	0	0	2	3	0	2
Dizzy Dean	0	0	18.00	1	1	0	1	3	0	1
	70	84	3.72	300	155	74	1,364⅔	1,431	449	548

Shutouts: Passeau 3, Olsen 2, Erickson 1, French 1, Mooty 1.

	G	AB	H	2B	3B	HR	R	RBI	SB	AVG
Regulars										
1B Babe Dahlgren	99	359	101	20	1	16	50	59	2	.281
2B Lou Stringer	145	512	126	31	4	5	59	53	3	.246
SS Bobby Sturgeon	129	433	106	15	3	0	45	25	5	.245
3B Stan Hack	151	586	(186)	33	5	7	111	45	10	.317
RF Bill Nicholson	147	532	135	26	1	26	74	98	1	.254
CF Phil Cavarretta	107	346	99	18	4	6	46	40	2	.286
LF Dom Dallessandro	140	486	132	36	2	6	73	85	3	.272
C Clyde McCullough	125	418	95	9	2	9	41	53	5	.227
Substitutes										
Johnny Hudson	50	99	20	4	0	0	8	6	3	.202
Billy Myers	24	63	14	1	0	1	10	4	1	.222
Billy Herman	11	36	7	0	1	0	4	0	0	.194
Eddie Waitkus	12	28	5	0	0	0	1	0	0	.179
Lennie Merullo	7	17	6	1	0	0	3	1	1	.353
Rip Russell	6	17	5	1	0	0	1	1	0	.294
Lou Novikoff	62	203	49	8	0	5	22	24	0	.241
Hank Leiber	53	162	35	5	0	7	20	25	0	.216
Augie Galan	65	120	25	3	0	1	18	13	0	.208
Charlie Gilbert	39	86	24	2	1	0	11	12	1	.279
Barney Olsen	24	73	21	6	1	1	13	4	0	.288
Frank Jelincich	4	8	1	0	0	0	0	2	0	.125
Bob Scheffing	51	132	32	8	0	1	9	20	2	.242
Greek George	35	64	10	2	0	0	4	6	0	.156
Al Todd	6	6	1	0	0	0	1	0	0	.167
Pitchers										
Claude Passeau	34	86	19	2	0	3	6	12	0	.221
Vern Olsen	37	63	15	2	0	1	7	5	0	.238
Bill Lee	28	59	11	0	0	2	8	5	0	.186
Jake Mooty	33	50	10	1	0	0	5	1	0	.200
Larry French	26	47	9	0	0	0	5	3	0	.191
Paul Erickson	32	46	7	4	0	1	5	2	0	.152
Charlie Root	19	33	5	1	0	1	4	4	0	.152
Vallie Eaves	12	20	2	0	0	0	0	0	0	.100
Tot Pressnell	29	15	3	0	0	0	1	0	0	.200
Vance Page	25	7	2	0	0	0	0	0	0	.286
Johnny Schmitz	6	7	4	0	0	0	1	2	0	.571
Ken Raffensberger	10	5	0	0	0	0	0	0	0	.000
Russ Meers	1	2	0	0	0	0	0	0	0	.000
Wimpy Quinn	3	2	1	0	0	0	0	0	0	.500
Emil Kush	2	1	0	0	0	0	0	0	0	.000
Walt Lanfranconi	2	1	0	0	0	0	0	0	0	.000
Dizzy Dean	1	0	0	0	0	0	0	0	0	—
Hank Gornicki	1	0	0	0	0	0	0	0	0	—
		5,230	1,323	239	25	99	666	610	39	.253

1942

Record: 68–86
Finish: Sixth
Games Behind: 38
Manager: Jimmie Wilson

President Franklin D. Roosevelt gave baseball the green light in the war year of 1942. In a letter to the baseball commissioner dated January 15, FDR advised Judge Kenesaw Mountain Landis, "I believe it best for the country to keep baseball going. Baseball provides a recreation which does not last over two hours or two hours and a half and which can be got for very little cost."

It was the first full season for Jim Gallagher as general manager. Awash with enthusiasm, Gallagher played the numbers game and invited 40 players to the spring camp, believed to be a record; 23 battery men were included—19 pitchers and four catchers, none of whom had opened the '41 season on the Cub roster.

But the result was the same, another dismal sixth-place finish, 38 games behind the pennant-winning Cardinals. Groping for power, the Cubs acquired Jimmy Foxx, the famed Double X, from the Red Sox in a June 1 waiver deal. Foxx had had five seasons with 40 or more home runs, including 58 in 1932, but now, at age 34, he was in the twilight. In 70 games with the Cubs, he batted .205 with only three home runs and 19 RBIs.

On July 30, after he had struck out on three pitches with two outs in the 12th inning against the Braves in Boston, Foxx blamed his failures on the new lightweight Cub uniforms. "The fabric is so thin I feel like a skinned monkey," Foxx insisted. Lou Novikoff agreed: "No wonder we're in sixth place. We look so skinny and weak to the other clubs they convince themselves they can blow us down."

Tutored in base running by coach Kiki Cuyler, Novikoff was still clumsy in the field but had his best season at the plate. He hit .300 to tie third baseman Stan Hack for the club lead. Bill Nicholson was the only power source. Nicholson had a three-home-run game on August 15 and for the third year in a row led in home runs, 21, and RBIs, 78. Lou Stringer, the new second baseman, was second in home runs with nine.

Wilson posted his spring training Ten Commandments when the club assembled at Catalina Island. Among them: "A 7:30 wake-up call; no poker; no fooling or wrestling in the clubhouse; no throwing ice water on nude players in the shower or elsewhere; the coaches are second in command and their instructions are to be obeyed: neither is a stool pigeon or house detective."

Except for opening day, the Cubs were never in first place. They had two five-game winning streaks, their longest of the season, the first capped on June 18 when Les Fleming one-hit the Braves in a 1–0 victory on a Nicholson triple. On July 10 they were 39–42, 17 games out, and they continued to fade thereafter.

Claude Passeau and Bill Lee were the only pitchers to win in double figures. Passeau, who the previous season had led the staff with 14 victories, lowest by a Cub leader since 1901, had a nine-game winning streak and finished with a 19–14 record. Lee was next at 13–13. None of Gallagher's "College of Pitchers" had more than one win on Memorial Day.

The Cubs were a copy editor's nightmare. On the same day, in late July, they claimed pitcher Dick Errickson on waivers from Boston and optioned pitcher Paul Erickson to the Southern Association. On June 30, in Cincinnati, Wilson was ejected by umpire George Magerkurth. Before departing, Wilson ran around the bases.

	W	L	ERA	G	GS	CG	IP	H	BB	K
Claude Passeau	19	14	2.68	35	34	24	278⅓	284	74	89
Bill Lee	13	13	3.85	32	30	18	219⅔	221	67	75
Hi Bithorn	9	14	3.68	38	16	9	171⅓	191	81	65
Vern Olsen	6	9	4.49	32	17	4	140⅓	161	55	46
Bill Fleming	5	6	3.01	33	14	4	134⅓	117	63	59
Lon Warneke	5	7	2.27	15	12	8	99	97	21	28
Johnny Schmitz	3	7	3.43	23	10	1	86⅔	70	45	51
Jake Mooty	2	5	4.70	19	10	1	84⅓	89	44	28
Paul Erickson	1	6	5.43	18	7	1	63	70	41	26
Tot Pressnell	1	1	5.49	27	0	0	39⅓	40	5	9
Hank Wyse	2	1	1.93	4	4	1	28	33	6	8
Dick Errickson	1	1	4.13	13	0	0	24	39	8	9
Ed Hanyzewski	1	1	3.79	6	1	0	19	17	8	6
Jesse Flores	0	1	3.38	4	0	0	5⅓	5	2	6
Vallie Eaves	0	0	9.00	2	0	0	3	4	2	0
Joe Berry	0	0	18.00	2	0	0	2	7	2	1
Emil Kush	0	0	0.00	1	0	0	2	1	1	1
Bob Bowman	0	0	0.00	1	0	0	1	1	0	0
	68	86	3.60	305	155	71	1,400⅔	1,447	525	507

Shutouts: Passeau 3, Fleming 2, Lee 1, Olsen 1, Warneke 1, Wyse 1.

	G	AB	H	2B	3B	HR	R	RBI	SB	AVG
Regulars										
1B Phil Cavarretta	136	482	130	28	4	3	59	54	7	.270
2B Lou Stringer	121	406	96	10	5	9	45	41	3	.236
SS Lennie Merullo	143	515	132	23	3	2	53	37	14	.256
3B Stan Hack	140	553	166	36	3	6	91	39	9	.300
RF Bill Nicholson	152	588	173	22	11	21	83	78	8	.294
CF Dom Dallessandro	96	264	69	12	4	4	30	43	4	.261
LF Lou Novikoff	128	483	145	25	5	7	48	64	3	.300
C Clyde McCullough	109	337	95	22	1	5	39	31	7	.282
Substitutes										
Rip Russell	102	302	73	9	0	8	32	41	0	.242
Jimmie Foxx	70	205	42	8	0	3	25	19	1	.205
Bobby Sturgeon	63	162	40	7	1	0	8	7	2	.247
Babe Dahlgren	17	56	12	1	0	0	4	6	0	.214
Cy Block	9	33	12	1	1	0	6	4	2	.364
Charlie Gilbert	74	179	33	6	3	0	18	7	1	.184
Peanuts Lowrey	27	58	11	0	0	1	4	4	0	.190
Marv Rickert	8	26	7	0	0	0	5	1	0	.269
Whitey Platt	4	16	1	0	0	0	1	2	0	.063
Chico Hernandez	47	118	27	5	0	0	6	7	0	.229
Bob Scheffing	44	102	20	3	0	2	7	12	2	.196
Paul Gillespie	5	16	4	0	0	2	3	4	0	.250
Marv Felderman	3	6	1	0	0	0	0	0	0	.167
Pitchers										
Claude Passeau	35	105	19	1	0	2	7	10	0	.181
Bill Lee	32	69	11	2	0	0	2	7	0	.159
Hi Bithorn	38	57	7	1	0	0	3	1	0	.123
Vern Olsen	32	48	9	1	0	0	4	4	0	.188
Bill Fleming	33	39	2	0	0	0	2	0	0	.051
Lon Warneke	12	32	6	0	0	0	1	1	0	.188
Jake Mooty	19	28	6	0	0	0	3	2	0	.214
Johnny Schmitz	23	26	4	0	0	0	1	0	0	.154
Paul Erickson	18	21	3	0	0	0	0	1	0	.143
Hank Wyse	4	8	1	0	0	0	1	1	0	.125
Dick Errickson	21	5	0	0	0	0	0	0	0	.000
Ed Hanyzewski	6	5	1	0	0	0	0	2	0	.200
Tot Pressnell	27	3	2	1	0	0	0	3	0	.667
Emil Kush	1	1	0	0	0	0	0	0	0	.000
Joe Berry	2	0	0	0	0	0	0	0	0	—
Bob Bowman	1	0	0	0	0	0	0	0	0	—
Vallie Eaves	0	0	0	0	0	0	0	0	0	—
Jesse Flores	4	0	0	0	0	0	0	0	0	—
		5,354	1,360	224	41	75	591	533	63	.254

1943

Record: 74–79
Finish: Fifth
Games Behind: 30½
Manager: Jimmie Wilson

In what may have been his only clubhouse speech, owner Philip Wrigley assembled the troops on the morning of May 27, 1943. The Cubs had lost nine games in a row, 21 of their first 30, and were in last place, 11 games out. It was not a harangue. Wrigley told the players he knew they were doing their best, but that they should understand there would be no immediate changes in the uniformed personnel. No individual would take the fall.

It was a vote of confidence for Jimmie Wilson, who had been on the grill the previous two summers and was among the most unpopular managers in Cub history. Ed Burns of the *Tribune* was unimpressed with Wrigley's panegyric. "Chicago is no cellar town," Burns wrote. "There will be some lusty yelping if the floperoo continues."

The Cubs had plunged into the second division to stay on April 28. And the floperoo continued. They were seventh on July 4 and straggled home in fifth place, 30½ games behind the champion Cardinals. Their longest winning streak was five games, offset by losing streaks of nine and 11 games.

Complying with the government's request that travel be curtailed, the Cubs (and the White Sox) trained in French Lick, Indiana, 279 miles from Chicago. A diamond was laid out between the practice fairway and the parallel 18th fairway of the golf links adjoining the elegant French Lick Springs Hotel, headquarters for both clubs. Spring training was delayed a month, with a reporting date of March 21.

Rookie Eddie Stanky, ticketed for shortstop, was among the holdouts. Acquired from the Milwaukee Brewers, Stanky was coming off a sensational season in the American Association. He led the league with a .342 average, 124 runs, and 53 doubles. The other principal holdouts were catcher Clyde McCullough and Lou Novikoff, who, when he did report, was of no help: homerless in 233 at bats with only 28 RBIs.

Eddie Waitkus, expected to be the regular first baseman, had enlisted in the service and was lost for the season. Several of the Cubs' veteran players took a sabbatical. Jimmy Foxx was among them. Though his power had diminished, Foxx might have feasted on the wartime pitching but refused to respond to the urgent calls of general manager Jim Gallagher and remained in Boston as an oil salesman.

Throughout the season many players insisted the ball had been deadened. Whatever, the Cubs submitted to an early burial. In late June came the most embarrassing blow of all: Lefty O'Doul, manager of the San Francisco Seals of the Pacific Coast League, told reporters the surest way for the Cubs to improve was to swap places with their Los Angeles farm club, which, at that point, had won 70 percent of its games.

The wolves were also howling for Wilson's blood. Newsboys displayed "Novikoff for Manager" signs at Wrigley Field. According to newspaper polls, many fans favored team captain Stan Hack as Wilson's successor, and if not Hack, Kiki Cuyler, who had been a Cub coach the two previous seasons and was currently managing in the International League.

Slugger Bill Nicholson and pitcher Hi Bithorn kept the club out of the cellar. Nicholson, who had no home runs and only 11 RBIs in his first 32 games, led the league with 29 home runs and both leagues in RBIs with 128. Bithorn was 18–12. He led the league with seven shutouts and pitched four one-run games.

	W	L	ERA	G	GS	CG	IP	H	BB	K
Claude Passeau	15	12	2.91	35	31	18	257	245	66	93
Hi Bithorn	18	12	2.60	39	30	19	249⅔	226	65	86
Paul Derringer	10	14	3.57	32	22	10	174	184	39	75
Hank Wyse	9	7	2.94	38	15	8	156	160	34	45
Ed Hanyzewski	8	7	2.56	33	16	3	130	120	45	55
Lon Warneke	4	5	3.16	21	10	4	88⅓	82	18	30
Bill Lee	3	7	3.56	13	12	4	78⅓	83	27	18
Ray Prim	4	3	2.55	29	5	0	60	67	14	27
Dick Barrett	0	4	4.80	15	4	0	45	52	28	20
Paul Erickson	1	3	6.12	15	4	0	42⅔	47	22	24
John Burrows	0	2	3.86	23	1	0	32⅔	25	16	18
Bill Fleming	0	1	6.40	11	0	0	32⅓	40	12	12
Walter Signer	2	1	2.88	4	2	1	25	24	4	5
Dale Alderson	0	1	6.43	4	2	0	14	21	3	4
Jake Mooty	0	0	0.00	2	0	0	1	2	1	1
	74	79	3.24	314	154	67	1,386	1,378	394	513

Shutouts: Bithorn (7), Derringer 2, Passeau 2, Wyse 2.

	G	AB	H	2B	3B	HR	R	RBI	SB	AVG
Regulars										
1B Phil Cavarretta	143	530	154	27	9	8	93	73	3	.291
2B Eddie Stanky	142	510	125	15	1	0	92	47	4	.245
SS Lennie Merullo	129	453	115	18	3	1	37	25	7	.254
3B Stan Hack	144	533	154	24	4	3	78	35	5	.289
RF Bill Nicholson	154	608	188	30	9	(29)	95	(128)	4	.309
CF Peanuts Lowrey	130	480	140	25	12	1	59	63	13	.292
LF Ival Goodman	80	225	72	10	5	3	31	45	4	.320
C Clyde McCullough	87	266	63	5	2	2	20	23	6	.237
Substitutes										
Stu Martin	64	118	26	4	0	0	13	5	1	.220
Heinz Becker	24	69	10	0	0	0	5	2	0	.145
Bill Schuster	13	51	15	2	1	0	3	0	0	.294
Don Johnson	10	42	8	2	0	0	5	1	0	.190
Pete Elko	9	30	4	0	0	0	1	0	0	.133
Lou Novikoff	78	233	65	7	3	0	22	28	0	.279
Dom Dallessandro	87	176	39	8	3	1	13	31	1	.222
Andy Pafko	13	58	22	3	0	0	7	10	1	.379
Ed Sauer	14	55	15	3	0	0	3	9	1	.273
Whitey Platt	20	41	7	3	0	0	2	2	0	.171
John Ostrowski	10	29	6	0	1	0	2	3	0	.207
Charlie Gilbert	8	20	3	0	0	0	1	0	1	.150
Chico Hernandez	43	126	34	4	0	0	10	9	0	.270
Mickey Livingston	36	111	29	5	1	4	11	16	1	.261
Al Todd	21	45	6	0	0	0	1	1	0	.133
Billy Holm	7	15	1	0	0	0	0	0	0	.067
Mickey Krietner	3	8	3	0	0	0	0	2	0	.375
Pitchers										
Claude Passeau	35	96	19	4	2	0	5	5	0	.198
Hi Bithorn	39	92	16	3	0	0	7	8	0	.174
Paul Derringer	32	58	13	3	0	0	4	2	0	.224
Hank Wyse	40	50	4	1	0	0	3	1	0	.080
Ed Hanyzewski	33	41	2	0	0	0	0	0	0	.049
Bill Lee	13	26	7	0	0	0	3	1	0	.269
Lon Warneke	21	26	5	1	0	0	2	0	1	.192
Paul Erickson	15	15	3	0	0	0	0	3	0	.200
Ray Prim	29	12	2	0	0	0	2	1	0	.167
Dick Barrett	15	9	1	0	0	0	1	0	0	.111
Bill Fleming	11	8	0	0	0	0	0	0	0	.000
Walter Signer	4	8	2	0	0	0	0	0	0	.250
Dale Alderson	4	3	0	0	0	0	0	0	0	.000
John Burrows	23	3	2	0	0	0	0	0	0	.667
Jake Mooty	2	0	0	0	0	0	0	0	0	—
		5,279	1,380	207	56	52	631	579	53	.261

1944

Record: 75–79
Finish: Fourth
Games Behind: 30
Managers: Jimmie Wilson, Roy Johnson, Charlie Grimm

Bill Nicholson led the league in home runs with 33 and runs batted in with 122, but there was more to the story. On July 23, 1944, in the second game of a Polo Grounds doubleheader against the Giants, he received the ultimate tribute—an intentional walk with the bases loaded. So far as has been determined it was only the third time a manager, to avoid pitching to a hitter, purposely forced in a run.

Nicholson had hit three home runs in the opener and had connected again in the seventh inning of the second game: four home runs in a doubleheader, a league record. He came to bat again with two outs in the eighth inning, the bases filled, the Giants leading 10–7. Another home run would put the Cubs ahead 11–10. Manager Mel Ott told his pitcher, Andy "Swede" Hansen, "He's killing us. Put him on." The strategy worked; the run was of no consequence. Andy Pafko flied out to end the inning.

As anticipated, Manager Jimmie Wilson got the ax. The Cubs opened with a 3–0 win at Cincinnati but lost their next nine games. Philip Wrigley and Jim Gallagher decided it was time for change. The call went out to Charlie Grimm, then the president, part owner, and field manager of the American Association Milwaukee Brewers.

Grimm didn't come on the run. He waited until his successor, Casey Stengel, who had been lured out of retirement, arrived in Milwaukee. During the delay, the Cubs were beaten again under coach Roy Johnson. The skid continued: three more losses with Grimm. The 13–game plunge is still the club record for most consecutive losses and wasn't equaled until 1982, 41 years later.

It was the second of Grimm's three managerial terms. He had managed the club from midseason 1932 to midseason 1938. In announcing Grimm's return, Wrigley told reporters, "I always regretted that we let him go. He was the best manager this club ever had."

Grimm was confronted with a long upward climb. When he took command, he predicted a first-division finish. Begining on June 23, the Cubs played their best ball, 26–14. Fourth place was clinched on September 26, their best showing since 1940. They were 74–69 under Grimm but four games under .500 for the season, 30 games behind the runaway Cardinals and 14 games out of third place.

It was Nicholson's best season. He was the first NL player to lead the league in home runs and RBIs two consecutive years. He also led in runs, 116, broke the league record with four home runs in a doubleheader, and equaled the major league mark with four home runs in four at bats. First baseman Phil Cavarretta, at .321, and left fielder Dom Dallessandro, at .304, were the only .300 hitters.

Stan Hack, who had had six .300 seasons, slumped to .282 and had only 108 hits, a 12-year low (1934–45). Hack advised the club he would report late and remained in Oregon, where he was managing a ranch. He didn't break into the starting lineup until June 28. With Hi Bithorn gone—he had enlisted in the navy—the Cubs had only two pitchers win in double figures: Hank Wyse, 16, and Claude Passeau, 15.

For the second consecutive year the Cubs trained in French Lick, Indiana. Tom Taggart, owner of the French Lick Springs Hotel, convinced the club management that the players would benefit if they drank two quarts of goat milk daily. Taggart insisted it would make them "more nimble" and "had great therapeutical value when mixed with mineral spring water."

	W	L	ERA	G	GS	CG	IP	H	BB	K
Hank Wyse	16	15	3.15	41	34	14	257⅓	(277)	57	86
Claude Passeau	15	9	2.89	34	27	18	227	234	50	89
Paul Derringer	7	13	4.15	42	16	7	180	205	39	69
Bill Fleming	9	10	3.13	39	18	9	158⅓	163	62	42
Bob Chipman	9	9	3.49	26	21	8	129	147	40	41
Hy Vandenberg	7	4	3.63	35	9	2	126⅓	123	51	54
Paul Erickson	5	9	3.55	33	15	5	124⅓	113	67	82
Red Lynn	5	4	4.06	22	7	4	84⅓	80	37	35
Ed Hanyzewski	2	5	4.47	14	7	3	58⅓	61	20	19
Dale Alderson	0	0	6.65	12	1	0	21⅔	31	9	7
Mack Stewart	0	0	1.46	8	0	0	12⅓	11	4	3
Charlie Gassaway	0	1	7.71	2	2	0	11⅔	20	10	7
John Miklos	0	0	7.71	2	0	0	7	9	3	0
John Burrows	0	0	18.00	3	0	0	3	7	3	1
	75	79	3.59	313	157	70	1,400⅔	1,481	452	535

Shutouts: Erickson 3, Wyse 3, Passeau 2, Chipman 1, Fleming 1, Lynn 1.

	G	AB	H	2B	3B	HR	R	RBI	SB	AVG
Regulars										
1B Phil Cavarretta	152	614	(197)	35	15	5	106	82	4	.321
2B Don Johnson	154	608	169	37	1	2	50	71	8	.278
SS Lennie Merullo	66	193	41	8	1	1	20	16	3	.212
3B Stan Hack	98	383	108	16	1	3	65	32	5	.282
RF Bill Nicholson	156	582	167	35	8	(33)	(116)	(122)	3	.287
CF Andy Pafko	128	469	126	16	2	6	47	62	2	.269
LF Dom Dallessandro	117	381	116	19	4	8	53	74	1	.304
C Dewey Williams	79	262	63	7	2	0	23	27	2	.240
Substitutes										
Roy Hughes	126	478	137	16	6	1	86	28	16	.287
Bill Schuster	60	154	34	7	1	1	14	14	4	.221
Tony York	28	85	20	1	0	0	4	7	0	.235
Charlie Brewster	10	44	11	2	0	0	4	2	0	.250
Eddie Stanky	13	25	6	0	1	0	4	0	1	.240
Pete Elko	7	22	5	1	0	0	2	0	0	.227
Jimmie Foxx	15	20	1	1	0	0	0	2	0	.050
Ival Goodman	62	141	37	8	1	1	24	16	0	.262
Lou Novikoff	71	139	39	4	2	3	15	19	1	.281
Frank Secory	22	56	18	1	0	4	10	17	1	.321
Ed Sauer	23	50	11	4	0	0	3	5	0	.220
John Ostrowski	8	13	2	1	0	0	2	2	0	.154
Billy Holm	54	132	18	2	0	0	10	6	1	.136
Mickey Krietner	39	85	13	2	0	0	3	1	0	.153
Roy Easterwood	17	33	7	2	0	1	1	2	0	.212
Paul Gillespie	9	26	7	1	0	1	2	2	0	.269
Joe Stephenson	4	8	1	0	0	0	1	0	1	.125
Ben Mann	1	0	0	0	0	0	1	0	0	—
Pitchers										
Hank Wyse	41	90	16	3	0	0	11	8	0	.178
Claude Passeau	34	80	13	3	0	0	6	3	0	.163
Paul Derringer	42	57	9	1	0	0	2	4	0	.158
Bill Fleming	40	53	9	2	0	0	4	6	0	.170
Bob Chipman	26	48	5	0	0	0	1	0	0	.104
Hy Vandenberg	35	38	9	0	0	0	3	5	0	.237
Paul Erickson	33	36	2	0	1	1	2	1	0	.056
Red Lynn	22	29	6	1	0	0	4	2	0	.207
Ed Hanyzewski	14	17	1	0	0	0	2	1	0	.059
Dale Alderson	12	4	0	0	0	0	0	0	0	.000
Charlie Gassaway	2	4	1	0	0	0	0	0	0	.250
John Miklos	2	2	0	0	0	0	0	0	0	.000
Mack Stewart	8	1	0	0	0	0	0	0	0	.000
John Burrows	3	0	0	0	0	0	0	0	0	—
		5,462	1,425	236	46	71	701	639	53	.261

1945

Record: 98–56
Finish: First
Games Ahead: 3
Manager: Charlie Grimm

Yankee owner Larry MacPhail, in trying to rationalize a crucial midseason waiver deal, described Hank Borowy, his star pitcher, as a "morning glory." MacPhail insisted Borowy couldn't win a complete game after July 4 and peddled him to the Cubs for $100,000. It was among the best investments in Cub history.

Not only did Borowy help the Cubs win a National League record 16th pennant in 1945, but he had the additional pleasure of making MacPhail choke on his words. He completed his first 10 starts with the Cubs, eight of them victories, two in extra innings. Combined, he was a 21-game winner, 10–5 with the Yankees, 11–2 with the Cubs. He finished 11 of his 14 Cub starts and led the NL in fewest hits allowed per nine innings and in earned run average, 2.13.

General manager Jim Gallagher made the Borowy deal. Gallagher was fearful that Hank Wyse, the Cub workhorse, would be inducted into the service. "We said goodbye to him with tears in our eyes," Gallagher recalled. But Wyse was declared unfit, returned nine days later, and led the staff with a 22–10 record.

Clubs from both leagues appealed to Commissioner Kenesaw Mountain Landis, insisting the Borowy deal be nullified because it gave the Cubs an unfair advantage. The National Leaguers charged that the Cubs had been given too big a boost. When the deal was made on July 27, they were in first place, 4½ games in front.

The complaints increased with every Borowy victory and every Yankee loss. Landis was silent. There was no rule violation. American League president Will Harridge, also asked to intervene, said it was a legitimate transaction. The clubs in his league had had the opportunity to claim Borowy. It may have been the first time one club had the two winningest pitchers in both leagues. When Borowy climbed aboard, Wyse had 12 victories. Number 11 came on July 12 when he broke Tommy Holmes' batting streak at 37 games, then the modern league record.

Half Cherokee with a mixture of Irish and English, Wyse was born in Lunsford, Arkansas, one of nine children. His father had been a professional player and had taught him the necessity of throwing strikes and how to pace himself. He sometimes worked with only two days of rest, and he was among the best control pitchers in the league—less than two walks a game.

The Cubs finished with a 98–56 record, most victories since Grimm's 1935 pennant winners. They were tied for fifth, nine games out on May 5, but won 32 of their next 47 games. They took the lead to stay on July 8—20 days before Borowy's first appearance—and finished three games ahead of St. Louis, which remained in pursuit until the final weekend. Head to head, they were 6–16 against the Cardinals but 21–1 against seventh-place Cincinnati.

The Cubs led the league in the three principal departments—pitching, hitting, and fielding. In addition to Wyse and Borowy, three other starters won in double figures: Claude Passeau, 17 wins; Paul Derringer, 16; and Pop Prim, a 38-year-old left-hander, 13. They also led in complete games with 86 and had the league batting champion in captain Phil Cavarretta, who hit .355 and won the Most Valuable Player award.

Bill Nicholson, the club RBI leader the previous five seasons, didn't hit with his usual power—only 13 home runs and 88 runs batted in. Outfielders Andy Pafko and Harry "Peanuts" Lowrey, both in their second big league season, made major contributions. Pafko hit .298 and led the club in RBIs with 110. Lowrey batted .283 and had a career high of 89 runs batted in.

	W	L	ERA	G	GS	CG	IP	H	BB	K
Hank Wyse	22	10	2.68	38	34	23	278⅓	272	55	77
Claude Passeau	17	9	2.46	34	27	19	227	205	59	98
Paul Derringer	16	11	3.45	35	30	15	213⅔	223	51	86
Ray Prim	13	8	2.40	34	19	9	165⅓	142	23	88
Hank Borowy	11	2	(2.13)	15	14	11	122⅓	47	47	47
Paul Erickson	7	4	3.32	28	9	3	108⅓	94	48	53
Hy Vandenberg	6	3	3.49	30	7	3	95⅓	91	33	35
Bob Chipman	4	5	3.50	25	10	3	72	63	34	29
Mack Stewart	0	1	4.76	16	1	0	28⅓	37	14	9
Lon Warneke	1	1	3.86	9	1	0	14	16	1	6
Ray Starr	1	0	7.43	9	1	0	13⅓	17	7	5
Jorg Comellas	0	2	4.50	7	1	0	12	11	6	6
Walter Signer	0	0	3.38	6	0	0	8	11	5	0
Ed Hanyzewski	0	0	5.79	2	1	0	4⅔	7	1	0
George Hennessey	0	0	7.36	2	0	0	3⅔	7	1	2
	98	56	(2.98)	290	155	(86)	1,366⅓	1,301	385	541

Shutouts: Passeau 5, Prim 2, Wyse 2, Borowy 1, Chipman 1, Derringer 1, Vandenberg 1.

	G	AB	H	2B	3B	HR	R	RBI	SB	AVG
Regulars										
1B Phil Cavarretta	132	498	177	34	10	6	94	97	5	(.355)
2B Don Johnson	138	557	168	23	2	2	94	58	9	.302
SS Lennie Merullo	121	394	94	18	0	2	40	37	7	.239
3B Stan Hack	150	597	193	29	7	2	110	43	12	.323
RF Bill Nicholson	151	559	136	28	4	13	82	88	4	.243
CF Andy Pafko	144	534	159	24	12	12	64	110	5	.298
LF Peanuts Lowrey	143	523	148	22	7	7	72	89	11	.283
C Mickey Livingston	71	224	57	4	2	2	19	23	2	.254
Substitutes										
Roy Hughes	69	222	58	8	1	0	34	8	6	.261
Heinz Becker	67	133	38	8	2	2	25	27	0	.286
Bill Schuster	45	47	9	2	1	0	8	2	2	.191
Reggie Otero	14	23	9	0	0	0	1	5	0	.391
John Ostrowski	7	10	3	2	0	0	4	1	0	.300
Cy Block	2	7	1	0	0	0	1	1	0	.143
Ed Sauer	49	93	24	4	1	2	8	11	2	.258
Frank Secory	35	57	9	1	0	0	4	6	0	.158
Lloyd Christopher	1	0	0	0	0	0	0	0	0	—
Paul Gillespie	75	163	47	6	0	3	12	25	2	.288
Dewey Williams	59	100	28	2	2	2	16	5	0	.280
Len Rice	32	99	23	3	0	0	10	7	2	.232
Johnny Moore	7	6	1	0	0	0	0	2	0	.167
Pitchers										
Hank Wyse	38	101	17	2	0	0	6	7	0	.168
Claude Passeau	34	91	17	2	0	2	10	9	0	.187
Paul Derringer	35	75	15	3	0	0	3	8	0	.200
Ray Prim	38	51	13	0	0	0	4	1	0	.255
Hank Borowy	15	41	7	1	0	0	5	0	0	.171
Paul Erickson	28	32	5	2	0	0	2	0	0	.156
Hy Vandenberg	30	32	4	0	1	0	4	2	0	.125
Bob Chipman	25	17	3	1	0	0	1	2	0	.176
Jorge Comellas	7	3	0	0	0	0	0	0	0	.000
Mack Stewart	16	3	1	0	0	0	0	0	0	.333
Ray Starr	9	2	1	0	0	0	0	1	0	.500
Lon Warneke	9	2	0	0	0	0	1	0	0	.000
Ed Hanyzewski	2	1	0	0	0	0	0	0	0	.000
Walter Signer	6	1	0	0	0	0	0	0	0	.000
George Hennessey	2	0	0	0	0	0	0	0	0	—
		5,298	1,465	229	52	57	735	674	69	(.277)

1946

Record: 82–71
Finish: Third
Games Behind: 14½
Manager: Charlie Grimm

During the pregame ceremonies on April 20, 1946, before the Cubs' home opener, National League president Ford Frick presented manager Charlie Grimm with the 1945 pennant. Grimm took the flag and said, "Mr. Frick, I hope you're here at home plate again next year."

It was wishful thinking. The Cubs were never a factor—except on the final day when rookie Johnny Schmitz beat the Cardinals with a three-hitter to force a St. Louis–Brooklyn pennant playoff. The Cubs finished a distant third, 14½ games behind the champion Cardinals and only one game ahead of the fourth-place Boston Braves.

For the second consecutive season, slugger Bill Nicholson was unable to hit with his accustomed power. But the biggest disappointment was Hank Borowy, who had been acquired in midseason the year before and had helped pitch the Cubs to a flag. Whereas Borowy had completed his first 10 games with the Cubs in 1945, this time he went the distance only once in his first 14 starts.

Borowy had a season-long problem with blisters on the fingers of his pitching hand and finished with a 12–10 record. Hank Wyse, coming off a 22-victory season, was 14–12, another disappointment. Schmitz, a gangling left-hander, was a pleasant surprise, 11–11 on the season, with a club-leading 2.61 earned run average. He also led the league in strikeouts with 135.

Eddie Waitkus was another rookie who had an outstanding season. Returning after three years in the army, decorated with four battle stars in the Pacific Theater, Waitkus was a defensive wizard and at the season's end was generally acknowledged as the best fielding first baseman in the league.

He also had a good season at the plate, batting .304, the club's only .300 hitter. Captain Phil Cavarretta, previously the regular first baseman, who also had a good glove, was pushed into an unsettled outfield. The slumping Nicholson was in and out of the lineup. Andy Pafko, who had been the regular center fielder, missed half the season with elbow and ankle injuries.

Pafko drove in 39 runs, 71 fewer than in '45. Nicholson, who had developed a hitch in his swing, had 41 RBIs and batted .220. Nicholson had only eight home runs, as many as he once hit in a good month. Cavarretta also had eight, tying him for the club high, the fewest home runs for a Cub leader since Max Flack and Ray Grimes each hit six in 1921.

Marv Rickert, 24, was originally ticketed to challenge Nicholson for the right-field job. Rickert had been discharged from the Coast Guard. He had served on an "explosives ship," hauling ammunition in the Aleutian Islands. He had five years of minor league experience and looked good in spring training, and manager Charlie Grimm was confident he was ready.

Rickert said the best advice he ever had was from Jimmy Mosolf, a former Pirate who had been among his teammates in Tacoma: "When you're in a slump go up to the plate and just whistle or hum any song you can think of." Rickert appeared in 111 games and sang his way to a .263 average, with seven home runs and 47 runs batted in.

The Cubs were also singing in praise of Billy Jurges, their one-time star shortstop who rejoined the club after being released by the Giants. Jurges, 38, didn't hit but was outstanding in the field. General manager Jim Gallagher gleefully told reporters, "Didn't I tell you we'd come up with another Jurges?" Two other former Cub heroes, pitchers Dizzy Dean and Lon Warneke, were also gainfully employed. Dean launched his career as a broadcaster; Warneke was a rookie umpire in the Pacific Coast League.

	W	L	ERA	G	GS	CG	IP	H	BB	K
Johnny Schmitz	11	11	2.61	41	31	14	224⅓	184	94	(135)
Hank Wyse	14	12	2.68	40	27	12	201⅓	206	52	52
Hank Borowy	12	10	3.76	32	28	8	201	220	61	95
Paul Erickson	9	7	2.43	32	14	5	137	119	65	70
Emil Kush	9	2	3.05	40	6	1	129⅔	120	43	50
Claude Passeau	9	8	3.13	21	21	10	129⅓	118	42	47
Bob Chipman	6	5	3.13	34	10	5	109⅓	103	54	42
Hi Bithorn	6	5	3.84	26	7	2	86⅔	97	25	34
Russ Bauers	2	1	3.53	15	2	2	43⅓	45	19	22
Bill Fleming	0	1	6.14	14	1	0	29⅓	37	12	10
Ray Prim	2	3	5.79	14	2	0	23⅓	28	10	10
Russ Meyer	0	0	3.18	4	1	0	17	21	10	10
Doyle Lade	0	2	4.11	3	2	0	15⅓	15	3	8
Red Adams	0	1	8.25	8	0	0	12	18	7	8
Russ Meers	1	2	3.18	7	2	0	11⅓	10	10	2
Vern Olsen	0	0	2.79	5	0	0	9⅔	10	9	8
Ed Hanyzewski	1	0	4.50	3	0	0	6	8	5	1
Hal Manders	0	1	9.00	2	1	0	6	11	3	4
Emmett O'Neill	0	0	0.00	1	0	0	1	0	3	1
	82	71	3.24	342	155	59	1,393	1,370	527	609

Shutouts: Chipman 3, Schmitz 3, Passeau 2, Wyse 2, Bithorn 1, Borowy 1, Erickson 1, Kush 1.

	G	AB	H	2B	3B	HR	R	RBI	SB	AVG
Regulars										
1B Eddie Waitkus	113	441	134	24	5	4	50	55	3	.304
2B Don Johnson	83	314	76	10	1	1	37	19	6	.242
SS Bill Jurges	82	221	49	9	2	0	26	17	3	.222
3B Stan Hack	92	323	92	13	4	0	55	26	3	.285
RF Phil Cavarretta	139	510	150	28	10	8	89	78	2	.294
CF Peanuts Lowrey	144	540	139	24	5	4	75	54	10	.257
LF Marv Rickert	111	392	103	18	3	7	44	47	3	.263
C Clyde McCullough	95	307	88	18	5	4	38	34	2	.287
Substitutes										
Bobby Sturgeon	100	294	87	12	2	1	26	21	0	.296
Lou Stringer	80	209	51	3	1	3	26	19	0	.244
John Ostrowski	64	160	34	4	2	3	20	12	1	.213
Lennie Merullo	65	126	19	8	0	0	14	7	2	.151
Cy Block	6	13	3	0	0	0	2	0	0	.231
Hank Schenz	6	11	2	0	0	0	0	1	1	.182
Al Glossop	4	10	0	0	0	0	2	0	0	.000
Bill Nicholson	105	296	65	13	2	8	36	41	1	.220
Andy Pafko	65	234	66	6	4	3	18	39	4	.282
Dom Dallessandro	65	89	20	2	2	1	4	9	1	.225
Frank Secory	33	43	10	3	0	3	6	12	0	.233
Charlie Gilbert	15	13	1	0	0	0	2	1	0	.077
Clarence Maddern	3	3	0	0	0	0	0	0	0	.000
Mickey Livingston	66	176	45	14	0	2	14	20	0	.256
Bob Scheffing	63	115	32	4	1	0	8	18	0	.278
Dewey Williams	4	5	1	0	0	0	0	0	0	.200
Ted Pawelek	4	4	1	1	0	0	0	0	0	.250
Heinz Becker	9	7	2	0	0	0	0	1	0	.286
Rabbit Garriott	6	5	0	0	0	0	1	0	0	.000
Pitchers										
Hank Wyse	40	74	18	1	0	0	4	7	1	.243
Hank Borowy	33	72	13	4	1	0	9	8	0	.181
Johnny Schmitz	42	70	9	0	0	1	3	3	0	.129
Claude Passeau	21	49	10	1	0	3	7	7	0	.204
Paul Erickson	32	40	2	1	0	0	1	0	0	.050
Emil Kush	40	38	8	1	0	0	3	1	0	.211
Bob Chipman	34	33	2	0	0	0	1	3	0	.061
Hi Bithorn	26	28	5	0	0	0	4	2	0	.179
Russ Bauers	15	10	3	1	0	0	1	2	0	.300
Doyle Lade	3	5	1	0	0	0	0	0	0	.200
Russ Meyer	4	5	1	0	0	0	0	0	0	.200

	G	AB	H	2B	3B	HR	R	RBI	SB	AVG
Ray Prim	14	5	1	0	0	0	0	1	0	.200
Bill Fleming	14	3	0	0	0	0	0	0	0	.000
Hal Manders	2	2	0	0	0	0	0	0	0	.000
Red Adams	8	1	0	0	0	0	0	0	0	.000
Ed Hanyzewski	3	1	0	0	0	0	0	0	0	.000
Russ Meers	7	1	1	0	0	0	0	1	0	1.000
Vern Olsen	5	0	0	0	0	0	0	0	0	—
Emmett O'Neill	1	0	0	0	0	0	0	0	0	—
	5,298	1,344	223	50	56	626	566	43	.254

1947

Record: 69–85
Finish: Sixth
Games Behind: 25
Manager: Charlie Grimm

Two years later Yankee owner Larry MacPhail's prophecy of 1945 came true: Hank Borowy was a "morning glory," without staying power, unlikely to pitch complete games in the second half. In 1947, Borowy was a disappointing 8–12 on the season, lost his last nine decisions and went the distance only seven times in 25 starts, once after July 4.

Borowy wasn't the Lone Ranger. The entire Cub pitching staff was ineffective, with the exception of some short runs—the longest winning streak was five games. Johnny Schmitz was high with 13 victories but led the league in losses, 18. Rookie Doyle Lade, 11–10, was the only other winner in double figures.

Hank Wyse, who had averaged 17 wins in the previous three seasons, won only six games; the victories were scattered, one for each month. Like the others, Wyse required constant bullpen help: five completions in 19 starts. Emil Kush, a rubber-armed right-hander, emerged as the Cubs' first heavy-duty closer. He appeared in 47 games, all but one in relief.

Kush, 8–3, worked four finishing innings and was the winner on July 24 when the Cubs broke a nine-game losing streak. Frantic for a stopper, Grimm used eight different starters in the nine games. It was the Cubs' longest skid of the season and dropped them into sixth place. A month earlier, on June 24, they had been in the lead, but it was a 24-hour mirage. They fell to second the next day and never recovered.

The Cubs finished in sixth place, the first of what was to be a succession of 20 years in the second division. Grimm's only comfort was a five-year contract extension and the comeback of slugger Bill Nicholson who was growing bald and had begun using hair restorer. He led the team in RBIs with 75 and home runs with 26, 19 on the road.

Most of the Chicago baseball Boswells, including the veteran Ed Burns, had been convinced Nicholson was on the discard pile. Nicholson's two-year slump was of such proportions that the previous summer a fan leaped from a box seat during batting practice and was in the midst of giving him a batting lesson before Grimm summoned security and had the volunteer professor gently led away.

In the May 21 *Sporting News*, Burns observed: "There have been times when we thought it would be best if William Beck Nicholson turn in his uniform, return to his home in Chestertown, Maryland, and spend the rest of his time helping his charming wife, Nancy, with the household chores and teaching his two robust sons the folly of trying to absorb a whole pack of chewing tobacco in a single stoking. But at 32 he has become as good as he was in '43 and '44 and we predict he will return to his former prowess."

It was the last hurrah for third baseman Stan Hack, who batted .271 in 76 games and ended his 16-year Cub career with a .301 lifetime. Bill Jurges also retired. And it was the farewell season for pitchers Bill Lee and Claude Passeau, as well as Wyse.

The only notable in-season acquisition was outfielder Cliff Aberson, who was recalled after he had hit 20 home runs with Des Moines of the Western League. Aberson appeared in 47 games with the Cubs and batted .279, with four home runs and 20 runs batted in. The Cubs had two .300 hitters: Phil Cavarretta, .314, and Andy Pafko, .302.

	W	L	ERA	G	GS	CG	IP	H	BB	K
Johnny Schmitz	13	(18)	3.22	38	28	10	207	209	80	97
Doyle Lade	11	10	3.94	34	25	7	187⅓	202	79	62
Hank Borowy	8	12	4.38	40	25	7	183	190	63	75
Paul Erickson	7	12	4.34	40	20	6	174	179	93	82
Hank Wyse	6	9	4.31	37	19	5	142	158	64	53
Bob Chipman	7	6	3.68	32	17	5	134⅔	135	66	51
Emil Kush	8	3	3.36	47	1	1	91	80	53	44
Russ Meers	2	0	4.48	35	1	0	64⅓	61	38	28
Claude Passeau	2	6	6.25	19	6	1	63⅓	97	24	26
Russ Meyer	3	2	3.40	23	2	1	45	43	14	22
Ralph Hamner	1	2	2.52	3	3	2	25	24	16	14
Bill Lee	0	2	4.50	14	2	0	24	26	14	9
Ox Miller	1	2	10.13	4	4	1	16	31	5	7
Bob Carpenter	0	1	4.91	4	1	0	7⅓	10	4	1
Freddy Schmidt	0	0	9.00	1	1	0	3	4	5	0
	69	85	4.10	371	155	46	1,367	1,449	618	571

Shutouts: Schmitz 3, Borowy 1, Chipman 1, Lade 1, Passeau 1, Wyse 1.

	G	AB	H	2B	3B	HR	R	RBI	SB	AVG
Regulars										
1B Eddie Waitkus	130	514	150	28	6	2	60	35	3	.292
2B Don Johnson	120	402	104	17	2	3	33	26	2	.259
SS Lennie Merullo	108	373	90	16	1	0	24	29	4	.241
3B Peanuts Lowrey	115	448	126	17	5	5	56	37	2	.281
RF Bill Nicholson	148	487	119	28	1	26	69	75	1	.244
CF Andy Pafko	129	513	155	25	7	13	68	66	4	.302
LF Phil Cavarretta	127	459	144	22	5	2	56	63	2	.314
C Bob Scheffing	110	363	96	11	5	5	33	50	2	.264
Substitutes										
Stan Hack	76	240	65	11	2	0	28	12	0	.271
Bobby Sturgeon	87	232	59	10	5	0	16	21	0	.254
Ray Mack	21	78	17	6	0	2	9	12	0	.218
Lonny Frey	24	43	9	0	0	0	4	3	0	.209
Bill Jurges	14	40	8	2	0	1	5	2	0	.200
Sal Madrid	8	24	3	1	0	0	0	1	0	.125
Hank Schenz	7	14	1	0	0	0	2	0	0	.071
Cliff Aberson	47	140	39	6	3	4	24	20	0	.279
Marv Rickert	71	137	20	0	0	2	7	15	0	.146
Dom Dallessandro	66	115	33	7	1	1	18	14	0	.287
Clyde McCullough	86	234	59	12	4	3	25	30	1	.252
Mickey Livingston	19	33	7	2	0	0	2	3	0	.212
Dewey Williams	3	2	0	0	0	0	0	0	0	.000
Pitchers										
Johnny Schmitz	38	68	9	0	0	0	3	3	0	.132
Paul Erickson	40	60	15	2	0	1	2	3	0	.250
Doyle Lade	35	60	13	2	0	0	3	4	1	.217
Hank Borowy	41	56	7	3	0	0	5	6	0	.125
Hank Wyse	37	45	5	0	1	0	3	4	0	.111
Bob Chipman	33	44	4	0	0	0	4	0	0	.091
Emil Kush	47	20	5	2	0	0	2	1	0	.250
Russ Meers	35	14	2	0	0	0	1	0	0	.143
Claude Passeau	19	14	0	0	0	0	0	0	0	.000
Russ Meyer	23	12	3	0	0	0	2	1	0	.250
Ralph Hamner	3	8	1	0	0	0	0	0	0	.125
Ox Miller	4	7	3	1	0	1	3	4	0	.429
Bill Lee	14	3	1	0	0	0	0	0	0	.333
Freddy Schmidt	1	2	0	0	0	0	0	0	0	.000
Bob Carpenter	4	1	1	0	0	0	0	0	0	1.000
		5,305	1,373	231	48	71	567	540	22	.259

1948

Record: 64–90
Finish: Eighth
Games Behind: 27½
Manager: Charlie Grimm

The 1948 race in Chicago wasn't for the pennant. It was the "Dungeon Derby" between the Cubs and crosstown White Sox. Both clubs obliged and for the first time finished last in the same season. It was not a record for a two-team city. Beginning in 1919, in tandem, the Philadelphia clubs finished last nine times.

For the Cubs it was an embarrassment without precedent. It wasn't their first cellar finish; they were last in 1925. But they lost 90 games, then a franchise record. It was a season of such futility that owner Philip Wrigley, in what may been another first, apologized to the fans in an August 30 paid advertisement published in all the Chicago newspapers. In part:

"The Cub Management wants you to know we appreciate the wonderful support you are giving the ball club. We want to have a winning team that can be up at the top—the kind you deserve. This year's rebuilding job has been a flop. But we are not content to just go along with an eye only to attendance. We want a winner just as you do and will do everything in our power to get one."

Three days earlier, the Cubs had passed the million mark in home attendance. They finished with a gate of 1,237,792—only 230,000 fewer than the club record set during the 1929 pennant season. It was a remarkable achievement considering that they were the only team that did not play night games, had no black players, and did not offer game-day promotions.

Except for the curve balling Johnny Schmitz, the starting pitching was a disaster. Schmitz led the staff with 18 wins, six against Brooklyn. He won his first five starts against the Dodgers, all complete games; in these 47 innings he allowed only seven runs and 34 hits. He was 6–3 against the Dodgers, 12–10 against the six other teams.

Russ Meyer was next at 10–10. Meyer was effective early. On April 25 he beat the Cardinals 3–1 allowing one hit, a scratch single off the glove of Andy Pafko. Previously an outfielder, Pafko played the full season at third base. Overall, Meyer was ineffective and made nine unsuccessful starts between his ninth and tenth victories. No other starter won more than five games.

Roy Smalley, purchased from Nashville of the Southern Association with a reputation as a long-ball hitter, was installed as the regular shortstop. He batted .216 and led all NL shortstops in errors with 34. Clarence Maddern, another highly advertised rookie, was expected to win a starting outfield berth but appeared in only 80 games—four home runs and 27 RBIs in 214 at bats.

Rookie left-hander Dutch McCall set a club record with 13 consecutive losses. Bob Rush, another first-year pitcher who was to become a star, was 5–11. Hank Borowy was of no help and won only five of 17 starts. Pafko led the offense with 26 home runs, 101 RBIs, and a .312 average. Bill Nicholson was next with 19 home runs and 67 RBIs.

At the end of the season general manager Jim Gallagher

began unloading. Nicholson was traded to the Phillies for Harry Walker, the 1947 NL batting champion. In mid-December, catcher Clyde McCullough was sent to Pittsburgh and Borowy and Eddie Waitkus to the Phillies. The Phillies also acquired Meyer in a straight sale.

After the early skirmishing, the Cubs were never higher than sixth. They were in last place almost continuously for three months, except for one day in July, climbed to seventh again in the first week of September after a sequence of nine wins in 13 games, and dropped into the cellar to stay on September 22. Owner Wrigley said the club finished last because the players "lacked spirit."

	W	L	ERA	G	GS	CG	IP	H	BB	K
Johnny Schmitz	18	13	2.64	34	30	18	242	186	97	100
Russ Meyer	10	10	3.66	29	26	8	164⅔	157	77	89
Dutch McCall	4	13	4.82	30	20	5	151⅓	158	85	89
Bob Rush	5	11	3.92	36	16	4	133⅓	153	37	72
Hank Borowy	5	10	4.89	39	17	2	127	156	49	50
Ralph Hamner	5	9	4.69	27	17	5	111⅓	110	69	53
Cliff Chambers	2	9	4.43	29	12	3	103⅔	100	48	51
Doyle Lade	5	6	4.02	19	12	6	87⅓	99	31	29
Jess Dobernic	7	2	3.15	54	0	0	85⅔	67	40	48
Emil Kush	1	4	4.38	34	1	0	72	70	37	31
Bob Chipman	2	1	3.58	34	3	0	60⅓	73	24	16
Paul Erickson	0	0	6.35	3	0	0	5⅔	7	6	4
Ben Wade	0	1	7.20	2	0	0	5	4	4	1
Warren Hacker	0	1	21.00	3	1	0	3	7	3	0
Tony Jacobs	0	0	4.50	1	0	0	2	3	0	2
Don Carlsen	0	0	36.00	1	0	0	1	5	2	1
	64	90	4.00	375	155	51	1,355⅓	1,355	609	636

Shutouts: Meyer 3, Schmitz 2, Borowy 1, Chambers 1.

	G	AB	H	2B	3B	HR	R	RBI	SB	AVG
Regulars										
1B Eddie Waitkus	139	562	166	27	10	7	87	44	11	.295
2B Hank Schenz	96	337	88	17	1	1	43	14	3	.261
SS Roy Smalley	124	361	78	11	4	4	25	36	0	.216
3B Andy Pafko	142	548	171	30	2	26	82	101	3	.312
RF Bill Nicholson	143	494	129	24	5	19	68	67	2	.261
CF Hal Jeffcoat	134	473	132	16	4	4	53	42	8	.279
LF Peanuts Lowrey	129	435	128	12	3	2	47	54	2	.294
C Bob Scheffing	102	293	88	18	2	5	23	45	0	.300
Substitutes										
Phil Cavarretta	111	334	93	16	5	3	41	40	4	.278
Emil Verban	56	248	73	15	1	1	37	16	4	.294
Gene Mauch	53	138	28	3	2	1	18	7	1	.203
Dick Culler	48	89	15	2	0	0	4	5	0	.169
Jeff Cross	16	20	2	0	0	0	1	0	0	.100
Don Johnson	6	12	3	0	0	0	0	0	1	.250
Dummy Lynch	7	7	2	0	0	1	3	1	0	.286
Clarence Maddern	80	214	54	12	1	4	16	27	0	.252
Cliff Aberson	12	32	6	1	0	1	1	6	0	.188
Carmen Mauro	3	5	1	0	0	1	2	1	0	.200
Clyde McCullough	69	172	36	4	2	1	10	7	0	.209
Rube Walker	79	171	47	8	0	5	17	26	0	.275
Carl Sawatski	2	2	0	0	0	0	0	0	0	.000
Pitchers										
Johnny Schmitz	34	84	11	1	1	0	3	4	0	.131
Russ Meyer	29	56	6	0	1	0	1	3	0	.107
Dutch McCall	30	53	9	2	0	0	3	6	0	.170
Bob Rush	38	39	5	1	0	0	1	0	0	.128
Hank Borowy	39	36	8	3	0	0	4	0	0	.222
Ralph Hamner	27	33	6	1	0	1	1	5	0	.182
Doyle Lade	19	32	5	0	0	0	3	2	0	.156
Cliff Chambers	29	30	4	1	0	0	0	3	0	.133
Bob Chipman	34	16	4	0	0	0	2	2	0	.250
Emil Kush	34	13	2	0	0	0	1	0	0	.154
Jess Dobernic	54	10	2	0	0	0	0	0	0	.200
Ben Wade	2	2	0	0	0	0	0	0	0	.000
Paul Erickson	3	1	0	0	0	0	0	0	0	.000
Don Carlsen	1	0	0	0	0	0	0	0	0	—
Warren Hacker	3	0	0	0	0	0	0	0	0	—
Tony Jacobs	1	0	0	0	0	0	0	0	0	—
		5,352	1,402	225	44	87	597	564	39	.262

Left to right: Bill Nicholson, Andy Pafko, Clarence Maddern, and Phil Cavarretta

1949

Record: 61–93
Finish: Eighth
Games Behind: 36
Managers: Charlie Grimm, Frankie Frisch

Nineteen forty-nine was the year when Leo Durocher, then managing the New York Giants, said "Nice guys finish last." Durocher wasn't referring to the Cubs, but they did finish last and were very nice about it, especially on June 10 when Frankie Frisch replaced Charlie Grimm as the Cub manager.

It was a remarkably cordial succession, possibly without precedent. Owner Philip Wrigley gave Grimm a "promotion"—vice president in charge of player operations, including the farm system, all of which had been the domain of general manager James Timothy Gallagher, who was named business manager.

In the kindest cut of all, Grimm was given the courtesy of choosing his successor. Grimm did so without hesitation. The baton was passed to Frisch, an old opponent, and a Grimm clone. They were the same age, 50; had broken into the big leagues together, in 1919; had begun their managerial careers one year apart; were of German descent; and were among baseball's leading raconteurs.

Frisch took command on June 14, the day before the trading deadline, and immediately made his major contribution. He recommended a four-player deal with the Cincinnati Reds. Grimm approved: outfielders Harry Walker and Peanuts Lowrey in exchange for outfielders Hank Sauer and Frank Baumholtz.

It was among the most judicious trades in Cub history. Sauer, who was soon to become the "Mayor of Wrigley Field," singled in his first Cub at bat, on June 17; he hit his first Cub home run three days later off Boston's Vern Bickford. In his first 39 games he whaled away at a .367 pace, with 15 home runs and 45 runs batted in. He led the club in batting with a .291 average, drove in 83 runs, and hit 31 roundtrippers, 27 for the Cubs.

Andy Pafko, who shuttled between third base and the outfield—49 games at third, 98 in the outfield—gave the Cubs a credible one-two punch: .281, 18 home runs, and 69 RBIs. The defense was erratic, especially in the infield. The pitching was undistinguished. Johnny Schmitz led the club in victories with 11, four against Brooklyn. Bob Rush was next with ten.

Roy Smalley, who had a sensational spring training, was a major disappointment. Smalley and Rush reported to Catalina Island a week ahead of the club and devoted most of their time to herding buffalo for Jack White, Wrigley's ranch boss. Pleased, and with a straight face, Grimm told reporters the daily roping of bison had improved Smalley's batting swing and Rush's control.

Grimm may have been jesting, but Smalley batted safely in all but two of the 15 exhibition games against major league opponents—a .403 average, six home runs, seven doubles, and two triples. Two weeks after the regular season began, Smalley was hitting .125. He finished with a .245 average, led the team in strikeouts with 77, and led all shortstops in errors with 39.

Pittsburgh's Rip Sewell, a 41-year-old junkballer, beat the Cubs 1–0 in their home opener on a ninth-inning Smalley error. It was the third time Sewell blanked the Cubs in their opener. The infield, expected to be airtight, was charged with seven errors in the first 12 games. The Cubs won only 11 of their first 30 games and on June 1 toppled into the cellar.

They were 19–31 under Grimm, 42–62 thereafter, dropping their first six games under Frisch en route to a record 93 losses. There was no friction between Grimm and Frisch. Grimm never descended from his front-office perch but on several occasions told reporters, "These hands were never meant to carry a briefcase."

	W	L	ERA	G	GS	CG	IP	H	BB	K
Johnny Schmitz	11	13	4.35	36	31	9	207	227	92	75
Bob Rush	10	18	4.07	35	27	9	201	197	79	80
Dutch Leonard	7	16	4.15	33	28	10	180	198	43	83
Monk Dubiel	6	9	4.14	32	20	3	147⅔	142	54	52
Doyle Lade	4	5	5.00	36	13	5	129⅔	141	58	43
Warren Hacker	5	8	4.23	30	12	3	125⅔	141	53	40
Bob Chipman	7	8	3.97	38	11	3	113⅓	110	63	46
Dewey Adkins	2	4	5.68	30	5	1	82⅓	98	39	43
Bob Muncrief	5	6	4.56	34	3	1	75	80	31	36
Emil Kush	3	3	3.78	26	0	0	47⅔	51	24	22
Cal McLish	1	1	5.87	8	2	0	23	31	12	6
Ralph Hamner	0	2	8.76	6	1	0	12⅓	22	8	3
Dwain Sloat	0	0	7.00	5	1	0	9	14	3	3
Jess Dobernic	0	0	20.25	4	0	0	4	9	4	0
Mort Cooper	0	0	0.00	1	0	0	0	2	1	0
	61	93	4.50	354	154	44	1,357⅔	1,463	564	532

Shutouts: Schmitz 3, Chipman 1, Dubiel 1, Lade 1, Leonard 1, Rush 1.

	G	AB	H	2B	3B	HR	R	RBI	SB	AVG
Regulars										
1B Herm Reich	108	386	108	18	2	3	43	34	4	.280
2B Emil Verban	98	343	99	11	1	0	38	22	3	.289
SS Roy Smalley	135	477	117	21	10	8	57	35	2	.245
3B Frankie Gustine	76	261	59	13	4	4	29	27	3	.226
RF Hal Jeffcoat	108	363	89	18	6	2	43	26	12	.245
CF Andy Pafko	144	519	146	29	2	18	79	69	4	.281
LF Hank Sauer	96	357	104	17	1	27	59	83	0	.291
C Mickey Owen	62	198	54	9	3	2	15	18	1	.273
Substitutes										
Phil Cavarretta	105	360	106	22	4	8	46	49	2	.294
Bob Ramazzotti	65	190	34	3	1	0	14	6	9	.179
Gene Mauch	72	150	37	6	2	1	15	7	3	.247
Wayne Terwilliger	36	112	25	2	1	2	11	10	0	.223
Bill Serena	12	37	8	3	0	1	3	7	0	.216
Hank Schenz	7	14	6	0	0	0	2	1	2	.429
Clarence Maddern	10	9	3	0	0	1	1	2	0	.333
Hank Edwards	58	176	51	8	4	7	25	21	0	.290
Frankie Baumholtz	58	164	37	4	2	1	15	15	2	.226
Harry Walker	42	159	42	6	3	1	20	14	2	.264
Peanuts Lowrey	38	111	30	5	0	2	18	10	3	.270
Cliff Aberson	4	7	0	0	0	0	0	0	0	.000
Rube Walker	56	172	42	4	1	3	11	22	0	.244
Bob Scheffing	55	149	40	6	1	3	12	19	0	.268
Rube Novotney	22	67	18	2	1	0	4	6	0	.269
Smoky Burgess	46	56	15	0	0	1	4	12	0	.268
Jim Kirby	3	2	1	0	0	0	0	0	0	.500
Pitchers										
Johnny Schmitz	36	70	10	2	1	0	4	4	0	.143
Bob Rush	35	63	2	0	0	0	4	2	0	.032
Dutch Leonard	33	59	12	1	0	0	4	5	0	.203
Warren Hacker	32	38	7	0	0	0	1	1	0	.184
Monk Dubiel	33	35	10	0	2	0	2	3	0	.286
Doyle Lade	36	32	7	0	0	0	4	4	1	.219
Bob Chipman	38	24	3	0	0	0	2	0	0	.125
Dewey Adkins	30	20	4	1	0	1	1	2	0	.200
Bob Muncrief	34	14	4	0	1	0	1	1	0	.286
Emil Kush	26	9	3	1	0	0	2	1	0	.333
Cal McLish	26	9	3	0	0	0	2	2	0	.333
Ralph Hamner	6	2	0	0	0	0	0	0	0	.000
Mort Cooper	1	0	0	0	0	0	0	0	0	—
Jess Dobernic	4	0	0	0	0	0	0	0	0	—
Dwain Sloat	5	0	0	0	0	0	0	0	0	—
		5,214	1,336	212	53	97	593	539	53	.256

1950

Record: 64–89
Finish: Seventh
Games Behind: 26½
Manager: Frankie Frisch

Manager Frankie Frisch posted his spring training regimen in late January: To strengthen their legs the players would climb mountains and take long hikes. The program would also include hard runs from home plate to the left- and right-field poles, the tempo increasing daily. Said Frisch: "I'll run them right down to their knees."

Charlie Grimm was the first to take a hike. Grimm, who had been kicked upstairs presumably to function as the general manager, resigned on January 6, 1950, reportedly because of differences with Jim Gallagher. Philip Wrigley accepted the resignation with the usual regrets. Two weeks later a delighted Grimm was back on the field. He signed a $30,000 contract to manage Dallas in the Texas League, highest wage ever for a minor league manager.

On February 18, Grimm was succeeded by Wid Mathews, who had been among Branch Rickey's disciples in Brooklyn. Like Rickey, Mathews was a .400 talker whose quiver overflowed with theoretical ramblings. On how he sized up a prospect: "When I shake hands with a boy and he has a good grip, that's one of the essentials. Then I pat him on the shoulder to see how muscular he is."

The 1950 Cubs were last in fielding, last in hitting, and next-to-last in pitching. But they were muscular: 161 home runs, 10 short of the club record. Andy Pafko was second in the league with 36, a career high. Hank Sauer was third with 32 but only hit two at night. Shortstop Roy Smalley, erratic as ever in the field, muscled up for 21 home runs. Third baseman Bill Serena, nicknamed "The Whip" because of his strong arm, hit 17.

It was the year the pennant was won by the Philadelphia "Whiz Kids." Halfway through the season the Cubs were being mocked as the "Whiff Kids." They set a one-season league record of 767 strikeouts, Smalley leading the whiff parade with 114. For the third year in a row Smalley led all NL shortstops in errors, 51. He also had the most total chances.

Frisch was committed to a so-called youth movement. He opened the season with three rookie infielders: Preston Ward at first base, Wayne Terwilliger at second, Serena at third. Excluding battery men, Sauer, age 31, and Pafko, 29, were the oldest regulars, and Frisch occasionally had them on the bench with the hope of developing newcomers Bob Borkowski and Carmen Mauro. Borkowski got into 85 games, Mauro 62. Neither was capable of delivering the long ball. Together, they had only five home runs and 39 RBIs.

Sauer and Pafko combined drove in 195 runs—Sauer 103, Pafko 92. Pafko led the club in hitting with a .304 average and was virtually slump-proof. He crashed his 30th home run on August 22. Sauer went 31 days without a home run, from mid-July until August 19. Each had a three-home-run game. The lumbering Sauer was also smiling on June 25 in Philadelphia when he scored from second on Pafko's sacrifice fly to deep center field.

Bob Rush, now throwing nothing but heat—Frisch told him to stuff his breaking pitches—won his first five decisions and led the staff with 13 victories but won only one game from June 19 through September 6, a stretch of 79 days. He lost a league-high 20 games, nine by one run. Johnny Schmitz, winless in starting assignments from June 24 through September 16, was 10–16.

Frank Hiller, age 30, was the most effective pitcher. Acquired in spring training from the Yankees on a look-see arrangement, Hiller was used both as a starter and out of the bullpen. He was 12–5 on the season with a club-leading 3.53 earned run average. The Cubs finished seventh, 26½ games out of first place.

	W	L	ERA	G	GS	CG	IP	H	BB	K
Bob Rush	13	(20)	3.71	39	34	19	254⅔	261	93	93
Johnny Schmitz	10	16	4.99	39	27	8	193	217	91	75
Paul Minner	8	13	4.11	39	24	9	190⅓	217	72	99
Frank Hiller	12	5	3.53	38	17	9	153	153	32	55
Monk Dubiel	6	10	4.16	39	12	4	142⅔	152	67	51
Doyle Lade	5	6	4.74	34	12	2	117⅔	126	50	36
Johnny Klippstein	2	9	5.25	33	11	3	104⅔	112	64	51
Dutch Leonard	5	1	3.77	35	1	0	74	70	27	28
Johnny Vander Meer	3	4	3.79	32	6	0	73⅔	60	59	41
Bill Voiselle	0	4	5.79	19	7	0	51⅓	64	29	25
Warren Hacker	0	1	5.28	5	3	1	15⅓	20	8	5
Andy Varga	0	0	0.00	1	0	0	1	0	1	0
	64	89	4.28	353	154	55	1,371⅓	1,452	593	559

Shutouts: Schmitz 3, Dubiel 2, Hiller 2, Minner 1, Rush 1.

	G	AB	H	2B	3B	HR	R	RBI	SB	AVG
Regulars										
1B Preston Ward	80	285	72	11	2	6	31	33	3	.253
2B Wayne Terwilliger	133	480	116	22	3	10	63	32	13	.242
SS Roy Smalley	154	557	128	21	9	21	58	85	2	.230
3B Bill Serena	127	435	104	20	4	17	56	61	1	.239
RF Bob Borkowski	85	256	70	7	4	4	27	29	1	.273
CF Andy Pafko	146	514	156	24	8	36	95	92	4	.304
LF Hank Sauer	145	540	148	32	2	32	85	103	1	.274
C Mickey Owen	86	259	63	11	0	2	22	21	2	.243
Substitutes										
Phil Cavarretta	82	256	70	11	1	10	49	31	1	.273
Bob Ramazzotti	61	145	38	3	3	1	19	6	3	.262
Randy Jackson	34	111	25	4	3	3	13	6	4	.225
Emil Verban	45	37	4	1	0	0	7	1	0	.108
Carmen Mauro	62	185	42	4	3	1	19	10	3	.227
Hal Jeffcoat	66	179	42	13	1	2	21	18	7	.235
Ron Northey	53	114	32	9	0	4	11	20	0	.281
Hank Edwards	41	110	40	11	1	2	13	21	0	.364
Rube Walker	74	213	49	7	1	6	19	16	0	.230
Carl Sawatski	38	103	18	1	0	1	4	7	0	.175
Bob Scheffing	12	16	3	1	0	0	0	1	0	.188
Harry Chiti	3	6	2	0	0	0	0	0	0	.333
Pitchers										
Bob Rush	40	90	15	2	0	1	6	5	1	.167
Johnny Schmitz	39	67	8	2	0	0	3	5	0	.119
Paul Minner	43	65	14	0	1	1	6	7	0	.215
Monk Dubiel	39	45	9	2	0	0	4	0	0	.200
Frank Hiller	38	44	5	0	0	0	2	1	0	.114
Doyle Lade	34	35	10	2	0	0	5	1	0	.286
Johnny Klippstein	35	33	11	3	0	1	4	3	0	.333
Dutch Leonard	35	16	1	0	0	0	0	0	0	.063
Johnny Vander Meer	35	16	2	0	1	0	1	0	0	.125
Bill Voiselle	19	13	1	0	0	0	0	0	0	.077
Warren Hacker	5	5	0	0	0	0	0	0	0	.000
Andy Varga	1	0	0	0	0	0	0	0	0	—
		5,230	1,298	224	47	161	643	615	46	.248

1951

Record: 62–92
Finish: Eighth
Games Behind: 34½
Managers: Frankie Frisch, Phil Cavarretta

Otis Shepard, chief artist for the worldwide Wrigley gum empire and a member of the Cubs' board of directors, arrived in spring training with a rag doll he had designed, "Clubby Chubby." According to Shepard, it had magical properties that would lift the Cubs out of seventh place.

But all the hocus-pocus, including a blockbuster eight-player deal with Brooklyn and another midseason managerial change, couldn't prevent the Cubs from toppling back into the cellar in 1951, their third last-place finish in four years. Under the combined leadership of Frankie Frisch and Phil Cavarretta, they lost 92 games, one less than the club record.

Cavarretta, the first native Chicagoan to manage the Cubs, took command on July 25 with the understanding he would only finish the season and go to the minors for more managerial experience. Cavarretta agreed. Stan Hack, then managing the Cubs' Los Angeles farm team, would be at the helm in 1952.

The Cubs weren't doing too badly under Frisch. They won 21 of their first 41 games and were only ten games under .500 when Frisch departed. The dismissal may have been triggered by the increasing frustration. According to some of the players, Frisch had become a veritable Captain Bligh in the dugout and in the clubhouse.

Frisch had also refused to align his starting pitchers into a regular rotation, believing they should be ready whenever summoned. Often, a pitcher who had been bombed out early in a game didn't appear again for a week, sometimes longer. Cavarretta, in his first move, went to a four-man rotation.

The big deal with Brooklyn was consummated on June 15, the last day of the trading deadline, when the Dodgers were leading the league by six games: Andy Pafko, Johnny Schmitz, Wayne Terwilliger, and catcher Al Walker went east in exchange for catcher Bruce Edwards, second baseman Eddie Miksis, outfielder Gene Hermanski, and pitcher Joe Hatten.

A Chicago sportswriter insisted the Cubs must have been "chloroformed." Home and aboard, it was described as "the biggest steal" since the Boston Red Sox sold Babe Ruth to the Yankees. J. G. Taylor Spink, the influential editor and publisher of the *Sporting News,* in a copyrighted story, reasoned there had to be more to the deal, that the Dodgers, when the season ended, had agreed to send outfielder Duke Snider to the Cubs for $200,000.

The Cubs regarded Edwards as the key player, but he soon hurt his arm and had only 141 at bats. Only Miksis, who had been rusting on the Brooklyn bench, was a better than average performer. A singles hitter, he batted .266 but was outstanding in the field. Hermanski, expected to be an everyday regular, was a reserve outfielder. Hatten, used mostly in relief, was 2–6 with a fat 5.14 ERA.

Center fielder Frankie Baumholtz, excellent defensively, led the club with a .284 average. Sauer had 30 home runs and 89 RBIs. Third baseman "Handsome" Ransom Jackson was an offensive force: 16 home runs, 76 RBIs. Kevin "Chuck"

Connors, who later had an enormously successful career as a cowboy actor, got into 57 games at first base but was inadequate in the field and without power. Bob Rush had the most victories, 11. On August 21, Cavarretta's contract was extended through 1952.

	W	L	ERA	G	GS	CG	IP	H	BB	K
Bob Rush	11	12	3.83	37	29	12	211⅓	219	68	129
Paul Minner	6	(17)	3.79	33	28	14	201⅔	219	64	68
Cal McLish	4	10	4.45	30	17	5	145⅔	159	52	46
Frank Hiller	6	12	4.84	24	21	6	141⅓	147	31	50
Turk Lown	4	9	5.46	31	18	3	127	80	90	39
Bob Kelly	7	4	4.66	35	11	4	123⅔	130	55	48
Johnny Klippstein	6	6	4.29	35	11	1	123⅔	121	53	56
Dutch Leonard	10	6	2.64	41	1	0	81⅓	69	28	30
Bob Schultz	3	6	5.24	17	10	2	77⅓	75	51	27
Joe Hatten	2	6	5.14	23	6	1	75¼	82	37	23
Monk Dubiel	2	2	2.30	22	0	0	54⅔	46	22	19
Johnny Schmitz	1	2	8.00	8	3	0	18	22	15	6
Andy Varga	0	0	3.00	2	0	0	3	2	6	1
Warren Hacker	0	0	13.50	2	0	0	1⅓	3	0	2
	62	92	4.34	340	155	48	1,385⅔	1,374	572	544

Shutouts: Minner 3, Hiller 2, Rush 2, Klippstein 1, Lown 1, McLish 1.

	G	AB	H	2B	3B	HR	R	RBI	SB	AVG
Regulars										
1B Chuck Connors	66	201	48	5	1	2	16	18	4	.239
2B Eddie Miksis	102	421	112	13	3	4	48	35	11	.266
SS Roy Smalley	79	238	55	7	4	8	24	31	0	.231
3B Randy Jackson	145	557	153	24	6	16	78	76	14	.275
RF Hal Jeffcoat	113	278	76	20	2	4	44	27	8	.273
CF Frankie Baumholtz	146	560	159	28	10	2	62	50	5	.284
LF Hank Sauer	141	525	138	19	4	30	77	89	2	.263
C Smoky Burgess	94	219	55	4	2	2	21	20	2	.251
Substitutes										
Phil Cavarretta	89	206	64	7	1	6	24	28	0	.311
Wayne Terwilliger	50	192	41	6	0	0	26	10	3	.214
Dee Fondy	49	170	46	7	2	3	23	20	5	.271
Jack Cusick	65	164	29	3	2	2	16	16	2	.177
Bob Ramazzotti	73	158	39	5	2	1	13	15	0	.247
Bill Serena	13	39	13	3	1	1	8	4	0	.333
Fred Richards	10	27	8	2	0	0	1	4	0	.296
Gene Hermanski	75	231	65	12	1	3	28	20	3	.281
Andy Pafko	49	178	47	5	3	12	26	35	1	.264
Bob Borkowski	58	89	14	1	0	0	9	10	0	.157
Carmen Mauro	13	29	5	1	0	0	3	3	0	.172
Bruce Edwards	51	141	33	9	2	3	19	17	1	.234
Mickey Owen	58	125	23	6	0	0	10	15	1	.184
Rube Walker	37	107	25	4	0	2	9	5	0	.234
Harry Chiti	9	31	11	2	0	0	1	5	0	.355
Pitchers										
Paul Minner	36	71	18	4	0	1	8	6	0	.254
Bob Rush	37	68	13	2	0	0	5	2	0	.191
Frank Hiller	24	48	6	0	0	0	4	2	1	.125
Cal McLish	31	42	5	0	1	0	2	1	0	.119
Turk Lown	31	39	8	1	0	0	4	1	0	.205
Johnny Klippstein	35	37	4	0	0	1	1	4	0	.108
Bob Kelly	35	31	5	0	0	0	1	0	0	.161
Bob Schultz	17	29	4	0	0	0	2	1	0	.138
Dutch Leonard	41	21	0	0	0	0	1	1	0	.000
Joe Hatten	23	17	4	0	0	0	0	1	0	.235
Monk Dubiel	22	12	0	0	0	0	0	0	0	.000
Johnny Schmitz	8	6	1	0	0	0	0	0	0	.167
Warren Hacker	2	0	0	0	0	0	0	0	0	—
Andy Varga	2	0	0	0	0	0	0	0	0	—
	5,307	1,327	200	47	103	614	572	63		.250

1952

Record: 77–77
Finish: Fifth
Games Behind: 19½
Manager: Phil Cavarretta

The Cubs switched their spring training base to Mesa, Arizona, in 1952, and the local chamber of commerce, delighted with the presence of a major league club, announced it would present a share of a gold mine in the magnificent Superstition Mountains to the player who hit the first home run. Harvey Gentry, a slender outfielder who didn't make the club, won the prize and was given a document certifying his claim.

But the most significant citation, the NL's Most Valuable Player trophy, was captured by Hank Sauer, who had a blockbuster year: 37 home runs, tied with Ralph Kiner for the league lead, and 121 runs batted in, which topped both leagues. Sauer also led the NL to victory in the All-Star Game in Philadelphia's Shibe Park with a rooftop home run, previously the private preserve of Jimmy Foxx.

The Cubs finished fifth, with a 77–77 record, their best showing in the last six years. Owner Philip Wrigley, inadvertently, may have been entitled to an assist. At a January press conference in Chicago, Wrigley embarrassed player personnel director Wid Mathews when he interrupted him while he was predicting that the Cubs would have a big season and that catcher Bruce Edwards, who came from the Dodgers in the Pafko deal, would be completely recovered from a sore arm and en route to stardom.

Upset by the buttery prediction, Wrigley said, "I believe it's about time we stopped our daydreaming and wishful thinking and faced things as they are. At the moment, I regard Edwards as no more than a patched-up ballplayer out of whom we hope to get as much service as possible until we can get somebody better."

Two months later, in the midst of spring training, Leo Durocher, then managing the Giants, also put the knock to Mathews. "The Cubs have only two good players, Eddie Miksis and Ransom Jackson," Durocher said, "and nobody else in sight who might help." Asked about Sauer, Durocher replied, "Well, he's Hank Sauer. He runs hot and cold."

Except for a minor September slump, Sauer was hot throughout. He led Kiner in the home run race for all but two days, and for the first time—in response to the "Boudreau shift," which stacked the infield and outfield to the left side—he began hitting to the opposite field. On June 14, Sauer led the league in batting with a .349 average. Four days later, in the Cubs' 50th game, he had 18 home runs and 58 RBIs. He also had his second career three-home run game, both against Curt Simmons of the Phillies, two years apart.

Center fielder Frank Baumholtz, disabled twice with injuries—he appeared in only 103 games—batted .325, second in the league. Dee Fondy, now the regular first baseman, was second to Sauer with 10 home runs and 67 RBIs. Catcher Maurice Daily "Toby" Atwell, the only rookie selected on either of the All-Star teams, batted .290. To conceal his balding dome, the 28-year-old Atwell kept his head covered; his teammates called him Mr. Hat.

Slugger Hank Sauer, the "Mayor of Wrigley Field," with some young admirers

Bob Rush led the pitchers with a 17–13 record. Warren Hacker, who didn't break into the rotation until June 7, was 15–9, with a 2.58 ERA. A control pitcher, Hacker had five shutouts and issued only 31 walks in 185 innings, an average of 1.5 for every nine innings. Left-hander Paul Minner won 14 games and Johnny Klippstein nine. Ancient Dutch Leonard, 42, anchored the bullpen: 45 appearances, all in relief, 11 saves, two victories, and a club-leading 2.16 ERA.

	W	L	ERA	G	GS	CG	IP	H	BB	K
Bob Rush	17	13	2.70	34	32	17	250⅓	205	81	157
Johnny Klippstein	9	14	4.44	41	25	7	202⅔	208	89	110
Warren Hacker	15	9	2.58	33	20	12	185	144	31	84
Paul Minner	14	9	3.74	28	27	12	180⅔	180	54	61
Turk Lown	4	11	4.37	33	19	5	156⅔	154	93	73
Bob Kelly	4	9	3.59	31	15	3	125⅓	114	46	50
Bob Schultz	6	3	4.01	29	5	1	74	63	51	31
Willie Ramsdell	2	3	2.42	19	4	0	67	41	24	30
Dutch Leonard	2	2	2.16	45	0	0	66⅔	56	24	37
Joe Hatten	4	4	6.08	13	8	2	50⅓	65	25	15
Dick Manville	0	0	7.94	11	0	0	17	25	12	6
Vern Fear	0	0	7.88	4	0	0	8	9	3	4
Cal Howe	0	0	0.00	1	0	0	2	0	1	2
Monk Dubiel	0	0	0.00	1	0	0	⅔	1	0	1
	77	77	3.58	323	155	59	1,386⅓	1,265	534	661

Shutouts: Hacker 5, Rush 4, Kelly 2, Klippstein 2, Minner 2.

	G	AB	H	2B	3B	HR	R	RBI	SB	AVG
Regulars										
1B Dee Fondy	145	554	166	21	9	10	69	67	13	.300
2B Eddie Miksis	93	383	89	20	1	2	44	19	4	.232
SS Roy Smalley	87	261	58	14	1	5	36	30	0	.222
3B Randy Jackson	116	379	88	8	5	9	44	34	6	.232
RF Frankie Baumholtz	103	409	133	17	4	4	59	35	5	.325
CF Hal Jeffcoat	102	297	65	17	2	4	29	30	7	.219
LF Hank Sauer	151	567	153	31	3	(37)	89	(121)	1	.270
C Toby Atwell	107	362	105	16	3	2	36	31	2	.290
Substitutes										
Bill Serena	122	390	107	21	5	15	49	61	1	.274
Tommy Brown	61	200	64	11	0	3	24	24	1	.320
Bob Ramazzotti	50	183	52	5	3	1	26	12	3	.284
Phil Cavarretta	41	63	15	1	1	1	7	8	0	.238
Leon Brinkopf	9	22	4	0	0	0	1	2	0	.182
Bud Hardin	3	7	1	0	0	0	1	0	0	.143
Bob Addis	93	292	86	13	2	1	38	20	4	.295
Gene Hermanski	99	275	70	6	0	4	28	34	2	.255
Harry Chiti	32	113	31	5	0	5	14	13	0	.274
Bruce Edwards	50	94	23	2	2	1	7	12	0	.245
Johnny Pramesa	22	46	13	1	0	1	1	5	0	.283
Ron Northey	1	1	0	0	0	0	0	0	0	.000
Bob Usher	1	0	0	0	0	0	0	0	0	—
Pitchers										
Bob Rush	34	96	28	5	1	0	5	15	0	.292
Paul Minner	29	64	15	5	1	1	8	5	0	.234
Johnny Klippstein	41	63	11	1	1	1	3	9	0	.175
Warren Hacker	34	58	7	0	0	0	1	4	1	.121
Turk Lown	33	50	7	1	1	0	3	2	0	.140
Bob Kelly	31	37	8	0	0	0	2	1	0	.216
Willie Ramsdell	19	18	1	1	0	0	0	0	0	.056
Bob Schultz	29	18	4	1	0	0	2	1	0	.222
Joe Hatten	17	15	1	0	0	0	2	0	0	.067
Dutch Leonard	45	10	2	0	0	0	0	0	0	.200
Dick Manville	11	2	1	0	0	0	0	0	0	.500
Vern Fear	4	1	0	0	0	0	0	0	0	.000
Monk Dubiel	1	0	0	0	0	0	0	0	0	—
Cal Howe	1	0	0	0	0	0	0	0	0	—
	5,330	1,408	223	45	107	628	595	50		.264

1953

Record: 65–89
Finish: Seventh
Games Behind: 40
Manager: Phil Cavarretta

It was September 17, 1953, in Wrigley Field; the Cubs were in seventh place, 37 games out of the lead, mopping up another dreary season. They unveiled their first black player, a 22-year-old, 160-pound shortstop purchased for $25,000 from the Kansas City Monarchs. It was an undistinguished debut: 0-for-3 with a walk. Three days later, in St. Louis, he hit a home run off Gerry Staley.

It was the first of 512 major league home runs for Ernie Banks, who for the next two decades, and beyond, was Mr. Cub. Banks played in all of the club's last 10 games, batted .314, with two home runs and six runs batted in, and began to set the first of his many records: 424 games without a miss, the most ever from the start of a major league career.

Gene Baker, six years older, with four full seasons in the club's farm system, was the first black player signed to a Cub contract. He was with the Cubs in spring training in 1953 but returned to Los Angeles before the regular season began. Also a shortstop, he made his big league bow on September 20, as a pinch hitter, and batted .227 in seven games. He was Banks' double-play partner for the next three seasons.

There was another significant day during the 1953 Cub season. On June 4 slugger Ralph Kiner, the National League's highest salaried player at $75,000 a year, who in the

seven previous seasons had led or tied for the National League in home runs, was acquired from Pittsburgh in a 10-player deal.

Kiner, pitcher Howard Pollet, catcher Joe Garagiola, and infielder-outfielder George Metkovich came to the Cubs in exchange for outfielders Gene Hermanski and Bob Addis, infielders Preston Ward and Gene Freese, catcher Toby Atwell, and pitcher Bob Schultz plus an estimated $200,000 in cash.

Except for Schultz, all of the departing Cubs had been in the Brooklyn farm system when Branch Rickey was running the Dodgers. Now in command in Pittsburgh, Rickey was reclaiming his players. The deal didn't help the Pirates. They lost 104 games and finished last, 15 games behind the Cubs. Neither did it vault the Cubs into contention, but it heightened the excitement. Kiner and Sauer were expected to be the most devastating duo since Hack Wilson and Gabby Hartnett hit 93 home runs in 1930.

In the field it presented a problem. Both were slow-footed left fielders. Sauer shifted to right. Frankie Baumholtz, who had good range, patrolled the middle and was constantly on the run. Once he caught a fly ball in foul territory. On June 21, for the first time, Kiner (batting third) and Sauer (fourth) connected for back-to-back home runs.

But neither approached expectations. Kiner had 28 home runs for the Cubs, Sauer 19, a career low. Sauer suffered three separate hand injuries and appeared in only 108 games. Infielders Ransom Jackson and Dee Fondy picked up some of the slack. Fondy, who led the club with a .309 average, hit 18 home runs, Jackson 19.

The Cubs were in seventh place continuously from June 28 until the end of the season. All the rotation starters had losing records: Hacker 12–19, led the league in losses; through June 13, he was 1–10, the victim of five shutouts. Minner was 12–15, Klippstein 10–11, Rush 9–14. On May 4, manager Phil Cavarretta, 35, who surfaced in 1934, became the youngest 20-year man in big league history. Two weeks before the season, the Boston Braves moved to Milwaukee. The Cubs were now the only original NL team to play in the same city without interruption.

Ernie Banks (left) and Gene Baker, who broke the Cub color line

	W	L	ERA	G	GS	CG	IP	H	BB	K
Warren Hacker	12	(19)	4.38	39	32	9	221⅔	225	54	106
Paul Minner	12	15	4.21	31	27	9	201	227	40	64
Johnny Klippstein	10	11	4.83	48	20	5	167⅔	169	107	113
Bob Rush	9	14	4.54	29	28	8	166⅔	177	66	84
Turk Lown	8	7	5.16	49	12	2	148⅓	166	84	76
Howie Pollet	5	6	4.12	25	16	2	111⅓	120	44	45
Bubba Church	4	5	5.00	27	11	1	104⅓	115	49	47
Dutch Leonard	2	3	4.60	45	0	0	62⅓	72	24	27
Duke Simpson	1	2	8.00	30	1	0	45	60	25	21
Jim Willis	2	1	3.12	13	3	2	43⅓	37	17	15
Sheldon Jones	0	2	5.40	22	2	0	38⅓	47	16	9
Bob Kelly	0	1	9.53	14	0	0	17	27	9	6
Bob Schultz	0	2	5.40	7	2	0	11⅔	13	11	4
Fred Baczewski	0	0	6.30	9	0	0	10	10	6	3
Don Elston	0	1	14.40	2	1	0	5	11	0	2
Bill Moisan	0	0	5.40	3	0	0	5	5	2	1
	65	89	4.79	393	155	38	1,359	1,491	554	623

Shutouts: Minner 2, Rush 1.

	G	AB	H	2B	3B	HR	R	RBI	SB	AVG
Regulars										
1B Dee Fondy	150	595	184	24	11	18	79	78	10	.309
2B Eddie Miksis	142	577	145	17	6	8	61	39	13	.251
SS Roy Smalley	82	253	63	9	0	6	20	25	0	.249
3B Randy Jackson	139	498	142	22	8	19	61	66	8	.285
RF Hank Sauer	108	395	104	16	5	19	61	60	0	.263
CF Frankie Baumholtz	133	520	159	36	7	3	75	25	3	.306
LF Ralph Kiner	117	414	117	14	2	28	73	87	1	.283
C Clyde McCullough	77	229	59	3	2	6	21	23	0	.258
Substitutes										
Bill Serena	93	275	69	10	5	10	30	52	0	.251
Tommy Brown	65	138	27	7	1	2	19	13	1	.196
Bob Ramazzotti	26	39	6	2	0	0	3	4	0	.154
Ernie Banks	10	35	11	1	1	2	3	6	0	.314
Gene Baker	7	22	5	1	0	0	1	0	1	.227
Hal Jeffcoat	106	183	43	3	1	4	22	22	5	.235
Catfish Melkovich	61	124	29	9	0	2	19	12	2	.234
Preston Ward	33	100	23	5	0	4	10	12	3	.230
Gene Hermanski	18	40	6	1	0	0	1	1	0	.150
Dale Talbot	8	30	10	0	1	0	5	0	1	.333
Bob Addis	10	12	2	1	0	0	2	1	0	.167
Paul Schramka	2	0	0	0	0	0	0	0	0	—
Joe Garagiola	74	228	62	9	4	1	21	21	0	.272
Toby Atwell	24	74	17	2	0	1	10	8	0	.230
Carl Sawatski	43	59	13	3	0	1	5	5	0	.220
Phil Cavarretta	27	21	6	3	0	0	3	3	0	.286
Pitchers										
Warren Hacker	42	78	17	1	1	0	8	4	0	.218
Paul Minner	31	68	15	1	1	1	5	6	0	.221
Johnny Klippstein	48	58	9	2	0	1	5	4	0	.155
Bob Rush	29	54	6	0	1	0	2	5	0	.111
Turk Lown	49	48	6	1	0	0	3	2	0	.125
Bubba Church	27	33	7	0	0	1	1	1	0	.212
Howie Pollet	25	31	4	0	0	0	2	0	0	.129
Dutch Leonard	45	10	3	1	0	0	0	2	0	.300
Jim Willis	13	9	0	0	0	0	1	1	0	.000
Duke Simpson	30	8	2	0	0	0	1	0	0	.250
Sheldon Jones	22	7	0	0	0	0	0	0	0	.000
Bob Schultz	7	3	0	0	0	0	0	0	0	.000
Fred Baczewski	9	2	1	0	0	0	0	0	0	.500
Don Elston	2	1	0	0	0	0	0	0	0	.000
Bob Kelly	14	1	0	0	0	0	0	0	0	.000
Bill Moisan	3	0	0	0	0	0	0	0	0	—
		5,272	1,372	204	57	137	633	588	49	.260

1954

Record: 64–90
Finish: Seventh
Games Behind: 33
Manager: Stan Hack

Bob Zick, a rookie knuckleballer out of Chicago, was recalled from Beaumont of the Texas League on July 28, 1954, when the Cubs, as usual, were languishing in seventh place. According to Dick Young of the *New York Daily News*, Zick approached manager Stan Hack and said, "I'm Zick." Replied Hack, "I don't feel so good myself."

It was another disappointing season but with an unusual beginning. Manager Phil Cavarretta was fired on March 29 when the club was still in spring training, dismissed because he had the courage to tell the truth to owner Phil Wrigley. In a conversation with Wrigley two weeks earlier, Cavarretta said the Cubs were doomed to another second-division finish because of a lack of quality pitching.

Wrigley charged Cavarretta with "negative thinking." Said Wrigley: "I believe managers should be moved just like players. Sometimes a manager might go a little stale, but he can still do a good job for you somewhere else. So why can't you capitalize on his experience and keep him in the system?" Cavarretta moved on, but the incident was an indication of things to come. Seven years later Wrigley would adopt an ill-fated system of rotating managers.

Hack succeeded Cavarretta. For seven years, the last three at Los Angeles, Hack had been managing Cub farm teams. At the season's end it was obvious Cavarretta's appraisal had been on the mark. The Cubs lost 90 games, finished 33 games out, and had a 4.51 ERA, second worst in the league.

Bob Rush, 13–15, was the only starter with more than 11 wins. Paul Minner was 11–11, Warren Hacker 6–13, Johnny Klippstein 4–11 and Howard Pollet 8–10. Combined, they were 42–60. Turk Lown, who replaced Dutch Leonard as the primary closer, was equally ineffective: 0–2, with no saves and a 6.14 ERA. The only pitcher above .500 was left-hander Jim Davis, who wasn't with the club in spring training.

Hal Jeffcoat, a weak-hitting outfielder, was converted into a pitcher and appeared in 43 games, 40 out of the bullpen, but had only modest success, a 5.19 ERA with five wins and six losses. Garagiola and Elvin Tappe shared the catching. Tappe, who was to become a Wrigley favorite, was strong defensively but was without power and batted only .185.

Hank Sauer, recovered from injuries, led the offense with a .288 average, 41 home runs, a career high, and 103 runs batted in. Ralph Kiner was in decline: 22 home runs, at that point a career low, and 73 RBIs. Ernie Banks, in his first full major league season, was being acknowledged as the league's best all-around shortstop. Banks hit 19 home runs and drove in 79 runs.

Third baseman Ransom Jackson, who got off to a glorious start, also had 19 home runs but was sidelined for a month with blood poisoning in his right hand. Before being stricken, Jackson was batting .293 with 63 RBIs. He returned on August 24; in the remaining 30 games he hit .202 with no home runs and four RBIs.

Wid Mathews, who had captured Wrigley's ear with his

fanciful optimism, had predicted the Cubs would be 40 percent better than in 1953. Mathews' "Five-Year Plan" was a disaster. The Cubs never finished higher than fifth, and then only once. Wrigley anointed 75-year-old Clarence Rowland, former president of the Pacific Coast League, as an executive vice president who would function as the general manager. Matthews kept his title as director of player personnel, but his responsibility was limited to the farm system.

	W	L	ERA	G	GS	CG	IP	H	BB	K
Bob Rush	13	15	3.77	33	32	11	236⅓	213	103	124
Paul Minner	11	11	3.96	32	29	12	218	236	50	79
Warren Hacker	6	13	4.25	39	18	4	158⅔	157	37	80
Johnny Klippstein	4	11	5.29	36	21	4	148	155	96	69
Howie Pollet	8	10	3.58	20	20	4	128⅓	131	54	58
Jim Davis	11	7	3.52	46	12	2	127⅔	114	51	58
Hal Jeffcoat	5	6	5.19	43	3	1	104	110	58	35
Dave Cole	3	8	5.36	18	14	2	84	74	62	37
Bill Tremel	1	2	4.21	33	0	0	51⅓	45	28	21
Jim Brosnan	1	0	9.45	18	0	0	33⅓	44	18	17
Jim Willis	0	1	3.91	14	1	0	23	22	18	5
Turk Lown	0	2	6.14	15	0	0	22	23	15	16
Bob Zick	0	0	8.27	8	0	0	16⅓	23	7	9
Bubba Church	1	3	9.82	7	3	1	14⅔	21	13	8
Al Lary	0	0	3.00	1	1	0	6	3	7	4
John Pyecha	0	1	10.13	1	0	0	2⅔	4	2	2
	64	90	4.51	364	154	41	1,374⅓	1,375	619	622

Shutouts: Pollet 2, Cole 1, Hacker 1.

	G	AB	H	2B	3B	HR	R	RBI	SB	AVG
Regulars										
1B Dee Fondy	141	568	162	30	4	9	77	49	20	.285
2B Gene Baker	135	541	149	32	5	13	68	61	4	.275
SS Ernie Banks	154	593	163	19	7	19	70	79	6	.275
3B Randy Jackson	126	484	132	17	6	19	77	67	2	.273
RF Hank Sauer	142	520	150	18	1	41	98	103	2	.288

Phil Cavarretta (left) and Stan Hack, his successor as the Cub manager

	G	AB	H	2B	3B	HR	R	RBI	SB	AVG
CF Dale Talbot	114	403	97	15	4	1	45	19	3	.241
LF Ralph Kiner	147	557	159	36	5	22	88	73	2	.285
C Joe Garagiola	63	153	43	5	0	5	16	21	0	.281
Substitutes										
Eddie Miksis	38	99	20	3	0	2	9	3	1	.202
Steve Bilko	47	92	22	8	1	4	11	12	0	.239
Vern Morgan	24	64	15	2	0	0	3	2	0	.234
Bill Serena	41	63	10	0	1	4	8	13	0	.159
Chris Kitsos	1	0	0	0	0	0	0	0	0	—
Frankie Baumholtz	90	303	90	12	6	4	38	28	1	.297
Hal Rice	51	72	11	0	0	0	5	5	0	.153
Luis Marquez	17	12	1	0	0	0	2	0	3	.083
Don Robertson	14	6	0	0	0	0	2	0	0	.000
Walker Cooper	57	158	49	10	2	7	21	32	0	.310
El Tappe	46	119	22	3	0	0	5	4	0	.185
Clyde McCullough	31	81	21	7	0	3	9	17	0	.259
Jim Fanning	11	38	7	0	0	0	2	1	0	.184
Bruce Edwards	4	3	0	0	0	0	1	1	0	.000
Pitchers										
Bob Rush	33	83	23	4	1	2	6	9	0	.277
Paul Minner	33	76	13	3	0	2	7	14	0	.171
Warren Hacker	43	55	13	0	1	0	4	6	0	.236
Howie Pollet	20	47	13	2	0	0	6	4	0	.277
Johnny Klippstein	36	45	6	1	0	0	2	3	0	.133
Jim Davis	46	32	2	0	0	0	3	0	0	.063
Hal Jeffcoat	56	31	8	2	1	1	13	6	2	.258
Dave Cole	19	28	6	0	0	1	1	4	0	.214
Jim Brosnan	18	8	1	0	0	0	1	2	0	.125
Bill Tremel	33	8	2	0	0	0	0	2	0	.250
Bubba Church	8	5	0	0	0	0	0	0	0	.000
Jim Willis	14	5	0	0	0	0	0	0	0	.000
Bob Zick	10	4	1	0	0	0	2	0	0	.250
Al Lary	2	2	1	0	0	0	0	0	0	.500
John Pyecha	1	1	0	0	0	0	0	0	0	.000
Turk Lown	16	0	0	0	0	0	0	0	0	—
		5,359	1,412	229	45	159	700	640	46	.263

1955

Record: 72–81
Finish: Sixth
Games Behind: 26
Manager: Stan Hack

Like Wid Mathews, Clarence "Pants" Rowland, the new general manager, majored in good cheer, and he was chided in the press as the Cub vice president in charge of "fine spirit." Two weeks after the players had assembled in Mesa, the 76-year-old Rowland said, "This is the best looking team I have ever seen in spring training, bar none."

Rowland, who had managed the 1917 White Sox, the last Chicago club to win a World Series, was still smiling seven months later. The Cubs finished sixth in 1955, 26 games behind the champion Dodgers, but were only 4½ games out of fourth place, the closest they had been to the first division since 1946.

For this lofty state, two players were responsible. Outfielder Bob Speake, who had a torrid month of May, and Ernie Banks, who was ablaze throughout. Banks hit 44 home runs, most ever in either league by a shortstop, and most by a Cub since Hack Wilson's 56 in 1930. Banks also had his first three-home-run game and hit five grand-slam home runs, a major league record that was broken 32 years later by Don Mattingly of the Yankees.

Veteran catcher Clyde McCullough likened Banks' short stroke to Jack Dempsey's knockout punch. "He doesn't swing the bat around very far," McCullough observed. "But he is quick and has strong wrists. This way he can take a little more time to judge a pitch."

"Toothpick" Sam Jones, a 29-year-old rookie acquired from Cleveland in a winter deal for Ralph Kiner, led the pitchers with 14 victories, including a breathtaking no-hitter May 12 against the Cardinals, the first on Cub soil since 1917. Jones faced 31 batters and issued seven walks. The last three passes came with no outs in the ninth inning, bringing the tying run to the plate. Jones recovered by striking out Dick Groat, Roberto Clemente, and Frank Thomas on 12 pitches—three to Groat, five to Clemente, four to Thomas.

Speake bloomed early. He had hit only .264 with Des Moines the previous season and joined the club as a backup outfielder. Prior to May 2, he had eight at bats. He then replaced the slumping Hank Sauer in the lineup with heroic results. At the end of May, Speake was hitting .304, with 10 home runs, four doubles, two triples, and 31 RBIs.

Then came the awful month of June, which in the Cub lexicon rhymes with "swoon." In the 12 games from June 1 to 11 his average plunged 43 points to .261, and during this stretch he struck out seven times in 17 at bats. He was benched the next day, hit only two home runs thereafter, and finished the season at .218. His 12 home runs were a Cub record for a rookie.

The Cubs started well and won 20 of 29 games in May, easily their best month. Speake supplied the principal blow in 10 of these victories. They were in second place after the Memorial Day action, only six games out of the lead. Their worst slump, 15 losses in 16 games, was sandwiched around the All-Star break. They lost 10 of 11 in mid-August and were eliminated on August 30.

For the second year in a row there were no .300 hitters. Nonetheless, the club had good power, seven players with 11 or more home runs. Used sparingly, Sauer batted .211, a career low, with only 12 home runs. He hit number one on May 2 but didn't connect again until June 29, a 56-game drought. Owner Wrigley expressed delight that the team was on the rise—eight more victories than the previous season. A semipro mechanic, Wrigley was applauded in spring training when he repaired the Iron Mike pitching machine.

	G	AB	H	2B	3B	HR	R	RBI	SB	AVG
Regulars										
1B Dee Fondy	150	574	152	23	8	17	69	65	8	.265
2B Gene Baker	154	609	163	29	7	11	82	52	9	.268
SS Ernie Banks	154	596	176	29	9	44	98	117	9	.295
3B Randy Jackson	138	499	132	13	7	21	73	70	0	.265
RF Jim King	113	301	77	12	3	11	43	45	2	.256
CF Eddie Miksis	131	481	113	14	2	9	52	41	3	.235
LF Hank Sauer	79	261	55	8	1	12	29	28	0	.211
C Harry Chiti	113	338	78	6	1	11	24	41	0	.231
Substitutes										
Owen Friend	6	10	1	0	0	0	0	0	0	.100
Vern Morgan	7	7	1	0	0	0	1	1	0	.143
Frankie Baumholtz	105	280	81	12	5	1	23	27	0	.289
Bob Speake	95	261	57	9	5	12	36	43	3	.218
Jim Bolger	64	160	33	5	4	0	19	7	2	.206
Lloyd Merriman	72	145	31	6	1	1	15	8	1	.214
Ted Tappe	23	50	13	2	0	4	12	10	0	.260
Gale Wade	9	33	6	1	0	1	5	1	0	.182
Walker Cooper	54	111	31	8	1	7	11	15	0	.279
Clyde McCullough	44	81	16	0	0	0	7	10	0	.198
Jim Fanning	5	10	0	0	0	0	0	0	0	.000
El Tappe	2	0	0	0	0	0	0	0	0	—
Al Lary	4	0	0	0	0	0	1	0	0	—
Pitchers										
Bob Rush	33	82	9	2	0	1	6	5	0	.110
Sam Jones	36	77	14	1	0	0	2	5	0	.182
Warren Hacker	35	72	18	3	1	0	6	3	0	.250
Paul Minner	22	56	13	2	0	0	5	1	0	.232
Jim Davis	42	37	1	0	0	0	1	1	0	.027
Hal Jeffcoat	52	23	4	0	0	1	3	1	0	.174
Howie Pollet	24	15	6	2	0	0	0	0	0	.400
Harry Perkowski	26	13	2	0	0	0	2	0	0	.154
Dave Hillman	26	10	1	0	0	0	1	0	0	.100
John Andre	22	9	1	0	0	0	0	0	0	.111
Bill Tremel	23	7	2	0	0	0	0	0	0	.286
Hy Cohen	7	3	0	0	0	0	0	0	0	.000
Don Kaiser	11	2	0	0	0	0	0	0	0	.000
Bubba Church	3	1	0	0	0	0	0	0	0	.000
Vincente Amor	4	0	0	0	0	0	0	0	0	—
Bob Thorpe	2	0	0	0	0	0	0	0	0	—
		5,214	1,287	187	55	164	626	597	37	.247

1956

Record: 60–94
Finish: Eighth
Games Behind: 33
Manager: Stan Hack

Wid Mathews' "Five-Year Plan" was the "Seven-Year Itch" in 1956 as the Cubs returned to last place. They lost a record 94 games, were never in first place, occupied second for only 24 hours, in the early skirmishing, and were last or next to last 102 days of the 158-day season. More embarrassing, the 94th loss was inflicted by Cincinnati's Hal Jeffcoat, who the season before had been the Cubs' most effective pitcher.

Mathews, who finally acknowledged he was wary about his cheery predictions, couldn't resist. "I am looking for the Cubs to crash into the first division," he insisted. Instead, it was the tenth consecutive season in the second division, the fourth time in the cellar during this sequence.

Hank Sauer, the most popular Cub since Bill Nicholson, was traded to the Cardinals on March 30 for outfielder Pete Whisenant, who in turn was traded at the season's end. Convinced a "holler guy" was needed in the infield, the Cubs acquired third baseman Don Hoak from Brooklyn. Hoak hollered, but his bat was silent. He hit .215; on May 2 against the Giants he struck out six times, equaling the major league record.

	W	L	ERA	G	GS	CG	IP	H	BB	K
Sam Jones	14	(20)	4.10	36	34	12	241⅓	175	(185)	(198)
Bob Rush	13	11	3.50	33	33	14	234	204	73	130
Warren Hacker	11	15	4.27	35	30	13	213	202	43	80
Paul Minner	9	9	3.48	22	22	7	157⅔	173	47	53
Jim Davis	7	11	4.44	42	16	0	133⅔	122	58	62
Hal Jeffcoat	8	6	2.95	50	1	0	100⅔	107	53	32
Howie Pollet	4	3	5.61	24	7	1	61	62	27	27
Dave Hillman	0	0	5.31	25	3	0	57⅔	63	25	23
Harry Perkowski	3	4	5.29	25	4	0	47⅔	53	25	28
John Andre	0	1	5.80	22	3	0	45	45	28	19
Bill Tremel	3	0	3.72	23	0	0	38⅔	33	18	13
Don Kaiser	0	0	5.40	11	0	0	18⅓	20	5	11
Hy Cohen	0	0	7.94	7	1	0	17	28	10	4
Vincente Amor	0	1	4.50	4	0	0	6	11	3	3
Bubba Church	0	0	5.40	2	0	0	3⅓	4	1	3
Bob Thorpe	0	0	3.00	2	0	0	3	4	0	0
	72	81	4.17	363	154	47	1,378⅓	1,306	601	686

Shutouts: Jones 4, Rush 3, Minner 1, Pollet 1.

There was more. Russ "Monk" Meyer, a 30-year-old right-handed pitcher who had a deserved reputation as a "Cub Killer," rejoined the Cubs in the same deal with the Dodgers. Since being traded in the fall of 1948, Meyer had had incredible success against the Cubs: 24 wins against only three losses. Upon arrival Meyer said, "At least I ought to repay them for all the times I've beaten them." He didn't. He was 1–6 and on September 1 was sold to Cincinnati.

In late May, after reliever Jim Hughes, 32, had climbed aboard, there were nine ex-Dodgers on the 25-man roster. The Cubs were now ridiculed as Brooklyn's B team. The son of a Chicago fire battalion chief, Hughes was 1–3 with no saves. His Cub debut was a disaster: home run, triple, two singles, and a walk in one-third of an inning.

Outfielder Walt Moryn was the only Brooklyn import who contributed to the hopeless cause. A husky, gregarious left-handed power hitter, Moryn was delighted with the opportunity to play every day. He drove in 67 runs and hit 23 home runs, second on the club to Ernie Banks' 28. Banks also led the club in batting, .297; Moryn was second at .285.

The Cubs scored the fewest runs in the league and were saddled with erratic pitching, especially from the starters. Bob Rush, 13–10, was the only starter to win in double figures. Sam Jones was 9–14 and for the second consecutive season led the league in walks and strikeouts. Closer Turk Lown, 9–8 with 13 saves, appeared in a club-record 61 games, all in relief.

Of the first 29 games played to a decision, the Cubs lost 21. Beginning on May 4, there was a stretch of 17 games in which the starter didn't go the distance. In mid-June, following Philip Wrigley's suggestion, oxygen was placed in the dugout "as a means of speedy restoration of energy after intensive periods of exercise."

On October 11, two weeks after the season had come to a welcome close, Wrigley decided the time had come for a change. Jim Gallagher resigned as business manager, and Matthews and field manager Stan Hack were fired, replaced by John Holland and Bob Scheffing, both of whom had been with the club's Los Angeles farm team. Charlie Grimm also returned for his fourth term with the club. The Cubs now led the league in vice presidents—Holland, Grimm, and holdover Clarence Rowland.

	W	L	ERA	G	GS	CG	IP	H	BB	K
Bob Rush	13	10	3.19	32	32	13	239⅔	210	59	104
Sam Jones	9	14	3.91	33	28	8	188⅔	155	(115)	(176)
Warren Hacker	3	13	4.66	34	24	4	168	190	44	65
Don Kaiser	4	9	3.59	27	22	5	150⅓	144	52	74
Jim Davis	5	7	3.66	46	11	2	120⅓	116	59	66
Turk Lown	9	8	3.58	61	0	0	110⅔	95	78	74
Vito Valentinetti	6	4	3.78	42	2	0	95⅓	84	36	26
Jim Brosnan	5	9	3.79	30	10	1	95	95	45	51
Russ Meyer	1	6	6.32	20	9	0	57	71	26	28
Moe Drabowsky	2	4	2.47	9	7	3	51	37	39	36
Paul Minner	2	5	6.89	10	9	1	47	60	19	14
Jim Hughes	1	3	5.16	25	1	0	45⅓	43	30	20
Dave Hillman	0	2	2.19	2	2	0	12⅓	11	5	6
Johnny Briggs	0	0	1.69	3	0	0	5⅓	5	4	1
George Piktuzis	0	0	7.20	2	0	0	5	6	2	3
Bill Tremel	0	0	13.50	1	0	0	⅔	3	0	0
	60	94	3.96	377	157	37	1,391⅔	1,325	613	744

Shutouts: Jones 2, Brosnan 1, Davis 1, Kaiser 1, Rush 1.

Pitchers Russ Meyer, Warren Hacker, Paul Minner, and Sad Sam Jones

	G	AB	H	2B	3B	HR	R	RBI	SB	AVG
Regulars										
1B Dee Fondy	137	543	146	22	9	9	52	46	9	.269
2B Gene Baker	140	546	141	23	3	12	65	57	4	.258
SS Ernie Banks	139	538	160	25	8	28	82	85	6	.297
3B Don Hoak	121	424	91	18	4	5	51	37	8	.215
RF Walt Moryn	147	529	151	27	3	23	69	67	4	.285
CF Pete Whisenant	103	314	75	16	3	11	37	46	8	.239
LF Monte Irvin	111	339	92	13	3	15	44	50	1	.271
C Hobie Landrith	111	312	69	10	3	4	22	32	0	.221
Substitutes										
Eddie Miksis	114	356	85	10	3	9	54	27	4	.239
Frank Kellert	71	129	24	3	1	4	10	17	0	.186
Jerry Kindall	32	55	9	1	1	0	7	0	1	.164
Ed Winceniak	15	17	2	0	0	0	1	0	0	.118
Jim King	118	317	79	13	2	15	32	54	1	.249
Solly Drake	65	215	55	9	1	2	29	15	9	.256
Gale Wade	10	12	0	0	0	0	0	0	0	.000
Harry Chiti	72	203	43	6	4	4	17	18	0	.212
Clyde McCullough	14	19	4	1	0	0	0	1	0	.211
Jim Fanning	1	4	1	0	0	0	0	0	0	.250
El Tappe	3	1	0	0	0	0	0	0	0	.000
Owen Friend	2	2	0	0	0	0	0	0	0	.000
Richie Myers	4	1	0	0	0	0	1	0	0	.000
Pitchers										
Bob Rush	38	82	8	1	0	0	6	2	0	.098
Sam Jones	33	57	10	0	0	0	3	1	0	.175
Warren Hacker	34	54	8	0	0	0	2	4	0	.148
Don Kaiser	27	47	2	0	0	0	1	1	0	.043
Jim Davis	46	28	5	0	0	0	3	0	0	.179
Turk Lown	61	23	5	0	1	1	2	2	0	.217
Jim Brosnan	30	22	4	1	0	0	2	0	0	.182
Vito Valentinetti	42	20	2	0	0	0	0	0	0	.100
Moe Drabowsky	9	16	4	0	0	0	1	0	0	.250
Russ Meyer	20	12	1	0	0	0	0	0	0	.083
Paul Minner	10	12	3	2	1	0	2	0	0	.250
Jim Hughes	25	7	2	1	0	0	2	1	0	.286
Dave Hilman	2	4	0	0	0	0	0	0	0	.000
Johnny Briggs	3	0	0	0	0	0	0	0	0	—
George Piktuzis	2	0	0	0	0	0	0	0	0	—
Bill Tremel	1	0	0	0	0	0	0	0	0	—
		5,260	1,281	202	50	142	597	563	55	.244

1957

Record: 62–92
Finish: Seventh (tie)
Games Behind: 33
Manager: Bob Scheffing

It was the year the Brooklyn Dodgers and New York Giants announced they were moving to California, but the Cub address remained the same in 1957: last place in the National League, which they shared with Pittsburgh, both straggling to the finish line with 62–92 records, 33 games out of the lead.

Still, a light appeared to be flickering at the end of the second-division tunnel principally because of the presence of rookie right-handers Dick Drott and Moe Drabowsky. Together, they won 28 games. With better support they might have won 40. Drott was 15–11, Drabowsky 13–15. Nobody else won more than six games.

Drott, a Cincinnati native, had the better stuff: a 90-mile-an-hour fastball and a hellacious curve, almost certain death to right-handed hitters. It came in high and tight and at the last instant split the plate at the knees. Dozens of hitters, including Willie Mays, took third strikes on their knees, after diving into the dirt.

At Wrigley Field on May 26, Drott had 15 strikeouts in the opener of a doubleheader against Milwaukee, two short of Dizzy Dean's league record. Hank Aaron was caught looking three times. Two months later, July 23 at the Polo Grounds,

two days after his 21st birthday, Drott fanned 14 Giants. Mays went down twice. The Cubs' previous single-game high was 13 by Lon Warneke in 1934.

Drabowsky was also a strikeout pitcher and, at the season's end, had 170 Ks, same as Drott, Drabowsky in 239⅔ innings, Drott in 229, second in the league behind Jack Sanford of Philadelphia, who won Rookie of the Year honors. Unlike Drott, who had ascended through the Cub system, Drabowsky, 22, signed for a $55,000 bonus out of Trinity College in Hartford, Connecticut. Drabowsky had a hard-luck first half but was 11–2 after the All-Star break.

The beneficient Philip Wrigley was so delighted he boosted Drott's salary in May from $6,000 to $15,000. Drabowsky was also awarded a sizable increase. Outfielders Chuck Tanner and Walt Moryn, and pitcher Dave Hillman had their salaries adjusted upward. To the dismay of the other owners, Wrigley, in reward for unanticipated achievement, had begun hiking salaries on the spot in the '30s, a practice subsequently discarded.

General manager John Holland, his rookie season in command, was a busy trader, almost always swapping veterans for younger players. The turnover was such that on May 1, after a big deal with the Pirates, only nine players remained from the '56 club. First baseman Dale Long and outfielder Lee Walls were acquired in the Pittsburgh trade for Dee Fondy and Gene Baker. Fondy and Long were almost the same age, but Walls was seven years younger than Baker.

Baker and Ernie Banks had been double-play partners for the previous three seasons, among the best in the league. But prior to Baker's departure Banks had been shifted to third base. Two months later, after 50 errorless games at the hot corner, Banks was back at short. It was typical of the unsettled lineup. The Cubs used 11 third basemen, six second basemen, and seven center fielders.

Banks finished strong after a sluggish start and drove in 102 runs, with 43 home runs, one fewer than Hank Aaron, who led the league. Long, who played a good first base, had

Frank Ernaga (right), who homered in his first major league at bat, and pitcher Moe Drabowsky

21 home runs and batted .305 in 123 games with the Cubs. Moryn had a five-hit game, hammered 19 home runs, and was second to Banks in RBIs with 88. Newcomer Cal Neeman, a catcher plucked out of the Yankee system in the winter draft, batted .258 but was outstanding on defense. Scheffing's contract was extended through the 1958 season.

	W	L	ERA	G	GS	CG	IP	H	BB	K
Moe Drabowsky	13	15	3.53	36	33	12	239⅔	214	94	170
Dick Drott	15	11	3.58	38	32	7	229	200	(129)	170
Bob Rush	6	16	4.38	31	29	5	205⅓	211	66	103
Don Elston	6	7	3.56	39	14	2	144	139	55	102
Dave Hillman	6	11	4.35	32	14	1	103⅓	115	37	53
Jim Brosnan	5	5	3.38	41	5	1	98⅔	79	46	73
Turk Lown	5	7	3.77	67	0	0	93	74	51	51
Tom Poholsky	1	7	4.93	28	11	1	84	117	22	28
Don Kaiser	2	6	5.00	20	13	1	72	91	28	23
Dick Littlefield	2	3	5.35	48	2	0	65⅔	76	37	51
Bob Anderson	0	1	7.71	8	0	0	16⅓	20	8	7
Elmer Singleton	0	1	6.75	5	2	0	13⅓	20	2	6
Vito Valentinetti	0	0	2.25	9	0	0	12	12	7	8
Jackie Collum	1	1	6.75	9	0	0	10⅔	8	9	7
Ed Mayer	0	0	5.87	3	1	0	7⅔	8	2	3
Johnny Briggs	0	1	12.46	3	0	0	4⅓	7	3	1
Glen Hobbie	0	0	10.38	2	0	0	4⅓	6	5	3
	62	92	4.13	419	156	30	1,403⅓	1,397	601	859

Shutouts: Drott 3, Drabowsky 2.

	G	AB	H	2B	3B	HR	R	RBI	SB	AVG
Regulars										
1B Dale Long	123	397	121	19	0	21	55	62	1	.305
2B Bobby Morgan	125	425	88	20	2	5	43	27	5	.207
3B Ernie Banks	156	594	169	34	6	43	113	102	8	.285
RF Walt Moryn	149	568	164	33	0	19	76	88	0	.289
CF Chuck Tanner	95	318	91	16	2	7	42	42	0	.286
LF Lee Walls	117	366	88	10	5	6	42	33	5	.240
C Cal Neeman	122	415	107	17	1	10	37	39	0	.258
Substitutes										
Bobby Adams	60	187	47	10	2	1	21	10	0	.251
Jerry Kindall	72	181	29	3	0	6	18	12	1	.160
Jack Littrell	61	153	29	4	2	1	8	13	0	.190
Casey Wise	43	106	19	3	1	0	12	7	0	.179
Dee Fondy	11	51	16	3	1	0	3	2	1	.314
Ed Winceniak	17	50	12	3	0	1	5	8	0	.240
Gene Baker	12	44	11	3	1	1	4	10	0	.250
John Goryl	9	38	8	2	0	0	7	1	0	.211
Ed Mickelson	6	12	0	0	0	0	0	1	0	.000
Bob Speake	129	418	97	14	5	16	65	50	5	.232
Jim Bolger	112	273	75	4	1	5	28	29	0	.275
Bob Will	70	112	25	3	0	1	13	10	1	.223
Bobby Del Greco	20	40	8	2	0	0	2	3	1	.200
Frank Ernaga	20	35	11	3	2	2	9	7	0	.314
Eddie Haas	14	24	5	1	0	0	1	4	0	.208
Bob Lennon	9	21	3	1	0	1	2	3	0	.143
Jim Fanning	47	89	16	2	0	0	3	4	0	.180
Charlie Silvera	26	53	11	3	0	0	1	2	0	.208
Gordon Massa	6	15	7	1	0	0	2	3	0	.467
Jim Woods	2	0	0	0	0	0	1	0	0	—
Pitchers										
Moe Drabowsky	36	82	15	2	0	1	3	10	0	.183
Dick Drott	38	80	8	0	0	0	3	0	0	.100
Bob Rush	31	69	14	3	0	0	3	3	0	.203
Don Elston	39	37	4	0	0	0	0	2	0	.108
Dave Hillman	36	24	0	0	0	0	1	0	0	.000
Jim Brosnan	41	20	5	4	0	0	2	0	0	.250
Don Kaiser	20	19	2	0	0	0	1	1	0	.105
Tom Poholsky	28	19	2	0	0	0	1	1	0	.105
Dick Littlefield	48	11	2	0	0	0	0	0	0	.182
Turk Lown	67	10	2	0	0	0	0	1	0	.200
Bob Anderson	8	4	0	0	0	0	0	0	0	.000
Elmer Singleton	6	3	0	0	0	0	0	0	0	.000
Glen Hobbie	2	2	0	0	0	0	1	0	0	.000
Ed Mayer	3	2	1	0	0	0	0	0	0	.500
Vito Valentinetti	9	2	0	0	0	0	0	0	0	.000
Johnny Briggs	3	0	0	0	0	0	0	0	0	—
Jackie Collum	9	0	0	0	0	0	0	0	0	—
		5,369	1,312	223	31	147	628	590	28	.244

1958

Record: 72–82
Finish: Fifth (tie)
Games Behind: 20
Manager: Bob Scheffing

The Cubs had power to burn in 1958. They broke the National League home run record for one season, with 182, had five sluggers with 20 or more, and boasted the number-one practitioner in Ernie Banks, who led the league in all four power categories: home runs, 47; runs batted in, 129; slugging percentage, .616; and total bases, 379.

Banks also led the club in batting with a .313 average, his first time over .300, and was a landslide winner of the league's Most Valuable Player award. His 47 home runs extended his major league record for shortstops and were the most by a Cub since Hack Wilson's 56 in 1930; the 129 RBIs were also major league record for shortstops; the previous high was 126 in 1930 by Brooklyn's Glenn Wright.

The other Cubs with 20 or more home runs were outfielders Walt Moryn with 26, Lee Walls with 24, and Bobby Thomson with 21, and first baseman Dale Long with 20. The Cubs were second in the league in runs and in team batting. Their handicap was a porous pitching staff, which held them to ten games under .500 and a fifth-place tie with the Cardinals, 20 games behind the champion Milwaukee Braves but only four games out of fourth place.

Dick Drott and Moe Drabowsky, who together won 28 games the previous season, were a disappointment. Troubled with injuries, they won only 16 games. Drabowsky was 9–11, Drott 7–11. Rookie Glen Hobbie, a 6-foot, 3-inch, 200-pound right-hander out of Witt, Illinois, purchased for $85,000 from Memphis of the Southern Association, led the staff with ten wins. Reliever Don Elston, who had a stretch of 9⅔ innings without giving up a hit, appeared in a league-high 69 games and was 9–8 with ten saves.

The Cubs had three new Taylors: second baseman Tony Taylor, 22, a native of Mantazas, Cuba, who was picked up in the winter draft; catcher Sammy Taylor; and left-handed pitcher Taylor "T-Bone" Phillips. The last two were acquired from Milwaukee in a winter trade for pitchers Bob Rush and Don Kaiser and infielder-outfielder Eddie Haas. It was a good deal; with the Cubs, the three Taylors became frontliners.

The veteran Thomson came aboard on April 3 in another beneficial exchange, for Bob Speake, and six weeks later Alvin Dark was acquired for pitcher Jim Brosnan. Thomson batted .283 and solved the center-field problem. Dark, who was also nearing the end of his playing career but was expert at advancing runners, particularly on the hit-and-run, batted .295 and gave the Cubs a strong infield leader.

The Cubs had good early foot. They won 12 of their first 19 games; six of the victories were won by the bullpen, four without defeat by Elston. They were in first place 24 days into the season but dropped seven in a row during the first two weeks in May and were never higher than third thereafter.

Walls and Moryn each had a three-home-run game, both against the Dodgers, Walls on April 24 and Moryn on May 30 in the second game of a doubleheader. On August 23, Banks hit number 41, matching Babe Ruth's record

A mellowed Rogers Hornsby in his final years as a Cub batting coach

Rogers Hornsby (left) and outfielder Lee Walls in the late '50s

pace, but with typical modesty insisted he didn't deserve comparison with the Babe. "You could put all my homers end to end and I wouldn't be able to match Ruth," Banks said.

First baseman Long was twice pressed into service as an emergency catcher. He caught two-thirds of an inning without incident on August 20 against Pittsburgh, and a full inning on September 11 against the Dodgers, when he was charged with a passed ball and dropped a third strike without harm. He was the NL's first left-handed catcher since 1902.

	W	L	ERA	G	GS	CG	IP	H	BB	K
Taylor Phillips	7	10	4.76	39	27	5	170⅓	178	79	102
Glen Hobbie	10	6	3.74	55	16	2	168⅓	163	93	91
Dick Drott	7	11	5.43	39	31	4	167⅓	156	99	127
Moe Drabowsky	9	11	4.51	22	20	4	125⅔	118	73	77
Dave Hillman	4	8	3.15	31	16	3	125⅔	132	31	65
Don Elston	9	8	2.88	69	0	0	97	75	39	84
Johnny Briggs	5	5	4.52	20	17	3	95⅔	99	45	46
Bill Henry	5	4	2.88	44	0	0	81⅓	63	17	58
Bob Anderson	3	3	3.97	17	8	2	65⅔	61	29	51
Marcelino Solis	3	3	6.06	15	4	0	52	74	20	15
Jim Brosnan	3	4	3.14	8	8	2	51⅓	41	29	24
Dolan Nichols	0	4	5.01	24	0	0	41⅓	46	16	9
Gene Fodge	1	1	4.76	16	4	1	39⅔	47	11	15
John Buzhardt	3	0	1.85	6	2	1	24⅓	16	7	9
Ed Mayer	2	2	3.80	19	0	0	23⅔	15	16	14
Hersh Freeman	0	1	8.31	9	0	0	13	23	3	7
Freddy Rodriguez	0	0	7.36	7	0	0	7⅓	8	5	5
Elmer Singleton	1	0	0.00	2	0	0	4⅔	1	1	2
Turk Lown	0	0	4.50	4	0	0	4	2	3	4
Disk Ellsworth	0	1	15.43	1	1	0	2⅓	4	3	0
	72	82	4.22	447	154	27	1,361	1,322	619	805

Shutouts: Briggs 1, Drabowsky 1, Hobbie 1, Phillips 1.

	G	AB	H	2B	3B	HR	R	RBI	SB	AVG
Regulars										
1B Dale Long	142	480	130	26	4	20	68	75	2	.271
2B Tony Taylor	140	497	117	15	3	6	63	27	21	.235
SS Ernie Banks	154	617	193	23	11	(47)	119	(129)	4	.313
3B Alvin Dark	114	464	137	16	4	3	54	43	1	.295
RF Lee Walls	136	513	156	19	3	24	80	72	4	.304
CF Bobby Thomson	152	547	155	27	5	21	67	82	0	.283
LF Walt Moryn	143	512	135	26	7	26	77	77	1	.264
C Sammy Taylor	96	301	78	12	2	6	30	36	2	.259
Substitutes										
John Goryl	83	219	53	9	3	4	27	14	0	.242
Bobby Adams	62	96	27	4	4	0	14	4	2	.281
Jim Marshall	26	81	22	2	0	5	12	11	1	.272
Paul Smith	18	20	3	0	0	0	1	1	0	.150
Jerry Kindall	3	6	1	1	0	0	0	0	0	.167
Jim Bolger	84	120	27	4	1	1	15	11	0	.225
Chuck Tanner	73	103	27	6	0	4	10	17	1	.262
Lou Jackson	24	35	6	2	1	1	5	6	0	.171
Charlie King	8	8	2	0	0	0	1	1	0	.250
Bob Will	6	4	1	0	0	0	1	0	0	.250
Cal Neeman	76	201	52	7	0	12	30	29	0	.259
El Tappe	17	28	6	0	0	0	2	4	0	.214
Moe Thacker	11	24	6	1	0	2	4	3	0	.250
Frank Ernaga	9	8	1	0	0	0	0	0	0	.125
Dick Johnson	8	5	0	0	0	0	1	0	0	.000
Bill Gabler	3	3	0	0	0	0	0	0	0	.000
Gordon Massa	2	2	0	0	0	0	0	0	0	.000
Bobby Morgan	1	1	0	0	0	0	0	0	0	.000
Pitchers										
Dick Drott	39	55	15	0	0	0	6	6	0	.273
Taylor Phillips	39	54	3	0	0	0	2	2	0	.056
Glen Hobbie	55	48	7	0	0	0	3	1	0	.146
Moe Drabowsky	22	45	7	1	0	0	3	3	0	.156
Dave Hillman	32	41	6	2	0	0	4	3	0	.146
Johnny Briggs	20	35	9	1	1	0	3	6	0	.257
Marcelino Solis	15	20	5	1	0	0	1	0	0	.250
Jim Brosnan	8	19	2	1	0	0	0	1	0	.105
Bob Anderson	17	17	2	0	0	0	1	0	0	.118
Bill Henry	44	17	4	1	0	0	2	1	0	.235
Don Elston	69	14	5	0	0	0	1	0	0	.357
John Buzhardt	6	8	1	0	0	0	0	0	0	.125
Gene Fodge	16	7	0	0	0	0	1	0	0	.000
Ed Mayer	19	5	1	0	0	0	1	1	0	.200
Dolan Nichols	24	5	0	0	0	0	0	0	0	.000
Dick Ellsworth	1	1	0	0	0	0	0	0	0	.000
Hersh Freeman	9	1	0	0	0	0	0	0	0	.000
Freddy Rodriguez	7	1	0	0	0	0	0	0	0	.000
Elmer Singleton	2	1	0	0	0	0	0	0	0	.000
Turk Lown	4	0	0	0	0	0	0	0	0	—
		5,289	1,402	207	49	(182)	709	666	39	.265

1959

Record: 74–80
Finish: Fifth (tie)
Games Behind: 13
Manager: Bob Scheffing

It was another heroic season for Ernie Banks. In 1959 he drove in a career-high 143 runs, hit 45 home runs (his third consecutive season of 40 or more), and in a display of his remarkable all-around excellence, broke the two most significant major league defensive records for a shortstop: fewest errors, 12, and highest fielding percentage, .985.

His total of 45 home runs matched the combined production of the first four Cub outfielders and was one fewer than Milwaukee's Eddie Mathews, who connected for number 46 in the second game of a two-game pennant playoff against the Dodgers. If the Braves and Dodgers had not finished in a first-place tie, Banks would have led the NL in home runs and RBIs two years in a row, an achievement accomplished only by Bill Nicholson, a Cub hero of the previous generation.

In midseason Banks was averaging almost one RBI a game—71 in the first 74 games. His 143 total was the highest by a Cub since Hack Wilson's record 190, and 91 more than Bobby Thomson, who was second on the club with 52. In reward, Banks again won the league's Most Valuable Player honor, the first time it had twice been awarded to a player from a second-division club.

The Cubs finished in a fifth-place tie, just as they had in 1958, with a 74–80 record; the 74 wins were their most since 1952. They were never in the lead; after six games they were in second place, then never higher than third. They were at the .500 level on 35 occasions and were only 4½ games out on July 29 before they went into a seven-game tailspin.

Once again the Cubs were betrayed by inadequate starting pitching and for the second consecutive season had the fewest complete games, 30. Glen Hobbie, who led the staff with a 16–13 record, had 10 completions. Rookie Bob Anderson was 12–13, the only other consistent starter. Dick Drott, who finally admitted that his arm had been ailing since the end of the '57 season, was 1–2. Moe Drabowsky was 5–10.

Don Elston and Bill Henry, a righty-lefty bullpen tandem, kept the club afloat. They combined for 19 victories and 25 saves and led the league with 65 appearances apiece. Hobbie and John Buzhardt pitched one-hitters, Hobbie on April 21 against St. Louis when he retired the first 20 batters, Buzhardt on June 21 against the Phillies.

Unlike the previous season, when five Cubs connected for 20 or more home runs, besides Banks only Dale Long and Walt Moryn had as many as 14. Banks led the club with a .304 average and passed Hank Sauer, 198, and Nicholson, 205, on the Cubs' all-time home run list. Banks hit number 206 on July 5, in his 847th game, 502 games sooner than Nicholson.

Moryn, often benched, criticized general manager John Holland for spending too much time playing poker with the players on the chartered flights. Owner Philip Wrigley revealed he and Gabby Hartnett had played penny-ante poker. Told the pots were as high as $100, Wrigley said the stakes should be reduced. Some players, in jest, said Taylor "T-Bone" Phillips was traded because he had beaten Holland out of a big hand.

In a surprise move, manager Bob Scheffing was fired at the end of the season and replaced by vice president Charlie

Grimm, who had had two previous terms at the helm. "Managers are expendable," Wrigley said. "I believe there should be relief managers just like relief pitchers." His remark was an indication of what was to come.

	W	L	ERA	G	GS	CG	IP	H	BB	K
Bob Anderson	12	13	4.13	37	36	7	235⅓	245	77	113
Glen Hobbie	16	13	3.69	46	33	10	234	204	106	138
Dave Hillman	8	11	3.53	39	24	4	191	178	43	88
Moe Drabowsky	5	10	4.13	31	23	3	141⅓	138	75	70
Bill Henry	9	8	2.68	(65)	0	0	134⅓	111	26	115
Art Ceccarelli	5	5	4.76	18	15	4	102	95	37	56
John Buzhardt	4	5	4.97	31	10	1	101⅓	107	29	33
Don Elston	10	8	3.32	(65)	0	0	97⅔	77	46	82
Elmer Singleton	2	1	2.72	21	1	0	43	40	12	25
Dick Drott	1	2	5.93	8	6	1	27⅓	25	26	15
Seth Morehead	0	1	4.82	11	2	0	18⅔	25	8	9
Ben Johnson	0	0	2.16	4	2	0	16⅔	17	4	6
Taylor Phillips	0	2	7.56	7	2	0	16⅔	22	11	5
Ed Donnelly	1	1	3.14	9	0	0	14⅓	18	9	6
Joe Schaffernoth	1	0	8.22	5	1	0	7⅔	11	4	3
Bob Porterfield	0	0	11.37	4	0	0	6⅓	14	3	0
Morrie Martin	0	0	19.29	3	0	0	2⅓	5	1	1
Riverboat Smith	0	0	81.00	1	0	0	⅓	5	2	0
	74	80	4.01	405	155	30	1,391	1,337	519	765

Shutouts: Hobbie 3, Ceccarelli 2, Anderson 1, Buzhardt 1, Drabowsky 1, Drott 1, Hillman 1.

	G	AB	H	2B	3B	HR	R	RBI	SB	AVG
Regulars										
1B Dale Long	110	296	70	10	3	14	34	37	0	.236
2B Tony Taylor	150	624	175	30	8	8	96	38	23	.280
SS Ernie Banks	155	589	179	25	6	45	97	(143)	2	.304
3B Alvin Dark	136	477	126	22	9	6	60	45	1	.264
RF Lee Walls	120	354	91	18	3	8	43	33	0	.257
CF George Altman	135	420	103	14	4	12	54	47	1	.245
LF Bobby Thomson	122	374	97	15	2	11	55	52	1	.259
C Sammy Taylor	110	353	95	13	2	13	41	43	1	.269
Substitutes										
Jim Marshall	108	294	74	10	1	11	39	40	0	.252
Art Schult	42	118	32	7	0	2	17	14	0	.271
Randy Jackson	41	74	18	5	1	1	7	10	0	.243
John Goryl	25	48	9	3	1	1	1	6	1	.188
Bobby Adams	3	2	0	0	0	0	0	0	0	.000
Don Eaddy	15	1	0	0	0	0	3	0	0	.000
Walt Moryn	117	381	89	14	1	14	41	48	0	.234
Irv Noren	65	156	50	6	2	4	27	19	2	.321
Billy Williams	18	33	5	0	1	0	0	2	0	.152
Charlie King	7	3	0	0	0	0	3	0	0	.000
Earl Averill	74	186	44	10	0	10	22	34	0	.237
Cal Neeman	44	105	17	2	0	3	7	9	0	.162
Lou Jackson	6	4	1	0	0	0	2	1	0	.250
Pitchers										
Bob Anderson	37	80	6	1	0	0	6	3	0	.075
Glen Hobbie	46	79	9	1	0	0	3	2	0	.114
Dave Hillman	42	60	9	0	0	0	0	3	0	.150
Moe Drabowsky	31	45	5	1	0	0	2	2	0	.111
Art Ceccarelli	18	33	3	0	0	0	2	0	0	.091
Bill Henry	65	31	6	0	0	0	4	2	0	.194
John Buzhardt	31	29	2	1	0	0	4	0	0	.069
Don Elston	65	19	4	0	0	0	2	1	0	.211
Dick Drott	8	8	1	0	0	0	0	0	0	.125
Elmer Singleton	21	6	0	0	0	0	0	0	0	.000
Ben Johnson	4	4	0	0	0	0	0	1	0	.000
Taylor Phillips	7	4	0	0	0	0	0	0	0	.000
Joe Schaffernoth	5	3	0	0	0	0	0	0	0	.000
Seth Morehead	11	2	1	1	0	0	0	0	0	.500
Bob Porterfield	4	1	0	0	0	0	0	1	0	.000
Ed Donnelly	9	0	0	0	0	0	0	0	0	—
Morrie Martin	3	0	0	0	0	0	0	0	0	—
Riverboat Smith	1	0	0	0	0	0	0	0	0	—
	5,296	1,321	209	44	163	673	635	32		.249

1960

Record: 60–94
Finish: Seventh
Games Behind: 35
Managers: Charlie Grimm, Lou Boudreau

Charlie Grimm's third and final managerial term was brief and unsuccessful. After 17 games of the new season, on May 4, 1960, he was transferred to the broadcasting squad in a straight swap for announcer Lou Boudreau, the one-time "boy manager" of the Cleveland Indians. When Grimm ascended to the radio booth, the Cubs were in last place with a 6–11 record.

Boudreau, who had been a star shortstop and innovator—he had developed the successful "Ted Williams shift"—said he had "seen more" from his heavenly perch because it provided "a better view," an indication that, armed with his new insights, he could turn the club around. He was wrong. The Cubs tied the franchise record for most losses, 94, and finished in seventh place, one game out of the cellar.

It was another big season for Ernie Banks—41 home runs and 117 runs batted in, his fourth consecutive 40-HR season and the fifth of his career, tying the league record. Banks was the first major leaguer to reach the 100-RBI plateau, on August 27, and played in all 156 games. At the season's end he had appeared in 652 consecutive games, longest steak of any active player.

Glen Hobbie led the club in victories with 16 but also led the league in losses, 20. Don Cardwell, a hard-throwing right-hander, pitched a no-hitter on May 15 in the second game of a doubleheader against the Cardinals, two days after he had arrived in a six-player deal with the Phillies. Left fielder Walt Moryn made a sensational shoe-top catch on Joe Cunningham's sinking line drive for the final out.

Said Boudreau: "He can become a 20-game winner."

Wrong again. Cardwell won eight games, one fewer than the apple-cheeked Bob Anderson. Dick Ellsworth, a rookie left-hander out of Fresno, California, who had been cut in spring training, was 7–13. Reliever Don Elston was 8–9 with 11 saves in 60 appearances, the third successive season he had been in 60 or more games; six more would have tied the all-time three-year record of 200 games.

On August 4 at Wrigley Field, lefty Jim Brewer suffered multiple facial bruises in an ugly incident with Billy Martin, then with Cincinnati. After Brewer walked Martin, Martin was seemingly strolling to first base. Halfway there, he turned, ran to the mound and assaulted Brewer with a sneak punch. Seven days later Brewer underwent eye surgery for the third time.

"Nobody, but nobody is going to throw at my head and get away with it," Martin said. The Chicago National League Club and Brewer jointly filed a $1 million civil suit against Martin. Said an unconcerned Martin, "How do they want it, cash or check?"

It was also a year of considerable change. Seven frontliners were sold or traded: Bill Henry to Cincinnati, Walt Moryn to St. Louis, Dale Long to San Francisco, and Tony Taylor, Lee Walls, John Buzhardt, and Cal Neeman to Philadelphia. The principal new arrivals in these exchanges, in addition to Cardwell, were outfielders Richie Ashburn and Frank Thomas and infielder Don Zimmer, aging veterans coming off poor seasons.

Ashburn, an excellent defensive center fielder and leadoff hitter, a former NL batting champion, hit .291 and stole 16 bases. Thomas had 21 home runs and 64 RBIs, second to Banks in both departments. Ron Santo was easily the best rookie. Recalled from the minors on June 26, Santo became the regular third baseman and batted .251 with nine home runs and 44 RBIs; 35 of his 121 hits were for extra bases. Boudreau was dismissed on October 4 and returned to the radio booth.

	W	L	ERA	G	GS	CG	IP	H	BB	K
Glen Hobbie	16	(20)	3.97	46	36	16	258⅔	253	101	134
Bob Anderson	9	11	4.11	38	30	5	203⅔	201	68	115
Don Cardwell	8	14	4.37	31	26	6	177	166	68	129
Dick Ellsworth	7	13	3.72	31	27	6	176⅔	170	72	94
Don Elston	8	9	3.40	60	0	0	127	109	55	85
Seth Morehead	2	9	3.94	45	7	2	123⅓	123	46	64
Mark Freeman	3	3	5.63	30	8	1	76⅔	70	33	50
Dick Drott	0	6	7.16	23	9	0	55⅓	63	42	32
Joe Schaffernoth	2	3	2.78	33	0	0	55	46	17	33
Moe Drabowsky	3	1	6.44	32	7	0	50⅓	71	23	26
Ben Johnson	2	1	4.91	17	0	0	29⅓	39	11	9
Jim Brewer	0	3	5.82	5	4	0	21⅓	25	6	7
Mel Wright	0	1	4.96	9	0	0	16⅓	17	3	8
Art Ceccarelli	0	0	5.54	7	1	0	13	16	4	10
Dick Burwell	0	0	5.59	3	1	0	9⅔	11	7	1
John Goetz	0	0	12.79	4	0	0	6⅓	10	4	6
Al Schroll	0	0	10.13	2	0	0	2⅔	3	5	2
	60	94	4.35	416	156	36	1,402⅔	1,393	565	805

Shutouts: Hobbie 4, Cardwell 1.

	G	AB	H	2B	3B	HR	R	RBI	SB	AVG
Regulars										
1B Ed Bouchee	98	299	71	11	1	5	33	44	2	.237
2B Jerry Kindall	89	246	59	16	2	2	17	23	4	.240
SS Ernie Banks	156	597	162	32	7	(41)	94	117	1	.271
3B Ron Santo	95	347	87	24	2	9	44	44	0	.251
RF Bob Will	138	475	121	20	9	6	58	53	1	.255
CF Richie Ashburn	151	547	159	16	5	0	99	40	16	.291
LF George Altman	119	334	89	16	4	13	50	51	4	.266
C Moe Thacker	54	90	14	1	0	0	5	6	1	.156
Substitutes										
Frank Thomas	135	479	114	12	1	21	54	64	1	.238
Don Zimmer	132	368	95	16	7	6	37	35	8	.258
Dick Gernert	52	96	24	3	0	6	8	11	1	.250
Tony Taylor	19	76	20	3	3	1	14	9	2	.263
Grady Hatton	28	38	13	0	0	0	3	7	0	.342
Sammy Drake	15	15	1	0	0	0	5	0	0	.067
Walt Moryri	38	109	32	4	0	2	12	11	2	.294
Al Heist	41	102	28	5	3	1	11	6	3	.275
Danny Murphy	31	75	9	2	0	1	7	6	0	.120
Lou Johnson	34	68	14	2	1	0	6	1	3	.206
Billy Williams	12	47	13	0	2	2	4	7	0	.277
Art Schult	12	15	2	1	0	0	1	1	0	.133
Irv Noren	12	11	1	0	0	0	0	1	0	.091
Nelson Mathews	3	8	2	0	0	0	1	0	0	.250
Jim McKnight	3	6	2	0	0	0	0	1	0	.333
Sammy Taylor	74	150	31	9	0	3	14	17	0	.207
El Tappe	51	103	24	7	0	0	11	3	0	.233
Earl Averill	52	102	24	4	0	1	14	13	1	.235
Del Rice	18	52	12	3	0	0	2	4	0	.231
Jim Hegan	24	43	9	2	1	1	4	5	0	.209
Dick Bertell	5	15	2	0	0	0	0	2	0	.133
Cal Neeman	9	13	2	1	0	0	0	0	0	.154
Pitchers										
Glen Hobbie	46	86	13	1	0	1	6	6	0	.151
Bob Anderson	39	71	12	0	0	0	4	1	0	.169
Don Cardwell	33	69	14	1	0	3	9	6	1	.203
Dick Ellsworth	31	48	2	0	0	0	3	1	0	.042
Seth Morehead	45	29	4	1	0	0	1	2	0	.138
Don Elston	60	24	3	0	0	0	0	0	0	.125
Mark Freeman	30	20	3	0	0	0	2	1	0	.150
Dick Drott	23	10	1	0	0	0	0	0	0	.100
Joe Schaffernoth	33	7	2	0	0	0	0	1	0	.286
Jim Brewer	6	6	1	0	0	0	0	0	0	.167

	G	AB	H	2B	3B	HR	R	RBI	SB	AVG
Moe Drabowsky	33	6	0	0	0	0	0	0	0	.000
Dick Burwell	3	3	1	0	0	0	1	0	0	.333
Ben Johnson	17	2	0	0	0	0	0	0	0	.000
Mel Wright	9	2	0	0	0	0	0	0	0	.000
John Goetz	4	1	0	0	0	0	0	0	0	.000
Al Schroll	2	1	1	0	0	0	0	0	0	1.000
Art Ceccarelli	7	0	0	0	0	0	0	0	0	—
		5,311	1,293	213	48	119	634	600	51	.243

1961

Record: 64–90
Finish: Seventh
Games Behind: 29
Manager: None

Owner Philip Wrigley, amateur lexicographer but professional pioneer, said he looked up the word "manager" in *his* dictionary and discovered the definition was "dictator." So on January 12, 1961, when the snow was on the ground, Wrigley announced he would rid himself and his players of this evil and embarked on a historic mission.

Instead of a manager there would be a platoon of coaches, all interchangeable and equal, who would rotate throughout the Cub system. For two weeks, possibly as long as a month, a head coach would be designated and function in the traditional role of a manager.

Commissioner Ford Frick wasn't enthralled: " If Mr. Wrigley wants to have eight coaches and no manager that's strictly his business. My only concern is that he has nine men on the field." National League president Warren Giles also expressed reluctant approval. "Certainly, Mr. Wrigley knows what he wants to do," Giles said, "but I've never heard of a team without a manager."

Neither had anyone else. Eleven coaches were signed, including two holdovers from the previous season. In alphabetical order they were Bobby Adams, Dick Cole, James "Rip" Collins, Harry Craft, Charlie Grimm, Vedie Himsl, Goldie Holt, Lou Klein, Fred Martin, Elvin Tappe, and Verlon Walker.

Only Himsl, Craft, Tappe, and Klein were anointed as head coaches. There were eight rotations. Himsl was the first head coach. He had three terms and a 10–21 won-lost record. Tappe, also up and down three times, had the longest reign, 102 games, and was 45–57. Craft had two shots and was 7–9. Klein was 2–3.

All the king's men were unable to lift the Cubs out of seventh place. Reliever Don Elston helped in six of the first seven victories, four wins and two saves. The Cubs were never more than one game over .500, three times in the first three weeks. On May 6, in the beginning of an eight-game tailspin, they plunged to seventh, and they held that position continuously for the rest of the season.

It was a difficult year for Ernie Banks, the Cubs' All-Star shortstop. Accustomed to playing the full schedule, Banks was troubled by a knee injury and, later, had a problem with the depth perception in his left eye. Banks missed 18 games. His consecutive-game streak, longest in either league, was broken at 717 games on June 23 when he benched himself because of his ailing knee.

Banks also suffered from the vagaries of the rotating head coaches. On May 23, Himsl sent him to left field, where he remained for 23 games. Tappe shifted him to first base on June 16. When Banks came back on July 1, recovered from his knee injury, Tappe told him he could return to short if that was his desire. It was.

For the first time in the last seven seasons, Banks did not lead the club in runs batted in. Outfielder George Altman was the new RBI leader with 96, 10 more than Billy Williams, the Rookie of the Year. Banks continued to lead in home runs with 29, followed by Altman with 27, Williams with 25, and Ron Santo with 23.

Outfielder Lou Brock, like Billy Williams a future Hall of Famer, was recalled from a Class C league. He made his big league debut on September 10 and hit .091 in four games. At the end of the season, Ashburn and Zimmer, the team leaders, criticized Wrigley's adventure. "It was a nutty idea," Ashburn said. Zimmer asked to be traded because "I can't play under that many bosses." They never played with the Cubs again.

	W	L	ERA	G	GS	CG	IP	H	BB	K
Don Cardwell	15	14	3.82	39	(38)	13	259⅓	243	88	156
Glen Hobbie	7	13	4.26	36	29	7	198⅔	207	54	103
Dick Ellsworth	10	11	3.86	37	31	7	186⅔	213	48	91
Jack Curtis	10	13	4.89	31	27	6	180⅓	220	51	57
Bob Anderson	7	10	4.26	57	12	1	152	162	56	96
Dick Drott	1	4	4.22	35	8	0	98	75	51	48
Don Elston	6	7	5.59	58	0	0	93⅓	108	45	59
Jim Brewer	1	7	5.82	36	11	0	86⅔	116	21	57
Barney Schultz	7	6	2.70	41	0	0	66⅔	57	25	59
Joe Schaffernoth	0	4	6.34	21	0	0	38⅓	43	18	23
Mel Wright	0	1	10.71	11	0	0	21	42	4	6
Dick Burwell	0	0	9.00	2	0	0	4	6	4	0
	64	90	4.48	404	156	34	1,385	1,492	465	755

Shutouts: Cardwell 3, Hobbie 2, Ellsworth 1.

	G	AB	H	2B	3B	HR	R	RBI	SB	AVG
Regulars										
1B Ed Bouchee	112	319	79	12	3	12	49	38	1	.248
2B Don Zimmer	128	477	120	25	4	13	57	40	5	.252
SS Ernie Banks	138	511	142	22	4	29	75	80	1	.278
3B Ron Santo	154	578	164	32	6	23	84	83	2	.284
RF George Altman	138	518	157	28	(12)	27	77	96	6	.303
CF Al Heist	109	321	82	14	3	7	48	37	3	.255
LF Billy Williams	146	529	147	20	7	25	75	86	6	.278
C Dick Bertell	92	267	73	7	1	2	20	33	0	.273
Substitutes										
Jerry Kindall	96	310	75	22	3	9	37	44	2	.242
Andre Rodgers	73	214	57	17	0	6	27	23	1	.266
Mel Roach	23	39	5	2	0	0	1	1	1	.128
Ken Hubbs	10	28	5	1	1	1	4	2	0	.179
Moe Morhardt	7	18	5	0	0	0	3	1	0	.278
Richie Ashburn	109	307	79	7	4	0	49	19	7	.257
Bob Will	86	113	29	9	0	0	9	8	0	.257
Frank Thomas	15	50	13	2	0	2	7	6	0	.260
Danny Murphy	4	13	5	0	0	2	3	3	0	.385
Lou Brock	4	11	1	0	0	0	1	0	0	.091
Jim McAnany	11	10	3	1	0	0	1	0	0	.300
Nelson Mathews	3	9	1	0	0	0	0	0	0	.111
Sammy Drake	13	5	0	0	0	0	1	0	0	.000
Sammy Taylor	89	235	56	8	2	8	26	23	0	.238
Moe Thacker	25	35	6	0	0	0	3	2	0	.171
Cuno Barragan	10	28	6	0	0	1	3	2	0	.214
George Freese	9	7	2	0	0	0	0	1	0	.286
Pitchers										
Don Cardwell	40	95	10	3	0	3	6	6	0	.105
Glen Hobbie	36	66	11	3	0	2	5	6	0	.167
Jack Curtis	31	60	10	2	0	2	8	4	0	.167
Dick Ellsworth	37	56	2	1	0	0	1	0	0	.036
Bob Anderson	57	42	6	0	0	2	5	5	0	.143
Jim Brewer	36	22	4	0	0	0	1	0	0	.182
Dick Drott	35	22	6	0	1	0	1	1	0	.273
Don Elston	58	11	2	0	0	0	1	0	0	.182
Barney Schultz	41	10	1	0	0	0	0	0	0	.100
Joe Schaffernoth	21	5	0	0	0	0	1	0	0	.000
Mel Wright	11	2	0	0	0	0	0	0	0	.000
Dick Burwell	2	1	0	0	0	0	0	0	0	.000
		5,344	1,364	238	51	176	689	650	35	.255

1962

Record: 59–103
Finish: Ninth
Games Behind: 42½
Manager: None

The revolving head coaching experiment continued in 1962, but the movement was minimal. Unlike the previous season, when there were eight exchanges, the baton was passed only twice: Lou Klein replaced Elvin Tappe on May 1, and on June 3, with the club in ninth place, Charlie Metro relieved Klein and directed play in the 112 remaining games.

Owner Philip Wrigley, who had been saying, "When the bulldozer breaks down, you should hire a new driver," didn't realize the driver wasn't the problem. It was the bulldozer that was in need of repair. Because of expansion, the National League now had ten teams, and the Cubs finished ninth—with all-time records of 103 losses and 59 victories.

The Cubs had four rookies in their opening-day lineup: outfielder Lou Brock, catcher Cuno Barragan, second baseman Ken Hubbs, and Elder White, who qualifies as a trivia question. When Ernie Banks moved to first base, this time to stay, White inherited Banks' shortstop position. He batted .151, appeared in only 23 games, was farmed out, and never again surfaced in the big leagues.

Hubbs, 20, recalled from a Class B league, had been signed out of Colton, California, for a $15,000 bonus. He was a landslide winner—19 of 20 first-place votes—for the league's Rookie of the Year award, the second successive season the honor fell to a Cub. Hubbs batted a thin .260 and led the league in strikeouts but was superior on defense. After gumming a Roberto Clemente groundball on June 13, he was errorless in his next 78 games, breaking the major league record for second basemen, 73 games, set by Bobby Doerr of the Red Sox in 1948.

Brock batted .263, with only nine home runs, but number 7 was a memorable wallop against Alvin Jackson of the Mets in the first game of a June 17 doubleheader in the spacious Polo Grounds. The estimated distance was 460–470 feet. The ball sailed over the head of Richie Ashburn (who had been sold to the Mets in December after he knocked Wrigley's system of rotating head coaches) then went over the fence 455 feet from the plate and landed on the right side of the center-field bleachers.

The last player to reach the bleachers had been Joe Adcock in 1953. Babe Ruth had also homered into that sector, twice, but the bleachers were then closer to the plate. It was only the 65th big league game for the left-handed hitting Brock, who had been platooned, and his first off a left-handed pitcher. Earlier, in spring training, Brock had connected for a near-500-foot home run off Cleveland's Barry Latman in a Tucson, Arizona, exhibition game.

Banks, who never had much more than average range at short, made an easy transition to first base. Said Banks: "Those ground balls aren't much different, and now I've got a bigger glove."

Free of injuries, Banks had his usual year at the plate: 37 home runs and 104 runs batted in. Outfielders Billy Williams and George Altman were next, each with 22 home runs, and with 91 and 74 RBIs, respectively. For the fourth year in a row, the Cub pitchers, collectively, had a 4.00-plus earned run average. Bob Buhl, 34, acquired in an April deal with Milwaukee, led the pitchers with 12 wins.

The Cubs were 4–16 with Tappe, 12–18 with Klein, and 43–69 under Metro, who refused to be rotated back to the minors. He was fired on November 8. Blunt and outspoken, Metro in midseason had punctured the fiction that the head coaches were "one-for-all and all-for-one." Wrigley insisted Metro, a disciplinarian, was dismissed because some of the players didn't like him.

The Cubs hired John "Buck" O'Neil, the major leagues' first black coach.

	W	L	ERA	G	GS	CG	IP	H	BB	K
Bob Buhl	12	13	3.69	34	30	8	212	204	94	109
Dick Ellsworth	9	20	5.09	37	33	6	208⅔	241	77	113
Don Cardwell	7	16	4.92	41	29	6	195⅔	205	60	104
Cal Koonce	10	10	3.97	35	30	3	190⅔	200	86	84
Glen Hobbie	5	14	5.22	42	23	5	162	198	62	87
Bob Anderson	2	7	5.02	57	4	0	107⅓	111	60	82
Barney Schultz	5	5	3.82	51	0	0	77⅓	66	23	58
Don Elston	4	8	2.44	57	0	0	66⅓	57	32	37
Jug Gerard	2	3	4.91	39	0	0	58⅔	67	28	30
Al Lary	0	1	7.15	15	3	0	34	42	15	18
Paul Toth	3	1	4.24	6	4	1	34	29	10	11
Tony Balsamo	0	1	6.44	18	0	0	29⅓	34	20	27
Jack Curtis	0	2	3.50	4	3	0	18	18	6	8
Morrie Steevens	0	1	2.40	12	1	0	15	10	11	5
Freddie Burdette	0	0	3.72	8	0	0	9¾	5	8	5
Jack Warner	0	0	7.71	7	0	0	7	9	0	3
Jim Brewer	0	1	9.53	6	1	0	5⅔	10	3	1
George Gerberman	0	0	1.69	1	1	0	5⅓	3	5	1
Don Prince	0	0	0.00	1	0	0	1	0	1	0
	59	103	4.54	471	162	29	1,438⅓	1,509	601	783

Shutouts: Buhl 1, Cardwell 1, Koonce 1.

	G	AB	H	2B	3B	HR	R	RBI	SB	AVG
Regulars										
1B Ernie Banks	154	610	164	20	6	37	87	104	5	.269
2B Ken Hubbs	160	661	172	24	9	5	90	49	3	.260
SS Andre Rodgers	138	461	128	20	8	5	40	44	5	.278
3B Ron Santo	162	604	137	20	4	17	44	83	4	.227
RF George Altman	147	534	170	27	5	22	74	74	19	.318
CF Lou Brock	123	434	114	24	7	9	73	35	16	.263
LF Billy Williams	159	618	184	22	8	22	94	91	9	.298
C Dick Bertell	77	215	65	6	2	2	19	18	0	.302
Substitutes										
Jim McKnight	60	85	19	0	1	0	6	5	0	.224
Alex Grammas	23	60	14	3	0	0	3	3	1	.233
Elder White	23	53	8	2	0	0	4	1	3	.151
Daryl Robertson	9	19	2	0	0	0	0	2	0	.105
Don Landrum	83	238	67	5	2	1	29	15	9	.282
Bob Will	87	92	22	3	0	2	6	15	0	.239
Nelson Mathews	15	49	15	2	0	2	5	13	3	.306
Danny Murphy	14	35	7	3	1	0	5	3	0	.200
Bobby Gene Smith	13	29	5	0	0	1	3	2	0	.172
Billy Ott	12	28	4	0	0	1	3	2	0	.143
Cuno Barragan	58	134	27	6	1	0	11	12	0	.201
Moe Thacker	65	107	20	5	0	0	8	9	0	.187
El Tappe	26	53	11	0	0	0	3	6	0	.208
Sammy Taylor	7	15	2	1	0	0	0	1	0	.133
Moe Morhardt	18	16	2	0	0	0	1	2	0	.125
Jim McAnany	7	6	0	0	0	0	0	0	0	.000
Pitchers										
Bob Buhl	34	69	0	0	0	0	2	1	1	.000
Cal Koonce	35	64	6	1	0	0	7	2	0	.094
Dick Ellsworth	37	62	7	1	0	0	5	2	0	.113
Don Cardwell	41	61	9	0	1	0	2	3	0	.148
Glen Hobbie	42	49	6	0	0	0	4	0	0	.122
Bob Anderson	57	23	3	0	1	0	1	1	0	.130
Paul Toth	6	11	2	0	0	0	1	1	0	.182
Don Elston	57	8	0	0	0	0	0	0	0	.000
Jug Gerard	39	8	3	0	0	0	0	0	0	.375
Al Lary	23	6	1	0	0	0	1	0	0	.167
Tony Balsamo	18	5	1	1	0	0	1	0	0	.200
Barney Schultz	51	5	0	0	0	0	0	1	0	.000
Jack Curtis	4	4	1	0	0	0	1	0	0	.250
Freddie Burdette	8	1	0	0	0	0	0	0	0	.000
George Gerberman	1	1	0	0	0	0	0	0	0	.000
Morrie Steevens	12	1	0	0	0	0	0	0	0	.000

	G	AB	H	2B	3B	HR	R	RBI	SB	AVG
Jim Brewer	6	0	0	0	0	0	0	0	0	—
Don Prince	1	0	0	0	0	0	0	0	0	—
Jack Warner	7	0	0	0	0	0	0	0	0	—
		5,534	1,398	196	56	126	632	600	78	.253

1963

Record: 82–80
Finish: Seventh
Games Behind: 17
Manager: Bob Kennedy

"We're trying to sign another man," owner Philip Wrigley told the press, "and if we get him he'll be our permanent head coach. Or if you fellows wish, you can call him manager." A week later Bob Kennedy, who had an extensive major league history, joined the circus and managed the Cubs, without relief, for the next two and a half years.

But Wrigley, an old fox, had another card to play and on January 10, 1963, hired Robert V. Whitlow, 43, who was given the title Athletic Director of the Chicago Cubs and Associated Clubs. It was another Wrigley innovation: baseball's first athletic director.

Whitlow, a retired Air Force colonel, had no baseball experience. More important, in Wrigley's view, was that he made a good appearance and was 6 feet, 4 inches and 240 pounds. Said Wrigley: "He has the size that commands respect."

Whitlow had been active in the astronaut training program and was aware of the newest physical fitness procedures and bodybuilding diets. During a visit to Chicago, in October, Whitlow stopped at the Wrigley Building to visit a chum, Bud Offield, Wrigley's nephew. Offield took him upstairs to meet his uncle. Impressed, Wrigley gave the colonel the keys to the kingdom, putting him in command of the entire baseball operation. Even John Holland, the Cub general manager for the six previous years, was under Whitlow's big foot.

No shy violet, Whitlow announced he might alternate with Kennedy and appoint himself the head coach and that he definitely would suit up and shag flies in spring training. The players were amused. Whitlow gave them chocolate balls spiked with mysterious quick-energy ingredients.

Remarkably, the Cubs responded with an 82–80 record, good enough for seventh place, the first time in 17 years the club had been above .500. It was a miracle improvement over the previous 59–103 log, the largest gain in either league, a jump of .142 in won-lost percentage. If Ernie Banks had been healthy, the Cubs probably would have finished in the first division.

It was a frustrating year for Banks, on and off the field. Campaigning as an independent, he ran for alderman in the Eighth Ward on Chicago's South Side and finished third in a four-man race. He had a recurrence of his eye problems along with subclinical mumps, and for the first time, on July 27, he was lifted for a pinch hitter. Merritt Ranew hit for him. Banks batted .227, with 18 home runs and 64 RBIs, career lows to that point.

Ron Santo and Billy Williams led the assault, both with 25 home runs; Santo drove in 99 runs, Williams 95. Lou Brock stole 24 bases, most by a Cub since Kiki Cuyler's 37 in 1930. But it was the pitching that turned the club around. The Cubs had the second-lowest ERA in the league, 3.04, and were led by Dick Ellsworth. A 20-game loser in '62, Ellsworth was 22–10 and had a one-hitter, two-hitter, three-hitter, and four-hitter in '63.

It was the most wins by a Cub left-hander since Hippo Vaughn also won 22 in 1918 and the first time since Cincinnati's Paul Derringer in 1935 that a pitcher had reversed 20-game seasons, going from 20 losses to 20 wins. Larry Jackson and Lindy McDaniel, acquired in a trade from the Cardinals, were also outstanding. Jackson won 14 games. McDaniel was 13–7 with 22 saves.

On June 6, McDaniel had a reliever's dream. He entered with the bases loaded and one out in the 10th, picked Willie Mays off second, retired Ed Bailey, and in the bottom half hit a game-winning home run. The Cubs were 10 games over .500 as late as August 2. They fell out of the first division on August 11.

	W	L	ERA	G	GS	CG	IP	H	BB	K
Dick Ellsworth	22	10	2.11	37	37	19	290⅔	223	75	185
Larry Jackson	14	18	2.55	37	37	13	275	256	54	153
Bob Buhl	11	14	3.38	37	34	6	226	219	62	108
Glen Hobbie	7	10	3.92	36	24	4	165⅓	172	49	94
Paul Toth	5	9	3.10	27	14	3	130⅔	115	35	66
Lindy McDaniel	13	7	2.86	57	0	0	88	82	27	75
Cal Koonce	2	6	4.58	21	13	0	72⅔	75	32	44
Don Elston	4	1	2.83	51	0	0	70	57	21	41
Jim Brewer	3	2	4.89	29	1	0	49⅔	59	15	35
Barney Schultz	1	0	3.62	15	0	0	27⅓	25	9	18
Jack Warner	0	1	2.78	8	0	0	22⅔	21	8	7
Tom Baker	0	1	3.00	10	1	0	18	20	7	14
Dick LeMay	0	1	5.28	9	1	0	15⅓	26	4	10
Freddie Burdette	0	0	3.86	4	0	0	4⅔	5	2	1
Phil Mudrock	0	0	9.00	1	0	0	1	2	0	0
	82	80	3.08	379	162	45	1,457	1,357	400	851

Shutouts: Ellsworth 4, Jackson 4, Toth 2, Hobbie 1.
Saves: McDaniel 22, Elston 4, Schultz 2.

	G	AB	H	2B	3B	HR	R	RBI	SB	AVG
Regulars										
1B Ernie Banks	130	432	98	20	1	18	41	64	0	.227
2B Ken Hubbs	154	566	133	19	3	8	54	47	8	.235
SS Andre Rodgers	150	516	118	17	4	5	51	33	5	.229
3B Ron Santo	162	630	187	29	6	25	79	99	6	.297
RF Lou Brock	148	547	141	19	11	9	79	37	24	.258
CF Ellis Burton	93	322	74	16	1	12	45	41	6	.230
LF Billy Williams	161	612	175	36	9	25	87	95	7	.286
C Dick Bertell	100	322	75	7	2	2	15	14	0	.233
Substitutes										
Steve Boros	41	90	19	5	1	3	9	7	0	.211
John Boccabella	24	74	14	4	1	1	7	5	0	.189
Leo Burke	27	49	9	0	0	2	4	7	0	.184
Jimmy Stewart	13	37	11	2	0	0	1	1	1	.297
Ken Aspromonte	20	34	5	3	0	0	2	4	0	.147
Alex Grammas	16	27	5	0	0	0	1	0	0	.185
Bob Will	23	23	4	0	0	0	0	1	0	.174
Don Landrum	84	227	55	4	1	1	27	10	6	.242
Nelson Mathews	61	155	24	3	2	4	12	10	3	.155
Billy Cowan	14	36	9	1	1	1	1	2	0	.250
Merritt Ranew	78	154	52	8	1	3	18	15	1	.338
Jimmie Schaffer	57	142	34	7	0	7	17	19	0	.239
Cuno Barragan	1	1	0	0	0	0	0	0	0	.000
Pitchers										
Dick Ellsworth	37	94	9	0	0	0	8	5	0	.096
Larry Jackson	37	87	17	5	0	0	5	6	0	.195
Bob Buhl	37	74	8	0	0	0	2	5	1	.108
Glen Hobbie	36	50	4	0	0	0	2	0	0	.080
Paul Toth	27	39	1	0	0	0	0	0	0	.026
Lindy McDaniel	57	22	2	0	0	1	1	2	0	.091
Cal Koonce	21	19	2	0	0	0	1	0	0	.105
Jim Brewer	29	6	0	0	0	0	0	1	0	.000
Don Elston	51	4	0	0	0	0	1	0	0	.000
Barney Schultz	15	4	0	0	0	0	0	0	0	.000
Jack Warner	8	4	1	0	0	0	0	0	0	.250
Tom Baker	10	3	0	0	0	0	0	0	0	.000
Dick LeMay	9	2	0	0	0	0	0	0	0	.000
Freddie Burdette	4	0	0	0	0	0	0	0	0	—
Phil Mudrock	1	0	0	0	0	0	0	0	0	—
		5,404	1,286	205	44	127	570	530	68	.238

1964

Record: 76–86
Finish: Eighth
Games Behind: 17
Manager: Bob Kennedy

The Lou Brock trade wasn't the tragedy of the year. On February 13, 1964, Ken Hubbs, 22, the Cubs' brilliant second baseman, died in an airplane accident, two weeks after he had obtained his pilot's license. The crash occurred when Hubbs, flying in a single-engine aircraft with one passenger, Dennis Doyle, a lifelong friend, were returning from Provo, Utah, to their home in Colton, California.

They took off in clear skies but encountered a snowstorm. According to investigators, Hubbs apparently lost the horizon and plunged into an ice-encrusted lake. The wreckage was not discovered until two days later. Said a distraught Ron Santo, "He was like the kid next door. He taught Sunday school and didn't smoke or drink."

The Brock deal, a six-player swap with the Cardinals consummated an hour before the June 15 trading deadline, is generally regarded as the worst in club history. For Brock and pitchers Paul Toth and Jack Spring the Cubs received pitchers Ernie Broglio and Bobby Shantz and outfielder Doug Clemens. Broglio and Brock were the centerpieces. "We're taking a shot at the pennant," said general manager John Holland. "The race is wide open."

It seemed like a good deal for the Cubs. In two and a half seasons with the Cubs, Brock was Mr. Anonymous, except for that one day, June 17, 1962, when he homered into the Polo Grounds bleachers. The St. Louis sportswriters knocked the deal with the complaint "Who is Lou Brock?" The Chicago scribes were delighted. Wrote Bob Smith in the *Chicago Daily News:* "Thank you, thank you, oh, you lovely St. Louis Cardinals. Nice doing business with you. Please call again."

An 18-game winner the previous season, Broglio was expected to solidify the Cub pitching. What Holland apparently didn't know was that he had a sore arm. Broglio won only four of 18 starts; overall he was 7–19 in two and a half seasons with the Cubs. Brock was an immediate sensation. He helped lead the Cardinals to the pennant and had a blockbuster 19-year major league career: 3,023 hits, a .293 lifetime average, and a record 938 stolen bases. He was inducted into the Hall of Fame in 1985.

In retrospect, Broglio wasn't needed. The Cubs had a good enough starting rotation but—and this was unusual—were lacking in the bullpen. No reliever won more than two games out of the pen. Lindy McDaniel, who had helped in the winning of 35 games in '63, had soreness in his pitching elbow much of the season and was 1–7 with 15 saves.

Larry Jackson had a career year, 24 victories, tops in both leagues, most by a Cub since Charley Root's 26 in 1927. Unlike the previous season, when Jackson lost his last seven decisions, he won nine in a row from August 22 through September 27. Bob Buhl won 15, Dick Ellsworth 14. Both were stuck on 12 for a while. Buhl won number 13 on his 11th try, Ellsworth on his eighth.

Ron Santo and Billy Williams, both of whom hit .300 for the first time, led the attack. Santo, now hitting to all fields, had 30 home runs and drove in 114 runs, becoming the Cubs' first 100-RBI man other than Banks since Hank Sauer in 1954.

Williams had 33 homers, 98 RBIs. Santo was seventh in the league in batting at .313, Williams eighth at .312. Banks, still not completely free of injuries, hit 23 home runs and drove in 95.

The Cubs won six fewer games than in '63 and finished eighth, 17 games out. They were 48–48 on July 26, only eight games out of the lead, lost their next five games, and were in eighth place thereafter. In August, a Chicago investment group offered to buy the club for $4.3 million. Wrigley refused.

	W	L	ERA	G	GS	CG	IP	H	BB	K
Larry Jackson	(24)	11	3.14	40	38	19	297⅔	265	58	148
Dick Ellsworth	14	18	3.75	37	36	16	256⅔	267	71	148
Bob Buhl	15	14	3.83	36	35	11	227⅔	208	68	107
Lew Burdette	9	9	4.88	28	17	8	131	152	19	40
Ernie Broglio	4	7	4.04	18	16	3	100⅓	111	30	46
Lindy McDaniel	1	7	3.88	63	0	0	95	104	23	71
Don Elston	2	5	5.30	48	0	0	54⅓	68	34	26
Sterling Slaughter	2	4	5.75	20	6	1	51⅓	64	32	32
Wayne Schurr	0	0	3.72	26	0	0	48⅓	57	11	29
Fred Norman	0	4	6.54	8	5	0	31⅓	34	21	20
Cal Koonce	3	0	2.03	6	2	0	31	30	7	17
Glen Hobbie	0	3	7.90	8	4	0	27⅓	39	10	14
Freddie Burdette	1	0	3.15	18	0	0	20	17	10	4
Lee Gregory	0	0	3.50	11	0	0	18	23	5	8
Bobby Shantz	0	1	5.56	20	0	0	11⅓	15	6	12
Paul Toth	0	2	8.44	4	2	0	10⅔	15	5	0
Jack Warner	0	0	2.89	7	0	0	9⅓	12	4	6
Paul Jaeckel	1	0	0.00	4	0	0	8	4	3	2
Jack Spring	0	0	6.00	7	0	0	6	4	2	1
John Flavin	0	1	13.50	5	1	0	4⅔	11	3	5
Dick Scott	0	0	12.46	3	0	0	4⅓	10	1	1
	76	86	4.08	417	162	58	1,445	1,510	423	737

Shutouts: Buhl 3, Jackson 3, Burdette 2, Ellsworth 1.
Saves: McDaniel 15, Broglio 1.

	G	AB	H	2B	3B	HR	R	RBI	SB	AVG
Regulars										
1B Ernie Banks	157	591	156	29	6	23	67	95	1	.264
2B Joey Amalfitano	100	324	78	19	6	4	51	27	2	.241
SS Andre Rodgers	129	448	107	17	3	12	50	46	5	.239
3B Ron Santo	161	592	185	33	(13)	30	94	114	3	.313
RF Len Gabrielson	89	272	67	11	2	5	22	23	9	.246
CF Billy Cowan	139	497	120	16	4	19	52	50	12	.241
LF Billy Williams	162	645	201	39	2	33	100	98	10	.312
C Dick Bertell	112	353	84	11	3	4	29	35	2	.238
Substitutes										
Jimmy Stewart	132	415	105	17	0	3	59	33	10	.253
Ron Campbell	26	92	25	6	1	1	7	10	0	.272
John Boccabella	9	23	9	2	1	0	4	6	0	.391
Don Kessinger	4	12	2	0	0	0	1	0	0	.167
Lou Brock	52	215	54	9	2	2	30	14	10	.251
Doug Clemens	54	140	39	10	2	2	23	12	0	.279
Ellis Burton	42	105	20	3	2	2	12	7	4	.190
Leo Burke	59	103	27	3	1	1	11	14	0	.262
Billy Ott	20	39	7	3	0	0	4	1	0	.179
Don Landrum	11	11	0	0	0	0	2	0	0	.000
Jimmie Schaffer	54	122	25	6	1	2	9	9	2	.205
Vic Roznovsky	35	76	15	1	0	0	2	2	0	.197
Merritt Ranew	16	33	3	0	0	0	0	1	0	.091
Paul Popovich	1	1	1	0	0	0	0	0	0	1.000
Pitchers										
Larry Jackson	40	114	20	3	0	0	2	6	0	.175
Dick Ellsworth	37	87	4	0	0	0	4	1	0	.046
Bob Buhl	36	73	7	0	0	0	3	1	0	.096
Lew Burdette	28	43	12	0	1	2	6	4	0	.279
Ernie Broglio	18	35	10	1	0	0	2	0	0	.286
Lindy McDaniel	63	16	2	0	0	0	0	0	0	.125
Lee Gregory	19	13	1	0	0	0	0	0	0	.077
Sterling Slaughter	20	12	1	0	0	0	1	0	0	.083
Fred Norman	8	11	1	0	0	0	1	0	0	.091
Cal Koonce	6	10	0	0	0	0	0	0	0	.000
Don Elston	48	6	1	0	0	0	0	1	0	.167
Glen Hobbie	8	5	0	0	0	0	0	0	0	.000
Wayne Schurr	26	5	0	0	0	0	0	0	0	.000
Paul Toth	4	3	1	0	0	0	0	0	0	.333
Freddie Burdette	18	1	1	0	0	0	0	0	0	1.000
John Flavin	5	1	0	0	0	0	0	0	0	.000

	G	AB	H	2B	3B	HR	R	RBI	SB	AVG
Paul Jaeckel	4	1	0	0	0	0	0	0	0	.000
Dick Scott	3	0	0	0	0	0	0	0	0	—
Bobby Shantz	20	0	0	0	0	0	0	0	0	—
Jack Spring	7	0	0	0	0	0	0	0	0	—
Jack Warner	7	0	0	0	0	0	0	0	0	—
		5,545	1,391	239	50	145	649	609	70	.251

1965

Record: 72–90
Finish: Eighth
Games Behind: 25
Managers: Bob Kennedy, Lou Klein

The cast was changing. The Cubs had a new double-play combination in rookies Glenn Beckert and Don Kessinger. Beckert, 24, in his fourth season of pro ball, had been picked up for $8,000 in the winter draft, plucked out of the Boston Red Sox organization. Kessinger, a year younger, had been signed out of the University of Mississippi, where he had also been a basketball star.

On opening day, 1965, Beckert was at second base, Roberto Pena, another rookie import, at shortstop. Pena opened with a sensational batting performance—3-for-6, a home run, double, single, and three runs batted in—but committed three errors. After 51 games Pena had been charged with 17 errors and was struggling at the plate: a .218 average, including an 0-for-23 drought.

Kessinger had looked good in spring training but was sent to Dallas–Fort Worth for more experience. On June 10, Kessinger and Pena exchanged places and Kessinger was up to stay; for eight seasons he and Beckert, both excellent in the field and subsequent All-Stars, were among the best double-play partners of the time. They played in their 1,000th game on the same day, August 21, 1971.

Reliever Ted Abernathy was another significant newcomer. Abernathy, 32, had been bouncing around the majors and minors for 15 seasons before the Cubs acquired him on April 11 from Cleveland for a player to be named later. A submarine-baller, he released the ball an inch or two above the knee with an underhand delivery just like a softball pitcher; it had the effect of a rising knuckleball.

Initially, Abernathy was to be Lindy McDaniel's assistant in the bullpen. But Abernathy was a huge surprise. He was in 84 games, breaking the league record for appearances, and led in saves, 31, with an additional four victories in relief. McDaniel was 5–6 with two saves. Together, they were in 155 games, most ever by two relievers with the same club.

Larry Jackson and Dick Ellsworth combined for 28 victories, 14 each, but lost a total of 36 games. Bob Buhl was 13–11. Left-hander Bob Hendley, 4–4, was matched against the Dodgers' Sandy Koufax on September 9, and the game was nearly a double no-hitter. Koufax pitched a perfect game, a record fourth no-hitter, one each in four successive seasons. Hendley gave up only one hit, a looping seventh-inning double down the right-field line by Lou Johnson.

The Cubs had three 100-RBI men for the first time in 35 years: Billy Williams, 108; Ernie Banks, 106; and Ron Santo, 101. Santo made it with two RBIs in the final game. For a stretch of 39 games, from August 6 through September 18, Williams batted .403. He led the club with a .315 average and 34 home runs. Santo had 33, Banks 28. Nobody else had more than six.

There were two changes at the top. Colonel Whitlow resigned as the club's athletic director on January 8 because, he said, he wasn't earning his $25,000 salary. Wrigley expressed regrets. "Baseball simply refused to accept his ideas," Wrigley said. "He was too far ahead of his time." More accurately, Whitlow was muscled out by the established vice presidential triumvirate of John Holland, Charlie Grimm, and Clarence Rowland, none of whom paid much attention to him.

Bob Kennedy's two-and-a-half-year managerial reign ended 56 games into the season, on June 14. Kennedy was replaced by Lou Klein, at that time a roving batting coach. The club was 24–32 under Kennedy, 48–58 with Klein, and only five games under .500 on July 15 but finished in eighth place 25 games out. Kennedy, who had agreed to remain as Holland's assistant, departed after the World Series. The Leo Durocher era was about to begin.

	W	L	ERA	G	GS	CG	IP	H	BB	K
Larry Jackson	14	21	3.85	39	39	12	257⅓	268	57	131
Dick Ellsworth	14	15	3.81	36	34	8	222⅓	227	57	130
Bob Buhl	13	11	4.39	32	31	2	184½	207	57	92
Cal Koonce	7	9	3.69	38	23	3	173	181	52	88
Ted Abernathy	4	6	2.57	(84)	0	0	136⅓	113	56	104
Lindy McDaniel	5	6	2.59	71	0	0	128⅔	115	47	92
Bill Faul	6	6	3.54	17	16	5	96⅔	83	18	59
Bob Humphreys	2	0	3.15	41	0	0	65⅔	59	27	38
Bob Hendley	4	4	4.35	18	10	2	62	59	25	38
Billy Hoeft	2	2	2.81	29	2	1	51⅓	41	20	44
Ernie Broglio	1	6	6.93	26	6	0	50⅔	63	46	22
Lew Burdette	0	2	5.31	7	3	0	20⅓	26	4	5
Jack Warner	0	1	8.62	11	0	0	15⅔	22	9	7
Ken Holtzman	0	0	2.25	3	0	0	4	2	3	3
Frank Baumann	0	1	7.36	4	0	0	3⅔	4	3	2
	72	90	3.78	456	164	33	1,472	1,470	481	855

Shutouts: Jackson 4, Faul 3, Koonce 1.
Saves: Abernathy 31, McDaniel 2, Ellsworth 1.

	G	AB	H	2B	3B	HR	R	RBI	SB	AVG
Regulars										
1B Ernie Banks	163	612	162	25	3	28	79	106	3	.265
2B Glenn Beckert	154	614	147	21	3	3	73	30	6	.239
SS Don Kessinger	106	309	62	4	3	0	19	14	1	.201
3B Ron Santo	164	608	173	30	4	33	88	101	3	.285
RF Billy Williams	164	645	203	39	6	34	115	108	10	.315
CF Don Landrum	131	425	96	20	4	6	60	34	14	.226
LF Doug Clemens	128	340	75	11	0	4	36	26	5	.221
C Vic Roznovsky	71	172	38	4	1	3	9	15	1	.221
Substitutes										
Roberto Pena	51	170	37	5	1	2	17	12	1	.218
Joey Amalfitano	67	96	26	4	0	0	13	8	2	.271
John Boccabella	6	12	4	0	0	2	2	4	0	.333
Jimmy Stewart	116	282	63	9	4	0	26	19	13	.223
George Altman	90	196	46	7	1	4	24	23	3	.235
Harvey Kuenn	54	120	26	5	0	0	11	6	1	.217
Len Gabrielson	28	48	12	0	0	3	4	5	0	.250
Ellis Burton	17	40	7	1	0	0	6	4	1	.175
Don Young	11	35	2	0	0	1	1	2	0	.057
Byron Browne	4	6	0	0	0	0	0	0	0	.000
Chris Krug	60	169	34	5	0	5	16	24	0	.201
Ed Bailey	66	150	38	6	0	5	13	23	0	.253
Dick Bertell	34	84	18	2	0	0	6	7	0	.214
Leo Burke	12	10	2	0	0	0	0	0	0	.200
Harry Bright	27	25	7	1	0	0	1	4	0	.280
Ron Campbell	2	2	0	0	0	0	0	0	0	.000
Chuck Hartenstein	1	0	0	0	0	0	0	0	0	—
Pitchers										
Larry Jackson	49	86	11	0	2	1	6	5	0	.128
Dick Ellsworth	36	73	7	0	1	0	1	2	0	.096
Bob Buhl	32	67	4	0	0	0	3	2	0	.060
Cal Koonce	38	49	5	1	0	0	2	1	0	.102
Bill Faul	17	30	3	1	0	0	2	2	0	.100
Ted Abernathy	84	18	3	0	0	0	1	2	0	.167
Bob Hendley	18	14	0	0	0	0	0	1	0	.000
Billy Hoeft	29	11	3	0	0	0	1	0	0	.273

continued

	G	AB	H	2B	3B	HR	R	RBI	SB	AVG
Lindy McDaniel	71	8	0	0	0	0	0	0	0	.000
Lew Burdette	8	6	2	1	0	0	0	0	1	.333
Ernie Broglio	26	4	0	0	0	0	0	0	0	.000
Bob Humphreys	41	3	0	0	0	0	0	0	0	.000
Jack Warner	11	1	0	0	0	0	0	0	0	.000
Frank Baumann	4	0	0	0	0	0	0	0	0	—
Ken Holtzman	3	0	0	0	0	0	0	0	0	—
		5,540	1,316	202	33	134	635	590	65	.238

1966

Record: 59–103
Finish: Tenth
Games Behind: 36
Manager: Leo Durocher

Leo Durocher was signed on October 25, two weeks after the 1965 World Series, and with his customary blather said, "This definitely is not an eighth-place club." He was right. The Cubs finished tenth in 1966, lowest in club history. They lost eight of their first nine games, won the next two behind rookie pitchers Ferguson Jenkins and Ken Holtzman, and on April 28, after their 13th game, dropped to the bottom to stay.

Durocher, 60, had managed the Brooklyn Dodgers and the New York Giants to three pennants in the previous two decades. He was given a three-year contract at annual salary of $50,000, highest wage for a Cub manager. "Having Durocher as our manager is a definite plus for us," said pitcher Dick Ellsworth, echoing the sentiments of his teammates. "But he needs playing talent to win."

Durocher began retooling, replacing veterans with younger players. Two deals were extremely beneficial: catcher Randy Hundley, 23, and pitcher Bill Hands, 25, rookies, from the Giants for Lindy McDaniel and Don Landrum; and Jenkins and center fielder Adolfo Phillips, both 22, from the Phillies for ancients Larry Jackson and Bob Buhl.

Enamored of Phillips' speed and occasional defensive brilliance, Durocher began pumping him up as "another Willie Mays." Phillips led the club in stolen bases with 32 but batted .262 and struck out 135 times, including nine in a row, a major league record for a nonpitcher. Byron Browne, another rookie outfielder, was the club's whiff king—143, the league high.

Phillips and Browne exceeded the club's strikeout mark of 129 set by Ken Hubbs in 1962. They were also erratic in the field and didn't add much punch to what otherwise could have been an adequate attack: 87 runs batted in between them, four fewer than Billy Williams, the club's only consistent threat in the outfield.

It was a glorious year under trying circumstances for Ron Santo. On June 26, Santo suffered a fractured left cheekbone, struck in the face by a pitch from Jack Fisher of the Mets. Immediate surgery was required. Santo missed only seven games, returned on July 4 and extended his batting streak to a club-record 28 games. He led the club in the three principal offensive categories: batting, .312; home runs, 30; and RBIs, 94, also topping all NL third basemen in assists, putouts, and chances.

Pitching was the problem. Groping for an effective rotation, Durocher tried 12 starters in the first 48 games. In order, they were Larry Jackson, Ernie Broglio, Bob Buhl, Dick Ellsworth, Bob Hendley, Bill Hands, Ken Holtzman, Bill

Faul, Ferguson Jenkins, Chuck Estrada, Calvin Koonce, and Curt Simmons. Before the season ended, three more were tested: Robin Roberts, 39, longtime star with the Phillies, and rookies Rich Nye and Dave Dowling.

The Cubs had a 4.33 earned run average, highest in the league; the fewest shutouts, six, and complete games, 28. Holtzman, a hard-throwing left-hander with a smooth delivery, led the staff in victories with 11. His last win came on September 25 in a highly publicized matchup with Sandy Koufax, his boyhood idol. Holtzman had a no-hitter into the ninth, gave up two hits, and won 2–1.

Jenkins won as a starter for the first time on September 6. Bill Faul was sent to the minors on July 6 after a clubhouse shouting match with Durocher. Hundley caught 149 games, including 31 in a row. On November 29, the Circuit Court of Cook County awarded Jim Brewer a $100,000 judgment for his 1960 altercation with Billy Martin. The Cubs were no longer a party in the suit. Martin paid in installments.

	W	L	ERA	G	GS	CG	IP	H	BB	K
Dick Ellsworth	8	(22)	3.98	38	37	9	269⅓	(321)	51	144
Ken Holtzman	11	16	3.79	34	33	9	220⅔	194	68	171
Ferguson Jenkins	6	8	3.31	60	12	2	182	147	51	148
Bill Hands	8	13	4.58	41	26	0	159	168	59	93
Cal Koonce	5	5	3.81	45	5	0	108⅔	113	35	65
Bob Hendley	4	5	3.91	43	6	0	89⅔	98	39	65
Curt Simmons	4	7	4.07	19	10	3	77⅓	79	21	24
Ernie Broglio	2	6	6.35	15	11	2	62⅓	70	38	34
Bill Faul	1	4	5.08	17	6	1	51⅓	47	18	32
Robin Roberts	2	3	6.14	11	9	1	48⅓	62	11	28
Billy Hoeft	1	2	4.61	36	0	0	41	43	14	30

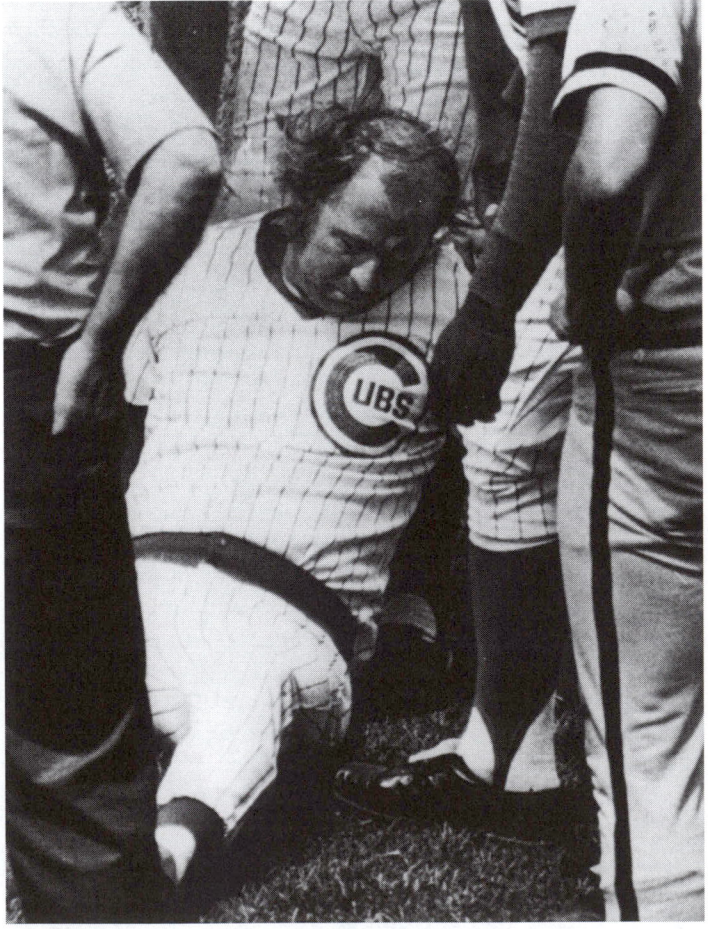

Ron Santo being helped after being hit by a pitch

	W	L	ERA	G	GS	CG	IP	H	BB	K
Ted Abernathy	1	3	6.18	20	0	0	27⅔	26	17	18
Don Lee	2	1	7.11	16	0	0	19	28	12	7
Arnie Earley	2	1	3.57	13	0	0	17⅔	14	9	12
Rich Nye	0	2	2.12	3	2	0	17	16	7	9
Bill Connors	0	1	7.31	11	0	0	16	20	7	3
Chuck Estrada	1	1	7.30	9	1	0	12⅓	16	5	3
Chuck Hartenstein	0	0	1.93	5	0	0	9⅓	8	3	4
Dave Dowling	1	0	2.00	1	1	1	9	10	0	3
Larry Jackson	0	2	13.50	3	2	0	8	14	4	5
Len Church	0	1	7.50	4	0	0	6	10	7	3
Fred Norman	0	0	4.50	2	0	0	4	5	2	6
Bob Buhl	0	0	15.43	1	1	0	2⅓	4	1	1
	59	103	4.33	447	162	28	1,458	1,513	479	908

Shutouts: Jenkins 1, Simmons 1.
Saves: Hendley 7, Jenkins 5, Abernathy 4, Hoeft 3, Hands 2, Koonce 2, Broglio 1.

	G	AB	H	2B	3B	HR	R	RBI	SB	AVG
Regulars										
1B Ernie Banks	141	511	139	23	7	15	52	75	0	.272
2B Glenn Beckert	153	656	188	23	7	1	73	59	10	.287
SS Don Kessinger	150	533	146	8	2	1	50	43	13	.274
3B Ron Santo	155	561	175	21	8	30	93	94	4	.312
RF Billy Williams	162	648	179	23	5	29	100	91	6	.276
CF Adolfo Phillips	116	416	109	29	1	16	68	36	32	.262
LF Byron Browne	120	419	102	15	7	16	46	51	3	.243
C Randy Hundley	149	526	124	22	3	19	50	63	1	.236
Substitutes										
Lee Thomas	75	149	36	4	0	1	15	9	0	.242
Ron Campbell	24	60	13	1	0	0	4	4	1	.217
Joey Amalfitano	41	38	6	2	0	0	8	3	0	.158
John Herrnstein	9	17	3	0	0	0	3	0	0	.176
Roberto Pena	6	17	3	2	0	0	0	1	0	.176
Paul Popovich	2	6	0	0	0	0	0	0	0	.000
John Boccabella	75	206	47	9	0	6	22	25	0	.228
George Altman	88	185	41	6	0	5	19	17	2	.222
Jimmy Stewart	57	90	16	4	1	0	4	4	1	.178
Bob Raudman	8	29	7	2	0	0	1	2	0	.241
Marty Keough	33	26	6	1	0	0	3	5	1	.231
Carl Warwick	16	22	5	0	0	0	3	0	0	.227
Ty Cline	7	17	6	0	0	0	3	2	1	.353
Wes Covington	9	11	1	0	0	0	0	0	0	.091
Harvey Kuenn	3	3	1	0	0	0	0	0	0	.333
Chris Krug	11	28	6	1	0	0	1	1	0	.214
Don Bryant	13	26	8	2	0	0	2	4	1	.308
Frank Thomas	5	5	0	0	0	0	0	0	0	.000
Pitchers										
Dick Ellsworth	38	90	14	0	1	0	7	5	0	.156
Ken Holtzman	34	73	9	1	0	0	2	2	0	.123
Ferguson Jenkins	60	51	7	0	1	1	6	2	0	.137
Bill Hands	41	49	2	1	0	0	2	1	0	.041
Cal Koonce	45	23	3	1	0	0	2	1	0	.130
Ernie Broglio	15	19	7	1	0	0	2	0	0	.368
Bob Hendley	43	18	3	1	0	0	2	2	0	.167
Curt Simmons	19	18	2	0	0	0	0	0	0	.111
Bill Faul	17	13	0	0	0	0	0	1	0	.000
Robin Roberts	11	10	2	0	0	0	1	0	0	.200
Ted Abernathy	20	4	0	0	0	0	0	0	0	.000
Billy Hoeft	36	4	1	0	0	0	0	0	0	.250
Rich Nye	3	4	1	0	0	0	0	0	0	.250
Chuck Estrada	9	3	0	0	0	0	0	0	0	.000
Larry Jackson	3	3	0	0	0	0	0	0	0	.000
Dave Dowling	1	2	0	0	0	0	0	0	0	.000
Bob Buhl	1	1	0	0	0	0	0	0	0	.000
Len Church	4	1	0	0	0	0	0	0	0	.000
Arnie Earley	13	1	0	0	0	0	0	0	0	.000
Bill Connors	11	0	0	0	0	0	0	0	0	—
Chuck Hartenstein	5	0	0	0	0	0	0	0	0	—
Don Lee	16	0	0	0	0	0	0	0	0	—
Fred Norman	2	0	0	0	0	0	0	0	0	—
		5,592	1,418	203	43	140	644	603	76	.254

1967

Record: 87–74
Finish: Third
Games Behind: 14
Manager: Leo Durocher

After wandering in the second-division wasteland for a major-league-record 20 consecutive years, the Cubs swept onward and upward. With Durocher at the whip, they led the league in runs and fielding, were third in batting, and soared from tenth place to third, 3½ games out of second place, their best showing since a third-place finish in 1946. They won 87 games, the most since the World War II year of 1945.

Ferguson Jenkins led the climb with a 20–13 record, the first of his six successive 20-victory seasons. Jenkins led the league with 20 complete games and broke the club's 59-year-old strikeout record with 236. Left-hander Kenny Holtzman, in the military, available for the equivalent of only six weeks, made 12 starts and was 9–0, the fifth pitcher in big league history with more than eight decisions to finish without a loss.

Durocher used 21 pitchers, many of whom were soon discarded; 12 made fewer than three starts. Aside from Jenkins, only Rich Nye and Joe Niekro won in double figures. Nye was 13–10, Niekro 10–7. Bill Hands, who the previous season was unable to complete any of his 26 starts, was the swing man, 11 starts and 38 relief appearances. He was 7–8 with six saves and a club-low 2.46 ERA.

The Cubs were at .500 eight times but never below. From June 16 through July 3, they won 14 out of 15, which included two seven-game winning streaks, their longest in 13 years. On July 3, following a 12–6 victory over Atlanta, they were 46–29, the high-water mark, 17 games over .500, and tied for the league lead.

To Durocher's dismay, Ernie Banks helped lead the surge. Though Durocher had many favorites, Banks was never among them. Envious, stewing in anger over Banks' enormous popularity, Durocher referred to him as "Mr. Cub, my ass!" At 36, Banks had lost much of his speed and never took more than a minimal lead when he was on base. In another attempt at embarrassment, Durocher repeatedly told him he would give him $100 each time he was picked off.

John Boccabella, Clarence Jones, Lee Thomas, and Norm Gigon all were candidates to succeed Banks at first base, but Banks was in the opening-day lineup and knocked out six hits in the first four games, two of them home runs. A fierce competitor beneath his cheerful disposition, Banks played in 151 games and batted .276 with 23 home runs and 95 runs batted in, 11 more RBIs than Billy Williams and within three of tying Ron Santo for the team lead.

Kessinger and Beckert were now acknowledged as the Cubs' best second base combination since Billy Herman and Bill Jurges. Randy Hundley, baseball's first one-handed catcher—he kept his bare hand behind his back to prevent injuries from foul tips—caught every inning in 56 consecutive games; he played in a record 152 games and was charged with only four errors, also a team record. Right field was the only trouble spot; 11 players were used at this position. Williams batted .278, with 28 home runs, and stretched his consecutive-game streak to 652.

Center fielder Adolfo Phillips, a 24-year-old Panamanian, was the early league leader in home runs, RBIs, and average. On June 11, in a doubleheader against the Mets, he was 6-for-9, including four home runs, three in the second game. He also made two diving catches. It was an unforgettable moment. Wrigley Field was suddenly a bull ring. The fans responded with six standing ovations: "Olé! Adolfo! Olé!" Phillips was hitting .328 going into a return series at Shea Stadium the following weekend. The Met pitchers repeatedly knocked him down. When he complained, other pitchers began throwing at him. He batted .229 thereafter.

	W	L	ERA	G	GS	CG	IP	H	BB	K
Ferguson Jenkins	20	13	2.80	38	38	(20)	289⅓	230	83	236
Rich Nye	13	10	3.20	35	30	7	205	179	52	119
Joe Niekro	10	7	3.34	36	22	7	169⅔	171	32	77
Ray Culp	8	11	3.89	30	22	4	152⅔	138	59	111
Bill Hands	7	8	2.46	49	11	3	150	134	48	84
Ken Holtzman	9	0	2.53	12	12	3	92⅔	76	44	62
Curt Simmons	3	7	4.94	17	14	3	82	100	23	31
Chuck Hartenstein	9	5	3.08	45	0	0	73	74	17	20
Bill Stoneman	2	4	3.29	28	2	0	63	51	22	52
Cal Koonce	2	2	4.59	34	0	0	51	52	21	28
Rob Gardner	0	2	3.98	18	5	0	31⅓	33	6	16
Dick Radatz	1	0	6.56	20	0	0	23⅓	12	24	18
Bob Shaw	0	2	6.04	9	3	0	22⅓	33	9	7
Jim Ellis	1	1	3.24	8	1	0	16⅔	20	9	8
Bob Hendley	2	0	6.57	7	0	0	12⅓	17	3	10
Pete Mikkelsen	0	0	6.43	7	0	0	7	9	5	0
Rick James	0	1	13.50	3	1	0	4⅔	9	2	2
Dick Calmus	0	0	8.31	1	1	0	4⅓	5	0	1
Don Larsen	0	0	9.00	3	0	0	4	5	2	1
John Upham	0	1	33.75	5	0	0	1⅓	4	2	2
Fred Norman	0	0	0.00	1	0	0	1	0	0	3
	87	74	3.48	406	162	47	1,457	1,352	463	888

Shutouts: Jenkins 3, Niekro 2, Culp 1, Hands 1.
Saves: Hartenstein 10, Hands 6, Radatz 5, Stoneman 4, Koonce 2, Hendley 1.

	G	AB	H	2B	3B	HR	R	RBI	SB	AVG
Regulars										
1B Ernie Banks	151	573	158	26	4	23	68	95	2	.276
2B Glenn Beckert	146	597	167	32	3	5	91	40	10	.280
SS Don Kessinger	145	580	134	10	7	0	61	42	6	.231
3B Ron Santo	161	586	176	23	4	31	107	98	1	.300
RF Ted Savage	96	225	49	10	1	5	40	33	7	.218
CF Adolfo Phillips	144	448	120	20	7	17	66	70	24	.268
LF Billy Williams	162	634	176	21	12	28	92	84	6	.278
C Randy Hundley	182	539	144	25	3	14	68	60	2	.267
Substitutes										
Paul Popovich	49	159	34	4	0	0	18	2	0	.214
Norm Gigon	34	70	12	3	1	1	8	6	0	.171
Lee Thomas	77	191	42	4	1	2	16	23	1	.220
Clarence Jones	53	135	34	7	0	2	13	16	0	.252
Al Spangler	62	130	33	7	0	0	18	13	2	.254
John Boccabella	25	35	6	1	1	0	0	8	0	.171
Bob Raudman	8	26	4	0	0	0	0	1	0	.154
Byron Browne	10	19	3	2	0	0	3	2	1	.158
George Altman	15	18	2	2	0	0	1	1	0	.111
Joe Campbell	1	3	0	0	0	0	0	0	0	.000
Johnny Stephenson	18	49	11	3	1	0	3	5	0	.224
Dick Bertell	2	6	1	0	1	0	1	0	0	.167
Jimmy Stewart	6	6	1	0	0	0	1	1	0	.167
Joey Amalfitano	4	1	0	0	0	0	0	0	0	.000

	G	AB	H	2B	3B	HR	R	RBI	SB	AVG
Pitchers										
Ferguson Jenkins	39	93	14	3	1	0	5	10	0	.151
Rich Nye	35	75	16	4	0	0	5	4	0	.213
Ray Culp	30	51	5	0	2	0	4	5	0	.098
Joe Niekro	36	46	9	2	0	0	5	11	1	.196
Bill Hands	49	38	4	0	0	0	0	3	0	.105
Ken Holtzman	12	35	7	1	0	0	4	2	0	.200
Curt Simmons	17	28	4	0	0	0	1	3	0	.143
Chuck Hartenstein	45	16	1	0	0	0	0	1	0	.063
Bill Stoneman	28	13	0	0	0	0	0	0	0	.000
Cal Koonce	34	7	0	0	0	0	0	0	0	.000
Rob Gardner	18	6	0	0	0	0	1	0	0	.000
Bob Hendley	7	6	0	0	0	0	0	0	0	.000
Jim Ellis	8	5	1	1	0	0	0	1	0	.200
Dick Radatz	20	4	1	0	0	0	0	0	0	.250
Bob Shaw	9	4	1	0	0	0	0	0	0	.250
John Upham	8	3	2	0	0	0	1	0	0	.667
Dick Calmus	1	2	1	0	0	0	1	2	0	.500
Rick James	3	1	0	0	0	0	0	0	0	.000
Don Larsen	3	0	0	0	0	0	0	0	0	—
Pete Mikkelsen	7	0	0	0	0	0	0	0	0	—
Fred Norman	1	0	0	0	0	0	0	0	0	—
		5,463	1,373	211	49	128	702	642	63	.251

1968

Record: 84–78
Finish: Third
Games Behind: 13
Manager: Leo Durocher

The irrepressible Ernie Banks, who had an annual pennant slogan, predicted, "Don't Fear, This Is the Year!" He was overly optimistic. The 1968 season wasn't *the* year, but it was another successful one: the first million home gate since 1952 and another third-place finish, 13 games behind the first-place Cardinals.

Despite a record five 1–0 losses, Ferguson Jenkins was 20–15, the club's first back-to-back 20-game winner since Lon Warneke in 1934–35. Jenkins led the league in starts, 40, and was second in innings pitched, 308, and strikeouts, 260, surpassing the club record of 236 he had set the previous season.

Bill Hands, now a rotation starter, was next with 16 wins, followed by Joe Niekro with 14. Ken Holtzman, coming off an undefeated season, was 11–14. Veteran reliever Phil Regan, acquired on April 24 in a beneficial deal with the Dodgers, kept the club afloat with a league-high 25 saves and 10 victories, all out of the bullpen. No other reliever had more than two saves.

According to off-season reports, Regan was suffering from an arthritic arm. He was sound throughout, appearing in 68 games, and subjected to repeated "strip searches." The umpires trudged to the mound, inspected his glove and cap for Vaseline or other outlawed lubricants and on several occasions had him remove his belt and shirt, all in unsuccessful efforts to locate a foreign substance.

On August 18, in the first game of a doubleheader against Cincinnati, plate umpire Chris Pelekoudas, in an unprecedented action, charged Regan with throwing three illegal pitches "by watching the break of the ball." In each instance, the count was changed and Regan was charged with a ball. Alex Johnson, in one at bat, was given two extra swings. Pete Rose, after striking out, was allowed to return and singled on the next pitch.

General manager John Holland protested, and the next morning league president Warren Giles flew in from Rochester, New York, where he had had a speaking engagement. An angry Giles advised the umpires that observing the "break of the ball" was not sufficient evidence of an illegal pitch. Pelekoudas was instructed to apologize to Regan, who taught Sunday school and, was, according to Giles, "a fine Christian gentleman."

The Cubs led the league in home runs with 130. Banks, still strong at 37, hit 32, followed by Billy Williams with 30 and Ron Santo with 26. There were no .300 hitters; Glenn Beckert's .294 was the club high. Beckert hit safely in 27 consecutive games, from June 26 through July 23, the longest streak in either league and one short of Santo's team record. For the third year in a row, Beckert led the NL in fewest strikeouts, 20 in 643 at bats.

The Cubs never won more than five games in succession and prior to the final weekend were in third place only one day, on April 28 after sweeping a doubleheader against Houston. From June 15 through June 29 they lost 12 out of 23. During this stretch they were scoreless for 48 consecutive innings, tying the major league record set in the dead-ball era by the 1906 Philadelphia Athletics.

On April 19, after a 9–2 loss to St. Louis, Durocher publicly criticized Banks when he failed to score from third on a ground ball. Said Durocher: "He should have been running, but he just won't get off the bag." Banks played in his 2,254th game on September 15, breaking Cap Anson's club record. After the season, Alderman John Hoellen recommended a statue of Banks be erected and placed in front of City Hall as a symbol of Chicago.

	W	L	ERA	G	GS	CG	IP	H	BB	K
Ferguson Jenkins	20	15	2.63	40	(40)	20	308	255	65	260
Bill Hands	16	10	2.89	38	34	11	258⅔	221	36	148
Ken Holtzman	11	14	3.35	34	32	6	215	201	76	151
Joe Niekro	14	10	4.31	34	29	2	177⅓	204	59	65
Rich Nye	7	12	3.80	27	20	6	132⅔	145	34	74
Phil Regan	10	5	2.20	68	0	0	127	109	24	60
Jack Lamabe	3	2	4.30	42	0	0	60⅔	68	24	30
Gary Ross	1	1	4.17	13	5	1	41	44	25	31
Chuck Hartenstein	2	4	4.54	28	0	0	35⅔	41	11	17
Bill Stoneman	0	1	5.52	18	0	0	29⅓	35	14	18
Bobby Tiefenauer	0	1	6.08	9	0	0	13⅓	20	2	9
Archie Reynolds	0	1	6.75	7	1	0	13⅓	14	7	6
Darcy Fast	0	1	5.40	8	1	0	10	8	8	10
Ramon Hernandez	0	0	9.00	8	0	0	9	14	0	3
John Upham	0	0	0.00	2	0	0	7	2	3	2
Frank Reberger	0	1	4.50	3	1	0	6	9	2	3
Pete Mikkelsen	0	0	7.71	3	0	0	4⅔	7	1	5
Willie Smith	0	0	0.00	1	0	0	2⅔	0	0	2
Jophery Brown	0	0	4.50	1	0	0	2	2	1	0
	84	78	3.41	384	163	46	1,453⅓	1,399	392	894

Shutouts: Hands 4, Holtzman 3, Jenkins 3, Niekro 1, Nye 1.
Saves: Regan (25), Niekro 2, Hartenstein 1, Holtzman 1, Lamabe 1, Nye 1, Tiefenauer 1.

	G	AB	H	2B	3B	HR	R	RBI	SB	AVG
Regulars										
1B Ernie Banks	150	552	136	27	0	32	71	83	2	.246
2B Glenn Beckert	155	643	189	28	4	4	(98)	37	8	.294
SS Don Kessinger	160	655	157	14	7	1	63	32	9	.240
3B Ron Santo	162	577	142	17	3	26	86	98	3	.246
RF Jim Hickman	75	188	42	6	3	5	22	23	1	.223
CF Adolfo Phillips	143	439	106	20	5	13	49	33	9	.241
LF Billy Williams	163	642	185	30	8	30	91	98	4	.288
C Randy Hundley	160	553	125	18	4	7	41	65	1	.226
Substitutes										
Dick Nen	81	94	17	1	1	2	8	16	0	.181
Lee Elia	15	17	3	0	0	0	1	3	0	.176
Gene Oliver	8	11	4	0	0	0	1	1	0	.364
Clarence Jones	5	2	0	0	0	0	0	0	0	.000
Vic LaRose	4	2	0	0	0	0	0	0	0	.000
Lou Johnson	62	205	50	14	3	1	14	14	3	.244
Al Spangler	88	177	48	9	3	2	21	18	0	.271
Willie Smith	55	142	39	8	2	5	13	25	0	.275

	G	AB	H	2B	3B	HR	R	RBI	SB	AVG
Jose Arcia	59	84	16	4	0	1	15	8	0	.190
Jimmy McMath	6	14	2	0	0	0	0	2	0	.143
John Upham	13	10	2	0	0	0	0	0	0	.200
Ted Savage	3	8	2	0	0	0	0	0	0	.250
John Boccabella	7	14	1	0	0	0	0	1	0	.071
Randy Bobb	7	8	1	0	0	0	0	0	0	.125
Bill Plummer	2	2	0	0	0	0	0	0	0	.000
John Felske	4	2	0	0	0	0	0	0	0	.000
Johnny Stephenson	2	2	0	0	0	0	0	0	0	.000
Pitchers										
Ferguson Jenkins	40	100	16	4	0	1	4	10	0	.160
Bill Hands	38	82	5	0	0	0	2	0	0	.061
Ken Holtzman	35	80	10	1	0	0	4	5	0	.125
Joe Niekro	34	60	6	0	0	0	2	0	0	.100
Rich Nye	27	44	8	0	0	0	0	2	0	.182
Phil Regan	68	20	3	1	0	0	3	1	0	.150
Gary Ross	13	11	1	0	0	0	1	1	0	.091
Jack Lamabe	42	5	1	0	0	0	0	0	1	.200
Bill Stoneman	18	4	0	0	0	0	0	0	0	.000
Darcy Fast	8	3	0	0	0	0	0	0	0	.000
Chuck Hartenstein	28	2	0	0	0	0	0	0	0	.000
Archie Reynolds	7	2	1	1	0	0	2	0	0	.500
Pete Mikkelsen	3	1	1	0	0	0	0	0	0	1.000
Bobby Tiefenauer	9	1	0	0	0	0	0	0	0	.000
Ramon Hernandez	8	0	0	0	0	0	0	0	0	—
Frank Reberger	3	0	0	0	0	0	0	0	0	—
Jophery Brown	1	0	0	0	0	0	0	0	0	—
	5,458	1,319	203	43		(130)	612	576	41	.242

1969

Record: 92–70
Finish: Second (East)
Games Behind: 8
Manager: Leo Durocher

It was the year of the Great Flop, among the most exciting seasons in Cub history and certainly the most disappointing. The Cubs were in first place 155 days without interruption, had the National League's All-Star infield including catcher Randy Hundley, had a pair of 20-game winners in Ferguson Jenkins and Bill Hands, and had the long-ball triumvirate of Ernie Banks, Billy Williams, and Roy Santo. Combined, the three batted .279 with an average of 24 home runs and 108 runs batted in.

The Cubs broke the Chicago attendance record in 1969 and were lionized daily by a Niagara of newspaper and broadcast publicity. The theme song, played incessantly, was "Hey, Hey, Holy Mackerel. No Doubt about It. The Cubs Are on the Way." But at the bitter finish there was no doubt the '69 Cubs were among the storied failures in diamond history.

They limped home in second place in the Eastern Division, eight games behind the Miracle Mets, who mauled them, head to head, and won 38 of their last 49 games. "I never saw anything like it," Durocher groaned. "Our offense went down the toilet, the defense went down the drain, and I'm still looking for a pitching staff."

Certain of success, the players agreed to divide the spoils. Jack Childers, a Chicago business agent, had free run of the clubhouse and was constantly returning with endorsement deals. In May player rep Phil Regan revealed that $30,000 was already in the till, in a special bank account, to be divided equally, similar to World Series swag. Prior to the collapse the pot had grown to $125,000.

The Cubs started fast, won their first four games and 14 of 20. From May 11 to 13, Ken Holtzman, Ferguson Jenkins, and Dick Selma pitched successive shutouts, 8–0 over the Giants, 2–0 and 19–0 against the Padres. The following week the Cubs launched an eight-game winning streak, and they were 21 over .500 with an 8½ game lead after sweeping a June 15 doubleheader from Cincinnati.

The first ominous sign came 11 days later. In the third inning of a game with the Dodgers, Durocher complained of a stomachache and left the club. But instead of going to his hotel he boarded a chartered plane and went to see his stepson at Camp Ojibwa in Eagle River, Wisconsin, 400 miles away. When he returned three days later, his secret mission discovered, Wrigley said, "The players have been showing wonderful spirit. Leo owes them an apology."

More dissension followed. On July 8 against the Mets in Shea Stadium, rookie center fielder Don Young misplayed two ninth-inning fly balls, both falling for doubles, which led to a 4–3 loss. Durocher and Santo came down hard on Young. "He had a bad day at the plate," Santo said, "so he's got his head down. He's worried about his batting average, not the team." The next day Santo called a press conference and said he was sorry; he didn't mean it.

When play began on August 14 the Cubs still had a commanding lead, 8½ games ahead of the second-place Cardinals, 9½ ahead of the third-place Mets. The pivotal game was a 3–2 loss to the Mets on September 8. Tommie Agee, who had hit a two-run home run in the third inning, scored the winning run from second on a single to right in the sixth. The throw came in on one bounce, on the right side. A quarter of a century later Hundley was still insisting, "I made the bloomin' tag."

The Mets won again the next night, 7–1 behind Seaver, to trim the Cub lead to a half game, followed with a September 10 doubleheader sweep against Montreal, and led the rest of the way. Dr. Harvey Mandel, a Chicago psychiatrist, said the Cubs had "an unconscious desire to lose the pennant."

	W	L	ERA	G	GS	CG	IP	H	BB	K
Ferguson Jenkins	21	15	3.21	43	(42)	23	311	284	71	(273)
Bill Hands	20	14	2.49	41	41	18	300	268	73	181
Ken Holtzman	17	13	3.59	39	39	12	261	248	93	176
Dick Selma	10	8	3.63	36	25	4	168⅔	137	72	161
Phil Regan	12	6	3.70	71	0	0	112	120	35	56
Ted Abernathy	4	3	3.18	56	0	0	85	75	42	55
Rich Nye	3	5	5.09	34	5	1	69	72	21	39
Hank Aguirre	1	0	2.60	41	0	0	45	45	12	19
Joe Niekro	0	1	3.72	4	3	0	19⅓	24	6	7
Ken Johnson	1	2	2.84	9	1	0	19	17	13	18
Don Nottebart	1	1	7.00	16	0	0	18	28	7	8
Jim Colborn	1	0	3.00	6	2	0	15	15	9	4
Joe Decker	1	0	3.00	4	1	0	12	10	6	13
Archie Reynolds	0	1	2.57	2	2	0	7	11	7	4
Alec Distaso	0	0	3.60	2	0	0	5	6	1	1
Dave Lemonds	0	1	3.60	2	1	0	5	5	5	0
Gary Ross	0	0	13.50	2	1	0	2	1	2	2
	92	70	3.34	408	163	58	1,454	1,366	475	1,017

Shutouts: Jenkins 7, Holtzman 6, Hands 3, Selma 2.
Saves: Regan 17, Abernathy 3, Nye 3, Aguirre 1, Jenkins 1, Selma 1, Johnson 1.

	G	AB	H	2B	3B	HR	R	RBI	SB	AVG
Regulars										
1B Ernie Banks	155	565	143	19	2	23	60	106	0	.253
2B Glenn Beckert	131	543	158	22	1	1	69	37	6	.291
SS Don Kessinger	158	664	181	38	6	4	109	53	11	.273
3B Ron Santo	160	575	166	18	4	29	97	123	1	.289
RF Jim Hickman	134	338	80	11	2	21	38	54	2	.237
CF Don Young	101	272	65	12	3	6	36	27	1	.239
LF Billy Williams	163	642	188	33	10	21	103	95	3	.293
C Randy Hundley	151	522	133	15	1	18	67	64	2	.255
Substitutes										
Paul Popovich	60	154	48	6	0	1	26	14	0	.312
Nate Oliver	44	44	7	3	0	1	15	4	0	.159
Rick Bladt	10	13	2	0	0	0	1	1	0	.154
Al Spangler	82	213	45	8	1	4	23	23	0	.211

	G	AB	H	2B	3B	HR	R	RBI	SB	AVG
Willie Smith	103	195	48	9	1	9	21	25	1	.246
Jim Qualls	43	120	30	5	3	0	12	9	2	.250
Oscar Gamble	24	71	16	1	1	1	6	5	0	.225
Adolfo Phillips	28	49	11	3	1	0	5	1	1	.224
Jimmie Hall	11	24	5	1	0	0	1	1	0	.208
Ken Rudolph	27	34	7	1	0	1	7	6	0	.206
Bill Heath	27	32	5	0	1	0	1	1	0	.156
Gene Oliver	23	27	6	3	0	0	0	0	0	.222
John Hairston	3	4	1	0	0	0	0	0	0	.250
Randy Bobb	3	2	0	0	0	0	0	0	0	.000
Manny Jimenez	6	6	1	0	0	0	0	0	0	.167
Charley Smith	1	2	0	0	0	0	0	0	0	.000
Pitchers										
Ferguson Jenkins	43	108	15	2	1	1	6	9	0	.139
Ken Holtzman	39	100	15	1	1	1	5	7	0	.150
Bill Hands	41	98	9	0	0	0	5	3	0	.092
Dick Selma	36	52	8	1	1	0	3	0	0	.154
Rich Nye	36	16	1	0	0	0	1	0	0	.063
Phil Regan	71	15	1	1	0	0	0	0	0	.067
Ted Abernathy	56	8	2	1	0	0	1	1	0	.250
Hank Aguirre	41	5	2	0	0	0	2	0	0	.400
Joe Niekro	4	5	1	1	0	0	0	2	0	.200
Ken Johnson	9	4	0	0	0	0	0	0	0	.000
Jim Colborn	6	3	0	0	0	0	0	0	0	.000
Joe Decker	4	2	0	0	0	0	0	0	0	.000
Don Nottebart	16	1	0	0	0	0	0	0	0	.000
Archie Reynolds	2	1	0	0	0	0	0	0	0	.000
Dave Lemonds	2	1	0	0	0	0	0	0	0	.000
Gary Ross	2	0	0	0	0	0	0	0	0	—
Alec Distaso	2	0	0	0	0	0	0	0	0	—
	5,530	1,400	215	40	142	720	671	30	.253

1970

Record: 84–78
Finish: Second (East)
Games Behind: 5
Manager: Leo Durocher

Often, one pennant begets another. If the Cubs had succeeded in '69, more than likely they would have won again the following year. But 1970 was more of the same, another second-place finish but without the hoopla. With lowered expectations, it was, comparatively, a season with cathedral-like silence.

There were similarities. Again they had good early foot. Beginning on April 14, six games into the new season, they launched an 11-game winning streak, longest in 34 years, and were in first place continuously from April 21 through June 3. A doubleheader loss to the hated Mets dropped them to second place. They never led again, though as late as September 4 they were within .004 percentage points of the lead.

As in the previous season, there were outstanding individual achievements. The Cubs were the only club in the league with three pitchers who won more than 15 games, also the only team with three sluggers with more than 25 home runs and 100 runs batted in. Ferguson Jenkins was 21–16, Ken Holtzman 17–11, and Bill Hands 18–15. Billy Williams had 42 home runs and 129 RBIs, Jim Hickman 32 and 115, Ron Santo 26 and 114.

It was Jenkins' fourth 20-victory season, making him the only active pitcher in either league to reach this plateau in four consecutive seasons. Holtzman had a one-hitter, two-hitter, three-hitter, and five-hitter after the All-Star break; in two of these games he carried a no-hitter into the eighth inning.

The problem was in the bullpen. Phil Regan led the club with only 12 saves and was 5–9 with a 4.74 earned run average. Wearying in his search for an effective reliever, Durocher locked the bullpen door or, as he often did, kept

May 9, 1970: Ernie Banks acknowledges the cheers of the crowd after hitting his 499th career home run.

it closed until it was too late. Relievers were summoned in 17 games with the tying or winning run on base, when there was no room for error; 15 of these games were lost.

Cub pitchers had a league-high 59 complete games, 50 of them victories. Jenkins led the league in completions, 24, was second in innings pitched, 313, and tied for second in strikeouts, 274, a Cub record. A control pitcher with a wide repertoire, he also led in fewest walks, 1.7 for every nine innings of toil.

It was a heroic year for Williams. Going into the September stretch he was among the batting leaders and was dueling Cincinnati's Johnny Bench for the home run and RBI leads, but his visions of a Triple Crown soon faded. He finished second to Bench in home runs, 45 to 42, and RBIs, 148 to 129, and was fourth in batting with a .322 average.

There were consolations. Williams tied Pete Rose for the most hits, 205, and led in runs, 137, the most in either league

in 23 years. He also extended his playing streak to an NL record 1,117 consecutive games. Durocher had been urging him to break the streak; a day off would be beneficial. Williams benched himself on September 3.

Hickman also had his best season. It was his ninth year in the big leagues but only his second as a regular. He batted .315, the club's only .300 hitter except for Williams. Hickman was also second to Williams in home runs and RBIs. Ernie Banks, 39, was nearing the end: 222 at bats, 12 home runs, and 44 RBIs.

Randy Hundley, the iron-man catcher, suffered a fractured left thumb in spring training and was hurt again, much more seriously, on April 18 in another collision at the plate: torn ligaments in his left knee. He was out for three months. The Cubs hung in and were only a game and a half back on September 19. They were eliminated eight days later.

	W	L	ERA	G	GS	CG	IP	H	BB	K
Ferguson Jenkins	22	16	3.39	40	39	(24)	313	265	60	274
Ken Holtzman	17	11	3.38	39	38	15	288	271	94	202
Bill Hands	18	15	3.70	39	38	12	265	278	76	170
Milt Pappas	10	8	2.68	21	20	6	144⅔	135	36	80
Joe Decker	2	7	4.62	24	17	1	109	108	56	79
Phil Regan	5	9	4.74	54	0	0	76	81	32	31
Jim Colborn	3	1	3.58	34	5	0	73	88	23	50
Roberto Rodriguez	3	2	5.82	26	0	0	43⅓	50	15	46
Larry Gura	1	3	3.79	20	3	1	38	35	23	21
Juan Pizarro	0	0	4.50	12	0	0	16	16	9	14
Archie Reynolds	0	2	6.60	7	1	0	15	17	9	9
Hank Aguirre	3	0	4.50	17	0	0	14	13	9	11
Jim Dunegan	0	2	4.85	7	0	0	13	13	12	3
Ted Abernathy	0	0	2.00	11	0	0	9	9	5	2
Bob Miller	0	0	5.00	7	1	0	9	6	6	4
Steve Barber	0	1	9.53	5	0	0	5⅔	10	6	3
Hoyt Wilhelm	0	1	9.82	3	0	0	3⅔	4	3	1
Jim Cosman	0	0	27.00	1	0	0	1	3	1	0
	84	78	3.76	367	162	(59)	1,436⅓	1,402	475	1,000

Shutouts: Jenkins 3, Hands 2, Pappas 2, Holtzman 1.
Saves: Regan 12, Colborn 4, Miller 2, Rodriguez 2, Abernathy 1, Aguirre 1, Gura 1, Hands 1, Pizarro 1.

	G	AB	H	2B	3B	HR	R	RBI	SB	AVG
Regulars										
1B Jim Hickman	149	514	162	33	4	32	102	115	0	.315
2B Glenn Beckert	143	591	170	15	6	3	99	36	4	.288
SS Don Kessinger	154	631	168	21	14	1	100	39	12	.266
3B Ron Santo	154	555	148	30	4	26	83	114	2	.267
RF Johnny Callison	147	477	126	23	2	19	65	68	7	.264
CF Cleo James	100	176	37	7	2	3	33	14	5	.210
LF Billy Williams	161	636	(205)	34	4	42	(137)	129	7	.322
C Randy Hundley	73	250	61	5	0	7	13	36	0	.244
Substitutes										
Ernie Banks	72	222	56	6	2	12	25	44	0	.252
paul popovich	78	186	47	5	1	4	22	20	0	.253
Willie Smith	87	167	36	9	4	5	15	24	2	.216
Phil Gagliano	26	40	6	0	0	0	5	3	0	.150
Roger Metzger	1	2	0	0	0	0	0	0	0	.000
Joe Pepitone	56	213	57	9	2	12	38	44	0	.268
Tommy Davis	11	42	11	2	0	2	4	8	0	.262
Jimmie Hall	28	32	3	1	0	0	2	1	0	.094
Al Spangler	21	14	2	1	0	1	2	1	0	.143
Boots Day	11	8	2	0	0	0	2	0	0	.250
Brock Davis	6	3	0	0	0	0	0	0	0	.000
Terry Hughes	2	3	1	0	0	0	0	0	0	.333
Jack Hiatt	66	178	43	12	1	2	19	22	0	.242
J. C. Martin	40	77	12	1	0	1	11	4	0	.156
Ken Rudolph	20	40	4	1	0	0	1	2	0	.100
Adrian Garrett	3	3	0	0	0	0	0	0	0	.000
Roe Skidmore	1	1	1	0	0	0	0	0	0	1.000
Pitchers										
Ferguson Jenkins	40	113	14	2	0	3	4	11	0	.124
Ken Holtzman	40	105	21	5	0	0	6	6	0	.200
Bill Hands	39	75	10	2	0	0	6	6	0	.133
Milt Pappas	21	50	12	2	1	2	7	5	0	.240

continued

	G	AB	H	2B	3B	HR	R	RBI	SB	AVG
Joe Decker	24	34	6	1	0	1	3	3	0	.176
Jim Colborn	34	15	1	0	0	0	0	1	0	.067
Larry Gura	20	10	0	0	0	0	0	0	0	.000
Phil Regan	54	9	0	0	0	0	1	0	0	.000
Roberto Rodriguez	26	8	1	0	0	1	1	1	0	.125
Jim Dunegan	10	4	1	1	0	0	0	2	0	.250
Juan Pizarro	12	3	0	0	0	0	0	0	0	.000
Hank Aguirre	17	2	0	0	0	0	0	0	0	.000
Archie Reynolds	7	2	0	0	0	0	0	0	0	.000
Ted Abernathy	11	0	0	0	0	0	0	0	0	—
Steve Barber	5	0	0	0	0	0	0	0	0	—
Jim Cosman	1	0	0	0	0	0	0	0	0	—
Bob Miller	7	0	0	0	0	0	0	0	0	—
Hoyt Wilhelm	3	0	0	0	0	0	0	0	0	—
		5,491	1,424	228	44	179	806	761	39	.259

1971

Record: 83–79
Finish: Third (tie) (East)
Games Behind: 14
Manager: Leo Durocher

It was another crisis, and owner Philip Wrigley, unwilling to make a conventional announcement and rely on a simultaneous interpretation by the press, delivered the message in a paid advertisement published in all four Chicago dailies. The sixth and final paragraph:

"Leo is the team manager and the 'Dump Durocher Clique' might as well give up. He is running the team, and if some of the players do not like it and lie down on the job, during the off-season, we will see what we can do to find them happier homes."

It was the third time Wrigley believed it necessary to advertise, either in apology or defense of the club. But this manifesto was without precedent. An owner, in effect, was firing the players, not the manager—in response to a festering player rebellion that erupted during a stormy August 23 clubhouse meeting.

The Cubs were not struggling. They had won 12 out of 20 and were only 4½ games out of the lead. But the day before Milt Pappas had been defeated by the Houston Astros when Doug Rader doubled on an 0–2 pitch. In that situation the pitcher must waste a pitch; to feed the batter another strike is unforgivable.

Durocher ripped into Pappas. Pappas remained silent. First baseman Joe Pepitone came to Pappas's defense. "He didn't want to do it," Pepitone said. "Why are you always blaming people?" Durocher then accused Ron Santo of malingering and front-office politics: "Ron, the only reason we're having a 'Ron Santo Day' is because Billy [Williams] and Ernie [Banks] had one and you asked John Holland for one." Screaming, Santo confronted Durocher, chin-to-chin, called him "a liar" and said it was John Holland's idea.

Initially, Wrigley, who had been cooling on Durocher, supported the players. "There is no question that the open quarreling between the players and manager leaves festering wounds," Wrigley observed. "It affects the players on the field and has hurt our chances in the pennant race."

The Cubs lost nine of their next 11 games after Wrigley's advertisement and finished in a third-place tie with the Cardinals, 14 games out. They shared the lead only once, on opening day, when Ferguson Jenkins beat the Cardinals in 10 innings. They were 10 games out at the All-Star break and 15½ back when they were mathematically eliminated on September 14.

Jenkins led the league with 24 wins, 30 complete games, and 325 innings. Pappas was 17–14 and Bill Hands 12–18. Ken Holtzman pitched his second no-hitter, June 3 against Cincinnati, 1–0, the first Cub with a pair of no-hitters since Larry Corcoran in the 19th century, but was only 9–15 on the season. The bullpen was bare, a league-low 13 saves, six by Phil Regan.

Glenn Beckert had his best year at the plate. He hit .342 and was challenging the Cardinals' Joe Torre for the batting title, but on September 3, trying to snare a line drive, he ruptured a tendon in his right thumb and was out for the rest of the season. Injuries continued to plague catcher Randy Hundley, the former iron man. Hundley tore cartilage in his right knee, "the good one," in spring training, and on April 12, in his first regular season at bat, suffered a recurrence and appeared in only nine games.

It was the 19th and farewell season for the glorious Mr. Cub. Ernie Banks appeared in 39 games, 18 as a pinch batter. He hit three home runs; the second, number 511, on July 21 off Tug McGraw of the Mets. Number 512, on August 24 against Cincinnati's Jim McGlothen, tied him with Eddie Mathews for sixth on the all-time list. Durocher, 65, began drawing his baseball pension, $1,945 a month.

	W	L	ERA	G	GS	CG	IP	H	BB	K
Ferguson Jenkins	(24)	13	2.77	39	(39)	(30)	(325)	(304)	37	263
Milt Pappas	17	14	3.52	35	35	14	261	279	62	99
Bill Hands	12	18	3.42	36	35	14	242	248	50	128
Ken Holtzman	9	15	4.48	30	29	9	195	213	64	143
Juan Pizarro	7	6	3.48	16	14	6	101	78	40	67
Phil Regan	5	5	3.95	48	1	0	73	84	33	28
Bill Bonham	2	1	4.65	33	2	0	60	63	36	41
Joe Decker	3	2	4.70	21	4	0	46	62	25	37
Ron Tompkins	0	2	4.05	35	0	0	40	31	21	20
Ray Newman	1	2	3.55	30	0	0	38	30	17	35
Burt Hooton	2	0	2.14	3	3	2	21	8	10	22
Earl Stephenson	1	0	4.50	16	0	0	20	24	11	11
Jim Colborn	0	1	7.20	14	0	0	10	18	3	2
Bob Miller	0	0	5.14	2	0	0	7	10	1	2
Larry Gura	0	0	6.00	6	0	0	3	6	1	2
	83	79	3.61	364	162	75	1,442	1,458	411	900

Shutouts: Pappas 5, Holtzman 3, Jenkins 3, Pizarro 3, Hands 1, Hooton 1.
Saves: Regan 6, Tompkins 3, Newman 2, Gura 1, Stephenson 1.

	G	AB	H	2B	3B	HR	R	RBI	SB	AVG
Regulars										
1B Joe Pepitone	115	427	131	19	4	16	50	61	1	.307
2B Glenn Beckert	131	530	181	18	5	2	80	42	3	.342
SS Don Kessinger	155	617	159	18	6	2	77	38	15	.258
3B Ron Santo	154	555	148	22	1	21	77	88	4	.267
RF Johnny Callison	103	290	61	12	1	8	27	38	2	.210
CF Brock Davis	106	301	77	7	5	0	22	28	0	.256
LF Billy Williams	157	594	179	27	5	28	86	93	7	.301
C Chris Cannizzaro	71	197	42	8	1	5	18	23	0	.213
Substitutes										
Paul Popovich	89	226	49	7	1	4	24	28	0	.217
Ernie Banks	39	83	16	2	0	3	4	6	0	.193
Hector Torres	31	58	13	3	0	0	4	2	0	.224
Pat Bourque	14	37	7	0	1	1	3	3	0	.189
Hal Breeden	23	36	5	1	0	1	1	2	0	.139
Ramon Webster	16	16	5	2	0	0	1	0	0	.313
Garry Jestadt	3	3	0	0	0	0	0	0	0	.000
Jim Hickman	117	383	98	13	2	19	50	60	0	.256
Cleo James	54	150	43	7	0	2	25	13	6	.287
Jose Ortiz	36	88	26	7	1	0	10	3	2	.295
Carmen Fanzone	12	43	8	2	0	2	5	5	0	.186
Gene Hiser	17	29	6	0	0	0	4	1	1	.207
Billy North	8	16	6	0	0	0	3	0	1	.375
J. C. Martin	47	125	33	5	0	2	13	17	1	.264
Ken Rudolph	25	76	15	3	0	0	5	7	0	.197
Danny Breeden	25	65	10	1	0	0	3	4	0	.154
Frank Fernandez	17	41	7	1	0	4	11	4	0	.171
Randy Hundley	9	21	7	1	0	0	1	2	0	.333
Al Spangler	5	5	2	0	0	0	0	0	0	.400

	G	AB	H	2B	3B	HR	R	RBI	SB	AVG
Pitchers										
Ferguson Jenkins	39	115	28	7	1	6	13	20	0	.243
Milt Pappas	35	91	14	2	0	0	6	2	1	.154
Bill Hands	36	72	6	3	0	0	3	6	0	.083
Ken Holtzman	30	69	9	2	0	1	4	5	0	.130
Juan Pizarro	16	34	6	1	0	1	3	2	0	.176
Bill Bonham	33	12	2	0	0	0	2	0	0	.167
Phil Regan	48	8	0	0	0	0	0	0	0	.000
Joe Decker	22	8	2	1	0	0	1	0	0	.250
Burt Hooton	3	7	0	0	0	0	0	0	0	.000
Ray Newman	30	6	0	0	0	0	1	0	0	.000
Earl Stephenson	16	2	0	0	0	0	0	0	0	.000
Bob Miller	2	1	0	0	0	0	0	0	0	.000
Larry Gura	6	1	0	0	0	0	0	0	0	.000
Ron Tompkins	35	0	0	0	0	0	0	0	0	—
Jim Colborn	14	0	0	0	0	0	0	0	0	—
		5,438	1,401	202	34	128	637	603	44	.258

1972

Record: 85–70
Finish: Second (East)
Games Behind: 11
Managers: Leo Durocher, Whitey Lockman

The "Dump Durocher Clique" dissolved on midnight July 24, 1972, when owner Philip Wrigley joined the movement. Durocher was dismissed in midseason, on the eve of the All-Star game in Atlanta. According to the official announcement, he "stepped aside." But he was pushed. Several days later Wrigley acknowledged he had approved the change because there was "friction between Leo and his players and . . . the team as a whole had not been playing to its full potential."

Durocher went quietly; a month later he was hired by the Houston Astros. In his six and a half seasons in Chicago he got the job done, lifting the Cubs out of the second division. The Cubs finished 10th in his first year, but in his next five full seasons they were never lower than third, including two second-place finishes. During his stormy reign the Cubs were 535–526, a .504 percentage.

Carroll "Whitey" Lockman, 46, was the new manager. The only player to hit home runs in his first and last major league at bats, Lockman had been the third base coach in 1966, Durocher's first year with the Cubs. He was "farmed out," at Durocher's suggestion, prior to the next season. Durocher didn't want him too close. He was a favorite with the players, who often went to him for counsel.

In the intervening years Lockman had managed the Cubs' Triple-A affiliates and had been Holland's principal lieutenant, in charge of player development. He had also been elevated to the position of vice president, a title Durocher never held. Lockman had played for Durocher for seven years when they were with the Giants, but he was opposite in manner: a quiet but firm leader. The Cubs were 46–44 with Durocher and 39–26 with Lockman, a .600 pace, often good enough for a pennant, but finished second, 11 games out.

Ferguson Jenkins was 20–12, the fourth pitcher since 1920 with six consecutive 20-victory seasons. The others: Lefty Grove, Robin Roberts, and Warren Spahn. Pappas was second to Jenkins with a 17–7 record, followed by Bill Hands, 11–8, and rookie Burt Hooton, 11–14. Another rookie, Rick Reuschel, who later was the Cubs' big winner, was 10–8. Ken Holtzman was gone. He was among the half dozen players who had asked to be traded during the off-season and was dealt to Oakland for center fielder Rick Monday.

Hooton and Pappas pitched no-hitters—Hooton against the Phillies on April 16 in his fourth major league start, Pappas against San Diego on September 2. Pappas came within one strike of a perfect game. He was ahead of Larry Stahl, one ball and two strikes, but lost him with a walk. Pappas's last two pitches were low and outside, close, but not close enough.

Billy Williams came close to winning the Triple Crown. He led the league with a .333 average but was second to Johnny Bench in home runs (40 to 37) and in runs batted in (125 to 122). With two weeks remaining, Williams appeared to have an excellent chance to lead in all three categories. Convinced the batting title was the jewel and fearful he would be unable to maintain his average, Williams began concentrating on making contact and stopped swinging for the long ball.

Randy Hundley, after two seasons curtailed by disabilities, caught 113 games but hit only .218. Glenn Beckert's average plunged 72 points to .270. Ron Santo, Jim Hickman, and newcomer Jose Cardenal, acquired from Milwaukee, each hit 17 home runs. Cardenal was an early-season sensation and batted .291. Rick Monday, adequate at the plate, was the club's best center fielder since Andy Pafko. It was also the

Leo Durocher exiting as the Cub manager in July 1972

Cub debut for utility infielder Carmen Fanzone, a professional trumpet player who later played in the Johnny Carson band. Williams was 8-for-8 in a July 11 doubleheader against Houston.

	W	L	ERA	G	GS	CG	IP	H	BB	K
Ferguson Jenkins	20	12	3.21	36	36	23	289	253	62	184
Burt Hooton	11	14	2.80	33	31	9	218⅓	201	81	132
Milt Pappas	17	7	2.77	29	28	10	195	187	29	80
Bill Hands	11	8	2.99	32	28	6	189⅓	168	47	96
Rick Reuschel	10	8	2.93	21	18	5	129	127	29	87
Tom Phoebus	3	3	3.78	37	1	0	83⅓	76	45	59
Jack Aker	6	6	2.96	48	0	0	67	65	23	36
Dan McGinn	0	5	5.86	42	2	0	63	78	29	42
Juan Pizarro	4	5	3.97	16	7	1	59	66	32	24
Bill Bonham	1	1	3.10	19	4	0	58	56	25	49
Steve Hamilton	1	0	4.76	22	0	0	17	24	8	13
Joe Decker	1	0	2.08	5	1	0	13	9	4	7
Larry Gura	0	0	3.75	7	0	0	12	11	3	13
Phil Regan	0	1	2.25	5	0	0	4	6	2	2
Clint Compton	0	0	9.00	1	0	0	2	2	2	0
	85	70	3.22	353	156	54	1,399	1,329	421	824

Shutouts: Jenkins 5, Reuschel 4, Hands 3, Hooton 3, Pappas 3.
Saves: Aker 17, Phoebus 6, Bonham 4, McGinn 4, Pizarro 1.

	G	AB	H	2B	3B	HR	R	RBI	SB	AVG
Regulars										
1B Jim Hickman	115	368	100	15	2	17	65	64	3	.272
2B Glenn Beckert	120	474	128	22	2	3	51	43	2	.270
SS Don Kessinger	149	577	158	20	6	1	77	39	8	.274
3B Ron Santo	133	464	140	25	5	17	68	74	1	.302
RF Jose Cardenal	143	533	155	24	6	17	96	70	25	.291
CF Rick Monday	138	434	108	22	5	11	68	42	12	.249
LF Billy Williams	150	574	191	34	6	37	95	122	3	(.333)
C Randy Hundley	114	357	78	12	0	5	23	30	1	.218
Substitutes										
Carmen Fanzone	86	222	50	11	0	8	26	42	2	.225
Joe Pepitone	66	214	56	5	0	8	23	21	1	.262
Paul Popovich	58	129	25	3	2	1	8	11	0	.194
Pat Bourque	11	27	7	1	0	0	3	5	0	.259
Tommy Davis	15	26	7	1	0	0	3	6	0	.269
Art Shamsky	15	16	2	0	0	0	1	1	0	.125
Dave Rosello	5	12	3	0	0	1	2	3	0	.250
Allan Montreuil	5	11	1	0	0	0	0	0	0	.091
Billy North	66	127	23	2	3	0	22	4	6	.181
Gene Hiser	32	46	9	0	0	0	2	4	1	.196
Jim Tyrone	13	8	0	0	0	0	1	0	1	.000
Pete LaCock	5	6	3	0	0	0	3	4	1	.500
Ken Rudolph	42	106	25	1	1	2	10	9	1	.236
J. C. Martin	25	50	12	3	0	0	3	7	1	.240
Ellie Hendricks	17	43	5	1	0	2	7	6	0	.116
Frank Fernandez	3	3	0	0	0	0	0	0	0	.000
Frank Coggins	6	1	0	0	0	0	1	0	0	.000
Chris Ward	1	1	0	0	0	0	0	0	0	.000
Pitchers										
Ferguson Jenkins	36	109	20	1	1	1	8	8	0	.183
Burt Hooton	33	72	9	1	0	1	4	6	0	.125
Milt Pappas	29	68	13	1	0	1	5	8	0	.191
Bill Hands	32	57	1	0	0	0	1	0	0	.018
Rick Reuschel	21	44	6	1	0	0	3	3	0	.136
Juan Pizarro	16	21	3	0	0	0	2	0	0	.143
Tom Phoebus	37	15	2	0	0	0	0	0	0	.133
Bill Bonham	19	14	4	0	0	0	3	1	0	.286
Dan McGinn	43	8	2	0	1	0	0	1	0	.250
Jack Aker	48	6	0	0	0	0	0	0	0	.000
Joe Decker	5	2	0	0	0	0	1	0	0	.000
Steve Hamilton	22	1	0	0	0	0	0	0	0	.000
Larry Gura	7	1	0	0	0	0	0	0	0	.000
Phil Regan	5	0	0	0	0	0	0	0	0	—
Clint Compton	1	0	0	0	0	0	0	0	0	—
		5,247	1,346	206	40	133	686	634	69	.257

1973

Record: 77–84
Finish: Fifth (East)
Games Behind: 5
Manager: Whitey Lockman

Whitey Lockman, in his first full season at the helm, emphasized the necessity for team balance in 1973. In spring training he repeatedly told reporters that he would use all his players and that he would be delighted if his ten pitchers won ten games apiece. It was fanciful thinking, a mathematical impossibility.

Even if each pitcher, starters and relievers, had an equal chance for victory, the odds for the first 10 wins would have been 3.6 million to 1; when considering the entire 162-game season and the fact that middle relievers, on an average, win only three or four games, the odds probably would have increased a thousandfold, perhaps more.

But it almost happened the first time around. The Cubs' first nine wins were won by nine different pitchers—Bob Locker, Jack Aker, Rick Reuschel, Bill Bonham, Ferguson Jenkins, Ray Burris, Burt Hooton, Larry Gura, and Milt Pappas in that order. The only nonwinner was reliever Dave LaRoche, and he wasn't too far behind. LaRoche won the club's 12th victory when he worked the eighth inning against the Dodgers on May 3.

Lockman had the Cubs in first place, without interruption, from May 9 through July 21. The batting stars during this surge were Ron Santo, who on May 14 was leading the league with a .369 average; Glenn Beckert, whose 26-game hitting streak was broken five days later; and Rick Monday, who had 21 home runs two weeks before the All-Star break, twice as many as his previous season total.

Monday went seven full weeks without another home run but nonetheless led the club with 26. He finished with only 56 RBIs, the lowest total ever by a player with 25 or more home runs. Santo and Billy Willliams were next with 20 each. The power shortage was such that the club was 10th in the league in scoring and eighth in home runs.

The Cubs were 46–31, 15 games over .500 and eight games in front on June 29, their biggest lead. But they were unable to maintain the pace; from June 30 through September 18, they lost 48 of 73 games, the worst record in either league. The skid included 13 of 15 losses from July 11 through the first game of a July 29 doubleheader and an 11-game slumber from August 4 through August 16, their longest losing streak in three years.

Still, the race was so close that on September 22, in fifth place, with seven games to play, they were only 2½ games out of the lead. But they won only two of these games and finished fifth, five games out. Jenkins won on September 25 against the Cardinals, and Locker on September 30 against the Mets when he worked the final two innings to complete a 1–0 Reuschel shutout.

Santo closed at .267, Beckert at .255. The only .300 hitter was Jose Cardenal at .303. After six consecutive 20-win seasons, Jenkins was 14–16, never winning more than two successive starts. There were two other 14-game winners: Reuschel, 14–15, and Hooton 14–17. Bonham, in his first full big league season, won seven of 15 starts. Locker, acquired from Oakland in a winter deal, was the star of the bullpen: 10 victories, all in relief, and 18 saves.

Ernie Banks, the longtime Mr. Cub who had retired to the coaching lines, added another distinction to his illustrious career. On May 8 he became the major leagues' first black manager—but only for an inning and a half in a 12-inning 3–2 win at San Diego. Lockman had been ejected, and his first two lieutenants were unavailable: Pete Reiser was recovering from an injury, and Larry Jansen was home with his wife, who had undergone surgery.

	W	L	ERA	G	GS	CG	IP	H	BB	K
Ferguson Jenkins	14	16	3.89	38	38	7	271	267	57	170
Burt Hooton	14	17	3.68	42	34	9	240	248	73	134
Rick Reuschel	14	15	3.00	36	36	7	237	244	62	168
Milt Pappas	7	12	4.28	30	29	1	162	192	40	48
Bill Bonham	7	5	3.02	44	15	3	152	126	64	121
Bob Locker	10	6	2.55	63	0	0	106	96	42	76
Larry Gura	2	4	4.85	21	7	0	65	79	11	43
Ray Burris	1	1	2.91	31	1	0	65	65	27	57
Jack Aker	4	5	4.08	47	0	0	64	76	23	25
Dave LaRoche	4	1	5.83	45	0	0	54	55	29	34
Mike Paul	0	1	3.50	11	1	0	18	17	9	6
Juan Pizarro	0	1	11.25	2	0	0	4	6	1	3
	77	84	3.66	410	161	27	1,438	1,471	438	885

Shutouts: Reuschel 3, Hooton 2, Jenkins 2, Pappas 1.
Saves: Locker 18, Aker 12, Bonham 6, LaRoche 4.

	G	AB	H	2B	3B	HR	R	RBI	SB	AVG
Regulars										
1B Jim Hickman	92	201	49	1	2	3	27	20	1	.244
2B Glenn Beckert	114	372	95	13	0	0	38	29	0	.255
SS Don Kessinger	160	577	151	22	3	0	52	43	6	.262
3B Ron Santo	149	536	143	29	2	20	65	77	1	.267
RF Jose Cardenal	145	522	158	33	2	11	80	68	19	.303
CF Rick Monday	149	554	148	24	5	26	93	56	5	.267
LF Billy Williams	156	576	166	22	2	20	72	86	4	.288
C Randy Hundley	124	368	83	11	1	10	35	43	5	.226
Substitutes										
Paul Popovich	99	280	66	6	3	2	24	24	3	.236
Carmen Fanzone	64	150	41	7	0	6	22	22	1	.273
Pat Bourque	57	139	29	6	0	7	11	20	1	.209
Joe Pepitone	31	112	30	3	0	3	16	18	3	.268
Gonzalo Marquez	19	58	13	2	0	1	5	4	0	.224
Dave Rosello	16	38	10	2	0	0	4	2	2	.263
Andre Thornton	17	35	7	3	0	0	3	2	0	.200
Gene Hiser	100	109	19	3	0	1	15	6	4	.174
Rico Carty	22	70	15	0	0	1	4	8	0	.214
Adrian Garrett	36	54	12	0	0	3	7	8	1	.222
Cleo James	44	45	5	0	0	0	9	0	5	.111
Pete LaCock	11	16	4	1	0	0	1	3	0	.250
Matt Alexander	12	5	1	0	0	0	4	1	2	.200
Ken Rudolph	64	170	35	8	1	2	12	17	1	.206
Tom Lundstedt	4	5	0	0	0	0	0	0	0	.000
Tony LaRussa	1	0	0	0	0	0	1	0	0	—
Pitchers										
Ferguson Jenkins	38	84	10	4	0	0	2	4	0	.119
Rick Reuschel	36	73	9	1	0	0	3	2	0	.123
Burt Hooton	42	70	9	0	0	0	4	3	0	.129
Milt Pappas	30	48	3	0	0	1	2	2	0	.063
Bill Bonham	44	43	4	0	0	0	1	1	0	.093
Bob Locker	63	15	1	0	0	0	0	0	1	.067
Larry Gura	22	15	3	0	0	0	1	1	0	.200
Jack Aker	47	7	0	0	0	0	0	0	0	.000
Ray Burris	31	7	1	0	0	0	0	0	0	.143
Mike Paul	11	4	0	0	0	0	0	0	0	.000
Dave LaRoche	45	4	2	0	0	0	1	0	0	.500
Juan Pizarro	2	1	0	0	0	0	0	0	0	.000
		5,363	1,322	201	21	117	614	570	65	.247

1974

Record: 66–96
Finish: Sixth (East)
Games Behind: 22
Managers: Whitey Lockman, Jim Marshall

It was a year of transition and more disappointment in 1974. General manager John Holland backed up the truck and unloaded four of the club's longtime heroes: pitcher Ferguson Jenkins was traded to Texas, second baseman Glenn Beckert to San Diego, catcher Randy Hundley to Minnesota, and third baseman Ron Santo to the crosstown White Sox.

Shortstop Don Kessinger, the only infield survivor, said, "This is the first time I'll be going to spring training not knowing what to expect."

Totally committed to rebuilding with younger players, the Cubs fielded what at times seemed to be an all-rookie team. They were never in contention and finished sixth and last in the Eastern Division, 30 games under .500. They didn't win more than two games in a row until July 5, spent the last 66 days in the cellar, and were at or near the bottom in all areas of play: last in fielding, next to last in pitching, eighth in hitting.

Only two players were among the league leaders. Third baseman Bill Madlock—a strong candidate for Rookie of the Year honors who came in the Jenkins trade and was to win four batting championships—hit .313, fifth best in the league; and outfielder Jose Cardenal tied for fifth in doubles with 35. Right-handed pitcher Bill Bonham was the lone Cub to lead in any department, tying for the most *losses,* 22.

The only holdovers were Kessinger and outfielders Billy Williams, Rick Monday, and Jose Cardenal. Manager Whitey Lockman juggled as best he could. To free left field for newcomer Jerry Morales, he moved Williams to first base. The experiment was abandoned in late June. Williams returned to the outfield, then went on the disabled list for the first time in his career on August 19 when he spiked himself on the ankle. He was out for a month, finishing with a low of 16 home runs and 68 runs batted in.

Rookie Andre Thornton, who showed well both in the field and at the plate, replaced Williams at first base. Second base was a season-long problem. Vic Harris, acquired from Texas in the Jenkins deal—regarded as a better prospect than Madlock—was a disaster, batting only .195. Dave Rosello and Rob Sperring also played second. They didn't hit, either: Rosello batted .203, Sperring .206.

Rookie catcher Steve Swisher, who was among the four players the White Sox delivered for Santo, also failed at the plate. Swisher had been touted as another Johnny Bench, but there was little resemblance. He hit .214 and shared the catching duties with George Mitterwald, who arrived in the Hundley deal. Mitterwald batted .251 with seven home runs, three of which came on April 17 in an 18–9 Wrigley Field rout of Pittsburgh.

The only strength was in the outfield. Monday batted .294, Cardenal .293, Williams .280, and Morales .273. No Cub had as many as 160 hits. Monday led in home runs with 20, lowest for a club leader in 28 years. Rick Reuschel, who lost two 1–0 games, led the pitchers with a 13–12 record. Bonham, 11–22, was the only other pitcher to win in double figures. Oscar Zamora, 29, rescued after ten years in the minors, joined the club on June 15 and was a pleasant surprise: 10 saves and three wins in relief.

Lockman resigned on July 24 and returned to the front office as Holland's top lieutenant. Third base coach Jim Marshall succeeded Lockman. The Cubs were 41–52 under Lockman, a .441 winning percentage; 25–44, .362, with Marshall. Asked why Ernie Banks was overlooked, owner Philip Wrigley said, "Being a major league manager is like being a Kamikaze pilot. It's suicide."

	W	L	ERA	G	GS	CG	IP	H	BB	K
Bill Bonham	11	(22)	3.85	44	36	10	243	246	109	191
Rick Reuschel	13	12	4.29	41	38	8	241	262	83	160
Burt Hooton	7	11	4.81	48	21	3	176	214	51	94
Steve Stone	8	6	4.13	38	23	1	170	185	64	90
Ken Frailing	6	9	3.89	55	16	1	125	150	43	71
Dave LaRoche	5	6	4.79	49	4	0	92	103	47	49
Jim Todd	4	2	3.89	43	6	0	88	82	41	42
Oscar Zamora	3	9	3.11	56	0	0	84	82	19	38
Ray Burris	3	5	6.60	40	5	0	75	91	26	40
Tom Dettore	3	5	4.15	16	9	0	65	64	31	43
Horacio Pina	3	4	4.02	34	0	0	47	49	28	32
Jim Kremmel	0	2	5.23	23	2	0	31	37	18	22
Herb Hutson	0	2	3.41	20	2	0	29	24	15	22
Mike Paul	0	1	36.00	2	0	0	1	4	1	1
	66	96	4.29	509	162	23	1,467	1,593	576	895

Shutouts: Bonham 2, Reuschel 2, Hooton 1.
Saves: Zamora 10, LaRoche 5, Pina 4, Bonham 1, Burris 1, Frailing 1, Hooton 1.

	G	AB	H	2B	3B	HR	R	RBI	SB	AVG
Regulars										
1B Andre Thornton	107	303	79	16	4	10	41	46	2	.261
2B Vic Harris	62	200	39	6	3	0	18	11	9	.195
SS Don Kessinger	153	599	155	20	7	1	83	42	7	.259
3B Bill Madlock	128	453	142	21	5	9	65	54	11	.313
RF Jose Cardenal	143	542	159	35	3	13	75	72	23	.293
CF Rick Monday	142	538	158	19	7	20	84	58	7	.294
LF Jerry Morales	151	534	146	21	7	15	70	82	2	.273
C Steve Swisher	90	280	60	5	0	5	21	27	0	.214
Substitutes										
Billy Williams	117	404	113	22	0	16	55	68	4	.280
Carmen Fanzone	65	158	30	6	0	4	13	22	0	.190
Dave Rosello	62	148	30	7	0	0	9	10	1	.203
Billy Grabarkewitz	53	125	31	3	2	1	21	12	1	.248
Rob Sperring	42	107	22	3	0	1	9	5	1	.206
Ron Dunn	23	68	20	7	0	2	6	15	0	.294
Matt Alexander	45	54	11	2	1	0	15	0	8	.204
Gonzalo Marquez	11	11	0	0	0	0	1	0	0	.000
Chris Ward	92	137	28	4	0	1	8	15	0	.204
Pete LaCock	35	110	20	4	1	1	9	8	0	.182
Jim Tyrone	57	81	15	0	1	3	19	3	1	.185
Gene Hiser	12	17	4	1	0	0	2	1	0	.235
George Mitterwald	78	215	54	7	0	7	17	28	1	.251
Rick Stelmaszek	25	44	10	2	0	1	2	7	0	.227
Tom Lundstedt	22	32	3	0	0	0	1	0	0	.094
Adrian Garrett	10	8	0	0	0	0	0	0	0	.000
Pitchers										
Rick Reuschel	41	86	19	4	1	0	4	2	0	.221
Bill Bonham	48	84	12	2	0	0	8	4	0	.143
Steve Stone	42	58	7	0	0	0	2	2	0	.121
Burt Hooton	48	50	3	1	0	0	1	1	0	.060
Ken Frailing	58	31	8	0	0	0	4	6	0	.258
Dave LaRoche	50	27	9	2	0	0	4	2	0	.333
Tom Dettore	16	20	5	1	0	0	1	5	0	.250
Jim Todd	43	16	1	0	0	0	0	1	0	.063
Ray Burris	41	13	1	0	0	0	0	0	0	.077
Oscar Zamora	56	11	2	0	0	0	0	1	0	.182
Horacio Pina	34	5	1	0	0	0	0	0	0	.200
Jim Kremmel	23	3	0	0	0	0	1	0	0	.000
Herb Hutson	20	2	0	0	0	0	0	0	0	.000
Mike Paul	2	0	0	0	0	0	0	0	0	—
		5,574	1,397	221	42	110	669	610	78	.251

1975

Record: 75–87
Finish: Fifth (tie) (East)
Games Behind: 17½
Manager: Jim Marshall

After the many major changes of 1974, Billy Williams was the next significant Cub player to go, traded to Oakland for second baseman Manny Trillo, who tightened the infield and drove in 70 runs. But for the first time in more than a quarter of a century the Cubs were without a consistent longball threat in 1975. There was a consolation: third baseman Bill Madlock won the batting title with a .354 average, highest since Phil Cavarretta's .355 MVP season in 1945.

But unlike Cavarretta, Madlock's heroics were unable to motivate the club to a flag. The Cubs did push off to a surprisingly fast start and went into first place on April 14 when they were in the midst of a seven-game winning streak. They held the lead for 46 consecutive days, dropped to second on May 30, and soared ahead again for four more days before Cincinnati pricked the pennant bubble with a four-game sweep.

Five losses in the next six games, including two more to the Reds on June 13 and 14, plunged the Cubs into the second division. They were fifth, 14 out, at the All-Star interlude and finished in a last-place tie with Montreal. A month later, on October 28, shortstop Don Kessinger, the last survivor from the Durocher era, was traded to St. Louis for Mike Garman, an undistinguished right-hander who remained with the Cubs for only one season, winning a total of two games.

Again, the pitching was inadequate—a collective 4.56 earned average, easily the highest in the league. None of the rotation starters had an ERA below 3.73, including Ray Burris, who led the staff with a 15–10 record. Rick Reuschel, 3.73, was 11–17; Bill Bonham, 4.72, 13–15; and Steve Stone, 3.95, 12–8. Stone was the only pitcher in either league to win his first five games.

The biggest embarrassment occurred on September 15, in Wrigley Field, a 22–0 loss to the Pirates, the widest shutout margin in diamond history. Rennie Stennett led the rout with seven hits, the first 7-for-7 performance in a nine-inning major league game since Wilbert Robinson of the old Baltimore Orioles did it in 1892. Rick Reuschel started the game and faced nine batters in the first inning, eight of whom scored. His brother Paul finished with two scoreless innings. A month earlier, on August 21, the Reuschels, who together weighed almost a fourth of a ton—Rick 230, Paul 225—combined for a 7–0 victory over the Dodgers, the first all-brother shutout.

Madlock and Jose Cardenal were the only .300 hitters. Madlock was on fire throughout. He was 14-for-18 from June 13 to 16, later in the month went 24-for-44, and was 6-for-6 against the Mets on July 26. He hit .425 in August and peaked at .363. Cardenal batted .317 and stole 34 bases, the most by a Cub since 1903. Andre Thornton and Rick Monday were the power hitters. Thornton, out for a month with injuries, had 18 home runs, Monday 17. Jerry Morales had 91 RBIs.

Manager Jim Marshall's contract was renewed, but two weeks after the season there was a surprise change. E. R.

"Salty" Saltwell, longtime organization man who had been in charge of park operations, including concessions, moved into the general manager's chair, succeeding the retiring John Holland, who remained as an adviser. Philip Wrigley's instructions to Saltwell: "Get tough with the players."

Before the season Wrigley had expressed dismay because of the rising player salaries. After pitcher Catfish Hunter, a free agent, signed with the Yankees for $3 million for five years, Wrigley warned, "The time is approaching when big league clubs will have to be subsidized by local subscription in the manner of opera companies and symphony orchestras."

	W	L	ERA	G	GS	CG	IP	H	BB	K
Ray Burris	15	10	4.12	36	35	8	238	259	73	108
Rick Reuschel	11	(17)	3.73	38	37	6	234	244	67	155
Bill Bonham	13	15	4.72	38	36	7	229	254	109	165
Steve Stone	12	8	3.95	33	32	6	214	198	80	139
Darold Knowles	6	9	5.83	58	0	0	88	107	36	63
Tom Dettore	5	4	5.40	36	5	0	85	88	31	46
Oscar Zamora	5	2	5.07	52	0	0	71	84	15	28
Geoff Zahn	2	7	4.45	16	10	0	62⅔	67	26	21
Ken Frailing	2	5	5.43	41	0	0	53	61	26	39
Milt Wilcox	0	1	5.68	25	0	0	38	50	17	21
Paul Reuschel	1	3	3.50	28	0	0	36	44	13	12
Bob Locker	0	1	4.91	22	0	0	33	38	16	14
Willie Prall	0	2	8.40	3	3	0	15	21	8	7
Burt Hooton	0	2	8.18	3	3	0	11	18	4	5
Donnie Moore	0	0	4.00	4	1	0	9	12	4	8
Ken Crosby	1	0	3.38	9	0	0	8	10	7	6
Eddie Solomon	0	0	1.29	6	0	0	7	7	6	3
Eddie Watt	0	1	13.50	6	0	0	6	14	8	6
Buddy Schultz	2	0	6.00	6	0	0	6	11	5	4
	75	87	4.56	460	162	27	1,443⅔	1,587	551	850

Shutouts: Bonham 2, Burris 2, Stone 1.
Saves: Knowles 15, Zamora 10, P. Reuschel 5, R. Reuschel 1, Frailing 1, Zahn 1.

	G	AB	H	2B	3B	HR	R	RBI	SB	AVG
Regulars										
1B Andre Thornton	120	372	109	21	4	18	70	60	3	.293
2B Manny Trillo	154	545	135	12	2	7	55	70	1	.248
SS Don Kessinger	154	601	146	26	10	0	77	46	4	.243
3B Bill Madlock	130	514	182	29	7	7	77	64	9	(.354)
RF Jose Cardenal	154	574	182	30	2	9	85	68	34	.317
CF Rick Monday	136	491	131	29	4	17	89	60	8	.267
LF Jerry Morales	153	578	156	21	0	12	62	91	3	.270
C Steve Swisher	93	254	54	16	2	1	20	22	1	.213
Substitutes										
Pete LaCock	106	249	57	8	1	6	30	30	0	.229
Rob Sperring	65	144	30	4	1	1	25	9	0	.208
Dave Rosello	19	58	15	2	0	1	7	8	0	.259
Ron Dunn	32	44	7	3	0	1	2	6	0	.159
Adrian Garrett	16	21	2	0	0	1	1	6	0	.095
Champ Summers	76	91	21	5	1	1	14	16	0	.231
Gene Hiser	45	62	15	3	0	0	11	6	0	.242
Joe Wallis	16	56	16	2	2	1	9	4	2	.286
Vic Harris	51	56	10	0	0	0	6	5	0	.179
Jim Tyrone	11	22	5	0	1	0	0	3	1	.227
George Mitterwald	84	200	44	4	3	5	19	26	0	.220
Tim Hosley	62	141	36	7	0	6	22	20	1	.255
Pitchers										
Bill Bonham	40	82	15	1	1	0	8	6	0	.183
Ray Burris	38	82	15	2	0	0	10	4	0	.183
Rick Reuschel	38	77	16	2	0	1	3	7	0	.208
Steve Stone	34	72	8	2	0	0	3	3	0	.111
Tom Dettore	36	24	6	0	0	0	2	2	0	.250
Darold Knowles	58	15	1	0	0	0	0	1	0	.067
Geoff Zahn	16	15	2	0	0	0	1	1	0	.133
Ken Frailing	41	7	1	0	0	0	2	0	0	.143
Oscar Zamora	52	6	1	0	0	0	0	0	0	.167
Willie Prall	3	4	0	0	0	0	1	1	0	.000
Paul Reuschel	28	4	0	0	0	0	0	0	0	.000
Donnie Moore	4	3	0	0	0	0	0	0	0	.000
Burt Hooton	3	3	0	0	0	0	0	0	0	.000
Milt Wilcox	25	3	1	0	0	0	0	0	0	.333
Bob Locker	22	0	0	0	0	0	0	0	0	—

	G	AB	H	2B	3B	HR	R	RBI	SB	AVG
Eddie Watt	6	0	0	0	0	0	0	0	0	—
Buddy Schultz	6	0	0	0	0	0	0	0	0	—
Ken Crosby	9	0	0	0	0	0	1	0	0	—
Eddie Solomon	6	0	0	0	0	0	0	0	0	—
		5,470	1,419	229	41	95	712	645	67	.259

1976

Record: 75–87
Finish: Fourth (East)
Games Behind: 26
Manager: Jim Marshall

The Cubs were unable to climb out of the second division in 1976 but were first in the hearts of their countrymen. On April 25, before a Sunday crowd of 25,167 at Dodger Stadium, Rick Monday prevented William Thomas of Eldon, Missouri, from burning the American flag in center field. Thomas, accompanied by his 11-year-old son, was protesting in behalf of the American Indians.

Monday was returning to his position in the fourth inning when they spread the flag on the grass like a picnic blanket. As they were fumbling with a lighter and a can of fluid, Monday swooped in—Paul Revere at full gallop—and snatched the flag. The crowd cheered wildly. The message board flashed, "Rick Monday . . . You made a great play."

Overnight, Monday became a national hero. Mayor Richard J. Daley invited him to serve as the grand marshall of Chicago's annual Flag Day parade. President Gerald Ford sent a message of congratulations. *The Sporting News* described Monday as "Francis Scott Key, Betsy Ross, Verdun, and Iwo Jima—all wrapped up in a fleeting moment of patriotism."

Monday also did his best to save the Cubs, hitting a career-high 32 home runs. At the close of the season he was asked if the flag incident had inspired his home run production. "I don't think so," he replied. "I wasn't swinging a red, white, and blue bat."

Bill Madlock continued swinging his magic wand and won the batting championship for the second year in a row, the first Cub to repeat since Cap Anson in the 19th century. Going into the final day Madlock was hitting .333, four points less than Cincinnati's Ken Griffey. Confident Madlock wouldn't catch him, Griffey didn't start the last game, but he entered in the seventh inning after learning Madlock had gone 4-for-4 against Montreal. Griffey was hitless in two trips. Madlock finished at .339, Griffey at .336.

The Cubs were never in first place and suffered their most embarrassing defeat in their seventh game, on April 17, when they blew a 13–2 lead to the Phillies, who rallied for an 18–16, 10-inning victory on a four-home-run performance by Mike Schmidt. Following a nine-game losing streak, from June 25 through the first game of a July 4 doubleheader, owner Philip Wrigley described his players as clowns.

They were also characterized as Marshall's Marshmallows and Crybabies because of their constant sniveling. Andre Thornton, who was among the first to challenge Marshall's authority, was traded to Montreal on May 17. First baseman Pete LaCock and outfielder Jerry Morales also expressed dissatisfaction with manager Jim Marshall, who was dismissed at the end of the season.

Ray Burris and Rick Reuschel were the only pitchers to win in double figures. Burris was 15–13 and Reuschel 14–12. The star of the staff was Bruce Sutter, a 23-year-old reliever. Recalled from the minors, Sutter made his debut on May 9. He appeared in 52 games, allowed only 63 hits in 83 innings and had 73 strikeouts while walking 26. He won six games, all in relief, with 10 saves. If not for Sutter's brilliance, the Cubs would have fallen deep into the second division.

They finished fourth with a 75–87 record, 26 games out of the lead. Marshall's two-and-a-half-year managerial term (175–218) came to an end. Bob Kennedy, who had managed the Cubs in the '60s, returned to the club, this time as the general manager, and immediately replaced Marshall with 63-year-old Herman Franks, who had been a coach with the Cubs during the Durocher era. Salty Saltwell resumed his duties as vice president, park operations.

	W	L	ERA	G	GS	CG	IP	H	BB	K
Rick Reuschel	14	12	3.46	38	37	9	260	260	64	146
Ray Burris	15	13	3.11	37	36	10	249	251	70	112
Bill Bonham	9	13	4.27	32	31	3	196	215	96	110
Steve Renko	8	11	3.86	28	27	4	163⅓	164	43	112
Paul Reuschel	4	2	4.55	50	2	0	87	94	33	55
Bruce Sutter	6	3	2.71	52	0	0	83	63	26	73
Joe Coleman	2	8	4.10	39	4	0	79	72	35	66
Mike Garman	2	4	4.97	47	2	0	76	79	35	37
Steve Stone	3	6	4.08	17	15	1	75	70	21	33
Darold Knowles	5	7	2.88	58	0	0	72	61	22	39
Oscar Zamora	5	3	5.24	40	2	0	55	70	17	27
Buddy Schultz	1	1	6.00	29	0	0	24	37	9	15
Ken Frailing	1	2	2.37	6	3	0	19	20	5	10
Ken Crosby	0	0	12.00	7	1	0	12	20	8	5
Geoff Zahn	0	1	11.25	3	2	0	8	16	2	4
Tom Dettore	0	1	10.29	4	0	0	7	11	2	4
Mike Krukow	0	0	9.00	2	0	0	4	6	2	1
Ramon Hernandez	0	0	0.00	2	0	0	1⅓	2	0	1
	75	87	3.94	491	162	27	1,471	1,511	490	850

Shutouts: Burris 4, R. Reuschel 2, Stone 1.
Saves: Sutter 10, Knowles 9, Coleman 4, P. Reuschel 3, Zamora 3, Schultz 2, Garman 1, R. Reuschel 1.

	G	AB	H	2B	3B	HR	R	RBI	SB	AVG
Regulars										
1B Pete LaCock	106	244	54	9	2	8	34	28	1	.221
2B Manny Trillo	158	582	139	24	3	4	42	59	17	.239
SS Mick Kelleher	124	337	77	12	1	0	28	22	0	.228
3B Bill Madlock	142	514	174	36	1	15	68	84	15	(.339)
RF Jerry Morales	140	537	147	17	0	16	66	67	3	.274
CF Rick Monday	137	534	145	20	5	32	107	77	5	.272
LF Jose Cardenal	136	521	156	25	2	8	64	47	23	.299
C Steve Swisher	109	377	89	13	3	5	25	42	2	.236
Substitutes										
Dave Rosello	91	227	55	5	1	1	27	11	1	.242
Larry Biittner	78	192	47	13	1	0	21	17	0	.245
Rob Sperring	43	93	24	3	0	0	8	7	0	.258
Andre Thornton	27	85	17	6	0	2	8	14	2	.200
Jerry Tabb	11	24	7	0	0	0	2	0	0	.292
Joe Wallis	121	338	86	11	5	5	51	21	3	.254
Champ Summers	83	126	26	2	0	3	11	13	1	.206
Wayne Tyrone	30	57	13	1	0	1	3	8	0	.228
Mike Adams	25	29	4	2	0	0	1	2	0	.138
George Mitterwald	101	303	65	7	0	5	19	28	1	.215
Randy Hundley	13	18	3	2	0	0	3	1	0	.167
Ed Putman	5	7	3	0	0	0	0	0	0	.429
Pitchers										
Rick Reuschel	38	83	19	4	0	0	9	6	0	.229
Ray Burris	39	81	9	0	0	0	4	1	0	.111
Bill Bonham	32	65	13	4	0	0	6	2	0	.200
Steve Renko	29	53	5	0	0	0	3	1	0	.094
Steve Stone	17	21	3	0	0	0	1	0	0	.143
Joe Coleman	39	13	2	0	0	0	0	0	0	.154
Paul Reuschel	50	13	2	0	0	0	0	1	0	.154
Oscar Zamora	40	9	0	0	0	0	0	0	0	.000
Bruce Sutter	52	8	0	0	0	0	0	0	0	.000
Darold Knowles	58	7	1	0	0	0	0	0	0	.143
Mike Garman	47	7	0	0	0	0	0	0	0	.000

	G	AB	H	2B	3B	HR	R	RBI	SB	AVG
Buddy Schultz	29	4	0	0	0	0	0	0	0	.000
Ken Frailing	6	3	0	0	0	0	0	0	0	.000
Geoff Zahn	3	3	0	0	0	0	0	0	0	.000
Ken Crosby	7	2	1	0	0	0	0	0	0	.500
Mike Krukow	2	1	0	0	0	0	0	0	0	.000
Ramon Hernandez	2	0	0	0	0	0	0	0	0	—
Tom Dettore	4	0	0	0	0	0	0	0	0	—
		5,518	1,386	216	24	105	611	559	74	.251

1977

Record: 81–81
Finish: Fourth (East)
Games Behind: 20
Manager: Herman Franks

"Soooter! Soooter! Soooter!" That was the chant at Wrigley Field in 1977 when the Cubs were tied in the late innings or trying to protect a thin lead. The urgent summons was in tribute to 24-year-old Bruce Sutter. None of the great relievers—not Rich Gossage, Rollie Fingers, Dennis Eckersley, or Lee Smith, who also surfaced with the Cubs—had a half season comparable to Sutter's first-half heroics.

Before he broke down on July 16, the weekend before the All-Star break, Sutter had made 45 appearances, with 24 saves and five wins, 55 percent of the Cubs' first 53 victories. His stats were dazzling: a 1.11 earned run average, 49 hits in 81⅓ innings, and 94 strikeouts—better than one strikeout an inning, and eight times as many Ks as walks.

A failed starter, Sutter's career was resurrected by Fred Martin, a roving minor league pitching instructor who taught him the forkball, the same pitch used by Elroy Face and Lindy McDaniel, who were among the bullpen stars of the previous generation. Because of Sutter's success the pitch was renamed the split-fingered fastball.

The grip and arm action are the same. The ball is wedged between the first and second fingers, which are spread as far apart as possible, forming a Y. The pitch has the action of a fastball but plunges downward at the last instant, usually out of the strike zone, sometimes into the dirt. The ball looked easy to hit, and the batters couldn't resist.

The Cubs didn't go above the .500 mark until May 6, their 21st game. They went into first place six days later. On June 28, after six consecutive victories, which included four Sutter saves, they peaked: 25 games over .500 (47–22), 8½ in front. When Sutter went down, their lead began to shrink. From August 27 on, they lost 25 of their last 35 games, including eight of the last nine, and finished 81–81, in fourth place, 20 games out.

After he returned from the disabled list, Sutter made 17 appearances. He went 40 days without a save but had some memorable moments: on September 8, against Montreal, he became the ninth pitcher in league history to strike out the side on nine pitches. He finished with a 1.35 ERA, 31 saves, and seven wins, and he had 36 consecutive games with at least one strikeout.

Losing Sutter was not the sole cause for the collapse. Only Bobby Murcer, acquired from the Giants for Bill Madlock in a preseason trade, hit with power, leading the club in home runs with 27. Nobody else hit more than 11. Greg Gross, a spray hitter who was platooned in the outfield, batted .322. Third baseman Steve Ontiveros, who also came in the Madlock deal, hit .299 with 10 home runs and 68 RBIs.

Madlock was traded because of a contract dispute. He requested a long-term million-dollar deal similar to those awarded to lesser players who went through the free-agent reentry draft, a new procedure, the fallout of the Messersmith decision, which forced modification of the reserve clause. Philip Wrigley's response: "No ballplayer is worth more than $100,000 and I'm not sure they're worth that much." Rick Monday, also holding out, was traded to the Dodgers. Bill Buckner and Ivan DeJesus arrived in the exchange.

Rick Reuschel, 15–3 on July 28, led the pitchers with a 20–10 record. Sutter finished eight of Reuschel's victories. Ray Burris was next in wins with 14. Owner Wrigley, who had been running the club since 1932, died on April 12 at the age of 82. He was succeeded by his son, William, who signed Dave Kingman on November 30 for $1.3 million for five years, the club's first reentry acquisition.

	W	L	ERA	G	GS	CG	IP	H	BB	K
Rick Reuschel	20	10	2.79	39	37	8	252	233	74	166
Ray Burris	14	16	4.72	39	39	5	221	270	67	105
Bill Bonham	10	13	4.35	34	34	1	215	207	82	134
Mike Krukow	8	14	4.40	34	33	1	172	195	61	106
Willie Hernandez	8	7	3.03	67	1	0	110	94	28	78
Paul Reuschel	5	6	4.37	69	0	0	107	105	40	62
Bruce Sutter	7	3	1.35	62	0	0	107	69	23	129
Dave Roberts	1	1	3.23	17	6	1	53	55	12	23
Steve Renko	2	2	4.59	13	8	0	51	51	21	34
Donnie Moore	4	2	4.04	27	1	0	49	51	18	34
Pete Broberg	1	2	4.75	22	0	0	36	34	18	20
Jim Todd	1	1	9.00	20	0	0	31	47	19	17
Dennis Lamp	0	2	6.30	11	3	0	30	43	8	12
Dave Giusti	0	2	6.12	20	0	0	25	30	14	15
Ramon Hernandez	0	0	7.88	6	0	0	8	11	3	4
Larry Biittner	0	0	54.00	1	0	0	1	5	1	3
	81	81	4.02	481	162	16	1,468	1,500	489	942

Shutouts: R. Reuschel 4, Burris 1, Krukow 1.
Saves: Sutter 31, W. Hernandez 4, P. Reuschel 4, Giusti 1, R. Hernandez 1, Renko 1, Roberts 1, R. Reuschel 1.

	G	AB	H	2B	3B	HR	R	RBI	SB	AVG
Regulars										
1B Bill Buckner	122	426	121	27	0	11	40	60	7	.284
2B Manny Trillo	152	504	141	18	5	7	51	57	3	.280
SS Ivan DeJesus	155	624	166	31	7	3	91	40	24	.266
3B Steve Ontiveros	156	546	163	32	3	10	54	68	3	.299
RF Bobby Murcer	154	554	147	18	3	27	90	89	16	.265
CF Jerry Morales	136	490	142	34	5	11	56	69	0	.290
LF Greg Gross	115	239	77	10	4	5	43	32	0	.322
C George Mitterwald	110	349	83	22	0	9	40	43	3	.238
Substitutes										
Larry Biittner	138	493	147	28	1	12	74	62	2	.298
Mick Kelleher	63	122	28	5	2	0	14	11	0	.230
Dave Rosello	56	82	18	2	1	1	18	9	0	.220
Mike Sember	3	4	1	0	0	0	0	0	0	.250
Gene Clines	101	239	70	12	2	3	27	41	1	.293
Jose Cardenal	100	226	54	12	1	3	33	18	5	.239
Joe Wallis	56	80	20	3	0	2	14	8	0	.250
Bobby Darwin	11	12	2	1	0	0	2	0	0	.167
Mike Adams	2	2	0	0	0	0	0	0	0	.000
Steve Swisher	74	205	39	7	0	5	21	15	0	.190
Mike Gordon	8	23	1	0	0	0	0	2	0	.043
Randy Hundley	2	4	0	0	0	0	0	0	0	.000
Pitchers										
Rick Reuschel	41	87	18	3	1	1	9	8	0	.207
Ray Burris	40	69	12	2	1	1	4	8	0	.174
Bill Bonham	35	65	15	3	0	0	3	3	0	.231
Mike Krukow	34	55	11	1	0	0	4	2	0	.200
Bruce Sutter	62	20	3	0	0	0	4	0	0	.150

	G	AB	H	2B	3B	HR	R	RBI	SB	AVG
Dave Roberts	17	17	1	0	0	0	0	1	0	.059
Willie Hernandez	67	16	1	0	0	0	0	0	0	.063
Steve Renko	13	12	2	0	0	0	0	0	0	.167
Paul Reuschel	69	11	0	0	0	0	0	0	0	.000
Donnie Moore	27	10	3	0	1	0	0	1	0	.300
Dennis Lamp	11	8	3	0	0	0	0	2	0	.375
Pete Broberg	22	6	0	0	0	0	0	0	0	.000
Dave Giusti	20	2	0	0	0	0	0	0	0	.000
Ramon Hernandez	6	1	0	0	0	0	0	0	0	.000
Jim Todd	20	1	0	0	0	0	0	0	0	.000
		5,604	1,489	271	37	111	692	649	64	.266

1978

Record: 79–83
Finish: Third (East)
Games Behind: 11
Manager: Herman Franks

General manager Bob Kennedy, a spit-and-polish former Marine Corps pilot who kept his hair short in the style of the military, expressed reluctant approval when a half dozen of his players, including bullpen star Bruce Sutter, began sprouting beards. "If they want to look like idiots that's all right with me," Kennedy barked.

Field manager Herman Franks, six years Kennedy's senior, was considerably more pragmatic. Remarked Franks: "I'll try to grow one myself if we're in first place in September."

The Cubs held the lead for 30 consecutive days—but not in September. They went into first place on May 24 with a 6–4 win over the Phillies on Manny Trillo's 10th-inning home run, dropped to second a month later, and never regained the lead.

They went into August without a 10-game winner or a 50-RBI man but as late as August 27 were only 2½ games behind the front-running Phillies. A modest surge at this point and Franks would have grown whiskers. Instead, the Cubs lost 16 of their next 26 games. They were nine back on September 23 and finished third with a 79–83 record, 11 games behind the champion Phillies.

Sutter grew a thick, black beard, common in Lancaster, Pennsylvania, Amish country, where he grew up. He finished with 27 saves, fourth in the league, but only three more than he had in the first half of the previous season. He continued to average better than one strikeout an inning but, overall, was not as consistently effective and had an 8–10 log, with a comparatively fat 3.18 earned run average.

Middle relievers Donnie Moore and Willie Hernandez, together, had 17 wins. Moore worked in 26 of the first 50 games and led the club in appearances with 71. Hernandez was in 54 games. Eight years later, with Detroit, Hernandez would set a major league record with 32 consecutive saves. Moore came to a tragic end. He committed suicide in 1989, still distraught after giving up a game-winning home run three years earlier in the American League playoffs.

Rick Reuschel, a 20-game winner the previous season, was 14–15, the only starter with more than nine victories. Rookie Mike Krukow was 9–3. Dennis Lamp, also on his maiden voyage, was 7–15 and could have sued for nonsupport. Lamp was the victim of five shutouts and lost three 1–0 games. Ken Holtzman, the prodigal son, returned on June 10 after a seven-year absence, acquired in a straight sale from the Yankees. He made six starts, finished none, and lost his three decisions.

The Cubs led the league in batting with a cumulative .264 average but were next to last in home runs with 72. Dave Kingman, the free-agent import, hit 28 home runs and was the only long-ball threat. Kingman also led in RBIs with 79 and hit .266 on the season. He played in only 119 games and was repeatedly engaged in disputes with manager Franks. As Tom Seaver, his former teammate with the Mets, had warned, Kingman had to be handled with "tender and loving care."

Bobby Murcer, who was in a season-long slump, had only nine home runs, one-third of his 1977 production. Bill Buckner, in and out of the lineup with severe leg injuries and muscle pulls, hit a courageous .323. Shortstop Ivan DeJesus led the league in runs, 104, and stole 41 bases, most by a Cub since Kiki Cuyler in 1930. Billy Williams returned as a minor league batting instructor. Ernie Banks, who had been in group sales, was named to the board of directors.

	W	L	ERA	G	GS	CG	IP	H	BB	K
Rick Reuschel	14	15	3.41	35	35	9	243	235	54	115
Dennis Lamp	7	15	3.29	37	36	6	224	221	56	73
Ray Burris	7	13	4.75	40	32	4	199	210	77	94
Dave Roberts	6	8	5.26	35	20	2	142	159	56	54
Mike Krukow	9	3	3.91	27	20	3	138	125	53	81
Donnie Moore	9	7	4.11	71	1	0	103	117	31	50
Bruce Sutter	8	10	3.18	64	0	0	99	82	34	106
Lynn McGlothen	5	3	3.04	49	1	0	80	77	39	60
Willie Hernandez	8	2	3.75	54	0	0	60	57	35	38
Woodie Fryman	2	4	5.17	13	9	0	55⅔	64	37	28
Ken Holtzman	0	3	6.11	23	6	0	53	61	35	36
Paul Reuschel	2	0	5.14	16	0	0	28	29	13	13
Dave Geisel	1	0	4.30	18	1	0	23	27	11	15
Manny Seoane	1	0	5.63	7	1	0	8	11	6	5
	79	83	4.06	489	162	24	1,455⅔	1,475	539	768

Shutouts: Lamp 3, Burris 1, Krukow 1, P. Reuschel 1, Roberts 1.
Saves: Sutter 27, Moore 4, Hernandez 3, Holtzman 2, Burris 1, Roberts 1.

	G	AB	H	2B	3B	HR	R	RBI	SB	AVG
Regulars										
1B Bill Buckner	117	446	144	26	1	5	47	74	7	.323
2B Manny Trillo	152	552	144	17	5	4	53	55	0	.261
SS Ivan DeJesus	160	619	172	24	7	3	(104)	35	41	.278
3B Steve Ontiveros	82	276	67	14	4	1	34	22	0	.243
RF Bobby Murcer	146	499	140	22	6	9	66	64	14	.281
CF Greg Gross	124	347	92	12	7	1	34	39	3	.265
LF Dave Kingman	119	395	105	17	4	28	65	79	3	.266
C Dave Rader	116	305	62	13	3	3	29	36	1	.203
Substitutes										
Larry Biittner	120	343	88	15	1	4	32	50	0	.257
Rodney Scott	78	227	64	5	1	0	41	15	27	.282
Mick Kelleher	68	95	24	1	0	0	8	6	4	.253
Davy Johnson	24	49	15	1	1	2	5	6	0	.306
Rudi Meoli	47	29	3	0	1	0	10	2	1	.103
Ed Putman	17	25	5	0	0	0	2	3	0	.200
Mike Sember	9	3	1	0	0	0	2	0	0	.333
Gene Clines	109	229	59	10	2	0	31	17	4	.258
Mike Vail	74	180	60	6	2	4	15	33	0	.333
Jerry White	59	136	37	6	0	1	22	10	4	.272
Hector Cruz	30	76	18	5	0	2	8	9	0	.237
Joe Wallis	28	55	17	2	1	1	7	6	0	.309
Scot Thompson	19	36	15	3	0	0	7	2	0	.417
Larry Cox	59	121	34	5	0	2	10	18	0	.281
Tim Blackwell	49	103	23	3	0	0	8	7	0	.223
Mike Gordon	4	5	1	0	0	0	0	0	0	.200
Pitchers										
Dennis Lamp	37	73	15	2	0	0	1	3	0	.205
Rick Reuschel	35	73	10	2	0	0	5	4	1	.137
Ray Burris	41	61	7	1	2	0	3	2	0	.115
Dave Roberts	37	52	17	3	0	2	4	7	0	.327
Mike Krukow	27	45	11	5	0	0	4	3	0	.244
Woodie Fryman	13	16	1	1	0	0	0	1	0	.063
Donnie Moore	71	15	4	1	0	0	2	4	0	.267
Bruce Sutter	64	13	1	0	0	0	1	0	0	.077

	G	AB	H	2B	3B	HR	R	RBI	SB	AVG
Lynn McGlothen	49	13	3	1	0	0	1	0	0	.231
Ken Holtzman	23	10	2	1	0	0	2	0	0	.200
Paul Reuschel	16	4	0	0	0	0	0	0	0	.000
Dave Geisel	18	3	0	0	0	0	0	0	0	.000
Willie Hernandez	55	1	0	0	0	0	1	0	0	.000
Manny Seoane	7	0	0	0	0	0	0	0	0	—
		5,530	1,461	224	48	72	664	612	110	(.264)

1979

Record: 80–82
Finish: Fifth (East)
Games Behind: 18
Managers: Herman Franks, Joey Amalfitano

Female sportswriters were beginning to invade the lair and were not always welcome. In 1979 the Cubs had their first brush with a lady reporter, Karen Chaderjian of the *Joliet News Herald*. She was allowed to enter the manager's office but was denied access to the players' quarters. Chaderjian appealed to the front office.

General manager Bob Kennedy was not sympathetic. "Either grow a beard or take the club to court," he advised.

Later, when Dave Kingman, the moody slugger, stopped talking to the press, the baseball writers asked manager Herman Franks to intervene. Replied Franks: "I've got my own problems. I've got a couple of players I don't talk to, too."

Eventually, communications improved, but there wasn't much to cheer about. The Cubs were never in first place and dropped back into the second division. A 9–22 September solidified the collapse. They finished fifth, two games under .500, 18 games behind the divisional champion Pittsburgh Pirates.

Franks quit a week before the season ended and was replaced by Joey Amalfitano, his third base coach. There was never any question about Franks' managerial ability. But he had a gruff exterior and didn't possess some of the niceties. He sprayed tobacco juice, and when some of it landed on his uniform blouse, he told reporters, "Hey, I ain't here to look pretty."

Kingman and reliever Bruce Sutter were the only Cubs among the league leaders. Kingman led in home runs, 48, and in slugging average, .613, and he was second in RBIs with 115. Sutter returned to his previous form and was directly involved in more than half of the club's victories. He won six games and equaled the league record with 37 saves. In 101 innings he struck out 110 batters and allowed only 67 hits.

Sutter won the Cy Young award and said, "I owe half my saves to Dick Tidrow." It was not an expression of modesty. Acquired from the Yankees for starter Ray Burris, Tidrow made his Cub debut on May 24 in the Cubs' 37th game. Working middle relief, Tidrow won 11 games and had four saves and a 2.71 ERA, but these numbers are insufficient in explaining his value. He appeared in 29 winning games, eight of which Sutter saved. Sutter finished eight of Tidrow's wins. Tidrow was in 63 games, one more than Sutter.

Rick Reuschel, 7–0 in August, led in victories with 18. The only other starters who won in double figures were Lynn McGlothen with 13 and Dennis Lamp with 11. Kenny Holtzman, who had been rusting on the bench—he had pitched a total of only 143 innings the previous two seasons—was the fifth starter. He was 6–9, had several outstanding performances, and retired at the end of the season.

Kingman provided most of the offense and was the principal lure for a record home gate of 1,648,587. He tied the league record of five home runs in two games and connected three times on May 17 in a memorable nine-inning 23–22 loss to the Phillies. Bobby Murcer, now under a constant shower of boos, had seven home runs and 22 RBIs when he was traded to the Yankees on June 26 for a minor league pitcher. Prior to his departure, Murcer stranded 47 of 52 base runners in scoring position.

Kennedy swung a beneficial eight-player preseason deal with the Phillies. Second baseman Manny Trillo and catcher Dave Rader were sacrificed. Center fielder Jerry Martin, catcher Barry Foote, and second baseman Ted Sizemore were the principals who came in the exchange. Martin had a good year, 19 home runs and 73 RBIs. Foote batted .254, with 16 home runs, and was adequate on defense. At the end of the season, Sizemore was traded back to the Phillies.

	W	L	ERA	G	GS	CG	IP	H	BB	K
Rick Reuschel	18	12	3.62	36	36	5	239	251	75	125
Lynn McGlothen	13	14	4.12	42	29	6	212	236	55	147
Dennis Lamp	11	10	3.51	38	32	6	200	223	46	86
Mike Krukow	9	9	4.20	28	28	0	165	172	81	119
Ken Holtzman	6	9	4.58	23	20	3	118	133	53	44
Dick Tidrow	11	5	2.71	63	0	0	103	86	42	68
Bruce Sutter	6	6	2.23	62	0	0	101	67	32	110
Bill Caudill	1	7	4.80	29	12	0	90	89	41	104
Willie Hernandez	4	4	5.01	51	2	0	79	85	39	53
Donnie Moore	1	4	5.18	39	1	0	73	95	25	43
Ray Burris	0	0	6.23	14	0	0	21⅔	23	15	14
Doug Capilla	0	1	2.60	13	1	0	17⅓	14	7	10
Dave Geisel	0	0	0.60	7	0	0	15	10	4	5
George Riley	0	1	5.54	4	1	0	13	16	6	5
	80	82	3.90	449	162	20	1,447	1,500	521	933

Shutouts: Holtzman 2, Lamp 1, McGlothen 1, Reuschel 1.
Saves: Sutter (37), Tidrow 4, McGlothen 2, Moore 1.

	G	AB	H	2B	3B	HR	R	RBI	SB	AVG
Regulars										
1B Bill Buckner	149	591	168	34	7	14	72	66	9	.284
2B Ted Sizemore	98	330	82	17	0	2	36	24	3	.248
SS Ivan DeJesus	160	636	180	26	10	5	92	52	24	.283
3B Steve Ontiveros	152	519	148	28	2	4	58	57	0	.285
RF Scot Thompson	128	346	100	13	5	2	36	29	4	.289
CF Jerry Martin	150	534	145	34	3	19	74	73	2	.272
LF Dave Kingman	145	532	153	19	5	(48)	97	115	4	.288
C Barry Foote	132	429	109	26	0	16	47	56	5	.254
Substitutes										
Steve Dillard	89	166	47	6	1	5	31	24	1	.283
Mick Kelleher	73	142	36	4	1	0	14	10	2	.254
Steve Macko	19	40	9	1	0	0	2	3	0	.225
Steve Davis	3	4	0	0	0	0	0	1	0	.000
Kurt Seibert	7	2	0	0	0	0	2	0	0	.000
Larry Biittner	111	272	79	13	3	3	35	50	1	.290
Bobby Murcer	58	190	49	4	1	7	22	22	2	.258
Mike Vail	87	179	60	8	2	7	28	35	0	.335
Ken Henderson	62	81	19	2	0	2	11	8	0	.235
Miguel Dilone	43	36	11	0	0	0	14	1	15	.306
Sam Mejias	31	11	2	0	0	0	4	0	0	.182
Tim Blackwell	63	122	20	3	1	0	8	12	0	.164
Bruce Kimm	9	11	1	0	0	0	0	0	0	.091

	G	AB	H	2B	3B	HR	R	RBI	SB	AVG
Pitchers										
Rick Reuschel	38	79	13	2	1	0	8	6	0	.165
Lynn McGlothen	42	71	16	3	0	0	6	3	0	.225
Dennis Lamp	38	58	9	1	0	0	2	1	0	.155
Mike Krukow	28	51	16	2	0	1	4	8	0	.314
Ken Holtzman	24	43	10	3	0	0	2	1	0	.233
Bill Caudill	29	17	1	0	0	0	0	0	0	.059
Donnie Moore	39	13	2	0	1	0	0	1	0	.154
Bruce Sutter	62	12	3	0	0	0	0	3	1	.250
Dick Tidrow	63	10	2	0	0	0	0	1	0	.200
Willie Hernandez	52	8	2	1	0	0	0	1	0	.250
George Riley	4	2	0	0	0	0	0	0	0	.000
Dave Geisel	7	1	0	0	0	0	0	0	0	.000
Ray Burris	14	1	0	0	0	0	1	0	0	.000
Doug Capilla	13	0	0	0	0	0	0	0	0	—
		5,539	1,492	250	43	135	706	663	73	.269

1980

Record: 64–98
Finish: Sixth (East)
Games Behind: 27
Managers: Preston Gomez, Joey Amalfitano

Slugger Dave Kingman opened the 1980 season by dumping a bucket of ice water on a sportswriter, later went AWOL, and prior to the All-Star break was mocked with a proliferation of bumper stickers announcing, "Hey! Hey! The Cubs Are on Their Way! Dave Ding Dong Went Fishing Today!"

Kingman played half the season, 81 games; the rest of the time he was either benched for failing at the plate or out with injuries. He fell on his right shoulder, was on the disabled list for 33 days, and went two and a half months without a home run. He had only 255 at bats and finished with 18 home runs, 30 fewer than the previous season. His RBIs dropped from 115 to 57.

His problems began when he doused Don Friske, 25, of the suburban Arlington Heights, Illinois, *Daily Herald*. "This will give you stories for two days," Kingman shouted. Later, he recanted and claimed he was "only kidding." National League president Charles Feeney dismissed the incident with a warning: Kingman would be punished if he did it again.

Kingman's troubles continued. When the Cubs left Houston on June 11, after a 2–8 road trip, the next day was an open date. Kingman was given permission to detour to his San Diego home. He would then rejoin the club in Chicago on June 13 for the beginning of a home stand. The wind was blowing out to left field, ideal for Kingman, but he failed to report. The Cubs lost to Atlanta 8–7.

When he arrived the following day he insisted his shoulder was hurting and he wouldn't have been able to play. Kingman was chastised at a postgame clubhouse meeting. He apologized to manager Preston Gomez and to his teammates. General manager Bob Kennedy fined Kingman $1,250, a day's pay. He was put on the disabled list three days later.

Jerry Martin picked up some of the slack with 23 home runs and led the club with 73 RBIs. Bill Buckner led the league in batting with a .324 average, the club's fourth batting champion in the last nine years. Going into the final day, Buckner held a five-percentage-point lead over the Mets' Keith Hernandez. Buckner was urged to sit out. He refused, saying, "If I win, I want to do it right." He went 0-for-4; Hernandez was 1-for-4 and finished at .321.

Shortstop Ivan DeJesus stole 44 bases and in the second game of an April 22 doubleheader against the Cardinals became the 12th Cub to hit for the cycle. Catcher Barry Foote hit a grand-slam home run and drove in eight runs in the opener, one short of the club's single-game RBI record. Foote was ailing most of the season and appeared in only 63 games.

None of the four rotation starters had winning records: Lynn McGlothen went 12–14, Rick Reuschel 11–13, Dennis Lamp 10–14, and Mike Krukow 10–15. Reuschel was 5–0 in August, lifting his career August record to 20–4. No other starter won more than one game.

The strength of the club was in the bullpen. Bruce Sutter led the league with 28 saves and again was ably supported by Dick Tidrow, who equaled the club record for appearances, 84. Rookie Bill Caudill, who had an explosive fastball, had 112 strikeouts in 128 innings. Lee Smith, later a premier reliever, bowed with a 2–0 record.

Preston Gomez, who had been a coach with the Dodgers, opened the season in the manager's chair but was dismissed on July 25. "Firing Preston is not the answer," Sutter insisted. "What this club needs is a major overhaul." The Cubs finished last, 27 games out of the lead. They were 38–52 under Gomez, 26–46 with Joey Amalfitano, who succeeded him.

	W	L	ERA	G	GS	CG	IP	H	BB	K
Rick Reuschel	11	13	3.40	38	38	6	257	(281)	76	140
Mike Krukow	10	15	4.39	34	34	3	205	200	80	130
Dennis Lamp	10	14	5.19	41	37	2	203	259	82	83
Lynn McGlothen	12	14	4.80	39	27	2	182	211	64	119
Bill Caudill	4	6	2.18	72	2	0	128	100	59	112
Dick Tidrow	6	5	2.79	(84)	0	0	116	97	53	97
Willie Hernandez	1	9	4.42	53	7	0	108	115	45	75
Bruce Sutter	5	8	2.65	60	0	0	102	90	34	76
Doug Capilla	2	8	4.10	39	11	0	90	82	51	51
George Riley	0	4	5.75	22	0	0	36	41	20	18
Randy Martz	1	2	2.10	6	6	0	30	28	11	5
Lee Smith	2	0	2.86	18	0	0	22	21	14	17
	64	98	3.89	506	162	13	1,479	1,525	589	923

Shutouts: McGlothen 2, Lamp 1.
Saves: Sutter (28), Tidrow 6, Reuschel 4, Caudill 1.

	G	AB	H	2B	3B	HR	R	RBI	SB	AVG
Regulars										
1B Bill Buckner	145	578	187	41	3	10	69	68	1	(.324)
2B Mike Tyson	123	341	81	19	3	3	34	23	1	.238
SS Ivan DeJesus	157	618	160	26	3	3	78	33	44	.259
3B Lenny Randle	130	489	135	19	6	5	67	39	19	.276
RF Scot Thompson	102	226	48	10	1	2	26	13	6	.212
CF Jerry Martin	141	494	112	22	2	23	57	73	8	.227
LF Dave Kingman	81	255	71	8	0	18	31	57	2	.278
C Tim Blackwell	103	320	87	16	4	5	24	30	0	.272
Substitutes										
Larry Biittner	127	273	68	12	2	1	21	34	1	.249
Steve Dillard	100	244	55	8	1	4	31	27	2	.225
Cliff Johnson	68	196	46	8	0	10	28	34	0	.235
Mick Kelleher	105	96	14	1	1	0	12	4	1	.146
Steve Ontiveros	31	77	16	3	0	1	7	3	0	.208
Steve Macko	6	20	6	2	0	0	2	2	0	.300
Mike Vail	114	312	93	17	2	6	30	47	2	.298
Jesus Figueroa	115	198	50	5	0	1	20	11	2	.253
Jim Tracy	42	122	31	3	3	3	12	9	2	.254
Carlos Lezcano	42	88	18	4	1	3	15	12	1	.205
Ken Henderson	44	82	16	3	0	2	7	9	0	.195
Barry Foote	63	202	48	13	1	6	16	28	1	.238
Mike O'Berry	19	48	10	1	0	0	7	5	0	.208
Bill Hayes	4	9	2	1	0	0	0	0	0	.222
Pitchers										
Rick Reuschel	44	82	13	3	1	0	4	5	0	.159
Mike Krukow	34	65	16	0	0	1	5	6	0	.246
Dennis Lamp	41	61	6	0	0	0	3	1	0	.098
Lynn McGlothen	41	51	10	4	0	0	6	1	0	.196
Doug Capilla	40	21	4	0	1	0	1	1	0	.190
Willie Hernandez	53	19	4	1	0	0	0	1	0	.211

	G	AB	H	2B	3B	HR	R	RBI	SB	AVG
Bruce Sutter	60	9	1	0	0	0	0	1	0	.111
Bill Caudill	72	9	2	1	0	0	0	1	0	.222
Randy Martz	6	9	1	0	0	0	0	0	0	.111
Dick Tidrow	84	4	0	0	0	0	1	0	0	.000
George Riley	22	1	0	0	0	0	0	0	0	.000
Lee Smith	18	0	0	0	0	0	0	0	0	—
		5,619	1,411	251	35	107	614	578	93	.251

1981

Record: 38–65
Finish: Sixth (East)
Games Behind: 21½
Manager: Joey Amalfitano

As Bruce Sutter had said, the Cubs needed a major overhaul. Surprise! Sutter was the first to go, traded to the Cardinals in the off-season. Dave Kingman was next, dealt to the Mets. Rick Reuschel went to the Yankees on June 12, 1981, and four days later came the biggest swap of all: Bill Wrigley sold the club to the Tribune Company, a media giant headquartered on Michigan Avenue, directly across the street from the Wrigley Building.

It was the year of the 50-day player strike, forcing cancellation of 712 games, then the longest stoppage in baseball history. The shutdown began on the morning of June 12. The result was a split season. The Cubs were 15–37 in the first half, which ended when the strike began; 23–28 in the second half after play resumed on August 10. Their combined 38–65 record was the worst in the league.

Kingman was traded to the Mets for Steve Henderson on February 28, the first day of spring training. To swing the deal the Cubs agreed to give the Mets $200,000, which represented almost all of Kingmans $240,000 salary. Many of the Cub players were delighted. Said pitcher Lynn McGlothen: "I'll be glad to throw at him."

Catcher Barry Foote was traded to the Yankees on April 27. The Reuschel deal, also with the Yankees, was the blockbuster, consummated because Wrigley was strapped for cash. The Yankees paid $400,000 and sent three players in the exchange: pitchers Doug Bird and Mike Griffith, and Pat Tabler, a promising second base prospect.

Because of the shortened season, none of the Cub pitchers won in double figures. Mike Krukow led the club with nine victories and was the only starter with a .500 record. With Sutter gone, Dick Tidrow was now the bullpen ace, with nine saves in 51 appearances and a 5.04 ERA. But he was perfect during the first week of May; in a four-game sequence he retired 22 batters in succession.

The Cubs were last in the league in complete games, six, and last in shutouts, two. They were also last in batting with a .236 team average and had only one .300 hitter, the reliable Bill Buckner, who hit .311. Buckner and Leon Durham, who came from the Cardinals in the Sutter deal, led the club in home runs, 10 each. Henderson, Kingman's replacement, didn't live up to expectations and showed only occasional power: five home runs and 35 RBIs.

General manager Bob Kennedy was dismissed on May 22 and was replaced by Herman Franks, his former field manager. Bill Wrigley, who owned 81 percent of the stock, sold the club three weeks later, on June 16, to the Tribune Company for a reported $20.5 million, bringing an end to the Wrigley family's 65-year ownership, which spanned three generations.

Andrew J. McKenna, a lifelong Chicagoan who six months earlier had guided the sale of the White Sox—he had been chairman of the White Sox board—also prompted the Tribune purchase. Wrigley was faced with $40 million in inheritance taxes; his parents had died within months of each other in 1977. The Tribune's WGN radio and television stations had for many years aired the Cub games, and McKenna correctly assumed it was an ideal match.

Stanton Cook, chief of the Tribune empire, named McKenna chairman of the Cub board, and after the season ended, on October 15, McKenna hired Dallas Green as the club's executive vice president and general manager—$1 million for five years. Green had managed the Phillies to a World Series victory in '80 and before that had been their farm director. Franks resigned. So did field manager Joey Amalfitano. Green immediately sent a letter to the players, scolding them for not being in shape, for lacking in fundamentals, and for using day baseball as an excuse for their late-season failures. A new era was about to begin.

	W	L	ERA	G	GS	CG	IP	H	BB	K
Mike Krukow	9	9	3.69	25	(25)	2	144	146	55	101
Randy Martz	5	7	3.67	33	14	1	108	103	49	32
Rick Reuschel	4	7	3.45	13	13	1	86	87	23	53
Ken Kravec	1	6	5.08	24	12	0	78	80	39	50
Dick Tidrow	3	10	5.04	51	0	0	75	73	30	39
Doug Bird	4	5	3.60	12	12	2	75	72	16	34
Bill Caudill	1	5	5.83	30	10	0	71	87	31	45
Lee Smith	3	6	3.49	40	1	0	67	57	31	50
Lynn McGlothen	1	4	4.75	20	6	0	55	71	28	26
Mike Griffin	2	5	4.50	16	9	0	52	64	9	20
Doug Capilla	1	0	3.18	42	0	0	51	52	34	28
Rawley Eastwick	0	1	2.30	30	0	0	43	43	15	24
Jay Howell	2	0	4.91	10	2	0	22	23	10	10
Dave Geisel	2	0	0.56	11	2	0	16	11	10	7
Willie Hernandez	0	0	3.86	12	0	0	14	14	8	13
	38	65	4.02	369	106	6	957	983	388	532

Shutouts: Bird 1, Krukow 1.
Saves: Tidrow 9, Martz 6, Hernandez 2, Eastwick 1, Griffin 1, Smith 1.

	G	AB	H	2B	3B	HR	R	RBI	SB	AVG
Regulars										
1B Bill Buckner	106	421	131	(35)	3	10	45	75	5	.311
2B Pat Tabler	35	101	19	3	1	1	11	5	0	.188
SS Ivan DeJesus	106	403	78	8	4	0	49	13	21	.194
3B Ken Reitz	82	260	56	9	1	2	10	28	0	.215
RF Leon Durham	87	328	95	14	6	10	42	35	25	.290
CF Steve Henderson	82	287	84	9	5	5	32	35	5	.293
LF Jerry Morales	84	245	70	6	2	1	27	25	1	.286
C Jody Davis	56	180	46	5	1	4	14	21	0	.256
Substitutes										
Steve Dillard	53	119	26	7	1	2	18	11	0	.218
Hector Cruz	53	109	25	5	0	7	15	15	2	.229
Mike Tyson	50	92	17	2	0	2	6	8	1	.185
Joe Strain	25	74	14	1	0	0	7	1	0	.189
Ty Waller	30	71	19	2	1	3	10	13	2	.268
Scott Fletcher	19	46	10	4	0	0	6	1	0	.217
Bobby Bonds	45	163	35	7	1	6	26	19	5	.215
Scot Thompson	57	115	19	5	0	0	8	8	2	.165
Jim Tracy	45	63	15	2	1	0	6	5	1	.238
Mike Lum	41	58	14	1	0	2	5	7	0	.241
Carlos Lezcano	7	14	1	0	0	0	1	2	0	.071
Mel Hall	10	11	1	0	0	1	1	2	0	.091
Tim Blackwell	58	158	37	10	2	1	21	11	2	.234
Barry Foote	9	22	0	0	0	0	0	1	0	.000
Bill Hayes	1	0	0	0	0	0	0	0	0	—
Pitchers										
Mike Krukow	25	50	9	2	0	0	5	3	0	.180
Randy Martz	34	28	6	0	0	0	0	2	0	.214
Rick Reuschel	16	25	2	0	0	0	1	1	0	.080
Doug Bird	12	20	2	0	0	0	0	0	0	.100
Ken Kravec	25	15	0	0	0	0	1	0	0	.000
Bill Caudill	30	14	2	0	0	0	0	1	0	.143

	G	AB	H	2B	3B	HR	R	RBI	SB	AVG
Mike Griffin	16	13	2	0	0	0	0	0	0	.154
Lynn McGlothen	20	12	1	1	0	0	1	0	0	.083
Lee Smith	40	9	0	0	0	0	0	0	0	.000
Dick Tidrow	51	5	0	0	0	0	0	0	0	.000
Doug Capilla	42	3	0	0	0	0	0	0	0	.000
Dave Geisel	11	3	0	0	0	0	0	0	0	.000
Rawley Eastwick	30	2	0	0	0	0	0	0	0	.000
Jay Howell	10	2	0	0	0	0	2	0	0	.000
Willie Hernandez	13	0	0	0	0	0	0	0	0	—
		3,541	836	138	29	57	370	348	72	.236

1982

Record: 73–89
Finish: Fifth (East)
Games Behind: 19
Manager: Lee Elia

Dallas Green's previous major league experience had been limited to the Philadelphia Phillies—as a player, farm director, and manager. When he began retooling for the long climb ahead, there was such an avalanche of arriving Phillies that the Cubs soon became known as the Phil-Cubs or the Cub-Phils.

Lee Elia, Green's third base coach in Philadelphia, was the new manager. Other Philly coaches also checked in, along with Ryne Sandberg (who was initially regarded as a center fielder), veteran shortstop Larry Bowa, outfielder Keith Moreland, and pitchers Dickie Noles, Mike Proly, and Dan Larson.

All of the Cub department heads were dismissed. In the first season of Green's command, 22 Philadelphia refugees were aboard at both the major and minor league levels. Green also adopted a new slogan, "Building a New Tradition." Except for those born yesterday, Cub fans were annoyed. Obviously, Green was unaware the Cubs had collected 16 pennants, a glorious tradition.

Sandberg was the only former Philly who would have a distinguished Cub career, and he was a throw-in in the deal that brought Bowa at the expense of shortstop Ivan DeJesus, seven years younger. Bowa steadied the infield and hit .246, a drop of 37 points from the previous season. Sandberg recovered from a dismal start. He was hitless in his first 20 at bats before he singled off the Cardinals' Joaquin Andujar. The slump grew to 1-for-32—.031. Sandberg finished with a .271 average, stole 32 bases, and scored 103 runs, most ever by a Cub rookie.

The Cubs won their 8,000th National League game on May 13 at Houston, and—"Believe It or Not"—right-hander Allen Ripley was the winner, his first victory of the season. The worst was yet to come. From May 30 through June 13, they dropped 13 in a row, their longest skid in 38 years. One more loss would have equaled the franchise record for consecutive defeats. They were charged with six errors in the next game but hung on, 12–11, against the Phillies. Steve Carlton was the loser.

During the losing streak, on May 24 in San Diego, Bill Buckner got into a dugout shoving match with Elia. Buckner, always contentious, was angry: he had been knocked down by pitcher Tim Lollar, and the Cubs did not retaliate. Buckner apologized two days later. There were no other major incidents. The Cubs finished fifth but were charging: 18–10 in July and 33–24 after August 1, from that point the fourth-best won-lost record in either league.

The bullpen kept the club afloat. Lee Smith, having failed in an experiment as a starter, had an 0.84 ERA and 15 of his 17 saves after he returned to the pen on July 8. Willie Hernandez had a 1.73 ERA over his last 31 games; Bill Campbell, 1.79 in his final 45 innings; and Dick Tidrow, 2.13 in his last 42 appearances.

In his rebuilding program, Green tried for a quick fix and went with several players who were in the twilight. In addition to the 36-year-old Bowa, pitchers Ferguson Jenkins, 38, and Campbell, 33, were signed as free agents. Jenkins returned after an eight-year absence and led the staff in victories, 14, and in losses, 15. Randy Martz, 11–10, was the only starter over .500.

Buckner had his first 200-hit season, batting .306 with 15 home runs and 105 RBIs. Outfielder Leon Durham led the club in hitting, .312, and in home runs, 22. Bump Wills, 30, acquired from Texas in a trade, opened the season at second base and hit a home run in his first appearance. Wills batted .272 and stole 35 bases but was inadequate in the field. Sandberg opened at third and moved to second on September 3.

	W	L	ERA	G	GS	CG	IP	H	BB	K
Ferguson Jenkins	14	15	3.15	34	34	4	217⅓	221	68	134
Doug Bird	9	14	5.14	35	33	2	191	230	30	71
Dickie Noles	10	13	4.42	31	30	2	171	180	61	85
Randy Martz	11	10	4.21	28	24	1	147⅔	157	36	40
Allen Ripley	5	7	4.26	28	19	0	122⅔	130	38	57
Lee Smith	2	5	2.69	72	5	0	117	105	37	99
Dick Tidrow	8	3	3.39	65	0	0	103⅔	106	29	62
Bill Campbell	3	6	3.69	62	0	0	100	89	40	71
Mike Proly	5	3	2.30	44	1	0	82	77	22	24
Willie Hernandez	4	6	3.00	75	0	0	75	74	24	54
Tom Filer	1	2	5.53	8	8	0	40⅔	50	18	15
Dan Larson	0	4	5.67	12	6	0	39¾	51	18	22
Ken Kravec	1	1	6.12	13	2	0	25	27	18	20
Randy Stein	0	0	3.48	6	0	0	10⅓	7	7	6
Herman Segelke	0	0	8.31	3	0	0	4⅓	6	6	4
	73	89	3.93	516	162	9	1,447⅓	1,510	452	764

Shutouts: Noles 2, Jenkins 1.
Saves: Smith 17, Hernandez 10, Campbell 8, Tidrow 6, Martz 1, Proly 1.

	G	AB	H	2B	3B	HR	R	RBI	SB	AVG
Regulars										
1B Bill Buckner	161	(657)	201	34	5	15	93	105	15	.306
2B Bump Wills	128	419	114	18	4	6	64	38	35	.272
SS Larry Bowa	142	499	123	15	7	0	50	29	8	.246
3B Ryne Sandberg	156	635	172	33	5	7	103	54	32	.271
RF Jay Johnstone	98	269	67	13	1	10	39	43	0	.249
CF Leon Durham	148	539	168	33	7	22	84	90	28	.312
LF Keith Moreland	138	476	124	17	2	15	50	68	0	.261
C Jody Davis	130	418	109	20	2	12	41	52	0	.261
Substitutes										
Junior Kennedy	105	242	53	3	1	2	22	25	1	.219
Pat Tabler	25	85	20	4	2	1	9	7	0	.235
Scott Fletcher	11	24	4	0	0	0	4	1	0	.167
Steve Henderson	92	257	60	12	4	2	23	29	6	.233
Gary Woods	117	245	66	15	1	4	28	30	3	.269
Jerry Morales	65	116	33	2	2	4	14	30	1	.284
Mel Hall	24	80	21	3	2	0	6	4	0	.263
Scot Thompson	49	74	27	5	1	0	11	7	0	.365
Bob Molinaro	65	66	13	1	0	1	6	12	1	.197
Dan Briggs	48	48	6	0	0	0	1	1	0	.125
Ty Waller	17	21	5	0	0	0	4	1	0	.238
Hector Cruz	17	19	4	1	0	0	1	0	0	.211
Butch Benton	4	7	1	0	0	0	0	1	0	.143
Larry Cox	2	4	0	0	0	0	1	0	0	.000
Pitchers										
Ferguson Jenkins	34	67	10	2	0	0	2	6	0	.149
Dickie Noles	31	56	6	3	0	0	5	2	0	.107
Doug Bird	35	56	8	1	0	0	0	3	0	.143
Randy Martz	28	42	6	2	0	0	6	6	0	.143
Allen Ripley	28	38	5	0	0	0	3	1	0	.132
Lee Smith	72	16	1	0	0	1	2	1	0	.063
Mike Proly	44	14	4	1	0	0	0	1	0	.286
Tom Filer	8	12	1	1	0	0	1	0	0	.083
Dan Larson	12	11	3	0	0	0	2	0	0	.273
Bill Campbell	62	7	1	0	0	0	0	0	0	.143
Dick Tidrow	65	6	0	0	0	0	0	0	0	.000
Ken Kravec	13	3	0	0	0	0	0	0	0	.000
Willie Hernandez	75	3	0	0	0	0	1	0	1	.000
Randy Stein	6	0	0	0	0	0	0	0	0	—
Herman Segelke	3	0	0	0	0	0	0	0	0	—
	5,531	1,436	239	46	102	676	647	132	.260	

1983

Record: 71–91
Finish: Fifth (East)
Games Behind: 19
Managers: Lee Elia, Charlie Fox

It was another season of frustration. On April 29, 1983, when they were 5–14 after a 4–3 loss to the Dodgers, the Cub players were trudging to the clubhouse. About a dozen fans, grouped down the left field line, doused outfielder Keith Moreland with stale beer and hurled verbal abuse at shortstop Larry Bowa.

Within minutes, manager Lee Elia was in his clubhouse office for what was expected to be a routine press conference. But Elia was unable to contain his rage and erupted with five minutes of blasphemy, a profane soliloquy that was to become an underground collector's item, the infamous "Elia Tape."

Among other things, Elia said: "Eight-five percent of the people in this country go to work. The other 15 percent come out here [to Wrigley Field] and boo the players." Later, Elia insisted he had been misinterpreted. "It sounded like I was cursing the entire Cub kingdom," he said. "But that's not true. I was talking about only those fans who were harassing Moreland and Bowa."

The Cubs were never higher than fourth. They stumbled at the gate, lost their first six games, were 38–41 at the All-Star break, and finished with a 71–91 record, in fifth place, 19 games out. Elia was fired on August 23, when the Cubs were 15 games under .500, and succeeded by Charlie Fox, 61, a gregarious singer of Irish ballads who previously had managed two big league clubs and was with the Cubs as an assistant to vice president Dallas Green.

That Green required assistance was evident. He left Ferguson Jenkins unprotected in the free-agent compensation pool. Jenkins was selected by the crosstown White Sox, but the Cubs "bought" him back 24 hours later with a hasty six-player trade—pitchers Dick Tidrow and Randy Martz and reserve infielders Pat Tabler and Scott Fletcher to the Sox for pitchers Steve Trout and Warren Brusstar. The commissioner's office investigated the deal but found no violation.

Green had another embarrassing moment. After a long and unsuccessful attempt to land the Dodgers' Steve Garvey, a free agent, Green was so eager for a replacement he used the "Garvey money"—$4.75 million, $950,000 a year for five years—and threw it at Dodger third baseman Ron Cey, a lesser player. Cey's agent took the money and ran and later admitted he was stunned; the offer was considerably beyond expectations.

Cey, who had a career total of 228 home runs, including 24 the previous year, had a sluggish start; he didn't hit his first Cub home run until his 89th at bat, was batting .171 going into May, but finished with 24 home runs and 90 RBIs. Jody Davis, a comparatively obscure catcher, almost matched Cey's production. Davis also hit 24 home runs and drove in 84 runs.

Ryne Sandberg, beginning to blossom, tightened the defense, participated in a league-high 126 double plays, and led the club in steals with 37, most by a Cub second baseman since Johnny Evers' 46 in 1907. The Cubs led the league in fielding but were unable to overcome a 4.08 team ERA, highest in the league.

Chuck Rainey, acquired in a deal with the Red Sox, led in victories with 14, one of which was a near no-hitter against Cincinnati on August 24; Eddie Milner singled with two outs in the ninth. Dick Ruthven, another Philadelphia import, was next with 12 wins. The Cubs were last in complete games, nine, and had a string of 67 incompletions, dating from September 15 of the previous season. The bullpen prevented a last-place finish. Lee Smith led the NL in saves, 29, and Bill Campbell in appearances, 82. Campbell lost both games of a June 20 doubleheader.

	W	L	ERA	G	GS	CG	IP	H	BB	K
Chuck Rainey	14	13	4.48	34	34	1	191	219	74	84
Steve Trout	10	14	4.65	34	32	1	180	217	59	80
Ferguson Jenkins	6	9	4.30	33	29	1	167⅓	176	46	96
Dick Ruthven	12	9	4.10	25	25	5	149⅓	156	28	73
Bill Campbell	6	8	4.49	(82)	0	0	122⅓	128	49	97
Dickie Noles	5	10	4.72	24	18	1	116⅓	133	37	59
Lee Smith	4	10	1.65	66	0	0	103⅓	70	41	91
Craig Lefferts	3	4	3.13	56	5	0	89	80	29	60
Mike Proly	1	5	3.58	60	0	0	83	79	38	31
Warren Brusstar	3	1	2.35	59	0	0	80⅓	67	37	46
Paul Moskau	3	2	6.75	8	8	0	32	44	14	16
Rich Bordi	0	2	4.97	11	1	0	25⅓	34	12	20
Rick Reuschel	1	1	3.92	4	4	0	20⅔	18	10	9
Willie Hernandez	1	0	3.20	11	1	0	19⅔	16	6	18
Reggie Patterson	1	2	4.82	5	2	0	18⅔	17	6	10
Don Schulze	0	1	7.07	4	3	0	14	19	7	8
Bill Johnson	1	0	4.38	10	0	0	12⅓	17	3	4
Alan Hargesheimer	0	0	9.00	5	0	0	4	6	2	5
	71	91	4.08	531	162	9	1,428⅔	1,496	498	807

Shutouts: Ruthven 2, Noles 1, Jenkins 1, Rainey 1.
Saves: Smith (29), Campbell 8, Bordi 1, Brusstar 1, Hernandez 1, Lefferts 1, Proly 1.

	G	AB	H	2B	3B	HR	R	RBI	SB	AVG
Regulars										
1B Bill Buckner	153	626	175	(38)	6	16	79	66	12	.280
2B Ryne Sandberg	158	633	165	25	4	8	94	48	37	.261
SS Larry Bowa	147	499	133	20	5	2	73	43	7	.267
3B Ron Cey	159	581	160	33	1	24	73	90	0	.275
RF Keith Moreland	154	533	161	30	3	16	76	70	0	.302
CF Mel Hall	112	410	116	23	5	17	60	56	6	.283
LF Leon Durham	100	337	87	18	8	12	58	55	12	.258
C Jody Davis	151	510	138	31	2	24	56	84	0	.271
Substitutes										
Carmelo Martinez	29	89	23	3	0	6	8	16	0	.258
Tom Veryzer	59	88	18	3	0	1	5	3	0	.205
Dan Rohn	23	31	12	3	2	0	3	6	1	.387
Junior Kennedy	17	22	3	0	0	0	3	3	0	.136
Dave Owen	16	22	2	0	1	0	1	2	1	.091
Fritz Connally	8	10	1	0	0	0	0	0	0	.100
Gary Woods	93	190	46	9	0	4	25	22	5	.242
Jay Johnstone	86	140	36	7	0	6	16	22	1	.257
Scot Thompson	53	88	17	3	1	0	4	10	0	.193
Jerry Morales	63	87	17	9	0	0	11	11	0	.195
Thad Bosley	43	72	21	4	1	2	12	12	1	.292
Joe Carter	23	51	9	1	1	0	6	1	1	.176
Wayne Nordhagen	21	35	5	1	0	1	1	4	0	.143
Tom Grant	16	20	3	1	0	0	2	2	0	.150
Steve Lake	38	85	22	4	1	1	9	7	0	.259
Mike Diaz	6	7	2	1	0	0	2	1	0	.286

	G	AB	H	2B	3B	HR	R	RBI	SB	AVG
Pitchers										
Steve Trout	34	62	12	0	0	0	6	1	0	.194
Chuck Rainey	34	56	9	0	0	0	4	0	0	.161
Ferguson Jenkins	33	53	13	2	1	0	3	5	0	.245
Dick Ruthven	25	53	12	1	0	0	5	3	0	.226
Dickie Noles	24	38	9	1	0	0	1	5	0	.237
Craig Lefferts	56	18	2	0	0	0	1	0	0	.111
Mike Proly	60	11	1	0	0	0	1	0	0	.091
Paul Moskau	8	11	2	1	0	0	2	0	0	.182
Bill Campbell	82	10	1	0	0	0	0	1	0	.100
Lee Smith	66	9	1	0	0	0	0	0	0	.111
Rick Reuschel	4	7	1	0	0	0	0	0	0	.143
Reggie Patterson	5	6	0	0	0	0	1	0	0	.000
Warren Brusstar	59	4	0	0	0	0	0	0	0	.000
Rich Bordi	11	4	0	0	0	0	0	0	0	.000
Willie Hernandez	11	2	1	0	0	0	0	0	0	.500
Don Schulze	4	1	0	0	0	0	0	0	0	.000
Alan Hargesheimer	5	0	0	0	0	0	0	0	0	—
Bill Johnson	10	0	0	0	0	0	0	0	0	—
		5,511	1,436	272	42	140	701	649	84	.261

1984

Record: 96–65
Finish: First (East)
Games Ahead: 6½
Manager: Jim Frey

History repeats. As general manager Jim Gallagher had done in 1945, the year of the last Cub pennant, Dallas Green made an interleague in-season waiver deal for Rick Sutcliffe, a quality pitcher. But whereas Gallagher's Cubs captured the flag and were in an eight-team league, with one winner, the '84 club won only a split divisional title. Still, the sleeping Cub giant had awakened. It was their first championship in 39 years.

Just as Gallagher had patched an ailing pitching staff with the acquisition of Hank Borowy, Green acquired Sutcliffe on June 14 in a seven-player trade with Cleveland because two Cub starters, Scott Sanderson and Dick Ruthven, were disabled. Aware he had a strong team, Green didn't wait, but to make the deal he had to sacrifice a pair of promising young outfielders, Joe Carter and Mel Hall.

Carter went on to stardom, but Green had the pitcher to put the Cubs across. Manager Jim Frey, who had succeeded Charlie Fox, later described Sutcliffe as a godsend. He won his first two starts, lost one, and finished with 14 consecutive victories, including the September 24 clincher in Pittsburgh. With a 16–1 record, Sutcliffe's .941 winning percentage was the highest in franchise history.

The Cubs swept the postseason awards. Sutcliffe was a unanimous choice for the Cy Young; second baseman Ryne Sandberg, who had a career year, was a landslide winner as the Most Valuable Player—22 of the 24 first-place votes; Frey was named Manager of the Year; and Green, Executive of the Year.

Remarkably, when the season opened, the consensus prediction was for another year of gloom and doom. The Cubs were 7–20 in spring training, the worst exhibition-game record in either league. On opening day, at the request of Charlie Grimm's widow, his ashes were scattered over Wrigley Field. It seemed an appropriate funeral beginning. More than likely, the Cubs soon would be buried in the second division.

But during the off-season there had been several significant adjustments. In another deal with the Phillies, Green acquired outfielders Gary Matthews and Bob Dernier. The cost was minimal: Bill Campbell, an aging reliever approaching retirement, and Mike Diaz, an obscure catcher ticketed for the minors.

The Cubs came out charging. They won their first two games and ten of the first 16. From April 19 on, they were never lower than third, and they held the lead for 15 days in May. Principally because of Sutcliffe—seven of his wins followed losses—the Cubs had a 22-game stretch, July 18 through August 8, when they never lost two in a row. They went ahead to stay on August 1 and were 96–65 at the finish, 6½ games in front of the Mets.

Sandberg narrowly missed becoming the first player with 200 or more hits, plus 20 or more doubles, triples, home runs, and stolen bases in the same season. He was short one triple and one home run. He batted .314, fourth in the league; was second in hits, 200; led in runs, 114; tied for the lead in triples; and was second in total bases. He also led all second baseman in chances, assists, and fielding percentage and went 61 consecutive games without an error.

Matthews, alias "The Sarge," was the inspirational force, and led the league in on-base percentage. Ron Cey had 25 home runs, 97 RBIs; Leon Durham, 23, 96. Dernier, batting leadoff, stole a career-high 45 bases. Sutcliffe, 4–5 with Cleveland, was 20–6 for the season and, in a wonderful coincidence, was the first 20-game winner who pitched in both leagues since Borowy. Dennis Eckersley, acquired from Boston in a trade for Bill Buckner, won 10 games. Ferguson Jenkins, 14 wins short of 300, was released.

	W	L	ERA	G	GS	CG	IP	H	BB	K
Steve Trout	13	7	3.41	32	31	6	190	205	59	81
Dennis Eckersley	10	8	3.03	24	24	2	160⅓	152	36	81
Rick Sutcliffe	16	1	2.69	20	20	7	150⅓	123	39	155
Scott Sanderson	8	5	3.14	24	24	3	140⅔	140	24	76
Dick Ruthven	6	10	5.04	23	22	0	126⅔	154	41	55
Lee Smith	9	7	3.65	69	0	0	101	98	35	86
Rick Reuschel	5	5	5.17	19	14	1	92⅔	123	23	43
Tim Stoddard	10	6	3.82	58	0	0	92	77	57	87
Chuck Rainey	5	7	4.28	17	16	0	88⅓	102	38	45
Rich Bordi	5	2	3.46	31	7	0	83⅓	78	20	41
Warren Brusstar	1	1	3.11	41	0	0	63⅔	57	21	36
George Frazier	6	3	4.10	37	0	0	63⅔	53	26	58
Dickie Noles	2	2	5.15	21	1	0	50⅓	60	16	14
Porfirio Altamirano	0	0	4.76	5	0	0	11⅓	8	1	7
Reggie Patterson	0	1	10.50	3	1	0	6	10	2	5
Bill Johnson	0	0	1.69	4	0	0	5⅓	4	1	3
Ron Meridith	0	0	3.38	3	0	0	5⅓	6	2	4
Don Schulze	0	0	12.00	1	1	0	3	8	1	2
	96	65	3.75	432	161	19	1,434	1,458	442	879

Shutouts: Sutcliffe 3, Trout 2.
Saves: Smith 33, Stoddard 7, Bordi 4, Brusstar 3, Frazier 3.

	G	AB	H	2B	3B	HR	R	RBI	SB	AVG
Regulars										
1B Leon Durham	137	473	132	30	4	23	86	96	16	.279
2B Ryne Sandberg	156	636	200	36	(19)	19	(114)	84	32	.314
SS Larry Bowa	133	391	87	14	2	0	33	17	10	.223
3B Ron Cey	146	505	121	27	0	25	71	97	3	.240
RF Keith Moreland	140	495	138	17	3	16	59	80	1	.279
CF Bob Dernier	143	536	149	26	5	3	94	32	45	.278
LF Gary Matthews	147	491	143	21	2	14	101	82	17	.291
C Jody Davis	150	523	134	24	2	19	55	94	5	.256
Substitutes										
Dave Owen	47	93	18	2	2	1	8	10	1	.194
Richie Hebner	44	81	27	3	0	2	12	8	1	.333
Tom Veryzer	44	74	14	1	0	0	5	4	0	.189
Bill Buckner	21	43	9	0	0	0	3	2	0	.209
Dan Rohn	25	31	4	0	0	1	1	3	0	.129
Mel Hall	48	150	42	11	3	4	25	22	2	.280
Henry Cotto	105	146	40	5	0	0	24	8	9	.274
Gary Woods	87	98	23	4	1	3	13	10	2	.235
Thad Bosley	55	98	29	2	2	2	17	14	5	.296
Jay Johnstone	52	73	21	2	2	0	8	3	0	.288
Billy Hatcher	8	9	1	0	0	0	1	0	2	.111

	G	AB	H	2B	3B	HR	R	RBI	SB	AVG
Steve Lake	25	54	12	4	0	2	4	7	0	.222
Ron Hassey	19	33	11	0	0	2	5	5	0	.333
Davey Lopes	16	17	4	1	0	0	5	0	3	.235
Pitchers										
Steve Trout	32	61	8	0	0	0	4	3	0	.131
Rick Sutcliffe	20	56	14	3	0	0	3	6	0	.250
Dennis Eckersley	24	55	6	0	0	0	1	1	0	.109
Dick Ruthven	25	44	7	3	0	0	2	2	0	.159
Scott Sanderson	24	42	5	0	0	0	3	5	0	.119
Chuck Rainey	17	31	3	0	0	0	2	3	0	.097
Rick Reuschel	20	29	7	3	0	0	2	3	0	.241
Rich Bordi	31	19	1	0	0	0	0	0	0	.053
Lee Smith	69	13	1	0	0	0	0	1	0	.077
Tim Stoddard	58	11	1	0	0	0	0	0	0	.091
Dickie Noles	21	10	0	0	0	0	0	0	0	.000
George Frazier	37	7	2	0	0	0	0	0	0	.286
Warren Brusstar	41	5	1	0	0	0	1	1	0	.200
Reggie Patterson	3	2	0	0	0	0	0	0	0	.000
Porfirio Altamirano	5	2	0	0	0	0	0	0	0	.000
Bill Johnson	4	0	0	0	0	0	0	0	0	—
Don Schulze	1	0	0	0	0	0	0	0	0	—
Ron Meridith	3	0	0	0	0	0	0	0	0	—
	5,437	1,415	239	47	136	762	703	154	.260

1985

Record: 77–84
Finish: Fourth (East)
Games Behind: 23½
Manager: Jim Frey

Records are not available for all freak occurrences but the 1985 Cubs may have been the first team with all five of its starting pitchers *simultaneously* on the disabled list. From this collective misfortune a trivia challenge emerges likely to stump the most knowledgeable Cub fan: Name the rotation for the nine-game sequence from August 14 to 23. The answer: Ray Fontenot, Steve Engel, Derek Botelho, Lary Sorensen, and Jay Baller.

It was a disastrous season, especially for Rick Sutcliffe. He went down three times, and finished at 8–8. Dennis Eckersley, 11–7, was the only pitcher to win in double figures. The other starters were Steve Trout, 9–7; Scott Sanderson, 5–6; and Dick Ruthven, 4–7. The "Big Four"—Sutcliffe, Trout, Eckersley, and Sanderson—combined, missed 51 starts, and won a total of 33 games.

Sutcliffe won his first two starts to lengthen his winning streak to 16 games, a franchise record. Trout was 6–1, Eckersley 4–1 before Sutcliffe was sidelined on May 20 with a leg injury, suffered running the bases. Still, there was no cause for alarm. The Cubs were sailing along, 15 games over .500 with a 34–19 record, in first place with a 3½-game lead.

Then came a 13-game losing streak, which equaled the club record. On June 26, after the skid had been broken, manager Jim Frey told reporters: "Here's the plan. We're going to win again tomorrow, hand tough on the road until we get back home, be in a strong position by the All-Star game, and then come out smokin'."

It was wishful thinking. Except for four days in late June and early July the Cubs were never higher than third. From that point on they didn't win more than three in a row, and they finished fourth with a 77–84 record, 19 fewer victories than the previous season. It was the fifth consecutive season that none of the American or National League's divisional champions was able to repeat.

Frey used 101 lineups and 20 pitchers, including 13 different starters, six of whom won their first major league game. The position players were not immune to injury: out-fielders Gary Matthews and Bob Dernier were also disabled. The only everyday players with nothing more than nagging injuries were third baseman Ron Cey, who failed to drive in a run in 35 consecutive games, and the shortstop tandem of Larry Bowa and Chris Speier.

Bowa was a season-long thorn. Once he realized Frey planned to open with rookie shortstop Shawon Dunston, Bowa began complaining. This plan would delay and possibly nullify Bowa's ambition to break Rabbit Maranville's NL shortstop record of 2,153 games. Coach Don Zimmer, wearying of Bowa's whining, described him as "the most selfish player I've ever seen." Dunston was farmed out on May 15 when he was hitting .194 but returned and finished at .260. Bowa broke Maranville's record and was released.

There was no stopping Sandberg. Frey, a major league batting coach for 12 years, didn't tamper with Sandberg's swing but convinced him he should be more aggressive at the plate and "attack" the ball. Following instructions, Sandberg raised his average to .305 and increased his power totals—26 home runs and 83 RBIs. Keith Moreland led the club in RBIs with 106 and batted .307.

Jim Finks resigned as the Cub president, a position he had assumed during the '84 season. Finks apparently was unwilling to be the point man in the club's push to install lights. Tribune executives, reading fanciful stories in the Philadelphia press that the Phillies wanted Dallas Green to return, hastily named Green the club's president, with a hefty salary increase.

	W	L	ERA	G	GS	CG	IP	H	BB	K
Dennis Eckersley	11	7	3.08	25	25	6	169⅓	145	19	117
Ray Fontenot	6	10	4.36	38	28	0	154⅔	177	45	70
Steve Trout	9	7	3.39	24	24	3	140⅔	142	63	44
Rick Sutcliffe	8	8	3.18	20	20	6	130	119	44	102
Scott Sanderson	5	6	3.12	19	19	2	121	100	27	80
Lee Smith	7	4	3.04	65	0	0	97⅔	87	32	112
Dick Ruthven	4	7	4.53	20	15	0	87⅓	103	37	26
Lary Sorensen	3	7	4.26	45	3	0	82⅓	86	24	34
George Frazier	7	8	6.39	51	0	0	76	88	52	46
Warren Brusstar	4	3	6.05	51	0	0	74⅓	87	36	34
Jay Baller	2	3	3.46	20	4	0	52	52	17	31
Steve Engel	1	5	5.57	11	8	1	51⅔	61	26	29
Ron Meridith	3	2	4.47	32	0	0	46⅓	53	24	23
Derek Botelho	1	3	5.32	11	7	1	44	52	23	23
Reggie Patterson	3	0	3.00	8	5	1	39	36	10	17
Johnny Abrego	1	1	6.38	6	5	0	24	32	12	13
Larry Gura	0	3	8.41	5	4	0	20⅓	34	6	7
Dave Beard	0	0	6.39	9	0	0	12⅔	16	7	4
Dave Gumpert	1	0	3.48	9	0	0	10⅓	12	7	4
Jon Perlman	1	0	11.42	6	0	0	8⅔	10	8	4
	77	84	4.17	475	162	20	1,442⅓	1,492	519	820

Shutouts: Sutcliffe 3, Eckersley 2, Trout 1.
Saves: Smith 33, Abrego 4, Brusstar 4, Gura 4, Frazier 2, Baller 1, Engel 1, Meridith 1.

	G	AB	H	2B	3B	HR	R	RBI	SB	AVG
Regulars										
1B Leon Durham	153	542	153	32	2	21	58	75	7	.282
2B Ryne Sandberg	153	609	186	31	6	26	113	83	54	.305
SS Shawon Dunston	74	250	65	12	4	4	40	18	11	.260
3B Ron Cey	145	500	116	18	2	22	64	63	1	.232
RF Keith Moreland	161	587	180	30	3	14	74	106	12	.307
CF Bob Dernier	121	469	119	20	3	1	63	21	31	.254
LF Gary Matthews	97	298	70	12	0	13	45	40	2	.235
C Jody Davis	142	482	112	30	0	17	47	58	1	.232
Substitutes										
Chris Speier	106	218	53	11	0	4	16	24	1	.243
Larry Bowa	72	195	48	6	4	0	13	13	5	.246
Richie Hebner	83	120	26	2	0	3	10	22	0	.217
Dave Owen	22	19	7	0	0	0	6	4	1	.368
Davey Lopes	99	275	78	11	0	11	52	44	47	.284

	G	AB	H	2B	3B	HR	R	RBI	SB	AVG
Thad Bosley	108	180	59	6	3	7	25	27	5	.328
Billy Hatcher	53	163	40	12	1	2	24	10	2	.245
Gary Woods	81	82	20	3	0	0	11	4	0	.244
Brian Dayett	22	26	6	0	0	1	1	4	0	.231
Chico Walker	21	12	1	0	0	0	3	0	1	.083
Darrin Jackson	5	11	1	0	0	0	0	0	0	.091
Steve Lake	58	119	18	2	0	1	5	11	1	.151
Pitchers										
Dennis Eckersley	26	56	7	0	0	1	1	1	0	.125
Steve Trout	24	46	5	1	0	0	2	2	0	.109
Rick Sutcliffe	20	43	10	0	0	1	4	3	0	.233
Ray Fontenot	38	41	2	0	0	0	2	0	0	.049
Scott Sanderson	19	31	2	0	0	0	1	1	0	.065
Dick Ruthven	20	24	5	0	0	0	1	1	0	.208
Steve Engel	11	16	3	0	0	1	1	4	0	.188
Derek Botelho	11	14	2	0	0	0	2	0	0	.143
Reggie Patterson	8	10	1	0	0	0	1	0	0	.100
Johnny Abrego	6	9	0	0	0	0	0	1	0	.000
Jay Baller	20	8	0	0	0	0	0	0	0	.000
Warren Brusstar	51	7	1	0	0	0	0	0	0	.143
Larry Gura	5	6	0	0	0	0	0	0	0	.000
Lary Sorensen	45	6	0	0	0	0	1	0	0	.000
George Frazier	51	6	0	0	0	0	0	0	0	.000
Lee Smith	65	6	0	0	0	0	0	0	0	.000
Ron Meridith	32	4	1	0	0	0	0	0	0	.250
Dave Gumpert	9	1	0	0	0	0	0	0	0	.000
Jon Perlman	6	1	0	0	0	0	0	0	0	.000
Dave Beard	9	0	0	0	0	0	0	0	0	—
	5,492	1,397	239	28	150	686	640	182	.254

1986

Record: 70–90
Finish: Fifth (East)
Games Behind: 37
Managers: Jim Frey, John Vukovich, Gene Michael

In spring training, during batting practice, manager Jim Frey was hit in the head by outfielder Brian Dayett's throw and was rushed to a hospital. Frey suffered severe headaches. It was an ominous beginning. The pain abated, but once the 1986 championship season began there was continued distress.

The Cubs opened poorly. They lost 20 of their first 34 games. When newspaper speculation indicated Frey was likely to be dismissed, general manager Dallas Green summoned the press and said, "I told Jim to forget all the baloney that's been going around and win some games. It amazes me that people want to fire the manager the minute you have a rough go."

Less than a month later, on June 12, with the Cubs in fifth place, 10 games under .500, Frey was gone. Coach John Vukovich handled the club for the next two games. Gene Michael, who had been the Yankees' third base coach, was anointed Green's fourth manager in five years. The managerial change was not of consequence. The Cubs finished fifth, 20 under .500, 37 games behind the first-place New York Mets.

In August, in another change accompanied by a blizzard of publicity, Green gave the boot to ball girl Marla Collins after she had bared all for a spread in *Playboy* magazine. While the curvaceous Collins was reviewing more than a dozen nationwide offers, Michael was trying, without success, to resuscitate his ailing pitching staff.

For the first time in their history—in 111 seasons—the Cubs were without a 10-game winner. Scott Sanderson and closer Lee Smith, who on July 18 combined for a one-hitter against the Giants, led with nine victories each. Two of Sanderson's wins came in relief, after he had been dropped from the rotation.

Of the pitchers, only Smith had a big year. The possessor of a 95-mile-an-hour fastball, Smith broke Bruce Sutter's club record of 133 saves on August 4 against the Phillies and was fourth in the league in saves, 31, the first NL reliever with three successive 30-save seasons.

Rick Sutcliffe, the hero of '84, hampered by shoulder ailments, lost six of his first seven decisions and was the majors' first 10-game loser. He finished with a 5–14 record. Right-hander Ed Lynch, acquired from the Mets in a midseason trade for two minor leaguers—and who nine years later would become the Cub general manager—was 7–5. Farmhand Greg Maddux, recalled for a late-season look, was 2–4.

The Cub starters completed only 11 games; the staff ERA was a bloated 4.49. Outfielder Jerry Mumphrey, .304 in 309 at bats, was the lone .300 hitter. The club had good power, 155 home runs, most in the league, and was third in batting. Gary Matthews and Jody Davis led the team in home runs, 21 each. Leon Durham had 20 and Shawon Dunston 17, most by a Cub shortstop since the days of Ernie Banks.

Green and Michael sparred in the press after the season. Green insisted Michael had failed to motivate the troops. Responded Michael: "You can get an ulcer managing this club. When you finish 37 games back, it can't be the fault of the manager and his coaches. Dallas probably doesn't want to hear this, but he didn't assemble a very good team."

Club executives continued to meet with neighborhood groups in an effort to promote a limited night-game schedule. Player rep Keith Moreland passed out key chains bearing the message "Let there be light." Michael's contract was renewed for 1987. Frey also remained and accepted an assignment as a broadcast analyst, a decision that a year later helped elevate him into the executive wing.

	W	L	ERA	G	GS	CG	IP	H	BB	K
Dennis Eckersley	6	11	4.57	33	32	1	201	226	43	137
Rick Sutcliffe	5	14	4.64	28	27	4	176⅔	166	96	122
Scott Sanderson	9	11	4.19	37	28	1	169⅔	165	37	124
Steve Trout	5	7	4.75	37	25	0	161	184	78	69
Ed Lynch	7	5	3.79	23	13	1	99⅔	105	23	57
Lee Smith	9	9	3.09	66	0	0	90⅓	69	42	93
Jamie Moyer	7	4	5.05	16	16	1	87⅓	107	42	45
Guy Hoffman	6	2	3.86	32	8	1	84	92	29	47
Dave Gumpert	2	0	4.37	38	0	0	59⅔	60	28	45
Ray Fontenot	3	5	3.86	42	0	0	56	57	21	24
Jay Baller	2	4	5.37	36	0	0	53⅓	58	28	42
George Frazier	2	4	5.40	35	0	0	51⅓	63	34	41
Frank DiPino	2	4	5.18	30	0	0	40	47	14	43
Greg Maddux	2	4	5.52	6	5	1	31	44	11	20
Matt Keough	2	2	4.97	19	2	0	29	36	12	19
Drew Hall	1	2	4.56	5	4	1	23⅔	24	10	21
Ron Davis	0	2	7.65	17	0	0	20	31	3	10
Dick Ruthven	0	0	5.06	6	0	0	10⅔	12	6	3
	70	90	4.49	506	160	11	1,445	1,546	557	962

Shutouts: Lynch 1, Sanderson 1, Sutcliffe 1, Moyer 1.
Saves: Smith 31, Baller 5, Fontenot 2, Gumpert 2, Frazier 2, Hall 1, Sanderson 1.

	G	AB	H	2B	3B	HR	R	RBI	SB	AVG
Regulars										
1B Leon Durham	141	484	127	18	7	20	66	65	8	.262
2B Ryne Sandberg	154	627	178	28	5	14	68	76	34	.284
SS Shawon Dunston	150	581	145	37	3	17	66	68	13	.250
3B Ron Cey	97	256	70	21	0	13	42	36	0	.273
OF Keith Moreland	156	586	159	30	0	12	72	79	3	.271
OF Gary Matthews	123	370	96	16	1	21	49	46	3	.259
OF Bob Dernier	108	324	73	14	1	4	32	18	27	.225
OF Jerry Mumprey	111	309	94	11	2	5	37	32	2	.304
C Jody Davis	148	528	132	27	2	21	66	74	0	.250

	G	AB	H	2B	3B	HR	R	RBI	SB	AVG
Substitutes										
Thad Bosley	87	120	33	4	1	1	15	9	3	.275
Steve Christmas	3	9	1	1	0	0	0	2	0	.111
Brian Dayett	24	67	18	4	0	4	7	11	0	.269
Terry Francona	86	124	31	3	0	2	13	8	0	.250
Steve Lake	10	19	8	1	0	0	4	4	0	.421
Davey Lopes	59	157	47	8	2	6	38	22	17	.299
Mike Martin	8	13	1	1	0	0	1	0	0	.077
Dave Martinez	53	108	15	1	1	1	13	7	4	.139
Rafael Palmeiro	22	73	18	4	0	3	9	12	1	.247
Chris Speier	95	155	44	8	0	6	21	23	2	.284
Manny Trillo	81	152	45	10	0	1	22	19	0	.296
Chico Walker	28	101	28	3	2	1	21	7	15	.277
Pitchers										
Jay Baller	36	5	0	0	0	0	0	0	0	.000
Ron Davis	17	2	0	0	0	0	0	0	0	.000
Frank DiPino	30	1	0	0	0	0	0	0	0	.000
Dennis Eckersley	33	69	11	3	0	2	7	10	0	.159
Ray Fontenot	42	6	1	0	0	0	1	0	0	.167
George Frazier	35	4	0	0	0	0	0	0	0	.000
Dave Gumpert	38	5	0	0	0	0	0	0	0	.000
Drew Hall	5	7	1	0	0	0	1	0	0	.143
Guy Hoffman	33	15	1	0	0	0	2	1	0	.067
Matt Keough	19	5	2	1	0	0	0	0	0	.400
Ed Lynch	23	30	1	0	0	0	0	0	0	.033
Greg Maddux	6	12	4	0	0	0	3	3	0	.333
Jamie Moyer	16	22	2	0	0	0	3	3	0	.091
Dick Ruthven	6	1	0	0	0	0	0	0	0	.000
Scott Sanderson	38	51	3	1	0	0	1	2	0	.059
Lee Smith	66	5	0	0	0	0	0	0	0	.000
Rick Sutcliffe	29	53	11	2	0	1	3	4	0	.208
Steve Trout	37	43	9	1	0	0	5	3	0	.209
	5,499	1,409	258	27		(155)	680	638	132	.256

Greg Maddux broke in with the Cubs in '86. In the '90s he won a record four consecutive Cy Young awards, the last three when he was with the Atlanta Braves.

1987

Record: 76–85
Finish: Sixth (East)
Games Behind: 18½
Managers: Gene Michael, Frank Lucchesi

For Andre Dawson, a veteran outfielder picked up for a song, it was the best of times. He led the league in home runs and runs batted in and was an overwhelming choice for the Most Valuable Player award, the first MVP from a last-place club. Dawson's popularity was such that by midseason the fans in the right-field bleachers stood and bowed in appreciation every time he took his position.

Otherwise, it was a season of disappointment and enormous change. Unable to resolve his differences with general manager Dallas Green, Gene Michael resigned as field manager on September 7. Michael beat Green to the punch and announced his resignation in a radio interview. Said Green: "It's nice he told somebody. He didn't tell me." Frank Lucchesi, the Cubs' "eye in the sky," who previously had managed the Phillies, replaced Michael.

Michael didn't leave quietly. "I have no respect for Dallas Green," Michael said. "He isn't very sharp and is always covering up for his mistakes. He's a big buffoon with a big mouth. He didn't make a mistake hiring me. His mistake was not listening to me."

In mid-September, after the club had plunged into the cellar, in a frantic effort to arouse the troops, Green issued what was to be his final manifesto. "The players have quit with a capital Q," Green declared. Five weeks later, on October 29, Green was gone.

Green was relieved of his command after he revealed his desire to take over as the club's field manager. The Tribune Company apparently approved on the condition he would be replaced as the front-office boss. Citing "philosophical differences," Green departed. He was succeeded by Jim Frey, who 17 months earlier had been fired by Green as the club's field manager.

The Dawson signing may have been the most unusual in club history. Dawson, 32, a free agent with a history of severe knee injuries, had been with the Montreal Expos for 10 seasons and had rejected the Expos' offer of a one-year, $1 million contract. He wanted to finish his career playing day ball on a grass field.

Pitcher Rick Sutcliffe announced he would donate $100,000 toward Dawson's salary. Green continued to resist. In a successful publicity coup, Dick Moss, Dawson's agent, advised him to go to the Cubs' Arizona spring camp. The Chicago newspapers ran photos of Dawson watching the Cub workouts from behind a chicken-wire fence. When the stalemate continued, Moss told Green he would submit a blank contract. Green could fill in the numbers.

Dawson was signed for $500,000, a comparative pittance, 15th on the club's player payroll, which was the second highest in baseball. There were two incentive bonuses: $50,000 if he was not on the disabled list prior to the All-Star game, and $150,000 if he made the All-Star team. Dawson earned both.

Dawson responded with a career year. He narrowly missed hitting a grand-slam home run in the opener, hit for the cycle on April 29, drove in 82 runs in the first 92 games, connected for three consecutive home runs on August 1, and set a club HR record for August with 15. He homered in his last at bat and finished with 49 home runs, second highest in club history, and 137 RBIs, most homers and RBIs by an NL player since 1977.

The Cubs led the league in home runs with 209, most in the NL since 1956. Sutcliffe had a comeback year: 18–10, five more wins than in the previous two seasons combined. Jamie Moyer, who had an eight-inning no-hitter in his first start, was 12–15. Greg Maddux continued his apprenticeship: 6–14 with a 5.61 ERA. There was another consolation: The Cubs were the NL's first last-place club with a home gate in excess of 2 million. They were 68–68 under Michael, 8–17 with Lucchesi.

	W	L	ERA	G	GS	CG	IP	H	BB	K
Rick Sutcliffe	18	10	3.68	34	34	6	237⅓	223	106	174
Jamie Moyer	12	15	5.10	35	33	1	201	210	97	147
Greg Maddux	6	14	5.61	30	27	1	155⅔	181	74	101
Scott Sanderson	8	9	4.29	32	22	0	144⅔	156	50	106
Les Lancaster	8	3	4.90	27	18	0	132⅓	138	51	78
Ed Lynch	2	9	5.38	58	8	0	110½	130	48	80
Lee Smith	4	10	3.12	62	0	0	83¾	84	32	96
Frank DiPino	3	3	3.15	69	0	0	80	75	34	61
Steve Trout	6	3	3.00	11	11	3	75	72	27	32
Dickie Noles	4	2	3.50	41	1	0	64⅓	59	27	33
Mike Mason	4	1	5.68	17	4	0	38	43	23	28
Drew Hall	1	1	6.89	21	0	0	32⅔	40	14	20
Ron Davis	0	0	5.85	21	0	0	32⅓	43	12	31
Jay Baller	0	1	6.75	23	0	0	29⅓	38	20	27
Bob Tewksbury	0	4	6.50	7	3	0	18	32	13	10
	76	85	4.55	488	161	11	1,434⅔	1,524	628	1,024

Shutouts: Trout 2, Maddux 1, Sutcliffe 1.
Saves: Smith 36, DiPino 4, Lynch 4, Noles 2, Sanderson 2.

	G	AB	H	2B	3B	HR	R	RBI	SB	AVG
Regulars										
1B Leon Durham	131	439	120	22	1	27	70	63	2	.273
2B Ryne Sandberg	132	523	154	25	2	16	81	59	21	.294
SS Shawon Dunston	95	346	85	18	3	5	40	22	12	.246
3B Keith Moreland	153	563	150	29	1	27	63	88	3	.266
OF Andre Dawson	153	621	178	24	2	(49)	90	(137)	11	.287
OF Dave Martinez	142	459	134	18	8	8	70	36	16	.292
OF Jerry Mumphrey	118	309	103	19	2	13	41	44	1	.333
C Jody Davis	125	428	106	12	2	19	57	51	1	.248
Substitutes										
Damon Berryhill	12	28	5	1	0	0	2	1	0	.179
Mike Brumley	39	104	21	2	2	1	8	9	7	.202
Brian Dayett	97	177	49	14	1	5	20	25	0	.277
Bob Dernier	93	199	63	4	4	8	38	21	16	.317
Darrin Jackson	7	5	4	1	0	0	2	0	0	.800
Gary Matthews	44	42	11	3	0	0	3	8	0	.262
Paul Noce	70	180	41	9	2	3	17	14	5	.228
Rafael Palmeiro	84	221	61	15	1	14	32	30	2	.276
Luis Quinones	49	101	22	6	0	0	12	8	0	.218
Wade Rowdon	11	31	7	1	1	1	2	4	0	.226
Jim Sundberg	61	139	28	2	0	4	9	15	0	.201
Manny Trillo	108	214	63	8	0	8	27	26	0	.294
Chico Walker	47	105	21	4	0	0	15	7	11	.200
Pitchers										
Jay Baller	23	1	1	0	0	0	0	0	0	1.000
Ron Davis	21	0	0	0	0	0	0	0	0	—
Frank DiPino	69	2	1	0	0	0	0	0	0	.500
Drew Hall	21	4	0	0	0	0	0	0	0	.000
Les Lancaster	27	49	4	1	0	0	2	2	0	.082
Ed Lynch	58	16	3	0	0	0	1	0	0	.188
Greg Maddux	34	42	5	0	0	0	3	2	0	.119
Mike Mason	18	9	2	0	0	0	1	0	0	.222
Jamie Moyer	39	61	14	1	0	0	3	3	0	.230
Dickie Noles	41	11	0	0	0	0	0	0	0	.000
Scott Sanderson	32	40	3	0	0	1	2	2	0	.075
Lee Smith	63	2	0	0	0	0	0	0	0	.000
Rick Sutcliffe	35	81	12	5	1	0	8	6	1	.148
Bob Tewksbury	7	5	0	0	0	0	0	0	0	.000
Steve Trout	11	26	4	0	0	0	1	0	0	.154
		5,583	1,475	244	33	(209)	720	683	109	.264

1988

Record: 77–85
Finish: Fourth (East)
Games Behind: 28
Manager: Don Zimmer

The Cubs succumbed to the bitch goddess of progress in 1988 and played seven night games. Mother Nature, in rebellion, responded with a torrential downpour, and the first scheduled Wrigley Field night game, August 8 against the Phillies, was called in the fourth inning because of rain.

When the lights were turned on again the next night, the Cubs beat the Phillies 6–4 and no longer were the only major league temple of day baseball. Night games had been introduced more than a half century earlier, in Cincinnati in 1935. The last big league park without lights, other than Wrigley Field, had been Briggs Stadium in Detroit, which submitted in 1948.

Don Zimmer, who had been fired by Dallas Green as the Cubs' third base coach in the middle of the 1986 season, dismissed in tandem with field manager Jim Frey, was the new manager. Frey, now in charge, hired Zimmer, his boyhood pal; they had grown up together in Cincinnati. It was Zimmer's fourth managerial assignment and the final irony of Green's departure.

The players responded with enthusiasm. The Cubs won only one more game than the previous season and finished fourth, 24 games back, but there were unmistakable indications better days were ahead. Left fielder Rafael Palmeiro and rookie first baseman Mark Grace showed especially well. Palmeiro hit .307, Grace .296.

The Cubs led the league in batting with a .261 team average and had four of the league's top eight hitters: Palmeiro, Grace, Andre Dawson, and Vance Law, a 33-year-old third baseman who came aboard as a free agent. Law batted safely in his first 13 games, hit .293 (40 points above his career average), and drove in 78 runs, a one-season high. Dawson led in home runs with 24 and in RBIs with 79.

The pitching, as usual, was shaky, but a new star emerged. Greg Maddux, the slender right-hander who would become the most dominant pitcher of his generation, was a dazzling 15–3, with a 2.14 earned run average, at the All-Star break, the best first-half NL showing since Randy Jones of the San Diego Padres was 16–3 in 1976.

Maddux opened with a three-hit shutout against Atlanta and was the first Cub pitcher in 25 years to launch a season with two consecutive complete-game victories. He had a string of 26⅔ scoreless innings, won nine in a row, and defeated every NL club, an achievement last accomplished on the Cubs by Ferguson Jenkins in '71.

The revitalized Sutcliffe, still troubled by injuries and now throwing a forkball, was 13–14. Jamie Moyer and Calvin Schiraldi each won nine. Moyer repeatedly suffered from thin offensive support. In his first six losses, the club scored only four runs while he was in the game.

The bullpen was a season-long disaster. Lee Smith, the first closer since Kansas City's Dan Quisenberry with four successive seasons of 30 or more saves, was sent to Boston in a winter trade. Goose Gossage, 36, for many years baseball's premier reliever, was acquired from San Diego but was ineffective: a 4.33 ERA and 13 saves, a 57 percent success ratio,

lowest in either league for relievers with 20 or more save opportunities.

Three other veterans, previously front-liners, were traded: Leon Durham, who yielded first base to Mark Grace, went to Cincinnati; catcher Jody Davis, also unhappy when Damon Berryhill replaced him, to Atlanta; and outfielder Keith Moreland, who during the off-season lost four front upper teeth in a deer-hunting accident, to San Diego in the Gossage deal. Manager Don Zimmer, brave man, was assigned uniform number 4, which had been worn by Lee Elia, Jim Frey, and Gene Michael.

	W	L	ERA	G	GS	CG	IP	H	BB	K
Greg Maddux	18	8	3.18	34	34	9	249	230	81	140
Rick Sutcliffe	13	14	3.86	32	32	12	226	232	70	144
Jamie Moyer	9	15	3.48	34	30	3	202	212	55	121
Calvin Schiraldi	9	13	4.38	29	27	2	166⅓	166	63	140
Jeff Pico	6	7	4.15	29	13	3	112⅔	108	37	57
Frank DiPino	2	3	4.98	63	0	0	90⅓	102	32	69
Les Lancaster	4	6	3.78	44	3	1	85⅔	89	34	36
Al Nipper	2	4	3.04	22	12	0	80	72	34	27
Mike Bielecki	2	2	3.35	19	5	0	48⅓	55	16	33
Goose Gossage	4	4	4.33	46	0	0	43⅔	50	15	30
Pat Perry	2	2	3.32	35	0	0	38	40	7	24
Mike Harkey	0	3	2.60	5	5	0	34⅔	33	15	18
Mike Capel	2	1	4.91	22	0	0	29⅓	34	13	19
Drew Hall	1	1	7.66	19	0	0	22⅓	26	9	22
Scott Sanderson	1	2	5.28	11	0	0	15⅓	13	3	6
Bill Landrum	1	0	5.84	7	0	0	12⅓	19	3	6
Kevin Blankenship	1	0	7.20	1	1	0	5	7	1	4
Bob Tewksbury	0	0	8.10	1	1	0	3⅓	6	2	1
	77	85	3.84	453	163	30	1,464⅓	1,494	490	897

Shutouts: Maddux 3, Pico 2, Sutcliffe 2, Moyer 1, Schiraldi 1.
Saves: Gossage 13, DiPino 6, Lancaster 5, Hall 1, Nipper 1, Perry 1, Pico 1, Schiraldi 1.

	G	AB	H	2B	3B	HR	R	RBI	SB	AVG
Regulars										
1B Mark Grace	134	486	144	23	4	7	65	57	3	.296
2B Ryne Sandberg	155	618	163	23	8	19	77	69	25	.264
SS Shawon Dunston	155	575	143	23	6	9	69	56	30	.249
3B Vance Law	151	556	163	29	2	11	73	78	1	.293
OF Andre Dawson	157	591	179	31	8	24	78	79	12	.303
OF Rafael Palmeiro	152	580	178	41	5	8	75	53	12	.307
OF Dave Martinez	75	256	65	10	1	4	27	34	7	.254
OF Darrin Jackson	100	188	50	11	3	6	29	20	4	.266
C Damon Berryhill	95	309	80	19	1	7	19	38	1	.259
C Jody Davis	88	249	57	9	0	6	19	33	0	.229
Substitutes										
Doug Dascenzo	26	75	16	3	0	0	9	4	6	.213
Leon Durham	24	73	16	6	1	3	10	6	0	.219
Dave Meier	2	5	2	0	0	0	0	1	0	.400
Jerry Mumphrey	63	66	9	2	0	0	3	9	0	.136
Rolando Roomes	17	16	3	0	0	0	3	0	0	.188
Angel Salazar	34	60	15	1	1	0	4	1	0	.250
Jim Sundberg	24	54	13	1	0	2	8	9	0	.241
Manny Trillo	76	164	41	5	0	1	15	14	2	.250
Gary Varsho	46	73	20	3	0	0	6	5	5	.274
Mitch Webster	70	264	70	11	6	4	36	26	10	.265
Rick Wrona	4	6	0	0	0	0	0	0	0	.000
Pitchers										
Mike Bielecki	19	10	1	0	0	0	0	0	0	.100
Kevin Blankenship	1	3	0	0	0	0	0	0	0	.000
Mike Capel	22	2	0	0	0	0	0	0	0	.000
Frank DiPino	63	10	1	0	0	0	2	0	0	.100
Goose Gossage	46	1	0	0	0	0	0	0	0	.000
Drew Hall	19	1	0	0	0	0	1	0	0	.000
Mike Harkey	5	11	1	0	0	0	1	0	0	.091
Les Lancaster	44	20	1	0	0	0	1	0	0	.050
Bill Landrum	7	2	0	0	0	0	0	0	0	.000
Greg Maddux	37	96	19	3	0	0	13	5	1	.198
Jamie Moyer	34	60	5	1	0	0	4	1	0	.083
Al Nipper	22	23	2	1	0	0	0	0	0	.087
Pat Perry	35	1	1	0	0	0	1	2	0	1.000
Jeff Pico	29	34	5	0	0	0	0	1	0	.147
Scott Sanderson	11	0	0	0	0	0	0	0	0	—

	G	AB	H	2B	3B	HR	R	RBI	SB	AVG
Calvin Schiraldi	29	60	6	1	0	0	4	5	0	.100
Rick Sutcliffe	33	75	12	5	0	1	8	6	1	.160
Bob Tewksbury	1	2	0	0	0	0	0	0	0	.000
		5,675	1,481	262	46	113	660	612	120	(.261)

1989

Record: 93–69
Finish: First (East)
Games Ahead: 6
Manager: Don Zimmer

Here's how the victorious 1989 season began: Ninth inning, Phillies load the bases with three consecutive singles off reliever Mitch Williams, acquired from Texas in a nine-player deal, making his Cub debut. Boos from the opening-day Wrigley Field crowd of 33,361. Williams strikes out Mike Schmidt. Chris James also strikes out. Mark Ryal goes out the same way. It was a perilous beginning, but the Cubs were on their way to a divisional championship, their second in six years.

Williams finished with 36 saves, one short of Bruce Sutter's club record. There were many other heroes. Second baseman Ryne Sandberg extended his errorless streak to 90 games and batted .290 with a career-high 30 home runs. Center fielder Jerome Walton, who won Rookie of the Year honors, had a 30-game hitting streak, longest by a Cub in the 20th century. Dwight Smith, another rookie outfielder, batted .324. First baseman Mark Grace, in his second full season, hit .314.

Greg Maddux led the pitchers with a 19–12 record. Mike Bielecki, who had won a total of 12 games in his previous five big league seasons, was next, 18–7, followed by Rick Sutcliffe, 16–11. Les Lancaster, working middle relief—he was Mitch Williams' setup man—had a 1.36 earned run average, eight saves, four wins, and a string of 30⅔ scoreless innings. Clearly, it was a team victory.

It was also a major triumph for general manager Jim Frey, who was constantly retooling. Frey's biggest deal was for Williams, an erratic left-handed closer with continual control problems who was appropriately tagged "The Wild Thing." Williams had converted only 18 saves in 26 opportunities with the Rangers in 1988, second-lowest ratio of success among relievers with 20 or more save opportunities.

For Williams, the Cubs had to part with outfielder Rafael Palmeiro, who in 1988, his first full season, was the National League's second leading hitter. Andre Dawson, the club elder, told newsmen it was a mistake, that Grace, not Palmeiro, should have been sacrificed. Palmeiro didn't like it either and in Texas and elsewhere in the American League often wore a T-shirt that read, "I was Frey-ed and Zimmer-ed."

Williams responded with his best season. He protected six of the club's first eight victories and had 13 saves by May 30, equaling Goose Gossage's club-leading total of the previous season. Williams' 36 saves were four more than he had had in his previous three major league seasons and a career mark for a Cub left-hander.

The Cubs had a good mix. The opening-day lineup included three players up from Class A: Walton, catcher Joe Gi-

rardi, and left-handed pitcher Steve Wilson, acquired in the Williams trade along with pitcher Paul Kilgus; both won six games. Outfielder Dwight Smith, up from the minors, replaced Palmeiro in left field. Smith's .324 average was the highest by a Cub rookie in 65 years. Utility man Curtis Wilkerson, obtained from Cincinnati in another beneficial deal, played four positions and batted .244, and Floyd McClendon had a .286 average.

Don Grenesko, a financial officer on loan from the Tribune Company, replaced Dallas Green as the club president and gave Sandberg, underpaid at $840,000, a four-year extension for a total of $6.3 million, largest haul ever for a second baseman. Andre Dawson was renewed for $2.1 million. Troubled with knee injuries, Dawson batted .252, a career low, but was second to Sandberg in home runs, 21, and drove in 77 runs. The Cubs went ahead to stay on August 6, finished six games in front, played their full schedule of 18 night games, and had a record home gate of 2,161,534.

	W	L	ERA	G	GS	CG	IP	H	BB	K
Greg Maddux	19	12	2.95	35	35	7	238⅓	222	82	135
Rick Sutcliffe	16	11	3.66	35	34	5	229	202	69	153
Mike Bielecki	18	7	3.14	33	33	4	212⅓	187	81	147
Scott Sanderson	11	9	3.94	37	23	2	146⅓	155	31	86
Paul Kilgus	6	10	4.39	35	23	0	145⅔	164	49	61
Jeff Pico	3	1	3.77	53	5	0	90⅔	99	31	38
Steve Wilson	6	4	4.20	53	8	0	85⅔	83	31	65
Mitch Williams	4	4	2.64	76	0	0	81⅓	71	52	67
Calvin Schiraldi	3	6	3.78	54	0	0	78⅔	60	50	54
Les Lancaster	4	2	1.36	42	0	0	72⅔	60	15	56
Pat Perry	0	1	1.77	19	0	0	35⅔	23	16	20
Paul Assenmacher	2	1	5.21	14	0	0	19	19	12	15
Dean Wilkins	1	0	5.17	11	0	0	15⅔	13	9	14
Kevin Blankenship	0	0	1.69	2	0	0	5⅓	4	2	2
Joe Kraemer	0	1	4.91	1	1	0	3⅔	7	2	5
	93	69	3.43	500	162	18	1,460⅓	1,369	532	918

Shutouts: Bielecki 3, Maddux 1, Sutcliffe 1.
Saves: Williams 36, Lancaster 8, Schiraldi 4, Kilgus 2, Pico 2, Wilson 2, Perry 1.

	G	AB	H	2B	3B	HR	R	RBI	SB	AVG
Regulars										
1B Mark Grace	142	510	160	28	3	13	74	79	14	.314
2B Ryne Sandberg	157	606	176	25	5	30	(104)	76	15	.290
SS Shawon Dunston	138	471	131	20	6	9	52	60	19	.278
3B Vance Law	130	408	96	22	3	7	38	42	2	.235
OF Andre Dawson	118	416	105	18	6	21	62	77	8	.252
OF Jerome Walton	116	475	139	23	3	5	64	46	24	.293
OF Dwight Smith	109	343	111	19	6	9	52	52	9	.324
OF Mitch Webster	98	272	70	12	4	3	40	19	14	.257
C Damon Berryhill	91	334	86	13	0	5	37	41	1	.257
C Joe Girardi	59	157	39	10	0	1	15	14	2	.248
Substitutes										
Doug Dascenzo	47	139	23	1	0	1	20	12	6	.165
Darrin Jackson	45	83	19	4	0	1	7	8	1	.229
Lloyd McClendon	92	259	74	12	1	12	47	40	6	.286
Domingo Ramos	85	179	47	6	2	1	18	19	1	.263
Luis Salazar	26	80	26	5	0	1	7	12	0	.325
Greg Smith	4	5	2	0	0	0	1	2	0	.400
Phil Stephenson	17	21	3	0	0	0	0	0	1	.143
Gary Varsho	61	87	16	4	2	0	10	6	3	.184
Curtis Wilkerson	77	160	39	4	2	1	18	10	4	.244
Rick Wrona	38	92	26	2	1	2	11	14	0	.283
Marvell Wynne	20	48	9	2	1	1	8	4	2	.188
Pitchers										
Paul Assenmacher	14	3	0	0	0	0	0	0	0	.000
Mike Bielecki	33	70	3	0	0	0	1	3	1	.043
Kevin Blankenship	2	1	0	0	0	0	0	0	0	.000
Paul Kilgus	35	41	3	0	0	0	1	2	0	.073
Joe Kraemer	1	1	0	0	0	0	0	0	0	.000
Les Lancaster	42	11	2	1	0	0	0	1	0	.182
Greg Maddux	35	81	17	2	0	0	6	4	1	.210

continued

	G	AB	H	2B	3B	HR	R	RBI	SB	AVG
Pat Perry	19	6	1	0	0	0	1	0	0	.167
Jeff Pico	53	10	1	0	0	0	0	0	0	.100
Scott Sanderson	37	43	2	0	0	0	1	1	0	.047
Calvin Schiraldi	54	9	0	0	0	0	0	1	0	.000
Rick Sutcliffe	37	70	10	2	0	0	5	5	2	.143
Dean Wilkins	11	1	0	0	0	0	0	0	0	.000
Mitch Williams	76	5	1	0	0	1	1	3	0	.200
Steve Wilson	53	16	1	0	0	0	1	0	0	.063
		5,513	1,438	235	45	124	702	653	136	.261

1990

Record: 77–85
Finish: Fourth (tie) (East)
Games Behind: 18
Manager: Don Zimmer

The Cubs' 1990 season wasn't all fun and games. But as manager Don Zimmer later admitted, July 18 was his most joyful day of a long and frustrating season. Greg Maddux, star of the Cub pitching staff, who had failed to win in his previous 13 starts, was about to take the mound against the San Diego Padres. "If he wins," Zimmer said, "I'll swim Lake Michigan."

Maddux, with late-inning help from Jeff Pico, beat the Padres 4–2, his fifth victory against 14 losses, and within 48 hours Zimmer was flooded with flotation devices—an orange life jacket, an inflated inner tube, goggles, and frog flippers. Laughing, Zimmer told reporters, "I guess I shouldn't have said that. I can't even swim."

It was the Cubs who drowned. Not only were they unable to repeat as the divisional champion, but they were never even a factor. They dropped into the second division to stay as early as April 12, after their 13th game, and surrendered at the All-Star break, in fifth place, 13 under .500, 15 games off the pace. They almost sank to the bottom and finished in a fourth-place tie, 18 games out.

The peerless Ryne Sandberg had an outstanding season. He won his eighth consecutive Gold Glove for defensive excellence and broke two major league records for second basemen—most games in a row, 123, and most chances, 582, without an error. He was also the first second baseman to lead the league in home runs, 40, since Rogers Hornsby in 1925, had a career high of 100 RBIs, led the league in total bases, and for the second successive season led in runs scored, 116, an achievement unmatched in the 20th century.

Three Cubs were among the top 10 batters—Andre Dawson, fifth, .310; Mark Grace, sixth, .309; and Sandberg, tenth, .306. Dawson, who underwent his fifth knee surgery in the off-season, drove in 100 runs and hit 27 home runs. Outfielders Jerome Walton and Dwight Smith, 1–2 in the balloting for the 1989 Rookie of the Year award, had disappointing seasons. Walton's average dropped from .293 to .263, Smith's from .324 to .262.

The pitching was a season-long problem. The staff's earned run average of 4.34 was second highest in the league. After winning four of his first five starts, Maddux went 73 days without a victory. He was the only pitcher to work more than 200 innings and he finished with a 15–15 record. Rookie Mike Harkey, out for five weeks with a shoulder injury, was 12–6.

It was a lost season for the aging Rick Sutcliffe. Prior to the arrival of Maddux, Sutcliffe had been the club's leading pitcher and in the previous three seasons had won 47 games. On the bench and in the hospital with shoulder miseries, he didn't appear until August 28, in the 128th game. He made

five starts, pitched 21⅓ innings, and was 0–2 with a 5.91 ERA. Mike Bielicki, 18–7 in '89, was 8–11.

Reliever Mitch Williams, coming off a dream season in '89, had success early—he saved the first four victories in '90. His season was a nightmare thereafter. He was 1–8 with 16 saves, 20 fewer than in '89. Groping, Zimmer twice used him as a starter, in mid-September. Williams failed to survive the fourth inning in either game, compiled a 9.95 ERA, and returned to the bullpen.

Paul Assenmacher replaced Williams as the closer and got the job done: 10 saves and seven wins, all in relief. Jeff Pico, who during the off-season had married Mark Grace's sister-in-law, was used as a starter and in relief; he was 4–4 before his major league career ended on September 9 when he was struck by a line drive. Five days later left-hander Steve Wilson suffered a cut that required six stitches while rescuing a woman who was assaulted in a St. Louis restaurant.

	W	L	ERA	G	GS	CG	IP	H	BB	K
Greg Maddux	15	15	3.46	35	35	8	237	242	71	144
Mike Harkey	12	6	3.26	27	27	2	173⅔	153	59	94
Mike Bielicki	8	11	4.93	36	29	0	168	188	70	103
Les Lancaster	9	5	4.62	55	6	1	109	121	40	65
Steve Wilson	4	9	4.79	45	15	1	139	140	43	95
Paul Assenmacher	7	2	2.80	74	1	0	103	90	36	95
Shawn Boskie	5	6	3.69	15	15	1	97⅔	99	31	49
Jeff Pico	4	4	4.79	31	8	0	92	20	4	4
Mitch Williams	1	8	3.93	59	2	0	66⅓	60	50	55
Jose Nunez	4	7	6.53	21	10	0	60⅔	61	34	40
Bill Long	6	1	4.37	42	0	0	55⅔	66	21	32
Joe Kraemer	0	0	7.20	18	0	0	25	31	14	16
Dave Pavlas	2	0	2.11	13	0	0	21⅓	23	6	12
Rick Sutcliffe	0	2	5.91	5	5	0	21⅓	25	12	7
Randy Kramer	0	2	3.98	10	2	0	20⅓	20	12	12
Kevin Coffman	0	2	11.29	8	2	0	18⅓	26	19	9
Lance Dickson	0	3	7.24	3	3	0	13⅔	20	4	4
Kevin Blankenship	0	2	5.84	3	2	0	12⅓	13	6	5
Dean Wilkins	0	0	9.82	7	0	0	7⅓	11	7	3
Doug Dascenzo	0	0	0.00	1	0	0	1	1	0	0
	77	85	4.34	508	162	13	1,442⅔	1,510	572	877

Shutouts: Maddux 2, Harkey 1, Lancaster 1.
Saves: Williams 16, Assenmacher 10, Lancaster 6, Long 5, Pico 2, Bielecki 1, Wilkins 1, Wilson 1.

	G	AB	H	2B	3B	HR	R	RBI	SB	AVG
Regulars										
1B Mark Grace	157	589	182	32	1	9	72	82	15	.309
2B Ryne Sandberg	155	615	188	30	3	(40)	(116)	100	25	.306
SS Shawon Dunston	146	545	143	22	8	17	73	66	25	.262
3B Luis Salazar	115	410	104	13	3	12	44	47	3	.254
OF Andre Dawson	147	529	164	28	5	27	72	100	16	.310
OF Dwight Smith	117	290	76	15	0	6	34	27	11	.262
OF Doug Dascenzo	113	241	61	9	5	1	27	26	15	.253
OF Jerome Walton	101	392	103	16	2	2	63	21	14	.263
C Joe Girardi	133	419	113	24	2	1	36	38	8	.270
Substitutes										
Damon Berryhill	17	53	10	4	0	1	6	9	0	.189
Dave Clark	84	171	47	4	2	5	22	20	7	.275
Derrick May	17	61	15	3	0	1	8	11	1	.246
Lloyd McClendon	49	107	17	3	0	1	5	10	1	.159
Domingo Ramos	98	226	60	5	0	2	22	17	0	.265
Greg Smith	18	44	9	2	1	0	4	5	1	.205
Gary Varsho	46	48	12	4	0	0	10	1	2	.250
Hector Villanueva	52	114	31	4	1	7	14	18	1	.272
Curt Wilkerson	77	186	41	5	1	0	21	16	2	.220
Rick Wrona	16	29	5	0	0	0	3	0	1	.172
Marvell Wynne	92	186	38	8	2	4	21	19	3	.204
Pitchers										
Paul Assenmacher	74	8	0	0	0	0	0	0	0	.000
Mike Bielecki	36	43	7	0	0	0	3	0	0	.163
Kevin Blankenship	3	4	0	0	0	0	0	0	0	.000
Shawn Boskie	15	36	8	3	0	0	1	3	0	.222
Kevin Coffman	8	5	1	0	0	0	0	0	0	.200
Lance Dickson	3	3	0	0	0	0	0	0	0	.000
Mike Harkey	27	56	14	4	0	0	4	4	0	.250
Joe Kraemer	18	0	0	0	0	0	0	0	0	—

	G	AB	H	2B	3B	HR	R	RBI	SB	AVG
Randy Kramer	10	1	0	0	0	0	0	0	0	.000
Les Lancaster	55	20	1	0	0	0	1	0	0	.050
Bill Long	42	5	0	0	0	0	0	0	0	.000
Greg Maddux	35	83	12	0	0	0	1	3	0	.145
Jose Nunez	21	11	0	0	0	0	1	1	0	.000
Dave Pavlas	13	1	0	0	0	0	0	0	0	.000
Jeff Pico	31	22	6	1	0	0	2	1	0	.273
Rick Sutcliffe	5	5	0	0	0	0	0	0	0	.000
Dean Wilkins	7	0	0	0	0	0	0	0	0	—
Mitch Williams	59	5	0	0	0	0	1	0	0	.000
Steve Wilson	45	37	6	1	0	0	3	3	0	.162
		5,600	1,474	240	36	136	690	649	151	.263

1991

Record: 77–83
Finish: Fourth (East)
Games Behind: 20
Managers: Don Zimmer, Joe Altobelli, Jim Essian

The Cubs nearly doubled their player payroll for 1991 from $14 to $27 million and plunged into the free-agent market with unaccustomed gusto—an aggregate, one-year outlay of $8 million to fading veterans George Bell, a slugging outfielder, and pitchers Danny Jackson and Dave Smith. Bell would bat fourth, situated among Ryne Sandberg, Andre Dawson, and Mark Grace, and provide a Murderers' Row attack. Jackson would patch the rotation. Smith would bolster the bullpen.

Bell, 31, wasn't a force but did well enough: 25 home runs and 86 RBIs, three homers and 16 RBIs below his previous seven-season average. Jackson, 29, and Smith, 36, were lemons. Each had two stretches on the disabled list, and they combined for one victory and 17 saves. Jackson was 1–5 with a 6.75 earned run average, so ineffective he was allowed only 14 starts. Smith was 0–6, with a 6.00 ERA, and had one save after June 14.

Manager Don Zimmer was relieved of his command early, on May 20, only 37 games into the season. Joe Altobelli stepped in to manage one game, an 8–6 loss to the Mets. He was succeeded the next day by Jim Essian, who had been managing the Cubs' Triple-A farm team. The initial response was good: five consecutive victories. It was a brief honeymoon; the team lost six of the next nine games, and at the finish it was the same old Cubs—fourth place, 20 games out of the lead.

Dallas Green, who had been dismissed as the front-office chief almost two years earlier, couldn't give it up. When it was apparent the Cubs were doomed, Green hurled a long-distance blast at Don Grenesko, his successor. "He knows absolutely nothing about baseball," Green charged. Green also labeled general manager Jim Frey a yes-man and predicted Grenesko would dump Frey as the scapegoat for the disappointing season.

Grenesko responded, "I have been with the Cubs since 1985, and even a dummy can learn something."

Green was 1-for-2. Frey was kicked upstairs, his title upgraded to "senior vice president," with the understanding he would remain as a consultant. Frey returned to his Maryland home, but the phone was dead. Nobody called. What Green failed to foresee was that Grenesko would also be dismissed, transferred back to his desk at the Tribune Tower with a promotion: vice president and chief financial officer of the Tribune Company media empire.

The Cubs led the league in home runs, 159. Dawson and Bell together had 56, the first time the club had an outfield

tandem with 25 or more home runs each since Billy Williams and George Altman in 1961. But the Cubs didn't have any hitters among the top 15. Sandberg was 16th with a .291 average, with 26 home runs and 100 RBIs, the first second baseman in either league to drive in 100 or more runs two years in succession since Boston's Bobby Doerr in 1959–60.

The switch-hitting Chico Walker, who had spent parts of 15 years in the minors, filled in at second and third base and in the outfield, and was the league's top pinch hitter—13-for-32, a .406 average. Doug Dascenzo set a major league fielding record for outfielders, 242 consecutive games and 442 chances without an error. A week later he was charged with two errors in one game.

Greg Maddux led the pitchers with 15 wins. Mike Bielecki was 13–11. Les Lancaster, alternating between starting and relief, won nine games. Paul Assenmacher was 7–8, with 15 saves, only two fewer than the costly Dave Smith. Lefty reliever Chuck McElroy, acquired from the Phillies in an April 7 trade for Mitch Williams, set a club rookie record for appearances, 71, and had a 1.95 ERA with six wins and three saves. Rick Sutcliffe, on the shelf most of the season, was 6–5 with a 4.10 ERA and was released. The Cubs were eliminated on September 18. Essian was fired on October 19.

	W	L	ERA	G	GS	CG	IP	H	BB	K
Greg Maddux	15	11	3.35	37	37	7	263	232	66	198
Mike Bielecki	13	11	4.50	39	25	0	172	169	54	72
Les Lancaster	9	7	3.52	64	11	1	156	150	49	102
Shawn Boskie	4	9	5.23	28	20	0	129	150	52	62
Frank Castillo	6	7	4.35	18	18	4	111⅓	107	33	73
Bob Scanlan	7	8	3.89	40	13	0	111	114	40	44
Paul Assenmacher	7	8	3.24	75	0	0	102⅔	85	31	117
Chuck McElroy	6	2	1.95	71	0	0	101⅓	73	57	92
Rick Sutcliffe	6	5	4.10	19	18	0	96⅔	96	45	52
Danny Jackson	1	5	6.75	17	14	0	70⅓	89	48	31
Heathcliff Slocumb	2	1	3.45	52	0	0	62⅔	53	30	34
Dave Smith	0	6	6.00	35	0	0	33	39	19	16
Mike Harkey	0	2	5.30	4	4	0	18⅔	21	6	15
Steve Wilson	0	0	4.38	8	0	0	12⅓	13	5	9
Laddie Renfroe	0	1	13.50	4	0	0	4⅔	11	2	4
Yorkis Perez	1	0	2.08	3	0	0	4⅓	2	2	3
Doug Dascenzo	0	0	0.00	3	0	0	4	2	2	2
Scott May	0	0	18.00	2	0	0	2	6	1	1
Dave Pavlas	0	0	18.00	1	0	0	1	3	0	0
	77	83	4.03	520	160	12	1,456⅔	1,415	542	927

Shutouts: Maddux 2.
Saves: Smith 17, Assenmacher 15, Lancaster 3, McElroy 3, Scanlan 1, Slocumb 1.

	G	AB	H	2B	3B	HR	R	RBI	SB	AVG
Regulars										
1B Mark Grace	160	619	169	28	5	8	87	58	3	.273
2B Ryne Sandberg	158	585	170	32	2	26	104	100	22	.291
SS Shawon Dunston	142	492	128	22	7	12	59	50	21	.260
3B Luis Salazar	103	333	86	14	1	14	34	38	0	.258
OF Andre Dawson	149	563	153	21	4	31	69	104	4	.272
OF George Bell	149	558	159	27	0	25	63	86	2	.285
OF Chico Walker	124	374	96	10	1	6	51	34	13	.257
OF Jerome Walton	123	270	59	13	1	5	42	17	7	.219
C Rick Wilkins	86	203	45	9	0	6	21	22	3	.222
Substitutes										
Damon Berryhill	62	159	30	7	0	5	13	14	1	.189
Doug Dascenzo	118	239	61	11	0	1	40	18	14	.255
Joe Girardi	21	47	9	2	0	0	3	6	0	.191
Ced Landrum	56	86	20	2	1	0	28	6	27	.233
Derrick May	15	22	5	2	0	1	4	3	0	.227
Erik Pappas	7	17	3	0	0	0	1	2	0	.176
Rey Sanchez	13	23	6	0	0	0	1	2	0	.261
Gary Scott	31	79	13	3	0	1	8	5	0	.165
Dwight Smith	90	167	38	7	2	3	16	21	2	.228
Doug Strange	3	9	4	1	0	0	0	1	1	.444
Hector Villanueva	71	192	53	10	1	13	23	32	0	.276
Jose Vizcaino	93	145	38	5	0	0	7	10	2	.262

continued

	G	AB	H	2B	3B	HR	R	RBI	SB	AVG
Pitchers										
Paul Assenmacher	75	4	1	0	0	0	1	0	0	.250
Mike Bielecki	39	46	3	0	0	0	1	7	0	.065
Shawn Boskie	30	41	7	0	1	1	3	2	0	.171
Frank Castillo	18	35	5	0	0	0	0	1	0	.143
Mike Harkey	4	5	2	0	0	0	2	0	0	.400
Danny Jackson	17	23	2	0	0	0	1	1	0	.087
Les Lancaster	64	28	5	2	0	0	2	2	0	.179
Greg Maddux	39	88	18	2	0	1	8	7	1	.205
Scott May	2	0	0	0	0	0	0	0	0	—
Chuck McElroy	71	10	3	1	0	0	1	2	0	.300
Dave Pavlas	1	0	0	0	0	0	0	0	0	—
Yorkis Perez	3	0	0	0	0	0	0	0	0	—
Laddie Renfroe	4	1	0	0	0	0	0	0	0	.000
Bob Scanlan	40	24	1	0	0	0	0	1	0	.042
Heathcliff Slocumb	52	1	0	0	0	0	0	0	0	.000
Dave Smith	35	1	0	0	0	0	0	0	0	.000
Rick Sutcliffe	20	32	3	1	0	0	2	2	0	.094
Steve Wilson	9	1	0	0	0	0	0	0	0	.000
		5,522	1,395	232	26	159	695	654	123	.253

1992

Record: 78–84
Finish: Fourth (East)
Games Behind: 18
Manager: Jim Lefebvre

Greg Maddux, the Cubs' pitching ace, had a bittersweet year in 1992. He tied for the league lead in victories, 20; led in innings pitched, 268; had the third lowest earned run average, 2.18; and won the first of what was to be an unprecedented four consecutive Cy Young awards.

But it was his last year with the Cubs. Angry because Larry Himes, the new general manager, had been reluctant to extend his contract, Maddux exercised his free-agency rights. Following a continuing dispute with Himes, he departed and hooked up with the Atlanta Braves—$28 million for five years, only $500,000 more than the Cub offer. It was the biggest front-office blunder in more than a quarter of a century, since the 1964 Brock-for-Broglio trade.

Once again there were changes at the top. Stanton R. Cook, who had reached the executive mandatory retirement age of 65 after a long and successful run as chief of the Tribune Company, changed hats and became the Cub chairman. In a surprise move, Cook hired Himes, who a year earlier had been dismissed as the general manager of the crosstown White Sox.

A failed minor league catcher whose principal expertise had been in scouting, Himes was honored a month later by the Chicago baseball writers at their annual winter banquet and presented with their "Comeback of the Year" award. He was the first person to have headed the baseball operations of both Chicago clubs.

Jim Lefebvre was the new field manager. There was no improvement. The Cubs finished fourth for the third year in a row, 78–84, one more win than the previous season. They started poorly and on May 4, after 24 games, were in last place with twice as many losses as victories. They won 32 of the next 52 games and on June 30, after Maddux had won nine of his first 17 starts, were second, five out. But they were never again a factor.

Ryne Sandberg was awarded a four-year contract extension during spring training for $30.5 million, to kick in with the 1993 season at a wage of $7.1 million, which would make him baseball's highest paid player. Satisfied, Sandberg led the offense. He batted .304, with 26 home runs and 87 RBIs, and scored 100

runs. It was his seventh season of 100 or more runs, equaling Stan Hack's club record. But Sandberg's streak of nine consecutive Gold Gloves was broken by Pittsburg's Jose Lind.

Shortstop Shawon Dunston, afflicted with an ailing back, appeared in only 18 games. Rey Sanchez and Jose Vizcaino, Dunston's primary replacements, were also out with injuries. Alex Arias, another reserve shortstop, was 5-for-5 on September 7, the first player since Cecil Travis in 1933 to collect five hits in his major league debut.

Himes made two excellent trades. He pried Sammy Sosa, a 24-year-old outfielder, from the White Sox in exchange for the disgruntled George Bell, seven years Sosa's senior. Other significant acquisitions were pitcher Mike Morgan, signed as a free agent, who won 16 games, and third baseman Steve Buechele, acquired from Pittsburgh in a July 10 deal for pitcher Danny Jackson, a costly free agent who had won only one game in his first 21 Cub starts.

Andre Dawson, who had a good year—22 home runs and 90 RBIs—departed at the end of the season. The Cubs rejected his request for $11 million for three years. Reliever Dave Smith, who had been signed for $5 million for two years, was also released. Plagued with injuries, Smith made 46 appearances in his two seasons with the Cubs, pitched 47⅓ innings and was 0–6 with 17 saves: $294,000 for each save, $106,000 an inning, and $109,000 for each appearance.

	W	L	ERA	G	GS	CG	IP	H	BB	K
Greg Maddux	(20)	11	2.18	35	35	9	(268)	201	70	199
Mike Morgan	16	8	2.55	34	34	6	240	203	79	123
Frank Castillo	10	11	3.46	33	33	0	205⅓	179	63	135
Danny Jackson	4	9	4.22	19	19	0	113	117	48	51
Shawn Boskie	5	11	5.01	23	18	0	91⅓	96	36	39
Bob Scanlan	3	6	2.89	69	0	0	87⅓	76	30	42
Jim Bullinger	2	8	4.66	39	9	1	85	72	54	36
Chuck McElroy	4	7	3.55	72	0	0	83⅔	73	51	83
Jeff Robinson	4	3	3.00	49	5	0	78	76	40	46
Paul Assenmacher	4	4	4.10	70	0	0	68	72	26	67
Ken Patterson	2	3	3.89	32	1	0	41⅓	41	27	23
Mike Harkey	4	0	1.89	7	7	0	38	34	15	21
Heathcliff Slocumb	0	3	6.50	30	0	0	36	52	21	27
Dave Smith	0	0	2.51	11	0	0	14⅓	15	4	3
Jeff Hartsock	0	0	6.75	4	0	0	9⅓	15	4	6
Dennis Rasmussen	0	0	10.80	3	1	0	5	7	2	0
Jessie Hollins	0	0	13.50	4	0	0	4⅔	8	5	0
	78	84	3.39	534	162	16	1,469	1,337	575	901

Shutouts: Maddux 4, Morgan 1.
Saves: Scanlan 14, Assenmacher 8, Bullinger 7, McElroy 6, Robinson 1, Slocumb 1.

	G	AB	H	2B	3B	HR	R	RBI	SB	AVG
Regulars										
1B Mark Grace	158	603	185	37	5	9	72	79	6	.307
2B Ryne Sandberg	158	612	186	32	8	26	100	87	17	.304
SS Jose Vizcaino	86	285	64	10	4	1	25	17	3	.225
SS Rey Sanchez	74	255	64	14	3	1	24	19	2	.251
3B Luis Salazar	98	255	53	7	2	5	20	25	1	.208
3B Steve Buechele	65	239	66	9	3	1	25	21	1	.276
OF Andre Dawson	143	542	150	27	2	22	60	90	6	.277
OF Doug Dascenzo	139	376	96	13	4	0	37	20	6	.255
OF Derrick May	124	351	96	11	0	8	33	45	5	.274
OF Dwight Smith	109	217	60	10	3	3	28	24	9	.276
C Joe Girardi	91	270	73	3	1	1	19	12	0	.270
C Rick Wilkins	83	244	66	9	1	8	20	22	0	.270
Substitutes										
Alex Arias	32	99	29	6	0	0	14	7	0	.293
Kal Daniels	48	108	27	6	0	4	12	17	0	.250
Shawon Dunston	18	73	23	3	1	0	8	2	2	.315
Jeff Kunkel	20	29	4	2	0	0	0	1	0	.138
George Pedre	4	4	0	0	0	0	0	0	0	.000
Fernando Ramsey	18	25	3	0	0	0	0	2	0	.120
Gary Scott	36	96	15	2	0	2	8	11	0	.156
Sammy Sosa	67	262	68	7	2	8	41	25	15	.260

	G	AB	H	2B	3B	HR	R	RBI	SB	AVG
Doug Strange	52	94	15	1	0	1	7	5	1	.160
Hector Villanueva	51	112	17	6	0	2	9	13	0	.152
Chico Walker	19	26	3	0	0	0	2	2	1	.115
Jerome Walton	30	55	7	0	1	0	7	1	1	.127
Pitchers										
Paul Assenmacher	70	4	0	0	0	0	1	0	0	.000
Shawn Boskie	23	27	5	1	0	0	1	1	0	.185
Jim Bullinger	39	20	5	0	0	1	3	2	1	.250
Frank Castillo	33	65	6	0	0	0	3	1	0	.092
Mike Harkey	8	15	4	0	0	0	4	0	0	.267
Jeff Hartsock	4	2	0	0	0	0	0	0	0	.000
Jessie Hollins	4	0	0	0	0	0	0	0	0	—
Danny Jackson	19	36	3	0	0	0	0	1	0	.083
Greg Maddux	35	88	15	3	0	1	6	8	0	.170
Chuck McElroy	72	6	4	2	1	0	2	1	0	.667
Mike Morgan	34	74	8	0	0	0	1	5	0	.108
Ken Patterson	32	1	0	0	0	0	0	0	0	.000
Dennis Rasmussen	3	0	0	0	0	0	0	0	0	—
Jeff Robinson	49	12	0	0	0	0	0	0	0	.000
Bob Scanlan	69	4	0	0	0	0	1	0	0	.000
Heathcliff Slocumb	30	4	0	0	0	0	0	0	0	.000
Dave Smith	11	0	0	0	0	0	0	0	0	—
		5,590	1,420	221	41	104	593	566	77	.254

1993

Record: 84–78
Finish: Fourth (East)
Games Behind: 13
Manager: Jim Lefebvre

As Greg Maddux was departing for Atlanta, general manager Larry Himes didn't seem overly concerned, obviously unaware that Maddux soon would be universally recognized as the best pitcher of his generation. After he signed free agent Jose Guzman, Himes announced: "I've now got the starter to replace him."

Guzman, previously with the Texas Rangers, came aboard for $14.4 million for four years. It wasn't a wise investment. Guzman pitched a near no-hitter in his first start—the only hit was a single with two outs in the ninth—but was erratic: 12–10 with a 4.34 earned run average. Afflicted with shoulder tendinitis, Guzman was constantly in rehab thereafter and won only two games in the next three seasons.

Greg Hibbard, a so-called cunny-thumb left-hander acquired in a trade with the White Sox, led the starters with 15 victories, a considerable achievement considering he was essentially a breaking-ball pitcher with a hittable fastball. Mike Morgan, 16–8 in '92, was 10–15. The only other pitchers to win in double figures were Jose Bautista, 10–3, and Mike Harkey, 10–10. No one else had more than five victories.

Reliever Randy Myers, signed as a free agent—$11 million for three years—was the star of the staff. A left-hander with an overpowering fastball, he logged 86 strikeouts in 75⅓ innings and set a National League record with 53 saves. He converted his first 13 opportunities, had 27 saves at the All-Star break, and in September accused his teammates of lackadaisical play. "Some of these guys aren't winners," Myers said. "All they care about is their stats."

Ryne Sandberg, who never before had expressed dissatisfaction, was publicly critical of the seemingly endless changes at the top. "I'd like to see more stability and continuity," Sandberg said. In his 12 seasons with the Cubs there had been four club presidents, three general managers, and seven field managers. He also criticized Himes for repeatedly telling manager Jim Lefebvre the club should be 10 games over .500 by the All-Star break.

"All that publicity is a distraction," Sandberg said. "Suddenly you're playing as if you're under a timetable, and what's going to happen if you don't? Where are we headed? And if there are questions about the manager, what's next?"

The Cubs were four under .500 at the break. They never won more than five games in a row or had a losing streak longer than four; 33 times they were at .500. They were six over at the finish—84–78—in fourth place for the fourth successive season, 13 games out. Sandberg missed most of the first and last months with hand injuries. Shortstop Shawon Dunston, who had undergone back surgery the previous May, didn't return until September, appearing in seven games with 10 at bats. Mark Grace hit for the cycle on May 9 and batted .325 with a career-high 98 RBIs. Candy Maldonado, Andre Dawson's outfield replacement—a costly free agent, $3.4 million for two years—hit .186 and was traded to Cleveland on August 18.

Rick Wilkins had 30 home runs and batted .303, the first Cub catcher since Gabby Hartnett in 1930 with 30 or more home runs and a .300 average in the same season. Outfielder Sammy Sosa, .261 with 135 strikeouts, became the first Cub to join the 30–30 club: 33 home runs and 36 stolen bases. Sosa also set a club record with nine consecutive hits, including six in a nine-inning game.

Lefebvre was dismissed. Angry, he told reporters, "This is what I get for busting my butt for two years." Lefebvre said when he asked Himes why he was fired, Himes told him, " 'I don't want to get into it.' He said he was doing it because it was best for him. He doesn't care what's in the best interest of the team."

	W	L	ERA	G	GS	CG	IP	H	BB	K
Mike Morgan	10	15	4.03	32	32	1	207⅔	206	74	111
Jose Guzman	12	10	4.34	30	30	2	191	188	74	163
Greg Hibbard	15	11	3.96	31	31	1	191	209	47	82
Mike Harkey	10	10	5.26	28	28	1	157⅓	187	43	67
Frank Castillo	5	8	4.84	29	25	2	141⅓	162	39	84
Jose Bautista	10	3	2.82	58	7	1	111⅔	105	27	63
Randy Myers	2	4	3.11	73	0	0	75⅓	65	26	86
Bob Scanlan	4	5	4.54	70	0	0	75⅓	79	28	44
Shawn Boskie	5	3	3.43	39	2	0	65⅔	63	21	39
Dan Plesac	2	1	4.74	57	0	0	62⅔	74	21	47
Chuck McElroy	2	2	4.56	49	0	0	47⅓	51	25	31
Paul Assenmacher	2	1	3.49	46	0	0	38⅔	44	13	34
Turk Wendell	1	2	4.37	7	4	0	22⅔	24	8	15
Steve Trachsel	0	2	4.58	3	3	0	19⅔	16	3	14
Jim Bullinger	1	0	4.32	15	0	0	16⅔	18	9	10
Bill Brennan	2	1	4.20	8	1	0	15	16	8	11
Heathcliff Slocumb	1	0	3.38	10	0	0	10⅔	7	4	4
	84	78	4.18	585	163	8	1,449⅔	1,514	470	905

Shutouts: Guzman 1, Morgan 1.
Saves: Myers (53), Bautista 2, Bullinger 1.

	G	AB	H	2B	3B	HR	R	RBI	SB	AVG
Regulars										
1B Mark Grace	155	594	193	39	4	14	86	98	8	.325
2B Ryne Sandberg	117	456	141	20	0	9	67	45	9	.309
SS Jose Vizcaino	151	551	158	19	4	4	74	54	12	.287
3B Steve Buechele	133	460	125	27	2	15	53	65	1	.272
OF Sammy Sosa	159	598	156	25	5	33	92	93	36	.261
OF Derrick May	128	465	137	25	2	10	62	77	10	.295
OF Dwight Smith	111	310	93	17	5	11	51	35	8	.300
OF Willie Wilson	105	221	57	11	3	1	29	11	7	.258
C Rick Wilkins	136	446	135	23	1	30	78	73	2	.303
Substitutes										
Shawon Dunston	7	10	4	2	0	0	3	2	0	.400
Glenallen Hill	31	87	30	7	0	10	14	22	1	.345
Doug Jennings	42	52	13	3	1	2	8	8	0	.250
Steve Lake	44	120	27	6	0	5	11	13	0	.225
Candy Maldonado	70	140	26	5	0	3	8	15	0	.186

continued

	G	AB	H	2B	3B	HR	R	RBI	SB	AVG
Karl Rhodes	15	52	15	2	1	3	12	7	2	.288
Kevin Roberson	62	180	34	4	1	9	23	27	0	.189
Rey Sanchez	105	344	97	11	2	0	35	28	1	.282
Tommy Shields	20	34	6	1	0	0	4	1	0	.176
Matt Walbeck	11	30	6	2	0	1	2	6	0	.200
Eric Yelding	69	108	22	5	1	1	14	10	3	.204
Eddie Zambrano	8	17	5	0	0	0	1	2	0	.294
Pitchers										
Paul Assenmacher	46	2	1	0	0	0	0	0	0	.500
Jose Bautista	61	21	4	0	0	0	1	1	0	.190
Shawn Boskie	39	11	3	0	0	0	2	0	0	.273
Bill Brennan	8	1	0	0	0	0	0	0	0	.000
Jim Bullinger	15	1	0	0	0	0	0	0	0	.000
Frank Castillo	29	43	7	0	0	0	1	3	0	.163
Jose Guzman	30	63	7	0	0	0	1	2	0	.111
Mike Harkey	28	54	5	1	0	0	0	0	0	.093
Greg Hibbard	32	65	6	1	0	0	4	3	0	.092
Chuck McElroy	49	6	0	0	0	0	0	0	0	.000
Mike Morgan	32	66	4	2	0	0	1	1	0	.061
Randy Myers	74	2	1	1	0	0	0	2	0	.500
Dan Plesac	57	1	0	0	0	0	0	0	0	.000
Bob Scanlan	70	2	1	0	0	0	0	2	0	.500
Heathcliff Slocumb	10	1	0	0	0	0	0	0	0	.000
Steve Trachsel	3	6	1	0	0	0	1	0	0	.167
Turk Wendell	7	7	1	0	0	0	0	0	0	.143
	5,627	1,521	259	32	161	738	706	100		.270

1994

Record: 49–64
Finish: Fifth (Central)
Games Behind: 16½
Manager: Tom Trebelhorn

Tom Trebelhorn, the new manager, had a troublesome season—a last-place finish—but will be forever remembered in Cub lore as the only manager to stand on a park bench adjacent to the Waveland Avenue Fire Station across the street from the left-field bleachers and address an estimated 200 fans who were asking the usual question: "What's wrong with the Cubs?"

Joseph A. Reaves wrote in the *Tribune:* "Not since Daniel went into the lions' den has anybody taken such a chance and lived to tell about it. One hour after the Cubs left the bases loaded in the ninth inning and had lost their ninth consecutive home game, Trebelhorn kept a vow and marched into an angry mob which had been burning copies of the *Tribune* in disgust with the Cub ownership. There were also repeated chants of 'Kill Larry Himes!'"

Trebelhorn, a former high school teacher, was accompanied by four security guards. He responded to questions for half an hour in what, in effect, turned into a town meeting. One fan drew a loud ovation when he told Trebelhorn: "I appreciate you coming here because it takes a lot of guts." Trebelhorn was applauded and cheered. At the finish the firefighters from Engine Company 78 invited him inside for a broiled chicken dinner.

The Cubs went through April without winning a home game, leading in only eight of 108 innings. It was the most embarrassing start in club history—12 successive Wrigley Field defeats beginning with a 12–8 opening-day loss to the Mets, who overcame a three-home-run performance by Karl "Dusty" Rhodes, an obscure outfielder formerly with the Houston Astros.

The first Wrigley Field victory came on May 4, 5–2 against Cincinnati, and was won by Steve Trachsel with late-inning help from Randy Myers. The Cubs won their next game behind Anthony Young, an unlikely winner who had been acquired from

the Mets for reserve shortstop Jose Vizcaino. Young reported with a string of 27 losses, a major league record for futility.

Mike Morgan pitched the opener and was expected to be the star of the staff. After he lost his first five decisions, Morgan went on the disabled list, suffering from "emotional distress." Morgan returned 19 days later, lost two more, and didn't win until June 23, in the club's 68th game.

In an astonishing announcement, Ryne Sandberg, the peerless second baseman, retired on June 13, insisting he had lost his "desire," that the game was "no longer fun." The problem was at home. A week later, Sandberg's wife, Cindy, filed for divorce, contending the marriage was "irretrievably broken."

The Cubs, who had been trimming the payroll, were freed of $16 million in salary: $4 million from Sandberg's $5.9 million 1994 pay and an additional commitment of $12 million for the next two seasons. Sandberg, at this point, had 245 home runs, fourth highest on the Cub list, and was sixth in hits and seventh in RBIs.

The major league players went on strike August 13, forcing cancellation of the final third of the season and the playoffs and World Series. Tribune executive Jim Dowdle took over the club and on September 4 named Andy MacPhail, 41, previously with the Minnesota Twins, president and CEO. Himes was gone a month later, succeeded by Ed Lynch, a former Cub pitcher with front office experience with the Mets and Padres. Trebelhorn was fired on October 17.

Karl Rhodes was repeatedly benched for light hitting and finished with eight home runs. Sammy Sosas was the only .300 hitter. Shawon Dunston, after a virtual two-year absence, appeared in 88 games. Morgan was 2–10. Myers had 21 saves, 32 fewer than the previous season. Trachsel led the pitchers with nine wins.

	W	L	ERA	G	GS	CG	IP	H	BB	K
Steve Trachsel	9	7	3.21	22	22	1	146	133	54	108
Willie Banks	8	12	5.40	23	23	1	138⅓	139	56	91
Anthony Young	4	6	3.92	20	19	0	114⅔	103	46	65
Jim Bullinger	6	2	3.60	33	10	1	100	87	34	72
Kevin Foster	3	4	2.89	13	13	0	81	70	35	75
Mike Morgan	2	10	6.69	15	15	1	80⅔	111	35	57
Jose Bautista	4	5	3.89	58	0	0	69⅓	75	17	45
Chuck Crim	5	4	4.48	49	1	0	64⅓	69	24	43
Dan Plesac	2	3	4.61	54	0	0	54⅔	61	13	53
Dave Otto	0	1	3.80	36	0	0	45	49	22	19
Randy Myers	1	5	3.79	38	0	0	40⅓	40	16	32
Frank Castillo	2	1	4.30	4	4	1	23	25	5	19
Jose Guzman	2	2	9.15	4	4	0	19⅔	22	13	11
Blaise Isley	0	0	7.80	10	0	0	15	25	9	9
Turk Wendell	0	1	11.93	6	2	0	14⅓	22	10	9
Randy Veres	1	1	5.59	10	0	0	9⅔	12	2	5
Donn Pall	0	0	4.50	2	0	0	4	8	1	2
Shawn Boskie	0	0	0.00	2	0	0	3⅔	3	0	2
	49	64	4.47	399	113	5	1,023⅔	1,054	392	717

Shutouts: Banks 1.
Saves: Myers 21, Bullinger 2, Crim 2, Bautista 1, Plesac 1.

	G	AB	H	2B	3B	HR	R	RBI	SB	AVG
Regulars										
1B Mark Grace	106	403	120	23	3	6	55	44	0	.298
2B Rey Sanchez	96	291	83	13	1	0	26	24	2	.285
2B Ryne Sandberg	57	223	53	9	5	5	36	24	2	.238
SS Shawon Dunston	88	331	92	19	0	11	38	35	3	.278
3B Steve Buechele	104	339	82	11	1	14	33	52	1	.242
OF Sammy Sosa	105	426	128	17	6	25	59	70	22	.300
OF Derrick May	100	345	98	19	2	8	43	51	3	.284
OF Karl Rhodes	95	269	63	17	0	8	39	19	6	.234
OF Glenallen Hill	89	269	80	12	1	10	48	38	19	.297
C Rick Wilkins	100	313	71	25	2	7	44	39	4	.227

	G	AB	H	2B	3B	HR	R	RBI	SB	AVG
Substitutes										
Todd Haney	17	37	6	0	0	1	6	2	2	.162
Jose Hernandez	56	132	32	2	3	1	18	9	2	.242
Mike Maksudian	26	26	7	2	0	0	6	4	0	.269
Mark Parent	44	99	26	4	0	3	8	16	0	.263
Kevin Roberson	44	55	12	4	0	4	8	9	0	.218
Willie Wilson	17	21	5	0	2	0	4	0	1	.238
Eddie Zambrano	67	116	30	7	0	6	17	18	2	.259
Pitchers										
Willie Banks	23	41	5	1	0	0	3	0	0	.122
Joe Bautista	58	2	0	0	0	0	0	0	0	.000
Shawn Boskie	2	0	0	0	0	0	0	0	0	—
Jim Bullinger	33	22	3	2	0	0	0	4	0	.136
Frank Castillo	4	9	0	0	0	0	0	0	0	.000
Chuck Crim	49	2	0	0	0	0	0	0	0	.000
Kevin Foster	13	27	2	0	0	0	2	0	0	.074
Jose Guzman	4	8	0	0	0	0	0	0	0	.000
Blaise Isley	10	1	0	0	0	0	0	0	0	.000
Mike Morgan	15	24	3	0	0	0	1	0	0	.125
Randy Myers	38	1	0	0	0	0	0	0	0	.000
Dave Otto	36	2	0	0	0	0	0	0	0	.000
Donn Pall	2	0	0	0	0	0	0	0	0	—
Dan Plesac	54	4	0	0	0	0	0	0	0	.000
Steve Trachsel	22	43	8	1	0	0	3	2	0	.186
Randy Veres	10	1	0	0	0	0	0	0	0	.000
Turk Wendell	6	2	0	0	0	0	0	0	0	.000
Anthony Young	20	34	6	1	0	0	3	4	0	.176
		3,918	1,015	189	26	109	500	464	69	.259

1995

Record: 73–71
Finish: Third (Central)
Games Behind: 12
Manager: Jim Riggleman

The baton was passed to Jim Riggleman, the 13th Cub manager in 15 years. A failed infielder, Riggleman, 42, had never played above Double A but had an abundance of managerial experience, nine years in the minors and more than two seasons with the San Diego Padres. General manager Ed Lynch, who had worked with Riggleman in San Diego, made the appointment.

The major league players were still on strike when the 1995 spring training camps opened. So-called replacement players—some retired major leaguers, but mostly former minor leaguers who had never climbed the ladder—were recruited by scouting director Jim Hendry. Many big league managers expressed disdain, but not Riggleman, who was of good cheer. "It was a learning experience," Riggleman said. "I enjoyed it."

On April 2, when the championship season was supposed to begin, the players agreed to return under the terms of the old Basic Agreement, the collective contract that binds the owners and players together. It was then decided that three weeks of spring drills were necessary for the players to get into shape. The schedule was reduced from 162 to 144 games, and no attempt was made to make up the cancellations. The season began on April 26.

While Jim Bullinger was pitching the Cubs to a 7–1 opening-day win over Cincinnati, an unidentified fan leaned over the left-field wall and, following death-bed instructions, spread his father's ashes on the warning track. "I hope it's a good luck omen," Lynch said.

It was. The Cubs won their next three games and were on their way. Except for one day, they held the lead without interruption until June 4. Sammy Sosa hit nine home runs in the first 29 games. Right-hander Jaime Navarro, a grizzled veteran previously with Milwaukee, won his first five decisions. A five-game skid dropped them to second place. They never fell into the second division and finished third, only 12 out.

Andy MacPhail and Ed Lynch began retooling with an April 5 trade: two minor league pitchers to Kansas City for Brian McRae, an outstanding defensive center fielder. McRae was among the five new principal acquisitions. The others: Navarro, signed as a free agent four days later; third baseman Todd Zeile, from St. Louis for pitcher Mike Morgan, June 16; and catcher Scott Servais and outfielder Luis Gonzalez, from Houston for catcher Rick Wilkins.

The first deal was the best. McRae, whose father had had an outstanding playing career and also managed the Royals, hit .288 with 92 runs, 12 home runs, and 27 stolen bases and led the league in at bats and putouts. More important, he emerged as a leader. On the club's first trip, in St. Louis, he arranged a team dinner that helped bring the troops together. Said McRae the next day: "I hope the rookies can play better than they sing."

Mark Grace, now playing at the $4 million level, led the club in batting, .326, and had 51 doubles, six short of the club record. Sossa was the offensive star: 36 home runs and 34 steals, his second 30–30 season. Sosa's 119 RBIs were second in the league. A total of six players had 10 or more home runs, not including catcher Mark Parent, who hit 15 of his 18 with Pittsburgh.

Navarro worked 200 innings and had a club-high 14 victories in 20 decisions. Steve Trachsel, 7–13, was a disappointment. Bullinger and Kevin Foster each won 12. Frank Castillo, also in the rotation, was 11–10, and almost pitched a no-hitter against the Cardinals in his last start, broken by a two-out, two-strike, ninth-inning triple. Randy Myers had a league-high 38 saves. Ryne Sandberg, on October 31, announced he was returning for the 1996 season.

	W	L	ERA	G	GS	CG	IP	H	BB	K
Jaime Navarro	14	6	3.28	29	29	1	200⅓	194	56	128
Frank Castillo	11	10	3.21	29	29	2	188	179	52	135
Kevin Foster	12	11	4.51	30	27	0	167⅔	149	65	146
Steve Trachsel	7	13	5.15	30	29	2	160⅔	174	76	117
Jim Bullinger	12	8	4.14	24	24	1	150	152	65	93
Mike Perez	2	6	3.66	68	0	0	71⅓	72	27	49
Turk Wendell	3	1	4.92	43	0	0	60⅓	71	24	50
Randy Myers	1	2	3.88	57	0	0	55⅔	49	28	59
Mike Walker	1	3	3.22	42	0	0	44⅔	45	24	20
Anthony Young	3	4	3.70	32	1	0	41⅓	47	14	15
Bryan Hickerson	2	3	6.82	38	0	0	31⅔	36	15	28
Larry Casian	1	0	1.93	42	0	0	23⅓	23	15	11
Mike Morgan	2	1	2.19	4	4	0	24⅔	19	9	15
Chris Nabholz	0	1	5.40	34	0	0	23⅓	22	14	21
Terry Adams	1	1	6.50	18	0	0	18	22	10	15
Willie Banks	0	1	15.43	10	0	0	11⅔	27	12	9
Rich Garces	0	0	3.27	7	0	0	11	11	3	6
Dave Swartzbaugh	0	0	0.00	7	0	0	7⅓	5	3	5
Roberto Rivera	0	0	5.40	7	0	0	5	8	2	2
Tom Edens	1	0	6.00	5	0	0	3	6	3	2
Tanyon Sturtze	0	0	9.00	2	0	0	2	2	1	0
	73	71	4.13	558	144	6	1,301	1,313	518	926

Shutouts: Castillo 2, Bullinger 1, Navarro 1.
Saves: Myers (38), Perez 2, Young 2, Adams 1, Hickerson 1, Walker 1.

	G	AB	H	2B	3B	HR	R	RBI	SB	AVG
Regulars										
1B Mark Grace	143	552	180	51	3	16	97	92	6	.326
2B Rey Sanchez	114	428	119	22	2	3	57	27	6	.278
SS Shawon Dunston	127	477	141	30	6	14	58	69	10	.296
3B Todd Zeile	79	299	68	16	0	9	34	30	0	.227
OF Sammy Sosa	144	564	151	17	3	36	89	119	34	.268
OF Brian McRae	137	(580)	167	38	7	12	92	48	27	.288
OF Luis Gonzalez	77	262	76	19	4	7	34	34	5	.290
OF Jose Hernandez	93	245	60	11	4	13	37	40	1	.245
C Scott Servais	52	175	50	12	0	12	31	35	2	.286
C Rick Wilkins	50	162	31	2	0	6	24	14	0	.191
Substitutes										
Steve Buechele	32	106	20	2	0	1	10	9	0	.189
Scott Bullett	104	150	41	5	7	3	19	22	8	.273
Matt Franco	16	17	5	1	0	0	3	1	0	.294
Todd Haney	25	73	30	8	0	2	11	6	0	.411
Mike Hubbard	15	23	4	0	0	0	2	1	0	.174
Howard Johnson	87	169	33	4	1	7	26	22	1	.195
Joe Kmak	19	53	13	3	0	1	7	6	0	.245
Mark Parent	12	32	8	2	0	3	5	5	0	.250
Todd Pratt	25	60	8	2	0	0	3	4	0	.133
Karl Rhodes	13	16	2	0	0	0	2	2	0	.125
Kevin Roberson	32	38	7	1	0	4	5	6	0	.184
Ozzie Timmons	77	171	45	10	1	8	30	28	3	.263
Pitchers										
Terry Adams	18	0	0	0	0	0	0	0	0	—
Willie Banks	10	1	0	0	0	0	0	0	0	.000
Jim Bullinger	25	47	6	3	0	0	1	5	0	.128
Larry Casian	42	2	0	0	0	0	0	0	0	.000
Frank Castillo	29	59	6	0	0	0	1	1	0	.102
Tom Edens	5	0	0	0	0	0	0	0	0	—
Kevin Foster	33	60	15	1	1	1	7	9	2	.250
Rich Garces	7	1	0	0	0	0	0	0	0	.000
Bryan Hickerson	38	2	1	0	0	0	1	1	0	.500
Mike Morgan	4	7	1	0	0	0	1	0	0	.143
Randy Myers	57	0	0	0	0	0	0	1	0	—
Chris Nabholz	34	1	0	0	0	0	0	0	0	.000
Jaime Navarro	29	65	12	5	0	0	0	7	0	.185
Mike Perez	68	4	0	0	0	0	1	0	0	.000
Roberto Rivera	7	0	0	0	0	0	0	0	0	—
Tanyon Sturtze	2	0	0	0	0	0	0	0	0	—
Dave Swartzbaugh	7	0	0	0	0	0	0	0	0	—
Steve Trachsel	30	49	13	2	0	0	3	4	0	.265
Mike Walker	42	3	0	0	0	0	0	0	0	.000
Turk Wendell	43	7	0	0	0	0	0	0	0	.000
Anthony Young	32	3	2	0	0	0	2	0	0	.667
		4,963	1,315	267	39	158	693	648	105	.265

1996

Record: 76–86
Finish: Fourth (Central)
Games Behind: 12
Manager: Jim Riggleman

It was a bittersweet season. The Cubs were in contention early and were tied for the divisional lead on May 6. They were only 3½ games out on August 21, but they crashed in mid-September, losing 14 of their last 16 games and finishing 10 games under .500, in fourth place, 12 games out. They were last in hitting, ninth in pitching. Only two pitchers won in double figures: Jaime Navarro, 15–12, and Steve Trachsel, 13–9.

But Ryne Sandberg, who had retired in June, 1994, returned in 1996 and at the age of 36 made a remarkable comeback. Although he had lost a step in the field, Sandberg hit with his accustomed power: 25 home runs and 92 RBIs. It was also another big year for outfielder Sammy Sosa, who was

challenging Hack Wilson's home run record when he was hit by a pitch on August 20 and disabled for the last six weeks of the season.

A 10-time All-Star, Sandberg batted .244, 45 points below his previous lifetime average, but he broke the National League home-run record for a second baseman with a career total of 265, two more than Rogers Hornsby's mark and only one short of Joe Morgan's major league record. Sandberg played in 150 games and was sound defensively; for the fifth time he went an entire season without a throwing error.

Sosa, batting cleanup and without the protection of a reliable number-five hitter, continued to emerge as one of the league's premier sluggers. On May 16, against Houston, he became the first Cub to hit two home runs in one inning. He had his first three–home run game, against Philadelphia, on June 5 and was leading the league in homers when Florida's Mark Hutton hit him on the right hand with a pitch. Sosa suffered a severe fracture. He finished with a .273 average, 40 home runs, 100 RBI's, and 18 stolen bases.

Sosa had been on a 52–home run pace; if he had maintained it, he would have been only four short of Wilson's heroic record. The injury deprived him of the opportunity of becoming the second major league player with 50 home runs and 20 stolen bases in the same season, a feat previously achieved by Willie Mays in 1955. It also deprived him of what could have been his third 30–30 season: 30 or more home runs and 30 or more stolen bases.

Shortstop Shawon Dunston, a 10-year Cub veteran, was released during the off-season after he had requested a three-year $10 million contract. Dunston took a hefty salary cut, was signed for one year for $1.5 million by San Francisco, and was replaced by Rey Sanchez, his understudy. Sanchez appeared in only 95 games and was a disappointment at the plate: .211 with one home run and 12 RBIs. Dave Magaden, ticketed for third base, was also troubled by injuries. Manager Jim Riggleman tried seven players at third, increasing the total of Cub third basemen to 76 since Ron Santo's departure in 1973.

First baseman Mark Grace had another solid season. He won his fourth Gold Glove, struck out only 41 times in 616 plate appearances, and batted .331, fifth best in the league and the highest by a Cub since Bill Madlock hit .339 in '76. It was the sixth .300-plus season for Grace, who was also among the league leaders in on-base percentage and doubles.

Center fielder Brian McRae was the only outfielder to play the full season. A team leader, McRae was often brilliant in the field. He batted .276 and led the club in five offensive categories, including career highs in home runs (17) and runs (111). Luis Gonzalez was the regular left fielder and batted .271 with 15 home runs and 79 RBIs.

The pitching was inadequate. After the departure of star closer Randy Myers, who had become a free agent, the Cubs acquired 38-year-old Doug Jones. Jones was ineffective and was released on June 15. The Cubs lost 34 one-run games and tied for last in the league in saves with 34. Turk Wendell led with 18 saves in 21 opportunities.

	W	L	ERA	G	GS	CG	IP	H	BB	K
Jaime Navarro	15	12	3.92	35	35	4	236⅔	244	72	158
Steve Trachsel	13	9	3.03	31	31	3	205	181	62	132
Frank Castillo	7	16	5.28	33	33	1	182⅓	209	46	139
Jim Bullinger	6	10	6.54	37	20	1	129⅓	144	68	90
Terry Adams	3	6	2.94	69	0	0	101	84	49	78
Amaury Telemaco	5	7	5.46	25	17	0	97⅓	108	31	64
Kevin Foster	7	6	6.21	17	16	1	87	98	35	53
Turk Wendell	4	5	2.84	70	0	0	79⅓	58	44	75
Rodney Myers	2	1	4.68	45	0	0	67⅓	61	38	50
Kent Bottenfield	3	5	2.63	48	0	0	61⅔	59	19	33
Bob Patterson	3	3	3.13	79	0	0	54⅔	46	22	53
Mike Campbell	3	1	4.46	13	5	0	36⅓	29	10	19
Doug Jones	2	2	5.01	28	0	0	32⅓	41	7	26
Mike Perez	1	0	4.67	24	0	0	27	29	13	22
Larry Casian	1	1	1.88	35	0	0	24	14	11	15
Dave Swartzbaugh	0	2	6.38	6	5	0	24	26	14	13
Tanyon Sturtze	1	0	9.00	6	0	0	11	16	5	7
	76	86	4.36	601	162	10	1,456⅓	1,447	546	1,027

Shutouts: Trachsel 2, Bullinger 1, Castillo 1, Navarro 1.
Saves: Wendell 18, Patterson 8, Adams 4, Jones 2, Bottenfield 1, Bullinger 1.

	G	AB	H	2B	3B	HR	R	RBI	SB	AVG
Regulars										
1B Mark Grace	142	547	181	39	1	9	88	75	2	.331
2B Ryne Sandberg	150	554	135	28	4	25	85	92	12	.244
SS Jose Hernandez	131	331	80	14	1	10	52	41	4	.242
SS Rey Sanchez	95	289	61	9	0	1	28	12	7	.211
3B Leo Gomez	136	362	86	19	0	17	44	56	1	.238
OF Brian McRae	157	624	172	32	5	17	111	66	37	.276
OF Sammy Sosa	124	498	136	21	2	40	84	100	18	.273
OF Luis Gonzalez	146	483	131	30	4	15	70	79	9	.271
C Scott Servais	129	445	118	20	0	11	42	63	0	.265
Substitutes										
Dave Magadan	78	169	43	10	0	3	23	17	0	.254
Scott Bullett	109	165	35	5	0	3	26	16	7	.212
Ozzie Timmons	65	140	28	4	0	7	18	16	1	.200
Tyler Houston	46	115	39	7	0	2	18	19	3	.339
Doug Glanville	49	83	20	5	1	1	10	10	2	.241
Todd Haney	49	82	11	1	0	0	11	3	1	.134
Brant Brown	29	69	21	1	0	5	11	9	3	.304
Robin Jennings	31	58	13	5	0	0	7	4	1	.224
Brian Dorsett	17	41	5	0	0	1	3	3	0	.122
Mike Hubbard	21	38	4	0	0	1	1	4	0	.105
Terry Shumpert	27	31	7	1	0	2	5	6	0	.226
Bret Barberie	15	29	1	0	0	1	4	2	0	.034
Brooks Kieschnick	25	29	10	2	0	1	6	6	0	.345
Felix Fermin	11	16	2	1	0	0	4	1	0	.125
Pitchers										
Jaime Navarro	35	77	10	1	0	0	1	3	0	.130
Steve Trachsel	31	66	7	2	0	1	3	5	0	.106
Frank Castillo	33	57	5	0	0	0	1	2	0	.088
Jim Bullinger	38	32	8	3	0	2	8	6	0	.250
Amaury Telemaco	25	29	3	0	0	0	1	1	0	.103
Kevin Foster	19	27	8	4	1	0	3	6	0	.296
Mike Campbell	13	11	4	2	0	0	2	1	0	.364
Pedro Valdes	9	8	1	1	0	0	2	1	0	.125
Terry Adams	69	6	0	0	0	0	0	0	0	.000
Dave Swartzbaugh	6	6	0	0	0	0	0	0	0	.000
Rodney Myers	45	5	0	0	0	0	0	0	0	.000
Bob Patterson	79	3	1	0	0	0	0	0	0	.333
Kent Bottenfield	48	2	1	0	0	0	0	0	0	.500
Turk Wendell	70	2	1	0	0	0	0	0	0	.500
Mike Perez	24	1	0	0	0	0	0	0	0	.000
Tanyon Sturtze	6	1	0	0	0	0	0	0	0	.000
		5,531	1,388	267	19	175	772	725	108	.251

Player Profiles

More than 1,600 players have worn Cub uniforms in the 122 seasons since the team's inception in 1876 as the Chicago White Stockings.

Some of them were among the greatest players in baseball history, such as Al Spalding, Cap Anson, Mike "King" Kelly, John Clarkson, Frank Chance, Three-Finger Brown, Ed Reulbach, Grover Cleveland Alexander, Hack Wilson, Riggs Stephenson, Charlie Root, Rogers Hornsby, Gabby Hartnett, Billy Herman, Dizzy Dean, Ernie Banks, Ron Santo, Billy Williams, Ferguson Jenkins, Andre Dawson, and Ryne Sandberg.

Many others also were exceptionally talented players, such as Johnny Evers, Heinie Zimmerman, Charlie Grimm, Lon Warneke, Phil Cavarretta, Augie Galan, Claude Passeau, Bill Nicholson, Hank Sauer, Andy Pafko, Don Kessinger, Bill Madlock, Rick Reuschel, Bruce Sutter, Lee Smith, Bill Buckner, Rick Sutcliffe, Greg Maddux, Shawon Dunston, and Mark Grace.

The majority, of course, as on any other team, were journeymen players, performing respectably several years for the Cubs either before or after stints elsewhere in the major leagues. And a good number of them appeared only briefly, in just one or two seasons, and in some cases in just a few games or even just one.

Many of them contributed to winning the 16 National League pennants the Cubs have hoisted in more than a century, sadly for their current fans all of them before 1946. A few players, a tiny band, even tasted victory in a World Series, in 1907 and 1908, the Cubs winning only two of baseball's championships in the 10 opportunities they have had since the Fall Classic began in 1903.

This section is devoted to profiles of 162 notable players who have performed for the Cubs. The selections were based on the contributions the players made to the Cubs, and not on their overall performance as major leaguers.

The year-by-year statistics for all players are only for games played as Cubs even if a player split the season with another team. Career statistics are for all major league games played. The statistics for pitchers differ for those used largely in relief as contrasted to those who were primarily starters in that saves (SV) instead of complete games (CG) are tabulated. Some statistics for 19th-century players, such as runs batted in and stolen bases, are incomplete.

Alexander, Grover Cleveland

Cubs: 1918–26
Pitcher
Nickname: Ol' Pete
Birthplace: Elba, Nebraska

B: February 26, 1887
D: November 4, 1950
Batted right, threw right
Ht. 6–1; **Wt.** 185

Alexander, Grover Cleveland

Cubs	W	L	Pct	ERA	G	CG	IP	H	BB	K	ShO
1918	2	1	.667	1.73	3	3	26	19	3	15	0
1919	16	11	.593	1.72	30	27	235	180	38	121	9
1920	27	14	.659	1.91	46	33	363⅓	335	69	173	7
1921	15	13	.536	3.39	31	21	252	286	33	77	3
1922	16	13	.552	3.63	33	20	245⅔	283	34	48	1
1923	22	12	.647	3.19	39	26	305	308	30	72	3
1924	12	5	.706	3.03	21	12	169⅓	183	25	33	0
1925	15	11	.577	3.39	32	20	236	270	29	63	1
1926	3	3	.500	3.46	7	4	52	55	7	12	0
Career	373	208	.642	2.56	696	439	5,189	4,868	953	2,199	90

Although Grover Cleveland Alexander's greatest success came with the Philadelphia Phillies and his most celebrated feat was performed for the St. Louis Cardinals, he actually spent more of his career with the Cubs than with either of the other two teams.

Ol' Pete, as he became known in his latter years, was a Cub from 1918 into the middle of the 1926 season when his irregular behavior, particularly his chronic alcoholism, became too much for manager Joe McCarthy, a strict disciplinarian. He was placed on waivers and picked up by the Cardinals, for whom he became the hero of the 1926 World Series when, pitching in relief, he struck out Tony Lazzeri of the New York Yankees with the bases loaded in the seventh inning of the seventh game and went on to preserve the victory.

Alexander had a magnificent if troubled career, eventually to be chronicled in a movie, *The Winning Team*, in which he was portrayed by a future president of the United States, Ronald Reagan. He won 373 games in 20 seasons to tie Christy Mathewson for the National League record for most games won in a career.

Hack Wilson still holds the one-season National League records for home runs, 56, and runs batted in, 190, set in 1930.

Grover Cleveland Alexander (George Brace photo)

He broke into the major leagues with the Phillies in 1911 with a sensational rookie season, compiling a record of 28–13, with 31 complete games and seven shutouts, four of them in succession. As the bulwark of the Phillies staff, he hit his peak with three consecutive 30-game winning seasons—31–10 in 1915, 33–12 in 1916, and 30–13 in 1917. In those three campaigns he pitched 36 shutouts, including 16 in 1916.

After the 1917 season, with the United States engaged in World War I, Phillies owner William Baker, fearing Alexander would be drafted by the military, traded him and catcher Bill Killefer to the Cubs for pitcher Mike Prendergast, catcher Pickles Dillhoefer, and $60,000. "I needed the money,"Baker candidly explained to the shocked Phillies fans.

The acquisition of Alexander proved one of the finest deals the Cubs ever made, though he missed most of the 1918 pennant-winning season. At season's start he was 2–1 and then entered the army. He was gassed and suffered a partial hearing loss while serving as an infantryman in France, and began to drink even more heavily. He also suffered from epilepsy. Despite these impediments, he remained an exceptional pitcher and never had a losing season in his 20-year career until his final campaign at the age of 43 in 1930.

He was a consistent winner with the Cubs, with two 20-game-winning seasons; 27–14 in 1920 when he led the NL in victories and 22–12 in 1923. Overall, his record with the Cubs was 128–83. In his first full year as a Cub, 1919, he was 16–11 and earned a share of the modern team record with nine shutouts.

As a Cub, Alexander won the 300th game of his career on September 20, 1924 and won number 301 on opening day, April 14, 1925, before a crowd of 38,000 at Wrigley Field. He contributed a single, double, and home run in an 8–2 victory over the Pittsburgh Pirates in the first regular-season Cubs game to be broadcast on radio (Quin Ryan was the announcer).

According to one source, Alexander wore out his welcome when he defied McCarthy's authority soon after the new manager took over at the start of the 1926 season. At a team meeting to which Alexander was late and obviously hungover, McCarthy noted that Brooklyn shortstop Rabbit Maranville had been with the Cubs as player-manager the previous season.

"No matter what you think about him," McCarthy said, "Rabbit is a smart baseball operator. He knows all the Chicago signs from last season, and we'll have to change those signs today. Otherwise, the first time Maranville gets to second base, he'll have every one of our signs."

Alexander roused himself from his stupor to comment, "I wouldn't worry about Rabbit, Joe. He won't even reach second base."

McCarthy, whom many of the players scorned as an unproven busher because he never had played or managed in the major leagues until the Cubs hired him, resented the mocking of his authority. And when Alexander showed up drunk six days in a 10-day stretch, McCarthy suspended him. On June 15, 1926, the Cubs placed Alexander on waivers, and the Cardinals bought his contract.

Alexander had been 3–3 with the Cubs. He was 9–7 the rest of the season for the Cardinals to help them to their first NL pennant. In the World Series against the Yankees he won his two starts and then achieved the most celebrated feat of his career, his appearance in relief of starter Pop Haines in the seventh game in which he struck out Lazzeri and went on to finish the 3–2 victory.

Allegedly, Alexander had been drunk the night before, celebrating his victory over the Yankees in Game 6, but he later denied it.

"I was cold sober the night before I relieved Haines in the seventh game," Alexander told an interviewer in 1950. "After Saturday's game, [manager Rogers] Hornsby asked me not to celebrate, telling me he might need me in the seventh game. So I stayed in my hotel room all night."

In 1927, at the age of 40, Alexander was 21–10 for the Cardinals and went on to have a couple more good seasons before his career ended in 1930 with an 0–3 record for the Phillies.

The one-time farm boy from Nebraska had enormous talent, possessing a wicked fastball in his early years, and he developed a fine curveball, screwball, sinker, and change-up as he matured. His control was legendary. He holds the Cubs record for 51 consecutive innings pitched without a walk. He pitched 90 shutouts in his career, an NL record, and twice won both ends of a doubleheader. He once won a game for the Cubs in 58 minutes.

Not even a life of continuous dissipation could rob him of his skills, though it caught up with him in his later years when he lived in abject poverty, earning pittances by appearing in vaudeville and in flea circuses on the strength of his name, before eventually receiving a small monthly subsidy from the estate of Sam Breadon, a former owner of the Cardinals. He suffered from epilepsy and delirium tremens and was in and out of sanatoriums.

In a 1939 interview with Frank Yeutter of the *Philadelphia Evening Bulletin*, Alexander admitted he had misspent his life.

"I had control of everything but myself," Alexander said. "Control of bats, but none with dollars. But that's the way I've been. I've made promises and broke them, the way I broke a curve outside to the heavy hitters. I've laughed as many times as I've cried so I guess I'm even with life."

Only one person, Aimee Durant, whom he married before sailing to France in 1918, ever influenced Alexander, and her influence was only spasmodic. They were divorced, remarried, and divorced again. When he was found dead on November 14, 1950, at the age of 63, in a rented room in St. Paul, Nebraska, an unfinished letter to Aimee was found in his typewriter.

Alexander was elected to the Hall of Fame in 1938.

Altman, George

Cubs: 1959–62, 1965–67
Outfielder
Birthplace: Goldsboro, North Carolina

B: March 20, 1933
Bats right, throws right
Ht. 6–4; **Wt.** 200

Altman, George Lee

Cubs	G	AB	H	AVG	RBI	R	2B	3B	HR	SLG	SB
1959	135	420	111	.245	47	56	14	4	12	.307	1
1960	119	334	89	.266	51	50	16	4	13	.455	4
1961	138	518	157	.303	96	77	28	12	27	.560	6
1962	147	534	170	.318	74	74	27	5	22	.511	19
1965	90	196	46	.235	23	24	7	1	4	.342	3
1966	88	185	41	.222	17	19	6	0	5	.335	2
1967	15	18	2	.111	1	1	2	0	0	.222	0
Career	991	3,091	832	.269	403	409	132	34	101	.432	52

George Altman

A power hitter who could play all three outfield positions, as well as first base occasionally, George Altman rounded out a strong offensive lineup for the Cubs in the early 1960s. He was big (6–4) and strong, and he had deceptive speed, enabling him to play center field as well as the flanking positions.

Altman was purchased by the Cubs in 1955 after showing promise with the powerful Kansas City Monarchs in Negro baseball. The Cubs earlier had obtained the double-play combination of shortstop Ernie Banks and second baseman Gene Baker from the Monarchs to give them their first black players.

In 1959, Altman broke into the Cubs lineup, heralding a new wave of promising youngsters that was soon to include Ron Santo and Billy Williams. As a rookie, he batted .245 in 135 games, with 12 home runs and 47 RBIs. An ankle injury and ailments, including mononucleosis, hampered Altman in 1960, although he increased his home run output to 13 and hiked his batting average to .266.

Altman's finest years with the Cubs came in 1961 and 1962 when he joined Banks and emerging stars Santo and Williams in a formidable Big Four in the middle of the lineup.

In 1961, Altman batted .303, with a slugging average of .560, led the league in triples with 12, had 28 doubles and 27 home runs, and drove in 96 runs. He hit 10 home runs dur-

ing June and was named to the NL All-Star team, hitting a pinch home run in his first plate appearance.

Altman maintained his productivity in 1962, batting .318 with 22 home runs and 74 RBIs on a Cubs team that was strong on power but doomed by pitching weakness to finish far out of contention with a record of 59–103.

The Cubs in an attempt to shore up their pitching staff traded Altman, catcher Moe Thacker, and pitcher Don Cardwell to the St. Louis Cardinals for star pitcher Larry Jackson, reliever Lindy McDaniel, and catcher Jimmie Schaffer after the 1962 season.

Altman spent 1963 with the Cardinals, then was traded to the New York Mets for the 1964 season, before rejoining the Cubs for the next three campaigns, 1965–67, largely in the role of a utility outfielder, hampered by a succession of injuries.

Released by the Cubs early in the 1967 season, Altman turned to baseball in Japan and was a standout there for the next eight years, batting .300 or better in six campaigns, with a high of .351, and pounding out 205 home runs.

He retired from baseball at the age of 42 to become a stockbroker.

Anson, Cap

White Stockings: 1876–97
First baseman
Birthplace: Marshalltown, Iowa
B: April 11, 1852

D: April 14, 1922
Batted right, threw right
Ht. 6–0; **Wt.** 227

Anson, Adrian Constantine

White Stockings	G	AB	H	AVG	RBI	R	2B	3B	HR	SLG	SB
1876	66	309	110	.356	59	63	9	7	1	.440	—
1877	59	255	86	.337	32	52	19	1	0	.420	—
1878	60	261	89	.341	40	55	12	2	0	.402	—
1879	51	227	72	.317	34	40	20	1	0	.414	—
1880	86	356	120	.337	74	54	24	1	1	.419	—
1881	84	343	137	.399	82	67	21	7	1	.510	—
1882	82	348	126	.362	83	69	29	8	1	.500	—
1883	98	413	127	.308	—	70	36	5	0	.419	—
1884	112	475	159	.335	—	108	30	3	21	.543	—
1885	112	464	144	.310	114	100	35	7	7	.461	—
1886	125	504	187	.371	147	117	35	11	10	.544	29
1887	122	472	164	.347	102	107	33	13	7	.517	27
1888	134	515	177	.344	84	101	20	12	12	.499	28
1889	134	518	161	.311	117	100	32	7	7	.440	27
1890	139	504	157	.312	107	95	14	5	7	.401	29
1891	136	540	157	.291	120	81	24	8	8	.409	17
1892	146	559	152	.272	74	62	25	9	1	.354	13
1893	103	398	125	.314	91	70	24	2	0	.384	13
1894	83	347	137	.395	99	82	28	4	5	.542	17
1895	122	474	159	.335	91	87	23	6	2	.422	12
1896	108	402	133	.331	90	72	18	2	2	.400	24
1897	114	424	121	.285	75	67	17	3	3	.361	11
Career	2,276	9,108	3,000	.329	1,715	1,719	528	124	96	.446	247

Cap Anson (George Brace photo)

If it seems appropriate to call Ernie Banks "Mr. Cub" in the 20th century, it would have been just as fitting to apply that label to Cap Anson in the 19th century when he was the bulwark and symbol of the team as well as one of early baseball's greatest and most durable stars.

Of course, he would have been "Mr. White Stockings" because that was the nickname of the team from its inception in 1876 to almost the end of Anson's tenure as player-manager after the 1897 season.

In his prime as a player, Anson was a national hero. Cigars, candy, and bats were named after him. He was a major crowd attraction in personal appearances, often on the vaudeville stage.

Anson was an extraordinary hitter who won NL batting championships with averages of .317 in 1879, .399 in 1881, and .344 in 1888. He compiled a career average of .329 in 22 seasons and was credited with being the first player to achieve 3,000 hits. For 19 seasons he batted .300 or over. A right-handed batter, he had a remarkable batting eye and never struck out more than 30 times in a season.

Powerfully built, at six feet and 220 pounds, and always in prime condition (he gave up alcohol early in his career), Anson was the first to hit three consecutive home runs and to hit five home runs in two games. Contemporaries considered him merely adequate as a fielder at first base, and he was not fast on the base paths, but he was undoubtedly the premier player at the position during his career.

When Anson died in 1922, John Sheridan of the *Sporting News,* who had seen him in his prime, was almost lyrical in the obituary he wrote:

"The giant of giants, most beautiful man on a club of beautiful men—the glorious Kelly, Williamson, Burns, Dalrymple, Gore, Pfeffer, the Adonis-like Clarkson—a man of the highest character and finest self-respect, a man who had the finest conception of honor and dignity of his profession . . ."

Adrian Constantine Anson reportedly was the first white child born at Marshalltown, Iowa, and was not named after Roman emperors but in honor of two towns in which his parents had lived in Michigan. As his career progressed, fans gave him various nicknames, starting with "Baby" Anson, "the Marshalltown Infant," then "Cap," alluding to his captaincy of the White Stockings, and finally "Pop" in his latter years as player-manager.

Anson briefly attended Notre Dame University, became captain of the baseball team, and decided to turn professional. He began his career as a catcher at minor league Rockford in 1871 at the age of 19, and moved up to the National Association Philadelphia Athletics as a third baseman the next year. He was an established star by the time Albert G. Spalding lured him to the White Stockings of the newly organized NL in 1876.

He became captain (synonymous then with manager) of

the team in 1879 and settled down at first base for the balance of his career. Self-confident and aggressive, Anson was a notorious umpire baiter but had a strict sense of honor and what was fitting. "He was a man whose word was as good as his bond," Spalding wrote of Anson.

Anson led the White Stockings to five pennants (his managerial career is discussed more extensively in Chapter 4, "The Skippers") as much by the example of his play as by his strategy. He batted over .300 in his first 15 years in the NL and remained a formidable batter to the end.

When critics suggested in 1895 that at the age of 43 it was time for him to retire as a player (he had batted .395 the previous year), Anson declared, "I will play first base or die in the attempt," then hit .335 that year.

By 1897, his final year as player-manager of the Cubs, he had slowed down so much at the age of 45—though he still batted .285—that a Chicago newspaperman mocked him in a long poem, one verse of which ran:

> *How old is Anson? When the ark*
> *First found once more a resting place,*
> *Old Noah, groping in the dark,*
> *Discovered Anson on first base—*
> *The grand old man had held it down*
> *In spite of floods that came to drown.*

On February 1, 1898, management dumped Anson after 19 years as manager and 22 seasons as a player with the Cubs. He managed the New York Giants briefly in 1898, then appeared in vaudeville, served a term as city clerk of Chicago, and later operated a billiard parlor until his death in 1922.

According to legend, even after the Cubs cut him loose he kept more than 400 bats in the cellar of his home in Chicago and oiled and dusted them daily, except Sundays, against the day he might return to baseball.

He was elected to the Hall of Fame in 1939.

Jimmy Archer

Archer, Jimmy

Cubs: 1909–17
Catcher
Birthplace: Dublin, Ireland
B: May 13, 1883

D: March 29, 1958
Batted right, threw right
Ht. 5–10; **Wt.** 168

Archer, James Peter

Cubs	G	AB	H	AVG	RBI	R	2B	3B	HR	SLG	SB
1909	80	261	60	.230	30	31	9	2	1	.291	5
1910	98	313	81	.259	41	36	17	6	2	.371	6
1911	116	387	98	.253	41	41	18	5	4	.357	5
1912	120	385	109	.283	58	35	20	2	5	.384	7
1913	110	367	98	.267	44	38	14	7	2	.360	4
1914	79	.248	64	.258	19	17	9	2	0	.310	1
1915	97	309	75	.243	27	21	11	5	1	.320	5
1916	77	205	45	.220	30	11	6	2	1	.283	3
1917	2	2	0	.000	0	0	0	0	0	.000	0
Career	846	2,645	660	.250	296	247	106	34	16	.333	36

When star catcher Johnny Kling staged a season-long holdout in 1909, manager Frank Chance acquired Jimmy Archer, who had failed in earlier trials with the Pittsburgh Pi-

rates and Detroit Tigers but had impressed him in an exhibition game at Buffalo, New York.

Archer was one of the finest defensive catchers in the game's history, as well as a decent hitter with a career average of .250. Sportswriter Ring Lardner bracketed Archer and Ray Schalk, the Hall of Famer with the White Sox, as the best catchers of that era.

Archer was the first catcher to make snap throws from a squatting position, speeding up his delivery when an opponent attempted to steal a base. Until he came along, catchers stood up to make a throw. His unorthodox style delayed his progress to the major leagues, but did not faze Chance.

"The object is to throw out the runner," Archer explained. "What difference does it make how you throw the ball just so you get it there in time."

An outstanding handler of pitchers, Archer played a key role in the Cubs' final pennant-winning season in the Chance era in 1910. His best season was 1912 when he batted .283, hit five home runs, drove in 58 runs, and threw out 81 runners attempting to steal.

Released by the Cubs in 1917, he finished his career the following season.

Baker, Gene

Cubs: 1953–57
Second baseman
Birthplace: Davenport, Iowa

B: June 15, 1925
Bats right, throws right
Ht. 6–1; Wt. 170

Baker, Eugene Walter

Cubs	G	AB	H	AVG	RBI	R	2B	3B	HR	SLG	SB
1953	7	22	5	.227	0	1	1	0	0	.273	1
1954	135	541	149	.275	61	68	32	5	13	.425	4
1955	154	609	163	.268	82	52	29	7	11	.392	9
1956	140	546	141	.258	57	65	22	3	12	.377	4
1957	12	44	11	.250	10	4	3	1	1	.432	0
Career	630	2,230	590	.265	227	265	109	21	39	.385	21

After Jackie Robinson broke the color barrier in 1947, the Cubs reluctantly began a search for promising black players and purchased shortstop Gene Baker from the Kansas City Monarchs of the Negro League in 1950.

Baker was a standout with the minor league Los Angeles Angels for four seasons before the Cubs finally called him up in September 1953. At the same time, they brought up another black shortstop, Ernie Banks, whom they had just purchased from the Monarchs, as if to provide a roommate on the road for Baker.

Baker and Banks played their first game for the Cubs on September 17, 1953. Baker was switched to second base, a position he never had played before, though scouts had considered him the outstanding shortstop in the minor leagues and wondered why the Cubs had delayed four years in giving him a chance. Baker was philosophical about the situation that had delayed his career until he was 28.

"I was just as good five years before I made the big leagues," he said. "Everybody who saw me play will tell you that. It's just that my time hadn't come."

Gene Baker

Baker was an immediate success as a second baseman, and batted .275 with 13 home runs in 1954, his first full season. The next year, he hit .268 and 11 home runs and 82 RBIs, and played in all of the Cubs' 154 games. He played in 140 games in 1956, batting .258, then was traded to Pittsburgh early in the 1957 season. Nagging injuries contributed to ending his career prematurely in 1960.

Banks, Ernie

Cubs: 1953–71
Shortstop, first baseman
Nickname: Mr. Cub
Birthplace: Dallas, Texas

B: January 31, 1931
Bats right, throws right
Ht. 6–1; Wt. 180

Banks, Ernest

Cubs	G	AB	H	AVG	RBI	R	2B	3B	HR	SLG	SB
1953	10	35	11	.314	6	3	1	1	2	.571	0
1954	154	593	163	.275	79	70	19	7	19	.427	6
1955	154	596	176	.295	117	98	29	9	44	.596	9
1956	139	538	160	.297	85	82	25	8	28	.530	6
1957	156	594	169	.285	102	112	34	6	43	.579	8
1958	154	617	193	.313	129	119	23	11	47	.614	4
1959	155	589	179	.304	143	97	25	6	45	.596	2
1960	156	597	162	.271	117	94	32	7	41	.554	1
1961	138	511	142	.278	80	75	22	4	29	.507	1
1962	154	610	164	.269	104	87	20	6	37	.503	5
1963	130	432	98	.227	64	41	20	1	18	.403	0
1964	157	591	156	.264	95	67	29	6	23	.450	1
1965	163	612	162	.265	106	79	25	3	28	.453	3
1966	141	511	139	.272	75	52	23	7	15	.432	0
1967	151	573	158	.276	95	68	26	4	23	.455	2
1968	150	552	136	.246	83	71	27	0	32	.469	2
1969	155	565	143	.253	106	60	19	2	23	.416	0
1970	72	222	56	.252	44	25	6	2	12	.459	0
1971	39	83	16	.193	6	4	2	0	3	.325	0
Career	2,528	9,421	2,583	.274	1,636	1,305	407	90	512	.500	50

Undoubtedly the most celebrated Cub player of the second half of the 20th century, Ernie Banks rode a crest of popularity throughout his 19-year career, all with one team, partly because of his effervescent, outgoing, optimistic nature but mostly because of his prodigious talent as a hitter.

On his retirement at the end of the 1971 season, Banks stood first on the all-time Cub list in games played (2,528), home runs (512), extra-base hits (1,009), and total bases (4,706); second in hits (2,583), RBIs (1,636), and doubles (407); fourth in runs scored (1,305) and slugging average (.500); and seventh in triples (90).

Banks twice led the NL in home runs, 47 in 1958—the most ever by a shortstop—and 41 in 1960, and twice led in RBIs with 129 in 1958 and 143 in 1959. He hit more than 40 home runs in five seasons, four of them consecutive, and in 1955 set a record with five grand slams.

His best two seasons came back-to-back. He batted .313 with 47 home runs and 129 RBIs in 1958 and hit .304 with 45 home runs and 143 RBIs in 1959. In both years he was voted the NL's Most Valuable Player, though the Cubs finished in fifth place each season.

The second in a family of 12 children, Banks caught the

Ernie Banks

attention of baseball scouts as an all-around sports star at Booker T. Washington High School in Dallas, Texas. Signed by the Kansas City Monarchs of the Negro League in 1950, he began his career after graduation, then spent two years in military service before returning to the Monarchs in 1953. The Cubs purchased his contract for $10,000 on September 8, 1953, almost as part of the preparation to call up their first black player, shortstop Gene Baker, from their Los Angeles farm team.

General manager Wid Mathews offhandedly mentioned to owner P. K. Wrigley that he had acquired another black player from the Monarchs.

"Who?" Wrigley asked.

"Fellow named Ernie Banks."

"Gee whiz!" Wrigley exclaimed. "We are bringing up one Negro player this year. Why did you go out and get another one?"

"Well," Mathews answered, "we had to have a roommate for the one we've got."

It was thus, almost casually, that the Cubs had just acquired their most beloved and greatest player since Cap Anson, a player who was to become the favorite not only of Cub fans in general, but of Philip Wrigley in particular.

Called up together, Banks, then 22, and Baker, the latter shifted to second base, played their first game for the Cubs on September 17, 1953. Three days later, Banks hit the first home run of the 512 he was to produce in his career, off Gerry Staley of the Cardinals in St. Louis.

In his first full season, 1954, Banks hit 19 home runs, the most ever by a Cub rookie, and in 1955 he emerged as a full-blown superstar, with a batting average of .295, 44 home runs, and 117 RBIs. Injuries hampered him in 1956, cutting his home run total to 28, but then came four consecutive seasons of 40 or more home runs, MVP awards in 1958 and 1959, and widespread acclaim both as an outstanding fielder and as the most devastating hitter ever to play the position.

Bob Scheffing, manager of the Cubs from 1957 to 1959, paid Banks a tremendous compliment, saying, "Right now Joe DiMaggio is the only player I'd ever consider in a trade for Banks, and I'm not forgetting it's a lot tougher playing shortstop than center field."

Banks was deceptively strong, a slender, willowy player who depended on exceptional wrist action as much as muscle for his power. He was very sure-handed, setting major league records for a shortstop at the time with a .985 fielding percentage and the fewest errors, 12, in 1957. He was durable, with consecutive playing streaks of 717 and 424 games.

By 1961 an arthritic knee condition had slowed Banks down in the field, and he was shifted to first base where he was to remain the rest of his career. He became an outstanding first baseman, especially on handling throws, and in 1969, at the age of 38, led the NL with a .997 fielding percentage—only four errors in 155 games. In the same year, he hit 23 home runs and topped the 100-RBI mark with 106 for the eighth time in his career.

During most of Banks' career, the Cubs were a woeful team, but they picked up in the late 1960s under fiery manager Leo Durocher, reaching their peak in 1969 with an ill-fated run for a division title. Banks anchored an All-Star infield with third baseman Ron Santo, shortstop Don Kessinger, and second baseman Glenn Beckert.

On May 12, 1970, Banks hit the 500th home run of his career off Pat Jarvis of the Atlanta Braves before a crowd of 5,264 at Wrigley Field. Reduced to part-time duty by age and ailments, Banks hit his final home run, number 512, on August 24, 1971, and retired at season's end.

Banks' enthusiasm for baseball was legendary, and his constant refrain became famous: "It's a beautiful day for baseball. . . . Let's play two."

He was elected to the Hall of Fame in 1977, and was involved with the Cubs off and on after his retirement as a player. But for the fans, he has always been "Mr. Cub."

Barnes, Ross

White Stockings: 1876–77   **D:** February 5, 1915
Second baseman   **Batted right, threw right**
Birthplace: Mount Morris, New York   **Ht.** 5–8; **Wt.** 145
B: May 8, 1850

Barnes, Roscoe Charles

White Stockings	G	AB	H	AVG	RBI	R	2B	3B	HR	SLG	SB
1876	66	322	138	.429	59	126	21	14	1	.590	—
1877	22	92	25	.272	5	16	1	0	0	.283	—
Career	234	1,032	329	.319	111	239	45	17	2	.401	—

The first home run in NL history was hit on May 2, 1876, by Ross Barnes, the second baseman of the White Stockings, who went on to win the league's first pennant that inaugural season. It was an inside-the-park drive off Bill "Cherokee" Fisher at Cincinnati. Barnes also went 6-for-6 in a game against Cincinnati.

Barnes was the NL's first batting champion in 1876 with a .429 average (or .404 if bases on balls are counted as times at bats as they were that season) as well as leading the league in hits (138), runs (126), doubles (21), and triples (14). Barnes benefited from the "fair-foul" rule, in effect only that season,

Ross Barnes

Frank Baumholtz

under which any ball that bounced in fair territory when first hit, even though it might roll foul while going down the baseline, was considered a hit as long as the batter made it to first base.

When the "fair-foul" was abolished after the 1876 season, depriving him of his specialty, Barnes dipped to .272 in 1877 and left the White Stockings. His playing career ended in 1881.

Baumholtz, Frankie

Cubs: 1949, 1951–55   **B:** October 7, 1918
Outfielder   **Bats left, throws left**
Birthplace: Midvale, Ohio   **Ht.** 5–10; **Wt.** 175

Baumholtz, Frank Conrad

Cubs	G	AB	H	AVG	RBI	R	2B	3B	HR	SLG	SB
1949	58	164	37	.226	15	15	4	2	1	.293	2
1951	146	560	159	.284	50	62	28	10	2	.380	5
1952	103	409	133	.325	35	59	17	4	4	.416	5
1953	133	520	159	.306	25	75	36	7	3	.419	3
1954	90	303	90	.297	28	38	12	6	4	.416	1
1955	105	280	81	.289	27	23	12	5	1	.379	0
Career	1,019	3,477	1,010	.290	272	450	165	51	25	.389	30

Few Cub center fielders have had to cover as much ground as Frankie Baumholtz, who was flanked for two seasons by lead-footed sluggers Ralph Kiner in left field and Hank Sauer

in right field. Baumholtz, 30, was obtained along with Sauer in trade from Cincinnati early in the 1949 season. He played 58 games with the Cubs that year, and spent all of 1950 in the minor leagues.

Fast and a good hitter with a career average of .290, Baumholtz batted .284 when recalled in 1951, and in 1952 challenged Stan Musial for the batting title, losing out with .325 to the St. Louis star's .336. Baumholtz batted .306 in 1953 and .297 in 1954. Sold to Philadelphia after the 1955 season, he ended his career with the Phillies in 1957.

Beckert, Glenn

Cubs: 1965–73
Second baseman
Birthplace: Pittsburgh, Pennsylvania

B: October 12, 1940
Bats right, throws right
Ht. 6–1; **Wt.** 190

Beckert, Glenn Alfred

Cubs	G	AB	H	AVG	RBI	R	2B	3B	HR	SLG	SB
1965	154	614	147	.239	30	73	21	3	3	.298	6
1966	153	656	188	.287	59	73	23	7	1	.348	10
1967	146	597	167	.280	40	91	32	3	5	.369	10
1968	155	643	189	.294	37	98	28	4	4	.369	8
1969	131	543	158	.291	37	69	22	1	1	.341	6
1970	143	591	170	.288	36	99	15	6	3	.349	4
1971	131	530	181	.342	42	80	18	5	2	.406	3
1972	120	474	128	.270	43	51	22	2	3	.344	2
1973	114	372	95	.255	29	38	13	0	0	.290	0
Career	1,320	5,208	1,473	.283	360	685	196	31	22	.345	49

For nine seasons, 1965–73, Glenn Beckert and shortstop Don Kessinger complemented each other's skills as one of the best double-play combinations in Cub history.

A dependable if not spectacular fielder, Beckert broke in with the Cubs in 1965 and quickly earned a reputation as a scrappy player who could be counted on to "get the job done." He seldom struck out, leading the NL in fewest strikeouts for five seasons. In 1968, Beckert struck out only 20 times in 643 official at bats, for an average of one strikeout per 32.15 plate appearances.

His ability to get the bat on the ball and move runners to scoring position was one of the talents that endeared him to manager Leo Durocher, whose favorite player he became on the pennant-contending teams of the late 1960s and early 1970s.

"He'll beat you so many ways, running, hitting, fielding,

stealing a base," Durocher said. "He's a hustler. He battles the heart out of you."

Although Beckert's career average was .283, he reached a peak of .342 in 1971 and three times hit safely in 20 or more consecutive games, topped by a 27-game streak in 1968. He was chosen the NL's All-Star second baseman for four consecutive seasons, beginning in 1968, and won the Gold Glove Award in 1971.

Injuries took their toll on Beckert by 1972, and he was traded to San Diego by the Cubs after the 1973 season. He finished his career in 1975.

Bithorn, Hi

Cubs: 1942–43, 1946
Pitcher
Birthplace: Santurce, Puerto Rico
B: March 18, 1916

D: January 1, 1952
Batted right, threw right
Ht. 6–1; **Wt.** 201

Bithorn, Hiram Gabriel

Cubs	W	L	Pct	ERA	G	CG	IP	H	BB	K	ShO
1942	9	14	.391	3.68	38	9	171⅓	191	81	65	0
1943	18	12	.600	2.60	39	19	249⅔	226	65	86	7
1946	6	5	.545	3.84	26	2	86⅔	97	35	34	1
Career	34	31	.523	3.16	105	30	509⅔	516	171	185	8

Drafted in the winter of 1942 from the New York Yankees system for $7,500, Hi Bithorn became briefly the Cubs' first Latin star, having been born in Puerto Rico of Spanish-Danish extraction.

As a rookie in 1942, Bithorn was 9–14 for a poor team. The

Glenn Beckert

Hi Bithorn

next year he emerged as a full-blown star with an 18–12 record and a 2.60 ERA, pitching a league-leading seven shutouts. Bithorn then joined the U.S. Navy and served two years, but came back with a sore arm when he resumed his career in 1946. He threw his final pitches for the White Sox in 1947, then retired.

Bithorn died on New Year's Day 1952 after being shot by a policeman in Mexico City. As a memorial, Hiram Bithorn Stadium in Puerto Rico was named after him.

Bonham, Bill

Cubs: 1971–77
Pitcher
Birthplace: Glendale, California

B: October 1, 1948
Bats right, throws right
Ht. 6–2; **Wt.** 190

Bonham, William Gordon

Cubs	W	L	Pct	ERA	G	CG	IP	H	BB	K	ShO
1971	2	1	.667	4.65	33	0	60	63	36	41	0
1972	1	1	.500	3.10	19	0	58	56	25	49	0
1973	7	5	.583	3.02	44	3	152	126	64	121	0
1974	11	22	.333	3.85	44	10	243	246	109	191	2
1975	13	15	.464	4.72	38	7	229	254	109	165	2
1976	9	13	.409	4.27	32	3	196	215	96	110	0
1977	10	13	.435	4.35	34	1	215	207	82	134	0
Career	75	83	.475	4.00	300	27	1,488	1,512	636	985	4

One of the "flower children" of the late 1960s and early 1970s, who admitted to sleeping on the floor and preferring an exotic, mostly vegetarian diet in his youth, Bill Bonham was a highly regarded pitching prospect whose most memorable achievement with the Cubs was to lead the NL in losses with an 11–22 record in 1974.

Bonham came up with the Cubs near the end of the Leo Durocher era in 1971, touted because of an excellent fastball and a good breaking pitch. He was part of the starting rotation from 1974 to 1977, averaging 34 starts a season, but failed to

Bill Bonham

reach .500 in any of those four campaigns. Lack of control and poor support from lackluster Cub teams were his undoing.

Traded to Cincinnati after the 1977 campaign, Bonham faded out of the major leagues after three seasons with the Reds.

Borowy, Hank

Cubs: 1945–48
Pitcher
Birthplace: Bloomfield, New Jersey

B: May 12, 1916
Bats right, throws right
Ht. 6–0; **Wt.** 175

Borowy, Henry Ludwig

Cubs	W	L	Pct	ERA	G	CG	IP	H	BB	K	ShO
1945	11	2	.846	2.13	15	14	132⅓	105	88	47	1
1946	12	10	.545	3.76	32	8	201	220	61	95	1
1947	8	12	.400	4.38	40	7	183	190	63	75	1
1948	5	10	.333	4.89	39	2	127	156	49	50	1
Career	108	82	.568	3.50	314	94	1,716	1,660	623	690	17

The Cubs purchased Hank Borowy for a reported $97,500 from the New York Yankees on July 27, 1945, to solidify their pitching staff for the pennant race with the St. Louis Cardinals. The deal was one of the best they ever made.

Borowy, who had been 10–5 with the Yankees that season, went on to a 11–2 record the rest of the season for the Cubs, who beat out the Cardinals to win the NL pennant. The games he lost were by scores of 2–1 and 1–0. With an overall record for the season of 21–7, Borowy became one of the few pitchers ever to win 20 or more games in a season while pitching in both major leagues.

The willingness of the Yankees to sell Borowy to the Cubs was a bit puzzling because he was the ace of their pitching staff. He had compiled a 15–4 record as a rookie in 1942, and he was 14–9 in 1943 and 17–10 in 1944.

Some skeptics suggested that Yankees general manager Larry MacPhail was repaying the Cubs for a deal several years earlier while he was at Brooklyn in which they had sent him second baseman Billy Herman, who helped win the pennant for the Dodgers in 1941.

Borowy pitched a 9–0 shutout to beat Hal Newhouser in the 1945 World Series opener against the Detroit Tigers, and won another game in relief, but also lost two as the Cubs went down to defeat in seven games.

Physical problems, particularly finger blisters, beset Borowy after 1945, and he never regained his former effectiveness. The Cubs traded him to Philadelphia after the 1948 season. He played in his last major league game in 1951.

Bowa, Larry

Cubs: 1982–85
Shortstop
Birthplace: Sacramento, California

B: December 6, 1945
Bats both, throws right
Ht. 5–10; **Wt.** 155

Bowa, Lawrence Robert

Cubs	G	AB	H	AVG	RBI	R	2B	3B	HR	SLG	SB
1982	142	499	123	.246	29	50	15	7	0	.305	8
1983	147	499	133	.267	43	70	20	5	1	.339	7
1984	133	391	87	.223	17	33	14	2	0	.269	10
1985	72	195	48	.246	13	13	6	4	0	.318	5
Career	2,247	8,418	2,191	.260	525	987	262	99	15	.320	318

Larry Bowa

A sure-handed shortstop with the Philadelphia Phillies for 12 seasons, Larry Bowa was acquired along with rookie infielder Ryne Sandberg by Cub general manager Dallas Green in exchange for shortstop Ivan DeJesus on January 27, 1982.

With that deal, the best of his Cub regime, Green had put in place two of the building blocks for the Cubs' first NL East Division title in 1984, and in Sandberg had obtained one of the greatest players in the team's history.

Bowa at 36 had slowed down by the time he became a Cub, but his fiery leadership and steady if no longer spectacular play in the field helped solidify the lineup that produced the division title winner in 1984. However, Bowa had faded as a hitter and in one stretch in 1984 went 130 consecutive times at bat without driving in a run.

A chronic complainer, who constantly feuded with his managers, Bowa wore out his welcome in 1985 and was sent to the New York Mets, with whom he ended his career that season.

Brock, Lou

Cubs: 1961–64
Outfielder
Birthplace: El Dorado, Arkansas

B: June 18, 1939
Bats left, throws left
Ht. 6–0; **Wt.** 170

Brock, Louis Clark

Cubs	G	AB	H	AVG	RBI	R	2B	3B	HR	SLG	SB
1961	4	11	1	.091	0	1	0	0	0	.091	0
1962	123	434	114	.263	35	73	24	7	9	.412	16
1963	148	547	141	.258	37	79	19	11	9	.382	24
1964	52	215	54	.251	14	30	9	2	2	.340	10
Career	2,816	10,332	3,023	.293	900	1,610	486	141	149	.410	938

In what has become the most infamous trade in Cub history, general manager John Holland on June 15, 1964, sent young outfielder Lou Brock and two journeymen pitchers to St. Louis for pitchers Ernie Broglio and Bobby Shantz and outfielder Doug Clemens. Holland was jubilant, saying, "We're taking more than a shot at the flag. We're cutting loose with both barrels."

Both barrels exploded in Holland's face, his acquisitions proving of minimal value while Brock went on to a Hall of Fame career with the Cardinals. During a 19-year career, he was a key component in three pennant-winning seasons for St. Louis, including World Series championships in 1964 and 1967.

Brock became one of baseball's greatest base stealers, with a career total of 938 and a peak of 118 in 1974, then a major league record. He finished his career in 1979 with a career average of .293 and 3,023 base hits, his 3,000th ironically coming against the Cubs.

The Cubs signed him for a reported $30,000 bonus out of Southern University in 1961; after an impressive minor league showing that year, he was promoted to the Cubs near the end of the season. His speed and batting ability were obvious, and the Cubs played him more or less regularly in the outfield. In 1962 he batted .263 in 123 games. The next season he hit .258 in 148 games and stole 24 bases.

All the while, however, his defensive play was suspect, and after trying him in left field and in center field, the Cubs shifted him to right field where he also had problems. Holland and his staff decided that he was expendable and made the deal with the Cardinals in midseason 1964.

Brock was an immediate success at St. Louis, batting .348 in 105 games for St. Louis to round out the season as the Cardinals rolled to a pennant and a World Series victory over the New York Yankees. He stole 50 or more bases during the next 12 straight seasons and was the first player to surpass Ty Cobb's career record of 892. He was elected to the Hall of Fame in 1985.

Brown, Mordecai

Cubs: 1904–12, 1916
Pitcher
Nickname: Three-Finger
Birthplace: Nyesville, Indiana

B: October 19, 1876
D: February 14, 1948
Batted right, threw right
Ht. 5–10; **Wt.** 175

Brown, Mordecai Peter Centennial

Cubs	W	L	Pct	ERA	G	CG	IP	H	BB	K	ShO
1904	15	10	.600	1.86	26	21	212⅓	155	50	81	4
1905	18	12	.600	2.17	30	24	249	219	44	89	4
1906	26	6	.813	1.04	36	27	277⅓	198	61	144	10
1907	20	6	.769	1.39	34	20	233	180	40	107	6
1908	29	9	.763	1.47	44	27	312⅓	214	49	123	9
1909	27	9	.750	1.31	50	32	342⅔	246	53	172	8
1910	25	13	.658	1.86	46	27	295⅓	256	64	143	7
1911	21	11	.656	2.80	53	21	270	267	55	129	0
1912	5	6	.455	2.64	15	5	88⅔	92	20	34	2
1916	2	3	.400	3.91	12	2	48½	52	9	21	0
Career	239	129	.649	2.06	481	271	3,172⅓	2,708	673	1,375	57

When Mordecai Peter Centennial Brown—his parents gave him the extra middle name because he was born in 1876, the centennial year of United States independence—

Three-Finger Brown

in which Giants rookie Fred Merkle failed to touch second base, costing his team the pennant. When the game was ruled a tie and the NL ordered it played over at season's end on October 8, 1908, Brown relieved starter Jack Pfiester in the first inning and earned a 4–2 victory as the Cubs won the pennant.

In 1906, when the Cubs won a record 116 games, Brown won 11 in a row and pitched 10 shutouts. He was 239–129 over his career, with 57 shutouts, as well as three in World Series competition.

Teammate Johnny Evers said of Brown that he had "plenty of nerve, ability and willingness to work at all times under any conditions; the crowds never bothered him."

When Evers left the Cubs to manage the Cincinnati Reds in 1913, he took Brown with him. Brown had one last burst of success in 1915 when he jumped to the Chicago Whales of the Federal League and compiled a 17–8 record. In 1916, Brown rejoined the Cubs briefly, won two games, then slipped into the minor leagues to end his career.

He was elected to the Hall of Fame in 1949.

Bryant, Clay

Cubs: 1935–40   **B:** November 26, 1911
Pitcher   **Bats right, throws right**
Birthplace: Madison Heights, Virginia   **Ht.** 6–2; **Wt.** 195

Bryant, Clay											
Cubs	W	L	Pct	ERA	G	CG	IP	H	BB	K	ShO
1935	1	2	.333	5.16	9	0	22⅔	34	7	13	0
1936	1	2	.333	3.30	26	0	57⅓	57	24	35	0
1937	9	3	.750	4.26	38	4	135⅓	117	78	75	1
1938	19	11	.633	3.10	44	17	270⅓	235	125	135	3
1939	2	1	.667	5.74	4	2	31⅓	42	14	9	0
1940	0	1	.000	4.78	8	0	26⅓	26	14	5	0
Career	32	20	.615	3.73	129	23	543⅓	511	262	272	4

was 7, he lost his right index finger above the knuckle in a farm accident. Another mishap gnarled the third and fourth fingers of his right hand, and the little finger also was useless the rest of his life.

The mangled hand proved a blessing in disguise when Brown turned to pitching for the coal-mining teams in southern Indiana. The stub of the finger enabled him to put more spin on the ball, his curve breaking down and out and inducing batters to beat the ball into the ground. "It gives me a bigger dip," he said. It also earned him the nickname of "Three-Finger."

Brown broke into the major leagues with the St. Louis Cardinals in 1903, then was traded to the Cubs and became the pitching mainstay of Frank Chance's pennant winners from 1906 to 1908 and in 1910. Brown was a 20-game winner in six consecutive seasons, from 1906 to 1911, with his peak in 1908 when he was 29–9. He was 2–0 over the Detroit Tigers in the 1908 World Series, the last one the Cubs have won.

Brown's duels with Christy Mathewson, the New York Giants ace, were legendary. They confronted each other 24 times, with Brown winning 13, nine of them consecutively.

One of those victories was the replay of one of the most famous games ever played, the contest at the Polo Grounds

Clay Bryant's brief career was cut short by arm trouble after six seasons in the major leagues, all with the Cubs, but his contribution was vital to the team winning the 1938 pennant in a campaign made memorable by Gabby Hartnett's celebrated "homer in the gloamin' " that crushed the second-place Pittsburgh Pirates.

The pennant would have been inconceivable without Bryant's 19–11 record, second only to Bill Lee's 22–11. Bryant also led the NL in strikeouts with 135—as well as in walks with 125.

A highlight of Bryant's career came on August 28, 1937, when he hit a grand-slam home run to win his own game in relief 10–7 over the Braves at Boston. He was 9–3 that year, and won a total of only four games over four seasons other than 1937 and 1938.

Bryant faded into the minor leagues in 1941, but continued his baseball career as a coach, pitching instructor, and minor league manager for another 30 years.

Buckner, Bill

Cubs: 1977–84
First baseman
Birthplace: Vallejo, California

B: December 14, 1949
Bats left, throws left
Ht. 6–0; **Wt.** 185

Buckner, William Joseph

Cubs	G	AB	H	AVG	RBI	R	2B	3B	HR	SLG	SB
1977	122	426	121	.284	60	40	27	0	11	.423	7
1978	117	446	144	.323	74	47	26	1	5	.419	7
1979	149	591	168	.284	66	72	34	7	14	.437	9
1980	145	578	187	.324	68	69	41	3	10	.457	1
1981	106	421	131	.311	75	45	35	3	10	.480	5
1982	161	657	201	.306	105	93	34	5	15	.441	15
1983	153	626	175	.280	66	79	38	6	16	.436	12
1984	21	43	9	.209	2	3	0	0	0	.209	0
Career	2,495	9,354	2,707	.289	1,205	1,073	498	49	173	.409	183

A hot-tempered, intense competitor, Bill Buckner was an outstanding left-handed batter who had slowed down because of a surgically repaired left ankle by the time he became a Cub in 1977, eight years after starting his major league career with the Los Angeles Dodgers.

General manager Bob Kennedy traded outfielder Rick Monday and reliever Mike Garman to the Los Angeles Dodgers for Buckner and shortstop Ivan DeJesus on January 11, 1977. It was Kennedy's first trade and one of his better

Bill Buckner

ones. Both Buckner and DeJesus became standouts for the Cubs for several seasons.

Buckner, then 28, had played mostly outfield with the Dodgers, but the Cubs put him on first base where he prospered for the next seven seasons. He batted .300 during his time with the Cubs, with 1,136 hits in 3,788 at bats. In 1980 he won the NL batting title with an average of .324, after finishing second among the league's hitters with .323 in 1978.

Buckner seldom struck out. In 1980 he struck out just 18 times in 614 plate appearances, a ratio of one strikeout for every 34.1 trips to the plate.

During Buckner's first season, the Cubs stirred excitement under manager Herman Franks, being in first place as late as August 4, before they fell back. Buckner was one of Franks' favorites at this point.

Two years later the Cubs made a similar futile charge at first place, and when they swooned, Franks resigned just before the season ended, with a parting blast in which he singled out Buckner as a "whiner" and malcontent.

Buckner's most memorable day as a Cub came on May 17, 1979, in one of the most unusual games ever played at Wrigley Field. Buckner hit a grand-slam home run and drove in seven runs, while teammate Dave Kingman hit three homers, as the Cubs lost 23–22 to Philadelphia on a home run by Mike Schmidt after the Phillies had blown a 21–9 lead.

Buckner survived Franks, but again engaged in a feud as well as a shoving match with another manager, Lee Elia, in 1982. Despite this, Buckner had another outstanding season, batting .306 with 201 hits, 15 home runs, and a career-high 105 RBIs.

His career with the Cubs ended on May 25, 1984, when he was traded by general manager Dallas Green to the Boston Red Sox for pitcher Dennis Eckersley and a minor leaguer, a move that opened the first base job for Leon Durham.

Buhl, Bob

Cubs: 1962–66
Pitcher
Birthplace: Saginaw, Michigan

B: August 12, 1928
Bats right, throws right
Ht. 6–2; **Wt.** 180

Buhl, Robert Ray

Cubs	W	L	Pct	ERA	G	CG	IP	H	BB	K	ShO
1962	12	13	.480	3.69	34	8	212	204	94	109	1
1963	11	14	.440	3.38	37	6	226	219	62	108	0
1964	15	14	.517	3.83	36	11	227⅔	208	68	107	3
1965	13	11	.542	4.39	32	2	184⅓	207	57	92	0
1966	0	0	.000	15.43	1	0	2⅓	4	1	1	0
Career	166	132	.557	3.55	457	111	2,586⅔	2.446	1,105	1.268	20

B ob Buhl had seen his best years with the powerful Milwaukee Braves in the late 1950s when the Cubs acquired him in a trade on April 30, 1962. He had been part of the Braves' "Big Three" rotation with Warren Spahn and Lew Burdette, and had put together exceptional back-to-back seasons with an 18–8 record in 1956 and 18–7 in 1957.

By the time he came to the Cubs at age 33, the right-hander had lost something off his fastball, but he had enough left to bolster their shaky pitching staff, along with Larry Jackson and Dick Ellsworth, in the mid-1960s. Buhl gave the Cubs plenty of innings and was in double digits in wins in each of his four seasons. In his best year, 1965, he was 15–14.

Bob Buhl

Buhl was 13–11 in 1965, but when manager Leo Durocher took over for the 1966 season, he decided to unload the veteran. Buhl's greatest contribution to the Cubs might have come in the ensuing deal on April 21, 1966. The Cubs traded Buhl and Jackson to Philadelphia for outfielder Adolfo Phillips and first baseman John Herrnstein, along with a lightly regarded rookie, Ferguson Jenkins, who was to become one of the greatest Cub pitchers of all time.

Burns, Tommy

White Stockings: 1880–91
Infielder
Birthplace: Honesdale, Pennsylvania
B: March 30, 1857
D: March 19, 1902
Batted right, threw right
Ht. 5–7; **Wt.** 152

Burns, Thomas Everett

White Stockings	G	AB	H	AVG	RBI	R	2B	3B	HR	SLG	SB
1880	85	333	103	.309	43	47	17	3	0	.378	—
1881	84	342	95	.278	42	41	20	3	4	.389	—
1882	84	355	88	.248	48	55	23	6	0	.346	—
1883	97	405	119	.294	—	69	37	7	2	.435	—
1884	83	343	84	.245	—	54	14	2	7	.359	—
1885	111	445	121	.272	70	82	23	9	7	.411	—
1886	112	445	123	.276	65	64	18	10	3	.382	—
1887	115	424	112	.264	60	57	20	10	3	.380	32
1888	134	483	115	.238	70	60	12	6	3	.306	34
1889	136	525	127	.242	66	64	27	6	4	.339	18
1890	139	538	149	.277	86	86	16	6	6	.362	44
1891	59	243	55	.226	17	36	8	1	1	.280	1
Career	1,251	4,920	1,299	.264	571	722	235	69	40	.364	147

Rookie shortstop Tommy Burns broke in with the White Stockings with a .309 batting average in 1880. He became part of the famous "Stonewall Infield" and was a fixture with the team for a dozen seasons.

Burns never again hit .300, but proved an exceptional fielder, switching full time to third base in 1886. In 1889 he led the league's third basemen in putouts, assists, and double plays. He was a particular favorite of the fans, especially for his head-first dives into bases.

Burns earned manager Cap Anson's respect with his hustle, as well as his abstinence from smoking and drinking, unusual for a player in that day. When almost all of Anson's players deserted to the Players League in 1890, Burns and pitcher Bill Hutchison were the only exceptions. His loyalty further solidified his standing with the manager and front office.

Released after the 1891 season, Burns was hired by Pittsburgh as player-manager for 1892. He lasted only 55 games into the season before being fired, then managed in the minor leagues for several years.

When the Cubs fired Anson early in 1898, Burns was named his successor as manager. (For details, turn to Chapter 4, "The Skippers.")

Burris, Ray

Cubs: 1973–79
Pitcher
Birthplace: Idabel, Oklahoma
B: August 22, 1950
Bats right, throws right
Ht. 6–5; **Wt.** 200

Burris, Bertram Ray

Cubs	W	L	Pct	ERA	G	CG	IP	H	BB	K	ShO
1973	1	1	.500	2.91	31	0	65⅔	65	27	57	0
1974	3	5	.375	6.60	40	0	75	91	26	40	0
1975	15	10	.600	4.12	36	8	238⅓	259	73	108	2
1976	15	13	.536	3.11	37	10	249	251	70	112	4
1977	14	16	.467	4.62	39	5	221	270	67	105	1
1978	7	13	.350	4.75	40	4	198⅔	210	79	94	1
1979	0	0	.000	6.23	14	0	21⅔	23	15	14	0
Career	108	134	.446	4.17	480	47	2,188⅓	2,310	764	1,065	10

Ray Burris

A big right-hander, who admittedly patterned his pitching style after Ferguson Jenkins, Ray Burris was a successful starter for some woeful Cub teams in the mid-1970s.

A graduate of the Cubs farm system, Burris hit his stride with a 15–10 record in 1975. His best showing doubtless came in 1976 when he started out 4–11, then won 11 of his last 13 decisions, including his last five in a row, to finish 15–13. He pitched four shutouts and compiled a 3.11 ERA.

After a 14–16 record in 1977, Burris slipped to 7–13 in 1978, his last full year with the Cubs. On May 23, 1979, Burris was traded to the New York Yankees for pitcher Dick Tidrow. He drifted from team to team during the final eight years of his career, and in 1987 he moved into the Milwaukee Brewers' front office.

Bush, Guy

Cubs: 1923–34　　　　**D:** July 2, 1985
Pitcher　　　　**Batted right, threw right**
Birthplace: Aberdeen, Mississippi　　**Ht.** 6–0; **Wt.** 175
B: August 23, 1901

Bush, Guy Terrell

Cubs	W	L	Pct	ERA	G	CG	IP	H	BB	K	ShO
1923	0	0	.000	0.00	1	0	1	1	0	2	0
1924	2	5	.286	4.02	16	4	80⅔	91	24	36	0
1925	6	13	.316	4.30	42	5	182	213	52	76	0
1926	13	9	.591	2.86	35	7	157⅓	149	42	32	2
1927	10	10	.500	3.03	36	9	193⅓	177	79	62	1
1928	15	6	.714	3.83	42	9	204⅓	229	86	61	2
1929	18	7	.720	3.66	50	18	270⅔	277	107	82	2
1930	15	10	.600	6.20	46	11	225	291	86	75	0
1931	16	8	.667	4.49	39	14	180⅓	190	66	54	1
1932	19	11	.633	3.21	40	15	238⅔	262	70	73	1
1933	20	12	.625	2.75	41	20	258⅔	261	68	84	4
1934	18	10	.643	3.83	40	15	209⅓	213	54	75	1
Career	176	136	.564	3.86	542	151	2,721	2,950	859	850	16

An exceptional starting pitcher, with seven consecutive seasons (1928–34) in which he won 15 or more games, Guy Bush was a major factor in two Cub pennant-winning seasons, 1929 and 1932. During 12 seasons with the Cubs (1923–34) he won 152 games and lost 101.

Discovered by long-time Cub scout Jack Doyle while pitching for Greenville, Mississippi in the Cotton States League, Bush was purchased from the minor league team owner for $1,200 and a jug of corn whiskey. Brought up to the Cubs in 1923, he was taught how to throw a curveball and a screwball by Grover Cleveland Alexander.

Bush began to come into his own in 1926 with an 13–9 record, and in 1929, when the Cubs won their first pennant since 1918, he was 18–7, combining with Charlie Root and Pat Malone in an outstanding pitching trio. Bush was the only Cub to win a game in the 1929 World Series, beating the Philadelphia Athletics 3–1 in the third game.

His contribution to the 1932 pennant winners was a 19–11 record, but he was hammered by the Yankees in two starts in the World Series, which New York swept in four games.

Though one of the outstanding pitchers in the NL for almost a decade, Bush was troubled before the 1933 season because he had never won 20 games. He asked Cub fans to improve his luck by sending him four-leaf clovers; he went 20–12 that year.

Guy Bush

He was 18–10 in 1934, his final campaign with the Cubs, who traded him to Pittsburgh after the season. At Pittsburgh, his chief claim to fame was to yield the final home runs of Babe Ruth's career, numbers 713 and 714, on May 25, 1935, when Ruth was finishing out his run with the Boston Braves.

During the manpower shortage of World War II, though Bush's career had apparently ended in 1938, he attempted a comeback in 1945 at the age of 43 with the Cincinnati Reds. He appeared in four games before giving up pitching for good.

Callahan, Nixey

Cubs: 1897–1900　　　　**D:** October 4, 1934
Pitcher, outfielder　　**Batted right, threw right**
Birthplace: Fitchburg, Massachusetts　**Ht.** 5–10; **Wt.** 180
B: March 18, 1874

Callahan, James Joseph

Cubs	W	L	Pct	ERA	G	CG	IP	H	BB	K	ShO
1897	12	9	.571	4.03	23	21	189⅔	221	55	52	1
1898	20	10	.667	2.46	31	30	274⅓	267	71	73	2
1899	21	12	.636	3.06	35	33	294⅓	327	76	77	3
1900	13	16	.448	3.82	32	32	285⅓	347	74	77	2
Career	99	73	.576	3.39	195	169	1,603	1,748	437	445	11

Cubs	G	AB	H	AVG	RBI	R	2B	3B	HR	SLG	SB
1897	94	360	105	.292	47	60	18	6	3	.400	12
1898	40	164	43	.262	22	27	7	3	0	.366	3
1899	47	150	39	.260	18	21	4	3	0	.327	9
1900	32	115	27	.235	9	16	3	2	0	.296	5
Career	923	3,295	901	.273	394	442	135	46	11	.352	186

Nixey Callahan

Jose Cardenal

Jimmy "Nixey" Callahan was a sensation when brought up from the minors to the Cubs in 1897, Cap Anson's last year as player-manager, because he was both an outstanding pitching prospect and a hard-hitting outfielder.

Callahan combined both talents in one of the Cubs' most memorable games on June 29, 1897, when they defeated Louisville by the record score of 36–7. Not only was he the winning pitcher, but he also had five hits in seven at bats, including two doubles, and scored four runs. For the season, Callahan was 12–9 and batted .292 in 360 at bats, playing four other positions when he wasn't pitching.

Callahan's record was 20–10, 21–12, and 13–16 for the Cubs the next three seasons, until he jumped to the White Sox of the new AL in 1901. Between pitching assignments, he continued to fill in at various positions. Callahan went on to two tenures as White Sox player-manager, mostly playing the outfield, and in his last baseball stint managed Pittsburgh in 1916 and part of 1917.

Cardenal, Jose

Cubs: 1972–77
Outfielder
Birthplace: Matanzas, Cuba

B: October 7, 1943
Bats right, throws right
Ht. 5–10; **Wt.** 170

Cardenal, Jose Rosario

Cubs	G	AB	H	AVG	RBI	R	2B	3B	HR	SLG	SB
1972	143	533	155	.291	70	96	24	6	17	.454	25
1973	145	522	158	.303	68	80	33	2	11	.437	19
1974	143	542	159	.293	72	75	35	3	13	.441	23
1975	154	574	182	.317	68	85	30	2	9	.423	34
1976	136	521	156	.299	47	64	25	2	8	.401	23
1977	199	226	54	.239	30	28	12	1	3	.341	3
Career	2,017	6,964	1,913	.275	775	936	333	46	138	.395	329

A likeable, colorful outfielder who quickly earned a reputation as a "hot dog," Jose Cardenal bounced around the major leagues for nine seasons before he was acquired at the age of 28 by the Cubs before the 1972 season. He quickly became a favorite of Chicago's Hispanic population and was a

standout defensively and offensively for most of his six seasons with the Cubs, playing right and left fields. Cardenal entertained the fans by doing juggling acts during batting practice and his teammates by playing the violin in the clubhouse.

With all that, he was a solid performer, batting over .290 in his first five seasons in Chicago, and bringing base-stealing skills to a usually lead-footed Cubs offense. In his best year, 1975, Cardenal batted .317 in 154 games and stole 34 bases, the most by a Cub since Kiki Cuyler's 37 in 1930. He batted .303 in 1973. Despite his light frame, Cardenal had some power, hitting a career-high 17 home runs in 1972.

Cardenal's biggest day as a Cub came on May 2, 1976, when he had six hits (four singles, a double, and a home run) and drove in four runs, including the game winner in the 14th inning in a 6–5 victory at San Francisco.

A knee injury sidelined Cardenal most of the 1977 season, and that fall he was traded to the Phillies. His playing career ended in 1980, and he turned to coaching.

Cardwell, Don

Cubs: 1960–62
Pitcher
Birthplace: Winston-Salem, North Carolina

B: December 7, 1935
Bats right, throws right
Ht. 6–4; **Wt.** 210

Cardwell, Donald Eugene

Cubs	W	L	Pct	ERA	G	CG	IP	H	BB	K	ShO
1960	8	14	.364	4.37	31	6	177	166	68	129	1
1961	15	14	.517	3.82	39	13	259⅓	243	88	156	3
1962	7	16	.360	4.92	41	6	195⅔	205	60	104	1
Career	102	138	.425	3.92	410	72	2,123	2,009	671	1,211	17

A much-traveled journeyman pitcher, Don Cardwell had one brief moment of glory with the Cubs after they acquired him from Philadelphia on May 13, 1960. Two days later, in his first start in a Cub uniform, Cardwell pitched a no-

Don Cardwell

A better-than-average pitcher, right-hander Tex Carleton contributed to two Cub pennants (1935, 1938) during his four seasons with the team. Acquired after the 1934 season from St. Louis, where he had been a stablemate of Dizzy Dean and his brother Paul on the World Series champion Gashouse Gang, Carleton tied for the NL lead in shutouts with four in 1936.

Carleton's best year with the Cubs was 1937, when he was 16–8, sharing the team lead in victories with Larry French, who was 16–10. He was the losing pitcher in his only World Series start for the Cubs in 1935. Carleton gave up just one hit and one earned run in seven innings, but lost the fourth game 2–1 to the Detroit Tigers.

By 1939, Carleton's career was near its end, though he pitched briefly for Brooklyn in 1940 before retiring.

Cavarretta, Phil

Cubs: 1934–53
First baseman, outfielder
Birthplace: Chicago

B: July 19, 1916
Bats left, throws left
Ht. 5–11; **Wt.** 175

Cavarretta, Philip Joseph

Cubs	G	AB	H	AVG	RBI	R	2B	3B	HR	SLG	SB
1934	7	21	8	.381	6	5	0	1	1	.619	1
1935	146	589	162	.275	82	85	28	12	8	.404	4
1936	124	458	125	.273	56	55	18	1	9	.376	8
1937	106	329	94	.286	56	43	18	7	5	.429	7
1938	92	268	64	.239	28	29	11	4	1	.321	4
1939	22	55	15	.273	0	4	3	1	0	.364	2
1940	65	193	54	.280	22	34	11	4	2	.409	3
1941	107	346	99	.286	40	46	18	4	6	.413	2
1942	136	482	130	.270	54	59	28	4	5	.363	7
1943	143	530	154	.291	73	93	27	9	8	.421	3
1944	152	614	197	.321	82	106	35	15	5	.451	4
1945	132	498	177	.355	97	94	34	10	6	.500	5
1946	139	510	150	.294	78	89	28	10	8	.444	2
1947	127	459	144	.314	63	58	22	5	2	.397	2
1948	111	334	93	.278	40	41	16	5	3	.383	4
1949	105	360	106	.294	49	46	22	4	8	.444	2
1950	82	256	70	.273	31	49	11	1	10	.441	1
1951	89	206	64	.311	28	24	7	1	6	.442	0
1952	41	63	15	.238	8	7	1	1	1	.333	0
1953	27	21	6	.286	3	3	3	0	0	.429	0
Career	2,030	6,754	1,977	.293	920	990	347	99	95	.416	65

Few Cub players have been as popular or had such long careers as Phil Cavarretta, who played 20 years for the Cubs and was player-manager the last three seasons, 1951–53, though ironically he ended his career on the South Side with the rival White Sox.

Cavarretta had a built-in advantage in fan appeal because he was a native Chicagoan and had been a baseball standout at Lane Technical High School on Chicago's North Side, leading his team to three consecutive city championships. Gruff and undiplomatic, nevertheless he was respected by the fans because of his workmanlike play and competitive spirit.

Cavarretta was signed by the Cubs out of high school in 1934 and sent to the minor leagues. Called up late in the season, at age 18 he was one of the youngest men ever to play for the Cubs.

In his first major league game, September 25, 1934, Cavar-

hit, no-run game in the second game of a Sunday double-header against St. Louis at Wrigley Field.

Cardwell walked the second man he faced in the game, then retired 26 batters in succession, though it took a spectacular, one-handed catch at his shoetops by Walt Moryn, a lead-footed outfielder, of a sinking line drive by Joe Cunningham to retire the final batter for a 4–0 victory.

Cardwell finished the season with an 8–14 record for the Cubs (9–16 overall), rose to 15–14 for a poor Cub team in 1961, and went 7–16 in 1962 before being traded to Pittsburgh to continue his career for another eight seasons.

Carleton, Tex

Cubs: 1935–38
Pitcher
Birthplace: Comanche, Texas
B: August 19, 1906

D: January 11, 1977
Batted right, threw right
Ht. 6–1; **Wt.** 180

Carleton, James Otto

Cubs	W	L	Pct	ERA	G	CG	IP	H	BB	K	ShO
1935	11	8	.579	3.89	31	8	171	169	60	84	0
1936	14	10	.583	3.65	35	12	197⅓	206	67	88	4
1937	16	8	.667	3.15	32	18	208⅔	183	94	105	4
1938	10	9	.526	5.42	33	9	167⅔	213	74	80	0
Career	100	76	.568	3.91	293	91	1,607⅓	1,630	561	808	16

retta hit a home run as the Cubs beat Cincinnati 1–0. He further impressed manager Charlie Grimm, who immediately gave him the nickname "Phillibuck," in six other games by batting .381 in 21 times at bat before the season ended.

In fact, Grimm was so impressed that the next spring he handed Cavarretta the first base job he had held down with the Cubs for more than a decade. The youngster responded by batting .275 in 146 games in his first full season, hitting eight home runs and driving in 82 runs. He played a large role in the 21-game late-season winning streak that carried the Cubs to the pennant.

Despite his strong start, Cavarretta was not to be as productive again until 1943. For the next seven seasons he moved in and out of the lineup, at first base or in the outfield, batting between .270 and .286 most years. He was a rare Cub standout in the 1938 World Series, swept in four games by the New York Yankees, with six hits in 13 at bats.

It wasn't until the age of 27, in 1943, that Cavarretta began to realize his full potential. He took over first base full-time again, batted .291 in 143 games, and was named team captain. In 1944 he raised his average to .321 in 152 games, with 15 home runs and 82 RBIs.

But 1945 was Cavarretta's career year. With Grimm at the helm again, he led the Cubs to another pennant, led the league in batting with .355, drove in 97 runs, and earned the NL Most Valuable Player award. He also sparkled in the World Series (though the Cubs lost in seven games to Detroit), batting .423 and tying for most hits with 11.

Cavarretta batted .294 in 1946 and .314 in 1947. By 1950 he was reduced to part-time duty, and when the Cubs fired manager Frankie Frisch midway in the 1951 season, Cavarretta was named his successor. (For details of Cavarretta's managerial career, turn to Chapter 4, "The Skippers.")

Fired as manager by owner P. K. Wrigley in spring training 1954, Cavarretta was signed by the White Sox as a utility player and responded by batting .316 in 71 games. His playing career ended early in 1955. He concluded his baseball career as a minor league manager and hitting instructor and as a major league coach.

Cey, Ron

Cubs: 1983–86
Third baseman
Nickname: Penguin
Birthplace: Tacoma, Washington

B: February 15, 1948
Bats right, throws right
Ht. 5–9; Wt. 185

Cey, Ronald Charles

Cubs	G	AB	H	AVG	RBI	R	2B	3B	HR	SLG	SB
1983	159	581	160	.275	90	73	33	1	24	.460	0
1984	146	505	121	.240	97	71	27	0	25	.442	3
1985	145	500	116	.232	63	64	18	2	22	.408	1
1986	97	256	70	.273	36	42	21	0	13	.508	0
Career	2,073	7,162	1,868	.261	1,139	977	328	21	316	.445	24

A veteran of 11 seasons with the Los Angeles Dodgers when he was acquired by the Cubs in a trade on January 20, 1983, power-hitting third baseman Ron Cey played a major role in general manager Dallas Green's rebuilding of the team into a pennant contender in the mid-1980s.

Though he had slowed down in the field by the age of 35 when he arrived in Chicago, Cey still had a home run swing

Ron Cey

and the ability to drive in runs. In his first year with the Cubs, 1983, Cey hit 24 home runs and drove in 90 runs. The next season his power helped lift the Cubs to the NL East Division championship and into postseason play for the first time since the 1945 World Series as he hit 25 home runs and drove in 97 runs, leading the team in both categories. Cey added 22 home runs in 1985, but age and injuries took their toll the next year and the Cubs in early 1987 traded him to Oakland, where he finished his career that season.

Chance, Frank

Cubs: 1898–1912
First baseman
Nicknames: Husk, The Peerless Leader
Birthplace: Fresno, California

B: September 9, 1877
D: September 15, 1924
Batted right, threw right
Ht. 6–0; Wt. 190

Chance, Frank Leroy

Cubs	G	AB	H	AVG	RBI	R	2B	3B	HR	SLG	SB
1898	53	147	41	.279	14	32	4	3	1	.367	7
1899	64	192	55	.286	22	37	6	2	1	.354	10
1900	56	149	44	.295	13	26	9	3	0	.396	8
1901	69	241	67	.278	36	38	12	4	0	.361	30
1902	75	236	67	.284	31	40	9	4	1	.369	28
1903	125	441	144	.327	81	83	24	10	2	.440	67
1904	124	451	140	.310	49	89	16	10	6	.430	42
1905	118	392	124	.316	70	92	16	12	2	.434	38
1906	136	474	151	.319	71	103	24	10	3	.430	57
1907	111	382	112	.293	49	58	19	2	1	.361	35
1908	129	452	123	.272	55	65	27	4	2	.363	27
1909	93	324	88	.272	46	53	16	4	0	.346	29
1910	88	295	88	.298	36	54	12	8	0	.393	16
1911	31	88	21	.239	17	23	6	3	1	.409	9
1912	2	5	1	.200	0	2	0	0	0	.200	1
Career	1,286	4,293	1,271	.296	596	798	200	79	20	.393	405

In the late 1890s, Bill Lange, the Cubs' star outfielder, visited the campus of what then was Washington College in Irvington, California, to attend a baseball game and was tremendously impressed by one of the youngsters, a solidly built catcher. Lange excitedly wrote to Cub manager Cap Anson, saying, "Here's the most promising player I ever saw. Some day he'll be a wonder."

Lange was to be proven right about the prospect, Frank Chance, the son of a Fresno banker. Chance had planned to study medicine, but on the recommendation of Lange, Cub president James Hart signed the youngster to a contract. By the time Chance reported to the Cub training camp at West Baden, Indiana, in 1898, Anson had been replaced as manager by Tommy Burns.

Burns, too, was impressed by Chance, then only 20 years old. He liked his intelligence, poise, and enormous strength—Chance's nickname at the time was "Husk" for his husky build—and played him in 53 games as a rookie in 1898. Chance hit .279.

For the next four seasons Chance played several positions. He turned out to be injury-prone behind the plate, often being laid up for weeks with broken fingers caused by foul tips. When Frank Selee became manager in 1902, he persuaded a reluctant Chance, who at first threatened to quit if he could no longer catch, to move permanently to first base.

The shift was the making of Chance's career. He became an adept fielder at first base and blossomed offensively, batting over .300 for four consecutive seasons (1903–1906), with a high of .327 in 1903. He was a dangerous hitter until he stopped playing regularly after 1910. He was an exceptional base runner and twice tied for the NL lead in stolen bases, with 67 in 1903 and 57 in 1906. His record of 67 steals remains a high for a Cub in the 20th century.

Chance was extremely aggressive, crowding the plate at bat, and was hit by pitches 37 times in his career, including five times in a doubleheader on May 30, 1904. He was hit in the head so often that he suffered from constant headaches and hearing loss, and in 1912 underwent brain surgery to relieve a blood clot. The constant battering curtailed his playing career.

When Chance replaced the ailing Selee as manager midway in the 1905 season, he quickly earned the nickname "The Peerless Leader," bestowed on him by Charlie Dryden, a Chicago sportswriter. He led the Cubs during their greatest era, winning four pennants in five years (1906–08, 1910), with World Series victories in 1907 and 1908, and to a record 116 victories (36 losses) in 1906. (For details of Chance's managerial career, see Chapter 4, "The Skippers.")

Chance left the Cubs after the 1912 season, then played in a few games for the New York Yankees, whom he also managed, the next two years before ending his playing career.

Cheney, Larry

Cubs: 1911–15		**D:** January 6, 1969
Pitcher		**Batted right, threw right**
Birthplace: Belleville, Kansas		**Ht.** 6–2; **Wt.** 185
B: May 2, 1886		

Cheney, Laurence Russell

Cubs	W	L	Pct	ERA	G	CG	IP	H	BB	K	ShO
1911	1	0	1.000	0.00	3	0	10	8	3	11	0
1912	26	10	.722	2.85	42	28	303⅓	262	111	140	4
1913	21	14	.600	2.57	54	25	305	271	98	136	2
1914	20	18	.526	2.54	50	21	311⅓	239	140	157	3
1915	8	9	.471	3.56	25	6	131⅓	120	55	68	2
Career	116	100	.537	2.70	313	132	1,881⅓	1,605	733	926	20

Wild but effective, spitballer Larry Cheney broke in spectacularly with the Cubs in 1912 with a 26–10 rookie record. He led the league in wins, complete games (28), and percentage (.722). In his next two seasons he was 21–14 and 20–18.

Cheney pitched one of the most unusual games in baseball history on September 14, 1913, beating the New York Giants 7–0 on 14 hits, the most ever allowed in a nine-inning, complete-game shutout.

Cheney slumped to 8–9 in 1915 and was traded to the Brooklyn Dodgers late in the season. His career ended in 1919.

Larry Cheney

Clarkson, John

White Stockings: 1884–87
Pitcher
Birthplace: Cambridge, Massachusetts
B: July 1, 1861

D: February 4, 1909
Batted right, threw right
Ht. 5–10; **Wt.** 155

Clarkson, John Gibson

White Stockings	W	L	Pct	ERA	G	CG	IP	H	BB	K	ShO
1884	10	3	.769	2.14	14	12	118	94	25	102	0
1885	53	16	.768	1.85	70	68	623	497	97	308	10
1886	35	17	.673	2.41	55	50	466⅔	419	86	313	3
1887	38	21	.644	3.08	60	56	523	513	92	237	2
Career	326	177	.648	2.81	531	485	4,536⅓	4,295	1,191	1,978	37

Almost single-handedly, slim, temperamental John Clarkson pitched the White Stockings to pennants in 1885 and 1886. The renamed Cubs would not win another until 1906.

Clarkson, who unlike most pitchers of his day threw overhand, relied on a fastball, curve, and change-up to win 53 games against 16 losses in 1885, his second year with the White Stockings. He was 35–17 in 1886 and 38–21 in 1887.

Before the 1887 season, owner Al Spalding sold Clarkson to Boston for $10,000, and he rejoined catcher Mike "King" Kelly, whom the White Stockings had sold to the same team for the same sum the year before. The pair became known as the $20,000 battery. Clarkson continued his fine career until 1894, winding up with a record of 326–177.

His manager, Cap Anson, said of Clarkson, after his high-strung former pitcher died in an insane asylum in 1909: "Clarkson was one of the greatest pitchers of all time, certainly the best Chicago ever had."

Clarkson was elected to the Hall of Fame in 1963.

John Clarkson

Cole, King

Cubs: 1909–12
Pitcher
Birthplace: Toledo, Iowa
B: April 15, 1886

D: January 6, 1916
Batted right, threw right
Ht. 6–1; **Wt.** 170

Cole, Leonard Leslie

Cubs	W	L	Pct	ERA	G	CG	IP	H	BB	K	ShO
1909	1	0	1.000	0.00	1	1	9	6	3	1	1
1910	20	4	.833	1.80	33	21	239⅔	174	130	114	4
1911	18	7	.720	3.13	32	13	221⅓	188	99	101	2
1912	1	2	.333	10.89	8	0	19	36	24	10	0
Career	56	27	.675	3.12	129	47	730⅔	657	331	298	9

Spectacular but brief sums up Leonard "King" Cole's career with the Cubs. The right-hander broke in with a six-hit shutout late in the 1909 season, then helped pitch the Cubs to a pennant as a rookie in 1910 with a 20–4 record and an .833 percentage, the second best by a Cub pitcher with 15 or more decisions in the 20th century.

Cole continued his fine pitching in 1911 with an 18–7 mark, but slipped in 1912 and was traded to Detroit. He wound up his career with the New York Yankees in 1915 and died the next year at the age of 29.

Corcoran, Larry

White Stockings: 1880–85
Pitcher
Birthplace: Brooklyn, New York

B: August 10, 1859
D: October 14, 1891
Batted left, threw right

Corcoran, Lawrence J.

White Stockings	W	L	Pct	ERA	G	CG	IP	H	BB	K	ShO
1880	43	14	.754	1.95	63	57	536⅓	404	99	268	5
1881	31	14	.689	2.31	45	43	396⅔	380	78	150	4
1882	27	13	.675	1.95	40	39	355⅔	281	63	170	3
1883	34	20	.630	2.49	56	51	473⅔	483	82	216	3
1884	35	23	.603	2.40	60	57	516⅔	473	116	272	7
1885	5	2	.714	3.64	7	6	59⅓	63	24	10	1
Career	177	90	.663	2.36	278	257	2,392⅓	2,147	496	1,103	23

The only Cub pitcher to throw three no-hitters, Larry Corcoran also was the first to pitch one, in 1880. He helped the White Stockings win three consecutive pennants, 1880–82, blazing into the league as a rookie in 1880 with a 43–14 record. He won 30 or more games in four of his five full seasons with the White Stockings.

Corcoran injured his pitching arm after winning five of his first seven decisions in 1885 and was released by the White Stockings. He was signed by the New York Giants but won just two more games. His career ended in 1887. An alcoholic, he died four years later.

Larry Corcoran

Cuyler, Kiki

Cubs: 1928–35
Outfielder
Birthplace: Harrisville, Michigan
B: August 30, 1899

D: February 11, 1950
Batted right, threw right
Ht. 5–11; **Wt.** 180

Cuyler, Hazen Shirley

Cubs	G	AB	H	AVG	RBI	R	2B	3B	HR	SLG	SB
1928	133	499	142	.285	79	92	25	9	17	.473	37
1929	139	509	183	.360	102	111	29	7	15	.532	43
1930	156	642	228	.355	134	155	50	17	13	.547	37
1931	154	613	202	.330	88	110	37	12	9	.473	13
1932	110	446	130	.291	77	58	19	9	10	.442	9
1933	70	262	83	.317	35	37	13	3	5	.447	4
1934	142	559	189	.338	69	89	42	8	6	.474	15
1935	45	157	42	.268	18	22	5	1	4	.389	3
Career	1,879	7,161	2,299	.321	1,065	1,305	394	157	127	.473	328

Kiki Cuyler was an established star when the Cubs acquired him in a trade with Pittsburgh after the 1927 season. A feud with manager Donie Bush, who angrily benched him during the 1927 World Series in which the Pirates were swept by the New York Yankees, made Cuyler expendable. That judgment proved a blessing for the Cubs; Cuyler, a superb outfielder and great hitter, helped them to pennants in 1929 and 1932.

Cub teammate Charlie Grimm spoke highly of Cuyler. "He was the most meticulous ballplayer I've ever known," Grimm wrote in his autobiography. "He was the closest ap-proach baseball ever had to a matinee idol. He wore his uni-form like a tuxedo."

Cuyler reached his peak in 1929 and 1930, batting .360 and .355. He played right field in one of the greatest outfields ever assembled, with Hack Wilson in center field and Riggs Stephenson in left. He had a great throwing arm and was an excellent base runner, four times leading the NL in stolen bases, with a high of 43 in 1929.

In Cuyler's best season with the Cubs, 1930, he batted .355, with 50 doubles, 17 triples, 13 home runs, and 37 stolen bases, while scoring 155 runs and driving in 134. He batted over .300 in five of his seven full seasons with the Cubs, in-cluding 1934, when he hit .338, but was released during a slump midway in the 1935 season. He played three more years in the major leagues.

He was elected to the Hall of Fame in 1968.

Dahlen, Bill

White Stockings: 1891–98
Shortstop
Birthplace: Nelliston, New York
B: January 5, 1870

D: December 3, 1950
Batted right, threw right
Ht. 5–9; **Wt.** 180

Dahlen, William Frederick

White Stockings	G	AB	H	AVG	RBI	R	2B	3B	HR	SLG	SB
1891	135	549	143	.260	76	114	18	13	9	.390	21
1892	143	581	169	.291	58	114	23	9	5	.422	60
1893	116	485	145	.301	64	113	28	15	5	.452	31
1894	121	508	184	.362	107	150	32	14	15	.569	42
1895	129	516	131	.254	62	106	19	10	7	.370	38
1896	125	474	167	.352	74	137	30	19	9	.553	51
1897	75	276	80	.290	40	67	18	8	6	.478	15
1898	142	521	151	.290	79	96	35	8	1	.393	27
Career	2,443	9,039	2,460	.272	1,233	1,590	414	163	84	.382	547

Bill Dahlen

In manager Cap Anson's words, shortstop Bill Dahlen was "quick as a cat" in the field, with good range and a strong arm. Dahlen joined the White Stockings in 1891 as a third baseman, quickly took over at shortstop, and developed into a fine hitter with power.

Dahlen's career year was 1894 when he batted .362 in 121 games and had two consecutive-game hitting streaks, one of 42 games, among the longest in the game's history. Held in check just one game, Dahlen embarked on another streak, this one of 28 games, thus batting safely in 70 of 71 games.

"Bad Bill" Dahlen also twice achieved the feat, unparalled among Cubs, of hitting three triples in a game. He stole 547 bases during his career, with a peak of 60 in 1892. He was traded to Brooklyn after the 1898 season and remained among the league's best shortstops for another decade. He managed the Dodgers from 1910 to 1913.

Dallessandro, Dom

Cubs: 1940–44, 1946–47
Outfielder
Birthplace: Reading, Pennsylvania
B: October 3, 1913

D: April 29, 1988
Batted left, threw left
Ht. 5–6; **Wt.** 168

Dallessandro, Nicholas Dominic

Cubs	G	AB	H	AVG	RBI	R	2B	3B	HR	SLG	SB
1940	107	287	77	.268	36	33	19	6	1	.387	4
1941	140	486	132	.272	85	73	36	2	6	.391	3
1942	96	264	69	.261	43	30	12	4	4	.383	4
1943	87	176	39	.222	31	13	8	3	1	.318	1
1944	117	381	116	.309	74	53	19	4	8	.438	1
1946	65	89	20	.225	9	4	2	2	1	.326	1
1947	66	115	33	.287	14	18	7	1	1	.391	0
Career	746	1,945	520	.267	303	242	110	23	22	.381	16

Dom Dallesandro

A powerful minor league batter who never lived up to his promise in the major leagues, Dominic Dallessandro became a crowd favorite when he joined the Cubs in 1940 after failing in an earlier trial with the Boston Red Sox. He quickly earned the nickname "Dim Dom" for Diminutive Dominic.

Built along the lines of the great Hack Wilson, short (5–6) and stocky, Dallessandro was an acceptable World War II outfield fill-in, playing seven seasons for the Cubs (1940–44 and 1946–47). Ironically, after he was rejected by the military several times because of poor eyesight, he was drafted into the U.S. Army and was absent in 1945 when the Cubs won a pennant, thus missing a chance to play in a World Series.

In Dallessandro's best year, 1941, he batted .272, with 36 doubles and 85 RBIs in 140 games, while playing left field. During most of his career he served in a utility role. He was released in 1947.

Dalrymple, Abner

White Stockings: 1879–86
Outfielder
Birthplace: Warren, Illinois
B: September 9, 1857

D: January 25, 1939
Batted left, threw right
Ht. 5–10; **Wt.** 175

Dalrymple, Abner Frank

White Stockings	G	AB	H	AVG	RBI	R	2B	3B	HR	SLG	SB
1879	71	333	97	.291	23	47	25	1	0	.372	—
1880	86	382	126	.330	36	91	25	12	0	.458	—
1881	82	362	117	.323	37	72	22	4	1	.414	—
1882	84	397	117	.295	36	96	25	11	1	.421	—
1883	80	363	108	.298	37	78	24	4	2	.402	—
1884	111	521	161	.309	69	111	18	9	22	.505	—
1885	113	492	135	.274	58	109	27	12	11	.445	—
1886	82	331	77	.233	26	62	7	12	3	.353	—
Career	951	4,172	1,202	.288	298	813	217	81	43	.410	42

The regular left fielder on Cap Anson's greatest teams, Abner Dalrymple contributed to five pennant winners (1880–82 and 1885–86), usually as the lead-off batter. The White Stockings signed him after he batted .354 in 1879 as a rookie with a Milwaukee team that folded after that season.

A mediocre fielder who three times led the NL in outfield errors, Abner compensated with his hitting. He had good power, leading the league in home runs with 11 in 1885. (His 22 home runs in 1884 were "tainted" because of the absurd dimensions of Lakefront Park.) His best season at bat was 1880 when he hit .330 in 86 games. He followed that up the next season with .323.

After his poor 1886 season, the White Stockings sold Dalrymple to Pittsburgh.

Abner Dalrymple

Jody Davis

Davis, Jody

Cubs: 1981–88
Catcher
Birthplace: Gainesville, Georgia

B: November 12, 1956
Bats right, throws right
Ht. 6–4; **Wt.** 192

Davis, Jody Richard

Cubs	G	AB	H	AVG	RBI	R	2B	3B	HR	SLG	SB
1981	56	180	46	.256	21	14	5	1	4	.361	0
1982	130	418	109	.261	52	41	20	2	12	.404	0
1983	151	510	138	.271	84	56	31	2	24	.480	0
1984	150	523	134	.256	94	55	24	2	19	.419	5
1985	142	482	112	.232	58	47	30	0	17	.400	1
1986	148	528	132	.250	74	61	27	2	21	.428	0
1987	125	428	106	.248	51	57	12	2	19	.418	1
1988	88	249	57	.229	33	19	9	0	6	.337	0
Career	1,070	3,557	875	.246	489	364	163	11	127	.405	7

A big, red-headed, power-hitting catcher, Jody Davis caught the fans' fancy during the 1980s. The cry "Jo-dee! Jo-dee! Jo-dee!" shook the rafters at Wrigley Field when he came to bat.

Davis broke in with the Cubs in 1981 after being purchased from St. Louis for $25,000 and became the number-one catcher the next year. He blossomed in 1983, tying Ron Cey for the team lead in home runs with 24, while batting .271 with 84 RBIs.

He was a major force when the Cubs finally broke through in 1984 to win the NL East title after a 39-year absence from postseason play. Davis drove in 94 runs and had 19 home runs while hitting .256. The highlight of his 1984 season, and probably of his career, came in a three-game mid-June series against the contending St. Louis Cardinals in which he hit three home runs, including a grand slam, and drove in 10 runs. The outburst triggered the beginning of the "Jo-dee!" chant by the fans.

Davis hit 17, 21, and 19 home runs his final three full seasons as a Cub, but injuries took their toll, and late in the '88 season he was traded to Atlanta, where he concluded his career the next year.

Dawson, Andre

Cubs: 1987–92
Outfielder
Nickname: The Hawk
Birthplace: Miami, Florida

B: July 10, 1954
Bats right, throws right
Ht. 6–3; **Wt.** 180

Dawson, Andre Fernando

Cubs	G	AB	H	AVG	RBI	R	2B	3B	HR	SLG	SB
1987	153	621	178	.287	137	90	24	2	49	.568	11
1988	157	591	179	.303	79	78	31	8	24	.504	12
1989	118	416	105	.252	77	62	18	6	21	.476	8
1990	147	529	164	.310	100	72	28	5	27	.535	16
1991	149	563	153	.272	104	69	21	4	31	.488	4
1992	143	542	150	.277	90	60	27	2	22	.456	6
Career	2,627	9,927	2,774	.279	1,591	1,373	503	98	438	.482	314

Andre Dawson

Extremely intense and dedicated, Andre Dawson almost forced the Cubs to sign him as a free agent after 10 seasons as an outstanding right fielder for the Montreal Expos. He had won the NL Rookie of the Year award in 1977 and had established himself as the league's premier right fielder with a strong, accurate throwing arm and a bat that produced a high of 32 home runs and 113 RBIs in 1983.

But Dawson's knees had been ravaged by playing on artificial turf in Montreal, and he hoped to extend his career on the grass at Wrigley Field. He besieged the Cubs in spring training of 1987 by offering his services at a discount. The Cubs signed for $500,000—a bargain price by the inflated standards of the late 1980s—and had no reason to regret it. Not only was Dawson a fine right fielder with an exceptional throwing arm, but also he exploded offensively in one of the greatest offensive displays in Cubs history.

Dawson batted .287, with 49 home runs and 137 RBIs, and won the NL Most Valuable Player award with a team that finished 76–85. His 49 home runs were second only to Hack Wilson's 56 in 1930 among Cubs, and the 137 RBIs were the most since Ernie Banks had driven in 143 in 1959.

Cub fans' adulation of Dawson found a new means of expression, "salaams"—bows from the waist with the arms extended.

Dawson's knee problems were chronic, but he continued to produce for the Cubs during his remaining five years with them, driving in more than 100 runs in two other seasons. In 1989, when the Cubs won the NL East title, he contributed 21 home runs and 77 RBIs despite missing one-third of the campaign, but he got just two hits in 19 at bats as they fell to San Francisco in the NL championship series.

In his final Cubs season, 1992, Dawson played 143 games, batting .277 with 22 home runs and 90 RBIs, but was allowed to depart as a free agent. He concluded his career with the Boston Red Sox and Florida Marlins.

Dean, Dizzy

Cubs: 1938–41　　　　　　　**D:** July 17, 1974
Pitcher　　　　　　　　　　　**Batted right, threw right**
Birthplace: Lucas, Arkansas　**Ht.** 6–2; **Wt.** 182
B: January 16, 1911

Dean, Jay Hanna

Cubs	W	L	Pct	ERA	G	CG	IP	H	BB	K	ShO
1938	7	1	.875	1.81	13	3	74⅔	63	8	22	1
1939	6	4	.600	3.36	19	7	96⅓	98	17	27	2
1940	3	3	.500	5.17	10	3	54	68	20	18	0
1941	0	0	.000	18.00	1	0	1	3	0	1	0
Career	150	83	.644	3.02	317	154	1,967⅓	1,925	453	1,163	26

Dizzy Dean's story properly belongs to the St. Louis Cardinals, for whom he became the last NL pitcher to win 30 games (1934). He was a true character, a larger-than-life personality whose native wit, despite lack of education, became legendary.

Still, he did contribute to a Cubs pennant in 1938 with a 7–1 record achieved purely on guile and experience. His once-great fastball had disappeared because of a lame arm suffered even before Cubs owner P. K. Wrigley acquired him in a deal for three players and $185,000 in cash, an enormous sum during the Great Depression.

"I never had nothing'," Dean admitted. "I couldn't break a pane of glass and I knew it."

Dean added to the legend in the second game of the 1938 World Series against the New York Yankees, clinging to a 3–2 lead going into the eighth inning with his "nothin' ball." The Yankees then exploded and went on to a four-game sweep.

Dean struggled on for three more seasons with the Cubs, with minimal success, before retiring to the broadcasting booth and adding to his legend when baseball began to be televised nationally.

He was elected to the Hall of Fame in 1953.

DeJesus, Ivan

Cubs: 1977–81　　　　　　　**B:** January 9, 1953
Shortstop　　　　　　　　　　**Bats right, throws right**
Birthplace: Santurce, Puerto Rico　**Ht.** 5–11; **Wt.** 178

DeJesus, Ivan

Cubs	G	AB	H	AVG	RBI	R	2B	3B	HR	SLG	SB
1977	155	624	166	.266	40	91	31	7	3	.353	24
1978	160	619	172	.278	35	104	24	7	3	.354	41
1979	160	636	180	.283	52	92	26	10	5	.379	24
1980	157	618	160	.259	33	78	26	3	3	.325	44
1981	106	403	78	.194	13	49	8	4	0	.233	21
Career	1,371	4,602	1,167	.254	324	595	175	48	21	.326	194

Ivan DeJesus figured in two of the best trades in Cubs history, and in between played exceptionally well at shortstop for them, teaming up with second baseman Manny Trillo for two years (1977–78) in what some called the Latin Connection.

Obtained as a throw-in along with Bill Buckner from Los Angeles on January 17, 1977, DeJesus became the best Cub

Ivan DeJesus

Frank Demaree

shortstop since Don Kessinger and held the job for five years. In his best season, 1978, DeJesus batted .278, led the NL in runs scored with 104, and stole 41 bases. In 1980 he stole 44 bases, a high for a Cub shortstop.

DeJesus slipped to .194 in 1981, and early in 1982 was traded to Philadelphia for veteran shortstop Larry Bowa and rookie infielder Ryne Sandberg. He completed his playing career in 1988.

Demaree, Frank

Cubs: 1932–33, 1935–38
Outfielder
Birthplace: Winters, California
B: June 10, 1910

D: August 30, 1958
Batted right, threw right
Ht. 5–11; **Wt.** 185

Demaree, Joseph Franklin

Cubs	G	AB	H	AVG	RBI	R	2B	3B	HR	SLG	SB
1932	23	56	14	.250	6	4	3	0	0	.304	0
1933	134	515	140	.272	51	68	24	6	6	.377	4
1935	107	385	125	.325	66	60	19	4	2	.410	6
1936	154	605	212	.350	96	93	34	3	16	.496	4
1937	154	615	199	.324	115	106	36	6	17	.485	6
1938	129	476	130	.273	62	63	15	7	8	.384	1
Career	1,155	4,144	1,241	.299	591	578	190	36	72	.415	33

During his six seasons with the Cubs (he spent 1934 in the minor leagues), hard-hitting outfielder Frank Demaree (born Joseph Franklin Dimaria) played in three World Series, contributing heavily to league championships in 1935 and 1938.

Demaree batted over .300 for three consecutive seasons, 1935–37, with a high of .350 in 1936, while playing mostly center field or right field. His best year overall was 1937 when he batted .324 with 17 home runs, 115 RBIs, and 106 runs scored.

Demaree hit his first major league home run in the 1932 World Series against the New York Yankees, and hit two more Series home runs in 1935 against Detroit. His total of three World Series home runs is the most by a Cub.

Demaree was traded to the New York Giants after the 1938 season and played his final major league game in 1944.

Dernier, Bob

Cubs: 1984–87
Outfielder
Birthplace: Kansas City, Missouri

B: January 5, 1957
Bats right, throws right
Ht. 6–0; **Wt.** 175

Dernier, Robert Eugene

Cubs	G	AB	H	AVG	RBI	R	2B	3B	HR	SLG	SB
1984	143	536	149	.278	32	94	26	5	3	.362	45
1985	121	469	119	.254	21	63	20	3	1	.316	31
1986	108	324	73	.225	18	32	14	1	4	.312	27
1987	93	199	63	.317	21	38	4	4	8	.497	16
Career	904	2,483	634	.255	152	374	92	16	23	.333	218

The prototype center fielder, lean and fast, Bob Dernier was slightly regarded when the Cubs acquired him in a spring training 1984 trade with Philadelphia as one of two throw-ins accompanying left fielder Gary Matthews, the man they wanted.

Dernier proved a revelation, taking over center field and the leadoff spot as the Cubs rolled to the NL East title. He batted .278 in 143 games; stole 45 bases, the most ever by a Cub center fielder; and played superbly in the outfield. He contributed two 5-for-5 games.

Dernier led off the opener of the NL Championship Series against San Diego with a home run to spark a 13–0 Cubs victory on October 2, 1984. It was the highlight of his career, though he stayed with the team another three seasons. Hampered by injuries, he was unable to regain his productivity and left the Cubs as a free agent after the 1987 season.

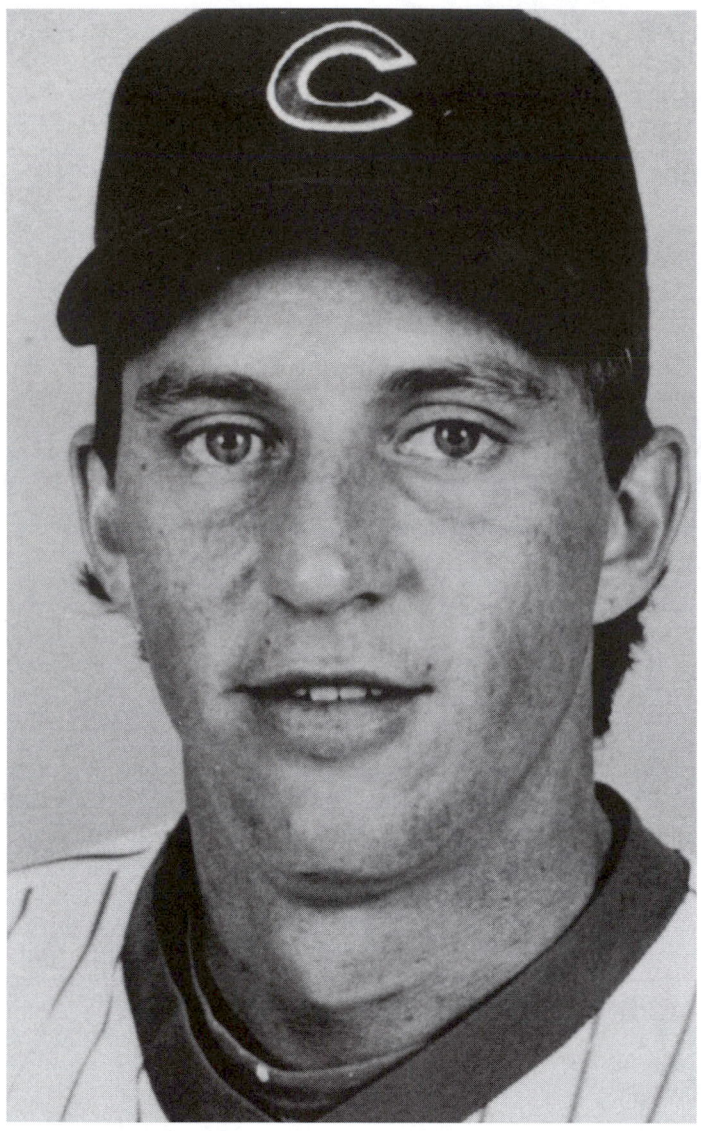

Bob Dernier

Paul Derringer

Derringer, Paul

Cubs: 1943–45
Pitcher
Birthplace: Springfield, Kentucky
B: October 17, 1906

D: November 17, 1987
Batted right, threw right
Ht. 6–3; **Wt.** 205

| Derringer, Samuel Paul | | | | | | | | | | | |
Cubs	W	L	Pct	ERA	G	CG	IP	H	BB	K	ShO
1943	10	14	.417	3.57	32	10	174	184	39	75	2
1944	7	13	.350	4.15	42	7	180	205	39	69	0
1945	16	11	.593	3.45	35	15	213⅔	223	53	86	1
Career	223	212	.513	3.46	579	251	3,645	3,912	761	1,507	32

Paul Derringer had his great years with the Cincinnati Reds, four times winning 20 or more games and helping them to pennants in 1939 and 1940. He was near the end of the trail when the Cubs purchased him in 1943, but he had enough left to pitch three more seasons.

After records of 10–14 and 7–13 in his first two years in Chicago, Derringer revived in 1945 for a 16–11 record with 15 complete games in 35 starts to help the Cubs win the pennant. Three appearances in the World Series defeat concluded his career.

Drabowsky, Moe

Cubs: 1956–60
Pitcher
Birthplace: Ozanna, Poland

B: July 21, 1935
Bats right, throws right
Ht. 6–3; **Wt.** 195

| Drabowsky, Myron Walter | | | | | | | | | | | |
Cubs	W	L	Pct	ERA	G	CG	IP	H	BB	K	ShO
1956	2	4	.333	2.47	9	3	51	37	39	36	0
1957	13	15	.464	3.53	36	12	239⅔	214	94	170	2
1958	9	11	.450	4.51	22	4	125⅔	118	73	77	1
1959	5	10	.333	4.13	31	3	141⅔	138	75	70	1
1960	3	1	.750	6.44	32	0	50⅓	71	23	26	0
Career	88	105	.456	3.71	589	33	1,640⅔	1,441	702	1,162	6

One of the dreariest periods in Cubs history was the late 1950s, but a couple of promising young pitchers, Moe Drabowsky and Dick Drott, known briefly as the Gold Dust Twins, gave them a glimmer of hope. Pitching for the '57 Cubs, a poor team, Drabowsky won 13 games in his first full season, and rookie Drott 15. Each struck out 170 batters.

However, both soon developed arm trouble, and Drott was never successful again. Drabowsky struggled for another three seasons with the Cubs, was traded to Milwaukee in 1961, and resuscitated his career as a much-traveled relief pitcher.

A rarity as a ballplayer born in Poland, and a notorious prankster, Drabowsky gained a few distinctions, dubious and otherwise, with the Cubs. He gave up Stan Musial's 3,000th

Moe Drabowsky

Dick Drott

hit, and he tied a major league record by hitting four batters in one inning. He also pitched a one-hitter.

The high spot of Drabowsky's 17-season major league career came with the Baltimore Orioles in the 1966 World Series against the Los Angeles Dodgers. In the opening game on October 5, Drabowsky relieved starter Dave McNally in the third inning. He struck out six consecutive batters and 11 men altogether and was the winning pitcher as the Orioles began their sweep of the Series.

Drabowsky returned to the Cubs briefly as the pitching coach in 1994.

Drott, Dick

Cubs: 1957–61
Pitcher
Nickname: Hammer
Birthplace: Cincinnati, Ohio

B: July 1, 1936
Bats right, throws right
Ht. 6–0; **Wt.** 185

Drott, Richard Fred

Cubs	W	L	Pct	ERA	G	CG	IP	H	BB	K	ShO
1957	15	11	.577	3.58	38	7	229	200	129	170	3
1958	7	11	.389	5.43	39	4	167⅓	156	99	127	0
1959	1	2	.333	5.93	8	1	27⅓	25	26	15	1
1960	0	6	.000	7.16	23	0	55⅓	63	42	32	0
1961	1	4	.200	4.22	35	0	98	75	51	48	0
Career	27	46	.370	4.78	176	14	687⅔	626	405	460	5

Hard-throwing right-hander Dick Drott appeared headed for a great career when he broke in with the Cubs in 1957 at the age of 20 and compiled a 15–11 record with 170 strike-outs. He struck out 15 Milwaukee Braves, including Hank Aaron four times, in one start to tie the Cub modern, single-game record at the time, and he struck out 14 in another game.

But the next season Drott hurt his arm and was never ef-

fective again, winning nine games and losing 23 in his final four years with the Cubs. Drafted by expansion Houston after the 1961 season, he was 3–12—ironically pitching a 1–0 shutout over the Cubs—in the next two years before drifting out of baseball.

Durham, Leon

Cubs: 1981–87
First baseman, outfielder
Nickname: Bull
Birthplace: Cincinnati, Ohio

B: July 31, 1957
Bats left, throws left
Ht. 6–1; **Wt.** 185

Durham, Leon

Cubs	G	AB	H	AVG	RBI	R	2B	3B	HR	SLG	SB
1981	87	328	95	.290	35	42	14	6	10	.460	25
1982	148	539	168	.312	90	84	33	7	22	.521	28
1983	100	337	87	.258	55	58	18	8	12	.466	12
1984	137	437	132	.279	96	86	30	4	23	.505	16
1985	153	542	153	.282	75	58	32	2	21	.465	7
1986	141	484	127	.262	65	66	18	7	20	.452	8
1987	131	439	120	.273	63	70	22	1	27	.513	2
1988	24	73	16	.219	6	10	6	1	3	.452	0
Career	1,067	3,587	992	.277	530	522	192	40	147	.475	106

Sturdily built and fleet-footed, Leon Durham appeared to have the potential to become an exceptional player, but never lived up to expectations partly because of a succession of injuries and eventually because of an alleged drug problem. Yet he had several good years with the Cubs and was a factor in winning the 1984 NL East title.

General manager Bob Kennedy obtained Durham and two other players from St. Louis in exchange for relief ace Bruce Sutter before the 1981 season. Durham played right field in the strike-curtailed campaign and batted .290 in 87 games, with 10 home runs. He continued to play in the out-

Leon Durham

Dennis Eckersley

field, batting .312 with 22 home runs and 90 RBIs in 1983, but injuries hampered his effectiveness the next year and he sank to .258.

When veteran Bill Buckner was traded early in the '84 season, Durham took over first base, batting .279 with 23 home runs and 96 RBIs, the latter two totals second only to Ron Cey, as the Cubs won the division title. Durham hit .351 with nine home runs and 34 RBIs in May to power the Cubs' early surge.

Durham played acceptably the next three seasons, even hitting a career-high 27 home runs in 1987 though driving in only 63 runs, but the Cubs were eager to make room for promising young first baseman Mark Grace. Early in the 1988 season, Durham was traded to Cincinnati, where his drug problems became public. He played his last major league game the next year.

Eckersley, Dennis

Cubs: 1984–86
Pitcher
Birthplace: Oakland, California

B: October 3, 1954
Bats right, throws right
Ht. 6–2; **Wt.** 190

Eckersley, Dennis Lee

Cubs	W	L	Pct	ERA	G	CG	IP	H	BB	K	ShO
1984	10	8	.556	3.03	24	2	160⅓	152	19	81	0
1985	11	7	.611	3.08	25	6	169⅓	145	19	117	2
1986	6	11	.453	4.57	33	1	201	226	43	137	0
Career	192	165	.538	3.48	964	100	3,193	2,981	722	2,334	20

A veteran who had been a 20-game winner with the Boston Red Sox in 1978, Dennis Eckersley was 29 when the Cubs traded for him on May 25, 1984, to bolster the starting rotation for their successful run for the NL East title.

Eckersley played a major role in the stretch drive with an 8–3 record in 15 starts after the All-Star Game break and was 10–8 with the Cubs, after starting the season with a 4–4 mark in Boston. He was 11–7 in 1985, then slumped to 6–11 the next year, his problems, it later turned out, having been partly due to admitted alcoholism.

The Cubs swapped Eckersley to Oakland for three minor leaguers before the 1987 season in what turned out to be one of the worst deals in their history. Eckersley conquered his drinking habit, switched to the bullpen, and became one of the greatest relief pitchers of all time.

Ellsworth, Dick

Cubs: 1958–66
Pitcher
Birthplace: Lusk, Wyoming

B: March 22, 1940
Bats left, throws left
Ht. 6–3; **Wt.** 180

Ellsworth, Richard Clark

Cubs	W	L	Pct	ERA	G	CG	IP	H	BB	K	ShO
1958	0	1	.000	15.43	1	0	2⅓	4	3	0	0
1960	7	13	.350	3.72	31	6	176⅔	170	72	94	0
1961	10	11	.476	3.86	37	7	186⅔	213	48	91	1
1962	9	20	.310	5.09	37	6	208⅓	241	77	113	0
1963	22	10	.688	2.11	37	19	290⅔	223	75	185	4
1964	14	18	.438	3.75	35	16	256⅔	267	71	148	1
1965	14	15	.483	3.81	36	8	222⅓	227	57	130	0
1966	8	22	.267	3.98	38	9	269⅓	321	51	144	0
Career	115	137	.456	3.72	407	87	2,156	2,274	595	1,140	9

T he only Cub left-hander to win 20 games in a season in the last 75 years, Dick Ellsworth was signed for $50,000 at the age of 18 as a bonus baby out of high school in the summer of 1958. He impressed immediately, shutting out the White Sox 1–0 on four hits in the annual Chicago crosstown game on June 16.

Dick Ellsworth

Don Elston

Success in the NL, however, came slowly to Ellsworth, as he struggled in the minor leagues and with the Cubs for several years. In 1962, his third full season with the Cubs, he suffered with a 9–20 record for a woeful team.

But in 1963, Ellsworth blossomed briefly into one of the best pitchers in baseball, with a 22–10 record for a team that finished just above .500 (82–80) and with an outstanding 2.11 ERA. He was the first Cub left-hander to win 20 games since Hippo Vaughn in 1919 and one of the few pitchers to follow up a 20-game-losing season with a 20-game-winning campaign. As a result, he won the Comeback of the Year award.

Ellsworth's success was short-lived. The next two years he was 14–18 and 14–15, and in 1966 he dropped to 8–22 to lead the NL in defeats. Traded to Philadelphia that winter, he wound up in Boston in 1968 and posted a 16–7 record for the Red Sox, becoming the first player to win two Comeback of the Year awards. His career ended in 1971.

Elston, Don

Cubs: 1953, 1957–64
Pitcher
Birthplace: Campbellstown, Ohio

B: April 6, 1929
Bats right, throws right
Ht. 6–0; **Wt.** 165

Elston, Donald Ray

Cubs	W	L	Pct	ERA	G	CG	IP	H	BB	K	ShO
1953	0	1	.000	15.43	1	0	2⅓	4	3	0	0
1957	6	7	.462	3.56	39	8	144	139	55	102	0
1958	9	8	.529	2.88	69	10	97	75	39	84	0
1959	10	8	.556	3.32	65	13	97⅔	77	46	82	0
1960	8	9	.471	3.40	60	11	127	109	55	85	0
1961	6	7	.462	5.59	58	8	93⅓	108	45	59	0
1962	4	8	.333	2.44	57	8	66⅓	57	32	37	0
1963	4	1	.800	2.83	51	4	70	57	21	41	0
1964	2	5	.286	5.30	48	1	54⅓	68	34	26	0
Career	49	54	.476	3.69	450	63	755⅔	702	327	519	0

Almost exclusively a relief pitcher during his career, slightly built Don Elston started out in the Cub organization and was traded to Brooklyn in 1955, but he was regained by the Cubs in May 1957 and became the ace of their bullpen for several seasons.

Elston twice led the league in games pitched, with 69 in 1958 and 65 in 1959. In his best season, 1959, he was 10–8 (all decisions in relief) with 13 saves and was named to the NL All-Star team. He made no starts after 1957, appearing in relief in all but 15 of 450 games until his retirement after the '64 season. He earned 63 career saves.

Everitt, Bill

Cubs: 1895–1900
Third baseman, first baseman
Nickname: Bad Bill
Birthplace: Fort Wayne, Indiana

B: December 13, 1868
D: January 19, 1938
Batted left, threw right
Ht. 6–1; **Wt.** 185

Everitt, William L.

Cubs	G	AB	H	AVG	RBI	R	2B	3B	HR	SLG	SB
1895	133	550	197	.358	88	129	16	10	3	.440	47
1896	132	575	184	.320	46	130	16	13	2	.403	46
1897	92	379	119	.314	39	63	14	7	5	.427	26
1898	149	596	190	.319	69	102	15	6	0	.364	28
1899	136	536	136	.310	74	87	17	5	1	.366	30
1900	23	91	24	.264	17	10	4	0	0	.308	2
Career	698	2,842	902	.317	341	535	85	43	11	.389	186

An atrocious fielder, even by the standards of the 19th century when playing fields were often ill-kept and bumpy, Bill Everitt was a fine hitter and exceptional base stealer. He broke in as a third baseman with Cap Anson's White Stockings in 1895, batting .358, the highest average ever for a Cub rookie, and hit over .300 the next four seasons.

Everitt made 75 errors at third base in 1897, and when switched to first base in 1898 in an effort to minimize the defensive damage, committed 42 errors that year and 47 the next. After six seasons, the Cubs traded him to minor league Kansas City in 1900; the next year with the Washington Senators was his last in the major leagues.

Evers, Johnny

Cubs: 1902–13
Second baseman
Birthplace: Troy, New York
B: July 21, 1881

D: March 28, 1947
Batted right, threw right
Ht. 5–9; **Wt.** 125

Evers, John Joseph

Cubs	G	AB	H	AVG	RBI	R	2B	3B	HR	SLG	SB
1902	26	89	20	.225	2	7	0	0	0	.225	1
1903	124	464	136	.293	52	70	27	7	0	.381	25
1904	152	532	141	.265	47	49	14	7	0	.318	26
1905	99	340	94	.276	37	44	11	2	1	.329	19
1906	154	533	136	.255	51	65	17	6	1	.315	49
1907	151	508	127	.250	51	66	18	4	2	.313	46
1908	126	416	125	.300	37	83	19	6	0	.375	36
1909	127	463	122	.263	24	88	19	6	1	.337	28
1910	125	433	114	.263	28	87	11	7	0	.321	28
1911	46	155	35	.226	7	29	4	3	0	.290	6
1912	143	478	163	.341	63	73	23	11	1	.441	16
1913	135	444	126	.284	49	81	20	5	3	.372	11
Career	1,783	6,134	1,658	.270	538	919	216	70	12	.334	324

The spark plug of the great Cub teams of the early 1900s, little Johnny Evers (he weighed 105 pounds when he joined the team in 1902) was hot-tempered, intense, and an ardent student of the game.

Evers would have welcomed the computer age with open arms. He reportedly went to bed each night with a rule book and a copy of the *Sporting News* to analyze the statistics of games, whether major league, minor league, or college, so that he could gain some advantage, however small, in the field. He aired his theories of the game in a book, *Touching Second,* cowritten with Hugh Fullerton and published in 1909.

Aggressive and determined, the lightly regarded Evers took over second base when veteran Bobby Lowe suffered a broken knee early in 1903 and kept the job for the next decade, during which the Cubs won four pennants. The first Tinkers-to-Evers-to-Chance double play—leading to the famous verses by Franklin P. Adams—had come the previous season, on September 15, 1902.

A pesky hitter with little power, Evers batted .293 in his first full season and produced a career average of .270, but broke out in 1912 with .341 in 141 games. He batted .316 in four World Series, three with the Cubs and one with the Boston Braves. A great base stealer, he stole 324 during his career, reaching a high of 49 in 1906.

Evers' passion for studying the rules led to the Merkle play, one of the most controversial plays in history. Fred Merkle's failure to touch second after a single that apparently won a game for the Giants over the Cubs in New York decided the pennant race of 1908. Evers' actions and protest

led to the ruling that the game had to be replayed, and when it was, the Cubs won and beat the Giants for the pennant.

Known as "The Crab" for his dour disposition, Evers' feud with shortstop Joe Tinker became legendary.

He managed the Cubs in 1913 after Frank Chance was fired, but finished third and signed with the Braves, whom he sparked to a pennant in 1914. He later managed the Cubs again for part of the 1921 season and the White Sox in 1924. (For details of his managerial career, see Chapter 4, "The Skippers.")

He was elected to the Hall of Fame in 1946.

Flack, Max

Cubs: 1916–22
Outfielder
Birthplace: Belleville, Illinois
B: February 5, 1890

D: July 31, 1975
Batted left, threw left
Ht. 5–7; **Wt.** 148

Flack, Max John

Cubs	G	AB	H	AVG	RBI	R	2B	3B	HR	SLG	SB
1916	141	465	120	.258	20	65	14	3	3	.320	24
1917	131	447	111	.248	21	65	18	7	0	.320	17
1918	123	478	123	.257	41	74	17	10	4	.360	17
1919	116	469	138	.294	35	71	20	4	6	.392	18
1920	135	520	157	.302	49	85	30	6	4	.406	13
1921	133	572	172	.301	37	80	31	4	6	.400	17
1922	17	54	12	.222	6	7	1	0	0	.241	2
Career	1,411	5,252	1,461	.278	391	783	212	72	35	.366	200

A fine right fielder with a strong arm, little Max Flack was one of the Cubs' stalwarts for more than six seasons from 1916 into 1922. He had arrived in the major leagues with the Chicago Whales of the Federal League in 1914. Twice he was the NL's top fielding outfielder.

Only a fair hitter, with little power, Flack barely topped

Max Flack

.300 in two of his seasons with the Cubs. He hit .263 in the futile World Series effort against the Boston Red Sox in 1918.

Among Flack's claims to fame was playing for two teams on the same day in Wrigley Field. Between games of a doubleheader with St. Louis on Memorial Day 1922, he was traded to the Cardinals for outfielder Cliff Heathcote. Flack finished his career with the Cardinals in 1925.

Flint, Silver

White Stockings: 1879–89	**D:** January 14, 1892
Catcher	**Batted right, threw right**
Birthplace: Philadelphia, Pennsylvania	**Ht.** 6–0; **Wt.** 180
B: August 3, 1855	

Flint, Frank Sylvester

White Stockings	G	AB	H	AVG	RBI	R	2B	3B	HR	SLG	SB
1879	79	324	72	.284	41	46	22	6	1	.398	—
1880	74	284	46	.162	17	30	10	4	0	.225	—
1881	80	306	95	.310	34	46	18	0	1	.379	—
1882	81	331	83	.251	44	48	18	8	4	.390	—
1883	85	332	88	.265	—	57	23	4	0	.358	—
1884	73	279	57	.204	—	35	5	2	9	.269	—
1885	68	249	52	.209	19	27	8	2	1	.269	—
1886	54	173	35	.202	13	30	6	2	1	.277	1
1887	49	187	50	.267	21	22	8	6	3	.422	7
1888	22	77	14	.182	3	6	3	0	0	.221	1
1889	15	56	13	.232	9	6	1	0	1	.304	1
Career	743	2,852	682	.239	219	376	129	34	21	.330	10

Hard-bitten, hard-drinking, and tough as nails, Frank "Old Silver" Flint was a catcher for five White Stockings pennant winners (1880–82 and 1885–86) during the regime of manager Cap Anson.

Refusing to wear a glove, which he considered sissy, Flint caught some of the hardest throwers of the era—Larry Goldsmith, Fred Corcoran, and John Clarkson—on the fly while other catchers were taking the ball on the bounce. During his 11 years with the White Stockings, he batted over .300 only once, hitting .310 in 1881, and finished with a career average of .239. His career ended in 1889, and he died three years later of tuberculosis.

Flint replaced Anson as manager briefly in 1879. (For details of his managerial career, turn to Chapter 4, "The Skippers.")

Fondy, Dee

Cubs: 1951–57	**B:** October 31, 1924
First baseman	**Bats left, throws left**
Birthplace: Marion, Illinois	**Ht.** 6–2; **Wt.** 215

Fondy, Dee Virgil

Cubs	G	AB	H	AVG	RBI	R	2B	3B	HR	SLG	SB
1951	49	170	46	.271	20	25	7	2	3	.388	5
1952	145	554	166	.300	67	69	21	9	10	.424	13
1953	150	595	184	.309	78	79	24	11	18	.477	10
1954	141	568	162	.285	49	77	30	4	9	.400	20
1955	150	574	152	.265	65	69	23	8	17	.422	8
1956	137	543	146	.269	46	52	22	9	9	.392	9
1957	11	51	16	.314	2	3	3	1	0	.412	1
Career	967	3,502	1,000	.286	373	437	144	47	69	.413	84

Dee Fondy

As the replacement for aging star first baseman Phil Cavarretta, Dee Fondy never lived up to expectations, possibly because his start in the major leagues was delayed until he was 27 years old by service in World War II.

Obtained in late 1950 from the Brooklyn organization, Fondy hit a bases-loaded triple in his first major league at bat on April 17, 1951. After a little more seasoning in the minor leagues, he took over first base for the Cubs in 1952 and kept the job until he was traded to Pittsburgh early in the 1957 season.

Fondy batted .300 and .309 in his first two full seasons with the Cubs, and reached his highs of 18 home runs and 78 RBIs in 1953. He finished his career with Cincinnati in 1958.

French, Larry

Cubs: 1935–41	**D:** February 9, 1987
Pitcher	**Batted right, threw left**
Birthplace: Visalia, California	**Ht.** 6–1; **Wt.** 195
B: November 1, 1907	

French, Lawrence Herbert

Cubs	W	L	Pct	ERA	G	CG	IP	H	BB	K	ShO
1935	17	10	.630	2.96	42	16	246⅓	279	44	90	4
1936	18	9	.667	3.39	43	16	252⅓	262	54	104	4
1937	16	10	.615	3.98	42	11	208	229	65	100	4
1938	10	19	.345	3.80	43	10	201⅓	210	62	83	3
1939	15	8	.652	3.29	36	10	194	205	50	98	2
1940	14	14	.500	3.29	40	18	246	240	64	107	3
1941	5	14	.263	4.63	26	6	138	161	43	60	1
Career	197	171	.535	3.44	570	199	3,152	3,375	819	1,187	40

Larry French was a rare commodity in Cub history, an outstanding left-handed starter and consistent winner. A veteran, he was obtained from Pittsburgh in a trade after the 1934 season. He won 17 and lost 10 in 1935 as the Cubs won a pennant. He lost both his starts to the Detroit Tigers in the World Series.

French won 18 and 16 games in the next two seasons, but slumped to 10–19 in 1938 when the Cubs again won a pen-

Larry French

Augie Galan

nant. He rebounded to 15–8 in 1939, was even at 14–14 in 1940, and slumped to 5–14 before the Cubs traded him to Brooklyn late in the 1941 season. He was 15–4 for the Dodgers in 1942, before rejoining the U.S. Navy. He continued his naval career as an officer until retiring in 1969.

Galan, Augie

Cubs: 1934–41
Outfielder
Birthplace: Berkeley, California
B: May 25, 1912

D: December 28, 1993
Batted both, threw right
Ht. 6–0; **Wt.**175

Galan, August John

Cubs	G	AB	H	AVG	RBI	R	2B	3B	HR	SLG	SB
1934	66	192	50	.260	22	31	6	2	5	.391	4
1935	154	646	203	.314	79	133	41	11	12	.467	22
1936	145	575	152	.264	81	74	26	4	8	.365	16
1937	147	611	154	.252	78	104	24	10	18	.412	23
1938	110	395	113	.286	69	52	16	9	6	.418	8
1939	148	549	167	.304	71	104	36	8	6	.432	8
1940	68	209	48	.230	22	33	14	2	3	.359	9
1941	65	120	25	.208	13	18	3	0	1	.258	1
Career	1,742	5,937	1,706	.287	830	1,004	336	74	100	.419	123

Manager Charlie Grimm converted rookie infielder Augie Galan into a switch-hitter after the 1934 season and uncovered a .314-hitting center fielder who helped the Cubs win a pennant in 1935. The switch-hitting Galan led the league in stolen bases with 22 and runs scored with 133, while hitting 41 doubles, 11 triples, and 12 home runs.

As a bonus, after the season it was discovered that Galan had become the first player to go an entire campaign (646 at bats) without hitting into a double play.

Galan never matched this production again for the Cubs, but he remained a solid outfielder for the next four seasons,

though Grimm switched him to left field in 1937 because of a weak arm. He hit a career-high 18 home runs in 1937 and again led the league in stolen bases with 23 while batting .252. In 1938 he batted .286 as the Cubs won another pennant. Galan also has the distinction of being the first batter to hit home runs from both sides of the plate in one game (June 25, 1937).

Injuries caught up with Galan in 1940, when he played in just 68 games. In 1941 he batted .208 in 65 games and was sold to Brooklyn for $2,500. It was a bargain for the Dodgers: Galan batted .300 in three of his six seasons with them. He completed a 16-year playing career in 1949.

Goldsmith, Larry

White Stockings: 1880–84
Pitcher
Birthplace: New Haven, Connecticut
B: May 15, 1852

D: March 28, 1939
Batted right, threw right
Ht. 6–1; **Wt.** 195

Goldsmith, Fred Ernest

White Stockings	W	L	Pct	ERA	G	CG	IP	H	BB	K	ShO
1880	21	3	.875	1.75	26	22	210⅓	189	18	90	4
1881	24	13	.649	2.59	39	37	330	328	44	76	5
1882	28	16	.636	2.42	44	44	405	377	38	109	4
1883	25	19	.568	3.15	46	40	383⅓	456	39	82	2
1884	9	11	.450	4.26	21	20	188	245	29	34	1
Career	112	67	.625	2.73	188	173	1,609⅔	1,685	171	433	16

By the time Fred Goldsmith joined the Cubs in 1880 he was 28 and considered the inventor of the curveball, which he had thrown underhand for years in semipro ball. He held a public demonstration in Brooklyn in 1870 when he was 18.

Pioneer baseball journalist Henry Chadwick of the *Brooklyn Eagle* was on hand to report that "what had been an optical illusion is now established fact."

Some reports have credited Arthur "Candy" Cummings with having originated the curveball, but researchers have concluded that the two men developed the pitch independently at about the same time.

Cap Anson is credited with being the first manager to use two starting pitchers regularly when he teamed Goldsmith with Larry Corcoran in rotation. The tandem pitched the White Stockings to three consecutive pennants (1880–82).

Goldsmith was 21–3 in 1880, won 24 games in 1881, 28 games in 1882, and 25 games in 1883 before slipping to 9–11 during the 1884 season when the White Stockings released him. He finished 1884 with Baltimore of the American Association, then quit baseball.

Gore, George

White Stockings: 1879–86
Outfielder
Birthplace: Saccarappa, Maine
B: May 3, 1857

D: September 16, 1933
Batted left, threw right
Ht. 5–11; **Wt.** 195

George Gore

Gore, George F.

White Stockings	G	AB	H	AVG	RBI	R	2B	3B	HR	SLG	SB
1879	63	266	70	.263	32	43	17	4	0	.357	—
1880	77	322	116	.360	47	70	23	2	2	.463	—
1881	73	309	92	.298	44	86	18	9	1	.424	—
1882	84	367	117	.319	51	99	15	7	3	.422	—
1883	92	392	131	.334	—	105	30	9	2	.472	—
1884	103	422	134	.318	—	104	18	4	5	.415	—
1885	109	441	138	.313	51	115	21	13	5	.454	—
1886	118	444	135	.304	63	150	20	12	6	.444	—
Career	1,310	5,357	1,612	.301	526	1,327	262	94	46	.411	147

Consistency on the field and inconsistency off it were George Gore's hallmarks as the center fielder of Cap Anson's great teams of the 1880s. Gore batted over .300 in six of his eight seasons with the White Stockings, and just missed in another season with .298 in 1881. He played on five pennant winners.

Anson later said of Gore that "wine and women were his downfall." But when not partying, Gore was an outstanding player, winning the NL batting title in 1880 with a .360 average after hitting .263 as a rookie. Although stolen bases were recorded irregularly at the time, with the result that his season and career totals are uncertain, Gore set a record by stealing seven against Providence on June 25, 1881.

Wearying of Gore's dissolute habits, especially after the White Stockings lost the "World Series" to the St. Louis Browns in 1886, team president Al Spalding sold him to the New York Giants that year. Gore's career ended with the 1892 season.

Griffith, Clark

Cubs: 1893–1900
Pitcher
Nickname: Old Fox
Birthplace: Clear Creek, Missouri

B: November 20, 1869
D: October 27, 1955
Batted right, threw right
Ht. 5–7; **Wt.** 155

Griffith, Clark Calvin

Cubs	W	L	Pct	ERA	G	CG	IP	H	BB	K	ShO
1893	1	2	.333	5.03	4	2	19⅔	24	5	9	0
1894	21	14	.600	4.92	36	28	261⅓	328	85	71	0
1895	26	14	.650	3.93	42	39	353	434	91	79	0
1896	23	11	.676	3.54	36	35	317⅔	370	70	81	0
1897	21	18	.538	3.72	41	38	343⅓	410	86	102	1
1898	24	10	.706	1.88	38	36	325⅔	305	64	97	4
1899	22	14	.611	2.79	38	35	319⅔	329	65	73	0
1900	14	13	.519	3.05	30	27	248	245	51	61	4
Career	240	144	.625	3.31	453	337	3,386⅓	3,670	774	955	23

Clark Griffith's greatest fame came from being the owner and manager of the Washington Senators in the 20th century, but earlier he was an outstanding pitcher for the Cubs and managed as well as pitched the White Sox to their first AL pennant in 1901.

Griffith caught on with Cap Anson's team in 1893 and became the ace of the staff the next season, starting a run of six consecutive seasons in which he won 20 games or more, with a high of 26–14 in 1895. The feat has been matched with the Cubs only by Three-Finger Brown and Ferguson Jenkins.

In 1901, Griffith jumped at an offer by Charles Comiskey to pitch for and manage the newly major league White Sox. Griffith also managed the New York Yankees and Cincinnati Reds before going to Washington in 1912.

He was named to the Hall of Fame in 1946.

Grimes, Ray

Cubs: 1921–24
First baseman
Birthplace: Bergholz, Ohio
B: September 11, 1893

D: May 25, 1953
Batted right, threw right
Ht. 5–11; **Wt.** 168

Grimes, Oscar Ray, Sr.

Cubs	G	AB	H	AVG	RBI	R	2B	3B	HR	SLG	SB
1921	147	530	170	.321	79	91	38	6	6	.449	5
1922	138	509	180	.354	99	99	45	12	14	.572	7
1923	64	216	71	.329	36	32	7	2	2	.407	5
1924	51	177	53	.299	34	33	6	5	5	.477	4
Career	433	1,537	505	.329	263	269	101	25	27	.480	21

Injury cut short what might have been a spectacular career, but Ray Grimes put together two outstanding seasons for the Cubs and set a major league record by batting in runs in 17 consecutive games in 1921, with a total of 27 RBIs in that stretch.

After just one major league game with the Boston Red Sox in 1920, Grimes was purchased by the Cubs for $5,500 and broke in with an impressive rookie season in 1921, batting .321 with 79 RBIs. He improved on those numbers in 1922, batting .354 with 45 doubles, 12 triples, 14 home runs, and 99 RBIs.

A slipped disc suffered in June 1923 eventually curtailed Grimes' career, though he batted .329 in 64 games. He played part time for the Cubs the next year, and was let go after the season. A comeback attempt with Pittsburgh in 1926 was futile.

Ray Grimes

Grimm, Charlie

Cubs: 1925–36
First baseman
Birthplace: St. Louis, Missouri
B: August 25, 1896

D: November 15, 1983
Batted left, threw left
Ht. 5–11; **Wt.** 173

Grimm, Charles John

Cubs	G	AB	H	AVG	RBI	R	2B	3B	HR	SLG	SB
1925	141	519	159	.306	76	73	29	5	10	.439	4
1926	147	524	145	.277	82	58	30	6	8	.403	3
1927	147	543	169	.311	74	68	29	6	2	.398	3
1928	147	547	161	.294	62	67	25	5	5	.386	7
1929	120	463	138	.298	91	66	28	3	10	.436	3
1930	114	429	124	.289	66	58	27	2	6	.403	1
1931	146	531	176	.311	66	65	33	11	4	.458	1
1932	149	570	175	.307	80	66	42	2	7	.425	2
1933	107	384	95	.247	37	38	15	2	3	.320	1
1934	75	267	79	.296	47	24	8	1	5	.390	1
1935	2	8	0	.000	0	0	0	0	0	.000	0
1936	39	132	33	.250	16	13	4	0	1	.303	0
Career	2,164	7,917	2,299	.290	1,078	908	394	108	79	.397	57

His name is inextricably intertwined with that of the Cubs as their three-time manager, but Charlie Grimm also was a solid regular first baseman and dangerous hitter at Pittsburgh for six seasons before he arrived at Wrigley Field in 1925. He reached career highs in 1923 by batting .345 with 194 hits and 99 RBIs for the Pirates.

The fun-loving Grimm, known as "Jolly Cholly," was an inveterate prankster and took pride in his playing of the banjo, yet was a dedicated player on the field. During nine seasons at the Cubs' regular first baseman, he contributed to two pennant winners, 1929 and 1932, as well as managing the team in 1932 and in 1935 when they won again.

In 1929, when the Cubs captured their first pennant since 1918, Grimm batted .298 with 91 RBIs as part of the supporting cast in the formidable offense headed by Rogers Hornsby, Hack Wilson, Riggs Stephenson, and Kiki Cuyler. Though the Cubs lost the World Series to Philadelphia, Grimm batted .389 with four RBIs in the five games.

In four of his nine years as the regular first baseman, Grimm batted over .300, with a peak of .331 in 1931. Manager Grimm cut his player duties to 75 games in 1934, and appeared in just a few games the next two years before retiring as a player.

(For details of Grimm's three terms as Cubs manager, see Chapter 4, "The Skippers.")

Hack, Stan

Cubs: 1932–47
Third baseman
Birthplace: Sacramento, California
B: December 6, 1909
D: December 15, 1979
Batted left, threw right
Ht. 6–0; **Wt.** 170

Hack, Stanley Camfield

Cubs	G	AB	H	AVG	RBI	R	2B	3B	HR	SLG	SB
1932	72	178	42	.236	19	32	5	6	2	.365	5
1933	20	60	21	.350	2	10	3	1	1	.483	4
1934	111	402	116	.289	21	54	16	6	1	.366	11
1935	124	427	133	.311	64	75	23	9	4	.436	14
1936	149	561	167	.298	78	102	27	4	6	.392	17
1937	154	582	173	.297	63	106	27	6	2	.375	16
1938	152	609	195	.320	67	109	34	11	4	.432	16
1939	156	641	191	.298	56	112	28	6	8	.398	17
1940	149	603	191	.317	40	101	38	6	8	.439	21
1941	151	586	186	.317	45	111	33	5	7	.427	10
1942	140	553	166	.300	39	91	36	3	6	.409	9
1943	144	533	154	.289	35	78	24	4	3	.366	5
1944	98	383	108	.282	32	65	16	1	3	.352	5
1945	150	597	193	.323	43	110	29	7	2	.405	12
1946	92	323	92	.285	26	55	13	4	0	.350	3
1947	76	240	65	.271	12	28	11	2	0	.333	0
Career	1,938	7,278	2,193	.301	642	1,239	363	81	57	.397	165

Probably the most popular Cub player of the 1930s and 1940s, with a pleasant and outgoing personality, Stan Hack also was one of the best fielding and hitting third basemen in the team's history.

During a 16-year career extending from 1932 through 1947, all with the Cubs, Smilin' Stan batted .301, hitting over .300 in six full seasons, with a high of .323 in 1945 when he helped the Cubs win their fourth pennant during his tenure. Though the Cubs lost all four World Series that Hack played in, he batted .348 in 18 games.

Hack tied an NL record by scoring 100 or more runs for six consecutive seasons (1936–41) and twice led the league in base hits. He also led the NL twice in stolen bases. Primarily a singles and doubles hitter, he never hit more than eight home runs in a season.

An exceptionally smooth fielder, with a strong arm and a sure glove, Hack set a NL record, since broken, by going 54 games without an error. He led the league several times in putouts, assists, and total chances.

He retired after the 1943 season partly because of a dispute with manager Jimmie Wilson. But when Wilson was fired the following May and Grimm returned for his third term as manager, Hack came back to play another four seasons.

Hack's playing career ended in 1947, and he managed in the Cubs' farm system for several years. He was named Cubs manager in 1954 and suffered through three poor seasons before being fired. (For details of managerial career, see Chapter 4, "The Skippers.")

Hacker, Warren

Cubs: 1948–56
Pitcher
Birthplace: Marissa, Illinois
B: November 21, 1924
Bats right, throws right
Ht. 6–1; **Wt.** 185

Hacker, Warren Louis

Cubs	W	L	Pct	ERA	G	CG	IP	H	BB	K	ShO
1948	0	1	.000	21.00	3	0	3	7	3	0	0
1949	5	8	.385	4.23	30	3	125⅔	141	53	40	0
1950	0	1	.000	5.28	5	1	15⅓	20	8	5	0
1951	0	0	.000	13.50	2	0	1⅓	3	0	2	0
1952	15	9	.625	2.58	33	12	185	144	31	84	5
1953	12	19	.387	4.38	39	9	221⅓	225	54	106	0
1954	6	13	.316	4.25	39	4	158⅔	157	37	80	1
1955	11	15	.423	4.27	35	13	213	202	43	80	0
1956	3	13	.188	4.66	34	4	168	190	44	65	0
Career	62	89	.411	4.21	306	47	1,283⅓	1,297	320	557	6

Poor pitching usually was the bane of the Cubs in the dreary 1950s, but occasionally a starter distinguished himself, even if briefly. That was the case with Warren Hacker, who had failed to stick with the Cubs in four earlier trials going back to 1948, but emerged as an outstanding starter in 1952.

Hacker didn't make his first start until June 7, but from then on put together an impressive season. He was 15–9, with five shutouts and 12 complete games in 20 starts, and his ERA of 2.58 was second in the NL. The next season, he pitched almost as well, losing two games 1–0, another pair 2–0, and falling to 12–19, partly for lack of batting support.

Warren Hacker

Hacker remained in the Cubs' rotation another four seasons without much success, then completed his career with the White Sox in 1961.

Hands, Bill

Cubs: 1966–72
Pitcher
Birthplace: Hackensack, New Jersey

B: May 6, 1940
Bats right, throws right
Ht. 6–2; Wt. 185

Hands, William Alfred

Cubs	W	L	Pct	ERA	G	CG	IP	H	BB	K	ShO
1966	8	13	.381	4.58	41	0	159	168	59	64	0
1967	7	8	.467	2.46	49	3	150	134	48	84	1
1968	16	10	.615	2.89	36	11	258⅔	221	36	148	4
1969	20	14	.588	2.49	41	18	300	268	73	181	3
1970	18	15	.545	3.70	39	12	265	278	76	170	2
1971	12	18	.400	3.42	36	14	242	248	50	128	1
1972	11	8	.579	2.99	32	6	189⅓	168	47	96	3
Career	111	110	.502	3.35	374	72	1,950⅔	1,895	492	1,128	17

Dogged determination and refusal to "give in" to batters, as well as natural talent, made Bill Hands one of the Cubs' "Big Three" starting pitchers, along with Ferguson Jenkins and Ken Holtzman, during the team's revival under manager Leo Durocher. One of Durocher's first actions on taking over as manager in late 1965 was to insist that the Cubs trade for Hands and catcher Randy Hundley, two prospects in the San Francisco organization. Both players became stars, although Hands took time to develop, while Hundley immediately established himself as a top-flight catcher.

After two learning seasons, Hands hit his stride in 1968 with a 16–10 record. He reached a peak with a 20–14 mark and a 2.49 ERA in 1969, the year the Cubs appeared to have an NL East title in their grasp until they faded before the onrush of the New York Mets. He was the "stopper" of the rotation, halting losing streaks four times, and was named Chicago Player of the year by the Baseball Writers.

Hands was 18–15 in 1970, but then began to slip, dropping to 12–18 the next year. He was 11–8 in 1972, then was traded to Minnesota over the winter. He pitched in his final major league game in 1975.

Hartnett, Gabby

Cubs: 1922–40
Catcher
Birthplace: Woonsocket, Rhode Island
B: December 20, 1900

D: December 20, 1972
Batted right, threw right
Ht. 6–1; Wt. 195

Hartnett, Charles Leo

Cubs	G	AB	H	AVG	RBI	R	2B	3B	HR	SLG	SB
1922	31	72	14	.236	4	4	1	1	0	.236	1
1923	85	231	62	.268	39	28	12	2	8	.442	4
1924	111	354	106	.299	67	56	17	7	16	.523	10
1925	117	398	115	.289	67	61	28	3	24	.555	1
1926	93	284	78	.275	41	35	25	3	8	.468	0
1927	127	449	132	.294	80	56	32	3	10	.454	2
1928	120	388	117	.302	57	61	26	9	14	.523	3
1929	25	22	6	.273	9	2	2	1	1	.591	1
1930	141	508	172	.339	122	84	31	3	37	.630	0
1931	116	380	107	.282	70	53	32	1	8	.434	3
1932	121	406	110	.271	52	52	25	3	12	.436	0
1933	140	490	135	.276	88	55	21	4	16	.502	1
1934	130	438	131	.299	90	58	21	1	22	.502	0
1935	116	413	142	.344	91	67	32	6	13	.545	1
1936	121	424	130	.307	64	49	25	6	7	.443	0
1937	110	356	126	.354	82	47	21	6	12	.548	0
1938	88	299	82	.274	59	40	19	1	10	.445	1
1939	97	306	85	.278	59	36	18	2	12	.467	0
1940	37	64	17	.266	12	3	3	0	1	.359	0
Career	1,990	6,432	1,912	.297	1,179	867	396	64	236	.489	28

Manager Bill Killefer got his first look at Gabby Hartnett when the moon-faced, solidly built rookie reported to the Cubs in 1922, and he had no doubts about his talent. "Boys, there's a catcher," Killefer raved, and Hartnett for 19 years proved that his manager's confidence was warranted. He hit for average, hit for power, had a rifle arm, blocked the plate like a bulldozer, and was durable, catching 100 or more games in 12 seasons, eight of them consecutive. He led the NL in fielding percentage seven seasons.

The Cubs won three pennants (1932, 1935, and 1938) with Hartnett behind the plate, the last when he also was managing. (He sat out most of the 1929 season, another Cubs pennant year, with an arm injury.) And the most famous home run in Cub history, "the homer in the gloamin'," came off Hartnett's bat to decide the pennant race of 1938.

The nickname "Gabby" was given early to Charles Leo Hartnett in mockery because as a youngster he was silent, although in later years he became extremely voluble, often yelling and shaking his fist from behind the plate to spur on his team.

Hartnett was the first catcher to hit more than 200 home runs, finishing with 236 for his career. In his greatest season, 1930, he batted .339 with 37 home runs and 122 RBIs, and in two other seasons he batted .354 and .344, finishing with a lifetime average of .297. Hartnett's rendezvous with history came at 5:37 P.M. on September 28, 1938, with darkness closing in on Wrigley Field and the Cubs and Pittsburgh Pirates deadlocked 5–5 in the bottom of the ninth. The first-place Pirates held a half-game lead on the Cubs in the pennant race. The umpires had decided to call the game after the Cubs' turn at bat.

With two out and nobody on, Hartnett, who had replaced Charlie Grimm as manager during the season, came to bat against Mace Brown. Hartnett swung and missed Brown's first pitch. He fouled off the second. Then he rocketed the third pitch into the twilight and the bleachers for a 6–5 Cub victory that lifted them into first place to stay.

"A lot of people have told me they didn't know the ball was in the bleachers [because of the darkness]," Hartnett later said. "Well, I did. Maybe I was the only one in the park who did. I knew it the moment I hit it." With one swing, Hartnett had created one of the most celebrated legends in baseball history, the "homer in the gloamin'."

Fired as the Cub manager in 1940 (see Chapter 4, "The Skippers"), Hartnett ended his playing career with the New York Giants in 1941 and later managed in the minor leagues.

He was elected to the Hall of Fame in 1955.

The early 1900s were heady times for the Cubs, especially the World Championship seasons of 1907 and 1908.

Billy Herman, Hank Wilson, Claude Passeau, Charlie Grimm, Gabby Hartnett, Rogers Hornsby, and Woody English were among Cubs favorites of the 1920s through the 1940s.

Billy Williams—"The Classic Hitter."

Fergie Jenkins was elected to the Hall of Fame in 1991.

Ron Santo spent his entire career in Chicago, playing his last year for the White Sox in 1974.

Cubs memorabilia from the 1980s' including Bill Buckner's "Big Stick."

WRIGLEY FIELD
HOME OF
CHICAGO CUBS

'84 N.L. EAST CHAMPS

Budweiser THIS BUD'S FOR YOU Budweiser

WORLD SERIES 1984

CUBS NATIONAL LEAGUE CHAMPIONS

Larry Bowa
Keith Moreland
Jody Davis
Johnny Oates
Leon Durham
Ron Cey
Ron Hassey
Steve Lake
Richie Hebner
Dave Owen
Bob Dernier
Jay Johnstone
Ryne Sandberg
Scott Sanderson
Gary Woods
Thad Bosley
Henry Cotto
Dennis Eckersley
Steve Trout
George Frazier
Gary Matthews
Rich Bordi
Rick Sutcliffe
Warren Brusstar
Dick Ruthven
Lee Smith
Tom Veryzer
Tim Stoddard
Rick Reuschel

Jim Frey, Mgr.

1984 PLAYOFFS GUIDE

Cubs rock 'em, sock 'em, 13 $3.00

CHICAGO

1984 NATIONAL LEAGUE CHAMPIONSHIP SERIES SAN DIEGO PADRES VS. CHICAGO CUBS

CUBS

Although banners proclaimed the Cubs pennant winners in 1984, they actually lost the LCS to the San Diego Padres, after winning the first two games.

The Cubs won the division championship again in 1989, only to lose to San Francisco in five games in the LCS.

ALL-STAR GAME
July 10, 1990
Wrigley Field
Chicago

Wrigley Field was the site of the 1990 All-Star Game

Ryne Sandberg came to be the Cubs player of the 1980s.

Venerable Wrigley Field was the last major league ballpark to install lights for playing night games.

Cub announcers Jack Brickhouse, Harry Caray (glasses), and Ronald Reagan.

Heathcote, Cliff

Cubs: 1922–30
Outfielder
Birthplace: Glen Rock, Pennsylvania
B: January 24, 1898

D: January 19, 1939
Batted left, threw left
Ht. 5–10; **Wt.** 160

Heathcote, Clifton Earl

Cubs	G	AB	H	AVG	RBI	R	2B	3B	HR	SLG	SB
1922	76	243	68	.280	34	37	8	7	1	.383	5
1923	117	393	98	.249	27	48	14	3	1	.308	32
1924	112	392	121	.309	30	66	19	7	0	.393	26
1925	109	380	100	.263	39	57	14	5	5	.366	15
1926	139	510	141	.276	53	98	33	3	10	.412	18
1927	83	228	67	.294	25	28	12	4	2	.408	6
1928	67	137	39	.285	18	26	8	0	3	.409	6
1929	82	224	70	.313	31	45	17	0	2	.415	9
1930	70	150	39	.260	18	30	10	1	9	.520	4
Career	1,415	4,443	1,222	.275	448	643	206	55	42	.375	190

Cliff Heathcote was a steady if unspectacular Cubs outfielder for nine seasons, but he played a major role in one of the most spectacular games ever. Heathcote went 5-for-5 (with two doubles), scored four runs, and drove in five on August 25, 1922, when the Cubs defeated Philadelphia 26–23 in the highest-scoring game in history.

Heathcote was obtained for Max Flack in the memorable Memorial Day 1922 trade with St. Louis between games of a doubleheader. Heathcote and Flack each played for both teams that day.

Heathcote was the Cubs' regular right fielder for several seasons. A good defensive outfielder and base runner (32 stolen bases in 1923 and 26 in 1924), he batted over .300 twice before being being traded to Cincinnati in 1931. His career ended in 1932.

Hendrix, Claude

Cubs: 1916–20
Pitcher
Birthplace: Olathe, Kansas
B: April 13, 1889

D: March 22, 1944
Batted right, threw right
Ht. 6–0; **Wt.** 195

Hendrix, Claude Raymond

Cubs	W	L	Pct	ERA	G	CG	IP	H	BB	K	ShO
1916	8	16	.333	2.68	36	15	218	193	67	117	3
1917	10	12	.455	2.60	40	13	215	202	72	81	1
1918	19	7	.731	2.78	32	21	233	229	54	86	3
1919	10	14	.417	2.62	33	15	206⅓	208	42	69	2
1920	9	12	.429	3.58	27	12	203⅔	216	54	72	0
Career	143	117	.550	2.65	360	184	2,371⅓	2,123	697	1,092	27

Among the players brought over from his Federal League Chicago Whales when new owner Charles Weeghman took over the Cubs in 1916 was veteran pitcher Claude Hendrix, who had won 29 games in 1914 and 16 in 1915.

Hendrix had losing records in his first two years with the Cubs, but in 1918 he was the ace of a pennant-winning staff with a 19–7 record and a league-leading percentage of .731.

Hendrix slumped the next two seasons with 10–14 and 9–12 records, then was implicated in a scandal revealed late in 1920. It was alleged that he had bet $5,000 against his own team in a game he had been scheduled to start but in which he had been replaced by Grover Cleveland Alexander. He was released by the Cubs before the 1921 season and never pitched again in the major leagues.

Cliff Heathcote

Claude Hendrix

Babe Herman

Herman, Babe

Cubs: 1933–35
Outfielder
Birthplace: Buffalo, New York
B: June 26, 1903

D: November 27, 1987
Batted left, threw left
Ht. 6–4; **Wt.** 190

Herman, Floyd Caves

Cubs	G	AB	H	AVG	RBI	R	2B	3B	HR	SLG	SB
1933	137	508	147	.289	93	77	36	12	16	.502	6
1934	125	467	142	.304	84	65	34	5	14	.488	1
Career	1,552	5,603	1,818	.324	997	882	399	110	181	.532	94

Gangling, power-hitting Babe Herman had been a great hitter and erratic outfielder in six seasons with Brooklyn and one with Cincinnati before the Cubs traded four players for him on November 30, 1932, in an effort to beef up the offense that had failed them in the World Series that year. Herman had hit .393 with 35 home runs and 130 RBIs for the Dodgers in 1930, and .381 the year before.

Herman spent two unhappy seasons with the Cubs, earning the fans' displeasure by failing to live up to high expectations, though he batted .289 with 16 home runs and 93 RBIs in 1933 and hit .304 the next year. He was traded to Pittsburgh after the 1934 season, had apparently finished his career at Detroit in 1937, but returned briefly to the Dodgers eight years later during the World War II player shortage.

Herman, Billy

Cubs: 1931–41
Second baseman
Birthplace: New Albany, Indiana

B: July 7, 1909
Bats right, throws right
Ht. 5–11; **Wt.** 180

Herman, William Jennings Bryan

Cubs	G	AB	H	AVG	RBI	R	2B	3B	HR	SLG	SB
1931	25	98	32	.327	16	14	7	0	0	.398	2
1932	154	656	206	.314	51	102	42	7	1	.404	14
1933	153	619	173	.279	44	82	35	2	0	.342	5
1934	113	456	138	.303	42	79	21	6	3	.395	6
1935	154	666	227	.341	83	113	57	6	7	.476	6
1936	153	632	211	.334	93	101	57	7	5	.470	5
1937	138	564	189	.335	65	106	35	11	8	.479	2
1938	152	624	173	.277	56	86	34	7	1	.359	3
1939	156	623	191	.307	70	111	34	18	7	.453	9
1940	135	558	163	.292	57	77	24	4	5	.376	1
1941	11	36	7	.194	0	4	0	1	0	.250	0
Career	1,922	7,707	2,345	.304	839	1,163	486	82	47	.407	67

A slick fielder and fine hitter, second baseman Billy Herman teamed up with shortstop Bill Jurges during most of the 1930s in one of the outstanding double-play combinations of the era. Purchased for $50,000 from the Louisville, Kentucky, minor league team in 1931 as an outstanding prospect, Herman quickly took over second base from the aging Rogers Hornsby and batted .327 in 25 games.

Herman proved he was "for real" by batting .314 with 206 hits in 154 games as the Cubs won a pennant in 1932. He reached a high of .341 in 1935 when he led the NL in hits with 227 and doubles with 57 as the Cubs won another pennant. Though no power hitter, never topping eight home runs in a season, Herman twice had 57 doubles and led the

Billy Herman

NL with 18 triples in 1939. He batted over .300 in seven seasons with the Cubs and played on three pennant-winners.

An exceptional fielder, Herman set a NL record for second basemen with 466 putouts in 1933. He topped 900 total chances in five different seasons.

Named Cubs captain in 1936, Herman sought the managerial job after Gabby Hartnett was fired in 1940. But the Cubs hired Jimmie Wilson, a coach with Cincinnati, and cleared the decks early in the 1941 season by trading Herman to Brooklyn for $25,000 and two prospects who turned out to be duds.

Herman helped the Dodgers to a pennant in 1941 and batted .330 in 1943 before going into the navy for two years. He played briefly after the war, and later managed the Pittsburgh Pirates and Boston Red Sox.

Herman was inducted into the Hall of Fame in 1975.

Hickman, Jim

Cubs: 1968–73
Outfielder, first baseman
Birthplace: Henning, Tennessee
B: May 10, 1937
Batted right, threw right
Ht. 6–3; **Wt.** 192

Hickman, James Lucius

Cubs	G	AB	H	AVG	RBI	R	2B	3B	HR	SLG	SB
1968	75	188	42	.223	23	22	6	3	5	.245	1
1969	134	338	80	.237	54	38	11	2	21	.467	2
1970	149	514	162	.315	115	102	33	4	32	.582	0
1971	117	383	98	.256	60	50	13	2	19	.449	0
1972	115	368	100	.272	64	65	15	2	17	.462	3
1973	92	201	49	.244	20	27	1	2	3	.313	1
Career	1,421	3,974	1,002	.252	560	518	163	25	159	.426	17

Jim Hickman

A tall, soft-spoken veteran journeyman outfielder who had never distinguished himself in six previous major league seasons, Jim Hickman proved a pleasant surprise to the Cubs after they acquired him in 1968. He was the regular right fielder during the abortive pennant chase in 1969, hitting 21 home runs, but really came alive the next year.

Hickman spelled the fading Ernie Banks at first base when he wasn't in right field, and had a "career year" in 1970 by batting .315 with 32 home runs and 115 RBIs, as well as driving in the winning run in the All-Star Game. Hickman's remaining three seasons with the Cubs were less distinguished. He ended his career at St. Louis in 1974.

Hobbie, Glen

Cubs: 1957–64
Pitcher
Birthplace: Witt, Illinois

B: April 24, 1936
Bats right, throws right
Ht. 6–2; **Wt.** 195

Hobbie, Glen Frederick

Cubs	W	L	Pct	ERA	G	CG	IP	H	BB	K	ShO
1957	0	0	.000	10.38	2	0	4⅓	6	5	3	0
1958	10	6	.625	3.74	55	2	168⅓	163	93	91	1
1959	16	13	.552	3.69	46	10	234	204	106	138	3
1960	16	20	.444	3.97	46	16	258⅔	253	101	134	4
1961	7	13	.350	4.26	36	7	198⅔	207	54	103	2
1962	5	14	.263	5.22	42	5	162	198	62	87	0
1963	7	10	.412	3.92	36	4	165⅓	172	49	94	1
1964	0	3	.000	7.90	8	0	27⅓	39	10	14	0
Career	62	81	.434	4.20	284	45	1,263	1,283	495	682	11

One of many promising young Cub pitchers whose careers ended prematurely during the cheerless 1950s and early 1960s, Glen Hobbie nevertheless put together a couple of decent seasons before fading. Brought up from the minor leagues at the age of 21 late in the 1957 season, Hobbie pitched a shutout against the Cincinnati Reds in his first major league start on May 6, 1958. He went on to a 10–6 record that season, came back in 1959 with a 16–13 record, and pitched well in 1960, though his 20 losses against 16 wins led the NL.

In his most memorable games, he pitched a one-hitter against St. Louis to beat the Cardinals 1–0 on April 22, 1959, and hit his first major league home run on August 25, 1960, to beat Pittsburgh 2–1.

Back and shoulder problems that developed in 1961 signaled the decline of Hobbie's career. He was 19–40 the rest of his stay with the Cubs until they traded him to St. Louis for veteran Lew Burdette on June 2, 1964. It was his last season.

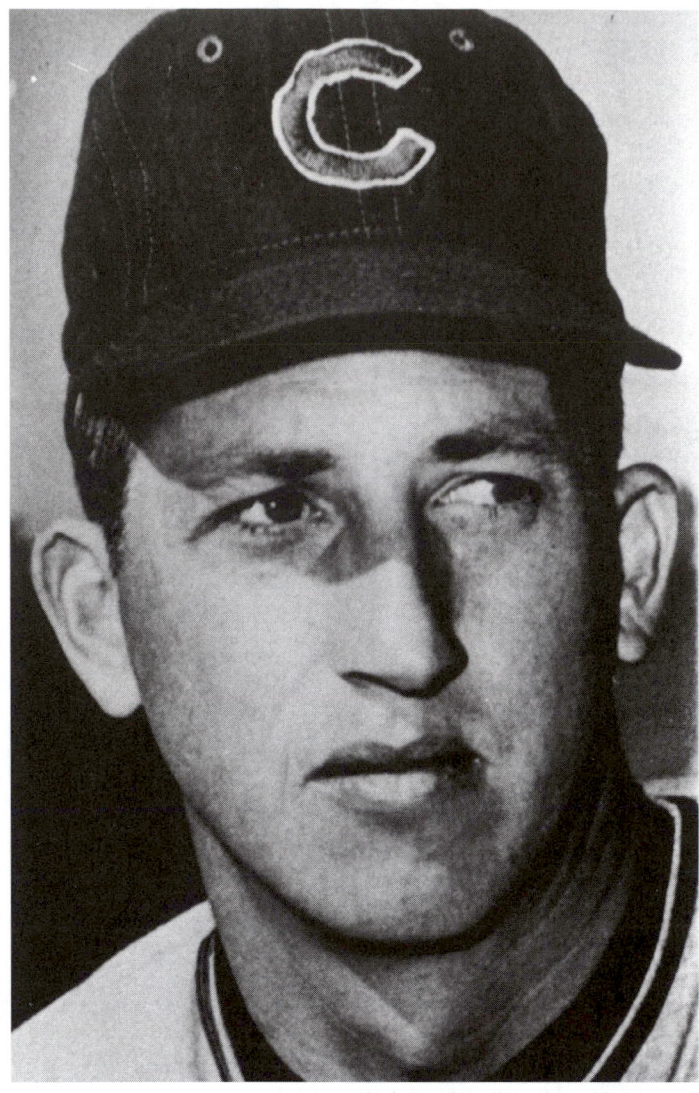

Glen Hobbie

Charlie Hollocher

his finest season, batting .340 in 152 games with 201 hits and 37 doubles and striking out just five times in 592 at bats. In 1923, though sidelined much of the season, he batted .342 in 66 games.

He retired after the 1924 season, during which his ailment reduced his play to 76 games and his average to .245. He committed suicide in 1940.

Hollocher, Charlie

Cubs: 1918–24
Shortstop
Birthplace: St. Louis, Missouri
B: June 11, 1896

D: August 14, 1940
Batted left, threw right
Ht. 5–7; Wt. 158

Hollocher, Charles Jacob

Cubs	G	AB	H	AVG	RBI	R	2B	3B	HR	SLG	SB
1918	139	509	161	.316	38	72	22	6	2	.397	26
1919	115	430	116	.270	26	51	14	5	3	.347	16
1920	80	301	96	.319	22	53	17	2	0	.389	20
1921	140	558	161	.289	37	71	28	8	3	.384	5
1922	152	592	201	.340	69	90	37	8	3	.444	19
1923	66	260	89	.342	28	46	14	2	1	.423	9
1924	76	286	70	.245	21	28	12	4	2	.336	4
Career	760	2,936	894	.304	241	411	145	35	14	.392	99

Deft in the field at shortstop and a fine hitter, Charlie Hollocher provided the spark in his rookie season of 1918 that the Cubs needed to win the pennant. He batted .316, led the league in hits with 161, and stole 26 bases.

Hollocher was troubled by a chronic stomach ailment that eventually ended his career prematurely at the age of 28. But when healthy, he was an exceptional player. In 1922 he had

Holtzman, Ken

Cubs: 1965–71, 1978–79
Pitcher
Birthplace: St. Louis, Missouri

B: November 3, 1945
Bats right, throws left
Ht. 6–2; Wt. 175

Holtzman, Kenneth Dale

Cubs	W	L	Pct	ERA	G	CG	IP	H	BB	K	ShO
1965	0	0	.000	2.25	3	0	4	2	3	3	0
1966	11	16	.407	3.79	34	9	220⅔	194	68	171	0
1967	9	0	1.000	2.53	12	3	92⅔	76	44	62	0
1968	11	14	.440	3.35	34	6	215	201	76	151	3
1969	17	13	.567	3.59	39	12	261	248	93	176	6
1970	17	11	.607	3.38	39	15	288	271	94	202	1
1971	9	15	.375	4.48	30	9	195	213	64	143	3
1978	0	3	.000	6.11	23	0	53	61	35	36	0
1979	6	9	.400	4.58	23	3	118	133	53	44	2
Career	174	150	.537	3.49	451	127	2,867⅓	2,787	910	1,601	31

Early in his career, Ken Holtzman was compared to Sandy Koufax because they both were Jewish and left-handed pitchers. While Holtzman never matched the feats of the overpowering Los Angeles Dodgers star, he was an outstanding pitcher in his own right for both the Cubs and the Oakland Athletics. During a 15-year major league career that began in 1965, Holtzman pitched two no-hitters, both for the Cubs, and won four World Series games, all for the A's.

After starring at the University of Illinois, Holtzman was drafted by the Cubs in 1965, sent briefly to the minor leagues, and thrust into the starting rotation in 1966 at the age of 20. He was 11–16 as a rookie for the last-place Cubs, and one of his wins came in a notable duel with Koufax, whom he outpitched 2–1, losing a no-hitter in the ninth inning. It was the only time he and Koufax faced each other.

Ken Holtzman

Burt Hooton

After going 9–0 in a season punctuated by military service in 1967, Holtzman continued to develop in 1968 when he was 11–14 and pitched three consecutive shutouts in 10 days.

In 1969, a year of disaster for the Cubs, Holtzman was one of the "Big Three" with Ferguson Jenkins and Bill Hands, winning 17 games, a total he matched the next season. And he pitched his first no-hitter on August 29, 1969, at Wrigley Field, beating Atlanta 3–0, helped by a stiff wind that kept a seeming home run by Hank Aaron from going into the bleachers in the sixth inning.

Holtzman's final season with the Cubs, 1971, was marred by a feud with manager Leo Durocher, whose "pet" he had been earlier in his career, and a 9–15 record. However, he pitched his second no-hitter on June 3, 1971, winning 1–0 over the Reds at Cincinnati.

Traded to Oakland for outfielder Rick Monday after the season, Holtzman played a major role in the A's tremendous success as they won three consecutive World Series from 1972 to 1974. He won 19 games, 21 games, 19 games, and 18 games in four seasons at Oakland, then had stints with Baltimore and the New York Yankees. In midseason 1978, Holtzman returned to the Cubs, but he retired after posting a 6–9 record in 1979.

Drafted in 1971 out of the University of Texas where he had been an All-American three years, Burt "Happy" Hooton served his apprenticeship with the Cubs, then went on to become a standout for the Los Angeles Dodgers. Before he left the Cubs, however, he pitched a no-hitter in his fourth major league start, on April 15, 1972, against the Phillies at Wrigley Field, winning 4–0.

Hooton threw a trick pitch, called the knuckle-curve, a cross between a curveball and a knuckler, but it didn't make him a winner with the Cubs. After a 2–0 record in late 1971, he was 11–14, 14–17, and 7–11 the next three seasons, and he was 0–2 when the Cubs traded him to the Dodgers on May 2, 1975.

Hooton's career immediately turned around, as he finished 1975 with an 18–7 record for L.A. His best year was 1978 with 19–10, and he helped the Dodgers into three World Series, 1977, 1978, and 1981. He finished his career at Texas in 1985.

Hooton, Burt

Cubs: 1971–75
Pitcher
Birthplace: Greenville, Texas

B: February 17, 1950
Bats right, throws right
Ht. 6–1; **Wt.** 210

Hooton, Burt Carlton

Cubs	W	L	Pct	ERA	G	CG	IP	H	BB	K	ShO
1971	2	0	1.000	2.14	3	2	21	8	10	22	1
1972	11	14	.440	2.80	33	9	218⅓	201	81	132	3
1973	14	17	.452	3.68	42	9	240	248	73	134	2
1974	7	11	.389	4.81	48	3	176	214	51	94	1
1975	0	2	.000	8.18	3	0	11	18	4	5	0
Career	151	136	.526	3.38	480	86	2,651⅓	2,497	799	1,491	29

Hornsby, Rogers

Cubs: 1929–32
Second baseman
Nickname: Rajah
Birthplace: Winters, Texas

B: April 27, 1896
D: January 5, 1963
Batted right, threw right
Ht. 5–11; **Wt.** 175

Hornsby, Rogers

Cubs	G	AB	H	AVG	RBI	R	2B	3B	HR	SLG	SB
1929	156	602	229	.380	149	156	47	8	39	.679	2
1930	42	104	32	.308	18	15	5	1	2	.433	0
1931	100	357	118	.331	90	64	37	1	16	.473	1
1932	19	58	13	.224	7	10	2	0	1	.310	0
Career	2,259	8,173	2,930	.358	1,584	1,579	541	169	301	.577	135

Widely regarded as the best right-handed hitter ever, Rogers Hornsby proved a bargain when the Cubs gave the Boston Braves $200,000 and five players for him on November 7, 1928. It was one of the Cubs' best deals.

Hornsby had won seven NL batting titles, had batted a composite .402 over a five-year period during which he had topped .400 three times with a 20th-century peak of .424 in 1924, and had managed the St. Louis Cardinals to a World Series title in 1926.

At 32, Hornsby remained a formidable hitter, having led the league in 1928 for the Braves with .387, and for the Cubs he rounded out a powerful attack with such sluggers as Hack Wilson, Riggs Stephenson, Kiki Cuyler, and Charlie Grimm. Hornsby came through immediately, batting .380 with 229 hits, 156 runs, 149 RBIs, and 39 home runs to lift the Cubs to a pennant in 1929.

An abrasive personality and a perfectionist, Hornsby had little tolerance for mediocrity—or authority. He clashed with manager Joe McCarthy and his teammates. Sidelined most of the 1930 season by a fractured ankle and playing only 42 games, in which he batted .308, Hornsby undermined McCarthy's authority, then replaced him as manager with four games left to play. (For details of his managerial career, see Chapter 4, "The Skippers.")

As player-manager in 1931, Hornsby batted .331 in 100 games, drove in 90 runs to lead the team, and in one game hit three home runs and drove in eight runs. But his alienation of the players played a part in a disappointing third-place finish. In 1932, with the Cubs lagging again after 89 games, Hornsby was fired as manager and replaced by Grimm, who rallied the Cubs to a surprise pennant.

Returning to the Cardinals in 1933, Hornsby wandered through baseball another 30 years, playing part-time until 1937, managing the St. Louis Browns (twice) and Cincinnati Reds, and coaching and managing in the minor leagues. He even served as a Cub television announcer in 1949. His career average of .358 was topped only by Ty Cobb's .367.

He was elected to the Hall of Fame in 1942.

Hubbs, Ken

Cubs: 1961–63
Second baseman
Birthplace: Riverside, California
B: December 23, 1941

D: February 15, 1964
Batted right, threw right
Ht. 6–2; **Wt.** 175

| Hubbs, Kenneth Douglass | | | | | | | | | | | |
Cubs	G	AB	H	AVG	RBI	R	2B	3B	HR	SLG	SB
1961	10	28	5	.179	2	4	1	1	1	.393	0
1962	160	661	172	.260	49	90	24	9	5	.346	3
1963	154	566	133	.235	47	54	19	3	8	.322	8
Career	324	1,255	310	.247	98	148	44	13	6	.336	11

Around 1960 the Cubs farm system began to be extremely fertile, producing such standouts as Ron Santo, Billy Williams, Dick Ellsworth, and a fine-fielding second baseman, Ken Hubbs.

Brought up late in 1961 for 10 games, Hubbs was so impressive that he was in the Cubs' opening-day lineup in 1962 at the age of 20. He didn't disappoint, not only batting a respectable .260 in 160 games, but also setting defensive

records for second basemen by handling 418 consecutive chances without error and playing 78 consecutive games without a miscue. He not only won the NL Rookie of the Year award, but also became the first rookie to win a Gold Glove award.

Hubbs' batting average slipped to .235 the following season, but he continued to be impressive in the field, and it appeared the Cubs had their second baseman for the rest of the 1960s. However, he was killed at the age of 22 in the crash of a private plane near Provo, Utah, on February 13, 1964.

Hundley, Randy

Cubs: 1966–73, 1976–77
Catcher
Birthplace: Martinsville, Virginia

B: June 1, 1942
Bats right, throws right
Ht. 5–11; **Wt.** 170

| Hundley, Cecil Randolph | | | | | | | | | | | |
Cubs	G	AB	H	AVG	RBI	R	2B	3B	HR	SLG	SB
1966	149	526	124	.236	63	50	22	3	19	.397	1
1967	152	539	144	.267	60	68	25	3	14	.403	2
1968	160	553	125	.226	65	41	18	4	7	.311	0
1969	151	522	133	.255	64	67	15	1	18	.391	2
1970	73	250	61	.244	36	13	5	0	3	.348	0
1971	9	21	7	.333	2	1	1	0	0	.381	0
1972	114	357	78	.218	30	23	12	0	5	.294	1
1973	124	368	83	.226	43	35	11	1	10	.342	5
1976	13	18	3	.167	1	3	2	0	0	.278	0
1977	2	4	0	.000	0	0	0	0	0	.000	0
Career	1,061	3,442	813	.236	381	311	118	13	82	.350	12

A fine defensive catcher and outstanding handler of pitchers, Randy Hundley also occasionally could hit for power, if seldom for a high batting average. He was acquired by the Cubs along with pitcher Bill Hands from the San Francisco Giants shortly after Leo Durocher was named manager late in 1965.

Randy Hundley

Durocher was sold on Hundley, who soon won accolades as the finest Cub catcher since Gabby Hartnett, 30 years earlier. As a rookie at the age of 24 in 1966, Hundley caught 149 games, batted .236, and hit 19 home runs. He had a fine arm and was fearless in blocking the plate on runners.

"He's my field general," Durocher said. "He runs my ball club out there."

Durocher's confidence in Hundley was such that he couldn't bear to rest him. Hundley became the first to catch 150 games or more for three consecutive seasons (1967–69) and often lost up to 15 pounds off of his normal weight of 170 because of overwork. Yet he played a major part in the success of the Cub pitching staff during the late 1960s when Hands, Ferguson Jenkins, and Ken Holtzman were the "Big Three."

A serious knee injury suffered in a collision at the plate early in the 1970 season triggered a succession of injuries and ailments that reduced Hundley's role to 73 games that year and nine the following. He was able to play 114 games in 1972 and 124 in 1973, but he had slowed down greatly, and his bat no longer had authority.

After the 1973 season, Hundley was traded to Minnesota, then returned to the Cubs as a player-coach in 1976 and 1977.

Hutchison, Bill

White Stockings: 1889–95
Pitcher
Birthplace: New Haven, Connecticut
B: December 17, 1859

D: March 19, 1926
Batted right, threw right
Ht. 5–9; **Wt.** 175

Hutchison, William Forrest

White Stockings	W	L	Pct	ERA	G	CG	IP	H	BB	K	ShO
1889	16	17	.485	3.54	37	33	318	306	117	136	3
1890	42	25	.627	2.70	71	65	603	505	199	289	5
1891	44	19	.698	2.81	66	56	561	508	178	261	4
1892	37	36	.507	2.74	75	67	627	572	187	316	5
1893	16	24	.400	4.75	44	38	348⅓	420	156	80	2
1894	14	16	.467	6.06	36	28	277⅔	373	140	59	0
1895	13	21	.382	4.73	38	30	291	371	129	85	2
Career	184	163	.530	3.58	375	321	3,083	3,124	1,129	1,236	21

Astocky, powerfully built right-hander, Bill Hutchison was manager Cap Anson's workhorse and the leading winner among NL pitchers for three consecutive seasons (1890–92). He pitched briefly for Kansas City of the Union Association in 1884 after graduating from Yale University, at which his father was a professor, and was signed by the White Stockings for 1889 during the crisis of the Players League.

After a 16–17 rookie season, Hutchison, known as Wild Bill because of control problems, reeled off campaigns of 42–25, 44–19, and 37–36, pitching a team record 627 innings in 1892. He began to fade with a 16–24 record in 1893 when the pitching distance was increased from 50 feet to 60 feet, 6 inches, but hung on for two more seasons before leaving the Cubs and finishing his career at St. Louis in 1897.

Jackson, Larry

Cubs: 1963–66
Pitcher
Birthplace: Nampa, Idaho

B: June 2, 1931
Bats right, throws right
Ht. 6–1; **Wt.** 175

Jackson, Lawrence Curtis

Cubs	W	L	Pct	ERA	G	CG	IP	H	BB	K	ShO
1963	14	18	.438	2.55	37	13	275	256	54	153	4
1964	24	11	.686	3.14	40	19	297⅔	265	58	148	3
1965	14	21	.400	3.85	39	12	257⅓	268	57	131	4
1966	0	2	.000	13.50	3	0	8	14	4	5	0
Career	194	183	.515	3.40	558	149	3,262⅔	3,206	924	1,709	37

Aconsistent winner for eight seasons at St. Louis before the Cubs acquired him in a six-player trade after the 1962 season, right-hander Larry Jackson pitched well for three seasons in Chicago. He came up with a "career year" in 1964 when with 24–11 he became the team's biggest winner since Charlie Root won 26 in 1927.

A hard-luck pitcher on a poor team his other two full years with the Cubs, Jackson was 14–18 in 1963, losing three 1–0 games and eight games by one run, and was 14–21 in 1965. His chief contribution to the Cubs, however, may have come early in the 1966 season when he was the bait for the Phillies in a deal that brought Ferguson Jenkins to the Cubs.

After three so-so seasons at Philadelphia, Jackson retired and eventually entered politics in his native Idaho, serving four terms in the state legislature.

Larry Jackson

Ransom Jackson

Jackson, Randy

Cubs: 1950–55, 1959
Third baseman
Birthplace: Little Rock, Arkansas

B: February 10, 1926
Bats right, throws right
Ht. 6–1; **Wt.** 180

Jackson, Ransom Joseph

Cubs	G	AB	H	AVG	RBI	R	2B	3B	HR	SLG	SB
1950	34	111	25	.225	6	13	4	3	3	.396	4
1951	145	553	138	.250	76	78	24	6	16	.452	14
1952	116	379	88	.232	34	44	8	5	9	.351	6
1953	139	498	142	.285	66	61	22	8	19	.476	8
1954	126	484	132	.273	67	77	17	6	19	.450	2
1955	138	499	132	.265	70	73	13	7	21	.445	0
1959	41	74	18	.243	10	7	5	1	1	.378	0
Career	955	3,203	835	.261	415	412	115	44	103	.421	36

Ransom "Randy" Jackson was brought along in the Cubs farm system in the late 1940s to replace aging third base star Stan Hack, and quickly earned the soubriquet of "Handsome Ransom."

After a disappointing trial run in 1950, Jackson got another chance when Bill Serena, his young competitor for the

third base job, was injured early the next season. Jackson hit four home runs and drove in 11 runs in a four-game stretch, and became the regular third baseman for five seasons.

Jackson had decent power and was a competent fielder. He hit his peak in home runs with 21 in 1955, and his best batting average was .285 in 1953. He was traded to Brooklyn for veteran third baseman Don Hoak and outfielder Walt Moryn and was largely a utility player the rest of his career, which ended with a return to the Cubs for 41 games in 1959.

Jeffcoat, Hal

Cubs: 1948–55
Outfielder, pitcher
Birthplace: West Columbia, South Carolina

B: September 6, 1924
Bats right, throws right
Ht. 5–10; **Wt.** 185

Jeffcoat, Harold Bentley

Cubs	G	AB	H	AVG	RBI	R	2B	3B	HR	SLG	SB
1948	134	473	132	.279	42	53	16	4	4	.355	8
1949	108	363	89	.245	26	43	18	6	2	.344	12
1950	66	179	42	.235	18	21	13	1	2	.352	7
1951	113	278	76	.273	27	44	20	2	4	.403	89
1952	102	297	65	.219	30	29	17	2	4	.330	7
1953	106	183	43	.235	22	22	3	1	4	.328	5
1954	56	31	8	.258	6	13	2	1	1	.484	2
1955	52	23	4	.148	1	3	0	0	1	.304	0
Career	918	1,963	487	.248	188	249	95	18	26	.355	49

Cubs	W	L	Pct	ERA	G	CG	IP	H	BB	K	ShO
1954	5	6	.455	5.19	43	1	104	110	58	35	0
1955	8	6	.571	2.95	50	0	100⅔	107	53	32	0
Career	39	37	.513	4.22	245	13	697	772	257	239	1

A great throwing arm and a light bat turned Hal Jeffcoat from an outfielder into a pitcher midway in his major league career. As a rookie sensation in 1948, Jeffcoat took center field away from veteran Andy Pafko, who was shifted

Hal Jeffcoat

to third base by Cub manager Charlie Grimm. Jeffcoat batted .279 in 134 games.

Jeffcoat tailed off the next season to .245 and lost his job as a regular, staying on as a utility outfielder until 1954 when manager Stan Hack saved his career by converting him into a pitcher. He was used mostly in relief for two seasons, with records of 5–6 in 1954 and 8–6 in 1955.

Traded to Cincinnati after the 1955 campaign, Jeffcoat had his best years as a pitcher with the Reds, used both in relief and as a starter. His career ended in 1959.

Jenkins, Ferguson

Cubs: 1966–73, 1982–83
Pitcher
Birthplace: Chatham, Ontario, Canada

B: December 13, 1943
Bats right, throws right
Ht. 6–5; **Wt.** 205

Ferguson Jenkins

Jenkins, Ferguson Arthur

Cubs	W	L	Pct	ERA	G	CG	IP	H	BB	K	ShO
1966	6	8	.429	3.31	60	2	182	147	51	148	1
1967	20	13	.606	2.80	38	20	289⅓	230	83	236	3
1968	20	15	.571	2.63	40	20	308	255	65	260	3
1969	21	15	.583	3.21	43	23	311⅓	284	71	273	7
1970	22	16	.579	3.39	40	24	313	265	60	274	3
1971	24	13	.649	2.77	39	30	325	304	37	263	3
1972	20	12	.625	3.21	36	23	289⅓	253	62	184	5
1973	14	16	.467	3.89	38	7	271	267	57	170	2
1982	14	15	.483	3.15	34	4	217⅓	221	68	134	1
1983	6	9	.400	4.30	33	1	167⅓	176	46	96	1
Career	284	226	.557	3.34	664	267	4,499⅔	4,142	997	3,192	49

It might have seemed hyperbole when *Chicago Sun-Times* baseball writer Edgar Munzel proclaimed "A Star Is Born" after rookie Ferguson Jenkins shut out Los Angeles for six innings and hit a home run en route to a 4–0 Cubs victory early in the 1966 season, but Munzel was not overstating the case. The development of a great pitcher was under way.

Jenkins was regarded almost as a throw-in in a trade on April 21, 1966, in which the Cubs also acquired outfielder Adolfo Phillips and first baseman John Herrnstein from Philadelphia in exchange for veteran pitchers Bob Buhl and Larry Jackson. It might have been the best deal the Cubs, notorious for bad ones, ever made.

A gangling 6–5, stoop-shouldered right-hander from Canada, where he became a national hero, Jenkins had a decent fastball and exceptional slider, but was lightly regarded in the Phillies' system even after a brief stint in Philadelphia in the '65 season. Considering Jenkins at best a reliever, the Phillies did not hesitate to send him to the Cubs. And he stayed in the bullpen much of the '66 season in Chicago, until manager Leo Durocher converted him into a starter in August.

The payoff was quick. Though Jenkins finished 6–8 for '66, he impressed Durocher with great control and 148 strikeouts in 182 innings. And in '67 his 20–13 record began one of the greatest runs of any Cub pitcher, six consecutive seasons of 20 or more victories, a streak matched only by Three-Finger Brown six decades earlier and Clark Griffith in the 1890s.

Jenkins was the "pied piper" who led the Cubs into an era of contention, including the disaster of 1969 when they faded in the stretch. He was 20–15 in '68 (when he lost five games 1–0), then 21–15, 22–16, 22–14, 24–13, and 20–12 to round out a run of six fine seasons. In that stretch he completed 140

of 236 starts, pitched 24 shutouts, including a high of seven in 1969, and led the NL in strikeouts with 273 the same year.

He was extremely durable, pitching more than 300 innings in four of the six seasons, with a high of 328 in 1971, when he set a club record with 274 strikeouts.

Though Jenkins frequently gave up home runs, most came with nobody on base because of his exceptional control. In 1971 he walked just 37 batters in 325 innings, and for his career became the only pitcher with more than 3,000 strikeouts (3,192) and less than 1,000 walks (997).

Randy Hundley, who caught Jenkins in most games, said of his battery mate: "If somebody hit one nine miles, it didn't upset him. Sometimes he would just laugh. He didn't walk hitters, so he was giving up solo home runs."

His peak with the Cubs was reached in '71, when he captured the NL Cy Young Award after winning 24 games, including two two-hitters, two three-hitters, and two four-hitters. A good hitter, Jenkins drove in the winning run in six games, finishing the season with six home runs and 20 RBIs.

Jenkins stumbled in 1973, his record dipping to 14–16 while the Cubs were breaking up the Durocher-era team. After the season he was traded to Texas for infielders Bill Madlock and Vic Harris. Madlock proved an exceptional hitter, leading the NL in batting twice for the Cubs, but Jenkins' revival at Texas made the trade seem a standoff.

Jenkins rebounded strongly in 1974 with a 25–12 record, the best of his career, and it could easily have been better because he again lost five 1–0 games. He just missed winning the AL Cy Young Award. He had several good seasons in the next seven years, including 18–8 for Texas in 1978, before returning to the Cubs as a free agent for the 1982 season.

He was the ace of an admittedly poor Cub staff, finishing 1982 with a 14–15 record and a 3.15 ERA at the age of 38. The next year he dropped to 6–9 to finish his playing career with a record of 284 and 226. He returned to the Cubs as pitching coach in 1995.

Jenkins was elected to the Hall of Fame in 1991.

Don Johnson

Tony Kaufmann

Johnson, Don

Cubs: 1943–48
Second baseman
Birthplace: Chicago

B: December 7, 1911
Bats right, throws right
Ht. 6–0; **Wt.** 170

Johnson, Donald Spore

Cubs	G	AB	H	AVG	RBI	R	2B	3B	HR	SLG	SB
1943	10	42	8	.190	1	5	2	0	0	.238	0
1944	154	608	169	.278	71	50	37	1	2	.352	8
1945	138	557	168	.302	58	94	23	2	2	.361	9
1946	83	314	76	.242	19	37	10	1	1	.290	6
1947	120	402	104	.259	26	33	17	2	3	.333	2
1948	6	12	3	.250	0	0	0	0	0	.250	1
Career	511	1,935	528	.273	175	219	89	6	8	.337	26

A steady fielder and decent hitter, Don Johnson was a vital component of the Cubs' pennant-winning 1945 team, when he batted a career-high .302 and scored 94 runs. The previous season he had beaten out Eddie Stanky for the second base job, batting .278 in 154 games. (Stanky was to become much more famous later.)

"Pep" Johnson, a late starter as a rookie at 32 in 1943, faded after the 1945 season, although he played in 120 games in 1947. His career ended the next year.

Kaufmann, Tony

Cubs: 1921–27
Pitcher
Birthplace: Chicago
B: December 16, 1900

D: June 4, 1982
Batted right, threw right
Ht. 5–11; **Wt.** 165

Kaufmann, Anthony Charles

Cubs	W	L	Pct	ERA	G	CG	IP	H	BB	K	ShO
1921	1	0	1.000	4.15	2	1	13	12	3	6	0
1922	7	13	.350	4.06	37	4	153	161	57	45	1
1923	14	10	.583	3.10	33	18	206⅓	209	67	72	2
1924	16	11	.593	4.02	34	16	208⅓	218	66	79	3
1925	13	13	.500	4.50	31	14	196	221	77	49	2
1926	9	7	.563	3.02	26	14	169⅔	169	44	52	1
1927	3	3	.500	6.41	9	3	53⅓	75	19	21	0
Career	64	62	.508	4.18	202	71	1,086⅓	1,198	368	345	9

A slightly built right-hander, Tony Kaufmann's most memorable accomplishment was that he was the starting and winning pitcher in the highest-scoring game ever, a 26–23 Cubs victory over Philadelphia on August 25, 1922.

Kaufmann enjoyed records of 14–10, 16–11, and 13–13 from 1923 through 1925 during almost six seasons with the Cubs, but had little success after being traded to Philadelphia during the 1927 season.

Kelly, King

White Stockings: 1880–86
Outfielder, catcher
Birthplace: Troy, New York
B: December 31, 1857

D: November 8, 1894
Batted right, threw right
Ht. 5–10; **Wt.** 170

Kelly, Michael Joseph

White Stockings	G	AB	H	AVG	RBI	R	2B	3B	HR	SLG	SB
1880	84	344	100	.291	60	72	17	9	1	.401	—
1881	82	353	114	.323	55	84	27	3	2	.433	—
1882	84	377	115	.305	55	81	37	4	1	.432	—
1883	98	428	109	.255	—	92	28	10	3	.388	—
1884	108	452	160	.354	—	120	28	5	13	.534	—
1885	107	438	126	.288	74	124	24	7	9	.436	—
1886	118	451	175	.388	79	155	32	11	4	.534	—
Career	1,455	5,894	1,813	.308	793	1,357	359	102	69	.438	315

He could play any position well, and often did, but Mike "King" Kelly was mostly a catcher and an outfielder, as well as a great hitter and fine base runner for manager Cap Anson's five championship teams of the 1880s. He has been celebrated as the Babe Ruth of the 19th century, the most colorful and popular ballplayer of his day.

Kelly won two batting titles with the White Stockings, hitting .354 in 1884 and .388 two years later. His daring on the base paths inspired a popular song of the period, "Slide, Kelly, Slide," which he capitalized on in vaudeville and music hall appearances. Records of stolen bases are vague for the period, but in 1887 he was credited with 84.

Kelly's major league career started with Cincinnati in 1878, but he became famous after joining the White Stockings in 1880. He often played right field, and allegedly was the first outfielder to take balls on the bounce and throw out runners at first base. His devil-may-care personality and

Mike "King" Kelly

handsome, mustachioed face made him a national figure, with commercial endorsements pouring in and his poster decorating public places all over the country.

Kelly's quick wit was legendary. He was responsible for the rule that a substitute player must report to the umpire. Sitting on the bench one day, Kelly jumped out on the field and caught a foul fly that nobody in the game could reach, shouting, "Kelly now catching!" Although the rules then specified that substitutions could be made at any time, the umpire refused to allow Kelly's ploy. But the rule was quickly changed to prevent the situation from coming up again.

Kelly was noted for his drinking and womanizing, which grated on the White Stockings management. After the 1886 season, the White Stockings sold him to Boston for the then colossal sum of $10,000, creating national headlines. Kelly had no objections, as Boston raised his salary as player-manager to $5,000, almost double what he had been paid in Chicago.

Kelly's career ended in 1893. He died a year later of pneumonia.

He was elected to the Hall of Fame in 1945.

Kessinger, Don

Cubs: 1964–75
Shortstop
Birthplace: Forrest City, Arkansas

B: July 17, 1942
Bats both, throws right
Ht. 6–1; **Wt.** 170

Kessinger, Donald Eulon

Cubs	G	AB	H	AVG	RBI	R	2B	3B	HR	SLG	SB
1964	4	12	2	.167	0	1	0	0	0	.167	0
1965	106	309	62	.201	14	19	4	3	0	.233	1
1966	150	533	146	.274	43	50	8	2	1	.302	13
1967	145	580	134	.231	42	61	10	7	0	.272	6
1968	160	655	157	.240	32	63	14	7	1	.287	9
1969	158	664	181	.273	53	109	38	6	4	.366	11
1970	154	631	168	.266	39	100	21	14	1	.349	12
1971	155	617	159	.258	38	77	18	6	2	.316	15
1972	149	577	158	.274	39	77	20	6	1	.334	8
1973	160	577	151	.262	43	52	22	3	0	.310	6
1974	153	599	155	.259	42	83	20	7	1	.321	7
1975	154	601	146	.243	46	77	26	10	0	.319	4
Career	2,078	7,651	1,931	.252	527	899	254	80	14	.312	100

An excellent fielder with great range and a strong arm, Don Kessinger was one of the premier shortstops in baseball for a decade with the Cubs, the glue of a great infield with first baseman Ernie Banks, second baseman Glenn Beckert, and third baseman Ron Santo.

Kessinger's batting ability was in doubt until manager Leo Durocher converted him into a switch-hitter in 1966. Kessinger responded immediately, batting .274 that season and again in 1972 for his career highs. He is also among a handful of major league players who have had six hits in six at bats in a game. "Leo's persuading me to switch-hit saved by career," Kessinger admitted.

As Kessinger matured, his power improved, and though he never hit more than four home runs in a season, he had career highs of 38 doubles and 14 triples, and twice scored 100 runs or more.

But it was fielding that made him a standout, earning him several Gold Gloves and selection to the NL All-Star team six

Don Kessinger

Ralph Kiner

times. He tied the NL record for shortstops by recording more than 500 assists in nine seasons.

Traded to St. Louis after the 1975 season, he finished his playing career with the White Sox in 1979, managing the team part of the season.

Kiner, Ralph

Cubs: 1953–54
Outfielder
Birthplace: Santa Rita, New Mexico

B: October 27, 1922
Bats right, throws right
Ht. 6–2; **Wt.** 195

Kiner, Ralph McPherran											
Cubs	G	AB	H	AVG	RBI	R	2B	3B	HR	SLG	SB
1953	117	414	117	.283	87	73	14	2	28	.529	1
1954	147	557	159	.285	73	88	36	5	22	.487	2
Career	1,472	5,205	1,451	.279	1,015	971	216	39	369	.548	22

Ralph Kiner had led the NL in home runs for seven consecutive seasons at Pittsburgh when the Cubs bundled up six players and $150,000 in exchange for him and two others on June 4, 1953. The Cubs teamed him with another slow, slugging outfielder, Hank Sauer, in the heart of their lineup.

A defensive liability, Kiner banged out 28 home runs for the Cubs the rest of that season, finishing with a total of 35 as well as 116 RBIs. The next year, however, it was evident he was nearing the end of his career, though he batted .285 with 22 home runs and 73 RBIs in 147 games. Kiner's career ended with Cleveland the next season. He later became a broadcaster with the New York Mets.

Kiner was elected to the Hall of Fame in 1975.

Kingman, Dave

Cubs: 1978–80
Outfielder
Birthplace: Pendleton, Oregon

B: December 21, 1948
Bats right, throws right
Ht. 6–6; **Wt.** 210

Kingman, David Arthur											
Cubs	G	AB	H	AVG	RBI	R	2B	3B	HR	SLG	SB
1978	119	395	105	.266	79	65	17	4	28	.542	3
1979	145	532	153	.288	115	97	19	5	48	.613	4
1980	81	255	71	.278	57	31	8	0	18	.522	2
Career	1,941	6,677	1,575	.236	1,210	901	240	25	442	.478	85

An unpredictable personality, Dave "Kong" Kingman was an atrocious fielding outfielder who hit with great power, if for low average, and yet put together a tremendous season for the Cubs in 1979. Kingman was signed by the Cubs as a free agent after the 1977 season. He had started his major league career at San Francisco in 1971, had hit as many as 37 home runs but had yet to bat over .238 in a season, and had made 1977 memorable by playing for four teams that year.

He was adequate in 1978, missing 43 games with an injury, yet led the Cubs with 28 home runs and 79 RBIs. But in 1979 he put together a sensational season, hitting 48 home runs to lead the NL, driving in 115 runs, and batting a respectable .288, the highest average of his 16-year career. He was named Chicago Player of the Year by the Baseball Writers' Association.

Briefly the Cubs' most popular player, Kingman quickly dispelled this esteem in 1979 with his eccentricities. He dumped a bucket of water on a sportswriter, declined to go to the ballpark while recovering from an injury, and even skipped a game at which fans were given a T-shirt in his honor. He played in just 81 games, hitting 18 home runs.

Early in 1981, Kingman was traded to the New York Mets, then played six more seasons in the major leagues. He finished his career with 442 home runs.

Klein, Chuck

Cubs: 1934–36
Outfielder
Birthplace: Indianapolis, Indiana
B: October 7, 1904

D: March 28, 1958
Batted left, threw right
Ht. 6–0; **Wt.** 185

Klein, Charles Herbert

Cubs	G	AB	H	AVG	RBI	R	2B	3B	HR	SLG	SB
1934	115	435	131	.301	80	78	27	2	20	.510	3
1935	119	434	127	.293	73	71	14	4	21	.488	4
1936	29	109	32	.294	18	19	5	0	5	.477	0
Career	1,753	6,486	2,076	.320	1,202	1,168	398	74	300	.543	79

By the time Chuck Klein joined the Cubs in 1934, he had led the NL four times in home runs, twice in RBIs, and with a batting average of .368 in 1933. In just over five seasons at Philadelphia, Klein had built his reputation in Baker Bowl, the Phillies' bandbox ballpark, with highs of .386 in batting average, 43 in home runs, and 170 in RBIs. (The last, incidentally, didn't lead the NL in 1930, the season of Hack Wilson's 190.)

In an effort to beef up power, the Cubs sent three players and $65,000 to the cash-strapped Phillies for Klein on November 21, 1933. As so often happened when they acquired a slugger from another team, Klein's power waned in Wrigley Field. He batted .301 with 20 home runs and 80 RBIs in 1934, and tailed off even more in 1935, with .293, 21 home runs, and 73 RBIs, with injuries dogging him both seasons.

Klein's bat, however, did help the Cubs win the pennant in 1935, and in the World Series he contributed a two-run homer to win the fifth game 3–1 before the Cubs fell to Detroit in six games. Early in the '36 season, they sent Klein back to the Phillies, contributing another player and $50,000 more in exchange for two men.

Klein continued to play until 1944, but he was no longer the force he had been in his earlier years, though he finished with a career average of .320 and 300 home runs.

He was elected to the Hall of Fame in 1980.

Kling, Johnny

Cubs: 1900–1908, 1910–11
Catcher
Birthplace: Kansas City, Missouri
B: February 25, 1875

D: January 31, 1947
Batted right, threw right
Ht. 5–9; **Wt.** 160

Kling, John

Cubs	G	AB	H	AVG	RBI	R	2B	3B	HR	SLG	SB
1900	15	51	15	.294	7	8	3	1	0	.392	0
1901	74	253	70	.277	21	26	6	3	0	.324	7
1902	114	434	124	.286	57	50	19	3	0	.343	23
1903	132	491	146	.297	68	67	29	13	3	.428	23
1904	123	452	110	.243	46	41	18	0	2	.296	7
1905	111	380	83	.218	52	26	8	6	1	.279	13
1906	107	343	107	.312	46	45	15	8	2	.420	14
1907	104	334	95	.284	43	44	15	8	1	.386	9
1908	126	424	117	.276	59	51	23	5	4	.382	15
1910	91	297	80	.269	32	31	17	2	2	.360	3
1911	27	80	14	.175	5	8	3	2	1	.250	0
Career	1,260	4,241	1,152	.272	513	475	181	61	20	.357	121

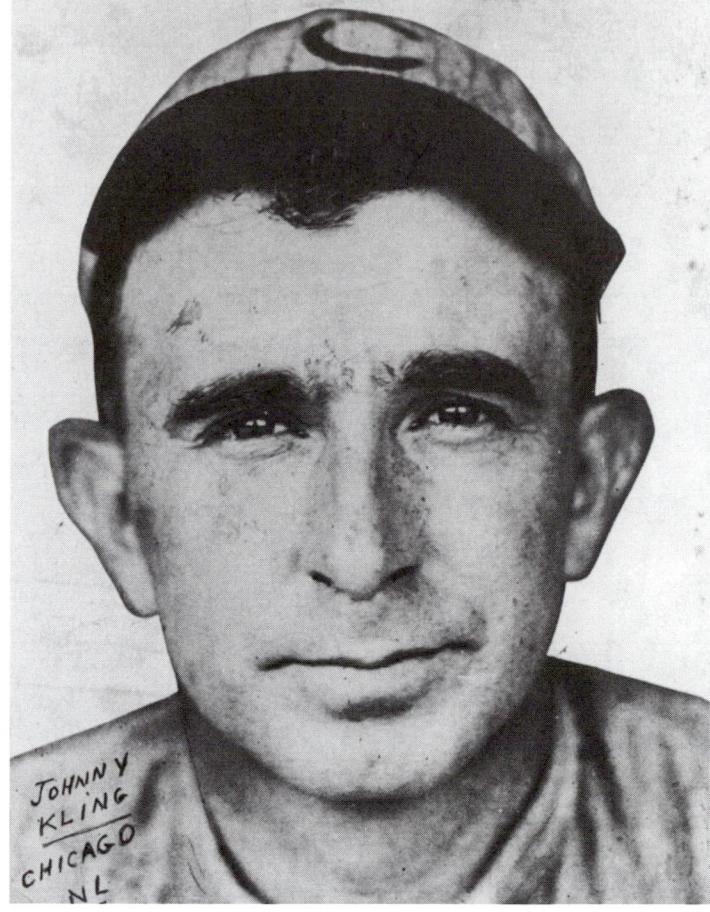

Johnny Kling

Johnny Kling was behind the plate for Frank Chance's four pennant winners early in the century, the receiver for such great pitchers as Three-Finger Brown, Ed Reulbach, and Orval Overall. Reulbach singled him out as "one of the greatest catchers who ever wore the mask."

The Cubs signed Kling out of the minor leagues in 1900, and by 1902 he was the regular catcher. A good hitter, in 1906 he reached a career-high with .312. Three years earlier he batted .297 with 29 doubles and 13 triples. Fast for a catcher, he twice stole 23 bases.

After the Cubs won three consecutive pennants (1906–08) and two World Series (1907–08) with Kling behind the plate, he quit baseball for a year to pursue his first love, billiards. He had won the world pocket billiard title in the winter of 1908–09. After losing the title, Kling returned to the Cubs for the 1910 season, and they won another pennant.

Early in the 1911 season Kling was traded to the Boston Braves, whom he managed in 1912. His career ended with Cincinnati the next year.

Mike Krukow

Krukow, Mike

Cubs: 1976–81 | **B:** January 21, 1952
Pitcher | **Bats right, throws right**
Birthplace: Long Beach, California | **Ht.** 6–5; **Wt.** 205

Krukow, Michael Edward											
Cubs	W	L	Pct	ERA	G	CG	IP	H	BB	K	ShO
1976	0	0	.000	9.00	2	0	4	6	2	1	0
1977	8	14	.364	4.40	34	1	172	195	61	106	1
1978	9	3	.750	3.91	27	3	138	125	53	81	1
1979	9	9	.500	4.20	28	0	165	172	81	119	0
1980	10	15	.400	4.39	34	3	205	200	80	130	0
1981	9	9	.500	3.69	25	2	144	146	55	101	1
Career	124	117	.515	3.90	369	41	2,190	2,188	767	1,478	10

One of the more promising pitchers the Cubs brought up from their farm system in the 1970s, Mike Krukow showed flashes of ability during five seasons in the starting rotation, but never quite emerged as a topflight pitcher until after he left Chicago.

Pitching for poor teams, Krukow finished above .500 only in 1978 with 9–3. During six seasons (1976–81) he had an overall record of 45–50 before being traded to Philadelphia. He emerged as a star in San Francisco, with a 20–9 record in 1986.

Lange, Bill

Cubs: 1893–99 | **D:** July 23, 1950
Outfielder | **Batted right, threw right**
Birthplace: San Francisco, California | **Ht.** 6–1; **Wt.** 190
B: June 6, 1871

Lange, William Alexander											
Cubs	G	AB	H	AVG	RBI	R	2B	3B	HR	SLG	SB
1893	117	469	132	.281	88	92	8	7	8	.380	47
1894	111	442	145	.328	90	84	16	9	6	.446	65
1895	123	478	186	.389	98	120	27	16	10	.575	67
1896	122	469	153	.326	92	114	21	16	4	.465	84
1897	118	479	163	.340	82	119	24	14	5	.480	73
1898	113	442	141	.319	69	79	16	10	6	.441	22
1899	107	416	135	.325	58	81	21	7	1	.416	41
Career	811	3,195	1,055	.330	578	689	133	79	40	.459	399

A standout hitter, with a career average of .330 for seven seasons, Bill "Little Eva" Lange reportedly was one of the finest center fielders in the game's history, teammate Clark Griffith saying that he was "the greatest outfielder I ever saw."

Manager Cap Anson handed the center field job to Lange in 1894, after he came up from the minor leagues in 1893 as a second baseman–outfielder. Lange responded by batting .319 or over for six consecutive seasons, with a high of .389 in 1895 when he hit 10 home runs, drove in 98 runs and scored 120. He stole 84 bases in 1896 and led the league with 73 in 1897 (though before 1898 runners were credited with a stolen base if they advanced from first to third on a single).

Lange, only 28, retired after the 1899 season, having married into wealth.

Lee, Bill

Cubs: 1934–43, 1947 | **D:** June 15, 1977
Pitcher | **Batted right, threw right**
Birthplace: Plaquemine, Louisiana | **Ht.** 6–3; **Wt.** 195
B: October 21, 1909

Lee, William Crutcher											
Cubs	W	L	Pct	ERA	G	CG	IP	H	BB	K	ShO
1934	13	14	.481	3.40	35	16	214⅓	218	74	104	4
1935	20	6	.769	2.96	39	18	252	241	84	100	3
1936	18	11	.621	3.31	43	20	258⅔	238	93	102	4
1937	14	15	.483	3.54	42	17	272⅓	289	73	108	2
1938	22	9	.710	2.66	44	19	291	281	74	121	9
1939	19	15	.559	3.44	37	20	282⅓	295	85	105	1
1940	9	17	.346	5.03	37	9	211⅓	246	70	70	1
1941	8	14	.364	3.76	28	12	167⅓	179	43	62	0
1942	13	13	.500	3.85	32	18	219⅔	221	67	75	1
1943	3	7	.300	3.56	13	4	78⅓	83	27	18	0
1947	0	2	.000	4.50	14	0	24	26	14	9	0
Career	169	157	.518	3.54	462	182	2,864	2,953	893	998	29

The Cubs seldom have put $40,000 to better use than in purchasing Bill Lee from the St. Louis Cardinals' farm system. They acquired a big right-handed pitcher who was their ace for almost a decade and helped them to pennants in 1935 and 1938.

"Big Bill" Lee wasted no time in displaying his credentials as a rookie in 1934, pitching shutouts in his first two major league starts. He finished 13–14. The next year, he won five games of the 21-game winning streak in the stretch drive that earned the Cubs the pennant and posted a 20–6 record, leading the league in percentage with .769.

Lee continued in top form for the next few years, reaching a peak in 1938. He led the NL in victories (22–9), percentage (.710), ERA (2.66), and shutouts (9), though he lost two World Series games to the New York Yankees. His last big year was 1939, when he was 19–15, but then he began to slip, and the Cubs traded him to Philadelphia for catcher Mickey Livingston on August 5, 1943.

Regained by the Cubs in 1947, Lee was 0–2 to end his career.

Leiber, Hank

Cubs: 1939–41
Outfielder
Birthplace: Phoenix, Arizona
B: January 17, 1911

D: November 8, 1993
Batted right, threw right
Ht. 6–1; **Wt.** 205

Leiber, Henry Edward

Cubs	G	AB	H	AVG	RBI	R	2B	3B	HR	SLG	SB
1939	112	365	113	.310	88	65	16	1	24	.556	1
1940	117	440	133	.302	86	68	24	2	17	.482	1
1941	53	162	35	.216	25	20	5	0	7	.377	0
Career	813	2,805	808	.288	518	410	137	24	101	.462	5

In their eternal quest for power, the Cubs acquired veteran outfielder Hank Leiber from the New York Giants in a six-player deal on December 6, 1938. Leiber did not disappoint as the the center fielder in 1939, batting .310 with 24 home runs and 88 RBIs in 112 games.

Leiber came back with .302 in 1940, with 17 home runs and 86 RBIs, though again missing many games with assorted injuries. But in 1941 he was beaned, suffered a severe brain concussion, played in only 53 games, and dropped to .216. Traded back to the Giants after the season, he was unable to regain his batting stroke and retired.

Dale Long

Hank Leiber

Long, Dale

Cubs: 1958–59
First baseman
Birthplace: Springfield, Missouri

B: February 26, 1926
Bats left, throws left
Ht. 6–4; **Wt.** 205

Long, Richard Dale

Cubs	G	AB	H	AVG	RBI	R	2B	3B	HR	SLG	SB
1958	142	480	130	.271	75	68	26	4	20	.467	2
1959	110	296	70	.236	37	34	10	3	14	.432	0
Career	1,013	3,020	805	.267	467	384	135	33	132	.464	10

Dale Long had put his name into the record books with the Pittsburgh Pirates in 1956 by becoming the first player to hit home runs in eight consecutive games before he joined the Cubs in 1958 in a four-player trade.

He added a footnote to the records with the Cubs, becoming one of the few left-handed catchers in the game's history by going behind the plate for a couple of putouts on August 20, 1958. More important, he batted .271 with 20 home runs and 75 RBIs in 1958, giving the Cubs five players to hit 20 or more homers that year.

The first baseman slumped to .236 in 1959, and the Cubs sold him to San Francisco. His career ended with the New York Yankees in 1963.

Lowrey, Peanuts

Cubs: 1942–43, 1945–49
Outfielder
Birthplace: Culver City, California
B: August 27, 1918

D: July 2, 1986
Batted right, threw right
Ht. 5–8; **Wt.** 170

Lowrey, Harry Lee

Cubs	G	AB	H	AVG	RBI	R	2B	3B	HR	SLG	SB
1942	27	58	11	.241	4	4	0	0	1	.241	0
1943	130	480	140	.292	63	59	25	12	1	.400	13
1945	143	523	148	.283	89	72	22	7	7	.392	11
1946	144	540	139	.257	54	75	24	5	4	.343	10
1947	115	448	126	.281	37	56	17	5	5	.375	2
1948	129	435	128	.294	54	47	12	3	2	.349	2
1949	38	111	30	.270	10	18	5	0	2	.369	3
Career	1,401	4,317	1,177	.273	479	564	186	45	37	.362	48

A child movie actor in small roles before he turned to baseball, Peanuts Lowrey was among the more interesting characters who have played for the Cubs. A good hitter and fielder, Lowrey was the left fielder for the pennant winner of 1945, batting .283 with seven home runs and 89 RBIs.

Lowrey became the Cubs' center fielder in 1943 and batted .292 in his first full major league season. After military service in 1944, he returned to find Andy Pafko in center field and moved to left. He batted .310 in the World Series loss to Detroit.

Lowrey, nicknamed Peanuts by a relative because he was a small baby, continued as a productive Cubs player for four more seasons, and batted .294 in 1948. Traded to Cincinnati early in 1949 in the deal that brought Hank Sauer and Frankie Baumholtz to the Cubs, he played respectably in the major leagues until 1955.

He also continued his movie career, appearing in minor roles in several baseball movies, including *The Pride of the Yankees, The Stratton Story,* and *The Winning Team.* During the late 1960s and 1970s he was a Cub coach.

Lundgren, Carl

Cubs: 1902–09
Pitcher
Birthplace: Marengo, Illinois
B: February 16, 1880

D: August 21, 1934
Batted right, threw right
Ht. 5–11; **Wt.** 175

Lundgren, Carl Leonard

Cubs	W	L	Pct	ERA	G	CG	IP	H	BB	K	ShO
1902	9	9	.500	1.97	18	17	160	158	45	68	1
1903	10	9	.526	2.94	27	16	193	191	60	67	0
1904	17	10	.630	2.60	31	25	242	203	77	106	2
1905	13	4	.765	2.24	23	16	169	132	53	69	3
1906	17	6	.739	2.21	27	21	207⅔	160	89	103	5
1907	18	7	.720	1.17	28	21	207	130	92	84	7
1908	6	9	.400	4.22	23	9	138⅔	149	56	38	1
1909	0	1	.000	4.15	2	0	4⅓	6	4	0	0
Career	90	55	.621	2.42	179	125	1,321⅓	1,129	476	535	19

In the Cubs' glory years of the early 1900s, Carl Lundgren was a consistent, impressive pitcher who contributed heavily to the pennant winners of 1906 and 1907.

In 1906, when the Cubs won a record 116 games, Lundgren was 17–6, and the next year, when they captured the pennant again, he was 18–7, with an ERA of 1.17 and seven shutouts. He didn't appear in the World Series in either year, or in 1908 when he fell off to 6–9 as the Cubs won their third consecutive pennant.

Lundgren's major league career ended in 1909. Later he became a noted college baseball coach, with his greatest years at the University of Illinois.

Peanuts Lowrey

Carl Lundgren

Madlock, Bill

Cubs: 1974–76
Third baseman
Birthplace: Memphis, Tennessee

B: January 2, 1951
Bats right, throws right
Ht. 5–11; **Wt.** 185

Madlock, William, Jr.

Cubs	G	AB	H	AVG	RBI	R	2B	3B	HR	SLG	SB
1974	128	453	142	.313	54	65	21	5	9	.442	11
1975	130	514	182	.354	64	77	29	7	7	.479	9
1976	142	514	174	.339	84	68	36	1	15	.500	15
Career	1,806	6,594	2,008	.305	860	920	348	34	163	.442	174

An exceptional hitter, with a compact, powerful stroke, Bill Madlock came to the Cubs from Texas in the trade that sent Ferguson Jenkins to the Rangers on October 25, 1973, and proved an exceptional replacement for Ron Santo at third base.

Madlock, nicknamed Mad Dog for his volatile personality, batted .313 as a rookie in 1974, the put together two straight batting titles, with .354 in 1975 and .339 the next year. He won the second batting championship by going 4-for-4 the final day of the season.

A contract dispute erupted after the season when Madlock reportedly sought $1 million for five years. The Cubs refused to yield, and he was traded to San Francisco on February 11, 1977, in a five-player deal. He left with a three-season average of .336 for the Cubs.

Madlock won two more NL batting titles during the following 11 seasons, played on a World Series winner at Pittsburgh in 1977, and retired with a .305 career average.

Malone, Pat

Cubs: 1928–34
Pitcher
Birthplace: Altoona, Pennsylvania
B: September 25, 1902

D: May 13, 1943
Batted left, threw right
Ht. 6–0; **Wt.** 200

Malone, Perce Leigh

Cubs	W	L	Pct	ERA	G	CG	IP	H	BB	K	ShO
1928	18	13	.581	2.84	42	16	250⅔	218	99	155	2
1929	22	10	.688	3.57	40	19	267	283	102	166	5
1930	20	9	.690	3.94	45	22	271¾	290	96	142	2
1931	16	9	.640	3.90	36	12	228⅓	229	88	112	2
1932	15	17	.469	3.38	37	17	237	222	78	120	2
1933	10	14	.417	3.91	31	13	186⅓	186	59	72	2
1934	14	7	.667	3.53	34	8	191	200	55	111	1
Career	134	92	.593	3.74	357	115	1,915	1,934	705	1,024	16

A true child of the Prohibition Era, Pat Malone may have shortened his career by being slugger Hack Wilson's drinking buddy, but for a brief period the hulking, red-faced, hard-throwing right-hander was the bellwether of the Cub staff.

Malone was 18–13 as a rookie in 1928 despite losing his first seven decisions, then led the NL in victories the next two seasons. He was 22–10 in 1929, the Cubs' pennant year, but lost two games to the Philadelphia A's in the World Series, then came back with 20–9 the next season. He also led the NL in strikeouts with 166 and in shutouts with five in 1929.

He continued to be a winner in 1931 with a 16–9 record, after which he faded to 15–17 and 10–14, before recovering to 14–7 in 1934. The Cubs traded him to the St. Louis Cardinals, who promptly sold him to the New York Yankees for $15,000. He finished his career in 1937 with the Yankees, and died six years later at the age of 40 of acute pancreatitis.

Bill Madlock (enlarge)

Pat Malone

Matthews, Gary

Cubs: 1984–87
Outfielder
Birthplace: San Fernando, California

B: July 5, 1950
Bats right, throws right
Ht. 6–2; Wt. 185

Matthews, Gary Nathaniel

Cubs	G	AB	H	AVG	RBI	R	2B	3B	HR	SLG	SB
1984	147	491	143	.291	82	101	21	2	14	.428	17
1985	97	298	70	.235	40	45	12	0	13	.406	2
1986	123	370	96	.259	46	49	16	1	21	.478	3
1987	44	42	11	.262	8	3	3	0	0	.33	0
Career	2,033	7,147	2,011	.281	978	1,083	319	51	234	.439	183

The Sarge, as Gary Matthews was nicknamed, was a veteran of 12 major league seasons when Cub general manager Dallas Green acquired him and Bobby Dernier in a five-man trade with Philadelphia on March 27, 1984. Matthews took over left field and Dernier center, and both were instrumental in the Cubs' winning the NL East title that season.

"We needed a screamer, a holler guy, a leader," Green said. "When I realized I could get him from the Phillies, I couldn't say yes fast enough."

A take-charge player, the enthusiastic Matthews immediately became wildly popular with the left-field fans in Wrigley Field. He drove in the winning run in 19 games, batted .291, hit 14 home runs, drove in 82 runs, and stole 17 bases as his contributions to the Cubs' first title of any sort in 39 years.

Matthews faded quickly at age 35 in 1985, dropping to .235, then .259 the next year, though he hit 21 home runs.

Gary Matthews

Traded to Seattle midway in the 1987 season, he finished his career that year.

McCormick, Jim

White Stockings: 1885–86
Pitcher
Birthplace: Glasgow, Scotland
B: 1856

D: March 10, 1918
Batted right, threw right
Ht. 5–10; Wt. 215

McCormick, James

White Stockings	W	L	Pct	ERA	G	CG	IP	H	BB	K	ShO
1885	20	4	.833	2.43	24	24	215	187	40	88	3
1886	31	11	.738	2.82	42	38	347⅔	341	100	72	2
Career	265	213	.554	2.43	494	466	4,275⅔	4,092	749	1,704	33

During a brief stint with the White Stockings, after an outstanding career with several teams, Jim McCormick contributed to pennant winners in 1885 and 1886. He was 20–4 for them in 1885 after starting the season in Providence, then 31–11 the next year, after which he departed to finish his career at Pittsburgh.

McCormick put together winning streaks of 14 games in 1885 and 16 games in 1886 with the White Stockings.

McCullough, Clyde

Cubs: 1940–43, 1945–48, 1953–56
Catcher
Birthplace: Nashville, Tennessee
B: March 4, 1917

D: September 18, 1982
Batted right, threw right
Ht. 5–11; Wt. 180

McCullough, Clyde Edward

Cubs	G	AB	H	AVG	RBI	R	2B	3B	HR	SLG	SB
1940	9	26	4	.154	1	4	1	0	0	.192	0
1941	125	418	95	.227	53	41	9	2	9	.323	5
1942	109	337	95	.282	31	39	22	1	5	.398	7
1943	87	266	63	.237	23	20	5	2	2	.293	6
1946	95	307	88	.287	34	38	18	5	4	.417	2
1947	86	234	59	.252	30	25	12	4	3	.376	1
1948	69	172	36	.209	7	10	4	2	1	.273	0
1953	77	229	59	.258	23	21	3	2	6	.367	0
1954	31	81	21	.259	17	9	7	0	3	.457	0
1955	44	81	16	.198	10	7	0	0	0	.198	0
1956	14	19	4	.211	1	0	1	0	0	.263	0
Career	1,098	3,121	785	.252	339	308	121	28	52	.358	27

A fine receiver and a natural leader, a peppery "holler guy," Clyde McCullough was mediocre at bat. He did hit three home runs in one game for the Cubs in 1942, though only 52 for a 15-year career in which he batted .252. He was the number-one catcher as a rookie in 1941, batting .227 in 125 games, and the following year, when he hit .282 in 109 games.

Sidelined the first seven weeks of the 1943 season by a broken ankle, McCullough regained his job, but then entered military service, returning just in time for one futile at bat in the 1945 World Series against Detroit. He shared the catching job for the next three years, then was traded to Pittsburgh after the 1948 season.

Another deal brought him back to the Cubs in 1953 as a reserve catcher. His career ended in 1956.

Clyde McCullough

Lindy McDaniel

McDaniel, Lindy

Cubs: 1963–65
Pitcher
Birthplace: Hollis, Oklahoma

B: December 13, 1935
Bats right, throws right
Ht. 6–3; **Wt.** 195

McDaniel, Lyndale Dale

Cubs	W	L	Pct	ERA	G	SV	IP	H	BB	K	ShO
1963	13	7	.650	2.86	57	22	88	82	27	75	0
1964	1	7	.125	3.88	63	15	95	104	23	71	0
1965	5	6	.455	2.59	71	2	128⅔	115	47	92	0
Career	141	119	.542	3.45	987	172	2,140⅓	2,099	623	1,361	0

After eight seasons with the St. Louis Cardinals, who converted him from a starter to a relief pitcher, Lindy McDaniel was acquired along with starter Larry Jackson after the 1962 season in one of the Cubs' better trades.

McDaniel, 27, was a sensation out of the bullpen in his first season with the Cubs, earning the Fireman of the Year award with a 13–7 record and an NL-leading 22 saves. Traded to the San Francisco Giants along with outfielder Don Landrum in late 1965, McDaniel may have performed an even more valuable service to the Cubs, the deal bringing them catcher Randy Hundley and pitcher Bill Hands.

McDaniel was a solid relief pitcher for another 10 years, retiring after the 1975 campaign with a 21-year career total of 141–119, 172 saves, and 987 appearances, second only to Hoyt Wilhelm's 1,070.

Merkle, Fred

Cubs: 1917–20
First baseman
Birthplace: Watertown, Wisconsin
B: December 20, 1888

D: March 2, 1956
Batted right, threw right
Ht. 6–1; **Wt.** 190

Merkle, Frederick Charles

Cubs	G	AB	H	AVG	RBI	R	2B	3B	HR	SLG	SB
1917	146	549	116	.266	57	65	30	9	3	.370	13
1918	129	482	143	.297	65	55	25	5	3	.388	21
1919	133	498	133	.267	62	52	20	6	3	.349	20
1920	92	330	94	.285	38	33	20	4	3	.397	3
Career	1,637	5,782	1,580	.273	733	720	290	83	61	.384	271

It is one of the ironies of baseball that Fred Merkle, whose baserunning "boner" with the New York Giants in 1908 gave the Cubs a pennant, helped them to another in 1918 as their first baseman. A better-than-average player, Merkle was acquired by the Cubs early in the 1917 season and took over first base for four years.

Merkle's best season with the Cubs was 1918, when he batted .297 with 65 RBIs in 129 games, and contributed a .278 average to a losing cause in the World Series. He retired in 1920, but took the field briefly as player-coach for the New York Yankees in 1925 and 1926.

Fred Merkle

Lennie Merullo

Merullo, Lennie

Cubs: 1941–47
Shortstop
Birthplace: Boston, Massachusetts

B: May 5, 1917
Bats right, throws right
Ht. 5–11; **Wt.** 166

Merullo, Leonard Richard

Cubs	G	AB	H	AVG	RBI	R	2B	3B	HR	SLG	SB
1941	7	17	6	.353	1	3	1	0	0	.412	1
1942	143	515	132	.256	37	53	23	3	2	.324	14
1943	129	453	115	.254	25	37	18	3	1	.313	7
1944	66	193	41	.212	16	20	8	1	1	.280	3
1945	121	394	94	.239	37	40	18	0	2	.299	7
1946	65	126	19	.151	7	14	8	0	0	.214	2
1947	108	373	90	.241	29	24	16	1	0	.290	4
Career	639	2,071	497	.240	152	191	92	8	6	.301	38

One of a seemingly endless succession of failed shortstops between Billy Jurges in the 1930s and Ernie Banks in the mid–1950s, Lennie Merullo is chiefly remembered for setting a major league record by committing four errors in an inning on four successive plays on September 13, 1942.

Merullo came highly touted out of the Cubs farm system in 1941 and held the regular shortstop job for the next two seasons, batting .256 and .254. He then shared the job with Roy Hughes, but played more in the pennant season of 1945. A back problem led to the end of Merullo's career after the 1947 season.

Miksis, Eddie

Cubs: 1951–56
Second baseman, outfielder
Birthplace: Burlington, New Jersey

B: September 11, 1926
Bats right, throws right
Ht. 6–0; **Wt.** 185

Miksis, Edward Thomas

Cubs	G	AB	H	AVG	RBI	R	2B	3B	HR	SLG	SB
1951	102	421	112	.266	35	48	13	3	4	.340	11
1952	93	383	89	.232	19	44	20	1	2	.305	4
1953	142	577	145	.251	39	61	17	6	8	.343	13
1954	38	99	20	.202	3	9	3	0	2	.293	1
1955	131	481	113	.235	41	52	14	2	9	.328	3
1956	114	356	85	.239	27	54	10	3	9	.360	4
Career	1,042	3,053	722	.236	228	383	95	17	44	.322	52

Obtained in a seven-player trade on June 15, 1951, that sent Andy Pafko to Brooklyn, Eddie Miksis was a career utility player with some power but a low batting average who never lived up to the Cubs' expectations as a second baseman.

Miksis teamed up with shortstop Roy Smalley as a double-play combination for his first three years with the Cubs, but went to the bench in 1954 when Gene Baker and Ernie Banks took over in the middle of the infield. An outfielder in 1955, Miksis filled in at various spots the next year, his last with the Cubs. His career ended in 1958.

Eddie Miksis

Miller, Hack

Cubs: 1922–25
Outfielder
Birthplace: New York City
B: January 11, 1894

D: September 17, 1971
Batted right, threw right
Ht. 5–9; **Wt.** 195

Miller, Lawrence H.

Cubs	G	AB	H	AVG	RBI	R	2B	3B	HR	SLG	SB
1922	122	466	164	.352	78	61	28	5	12	.511	3
1923	135	485	146	.301	88	74	24	2	20	.482	6
1924	53	131	44	.336	25	17	8	1	4	.504	1
1925	24	86	24	.279	9	10	3	2	2	.430	0
Career	349	1,200	387	.323	205	164	65	11	38	.490	10

Compact yet powerfully built, Hack Miller failed in earlier trials in the major leagues, but quickly became a Cub hero with his slugging and weight-lifting exhibitions after he joined the team in 1922. As a rookie, he batted .352 with 12 home runs and 78 RBIs, and in 1923 he hit .301 with 20 home runs and 88 RBIs. Miller contributed two three-run home runs to the highest scoring game of all time, a 26–23 victory over Philadelphia on August 25, 1922.

Unable to cover much ground in the outfield, Miller's fielding deficiencies cut his playing time in his final two years with the Cubs. He batted .336 in 53 games in 1924, then sank to .279 before being released in May 1925. His career ended in the minor leagues.

His nickname "Hack" derived from his resemblance to a famous wrestler of the day, Hackenschmidt.

Hack Miller

Minner, Paul

Cubs: 1950–56
Pitcher
Birthplace: New Wilmington, Pennsylvania

B: July 30, 1923
Bats left, throws left
Ht. 6–5; **Wt.** 200

Minner, Paul Edison

Cubs	W	L	Pct	ERA	G	CG	IP	H	BB	K	ShO
1950	8	13	.381	4.11	39	9	190⅓	217	72	99	1
1951	6	17	.261	3.79	33	14	201⅔	219	64	68	3
1952	14	9	.609	3.74	28	12	180⅔	180	54	61	2
1953	12	15	.444	4.21	31	9	201	227	40	64	2
1954	11	11	.500	3.96	32	12	218	236	79	50	0
1955	9	9	.500	3.48	22	7	157⅔	173	47	53	1
1956	2	5	.286	6.89	10	1	47	60	19	14	0
Career	69	84	.451	3.94	253	64	1,310⅓	1,428	393	481	9

One of the more successful Cub left-handers between Larry French in the 1930s and Dick Ellsworth in the 1960s, Paul "Lefty" Minner had lost his fastball by the time he was obtained from Brooklyn in a deal on October 14, 1949. He made do with off-speed pitches, including a palm ball.

After starting slowly with the Cubs with 8–13 in 1950 and 6–17 in 1951, Minner put together three good seasons, his best being 14–9 in 1952. He was noted for his mastery of St. Louis, with a career record of 21–8 over the Cardinals. A back injury ended his career in 1956.

Paul Minner

Rick Monday

Monday, Rick

Cubs: 1972–76
Outfielder
Birthplace: Batesville, Arkansas

B: November 20, 1945
Bats left, throws left
Ht. 6–3; **Wt.** 195

Monday, Robert James

Cubs	G	AB	H	AVG	RBI	R	2B	3B	HR	SLG	SB
1972	138	434	108	.249	42	68	22	5	11	.399	12
1973	149	554	148	.267	56	93	24	5	26	.469	5
1974	142	538	158	.294	58	84	19	7	20	.467	7
1975	136	491	131	.267	60	89	29	4	17	.446	8
1976	137	534	135	.272	77	60	20	5	32	.507	5
Career	1,986	6,136	1,619	.264	775	950	248	64	241	.443	98

When the Cubs traded Ken Holtzman to Oakland for Rick Monday after the 1971 season, they acquired their best center fielder since Andy Pafko, two decades earlier. Monday gave them left-handed power and consistently good defense.

A six-year major league veteran, Monday was in his prime during his five seasons with the Cubs. He produced his peak batting average of .294 in 1974, and achieved his high in home runs (32) and RBIs (77) in 1976. He hit 20 or more home runs three times, and on on May 16, 1972, hit three consecutively in a game at Philadelphia.

His most publicized feat, however, was not achieved with bat or glove, but came on April 25, 1976, when he rescued an American flag from two demonstrators who were about to burn it as a political protest after running on the field at Los Angeles.

Traded to the Dodgers after the 1976 season in the deal that brought Bill Buckner and Ivan DeJesus to the Cubs, Monday played eight more seasons and in three World Series at Los Angeles. He became a broadcaster after retiring as a player in 1984.

Morales, Jerry

Cubs: 1974–77, 1981–83
Outfielder
Birthplace: Yabucoa, Puerto Rico

B: February 18, 1949
Bats right, throws right
Ht. 5–10; **Wt.** 155

Morales, Julio Ruben

Cubs	G	AB	H	AVG	RBI	R	2B	3B	HR	SLG	SB
1974	151	534	146	.273	82	70	21	7	15	.423	2
1975	153	578	156	.270	91	62	21	0	12	.369	3
1976	140	537	147	.274	67	66	17	0	16	.395	3
1977	136	490	142	.290	69	56	34	5	11	.447	0
1981	84	245	70	.286	25	27	6	2	1	.339	1
1982	65	116	33	.284	30	14	2	2	4	.440	1
1983	63	87	17	.195	11	11	9	0	0	.299	0
Career	1,441	4,528	1,173	.259	570	516	199	36	95	.382	37

A competent outfielder with some power, Jerry Morales had two terms with the Cubs, his first starting in 1974 after aging second baseman Glenn Beckert was traded to San Diego for him.

Arriving as a four-year veteran, Morales enjoyed four good seasons with the Cubs, batting as high as .290 in 1977, and reaching highs in home runs with 16 in 1976 and RBIs with 91 in 1975. Traded to St. Louis after the 1977 season, Morales was reacquired three years later, and was a utility outfielder from 1981 to 1983 before being released.

Jerry Morales

Keith Moreland

Moreland, Keith

Cubs: 1982–87
Outfielder, catcher
Birthplace: Dallas, Texas

B: May 2, 1954
Bats right, throws right
Ht. 6–0; **Wt.** 190

Moreland, Bobby Keith

Cubs	G	AB	H	AVG	RBI	R	2B	3B	HR	SLG	SB
1982	138	476	124	.261	68	50	17	2	15	.399	0
1983	154	533	161	.302	70	76	30	3	16	.460	0
1984	140	495	138	.279	80	59	17	3	16	.422	1
1985	161	587	180	.307	106	74	30	3	14	.440	12
1986	156	586	159	.271	79	72	30	0	12	.384	3
1987	153	563	150	.266	88	63	29	1	27	.465	3
Career	1,306	4,581	1,279	.279	674	511	214	14	121	.411	28

A second-string catcher at Philadelphia, husky, red-headed Keith Moreland was converted into an outfielder by the Cubs after joining them in 1982. He was the regular right fielder when they won the East Division championship in 1984.

After batting .261 in 138 games in 1982, Moreland lifted his average to .302 the next season. He started slowly in 1984, then caught fire in July, and in August won NL Player of the Month honors. He batted .360 in August, with five home runs, 32 RBIs, and eight game-winning hits. He finished the season with .279, 16 home runs, and 80 RBIs.

Moreland had three more good seasons with the Cubs, reaching career highs with .307 and 106 RBIs in 1985, and with 27 home runs in 1987. The latter season he was switched to third base, but proved inadequate in the field. He was traded after the season to San Diego, and two years later retired.

Moryn, Walt

Cubs: 1956–60
Outfielder
Birthplace: St. Paul, Minnesota
B: April 12, 1926

D: July 21, 1996
Batted right, threw right
Ht. 6–2; **Wt.** 205

Moryn, Walter Joseph

Cubs	G	AB	H	AVG	RBI	R	2B	3B	HR	SLG	SB
1956	147	529	151	.285	67	69	27	3	23	.478	4
1957	149	568	164	.289	88	76	33	0	19	.447	0
1958	143	512	135	.264	77	77	26	7	26	.494	1
1959	117	381	89	.234	48	41	14	1	14	.386	0
1960	38	109	32	.294	11	12	4	0	2	.385	2
Career	785	2,506	667	.266	354	324	116	16	101	.446	7

A fan favorite at Wrigley Field, Walt Moryn earned his nickname of "Moose" because of his physique and power as well as lack of speed. The Cubs acquired Moryn out of the Brooklyn farm system in a trade that sent first baseman Ransom Jackson to the Dodgers after the 1955 season.

An outfielder with a strong arm, Moryn was a potent hitter, batting .285 with 23 home runs in 1956. In 1957 he batted .289 with 19 home runs and 88 RBIs. And in 1958 he was chosen for the All-Star team as he batted .264 with 26 home runs and hit three home runs in a game. He slumped to .234 the next year, with just 14 home runs.

Moryn's most memorable moment as a Cub might have come when he made a spectacular shoestring catch with two outs in the ninth inning to save a no-hitter for Don Cardwell on May 15, 1960.

A month later, though he was batting .294 in 38 games, he was traded to St. Louis. His career ended in 1961.

Moose Moryn

Bobby Murcer

Murcer, Bobby

Cubs: 1977–79
Outfielder
Birthplace: Oklahoma City, Oklahoma

B: May 20, 1946
Bats left, throws right
Ht. 5–11; **Wt.** 160

Murcer, Bobby Ray

Cubs	G	AB	H	AVG	RBI	R	2B	3B	HR	SLG	SB
1977	154	554	147	.265	89	90	18	3	27	.455	16
1978	146	499	140	.281	64	66	22	6	9	.403	14
1979	58	190	49	.258	22	22	4	1	7	.400	2
Career	1,908	6,730	1,862	.277	1,043	972	285	45	252	.445	127

A star with the New York Yankees before moving in 1975 to San Francisco for two seasons, Bobby Murcer came to the Cubs in the February 11, 1977, trade that sent two-time NL batting champion Bill Madlock to the Giants. Murcer became the highest-paid Cub up to that time, with a five-year contract.

In Murcer's first season with the Cubs, 1977, he played right field and led the team in home runs with 27 and RBIs with 89, though he batted only .265. But in 1978, though his average rose to .281, his home run production declined to nine. After another slow start in 1979, Murcer was traded after 58 games to the Yankees, with whom he finished his career in 1983.

Nicholson, Bill

Cubs: 1939–48
Outfielder
Birthplace: Chestertown, Maryland
B: December 11, 1914

D: March 8, 1996
Batted left, threw right
Ht. 6–0; **Wt.** 205

Nicholson, William Beck

Cubs	G	AB	H	AVG	RBI	R	2B	3B	HR	SLG	SB
1939	58	220	65	.295	38	37	12	5	5	.464	0
1940	135	491	146	.297	98	78	27	7	25	.534	2
1941	147	532	135	.254	98	74	26	1	26	.453	1
1942	152	588	173	.294	78	83	22	11	21	.476	8
1943	154	608	188	.309	128	95	30	9	29	.531	4
1944	156	582	167	.287	122	116	35	8	33	.545	3
1945	151	559	136	.243	88	82	28	4	13	.377	4
1946	105	296	65	.220	41	36	13	2	8	.358	1
1947	148	487	119	.244	75	69	28	1	26	.466	1
1948	143	494	129	.261	67	68	24	5	19	.445	2
Career	1,677	5,546	1,484	.268	948	837	272	60	235	.465	27

A powerfully built farm boy from Maryland, Bill Nicholson failed in an early trial with the Philadelphia Athletics, but three years later, in 1939, he made his debut with the Cubs and went on to become a legendary slugger for most of the 1940s.

Nicholson erupted in his first full season, 1940, for 25 home runs and 98 RBIs, while batting .297. He quickly was given the nickname "Swish" because of his bat speed and propensity to homer or strikeout—though by current standards his career high of 91 strikeouts in a season would be considered modest.

Nicholson's best seasons were 1943 and 1944, when he hit 29 and 33 home runs and batted in 128 and 122 runs to lead the league in both categories. He also reached his career-high batting average with .309 in 1943, and the next year batted .287 and was named the NL's Most Valuable Player.

Nicholson in 1944 also became one of the few batters in the history of the game to be walked intentionally with the bases loaded. He had hit four home runs in a doubleheader against the Giants on July 23, and when he came to bat with the bases loaded in the seventh inning of the second game, New York manager Mel Ott ordered him walked. The strategy worked, the Giants winning 12–10, but dumbfounded Nicholson. "I couldn't believe it," Nicholson said. "I was the most surprised guy in the ballpark."

Nicholson fell off drastically after his banner 1944 season, contributing just 13 home runs to the Cubs' pennant victory of 1945, though he batted in 88 runs. However, he drove in eight runs and hit a home run in the losing World Series effort against Detroit.

Nicholson's final big power year was 1947, when he hit 26 home runs. A year later he was traded to the Phillies, with whom he spent four years before retiring in 1953. During 10 seasons with the Cubs, he hit 205 home runs.

Novikoff, Lou

Cubs: 1941–44
Outfielder
Birthplace: Glendale, Arizona
B: October 12, 1915
D: September 30, 1970
Batted right, threw right
Ht. 5–10; **Wt.** 185

Novikoff, Louis Alexander

Cubs	G	AB	H	AVG	RBI	R	2B	3B	HR	SLG	SB
1941	62	203	49	.241	24	22	8	0	5	.355	0
1942	128	483	145	.300	64	48	25	5	7	.416	3
1943	78	233	65	.279	28	22	7	3	0	.335	0
1944	71	139	39	.281	19	15	4	2	3	.403	1
Career	356	1,081	305	.282	138	107	45	10	15	.384	4

"The Mad Russian," the moniker by which he quickly became known, contributed very little to the Cubs as a player but a great deal as a "screwball." Lou Novikoff's antics and idiosyncrasies, such as complaining that he couldn't play left field at Wrigley Field because the "foul lines were crooked," became grist for the media mills.

Novikoff, an atrocious outfielder, had led four minor leagues in batting by the time the Cubs decided to play him regularly in left field in 1942 no matter how badly he fielded. Though he was hitting only .206 in June, he pushed his average up to .300 by season's end, allegedly revitalized because his wife had started feeding him ground meat wrapped in cabbage leaves.

Because his fielding didn't improve, the Cubs played him less and less the next two seasons, though he batted .279 and .281, and sent him to the minor leagues for 1945. He later was sold to the Phillies and released after 17 games in 1946. A great softball player, he was enshrined in the Softball Hall of Fame.

Overall, Orval

Cubs: 1906–1910, 1913
Pitcher
Birthplace: Farmersville, California
B: February 2, 1881
D: July 14, 1947
Batted both, threw right
Ht. 6–2; **Wt.** 214

Overall, Orval

Cubs	W	L	Pct	ERA	G	CG	IP	H	BB	K	ShO
1906	12	3	.800	1.88	18	13	144	116	51	94	2
1907	23	8	.742	1.70	35	26	265⅓	199	69	139	8
1908	15	11	.577	1.92	37	16	225	165	78	167	4
1909	20	11	.645	1.42	38	23	285	204	80	205	9
1910	12	6	.667	2.68	23	11	144⅔	106	54	92	4
1913	4	5	.444	3.31	11	6	68	73	26	30	1
Career	106	71	.599	2.24	217	133	1,532⅓	1,230	551	933	30

Obtained in a deal with Cincinnati in midseason 1906, Orval Overall rounded out the formidable pitching staff that won four pennants in five seasons for Frank Chance's Cubs. Overall was 12–3 for the Cubs in 1906 when they won a major league record 116 games to capture their first pennant in 20 years.

His greatest season was 1907 when he was 23–8, led the league with eight shutouts, and was 1–0 in the World Series triumph over Detroit. Although he dropped to 15–11 in 1908, he was 2–0 in the World Series as the Cubs again handled the Tigers.

Overall rebounded to 20–11 in 1909, leading the league in shutouts with nine and strikeouts with 205. He was fading by 1910, but was 12–6 when the Cubs won their fourth pennant in five years.

Upset by a contract dispute with management, Overall quit baseball after the 1910 season. He attempted a comeback in 1913, struggled to a 4–5 record, and retired at season's end.

Lou Novikoff

Orval Overall

Andy Pafko

Pafko, Andy

Cubs: 1943–51
Outfielder, third baseman
Birthplace: Boyceville, Wisconsin

B: February 25, 1921
Bats right, throws right
Ht. 6–0; **Wt.** 190

Pafko, Andrew

Cubs	G	AB	H	AVG	RBI	R	2B	3B	HR	SLG	SB
1943	13	58	22	.379	10	7	3	0	0	.431	1
1944	128	469	126	.269	62	47	16	2	6	.350	2
1945	144	534	159	.298	110	64	24	12	12	.455	5
1946	65	234	66	.282	39	18	6	4	3	.380	4
1947	129	513	155	.302	66	68	25	7	13	.454	4
1948	142	548	171	.312	101	82	30	2	26	.516	3
1949	144	519	146	.281	69	79	29	2	18	.449	4
1950	146	514	156	.304	92	95	24	8	36	.591	4
1951	49	178	47	.264	35	26	5	3	12	.528	1
Career	1,852	6,292	1,796	.285	976	844	264	62	213	.449	38

Andy Pafko ranks high among the Cubs' finest center fielders. He could run and hit for distance, and he had a powerful throwing arm. He was called up from Los Angeles of the Pacific Coast League, where he had won the batting championship in 1943 by hitting .356. He batted .269 as the Cubs' regular center fielder in 1944.

Pafko blossomed the next year, lifting his average to .298 and driving in 110 runs in 144 games; he had a big hand in the Cubs' march to the pennant. Injuries hampered him in 1946, but the next four seasons were among the best of his career. He batted .302 in 1947, .312 the next year, and .304 in 1950. He hit 26 home runs in 1948 with 101 RBIs, and 36 with 92 RBIs in 1950.

A versatile player, Pafko switched to third base in 1948 to make room for rookie Hal Jeffcoat in center, then switched back again the following year, gaining the nickname of "Handy Andy."

His other nickname, "Prushka," was bestowed on him by manager Charlie Grimm because "he looked like a Prushka to me. My thought was that if he had a carpet bag in his hand he'd look like he'd just got off the boat from one of those old countries. But what a ballplayer."

Pafko's tenure with the Cubs ended on June 15, 1951, in an eight-player trade with Brooklyn. The deal proved a bust for the Cubs, but the Dodgers now had one of the better all-time outfields with Pafko in left, Duke Snider in center, and Carl Furillo in right. Pafko helped the Dodgers win a pennant in 1952, and after being traded to Milwaukee played in two more World Series with the Braves. He retired after the 1959 season.

Pappas, Milt

Cubs: 1970–73
Pitcher
Birthplace: Detroit, Michigan

B: May 11, 1939
Bats right, throws right
Ht. 6–3; **Wt.** 190

Pappas, Milton Stephen

Cubs	W	L	Pct	ERA	G	CG	IP	H	BB	K	ShO
1970	10	8	.556	2.68	21	6	144⅔	135	36	80	2
1971	17	14	.548	3.42	35	14	261	279	62	99	5
1972	17	7	.708	2.77	29	10	195	187	29	80	3
1973	7	12	.368	4.38	30	1	162	192	40	48	1
Career	209	164	.560	3.40	520	129	3,185⅔	3,046	858	1,728	43

Milt Pappas

Milt Pappas holds a unique distinction in that he is the only pitcher to win 200 major league games without ever winning 20 in a season. However, he was a consistent winner for three teams over 13 seasons, most of them with Baltimore, before the Cubs bought him at the age of 31 from Atlanta in June 1970.

Manager Leo Durocher thrust him into the starting rotation with Ferguson Jenkins, Bill Hands, and Ken Holtzman, and Pappas rose to the occasion. He was 10–8 the rest of 1970 with the Cubs. He reached career highs in wins with 17–14 in 1971 and 17–7 in 1972, when he won his last 11 decisions in a row, the final being a no-hitter that came within a pitch of a perfect game. On September 2, 1970, Pappas faced San Diego at Wrigley Field and retired the first 26 Padres in order, then walked Larry Stahl on a full count to end his bid for a perfect game. The next batter popped up to give Pappas his no-hitter.

Pappas, who was born Miltiades Stergios Papastegios and sometimes called Gimpy, faded to 7–12 in 1973 and was released after the season.

Passeau, Claude

Cubs: 1939–47
Pitcher
Birthplace: Waynesboro, Mississippi

B: April 9, 1909
Bats right, throws right
Ht. 6–3; **Wt.** 198

Passeau, Claude William

Cubs	W	L	Pct	ERA	G	CG	IP	H	BB	K	ShO
1939	13	9	.591	3.05	34	13	221	215	48	108	1
1940	20	13	.606	2.50	46	20	280⅔	259	59	124	4
1941	14	14	.500	3.35	34	20	231	262	52	80	3
1942	19	14	.576	2.68	35	24	278⅓	284	74	89	3
1943	15	12	.556	2.91	35	18	257	245	66	93	2
1944	15	9	.625	2.89	34	18	227	234	50	89	2
1945	17	9	.654	2.46	34	19	227	205	59	98	5
1946	9	8	.529	3.13	21	10	129⅓	118	42	47	2
1947	2	6	.250	6.25	19	1	63⅓	97	24	26	1
Career	162	150	.519	3.37	444	188	2,719⅔	2,856	728	1,104	27

Claude Passeau never lost more than he won in eight consecutive seasons, a major feat considering the poor Cubs teams of the early 1940s. He was the ace of the staff, with five seasons of 15 wins or more, including 20–13 in 1940, his first full season as a Cub.

In one of their better deals, the Cubs sent three players and $50,000 to Philadelphia early in the 1939 campaign for Passeau. He consistently ignored injuries and ailments, including an appendix problem in 1942 when he won 19 games. In 1945 he led the Cubs to a pennant with a 17–9 record despite bone chips in his elbow. "Every time I threw a ball it was like a dozen needles shooting through my arm," Passeau admitted.

Despite the pain, he pitched a one-hitter and a 3–0 shutout over Detroit in the third game of the 1945 World Series. And he held a 5–1 lead into the seventh inning of the sixth game when a line drive that tore off a fingernail forced him from the mound. The Cubs won that game, but lost the seventh.

Age and injuries held Passeau to 9–8 in 1946, and after spinal surgery and a 2–6 record in 1947 he retired. He later served as a sheriff in Mississippi.

Pepitone, Joe

Cubs: 1970–73
First baseman, outfielder
Birthplace: Brooklyn, New York

B: October 9, 1940
Bats left, throws left
Ht. 6–2; **Wt.** 185

Pepitone, Joseph Anthony

Cubs	G	AB	H	AVG	RBI	R	2B	3B	HR	SLG	SB
1970	56	213	57	.268	44	38	9	2	12	.498	0
1971	115	427	131	.307	61	50	19	4	16	.482	1
1972	66	214	56	.262	21	23	5	0	8	.397	1
1973	31	112	30	.268	18	16	3	0	3	.375	3
Career	1,397	5,097	1,315	.258	721	606	158	39	215	.432	41

Better known for his antics than his undoubted talent, Joe Pepitone was picked up from Houston by the Cubs in midseason 1970 in an effort to bolster their lineup for what proved a futile pennant bid. "Pepi" had been a competent first baseman for the New York Yankees from 1962 to 1969. Cub manager Leo Durocher switched him to center field, where he played well the rest of the 1970 season, batted .268, and finished the campaign with 26 home runs overall. He was a fan favorite because of his idiosyncrasies, which included arriving at Wrigley Field on a motorcycle or in a limousine and flaunting a toupee that he wore to cover his baldness.

He played mostly first base the next two years, batting .307 with 16 home runs in 1971, then dwindling to .262 in 1972. He wore out his welcome the next year after 31 games and was traded to Atlanta, which he quit after three games.

Pfeffer, Fred

White Stockings: 1883–89, 1891, 1896–97
Second baseman
Birthplace: Louisville, Kentucky

B: March 17, 1860
D: April 10, 1932
Batted right, threw right
Ht. 5–10; **Wt.** 184

Pfeffer, Nathaniel Frederick

White Stockings	G	AB	H	AVG	RBI	R	2B	3B	HR	SA	SB
1883	96	371	87	.235	—	41	22	7	1	.340	—
1884	112	467	135	.289	—	105	10	10	25	.514	—
1885	112	469	113	.241	71	90	12	6	6	.330	—
1886	118	474	125	.264	95	88	17	8	7	.378	—
1887	123	479	133	.278	89	95	21	6	16	.447	57
1888	135	517	129	.250	57	90	22	10	8	.377	64
1889	134	531	121	.228	77	85	15	7	7	.322	45
1891	137	498	123	.247	77	93	12	9	7	.349	40
1896	94	360	88	.244	52	45	16	7	2	.344	22
1897	32	114	26	.228	11	10	0	1	0	.246	5
Career	1,670	6,555	1,671	.255	859	1,094	231	118	95	.370	352

An outstanding fielder of his day, who refused to wear a glove until near the end of his career, Fred Pfeffer was rated by his contemporary Charles Comiskey as the equal of such later great second basemen as Nap Lajoie and Eddie Collins. Pfeffer had a strong arm and great range, and usually led the league's second basemen in putouts.

Pfeffer (nicknamed Dandelion or Fritz) joined the White Stockings in 1883 and became the glue of the infield that helped them to pennants in 1885 and 1886. As a batter, he had his best season in 1884 when he hit .289, as well as 25 home runs, second only to teammate Ned Williamson's league-leading 27 but just as counterfeit because of the rule that for one season allowed home runs on balls hit less than 200 feet at Lakefront Park. Pfeffer, however, did hit 16 home runs in 1887 when ballpark dimensions were less absurd.

An activist in player-management relations, Pfeffer jumped to the Players League for its only season in 1890. Forgiven by manager Cap Anson, he returned to Chicago for one season, was traded to Louisville where he played through 1895, and was regained by the White Stockings in 1896. He finished his career the next year.

Fred Pfeffer

Pfiester, Jack

Cubs: 1906–11
Pitcher
Birthplace: Cincinnati, Ohio
B: May 24, 1878

D: September 3, 1953
Batted right, threw left
Ht. 5–11; **Wt.** 180

Pfiester, John Albert

Cubs	W	L	Pct	ERA	G	CG	IP	H	BB	K	ShO
1906	20	8	.714	1.56	31	20	242⅔	173	63	153	4
1907	15	9	.625	1.15	30	13	195	143	48	90	3
1908	12	10	.545	2.00	33	18	252	204	70	117	3
1909	17	6	.739	2.43	29	13	196⅔	179	49	73	5
1910	6	3	.667	1.79	14	5	100⅓	82	26	34	2
1911	0	4	.000	4.01	6	3	33⅓	34	18	15	0
Career	71	44	.647	2.04	149	75	1,058⅓	869	293	503	17

A failure in two earlier trials with Pittsburgh, Jack Pfiester, an outstanding left-hander, found a role on the Cubs' great pitching staff of the early 1900s. He broke in with a 20–8 record in 1906 when the Cubs won the first of their four pennants in five years and was a consistent winner until 1911.

In an early start he became known as Jack the Giant Killer after the Cubs drubbed their greatest rivals, the New York Giants, 19–0, in a game in which they scored 11 runs in the first inning. He dominated the Giants until his career tailed off with a 0–4 record in 1911.

Jack Pfiester

Phil Regan

Regan, Phil

Cubs: 1968–72
Pitcher
Birthplace: Ostego, Michigan

B: April 6, 1937
Bats right, throws right
Ht. 6–3; **Wt.** 200

Regan, Philip Raymond

Cubs	W	L	Pct	ERA	G	SV	IP	H	BB	K	ShO
1968	10	5	.667	2.20	68	25	127	109	24	60	0
1969	12	6	.667	3.70	71	17	112	120	35	56	0
1970	5	9	.357	4.74	54	12	76	81	32	31	0
1971	5	5	.500	3.95	48	6	73	84	33	28	0
1972	0	1	.000	2.25	5	0	4	6	2	2	0
Career	96	81	.542	3.48	551	92	1,372⅔	1,392	447	743	1

During the regeneration of the Cubs in the Leo Durocher era, Phil Regan was the "stopper" who bailed out the "Big Three" starters, Ferguson Jenkins, Bill Hands, and Ken Holtzman.

Regan began his career in Detroit as a starting pitcher, but didn't achieve major success until he was converted to relief by the Los Angeles Dodgers. In 1966 he was 14–1 with a league-leading 21 saves. He earned the Fireman of the Year and Comeback Player of the Year awards, as well as the nickname "The Vulture" for earning wins in the late innings.

Obtained by the Cubs in a deal that also brought Jim Hickman on April 23, 1968, Regan was the ace of Durocher's

bullpen that season. He led the league again in saves with 25, and had a 10–5 record for the Cubs, despite "harassment" by the umpires, who charged he was throwing a "Vaseline ball." He won his second Fireman of the Year award.

He continued to be successful for most of 1969 but began to show the effects of wear and tear late in the season as the Cubs faded before the onrush of the New York Mets. He finished 12–6 with 17 saves, but it was his last good year. He struggled for the next three seasons until he was released in 1972.

Regan continued in baseball and became manager at Baltimore in 1995.

Reulbach, Ed

Cubs: 1905–13
Pitcher
Birthplace: Detroit, Michigan
B: December 1, 1882

D: July 17, 1961
Batted right, threw right
Ht. 6–1; **Wt.** 190

Reulbach, Edward Martin

Cubs	W	L	Pct	ERA	G	CG	IP	H	BB	K	ShO
1905	18	13	.581	1.42	34	28	292	208	73	152	5
1906	19	4	.826	1.65	33	20	218	129	92	94	6
1907	17	4	.810	1.69	27	16	192	147	64	96	4
1908	24	7	.774	2.03	46	25	297⅔	227	106	133	7
1909	19	10	.655	1.78	35	23	262⅔	194	82	105	6
1910	12	8	.600	3.12	24	13	173⅓	61	49	55	1
1911	16	9	.640	2.96	33	15	221⅓	191	103	79	2
1912	10	6	.625	3.78	39	8	169	161	60	75	0
1913	1	3	.250	4.42	5	0	38⅔	41	21	10	0
Career	181	105	.633	2.28	398	200	2,632⅔	2,117	892	1,137	40

No one is likely to match Ed Reulbach's most unusual feat for the Cubs, shutting out Brooklyn in both ends of a doubleheader on September 26, 1908, 5–0 on five hits in the first

Ed Reulbach

Cubs	W	L	Pct	ERA	G	CG	IP	H	BB	K	ShO
1979	18	12	.600	3.62	36	5	239	251	75	125	1
1980	11	13	.458	3.40	38	6	257	281	76	140	0
1981	4	7	.364	3.47	13	1	85⅔	87	23	53	0
1983	1	1	.500	3.92	4	0	20⅔	18	10	9	0
1984	5	5	.500	5.17	19	1	92⅓	123	23	43	0
Career	214	191	.528	3.37	557	102	3,549⅔	3,588	935	2,015	26

A burly right-hander, Rick "Big Daddy" Reuschel was deceptively athletic—an excellent fielder, hitter, and base runner as well as the most consistent Cubs starting pitcher of the 1970s. While the Cubs languished during most of his tenure, Reuschel was consistently in double figures as a winner, reaching a peak of 20–10 in 1977 and posting a record of 18–12 in 1979.

Reuschel arrived near the end of manager Leo Durocher's regime in 1972, was 10–8 as a rookie, and settled in as the number-one starter for the rest of the decade when Ferguson Jenkins was traded after the 1973 season.

Reuschel was joined on the Cubs for almost four seasons by his even bigger older brother Paul in 1975, and the two entered the record books by beating Los Angeles 7–0 on August 21, 1975. Rick started the game but had to leave in the seventh inning because of a blister on his pitching hand. Paul relieved and completed the shutout, the first ever by brothers.

Reuschel left the Cubs for the New York Yankees in a major deal on June 12, 1981, but soon developed arm trouble in New York and missed the entire 1982 season. Released by the Yankees, he rejoined the Cubs in 1983, but struggled for two seasons, contributing a 5–5 record to the team's East Division title campaign in 1984.

The Cubs decided to let him go as a free agent. The decision proved a blunder. He came back with a vengeance for Pittsburgh, then San Francisco. For the Giants, he was 19–11 in 1988 and 17–9 in 1989. His career ended in 1991.

game, and 3–0 on three hits in the second. And Reulbach sandwiched those shutouts between two others, giving him four in a row.

"Big Ed" Reulbach was a winner from the beginning: 18–13 as a rookie in 1905, as well as every season through 1912. He led the league in winning percentage for three consecutive seasons when the Cubs won pennants in 1906, 1907, and 1908, with records of 19–4, 17–4, and 24–7. While the Cubs finished second in 1909 despite winning 104 games, Reulbach was 19–10, and he went 12–8 when they won their fourth pennant in five years in 1910.

Though the Cubs lost the World Series of 1906 to the White Sox, Reulbach pitched a one-hitter to win 7–1 in his only decision. He beat Detroit in 1907 in his only other World Series decision.

In his last two full seasons with the Cubs, Reulbach was 16–9 and 10–6, then was traded to Brooklyn after a 1–3 record early in 1913. He made a comeback with Newark of the Federal League in 1915 with a 20–10 record, then completed his career with the Boston Braves in 1917.

Reuschel, Rick

Cubs: 1972–81, 1983–84
Pitcher
Birthplace: Quincy, Illinois

B: May 16, 1949
Bats right, throws right
Ht. 6–3; **Wt.** 230

Reuschel, Rickey Eugene

Cubs	W	L	Pct	ERA	G	CG	IP	H	BB	K	ShO
1972	10	8	.556	2.93	21	5	129	127	29	87	4
1973	14	13	.483	3.00	36	7	237	244	62	168	3
1974	13	12	.520	4.29	41	8	241	262	83	160	2
1975	11	17	.393	3.73	38	6	234	244	67	155	0
1976	14	12	.538	3.46	38	9	260	260	64	146	2
1977	20	10	.667	2.79	39	8	252	233	74	166	4
1978	14	15	.483	3.41	35	9	243	235	54	115	1

Rick Reuschel

Andre Rodgers

Rodgers, Andre

Cubs: 1961–64
Shortstop
Birthplace: Nassau, Bahamas

B: December 2, 1934
Bats right, throws right
Ht. 6–3; **Wt.** 200

Rodgers, Kenneth Andre Ian

Cubs	G	AB	H	AVG	RBI	R	2B	3B	HR	SLG	SB
1961	73	228	57	.266	23	27	17	0	6	.430	1
1962	138	461	128	.278	44	40	20	8	5	.388	5
1963	150	516	118	.229	33	51	17	4	5	.306	5
1964	129	448	107	.239	46	50	17	3	12	.371	5
Career	854	2,521	628	.249	245	268	112	23	45	.365	22

When an arthritic knee condition slowed down Ernie Banks in the early 1960s, necessitating a switch to first base, the Cubs were back to square one in their customary hunt for a shortstop. They turned to Andre Rodgers, a former cricket player from the Bahamas, whom they acquired in a trade with Milwaukee before the 1961 season.

Rodgers hit with occasional power during his three seasons as the regular shortstop, hitting a high of 12 home runs in 1964, but his play in the field was erratic. Andy was traded to Pittsburgh on December 9, 1964 for Roberto Pena, another shortstop who didn't pan out. Pena was quickly replaced by Don Kessinger.

Root, Charlie

Cubs: 1926–41
Pitcher
Birthplace: Middletown, Ohio
B: March 17, 1899

D: November 5, 1970
Batted right, threw right
Ht. 5–10; **Wt.** 190

Root, Charles Henry

Cubs	W	L	Pct	ERA	G	CG	IP	H	BB	K	ShO
1926	18	17	.514	2.82	42	21	271⅓	267	62	127	2
1927	26	15	.634	3.76	48	21	309	296	117	145	4
1928	14	18	.438	3.57	40	13	237	214	73	122	1
1929	19	6	.760	3.47	43	19	272	286	83	124	4
1930	16	14	.533	4.33	37	15	220⅓	247	63	124	4
1931	17	14	.548	3.48	39	19	251	240	71	131	3
1932	15	10	.600	3.58	39	11	216⅓	211	55	96	0
1933	15	10	.600	2.60	35	20	242⅓	232	61	86	2
1934	4	7	.364	4.28	34	2	117⅔	141	53	46	0
1935	15	8	.652	3.08	38	11	201⅓	193	47	94	1
1936	3	6	.333	4.15	33	0	73⅔	81	20	32	0
1937	13	5	.722	3.38	43	5	178⅔	173	32	74	0
1938	8	7	.533	2.86	44	5	160⅔	163	30	70	0
1939	8	8	.500	4.03	35	8	167⅓	189	34	65	0
1940	2	4	.333	3.82	36	1	113	118	33	50	0
1941	8	7	.533	5.40	19	6	106⅔	133	37	46	0
Career	201	160	.557	3.58	632	177	3,198⅓	3,252	889	1,459	21

The names Charlie Root and Babe Ruth are linked in legend. Root was pitching for the Cubs in the third game of the 1932 World Series against the New York Yankees when in the fifth inning, Ruth allegedly pointed to the right-centerfield bleachers at Wrigley Field and hit his "called shot" home run.

"Chinski" Root vehemently denied that Ruth, who had hit a three-run home run in the first inning, had made the widely publicized gesture. "He didn't point," Root insisted. "If he had, I'd have knocked him on his fanny."

Root deserves to be remembered apart from that incident because he was one of the best Cub pitchers, with a career 201–160 record, and in 16 years with the team (1926–1941) helped it to four pennants.

After failing in an earlier trial with the St. Louis Browns, Root was brought up by the Cubs in 1926 and immediately established himself as a quality starting pitcher with a record of 18–17. The next season was his most productive, with a

Charlie Root

26–15 record. During his career, he won 15 or more games eight times.

He was a major contributor in three pennant seasons, with 19–6 in 1929, then 15–10 in 1932, and 15–8 in 1935. By 1938 he was only an occasional starter, but had an 8–7 record as the Cubs again won the pennant. His 0–3 record in four World Series, however, matched that of his team.

Released at the age of 42 after the 1941 season, Root continued to pitch in the minor leagues until he was 49, then managed in the minors, and from 1951 to 1953 was the Cubs' pitching coach.

Rush, Bob

Cubs: 1948–57
Pitcher
Birthplace: Battle Creek, Michigan

B: December 21, 1925
Bats right, throws right
Ht. 6–4; **Wt.** 225

Rush, Robert Ransom

Cubs	W	L	Pct	ERA	G	CG	IP	H	BB	K	ShO
1948	5	11	.313	3.92	36	4	133⅓	153	37	72	0
1949	10	18	.357	4.07	35	9	201	197	79	80	1
1950	13	20	.394	3.71	39	19	254⅔	261	93	93	1
1951	11	12	.478	3.83	37	12	211⅓	212	68	129	3
1952	17	13	.567	2.70	34	17	250⅓	205	81	157	4
1953	9	14	.391	4.54	29	8	166⅔	172	66	84	1
1954	13	15	.464	3.77	33	11	236¼	213	103	124	0
1955	13	11	.542	3.50	33	14	234	204	73	130	3
1956	13	10	.565	3.19	32	13	239⅔	210	59	104	1
1957	6	16	.273	4.38	31	5	205¼	211	66	103	0
Career	127	152	.455	3.65	417	118	2,410⅔	2,327	789	1,244	16

The workhorse of the pitching staff during the Cubs' most forlorn decade, the 1950s, Bob Rush might have had more outstanding season records with better teams, but he managed to win in double figures eight times.

Rush was considered huge for a pitcher in his day, towering over 6–4, and threw an exceptional fastball with a high leg kick. Control problems hampered him at first, and he had to modify the leg kick before he became successful.

Bob Rush

Rush reached a career high in 1952 with a 17–13 record for a team that was exactly .500. He lost two 1–0 games, two 2–0 games, one 3–0 game, and several other low-scoring games by one run. He overcame lack of offensive support by pitching three consecutive shutouts, and ran up a seven-game winning streak at one point. He also was the winning pitcher in the All-Star Game, 2–1, on a two-run home run by teammate Hank Sauer.

It was quite a turnabout for Rush, who broke in with a 5–11 record as a rookie in 1948, lost 18 games the next season, and led the league in losses with 20 in 1950. After dropping to 9–14 in 1953, Rush won 13 games in each of the next three seasons before dwindling to 6–16 in 1957, his final year with the Cubs.

Traded to Milwaukee after the 1957 season, he helped pitch the Braves to a pennant in 1958, started and lost a World Series game, and finished his career in 1960.

Ryan, Jimmy

White Stockings: 1885–89, 1891–1900
Outfielder
Birthplace: Clinton, Massachusetts

B: February 11, 1863
D: October 26, 1923
Batted right, threw left
Ht. 5–9; **Wt.** 162

Ryan, James Edward

White Stockings	G	AB	H	AVG	RBI	R	2B	3B	HR	SLG	SB
1885	3	13	6	.462	2	2	1	0	0	.538	—
1886	84	327	100	.306	53	58	17	6	4	.431	—
1887	126	508	145	.285	74	117	23	10	11	.435	50
1888	129	549	182	.332	64	115	33	10	16	.515	60
1889	135	576	177	.307	72	140	31	14	17	.498	45
1891	118	505	140	.277	66	110	22	15	9	.434	27
1892	128	505	148	.293	65	105	21	11	10	.438	27
1893	83	341	102	.299	30	82	21	7	3	.428	8
1894	108	481	173	.360	62	133	37	7	3	.484	11
1895	108	438	139	.317	49	83	22	8	6	.445	18
1896	128	489	153	.313	86	83	24	10	2	.421	29
1897	136	520	156	.300	85	103	33	17	5	.458	27
1898	144	572	185	.323	79	122	32	13	4	.446	29
1899	125	525	158	.301	68	91	20	10	3	.394	9
1900	105	415	115	.277	59	66	25	4	5	.393	19
Career	2,012	8,171	2,506	.307	1,093	1,643	451	157	118	.444	408

A consistent .300 hitter with great power for his day, Jimmy Ryan was an exceptional outfielder with a strong throwing arm. He broke in with Cap Anson's White Stockings in 1885, after starring at Holy Cross University, and the next season, his first full year, batted .306 playing right field for Anson's second straight pennant winners.

"Pony" Ryan led the NL in home runs with 16 in 1888, and he hit 17 the next season. During his 18-year career, he hit 118 home runs, a total surpassed by only four players before the end of the dead-ball era in 1920. He led off six games with home runs in 1889, a record only surpassed 84 years later by Bobby Bonds of San Francisco.

Ryan batted .360 in 1894, but his best season overall was 1888 when he batted .332 and led the league in hits (182), doubles (33), and home runs (16), as well as outfield assists (34). He was particularly admired for the strength and accuracy of his throws. He was a good base runner, stealing 408 bases in his career.

Jimmy Ryan

Cubs	G	AB	H	AVG	RBI	R	2B	3B	HR	SLG	SB
1991	158	585	170	.291	100	104	32	2	26	.485	22
1992	158	612	186	.304	87	100	32	8	26	.507	17
1993	117	456	141	.309	45	67	20	0	9	.412	9
1994	57	223	53	.238	24	36	9	5	5	.390	2
1996	150	554	135	.244	92	85	28	4	25	.444	12
Career	3,029	7,938	2,268	.286	997	1,264	377	76	270	.454	337

Among baseball insiders, Ryne Sandberg is known as a five-point player: hit for average, hit with power, catch, run, and throw. The undervalued minor league shortstop who came to the Cubs almost as a "throw-in" in a trade with Philadelphia on January 27, 1982, and played third base that season, became the finest second baseman of his era both as a fielder and as a formidable hitter.

Although he had played less than 13 full seasons with the Cubs when he retired prematurely on June 13, 1994, Sandberg stood at number four on the team's all-time home run list, second to Frank Chance in stolen bases, fifth in total bases, and sixth in hits. He had appeared in eight All-Star Games, including eight consecutive starts.

Defensively, "Ryno" Sandberg was without compare. He was the first second baseman to win nine consecutive Gold Glove awards. He played a record 123 consecutive games without an error and four seasons without a throwing error. For three years he had the highest fielding percentage in the major leagues.

He had five errorless stretches of 50 games or more, 10 of 40 games or more. He retired in '94 with a career .990 fielding percentage, best of any second baseman in major league history. Sandberg had exceptional range. He was outstanding on balls hit to his left or right, and he consistently made plays on balls seemingly out of his reach.

Even his teammates were awed by his fielding proficiency. After Sandberg had made an error in two consecutive games, his double-play partner, shortstop Shawon Dunston, commented to him, "Hey, you're human." Dunston later said, "He just looked at me. Didn't smile or anything."

Ryan was occasionally called on by Anson to pitch, either as a starter or in relief. He appeared in only 24 games, with a record of 6–1.

Ryan served two terms with the White Stockings, jumping to the Players League for the 1890 season, then returning to Anson's team in 1891. He was released by the Cubs after the 1900 season, in which he dipped to .277. He completed his career at Washington in the new AL in 1903.

Sandberg, Ryne

Cubs: 1982–94, 1996
Second baseman
Birthplace: Spokane, Washington

B: September 18, 1959
Bats right, throws right
Ht. 6–1; **Wt.** 175

Sandberg, Ryne Dee

Cubs	G	AB	H	AVG	RBI	R	2B	3B	HR	SLG	SB
1982	156	635	172	.271	54	103	33	5	7	.372	32
1983	158	633	165	.261	48	94	25	4	8	.351	37
1984	156	636	200	.314	84	114	36	19	19	.520	32
1985	153	609	186	.305	83	113	31	6	26	.504	54
1986	154	627	178	.284	76	68	28	5	14	.411	34
1987	132	523	154	.294	59	81	25	2	16	.442	21
1988	155	618	163	.264	69	77	23	8	19	.419	25
1989	157	606	176	.290	76	104	25	5	30	.497	15
1990	155	615	188	.306	100	116	30	3	40	.559	25

Ryne Sandberg

Sandberg's silence and apparent lack of emotion was falsely interpreted in the beginning as lack of desire. Worse yet, in 1982, during his first weeks with the Cubs, he had only one hit in his first 32 at bats, though he ended up hitting .271 for the season. But veteran shortstop Larry Bowa, who accompanied Sandberg from Philadelphia in the trade for shortstop Ivan DeJesus, never had a doubt that Sandberg was fiercely competitive. "This kid wants it," Bowa said.

The ultimate proof of that came on June 23, 1984, in a game against St. Louis at Wrigley Field that Sandberg considered his most memorable. Sandberg hit a ninth-inning, game-tying home run off Cardinals ace reliever Bruce Sutter, then a game-tying, 11th-inning home run again off Sutter. The Cubs won 12–11 and went on to win the East Division title, and Sandberg captured the 1984 Most Valuable Player award. He batted .314 with 19 triples, 19 home runs, 32 stolen bases, 84 RBIs, and a league-leading 114 runs scored.

Sandberg also had a great season in 1989, hitting 30 home runs, when the Cubs again won the East Division title. But his best season was 1990, when he batted .306 with 40 home runs and 100 RBIs. He matched that RBI figure in 1991, hitting 26 home runs for the second time in his career. In 1992 he again hit 26 home runs.

Two hand injuries limited him to 117 games in 1993, and his home run output dropped to nine, though he batted .309. In 1994 both he and the Cubs got off to bad starts, and after playing 57 games he was batting only .238 with five home runs. Worse, he believed he no longer had the "competitive fire" that had driven him in his great years.

On June 13, 1994, Sandberg announced his retirement at the relatively early age of 34, despite the fact that as one of the most highly paid players in the game he was walking away from about $15 million in pay for future seasons.

"I always felt I would wake up the next day and have it back," he said of his decreasing skill. "But the drive and the edge were not there. I am not willing and do not want to just hang around."

A year and a half later he changed his mind and returned to the Cubs. He had remarried, and he was apparently convinced that the new Cub regime of president Andy MacPhail, general manager Ed Lynch, and manager Jim Riggleman was committed to building a winning team.

Santo, Ron

Cubs: 1960–73
Third baseman
Birthplace: Seattle, Washington

B: February 25, 1940
Bats right, throws right
Ht. 6–0; **Wt.** 190

Santo, Ronald Edward

Cubs	G	AB	H	AVG	RBI	R	2B	3B	HR	SLG	SB
1960	95	347	87	.251	44	44	24	2	9	.409	0
1961	154	578	164	.284	83	84	32	6	23	.479	2
1962	162	604	137	.227	83	44	20	4	17	.358	4
1963	162	630	187	.297	99	79	29	6	25	.481	6
1964	161	592	185	.313	114	94	33	13	30	.564	32
1965	164	608	173	.285	101	88	30	4	33	.510	3
1966	155	561	175	.312	94	93	21	8	30	.538	4
1967	161	586	176	.300	98	107	23	4	31	.512	1
1968	162	577	142	.246	98	86	17	3	26	.421	3
1969	160	575	166	.289	123	97	18	4	29	.485	1

Cubs	G	AB	H	AVG	RBI	R	2B	3B	HR	SLG	SB
1970	154	555	148	.267	114	83	30	4	26	.476	2
1971	154	555	148	.267	88	77	22	1	21	.423	4
1972	133	464	140	.302	74	68	25	5	17	.487	1
1973	149	536	143	.267	77	65	29	2	20	.440	1
Career	2,243	8,143	2,254	.277	1,331	1,138	365	67	342	.464	35

Few rookies have broken in as impressively for the Cubs as third baseman Ron Santo did as a 20-year-old just called up from the minor leagues. On June 26, 1960, Santo keyed a doubleheader victory at Pittsburgh by driving in five runs with three hits. The third base job was his for the next 14 seasons.

Agile and sure-handed, Santo won five Gold Gloves as a fielder. He led the league in assists seven consecutive seasons, in putouts seven seasons (six consecutive), and in double plays six times.

He was a slow base runner but a powerful hitter, reaching career highs in batting with .313 in 1964, in home runs with 33 in 1965, and in RBIs with 123 in 1969. He hit 30 or more home runs in four consecutive seasons (1964–67) and 25 or more in eight seasons. He drove in more than 100 runs four times and more than 90 eight times. He batted over .300 in four seasons. He finished his career with 342 home runs and a batting average of .277.

Santo "came of age" in his fourth season after performing creditably in his first three. In 1963 he led the team with a .297 average and in RBIs with 99, and tied Billy Williams with 25 home runs. He also was chosen to the All-Star Team for the first of eight selections during his career.

His best overall season was 1964, when he batted .313, hit 30 home runs, and drove in 114 runs. The next season he hit 33 home runs, drove in 101 runs, and at the age of 25 was named team captain.

All this time the Cubs had been in the doldrums that had taken hold after their last pennant in 1945, but the naming of Leo Durocher as manager after the 1965 season heralded a new era, and Santo welcomed it. "I'm a Leo Durocher–type

Ron Santo

ballplayer," Santo declared, referring to his aggressive, hustling type of play.

After a disappointing start to the Durocher regime with a 10th-place finish in 1966, the pieces started to come together, including one of the best of all Cub infields: Santo at third base, Don Kessinger at shortstop, Glenn Beckert at second base, and Ernie Banks at first.

The Cubs jumped to third place in 1967, Santo contributing heavily with .300, 31 home runs, and 98 RBIs. They stayed in third place the next season, then caught fire in 1969, leading the East Division most of the way until they yielded to the New York Mets at the finish.

Santo reached his career high of 123 RBIs in that ill-fated 1969 bid, but his most memorable action may have started after a victory over Pittsburgh in June. On his way to the clubhouse, Santo leaped into the air and clicked his heels several times. It became part of his routine every time the Cubs won until they began to fade late in the season.

After 1969, Santo's admiration of Durocher began to wane, and by 1971 they were at odds. In a widely publicized clubhouse incident on August 23, 1971, Santo had to be restrained from attacking Durocher, who had suggested that the third baseman had asked for a "day."

Ron Santo Day was held at Wrigley Field five days later, on August 28. Santo revealed that he had been a lifelong diabetic and arranged for the proceeds to be donated to the Diabetic Association of Chicago.

By 1971, Santo's best years were behind him, though he batted .302 the next year, and after the 1973 season he was traded to the White Sox, with whom he finished his career in 1974.

Some 15 years later, Santo became a broadcaster for the Cubs.

Sauer, Hank

Cubs: 1949–55
Outfielder
Birthplace: Pittsburgh, Pennsylvania

B: March 17, 1917
Bats right, throws right
Ht. 6–3; **Wt.** 198

Sauer, Henry John

Cubs	G	AB	H	AVG	RBI	R	2B	3B	HR	SLG	SB
1949	96	357	104	.291	83	59	17	1	27	.571	0
1950	145	540	148	.274	103	85	32	2	32	.519	1
1951	141	525	138	.263	89	77	19	4	30	.486	2
1952	151	567	153	.270	121	89	31	3	37	.531	1
1953	108	395	104	.263	60	61	16	5	19	.473	0
1954	142	520	150	.288	103	98	18	1	41	.563	2
1955	79	261	55	.211	28	29	8	1	12	.387	0
Career	1,399	4,796	1,278	.266	876	709	200	19	288	.496	11

For almost seven seasons, Hank Sauer was the idol of the fans in Wrigley Field, a big-nosed, powerfully built slugger who pounded home runs with awesome regularity. While no great shakes as an outfielder, Sauer performed adequately, his big bat making up for slowness afoot.

Sauer was 31 when he crashed into the big leagues to stay by hitting 35 home runs for Cincinnati in 1948. When his bat wavered early the next year, the Reds traded him along with Frankie Baumholtz to the Cubs for Peanuts Lowrey and Harry "the Hat" Walker. It was one of the Cubs' better trades.

Sauer reeled off a string of three consecutive seasons in which he hit 30 or more home runs for the Cubs, lapsed to

Hank Sauer

19 in 1953, when injuries limited him to 108 games, then came back with a career high of 41 in 1954. His best season overall was 1952 when he batted .270 with 37 home runs to tie Pittsburgh's Ralph Kiner for the league lead, and drove in 121 runs. The barrage earned him the Most Valuable Player award, though the Cubs finished in fifth place.

Sauer played left field until the Cubs acquired Kiner in midseason 1952, then moved to right field to make room in left for Kiner, who had led the league in home runs for seven consecutive seasons. With Baumholtz in center field, the two lead-foots were together in the outfield for almost two seasons, but the twin home run punch failed to lift the Cubs from also-ran status.

Kiner departed after the 1954 season, and Sauer began to wane at the age of 38 in 1955, playing in only 79 games, with 12 home runs. Traded to St. Louis for outfielder Pete Whisenant after the 1955 season, Sauer continued his career four more years before retiring.

As a Cub, Sauer hit 198 home runs and for a time held the team record for most home runs by a left fielder (37) and for a right fielder (41), both later broken.

Scheffing, Bob

Cubs: 1941–42, 1946–50
Catcher
Birthplace: Overland, Missouri
B: August 11, 1913

D: October 26, 1985
Batted right, threw right
Ht. 6–2; **Wt.** 180

Scheffing, Robert Boden

Cubs	G	AB	H	AVG	RBI	R	2B	3B	HR	SLG	SB
1941	51	132	32	.242	20	9	8	0	1	.326	2
1942	44	102	20	.196	12	7	3	0	2	.284	2
1946	63	115	32	.278	18	8	4	1	0	.330	0
1947	110	363	96	.264	50	33	11	5	5	.364	2
1948	102	293	88	.300	45	23	18	2	5	.427	0
1949	55	149	40	.268	19	12	6	1	3	.383	0
1950	12	16	3	.188	1	0	1	0	0	.250	0
Career	517	1,357	357	.263	187	105	53	9	20	.360	6

Never more than a journeyman, Bob Scheffing shared the catching duties with harder-throwing Clyde McCullough during most of his stay with the Cubs in the 1940s. He joined the Cubs in 1941, lost three seasons (1943–45) to military service, and played in more than 100 games only in 1947 and 1948, hitting .300 the latter season.

In midseason 1950, Scheffing was traded to Cincinnati, and the next season finished his playing career.

Scheffing had been a player-manager in the minor leagues at the age of 23. This experience paved the way for his subsequent career as a Cub coach, then minor league manager, and then manager of the Cubs from 1957 through 1959. He later managed the Detroit Tigers and became vice president and general manager of the New York Mets in the 1970s. (For details of his managerial career, turn to Chapter 4, "The Skippers.")

Schmitz, Johnny

Cubs: 1941–42, 1946–51
Pitcher
Birthplace: Wausau, Wisconsin

B: November 27, 1920
Bats right, throws left
Ht. 6–0; **Wt.** 170

Schmitz, John Albert

Cubs	W	L	Pct	ERA	G	CG	IP	H	BB	K	ShO
1941	2	0	1.000	1.31	5	1	20⅔	12	9	11	0
1942	3	7	.300	3.43	23	1	86⅔	70	45	51	0
1946	11	11	.500	2.61	41	14	224⅓	84	94	135	3
1947	13	18	.419	3.22	38	10	207	209	80	97	3
1948	18	13	.581	2.64	34	18	242	186	97	100	2
1949	11	13	.458	4.35	36	9	207	227	92	75	3
1950	10	16	.385	4.99	39	8	193	217	91	75	3
1951	1	2	.333	8.00	8	0	18	22	15	6	0
Career	93	114	.449	3.55	366	86	1,812⅔	1,766	757	746	17

At one time it appeared that Johnny Schmitz might develop into one of the better left-handers in Cub history, but he wound up with merely a respectable career that featured only one outstanding season. He wore size 14 shoes, leading to the nickname of "Bear Tracks."

Johnny Schmitz

After trial seasons in 1941 and 1942, Schmitz served in the military for three years before emerging as a full-time starting pitcher in 1946. He led the league in losses in 1947 with a 13–18 record, but turned the figures around the next year with a last-place team.

His 18–13 record in 1948 with a 2.64 ERA included two shutouts, 18 complete games in 34 starts, a one-hitter, and 13 other games in which he allowed six hits or less. But Schmitz faded the next two seasons with 11–13 and 10–16 records, and in May 1951 was traded to Brooklyn. During the remaining six years of his career, he pitched for seven teams with only occasional success.

Schulte, Frank

Cubs: 1904–16
Outfielder
Birthplace: Cohocton, New York
B: September 17, 1882

D: October 2, 1949
Batted left, threw right
Ht. 5–11; **Wt.** 170

Schulte, Frank M.

Cubs	G	AB	H	AVG	RBI	R	2B	3B	HR	SLG	SB
1904	20	84	24	.286	13	16	4	3	2	.476	1
1905	123	493	135	.274	47	67	15	14	1	.367	16
1906	146	563	158	.281	60	77	18	13	7	.396	25
1907	97	342	98	.287	32	44	14	7	2	.386	7
1908	102	386	91	.236	43	42	20	2	1	.306	15
1909	140	538	142	.264	60	57	16	11	4	.357	23
1910	151	559	168	.301	68	93	29	15	10	.460	22
1911	154	577	173	.300	121	105	30	21	21	.534	23
1912	139	553	146	.264	70	90	27	11	13	.423	17
1913	132	495	138	.279	72	85	28	6	9	.414	21
1914	137	465	112	.241	61	54	22	7	5	.351	16
1915	151	550	137	.249	69	66	20	6	12	.373	19
1916	72	230	68	.296	27	31	11	1	5	.417	9
Career	1,806	6,531	1,766	.270	823	906	288	124	93	.395	233

A vital part of the great Cubs teams of the early 1900s, Frank "Wildfire" Schulte hit .309 in four World Series (1906–08, 1910) and was a regular, first in left field, then in right, from 1905 to 1916, when he was traded in midseason to Pittsburgh.

Schulte reached his peak in 1910 and 1911, batting .301 and .300, and leading the league in home runs with 10 the first year and 21 the second. In 1911 he had 30 doubles, 21 triples, and 23 stolen bases, as well as the 21 home runs, to become the first player ever to reach 20 in all four categories, a feat that was not duplicated until Willie Mays achieved it in 1957. He also led the league with 121 RBIs and won the 1911 version of the Most Valuable Player award.

Schulte's career ended with the 1918 season.

Frank "Wildfire" Schulte

Jimmy Sheckard

121 runs scored, 149 hits, 147 walks, and 32 stolen bases. He slipped to .245 the next year, despite drawing 122 walks, and in 1913 he finished his career at St. Louis and Cincinnati.

Sheckard, Jimmy

Cubs: 1906–12
Outfielder
Birthplace: Upper Chanceford, Pennsylvania

B: November 23, 1878
D: January 15, 1947
Batted left, threw right
Ht. 5–9; **Wt.** 175

Sheckard, Samuel James Tilden

Cubs	G	AB	H	AVG	RBI	R	2B	3B	HR	SLG	SB
1906	149	544	149	.262	45	90	27	10	1	.353	30
1907	142	484	129	.267	36	76	23	1	1	.324	31
1908	115	403	93	.231	22	54	18	3	2	.305	18
1909	148	525	134	.255	43	81	29	5	1	.335	15
1910	144	507	130	.256	51	82	27	6	5	.363	22
1911	156	539	149	.276	50	121	26	11	4	.388	32
1912	146	523	128	.245	47	85	22	10	3	.342	15
Career	2,121	7,609	2,085	.274	813	1,296	356	136	56	.379	465

By the time he got to the Cubs in 1906, Jimmy Sheckard was a veteran who had batted .353 and .332 for Brooklyn, yet never reached .300 again during seven seasons in Chicago. But he was a solid left fielder with a great throwing arm and also had an exceptional knack for drawing walks, reaching highs of 147 in 1911 and 122 in 1912.

Sheckard rounded out the outfield that helped bring four pennants to the Cubs in the Frank Chance era. He fared poorly in World Series play, batting just .182 in 21 games. His peak year with the Cubs was 1911, when he batted .276 with

Slagle, Jimmy

Cubs: 1902–08
Outfielder
Birthplace: Worthville, Pennsylvania

B: July 11, 1873
D: May 10, 1956
Ht. 5–7; **Wt.** 144

Slagle, James Franklin

Cubs	G	AB	H	AVG	RBI	R	2B	3B	HR	SLG	SB
1902	115	454	143	.315	28	64	11	4	0	.357	40
1903	139	543	162	.298	44	104	20	6	0	.357	33
1904	120	481	125	.260	31	73	12	10	1	.333	28
1905	155	568	153	.269	37	96	19	4	0	.317	27
1906	127	498	119	.239	33	71	8	6	0	.279	25
1907	136	489	126	.258	32	71	6	6	0	.294	28
1908	104	352	78	.222	26	38	4	1	0	.239	17
Career	1,298	4,996	1,340	.268	344	779	124	56	2	.317	273

Speed and defensive skill, including a fine arm, put Jimmy Slagle between Wildfire Schulte in right field and Jimmy Sheckard in left as a "three S" outfield on three consecutive Cub pennant winners from 1906 to 1908.

A line-drive hitter, with little power, Slagle arrived in 1902 from the Boston Red Sox along with manager Frank Selee as part of the latter's scheme to rebuild the Cubs. Slagle never again matched the .315 batting average of his first year with the Cubs, but he was a great asset with his defensive skills and base-stealing ability. He was nicknamed Shorty because of his size, as well as Rabbit because of his speed, and even "The Human Mosquito" because of his peskiness.

An injury kept Slagle out of the 1906 World Series, but in 1907 he stole six bases against Detroit for a World Series record that stood until Lou Brock of St. Louis broke it in

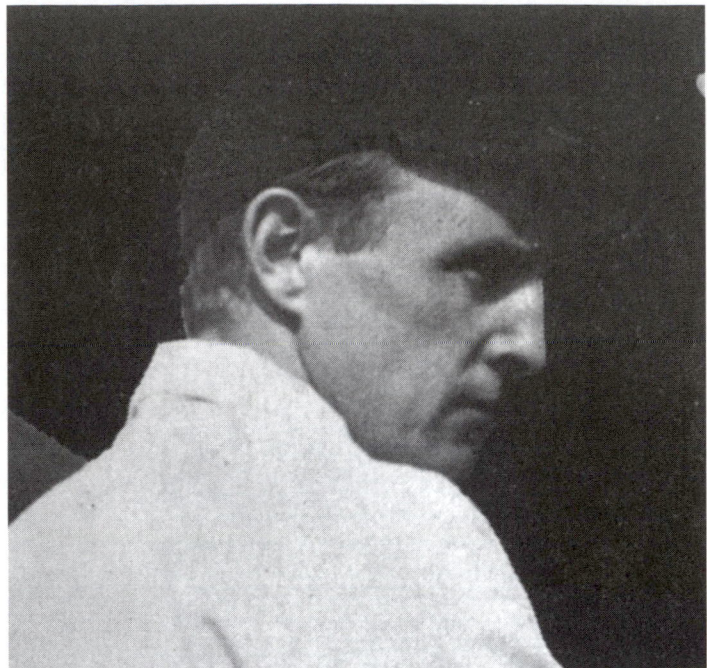

Jimmy Slagle

1967. Slagle slumped to .222 in 1908 and was released before the World Series.

Smalley, Roy

Cubs: 1948–53
Shortstop
Birthplace: Springfield, Missouri

B: June 9, 1926
Bats right, throws right
Ht. 6–3; **Wt.** 190

Smalley, Roy Frederick, Jr.

Cubs	G	AB	H	AVG	RBI	R	2B	3B	HR	SLG	SB
1948	124	361	78	.216	36	25	11	4	4	.302	2
1949	135	477	117	.245	35	57	21	10	8	.382	2
1950	154	557	128	.230	85	58	21	9	21	.413	2
1951	79	238	55	.231	31	24	7	4	8	.395	0
1952	87	261	58	.222	30	36	14	1	5	.341	0
1953	82	253	63	.249	25	20	9	0	6	.356	0
Career	872	2,644	601	.227	305	277	103	33	61	.360	4

Like Lennie Merullo, whom he replaced at shortstop in 1948, Roy Smalley came up from the minor leagues with high expectations but was a disappointment in his six seasons with the Cubs.

Smalley had excellent range and a strong arm, but a deformed finger might have contributed to his tendency to make wild throws. He led NL shortstops in errors several seasons, including a career high of 51 in 1950. The same year was his best at bat, with 21 home runs and 85 RBIs, although he hit only .230.

A broken ankle suffered early in 1951 reduced his effectiveness, and he played mostly in a utility role the next three seasons before the Cubs traded him to Philadelphia to clear the deck for Ernie Banks. Smalley's career ended in 1958.

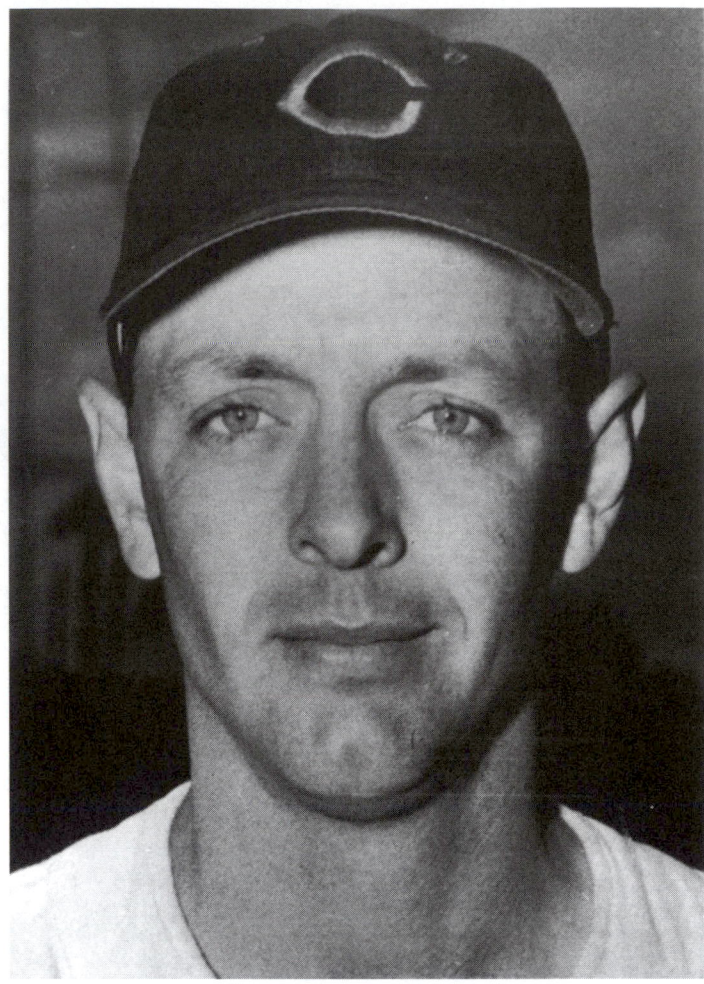

Roy Smalley

Spalding, Al

White Stockings: 1876–78
Pitcher
Birthplace: Byron, Illinois

B: September 2, 1850
D: September 9, 1915
Ht. 6–1; **Wt.** 170

Spalding, Albert Goodwill

White Stockings	W	L	Pct	ERA	G	CG	IP	H	BB	K	ShO
1876	47	13	.783	1.75	61	53	528⅔	542	26	39	8
1877	1	0	1.000	3.27	4	0	11	17	0	2	0
Career	48	13	.787	1.78	65	53	539⅔	559	26	41	8

White Stockings	G	AB	H	AVG	RBI	R	2B	3B	HR	SLG	SB
1876	66	292	91	.312	44	54	14	2	0	.373	—
1877	60	254	65	.256	35	29	7	6	0	.331	—
1878	1	4	2	.500	0	0	0	0	0	.500	—
Career	127	550	158	.287	79	83	21	8	0	.355	—

No man has worn as many hats with the Cubs as did Albert G. Spalding. He was player, manager, club secretary, president, and eventually chief owner after being lured from Boston by White Stockings founder William G. Hulbert for the initial 1876 season of the National League.

Spalding was the greatest pitcher of his day, and he proved it in 1876 when he started 60 of the White Stockings' 66 games, completing 53, and achieved a record of 47–13 while managing the team to the first NL pennant. When not pitching, Spalding played first base and batted .312.

Spalding hurt his arm before the 1877 season, forcing him to give up pitching early that year. He filled in where needed, batting .256 in 60 games, and after appearing in one game in 1878, retired as a player to pursue his off-the-field career. (For details of Spalding's career as manager, team official, and owner, see Chapters 4 and 5.)

He was elected to the Hall of Fame in 1939.

Steinfeldt, Harry

Cubs: 1906–10
Third baseman
Birthplace: St. Louis, Missouri
B: September 29, 1877

D: August 17, 1914
Batted right, threw right
Ht. 5–9; **Wt.** 180

Steinfeldt, Harry M.

Cubs	G	AB	H	AVG	RBI	R	2B	3B	HR	SLG	SB
1906	151	539	176	.327	83	81	27	10	3	.430	29
1907	152	544	144	.266	70	52	25	5	1	.336	19
1908	150	539	130	.241	62	63	20	6	1	.306	12
1909	151	528	133	.252	59	73	27	6	2	.337	22
1910	129	448	113	.252	58	70	21	1	2	.317	10
Career	1,648	5,889	1,578	.268	762	759	284	90	27	.360	194

Like many of his teammates on Frank Chance's championship teams of the early 1900s, third baseman Harry Steinfeldt was a veteran who already had played eight seasons at Cincinnati before the Cubs acquired him in 1906. Steinfeldt played in four World Series in his five seasons as a Cub.

A good fielder, Steinfeldt had his finest offensive season in 1906 when the Cubs swept to the pennant by winning a record 116 games. He led the club in batting with .327 and the league in hits with 176 and RBIs with 83. He did not bat over .266 in his remaining four years in Chicago, though he led the team in RBIs with 70 in 1907, but contributed heavily as the Cubs won three more pennants as well as the World Series in 1907 and 1908.

Steinfeldt was one of the heroes of the 1907 World Series victory over Detroit, with eight hits in 17 at bats for a .471 average. He was traded to the Boston Braves in 1911.

Stephenson, Riggs

Cubs: 1926–34
Outfielder
Birthplace: Akron, Alabama
B: January 5, 1898

D: November 15, 1985
Batted right, threw right
Ht. 5–10; **Wt.** 185

Stephenson, Jackson Riggs

Cubs	G	AB	H	AVG	RBI	R	2B	3B	HR	SLG	SB
1926	82	281	95	.338	44	40	18	3	3	.456	2
1927	152	579	199	.344	82	101	46	9	7	.491	8
1928	137	512	166	.324	90	75	36	9	8	.477	8
1929	136	495	179	.362	110	91	36	6	17	.562	10
1930	109	341	125	.367	68	56	21	1	5	.478	2
1931	80	263	84	.319	52	34	14	4	1	.414	1
1932	147	583	189	.324	85	86	49	4	4	.443	3
1933	97	346	114	.329	51	45	17	4	4	.436	5
1934	38	74	16	.216	7	5	0	0	0	.216	0
Career	1,310	4,508	1,515	.336	773	714	321	54	63	.473	54

A great fullback at the University of Alabama in the early 1920s, Riggs "Old Hoss" Stephenson also was a basketball and baseball standout in college. He broke into the major leagues with Cleveland in 1921, but remained in a utility role because of his shortcomings in the field, despite his obvious talent as a hitter.

After Joe McCarthy was summoned from the minor leagues to manage the Cubs in 1926, he brought up two minor league outfielders, Stephenson and Hack Wilson. Both emerged as among the greatest of all Cub hitters, and when

Harry Steinfeldt

Riggs Stephenson

Kiki Cuyler joined them in 1929, formed two-thirds of one of the most formidable outfields in history.

Stephenson batted .338 in 82 games in 1926, then during the next seven seasons batted .344, .324, .362, .367, .319, .324, and .329. A line-drive hitter, he reached his high in home runs with 17 in 1929 and drove in 110 runs to contribute to the Cubs' pennant winner, and also played on the championship team of 1932.

By 1934, Stephenson was reduced to part-time duty and batted only .216. He was released after the season to end his major league career.

Sunday, Billy

White Stockings: 1883–87
Outfielder
Birthplace: Ames, Iowa
B: November 19, 1862

D: November 6, 1935
Batted left, threw right
Ht. 5–10; **Wt.** 160

Sunday, William Ashley

White Stockings	G	AB	H	AVG	RBI	R	2B	3B	HR	SLG	SB
1883	14	54	13	.241	—	6	4	0	0	.315	—
1884	43	176	39	.222	—	25	4	1	4	.324	—
1885	46	172	44	.256	20	36	3	3	2	.343	—
1886	28	103	25	.243	6	16	2	2	0	.301	—
1887	50	199	58	.291	32	41	6	6	3	.427	34
Career	499	2,007	498	.248	137	339	55	24	12	.317	236

Billy Sunday was Cap Anson's protégé, attracting his attention while playing outfield for a team in Marshalltown, Iowa, the White Stockings manager's hometown. A superb fielder and fine base runner, Sunday was at best an average hitter, and it turned out his ultimate calling was not to baseball but to evangelism.

All the same, Sunday had a respectable career, playing mostly as a reserve outfielder for the White Stockings from 1883 through 1887, and twice helping them to pennants. His peak season was 1887, when he batted .291 in 50 games.

Sunday was traded to Pittsburgh in 1888, played his last game in 1890, and then plunged into a 40-year career as an evangelist with a fervor and eloquence that made him a national figure.

Sutcliffe, Rick

Cubs: 1984–91
Pitcher
Birthplace: Independence, Missouri

B: June 21, 1956
Bats right, throws right
Ht. 6–7; **Wt.** 215

Sutcliffe, Richard Lee

Cubs	W	L	Pct	ERA	G	CG	IP	H	BB	K	ShO
1984	16	1	.941	2.68	20	7	150⅓	123	39	155	3
1985	8	8	.500	3.18	20	6	130	119	44	102	3
1986	5	14	.263	4.64	28	4	176⅔	166	96	122	1
1987	18	10	.643	3.68	34	6	237⅓	223	106	174	1
1988	13	14	.481	3.86	32	12	226	232	70	144	2
1989	16	11	.593	3.66	35	5	229	202	69	153	1
1990	0	2	.000	5.82	5	0	21⅔	25	12	7	0
1991	6	5	.545	4.10	19	0	96⅔	96	45	52	0
Career	171	139	.552	4.08	457	72	2,698⅓	2,662	1,081	1,679	18

Billy Sunday

The media quickly named him "The Red Baron" because of the luxuriant red beard he wore while with the Cubs from 1984 through 1991. But Rick Sutcliffe looked more like a Viking warrior than the German aerial ace of World War I. One of the tallest Cubs ever at 6–7, Sutcliffe also contributed one of the team's most spectacular performances by a pitcher over more than half a season in 1984.

Sutcliffe had come up through the Los Angeles system, and he was the NL Rookie of the Year in 1979 with a 17–11 record. He soon lost favor and was traded to Cleveland, for whom he was 14–8 in 1982 and 17–10 in 1983. The Cubs, desperately in need of starting pitching, acquired him in a seven-player trade on June 13, 1984.

The deal was the biggest single step toward the Cubs' successful NL East title drive in 1984, with Sutcliffe winning 16 of 17 decisions for them. He had been 4–5 for Cleveland, and his combined 20–6 record made him the first pitcher since Hank Borowy—who switched from the New York Yankees to the Cubs in midseason 1945—to win 20 games in a season pitching in both leagues. It also earned him the Cy Young Award.

Sutcliffe's 14th consecutive win, a 4–1 victory at Pittsburgh in which he yielded just two hits, clinched the division title for the Cubs on September 23, 1984.

It also set up one of Sutcliffe's most spectacular perfor-

Rick Sutcliffe

Sutter, Bruce

Cubs: 1976–80
Pitcher
Birthplace: Lancaster, Pennsylvania

B: January 8, 1953
Bats right, throws right
Ht. 6–2; **Wt.** 190

Sutter, Howard Bruce

Cubs	W	L	Pct	ERA	G	CG	IP	H	BB	K	ShO
1976	6	3	.667	2.71	52	10	83	63	26	73	0
1977	7	3	.700	1.35	62	31	107	69	23	129	0
1978	8	10	.444	3.18	64	27	99	82	34	106	0
1979	6	6	.500	2.23	62	37	101	67	32	110	0
1980	5	8	.385	2.65	60	28	102	90	34	76	0
Career	68	71	.489	2.84	661	300	1,040⅔	879	309	861	0

An elbow injury suffered while pitching in the Cubs minor league system cost Bruce Sutter his fastball but was the making of him as an outstanding reliever. Fred Martin, a roving pitching instructor, introduced him to a trick pitch, the split-finger fastball. The pitch seemed to dive as it crossed the plate, and batters swung over it.

Armed with his new weapon, along with exceptional control, Sutter was promoted to the Cubs in 1976, and earned 10 saves with a 6–3 record. In 1977 he had 31 saves and was 7–3 with a 1.35 ERA, and in 1978 he earned 27 saves. His peak year for the Cubs was 1979 when he won the Cy Young Award with 37 saves, a 6–6 record, and a 2.23 ERA. In both 1978 and 1979 Sutter was the winning pitcher in the All-Star Game.

While Sutter led the league in saves with 28 in 1980 for the second consecutive year—he was to run the string to four—his Cub days already were numbered. The previous winter he had won a salary of $700,000 in arbitration, and the Cubs thought it was too much. They traded him to St. Louis on December 9, 1980.

mances, a 13–0 victory over the San Diego Padres in the League Championship Series at Wrigley Field in which he pitched seven innings and hit a home run. However, he lost the fifth game of the best-of-five series at San Diego a few days later.

Sutcliffe as a free agent was the object of a fierce bidding war after the 1984 season, but finally signed with the Cubs for $9.5 million over five years, becoming their highest-paid player up to that time.

"I owe it to Chicago," he explained. "Call it a sense of loyalty or whatever you want to call it, but something happened the three and a half months I was here. It was the fans, the players, the city."

The Cubs failed to capitalize on their investment in Sutcliffe for the next two seasons as, beset by injuries, he struggled through seasons of 8–8 in 1985 and 5–14 the next year. He snapped back to lead the league in victories with an 18–10 record in 1987, was 13–14 in 1988, and again was a big factor with a 16–11 record in 1989 when the Cubs won a division title for the second time.

A succession of injuries sidelined him much of the next two seasons, and the Cubs decided to let him go as a free agent after a 6–5 record in 1991. He came back strongly in Baltimore with a 16–15 record in 1992, but he ended his career with St. Louis in 1994.

Bruce Sutter

Sutter's success continued through four seasons with the Cardinals, after which he moved to Atlanta, where he soon suffered the injury that brought his career to an end in 1988.

Taylor, Jack

Cubs: 1898–1903, 1906–07
Pitcher
Birthplace: New Straightsville, Ohio
B: January 14, 1874

D: March 4, 1938
Batted right, threw right
Ht. 5–10; **Wt.** 170

Taylor, John W.

Cubs	W	L	Pct	ERA	G	CG	IP	H	BB	K	ShO
1898	5	0	1.000	2.20	5	5	41	32	10	11	0
1899	18	21	.462	3.76	41	39	354⅔	380	84	67	1
1900	10	17	.370	2.55	28	25	222⅓	226	58	57	2
1901	13	19	.406	3.36	33	30	275⅔	341	44	68	0
1902	22	11	.667	1.33	396	33	324⅔	271	43	83	8
1903	21	14	.600	2.45	37	33	312⅓	277	57	83	1
1906	12	3	.800	1.83	17	15	147⅓	116	39	34	2
1907	6	5	.545	3.29	18	8	123	127	33	22	0
Career	151	139	.521	2.66	310	278	2,617	2,502	581	528	20

Jack Taylor almost always finished what he started, completing 278 of his 287 major league starts for an unmatched 97 percent completion record. During one stretch he pitched 187 consecutive complete games—as well as relieving in 17 games.

Control problems hampered Taylor in his first four Cub seasons after he came up in 1898, but he turned into a winner with 22–11 in 1902 and 21–14 in 1903. He led the league with an 1.33 ERA and eight shutouts in 1902. Taylor wore out his Cub welcome after the 1903 season when it was suspected

that he had thrown games to the White Sox in the "City Series" and he was fined by the management.

On December 12, 1903, Taylor was traded to St. Louis in a deal that brought Three-Finger Brown to the Cubs. He pitched well in St. Louis, winning 21 games in 1904, and on July 1, 1906, was reacquired by the Cubs. He won 12 of 15 decisions to help in the pennant push, but dwindled to 6–5 the next year and was released.

Taylor, Tony

Cubs: 1958–60
Second baseman
Birthplace: Central Alara, Cuba

B: December 19, 1935
Bats right, throws right
Ht. 5–9; **Wt.** 175

Taylor, Antonio Nemesio

Cubs	G	AB	H	AVG	RBI	R	2B	3B	HR	SLG	SB
1958	140	497	117	.235	27	63	15	3	6	.314	21
1959	150	624	175	.280	38	96	30	8	8	.393	23
1960	19	76	20	.263	9	14	3	3	1	.421	2
Career	2,195	7,680	2,007	.261	598	1,005	298	86	75	.352	234

Tony Taylor's career with the Cubs in a way symbolized their disarray in the early 1960s. He broke in with them as a rookie in 1958 and by 1959 had established himself among the better second basemen in the league as he batted .280,

Brakeman Jack Taylor

Tony Taylor

scored 96 runs, and led the team in stolen bases with 23 while forming a double-play combination with Ernie Banks.

The Cubs, however, decided to trade Taylor early in the 1960 season to Philadelphia for pitcher Don Cardwell and first baseman Ed Bouchee, neither of whom had extended success in Chicago. Taylor played for 17 more seasons, most of them with the Phillies, and became one of the most versatile players and outstanding clutch hitters in the game.

Tinker, Joe

Cubs: 1902–12, 1916
Shortstop
Birthplace: Muscotah, Kansas
B: July 27, 1880

D: July 27, 1948
Batted right, threw right
Ht. 5–9; **Wt.** 175

Tinker, Joseph Bert

Cubs	G	AB	H	AVG	RBI	R	2B	3B	HR	SLG	SB
1902	133	501	137	.273	54	54	19	5	2	.343	27
1903	124	460	134	.291	70	67	21	7	2	.380	27
1904	141	488	108	.221	41	55	12	13	3	.318	41
1905	149	547	135	.247	66	70	18	8	2	.320	31
1906	148	523	122	.233	64	75	18	4	1	.289	30
1907	117	402	89	.221	36	36	11	3	1	.271	20
1908	157	548	146	.266	68	67	23	14	6	.392	30
1909	143	516	132	.256	57	56	26	11	4	.372	23
1910	133	473	136	.288	69	48	25	9	3	.397	20
1911	144	536	149	.278	69	61	24	12	4	.390	30
1912	142	550	155	.282	75	80	24	7	0	.351	25
1916	7	10	1	.100	1	0	0	0	0	.100	0
Career	1,805	6,441	1,695	.263	782	773	264	114	31	.354	336

Joe Tinker's ability to hit in the clutch became proverbial, and there was never a more celebrated instance of it than in the second game of the World Series of 1908 between the Cubs and Detroit. Tinker came to bat in the eighth inning of the scoreless game at Detroit after Solly Hofman led off with a single. Tinker followed with a home run into the temporary right-field stands, and the Cubs went on to win 6–1 and take the Series in six games. It was the first home run hit in a World Series in five years.

Tinker, though just a capable hitter with a career average of .263, was noted for rising to the occasion, particularly when facing Christy Mathewson, the greatest pitcher of the era, against whom he batted .291. Mathewson considered him "one of the most dangerous batters I have ever faced."

Tinker took over at shortstop as a rookie in 1902 and soon was teamed with second baseman Johnny Evers, with Frank Chance moving to first base after several seasons as a catcher. Thus was formed the Tinker-to-Evers-to-Chance double-play combination, celebrated in verse by Franklin P. Adams, a New York newspaper columnist.

Tinker's best year at bat as a Cub was 1903, when he hit .291. But he always was a pesky hitter, and fine base stealer—he stole home twice in one game—as well as one of the best fielding shortstops of his era, rated second only to Honus Wagner. Tinker led the league shortstops in every category except double plays in 1911, and led in various other areas in several seasons.

The scrappy Tinker and the dour Evers carried on a notorious feud in which they didn't speak to each other during most of their partnership around second base, but they were the heart of a team that won four pennants in five seasons under Chance's leadership.

When Evers succeeded Chance as the Cub manager in the winter of 1912–13, Tinker asked to be traded to Cincinnati. He batted a career-high .317 for the Reds as player-manager in 1913, skipped to the Chicago Whales of the new Federal League in 1914, and led them to the pennant in 1915.

When the Whales disappeared after the 1915 campaign, owner Charles Weeghman took control of the Cubs and brought Tinker back as player-manager. Tinker played just seven games in 1916, finished fifth and was fired. (For details of his managerial career, turn to Chapter 4, "The Skippers.") He played and managed in the minor leagues briefly after that.

Tinker entered the Hall of Fame in 1946.

Trillo, Manny

Cubs: 1975–78, 1986–88
Second baseman
Birthplace: Carapito, Venezuela

B: December 25, 1950
Bats right, throws right
Ht. 6–1; **Wt.** 150

Trillo, Jesus Manuel

Cubs	G	AB	H	AVG	RBI	R	2B	3B	HR	SA	SB
1975	154	545	135	.248	70	55	12	2	7	.316	1
1976	158	582	139	.239	59	42	24	3	4	.311	17
1977	152	504	141	.280	57	51	18	5	7	.377	3
1978	152	552	144	.261	55	53	17	5	4	.332	0
1986	81	152	45	.296	19	22	10	0	1	.382	0
1987	108	214	63	.294	26	27	8	0	8	.444	0
1988	76	164	41	.250	14	15	5	0	1	.299	2
Career	1,780	5,950	1,562	.263	571	598	239	33	61	.345	56

Manny Trillo

A smooth fielder with an exceptional throwing arm, Manny Trillo was acquired by the Cubs from Oakland, along with relievers Darold Knowles and Bob Locker, on October 23, 1974, in a trade that was highly publicized because Billy Williams was sent to the Athletics.

Trillo played superbly at second base for four years, teaming up the last two seasons with shortstop Ivan DeJesus in what was called the Latin Connection. A productive hitter low in the batting order, Trillo drove in 70 runs in 1975 and reached his Cubs high of .280 in 1977.

It wasn't until Trillo was traded by the Cubs to Philadelphia in an eight-player deal before the 1979 season that his talents were fully appreciated. He won four Gold Gloves in four seasons with the Phillies, was voted the Most Valuable Player of the NL Championship Series of 1980, and batted .381 in the World Series victory over Kansas City.

Injuries reduced Trillo's playing time in subsequent seasons. He played for Cleveland, Montreal, and San Francisco before returning to the Cubs for three seasons (1986–88) as a utility player. He finished his career at Cincinnati in 1989.

Trout, Steve

Cubs: 1983–87
Pitcher
Birthplace: Detroit, Michigan

B: July 30, 1957
Bats left, throws left
Ht. 6–4; **Wt.** 195

Trout, Steven Russell

Cubs	W	L	Pct	ERA	G	CG	IP	H	BB	K	ShO
1983	10	14	.417	4.65	34	1	180	217	59	80	0
1984	13	7	.650	3.41	32	6	190	205	59	81	2
1985	9	7	.563	3.39	24	3	140⅔	142	63	44	1
1986	5	7	.415	4.75	37	0	161	184	78	69	0

Steve Trout

Cubs	W	L	Pct	ERA	G	CG	IP	H	BB	K	ShO
1987	6	3	.667	3.00	11	3	75	72	27	32	2
Career	88	92	.489	4.18	301	32	1,502	1,665	578	656	9

Steve Trout enjoyed a brief span as the Cubs' obligatory left-handed starter in the mid-1980s, contributing the best record of his career, 13–7, to the winning of the East Division title in 1984.

Obtained in a deal in January 1983, after five indifferent seasons with the White Sox, "Rainbow" Trout was 10–14 that year. The next season he mastered his control problems long enough to help the Cubs to the East title. He pitched two shutouts and had an ERA of 3.41. He started and won the second game of the League Championship Series over San Diego before the Cubs lost the final three.

Trout slipped to 9–7 in 1985 and 5–7 the next year, and in midseason 1987 was traded to the New York Yankees. His career ended two years later.

Vaughn, Hippo

Cubs: 1913–21
Pitcher
Birthplace: Weatherford, Texas
B: April 9, 1888

D: May 29, 1966
Batted both, threw left
Ht. 6–4; **Wt.** 215

Vaughn, James Leslie

Cubs	W	L	Pct	ERA	G	CG	IP	H	BB	K	ShO
1913	5	1	.833	1.45	7	5	56	37	27	36	1
1914	21	13	.618	2.05	42	23	293⅓	236	109	165	4
1915	20	12	.625	2.87	41	18	269⅔	240	77	148	4
1916	17	15	.531	2.20	44	21	294	269	67	144	4
1917	23	13	.639	2.01	41	27	295⅔	255	91	195	5
1918	22	11	.667	1.74	35	27	290⅓	216	76	148	8
1919	21	14	.600	1.79	38	25	306⅔	264	62	141	4
1920	19	16	.543	2.54	40	24	301	301	81	131	4
1921	3	11	.214	6.01	17	7	109⅓	153	31	20	0
Career	178	137	.565	2.49	390	215	2,730	2,461	817	1,416	41

Frequently recalled as the loser for the Cubs in the double no-hitter for nine innings in which Cincinnati's Fred Toney (a former Cub) prevailed 1–0 in 10 innings on May 22, 1917, Hippo Vaughn was possibly the best left-handed pitcher in the team's history. Vaughn gave up a hit in the 10th inning while Toney completed the no-hitter.

After indifferent success in the American League for four seasons, Vaughn was in the minor leagues when the Cubs acquired him in August 1913. He quickly became a winner, recording five 20-victory seasons in the next six years. He won 23 games in 1917, but 1918 was his zenith as he led the Cubs to a pennant with a 22–10 mark, leading the league in wins, ERA (1.74), strikeouts (148), and shutouts (8).

Vaughn ran out of luck in the World Series against the Boston Red Sox despite pitching a 3–0 shutout in the fifth game. He lost the first game 1–0 to Babe Ruth and the third game 2–1 to Carl Mays, finishing the Series with a 1.00 ERA and a 1–2 record.

Vaughn's fifth 20-victory season came in 1919 with a 21–14 record as he led the league in strikeouts again with 141, and he was 19–16 in 1920. In midseason 1921 he retired with a 3–11 record after a dispute with manager Johnny Evers.

Hippo Vaughn

Emil Verban

Verban, Emil

Cubs: 1948–50
Second baseman
Nicknames: Dutch, The Antelope
Birthplace: Lincoln, Illinois

B: August 27, 1915
D: June 8, 1989
Batted right, threw right
Ht. 5–11; **Wt.** 165

Verban, Emil Matthew

Cubs	G	AB	H	AVG	RBI	R	2B	3B	HR	SLG	SB
1948	56	248	73	.294	16	37	15	1	1	.375	4
1949	98	343	99	.289	22	38	11	1	0	.327	3
1950	45	37	4	.108	1	7	1	0	0	.135	0
Career	853	2,911	793	.272	241	301	99	26	1	.325	21

Despite the adoption of his name as a symbol of Cub mediocrity by the Emil Verban Society, a well-publicized group of Washington, D.C., intellectuals, Verban was a competent player, good enough to be the regular second baseman of the 1944 St. Louis Cardinals, who won a World Series.

Verban was a smooth fielder and fast base runner, batted .272 during his seven-year major league career, and seldom failed to get the bat on the ball. In 1947 he struck out only eight times in 540 at bats for the Philadelphia Phillies, still the major league record for fewest strikeouts by a right-handed batter in 150 or more games. His fielding ability drew the praise of Cub manager Charlie Grimm, who said, "Verban is the best in the National League, and there is no one even close to him."

Verban was acquired by the Cubs from Philadelphia in midseason 1948, hit .294 in 56 games, batted .289 in 98 games in 1949, and faded out the next season after a hand injury, finishing with the Boston Braves.

Waitkus, Eddie

Cubs: 1941, 1946–48
First baseman
Birthplace: Cambridge, Massachusetts
B: September 4, 1919

D: September 15, 1972
Batted left, threw left
Ht. 6–0; **Wt.** 170

Waitkus, Edward Stephen

Cubs	G	AB	H	AVG	RBI	R	2B	3B	HR	SLG	SB
1941	12	28	5	.179	0	1	0	0	0	.179	0
1946	113	441	134	.304	55	50	24	5	4	.408	3
1947	130	514	150	.292	35	60	28	6	2	.381	3
1948	139	562	166	.295	44	87	27	10	7	.416	11
Career	1,140	4,254	1,214	.285	373	528	215	44	24	.374	28

After a brief test with the Cubs in 1941, Eddie Waitkus spent three years in military service and didn't return until 1946 when he took over at first base. Waitkus lacked the home run power that is expected of a first baseman, but he hit well for average and was a fine fielder, especially good at handling throws into the dirt.

With the arrival of Waitkus, long-time Cub first baseman Phil Cavarretta was shifted to the outfield. Waitkus was among the top rookies in 1946 and batted .304 in 113 games. A line-drive hitter, he batted .292 and .295 the next two seasons, but reached a peak of only seven home runs in 1948.

Deciding they needed more power at first base, as well as pitching help, the Cubs traded Waitkus and Hank Borowy to Philadelphia for pitchers Monk Dubiel and Dutch Leonard after the 1948 season. The trade didn't help the Cubs much, but Waitkus went on to several productive seasons with the Phillies, especially in 1950 when he batted .284 as they won a pennant for the first time in 35 years.

Eddie Waitkus

Waitkus's performance in 1950 was all the more remarkable because of a bizarre incident that almost cost him his life on June 15, 1949. An infatuated young woman persuaded him to come to her hotel room in Chicago, then shot him in the chest. The bullet passed through his chest and lung and lodged in his back near the spine. Five operations were needed to repair the damage, but he was back on the field in 1950.

Waitkus played in the major leagues until 1955, finishing his career with the Phillies after a brief stint in Baltimore.

Warneke, Lon

Cubs: 1930–36, 1942–43, 1945
Pitcher
Birthplace: Mt. Ida, Arkansas
B: March 28, 1909

D: June 23, 1976
Batted right, threw right
Ht. 6–2; **Wt.** 185

A lanky, right-handed country boy from Arkansas who threw hard and kept his pitches low, Lon Warneke was the Cub ace and their most consistent starting pitcher from 1932 to 1936, winning 20 or more games in three out of five seasons.

After brief trials the previous two seasons, Warneke blossomed in 1932 with a 22–6 record to lead the league in victories, percentage (.786), ERA (2.37), and shutouts (4), as well as helping the Cubs to win a pennant. He won 18 games in 1933, then again reached 22 wins the next season, which he started out with back-to-back one-hitters.

In 1935, as the Cubs surged to another pennant with a late-season 21-game winning streak, Warneke was 20–13, with four of his wins coming during the stretch drive. He stood out for the Cubs in the losing World Series effort against Detroit, beating the Tigers twice, including a 3–0 four-hitter in the opening game.

Although he dipped to 16–13 in 1936, he again led the league in shutouts with four, then was traded after the season to St. Louis for slugging first baseman Rip Collins and pitcher Tarzan Parmelee. He was a consistent winner with the Cardinals for the next five seasons, then returned to the Cubs in a midseason trade in 1942, but was in decline. He pitched his final game in 1945.

Lon Warneke

Warneke, Lonnie											
Cubs	W	L	Pct	ERA	G	CG	IP	H	BB	K	ShO
1930	0	0	.000	33.75	1	0	1⅓	2	5	0	0
1931	2	4	.333	3.22	20	3	64⅔	67	37	27	0
1932	22	6	.786	2.37	35	25	277	247	64	106	4
1933	18	13	.581	2.00	36	26	287⅓	262	74	133	4
1934	22	10	.688	3.21	43	23	291⅓	273	66	143	3
1935	20	13	.606	3.06	42	20	261⅓	257	50	120	1
1936	16	13	.552	3.44	40	13	240⅔	246	76	113	4
1942	5	7	.417	2.27	12	8	99	97	21	28	1
1943	4	5	.444	3.16	21	4	88⅓	82	18	30	0
1945	1	1	.500	3.86	9	0	14	16	1	6	0
Career	193	121	.615	3.18	445	192	2,782⅔	2,726	739	1,140	31

Four years later, Warneke—"The Arkansas Hummingbird"—returned to the major leagues as an umpire, a career he pursued for a decade before returning to his home state and winning election as a county judge.

Williams, Billy

Cubs: 1959–74
Outfielder
Birthplace: Whistler, Alabama

B: June 15, 1938
Bats left, throws right
Ht. 6–1; **Wt.** 175

Williams, Billy Leo

Cubs	G	AB	H	AVG	RBI	R	2B	3B	HR	SLG	SB
1959	18	33	5	.182	2	0	0	1	0	.212	0
1960	12	47	13	.277	7	4	0	2	2	.489	0
1961	146	529	147	.278	86	75	20	7	25	.484	6
1962	159	618	184	.298	91	94	22	8	22	.466	9
1963	161	612	175	.286	95	87	36	9	25	.497	7
1964	162	645	201	.312	98	100	39	2	33	.532	10
1965	164	645	203	.315	108	115	39	6	34	.552	10
1966	162	648	179	.276	91	100	23	5	29	.461	6
1967	162	634	176	.278	84	92	21	12	28	.481	6
1968	163	642	185	.288	98	91	30	8	30	.500	4
1969	163	642	188	.293	95	103	33	10	21	.474	3
1970	161	636	205	.322	129	137	34	4	42	.586	7
1971	157	594	179	.301	93	86	27	5	28	.505	7
1972	150	574	191	.333	122	95	34	6	37	.606	3
1973	156	576	166	.288	86	72	22	2	20	.438	4
1974	117	404	113	.280	68	55	22	0	16	.453	4
Career	2,488	9,350	2,711	.290	1,475	1,410	434	88	426	.492	90

Consistent and durable, Billy Williams established himself as one of the finest of Cub outfielders during a long career that took him to the Hall of Fame in 1987. An outstanding left-handed batter with great power, Williams played competently in left field during most of his term with the Cubs from 1959 through 1974.

Nicknamed "Whistler" for his Alabama hometown, Williams was overshadowed most of his career by teammate Ernie Banks and his own subdued, calm personality. Yet his statistics speak loudly for his ability and achievements.

After brief trials in 1959 and 1960, Williams broke in as an outfield regular in 1961 and was selected the NL Rookie of the Year after batting .278 with 25 home runs and driving in 86 runs. He hit 20 or more home runs for 13 consecutive seasons, and topped 30 five times during that span, reaching a high of 42 in 1970. Known for his "sweet swing," Williams batted over .300 five times, scored more than 100 runs on five occasions, and drove in more than 100 runs in three seasons.

Labeled an iron man, Williams' proudest achievement might have been his consecutive-games-played streak of 1,117, which set a NL record, since surpassed by Steve Garvey. The streak started on September 22, 1963, and ended on September 3, 1970, when Williams sat out a game at his own request. Williams admitted it had been an ordeal.

"Never until they do it will anybody realize the pressure involved in keeping such a streak alive," Williams said. "Every day it's the same routine, going to the ballpark and saying to yourself, 'You must concentrate on the game. You gotta be ready to play both mentally and physically.' It was during this time that I learned to play every game like it was my last."

Williams' finest years came during the Leo Durocher era

Billy Williams

from 1966 to 1972 when the Cubs, reinforced with such outstanding players as Banks, Ron Santo, Glenn Beckert, and Don Kessinger and pitchers Ferguson Jenkins, Bill Hands, and Ken Holtzman, rose from decades of stagnation to challenge for division titles for several years.

Williams batted .322 with 42 home runs and 129 RBIs in 1970, tied for the league lead in hits with 205, and led in runs scored with 137—the highest total in the NL in 38 years. After batting .301 in 1971, in 1972 he led the league in batting with .333, hit 37 home runs, and drove in 122 runs, and he just missed winning the Most Valuable Player award. He finished second in the voting to Cincinnati's Johnny Bench, who had batted just .270, though he had surpassed Williams in home runs with 40 and RBIs with 125. It was the greatest disappointment in Williams' career. "When I saw how it turned out," he said, "I was so disgusted that I just stopped reading [the newspaper]."

Turning 35 years of age in 1973, Williams began to slow down, batting just .288 with 20 home runs. In 1974, his last with the Cubs, he played more at first base than in the outfield and in 117 games batted .280 with 16 home runs.

On October 23, 1974, Williams was traded to the Oakland A's. After two seasons with the A's, he retired as a player, finishing with a career batting average of .290 and 426 home runs. He later returned to the Cubs as the team's batting coach.

Williams, Cy

Cubs: 1912–17
Outfielder
Birthplace: Wadena, Indiana
B: December 21, 1887

D: April 23, 1974
Batted left, threw left
Ht. 6–2; **Wt.** 180

Williams Fred

Cubs	G	AB	H	AVG	RBI	R	2B	3B	HR	SLG	SB
1912	28	62	15	.242	1	3	1	1	0	.290	2
1913	49	156	35	.224	32	17	3	3	4	.359	5

Cubs	G	AB	H	AVG	RBI	R	2B	3B	HR	SLG	SB
1914	55	94	19	.202	5	12	2	2	0	.266	2
1915	151	518	133	.257	64	59	22	6	13	.398	15
1916	118	405	113	.279	66	55	19	9	12	.459	6
1917	138	468	113	.241	42	53	22	4	5	.338	8
Career	2,002	6,780	1,981	.292	1,005	1,024	306	74	251	.470	115

Although the Cubs' trade of young outfielder Fred "Cy" Williams to Philadelphia on December 26, 1917 sometimes has been compared to the infamous Lou Brock deal half a century later, the parallel is probably unfair. In exchange for Williams, the Cubs got George "Dode" Paskert, a veteran center fielder who helped them win the 1918 pennant.

What isn't debatable, however, is that Williams, who had slumped to .241 in 1917 after batting .279 and tying for the NL lead in home runs with 12 in 1916 (he hit 13 in 1915), developed into one of the most fearsome sluggers in the league with the Phillies. Williams led the NL in home runs three times at Philadelphia, with 15 in 1920, 41 in 1923, and 30 in 1927. He batted over .300 in six seasons, with a high of .345 in 1926.

Williams had the advantage of playing in bandbox Baker Bowl, though many of his line drives that bounced off the high tin fence in right field for doubles would have been home runs in a more conventional park.

Although the "Williams shift" in which players were bunched on the right side by Cleveland against Boston's Ted Williams in the 1940s and 1950s is credited to Indians manager Lou Boudreau, a similar alignment was often used in the 1920s against Cy Williams.

Cy Williams finished his playing career in 1930. A graduate of Notre Dame University, he later won a reputation as an architect.

Williams, Mitch

Cubs: 1989–90
Pitcher
Birthplace: Santa Ana, California

B: November 17, 1964
Bats left, throws left
Ht. 6–4; **Wt.** 205

Williams, Mitchell Steven

Cubs	W	L	Pct	ERA	G	CG	IP	H	BB	K	ShO
1989	4	4	.500	2.64	76	36	81⅔	71	52	67	0
1990	1	8	.111	3.93	59	16	66⅓	60	50	55	0
Career	45	57	.441	3.56	212	192	684⅔	526	537	650	0

Lack of control might have been an asset to Mitch Williams in intimidating batters as a hard-throwing, left-handed relief "stopper" who was quickly nicknamed the Wild Thing during his heroics for the 1989 Cubs, for whom he made an East Division title a reality. Williams contributed 36 saves and a 4–4 record to the team's success.

Williams was the prize in an nine-player trade the Cubs made with Texas on December 5, 1988, in which the Rangers' most notable acquisition was first baseman Rafael Palmeiro, who was to become a star. The deal paid off for the Cubs for just one season because Williams fell in 1990 to a 1–8 record with only 16 saves. He was traded to Philadelphia before the 1991 season.

Williams resumed his effectiveness for three seasons with the Phillies, having a big hand in their 1993 capture of the

Cy Williams

Mitch Williams

pennant with 43 saves. But failures in the World Series, particularly when Toronto's Joe Carter won the sixth and deciding game with a three-run homer run off him in the bottom of the ninth, apparently sapped Williams' confidence.

He was traded to Houston after the 1993 season, but was released by the Astros on May 31, 1994. A comeback attempt with the California Angels in 1995 also failed.

Williamson, Ned

White Stockings: 1879–89
Third baseman
Birthplace: Philadelphia, Pennsylvania
B: October 24, 1857

D: March 3, 1894
Batted right, threw right
Ht. 5–11; **Wt.** 175

Williamson, Edward Nagle

White Stockings	G	AB	H	AVG	RBI	R	2B	3B	HR	SLG	SB
1879	80	320	94	.294	36	66	20	13	1	.447	—
1880	75	311	78	.251	31	65	20	2	0	.328	—
1881	82	343	92	.268	48	56	12	6	1	.347	—
1882	83	348	98	.282	60	66	27	4	3	.408	—
1883	98	402	111	.276	—	83	49	5	2	.438	—
1884	107	417	116	.278	—	84	18	8	27	.554	—
1885	113	407	97	.238	64	87	16	5	3	.324	—
1886	121	430	93	.216	58	69	17	8	6	.335	—
1887	127	439	117	.267	78	77	20	14	9	.437	45
1888	132	452	113	.250	73	75	9	14	8	.385	25
1889	47	173	41	.237	30	16	3	1	1	.283	2
Career	1,201	4,553	1,159	.255	523	809	228	86	63	.384	75

Ned Williamson contributed to five White Stockings pennant winners, four as a third baseman and the fifth as a shortstop in 1886. And for 35 years, until Babe Ruth hit 29 in 1919, Williamson held a dubious record for home runs in a season with 27 in 1884.

While a decent hitter, batting a career high of .294 in 1879, Williamson never demonstrated extraordinary power in any year other than 1884. He was helped by a ground rule at Lakefront Park that for one season was changed to allow home runs on balls hit over a fence less than 200 feet away. Previously they had been ground-rule doubles.

Williamson had hit 49 doubles and two home runs in 1883, and in 1884 the ratio was reversed to 18 doubles and 27 home runs. Only three of his home runs came on the road. He also was the first player to hit three home runs in a game.

Williamson's greatest asset was his fielding skill as part of the "Stonewall Infield" of the 1880s. He consistently led the league in various fielding categories, both at third base and shortstop, from the time he joined the White Stockings in 1879.

Williamson's career was cut short after he injured a kneecap during the White Stockings' 1889 world tour. He struggled through the 1889 season, jumped to the Players League in 1890, then retired after batting only .195.

Wilmot, Walt

White Stockings: 1890–95
Outfielder
Birthplace: Plover, Wisconsin

B: October 18, 1863
D: February 21, 1929
Batted both, threw right

Ned Williamson

Walter Wilmot

Wilmot, Walter Robert

White Stockings	G	AB	H	AVG	RBI	R	2B	3B	HR	SLG	SB
1890	139	571	159	.278	99	114	15	12	14	.420	7
1891	121	498	139	.279	71	102	14	10	11	.414	42
1892	92	380	82	.216	35	47	7	7	2	.287	31
1893	94	392	118	.301	61	69	14	14	2	.431	39
1894	133	597	197	.330	130	134	45	12	5	.471	74
1895	108	466	132	.283	72	86	16	6	8	.395	28
Career	960	3,981	1,100	.276	594	725	152	91	59	.405	349

An outfielder for Cap Anson for six seasons in the 1890s, Walt Wilmot's chief claim to fame was drawing six walks in a game on August 22, 1891, a major league record matched only by Jimmy Foxx and Andre Thornton many years later.

Picked up from the Washington franchise that had dissolved after the 1889 season, Wilmot was a find for the Cubs, who had been hit hard by Players League defections. In 1890 he led the NL in home runs with 14 and batted .278 with 99 RBIs. His career high was .330 in 1894, when he also drove in 130 runs and scored 134.

Released after the 1895 season, Wilmot tried to come back with the New York Giants in 1897 and 1898, but faded into the minor leagues.

Wilson, Hack

Cubs: 1926–31
Outfielder
Birthplace: Ellwood City, Pennsylvania
B: April 26, 1900

D: November 23, 1948
Batted right, threw right
Ht. 5–6; **Wt.** 190

Hack Wilson

Wilson, Lewis Robert

Cubs	G	AB	H	AVG	RBI	R	2B	3B	HR	SLG	SB
1926	142	529	170	.321	109	97	36	8	21	.539	10
1927	146	551	175	.318	129	119	30	12	30	.579	13
1928	145	520	163	.313	120	89	32	9	31	.588	4
1929	150	574	198	.345	159	135	30	5	39	.618	3
1930	155	585	208	.356	190	146	35	5	56	.723	3
1931	112	395	103	.261	61	66	22	4	13	.435	1
Career	1,348	4,760	1,461	.307	884	1,062	266	67	244	.545	52

An oversight by the New York Giants made it possible for the Cubs to acquire Hack Wilson, one of the most powerful hitters in the game's history, for a mere $5,000 in the draft of minor leaguers held shortly after the 1925 World Series. Wilson had been up with the Giants for varying periods the previous three years but had been returned to the minor leagues for further seasoning. New York inadvertently failed to protect him in the postseason draft.

New Cub manager Joe McCarthy, who had been hired out of the minor leagues, had been impressed with Wilson's play at Toledo in 1925 and made sure the Cubs drafted him. The bargain quickly became apparent when Wilson led the NL in home runs with 21 in 1926, batting .321 and driving in 109 runs. Cub fans rhapsodized about "the Million Dollar Slugger from the Five and Ten Cent Store."

"I wouldn't trade him for any other outfielder in baseball," McCarthy said. "He can hit, field, run, and throw."

Built like a barrel on legs, stumpy with short lower limbs and a powerful upper torso, Wilson nevertheless was fast enough to play an outstanding center field, as well as hit what are today called tape-measure home runs in clusters. He went

from strength to strength despite an addiction to alcohol, improving his home run output for five consecutive seasons with the Cubs and leading the league four times.

He surpassed the 21 home runs of 1926 with 30 in 1927, 31 in 1928, 39 in 1929, and 56 in 1930, the last still a record for an NL hitter. The RBI totals for each year were 109, 129, 120, 159, and 190, the last a major league record that has been approached only by Lou Gehrig with 184 and Hank Greenberg with 183.

Wilson reached his zenith as a slugger in 1929 and 1930. In 1929, as the centerpiece of one of the greatest of all outfields, with Kiki Cuyler and Riggs Stephenson, Wilson batted .345 with 39 home runs and 159 RBIs. He and Rogers Hornsby, who batted .380 with 39 home runs and 149 RBIs, powered the Cubs to a pennant. In 1930, Wilson surpassed even himself, batting .356 with 56 home runs and 190 RBIs.

He was dogged, and perhaps driven, throughout 1930, however, by a misplay in the 1929 World Series loss to the Philadelphia Athletics. The Cubs squandered an 8–0 lead in the seventh inning of the fourth game when the Athletics scored 10 runs. Three of the runs scored when Wilson lost Mule Haas's flyball in the sun and the ball went for an inside-the-park home run. Throughout the 1930 season the fans greeted Wilson with a new nickname, "Sunny Boy." Overlooked was the fact that Wilson had batted .471 in the 1929 Series.

With the replacement of McCarthy by Rogers Hornsby as manager late in the 1930 season, Wilson's fortunes with the Cubs began to fade. The easygoing, hard-drinking "Li'l Round Man" complained that he was harassed by the dictatorial Hornsby. His output plummeted in 1931 to .261 with 13 home runs and 61 RBIs in just 112 games.

Wilson blamed Hornsby for "ruining my career" and was relieved when he was traded to St. Louis after the 1931 season. The Cardinals immediately traded him to Brooklyn, and he revived slightly in 1932, batting .297 with 23 home runs and 123 RBIs. He wound up his career two years later. Ending up as a laborer in Baltimore, he died penniless in 1948.

After a long delay in admittance to the Hall of Fame "on moral grounds," Wilson was elected in 1979.

Wyse, Hank

Cubs: 1942, 1943–47
Pitcher
Birthplace: Lunsford, Arkansas

B: March 1, 1918
Bats right, throws right
Ht. 5–11; **Wt.** 185

Wyse, Henry Washington

Cubs	W	L	Pct	ERA	G	CG	IP	H	BB	K	ShO
1942	2	1	.667	1.93	4	1	28	33	6	8	1
1943	9	7	.563	2.94	38	8	156	160	34	45	2
1944	16	15	.516	3.15	41	14	257⅓	277	57	86	3
1945	22	10	.688	2.68	38	23	278⅓	272	55	77	2
1946	14	12	.538	2.68	40	12	201⅓	206	52	52	2
1947	6	9	.400	4.31	37	5	142	158	64	53	1
Career	79	70	.530	3.52	251	67	1,257⅔	1,339	373	362	11

Control and changing speeds, as well as a good sinker, were Hank Wyse's stock in trade during the mid-1940s, and those assets served him and the Cubs well. He was the workhorse of the pitching staff from 1944 to 1946, after which back problems that had plagued him throughout his career got the best of him.

"Hooks" Wyse's long minor league apprenticeship ended when he was called up late in the 1942 season by the Cubs. He hit his stride in 1944 with a 16–15 record, then became the kingpin of the staff with a 22–10 record, an ERA of 2.68, and 23 complete games in 34 starts as he lifted the Cubs to a pennant.

After back surgery following the 1945 season, Wyse pitched well one more year, with a 14–12 record in 1946, before dropping to 6–9 the next season. Released by the Cubs, he slipped into the minor leagues, and resurfaced in the major leagues in 1950 with the Philadelphia Athletics in 1950 before his career ended the next year.

Zimmer, Don

Cubs: 1960–61
Second baseman
Birthplace: Cincinnati, Ohio

B: January 17, 1931
Bats right, throws right
Ht. 5–9; **Wt.** 165

Zimmer, Donald William

Cubs	G	AB	H	AVG	RBI	R	2B	3B	HR	SLG	SB
1960	132	368	95	.258	35	37	16	7	6	.389	8
1961	128	477	120	.252	40	57	25	4	13	.403	5
Career	1,095	3,283	773	.235	352	353	130	22	91	.372	45

A utility infielder with the Brooklyn–Los Angeles Dodgers for six seasons before the Cubs traded three players and $25,000 for him on April 8, 1960, Don Zimmer found a home briefly at second base. He batted .258 in 1960 and .252 in 1961 as the regular second baseman, hitting 13 home runs in the second year.

A hustling player, who continued his career despite having suffered a serious head injury from being hit by a pitch, Zimmer was traded to the New York Mets before the 1962 season. He completed a 12-season playing career with the Washington Senators in 1965.

He continued in major league baseball as a coach for several teams, as well as manager of the San Diego Padres (1972–73), Boston Red Sox (1976–80), and Texas Rangers (1981–82) before the Cubs hired him as a coach in 1984. He managed the Cubs from 1988 until early into the 1991 season. (For details of his managerial career, see Chapter 4, "The Skippers.")

Zimmerman, Heinie

Cubs: 1907–16
Third baseman
Birthplace: New York City
B: February 9, 1887

D: March 14, 1969
Batted right, threw right
Ht. 5–11; **Wt.** 176

Zimmerman, Henry

Cubs	G	AB	H	AVG	RBI	R	2B	3B	HR	SLG	SB
1907	5	9	2	.222	1	0	1	0	0	.333	0
1908	46	113	33	.292	9	17	4	1	0	.345	2
1909	65	183	50	.273	21	23	9	2	0	.344	7
1910	99	335	95	.384	38	35	16	6	3	.394	7
1911	143	535	164	.307	85	80	22	17	9	.462	23
1912	145	557	207	.372	103	95	41	14	14	.571	23
1913	127	447	140	.313	95	69	28	12	9	.490	18
1914	146	564	167	.296	87	75	36	12	4	.424	17
1915	139	520	138	.265	62	65	28	11	3	.379	19
1916	107	398	116	.291	64	54	25	5	6	.425	15
Career	1,456	5,304	1,566	.295	800	695	275	105	58	.419	175

Among baseball's rarest batting achievements is the winning of the Triple Crown—leading the league in average, home runs, and RBIs—and by some modern estimates Heinie Zimmerman is one of only 12 players to accomplish it. (Ted Williams and Rogers Hornsby did it twice.)

Zimmerman joined the Cubs in 1907 and for four seasons was largely a utility player. It wasn't until he replaced Harry Steinfeldt in 1911 as the regular third baseman that he broke through as a star, batting .307, .372, .313, and .296 the next four seasons.

Zimmerman's miraculous season was 1912, when he led the league not only in batting with .372, hits with 207, and doubles with 41, but also in home runs with 14 and RBIs with 103, though the last figure has been disputed. At the time RBIs were recorded haphazardly, and some record books credit Zimmerman with only 98 or 99 while Honus Wagner is credited with 102. If the figure of 103 is accepted, Zimmerman must be listed among the rare Triple Crown winners.

Among other feats, Zimmerman had a 23-game hitting streak in 1912 and set a still-current Cubs record with nine RBIs in a game in 1911.

Zimmerman was traded to the New York Giants in August 1916 and had several more good years, leading the league in RBIs with 83 that year and 102 the next. He became the "goat" of the 1917 World Series when he chased Eddie Collins of the White Sox across home plate with the winning run in the sixth and final game.

His career was abruptly terminated after the 1919 season when he was implicated in a betting scandal.

3

All the Team's Men

Pre-1900 Players

A total of 1,596 men have played for Chicago's National League franchise, from Bert Abbey, a 19th-century pitcher who won six games, to Dutch Zwilling, a weak-hitting outfielder who had the distinction of playing with all three of Chicago's major league teams—the Cubs, White Sox, and the Whales of the short-lived Federal League.

The Cubs have been the National League's anchor team: they are the only club to have played every season in the same city without interruption since the league's birth in 1876. They were originally known as the White Stockings. Prior to 1902, they had a variety of nicknames, such as Cap Anson's Colts, Anson's Orphans, Rainmakers, Cowboys, Rough Riders, and Remnants.

On March 27, 1902, in an unsigned story, the *Chicago Daily News* reported, "Manager Frank Selee this year will devote his strongest efforts on the teamwork of the new Cubs." The *Chicago Inter-Ocean* and the *Chicago Journal* began using the name Cubs in 1905.

A

Abbey, Bert (1893–95) pitcher: 6–11 with 5.01 ERA in 19 games.

Addy, Bob (1876) outfielder: 40-for-142, .282, in 32 games.

Andrews, Jim (1890) outfielder: 38-for-202, .188, in 53 games.

Andrus, Fred (1876, '84) outfielder-pitcher: 12-for-41, .293, in 41 games; 1–0 with 2.00 ERA in 5 games.

Anson, Adrian Constantine (Cap, Pop) (1876–97) first baseman–outfielder–catcher: 3,041-for-9,120, .333, in 2,276 games, 22 seasons.

B

Baldwin, Mark (1887–88) pitcher: 31–32 with 3.08 ERA in 70 games.

Barnes, Ross (1876–77) infielder-pitcher: 163-for-414, .394, in 88 games; 0–0 with 20.25 ERA in 1 game.

Bastian, Charlie (1889) infielder: 21-for-155, .135, in 46 games.

Beals, Tommy (1880) infielder-outfielder: 7-for-46, .152, in 13 games.

Bielaski, Oscar (1876) outfielder: 78-for-335, .233, in 83 games.

Bishop, Bill (1889) pitcher: 0–0, with 18.00 ERA in 2 games.

Borchers, George (1888) pitcher: 4–4 with 3.49 ERA in 10 games.

Bowman, Bill (1891) catcher: 4-for-45, .089, in 15 games.

Bradley, George (1887) pitcher: 18–23 with 3.31 ERA in 50 games.

Brown, Joe (1884) pitcher: 4–2 with 4.68 ERA in 7 games.

Brown, Lew (1879) infielder: 6-for-21, .286, in 6 games.

Brynan, Charlie (1888) pitcher: 2–1 with 6.48 ERA in 3 games.

Burns, Tom (1880–91) infielder: 1,291-for-4,881, .264, in 1,239 games.

C

Camp, Kid (1894) pitcher: 0–1 with 6.26 ERA in 4 games.

Camp, Llewellan (1893–94) infielder: 47-for-189, .249, in 46 games.

Canavan, Jimmy (1892) infielder-outfielder: 73-for-439, .166, in 118 games.

Carroll, Cliff (1890–91) outfielder: 298-for-1,097, .272, in 266 games.

Caruthers, Bob (1893) outfielder: 0-for-3, .000, in 1 game.

Cassidy, John (1878) outfielder: 68-for-256, .266, in 60 game.

Clarke, Henry (1898) pitcher: 1–0 with 2.00 ERA in 1 game.

Clarke, William (1888) pitcher-outfielder: 2-1 with 4.54 ERA in 5 games; 1-for-4, .250, in 1 game.

Clarkson, John (1884–87) pitcher: 137–57 (no ERA) in 189 games.

Clausen, Fritz (1893–94) pitcher: 6–3 (no ERA) in 11 games.

Cogan, Dick (1899) pitcher: 2–3 with 4.30 ERA in 5 games.

Connor, Jim (1892, '97–99) infielder: 247-for-1,058, .233, in 293 games.

Cooney, Jimmy (1890–92) infielder: 311-for-1,277, .244, in 318 games.

Corcoran, Larry (1880–85) pitcher: 175–86 (no ERA) in 271 games.

Corcoran, Mike (1884) pitcher: 0–1 with 4.00 ERA in 1 game.

Coughlin, Roscoe (1890) pitcher: 4–6 with 4.26 ERA in 11 games.

Crosby, George (1884) pitcher: 1–2 with 3.54 ERA in 3 games.

Curley, Doc (1899) infielder: 4-for-37, .108, in 10 games.

D

Dahlen, Bill (1891–98) infielder-outfielder: 1,166-for-3,904, .299, in 986 games.

Daily, Cornelius (1896) outfielder: 2-for-27, .074, in 9 games.

Dalrymple, Abner (1879–86) outfielder: 938-for-3,181, .295, in 709 games.

Daly, Tom (1887–88) catcher-infielder: 95-for-475, .200, in 139 games.

Darling, Dell (1887–89) catcher-infielder: 84-for-336, .250, in 94 games.

Decker, George (1892–97) outfielder-infielder: 599-for-2,149, .279, in 541 games.

Demarais, Fred (1890) pitcher: 0–0 with 0.00 ERA in 1 game.

DeMiller, Harry (1892) pitcher: 1–1 with 6.38 ERA in 4 games.

DeMontreville, Gene (1899) infielder: 87-for-310, .281, in 82 games.

Denzer, Roger (1897) pitcher: 2–8 with 5.13 ERA in 12 games.

Dolan, John (1895) pitcher: 0–1 with 6.55 ERA in 2 games.

Dolan, Tom (1879) catcher: 0-for-4, .000, in 1 game.

Donnelly, Frank (1893) pitcher: 3–1 with 25.36 ERA in 7 games.

Doscher, John Henry, Sr. (1879) outfielder-infielder: 2-for-25, .182, in 3 games.

Duffy, Hugh (1888–89) outfielder: 256-for-882, .290, in 207 games.

Dwyer, Frank (1888–89) pitcher: 20–14 (no ERA) in 32 games.

E

Eagan, Bill (1893) infielder: 5-for-19, .263, in 6 games.

Earl, Howard (1890) outfielder-infielder: 95-for-384, .247, in 92 games.

Eden, Charlie (1877) outfielder: 12-for-55, .218, in 15 games.

Eggler, Dave (1877) outfielder: 36-for-136, .265, in 33 games.

Eiteljorg, Ed (1890) pitcher: 0–1 with 22.50 ERA in 1 game.

F

Farrell, Duke (1888–89) catcher-infielder: 157-for-648, .242, in 165 games.

Ferguson, Bob (1878) infielder: 91-for-259, .351, in 61 games.

Fisher, Cherokee (1877) infielder: 0-for-4, .000, in 1 game.

Flint, Frank (1879–89) catcher-outfielder: 620-for-2,537, .244, in 673 games.

Flynn, Dibby (1896) outfielder: 27-for-106, .255, in 29 games.

Flynn, Jocko (1886–87) pitcher-outfielder: 23–6 with 2.24 ERA in 32 games; 41-for-205, .200, in 58 games.

Foster, Elmer (1890–91) outfielder-catcher: 29-for-121, .240, in 31 games.

France, Ossie (1890) pitcher: 0–0 with 13.50 ERA in 1 game.

Friend, Danny (1895–98) pitcher: 32–29 with 4.71 ERA in 67 games.

G

Gastfield, Ed (1885) catcher: 0-for-3, .000, in 1 game.

Geiss, Emil (1887) pitcher: 0–1 with 8.00 ERA in 1 game.

Gibson, Bob (1890) pitcher: 1–0 with 0.00 ERA in 1 game.

Glenalvin, Bob (1890, '93) infielder: 88-for-311, .283, in 82 games.

Glenn, John (1876–77) outfielder: 130-for-478, .272, in 116 games.

Goldsmith, Fred (1880–84) pitcher: 107–63 (no ERA) in 177 games.

Gore, George (1879–86) outfielder: 933-for-2,963, .315, in 719 games.

Griffith, Frank (1892) pitcher: 0–1 with 11.25 ERA in 1 game.

Gumbert, Ad (1888–89, '91–92) pitcher: 58–56 (no ERA) in 115 games.

Guth, Charles (1880) pitcher: 1–0 with 5.00 ERA in 1 game.

H

Hallinan, James (1877–78) infielder-outfielder: 44-for-140, .306, in 35 games.

Hankinson, Frank (1878–79) pitcher: 15–11 (no ERA) in 27 games.

Harbridge, Bill (1878–79) outfielder-catcher: 73-for-258, .283, in 58 games.

Hardie, Lew (1886) catcher-outfielder-infielder: 9-for-51, .176, in 16 games.

Healy, John (1889) pitcher: 1–4 with 2.50 ERA in 5 games.

Hernon, Tom (1897) outfielder: 1-for-16, .063, in 4 games.

Hibbard, John (1884) pitcher: 1–1 with 2.65 ERA in 2 games.

Hines, Paul (1876–77) outfielder: 174-for-566, .307, in 124 games.

Hollison, John Henry (1892) pitcher: 0–0 with 2.25 ERA in 1 game.

Honan, Marty (1890–91) catcher: 2-for-15, .133, in 6 games.

Houseman, John (1894) infielder: 6-for-15, .400, in 4 games.

Hughey, Jim (1893) pitcher: 0–1 with 11.00 ERA in 2 games.

Hutchinson, Bill (1899–95) pitcher: 182–158 (no ERA) in 367 games.

Hutchinson, Ed (1890) infielder: 1-for-17, .059, in 4 games.

I

Irwin, Charlie (1893–95) infielder: 171-for-590, .290, in 152 games

Isbell, William (1898) pitcher: 4–7 with 3.56 ERA in 13 games.

J

Johnson, Abe (1893) pitcher: 0–0 with 36.00 ERA in 1 game.

Jones, Charley (1877) outfielder: 3-for-8, .375, in 2 games.

K

Katoll, John (1898–99) pitcher: 1–2 (no ERA) in 4 games.

Kelly, King (1880–86) outfielder-catcher: 899-for-2,843, .316, in 681 games.

Kennedy, Ted (1885) pitcher: 7–2 with 3.43 ERA in 9 games.

Kilroy, Matt (1898) pitcher: 6–7 with 4.31 ERA in 13 games.

Kinzie, Walt (1884) infielder: 13-for-82, .159, in 19 games.

Kittridge, Malachi (1890–97) catcher: 431-for-1,970, .219, in 569 games.

Korwan, Jim (1897) pitcher: 1–2 (no ERA) in 5 games.

Kraemer, Joel (1889–90) pitcher: 0–1 with 6.91 ERA in 19 games.

Krieg, Bill (1885) catcher–first baseman: 0-for-3, .000, in 1 game.

Krock, Gus (1888–89) pitcher: 28–17 (no ERA) in 46 games.

L

Lange, Bill (1893–99) outfielder-infielder: 1,055-for-3,195, .330, in 811 games.

Larkin, Terry (1878–79) pitcher-outfielder: 60–49 (no ERA) in 114 games; 115-for-454, .253, in 118 games.

Lauer, Chuck (1890) catcher: 2-for-8, .250, in 2 games.

Lee, Tom (1884) pitcher: 1–4 with 3.77 ERA in 5 games.

Luby, Pat (1890–92) pitcher: 38–36 (no ERA) in 95 games.

Lynch, Henry (1893) outfielder: 3-for-14, .214, in 4 games.

Lynch, Tom (1884) pitcher: 0–0 with 2.57 ERA in 1 game.

Lytle, Pop (1890) outfielder-infielder: 0-for-4, .000, in 1 game.

M

Magoon, George (1899) infielder: 43-for-189, .228, in 59 games.

Mains, Grasshopper (1888) pitcher: 1–1 with 4.91 ERA in 2 games.

Malarkey, John (1899) pitcher: 0–1 with 13.00 ERA in 1 game.

Martin, Frank (1898) infielder: 0-for-4, .000, in 1 game.

Mauck, Hal (1893) pitcher: 8–10 with 4.41 ERA in 23 games.

McBride, Algie (1896) outfielder: 7-for-29, .241, in 9 games.

McCauley, Jim (1885) catcher: 1-for-6, .167, in 3 games.

McClellan, Bill (1878) infielder: 46-for-205, .224, in 48 games.

McCormick, Jim (1885–86) pitcher: 51–15 (no ERA) in 66 games.

McFarland, Monte (1895–96) pitcher: 2–4 with 6.46 ERA in 6 games.

McGill, Willie (1893–94) pitcher: 24–37 (no ERA) in 66 games.

McGinnis, August (1893) pitcher: 2–5 (no ERA) in 13 games.

McVey, Cal (1876–77) catcher-infielder-pitcher: 205-for-574, .357, in 123 games; 9–10 (no ERA) in 28 games.

Meakim, George (1892) pitcher: 0–1 with 11.00 ERA in 1 game.

Merritt, Bill (1891) catcher: 9-for-42, .214, in 11 games.

Moolic, George (1886) catcher-outfielder: 8-for-56, .143, in 16 games.

Moran, Bill (1895) infielder: 9-for-55, .164, in 15 games.

N

Nagle, Tom (1890–91) catcher: 42-for-169, .249 in 46 games.

Newman, Charlie (1892) outfielder: 10-for-61, .164, in 16 games.

Nicol, George (1891) pitcher: 0–1 with 4.91 ERA in 3 games.

Nicol, Hugh (1881–82) outfielder-infielder: 59-for-294, .201, in 73 games.

O

O'Brien, John (1893) infielder: 5-for-14, .357, in 4 games.

O'Brien, Pete (1890) second baseman: 30-for-106, .283, in 27 games.

P

Parker, Doc (1893, '95–96) pitcher: 5–7 (no ERA) in 17 games.

Parrott, Jiggs (1892-95) infielder: 307-for-1,309, .235, in 315 games.

Parrott, Tom (1893) catcher-pitcher; 7-for-27, .259, in 7 games; 0–3 with 6.67 ERA in 4 games.

Peters, Johnny (1876–77, '79) infielder-pitcher: 288-for-960, .300, in 209 games; 0–0 with 0.00 ERA in 1 game.

Pettit, Bob (1887) pitcher: 0–0 with 0.00 ERA in 1 game.

Pfeffer, Fred (1883, '89, '91, '96–97) infielder: 1,078-for-4,280, .250, in 1,093 games.

Phyle, Bill (1898–99) pitcher: 3–9 (no ERA) in 13 games.

Piercy, Andy (1881) infielder: 2-for-8, .250, in 2 games.

Poorman, Tom (1880) pitcher: 2–0 with 2.40 ERA in 2 games.

Powers, Phil (1878) catcher: 5-for-31, .161, in 8 games.

Pyle, Shadow (1887) pitcher: 1–3 with 4.73 ERA in 4 games.

Q

Quest, Joe (1879–82) infielder: 244-for-1,086, .225, in 285 games.

Quinn, Frank (1899) outfielder-infielder: 6-for-34, .176, in 12 games.

Quinn, Joe (1877) outfielder: 1-for-14, .071, in 4 games.

R

Reilly, Josh (1896) infielder: 9-for-42, .214, in 9 games.

Reis, Laurie (1877–78) pitcher: 4–4 with 2.00 ERA in 8 games.

Remsen, Jack (1878–79) outfielder-infielder: 85-for-376, .226, in 98 games.

Roach, Skell (1899) pitcher: 1–0 with 3.00 ERA in 1 game.

Roat, Fred (1892) infielder: 6-for-31, .194, in 8 games.

Rowe, Dave (1877) pitcher: 0–1 with 18.00 ERA in 1 game.

S

Schriver, Pop (1891–94) catcher-outfielder: 264-for-994, .266, in 279 games.

Scott, Milt (1882) first baseman: 2-for-5, .400, in 1 game.

Shaffer, George (1879) infielder-outfielder: 96-for-316, .304, in 73 games.

Shaw, Sam (1893) pitcher: 1–0 with 5.63 ERA in 2 games.

Smith, Harry (1897) infielder-catcher: 19-for-94, .202, in 24 games.

Sommers, Pete (1889) catcher-outfielder: 10-for-45, .222, in 12 games.

Spalding, Albert (1876–78) pitcher–first baseman: 48–13 with 1.78 ERA in 65 games; 158-for-550, .287, in 79 games.

Sprague, Charlie (1887) pitcher: 1–0 with 4.91 ERA in 3 games.

Start, Joe (1878) first baseman: 100-for-285, .351, in 61 games.

Stedronsky, John (1879) third baseman: 1-for-12, .083, in 4 games.

Stein, Ed (1890–91) pitcher: 19–12 (no ERA) in 34 games.

Stenzel, Jake (1890) outfielder-catcher: 11-for-41, .268, in 11 games.

Stewart, Asa (1895) second baseman: 88-for-365, .241, in 97 games.

Stratton, Scott (1894–95) pitcher: 10–8 (no ERA) in 20 games.

Sullivan, Bill (1878) outfielder: 1-for-6, .167, in 2 games.

Sunday, Billy (1883–87) outfielder: 179-for-705, .254, in 181 games.

Sullivan, Marty (1887–88) outfielder: 208-for-786, .265, in 190 games.

Sullivan, Mike (1890) pitcher: 5–6 with 4.59 ERA in 12 games.

Sutcliffe, Sy (1884–85) catcher-outfielder: 11-for-58, .190, in 15 games.

T

Tebeau, Patsy (1887) infielder: 11-for-68, .162, in 20 games.

Tener, John (1888–89) pitcher: 22–20 (no ERA) in 37 games.

Terry, Adonis (1894–97) pitcher: 41–40 (no ERA) in 92 games.

Thornton, Walt (1895–98) pitcher: 23–18 with 4.18 ERA in 56 games.

Traffley, Bill (1878) catcher: 1-for-9, .111, in 2 games.

Truby, Harry (1895–96) second baseman: 68-for-228, .298, in 62 games.

V

Van Haltren, George (1887–89) pitcher: 24–20 (no ERA) in 50 games.

Vickery, Tom (1891) pitcher: 6–5 with 4.07 ERA in 14 games.

W

Waitt, Charlie (1877) outfielder: 4-for-41, .098, in 10 games.

White, Deacon (1876) catcher-infielder-outfielder: 104-for-303, .343, in 66 games.

Williams, Wash (1885) pitcher: 0–0 with 13.50 ERA in 1 game.

Williamson, Ned (1879–89) infielder-catcher-pitcher: 1,050-for-4,042, .260, in 1,065 games; 1–1 with 3.34 ERA in 12 games.

Wilmot, Walt (1890–95) outfielder: 827-for-2,904, .284, in 687 games.

Woods, Walt (1898) pitcher: 9–13 with 3.14 ERA in 27 games.

Wright, Dave (1897) pitcher: 1–0 with 15.43 ERA in 1 game.

Wright, Pat (1890) second baseman: 0-for-2, .000, in 1 game.

Y

Yost, Gus (1893) pitcher: 0–1 with 13.50 ERA in 1 game.

Post-1900 Players

A

Abernathy, Ted (1965–66, '69–70) pitcher: 9–12 with 3.14 ERA in 171 games.

Aberson, Cliff (1947–49) outfielder: 45-for-179, .251, in 63 games.

Abrego, Johnny (1985) pitcher: 1–1 with 6.38 ERA in 6 games.

Adair, Jimmy (1931) infielder: 21-for-76, .276, in 18 games.

Adams, Bobby (1957–59) infielder: 74-for-285, .260, in 125 games.

Adams, Mike (1976–77) infielder-outfielder: 4-for-31, .129, in 27 games.

Adams, Rebel (1915) pitcher: 1–9 with 5.01 ERA in 30 games.

Adams, Red (1946) pitcher: 0–1 with 8.25 ERA in 8 games.

Adams, Sparky (1922–27) infielder: 777-for-2,659, .292, in 672 games.

Adams, Terry (1995–96) pitcher: 4–7 with 3.48 ERA in 87 games.

Addis, Bob (1952–53) outfielder: 88-for-304, .289, in 103 games.

Adkins, John (1949) 2–4 with 5.68 ERA in 30 games.

Aguirre, Hank (1969–70) pitcher: 4–0 with 3.05 ERA in 58 games.

Aker, Jack (1972–73) pitcher: 10–11 with 3.50 ERA in 95 games.

Alderson, Dale (1943–44) 0–1 with 6.56 ERA in 16 games.

Aldrige, Vic (1917–18, '22–24)

Bobby Adams

Jack Aker

pitcher: 53–43 with 3.43 ERA in 131 games.

Alexander, Grover Cleveland (1918–26) pitcher: 128–83 with 2.84 ERA in 232 games.

Alexander, Matt (1973–74) infielder-outfielder: 12-for-59, .203, in 57 games.

Allen, Artemus Ward (1916) catcher: 1-for-16, .063, in 5 games.

Allen, Ethan (1936) outfielder: 110-for-373, .295, in 91 games.

Allison, Pete (1913–14) outfielder: 3-for-7, .429, in 3 games.

Altamirano, Porfirio (1984) pitcher: 0–0 with 4.76 ERA in 5 games.

Altman, George (1959–62, '65–67) outfielder–first baseman: 608-for-2,205, .276, in 732 games.

Amalfitano, Joey (1964–67) infielder: 110-for-458, .240, in 208 games.

Amor, Vicente (1965) pitcher: 0–1 with 4.50 ERA in 4 games.

Anderson, Bob (1957–62) pitcher: 33–45 with 4.33 ERA in 214 games.

Andre, John (1955) pitcher: 0–1 with 5.80 ERA in 22 games.

Angley, Tom (1929) catcher: 4-for-16, .250, in 5 games.

Archer, Jimmy (1909–17) catcher: 673-for-2,582, .261, in 782 games.

Arcia, Jose (1968) outfielder-infielder: 16-for-84, .190, in 59 games.

Ted Abernathy

Terry Adams

Ethan Allen

Paul Assenmacher

Cuno Barragan

George Bell

Arias, Alex (1992) infielder: 29-for-99, .293, in 32 games.

Asbell, Jimmy (1938) outfielder: 6-for-17, .182, in 17 games.

Ashburn, Richie (1960–61) outfielder: 238-for-854, .279, in 260 games.

Aspromonte, Ken (1963) infielder: 5-for-34, .147, in 20 games.

Assenmacher, Paul (1989–93) pitcher: 22–1 with 3.42 ERA in 279 games.

Atwell, Toby (1952–53) catcher: 122-for-436, .280, in 131 games.

Averill, Earl, Jr. (1959–60) catcher-infielder-outfielder: 68-for-288, .236, in 126 games.

B

Baczewski, Fred (1960) pitcher: 0–0 with 6.30 ERA in 9 games.

Baecht, Ed (1931–32) pitcher: 2–4 with 3.76 ERA in 23 games.

Bailey, Ed (1965) catcher–first baseman: 38-for-150, .253, in 66 games.

Bailey, Sweetbreads (1919–21) pitcher: 4–7 with 4.59 ERA in 52 games.

Baker, Gene (1953–57) infielder: 469-for-1,782, .263, in 448 games.

Baker, Tom (1963) 0–1 with 3.00 ERA in 10 games.

Baller, Jay (1985–87) pitcher: 4–8 with 4.93 ERA in 79 games.

Balsamo, Tony (1962) pitcher: 0–1 with 6.44 ERA in 18 games.

Banks, (Mr. Cub) Ernie (1953–71) infielder-outfielder: 2,583-for-9,421, .274, in 2,528 games.

Banks, Willie (1994–95) pitcher: 8–13 with 6.18 ERA in 33 games.

Barber, Steve (1970) pitcher: 0–1 with 9.53 ERA in 5 games.

Barber, Ty (1917–22) outfielder–first baseman: 409-for-1,399, .292, in 443 games.

Barberie, Brett (1996) infielder: 1-for-29, .034, in 15 games.

Barragan, Cuno (1961–63) catcher: 33-for-163, .202, in 69 games.

Barrett, Bob (1923–25) infielder: 43-for-168, .256, in 71 games.

Barrett, Kewpie (1943) pitcher: 0–4 with 4.80 ERA in 15 games.

Barry, Shad (1904–05) outfielder-infielder: 91-for-367, .248, in 100 games.

Bartell, Dick (1939) infielder: 80-for-336, .238, in 105 games.

Barton, Vince (1931–32) outfielder: 87-for-373, .233, in 102 games.

Bates, John (1914) outfielder: 1-for-8, .125, in 9 games.

Bauers, Russ (1946) pitcher: 2–1 with 3.53 ERA in 15 games.

Baumann, Frank (1965) pitcher: 0–1 with 7.36 ERA in 4 games.

Baumholtz, Frankie (1949, '51–55) outfielder: 659-for-2,236, .295, in 635 games.

Bautista, Jose (1993–94) pitcher: 14–8 with 3.23 ERA in 116 games.

Beard, Dave (1985) pitcher: 0–0 with 6.39 ERA in 9 games.

Beaumont, Ginger (1910) outfielder: 46-for-172, .267, in 76 games.

Beck, Clyde (1926–30) infielder: 333-for-1,389, .240, in 425 games.

Becker, Heinz (1943, '45–46) first baseman: 50-for-209, .239, in 100 games.

Beckert, Glenn (1965–73) infielder:

1,423-for-5,020, .283, in 1,247 games.

Beebe, Fred (1906) pitcher: 6–1 with 2.70 ERA in 14 games.

Bell, George (1991) outfielder: 159-for-558, .285, in 149 games.

Bell, Les (1930–31) infielder: 140-for-500, .280, 149 games.

Benton, Butch (1982) catcher: 1-for-7, .143, in 4 games.

Berry, Joe (1942) pitcher: 0–0 with 18.00 ERA in 2 games.

Berryhill, Damon (1987–91) catcher: 201-for-883, .227, in 277 games.

Bertell, Dick (1960–65, '67) catcher: 318-for-1,262, .252, in 422 games.

Damon Berryhill

Mike Bielecki

Cy Block

Thad Bosley

Bielecki, Mike (1988–91) pitcher: 41–31 with 4.05 ERA in 127 games.

Biittner, Larry (1976–80) infielder-outfielder: 429-for-1,573, .273, in 544 games.

Bilko, Steve (1954) first baseman: 22-for-92, .239, in 47 games.

Bird, Doug (1981–82) pitcher: 13–19 with 4.70 ERA in 47 games.

Bithorn, Hi (1942–43, '46) pitcher: 33–31 with 3.17 ERA in 103 games.

Blackburn, Earl (1917) pinch hitter: 0-for-2, .000, in 2 games.

Blackwell, Tim (1978–81) catcher: 167-for-703, .238, in 273 games.

Bladt, Rick (1969) outfielder: 2-for-13, .154, in 10 games.

Blair, Footsie (1929–31) infielder: 243-for-890, .273, in 246 games.

Blake, Sheriff (1924–31) pitcher: 81–92 with 3.95 ERA in 255 games.

Blankenship, Kevin (1988–90) pitcher: 1–2 with 5.16 ERA in 6 games.

Block, Cy (1942, '45–46) infielder: 16-for-53, .302, in 17 games.

Bobb, Randy (1968–69) catcher: 1-for-10, .100, in 10 games.

Boccabella, John (1963–68) first baseman–outfielder–catcher: 81-for-364, .223, in 146 games.

Bolger, Jim (1955, '57–58) outfielder-infielder: 135-for-553, .244, in 260 games.

Bonds, Bobby (1981) outfielder: 35-for-163, .215, in 45 games.

Bonetti, Paul (1940) pitcher: 0–0 with 20.25 ERA in 1 game.

Bonham, Bill (1971–77) pitcher: 53–70 with 4.08 ERA in 244 games.

Bonura, Zeke (1940) first baseman: 48-for-182, .264, in 48 games.

Bordi, Rich (1983–84) pitcher: 5–4 with 3.81 ERA in 42 games.

Borkowski, Bob (1950–51) outfielder–first baseman: 84-for-345, .243, in 143 games.

Boros, Steve (1963) infielder: 19-for-90, .211, in 41 games.

Borowy, Hank (1945–48) pitcher: 36–34 with 3.85 ERA in 126 games.

Boskie, Shawn (1990–94) pitcher: 19–29 with 4.43 ERA in 107 games.

Bosley, Thad (1983–86) outfielder: 142-for-470, .302, in 293 games.

Bothelo, Derek (1985) pitcher: 1–3 with 5.32 ERA in 11 games.

Bottarini, John (1937) catcher: 11-for-40, .275, in 26 games.

Bottenfield, Kent (1996) pitcher: 3–5 with 2.63 ERA in 48 games.

Bouchee, Ed (1960–61) first baseman: 150-for-618, .243, in 210 games.

Bourque, Pat (1971–73) first baseman: 43-for-203, .212, in 82 games.

Bowa, Larry (1982–85) shortstop: 391-for-1,584, .247, in 494 games.

Bowman, Bob (1942) pitcher: 0–0 with 0.00 ERA in 1 game.

Bradley, Bill (1899–1900) infielder: 174-for-595, .292, in 155 games.

Bransfield, Kitty (1911) first baseman: 4-for-10, .400, in 3 games.

Breeden, Danny (1971) catcher: 10-for-65, .154, in 25 games.

Breeden, Hal (1971) first baseman: 5-for-36, .139, in 23 games.

Brennan, Bill (1993) pitcher: 2–1 with 4.20 ERA in 8 games.

Bresnahan, Roger (1900, '13–15)

Tim Blackwell

Zeke Bonura

Al Bridwell

Ernie Broglio

Warren Brusstar

catcher: 151-for-633, .239, in 248 games.

Brett, Herbert (1924–25) pitcher: 1–1 with 3.97 ERA in 11 games.

Brewer, Jim (1960–63) pitcher: 4–13 with 5.62 ERA in 76 games.

Brewster, Charlie (1944) shortstop: 11-for-44, .250, in 10 games.

Bridwell, Al (1913) shortstop: 97-for-405, .240, in 136 games.

Briggs, Buttons (1896–98, 1904–05) pitcher: 44–47 with 3.41 ERA in 106 games.

Briggs, Dan (1982) outfielder–first baseman: 6-for-48, .125, in 48 games.

Briggs, Johnny (1956–58) pitcher: 5–6 with 4.71 ERA in 26 games.

Bright, Harry (1965) pinch hitter: 7-for-25, .280, in 27 games.

Brillheart, Jim (1927) pitcher: 4–2 with 4.13 ERA in 32 games.

Brinkopf, Leon (1952) shortstop: 4-for-22, .182, in 9 games.

Broberg, Pete (1977) pitcher: 1–2 with 4.75 ERA in 22 games.

Brock, Lou (1961–64) outfielder: 310-for-1,207, .257, in 327 games.

Broglio, Ernie (1964–66) pitcher: 7–19 with 5.41 ERA in 59 games.

Bronkie, Dutch (1914) third baseman: 1-for-1, 1.000, in 1 game.

Brooks, Mandy (1925–26) outfielder: 107-for-397, .270, in 116 games.

Brosnan, Jim (1954, '56–58) pitcher: 14–18 with 4.19 ERA in 97 games.

Brown, Brant (1996) first baseman: 21-for-69, .304, in 29 games.

Brown, Jophery (1968) pitcher: 0–0 with 4.50 ERA in 1 game.

Brown, Jumbo (1925) pitcher: 0–0 with 3.00 ERA in 2 games.

Brown, Mordecai (1904–12, '16) pitcher: 188–86 with 1.80 ERA in 346 games.

Brown, Ray (1909) pitcher: 1–0 with 2.00 ERA in 1 game.

Brown, Tommy (1952–53) infielder-outfielder: 91-for-338, .269, in 126 games.

Browne, Byron (1965–67) outfielder: 105-for-444, .236, in 134 games.

Browne, George (1909) outfielder: 8-for-39, .205, in 12 games.

Brumley, Mike (1987) infielder: 21-for-104, .202, in 39 games.

Brusstar, Warren (1983–85) pitcher: 8–5 with 3.83 ERA in 151 games.

Bryant, Clay (1935–40) pitcher: 32–20 with 3.73 ERA in 129 games.

Bryant, Don (1966) catcher: 8-for-26, .308, in 13 games.

Buckner, Bill (1977–84) first baseman–outfielder: 1,136-for-3,788, .300, in 974 games.

Buechele, Steve (1992–95) infielder: 293-for-1,144, .257, in 331 games.

Bues, Art (1914) infielder: 10-for-45, .222, in 14 games.

Buhl, Bob (1962–66) pitcher: 51–52 with 3.83 ERA in 140 games.

Bullett, Scott (1995–96) outfielder: 78-for-315, .241, in 213 games.

Bullinger, Jim (1992–96) pitcher: 27–28 with 4.77 ERA in 148 games.

Burdette, Fred (1962–64) pitcher: 1–0 with 3.40 ERA in 30 games.

Burdette, Lew (1964–65) pitcher: 9–11 with 4.95 ERA in 35 games.

Burgess, Smoky (1949, '51) catcher: 70-for-275, .255, in 142 games.

Jim Brosnan

Scott Bullett

Jim Bullinger

Lew Burdette

Burke, Leo (1963–65) infielder-outfielder-catcher: 38-for-162, .235, in 98 games.

Burris, Ray (1973–79) pitcher: 55–68 with 4.27 ERA in 237 games.

Burrows, John (1943–44) pitcher: 0–2 with 5.00 ERA in 26 games.

Burton, Ellis (1963–65) outfielder: 101-for-467, .216, in 152 games.

Burwell, Dick Matthew (1960–61) pitcher: 0–0 with 6.59 ERA in 5 games.

Bush, Guy (1923–34) pitcher: 152–101 with 3.82 ERA in 428 games.

Butler, John (1928) infielder: 47-for-174, .270, in 62 games.

Buzhardt, John (1958–59) pitcher: 7–5 with 4.39 ERA in 37 games.

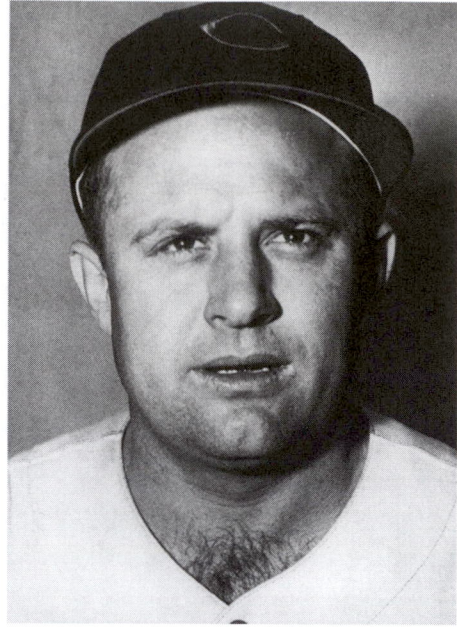

Smoky Burgess

C

Callaghan, Marty (1922–23) outfielder: 74-for-304, .243, in 135 games.

Callahan, Nixey (1897–1900) pitcher: 66–47 with 3.29 ERA in 121 games.

Callison, John (1970–71) outfielder: 187-for-767, .244, in 240 games.

Calmus, Dick (1967) pitcher: 0–0 with 8.31 ERA in 1 game.

Camilli, Dolph (1933–34) first baseman: 46-for-178, .258, in 48 games.

Johnny Callison

Campbell, Bill (1982–83) pitcher: 9–14 with 4.13 ERA in 144 games.

Campbell, Gilly (1933) catcher: 25-for-89, .281, in 46 games.

Campbell, Joe (1967) outfielder: 0-for-3, .000, in 1 game.

Campbell, Mike (1996) pitcher: 3–1 with 4.46 ERA in 13 games.

Campbell, Ron (1964–66) infielder: 38-for-154, .247, in 52 games.

Campbell, Vin (1908) outfielder: 0-for-1, .000, in 1 game.

Cannizzaro, Chris (1971) catcher: 42-for-197, .213, in 71 games.

Capel, Mike (1988) pitcher: 2–1 with 4.91 ERA in 22 games.

Capilla, Doug (1979–81) pitcher: 2–9 with 3.65 ERA in 94 games.

Cardenal, Jose (1972–77) outfielder-infielder: 864-for-2,918, .296, in 821 games.

Cardwell, Don (1960–62) pitcher: 30–44 with 4.31 ERA in 111 games.

Carleton, Tex (1935–38) pitcher: 51–45 with 3.97 ERA in 131 games.

Carlsen, Don (1948) pitcher: 0–0 with 36.00 ERA in 1 game.

Carlson, Hal (1927–30) pitcher: 30–17 with 4.34 ERA in 86 games.

Carney, Bill (1904) outfielder: 0-for-7, .000, in 2 games.

Carpenter, Bob (1947) pitcher: 0–1 with 4.91 ERA in 4 games.

Carson, Soldier (1910) pitcher: 0–0 with 4.05 ERA in 2 games.

Carter, Joe (1983) outfielder: 9-for-51, .176, in 23 games.

Carter, Nick (1916–20) pitcher: 18–22 with 3.36 ERA in 111 games.

Carty, Rico (1973) outfielder: 15-for-70, .214, in 22 games.

Joe Carter

Hugh Casey

Bill Caudill

Harry Chiti

Casey, Doc (1903–05) infielder-catcher: 395-for-1,509, .262, in 392 games.

Casey, Hugh (1935) pitcher: 0–0 with 3.86 ERA in 13 games.

Casian, Larry (1995–96) pitcher: 2–1 with 1.90 ERA in 77 games.

Castillo, Frank (1991–96) pitcher: 41–53 with 4.16 ERA in 146 games

Caudill, Bill (1979–81) pitcher: 6–18, 1 save, with 3.89 ERA in 131 games.

Cavarretta, Phil (1934–53) first baseman–outfielder: 1,927-for-6,592, .292, in 1,953 games.

Ceccarelli, Art (1959–60) pitcher: 5–0 with 4.85 ERA in 25 games.

Cey, Ron (1983–86) third baseman: 467-for-1,842, .252, in 542 games.

Chambers, Cliff (1948) pitcher: 2–9 with 4.43 ERA in 29 games.

Chance, Frank (1898–1912) first baseman–catcher–outfielder: 1,267-for-4,250, .298, in 1,273 games.

Chapman, Harry (1912) catcher: 1-for-4, .250, in 1 game.

Cheeves, Chief (1920–23) pitcher: 26–27 with 4.61 ERA in 100 games.

Cheney, Larry (1911–15) pitcher: 76–51 with 2.74 ERA in 174 games.

Childs, Cupid (1900–01) second baseman: 189-for-764, .248, in 199 games.

Childs, Pete (1901) infielder: 48-for-210, .229, in 60 games.

Chipman, Bob (1944–49) pitcher: 35–34 with 3.57 ERA in 189 games.

Chiti, Harry (1950–52, '55–56) catcher: 165-for-711, .232, in 329 games.

Christmas, Steve (1986) catcher–first baseman: 1-for-9, .111, in 3 games.

Christopher, Loyd (1945) outfielder: 0-for-0, .000, 1 game.

Church, Bubba (1953–55) pitcher: 5–8 with 5.61 ERA in 36 games.

Church, Len (1966) pitcher: 0–1 with 7.50 ERA in 4 games.

Churry, John (1924–27) catcher: 5-for-18, .278, in 12 games.

Clark, David (1990) outfielder: 47-for-171, .275, in 84 games.

Clark, Fred (1902) first baseman: 8-for-43, .186, in 12 games.

Clarke, Sumpter (1920) third baseman: 1-for-3, .333, in 1 game.

Clarke, Tommy (1918) catcher: 0-for-0, .000, in 1 game.

Clemens, Clem (1916) catcher: 0-for-15, .000, in 10 games.

Clemens, Doug (1964–65) outfielder: 114-for-480, .238, in 182 games.

Cline, Ty (1966) outfielder: 6-for-17, .353, in 7 games.

Clines, Gene (1977–79) outfielder: 131-for-478, .274, in 220 games.

Clingman, Billy (1900) shortstop: 33-for-159, .262, in 47 games.

Clymer, Otis (1913) outfielder: 24-for-105, .229, in 30 games.

Coakley, Andy (1908–09) pitcher: 2–1 with 2.45 ERA in 5 games.

Coffman, Kevin (1990) pitcher: 0–2 with 11.29 ERA in 8 games.

Coggins, Frank (1972) infielder: 0-for-1, .000, in 6 games.

Cohen, Hy (1955) pitcher: 0–0 with 7.94 ERA in 7 games.

Colborn, Jim (1969–71) pitcher: 4–2 with 3.86 ERA in 54 games.

Cole, Dave (1954) pitcher: 3–8 with 5.36 ERA in 18 games.

Frank Castillo

Cliff Chambers

Gene Clines

Jim Colborn

Rip Collins

Jim Cooney

Chuck Connors

Walker Cooper

Cole, King (1909–12) pitcher: 40–13 with 2.72 ERA in 74 games.

Coleman, Joe (1976) pitcher: 2–8 with 4.10 ERA in 39 games.

Collins, Bill (1911) outfielder: 1-for-5, .200, in 7 games.

Collins, Bob (1940) catcher: 25-for-120, .208, in 47 games.

Collins, Fidgety Phil (1923) pitcher: 1–0 with 3.60 ERA in 1 game.

Collins, Rip (1937–38) first baseman: 256-for-946, .271, in 258 games.

Collum, Jackie (1957) pitcher: 1–1 with 6.75 ERA in 9 games.

Comellas, Jorge (1945) pitcher: 0–2 with 4.50 ERA in 7 games.

Compton, Clint (1972) pitcher: 0–0 with 9.00 ERA in 1 game.

Congalton, Bunk (1902) outfielder: 40-for-179, .223, in 45 games.

Connally, Fritz (1983) third baseman: 1-for-10, .100, in 8 games.

Connors, Bill (1966) pitcher: 0–1 with 7.31 ERA in 11 games.

Connors, Chuck (1951) first baseman: 48-for-201, .239, in 66 games.

Cook, Jim (1903) outfielder-infielder: 4-for-26, .154, in 8 games.

Cooney, Jimmy (1926–27) shortstop: 161-for-645, .250, in 174 games.

Cooper, Mort (1949) pitcher: 0–0 with ∞ ERA in 1 game.

Cooper, Walker (1954–55) catcher: 80-for-269, .297, in 111 games.

Cooper, Wilbur (1925–26) pitcher: 14–15 with 4.31 ERA in 40 games.

Corriden, Red (1913–15) infielder: 90-for-418, .215, in 158 games.

Corridon, Frank (1904) pitcher: 5–5 with 3.05 ERA in 12 games.

Cosman, Jim (1970) pitcher: 0–0 with 27.00 ERA in 1 game.

Cotter, Dick (1912) catcher: 15-for-54, .278, in 26 games.

Cotter, Hooks (1922, '24) first baseman: 82-for-311, .264, in 99 games.

Cotto, Henry (1984) outfielder: 40-for-146, .274, in 105 games.

Cottrell, Ensign (1912) pitcher: 0–0 with 9.00 ERA in 1 game.

Covington, Wes (1966) outfielder: 1-for-11, .091, in 9 games.

Cowan, Billy (1963–64) outfielder: 129-for-533, .242, in 153 games.

Cox, Larry (1978, '82) catcher: 34-for-125, .272, in 61 games.

Henry Cotto

Babe Dahlgren

Doug Dascenzo

Crim, Chuck (1994) pitcher: 5–4 with 4.48 ERA in 49 games.

Croft, Henry (1901) outfielder: 4-for-12, .333, in 3 games.

Crosby, Ken (1975–76) pitcher: 1–0 with 8.41 ERA in 16 games.

Cross, Jeff (1948) infielder: 2-for-20, .100, in 16 games.

Cruz, Heity (1978–82) infielder-outfielder: 47-for-204, .230, in 100 games.

Culler, Dick (1948) infielder: 15-for-89, .169, in 48 games.

Culp, Ray (1967) pitcher: 8–11 with 3.89 ERA in 30 games.

Cunningham, Bert (1900–01) pitcher: 4–4 with 4.44 ERA in 9 games.

Currie, Clarence (1903) pitcher: 1–2 with 2.97 ERA in 6 games.

Curtis, Cliff (1911) pitcher: 1–2 with 3.86 ERA in 4 games.

Curtis, Jackie (1961–62) pitcher: 10–15 with 4.77 ERA in 35 games.

Cusick, Jack (1951) shortstop: 29-for-164, .177, in 65 games.

Cuyler, Kiki (1928–35) outfielder: 1,199-for-3,687, .325, in 949 games.

Cvengros, Mike (1929) pitcher: 5–4 with 4.64 ERA in 32 games.

D

Dahlgren, Babe (1941–42) first baseman: 113-for-415, .272, in 116 games.

Dallessandro, Dom (1940–44, '46–47) outfielder: 486-for-1,798, .270, in 678 games.

Daly, Tom (1918–21) catcher: 73-for-284, .257, in 121 games.

Daniels, Kal (1992) outfielder: 27-for-48, .250, in 48 games.

Dark, Alvin (1958–59) infielder: 263-for-941, .279, in 250 games.

Darwin, Arthur (1977) outfielder: 2-for-12, .167, in 11 games.

Dascenzo, Doug (1988–92) outfielder-pitcher: 257-for-1,070, .240, in 443 games; 0–0 with 0.00 ERA in 4 games.

Davidson, Bill (1909) outfielder: 1-for-7, .143, in 2 games.

Davis, Brock (1970–71) outfielder: 77-for-304, .253, in 112 games.

Davis, Curt (1936–37) pitcher: 21–14 with 3.48 ERA in 52 games.

Davis, Jim (1954–56) pitcher: 23–25 with 3.89 ERA in 134 games.

Davis, Jody (1981–88) catcher: 834-for-3,318, .248, in 990 games.

Davis, Ron (1986–87) pitcher: 0–2 with 6.54 ERA in 38 games.

Davis, Steve (1979) infielder: 0-for-4, .000, in 3 games.

Davis, Tommy (1970, '72) first baseman–outfielder: 18-for-68, .265, in 26 games.

Dawson, Andre (1987–92) outfielder: 929-for-3,262, .285, in 867 games.

Day, Boots (1970) outfielder: 2-for-8, .250, in 11 games.

Dayett, Brian (1985–87) outfielder: 73-for-270, .270, in 133 games.

Deal, Charlie (1916–21) third baseman: 562-for-2,148, .262, in 616 games.

Dean, Dizzy (1938–41) pitcher: 16–8 with 3.35 ERA in 43 games.

Dean, Wayland (1927) pitcher: 0–0 with 0.00 ERA in 2 games.

Decker, Joe (1969–72) pitcher: 7–9 with 4.35 ERA in 54 games.

Ray Culp

Boots Day

Brian Dayett

Joe Decker

Andy Dobernic

Larry Doyle

DeJesus, Ivan (1977–81) shortstop: 756-for-2,900, .261, in 738 games.

Delahanty, Jim (1901) infielder: 12-for-63, .190, in 17 games.

DelGreco, Bobby (1957) outfielder: 8-for-40, .200, in 20 games.

Demaree, Al (1917) pitcher: 5–9 with 2.55 ERA in 24 games.

Demaree, Frank (1932–38) outfielder: 820-for-2,652, .308, in 701 games.

Dernier, Bob (1984–87) outfielder: 404-for-1,528, .265, in 565 games.

Derrick, Claud (1914) shortstop: 21-for-96, .219, in 28 games.

Derringer, Paul (1943–45) pitcher: 33–28 with 3.71 ERA in 109 games.

Dettore, Tom (1974–76) pitcher: 8–10 with 5.10 ERA in 56 games.

Dexter, Charlie (1900–02) catcher-infielder-outfielder: 208-for-851, .244, in 225 games.

Diaz, Mike (1983) catcher: 2-for-7, .286, in 6 games.

Dickson, Lance (1990) pitcher: 0–3 with 7.24 ERA in 3 games.

Dillard, Steve (1979–81) infielder: 128-for-529, .242, in 242 games.

Dillhoefer, Pickles (1917) catcher: 12-for-95, .126, in 42 games.

Dilone, Miguel (1979) outfielder: 11-for-36, .306, in 43 games.

DiPino, Frank (1986–88) pitcher: 7–10 with 4.32 ERA in 162 games.

Distaso, Alec (1969) pitcher: 0–0 with 3.60 ERA in 2 games.

Dobbs, John (1902–03) outfielder: 85-for-296, .287, in 75 games.

Dobernic, Andy (Jess) (1948–49) pitcher: 7–2 with 3.90 ERA in 58 games.

Dolan, Cozy (1900–01) outfielder: 58-for-219, .265, in 56 games.

Donahue, Tim (1895–1900) catcher-infielder: 352-for-1,485, .237, in 459 games.

Donnelly, Ed (1959) pitcher: 1–1 with 3.14 ERA in 7 games.

Doolan, Mickey (1916) infielder: 15-for-70, .214, in 28 games.

Dorsett, Brian (1996) catcher: 5-for-41, .122, in 17 games.

Doscher, Jack (1903) pitcher: 0–1 with 12.00 ERA in 1 game.

Douglas, Shuffling Phil (1915, '17, '18–19) pitcher: 35–36 with 2.29 ERA in 105 games.

Douthit, Tay (1933) outfielder: 16-for-71, .225, in 27 games.

Dowling, Dave (1966) pitcher: 1–0 with 2.00 ERA in 1 game.

Downey, Tom (1912) infielder: 4-for-22, .182, in 13 games.

Downs, Red (1912) infielder: 25-for-95, .263, in 43 games.

Doyle, Jim (1911) third baseman: 133-for-472, .282, in 127 games.

Doyle, John (1901) first baseman: 66-for-285, .232, in 75 games.

Doyle, Larry (1916–17) infielder: 134-for-510, .263, in 143 games.

Drabowsky, Moe (1956–60) pitcher: 32–41 with 4.02 ERA in 130 games.

Drake, Sammy (1960–61) infielder-outfielder: 1-for-20, .050, in 28 games.

Drake, Solly (1956) outfielder: 55-for-215, .256, in 65 games.

Driscoll, Paddy (1917) infielder: 3-for-28, .107, in 13 games.

Drott, Dick (1957–61) pitcher: 24–34 with 4.69 ERA in 141 games.

Dubiel, Walt (1949–52) pitcher: 14–21 with 3.84 ERA in 94 games.

Dumovich, Nick (1923) pitcher: 3–5 with 4.60 ERA in 28 games.

Dunegan, Jim (1970) pitcher: 0–2 with 4.73 ERA in 7 games.

Dungan, Sam (1892–94, 1900) outfielder: 274-for-952, .288, in 436 games.

Dunn, Ron (1974–75) infielder-outfielder: 27-for-112, .241, in 55 games.

Dunston, Shawon (1985–95)

Shawon Dunston

Rawley Eastwick

Woody English

shortstop: 1,100-for-4,151, .265, in 1,140 games.

Durbin, Kid (1907–08) outfielder-pitcher: 0–1 with 5.40 ERA in 5 games; 13-for-46, .283, in 25 games.

Durham, Leon (1981–88) first baseman–outfielder: 898-for-3,215, .276, in 921 games.

E

Eaddy, Don (1959) third baseman: 0–1, .000, in 15 games.

Earley, Arnold (1966) pitcher: 2–1 with 3.57 ERA in 13 games.

Eason, Mal (1900–02) pitcher: 10–18 with 3.30 ERA in 30 games.

Easterwood, Roy (1944) catcher: 7-for-33, .212, in 17 games.

Eastwick, Rawley (1981) pitcher: 0–1 with 2.28 ERA in 30 games.

Eaves, Vallie (1941–42) pitcher: 3–6 with 3.77 ERA in 21 games.

Eckersley, Dennis (1984–86) pitcher: 17–26, 0 saves, with 3.63 ERA in 82 games.

Edens, Charlie (1995) pitcher: 1–0 with 6.00 ERA in 5 games.

Edwards, Bruce (1951–52, '54) catcher-infielder: 56-for-238, .235, in 105 games.

Edwards, Hank (1949–50) outfielder: 91-for-286, .318, in 99 games.

Elia, Lee (1968) infielder: 3-for-17, .176, in 15 games.

Elko, Peter (1943–44) third baseman: 9-for-52, .173, in 16 games.

Elliott, Allen (1923–24) first baseman: 44-for-182, .242, in 63 games.

Elliott, Carter (1921) shortstop: 7-for-28, .250, in 12 games.

Elliott, Rowdy (1916–18) catcher: 70-for-288, .243, in 113 games.

Ellis, Jim (1967) pitcher: 1–1 with 3.24 ERA in 8 games.

Ellsworth, Dick (1958, '60–66) pitcher: 84–110 with 3.70 ERA in 254 games.

Elston, Don (1953,'57–64) pitcher: 49–54, 63 saves, with 3.70 ERA in 449 games.

Engel, Steve (1985) pitcher: 1–5 with 5.57 ERA in 11 games.

English, Woody (1927–36) infielder: 1,248-for-4,296, .291, in 1,098 games.

Epperly, Al (1938) pitcher: 2–0 with 3.67 ERA in 9 games.

Erickson, Paul (1941–48) pitcher: 33–48 with 3.83 ERA in 201 games.

Ernaga, Frank (1957–58) outfielder: 12-for-43, .279, in 29 games.

Errickson, Dick (1942) pitcher: 1–1 with 4.13 ERA in 13 games.

Hank Edwards

Paul Erickson

Estrada, Chuck (1966) pitcher: 1–1 with 7.30 ERA in 9 games.

Eubanks, Uel (1922) pitcher: 0–0 with 27.00 ERA in 1 game.

Everitt, Bill (1895–1900) infielder-outfielder: 880-for-2,727, .323, in 659 games.

Evers, Johnny (1902–13) infielder: 1,339-for-4,855, .276, in 1,407 games.

F

Fanning, Jim (1954–57) catcher: 24-for-141, .170, in 64 games.

Fanzone, Carmen (1971–74) infielder-outfielder: 129-for-573, .225, in 227 games.

Farrell, Ed (1930) infielder: 33-for-113, .292, in 46 games.

Fast, Darcy (1968) pitcher: 0–1 with 5.40 ERA in 8 games.

Carmen Fanzone

Tom Filer

Kevin Foster

Faul, Bill (1965–66) pitcher: 7–10 with 4.07 ERA in 34 games.

Fear, Vern (1952) pitcher: 0–0 with 7.88 ERA in 4 games.

Felderman, Marv (1942) catcher: 1-for-6, .167, in 3 games.

Felske, John (1968) catcher: 0-for-2, .000, in 4 games.

Ferguson, Charlie (1901) pitcher: 0–0 with 0.00 ERA in 1 game.

Fermin, Felix (1996) infielder: 2-for-16, .125, in 11 games.

Fernandez, Frank (1971) catcher: 7-for-41, .171, in 17 games.

Figueroa, Jesus (1980) outfielder: 50-for-198, .253, in 115 games.

Filer, Tom (1982) pitcher: 1–2 with 5.53 ERA in 8 games.

Fischer, Bill (1916) catcher: 35-for-179, .196, in 65 games.

Fisher, Bob (1914–15) infielder: 178-for-618, .288, in 162 games.

Fitzgerald, Howie (1922, '24) outfielder: 11-for-43, .256, in 17 games.

Flack, Max (1916–22) outfielder: 883-for-3,005, .274, in 796 games.

Flavin, John (1964) pitcher: 0–1 with 13.50 ERA in 5 games.

Fleming, Les (1942–44, '46) pitcher: 14–18 with 3.65 ERA in 97 games.

Fletcher, Scott (1981–82) infielder: 14-for-70, .200, in 30 games.

Flores, Jesse (1942) pitcher: 0–1 with 3.38 ERA in 4 games.

Fluhrer, John (1915) outfielder: 2-for-6, .333, in 6 games.

Fodge, Gene (1958) pitcher: 1–1 with 4.76 ERA in 16 games.

Fondy, Dee (1951–57) first baseman: 872-for-3,055, .286, in 783 games.

Fontenot, Ray (1985–86) pitcher: 9–15 with 4.23 ERA in 80 games.

Foote, Barry (1979–81) catcher: 157-for-653, .240, in 204 games.

Foster, Kevin (1994–96) pitcher: 22–21 with 4.56 ERA in 60 games.

Foxen, Bill (1910–11) pitcher: 5–5 with 4.00 ERA in 18 games.

Foxx, Jimmy (1942, '44) catcher–first baseman: 43-for-225, .191, in 85 games.

Frailing, Ken (1974–76) pitcher: 9–16 with 4.16 ERA in 102 games.

Franco, Matt (1995) infielder: 5-for-17, .294, in 16 games.

Francona, Terry (1986) outfielder–first baseman: 31-for-124, .250, in 86 games.

Fraser, Chick (1907–09) pitcher: 19–14 with 2.25 ERA in 49 games.

Frazier, George (1984–86) pitcher: 15–15 with 5.36 ERA in 123 games.

Freeman, Buck (1921–22) pitcher: 9–11 with 4.70 ERA in 49 games.

Freeman, Hersh (1958) pitcher: 0–1 with 8.31 ERA in 9 games.

Freeman, Mark (1960) pitcher: 3–3 with 5.63 ERA in 30 games.

Freese, George (1961) pinch hitter: 2-for-7, .286, in 9 games.

Freigau, Howie (1925–27) infielder: 303-for-1,070, .283, in 287 games.

French, Larry (1935–41) pitcher: 95–84 with 3.55 ERA in 272 games.

Frey, Lonnie (1937, '47) infielder: 64-for-241, .266, in 102 games.

Friberg, Barney (1919–25) infielder–

John Felske

Scott Fletcher

George Frazier

Oscar Gamble

Dick Gernert

outfielder: 471-for-1,624, .290, in 487 games.

Friend, Owen (1955–56) infielder: 1-for-12, .083, in 8 games.

Fryman, Woody (1978) pitcher: 2–4 with 5.17 ERA in 13 games.

Fuhr, Oscar (1921) pitcher: 0–0 with 9.00 ERA in 1 game.

Fussell, Fred (1922–23) pitcher: 4–6 with 5.40 ERA in 31 games.

G

Gabler, Bill (1958) pinch hitter: 0-for-3, .000, in 3 games.

Gabrielson, Len (1964–65) outfielder–first baseman: 79-for-320, .247, in 117 games.

Gagliano, Phil (1970) infielder: 6-for-40, .150, in 26 games.

Galan, Augie (1934–41) outfielder-infielder: 912-for-3,297, .277, in 903 games.

Gamble, Oscar (1969) outfielder: 16-for-71, .225, in 24 games.

Gannon, William (1901) outfielder: 9-for-61, .148, in 15 games.

Ganzel, John (1900) first baseman: 78-for-284, .275, in 78 games.

Garagiola, Joe (1953–54) catcher: 105-for-381, .276, in 137 games.

Garbark, Bob (1937–39) catcher–first baseman: 17-for-75, .227, in 48 games.

Garces, Rich (1995) pitcher: 0–0 with 3.27 ERA in 7 games.

Gardner, Jim (1902) pitcher: 1–2 with 2.88 ERA in 3 games.

Gardner, Rob (1967) pitcher: 0–2 with 3.98 ERA in 18 games.

Garman, Mike (1976) pitcher: 2–4 with 4.95 ERA in 47 games.

Garrett, Adrian (1970, '73–75) outfielder-catcher: 14-for-86, .163, in 65 games.

Garriott, Rabbit (1946) pinch hitter: 0-for-5, .000, in 6 games.

Garvin, Ned (1899–1900) pitcher: 19–31 with 2.61 ERA in 54 games.

Gassaway, Charlie (1944) pitcher: 0–1 with 7.71 ERA in 2 games.

Gaw, Chippy (1920) pitcher: 1–1 with 4.85 ERA in 6 games.

Geisel, Dave (1978–79, '81) pitcher: 3–0 with 2.17 ERA in 36 games.

George, Greek (1941) catcher: 10-for-64, .156, in 35 games.

Gerard, Dave (1962) pitcher: 2–3 with 4.91 ERA in 39 games.

Gerberman, George (1962) pitcher: 0–1 with 1.69 ERA in 1 game.

Gernert, Dick (1960) infielder-outfielder: 24-for-96, .250, in 52 games.

Gessler, Doc (1906) outfielder–first baseman: 21-for-83, .253, in 34 games.

Gigon, Norm (1967) infielder: 12-for-70, .171, in 34 games.

Gilbert, Charlie (1941–43, '46) outfielder: 61-for-298, .205, in 136 games.

Gill, John (1935–36) outfielder: 45-for-177, .254, in 74 games.

Gillespie, Paul (1942, '44–45) catcher-outfielder: 58-for-205, .283, in 89 games.

Girardi, Joe (1989–92) catcher: 234-for-893, .262, in 304 games.

Giusti, Dave (1977) pitcher: 0–2 with 6.04 ERA in 20 games.

Glade, Fred (1902) pitcher: 0–1 with 9.00 ERA in 1 game.

Glanville, Doug (1996) outfielder: 20-for-83, .241, in 49 games.

Gleeson, Jimmy (1939–40) outfielder: 226-for-817, .277, in 240 games.

Glenn, Ed (1902) shortstop: 0-for-7, .000, in 2 games.

Glossop, Albie (1946) second baseman: 0-for-10, .000, in 4 games.

Goetz, John (1960) pitcher: 0–0 with 12.79 ERA in 4 games.

Golvin, Walt (1922) first baseman: 0-for-2, .000, in 2 games.

Gomez, Leo (1996) infielder: 86-for-362, .238, in 136 games.

Gonzalez, Luis (1995–96) outfielder-infielder: 207-for 745, .278, in 223 games.

Gonzalez, Mike (1925–29) catcher: 224-for-883, .254, in 298 games.

Joe Girardi

Leo Gomez

Ival Goodman

Johnny Goryl

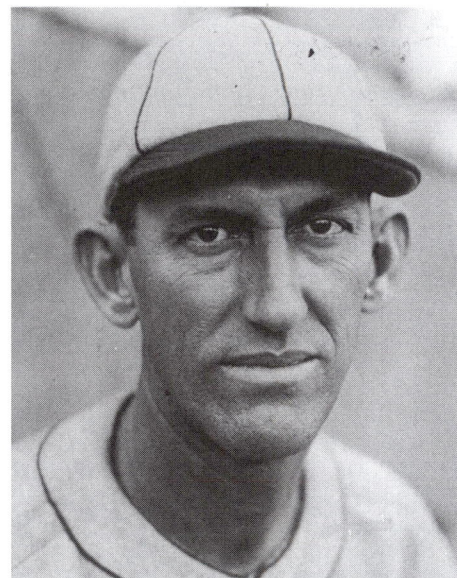

Miguel Gonzalez

Good, Lefty (1911–15) outfielder: 351-for-1,349, .260, in 428 games.

Goodman, Ival (1943–44) outfielder: 109-for-366, .298, in 142 games.

Gordon, Mike (1977–78) catcher: 2-for-28, .071, in 12 games.

Gornicki, Hank (1941) pitcher: 0–0 with 4.50 ERA in 1 game.

Goryl, John (1957–59) infielder: 70-for-305, .230, in 117 games.

Gossage, Goose (1988) pitcher: 4–4 with 4.33 ERA in 46 games.

Grabarkewitz, Billy (1974) infielder: 31-for-125, .248, in 53 games.

Grace, Mark (1988–1996) first baseman: 1,514-for-4,903, .309, in 1,297 games.

Grace, Robert (1929, '31) catcher: 21-for-89, .236, in 34 games.

Graham, Peaches (1903, '11) catcher: 17-for-71, .239, in 36 games.

Grammas, Alex (1962–63) infielder: 19-for-87, .218, in 39 games.

Grampp, Hank (1927, '29) pitcher: 0–1 with 16.20 ERA in 3 games.

Grant, Tom (1983) outfielder: 3-for-20, .150, in 16 games.

Grantham, Boots (1922–24) infielder: 312-for-1,062, .295, in 286 games.

Graves, Joe (1926) third baseman: 0-for-5, .000, in 2 games.

Green, Danny (1898–1901) outfielder: 483-for-1,589, .304, in 400 games.

Gregory, Lee (1964) pitcher: 0–0 with 3.50 ERA in 11 games.

Griffin, Hank (1911) pitcher: 0–0 with 18.00 ERA in 1 game.

Griffin, Mike (1981) pitcher: 2–5 with 4.50 ERA in 16 games.

Griffith, Clark (1893–1900) pitcher: 152–96 with 3.39 ERA in 265 games.

Luis Gonzalez

Mike Gordon

Mark Grace

Burleigh Grimes

Griffith, Tommy (1925) outfielder: 67-for-235, .285, in 76 games.

Grigsby, Denver (1923–25) outfielder: 179-for-620, .289, in 199 games.

Grimes, Burleigh (1932–33) pitcher: 9–17 with 4.35 ERA in 47 games.

Grimes, Ray (1921–24) first baseman: 474-for 1,432, .331, in 400 games.

Grimm, Charlie (1925–36) first baseman: 1,454-for-4,917, .296, in 1,334 games.

Gross, Greg (1977–78) outfielder: 169-for-586, .288, in 239 games.

Groth, Ernie (1904) pitcher: 0–2 with 5.63 ERA in 3 games.

Gudat, Marv (1932) outfielder: 24-for-94, .255, in 60 games.

Gumpert, Dave (1985–86) pitcher: 3–0 with 4.24 ERA in 47 games.

Gura, Larry (1970–73, '85) pitcher: 3–7 with 5.01 ERA in 54 games.

Greg Gross

Mel Hall

Gustine, Frank (1949) infielder: 59-for-261, .226, in 76 games.

Guzman, Jose (1993–94) pitcher: 14–12 with 4.34 ERA in 34 games.

H

Haas, Eddie (1957) outfielder: 5-for-24, .208, in 14 games.

Hack, Stan (1932–47) infielder: 2,193-for-7,278, .301, in 1,938 games.

Hacker, Warren (1948–56) pitcher: 55–81 with 4.13 ERA in 235 games.

Hageman, Casey (1914) pitcher: 1–1 with 3.47 ERA in 16 games.

Hagerman, Rip (1909) pitcher: 4–4 with 1.82 ERA in 13 games.

Hairston, John (1969) catcher: 1-for-4, .250, in 3 games.

Hall, Drew (1986–88) pitcher: 3–4 with 6.41 ERA in 45 games.

Hall, Jimmie (1969–70) outfielder: 8-for-56, .143, in 39 games.

Hall, Mel (1981–84) outfielder: 180-for-651, .276, in 194 games.

Hamilton, Steve (1972) pitcher: 1–0 with 4.76 ERA in 22 games.

Hamner, Ralph (1947–49) pitcher: 6–3 with 4.68 ERA in 36 games.

Hands, Bill (1966–72) pitcher: 92–86 with 3.18 ERA in 276 games.

Haney, Fred (1927) pinch hitter: 0-for-3, .000, in 4 games.

Haney, Todd (1994–96) infielder: 47-for-192, .245, in 91 games.

Hanlon, Big Bill (1903) first baseman: 2-for-21, .095, in 8 games.

Hanson, Ollie (1921) pitcher: 0–2 with 7.00 ERA in 2 games.

Hanyzewski, Ed (1942–46) pitcher: 12–13 with 3.30 ERA in 58 games.

Hardin, Bill (1952) infielder: 1-for-7, .143, in 3 games.

Mike Harkey

Hardy, Alex (1902–03) pitcher: 3–3 with 4.34 ERA in 7 games.

Hardy, Jack (1907) catcher: 1-for-4, .250, in 1 game.

Hargesheimer, Alan (1983) pitcher: 0–0 with 9.00 ERA in 5 games.

Hargrave, Bubbles (1913–15) catcher: 12-for-48, .250, in 41 games.

Harkey, Mike (1988–1993) pitcher: 26–21 with 3.92 ERA in 71 games.

Harley, Dick (1903) outfielder: 89-for-389, .231, in 104 games.

Harper, Jack (1906) pitcher: 0–0 with 0.00 ERA in 1 game.

Harrell, Ray (1939) pitcher: 0–2 with 8.31 ERA in 4 games.

Harris, Vic (1974–75) infielder-outfielder: 49-for-256, .191, in 113 games.

Hartenstein, Chuck (1965–68) pitcher: 11–9 with 3.43 ERA in 78 games.

Chuck Hartenstein

Hartnett, Gabby (1922–40) catcher: 1,867-for-6,282, .297, in 1,926 games.

Hartsell, Topsy (1901) outfielder: 187-for-558, .335, in 140 games.

Hartsock, Jeff (1992) pitcher: 0–0 with 6.75 ERA in 4 games.

Harvey, Erwin (1900) pitcher: 0–0 with 0.00 ERA in 1 game.

Hassey, Ron (1984) catcher: 11-for-33, .333, in 19 games.

Hatcher, Billy (1984) outfielder: 41-for-172, .238, in 61 games.

Hatten, Joe (1951–52) pitcher: 6–10 with 5.54 ERA in 36 games.

Hatton, Grady (1960) second baseman: 13-for-38, .342, in 28 games.

Hayden, Jack (1908) outfielder: 9-for-45, .200, in 11 games.

Hayes, Bill (1980–81) catcher: 2-for-9, .222, in 5 games.

Heath, Bill (1969) catcher: 5-for-32, .156, in 27 games.

Heathcote, Cliff (1922–30) outfielder: 743-for-2,657, .280, in 856 games.

Hebner, Richie (1984–85) infielder-outfielder: 53-for-201, .276, in 127 games.

Hechinger, Mike (1912–13) catcher: 0-for-3, .000, in 4 games.

Hegan, Jim (1960) catcher: 9-for-43, .209, in 24 games.

Heist, Al (1960–61) outfielder: 110-for-423, .260, in 150 games.

Hemsley, Rollie (1931–32) catcher: 99-for-355, .279, in 126 games.

Henderson, Ken (1979–80) outfielder: 35-for-163, .215, in 106 games.

Henderson, Steve (1981–82) outfielder: 144-for-544, .265, in 174 games.

Bob Hendley

Hendley, Bob (1965–67) pitcher: 10–9 with 4.28 ERA in 68 games.

Hendrick, Harvey (1933) infielder-outfielder: 55-for-189, .291, in 69 games.

Hendricks, Elrod (1972) catcher: 5-for-43, .116, in 17 games.

Hendricks, Jack (1902) outfielder: 4-for-7, .571, in 2 games.

Hendrix, Claude (1916–20) pitcher: 56–61 with 2.84 ERA in 168 games.

Hennessey, George (1945) pitcher: 0–0 with 7.36 ERA in 2 games.

Henry, Bill (1958–59) pitcher: 14–12, 14 saves, with 2.76 ERA in 109 games.

Henshaw, Roy (1933–36) pitcher: 21–11 wtih 3.68 ERA in 91 games.

Herman, Babe (1933–34) outfielder: 289-for-975, .296, in 262 games.

Herman, Billy (1931–41) second

Gene Hermanski

baseman: 1,710-for-5,532, .309, in 1,344 games.

Hermanski, Gene (1951–53) outfielder: 141-for-546, .258, in 192 games.

Hernandez, Chico (1942–43) catcher: 61-for-244, .250, in 90 games.

Hernandez, Jose (1994–96) infielder: 172-for-708, .243, in 280 games.

Hernandez, Ramon (1968, '76–77) pitcher: 0–0 with 7.58 ERA in 8 games.

Hernandez, Willie (1977–83) pitcher: 26–28, 20 saves, with 3.18 ERA in 323 games.

Herrmann, LeRoy (1932–33) pitcher: 2–2 with 5.82 ERA in 16 games.

Herrnstein, John (1966) first baseman–outfielder: 3-for-17, .176, in 9 games.

Herzog, Buck (1919–20) infielder: 113-for-498, .227, in 143 games.

Al Heist

Roy Henshaw

Jose Hernandez

Hiatt, Jack (1970) catcher–first baseman: 43-for-178, .242, in 66 games.

Hibbard, Greg (1993) pitcher: 15–11 with 3.96 ERA in 31 games.

Hibbard, Mike (1995–96) catcher: 8-for-61, .131, in 36 games.

Hickerson, Brian (1995) pitcher: 2–3 with 6.82 ERA in 38 games.

Hickey, Mike (1901) third baseman: 6-for-37, .162, in 10 games.

Hickman, Jim (1968–73) outfielder–first baseman: 531-for-1,992, .267, in 682 games.

Higbe, Kirby (1937–39) pitcher: 3–1 with 4.03 ERA in 12 games.

Higginbotham, Irv (1909) pitcher: 5–2 with 2.19 ERA in 19 games.

Hildebrand, R. E. (1902) outfielder: 0-for-4, .000, in 1 game.

Hill, Glenallen (1993–94) outfielder: 110-for-356, .309, in 120 games.

Hiller, Frank (1950–51) pitcher: 18–17 with 4.16 ERA in 62 games.

Hillman, Dave (1955–59) pitcher: 18–32 with 3.78 ERA in 129 games.

Hiser, Gene (1971–75) outfielder: 53-for-263, .201, in 206 games.

Hoak, Don (1956) third baseman: 91-for-424, .215, in 121 games.

Hobbie, Glen (1957–64) pitcher: 61–79 with 4.20 ERA in 271 games.

Hoeft, Billy (1965–66) pitcher: 3–4 with 3.62 ERA in 65 games.

Gene Hiser

Hoffman, Guy (1986) pitcher: 6–2 with 3.86 ERA in 32 games.

Hoffman, Larry (1901) infielder: 7-for-22, .318, in 6 games.

Hofman, Solly (1904–12, '16) outfielder-infielder: 838-for-3,097, .272, in 883 games.

Hogg, Brad (1915) pitcher: 1–0 with 2.08 ERA in 2 games.

Holley, Ed (1928) pitcher: 0–0 with 3.77 ERA in 13 games.

Hollins, Jessie (1992) pitcher: 0–0 with 13.50 ERA in 4 games.

Hollocher, Charlie (1918–24)

shortstop: 894-for-2,936, .304, in 760 games.

Holm, Billy (1943–44) catcher: 19-for-147, .129, in 61 games.

Holmes, Fred (1904) catcher: 1-for-3, .333, in 1 game.

Holtzman, Ken (1965–71, '78–79) pitcher: 80–81 with 3.76 ERA in 237 games.

Hooton, Burt (1971–75) pitcher: 34–44 with 3.72 ERA in 129 games.

Horne, Trader (1929) pitcher: 1–1 with 5.09 ERA in 11 games.

Hornsby, Rogers (1929–32) infielder-outfielder: 392-for-1,121, .350, in 317 games.

Hosley, Tim (1975–76) catcher: 36-for-142, .253, in 63 games.

Houston, Tyler (1996) catcher: 39-for-115, .339, in 79 games.

Howard, George (1907–09) infielder-outfielder: 162-for-666, .243, in 216 games.

Howe, Cal (1952) pitcher: 0–0 with 0.00 ERA in 1 game.

Howell, Jay (1981) pitcher: 2–0 with 4.84 ERA in 10 games.

Hubbard, Michael (1995–96) catcher: 8-for-61, .131, in 36 games

Hubbs, Kenny (1961–63) second baseman: 310-for-1,255, .247, in 324 games.

Hudson, John (1941) infielder: 20-for-99, .202, in 50 games.

Hughes, Ed (1902) outfielder: 0-for-3, .000, in 1 game.

Hughes, Jim (1956) pitcher: 1–3 with 5.16 ERA in 25 games.

Hughes, Roy (1944–45) infielder: 195-for-700, .279, in 195 games.

Hughes, Terry (1970) third baseman: 1-for-3, .333, in 2 games.

Hughes, Long Tom (1901–02) pitcher: 12–22 with 3.44 ERA in 40 games.

Humphreys, Bob (1965) pitcher: 2–0 with 3.15 ERA in 41 games.

Humphries, Bert (1913–15) pitcher: 34–28 with 2.56 ERA in 93 games.

Hundley, Randy (1966–73, '76–77) catcher: 758-for-3,158, .240, in 947 games.

Hunter, Herb (1916–17) infielder: 0-for-7, .000, in 5 games.

Huntzinger, Walt (1926) pitcher: 1–1 with 0.94 ERA in 11 games.

Hurst, Don (1934) first baseman: 31-for-156, .199, in 51 games.

Hutson, Herb (1974) pitcher: 0–2 with 3.45 ERA in 20 games.

Dave Hillman

Solly Hofman

Roy Hughes

I

Ilsey, Blaise (1994) pitcher: 0–0 with 7.80 ERA in 10 games.

Irvin, Monte (1956) outfielder: 92-for-339, .271, in 111 games.

J

Jackson, Danny (1991–92) pitcher: 5–14 with 5.19 ERA in 36 games.

Jackson, Darrin (1985–89) outfielder: 74-for-249, .323, in 157 games.

Jackson, Larry (1963–66) pitcher: 52–52 with 3.26 ERA in 119 games.

Jackson, Lou (1958–59) outfielder: 7-for-39, .179, in 30 games.

Darrin Jackson

Cleo James

Jackson, Randy (1950–55, '59) infielder-outfielder: 690-for-2,602, .265, in 739 games.

Jacobs, Elmer (1924–25) pitcher: 13–15 with 4.06 ERA in 56 games.

Jacobs, Mike (1902) shortstop: 4-for-19, .211, in 5 games.

Jacobs, Ray (1928) pinch hitter: 0-for-2, .000, in 2 games.

Jacobs, Tony (1948) pitcher: 0–0 with 4.50 ERA in 1 game.

Jacobson, Jake (1916) outfielder: 3-for-13, .231, in 4 games.

Jaeckel, Paul (1964) pitcher: 1–0 with 0.00 ERA in 4 games.

Jaeger, Joe (1920) pitcher: 0–0 with 12.00 ERA in 2 games.

Jahn, Art (1925) outfielder: 68-for-226, .301, in 58 games.

James, Cleo (1970–71, '73) outfielder-infielder: 85-for-371, .229, in 198 games.

James, Rick (1967) pitcher: 0–1 with 13.50 ERA in 3 games.

Jeffcoat, Hal (1948–55) outfielder-pitcher: 459-for-1,797, .255, in 637 games; 13–12 with 4.08 ERA in 93 games.

Jelincich, Frank (1941) outfielder: 1-for-8, .125, in 4 games.

Jenkins, Fergie (1966–73, '82–83) pitcher: 167–132 with 3.21 ERA in 401 games.

Jennings, Doug (1993) first baseman: 13-for-52, .250, in 42 games.

Jennings, Robin (1996) outfielder: 13-for-58, .224, in 31 games.

Jestadt, Garry (1971) third baseman: 0-for-3, .000, in 3 games.

Jimenez, Manny (1969) pinch hitter: 1-for-6, .167, in 6 games.

Howard Johnson

Johnson, Ben (1959–60) pitcher: 2–1 with 3.91 ERA in 21 games.

Johnson, Bill (1983–84) pitcher: 1–0 with 3.57 ERA in 14 games.

Johnson, Cliff (1980) infielder-outfielder-catcher: 46-for-96, .258, in 68 games.

Johnson, Dave (1978) third baseman: 15-for-49, .306, in 24 games.

Johnson, Don (1943–48) infielder: 528-for-1,935, .273, in 511 games.

Johnson, Howard (1995) infielder: 33-for-169, .195, in 87 games.

Johnson, Ken (1969) pitcher: 1–2 with 2.84 ERA in 9 games.

Johnson, Lou (1960, '68) outfielder: 64-for-273, .234, in 96 games.

Johnson, Richard (1958) pinch hitter: 0-for-5, .000, in 8 games.

Johnston, Jimmy (1914) outfielder: 23-for-101, .228, in 50 games.

Johnstone, Jay (1982–84) outfielder: 124-for-482, .257, in 236 games.

Joiner, Roy (1934–35) pitcher: 0–1 with 8.03 ERA in 22 games.

Jones, Clarence (1967–68) first baseman–outfielder: 34-for-137, .248, in 58 games.

Jones, Davy (1902–04) outfielder: 296-for-1,076, .275, in 292 games.

Jones, Doug (1996) pitcher: 2-2 with 5.01 ERA in 28 games.

Jones, Percy (1920–28) pitcher: 46–41 with 4.21 ERA in 207 games.

Jones, Sheldon (1953) pitcher: 0–2 with 5.40 ERA in 22 games.

Jones, Toothpick Sam (1955–56) pitcher: 23–34 with 4.01 ERA in 69 games.

Jonnard, Claude (1929) pitcher: 0–1 with 7.48 ERA in 12 games.

David Jones

Vic Keen

Jerry Kindall

Bill Jurges

Jurges, Billy (1931–38, '46–47) infielder: 928-for-3,658, .254, in 1,072 games.

K

Kahoe, Mike (1901–02, '07) catcher–first baseman: 61-for-265, .230, in 79 games.

Kaiser, Al (1911) outfielder: 21-for-84, .250, in 27 games.

Kaiser, Don (1955–57) pitcher: 6–15 with 4.15 ERA in 58 games.

Kane, John Francis (1909–10) outfielder-infielder: 19-for-107, .178, in 52 games.

Kaufmann, Tony (1921–27) pitcher: 63–57 with 3.89 ERA in 172 games.

Kearns, Ted (1924–25) first baseman: 5-for-18, .278, in 7 games.

Keating, Walter (1913–15) shortstop: 4-for-43, .093, in 26 games.

Keen, Vic (1921–25) pitcher: 30–33 with 3.96 ERA in 117 games.

Kelleher, John (1921–23) infielder: 202-for-687, .294, in 224 games.

Kelleher, Mick (1976–80) infielder: 179-for-792, .226, in 430 games.

Kellert, Frank (1956) first baseman: 24-for-129, .186, in 71 games.

Kelly, Bob (1951–53) pitcher: 11–14 with 4.47 ERA in 80 games.

Kelly, Highpockets (1930) first baseman: 55-for-166, .331, in 39 games.

Kelly, Joe (1916) outfielder: 43-for-169, .254, in 54 games.

Kelly, Joseph James (1926, '28) outfielder–first baseman: 70-for-228, .307, in 97 games.

Kennedy, Junior (1982–83) infielder: 56-for-264, .212, in 122 games.

Kennedy, Snapper (1902) outfielder: 0-for-5, .000, in 1 game.

Keough, Marty (1966) outfielder: 6-for-26, .231, in 33 games.

Keough, Matt (1986) pitcher: 2–2 with 4.97 ERA in 19 games.

Kerr, John (1925) pinch hitter: 0-for-0, .000, in 1 game.

Kessinger, Don (1964–75) shortstop–third baseman: 1,619-for-6,355, .255, in 1,648 games.

Kieshnick, Brooks (1996) outfielder: 10-for-29, .345, in 25 games.

Kilduff, Pete (1917–19) infielder: 99-for-383, .258, in 117 games.

Kilgus, Paul (1989) pitcher: 6–10 with 4.39 ERA in 35 games.

Killefer, Bill (1918–21) catcher: 252-for-970, .260, in 316 games.

Killen, Frank (1900) pitcher: 3–3 with 4.67 ERA in 6 games.

Kimball, Newt (1937–38) pitcher: 0–0 with 10.50 ERA in 3 games.

Kimm, Bruce (1979) catcher: 1-for-11, .091, in 9 games.

Kindall, Jerry (1956–58, '60–61) infielder: 173-for-798, .217, in 292 games.

Kiner, Ralph (1953–54) outfielder: 276-for-971, .284, in 264 games.

King, Chuck (1958) outfielder: 2-for-8, .250, in 8 games.

King, Jim (1955–56) outfielder: 156-for-618, .252, in 231 games.

Kingman, Dave (1978–80) outfielder–first baseman: 329-for-1,182, .278, in 345 games.

Kirby, Jim (1949) pinch hitter: 1-for-2, .500, in 3 games.

Kitsos, Chris (1954) shortstop: 0–0 .000, in 1 game.

Kling, Johnny (1900–11) catcher–outfielder–first baseman: 960-for-3,539, .271, in 1,025 games.

Klein, Chuck (1934–36) outfielder: 290-for-978, .297, in 263 games.

Klippstein, John (1950–54) pitcher: 31–51 with 4.78 ERA in 193 games.

Klugman, Joe (1921–22) second baseman: 6-for-23, .261, in 8 games.

Kmak, Joe (1995) catcher–third baseman: 13-for-53, .245, in 19 games.

Knabe, Dutch (1916) second baseman: 40-for-145, .276, in 51 games.

Knisely, Pete (1913–15) outfielder-infielder: 42-for-205, .205, in 103 games.

Knowles, Darold (1975–76) pitcher: 11–16 with 4.50 ERA in 116 games.

Koenig, Mark (1932–33) infielder: 98-for-320, .306, in 113 games.

Johnny Klippstein

Ken Kravec

Emil Kush

Darold Knowles

Calvin Koonce

Koestner, Bob (1914) pitcher: 0–0 with 2.84 ERA in 4 games.

Koonce, Calvin (1962–67) pitcher: 29–32 with 3.88 ERA in 179 games.

Kowalik, Fabian (1935–36) pitcher: 2–4 with 4.94 ERA in 26 games.

Kramer, Randy (1990) pitcher: 0–2 with 3.98 ERA in 10 games.

Kravec, Ken (1981–82) pitcher: 2–7 with 5.33 ERA in 37 games.

Kreevich, Mike (1931) outfielder: 2-for-12, .167, in 5 games.

Kreitner, Mickey (1943–44) catcher: 16-for-93, .172, in 42 games.

Kremmel, Jim (1974) pitcher: 0–2 with 5.23 ERA in 23 games.

Kroh, Rube (1908–10) pitcher: 12–5 with 2.22 ERA in 25 games.

Krug, Chris (1965–66) catcher: 40-for-197, .203, in 71 games.

Krug, Gary (1981) pinch hitter: 2-for-5, .400, in 7 games.

Krug, Marty (1922) infielder: 124-for-450, .275, in 127 games.

Krukow, Mike (1976–81) pitcher: 45–50 with 4.17 ERA in 150 games.

Kuenn, Harvey (1965–66) outfielder: 27-for-123, .220, in 57 games.

Kunkel, Jeff (1992) outfielder: 13-for-53, .245, in 20 games.

Kush, Emil (1941–49) pitcher: 21–12 with 3.48 ERA in 150 games.

L

LaCock, Peter (1972–76) outfielder–first baseman: 138-for-625, .221, in 263 games.

Lade, Doyle (1946–50) pitcher: 25–29 with 4.39 ERA in 126 games.

Lamabe, Jack (1968) pitcher: 3–2 with 4.26 ERA in 42 games.

Lamar, Pete (1902) catcher: 2-for-9, .222, in 2 games.

Lamp, Dennis (1977–80) pitcher: 28–41 with 4.08 ERA in 127 games.

Lancaster, Les (1987–91) pitcher: 34–23, 22 saves, with 3.82 ERA in 232 games.

Harvey Kuenn

Dennis Lamp

Les Lancaster

Landrith, Hobie (1956) catcher: 69-for-312, .221, in 111 games.

Landrum, Bill (1988) pitcher: 1–0 with 5.84 ERA in 7 games.

Landrum, Cedric (1991) outfielder: 20-for-86, .233, in 56 games.

Landrum, Don (1962–65) outfielder: 218-for-901, .242, in 309 games.

LanFranconi, Walter (1941) pitcher: 0–1 with 3.00 ERA in 2 games.

Lake, Steve (1983–86, '93) catcher: 87-for-397, .219, in 175 games.

LaRoche, Dave (1973–74) pitcher: 9–7 with 5.18 ERA in 94 games.

LaRose, Vic (1968) infielder: 0-for-2, .000, in 4 games.

Larsen, Don (1967) pitcher: 0–0 with 9.00 ERA in 3 games.

Larson, Dan (1982) pitcher: 0–4 with 5.67 ERA in 12 games.

Tony LaRussa

LaRussa, Tony (1973) pinch runner: 0-for-0, .000, in 1 game.

Lary, Al (1954, '62) pitcher: 0–1 with 6.52 ERA in 16 games.

Lavender, Jimmy (1912–16) pitcher: 57–68 with 3.03 ERA in 196 games.

Law, Vance (1988–89) third baseman: 259-for-964, .278, in 281 games.

Lazzeri, Tony (1938) shortstop: 32-for-120, .267, in 54 games.

Leach, Tommy (1912–14) outfielder-infielder: 347-for-1,296, .268, in 365 games.

Lear, King (1918–19) infielder: 17-for-77, .221, in 42 games.

Leathers, Hal (1920) infielder: 7-for-23, .304, in 9 games.

Lee, Bill (1934–43, '47) pitcher: 139–121 with 3.51 ERA in 350 games.

Lee, Don (1966) pitcher: 2–1 with 7.11 ERA in 16 games.

Lefferts, Craig (1983) pitcher: 3–4 with 3.13 ERA in 56 games.

Leiber, Hank (1939–41) outfielder–first baseman: 281-for-967, .292, in 382 games.

Leifield, Lefty (1912–13) pitcher: 7–3 with 3.13 ERA in 19 games.

LeMay, Dick (1963) pitcher: 0–1 with 5.28 ERA in 9 games.

Lemonds, Dave (1969) pitcher: 0–1 with 3.86 ERA in 2 games.

Lennon, Bob (1957) outfielder: 3-for-21, .143, in 9 games.

Lennox, Edgar (1912) third baseman: 19-for-81, .235, in 27 games.

Craig Lefferts

Dutch Leonard

Leonard, Dutch (1949–53) pitcher: 26–30, 28 saves, with 3.59 ERA in 199 games.

Leslie, Roy (1917) first baseman: 4-for-19, .211, in 7 games.

Lezcano, Carlos (1980–81) outfielder: 19-for-102, .186, in 49 games.

Lillard, Gene (1936, '39) pitcher: 3–5 with 6.55 ERA in 20 games.

Lindstrom, Chuck (1935) outfielder-infielder: 94-for-342, .275, in 90 games.

Littlefield, Dick (1957) pitcher: 2–3 with 5.35 ERA in 48 games.

Littrell, Jack (1957) infielder: 29-for-153, .190, in 61 games.

Livingston, Mickey (1943–47) catcher–first baseman: 138-for-544, .254, in 192 games.

Lobert, Hans (1905) third baseman: 9-for-46, .196, in 14 games.

Locker, Bob (1973, '75) pitcher: 10–7, 18 saves, with 3.11 ERA in 85 games.

Bob Locker

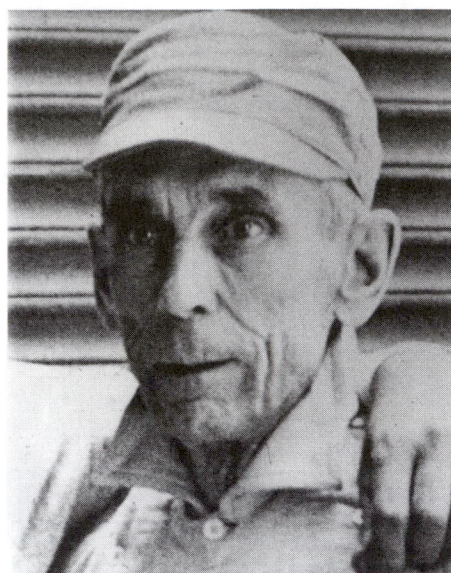

Bobby Lowe

Logan, Bob (1937–38) pitcher: 0–2 with 2.48 ERA in 18 games.

Long, Bill (1990) pitcher: 6–1 with 4.37 ERA in 42 games.

Long, Dale (1957–59) first baseman–catcher: 321-for-1,173, .274, in 375 games.

Lopes, Davey (1984–86) infielder-outfielder: 129-for-449, .287, in 174 games.

Loviglio, Jay (1983) pinch hitter: 0-for-1, .000, in 1 game.

Lowdermilk, Slim (1912) pitcher: 0–1 with 9.69 ERA in 2 games.

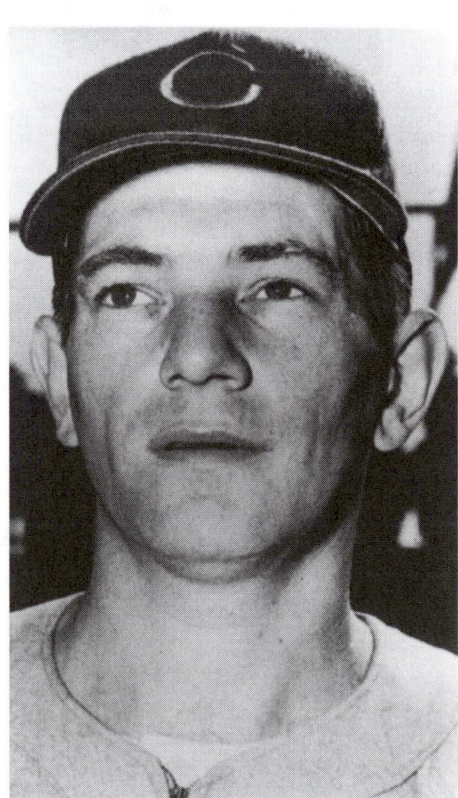

Turk Lown

Lowe, Bobby (1902–03) infielder: 144-for-577, .250, in 151 games.

Lown, Turk (1951–58) pitcher: 30–44, 28 saves, with 4.60 ERA in 260 games.

Lowrey, Peanuts (1942–49) infielder-outfielder: 722-for-2,595, .278, in 726 games.

Luderus, Fred (1909–10) first baseman: 22-for-91, .242, in 35 games.

Lum, Mike (1980–81) outfielder–first baseman: 14-for-58, .241, in 41 games.

Lundgren, Carl (1902–09) pitcher: 90–55 with 2.42 ERA in 179 games.

Lundstedt, Tom (1973–74) catcher: 3-for-37, .081, in 26 games.

Lynch, Danny (1948) second baseman: 2-for-7, .286, in 7 games.

Lynch, Ed (1986–87) pitcher: 9–14 with 4.63 ERA in 81 games.

Lynch, Mike (1902) outfielder: 4-for-28, .143, in 7 games.

Lynn, Red (1944) pitcher: 5–4 with 4.06 ERA in 22 games.

M

Mack, Bill (1908) pitcher: 0–0 with 3.00 ERA in 2 games.

Mack, Ray (1947) second baseman: 17-for-78, .218, in 21 games.

Macko, Steve (1979–80) infielder: 15-for-60, .250, in 25 games.

Madden, Len (1912) pitcher: 0–1 with 2.92 ERA in 6 games.

Maddern, Clarence (1946–49) outfielder–first baseman: 57-for-226, .252, in 93 games.

Maddux, Greg (1986–92) pitcher: 95–75 with 3.35 ERA in 212 games.

Madlock, Bill (1974–76) third baseman: 498-for-1,481, .336, in 400 games.

Madrid, Sal (1947) shortstop: 3-for-24, .125, in 8 games.

Magadan, Dave (1996) infielder: 43-for-169, .254, in 78 games.

Magee, Lee (1919) outfielder-infielder: 78-for-267, .292, in 79 games.

Maguire, Fred (1928) second baseman: 160-for-574, .279, in 140 games.

Maisel, George (1921–22) outfielder: 138-for-477, .289, in 149 games.

Maksudian, Mike (1994) catcher-infielder: 7-for-26, .269, in 26 games.

Maldonado, Candy (1993) outfielder: 26-for-140, .186, in 70 games.

Malone, Pat (1928–34) pitcher: 115–79 with 3.57 ERA in 265 games.

Dave Magadan

Maloney, Billy (1905) outfielder: 145-for-558, .260, in 145 games.

Mancuso, Gus (1939) catcher: 58-for-251, .231, in 80 games.

Manders, Hal (1946) pitcher: 0–1 with 9.00 ERA in 2 games.

Mann, Ben (1944) pinch runner: 0–0, .000, in 1 game.

Mann, Les (1916–19) outfielder: 443-for-1,647, .269, in 453 games.

Manville, Dick (1952) pitcher: 0–0 with 7.94 ERA in 11 games.

Maranville, Rabbit (1925) infielder: 62-for-266, .233, in 75 games.

Marquez, Gonzalo (1973–74) first baseman: 13-for-69, .188, in 30 games.

Marquez, Luis (1954) outfielder: 1-for-12, .083, in 17 games.

Marriott, Bill (1917, '20–21)

Gus Mancuso

Jerry Martin

David Martinez

Bobby Mattick

outfielder-infielder: 24-for-87, .276, in 46 games.

Marshall, Doc (1908) catcher-outfielder: 6-for-20, .300, in 12 games.

Marshall, Jim (1958–59) first baseman–outfielder: 96-for-375, .256, in 134 games.

Martin, J. C. (1970–72) catcher–first baseman: 57-for-252, .225, in 112 games.

Martin, Jerry (1979–80) outfielder: 257-for-1,028, .250, in 291 games.

Martin, Mike (1986) catcher: 1-for-13, .077, in 8 games.

Martin, Morrie (1959) pitcher: 0–0 with 19.29 ERA in 3 games.

Martin, Speed (1918–22) pitcher: 29–40 with 3.73 ERA in 117 games.

Martin, Stu (1943) infielder: 26-for-118, .220, in 64 games.

Martinez, Carmelo (1983) first baseman–outfielder: 23-for-89, .258, in 29 games.

Martinez, Dave (1986–88) outfielder: 214-for-823, .260, in 270 games.

Marty, Joe (1937–39) outfielder: 151-for-601, .251, in 187 games.

Martz, Randy (1980–82) pitcher: 17–19 with 3.78 ERA in 67 games.

Mason, Mike (1987) pitcher: 4–1 with 5.68 ERA in 17 games.

Massa, Gordon (1957–58) catcher: 7-for-17, .412, in 8 games.

Matthews, Nellie (1960–63) outfielder: 42-for-221, .190, in 82 games.

Matthews, Sarge (1984–87) outfielder: 320-for-1,201, .266, in 411 games.

Mattick, Bobby (1938–40) infielder: 148-for-620, .239, in 180 games.

Mauch, Gene (1948–49) infielder: 65-for-288, .226, in 125 games.

Mauro, Carmen (1948–51) outfielder: 48-for-219, .219, in 78 games.

May, Derrick (1990–94) outfielder: 351-for-1,244, .282, in 384 games.

May, Jake (1931–32) pitcher: 7–7 with 4.06 ERA in 66 games.

May, Scott (1991) pitcher: 0–0 with 18.00 ERA in 2 games.

Mayer, Eddie (1957–58) pitcher: 2–2 with 4.31 ERA in 22 games.

McAfee, Bill (1930) pitcher: 0–0 with 0.00 ERA in 2 games.

McAnany, Jim (1961–62) outfielder: 3-for-16, .188, in 18 games.

McAuley, Mike (1925) shortstop: 35-for-125, .280, in 37 games.

McCabe, Bill (1918–20) infielder-outfielder: 22-for-131, .168, in 65 games.

McCall, Dutch (1948) pitcher: 4–13 with 4.82 ERA in 30 games.

McCarthy, Alex (1915–16) infielder: 45-for-179, .251, in 60 games.

McCarthy, Jack (1900–05) outfielder-first baseman: 337-for-1,206, .279, in 322 games.

McChesney, Pud (1904) outfielder: 23-for-88, .261, in 22 games.

McClendon, Lloyd (1989–90) outfielder-infielder: 91-for-366, .249, in 141 games.

McConnell, George (1914, '16) pitcher: 4–13 with 2.53 ERA in 29 games.

J. C. Martin

Joe Marty

Chuck McElroy

McCormick, Barry (1896–1901) infielder: 560-for-2,299, .244, in 610 games.

McCullough, Clyde (1940–43, '46–48, '53–56) catcher: 540-for-2,170, .249, in 746 games.

McDaniel, Lindy (1963–65) pitcher: 19–20, 39 saves, with 3.06 ERA in 191 games.

McDonald, Ed (1913) pinch hitter: 0-for-0, .000 in 1 game.

McElroy, Chuck (1991–93) pitcher: 12–11 with 3.06 ERA in 192 games.

McGinn, Dan (1972) pitcher: 0–5 with 5.89 ERA in 13 games.

McGlothen, Lynn (1978–81) pitcher: 31–35 with 4.25 ERA in 150 games.

McIntyre, Harry (1910–12) pitcher: 25–18 with 3.56 ERA in 57 games.

McKnight, Jim (1960, '62) infielder: 21-for-91, .231, in 63 games.

McLarry, Paul (1915) infielder: 25-for-127, .197, in 68 games.

McLean, Larry (1903) catcher: 0-for-4, .000, in 1 game.

McLish, Cal (1949, '51) pitcher: 5–11 with 4.63 ERA in 38 games.

McMath, Jimmy (1968) outfielder: 2-for-14, .143, in 6 games.

McMillan, Bub (1928–29) infielder: 161-for-618, .261, in 173 games.

McRae, Brian (1995–96) outfielder: 339-for-1,204, .282, in 294 games.

Meers, Russ (1941, '46–47) pitcher: 3–3 with 3.98 ERA in 43 games.

Meier, Dave (1988) third baseman: 2-for-5, .400, in 2 games.

Mejias, Sam (1979) outfielder: 2-for-11, .182, in 31 games.

Menefee, Jocko (1900–03) pitcher-outfielder-infielder: 37–35 with 3.21 ERA in 79 games; 107-for-478, .224, in 152 games.

Meoli, Rudy (1978) infielder: 3-for-29, .103, in 47 games.

Meridith, Ron (1984–85) pitcher: 3–2 with 4.35 ERA in 35 games.

Merkle, Fred (1917–20) first baseman: 516-for-1,859, .278, in 500 games.

Merriman, Lloyd (1955) outfielder: 31-for-145, .214, in 72 games.

Mertes, Sandow (1898–1900) outfielder-infielder: 349-for-1,176, .297, in 327 games.

Merullo, Lennie (1941–47) shortstop: 497-for-2,071, .240, in 639 games.

Mesner, Steve (1938–39) shortstop: 13-for-47, .277, in 19 games.

Metkovich, George (1953) outfielder–first baseman: 29-for-124, .234, in 61 games.

Metzger, Roger (1970) shortstop: 0-for-2, .000, in 1 game.

Metzler, Alex (1925) outfielder: 7-for-38, .184, in 9 games.

Meyer, Dutch (1937) pinch runner: 0-for-0, .000, in 1 game.

Meyer, Russ (1946–48, '56) pitcher: 14–20 with 4.12 ERA in 86 games.

Michaels, Ralph (1924–26) infielder: 18-for-61, .295, in 32 games.

Mickelson, Ed (1957) first baseman: 0-for-12, .000, in 6 games.

Mikkelsen, Pete (1967–68) pitcher: 0–0 with 6.75 ERA in 10 games.

Miklos, Hank (1944) pitcher: 0–0 with 7.71 ERA in 2 games.

Miksis, Eddie (1951–56) infielder: 564-for-2,317, .243, in 620 games.

Miller, Bob (R. L.) (1970–71) pitcher: 0–0 with 5.06 ERA in 9 games.

Miller, Dakin (1902) outfielder: 46-for-187, .246, in 51 games.

Russ Meyer

Miller, Doc (1910) outfielder: 0-for-0, .000, in 1 game.

Miller, Hack (1922–25) outfielder: 378-for-1,168, .324, in 334 games.

Miller, Ox (1947) pitcher: 1–2 with 10.13 ERA in 4 games.

Miller, Ward (1912–13) outfielder: 122-for-444, .275, in 166 games.

Milstead, George (1924–26) pitcher: 3–7 with 4.16 ERA in 36 games.

Minner, Paul (1950–56) pitcher: 62–79 with 4.02 ERA in 195 games.

Mitchell, Mike (1913) outfielder: 72-for-278, .259, in 81 games.

Mitterwald, George (1974–77) catcher–first baseman: 246-for-1,067, .230, in 373 games.

Moisan, Bill (1953) pitcher: 0–0 with 5.40 ERA in 3 games.

Molinaro, Bob (1982) outfielder: 13-for-66, .197, in 65 games.

Mollwitz, Fritz (1913–14, '16) first

Lynn McGlothen

George Mitterwald

Donnie Moore

Jamie Moyer

Randy Myers

baseman: 25-for-98, .255, in 48 games.

Monday, Rick (1972–76) outfielder–first baseman: 690-for-2,551, .270, in 702 games.

Montreuil, Allan (1972) second baseman: 1-for-11, .091, in 5 games.

Moore, Charlie (1912) infielder: 2-for-9, .222, in 5 games.

Moore, Donnie (1975, '77–79) pitcher: 14–13, 5 saves, with 4.42 ERA in 141 games.

Moore, Earl (1913) pitcher: 1–1 with 4.45 ERA in 7 games.

Moore, Johnny (1928–29, '31–32, '45) outfielder: 179-for-620, .289, in 206 games.

Mooty, Jake (1940–43) pitcher: 16–20 with 3.53 ERA in 74 games.

Morales, Jerry (1974–77, '81–83) outfielder: 711-for-2,587, .275, in 792 games.

Moran, Pat (1906–09) catcher: 195-for-818, .238, in 261 games.

Morehead, Seth (1959–60) pitcher: 2–10 with 4.06 ERA in 56 games.

Moreland, Keith (1982–87) outfielder-infielder-catcher: 912-for-3,240, .280, in 902 games.

Morgan, Bobby (1957–58) infielder: 88-for-426, .206, in 126 games.

Morgan, Mike (1992–95) pitcher: 30–34 with 3.69 in 85 games.

Morgan, Vern (1955) third baseman: 1-for-7, .143, in 7 games.

Morhardt, Moe (1961–62) first baseman: 7-for-34, .206, in 25 games.

Moriarity, George (1903–04) third baseman–outfielder: 0-for-18, .000, in 5 games.

Moroney, Jim (1902) pitcher: 1–1 with 4.56 ERA in 10 games.

Morris, Ed (1922) pitcher: 0–0 with 8.25 ERA in 5 games.

Morrissey, Deacon (1902) pitcher: 1–3 with 2.25 ERA in 5 games.

Moryn, Moose (1956–60) outfielder: 571-for-2,099, .272, in 594 games.

Moskau, Paul (1983) pitcher: 3–2 with 6.75 ERA in 8 games.

Mosolf, Jim (1933) outfielder: 22-for-82, .268, in 31 games.

Moss, Mal (1930) pitcher: 0–0 with 6.27 ERA in 12 games.

Moyer, Jamie (1986–88) pitcher: 28–34 with 4.42 ERA in 85 games.

Mudrock, Phil (1963) pitcher: 0–0 with 9.00 ERA in 1 game.

Mulligan, Eddie (1915–16) infielder: 37-for-211, .175, in 69 games.

Mumphrey, Jerry (1986–88) outfielder: 206-for-684, .316, in 292 games.

Muncrief, Bob (1949) pitcher: 5–6 with 4.56 ERA in 34 games.

Munson, Joe (1925–26) outfielder: 39-for-136, .287, in 42 games.

Murcer, Bobby (1978–80) outfielder-infielder: 336-for-1,243, .270, in 358 games.

Murphy, Danny (1960–62) outfielder: 21-for-123, .171, in 49 games.

Murray, Jim (1902) outfielder: 8-for-47, .170 in 12 games.

Murray, Red (1915) outfielder-infielder: 43-for-144, .299, in 51 games.

Murray, Tony (1923) outfielder: 1-for-4, .250, in 2 games.

Myers, Billy (1941) infielder: 14-for-63, .222, in 24 games.

Myers, Dick (1956) pinch hitter: 0-for-1, .000, in 4 games.

Myers, Randy (1993–95) pitcher: 4–11, 112 saves, with 3.52 ERA in 168 games.

Myers, Rodney (1996) pitcher: 2–1 with 4.68 ERA in 45 games.

N

Nabholz, Chris (1995) pitcher: 0–1 with 5.40 ERA in 34 games.

Napier, Buddy (1918) pitcher: 0–0 with 5.40 ERA in 1 game.

Navarro, Jaime (1995–96) pitcher: 29–18 with 3.62 ERA in 64 games.

Needham, Tom (1909–14) catcher–first baseman: 58-for-315, .184, in 133 games.

Jaime Navarro

Cal Neeman

Neeman, Cal (1957–60) catcher: 178-for-734, .243, in 251 games.

Nehf, Art (1927–29) pitcher: 22–13 with 3.64 ERA in 71 games.

Nelson, Lynn (1930, '33–34) pitcher: 8–8 with 4.39 ERA in 63 games.

Nen, Dick (1968) first baseman: 17-for-94, .181, in 81 games.

Newkirk, Joel (1919–29) pitcher: 0–1 with 7.27 ERA in 3 games.

Newman, Ray (1971) pitcher: 1–2 with 3.52 ERA in 30 games.

Newsom, Bobo (1932) pitcher: 0–0 with 0.00 ERA in 1 game.

Nichols, Art (1898–1900) catcher: 29-for-114, .254, in 39 games.

Nichols, Dolan (1958) pitcher: 0–4 with 5.01 ERA in 24 games.

Nicholson, Bill (1939–48) outfielder: 1,323-for-4,857, .272, in 1,349 games.

Niekro, Joe (1967–69) pitcher: 24–18 with 3.84 ERA in 74 games.

Joe Niekro

Rich Nye

Nipper, Al (1988) pitcher: 2–4 with 3.04 ERA in 22 games.

Noce, Paul (1987) infielder: 41-for-180, .228, in 70 games.

Noles, Dickie (1982–84, '87) pitcher: 21–27 with 4.45 ERA in 117 games.

Noonan, Pete (1906) catcher–first baseman: 1-for-3, .333, in 5 games.

Nordhagen, Wayne (1983) outfielder–first baseman: 5-for-35, .143, in 21 games.

Noren, Irv (1959–60) outfielder–first baseman: 51-for-167, .305, in 77 games.

Norman, Fred (1964, '66–67) pitcher: 0–4 with 6.08 ERA in 11 games.

North, Billy (1971–72) outfielder: 29-for-143, .203, in 74 games.

Northey, Ron (1950, '52) outfielder: 32-for-115, .278, in 54 games.

Nottebart, Don (1969) pitcher: 1–1 with 7.00 ERA in 16 games.

Novikoff, Lou (1941–44) outfielder: 298-for-1,058, .282, in 339 games.

Novotney, Ralph (1949) catcher: 18-for-67, .269, in 22 games.

Nunez, Joe (1990) pitcher: 4–7 with 6.53 ERA in 21 games.

Nye, Rich (1966–69) pitcher: 23–29 with 3.65 ERA in 99 games.

O

O'Berry, Mike (1980) catcher: 10-for-48, .208, in 19 games.

O'Connor, John (1916) catcher: 0-for-0, .000, in 1 game.

O'Dea, Ken (1935–38) catcher: 241-for-857, .281, in 325 games.

O'Farrell, Bob (1915–25, '34) catcher: 529-for-1,895, .279, in 666 games.

Bob O'Farrell

O'Hagan, Hal (1902) first baseman–outfielder: 21-for-108, .194, in 31 games.

Oliver, Gene (1968–69) catcher–first baseman: 10-for-38, .263, in 31 games.

Oliver, Nate (1969) second baseman: 7-for-44, .159, in 44 games.

Olsen, Bernie (1941) outfielder: 21-for-73, .288, in 24 games.

Olsen, Vern (1939–42, '46) pitcher: 30–26 with 3.40 ERA in 112 games.

O'Neill, Emmett (1946) pitcher: 0–0 with 0.00 ERA in 1 game.

O'Neill, Jack (1904–05) catcher: 70-for-340, .206, in 104 games.

Ontiveros, Steve (1977–80) infielder: 394-for-1,418, .279, in 421 games.

Ortiz, Jose (1971) outfielder: 26-for-88, .295, in 36 games.

Osborn, Bob (1925–27, '29–30) pitcher: 21–16 with 4.19 ERA in 94 games.

Osborne, Tiny (1922–24) pitcher: 17–20 with 4.51 ERA in 80 games.

Ostrowski, Johnny (1943–46) infielder-outfielder: 45-for-212, .212, in 89 games.

Otero, Reggie (1945) first baseman: 9-for-23, .391, in 14 games.

Ott, Billy (1962, '64) outfielder: 11-for-67, .164, in 32 games.

Otto, Dave (1994) pitcher: 0–1 with 3.80 ERA in 36 games.

Overall, Orval (1906–10, '13) pitcher: 84–43 with 1.92 ERA in 163 games.

Ovitz, Ernie (1911) pitcher: 0–0 with 4.50 ERA in 1 game.

Owen, Dave (1983–85) infielder: 27-for-134, .201, in 85 games.

Owen, Mickey (1949–51) catcher: 140-for-582, .241, in 206 games.

Mickey Owen

P

Packard, Gene (1916–17) pitcher: 10–6 with 2.87 ERA in 39 games.

Pafko, Andy (1943–51) outfielder–third baseman: 1,048-for-3,567, .294, in 960 games.

Page, Vance (1938–41) pitcher: 15–16 with 4.03 ERA in 95 games.

Pagel, Karl (1978–79) pinch hitter: 0-for-3, .000, in 3 games.

Andy Pafko

Rafael Palmeiro

Pall, Donn (1994) pitcher: 0–0 with 4.50 ERA in 2 games.

Palmeiro, Rafael (1986–88) infielder: 257-for-874, .294, in 258 games.

Pappas, Erik Daniel (1991) catcher: 3-for-17, .176, in 7 games.

Pappas, Milt (1970–73) pitcher: 51–41 with 3.33 ERA in 115 games.

Parent, Mark (1994–95) catcher: 34-for-131, .260, in 56 games.

Parmelee, Roy (1937) pitcher: 7–8 with 5.13 ERA in 33 games.

Paskert, George (1918–20) outfielder-infielder: 321-for-1,218, .264, in 354 games.

Passeau, Claude (1939–47) pitcher: 124–94 with 2.96 ERA in 292 games.

Patterson, Bob (1996) pitcher: 3–3 with 3.13 ERA in 79 games.

Patterson, Ken (1992) pitcher: 2–3 with 3.89 ERA in 32 games.

Patterson, Reggie (1983–85) pitcher: 4–3 with 4.24 ERA in 16 games.

Paul, Mike (1973–74) pitcher: 0–2 with 5.21 ERA in 13 games.

Pavlas, Dave (1990–91) pitcher: 2–0 with 2.82 ERA in 14 games.

Pawelek, Ted (1946) catcher: 1-for-4, .250, in 4 games.

Pearce, George (1912–16) pitcher: 34–26 with 3.10 ERA in 98 games.

Pechous, Charlie (1916–17) infielder: 20-for-110, .182, in 35 games.

Pedre, Jorge (1992) catcher: 0-for-4, .000, in 4 games.

Pedroes, Chick (1902) outfielder: 0-for-6, .000, in 2 games.

Pena, Roberto (1965–66) shortstop: 40-for-187, .214, in 57 games.

Penner, Ken (1929) pitcher: 0–1 with 2.84 ERA in 5 games.

Pepitone, Joe (1970–73) first baseman–outfielder: 274-for-966, .284, in 268 games.

Perez, Mike (1995–96) pitcher: 3–6 with 3.94 ERA in 92 games.

Perez, Yorkis (1991) pitcher: 1–0 with 2.08 ERA in 3 games.

Perkowski, Harry (1955) pitcher: 3–4 with 5.29 ERA in 25 games.

Perlman, Jon (1985) pitcher: 1–0 with 11.42 ERA in 6 games.

Perry, Pat (1988–89) pitcher: 2–3 with 2.57 ERA in 54 games.

Perry, Scott (1916) pitcher: 2–1 with 2.54 ERA in 54 games.

Petty, Jess (1930) pitcher: 1–3 with 2.97 ERA in 9 games.

Pfeffer, Big Jeff (1905, '10) pitcher: 5–5 with 2.73 ERA in 28 games.

Pfiester, Jack the Giant Killer (1906–11) pitcher: 70–40 with 1.86 ERA in 143 games.

Phelan, Art (1913–15) infielder: 176-for-755, .233, in 549 games.

Phelps, Babe (1933–34) catcher: 22-for-77, .286, in 47 games.

Phillips, Adolfo (1966–69) outfielder: 346-for-1,352, .256, in 431 games.

Phillips, Taylor (1958–59) pitcher: 7–12 with 5.01 ERA in 46 games.

Phoebus, Tom (1972) pitcher: 3–3 with 3.78 ERA in 37 games.

Pick, Charlie (1918–19) infielder-outfielder: 94-for-358, .263, in 104 games.

Adolfo Phillips

Juan Pizarro

Howard Pollet

Paul Popovich

Mike Proly

Jimmy Qualls

Pick, Eddie (1927) infielder: 31-for-181, .171, in 54 games.

Pico, Jeffrey (1988–90) pitcher: 13–12 with 4.24 ERA in 113 games.

Pierce, Ray (1924) pitcher: 0–0 with 7.36 ERA in 6 games.

Piercy, Bill (1926) pitcher: 6–5 with 4.48 in 19 games.

Piktuzis, George (1956) pitcher: 0–0 with 7.20 ERA in 2 games.

Pina, Horacio (1974) pitcher: 3–4 with 3.99 ERA in 34 games.

Pittinger, Clarke (1925) infielder: 54-for-173, .312, in 59 games.

Pizarro, Juan (1970–73) pitcher: 11–12 with 3.90 ERA in 46 games.

Platt, Whitey (1942–43) outfielder: 8-for-57, .140, in 24 games.

Plesac, Dan (1993–94) pitcher: 4–4 with 4.68 ERA in 111 games.

Plummer, Bill (1968) catcher: 0-for-2, .000, in 2 games.

Poholsky, Tom (1957) pitcher: 1–7 with 4.93 ERA in 28 games.

Pollet, Howie (1953–55) pitcher: 17–19 with 4.20 ERA in 69 games.

Ponder, Elmer (1921) pitcher: 3–6 with 4.74 ERA in 16 games.

Popovich, Paul (1964, '66–67, '69–73) infielder: 270-for-1,141, .236, in 436 games.

Porterfield, Bob (1959) pitcher: 0–0 with 11.37 ERA in 4 games.

Powell, Bill (1912) pitcher: 0–0 with 9.00 ERA in 1 game.

Prall, Willie (1975) pitcher: 0–2 with 8.59 ERA in 3 games.

Pramesa, John (1952) catcher: 13-for-46, .283, in 22 games.

Pratt, Todd (1995) catcher: 8-for-60, .133, in 25 games.

Prendergast, Mike (1916–17) pitcher: 9–17 with 2.73 ERA in 70 games.

Pressnell, Tot (1941–42) pitcher: 6–4 with 3.96 ERA in 56 games.

Prim, Ray (1943–46) pitcher: 19–14 with 2.76 ERA in 77 games.

Prince, Don (1962) pitcher: 0–0 with 0.00 ERA in 1 game.

Proly, Mike (1982–83) pitcher: 6–8 with 2.95 ERA in 104 games.

Putman, Ed (1976) catcher-first baseman: 3-for-7, .429, in 5 games.

Pyecha, Johnny (1954) pitcher: 0–1 with 10.13 ERA in 1 game.

Q

Qualls, Jimmy (1969) outfielder-infielder: 30-for-120, .250, in 43 games.

Quinn, Wimpy (1941) pitcher: 0–0 with 7.20 ERA in 3 games.

Quinones, Luis (1987) shortstop: 22-for-101, .218, 49 games.

R

Radatz, Dick (1967) pitcher: 1–0 with 6.56 ERA in 20 games.

Rader, Dave (1978) catcher: 62-for-305, .203, in 116 games.

Raffensberger, Ken (1940–41) pitcher: 7–10 with 3.52 ERA in 53 games.

Ragan, Pat (1909) pitcher: 0–0 with 2.45 ERA in 2 games.

Rainey, Chuck (1983–84) pitcher: 19–20 with 4.41 ERA in 51 games.

Ramazotti, Bob (1949–53) infielder: 169-for-715, .236, in 275 games.

Ramos, Domingo (1989) infielder: 47-for-179, .283, in 85 games.

Lenny Randle

Ken Reitz

Carl Reynolds

Ramsdell, Jim (1952) pitcher: 2–3 with 2.42 ERA in 19 games.

Ramsey, Fernando (1962) outfielder: 3-for-25, .120, in 18 games.

Randall, Newt (1907) outfielder: 16-for-78, .205, in 22 games.

Randle, Lenny (1980) infielder: 135-for-489, .276, in 130 games.

Ranew, Merritt (1963–64) catcher–first baseman: 55-for-187, .294, in 94 games.

Rasmussen, Dennis (1992) pitcher: 0–0 with 10.80 ERA in 3 games.

Raub, Tommy (1903) catcher-infielder-outfielder: 22-for-78, .282, in 24 games.

Raudman, Shorty (1966–67) outfielder: 11-for-55, .200, in 16 games.

Raymer, Fred (1901) infielder: 108-for-463, .233, in 120 games.

Reberger, Frank (1968) pitcher: 0–1 with 4.50 ERA in 3 games.

Regan, Phil (1968–72) pitcher: 32–26, 60 saves, with 3.44 ERA in 246 games.

Reich, Herman (1949) first baseman–outfielder: 108-for-386, .280, in 108 games.

Reilly, Hal (1919) outfielder: 0-for-3, .000, in 1 game.

Reitz, Ken (1981) third baseman: 56-for-260, .215, in 82 games.

Renfroe, Laddie (1991) pitcher: 0–1 with 13.50 ERA in 4 games.

Renko, Steve (1977–78) pitcher: 10–13 with 4.04 ERA in 41 games.

Reulbach, Ed (1905–13) pitcher: 136–65 with 2.24 ERA in 281 games.

Reuschel, Paul (1975–78) pitcher: 12–11 with 4.40 ERA in 163 games.

Reuschel, Rick (1972–81, '83–84) pitcher: 129–121 with 3.50 ERA in 335 games.

Reynolds, Archie (1968–70) pitcher: 0–4 with 5.91 ERA in 16 games.

Reynolds, Carl (1937–39) outfielder: 222-for-789, .282, in 220 games.

Rhoads, Bob (1902) pitcher: 4–8 with 3.20 ERA in 16 games.

Rhodes, Tuffy (1993–95) outfielder: 80-for-337, .237, in 123 games.

Rice, Del (1960) catcher: 12-for-52, .231, in 18 games.

Rice, Hal (1954) outfielder: 11-for-72, .153, in 51 games.

Rice, Leonard (1945) catcher: 23-for-99, .232, in 32 games.

Richards, Fred (1951) first baseman: 8-for-27, .296, in 10 games.

Richbourg, Lance (1932) outfielder: 38-for-148, .257, in 44 games.

Richie, Lew (1910–13) pitcher: 44–27 with 2.94 ERA in 121 games.

Richmond, Berly (1933) pitcher: 0–0 with 1.93 ERA in 4 games.

Richter, Reggie (1911) pitcher: 1–3 with 3.13 ERA in 22 games.

Rickert, Marv (1942, '46–47) outfielder–first baseman: 130-for-555, .234, in 190 games.

Riley, George (1979–80) pitcher: 0–5 with 5.69 ERA in 26 games.

Ripley, Allen (1982) pitcher: 5–7 with 4.26 ERA in 28 games.

Rivera, Roberto (1995) pitcher: 0–0 with 5.40 ERA in 7 games.

Roach, Mel (1961) infielder: 5-for-39, .128, in 23 games.

Paul Reuschel

Tuffy Rhodes

Kevin Roberson

Dave Rosello

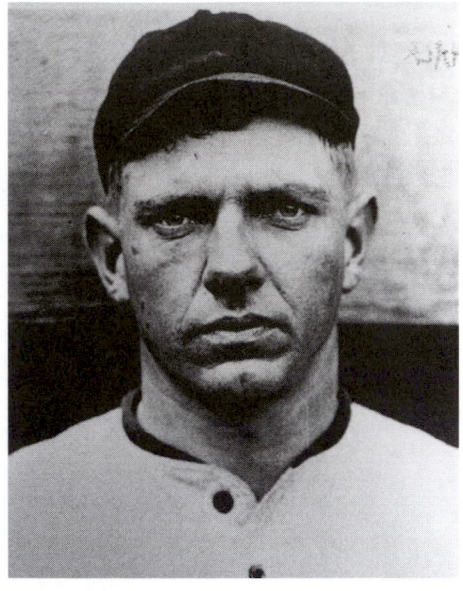

Vic Saier

Roberson, Kevin (1993–95) outfielder: 53-for-273, .194, in 138 games.

Roberts, Dave (1977–78) pitcher: 7–9 with 4.71 ERA in 52 games.

Roberts, Robin (1966) pitcher: 2–3 with 6.14 ERA in 11 games.

Robertson, Daryl (1962) infielder: 2-for-19, .105, in 9 games.

Robertson, Dave (1919–21) outfielder: 178-for-632, .282, in 183 games.

Robertson, Don (1954) outfielder: 0-for-6, .000, in 14 games.

Robinson, Jeff (1992) pitcher: 4–3 with 3.00 ERA in 49 games.

Rodgers, Andre (1961–64) infielder-outfielder: 410-for-1,639, .250, in 490 games.

Rodriguez, Freddy (1958) pitcher: 0–0 with 7.36 ERA in 7 games.

Rodriguez, Roberto (1970) pitcher: 3–2 with 5.82 ERA in 26 games.

Rogell, Billy (1940) infielder: 8-for-59, .136, in 33 games.

Rohn, Dan (1983–84) infielder: 16-for-62, .238, in 48 games.

Roomes, Rolando (1988) outfielder: 3-for-16, .188, in 17 games.

Root, Charlie (1926–41) pitcher: 201–156 with 3.54 ERA in 605 games.

Rosello, Dave (1972–77) infielder: 131-for-565, .232, in 249 games.

Ross, Gary (1968–69) pitcher: 1–1 with 4.60 ERA in 15 games.

Rowan, Jack (1911) pitcher: 0–0 with 4.50 ERA in 1 game.

Rowdon, Wade (1987) third baseman: 7-for-31, .226, in 11 games.

Roy, Luther (1927) pitcher: 3–1 with 2.29 ERA in 11 games.

Roznovsky, Vic (1964–65) catcher: 53-for-248, .214, in 106 games.

Rudolph, Ken (1969–73) catcher: 86-for-426, .202, in 178 games.

Rudolph, Marty (1904) outfielder: 1-for-3, .333, in 2 games.

Ruether, Dutch (1917) pitcher: 2–0 with 2.50 ERA in 10 games.

Rush, Bob (1948–57) pitcher: 110–140 with 3.71 ERA in 339 games.

Russell, Jack (1938–39) pitcher: 10–4 with 3.47 ERA in 81 games.

Russell, Rip (1939–42) infielder: 279-for-1,076, .259, in 319 games.

Ruthven, Dick (1983–85) pitcher: 22–26 with 4.55 ERA in 74 games.

Ryan, Jimmy (1885–89, 1891–1900) outfielder: 2,102-for-6,770, .310, in 1,660 games.

S

Saier, Vic (1911–17) first baseman: 738-for-2,782, .265, in 794 games.

Salazar, Angel (1988) infielder: 15-for-60, .250, in 34 games.

Salazar, Luis (1989–92) infielder-outfielder: 269-for-1,078, .250, in 341 games.

Sanchez, Rey (1991–96) infielder: 430-for-1,630, .264, in 497 games.

Sandberg, Ryne (1982–94, '96) infielder: 2,267-for-7,932, .286, in 2,016 games.

Sanderson, Scott (1984–89) pitcher: 42–42 with 3.81 ERA in 160 games.

Santo, Ron (1960–73) infielder: 2,171-for-7,768, .279, in 2,126 games.

Ken Rudolph

Rey Sanchez

Eddie Sauer

Sauer, Eddie (1943–45) outfielder: 50-for-198, .253, in 86 games.

Sauer, Hank (1949–55) outfielder–first baseman: 852-for-3,165, .269, in 862 games.

Savage, Ted (1967–68) outfielder-infielder: 51-for-233, .219, in 99 games.

Sawatski, Carl (1948, '50, '53) catcher: 31-for-164, .189, in 83 games.

Scanlan, Bob (1991–93) pitcher: 14–19 with 3.75 ERA in 179 games.

Schaefer, Germany (1901–02) infielder-outfielder: 60-for-296, .203, in 83 games.

Schaffer, Jim (1963–64) catcher: 59-for-264, .223, in 111 games.

Schaffernoth, Joe (1959–61) pitcher: 3–7 with 4.54 ERA in 59 games.

Scheffing, Bob (1941–42, '46–50) catcher: 311-for-1,170, .266, in 437 games.

Schenz, Hank (1946–49) infielder: 97-for-376, .258, in 116 games.

Schick, Morrie (1917) outfielder: 5-for-34, .147, in 14 games.

Schiraldi, Calvin (1988–89) pitcher: 12–19 with 4.19 ERA in 83 games.

Schlafly, Larry (1902) outfielder-infielder: 10-for-31, .323, in 10 games.

Schmidt, Fred (1947) pitcher: 0–0 with 9.00 ERA in 1 game.

Schmitz, Johnny (1941–42, '46–51) pitcher: 69–70 with 3.52 ERA in 224 games.

Schorr, Ed (1915) pitcher: 0–0 with 7.50 ERA in 2 games.

Schramka, Paul (1953) outfielder: 0–0, .000, in 2 games.

Schrieber, Henry (1926) infielder: 1-for-18, .056, in 10 games.

Schroll, Al (1960) pitcher: 0–0 with 10.13 ERA in 2 games.

Schult, Art (1959–60) outfielder–first baseman: 34-for-133, .256, in 54 games.

Schulte, Johnny (1929) catcher: 18-for-69, .261, in 31 games.

Schulte, Wildfire (1904–16) outfielder: 1,590-for-5,835, .273, in 1,523 games.

Schultz, Barney (1961–63) pitcher: 13–11, 14 saves, with 3.35 ERA in 107 games.

Schultz, Bob (1951–53) pitcher: 9–11 with 4.69 ERA in 53 games.

Schultz, Buddy (1975–76) pitcher: 3–1 with 6.00 ERA in 35 games.

Schultz, Joe (1915) third baseman: 2-for-8, .250, in 7 games.

Schulze, Don (1984–85) pitcher: 0–1 with 7.94 ERA in 5 games.

Schumpert, Terry (1996) infielder: 7-for-31, .226, in 27 games.

Schurr, Wayne (1964) pitcher: 0–0 with 3.72 ERA in 26 games.

Schuster, Billy (1943–45) infielder: 58-for-252, .230, in 118 games.

Schwenck, Rudy (1909) pitcher: 1–1 with 13.50 ERA in 3 games.

Scott, Dick (1964) pitcher: 0–0 with 12.46 ERA in 3 games.

Scott, Gary (1991–92) infielder: 28-for-175, .160, in 67 games.

Scott, Pete (1926–27) outfielder: 103-for-345, .299, in 148 games.

Scott, Rodney (1978) infielder: 64-for-227, .282, in 78 games.

Seaton, Tom (1916–17) pitcher: 11–10 with 2.98 ERA in 47 games.

Secory, Frank (1944–46) outfielder: 37-for-156, .237, in 90 games.

Segelke, Herman (1982) pitcher: 0–0 with 8.31 ERA in 3 games.

Siebert, Kurt (1979) 0-for-2, .000, in 7 games.

Selma, Dick (1969) pitcher: 10–8 with 3.63 ERA in 36 games.

Sember, Mike (1977–78) infielder: 2-for-7, .286, in 12 games.

Seoane, Manny (1978) pitcher: 1–0 with 5.40 ERA in 7 games.

Serena, Bill (1949–54) infielder: 311-for-1,239, .251, in 508 games.

Servais, Scott (1995–96) catcher: 168-for-620, .271, in 181 games.

Sewell, Tommy (1927) pinch hitter: 0-for-1, .000, in 1 game.

Shamsky, Art (1972) first baseman: 2-for-16, .125, in 15 games.

Shannon, Red (1926) shortstop: 17-for-51, .333, in 19 games.

Shantz, Bobby (1964) pitcher: 0–1 with 5.56 ERA in 20 games.

Bob Scanlan

Barney Schultz

Scott Servais

Clyde Shoun

Lee Smith

Willie Smith

Shaw, Bob (1967) pitcher: 0–2 with 6.04 ERA in 9 games.

Shay, Marty (1916) shortstop: 2-for-7, .286, in 2 games.

Shealy, Al (1930) pitcher: 0–0 with 8.00 ERA in 24 games.

Shean, David (1911) infielder: 28-for-145, .193, in 43 games.

Sheckard, Jimmy (1906–12) outfielder: 905-for-3,528, .257, in 1,000 games.

Shields, Tommy (1993) infielder-outfielder: 1-for-7, .143, in 7 games.

Shoun, Clyde (1935–37) pitcher: 8–7 with 5.56 ERA in 46 games.

Sicking, Eddie (1916) pinch hitter: 0-for-1, .000, in 1 game.

Signer, Walt (1943, '45) pitcher: 2–1 with 3.00 ERA in 10 games.

Silvera, Charlie (1957) catcher: 11-for-53, .208, in 26 games.

Simmons, Curt (1966–67) pitcher: 7–14 with 4.53 ERA in 36 games.

Simpson, Duke (1953) pitcher: 1–2 with 8.00 ERA in 30 games.

Singleton, Elmer (1957–59) pitcher: 3–2 with 3.39 ERA in 28 games.

Sizemore, Ted (1979) second baseman: 82-for-330, .248, in 98 games.

Skidmore, Roe (1970) pinch hitter: 1-for-1, 1.000, in 1 game.

Slagle, Jimmy (1902–08) outfielder: 905-for-3,383, .268, in 895 games.

Slapnicka, Cy (1911) pitcher: 0–2 with 3.38 ERA in 3 games.

Slaughter, Sterling (1964) pitcher: 2–4 with 5.75 ERA in 20 games.

Sloat, Lefty (1949) pitcher: 0–0 with 7.00 ERA in 5 games.

Slocumb, Heathcliffe (1991–92) pitcher: 3–4 with 4.45 ERA in 92 games.

Smalley, Roy (1948–53) shortstop: 499-for-2,147, .232, in 661 games.

Smith, Alec (1904) outfielder-infielder: 6-for-29, .207, in 10 games.

Smith, Bob (1931–32) pitcher: 19–15 with 3.69 ERA in 70 games.

Smith, Bobby Gene (1962) outfielder: 5-for-29, .172, in 13 games.

Smith, Charley (1969) pinch hitter: 0-for-2, .000, in 2 games.

Smith, Charlie (1911–14) pitcher: 19–19 with 3.11 ERA in 63 games.

Smith, Dave (1991–92) pitcher: 0–6, 17 saves, with 4.94 ERA in 46 games.

Smith, Dwight (1989–93) outfielder: 382-for-1,327, .288, in 536 games.

Smith, Earl (1916) outfielder: 7-for-27, .259, in 14 games.

Smith, Greg (1989–90) infielder: 11-for-49, .224, in 22 games.

Smith, Lee (1980–87) pitcher: 40–51 with 2.92 ERA, 180 saves, in 458 games.

Smith, Lewis (1906) pinch hitter: 0-for-1, .000, in 1 game.

Smith, Paul (1958) first baseman: 3-for-20, .150, in 18 games.

Smith, Riverboat (1959) pitcher: 0–0 with 81.00 ERA in 1 game.

Smith, Willie (1968–70) outfielder–first baseman: 123-for-504, .244, in 245 games.

Solis, Marcelino (1958) pitcher: 3–3 with 6.06 ERA in 15 games.

Solomon, Eddie (1975) pitcher: 0–0 with 1.35 ERA in 6 games.

Sommers, Rudy (1912) pitcher: 0–1 with 3.00 ERA in 1 game.

Sorensen, Lary (1985) pitcher: 3–7 with 4.26 ERA in 45 games.

Sosa, Sammy (1992–96) outfielder: 639-for-2,348, .272, in 599 games.

Spangler, Al (1967–71) outfielder: 130-for-539, .246, in 258 games.

Speake, Bob (1955, '57) outfielder–first baseman: 154-for-679, .227, in 224 games.

Speier, Chris (1985–86) infielder: 97-for-373, .260, in 201 games.

Sperring, Rob (1974–76) infielder: 76-for-344, .221, in 150 games.

Sponsberg, Carl (1908) pitcher: 0–0 with 9.00 ERA in 1 game.

Spring, Jack (1964) pitcher: 0–0 with 6.00 ERA in 7 games.

St. Vrain, Jim (1902) pitcher: 4–6 with 2.08 ERA in 12 games.

Stack, Eddie (1913–14) pitcher: 4–3 with 4.43 ERA in 18 games.

Stainback, Tuck (1934–37) outfielder: 184-for-688, .267, in 267 games.

Sammy Sosa

Eddie Stanky

Jimmy Stewart

Steve Stone

Staley, Gale (1925) second baseman: 11-for-26, .423, in 7 games.

Standridge, Pete (1915) pitcher: 4–1 with 3.61 ERA in 29 games.

Stanky, Eddie (1943–44) infielder: 131-for-535, .245, in 155 games.

Stanley, Joe (1909) outfielder: 7-for-52, .135, in 22 games.

Stanton, Harry (1904) catcher: 0-for-3, .000, in 1 game.

Starr, Ray (1945) pitcher: 1–0 with 7.43 ERA in 9 games.

Statz, Jigger (1922–25) outfielder-infielder: 536-for-1,814, .295, in 437 games.

Stauffer, Ed (1923) pitcher: 0–0 with 13.50 ERA in 1 game.

Steevens, Morris (1962) pitcher: 0–1 with 2.40 ERA in 12 games.

Stein, Randy (1982) pitcher: 0–0 with 3.48 ERA in 6 games.

Steinfeldt, Harry (1906–10) infielder: 696-for-2,594, .269, in 732 games.

Stelmaszek, Rick (1974) catcher: 10-for-44, .227, in 25 games.

Stephenson, Earl (1971) pitcher: 1–0 with 4.43 ERA in 16 games.

Stephenson, Joe (1944) catcher: 1-for-8, .125, in 4 games.

Stephenson, Johnny (1967–68) catcher: 11-for-51, .216, in 20 games.

Stephenson, Philip (1989) first baseman: 3-for-21, .143, in 17 games.

Stephenson, Riggs (1926–34) outfielder: 1,167-for-3,474, .336, in 978 games.

Stephenson, Stevie (1935–36) catcher: 11-for-38, .289, in 22 games.

Stewart, Jimmy (1963–67) infielder-outfielder: 196-for-830, .236, in 324 games.

Stewart, Mack (1944–45) pitcher: 0–1 with 3.76 ERA in 24 games.

Stewart, Tuffy (1913–14) outfielder: 1-for-9, .111, in 11 games.

Stoddard, Tim (1984) pitcher: 10–6 with 3.82 ERA in 58 games.

Stone, Steve (1974–76) pitcher: 23–20 with 4.04 ERA in 88 games.

Stoneman, Bill (1967–68) pitcher: 2–5 with 4.01 ERA in 46 games.

Strain, Joe (1981) catcher: 14-for-74, .189, in 25 games.

Strang, Sammy (1900–02) infielder: 33-for-113, .292, in 30 games.

Strange, Doug (1991–92) infielder: 19-for-103, .184, in 55 games.

Stringer, Lou (1941–42, '46) infielder: 273-for-1,127, .242, in 346 games.

Stueland, George (1921–23, '25) pitcher: 9–6 with 5.73 ERA in 45 games.

Sturgeon, Bobby (1940–42, '46–47) infielder: 296-for-1,142, .259, in 386 games.

Sturtze, Tanyon (1995–96) pitcher: 1–0 with 9.00 ERA in 8 games.

Sullivan, John L. (1921) outfielder: 79-for-240, .329, in 76 games.

Summers, Champ (1975–76) outfielder–first baseman: 47-for-217, .217, in 159 games.

Sundberg, Jim (1987–88) catcher: 41-for-193, .212, in 85 games.

Sutcliffe, Rick (1984–91) pitcher: 82–65 with 3.74 ERA in 193 games.

Sutter, Bruce (1976–80) pitcher: 32–30, 133 saves, with 2.40 ERA in 300 games.

Swartzbaugh, David (1995) 0–0 with 0.00 ERA in 7 games.

Sweeney, Bill (1907, '14) 102-for-473, .216, in 137 games.

Jigger Statz

Bobby Sturgeon

Sweetland, Les (1931) pitcher: 8–7 with 5.04 ERA in 26 games.

Swisher, Steve (1974–77) catcher: 242-for-1,116, .217, in 346 games.

T

Tabb, Jerry (1976) first baseman: 7-for-24, .292, in 11 games.

Tabler, Pat (1981–82) infielder: 39-for-186, .210, in 60 games.

Talbot, Bob (1953–54) outfielder: 107-for-433, .247, in 122 games.

Tanner, Chuck (1957–58) outfielder: 118-for-421, .280, in 168 games.

Tappe, Elvin (1954–56, '58, '60, '62) catcher: 63-for-304, .207, in 145 games.

Tappe, Ted (1955) outfielder: 13-for-50, .260, in 23 games.

Tate, Bennie (1934) outfielder: 3-for-24, .125, in 11 games.

Taylor, Chink (1925) outfielder: 0-for-6, .000, in 8 games.

Taylor, Danny (1929–32) outfielder: 148-for-514, .288, in 170 games.

Taylor, Harry (1932) first baseman: 1-for-8, .125, in 10 games.

Taylor, Jack (1898–1903, '06–07) pitcher: 89–82 with 2.66 ERA in 180 games.

Taylor, Sammy (1958–62) catcher: 262-for-1,054, .249, in 376 games.

Taylor, Tony (1958–60) infielder: 312-for-1,197, .261, in 309 games.

Taylor, Zack (1929–33) catcher: 88-for-355, .248, in 141 games.

Teachout, Bud (1930–31) pitcher: 12–6 with 4.54 ERA in 67 games.

Telemaco, Amaury (1996) pitcher: 5–7 with 5.46 ERA in 25 games.

Terry, Zeb (1920–22) infielder: 415-for-1,480, .280, in 387 games.

Terwilliger, Wayne (1949–51) 182-for-784, .232, in 219 games.

Tewksbury, Bob (1987–88) pitcher: 0–4 with 6.75 ERA in 8 games.

Thacker, Moe (1958, '60–62) catcher: 46-for-256, .180, in 155 games.

Thomas, Frank (1960–61, '66) infielder-outfielder: 127-for-529, .240, in 155 games.

Thomas, Lee (1966–67) first baseman–outfielder: 78-for-340, .229, in 152 games.

Thomas, Red (1921) outfielder: 8-for-30, .267, in 8 games.

Thompson, Scot (1978–83) outfielder–first baseman: 226-for-885, .255, in 408 games.

Thomson, Bobby (1958–59) outfielder–third baseman: 252-for-921, .274, in 374 games.

Wayne Terwilliger

Thornton, Andre (1973–76) infielder: 212-for-795, .267, in 271 games.

Thorpe, Bob (1955) pitcher: 0–0 with 3.00 ERA in 2 games.

Tidrow, Dick (1979–82) pitcher: 28–23 with 3.35 ERA in 263 games.

Tiefenauer, Bobby (1968) pitcher: 0–1 with 6.08 ERA in 9 games.

Timmons, Ozzie (1995–96) outfielder: 73-for-311, .235, in 142 games.

Tincup, Ben (1928) pitcher: 0–0 with 7.00 ERA in 2 games.

Tinker, Joe (1902–12, '16) infielder: 1,435-for-5,545, .259, in 1,535 games.

Bobby Thomson

Andre Thornton

Dick Tidrow

Tinning, Bud (1932–34) pitcher: 22–15 with 3.15 ERA in 95 games.

Todd, Al (1940–41, '43) catcher: 104-for-432, .241, in 131 games.

Todd, Jim (1974, '77) pitcher: 5–3 with 5.22 ERA in 63 games.

Tolson, Charles Julius (1926–27, '29–30) first baseman: 75-for-263, .285, in 141 games.

Tompkins, Ron (1971) pitcher: 0–2 with 4.08 ERA in 35 games.

Toney, Fred (1911–13) pitcher: 4–5 with 4.02 ERA in 34 games.

Torres, Hector (1971) infielder: 13-for-58, .224, in 31 games.

Toth, Paul (1962–64) pitcher: 8–12 with 3.63 ERA in 37 games.

Trachsel, Steve (1993–96) pitcher: 29–31 with 3.78 ERA in 86 games.

Tracy, Jim (1980–81) outfielder-infielder: 46-for-185, .249, in 87 games.

Steve Trachsel

Tremel, Bill (1954–56) pitcher: 4–2 with 4.05 ERA in 57 games.

Trillo, Manny (1975–78, '86–88) infielder: 708-for-2,713, .261, in 881 games.

Triplett, Coaker (1938) outfielder: 9-for-36, .250, in 12 games.

Trout, Steve (1983–87) pitcher: 43–38 with 3.95 ERA in 138 games.

Turgeon, Pete (1923) shortstop: 1-for-6, .167, in 3 games.

Turner, Ted (1920) pitcher: 0–0 with 13.50 ERA in 1 game.

Twombly, Clarence (1920–21) outfielder: 109-for-358, .304, in 165 games.

Tyler, George (1918–21) pitcher: 35–24 with 2.59 ERA in 76 games.

Tyree, Earl (1914) catcher: 0-for-4, .000, in 1 game.

Tyrone, Jim (1972, '74–75) outfielder-infielder: 20-for-111, .180, in 81 games.

Tyrone, Wayne (1976) outfielder-infielder: 13-for-57, .228, in 30 games.

Tyson, Mike (1980–81) infielder: 98-for-433, .226, in 173 games.

U

Upham, John (1967–68) pitcher-outfielder: 0–1 with 5.40 ERA in 7 games; 4-for-13, .308, in 21 games.

Usher, Bob (1952) outfielder: 0-for-0, .000, in 1 game.

V

Vail, Mike (1978–80) outfielder: 213-for-671, .317, in 275 games.

Valdes, Pedro (1996) outfielder: 1-for-8, .125, in 9 games.

Valentinetti, Vito (1956–57) pitcher: 6–4 with 3.62 ERA in 51 games.

Vandenberg, Hy (1944–45) pitcher: 14–7 with 3.58 ERA in 65 games.

Vander Meer, Johnny (1950) pitcher: 3–4 with 3.79 ERA in 32 games.

VanZandt, Ike (1904) outfielder: 0-for-11, .000, in 3 games.

Varga, Andy (1950–51) pitcher: 0–2 with 2.25 ERA in 3 games.

Varsho, Gary (1988–90) outfielder: 48-for-208, .231, in 153 games.

Vaughn, Hippo (1913–21) pitcher: 151–105 with 2.33 ERA in 305 games.

Verban, Emil (1948–50) infielder: 176-for-628, .280, in 199 games.

Veres, Randy (1994) pitcher: 1–1 with 5.59 ERA in 10 games.

Vernon, Joe (1912) pitcher: 0–0 with 11.25 ERA in 1 game.

Veryzer, Tom (1983–84) infielder: 32-for-162, .198, in 103 games.

Villaneuva, Hector (1990–92) catcher–first baseman: 101-for-418, .242, in 174 games.

Vizcaino, Jose (1991–93) infielder: 260-for-981, .265, in 330 games.

Vogel, Otto (1923–24) outfielder-infielder: 63-for-253, .249, in 111 games.

Voiselle, Bill (1950) pitcher: 0–4 with 5.79 ERA in 19 games.

W

Waddell, Rube (1901) pitcher: 14–14 with 2.81 ERA in 29 games.

Wade, Ben (1948) pitcher: 0–1 with 7.20 ERA in 2 games.

Wade, Gale (1955–56) outfielder: 6-for-45, .133, in 19 games.

Waitkus, Eddie (1941, '46–48) first baseman–outfielder: 455-for-1,545, .294, in 394 games.

Roy Walker

Walbeck, Matt (1993) catcher: 6-for-30, .200, in 11 games.

Walker, Al (Rube) (1948–51) catcher: 163-for-663, .246, in 246 games.

Walker, Chico (1985–87, '91–92) infielder-outfielder: 149-for-618, .241, in 239 games.

Walker, Harry (1949) outfielder: 42-for-159, .264, in 42 games.

Walker, Mike (1995) pitcher: 1–3 with 3.22 ERA in 42 games.

Walker, Roy (1917–18) pitcher: 1–4 with 2.88 ERA in 42 games.

Wallace, Jack (1915) catcher: 2-for-7, .286, in 2 games.

Waller, Tye (1981–82) infielder—outfielder: 24-for-92, .261, in 47 games.

Wallis, Joe (1975–78) outfielder: 139-for-529, .263, in 221 games.

Jose Vizcaino

Joe Wallis

Jerome Walton

Mitch Webster

Turk Wendell

Walls, Lee (1957–59) outfielder–third baseman: 335-for 1,233, .272, in 373 games.

Walsh, Tom (1906) catcher: 0-for-1, .000, in 2 games.

Walton, Jerome (1989–92) outfielder: 308-for-1,192, .258, in 370 games.

Ward, Chris (1972, '74) outfielder–first baseman: 28-for-138, .203, in 93 games.

Ward, Dick (1934) pitcher: 0–0 with 3.00 ERA in 3 games.

Ward, Preston (1950, '53) first baseman–outfielder: 95-for 385, .247, in 113 games.

Warneke, Lon (1930–36, '42–43, '45) pitcher: 109–73 with 2.84 ERA in 262 games.

Warner, Hooks (1921) third baseman: 8-for-38, .211, in 14 games.

Warner, Jack (1962–65) pitcher: 0–2 with 5.10 ERA in 33 games.

Warstler, Rabbit (1940) infielder: 36-for-159, .226, in 45 games.

Warwick, Carl (1966) outfielder: 5-for-22, .227, in 16 games.

Watson, Doc (1913) pitcher: 1–0 with 0.00 ERA in 1 game.

Watt, Eddie (1975) pitcher: 0–1 with 13.50 ERA in 6 games.

Weaver, Harry (1917–19) pitcher: 3–4 with 3.91 ERA in 14 games.

Weaver, Big Jim (1934) pitcher: 11–9 with 3.91 ERA in 27 games.

Weaver, Orlie (1910–11) pitcher: 3–3 with 2.72 ERA in 13 games.

Webb, Earl (1927–28) outfielder: 135-for-472, .286, in 164 games.

Webster, Mitch (1988–89) 140-for-536, .261, in 168 games.

Webster, Ray (1971) first baseman: 5-for-16, .313, in 16 games.

Weimer, Jake (1903–05) pitcher: 58–34 with 2.15 ERA in 105 games.

Weinert, Lefty (1927–28) pitcher: 2–1 with 4.86 ERA in 15 games.

Weis, Butch (1922–25) outfielder: 92-for-341, .270, in 128 games.

Welch, Johnny (1926–28, '31) pitcher: 2–1 with 4.81 ERA in 15 games.

Wendell, Turk (1993–96) pitcher: 8–9 with 4.48 ERA in 126 games.

Wheeler, Rip (1923–24) pitcher: 4–8 with 4.10 ERA in 32 games.

Whisenant, Pete (1956) outfielder: 75-for-314, .239, in 103 games.

White, Elder (1962) infielder: 8-for-53, .151, in 23 games.

White, Jerry (1978) outfielder: 37-for-136, .272, in 59 games.

Whitehill, Earl (1939) pitcher: 4–7 with 5.14 ERA in 24 games.

Wicker, Bob (1903–06) pitcher-outfielder: 53–29 with 2.67 ERA in

Preston Ward

Jake Weimer

Pete Whisenant

Bob Will

94 games; 34-for-155, .219, in 50 games.

Wiedemeyer, Charlie (1934) pitcher: 0–0 with 9.72 ERA in 4 games.

Wilcox, Milt (1975) pitcher: 0–1 with 5.63 ERA in 25 games.

Wilhelm, Hoyt (1970) pitcher: 0–1 with 9.82 ERA in 3 games.

Wilke, Harry (1927) third baseman: 0-for-9, .000, in 3 games.

Wilkerson, Curt (1989–90) infielder: 80-for-346, .231, in 154 games.

Wilkins, Dean (1989–90) pitcher: 1–0 with 6.65 ERA in 18 games.

Wilkins, Rick (1991–95) catcher: 348-for 1,368, .254, in 455 games.

Will, Bob (1957–58, '60–63) outfielder–first baseman: 202-for-819, .247, in 410 games.

Williams, Art (1902) outfielder–first baseman: 37-for-160, .231, in 47 games.

Williams, Billy (1959–74) outfielder–first baseman: 2,510-for-8,479, .296, in 2,213 games.

Williams, Cy (1912–17) outfielder: 428-for-1,706, .251, in 539 games.

Williams, Dewey (1944–47) catcher: 92-for-369, .249, in 145 games.

Williams, Mitch (1989–90) pitcher: 5–12, 52 saves, with 3.22 ERA in 135 games.

Williams, Otto (1903–04) infielder-outfielder: 66-for-315, .210, in 95 games.

Williams, Pop (1902–03) pitcher: 11–17 with 2.57 ERA in 32 games.

Wills, Bump (1982) second baseman: 114-for-419, .272, in 128 games.

Willis, Jim (1953–54) pitcher: 2–2 with 3.39 ERA in 27 games.

Wilson, Art (1916–17) catcher: 67-for-325, .206, in 117 games.

Wilson, Hack (1926–31) outfielder: 1,017-for-3,154, .322, in 850 games.

Wilson, Steve (1989–91) pitcher: 10–19 with 4.56 ERA in 98 games.

Wilson, Willie (1993–94) outfielder: 62-for-242, .256, in 115 games.

Winceniak, Ed (1956–57) infielder: 14-for-67, .209, in 32 games.

Wirtz, Kettle (1921–23) catcher: 13-for-74, .176, in 43 games.

Wise, Casey (1957) infielder: 19-for-106, .179, in 43 games.

Wolfe, Harry (1917) outfielder-infielder: 2-for-5, .400, in 9 games.

Wolter, Harry (1917) outfielder–first baseman: 88-for-353, .249, in 117 games.

Wolverton, Harry (1898–1900) infielder: 129-for-449, .287, in 115 games.

Woods, Gary (1982–85) outfielder-infielder: 155-for-615, .252, in 278 games.

Woods, Jim (1957) pinch hitter: 0-for-0, .000, in 2 games.

Wortman, Chuck (1916–18) infielder: 82-for-441, .186, in 161 games.

Wright, Bob (1915) pitcher: 0–0 with 2.25 ERA in 2 games.

Wright, Mel (1960–61) pitcher: 0–1 with 8.27 ERA in 20 games.

Wrona, Rick (1988–90) catcher: 31-for-127, .244, in 58 games.

Wynne, Marvell (1989–90) outfielder: 47-for-234, .201, in 112 games.

Wyse, Hank (1942–47) pitcher: 69–54 with 3.03 ERA in 198 games.

Y

Yantz, George (1912) catcher: 1-for-1, 1.000, in 1 game.

Yelding, Eric (1993) infielder: 22-for-108, .204, in 69 games.

Yerkes, Carroll (1932–33) pitcher: 0–0 with 3.27 ERA in 3 games.

Yerkes, Steve (1916) second baseman: 36-for-137, .263, in 44 games.

York, Lefty (1921) pitcher: 5–9 with 4.73 ERA in 40 games.

York, Tony (1944) infielder: 20-for-85, .235, in 28 games.

Yoter, Elmer (1927–28) third baseman: 6-for-27, .222, in 14 games.

Young, Anthony (1994–95) pitcher: 3–4 with 3.70 ERA in 32 games.

Young, Don (1965, '69) outfielder: 67-for-307, .218, in 112 games.

Z

Zabel, Zip (1913–15) pitcher: 12–14 with 2.71 ERA in 66 games.

Don Young

Zahn, Geoff (1975–76) pitcher: 2–8 with 5.20 ERA in 19 games.

Zambrano, Eddie (1993–94) outfielder-infielder: 35-for-133, .263, in 75 games.

Zamora, Oscar (1974–76) pitcher: 13–14, 23 saves, with 4.33 ERA in 148 games.

Zeider, Polly (1916–18) infielder: 223-for-950, .235, in 288 games.

Zeile, Todd (1995) infielder: 105-for-426, .245, in 113 games.

Zick, Bob (1954) pitcher: 0–0 with 8.27 ERA in 8 games.

Zimmer, Don (1960–61) infielder: 215-for-845, .254, in 260 games.

Zimmerman, Heinie (1907–16) infielder-outfielder: 1,112-for-3,661, .304, in 1,022 games.

Zwilling, Dutch (1916) outfielder: 6-for-53, .113, in 35 games.

Oscar Zamora

4

The Skippers

Among 50 men who have held the occasionally triumphant but far more often trying and thankless job of Cub manager, Albert G. Spalding was not only the first, in 1876, but in the wider view of the world, the most successful. He not only was never fired but also became the chief owner of the team.

Among his many successors as field pilots of the team that at first was named the Chicago White Stockings and subsequently became the Colts, Orphans, and permanently the Cubs, there have been a few who are comparably famous in baseball history but many whose tenures were as unmemorable as they were brief.

Among the most notable skippers have been Cap Anson, Frank Chance, Joe McCarthy, Rogers Hornsby, Charlie Grimm, Gabby Hartnett, Frankie Frisch, Lou Boudreau, and Leo Durocher. Some, like Anson, Chance, Hornsby, Hartnett, Frisch, and Boudreau, rank among the greatest players in the game's history. Others, like McCarthy and Durocher, were among the most successful and colorful of all managers and had notable careers apart from leading the Cubs.

No successor has been as versatile in several fields as Spalding, who in youth was probably the greatest pitcher of his time and after a brief period as the first manager of the White Stockings became owner of the team as well as the founder of one of the great sporting goods businesses in the United States.

Some managed the Cubs more than once. Grimm took the helm three times between 1932 and 1960 and Johnny Evers of Tinkers-to-Evers-to-Chance fame managed the Cubs in 1913, was fired, then was brought back for the 1921 season.

A few had been star players with the Cubs. Among that group were Spalding, Anson, Chance, Evers, Hornsby, Grimm, Hartnett, Phil Cavarretta, and Stan Hack.

Though the average length of tenure of a Cub manager is less than 2.5 years, a few have lasted far longer. Anson was in the driver's seat for 19 seasons; Grimm in his three terms was in charge a total of almost 12 seasons; Chance called the shots for almost eight campaigns; and Durocher lasted more than six years.

Some of the 50 even were successful in leading the Cubs to National League pennants, though none who managed after 1945 can make that claim. Anson won five pennants, Chance four, and Grimm three. Spalding, Fred Mitchell, McCarthy, and Hartnett each finished on top once. Chance was the only one to lead the Cubs to a World Series victory, in 1907 and 1908.

Since the institution of divisional play in 1969, no Cub manager has won a National League pennant, though Jim Frey gained a divisional title in 1984, as did Don Zimmer in 1989.

No manager in the game's history during a tenure of more than five years with one team has been as successful in winning percentages as Chance in more than seven seasons with the Cubs (1905–12). His teams won not only four pennants but virtually two-thirds of their games for a winning percentage of .664.

On the other hand, among those who managed the Cubs more than one season, Joey Amalfitano recorded the lowest percentage, .363 in 1979, 1980, and 1981.

Additionally, the Cubs are the only team in major league history to compete without an official "manager," which they did from 1961 through 1962 when they were led by rotating "head coaches." The experiment, ostensibly continuing through 1965, in reality was abandoned after the first two years. (For our purposes, the "head coaches" are here ranked as managers during the periods when they called the shots for the team.)

Frank Chance, the Peerless Leader, the most successful of all Cub managers. His teams won four pennants and two World Series in a five-year sequence. (George Brace photo)

1876–77

Albert G. Spalding

Record: 78–47 (.624)
B: September 2, 1850, Byron, Illinois
D: September 9, 1915, San Diego, California

Spalding, Albert G.

	W	L	T	Pct
1876	52	14	0	.788
1877	26	33	1	.441
White Stockings	78	47	1	.624
Career	78	47	1	.624

If there ever was a "universal man" in Cubs history, it was Spalding, who in his early twenties became a great pitcher, won a pennant in his first year as manager in 1876, and went on to become the principal owner of the team in his early thirties while at the same time making a fortune in the sporting goods business. In his later years he even became a candidate (unsuccessful) for the United States Senate from California.

Spalding was fortunate in that his mentor as a young professional was Harry Wright, a onetime English cricketeer. Wright was the pivotal figure in the founding in 1871 of the National Association of Professional Base Ball Players (NA), the first avowedly professional league. Wright was a part owner of the Boston franchise and also the team's manager. He was a pioneer in defining the manager's role, though it was quite different from what it was to become as baseball developed.

Wright had become baseball's first manager, as we now understand the term, in 1869, turning the Cincinnati Red Stockings into the first truly professional baseball team, with every player under contract for a full season. It was a revolutionary concept for the time, because up to then teams had been made up of a mixture of amateurs and thinly disguised professionals. The Red Stockings, traveling coast to coast and playing all comers, went almost unbeatable during the 1869 and 1870 seasons, winning 65 consecutive games during one stretch.

Among Wright's contributions to the game was the notion of using players in positions adapted to their skills in the field, which he based on his experience in cricket. He put his best fielders at shortstop and second base because most batters were right-handed and would hit the ball to the left side of the middle of the infield. He constantly tinkered with and adjusted his team, basing his changes on the situations and the players' skills.

Wright also was a stickler for discipline and training, determined to make the oft-unruly players of that day toe the line on and off the field. He understood the manager's role to include making the tactical and strategic decisions of the game as a virtual "dictator," reducing the role of team captain that had been so prominent prior to his advent.

When the Cincinnati club was disbanded after the 1870 season, Wright was lured to Boston by a group of businessmen as player-manager with a share of team ownership and the mandate to spearhead the formation of an all-professional league, the NA.

When Wright signed Spalding, only 20 years old, to a Red Stockings contract for an annual salary of $1,500 before the 1871 season, he was confident he was acquiring one of the promising young pitchers in the game. It is doubtful if he realized that he was also launching one of the most spectacular careers baseball ever has seen.

Spalding certainly more than realized Wright's hopes for him as a player, quickly established himself as the premier pitcher in the league and leading the Red Stockings to four consecutive league championships between 1872 and 1875.

Even more significantly for his future, Spalding impressed Wright with his intelligence and levelheadedness for one so young. In 1874, Wright sent him to England as an "advance man" to set up a tour by the Red Stockings. In July and August 1874 the Red Stockings crossed the Atlantic to play a series of baseball exhibition games and cricket matches against English clubs in the first overseas tour of a baseball team, something Spalding was to emulate with his Chicago club almost 15 years later with a trip around the world.

Spalding also proved an apt pupil in learning the manager's role, which in those days often included arranging schedules, scouting and signing players to contracts, handling the annual club budget, and even making travel arrangements, as well as the conduct of games and the training and disciplining of players. Wright, as Spalding was to become, had to be a master of all trades connected with baseball, a manager's role in the early days not being chiefly to "bring the best" out of the players he was given as eventually became the case when club presidents and later general managers took over.

The Red Stockings continued their success, with a record of 71–8 in 1875, Spalding contributing 56 victories as a pitcher, but the NA was falling apart, beset by scandals and financial crises as well as Boston's overwhelming success. The decisive blow to the league came on July 24, 1875 when it was disclosed that Spalding and three other star players were deserting the Red Sox for the Chicago franchise, whose chief owner was William Hulbert, a wealthy businessman. Hulbert signed Spalding to a contract for 1876 calling for $2,000 and the promise of 25 percent of the gate receipts as manager-captain and star pitcher of the White Stockings.

Hulbert made Spalding his chief lieutenant in his ambition to organize a new structure for professional baseball, the National League of Professional Base Ball Clubs, later known simply as the National League (NL). The two worked closely together in the formation of the new league, with Spalding entrusted to write much of the correspondence, arrange meetings, and help draw up the league's constitution and bylaws in addition to his managerial tasks, which included scheduling games and acquiring and signing players.

Hulbert and Spalding had assembled a powerhouse by the opening of the NL's inaugural season, and the Chicago White Stockings (an entirely new entity with no link to the former NAPBBP franchise) easily swept to a championship. As a pitcher, Spalding contributed a 47–13 record to the team's overall 52–14 mark. He also batted .312 as part of a lineup that included second baseman Ross Barnes, who led the league with .403, shortstop Johnny Peters at .351, first baseman Cal McVey at .347, and third baseman Cap Anson, who batted .309.

Spalding's leadership as manager was duly noted in the press, the *Chicago Evening Journal* commenting that "every man on the club has shown himself to be a gentleman as well as a ball player, and there never has been a breath of suspicion against them. They have made friends in and out of the profession, and are a credit to the city of their adoption."

Such kudos, while gratifying, did not disguise the fact that Spalding's chief asset as a manager was his ability as a pitcher. That fact became painfully apparent in 1877 when he injured his arm early in the season, limiting him to four starts, and moved himself to first base. The team staggered to a fifth-place finish. A pack of critics volubly suggested that he had spread himself too thin and was responsible for the team's failure.

Henry Chadwick wrote in the *New York Clipper* that Spalding had "too many irons in the fire and in his attempt to captain the nine, to run the general business of the club, and at the same time to manage his own baseball business and store, he undertook more than any one man could properly attend to, and the result was a measureable [*sic*], failure."

Spalding took the criticism to heart, realizing its validity, and with Hulbert's acquiescence ended his careers as pitcher and manager, turning over the team for 1878 to Bob Ferguson, who had managed the Hartford team for two seasons before it had dropped out of the NL after the 1877 campaign.

Spalding's managerial career had been brief but significant, not only because he had led the White Stockings to a pennant, something most of his successors failed to accomplish, but also because he had set the pattern for the job. Not the least important of his contributions was the realization that baseball had reached a point at which the field and "front office" elements of the game had to be separated.

And, unlike that of most managers, his fortunes were still on the rise.

1878

Bob Ferguson

Record: 30–30 (.500)
B: January 31, 1845, Brooklyn, New York
D: May 3, 1894, Brooklyn, New York

Bob Ferguson

Ferguson, Robert

	W	L	T	Pct
1878	30	30	1	.500
White Stockings	30	30	1	.500
Career	299	373	10	.445

Among the most respected players of the game's early days, in an era when many players were raucously unrespectable, was Bob Ferguson, whom Spalding chose as his successor for the 1878 season.

Ferguson was so highly regarded for his character that he had served two terms as president of the recently defunct NAPBBP, a largely honorary position. A shortstop, he had been the playing manager of several teams, the New York Mutuals, the Brooklyn Atlantics, and the Hartfords. As captain and manager of his teams, it was said of Ferguson that he would "insist upon implicit obedience from his men." His players, it was reported, "went about their business quietly."

At 33 when he took over the White Stockings, Ferguson was in the middle of a solid career as a middle infielder. His fielding skill had earned him the nickname "Death to Flying Things" (though he made 88 errors in 86 games in one season) and he compiled a career batting average of .271 in nine seasons as a player.

Ferguson took over a team decimated by the departures of Cal McVey and Johnny Peters, the decline of Ross Barnes and others, and most tellingly the absence of Al Spalding from the mound. He moved Cap Anson to left field, played shortstop himself (batting .351, by far the highest average of his career), and led the White Stockings to a fourth-place finish. It wasn't good enough for Spalding and owner William Hulbert, and Ferguson was out of a job.

But not for long. He managed Troy (New York) for the next four years, then the Philadelphia Phillies for part of the 1883 season. In 1884 he showed up in the American Association, then a major league, as manager of the Pittsburgh Alleghenies before finishing his career with two years as skipper of the AA's New York Metropolitans.

Ferguson played an important role in defining the manager's authority and in developing the tactics of the early game. But he was only moderately successful on the field, none of his teams finishing above third place in 11 years as manager.

He completed his baseball career as an umpire.

1879

Frank "Old Silver" Flint

Record: 5–12 (.294)
B: August 3, 1855, Philadelphia, Pennsylvania
D: January 14, 1892, Chicago, Illinois

Flint, Frank "Old Silver"				
	W	L	T	Pct
1879	5	12	2	.294
White Stockings	5	12	2	.294
Career	5	12	2	.294

When Spalding moved to Chicago after the 1875 season, he made a point of acquiring one of the game's most promising young hitters, Adrian "Cap" Anson, who had made a name for himself in four years at Philadelphia. He chose Anson, then 26, as Ferguson's successor for 1879. Anson was to keep the job for 19 seasons, the longest tenure by far of any Cub manager and one of the longest tenures in baseball history.

But Anson's rule wasn't uninterrupted. For a brief period in 1879 he stepped aside and turned the manager's job to Frank Flint, the tough young catcher whom Spalding had signed after his former team, Indianapolis, had folded after the 1878 season.

Flint was one of the premier catchers of the game's early days, allegedly the first to station himself right behind the batter and catch the ball on the fly while others preferred to take it on the bounce. He refused to wear a glove, consider-

ing it demeaning to his manhood. He was a great handler of pitchers, and caught some of the best during his 11 seasons with the White Stockings, among them Larry Corcoran, Fred Goldsmith, and John Clarkson.

Yet at this distant remove he seems a curious choice even as an interim manager. He was a hard drinker, once fined $50 by Spalding for "dissipation" that allegedly had lessened his "skill." On another occasion, Spalding warned Flint to pay a long overdue debt or be fired.

All the same, Anson entrusted the team to Flint for 19 games for the tail end of the 1879 season. The White Stockings were in fourth place at the time and under Flint's direction won only 5 of 19 games, losing 12 and tying two. It made no difference, the team hanging onto fourth place. Flint remained with the White Stockings for another 11 years as a catcher and never managed again.

1879–97

Adrian "Cap" Anson

Record: 1,283–932 (.579)
B: April 11, 1852, Marshalltown, Iowa
D: April 14, 1922, Chicago, Illinois

Anson, Adrian C. "Cap"				
	W	L	T	Pct
1879	41	21	2	.661
1880	67	17	2	.798
1881	56	28	0	.667
1882	55	29	0	.655
1883	59	39	0	.602
1884	62	50	1	.554
1885	87	25	1	.777
1886	90	34	2	.726
1887	71	50	3	.587
1888	77	58	1	.570
1889	67	65	5	.508
1890	84	53	2	.613
1891	82	53	2	.607
1892	70	76	1	.479
1893	56	71	1	.441
1894	57	75	3	.432
1895	72	58	3	.554
1896	71	57	4	.555
1897	59	73	6	.447
White Stockings	1,283	932	38	.579
Career	1,292	945	38	.578

Adrian "Cap" Anson's plaque in the Baseball Hall of Fame at Cooperstown, New York, is inscribed: "Greatest Hitter and Greatest Player-Manager of the Nineteenth Century." Strong evidence can be presented to back the validity of this judgment.

During his 22 seasons as a player, mostly as a first baseman, Anson compiled a .329 batting average, won three NL batting championships, became the first man to accumulate 3,000 hits, and was the first to hit three consecutive home runs in one game and five consecutive home runs in two games. For 20 seasons he hit .300 or over.

A powerfully built, right-handed batter, standing 6–1 and weighing 220 pounds, Anson was the prototypical first base-

Frank "Old Silver" Flint

Cap Anson died in 1922, three days after his 70th birthday (the birth date on the stone is incorrect), and was buried in Chicago's Oakwood Cemetery. The National League contributed funds for the monument.

man, the position he switched to in 1879 because he said he would be better able to manage from that perspective.

Born in Marshalltown, Iowa, a town reportedly founded by his father, Anson briefly attended Notre Dame University, captaining the baseball team. At age 20 he dropped out of college to turn pro, then established himself as a star player at Philadelphia before Spalding lured him to Chicago for the 1876 season. Three years later, at 27, Anson began his long managerial reign.

His formula for managerial success was simply stated: "Round up the strongest men who can knock a baseball the farthest the most often, put yourself on first base and win." In his early years as manager, the formula worked superbly, the White Stockings winning five pennants in the first eight years of his reign.

An all-around athlete, who excelled in billiards, golf, and bowling and was a crack shot with both pistol and rifle, Anson was a stickler for staying in condition, demanding the same from his players. A heavy drinker in his early 20s, he became a teetotaler, frowned on those who let drink impair their skill, and condemned "the curse of liquor." He was a pioneer advocate of healthful diets, abstaining from fried food, starches, and rich desserts.

He instituted daily physical training sessions, required his players to dress appropriately off the field, enforced his demands with his fists if necessary, and kept them on a generally tight rein. He attempted to elevate their social status by demanding that the management house them at the best hotels on the road and that they reciprocate by wearing formal garments for dinner. A stickler for hard work, he would not tolerate laziness and kicked slackers off the team.

A born showman, Anson often took the White Stockings on exhibition tours to small towns and villages, transporting them in handsome open carriages drawn by white horses, the players clad in white-bosomed shirts and dark dress suits.

Eminently self-confident, even cocky at times, the aggressive Anson tolerated no backchat from his players, umpires, and even his bosses. In one notable incident, after the White Stockings lost a game, Spalding confronted Anson to second-guess his strategy. Anson responded with a string of obscenities, and Spalding allegedly never questioned his manager again.

Umpires were the most frequent objects of his wrath. "That ain't no shadow," a fan commented when Anson's huge figure was outlined by the sun on the playing field as he protested an umpire's decision. "That's an argument. Everywhere Cap goes, the argument goes."

Anson was also an innovator, instituting the first "pitching rotation" by using the two pitchers on a regular basis instead of one, as had been the case. He was one of the early advocates of "spring training," taking the White Stockings to Hot Springs, Arkansas, in March 1886 to "boil out their fat." He reportedly was the first manager to coordinate infield and outfield play and the first to coach from the baselines. He was a proponent of a rudimentary form of "inside baseball," though he eschewed the sacrifice bunt, preferring base stealing and the hit-and-run.

The greatest blot on Anson's subsequent reputation has been his well-attested racial bigotry. He was directly responsible—though supported by many of like mind—for driving out and barring black players from organized baseball in the 1880s. His refusal to play even exhibition games against teams that had blacks on their rosters helped erect the barriers that did not break down until the arrival of Jackie Robinson in the mid-1940s.

When Anson took over as manager, he was enabled to make his formula of rounding up "the strongest men" work with the cooperation of Spalding, who rebuilt the White Stockings into a powerhouse, acquiring Ned Williamson, George Gore, Abner Dalrymple, and Frank Flint in 1879. The next year, two great pitchers, Larry Corcoran and Fred Goldsmith, came aboard, as well as Mike "King" Kelly and Tommy Burns.

The legendary Kelly, who also backed up catcher Flint, has been labeled the Babe Ruth of the 19th century. With Gore and Wiliamson, Kelly formed the finest outfield of the time. Corcoran never won less than 27 games in each of the next five seasons, with a peak of 43 in 1880. Goldsmith was a 20-game winner for four consecutive years.

The White Stockings captured three consecutive pennants, 1880–82. In '80 they won 21 consecutive games, a feat unsurpassed for 36 years, until the 1916 New York Giants had a string of 26. The team's winning percentage of .798 in '80, on a record of 67–17, never has been matched.

In '83 and '84, Anson's team faded, but fresh blood, particularly another great pitcher, John Clarkson, and the swift Billy Sunday, who later became world famous as an evangelist, restored the White Stockings to the top as they again won pennants in '85 and '86. Clarkson was 53–16 in '85 and 35–17 in '86.

Anson sparkled both as hitter and manager while the White Stockings won five pennants in seven years, leading the league in batting three times. Gore led the league with .360 in '80, and Kelly was the top hitter with .354 in '84 and .388 in '86. Williamson's 27 home runs in '84, though tainted by the short distance to the outfield wall, stood as a record until Babe Ruth hit 29 in 1919.

The '86 season marked the zenith of Anson's managerial career. The White Stockings began to fade, and he was unable to win another pennant in his remaining 11 years at the helm. Kelly and Gore were gone after the '86 campaign, Clarkson after the '87 season.

Gore was sold to New York despite his vociferous objections. When Anson told him he would have to leave Chicago, Gore burst out, "I'll go if I have to, but if I do I promise you'll never win another pennant." He was right.

Kelly was sold to Boston for $10,000, the most ever paid in a player transaction to that time. He had no objections as the Red Stockings raised his salary to $5,000, almost double what the White Stockings had paid him.

Anson was able to keep the White Stockings respectable for several more years, despite pitching problems and an infusion of new players who fell short of expectations. In '89, despite the defection of several stars to the newly formed Brotherhood, or Players League, his team finished second with a cast of over-the-hill, minor league, and sandlot players. They received the label of "Anson's orphans," quickly transmuted to the new nickname, Orphans, replacing White Stockings.

The Players League collapsed after one season, 1890, and many of the stars returned to their former teams. But Anson's problems were compounding when Spalding stepped down as team president after the '91 season and James Hart took his place. Anson and Hart couldn't get along, the manager charging that his new boss was tightfisted, was unwilling to approve good trades, and undermined his authority with the players. When club officials asked him to contribute to a gift of diamond cuff links for Hart, Anson snapped, "Why should I? Why should Hart get a gift like that? I'm doing the main work around here."

Anson struggled on with new, young players, among them such future stars as Clark Griffith, Bill Dahlen, and Bill Lange, joining the team, which now briefly was known as Anson's Colts because of its overall youth. After a second-place finish in 1891,

the Colts slid to seventh the next year, and never finished higher until after Anson's ouster following the '97 season.

At the same time, Anson's great days as a player were over. He was 40 in 1892, and his average dropped to .272. Amazingly, he bounced back to bat over .300 the next four seasons, with a high of .395 in 83 games in 1894, but he had slowed down and now significantly was called Pop rather than Cap. As his team languished, the critics ganged up, calling him too old to play and behind the times as a manager.

He responded to form, wearing a gray beard and a white wig for one game, then smashing three hits. He denounced his players, as well as Hart, cajoling sportswriter Hugh Fullerton of Chicago's *Inter-Ocean* to lead off his column with the following:

"Captain A. C. Anson desires me to announce, in black type, at the head of this column, that the Chicago Baseball Club is composed of a bunch of drunkards and loafers who are throwing him down."

It was too much for the new principal owner of the team, John Walsh, who declared, "That damn old Swede's contract is up. He's through."

Anson replied, "Hell, Swede. I'm English and Irish."

After the Colts finished ninth in 1897, Walsh and Hart saw their chance and on February 1, 1898, dumped the manager of 19 seasons. Anson tried to raise enough money to buy the team, but fell short and became manager of the Giants for 1898. This tenure, in which his team was 9–13, lasted only a few weeks because of friction with the owners. A brief term followed as chief of the NL umpires, before he turned to politics, winning election to the office of city clerk in Chicago.

Anson never returned to baseball, though he made several attempts to purchase franchises and had an offer from the new American League in 1900 to manage and be part owner of the Chicago franchise that was to become the White Sox.

"I won't insult my record of 22 big-league years by joining a minor league club," he said.

The rest of his life until his death at 70 in 1922, Anson was involved in a number of business ventures, many connected with sports, such as billiard parlors, bowling alleys, and golf courses. He even took a fling in vaudeville, building his act around his fame as a ballplayer.

His baseball legacy was the most pennants, five, of any Cubs manager, the most victories, 1,283, and a reputation as the greatest hitter of the 19th century. More notoriously, he is recalled as an unrepentant racist, who was directly responsible for keeping black players out of baseball for more than a half century.

1898–99

Tommy Burns

Record: 160–138 (.537)
B: March 30, 1857, Honesdale, Pennsylvania
D: March 19, 1902, Jersey City, New Jersey

Burns, Thomas E.

	W	L	T	Pct
1898	85	65	2	.567
1899	75	73	4	.507
Cubs	160	138	6	.537
Career	185	168	7	.524

Tommy Burns

J ames Hart's choice as Anson's successor was Tommy Burns, a steady if seldom spectacular infielder for a dozen seasons, from 1880 to 1891, for the team that he was taking over, which now was beginning to be called the Cubs.

Burns had broken in as a rookie under Anson in 1880, batting .309 and became an integral component of the "Stonewall Infield," first as a shortstop then as third baseman, for his five pennant winners. He compiled a career average of .264 before retiring as a player after the 1892 season, in part of which he had been player-manager at Pittsburgh.

Among his recommendations for the Cub managerial job had been his loyalty during the Players League raid; he had been one of only three of Anson's players who refused to defect. He was a teetotaler who also abstained from smoking, which helped make him a favorite of Anson's. As a player he had been a hustler who stole 44 bases one season, and he endeared himself to the fans with his aggressive play.

Burn's otherwise routine playing career did have one highlight, his part in a 26–6 White Stockings massacre of Detroit on September 6, 1883.

The White Stockings scored 18 runs in the bottom of the seventh inning, and Burns set six batting records, all of which still stand more than a century later. In the inning he had three hits, scored three runs, faced a pitcher three times, had three extra-base hits (two doubles and a home run), and accumulated eight total bases. None of these records has been surpassed though the only one that hasn't been tied is that of three extra-base hits in one inning.

In 1892, Burns left Chicago, signing with Pittsburgh as player-manager, but was dismissed 55 games into the season. He spent the next five seasons as a minor league manager before being called on to succeed Anson.

His first season at the helm was moderately successful, the Cubs finishing fourth in a 12-team league. Such veteran standouts as outfielders Jimmy Ryan, who batted .323, and Bill Lange, who hit .319, as well as pitchers Clark Griffith (24–10) and Nixey Callahan (20–10) made it seem as if the team was on the rise.

But in 1899 the Cubs and Burns fell on hard times, dropping to eighth despite a 75–73 record, and Hart decided to find a new manager.

Burns' subsequent career was brief. He managed a minor league team for part of the 1901 season. He died of a heart attack the next year.

1900–01

Tom Loftus

Record: 118–161 (.423)
B: November 15, 1856, St. Louis, Missouri
D: April 16, 1910, Dubuque, Iowa

Loftus, Thomas J.				
	W	**L**	**T**	**Pct**
1900	65	75	6	.464
1901	53	86	1	.381
Cubs	118	161	7	.423
Career	454	580	21	.439

F or Tommy Burns' successor, the Cubs turned to Tom Loftus, an experienced manager for several teams before he came to Chicago.

Loftus was somewhat of a new departure in that he was among the first managers who had little or no experience as a major league player. He played in a total of only nine games as an outfielder with St. Louis teams in the NL and American Association but soon hung up his glove to turn to managing in the major leagues and the minors.

His major league managerial experience began with the short-lived Milwaukee team of the Union Association in 1884. He managed Cleveland in the AA in '88 and Cleveland in the NL the next year, then Cincinnati of the NL the following two seasons before returning to the minor leagues, from where he was summoned by James Hart to the Cubs.

Loftus was unfortunate in that he arrived in Chicago at the same time as did the new American League, which soon began to raid the NL of its star players. Among the Cubs defectors were the heart of the pitching staff, Nixey Callahan and Clark Griffith, the latter of whom in 1901 became manager of the crosstown White Sox and pitched and led them to the first AL pennant as a major league.

The Cubs were hit hard, and so was Loftus. He guided them to fifth place in 1900, and they dropped a notch in 1901 before he was fired.

Tom Loftus

He managed Washington of the AL the next two years before dropping out of the major leagues for good.

1902–05

Frank Selee

Record: 280–223 (.557)
B: October 26, 1859, Amherst, New Hampshire
D: July 5, 1909, Denver, Colorado

Selee, Frank G.

1902	68	69	4	.496
1903	82	56	1	.594
1904	93	60	3	.608
1905	37	28	0	.569
Cubs	280	223	8	.557
Career	1,284	862	30	.598

An adverse fate has unjustly obscured the remarkable qualities of James Hart's choice as the new manager. Frank Selee had never played in the major leagues, but he had devel-

Frank Selee

oped a reputation for being one of the shrewdest judges of talent in the game.

By the time he came to the Cubs, Selee had managed 12 years in the big leagues, his Boston Beaneaters (later Braves) winning five pennants in the '90s with such stars as Bobby Lowe, Jimmy Collins, Hugh Duffy, and Herman Long. Hart counted on him to develop the Cubs into a contender, and he did, molding one of the greatest teams of all time.

Selee began by switching a backup catcher, Frank Chance, to first base. In less than four seasons he also put young Joe Tinker at shortstop, purchased Johnny Evers to play second base, gave Johnny Kling the catcher's job, and brought in—among others—outfielders Jimmy Slagle and Frank Schulte, and pitchers Jack Taylor, Carl Lundgren, Jake Weimer, Bob Wicker, Ed Reulbach, and Mordecai "Three-Finger" Brown.

As the Cubs began to shape up, they jumped from fifth place in 1902 to third place in 1903, their best finish in 12 years, then to second place in 1904. The team also played well in 1905, and was under new ownership, James Hart selling out to Charles W. Murphy. But stricken by tuberculosis, Selee resigned in midseason to be replaced by Chance, who guided the team to third place.

The "Tinkers-to-Evers-to-Chance" Cubs were in place, and were to go on to four pennants in the next five seasons, but Selee, who had laid the foundations of the team, had no part in its glory. He died in 1909.

1905–12

Frank Chance

Record: 768–389 (.664)
B: September 9, 1877, Fresno, California
D: September 15, 1924, Los Angeles, California

Chance, Frank L.				
	W	L	T	Pct
1905	55	33	2	.625
1906	116	36	3	.763
1907	107	45	3	.704
1908	99	55	4	.643
1909	104	49	2	.680
1910	104	50	0	.675
1911	92	62	3	.597
1912	91	59	2	.607
Cubs	768	389	19	.664
Career	946	648	26	.593

Frank Chance

In one of the more unusual methods of choosing a manager, management left it up to the players to name Selee's successor. Chance, only 27, won the election, getting 11 votes to four for Selee's choice, third baseman Doc Casey. Johnny Kling got two votes.

Chance was nicknamed Husk because of his imposing physique. He was bullnecked and broad-shouldered, a six-foot 200-pounder who used his strength to impose his will with his fists, if necessary. His dictum to his players: "You do things my way, or you meet me after the game."

Onetime heavyweight champion Gentleman Jim Corbett called him "the greatest amateur brawler in the world." In one notable fight, Chance leveled New York Giants pitcher Iron Man McGinnity, precipitating a riot on the playing field. In a 1907 incident at Brooklyn, when fans hurled pop bottles at him, Chance flung them back into the stands. He had to be protected by a police escort when he left the ballpark.

Oddly, he was no tough from the slums, but the well-educated son of a bank president. In addition, he was a charismatic leader, a fine judge of talent, and a sound tactician. Selee had laid the foundations and Chance completed the structure of a great team. A series of trades brought third baseman Harry Steinfeldt to round out a memorable infield, Jimmy Sheckard for the outfield, and right-hander Orval Overall and left-hander Jack Pfiester to solidify the pitching staff.

The Cubs were ready for the most successful period of their history, and in 1906 astonished the baseball world by winning a record 116 games while losing only 36 to finish 20 games ahead of the second-place New York Giants. Chance led not only as a manager but also by example, topping the league in stolen bases with 57 while batting .319. Newcomer Steinfeldt batted .327 and led the league in RBIs and hits. Mordecai Brown was 26–6 with a league-leading and record 1.04 ERA. Pfiester and Ed Reulbach also won 20 games.

No team has dominated its league as the Cubs did in 1906, but overconfidence might have done them in as they fell in the World Series to the slightly regarded crosstown rival White Sox, the "Hitless Wonders."

Nevertheless, they shook off the humiliation to capture the pennant again in 1907, this time winning 107 games with largely the same cast. They made it three straight in 1908, with 99 victories. They also won the World Series in 1907 and 1908, both times over the Detroit Tigers. Despite winning 104 games, they slipped to second place in 1909 before again winning the pennant in 1910 with the same total, though they lost the World Series to Philadelphia Athletics.

Despite the outstanding feats of his players, much of the credit for such overwhelming success went to Chance, who became known as the Peerless Leader. John McGraw, his bitter rival as manager of the Giants, had no doubts about Chance's abilities. "Frank Chance was a great baseball manager," McGraw said. "He could fight on the field and forget his enemies afterward. He was a great leader. He asked no man to take any chance he would not take himself. He had the power to instill enthusiasm even in a losing cause."

The ownership was so impressed with Chance in 1906 that it gave him the opportunity to purchase a 10 percent share of the team. When he left after the 1912 season, he was able to cash in on his investment of $10,000 for a $130,000 profit.

His aggressiveness as both player and manager was proverbial. He defied the pitchers as a batter by leaning over the plate and was hit five times by pitches in one doubleheader. He was beaned 37 times in his career and was plagued by hearing loss and headaches. Other injuries, including a broken shoulder in 1909, took their toll, and by 1911 he was virtually a bench manager.

At 34, his greatest days were behind him, as were those of the Cubs, though they won 92 games in 1911 and 91 in 1912, finishing second and third, respectively. By that time Chance long had been feuding with the management, even leaving his post briefly. Charles W. Murphy fired him on September 28, 1912, while Chance was recuperating from brain surgery for a blood clot ostensibly caused by being hit by so many pitches. Murphy contended that Chance had resigned, but the Peerless Leader cleared the air with an angry parting blast, claiming Murphy was interested solely in milking the team for profit.

"In all the years I have been with this club," Chance said, "I have had to fight to get the players I wanted. Murphy has not spent one-third as much for players as have other magnates. How can he expect to win championships without players?"

Chance went on to manage the New York Yankees the next two seasons, at an unheard-of salary of $40,000 a year. He later became owner-manager of the Los Angeles franchise in the Pacific Coast League before one last fling in the major leagues as manager of the Boston Red Sox in 1923. He died a year later, only 47, of tuberculosis just as he was about to accept a job as manager of the White Sox.

His record as Cub manager is unparalled, with four pennants and two World Series championships in his first five full years. During that stretch, his teams won 530 games, an average of 106 per season, while losing 235, an average of 47. The Cub W-L percentage from 1906 through 1910 was .693. Overall, during his almost eight-year tenure, the Cubs were 768–389 for a percentage of .664.

Johnny Evers

1913, 1921

Johnny Evers

Record: 129–120 (.518)
B: July 21, 1883, Troy, New York
D: March 28, 1947, Albany, New York

Evers, John J.

	W	L	T	Pct
1913	88	65	2	.575
1921	41	55	0	.427
Cubs	129	120	2	.518
Career	180	192	3	.484

Charles W. Murphy turned to veteran star second baseman Johnny Evers as player-manager partly in order to dampen the public relations damage caused by his dismissal of the popular Frank Chance.

An intense, nervous man, "Crab" Evers had earned a reputation for brawling, most notably in an on-the-field fight with shortstop Joe Tinker in 1905 that resulted in them not speaking to each other for the rest of their playing careers. A standout fielder in his earlier days, he had been a spark plug of the championship teams, contributing 49 stolen bases in 1906 and 46 the next year, and his .300 batting average led the club in 1908.

He sat out the 1910 World Series with a broken leg and missed most of the 1911 season with a nervous breakdown,

but had his finest offensive season in 1912, batting .341 in 143 games.

In 1913 he took over a team decimated by trades Murphy had made to cut the payroll. Gone were such veterans as Three-Finger Brown, Ed Reulbach, and Joe Tinker. Nevertheless, Evers led the Cubs to third place. He demanded a raise on his four-year contract, which already called for $10,000 per season, at the same time as he was negotiating with the newly formed Federal League (FL) to manage one of its teams.

Murphy saw an excuse to relieve himself of Evers' expensive contract and fired him. But the other NL owners, fearful of losing Evers to the FL, which already had captured several of its stars, including Tinker, demanded Murphy honor Evers' contract. Murphy's response was to trade Evers to the Boston Braves. The NL reacted by forcing Murphy to sell his 53 percent share of the Cubs to a partner, Charles Taft of Cincinnati. Evers was declared a free agent and signed with the Braves, whom in 1914 he led to the NL pennant, winning a Chalmers automobile as the league's Most Valuable Player.

After Evers' playing career wound down in 1917, he was resurrected to manage the Cubs again in 1921, but was fired when the team was in sixth place with a 41–55 record.

Evers' last managerial chance came in 1924 with the White Sox, who oddly enough had been counting on Chance to manage them. But Chance was mortally ill, and Evers got the job. He also became ill and after a 10–11 start stepped aside for a time, then resumed the post for a further 41–61 record before quitting for good. He never managed again.

1914

Hank O'Day

Record: 78–76 (.506)
B: July 8, 1862, Chicago, Illinois
D: July 2, 1935, Chicago, Illinois

O'Day, Henry F.				
	W	L	T	Pct
1914	78	76	2	.506
Cubs	78	76	2	.506
Career	153	154	4	.498

Hank "Peep" O'Day is among the rare instances of a career umpire being named manager. He interspersed a 35-year run as a major league umpire with one-year managerial stints at Cincinnati in 1912 and the Cubs in 1914.

A former big-league pitcher, O'Day became an umpire in 1891. His most lasting fame came from the decision to declare the Fred "Bonehead" Merkle game between the Cubs and Giants a draw, forcing a playoff for the pennant at the end of the 1908 season.

After managing Cincinnati in 1912, O'Day returned to umpiring before the Cubs named him to succeed Evers. He took over a decent team, with pitchers Fred "Hippo" Vaughn (21–13) and Larry Cheney (20–18), as well as third baseman Heinie Zimmerman, catcher Roger Bresnahan, and outfielder Frank Schulte, but they weren't enough. The Cubs finished 78–76 and in fourth place, and O'Day resumed his umpiring career until his retirement in 1927.

Hank O'Day, the umpire who called the Merkle play, managed the Cubs for one season. (George Brace photo)

1915

Roger Bresnahan

Record: 73–80 (.477)
B: June 11, 1879, Toledo, Ohio
D: December 4, 1944, Toledo, Ohio

Bresnahan, Roger P.				
	W	L	T	Pct
1915	73	80	3	.477
Cubs	73	80	3	.477
Career	328	432	14	.432

Considered the premier catcher of his era, Roger Bresnahan, "The Duke of Tralee," had managed the St. Louis Cardinals for four seasons (1909–12) with indifferent results before he was signed as a player by the Cubs for the 1913 season. He was at the tail end of a career in which he had been the battery mate of Christy Mathewson and other great pitchers for John McGraw's New York Giants in the first decade of the century.

In 1915 the Cubs signed Bresnahan, who had been sharing the catcher's duties with Jimmy Archer, to a three-year contract as player-manager. He took over a mediocre team beset by a range of troubles, including defections to the "outlaw" Federal League and lack of pitching depth and hitting

Roger Bresnahan

punch. The Cubs were locked in a three-way battle for fan support with the White Sox and the Federal League Chicago Whales, managed by Joe Tinker and owned by the flamboyant Charles Weeghman, with his new ballpark at Addison and Clark.

Bresnahan's Cubs floundered to fourth place in the team's last stand at old West Side Park. His three-year contract couldn't save him when the Federal League and the older leagues made a deal. The Federal League disappeared, and Weeghman and a consortium of partners were permitted to buy the Cubs. Tinker was to manage the team. One of the new minority owners was William Wrigley, Jr., the chewing gum magnate.

Weeghman bought out Bresnahan's contract, and with the proceeds Bresnahan was able to buy a minor league team. He later became a coach with the Giants and Detroit Tigers.

1916

Joe Tinker

Record: 67–86 (.438)
B: July 27, 1880, Muscotah, Kansas
D: July 27, 1948, Orlando, Florida

Tinker, Joseph B.

	W	L	T	Pct
1916	67	86	3	.438
Cubs	67	86	3	.438
Career	304	308	12	.497

Outgoing, good-natured Joe Tinker, who owned a saloon in Chicago, was an extreme contrast to Johnny Evers, his hated double-play partner of the Cub glory days, though he, too, had a reputation as a brawler. A fine-fielding shortstop, he had been a light hitter but had been a key ingredient in the team's four pennant-winning years.

He began his managerial career in 1913 with the Cincinnati Reds, then jumped to the Federal League, where he led the Chicago Whalers to second place in 1914 and a pennant in 1915, the only two years of the league's existence. He seemed a natural fit as manager when the Cubs moved to Weeghman Field (renamed Cubs Park and eventually to become Wrigley Field) for the 1916 season.

He inherited a poor team from Roger Bresnahan, and it didn't get any better as the Cubs finished fifth in 1916. Among the few bright spots were pitcher Hippo Vaughn (17–15), third baseman Heinie Zimmerman, and center fielder Cy Williams, who led the NL in home runs with 12. Tinker's playing days were near an end; he appeared in only seven games.

His major league managerial career also came to an end after the season when he was fired. He eventually settled down in Orlando, Florida, where he kept up his baseball interests as owner and manager of a team and where a ballpark is named after him.

Joe Tinker

1917–20

Fred Mitchell

Record: 308–269 (.534)
B: June 5, 1878, Cambridge, Massachusetts
D: October 13, 1970, Newton, Massachusetts

Mitchell, Frederick F.

	W	L	T	Pct
1917	74	80	3	.481
1918	84	45	2	.651
1919	75	65	0	.536
1920	75	79	0	.487
Cubs	308	269	5	.534
Career	494	543	7	.476

An undistinguished career as a utility player preceded Fred Mitchell's four-year tenure as Cubs manager, but he was to gain fame as the longtime baseball coach at Harvard University after he left Chicago. Mitchell was his baseball pseudonym. His real name was Frederick Yapp.

Charles Weeghman hired Mitchell because he had been highly regarded as a coach with the "Miracle" Boston Braves

Fred Mitchell (George Brace photo)

of 1914 and had a solid reputation as a strategist and a gentlemanly, soft-spoken man. Mitchell had a difficult task because of players going into the armed services as the United States entered World War I, and also because of renewed eruptions of the gambling problems that had plagued the game from its inception.

The highlight of Mitchell's first season, 1917, was the double no-hit, no-run game that Hippo Vaughn of the Cubs and Fred Toney of Cincinnati pitched through nine innings on May 2, with the Reds winning 1–0 as Toney held the Cubs hitless through 10 innings. The team, however, finished fifth.

The next year, with the war taking its toll of personnel, Mitchell brought the Cubs home in first place in a shortened season that ended on Labor Day, perhaps because they had fewer players fit for military duty, as was to be the case 27 years later in 1945. Vaughn (22–10) and rookie shortstop Charlie Hollocher, who led the team with a .316 average, were the standouts in the Cubs' first championship since 1910.

The Cubs lost the World Series, with the Chicago end being played in Comiskey Park, in six games to the Boston Red Sox and their star pitcher, Babe Ruth.

Weeghman savored his first NL pennant, but financial difficulties forced him to sell his majority share to William Wrigley, Jr., during the winter. Wrigley not only retained Mitchell as manager but also named him team president before the NL pointed out that such a dual role was a violation of league rules. Wrigley then named William Veeck, a Chicago sportswriter, team president.

Mitchell guided the Cubs to third place in 1919 and fifth in 1920 during a troubled period in which two of his pitchers, Paul Douglas and Claude Hendrix, were accused of conspiring with gamblers to throw games. It was the time of the Black Sox scandal, which came to a head in 1920, and corruption and "fixes" seemed rife.

Veeck fired Mitchell after the 1920 season, and for the

next three years Mitchell managed the Boston Braves before becoming coach at Harvard until 1939. He died at the age of 92 in 1970.

1921–25

Bill Killefer

Record: 300–293 (.506)
B: October 10, 1887, Bloomingdale, Michigan
D: July 3, 1960, Elmsmere, Delaware

Killefer, William L.

	W	L	T	Pct
1921	23	34	0	.404
1922	80	74	2	.519
1923	83	71	0	.539
1924	81	72	0	.529
1925	33	42	0	.440
Cubs	300	293	2	.506
Career	524	622	2	.457

Perhaps in hopes of recapturing the spirit of the Frank Chance teams, William Veeck named Johnny Evers to a second term as manager. It didn't work, Evers being unable to lift the team above .500, and he departed because of illness on August 21, 1921, Bill Killefer taking over with the Cubs 41–55 and in sixth place. They finished seventh.

Killefer had been an outstanding catcher with the Philadelphia Phillies until the Cubs obtained him in trade

Bill Killefer

along with his great battery mate Grover Cleveland Alexander after the 1917 season. He was the number-one catcher for a couple of years, though a "dead" throwing arm had reduced his effectiveness.

He inherited a team whose chief assets were Alexander, who had been 27–14 in 1920, and shortstop Hollocher. In 1922 the Cubs added a power-hitting rookie outfielder, Hack Miller, and promising young catcher Gabby Hartnett. In 1925 they dealt for first baseman Charlie Grimm and veteran shortstop Rabbit Maranville. Hartnett and Grimm were to play major roles in Cub history.

Killefer guided the Cubs to fifth place in 1922, fourth in 1923, and fifth in 1924, but he was fired when they slid to last place in midseason 1925. He resurfaced in 1930 as manager of the St. Louis Browns, a job he held for four years.

1925

Rabbit Maranville

Record: 23–30 (.434)
B: November 11, 1892, Springfield, Massachusetts
D: January 5, 1954, New York, New York

Maranville, Walter J. V.

	W	L	T	Pct
1925	23	30	0	.434
Cubs	23	30	0	.434
Career	23	30	0	.434

The hard-drinking Maranville was in midcareer as one of the best fielding shortstops of his era, though injuries restricted his play in 1925. Unexpectedly, and it turned out inappropriately, he was Veeck's choice to succeed Killefer as manager.

His fondness for alcohol, practical jokes, and juvenile pranks quickly made it clear that Maranville was not managerial material. The final blow came when he ran through a Pullman car of a train sprinkling the passengers from a spittoon. On September 3, William Veeck replaced him as manager with coach George Gibson.

The Cub record under Maranville was 23–30. He finished the season as a utility player, then was sold on waivers to the Brooklyn Dodgers. He extended his playing career for another 10 seasons but never managed again.

1925

George Gibson

Record: 12–14 (.462)
B: July 22, 1880, London, Ontario, Canada
D: January 25, 1967, London, Ontario, Canada

Gibson, George C.

	W	L	T	Pct
1925	12	14	0	.462
Cubs	12	14	0	.462
Career	413	344	2	.546

Rabbit Maranville (George Brace photo)

George Gibson

George "Moon" Gibson, a former catcher, had managed the Pittsburgh Pirates for almost three seasons (1920–22) before joining the Cubs as a coach. He had earned a reputation as a disciplinarian. Veeck thought he could restore order from the chaos wrought by Maranville.

Gibson, the first Canadian to become a major league manager, was permitted only to finish the season with the Cubs, who already had decided on another man to manage the team in 1926. They were 12–14 under Gibson's command and finished in last place for the first time in their 50-year history.

The Pirates rehired him as manager in 1932, and he lasted until midway into the 1934 season, when his major league career ended.

Joe McCarthy

1926–30

Joe McCarthy

Record: 442–321 (.579)
B: April 21, 1887, Philadelphia, Pennsylvania
D: January 3, 1978, Buffalo, New York

McCarthy, Joseph V.

	W	L	T	Pct
1926	82	72	1	.532
1927	85	68	0	.556
1928	91	63	0	.591
1929	98	54	4	.645
1930	86	64	2	.573
Cubs	442	321	7	.579
Career	2,125	1,333	26	.615

In September 1925, William Veeck met secretly at French Lick, Indiana, with Joe McCarthy, then managing the Louisville, Kentucky, minor league team, and offered him the Cub job. "Marse Joe" McCarthy had built a solid reputation for managerial acumen, and the New York Yankees reportedly were after him to replace ailing Miller Huggins. The Cubs won out.

A second baseman, McCarthy had never played a day in the major leagues and had turned to managing at the age of 26 in 1913. He had been uniformly successful in developing young players and winning teams wherever he went. He was tough in an understated way, efficient, highly organized, and extremely sharp in evaluating talent.

He lived by 10 commandments—his own, the formula he set down for success in baseball:

1. Nobody ever became a ballplayer by walking after a ball.

2. You will never become a .300 hitter unless you take the bat off your shoulder.

3. An outfielder who throws back of the runner is locking the barn after the horse is stolen.

4. Keep your head up and you may not have to keep it down.

5. When you start a slide, S-L-I-D-E. He who changes his mind may have to change a good leg for a bad one.

6. Do not alibi on bad hops. Anybody can field the good ones.

7. Always run them out. You can never tell.

8. Do not quit.

9. Do not find too much fault with umpires. You cannot expect them to be as perfect as you are.

10. A pitcher who hasn't control hasn't anything.

With Veeck's support, McCarthy in 1926 began to restructure the Cubs, whose chief assets on his arrival were Charlie Grimm, Gabby Hartnett, and pitchers Charlie Root and Guy Bush. He got rid of Grover Cleveland Alexander, whose chronic alcoholism was a threat to team discipline. He persuaded Veeck to acquire minor league outfielders Hack Wilson and Riggs Stephenson. The Cubs moved up to fourth place, Wilson leading the league in home runs with 21 and Stephenson batting .338.

For 1927, McCarthy added shortstop Woody English. Wilson again led the league in home runs with 30, and Stephenson batted .344, as the Cubs again finished fourth. The next year, the Cubs made a deal for veteran outfielder Kiki Cuyler to round out an all-star outfield and brought up rookie pitcher Pat Malone; they moved up to third place.

McCarthy was convinced that one more solid hitter, preferably an infielder, could give the Cubs a chance at the pennant in 1929. William Wrigley, Jr., and Veeck obliged by acquiring second baseman Rogers Hornsby, possibly the finest right-handed hitter of all time, for $200,000 plus five players, from the Boston Braves.

Hornsby met McCarthy's expectations, batting .380 in 1929 to lead the Cubs to their first pennant in 11 years, and hit 39 home runs with 149 RBIs. Wilson matched Hornsby's home run output and drove in 159 runs. Malone led the pitching staff with a 22–10 record. The team batting average was .303.

The powerhouse Cubs, however, fell victim to the Philadelphia Athletics in the World Series. They lost in five games, and their greatest humiliation came in game 4 as they took an 8–0 lead into the seventh inning when the A's scored 10 runs.

Wrigley wasn't just the owner of the team—he was a fan, and he took the World Series defeat to heart. He had hungered for a World Series championship and blamed McCarthy for having failed to win it.

Wrigley's disappointment festered during the 1930 season and was constantly stirred up by Hornsby, who considered McCarthy a "busher" because he had never played in the major leagues. Many of the other players felt the same. Hornsby, who had managed before in the NL at St. Louis, New York, and Boston, was eager to supplant McCarthy.

Despite the greatest turnout of fans in Cubs history, despite Wilson's march to a major league record 190 RBIs and a NL record 56 home runs, Wrigley fired McCarthy with four games left in the 1930 season and the team in second place, just missing another pennant partly because Hornsby had been injured and had played in only 42 games. Wrigley's stated reason: "McCarthy lacks enough desire for a world championship." He gave the job to Hornsby.

The misfortune was more that of the Cubs than of McCarthy. Shortly after the 1930 season, he was hired to manage the Yankees. Before his career ended in 1950 after a final managerial stint with the Boston Red Sox, his teams had won seven World Series and nine pennants. He ranks among the greatest of all managers.

1930–32

Rogers Hornsby

Record: 141–116 (.549)
B: April 27, 1896, Winters, Texas
D: January 5, 1963, Chicago, Illinois

Hornsby, Rogers

	W	L	T	Pct
1930	4	0	0	1.000
1931	84	70	2	.545
1932	53	46	0	.535
Cubs	141	116	2	.549
Career	701	812	17	.463

Rogers Hornsby

Impatient, outspoken, and dictatorial, Rogers "Rajah" Hornsby was hardly an ideal manager for a team composed largely of veterans when he took over the Cubs with four games left in the 1930 season. The apex of his tenure might have been the four consecutive victories with which the Cubs ended the campaign.

Hornsby holds the modern major league record with the .424 he batted in 1924. Over a stretch of five seasons (1921–25) his batting average was .402. Only Ty Cobb's .367 surpasses his career average of .358. Hornsby hit with power, leading the NL in home runs with 42 in 1922 and with 39 in 1925, a figure he matched for the Cubs in 1929. He was a competent if not spectacular fielding second baseman.

While a great player, Hornsby was his own worst enemy as a manager. He did lead the St. Louis Cardinals to a pennant in 1926 in his first year as player-manager, but created havoc with his abrasive, arrogant manner in following stints with the Giants and Braves before William Veeck named him to manage the Cubs.

He soon disenchanted Veeck and William Wrigley in 1931 when the Cubs dropped to third place. His players, including Wilson, whose home run output declined to 13, were driven to distraction by Hornsby's bluntness and impatience. He was intolerant of failure; perfection was demanded.

The situation festered well into the 1932 season, despite changes over the winter, including the death of William Wrigley, Jr., on January 26. The new double-play combination of second baseman Billy Herman and Bill Jurges sparkled, and Wilson, who had been traded to St. Louis, was replaced in center field by journeyman Joe Moore. Lon Warneke emerged as the ace of the pitching staff. Still, the Cubs trod water with a record of 53–46 on August 1.

Adding to Hornsby's problems were allegations that he consorted with gamblers and bookmakers, originating in his obsession with horse racing. On August 2, Veeck and new owner Philip K. Wrigley decided they had had enough. They fired Hornsby, replacing him with Grimm.

Hornsby's connection with the Cubs, however, was far from over. After other managerial stints, he served as a television announcer for Cub games in 1949, managed elsewhere again in the 1950s, and from 1958 until his death in 1963 was the team's batting instructor and coach.

1932–38

Charlie Grimm (First Term)

Overall Record: 946–784 (.547)
B: August 25, 1896, St. Louis, Missouri
D: November 15, 1983, Scottsdale, Arizona

Grimm, Charles J.

	W	L	T	Pct
1932	37	18	0	.673
1933	86	68	0	.558
1934	86	65	1	.570
1935	100	54	0	.649
1936	87	67	0	.565
1937	93	61	0	.604
1938	45	36	0	.556
1944	74	69	3	.517
1945	98	56	1	.636
1946	82	71	2	.536
1947	69	85	1	.448
1948	64	90	1	.416
1949	19	31	0	.380
1960	6	11	0	.353
Cubs	946	784	9	.547
Career	1,287	1,067	14	.547

Off the field, Charlie Grimm was a free spirit, nicknamed Jolly Cholly. On the field, he was all business, one of the outstanding first basemen of the 1920s and early 1930s, a good hitter and fielder. He finished with a career batting average of .290. He contributed to the 1929 NL championship with a batting average of .298, 10 home runs, and 91 RBIs.

The son of a German immigrant, he started his 20-year career as a player with the Athletics in 1916 and was acquired by the Cubs in 1925 after six solid seasons at Pittsburgh. A favorite with the players, he succeeded Hornsby on August 2, 1932, and the team immediately perked up under his relaxed style of managing.

It was apropos that the Cubs celebrated Charlie Grimm Day on August 16 at Wrigley Field. The team went on a 14-game winning streak, clinched the pennant on September 20, and finished with a record of 37–18 under Grimm to round out the season at 90–64. The World Series, however, was another matter. The Yankees crushed the Cubs in four straight, the highlight being Babe Ruth's alleged "called shot" home run.

Nevertheless, Grimm had solidified his standing with P. K. Wrigley and for the rest of his life was a favorite of the owner, serving the team in many capacities, including that of manager an unmatched three terms in all or part of 14 seasons.

Two third-place finishes followed the 1932 championship while Grimm replaced most of the veterans from the 1929 and 1932 pennant winners. When William Veeck died in 1933, Wrigley turned to James "Boots" Weber as general manager, with Grimm combining an advisory role with his field job. By 1935, Weber and Grimm had rebuilt the team with such young stars as third baseman Stan Hack, first baseman Phil Cavaretta, outfielders Augie Galan and Frank Demaree, and pitchers Bill Lee, Larry French, and Tex Carleton in place.

Despite the new talent, the Cubs appeared to be falling out of the pennant race by Labor Day, but then put together a 21-game winning streak, their longest since 1880, to finish four games ahead of second-place St. Louis. They again lost the World Series, this time to the Detroit Tigers in six games.

The next two years they finished second. In 1938 it seemed as if they again were to be out of the running with a record of 45–38 on July 26, despite such additions to the team as pitcher Dizzy Dean (whose ailing arm signaled the approaching end of his career, though he was 7–1 that year) and slugging first baseman Rip Collins.

Grimm turned the team over to veteran catcher Gabby Hartnett, hoping the change would spark the players. The ploy worked, the Cubs winning 44 of their final 71 games. Hartnett himself provided the decisive moment with his famous "Homer in the Gloamin'" on September 28 to take the heart out of the Pittsburgh Pirates and propel the Cubs into first place and another pennant.

The World Series was the customary disaster, the Yankees sweeping the Cubs once more.

Wrigley decided to take the pressure off Grimm in 1939, replacing him as Weber's associate as general manager with Clarence "Pants" Rowland, a veteran baseball man who had managed the White Sox to a World Series championship in 1917. For the next two years Grimm was a radio broadcaster of Cub games. He started 1941 as a coach, but in June left the Cubs to manage for Bill Veeck, Jr., who had just purchased the minor league Milwaukee Brewers. It was the beginning of Veeck's entrepeneurial career.

Grimm's first term as the Cub manager had helped the Cubs to three pennants, and his connection with the team was far from over.

1938–40

Gabby Hartnett

Record: 203–176 (.536)
B: December 20, 1900, Woonsocket, Rhode Island
D: December 10, 1972, Park Ridge, Illinois

Hartnett, Charles L.

	W	L	T	Pct
1938	44	27	2	.620
1939	84	70	2	.545
1940	75	79	0	.487
Cubs	203	176	4	.536
Career	203	176	4	.536

A constant chatterer behind the plate, deserving of his nickname "Gabby," Hartnett was a great catcher both as a receiver and power hitter. He had a career batting average of .297 during 20 seasons (1922–41), the first 19 with the Cubs. In his best years he batted .339, with 37 home runs and 122 RBIs in 1930 and .354 in 1937, his last full season as a catcher.

As a manager, Hartnett was at best adequate. He seemed as lacking in tact as Rogers Hornsby had been before him. When angry, his face turned red, earning him the nickname of "Tomato Face."

He did have a sense of humor, though. When Commis-

Gabby Hartnett

1941–44

Jimmie Wilson

Record: 213–258 (.452)
B: July 23, 1900, Philadelphia, Pennsylvania
D: May 31, 1947, Bradenton, Florida

Wilson, James

	W	L	T	Pct
1941	70	84	1	.455
1942	68	86	1	.442
1943	74	79	1	.484
1944	1	9	0	.100
Cubs	213	258	3	.452
Career	493	735	9	.401

A fine catcher, Jimmie "Ace" Wilson had gained managerial experience in guiding the hapless Philadelphia Phillies for five seasons (1934–38) with little success, the team finishing in last or seventh place every year. He quit in disgust with two games remaining in the 1938 season. "Even Connie Mack finishes last when he has no players," Wilson said on quitting.

He was a coach for Cincinnati in 1940 when he was pressed into service behind the plate again for the World Series against Detroit when Reds' star Ernie Lombardi was injured. The 40-year-old Wilson helped the Reds win the Series, and also won himself a job as the new manager of the Cubs, succeeding Gabby Hartnett. P. K. Wrigley and Boots Weber were impressed by his "guts" in the Series.

Before the announcement was made that Wilson had been hired, Wrigley made a major change in the front office, replacing Weber and Pants Rowland with Jim Gallagher, a sportswriter who had caught his attention by criti-

sioner Kenesaw M. Landis reprimanded him for a newspaper photograph that showed him leaning over a box seat to exchange pleasantries with gangster Al Capone, Hartnett replied, "If you don't want anybody to talk to the Big Guy, Judge, you tell him."

The precipitous decline of the Cubs after the 1938 pennant was hardly all Hartnett's fault. Ill-advised trades played a part. The most notorious was an exchange with the Giants. The Cubs gave up brilliant shortstop Bill Jurges, outfielder Frank Demaree, and catcher Ken O'Dea for outfielder Hank Leiber, shortstop Dick Bartell, and catcher Ken Mancuso. Jurges was to be sorely missed.

Early in the 1939 season, however, the Cubs scored high with another trade, getting pitcher Claude Passeau, who was to be a mainstay of the staff for years. Passeau (13–9) helped slow the Cub slide as they finished in fourth place. He was also a bright spot in 1940 with a 20–13 record when the Cubs slipped into fifth place. That performance didn't save Hartnett's job, as P. K. Wrigley and Boots Weber decided it was time for a change.

Hartnett finished his playing career with the Giants in 1941, then managed for several years in the minor leagues. In 1965 he coached for the Kansas City A's.

Jimmie Wilson (George Brace photo)

cizing the team. (It was a repeat of the hiring of William Veeck, Sr., also a newspaper critic, by P.K.'s father two decades earlier.) Gallagher came in with a five-year plan to rebuild the Cubs.

New general manager Gallagher and manager Wilson combined to dismantle the Cubs, trading away some of the team's established players, including Billy Herman, Augie Galan, and Larry French. Among the newcomers were outfielders Bill "Swish" Nicholson, Lou Novikoff, and Dominic Dallessandro, shortstop Len Merullo, catcher Clyde McCullough, and pitcher Hi Bithorn. Nicholson was a genuine slugger who twice led the NL in home runs, with 29 in 1943 and 33 in 1944.

World War II which the United States entered on December 7, 1941, complicated Gallagher's five-year plan as competent manpower became scarce. The Cubs, like other teams, scrambled for players who were not suited for military service.

The Cubs floundered, finished sixth in 1941 and 1942, rising to fifth in 1943. When they started out the 1944 season with a 1–9 record, Gallagher fired Wilson in May and brought back Charlie Grimm after coach Roy Johnson led the team for one day as interim manager.

Wilson returned to coaching with the Reds for another two years, and then retired.

1944

Roy Johnson

Record: 0–1 (.000)
B: February 23, 1903, Pryor, Oklahoma
D: September 10, 1973, Tacoma, Washington

Johnson, Roy C.

	W	L	T	Pct
1944	0	1	0	.000
Cubs	0	1	0	.000
Career	0	1	0	.000

A major league outfielder for 10 seasons, mostly with the Detroit Tigers and Boston Red Sox, Roy Johnson was a coach under Jimmie Wilson when Jim Gallagher named him to take over the team as manager for a day. The Cubs had won on opening day, then had lost nine consecutive games when Wilson was dismissed.

Johnson presided over a defeat, extending the Cubs' losing streak to 10 (it reached 13), and returned to coaching when Grimm took over for his second term as Cub manager. Johnson remained with the Cubs as a coach until 1953.

1944–49

Charlie Grimm (Second Term)

Charlie Grimm's managerial stint under Bill Veeck's ownership of the Milwaukee Brewers had been exhilarating. The outgoing, playful Grimm, who took joyous part in Veeck's outlandish promotions, perfectly suited the circus atmosphere in which baseball's newest showman operated. Attendance soared in Milwaukee as Veeck established himself as the rising young entrepeneur of the game.

Grimm took over a Cub team that had possibilities despite the manpower shortage caused by the war. Among the holdovers from the 1938 championship team were Stan Hack and Phil Cavaretta. A new center fielder, Andy Pafko, was a standout, as were pitchers Claude Passeau and Hank

Charlie Grimm (left) with Frank Frisch, who was among his three successors

Wyse. Despite the poor start, Grimm dragged the Cubs to fourth place in 1944.

And 1945 proved to be the year of a "miracle," aided undoubtedly by continuing player shortages that hit other teams harder than they did the Cubs. The newcomers who played major roles were Pafko, second baseman Don Johnson, and the key midseason acquisition, pitcher Hank Borowy, who finished the season 11–2 for the Cubs after a 10–5 start with the New York Yankees.

Cavarretta had a "career season," batting .355 to lead the league, driving in 97 runs, and earning the Most Valuable Player award. Pafko batted .302 and drove in 110 runs. Wyse was 22–10, Passeau was 17–9, and retread Paul Derringer was 16–11 as the Cubs won the pennant, partly because they won 21 of 22 games from Cincinnati.

The World Series against Detroit was hard fought, going to seven games, but was the same old story, the Cubs losing for their seventh consecutive defeat in the bid for baseball's championship.

Yet in winning a pennant, Grimm had done it again, reinforcing his standing as P. K. Wrigley's favorite manager. He kept his job almost four more seasons as the Cubs entered another dark era that was to last two decades.

The downturn started slowly, the Cubs finishing third in 1946, then snowballed as they dropped to sixth in 1947 and to last place in 1948. New players, such as first baseman Eddie Waitkus, shortstop Roy Smalley, catcher Bob Scheffing, and pitcher Johnny Schmitz, didn't seem to make any difference.

The 1949 season started out the way the 1948 season ended, the Cubs in last place with a 19–31 record, when Wrigley decided Grimm needed another respite from the rigors of managing. He appointed him vice president in charge of player personnel, commenting, "I think Charlie will live longer this way."

Grimm's major fault in Wrigley's view was that he was too agreeable. Wrigley said of him, "He's such a good guy that when you ask him whether such and such a player would be all right, he agrees, even though he doesn't mean it and regrets it later."

Accordingly, Wrigley's choice to manage the Cubs was a fiery veteran, Frankie Frisch, whose aggressive, abrasive manner left no hint of being "nice."

Grimm remained a vice president for a few months, then yielded to a renewed hunger to manage, first in the minor leagues, then for the Boston Braves in midseason 1952, moving with them to Milwaukee in 1953. He kept that job until well into the 1956 season.

As before, he was not yet through with the Cubs. (For career summary see 1932–38.)

1949–51

Frankie Frisch

Record: 141–196 (.418)
B: September 9, 1898, Bronx, New York
D: March 12, 1973, Wilmington, Delaware

Frisch, Frank F.

	W	L	T	Pct
1949	42	62	0	.404
1950	64	89	1	.418
1951	35	45	1	.438
Cubs	141	196	2	.418
Career	1,138	1,078	30	.514

Frankie Frisch had been a great second baseman with a career batting average of .316 in 19 seasons (1919–37) with the Giants and Cardinals. He was nicknamed the Fordham Flash, a tribute both to his speed and to his attendance at Fordham University.

His first managerial tenure, with the Cardinals from 1933 to 1938, had been highlighted by the World Series champion Gashouse Gang of '34. His second managerial stint, with the Pittsburgh Pirates from 1940 to 1946, had been less successful but competent. When the Cubs hired him in 1949, he was chafing in a job as radio broadcaster.

Frisch was extremely aggressive as player and manager while being witty and articulate. And he had no tolerance for less than the best from his players, who unfortunately were incapable of meeting his expectations. He took over a team in last place in 1949, and that's where it finished the season.

The next season was a little better, the Cubs rising to seventh place in 1950 with a new star emerging in left fielder Hank Sauer, obtained from the Reds the year before. Sauer hit 32 home runs and drove in 103 runs. But his slugging didn't make much difference.

In an effort to shake things up after the 1951 season got under way, the Cubs made another of their ill-advised trades. They bundled their fine center fielder Andy Pafko into a four-player package in exchange for four players from the Brooklyn Dodgers. Pafko helped the Dodgers to a pennant in 1952; the Cubs got little benefit from the deal.

The Cubs listlessly moved into the middle of the 1951 season with a 35–45 record when P. K. Wrigley decided Frisch was not the answer. Frisch had lost interest in his players and allegedly flipped absentmindedly through the pages of a book during games so he wouldn't have to watch them. He finally resigned on July 21, 1951.

Wrigley's choice to succeed Frisch was Phil Cavarretta, the veteran first baseman–outfielder who had been a Cub since 1934. And there was no doubt he was Wrigley's choice, though the ostensible front office chief was Wid Matthews, who had taken over Grimm's job as director of player personnel in 1950 with Jim Gallagher "promoted" into a less prominent role.

1951–53

Phil Cavarretta

Record: 169–213 (.442)
B: July 9, 1916, Chicago, Illinois

Cavarretta, Philip J.

	W	L	T	Pct
1951	27	47	0	.365
1952	77	77	1	.500
1954	65	89	1	.422
Cubs	169	213	2	.442
Career	169	213	2	.442

In naming Phil Cavarretta manager, owner Philip Wrigley appealed to team tradition and local pride. Cavarretta had been a baseball standout at Lane Technical High School in Chicago and had joined the Cubs on September 25, 1934, at the age of 18. He literally grew up in a Cub uniform, and he helped bring three pennant winners to Wrigley Field.

His finest seasons came in 1944 when he batted .321 in 152

Phil Cavarretta

games and in 1945 when he led the league in batting with .355 and was the NL's Most Valuable Player. When he took charge in midseason 1951, it was as a player-manager, and he batted .311 in 53 games that year.

He had a pleasant but not easy going personality and, as it turned out, was too candid for his own good about the players he was given. And most of the players under his command during his less than three seasons at the helm were second-rate.

Cavarretta finished out the 1951 season dismally, the Cubs going 27–47 after Frankie Frisch's departure and dropping into last place. But 1952 seemed to promise a brighter future, though it proved illusory. Sauer hit 37 home runs and drove in 121 runs to win the Most Valuable Player award, and pitchers Bob Rush and Warren Hacker won 17 and 15 games, respectively. First baseman Dee Fondy, who batted .300, looked like a comer. The Cubs finished in fifth place but with a .500 record (77–77) for the first time since 1945—and for the last time until 1963.

Seeing progress, Wid Matthews sought to bolster the Cubs' power after the 1953 season opened. The chief prize in a 10-player trade on June 4 with the Pittsburgh Pirates was slugger Ralph Kiner, who had led the NL in home runs seven consecutive seasons (1946–52). The thought of Sauer and Kiner in the same lineup dazzled Matthews.

The combination wore down center fielder Frankie Baumholtz, who was burdened with covering extra ground between the two lead-foots, Sauer and Kiner, who flanked

him. Additionally, Sauer missed more than 40 games with a broken thumb, and his home run total fell to 19. Kiner hit 35 home runs that season, 28 of them as a Cub, but the team sank to seventh place. The real highlight of the season was the arrival of the Cubs' first two black players, shortstop Ernie Banks and second baseman Gene Baker.

Sauer and Kiner both were healthy by spring training of '54, and the new double-play combination of Baker and Banks was promising, but Cavarretta wasn't as sanguine about the team's prospects as were Wrigley and Matthews. He despaired of the pitching staff, the outfield defense, and the numerous other shortcomings of the team. He reported to Wrigley that the Cubs had few first-rate players and that the team would probably finish in the second division.

Wrigley's reaction was to give Cavarretta the unique distinction of being the first manager to be fired in spring training. Rather than appreciating Cavarretta's candor, Wrigley termed it "defeatism."

Instead of opening the 1954 season as manager of the Cubs, Cavarretta began it as a utility player and pinch hitter for the White Sox, who signed him to capitalize on his popularity in Chicago. Cavarretta batted .316 in 71 games for the Sox in '54. He was released early the next season. He continued his baseball career for a few more years as coach and batting instructor for several teams.

1954–56

Stan Hack

Record: 196–265 (.425)
B: December 6, 1909, Sacramento, California
D: December 15, 1979, Dixon, Illinois

Hack, Stanley C.

	W	L	T	Pct
1954	64	90	0	.416
1955	72	81	1	.471
1956	60	94	3	.390
Cubs	196	265	4	.425
Career	199	272	4	.423

Like Phil Cavarretta, Stan Hack, his successor, was a gifted and popular player for many years. An outstanding third baseman, he finished his career with a batting average of .301 for 16 seasons and contributed to four pennant winners. His career high was .323 in 1945, and he twice led the NL in base hits.

Known as Smiling Stan because of his pleasant personality, Hack had been managing in the Cubs' minor league system for several years before he was chosen in spring training of 1954 to replace Cavarretta. He may have kept smiling for the next three years as manager, but it must have required extreme effort.

The mid-'50s were among the Cubs' most dismal periods, the team finishing in seventh place in 1954, sixth in 1955, and last in 1956 as Hack struggled with a roster mostly composed of castoffs from other teams and youngsters who never lived up to their promise.

Although Sauer hit 41 home runs and drove in 103 runs, Kiner contributed 22 home runs, and Banks hit 19 home runs as a rookie shortstop in 1954, the defense and pitching were pathetic. In '55, Banks blossomed with 44 home runs (the most ever by a shortstop) and 117 RBIs, but Sauer was almost through and Kiner was gone. The next year, Banks led

Stan Hack

Bob Scheffing

the team with 28 home runs, the only bright spot in a last-place finish.

P. K. Wrigley's patience again was exhausted, and Hack was fired as part of a major shakeup that included the departures of Jim Gallagher and Wid Matthews. John Holland, who had been general manager of the Cubs' minor league affiliate at Los Angeles, began a long reign as general manager of the Cubs, with Pants Rowland and Charlie Grimm, who had worn out his welcome in Milwaukee, as his advisers in vice presidential posts.

Hack continued his career as a coach with the Cardinals and was their interim manager for 10 games in 1958. He managed for a few more years in the minor leagues before retiring from baseball in 1966.

1957–59

Bob Scheffing

Record: 208–254 (.450)
B: August 11, 1913, Overland, Missouri
D: October 26, 1985, Phoenix, Arizona

Scheffing, Robert B.

	W	L	T	Pct
1957	62	92	2	.403
1958	72	82	0	.468
1959	74	80	1	.481
Cubs	208	254	3	.450
Career	418	427	4	.495

John Holland's choice as manager of the Cubs was simple enough. The new general manager brought Bob Scheffing along with him from Los Angeles, where his team had won the Pacific Coast League pennant by 16 games in 1956.

Scheffing long had been associated with the Cubs, from 1941 to 1950 as catcher, then as a coach in 1954 before his managerial assignment in Los Angeles. He represented a radical change from "Smiling Stan" Hack, being rough and tough. He was known as Grump, though he had his players' respect for the three years of his tenure even if their talent was limited.

Holland and Scheffing rebuilt the team around Banks chiefly to take advantage of Wrigley Field's reputation as a home run heaven. Slow but powerful hitters such as Walt "Moose" Moryn, Dale Long, Bobby Thomson, Lee Walls, and George Altman appeared on the scene. Banks had his greatest seasons, hitting 43 home runs with 102 RBIs in 1957, banging out 47 home runs in 1958 with 129 RBIs, and coming back with 45 home runs and 143 RBIs in 1959. He won the Most Valuable Player award in 1958 and again in 1959.

As part of his emphasis on hitting, Holland brought back Rogers Hornsby as batting coach. Hornsby's chief contribution was to discern that among the host of Cub minor leaguers Ron Santo and Billy Williams had the greatest potential.

Despite the cannonade, the Cubs made no real headway, the pitching and defense falling far behind the power hitting. From seventh place in 1957, the Cubs rose to fifth place the next two years but were never really in contention, though they finished the 1959 season only 13 games out of first place.

Wrigley wasn't impressed. He congratulated Scheffing on "a helluva fine job" but fired him because it was time to "make a change." Scheffing was shocked because he thought he had done well, considering the mediocre talent at his disposal. "I figured I'd get both a new contract and a raise," Scheffing said. "When I got to his office, Mr. Wrigley said they had decided to make a change and would bring Charlie Grimm back in an effort to loosen up the club because it was too tense."

Scheffing became manager of the Detroit Tigers in 1961 and led his team to a 101–61 record, which was good only for second place behind the Yankees. He kept the job until the middle of the '63 season. Later he became the New York Mets' farm director and finished his baseball career as the Mets' vice president and general manager.

1960

Charlie Grimm (Third Term)

At the end of the 1959 season, owner P. K. Wrigley turned to Charlie Grimm for a third time as manager, explaining that "every time we call on Charlie we win a pennant."

Grimm had his doubts about whether he was physically up to the demands of managing at the age of 63, but he acceded to his good friend Wrigley's request. He brought in Charlie Root as pitching coach, and among the new players were rookie third baseman Ron Santo and veteran outfielder Richie Ashburn.

After three weeks of the 1960 season, Grimm realized his infirmities made managing impossible, and he stepped down. The team was in last place with a 6–11 record.

In one of the more unusual moves in the game's history, Grimm was "traded" to WGN Radio for Lou Boudreau, a veteran manager who had been broadcasting Cub games for two years. Boudreau took over as manager and Grimm as a radio commentator.

Grimm returned to the field for much of the next three seasons as a Cub coach, under a new system devised by Wrigley. Later he was part scout, part consultant, and honorary vice president until his death on November 15, 1983. His ashes were scattered at Wrigley Field. (For career summary see 1932–38.)

1960

Lou Boudreau

Record: 54–83 (.394)
B: July 17, 1917, Harvey, Illinois

Boudreau, Louis

	W	L	T	Pct
1960	54	83	2	.394
Cubs	54	83	2	.394
Career	1,162	1,224	18	.487

Personable Lou Boudreau was a veteran manager at the age of 43 when he was summoned to replace Grimm early in the 1960 season. A heady shortstop and outstanding batter, Boudreau starred as a player for the Cleveland Indians from 1939 to 1950. In 1942 the Indians made him the youngest manager in major league history at the age of 24. He won the AL batting title in 1944 with an average of .327 and reached the peak of his career as both player and manager in 1948 when he led the Indians to a pennant and World Series championship while batting .355 with 18 home runs and 106 RBIs.

Fired by the Indians after the 1950 season, Boudreau concluded his playing career with the Boston Red Sox, for whom he became manager in 1952. He managed the Red Sox for three seasons, then the Kansas City Athletics for another three, with indifferent success before moving to the Cub broadcast booth.

Charlie Grimm anoints Lou Boudreau, who succeeded him after 17 games of the 1960 season.

As a broadcaster with the team he was taking over, Boudreau was well aware of its shortcomings. But he could do nothing to improve it, and the Cubs were 54–83 under his command to finish seventh in 1960.

P. K. Wrigley advised Boudreau to retreat to the broadcasting booth. He did so, much to his advantage, and continued as a commentator on Cub games for another two decades before retiring.

The owner was "going in a different direction," as the saying goes, and it proved one of the more bizarre adventures in baseball history.

1961–62

College of Coaches

On December 21, 1960, P. K. Wrigley unveiled a new scheme for the on-field direction of his stagnant team. It was a radical departure from the traditional organization in which a specific manager, assisted by two or three coaches, had total control to make all decisions on whom to play, on how to play, and on game tactics.

Wrigley's plan in essence called for a staff of eight "rotating" coaches who would take turns directing the team for varying periods. Three or four would be with the Cubs at one time; the others would travel through the team's minor league system to develop a uniform approach to the game. All would be interchangeable, sometimes serving as "head coach," other times as coaches with the Cubs or in the minor leagues.

The most revolutionary aspect of Wrigley's plan was that a temporary "head coach" rather than a "manager" would be selected by the coaches rather than by the front office. It was a sort of a democratic council, though critics referred to it as "anarchy."

The much-ridiculed scheme was in effect for two seasons. It was abandoned by 1963, though the term "head coach" lingered until the appointment of Leo Durocher as manager in late 1965.

The eight original members of what became known as the College of Coaches were Charlie Grimm, Rip Collins, Rube Walker, Vedie Himsl, Elvin Tappe, Goldie Holt, Harry Craft, and Bobby Adams. Later members were Bob Kennedy, Lou Klein, Charlie Metro, Al Dark, Freddie Martin, Mel Wright, Mel Harder, and Buck O'Neill.

During 1961, four men—Himsl, Craft, Tappe, and Klein—served as head coaches. The Cubs finished in seventh place with a 64–90 record.

In 1962 the post passed from Tappe to Klein to Metro. The NL had expanded to 10 teams, and the Cubs embarrassed themselves by finishing in ninth place, even behind the new Houston Colt .45s (managed by Craft).

During the two years of the head coach system, five men served in the post for various stretches, and the Cubs were no better off than they had been under managers.

After the '62 season, Kennedy was named "head coach" for 1963, and it was understood that to all intents and purposes he was the manager, Wrigley having covertly abandoned his College of Coaches.

The only positive aspects of the two seasons under the College of Coaches were the development of several young players, outfielder Billy Williams (Rookie of the Year in 1961), third baseman Ron Santo, second baseman Ken Hubbs (Rookie of the Year in 1962), and left-handed pitcher Dick Ellsworth.

Vedie Himsl

Record: 10–21 (.323)
B: April 2, 1917, Plevna, Montana

Himsl, Avitus B.

	W	L	T	Pct
1961	10	21	0	.323
Cubs	10	21	0	.323
Career	10	21	0	.323

As a pitcher, Vedie Himsl had a modest career, never rising above Class AAA competition. His only managerial experience had been two years at the lowest minor league level. But his diligence in spring training impressed P. K. Wrigley, and the owner, disregarding his own plan to have the head coach selected by his peers, chose Himsl as the first team leader under the College of Coaches system.

The Cubs started out 1961 with a 5–6 record before Himsl was transferred to San Antonio. Two weeks later he returned for a second stint as head coach with a 5–12 record. A third term produced a 0–3 record before Himsl receded forever from the top spot with a total mark of 10–21. He remained on the coaching staff until 1964 and later became director of scouting.

Vedie Himsl, the first of the rotating head coaches

Harry Craft

Harry Craft

Record: 7–9 (.438)
B: April 9, 1915, Ellisville, Mississippi
D: August 3, 1995, Conroe, Texas

Craft, Harry F.

	W	L	T	Pct
1961	7	9	0	.438
Cubs	7	9	0	.438
Career	360	485	4	.426

Harry Craft's respectable career as a Cincinnati Reds outfielder from 1937 to 1942 was curtailed by military service in World War II. He turned to coaching and managing after the war. He was named manager of the Kansas City Athletics during the 1957 season, a job he kept through the 1959 season. He joined the Cubs as a coach in 1960.

Craft took over as head coach from Himsl after the first 11 games in 1961, then guided the Cubs to a 7–9 record during his two-week tenure. It was his only chance to direct the Cubs, and he left after the 1961 season to become manager of the expansion Houston Colt .45s. He managed at Houston, with little success, until he was fired with two weeks left in the 1964 season.

Elvin Tappe

El Tappe

Record: 46–70 (.397)
B: May 21, 1927, Chicago, Illinois

Tappe, Elvin W.

	W	L	T	Pct
1961	42	54	1	.458
1962	4	16	0	.200
Cubs	46	70	1	.397

The most memorable aspect of El Tappe's tenure was that he was the only player–head coach, catching in 26 games in 1962. A good receiver, he was a light hitter, with a career average of .207 in 145 games as a major leaguer from 1954 to 1962, all with the Cubs. His twin brother Ted was an outfielder with the Cubs in 1955.

Tappe had three tenures as head coach in 1961. He succeeded Himsl after 40 games and compiled a 2–0 record before stepping down in favor of Craft. In his second term, the Cubs were 35–43 before he yielded to Klein for 12 games. He finished the season with a 5–11 mark for a total of 42–54 for 1961.

On the strength of his 1961 work, he was chosen to lead off 1962, but the Cubs started out 4–16, and Tappe had directed a major league team for the last time. He remained as a coach until 1965.

Lou Klein

Record: 65–82 (.442)
B: October 22, 1918, New Orleans, Louisiana
D: June 20, 1976, Metairie, Louisiana

Klein, Louis F.

	W	L	T	Pct
1961	5	6	0	.455
1962	12	18	0	.400
1965	48	58	0	.453
Cubs	65	82	0	.442

An exceptional minor league hitter, Lou Klein was a utility infielder most of his major league career from 1943 to 1951 with the St. Louis Cardinals. As a coach, his specialty was as an instructor in infield play and batting. He had a bland, uninspiring personality.

As the 1961 season rounded into its last month, Klein replaced El Tappe for 11 games, the Cubs winning five of them. After less than two weeks, he gave way to Tappe, who completed the season with the Cubs in seventh place.

The next year, Klein got a longer shift as head coach, leading the Cubs for a month after Tappe opened the season with a 4–16 record. The team was 12–18 under Klein, who then gave way to Charlie Metro, who was head coach for the rest of the season.

By 1963, P. K. Wrigley had covertly abandoned the "head coach" system with the appointment of Bob Kennedy, and Klein lingered on as a coach. But Wrigley must have seen something he liked about Klein's direction of the team under the head-coach system because when he fired Kennedy in June 1965, he named Klein his successor.

Klein, now considered a manager rather than a head coach, led the Cubs about two-thirds of the season, with a record of 48–58. He couldn't get them out of eighth place (in a 10-team league) and was dismissed.

Charlie Metro

Record: 43–69 (.384)
B: April 29, 1919, Nanty Glo, Pennsylvania

Metro, Charles

	W	L	T	Pct
1962	43	69	0	.384
Cubs	43	69	9	.384
Career	62	102	0	.378

Charlie Metro had a brief career (1943–45) as a reserve outfielder with the Detroit Tigers and Philadelphia Athletics, and a much longer term of service as a highly respected coach and major league scout.

Metro took over as head coach of the Cubs in June 1962 after they had gotten off to a horrendous 16–34 start under El Tappe and Lou Klein. He was a strict disciplinarian, a characteristic that may have pleased owner P. K. Wrigley more than it did the players, but he could not right the ship, and the Cubs finished with a 43–69 record, in ninth place. In reality, he was the last head coach.

Metro quit the Cubs after the 1962 season and returned to coaching for the White Sox and other teams. He was named manager of the Kansas City Athletics in 1970 but was fired after the team started out 19–33.

1963–65

Bob Kennedy

Record: 182–198 (.479)
B: August 18, 1920, Chicago, Illinois

Lou Klein

Charlie Metro

Kennedy, Robert D.

	W	L	T	Pct
1963	82	80	0	.506
1964	76	86	0	.469
1965	24	32	2	.429
Cubs	182	198	2	.479
Career	264	278	3	.478

Philip K. Wrigley unveiled a new wrinkle for 1963, without admitting he was abandoning the College of Coaches. He hired Robert Whitlow, a retired Air Force colonel, as "athletic director." Among Whitlow's duties, in addition to ensuring that the players were kept in good physical condition, was to "supervise assignments of head coaches and managers in the organization in consultation with other members of the management team." Whitlow had little impact on the team for the two years he held the unusual post other than perhaps to concur in Wrigley's decision to appoint Bob Kennedy head coach for 1963. The choice of Kennedy in effect ended the College of Coaches.

A gruff, purposeful leader, Kennedy had become the regular third baseman for the White Sox at the age of 19 in 1940. He enjoyed a 16-year major league career as an outfielder and third baseman with a rifle arm for several teams, finishing in 1957 with a career batting average of .254.

He became a coach and a minor league manager, and his reputation caught Wrigley's attention. Kennedy was added to the coaching staff, then named head coach. But in all except name he was the manager from 1963 to mid-1965.

Kennedy's first season was modestly successful, the Cubs going over .500 for the first time in 17 years with an 82–80 record, though they finished in seventh place. The most notable developments were the shift of Ernie Banks, who was slowing down, from shortstop to first base, where he was to

Bob Kennedy

remain the rest of his career, and an outstanding season by Dick Ellsworth, who was 22–10. Ron Santo and Billy Williams each hit 25 home runs. The Cubs also got help from relief pitcher Lindy McDaniel and starting pitcher Larry Jackson, who had been acquired in a preseason trade.

The 1964 campaign was marred by a preseason tragedy in which second baseman Ken Hubbs, who had been developing into a star, was killed in an airplane crash. The Cubs floundered to a 78–86 record and eighth place, one of the few bright spots of the season being Jackson's 24–11 record. He led the NL in victories.

By the time the 1965 season started, athletic director Whitlow was gone, Wrigley admitting to another failed experiment. Kennedy lasted two months into the season, leading the Cubs to a 24–32 record until Wrigley replaced him with Lou Klein. The Cubs finished the season 72–90 and in eighth place.

Kennedy's subsequent career earned him a reputation as an astute developer of young talent. He managed the Oakland Athletics in 1968, spent some years as a farm director, and from 1977 to 1981 was back with the Cubs as general manager.

1966–72

Leo Durocher

Record: 535–526 (.504)
B: July 27, 1905, West Springfield, Massachusetts
D: October 7, 1991, Palm Springs, California

Durocher, Leo E.

	W	L	T	Pct
1966	59	103	0	.364
1967	87	74	1	.540
1968	84	78	1	.519
1969	92	70	1	.568
1970	84	78	0	.519
1971	83	79	0	.512
1972	46	44	1	.511
Cubs	535	526	4	.504
Career	2,008	1,709	22	.540

Few managers have earned such a checkered reputation as Leo Durocher, a prototypical "dead-end kid" who parlayed a sharp baseball mind, a gift for gab that earned him the nickname "The Lip," and a cocky, aggressive, and truculent nature into a career that transcended baseball. He was a national figure, his name familiar even to people who did not follow the game, a television celebrity, one of whose four wives, Laraine Day, was a movie star.

Feisty, egotistic, ever combative, Durocher was an outstanding fielding shortstop though a weak hitter for 17 seasons. As a brash rookie in 1926 with the New York Yankees, he earned the hostility of teammate Babe Ruth, and in the mid-1930s he was a key component of the St. Louis Cardinals' Gashouse Gang.

As manager he led the 1941 Brooklyn Dodgers to a pennant, then after a period of eclipse, including suspension from baseball for one year (1947) for allegedly associating with gangsters, he managed the New York Giants to two pen-

Leo Durocher

nants, in 1951 and 1954, including a World Series championship the latter year.

Durocher's approach to the game, as to life, could be summed up by a quotation attributed to him, "Nice guys finish last," though his precise words had been refined by an adroit sportswriter. He was an outstanding "situations" manager and a daring "gambler" in a baseball sense, never afraid to play a hunch.

Jackie Robinson, who played for Durocher in 1948 as well as against his teams in subsequent years, summed up the fiery manager's style of direction: "If you had a winning team," Robinson said, "nobody was better than Durocher. He had the knack of stimulating winning ballplayers, pushing them to heights that were sometimes beyond their ability. But with a losing team, Durocher would lose his composure. He got upset, he made players angry, causing some to play below their ability."

All these aspects of Durocher's managerial style came into play during his almost seven-year tenure with the Cubs. Durocher's abrasive baseball personality—though he could be charming if it was to his advantage—was anathema to the gentlemanly P. K. Wrigley, as it was to the umpires with whom "The Lip" carried on an endless feud.

Yet Wrigley, with his infinite capacity for astonishing baseball, in late 1965 chose Durocher to manage the Cubs, signing him to a three-year contract though Durocher had been out of the game for a year and was 60 years old. It was a reprise of his hiring almost two decades earlier of Frisch, whose personality and methods he also had disliked. (Perhaps significantly, Frisch and Durocher had formed the double-play combination of the turbulent Gashouse Gang in 1934.)

The Cubs had suffered ruinous financial losses in the last two seasons, but Wrigley was bothered more by the stagnation of the team and ill-advised trades in which young players, such as outfielder Lou Brock in 1964, had been deigned failures and traded to other teams for whom they became standouts.

In announcing the hiring of Durocher, Wrigley admitted

that the College of Coaches had been a failure and that the players needed a rude awakening and a firm hand. Duroocher, he said, was "the manager." The choice of Durocher, he later said, was entirely his, with the concurrence of general manager John Holland.

"I decided what we needed was somebody with the drive, the toughness, and the leadership of Durocher to get their best out of them [the players]," Wrigley said. "Somebody had to wake them up."

That Durocher woke up the Cubs, none could dispute, though his first season of 1966 was a disaster, the team finishing in 10th place with a 59–103 record. This result provided some media merriment, Durocher having said before the season that "this is not an eighth-place team."

But with Durocher's advice and urging, Holland made trades that shaped the Cubs into a contending team for several seasons. The most significant trades were with the San Francisco Giants on December 2, 1965, in which the Cubs got pitcher Bill Hands and catcher Randy Hundley, and with the Philadelphia Phillies on April 21, 1966, in which they obtained pitcher Ferguson Jenkins and center fielder Adolfo Phillips.

Jenkins, a reliever whom Durocher converted into a starter, became a 20-game winner for six consecutive seasons (1967–72). Hands also was a first-rate starter for several years, winning 20 games in 1969. Hundley became the best Cub catcher since Hartnett, and Phillips had a brief burst of stardom before quickly fading.

Under Durocher's guidance, second baseman Glenn Beckert and shortstop Don Kessinger became the best Cub double-play combination since Billy Herman and Bill Jurges. With power hitters Ron Santo at third base and Ernie Banks at first, the Cubs had a all-star infield. Billy Williams in left field was a great hitter, and a young left-hander, Ken Holtzman, helped balance the starting pitching. Though the two other outfield positions were never satisfactorily filled for any length of time, Durocher and Holland had fashioned the Cubs into a genuine pennant contender.

Fan excitement and attendance soared in 1967 and 1968 as the Cubs ascended to third place both seasons with Durocher playing the pied piper as he alternately tongue-lashed and petted his players, while entertaining the fans and media with outrageous statements and combats with umpires and opposing teams. He gloried in the spotlight, though often displaying jealousy of Banks, who was the darling of the fans as "Mr. Cub" and remained a productive hitter, with 32 home runs in 1968.

The zenith of Duricher's reign came in 1969 when the Cubs seemed to be en route to easily winning the division title (the NL had expanded to 12 teams for 1969, with two divisions). They held a five-game lead over the second-place New York Mets on September 5, and a stereo in the clubhouse that morning was blaring their song: "Holy Mackerel, No Doubt about It, The Cubs Are on Their Way."

An overconfident Durocher had taken advantage of his seeming success by leaving the team on June 18 for a bachelor's party prior to his fourth marriage, to Mrs. Lynn Walker Goldblatt. In his absence, coach Pete Reiser presided over a defeat. Wrigley was upset. "I don't like the way Leo walked away from the team without saying anything," Wrigley barked, "but we'll have to forgive him this time."

All the same, Durocher repeated his misconduct on July 26, disappearing during a game. A rumor that he had taken ill was dispelled by the revelation that he had left the team to spend the weekend with his new stepson at a Wisconsin boy's camp. Wrigley bit his tongue and kept silent as Durocher continued his waywardness with umpire baiting, shouting matches with his players, and hostility toward the media.

And on September 5 the sweet season turned sour. The Cubs went into a tailspin, losing eight consecutive games, and the Mets vaulted over them into first place on September 10. The "Miracle Mets" went on to a pennant and a World Series championship. The Cubs finished second with a record of 92–70, their best since the pennant year of 1945. Attendance reached a record 1,674,993.

Durocher's explanation for the Cubs' late-season collapse: "We went into a composite slump. It wasn't just one or two guys. It was everybody and every department. Hitting, pitching, and fielding all went bad." Others blamed the Cubs' lack of depth behind their lineup of stars and Durocher's persistence in playing his regulars without rest to the point of weariness. The Cubs were saddled with the reputation of "the best team that never won a pennant," and there was some validity to it. Santo drove in 123 runs, Banks 106, and Williams 95; Jenkins won 21 games, Hands 20, and Holtzman 17.

The next two years brought no solace as the Cubs finished second in 1970 and third in 1971 under Durocher. The stars shone brightly in 1970, though Banks was at the end of his string. Williams stood out in 1970 with .322, 42 home runs, and 129 RBIs; Santo hit 36 home runs and drove in 114 runs; and veteran retread Jim Hickman at first base contributed .315 with 32 home runs and 115 RBIs. Jenkins was 22–16.

In 1971, Durocher's team finished just above .500 with an 83–79 record despite a 24–13 contribution by Jenkins. A player revolt against the manager in the clubhouse on August 30 in which Santo had to be restrained from attacking Durocher was the highlight of the campaign.

Wrigley defended Durocher, even taking out newspaper advertisements in which he upheld the manager's authority and vowed to trade away the disgruntled players. Among those gone by the start of the '72 season were Holtzman and Hands.

As the Cubs floundered in 1972, unable to get much over .500 and clearly out of contention, Durocher decided, with Wrigley's assent, that it was time to leave. He quit on July 24, turning over the team to Whitey Lockman, formerly one of his coaches. The Cubs had a 46–44 record and were in fourth place.

Durocher's long managerial career, however, was not over. A month after leaving the Cubs he bacame manager of the Houston Astros, a job he held through the 1973 season before he retired from baseball at the age of 68.

1972–74

Whitey Lockman

Record: 157–162 (.492)
B: July 25, 1926, Lowell, North Carolina

Lockman, Carroll W.

	W	L	T	Pct
1972	39	26	0	.600
1973	77	84	0	.478
1974	41	52	0	.441
Cubs	157	162	0	.492
Career	157	162	0	.492

Whitey Lockman

At the time of his appointment as successor to Leo Durocher, Whitey Lockman had been director of player development in the Cubs' organization. He had had a distinguished 15-year major league career as an outfielder, mostly with the Giants, and was the regular first baseman for Durocher's pennant winners in 1951 and 1954. His career batting average was .279. After his playing days, Lockman concentrated on player development, though he was a coach under Durocher with the Cubs in 1965 and 1966.

When he took over as manager on July 24, 1972, the Cubs were 46–44. They played at a .600 pace the rest of the season, winning 39 games and losing 26. They finished second, and it appeared they were responding to Lockman's congenial personality, much more relaxed than that of Durocher. Ferguson Jenkins again was a 20-game winner, and Billy Williams had a "career year" with .332 to lead the league in batting, with 37 home runs and 122 RBIs. Two young pitchers, Burt Hooton and Rick Reuschel, seemed to hold promise for the future.

For a time it appeared that the future had arrived in 1973 as the Cubs led the division on July 4 and Lockman's gentler touch seemed sure. But the wheels came off after that: an 11-game losing streak sank the Cubs into fifth place. Some of the players were getting old—Williams, Jim Hickman, and Ron Santo among them—and an unhappy Jenkins was 14–14 after six consecutive 20-game winning years.

Santo, Glenn Beckert, Randy Hundley, and Jenkins were gone by 1974, the latter bringing Bill Madlock, a fine hitting third baseman, from the Texas Rangers in the trade. But the Cubs were in the doldrums again and would remain so for another decade. Lockman quit after 93 games, leaving a 41–52 record, and handed the job to Jim Marshall, who had little better luck as the Cubs finished last.

Lockman returned to his role as director of player development. After the 1976 season he left the Cubs to continue a successful career in scouting and player development.

1974–76

Jim Marshall

Record: 175–218 (.445)
B: May 25, 1931, Danville, Illinois

Marshall, Rufus J.				
	W	L	T	Pct
1974	25	44	0	.362
1975	75	87	0	.463
1976	75	87	0	.463
Cubs	175	218	0	.445
Career	229	326	1	.413

Jim Marshall's career as a first baseman was distinguished mainly by his travels from team to team in both the minor and major leagues during the 1950s and 1960s. He spent parts of five seasons in the majors, including 1958 and 1959 with the Cubs, but mainly in a utility role. He even played three years in Japan before retiring as a player in 1965 to become a minor league manager in the Cub system.

After a creditable job at Wichita of the American Association, Marshall became Lockman's third base coach in 1974

Jim Marshall

and was named manager on July 24 when the Cubs were 41–52. Marshall couldn't budge them, and they finished 25–44, in sixth place.

It was much the same the next two seasons, the Cubs finishing 75–87 and in fifth place in 1975 and with the same record but in fourth place in 1976. Both seasons were distinguished chiefly by NL batting titles for Madlock, with .354 and .339, and some decent pitching by Rick Reuschel and Ray Burris. After the season, Don Kessinger was traded away to complete the breakup of the 1969 team.

Meanwhile, general manager John Holland was semiretired to a consultant role, and owner Philip K. Wrigley in 1976 named E. R. "Salty" Saltwell, whose expertise lay in operating Wrigley Field, concessions and the like, to the post despite Saltwell's admitted lack of knowledge about players. Wrigley on November 24, 1976, turned direction of the Cubs over to Bob Kennedy, the "head coach" of a decade earlier, as vice president in charge of baseball operations.

Kennedy dismissed Marshall and hired Herman Franks as manager. Marshall continued his career in both the minor leagues and in the majors, managing the Oakland A's in the 1979 season. In 1981 he managed a team in Japan.

1977–79

Herman Franks

Record: 238–241 (.497)
B: January 4, 1914, Price, Utah

Franks, Herman L.				
	W	L	T	Pct
1977	81	81	0	.500
1978	79	83	0	.488
1979	78	77	0	.503
Cubs	238	241	0	.497
Career	605	521	2	.537

Herman Franks, who had become a millionaire in real estate, represented a return to the Durocher era, shrewd if crude, loud and outspoken, a protégé and close friend of "The Lip."

Franks had been a reserve catcher for Leo Durocher at Brooklyn and New York, as well as for other teams during a six-year major league playing career (1939–49) that produced a batting average of .199. A four-year term as manager of the San Francisco Giants (1965–68) had resulted in four consecutive second-place finishes, and in 1969 Franks briefly had been a Cub coach, acting as a buffer between the volatile Durocher and his players as well as the media.

Bob Kennedy presented Franks with a reconstructed team, tearing up the Cubs of '76 with a flurry of trades, the chief acquisitions being center fielder Bobby Murcer, a former Yankees star, and first baseman Bill Buckner, a standout for the Dodgers. The most notable departure was that of Bill Madlock after a contract dispute.

P. K. Wrigley died on April 12, 1977, just after the season started, and the team passed into the hand of his son, William, who apparently had little interest in the Cubs, and less in the public attention that accompanies the ownership of a sports franchise.

Franks appeared to have the magic touch until August, as

Herman Franks

1980

Preston Gomez

Record: 38–52 (.422)
B: April 20, 1923, Central Preston, Cuba

Gomez y Martinez, Pedro

	W	L	T	Pct
1980	38	52	0	.422
Cubs	38	52	0	.422
Career	346	529	0	.395

Outwardly congenial, Preston Gomez had earned a reputation as a disciplinarian in previous managerial posts at San Diego and Houston, a quality that recommended him to Bob Kennedy after Herman Frank's accusations that the players were coddled and complacent.

Gomez had been one of many players recruited in Cuba by the old Washington Senators during the 1930s and 1940s. His major league playing career consisted of eight games at shortstop for the Senators in 1944, after which he spent 10 years in the minor leagues as a player. A successful minor league managing career that began in 1957 led to managerial jobs with the Padres and Astros, the latter as successor to Leo Durocher in 1974. He came to the Cubs after three years as a coach with the Dodgers.

Gomez stressed speed and defense. The Cubs he took over had very little of either, other than shortstop Ivan DeJesus and center fielder Miguel Dilone, who was promptly traded away. The team was slow and the defense porous. Kingman missed half the season with a shoulder injury and created dissension with several highly publicized antics. The Cubs got off to a poor start and never looked back. Gomez was fired in July with a 38–52 record, Joey Amalfitano again taking over the team, which completed the season 64–98 and in last place.

the Cubs fired up their fans by making a run for the division title. They were in first place as late as August 4 when twin blows destroyed their chances. Rick Reuschel, 14–3 at that point, injured his back, and Bruce Sutter, the sensational reliever, also was hurt. The Cubs slid into fourth place with an 81–81 record, though Reuschel finished 20–10 and Murcer led the team in home runs with 27 and RBIs with 95.

Over the winter, Kennedy signed Dave Kingman, a much-traveled slugger and defensive liability as a left fielder, and he helped provide a similar early rush in 1978, the Cubs leading the division until late June before the collapse began. They finished 70–83 and in third place.

The main excitement in 1979 was provided by Kingman, as he led the major leagues with 48 home runs, and by Sutter, who won the NL Cy Young Award with 37 saves. Nevertheless, the Cubs struggled, and Franks resigned with a week to go in the season to resume his business interests, but in a parting shot accused the players of being selfish and uninspired. Still, he was not quite through with the Cubs.

Coach Joey Amalfitano took over a team with a 78–77 record and won two of the final seven games. The Cubs finished in fifth place.

Preston Gomez

1979–81

Joey Amalfitano

Record: 66–116 (.363)
B: January 23, 1934, San Pedro, California

Amalfitano, John J.

	W	L	T	Pct
1979	2	5	0	.286
1980	26	46	0	.361
1981 (first half)	15	37	0	.288
1981 (second half)	23	28	0	.451
Cubs	66	116	0	.363
Career	66	116	0	.363

As a career coach, Joey Amalfitano was well regarded, and almost always employed. As a manager, he was saddled with one of the worst Cubs teams in one of the most difficult periods of the team's history.

As a journeyman major league infielder, Amalfitano had won Leo Durocher's respect during a playing career that extended from 1954 to 1967, much of it with the Giants and Cubs. He was a Cub coach from 1967 to 1971 and returned to the team in 1978.

His interim role as successor to Herman Franks in 1979 had produced a 2–5 record to close out the season. In 1980 he again answered the call to manage a demoralized team, taking over from the dismissed Preston Gomez. The Cubs stumbled to a 26–46 record to complete the season in last place. Their only solace was Buckner's league-leading .324 batting average.

As the 1981 season approached, Bob Kennedy traded away Dave Kingman and Bruce Sutter, then resigned to be replaced briefly as general manager by Franks. Rumors were current of the impending sale of the Cubs by William Wrigley to the Tribune Company, the deal being consummated on June 16. In the interim, nobody else seemed to want the job of managing what was undeniably a poor team, and Amalfitano was kept on.

On top of these problems, the chronic dispute between the players and the major league owners reached new heights of acrimony, and the players went on strike on June 12 after the Cubs had started out 1–12 before "improving" to 15–37. When play resumed after the All-Star Game, in what had been declared a split season, the Cubs were slightly better, with a 23–28 record and in fifth place in the second half.

Amalfitano was swept out in the general housecleaning as a new regime took over the Cubs. He resumed his career as a coach, mainly with the Dodgers.

1982–83

Lee Elia

Record: 127–158 (.446)
B: July 16, 1937, Philadelphia, Pennsylvania

Elia, Lee C.

	W	L	T	Pct
1982	73	89	0	.451
1983	54	69	0	.439
Cubs	127	158	0	.446
Career	238	300	1	.442

Gruff, outspoken, no-nonsense Dallas Green took command of the Cubs as general manager for 1982, pledging that he would "build a new tradition." A former pitcher, he had earned a reputation for toughness as manager of the 1980 World Series champion Philadelphia Phillies.

He brought with him from Philadelphia a new manager, Lee Elia, and more significantly made a trade with his old

Joe Amalfitano

Lee Elia

team to acquire veteran shortstop Larry Bowa and rookie in-fielder Ryne Sandberg. Another trade regained Fergie Jenkins. On hand already were some promising youngsters, catcher Jody Davis, first baseman Leon Durham, and reliever Lee Smith.

Elia had been a minor league shortstop though he had brief stints with the White Sox in 1966 and the Cubs in 1968. During off-season he was a schoolteacher. He became a manager in the Phillies' minor league system and was a coach with the Phillies when Green named him manager of the Cubs.

A typical baseball "lifer," Elia, despite his emotional approach, had no ready solution for the Cubs' problems and suffered through a dreary first season, including a 13-game losing streak. The Cubs finished 73–89 and in fifth place in 1982. Jenkins led a poor pitching staff with 14 wins, but at 39 years of age was clearly winding down. Sandberg, however, surprised at third base, and Smith, Davis, and Durham clearly provided hope for the future.

The Cubs fared even worse in 1983 with a 71–91 record and fifth place despite the addition of expensive free-agent veteran Ron Cey, a power-hitting third baseman from the Dodgers. However, Sandberg emerged as an outstanding fielder and hitter at second base, and Smith earned 29 saves.

Elia, in any case, had put the nail in his own coffin and wasn't around to see the finish, even though he earned a measure of lasting notoriety with a clubhouse tirade during a losing streak in which he blamed the fans rather than his players for the Cubs' problems. According to Elia, "Eighty-five percent of the world's workin'; the other 15 come out here [to Wrigley Field] to boo the Cubs."

Green replaced Elia on August 12, 1983, when they were 54–69, with Charlie Fox, who could not turn them around as they went 17–22 to the finish line.

Elia returned to the Philadelphia organization, and in 1987 and 1988 managed the Phillies.

1983

Charlie Fox

Record: 17–22 (.436)
B: October 7, 1921, New York, New York

Fox, Charles F.

	W	L	T	Pct
1983	17	22	0	.436
Cubs	17	22	0	.436
Career	377	371	0	.504

A keen evaluator of baseball talent, Charlie Fox was an adviser to Dallas Green when he was asked to return to the field as interim manager in place of Lee Elia on August 12, 1983.

A minor league catcher virtually all his playing career, "Irish" Fox, 61, had managed the Giants from 1970 to 1974, with a division title to his credit in 1971. He also had a brief managerial term with the Montreal Expos. He finished the 1983 season as interim manager of the Cubs, who were 17–22 under his guidance, then returned to his off-field career.

Charlie Fox

1984–86

Jim Frey

Record: 196–182 (.519)
B: May 26, 1931, Cleveland, Ohio

Frey, James G.

	W	L	T	Pct
1984	96	65	0	.596
1985	77	84	1	.478
1986	23	33	0	.411
Cubs	196	182	1	.519
Career	323	287	1	.530

When Jim Frey, 53, a former outfielder who had spent his entire career in the minor leagues, was named manager for 1984, the announcement didn't arouse high expectations for the Cubs. They were coing off a 71–91 record in 1983 and looked even worse in spring training under Frey, winning just seven of 27 games.

Frey, a tough little man who was highly demanding of players, had earned Dallas Green's respect as manager of the Kansas City Royals. He led the Royals to the 1980 World Series after a long career as minor league manager and major league coach, but was fired the next season after difficulties with some of his players. He was a coach with the New York Mets when Green hired him.

Though Green's Phillies defeated the Royals in the World Series, he was impressed with Frey's ability and no-nonsense

Jim Frey

personality. "I like the way he looks you square in the eye," Green said.

More concretely, a series of trades by Green before the '84 season and early in the season transformed the Cubs from a plodding team with poor defense and weak pitching into an instant contender. Green obtained pitcher Scott Sanderson from Montreal and landed two-thirds of an outfield from Philadelphia in swift center fielder Bobby Dernier and hard-hitting left fielder Gary Matthews. He traded Bill Buckner, the first baseman for seven years, to Boston for another solid starter, Dennis Eckersley, at the same time creating an opening at first base for Leon Durham, an indifferent outfielder.

Green's coup came on June 13. He solidified the pitching staff in a major trade with Cleveland in which the chief acquisition was right-hander Rick Sutcliffe. The deal was costly, Green giving up young outfielders Joe Carter and Mel Hall, the first of whom became a major star, but it was the making of the '84 Cubs.

Green had given Frey a competitive team, and the manager made the most of it, the Cubs taking off on their way to a division championship, their first title since the 1945 pennant.

Sutcliffe led the starting pitchers with a 16–1 record (he had been 4–5 for Cleveland) to win the Cy Young Award, and Lee Smith earned 33 saves as the ace of the bullpen. Cey led the team with 25 home runs and 97 RBIs, and Durham was right behind with 23 home runs and 96 RBIs.

Most spectacular, however, was Sandberg, a revelation in his second year as a second baseman. He batted .314 and showed unexpected power with 19 home runs and 84 RBIs to win the Most Valuable Player award. Frey had sensed Sandberg's power potential and urged him to pull the ball more often.

On June 23, 1984, Sandberg's batting pyrotechnics gave the Cubs a 12–11 come-from-behind victory over St. Louis

that convinced themselves, the league, and the fans they were "for real." He drove in seven runs and hit two home runs to tie the game twice in a five-for-six outburst. The game was probably the turning point of the season.

As the Cubs gathered momentum, taking over first place for good on August 1, "Cub fever" swept Chicago, as well as the huge national following the team had gathered through cable television. Attendance for 1984 soared to a Wrigley Field record of 2,107,665.

The Cubs clinched the NL East Division title on September 24 and finished the regular season with a 96–65 record and a wide margin over the second-place New York Mets, Frey earning the Manager of the Year award.

Despite high expectations for the first World Series in Wrigley Field for 39 years, not even Frey could change the Cubs' penchant for failure in postseason play. They were favored to waltz past the San Diego Padres in the NL Championship Series and fired up "Cub fever" to an even more intense pitch by winning the first two games at Wrigley Field. But when the series moved to San Diego, the Padres won the final three games and went to the World Series while the Cubs scattered to their homes.

Frey's second year as manager, 1985, was marred by an early 13-game losing streak and an epidemic of injuries to his best pitchers, Sutcliffe, Sanderson, and Eckersley. The aging Ron Cey and Larry Bowa were near the end of their careers. The replacements proved inadequate, and the Cubs skidded to a 77–84 record and fourth place.

A patch-up job over the winter of 1985–86 didn't help, the Cubs continuing to flounder. They were 23–33 and in fifth place in June 12, 1986, when Green relieved Frey as manager, replacing him with Gene Michael. (Coach John Vukovich served as interim manager for two games until Michael arrived.) Frey retreated to the broadcasting booth for 1987 as a color commentator for WGN Radio.

Unexpectedly, Frey returned in triumph after Green was forced out following the 1987 season, becoming his successor as general manager. Frey hired Don Zimmer as manager and directed the Cubs to another division title winner in 1989. He gave way to Larry Himes as general manager after the 1991 season.

1986

John Vukovich

Record: 1–1 (.500)
B: July 31, 1947, Sacramento, California

Vukovich, John C.

	W	L	T	Pct
1986	1	1	0	.500
Cubs	1	1	0	.500
Career	6	5	0	.545

A good-field, no-hit utility infielder (with a career batting average of .161) in the major leagues for 10 seasons (1970–81), mostly with the Phillies, John Vukovich spent six years (1982–87) with the Cubs as a coach.

After Don Zimmer was fired as manager by Dallas Green on June 12, 1986, Vukovich served as interim manager on June 13 during a doubleheader split with St. Louis.

John Vukovich

Vukovich left the Cubs after the 1987 season to coach for the Phillies, for whom he also served as interim manager in 1988 for nine games.

1986

Gene Michael

Record: 114–124 (.479)
B: June 2, 1938, Kent, Ohio

Michael, Eugene R.

	W	L	T	Pct
1986	46	56	0	.451
1987	68	68	0	.500
Cubs	114	124	0	.479
Career	206	200	0	.507

Tall and lean (hence his nickname "Stick"), Gene Michael was a steady-fielding shortstop for 10 major league seasons, mostly with the Yankees from 1968 to 1974. He had a reputation for being calm and dependable.

Michael was a coach with the Yankees when Dallas Green called on him on June 12, 1986, to manage the Cubs. Previously, he had managed the Yankees on two occasions, during most of the 1981 split-season until replaced by Bob Lemon with 25 games to go, and again the next year, when he replaced Lemon after 14 games. He held on for 86 games, with a 44–42 record, before in turn being replaced by Clyde King for the rest of the season.

Michael's managerial experience didn't help him much with the '86 Cubs, as they continued at the pace they had set under Frey, winning 46 of the remaining 102 games and finishing in fifth place.

Gene Michael

Green became impatient with Michael's calm managerial style, but made allowances for a total pitching collapse, with no Cub winning as many as 10 games, the worst showing of the century other than in the strike year of 1981. Sutcliffe sagged to 5–14 with shoulder problems. Only Lee Smith, with 30 saves, stood out, becoming the first NL reliever to record 30 or more saves for three consecutive seasons.

But Green kept Michael for the '87 season and came up with the final coup of his regime, signing free-agent right fielder Andre Dawson, who had starred at Montreal. Dawson came through spectacularly, batting .289 with 49 home runs and 137 RBIs to earn the NL Most Valuable Player award. Sutcliffe bounced back to an 18–10 record, and Smith saved 36 games. None of this helped Michael's cause, and with the team at 68–68 and in fifth place on September 7, he decided to resign before he could be fired.

Green, after appointing coach Frank Lucchesi as manager, responded with a blast at the players, saying he was "slapped in the face, and so were the Cub fans." "We quit with a capital Q," he barked. It was a parting shot. Green resigned a few weeks later, having been stripped of much of his authority by his superiors.

Under Lucchesi, the Cubs finished the season 8–17 to end up with a 76–85 record and in last place. The unperturbed Michael eventually returned to the Yankees organization and became general manager.

Frank Lucchesi

Don Zimmer

1987

Frank Lucchesi

Record: 8–17 (.320)
B: April 24, 1927, San Francisco, California

Lucchesi, Frank J.

	W	L	T	Pct
1987	8	17	0	.320
Cubs	8	17	0	.320
Career	316	399	0	.442

Patient, nice guy Frank Lucchesi was serving as the Cubs' "eye-in-the-sky" coach when Dallas Green named him to follow Gene Michael as manager on September 7, 1987.

Lucchesi had managerial experience. He had served 19 years in the minor leagues as player and manager before he was named to manage the Phillies after the 1969 season. He held the job with little success until he was fired in midseason 1972. He also managed the Texas Rangers from midseason 1975 to midseason 1977 without much luck before returning to minor league managing, coaching, and scouting.

Lucchesi's brief tenure to close the 1987 season, with an 8–17 record, ended his association with the Cubs.

1988–91

Don Zimmer

Record: 265–258 (.507)
B: January 17, 1931, Cincinnati, Ohio

Zimmer, Donald W.

	W	L	T	Pct
1988	77	85	1	.475
1989	93	69	0	.574
1990	77	85	0	.475
1991	18	19	0	.486
Cubs	265	258	1	.507
Career	885	858	2	.508

The friendship of Jim Frey and Don Zimmer went back to the late 1930s when they were teammates in baseball and basketball at Western Hills High School in Cincinnati. But while Frey's subsequent playing career was strictly minor league, Zimmer was a major league infielder for 12 seasons (1954–65), with a career batting average of .235. He was mostly a utility player, though he was the Cubs' regular second baseman in 1960 and 1961. Known for his scrappiness, Zimmer had not let a beaning end his career, though he wore a metal plate in his skull as a memento of the almost fatal incident.

After his playing days, Zimmer earned a reputation as a coach, then was named manager of the San Diego Padres in 1972, keeping the job for two seasons. He went on to manage the Boston Red Sox for almost five seasons and the Texas Rangers for almost three during the next decade before Frey surprised no one by hiring him as third base coach in 1984. When Frey was elevated to general manager in 1987, it was inevitable that he would choose Zimmer as manager.

Outgoing, outspoken, and aggressive, Zimmer was a "hunch" manager and had been moderately successful with the Red Sox, with two second-place finishes, including the memorable 1978 tie for first place that had been decided in favor of the Yankees by Bucky Dent's home run in a single-game playoff.

Zimmer's managerial style, however, failed to inspire the Cubs of 1988. They continued to stumble and finished 77–85, in fifth place. Frey contributed to the debacle with one of the poorest trades in the team's history, sending Lee Smith to Boston before the season for pitchers Calvin Schiraldi and Al Nipper, both failures. In retrospect, the most memorable event for the Cubs in 1988 was the first night game at Wrigley Field on August 9.

Nevertheless, the farm system finally came up with some promising youngsters, Mark Grace replacing Durham at first base and batting .296, Rafael Palmeiro batting .307 in left field, and young right-hander Greg Maddux recording an 18–8 season.

Just as in 1984, not much was expected of the Cubs in 1989, but a trade by Frey on December 5, 1988, and the surprise development of two rookie outfielders, Jerome Walton and Dwight Smith, paved the way to success. The Cubs traded Palmeiro and five others to Texas, getting three players in return, the most important being relief pitcher Mitch Williams, who earned 36 saves in 1989.

With Sandberg (30 home runs) and Dawson (23 home runs) providing much of the firepower, Rookie of the Year Walton (.293) some speed, and Maddux (19–12), Rick Sutcliffe (16–11), Mike Bielecki (18–7), and Williams (36 saves) most of the pitching, Zimmer's team reignited Cub fever in 1989, with attendance at Wrigley Field reaching a record 2,491,942.

The fans saw the Cubs win 16 games in their final at bats as they fought off three other contenders to win the NL East title with a 93–69 record. Zimmer's hunches seemed inspired as the Cubs came from behind in 33 victories.

But fan fever quickly cooled as the Cubs fell easily to the San Francisco Giants in the NL Championship Series, winning just one game in the best-of-seven set.

Zimmer returned to battle with much the same team in 1990, but the season proved a disaster because of almost total collapse of the pitching despite individual batting heroics such as those of Sandberg, who hit a career-high 40 home runs, and Dawson, who batted a career-high .310 with 27 home runs, while driving in 100 runs to match Sandberg. Walton, after his fine rookie year, faded away.

The Cubs sank to 77–85 and fourth place as Maddux, Bielecki, and Sutcliffe, who had been 53–30 among them in '89, slid to a combined 23–30 in '90.

Frey's chief acquisitions for 1991 were three free agents, starting left-hander Danny Jackson, reliever Dave Smith, and slugging left fielder George Bell. They were little help to Zimmer, though his firing on May 22 was unexpected because the Cubs were 18–19. But after coach Joe Altobelli's one-game stint as interim manager, Frey brought in Jim Essian as the new field boss.

Zimmer readily continued his career as one of the premier third base coaches.

1991

Joe Altobelli

Record: 0–1 (.000)
B: May 26, 1932, Detroit, Michigan

Altobelli, Joseph S.

	W	L	T	Pct
1991	0	1	0	.000
Cubs	0	1	0	.000
Career	437	407	0	.518

A couple of brief stretches in the major leagues had sweetened Joe Altobelli's mostly minor league career as a first baseman, but he had managed the San Francisco Giants and Baltimore Orioles before he came to the Cubs as a coach in 1988. In fact, he had led the Orioles to a World Series championship in 1983, which did not preclude his being fired less than two seasons later.

Altobelli was called on to manage the Cubs for one game after Zimmer was fired on May 22, 1991. The Cubs lost 8–6 to the Mets in New York, and Altobelli's career as Cub manager was more short than sweet. After the season, he left the Cubs to continue his coaching career.

1991

Jim Essian

Record: 59–63 (.484)
B: January 2, 1951, Detroit, Michigan

Essian, James S.

	W	L	T	Pct
1991	59	63	0	.484
Cubs	59	63	0	.484
Career	59	63	0	.484

Jim Essian was a hard-working, intense major league catcher, mainly as the number-two man, for 12 seasons (1973–85) for four major league teams, compiling a career batting average of .244. He was managing the Cubs' top minor league team at Iowa when he was summoned to replace Don Zimmer.

Just turned 40, Essian was of a newer generation than his immediate predecessors, and it was expected he would have better rapport with the players, many of whom had played for him at Iowa. An outgoing, cheerleading sort of person, Essian's enthusiasm was genuine if considered somewhat odd in the "laid-back" environment of baseball in the 1990s.

Essian got off to a good start, the Cubs winning their first five games after his arrival. But reality set in on a 13-game road trip that started in mid-June, the Cubs returning home 2–11. The season also finished in a swoon, the Cubs losing 21 of their final 33 games to finish fourth with a 77–83 record. They were 59–63 under Essian.

Essian's fate was sealed, and he was fired, though the Cubs' failure was due as much to the flop of free agents Danny Jackson and Dave Smith as to anything else. Jackson spent two periods on the disabled list, started just 14 games,

Jim Essian

and had a record of 1–5. Smith was 0–6, with a 6.00 earned run average and 17 saves, far short of expectations.

At least George Bell came through. He hit 25 home runs and drove in 86 runs to give the Cubs a solid offensive middle of the lineup, with Dawson contributing 31 home runs and 104 RBIs and Sandberg 26 home runs and 100 RBIs. Maddux led a shaky pitching staff with a 15–11 record.

Jim Frey joined Essian in the discard pile, relegated to a consulting role after being replaced as general manager on November 14, 1991, by Larry Himes, former general manager of the White Sox. Essian continued to pursue a managerial and coaching career in the minor leagues.

1992–93

Jim Lefebvre

Record: 162–162 (.500)
B: January 7, 1942, Inglewood, California

Lefebvre, James K.

	W	L	T	Pct
1992	78	84	0	.481
1993	84	78	0	.519
Cubs	162	162	0	.500
Career	395	415	0	.488

New GM Larry Himes' choice as Jim Essian's successor was Jim Lefebvre, 50, whose intensity as manager of the Seattle Mariners he had admired while he was general manager of the White Sox. "Frenchy" Lefebvre, like Essian, was overflowing with enthusiasm, quick to laugh, and sometimes prone to angry outbursts at incompetence or neglect by his players.

He had enjoyed a career as a solid, decent-hitting second baseman with the Dodgers from 1965 to 1972, compiling a career batting average of .258, and later had become a coach for the Dodgers, often specializing as a batting instructor. Clashes with manager Tom Lasorda led to his parting with the Dodgers.

A three-year term as manager at Seattle from 1989 to 1991 produced mixed results, though in the final season the Mariners finished above .500 at 83–79 for the first time in their 15-year history. Nevertheless, he was fired, reportedly because of dissension between Lefebvre and some of his best players.

Jim Lefebvre

Attempting to rebuild the team, Himes traded George Bell to the White Sox for promising young right fielder Sammy Sosa, and presented Lefebvre with starting pitcher Mike Morgan, a high-priced free agent. Despite numerous other changes, the result was no improvement over 1991, the Cubs finishing 78–84 and in fourth place in Lefebvre's first year despite a 20–11 record and a Cy Young Award for Maddux, Morgan's 16–8 record, another 26 home runs and 87 RBIs by Sandberg, and 22 home runs and 90 RBIs by Dawson.

A back injury that sidelined regular shortstop Shawon Dunston for most of the season contributed to the disappointing performance of the team, which included the customary 9–20 swoon in September.

During the winter of 1992–93, the Cubs let Maddux get away as a free agent and dropped Dawson. For '93, Himes presented Lefebvre with three high-priced free-agent pitchers, starters Jose Guzman and Greg Hibbard and reliever Randy Myers, as well as outfielder Candy Maldonado, who proved a bust. Young outfielder Derrick May, infielders Jose Vizcaino and Rey Sanchez, and catcher Rick Wilkins also were expected to contribute.

The Cubs improved slightly in '93, finishing 84–78 and in fourth place in what with expansion was now a seven-team NL East Division. They set a Wrigley Field attendance record with a turnout of 2,653,763, though never really in contention, getting above .500 only with an uncharacteristic 20–8 push to close the season.

Myers set an NL record with 53 saves. Wilkins became the first Cub catcher since Gabby Hartnett to bat .300 with 30 home runs, Sosa became the first Cub to steal 30 bases and hit 30 home runs in a season, Hibbard won 15 games and Guzman 12.

Lefebvre and Himes, however, were at odds most of the season over the quality of the personnel, and despite a call-in vote conducted by a newspaper that showed the fans in favor of keeping the manager, Lefebvre was fired after the '93 season. He returned to coaching and instructing batters.

1994

Tom Trebelhorn

Record: 49–64 (.434)
B: January 27, 1948, Portland, Oregon

Trebelhorn, Thomas L.

	W	L	T	Pct
1994	49	64	0	.434
Cubs	49	64	0	.434
Career	471	461	0	.505

Larry Himes had chosen Tom Trebelhorn as one of Jim Lefebvre's coaches in 1992, and it was no surprise when he was elevated to manager for 1994. Well-educated and personable, Treblehorn had had a brief minor league career as a player before turning to managing in the minors at the age of 27 in 1975. By 1986 he was a coach for the Milwaukee Brewers, and he became their manager on September 26, succeeding George Bamberger. He held the job for the next five full seasons, with reasonable success, though no division titles. He was fired after the 1991 campaign.

Like Jim Essian and Lefebvre before him, Trebelhorn

Tom Trebelhorn

brought a highly enthusiastic, upbeat approach to managing the Cubs, something that was sorely tested as the unfortunate 1994 season proceeded toward its unpredictable and abrupt end.

Himes' major effort to shore up the team had been trades for two right-handed starting pitchers, Anthony Young and Willie Banks, neither of whom could pick up the slack when injuries wiped out Mike Morgan, who was 2–10, and Jose Guzman, 2–2.

Rookies Steve Trachsel (9–7) and Kevin Foster (3–4) showed promise for the future, but in general the pitching was dismal, other than that of Randy Myers, who had 34 saves in the bobtailed 113-game season the Cubs played before competition was ended by a strike on August 12. Overall play was also dismal, despite a .300 average, 25 home runs, and 92 RBIs by Sosa and a .298 average for Grace.

Trebelhorn's Cubs were in trouble from the beginning of the season in the new Central Division created when the NL split into three divisions for 1994. Although they played well on the road, they lost their first 12 games at home, virtually burying them for the season. Trebelhorn attempted to mollify the disgruntled fans by conducting "fireside chats" near Firehouse 78 across the street from Wrigley Field. "A lot of heart and emotions comes with the Cubs," Trebelhorn said. "The fans are terrific. They root hard, but they root fair. You've gotta love it." He added a word for his players. "I'm tired of guys yelling and screaming and trashing things when we come into the clubhouse after a game just because we didn't execute during it. Get mad before a game, not after it."

All this may have eased Trebelhorn's troubled mind, but things went from bad to worse for the Cubs, the greatest blow falling on June 13 when Ryne Sandberg abruptly announced his retirement at the early age of 34 after 13 seasons. He was only in the second year of a four-year, $28 million contract.

He had won nine Gold Gloves for his fielding at second base and been one of the most productive batters in Cub history with 245 home runs.

It was alleged that one reason for his decision to quit was dissatisfaction with the Cub management's failure to produce a winning team. In any case, it was another blow to the team's sagging fortunes, and the Cubs were buried deep in fifth and last place with a 49–64 record on August 12 when the season was abruptly terminated by the players' strike.

Trebelhorn's career as Cubs manager was terminated shortly thereafter, as was that of Himes as general manager, with a new executive team taking over. Andy MacPhail, who had made a name for himself at Minnesota, was named Cub president, and he appointed Ed Lynch, a former Cub pitcher who had gone into the front office at San Diego and New York, the new general manager. Lynch hired Jim Riggleman, who had managed San Diego from late in the 1992 season through 1994 to manage the Cubs in 1995.

1995–

Jim Riggleman

Record: 149–157 (.487)
B: December 9, 1952, Fort Dix, New Jersey

Riggleman, James David

	W	L	T	Pct
1995	73	71	0	.507
1996	76	86	0	.469
Cubs	149	157	0	.487
Career	261	336	0	.437

A journeyman minor league player, a third baseman for the most part, Jim Riggleman began his managerial career with the St. Louis Cardinals organization in 1982 at age 29; in 1989, he became a coach with the major league team.

In 1991, Riggleman was hired by the San Diego Padres to manage their Class AAA affiliate in Las Vegas. He led the team to the Pacific Coast League playoffs in 1992, and on September 23 was rewarded with Greg Riddoch's job as manager of the Padres. He finished the season as Padres manager with a 4–8 record.

During the next two seasons, Riggleman earned respect for his managerial ability, despite a cost-cutting program in which the Padres traded such high-priced players as Gary Sheffield, Fred McGriff, Randy Myers, Benito Santiago, Bruce Hurst, and Tony Fernandez to make the financially-strapped franchise more attractive to prospective new ownership.

Under Riggleman, the Padres finished at 61–101 in 1993 and 47–70 in 1994, a decent showing considering the depleted talent pool with which he had to work. Ed Lynch, who took over as Cub general manager for the 1995 season and had been in the Padres' front office before switching to the New York Mets as assistant general manager for 1994, was so impressed by Riggleman the he turned to him as his choice to manage the Cubs.

Riggleman's approach as manager was to inculcate strong fundamental play, impose discipline without being a mar-

Jim Riggleman

tinet, communicate with his players, and demand all-out effort from them.

"Jimmy epitomizes the manager of the 1990s because the bottom line with him is that he's reasonable," Lynch said. "He's an outstanding communicator, not confrontational. He always has a rationale behind his decisions. People ask me, 'Why did he do that?' I'll occasionally say, 'I don't know, but I know he has his reasons.'

"But even though he wants compromise and is a good mediator, that doesn't mean he won't draw the line."

Lynch signed two major free-agent players, starting pitcher Jaime Navarro and center fielder Brian McRae, to ease Riggleman's task going into the '95 season. Both proved outstanding. Navarro led the rotation with a 14–6 record and a 3.30 ERA. McRae became the Cubs' best leadoff man in two decades, batting .288 with 12 home runs and 27 stolen bases, and he fielded spectacularly. Catcher Scott Servais and left fielder Luis Gonzalez, acquired in a mid-season deal with Houston, also were capable additions.

In a 1995 season limited to 144 games because of the late settlement of the players' strike that had begun in 1994, Riggleman led the Cubs to a 73–71 record, although they were never seriously in contention for the NL Central Division title. They reached their high point by going five games over .500 after the All-Star break, but fell back. A late surge kept them in the running for the new "wild card" playoff berth until the last week of the season.

Outstanding seasons were turned in by first baseman Mark Grace, right fielder Sammy Sosa, and stopper Randy Myers. Grace batted .326, with 16 home runs and 92 RBIs. Sosa batted .268, with 36 home runs and 119 RBIs, and he stole 34 bases. Myers (1–2) led the NL in saves with 38.

Bolstered by the return of second baseman Ryne Sandberg and the signing of reliever Doug Jones and third baseman Dave Magadan, the Cubs had high hopes for 1996. But Jones, who had been counted on to replace Myers (who had been lost to free agency) proved a bust and was released early in the season, and Magadan was sidelined by injuries for much of the campaign.

With inadequate hitting and insufficient starting pitching, Riggleman struggled to keep the Cubs around .500 much of the 1996 season. But the death knell to the team's hopes came on August 20, when Sosa, who appeared to be threatening Hack Wilson's NL record of 56 home runs set in 1930 was hit by a pitch. He suffered a broken bone in his hand and was out for the rest of the year. Sosa batted .273 with 40 home runs and 100 RBIs in 124 games.

The Cubs were two games over .500 with a 74–72 record in early September, but then went into a coma, losing 14 of their 16 last games for a final 76–86 record. They finished in fourth place in the five-team Central Division, 12 games behind the champion St. Louis Cardinals.

Riggleman, however, earned a contract extension through the 1998 season. In addition to Sosa's slugging, other highlights of the disappointing 1996 season were provided by Grace, Sandberg, Navarro, and starter Steve Trachsel. Grace batted .331. Sandberg provided 25 home runs and 92 RBIs, though his batting average slumped to an uncharacteristic .244. Navarro was 15–12, and Trachsel was 13–9 with an exceptional 3.03 earned run average.

Among the lowlights were several much-publicized squabbles between Riggleman and Navarro, who protested about being relieved "too early" in several starts, and one involving starter Frank Castillo (7–16) over a similar complaint.

The Front Office

In the beginning, professional baseball was small business indeed, especially among the rampaging dinosaurs of the Gilded Age, the era of the "robber barons: who gorged themselves on the post–Civil War boom of American enterprise.

When the National League of Professional Base Ball Clubs (NL) was formed in 1876, an annual team budget of $25,000 was adequate, with $10,000 or so going to the salaries of the players. A rudimentary baseball stadium, with a basic wooden grandstand and fence, could be constructed for a few thousand dollars. A franchise could be purchased or founded for less than $50,000.

This figure grew quickly as baseball's popularity soared, with the White Stockings reportedly pulling in annual profits of more than $30,000 within a few years of their birth. The value of franchises began to rocket. A team that was valued at $100,000 in the mid-1880s was worth five times as much two decades later.

Much slower to change were the structure and size of the nonplaying staff required to operate a team. The large bureaucracy, or "front office," that every major league team currently employs developed after World War II for the most part, with its roots firmly planted in the tables of organization beloved by the armed services.

In 1876, and long after, a few key men could run the entire operation. An owner or syndicate of owners, a president, a secretary-treasurer, a road secretary, a couple of scouts, and a few year-round office employees sufficed for a team's needs, other than seasonal hires such as ticket takers, musicians, groundskeepers, cushion renters, and concessionaires. At a time when $3 a day was a decent wage, the compensation to nonplaying personnel represented a small part of the budget.

From their inception, the White Stockings were one of the soundest financial franchises of the NL. Their first president, William Hulbert, was wealthy in his own right and the leader of a syndicate of similarly deep-pocketed fellow Chicagoans. His successor as principal owner and team president, Albert G. Spalding, also was rich independently of baseball, building an ever-burgeoning fortune from his sporting goods firm and real estate transactions.

During the more than 120 years of their existence, the Cubs (as the White Stockings eventually were named) have been under ownership that almost invariably could fall back on income from sources other than baseball. That statement held true particularly during their long ownership by the Wrigley family from 1918 to 1981, and it became indisputable when the Cubs were acquired by the Tribune Company, a huge conglomerate.

From the beginning until recently, team presidents played active roles in guiding the Cubs, from making the major judgements to deciding even the most minor questions. The presidents set policy for the franchise, handled league matters, ordered the building or renovation of ballparks, often hired managers, approved or even initiated player acquisitions, and ran the entire structure from top to bottom. In effect, the team president was also what later became known as general manager.

Eventually the president's role changed as new officers, including general managers, began to direct separate departments. Among them were ballpark supervisors, ticket managers, chiefs of scouting, public relations directors, concessions chiefs, and so on. The baseball bureaucracy was born and flourished.

The office and title of general manager did not come into widespread use until the early part of the 20th century, though before that time men such as Spalding had been employed in a similar capacity under team presidents. Spalding served as Hulbert's right-hand man from 1876 to the latter's death in 1882, carrying on much of the day-to-day supervision of the team, particularly in player acquisition, compensation, scheduling, transport, and hotel accommodations. In all but title, he was the Cub's first general manager before becoming president.

Philip K. Wrigley, Cub president and owner for 43 years, takes a turn at bat during spring training at Catalina Island.

However, it was not until the hiring in 1918 by owner William Wrigley of William Veeck, Sr., that the Cubs had what today would be called a general manager, though he, too, served as team president from 1919 until his death in 1933.

Like most teams, the Cubs over their long history have been blessed with capable presidents and general managers as well as cursed with unfit mediocrities. Their tenures were frequently mirrored in the fluctuations of the team's fortunes.

The Presidents

1876–82

William A. Hulbert

By any measure, William A. Hulbert, a successful grain and coal merchant and member of the Chicago Board of Trade, was the founding father of the National League, the organization that stabilized professional baseball and directed it toward a prosperous future. As their first president, he also created the Cubs.

Albert G. Spalding in his autobiography paid tribute to his mentor and predecessor as White Stockings president. He was "strong, forceful and self-reliant . . . a man of tremendous energy—and courage" who did things in a "business-like way."

Wealthy by his early 40s, Hulbert's twin passions were baseball and making money. He combined them by buying a minority interest in the Chicago White Stockings of the National Association of Professional Base Ball Players (NA) in the early 1870s. He soon discovered that the undisciplined organization with its underfinanced franchises, as well as the loose ethics of many irresponsible players—some of whom were not averse to "throwing" games, and more of whom were alcoholics—made baseball a shaky proposition.

By 1875, the White Stockings were near financial and artistic collapse, and Hulbert was offered the team presidency. With his usual directness, he set out to restructure the team as well as the league. He persuaded the four major stars of the dominant Boston Red Stockings—Spalding, Ross Barnes, Deacon White, and Cal McVey—as well as Cap Anson from Philadelphia, to defect to the White Stockings for the 1876 season.

When his colleagues in the NAPBBP responded by threatening to expel the players and the White Stockings, Hulbert retaliated by floating the conception of a new league to be run on "business principles"—in other words, to be controlled totally by the owners rather than with the input of the players as had been the basis of the NAPBBP.

With Spalding's collaboration, Hulbert recruited potential team owners around the country during the winter of 1875–76 with the promise to reduce the game, as Spalding put it, "to a business system such as heretofore had never obtained." A complete league structure was projected, with president, secretary-treasurer, and board of directors having authority to supervise league operations and enforce rules. Player contracts, fixed schedules, ticket prices, paid umpires, and other facets were to be regulated.

The project came to fruition on February 2, 1876, when a gathering of owners in New York approved Hulbert's proposals and objectives and founded the National League of Professional Base Ball Clubs (NL). A prominent banker and political figure, Morgan G. Bulkeley, was elected president of the new organization to reinforce its respectability.

Hulbert stated three major objectives in his plan to revitalize baseball:

1. To encourage, foster, and elevate the game.
2. To enact and enforce proper rules for the exhibition and conduct of the game.
3. To make baseball playing respectable and honorable.

As a result of the founding of the NL, the NAPBBP disintegrated, and the White Stockings were reconstituted as a new franchise. The Cubs had been born, with Hulbert as their first president.

The NL's success was not immediate. In the first year, the New York and Philadelphia teams declined to complete their schedules with road trips that they feared would lose money. In 1877, four Louisville players were discovered to have thrown games. When Bulkeley, unwilling or unable to cope with the problems, resigned as league president, Hulbert assumed the office, expelled the New York and Philadelphia teams, banned the four Louisville players for life and forfeited the franchise. The NL began to coalesce as a viable proposition as Hulbert warred on gamblers, drunks, and noncomplying franchises.

William Hulbert, first White Stockings president and founder of the National League

One of the most significant actions of Hulbert's tenure was the introduction in 1879 of the later-infamous reserve clause, which in effect bound players to their original teams for life unless they were sold or traded to another club.

Hulbert's reign as White Stockings president began with a pennant in 1876, and even while he simultaneously held the office of NL president from 1877 on, the team prospered under his hand. After the 1877 season, Spalding relinquished his role as manager to become the team's secretary and lighten the double load on Hulberg.

The White Stockings were doing so well that Hulbert decided to build a new ballpark to replace the 23rd Street Grounds, which they had inherited from their NA precursors and in which they played their first two seasons. In 1878 they moved to new Lakefront Park on Michigan Avenue, where they produced three more pennant winners, from 1880 to 1882, under the leadership of player-manager Cap Anson and with such stars as Mike "King" Kelly and Pitchers Larry Corcoran and Fred Goldsmith.

Hulbert and Spalding in tandem produced these results, cooperating harmoniously to procure the outstanding talent that characterized the teams of the period. In a way, Spalding was the original Cub "general manager," while Hulbert held the purse strings in his role as team president.

Hulbert was not around to see the "three-peat" completed. He died on April 10, 1882, at the age of 49, leaving as his twin legacies a stable National League and a solid franchise in the team to be called the Cubs.

1882–91

Albert G. Spalding

A small-town boy from Byron, Illinois, Albert G. Spalding had a golden touch, succeeding in virtually everything he attempted. He was baseball's premier pitcher in his early twenties, a pennant-winning rookie manager at 26, the majority owner of a major league team at 32, the head of the largest sporting goods business in the United States, and the respected "elder statesman" of the game by the turn of the century. Only a bid for a U.S. Senate seat in late life eluded him.

Spalding was William Hulbert's right-hand man in founding the NL and the White Stockings, and he managed, pitched, and contributed three hits in their first game, a 4–0 shutout of Louisville on April 25, 1876. After guiding the team to the NL's first pennant in 1876 and to fourth place in 1877, he left the field to become club secretary (in effect, general manager) and provided manager Cap Anson with the talent that resulted in five more pennants in 1880–82 and 1885–86.

At the same time, Spalding, with the involvement of members of his family, was building a sporting goods business, beginning with a small store in Chicago. A major coup came when Hulbert agreed that Spalding would supply baseballs to the new NL, as well as publish an annual guide. In 1883, Spalding bought out another supplier of baseballs, Al Reach, to create a virtual monopoly. By the late 1880s, A. G. Spalding & Brothers dominated the sporting goods industry.

This versatility was in keeping with Spalding's motto: "Everything is possible to him who dares." A born promoter with a flamboyant personality, Spalding never hesitated to

Albert Goodwill Spalding

speak out for what he believed, or considered to be in his interest. He acted decisively the moment he smelled success. He knew baseball inside out, and his huge ego had convinced him he knew more about it than anyone else.

Almost inevitably then on April 26, 1882, when the White Stockings' board of directors met after Hulbert's death, Spalding was elected president and became one of the two principal owners, the other being banker John L. Walsh. Spalding ran the club with an iron hand the next five years, occasionally even dressing down Anson for sloppy play by the team, and retained a major voice until he finally sold out his interest in 1902.

Spalding never relented in his demand for dedication and sobriety from the players. He waged an unceasing war on alcoholism, frequently fining and sometimes suspending those who strayed. One reason he gave for selling Mike "King" Kelly, the foremost player of the day, to Boston for $10,000 after the 1886 season was the star player's propensity to go on "benders."

The White Stockings had been highly profitable during Hulbert's tenure and became even more so under that of Spalding. In 1887 the stockholders reportedly each received a dividend of 20 percent. In 1888 the team's profits rose to $60,000, a huge sum for the still-fledgling baseball business.

Spalding did not hesitate to reinvest the money. He replaced Lakefront Park by building West Side Park for the 1885 season, yet by the end of the decade he had laid plans for a new venue, the West Side Grounds. It opened in May 1893 as the splashiest ballpark in the National League, with a capacity of 16,000.

Spalding also had a bent for experiment, innovating spring training by taking his team at Anson's suggestion to Hot Springs, Arkansas, in 1886, and leading it on a world tour in 1887, with exhibition games on several continents as well as cricket matches in England. He installed the recently invented telephone in his box seat at the ballpark so that he could communicate instantly with his employees and carry on business interests while watching games.

He was foiled, however, in his attempt to introduce baseball under the lights in 1883, anticipating by more than a century the Cubs' first home night game in 1988.

Spalding apparently became more preoccupied by his sporting goods and real estate businesses by the late 1880s than was good for the team, and the 1886 pennant was the last of his regime. Player sales such as that of Mike "King" Kelly in 1887 for the staggering sum of $10,000 drew fire from critics who charged Spalding was out purely for the money and questioned his dedication to providing a winning team.

The White Stockings' decline was accelerated by the outbreak of disputes between players and owners that resulted in formation of the Players League for the 1890 season. After the revolt was quelled, partly because of Spalding's leadership of the owners, he decided in 1891 to devote himself to his other interests and relinquish the team presidency, though he remained a major stockholder.

All the same, for the next dozen years Spalding continued as the sometimes official, often self-appointed, spokesman for baseball in a variety of crises, even after he finally sold out his holdings in the Cubs. As the instigator of a commission in 1907 to investigate the origins of the game, he also was chiefly responsible for the propagation of the myth that Abner Doubleday had "invented baseball."

Spalding died on September 9, 1915, at the age of 65, leaving a mixed reputation but general agreement that he was one of the founding fathers of modern baseball.

1892–1905

James A. Hart

Chicago businessman James A. Hart was an early minority investor in the White Stockings. After Albert G. Spalding retired as president of the team at the end of 1891, he and John Walsh, the other principal owner, turned to Hart as the new chief executive.

The first significant event of Hart's 13-year incumbency as president was a major restructuring of the White Stockings in late 1892, with the original corporation becoming responsible solely for investments in real estate, including property in Hot Springs, Arkansas, where the team went for spring training, and a site in Chicago where the new West Side Grounds was to be built. The team itself was incorporated as a separate firm, with a capital of $100,000.

Hart explained that "the old corporation [will] look after the land end of the business, while the new corporation will do nothing but hunt the pennant." The hunt, however, bagged no game for the rest of Hart's long regime.

From the beginning Hart's relations with manager Cap Anson were strained because the latter believed he had been denied an opportunity to buy into the team through the president's machinations. The situation went from bad to worse during the next five years as the White Stockings steadily went downhill on the field, never finishing above fourth place after 1891.

Anson constantly complained that Hart's penny-pinching made it difficult to obtain quality players in trades because the president was unwilling to pay high salaries. He also alleged that the president constantly undermined his authority with the players. It is uncertain how much tightening of the purse strings was due to Hart rather than to Spalding, who allegedly still was controlling the team through his successor. Spalding had made a practice in the past of unloading such stars as Kelly, John Clarkson, and Abner Dalrymple to be replaced by young, less well-paid players.

In 1896 a writer in *The Sporting News* commented, "Everyone knows Al Spalding, the owner of the Chicago Club. Al's mouthpiece is Jim Hart, the nominal president of the club. Al pulls the string and Jim spiels."

Whatever the truth, relations between Hart and Anson deteriorated to the point where in 1897 the manager even denounced the club president in the press. When the team finished in ninth place in 1897, Hart saw his opportunity and fired Anson on February 1, 1898. He undoubtedly had Spalding's consent.

Though the Cubs, as they now were called, languished the next four years under managers Tommy Burns and Tom Loftus, Hart did well financially despite the battle that began with the new American League in 1900. He was able to buy out Spalding and others in 1902 to become the majority owner of the team.

Hart was fortunate or shrewd in his third choice of a manager, naming Frank Selee, who had won five NL pennants in the 1890s with Boston, to manage the Cubs in 1902. Selee began to assemble the team that was to dominate the NL in the latter half of the decade, winning pennants in 1906, 1907, 1908, and 1910.

Such players as Frank Chance, Joe Tinker, Johnny Evers, Johnny Kling, Frank Schulte, Ed Reulbach, and Mordecai "Three-Finger" Brown developed under Selee. Illness, however, forced Selee to resign during the 1905 season, just as the team was about to coalesce into a powerhouse, and it went on to win four pennants in the next five years under Chance as manager.

Hart, who oddly enough let the players vote on a successor to Selee, also left on the verge of one of the Cubs' great eras, selling out after the 1905 season to a syndicate led by Charles W. Murphy, who succeeded him as president.

1906–14

Charles W. Murphy

Charles W. Murphy, a onetime newspaperman, by 1905 had turned his talents to baseball press agentry. He was a sort of advance man for the New York Giants. He preceded the team on road trips and drummed up publicity to boost attendance when the Giants played the home time. His colleagues called him "Chubby Charlie," not a totally endearing nickname because Murphy was freewheeling and often obstreperous.

Murphy was on a publicity assignment in Chicago in 1905 when he learned that Hart was about to put the Cubs up for sale and was likely to settle for $100,000. A born opportunist, Murphy, though he had only $15,000 himself, saw his chance to make a fortune. As it turned out, he stumbled on the Cubs at an opportune moment, and he was to preside over the second great era of their history.

Charlie Murphy

Earlier in his career Murphy had worked for the *Cincinnati Times-Star*, a newspaper owned by Charles P. Taft, the elder half-brother of future U.S. President William Howard Taft. He persuaded Charles Taft to "bankroll" his purchase of the Cubs. The deal was consummated, with the price reportedly $125,000, of which $5,000 was a bonus to Hart for handling the deal.

(Taft's wife owned the Philadelphia ballpark, and Taft secretly advanced the money through Murphy that enabled another newspaperman, Horace S. Fogel, to buy the Phillies in 1909. In 1912 matters came to a head with allegations of "interlocking" ownership and a reckless charge by Fogel of game throwing that resulted in his banishment for life from baseball.)

Murphy assumed the Cubs presidency just before they embarked on their great season of 1906, in which they won a record 116 games, losing only 36. He had caught a shooting star and did his best to line his vault while the going was great.

While Frank Chance, "The Peerless Leader," was wreaking havoc on the field with his Cubs, winning four pennants in five years (1906–08, 1910) and two World Series, Murphy was doing the same among his fellow owners, feuding with them endlessly. Additionally, he antagonized his manager, his players, and anyone else who came in contact with him. He was freewheeling, impulsive, turbulent, contentious, and loud mouthed. His large supply of enemies charged that he was "cheap" and not impeccably honest. Pittsburgh Pirates owner Barney Dreyfuss called Murphy a "rat" and a "sneak." Roger Bresnahan, manager of the St. Louis Cardinals, termed him a "windbag."

Murphy's conduct of the sale of World Series tickets in 1908 created a scandal, though he was cleared of collusion with scalpers. In 1911 he accused Bresnahan of throwing games. In 1912 he was suspected of being Fogel's "ghost" in the scandal that resulted in the latter's expulsion from baseball, but was let off the hook for the moment.

During these tumultuously triumphant years, Murphy reaped the profits of the Cubs' success and at the same time started to break up the team that was making them possible. A salary dispute with Orval Overall resulted in the pitcher quitting baseball for two years. Murphy traded away catcher Johnny Kling, Joe Tinker, Ed Reulbach, and other mainstays, and sent Mordecai Brown to the minor leagues to antagonize the fans even further (though Cincinnati eventually brought Brown back).

As the Cubs faltered, finishing second in 1911 and 1912, Chance was enraged by the housecleaning, as well as by difficulties over his own contract, and even left his post briefly, returning only reluctantly. On September 28, 1912, while Chance was recuperating from surgery, Murphy announced he had been fired as manager. However, he cannily retained the rights to Chance as a player and tried to block him from becoming manager of the New York Yankees until the other owners forced his hand.

Murphy sought to soothe the restless Cub fans by naming Johnny Evers manager for 1913 with a four-year contract at $10,000 a season. Evers achieved a third-place finish, but then Murphy made his fatal misstep. When Evers, who also was negotiating with the new Federal League, demanded more money to play for the Cubs, Murphy interpreted the demand as a statement of resignation. Without giving Evers the required 10 days notice, Murphy fired him, then tried to trade him to Boston. Evers balked, threatening to jump to the Federal League, but eventually the trade was completed with the intervention of other NL owners to keep one of the game's biggest stars from defecting.

The upshot was that Murphy was ousted in February 1914 by the other major league owners, who had seen enough of him and regarded the Evers matter as the last straw. They persuaded Taft, who had foisted Murphy on them in the first place, to buy Murphy's 53 percent of the Cubs for about $500,000. It represented a handsome return on Murphy's investment of $15,000 made just eight years before.

1914–15

Charles H. Thomas

Charles Taft's choice of Charlie Murphy's assistant, Charles H. Thomas, as the Cubs' new president did not sit well with the other NL owners, who felt they were the victims of a ruse that they suspected Murphy had merely retreated to the background and would continue to pull the strings with his henchman as the puppet.

Pittsburgh's Barney Dreyfuss scathingly protested that making a mere "office boy" the chief Cub executive was an insult to the other club owners. He added that "the record and reputation of Mr. Thomas are not of the best, and at this time we cannot afford to carry men of his character."

Taft reassured the owners that he had bought out Murphy completely and that the appointment of Thomas was a stop-gap measure. He intended to sell the team as soon as a suitable buyer could be found.

Thomas held the fort in a difficult period. His team had been decimated by Murphy's deals, though it had some standouts in third baseman Heinie Zimmerman and pitchers Fred "Hippo" Vaughn and Larry Cheney. Competition by the new Federal League Chifeds, soon renamed the Whales, managed by former Cub hero Joe Tinker and with a new ballpark on the North Side, cut heavily into attendance at West Side Grounds.

Thomas' manager, Hank O'Day, kept the Cubs above .500 in 1914, but that result didn't satisfy his boss. Thomas hired Roger Bresnahan, a veteran reserve catcher and former Cardinals manager, to replace O'Day (as if to signify that his ties with Murphy had been cut because the former owner had been involved in an ugly confrontation with Bresnahan in 1911). Bresnahan's Cubs finished 73–80 and in fourth place in 1915.

By the opening of the 1916 season, both Bresnahan and Thomas were gone, with the Cubs under new ownership. In late 1915, as part of a deal that dissolved the Federal League, Charles A. Weeghman, owner of the Chicago Whales, was permitted to form a syndicate to buy 90 percent of the Cub shares for $500,000. Significantly for the future, one minority investor was chewing gum millionaire William Wrigley, who put up $100,000 for two shares of the 10-portion syndicate. Another, for $50,000, was sold to William Walker, a Chicago fish wholesaler.

Charlie Weeghman

1916–18

Charles A. Weeghman

Armed with an $8 million fortune made early in the century by developing a chain of lunchrooms in Chicago, Charles H. Weeghman had indulged himself by venturing into baseball by 1913. He started small, with the Chifeds of the Federal League, then a minor league. But both Weeghman and the Federal League had greater ambitions.

By 1914 the Federal League owners had decided to force their way into the major leagues and declared war with player raids. Weeghman was in the forefront, pouring $250,000 into a new ballpark on Chicago's near North Side and hiring one of the NL's brightest stars, ex-Cub shortstop Joe Tinker, as player-manager.

Weeghman was a shrewd promoter and showman. His Chifeds, soon renamed the Whales in a fans' contest, introduced such innovations as permanent refreshment stands and giving balls hit into the stands to the fans. His Whales were stiff competition for the Cubs and White Sox, finishing second in 1914 under Tinker and winning the pennant in 1915. Hardest hit were the Cubs, whose attendance dropped to just over 200,000 in each of the 1914 and 1915 seasons, the Whales outdrawing them.

On January 20, 1916, Weeghman and his group took control of the Cubs. He was named president, and he brought Tinker with him as manager, but his most lasting contribution was Whales Park, eventually to be renamed Wrigley Field.

In the first season under Weeghman's control, attendance more than doubled over what it had been at the West Side Grounds in 1915, though the Cubs finished fifth under Tinker. Young center fielder Fred "Cy" Williams was a bright spot, tying for the league lead in home runs with 12. He had hit 13 the year before in his first full major league season.

Weeghman fired Tinker and brought in Fred Mitchell, a highly regarded, gentlemanly coach for the "Miracle" Boston

Braves of 1914. Mitchell's task was aggravated by the entry of the United States into World War I, with its resulting manpower drain, and the Cubs finished fifth again.

Weeghman was determined to produce a winner and willing to spend money to get one. A major deal on December 11, 1917, brought the battery of Grover Cleveland Alexander, a 30-game winner the previous three seasons, and Bill Killefer to the Cubs for $55,000 and two players. In another deal, the Cubs acquired veteran pitcher Lefty Tyler.

A third trade a couple of weeks later, however, ranks with the one that sent Lou Brock to the Cardinals almost 50 years later as among the worst in the team's history. Williams slumped in 1917, and Weeghman traded him to the Phillies for veteran outfielder George "Dode" Paskert. Williams played 13 seasons with the Phillies and led the league in home runs three more times, with a peak of 41. Some called him the Babe Ruth of the NL.

Alexander was of little help in 1918, with a 2–1 record before he entered military service, but the Cubs surprisingly achieved Weeghman's goal of an NL pennant. Rookie shortstop Charlie Hollocher, who hit a .316, and pitchers Hippo Vaughn (22–10), Claude Hendrix (19–7), and Lefty Tyler (19–9) led the charge in a season brought to an end on Labor Day by war concerns.

The Chicago games of the World Series against the Boston Red Sox were shifted to the White Sox' Comiskey Park because of its greater capacity. Babe Ruth led the Red Sox past the Cubs both as pitcher and hitter, and the Cubs fell four games to two.

Weeghman had brought a pennant to the Cubs, but it was his swan song. Financial problems forced him to borrow heavily, mostly from Wrigley, with his Cub stock as collateral. In December 1918, Weeghman sold out completely to Wrigley and resigned as president, ending his involvement with baseball.

William Wrigley, Jr., who gained sole control of the Cubs after the 1918 World Series

1919

Fred Mitchell

With his original $100,000 investment and what had been Charles Weeghman's stock in the Cubs in hand, William Wrigley, Jr., owned the most shares in the team at the close of 1918. By 1921 he had made further purchases to become by far the majority owner.

The son of a Philadelphia soap manufacturer, Wrigley as a young man in the 1880s had gone into business for himself, eventually moving to Chicago. After wholesaling soap and baking powder, he discovered the chewing gum business that was to earn his family a great fortune.

His involvement with the Cubs began in 1915 when he joined Weeghman's syndicate to buy the team from Charles Taft. It heightened in 1917, when he was able to convince the team to train in California, where he owned a great deal of property, including a residence in Pasadena. The upshot was his purchase of control in December 1918.

His choice as president to succeed Weeghman was Fred Mitchell, who also was to continue as manager. Mitchell's term as president was brief, lasting only until June, because the NL decreed that it was against the rules for anyone to be concurrently president and manager of a team.

Mitchell continued as manager through the 1920 season, managed the Boston Braves the following three years, and eventually became a long-serving coach at Harvard University.

1919–33

William L. Veeck, Sr.

During the spring of 1918, William Wrigley invited the baseball writers covering the Cubs to a dinner at his home in Pasadena, California, and was impressed by William Veeck, whom readers of the *Chicago American* knew under the pen name of Bill Bailey. Veeck had been among the more thoughtful critics of the way the Cubs were operating.

Wrigley hired Veeck as vice president of the Cubs and another sportswriter, John O. Seys, as club secretary. In June 1919, Veeck succeeded Fred Mitchell as president. He was to run the team, with frequent input from Wrigley, for the next 14 years. For all practical purposes, he was the Cubs' first general manager in today's terminology.

Fred Mitchell

William L. Veeck, Sr.

A dignified, thoughtful, patient man, Veeck lacked the promotional flair his son Bill was to display during the next generation, though he was not hidebound, introducing radio broadcasts of his team's games in 1925 despite fierce protests from other teams. (At one time, five stations were broadcasting the games.) He was steady and capable, and brought order from the chaos that had enveloped the Cubs since the heyday of the Frank Chance teams.

Among his earlier tasks was to supervise the installation of baseball facilities on Catalina Island, California, which Wrigley purchased in 1919. It was to be the Cubs' spring training site for most of the next four decades. He also advised Wrigley in 1921 to buy the minor league Los Angeles Angels as a nursery for prospective Cubs.

Veeck's first major problem, other than to rebuild the team, was the revelation that Cub pitcher Claude Hendrix was implicated in a gambler's scheme to lose a game to the Phillies on August 31. Alerted to the plot, Veeck ordered manager Mitchell to start Grover Cleveland Alexander instead of Hendrix. He even offered Alexander a $500 bonus if he won. The Cubs lost the game anyway, but the revelation and Veeck's decisive action helped trigger the investigation of charges that the White Sox had "thrown" the 1919 World Series to Cincinnati. Veeck released Hendrix after the season, and he never pitched again in the major leagues.

Veeck took a major role in the reorganization of baseball's governing structure after the Black Sox scandal. He deplored the ineffective three-man commission that ruled the game and supported the appointment of a single commissioner with absolute power. His candidate for the job, Judge Kenesaw M. Landis, a close friend, was appointed to the post in 1921.

While Veeck was successfully attending to baseball's larger problems, he was not having as much luck with the Cubs. After finishing third in 1919, they slipped to fifth in 1920. Veeck replaced Mitchell with Joe Tinker, but the onetime great shortstop's second term lasted only part of the 1921 season, after which coach Bill Killefer took over as manager and the Cubs dropped into seventh place.

During the summer of 1921, Veeck was approached by George Halas and Edward Sternaman, co-owners of a young football franchise, the Decatur Staleys, who were about to move the team to Chicago and wanted to play in Wrigley Field. Veeck agreed to rent the park to the partners, and the Bears had found a home they would stay in for 50 years until they moved to Soldier Field in 1971.

Among the better Cub players during the early 1920s were Alexander, who won 27 games to the lead NL in 1920, shortstop Charlie Hollocher, a consistently good hitter and fielder, and first baseman Ray Grimes. In 1922, a couple of promising rookies, slugging outfielder Hack Miller and catcher Gabby Hartnett, helped ease Killefer's task.

The Cubs rose to fifth place in 1922 and fourth place in 1923, when Alexander was 22–12 and Miller hit 20 home runs. Still, despite a constant traffic in players, either rookies or those acquired in trades, Veeck's program seemed stalled when the Cubs again sank to fifth place in 1924. Veeck tried another trade, this one to have long-term significance. He got first baseman Charlie Grimm and shortstop Rabbit Maranville, two free spirits, from the Pittsburgh Pirates, who were eager to get rid of them.

Grimm played well in 1925, and Maranville was a fine fielder, but Killefer lost control of the players, and in mid-season, with the Cubs in seventh place, Veeck relieved him as manager. Inexplicably, considering Maranville's propensity for alcohol and pranks, Veeck gave the job to him. Maranville made matters even worse and had to be replaced by coach George Gibson with just 12 games left in the season and the Cubs stuck in last place.

The situation seemed bleak, the Cubs having made no real progress since Veeck's installation as president in 1919. But his first masterstroke was at hand. Gibson was a stopgap, and in September 1925, Veeck met with Joe McCarthy, a career minor leaguer who had earned a good reputation as a manger at Louisville, Kentucky. In an almost unprecedented move, he hired McCarthy, who had never spent a day in the major leagues, to manage the Cubs in 1926.

Less publicized, but almost as significant, were Veeck's selection of Hack Wilson, an oddly shaped, barrel-chested outfielder, in the minor league draft after the 1925 season and the promotion of another minor league outfielder, Riggs Stephenson.

McCarthy, a no-nonsense manager, soon got rid of Maranville and the alcoholic and fading Alexander, and the Cubs showed promise in 1926. Stephenson batted .338, Wilson led the NL in home runs with 21, and some of the younger holdovers, such as Grimm, Hartnett, and pitcher Charlie Root, moved the Cubs up to fourth place.

Encouraged by the team's improvement and the increase in fan interest, Wrigley launched a second major renovation and enlargement of Wrigley Field after the 1926 campaign. This time the park was double-decked and its capacity increased in 38,396, just in time for the start of one of the Cubs' greatest eras. They were fourth again in 1927, with Wilson hitting 30 home runs and Root compiling a 26–15 record.

In 1928, after Veeck rounded out a great outfield by trading for Kiki Cuyler from Pittsburgh, the Cubs were in a pennant race for the first time in a decade, and though they finished third, they won 91 games.

Veeck, Wrigley, and McCarthy agreed that a hard-hitting player, preferably a second baseman, might put the Cubs over the top in 1929. But when Wrigley, who seldom interfered in such matters, went behind his back to make a deal with Boston for Rogers Hornsby, widely regarded as the finest right-handed hitter in the game's history, giving up $120,000 as well as five players, Veeck was outraged and resigned. He thought that the price was too high and that Hornsby had a reputation for being troublesome.

Only a promise by Wrigley never to interfere again persuaded Veeck to rescind his resignation. Ironically, Hornsby was just what was needed, at least for 1929, as he batted. 380, hit 39 home runs, and drove in 149 to lead the Cubs to their first pennant since 1918. Wilson also hit 39 home runs and drove in 159 runs. Young Pat Malone led the pitching staff with a 22–10 record, and Root won 19.

Veeck finally had achieved his goal—almost. To Wrigley's anguish, the Cubs fell to the Philadelphia A's in the World Series, something for which he never forgave McCarthy. And late in the 1930 season, despite an NL-record 56 home runs and major-league-record 190-RBI output by Wilson, as the Cubs' hopes vanished, Wrigley cajoled Veeck into firing McCarthy and replacing him with Hornsby.

Wrigley and Veeck were soon disenchanted by Hornsby's martinet methods in 1931 as the players grumbled under his lash, Wilson in particular fading, with just 13 home runs. The team slumped to third place.

William Wrigley died on January 26, 1932, and Veeck was still stuck with Hornsby. He had reinforced the team with a sparkling new double-day combination of shortstop Billy Jurges and second baseman Billy Herman, as well as making other changes, but Hornsby's team was going nowhere on August 1, so Veeck finally fired him. His choice as the new manager was Grimm, in the hopes that a more easygoing leader would relax the players. It worked, the Cubs soon embarking on a 14-game winning streak and going on to win a pennant, though they lost the World Series in four games to the New York Yankees.

Veeck decided that the Cubs needed more power. After the 1932 season, he swung his last major trade, acquiring slugger Babe Herman, a notable eccentric, from Cincinnati for four players and a bundle of cash. The deal didn't bring the Cubs a pennant in 1933; they finished third. Veeck died of leukemia before the year was out.

During his presidency, Veeck had brought the Cubs two pennants and unaccustomed prosperity. From 1918 to 1924, the Cubs's attendance averaged 512,505 per season. From 1925 through 1931, the average rose to 1,120,814, a gain of 119 percent, with a high of 1,485,166 in 1929, a Wrigley Field record that held for almost 40 years. In comparison, the other seven teams in the league gained 27 percent over the same period.

When Veeck died, the nation was in the depths of the Great Depression, and attendance was again falling off, dropping to 594,879 in 1933. He left the Cubs with the framework of a good team, one that was to win two more pennants in the 1930s.

1933–34

William H. Walker

Legend has it that Philip K. Wrigley promised his father, William, on his deathbed in 1932 that he would never sell the Cubs. What is certain is that P. K. Wrigley, on taking over the widespread Wrigley holdings, of which the Cubs were a small part, never did relinquish the team. It is perhaps significant that the Cubs, unlike the other properties, were a personal bequest to P. K. Wrigley.

On William Veeck's death in 1933, the younger Wrigley turned to William H. Walker, who had been a substantial stockholder in the Cubs since the Charles Weeghman days, to take over the presidency. Walker, a large florid man, was a fan rather than baseball expert, having made his fortune in wholesaling seafood, but eagerly accepted the job. The mistake was both his and Wrigley's.

Walker's first move was to acquire another slugger, Chuck Klein, from Philadelphia in a deal that cost the Cubs three players and $65,000. On the face of it, Klein seemed a worthwhile acquisition. He had led the NL in batting with .368 in 1933, hitting 28 home runs and batting in 120 runs, though in a park whose dimensions were even cozier than those of Wrigley Field.

Klein was a disappointment in left field in 1934, though Babe Herman was competent in right field, and the Cubs won 86 games, as they had the previous year, again finishing third. The volatile Walker harassed manager Charlie Grimm,

firing and rehiring him several times during the season, then made a monumental blunder. He traded promising Dolph Camilli, who had taken over for the aging Grimm at first base, to Philadelphia for veteran first baseman Don Hurst. Camilli developed into a star, but Hurst finished the season with the Cubs and his career that year.

Walker's bumbling incompetence not only annoyed Grimm but also displeased Wrigley, a more serious matter. Wrigley suggested innovations, such as reduced admission prices for children, but was told it couldn't be done. He decided that if Walker were shown the door, he could do what he pleased. He bought out Walker's interest for $191,100 and took over the presidency himself.

1934–77

Philip K. Wrigley

At the age of 40 in 1934, P. K. Wrigley reluctantly became president of the Cubs, then held the post for almost 43 years, until his death in 1977. Though he hired many general managers during his long regime, there was never any doubt about who made the ultimate decisions in almost every major facet of operating the franchise.

Wrigley considered the Cubs and Wrigley Field to be testimonials to his father, a sacred trust, never to be relinquished as long as he could afford to keep them. With the Wrigley Company's huge income, he was able to indulge his sentimental viewpoint for the rest of his life, even during stretches in which the Cubs lost much money.

Reserved and introspective, a contrast to his dynamic father, Wrigley did not court the limelight that shines on the owner of a major sports team but never retreated from what he considered his duty—to explain and clarify his actions to the media and the fans. He even felt he had to explain his decision to succeed Walker a president.

"God knows, I don't want the job," Wrigley said. "If I could find another Bill Veeck [senior], I'd put him in there in a minute, but he doesn't seem to be available. No matter who's in there, if anything goes wrong, I'm going to get blamed for it, so I might as well take the job myself."

Wrigley was prescient. For the next four decades, he was under fire whenever something went wrong with the Cubs, a frequent occurrence. He seldom resorted to the "no comment" tactic of many owners, but explained his actions, sometimes even resorting to newspaper advertisements in order to make certain he was not misquoted.

While he believed in actively advertising and publicizing the team, he disdained the "circus atmosphere" that one of his employees, the younger Bill Veeck, whom he hired at $18 a week as an office boy in 1935, was to so successfully exploit in the future. Wrigley told a newspaper reporter that "baseball can't sit still and watch the parade pass its windows. We've got to merchandise our stuff, just like the gum business."

His emphasis, however, was on Wrigley Field, even more than on the team itself, on the rationale that the fans must be wooed to come out whether the Cubs were winning or losing. It proved a potent appeal, even after his death. His explanation: "Our idea is advertising the game, and the fun, and the healthfulness of it, the sunshine and the relaxation, is to get the public to see ball games, win or lose."

"Beautiful Wrigley Field" became the watchword of the Wrigley regime and remained so under its successor, the Tribune Company. Wrigley's approach was to cater to the fans by offering entertainment in a comfortable, affordable, and enticing atmosphere. Among his first moves was to admit children for half price and to reduce the number of seats in a box from eight to six, making them more comfortable for the fans. At frequent intervals, the ambiance of Wrigley Field was enhanced by costly renovations and improvements.

Wrigley introduced statistical analysis and surveys, commonplace in his other business interests, into baseball, subjecting players, fans, and almost every aspect of the game to rigid examination. He encouraged the radio broadcasting and later televising of games, reasoning that it would maintain and increase interest in the team.

Even his resistance to night baseball, which he dismissed in the early 1930s as "a fad," had softened by 1941 when he ordered the installation of lights. But with the outbreak of World War II he donated the unused equipment to the war effort, and later justified his continued opposition to night games by extolling the charms of "day baseball" at Wrigley Field as a strong selling point.

On taking the presidency, Wrigley admitted he had seen fewer than 50 games during his father's long ownership of the Cubs. For the next few years he attended games from time to time, but later on he seldom appeared at the ballpark, preferring to listen to the games over the radio or watch them on television.

At first everything went well for the new regime, which included Charles "Boots" Weber, whom the organization had inherited in buying the Los Angeles minor league team. Wrigley named Weber general manager. Other key men in the organization were manager Charlie Grimm, vice president and secretary John O. Seys, and top scouts Clarence "Pants" Rowland, a former White Sox manager, and Jack Doyle, a major league player from 1889 to 1905.

Wrigley defined his role as maker of the ultimate decision after a general discussion on player trades and other proposals initiated by any member of his council, including himself. He did not pretend to be an authority on player talent, but he knew his subordinates and sought to balance their bursts of misplaced enthusiasm.

The Cubs started the 1935 season slowly, then caught fire in the stretch, winning 21 consecutive games and the pennant. Rookie first baseman Phil Cavaretta, young outfielders Augie Galan and Frank Demaree, and two 20-game winning pitchers, Lon Warneke and Bill Lee, contributed heavily to the 100 victories. The World Series, however, was the usual disappointment, though it went seven games before the Cubs succumbed to the Detroit Tigers.

Second-place finishes the next two years put Grimm's managerial job in jeopardy, though Wrigley had come to think the world of him and even had made him a sort of assistant general manager, along with Rowland, to stiffen the resolve of the oft-indecisive Weber. All members of the council, including Wrigley, were involved in one of the more astonishing deals in Cubs history just before the start of the 1938 season, the acquisition of lame-armed pitcher Dizzy Dean from the St. Louis Cardinals.

Grimm said he needed a "stopper" for 1938, a pitcher who could win the "big" games and halt losing streaks. Rowland said that Dean was available and that he was recovering from

an arm injury suffered in 1937 when it appeared that his career as one of the finest pitchers in baseball history (a 30-game winner in 1934) was over. Weber scoffed, saying everyone knew Dean's arm "was gone." Rowland replied that Dean was still young at 27, and young pitchers often recovered from injuries.

The price set by the Cardinals was enormous for those depression days: $185,000 and three players, but Wrigley did not hesitate. "Dean's the man the boys want. Let's go get him," he told Weber, who kept muttering, "This is crazy . . . this is crazy." The deal was made, without even a stipulation Weber had sought that the Cardinals guarantee Dean was sound.

Wrigley's rationale: "We don't need a guarantee. Even if he can't pitch very well, we'll get a lot of publicity from him. If he can pitch even a little bit, we'll get the money back at the box office. And if his arm ever comes back, we've got a bargain."

Dean's arm was gone, but he helped the Cubs to the 1938 pennant with a 7–1 record, pitching on memory. Grimm, however, voluntarily stepped aside in midseason during a team slump, with catcher Gabby Hartnett taking over as manager. It was the first managerial change during Wrigley's presidency, but just the first of many. And Grimm, Wrigley's favorite manager, was to reappear twice in the role.

Hartnett's celebrated "Homer in the Gloamin'" put the Cubs across in '38, but the World Series was the usual debacle, the New York Yankees sweeping four games.

The Cubs were about to enter the "dark ages" of their history, though it wasn't readily apparent at first, the false dawn of a wartime pennant in 1945 momentarily dispelling the gloom. Wrigley was to wear the hair shirt of the "sacred trust" from his father for almost 40 more years as the team floundered seemingly endlessly no matter whom he named general manager or manager, no matter what player deals he approved.

Frequent offers to buy the team were summarily rejected, no matter how generous. Wrigley once commented "There's no price tag on the Cubs. I'm not that hard up. I suppose that is difficult for some people to understand because many have the impression that money can buy everything." It didn't buy the Cubs great talent, though Wrigley belatedly set up a farm system of minor league teams in the 1940s, long after other teams had done so.

When Weber retired in 1940, Philip Wrigley, as his father had done two decades earlier in hiring the elder Veeck, reached into the newspaper ranks for a replacement, naming sportswriter Jim Gallagher as his general manager. Concurrently, catcher Jimmie Wilson replaced Hartnett as manager after the Cubs finished fourth in 1939.

Gallagher announced "a five-year" plan to rebuild the team, and a succession of trades followed, in which such stars as Billy Herman, Billy Jurges, and pitcher Larry French departed to help other teams win. Among the replacements, only slugging outfielder Bill Nicholson was a first-rate talent.

After three dismal campaigns under Wilson, Wrigley brought Grimm back to manage midway in the '44 season, and with the manpower demands of World War II hurting the Cubs less than they did other NL teams, Grimm guided them to a pennant in 1945. One of the Gallagher's deals, the purchase of pitcher Hank Borowy from the Yankees in midseason, made the achievement possible.

It was to be Wrigley's last taste of success, and even that was soured when the Cubs lost to the Tigers once more in the World Series.

Typical of Wrigley, when a ticket-scalping scandal broke out during the World Series, he apologized to the fans in a paid newspaper advertisement, concluding, "Unfortunately, there are always a few people who prefer a quick profit to anything else. We all know this to be true, but as we said to start with—we still do not like it."

He later took out many such ads to explain his views or to apologize for his team, but never again for World Series ticket scalping—the Cubs were to be also-rans for the final 31 years of his presidency.

After the 1945 pennant and a third-place finish with a record of 82–71 in 1946, the Cubs never won more games than they lost during the following 16 seasons. A constant turnover of managers, heavy expenditures on a farm system including the signing of youngsters to large bonuses, and numerous trades failed to change the team's sagging fortunes.

Grimm gave way to Frankie Frisch in 1949, Phil Cavaretta yielded to Stan Hack in 1954, Bob Scheffing took over in 1957, and Grimm made a brief and final appearance in 1960 before being replaced by Lou Boudreau early in the season.

The summary dismissal of Cavarretta in spring training of 1954 because he had been pessimistic over the team's chances created controversy, which Wrigley addressed directly by replying to a disaffected fan's letter, explaining that he fired the manager because of his "defeatism."

Wrigley was slow to come around to the signing of blacks by the Cubs arguing that the first black player would have to have extraordinary talent to surmount the pressures that he would face in Chicago. It wasn't until 1953, six years after Jackie Robinson had broken the color barrier with the Brooklyn Dodgers, that the Cubs added two black players, one of whom, shortstop Ernie Banks, did have extraordinary talent; the other, Gene Baker, was a solid second baseman.

Along with playing managerial roulette, Wrigley changed general managers after the 1949 season, hiring Wid Matthews, who had been farm director of the Brooklyn Dodgers, and kicking Gallagher upstairs as a vice president. Wrigley's penchant for keeping old hands on the payroll was notable, such longtime hired hands as Rowland and Grimm, when not employed elsewhere, retreating to vice presidential status. One of his chauffeurs in old age was pensioned off as an assistant traveling secretary, a post that involved no duties other than staying in good hotels and dining at the Cubs' expense.

Matthews' most memorable transactions came on June 4, 1953, when he acquired slow but hard-hitting outfielder Ralph Kiner in a 10-player trade with the Pittsburgh Pirates. Teaming up Kiner in an outfield with the equally slow and hard-hitting Hank Sauer proved a trial for the Cub pitchers as well as those of other teams.

After similar ill-fated deals, Wrigley in 1956 decided Matthews was not the answer and dismissed both him and Gallagher, bringing in John Holland as general manager. Holland had been successful with the Los Angeles farm team, which was about to be displaced by the move of the Dodgers from Brooklyn to Los Angeles.

Hard-hitting but slow teams that lacked pitching depth were the norm during this period, though individual stars such as Banks, who won the NL Most Valuable Player awards in 1958 and 1959, lightened the gloom somewhat.

After the 1960 season, casting about for some way to revive his team, Wrigley came up with the multiple-coach plan: the celebrated and oft-criticized "College of Coaches" that was to run the Cubs in 1960 and 1961 and whose ghost wasn't laid to rest until the hiring of Leo Durocher as manager in late 1965. (For details, turn to Chapter 4, "The Skippers," under 1961–62.)

A barrage of ridicule greeted Wrigley's plan to replace the time-honored managerial system with a platoon of coaches one of whom would serve briefly as "head coach" on a revolving basis. Wrigley was stung by the assault and even took out ads to defend and explain his ideas. In the end, the critics' view prevailed, the system failing as the Cubs finished seventh in 1961 and ninth in the expanded 10-team NL in 1962. In 1963, Wrigley covertly abandoned the College of Coaches, though Bob Kennedy, in actuality the manager, still bore the title of head coach.

Despite the setback, Wrigley came up with another novel idea in 1963, when he hired Colonel Robert V. Whitlow, a former athletic director of the Air Force Academy, as athletic director, the post making him an overseer of the entire operation. This novelty also underwent a baptism of criticism and proved a failure, Whitlow's chief impact being the creation of dissension in the Cub councils as he was largely ignored by Holland and Kennedy. He resigned after two years, admitting that he was not earning his salary.

Wrigley, however, had not ceased to astonish the baseball world. His next move after the 1965 season was to hire as manager the old firebrand Leo Durocher, whose flashy, aggressive, and adventurous lifestyle ran contrary to the owner's most deep-seated beliefs about personal behavior.

Wrigley had concluded that the Cub players were too complacent, that they needed someone with Durocher's driving, demanding personality to wake them up. Attendance had declined severely the previous two years, the team losing money heavily in 1965, when Kennedy was replaced as manager at midseason by Lou Klein, who brought them to the finish line in eighth place.

There was never any doubt as to who hired Durocher, although Wrigley had consulted Holland before making the decision. It wasn't losing money that bothered him, Wrigley contended, it was the sad state of the team and lack of progress. "Losses at the gate don't worry me," Wrigley said, "but losses on the field do, and that't why we got Durocher. I felt that the team wasn't putting out."

Durocher's arrival launched the Cubs into a sort of "silver age" as they provided excitement, if not pennants, under his rule until mid-1972. Contributing to the revival was the finally productive farm system, which graduated such stars as outfielder Billy Williams, third baseman Ron Santo, shortstop Don Kessinger, and pitcher Ken Holtzman, along with Holland's trades, which added pitchers Ferguson Jenkins and Bill Hands and second baseman Glenn Beckert.

After a faltering start, including a 10th-place finish in 1966, the Cubs became contenders under Durocher, the excitement reaching its peak in 1969 when they led their division by five games in early September only to yield to the furious assault of the New York Mets. Attendance soared, reaching a team-record 1,674,993, and the Cubs became profitable again.

Wrigley even calmly put up with Durocher's escapades, including two unexcused absences from the team during the pennant race, and his feuds with sportswriters, broadcasters, and umpires. It was as if he had made a "pact with the devil" and meant to keep it at all costs.

In 1971 when the players revolted against the manager in a highly publicized clubhouse incident, Wrigley strongly defended Durocher, using his customary pulpit of a newspaper ad on September 3. He concluded his support of Durocher by writing, "Leo is the team manager, and the 'Dump Durocher Clique' might as well give up. He is running the team, and if some of the players do not like it and lie down on the job, during the off-season we'll see what we can do to find them happier homes."

Durocher appreciated the support, but the following July, with the team aging and apparently going nowhere, he agreed to resign. Wrigley named Whitey Lockman, the player development director, as the new manager, a job he held until 1974, when he was replaced at midseason by coach Jim Marshall. The Cubs muddled along as also-rans despite batting championships in 1975 and 1976 for third baseman Bill Madlock.

In 1975, Holland was ailing, and asked to be relieved as general manager. Wrigley pensioned him off as a consultant and handed the job for 1976 to E. R. "Salty" Saltwell, whose chief role previously had been to manage Wrigley Field and concessions. Saltwell's tenure ended after one year, and Wrigley's final choice as general manager was Bob Kennedy, his manager of a decade earlier.

Kennedy, with Wrigley's approval, hired Herman Franks, a baseball warhorse and a close friend of Durocher, to manage the Cubs in 1977. It was the last major decision Wrigley was to make for the Cubs.

Philip K. Wrigley died on April 12, 1977, after more than four decades of running the Cubs as owner and president—and in most respects as general manager—in what many critics considered an eccentric fashion. Some questioned his devotion to baseball as a fan and his competence as an owner, but none ever doubted his tenacity, his willingness to accept financial losses, or his integrity, honesty, and forthrightness.

1977–81

William J. Hagenah

On the death of Philip K. Wrigley, control of the Wrigley empire, including the Cubs, passed to his only son, William, who pledged to continue along the lines his father had pursued and to keep the team in the family.

His father had not permitted William Wrigley, 44, to take more than a minimal role in the affairs of the team. William attended games and even occasionally accompanied the team on road trips, but his involvement did not go far beyond that. His father insisted that he concentrate on preparing to take a major role in running the other Wrigley enterprises, chiefly the gum company.

When P. K. Wrigley was asked by a reporter in 1958 whether he foresaw a time when his son would work full-time with the Cubs, he replied that he was training him to work for the gum company, not spend time at the ballpark. "If he wants to eat regularly, he'd better do it that way," Wrigley concluded.

William Wrigley respected his father's wishes, and on his death appointed William Hagenah, Jr. president of the Cubs, himself taking the less visible role of chairman of the executive committee. His involvement with the team was chiefly in a supervisory capacity. Shunning the limelight of sports team ownership, he immersed himself in the affairs of the Wrigley Company as well as the complications created in estate taxes by the deaths of his mother and father, which followed closely upon one another.

Hagenah, at one time a son-in-law of P. K. Wrigley, was a financial expert and treasurer of the Wrigley Company. No baseball man, his role as president of the team was mostly limited to matters demanding financial expertise. He left the baseball part of the business to Bob Kennedy, the general manager inherited from P. K. Wrigley.

Wildly escalating player salaries spurred by the advent of free agency in the 1970s were changing the baseball business and straining the Cubs' resources. Hagenah's major contribution during the period 1977–81 was to approve Kennedy's deals, the most widely publicized of which was the signing of slugger Dave Kingman for the 1978 season. Kingman had a spectacular 1979 season, leading the league with 48 home runs and driving in 115 runs.

Overall, though, despite occasional flashes of exciting play by the Cubs, the Hagenah-Kennedy team could not lift them from the doldrums. In none of the four seasons of Hagenah's presidency did they win more games than they lost. In 1980 they sank to last place with a record of 64–98 and lost $1.7 million.

Early in the 1981 season there were unconfirmed reports that the Wrigley ownership was nearing its end. The resignation of Kennedy on May 22, with Herman Franks taking over as general manager, spurred the speculation. On June 16, just a few days after the major league players began what was to be a long strike, Wrigley sold the Cubs to the Tribune Company, a media conglomerate that saw great financial advantages in combining its ownership of TV and radio stations with ownership of the team whose games they were broadcasting. The price was $20.5 million for Wrigley's 81 percent holdings and all remaining 1,900 shares, owned by 600 stockholders. The separate purchase of Wrigley Field came later.

Wrigley cited estate tax problems resulting from the death of his parents and his desire to find a solution to the team's financial needs as factors in his decision to end his family's 65-year association with the Cubs. Hagenah's reign ended with the sale. His term in office foreshadowed the future when most team presidents would be "money men" rather than "baseball men."

1981–83

Andrew J. McKenna

Like William Hagenah, Andy McKenna was chiefly a businessman, whose interest in baseball, while genuine, was tempered by practical financial considerations. Trained in the law, he had become president of a paper company and had drifted into baseball as a part owner and member of the board of the White Sox in 1975, becoming acting chairman in August 1980. When the Tribune Company purchased the Cubs on June 16, 1981, McKenna was appointed chairman of the board and president of the team.

McKenna's chief contribution to the Cubs was to set the team's financial affairs in order and to hire Dallas Green as general manager on October 15, 1981. The hard-driving

Andrew McKenna

Jim Finks

Green had been the manager of the World Series champion Philadelphia Phillies in 1980, and McKenna wanted strong leadership to bring the long-dormant Cubs to life.

"He's a strong leader," McKenna said. "Dallas is who we wanted . . . we needed."

McKenna backed Green to the hilt during the next two years as Green transformed the team through trades and the signing of expensive free agents, such as veteran third baseman Ron Cey after the 1982 season.

The payoff was not immediately apparent, the Cubs finishing fifth in both of McKenna's almost two full seasons (1982–83) as president. In September 1983, McKenna, though continuing as chairman of the board, gave up the presidency.

1983–84

Jim Finks

A former National Football League quarterback, Jim Finks had become in succession general manager of the Minnesota Vikings and the Chicago Bears, resigning the latter job in 1983. A highly respected and low-key executive, Finks had a reputation for toughness and candor. Though Finks had no baseball executive experience, Andy McKenna thought he was strong enough to balance Dallas Green's volatility. He hired him as team president in September 1983, in the process stripping the free-spending Green of some of his power.

Finks thus played a role in the Cubs' most exciting season since 1969. They swept to their first division title under Green's choice of a new manager, Jim Frey. With Finks' approval, Green swung several key trades in which the Cubs acquired pitchers Rick Sutcliffe, Scott Sanderson, and Dennis Eckersley and outfielders Gary Matthews and Bob Dernier,

who combined with such holdovers as second baseman Ryne Sandberg, third baseman Ron Cey, and shortstop Larry Bowa to move the Cubs to the top. For the first time, attendance at Wrigley Field surpassed 2 million, with a record turnout of 2,107,655.

After the Cubs fell to the San Diego Padres in the NL Championship Series, Finks decided to leave the club and return to the more congenial field of football, becoming the general manager of the New Orleans Saints. He resigned in October 1984.

1984–87

Dallas Green

From 1981 to 1987, Dallas Green was the driving force of the Cubs, first as executive vice-president and general manager, and after Jim Finks' resignation in October 1984, as president and general manager until after the 1987 season.

A former journeyman pitcher, Green had worked his way up through the Philadelphia organization, occupying the post of farm director when he was named Phillies manager on September 1, 1979. The next season he led the Phillies to a World Series victory, then managed through the strike-curtailed 1981 season, before accepting the Cubs' offer to become their general manager with a five-year contract worth over $1 million.

Green's approach to his players, as well as to almost everyone else, was that of a sledgehammer—loud, dictatorial, and unrelenting. "I come on hard, real hard," he said. "My way of doing things is to go right after it."

His six-year regime was both exciting and turbulent, as he clashed with his Tribune Company superiors as well as his managers—Lee Elia, Jim Frey, Gene Michael—and openly scolded his players when he felt they were not giving their best. "My trouble was I have a big mouth, and I pop off about a lot of things," he admitted.

He started with the proclamation that he would "Build a New Tradition" for the Cubs and throughout his regime set about it with a frenzy of trades and free-agent signings, the cost of some of which appalled his money-conscious superiors.

His two best deals were the acquisition of shortstop Larry Bowa and future superstar second baseman Ryne Sandberg in 1982 and that of pitcher Rick Sutcliffe early in the 1984 season, the latter triggering the run to the division title in which Sutcliffe was 16–1 with the Cubs that year.

His first two seasons in command, 1982 and 1983, made it seem as if the "New Tradition" was much the same as the old, the Cubs finishing fifth both years under Elia. For 1984, Green brought in Frey, who had been his foe as the manager of Kansas City in the 1980 World Series, and the Cubs came to life and won the NL East title.

The zenith of Green's term with the Cubs had been reached, and it was mostly downhill from then on as injuries and age took their toll on the team. Green fired Frey in 1986, then criticized his handpicked successor, Gene Michael, before firing him in 1987.

One final coup remained. Before the 1987 season, Green signed free-agent outfielder Andre Dawson, who responded that year with 49 home runs, 137 RBIs, and the NL Most Valuable Player award and was to continue as a major asset to the Cubs for another six seasons.

The Cubs had finished fourth, fifth, and sixth in the last three years of Green's reign, and his brusque and ungovernable manner had worn out his credit with his bosses. He severed his connections with the Cubs after the 1987 season, resigning on October 29, with two years remaining on his contract. He said he quit because of "basic philosophical differences with the management." It was reported that his Tribune Company superiors had planned to strip him of much of his authority.

Green later managed the New York Yankees and the New York Mets.

1988–91

Donald Gronesko

The Cub hierarchy dispensed with a team president for a year, with John Madigan, a Tribune Company executive, holding the chairmanship and supervising former manager Jim Frey, who succeeded Dallas Green as general manager.

Madigan also supervised the installation of lights at Wrigley Field, and the first complete night game in the old ballpark was played on August 9, 1988 after a false start the previous day when the planned debut was rained out in the fourth inning.

The '88 season in general was a washout, the Cubs finishing a poor fourth with a 77–85 record under Don Zimmer, Frey's choice as manager. But such young players as first baseman Mark Grace, left fielder Rafael Palmeiro, and pitcher Greg Maddux, as well as veteran stars Ryne Sandberg and Andre Dawson, stirred hopes for the future.

The promise was kept, at least in part, in 1989, with Don Gronesko, a veteran Tribune executive finally installed as

John Madigan

president. Gronesko's role with the Cubs was much like that of some of his predecessors, such as William Hagenah and Andrew McKenna, chiefly to take care of the finances. Presumably, they were in pretty good shape, the Cubs having drawn over 2 million fans with a last-place team in 1988.

Despite some dismal trades by Frey, such as that of ace reliever Lee Smith, who continued a spectacular career into the mid-1990s, for journeymen pitchers Al Nipper and Calvin Schiraldi, the Cubs came alive again in 1989. Led by Sandberg, Grace, Dawson, Maddux, a revived Rick Sutcliffe, and reliever Mitch Williams, a Frey acquisition, the Cubs made Gronesko's first year a success with a division title. They proved no match for the San Francisco Giants in the NL Championship Series.

The rest of Gronesko's regime was no bargain, as the Cubs sank back to fourth place, a spot they were to monopolize through 1993, though attendance continued firmly over 2 million.

In May 1991, the Cubs were floundering. Gronesko took a hand, meeting with Zimmer, who demanded to know his status for the following season. Another heated meeting 10 days later concluded with Zimmer threatening to quit on July 1 unless he was given a contract for 1992. Gronesko refused, and Zimmer was out on May 22, replaced by Jim Essian, who had been managing the Iowa farm team.

Gronesko's tenure as president ended after the 1991 season in a reshuffling of the Cub management that included the sidetracking of Frey and the hiring of Larry Himes as general manager, a job from which he had been fired by the White Sox. Gronesko retreated to the relative anonymity of the board of directors.

For the next three years, the Cubs were without a president, governed more or less by committee, with board chairman Stanton R. Cook seemingly taking the leading role. Under this regime, the Cubs plunged more heavily into the

The money the committee didn't choose to spend was more significant. Maddux departed as a free agent when his demands were not met for a five-year contract worth $28.5 million after the 1992 season in which he had led the NL with a 20–11 record and won the Cy Young Award. He went to the Atlanta Braves and captured his second, third, and fourth consecutive Cy Young Awards in 1993, 1994, and 1995.

The final year of the presidential vacuum, 1994, a strike-shortened season, was the worst, the Cubs finishing fifth in the new five-team Central Division. The directors decided to shuffle the cards. They fired general manager Larry Himes and his manager, Tom Trebelhorn, and imported Andrew MacPhail, a young executive who had added two World Series championships for the Minnesota Twins in his portfolio, to preside over the team with which he had started his career in baseball.

1994–

Andy MacPhail

If heredity counted, Andrew MacPhail, who assumed the presidency in late 1994, was ideally equipped for his job. His father, Lee MacPhail, had been president of the American League. His grandfather, Larry MacPhail, had been manager of the Cincinnati Reds, Brooklyn Dodgers, and New York Yankees.

Andy MacPhail's credentials to govern the Cubs went beyond family affiliations. He started his front-office career with the Cub organization in 1976 as business manager of a team on the lowest rung of the minor leagues. By 1981 he had become assistant director of scouting, then in 1982 moved to the Houston Astros as assistant general manager. In 1985, at the age of 33, he became general manager of the Minnesota Twins, whom he built into World Series winners in 1985 and 1987.

Don Grenesko

free-agent market, which they had started to do in 1991 with starting pitcher Danny Jackson and reliever Dave Smith, both of whom were busts. In '92 they expended more than $25 million, chiefly for starting pitcher Mike Morgan and outfielder George Bell with fair results. Starting pitcher Jose Guzman, reliever Randy Myers, and outfielder Candy Maldonado cost big money in 1993, with only Myers producing up to expectations.

Stanton Cook

Andy MacPhail

Tribune Company executive Jim Dowdle persuaded Mac-Phail to take the Cub job after the disastrous 1994 season. MacPhail's first move was to hire Ed Lynch, a former Cub pitcher who had gained front-office experience with the San Diego Padres and New York Mets, as general manager. Lynch brought in Jim Riggleman, who had managed the Padres in 1994, as the Cub manager to round out the new regime.

MacPhail defined his task: "I know some people think of the Cubs as lovable losers. Some people think that through the years, that's what's made the team so popular. I don't agree, but if that's the case, it's good to be less popular. Or maybe we can come up with some better reasons for people to like us."

MacPhail entered on his new job saddled with the financial constraints caused by the players' strike that had wiped the final third of the 1994 season and delayed the 1995 season by three weeks, as well as the lingering costs of huge long-term contracts entered on by the preceding regime.

His first major player move was an attempt to correct a long-standing problem in center field by signing free agent Brian McRae, a standout with the Kansas City Royals, to a one-year contract for $2.65 million. Another important free-agent acquisition for 1995 was starting pitcher Jaime Navarro.

Despite the encouraging 1995 finish of 73–71, MacPhail kept tight control of free-agent expenditures for the next campaign. Lynch was permitted to pick up a few bargains such as reliever Doug Jones, who proved a bust as a replacement for ace stopper Randy Myers, who had left for Baltimore. Infielders Dave Magadan and Leo Gomez proved more useful.

MacPhail had made it clear that the Cubs' emphasis was to build with youth from within the organization, but after

Jim Dowdle

another disappointing finish in 1996 (76–86), he signaled a change in course. MacPhail said the Tribune Company would give Lynch a bigger budget in '97, "a significant bump-up," apparently to pay for several higher-priced free-agent players.

The General Managers

1934–40

Charles "Boots" Weber

From 1918 until his death in 1933, William Veeck, Sr., was in effect the general manager of the Cubs, though he held the title of president. For the next year, William Walker, a minority Cubs stockholder, played much the same role until he was ousted after the 1934 season by Philip K. Wrigley, who appointed veteran baseball man Charles "Boots" Weber as general manager.

Weber had been running the minor league Los Angeles team when Wrigley's father, William, bought it in 1921, and he stayed on as general manger. (Oddly, the Angels remained a separate, virtually autonomous organization until the 1940s, operated by Wrigley's Santa Catalina Island Company.)

Weber was personable though not forceful, if anything extremely cautious and often indecisive. These characteristics made him well suited for his job, because P. K. Wrigley believed in making decisions "in council," with himself having the final word.

Weber was just one member of the council from 1934 to 1940, the others, in addition to Wrigley, being the team manager, the vice president and secretary John O. Seys, and scouts Clarence "Pants" Rowland and Jack Doyle. Rowland and Charlie Grimm, the manager from mid-1932 to mid-1938, were virtual assistant general managers and eventually became vice presidents.

Weber's tenure was a success, measured by Cub pennants in 1935 and 1938. His trades, often engineered by Rowland and Doyle, were mostly successful. Pitchers Larry French and Tex Carleton and veteran outfielder–third baseman Freddie Lindstrom, who helped the Cubs to the 1935 pennant, were among his best acquisitions. Pitcher Dizzy Dean and first baseman Rip Collins helped bring another pennant in 1938.

Typically, the deal with St. Louis for Dean, who had suffered an arm injury in 1937, was allegedly consummated by Wrigley despite Weber's objections. The general manager reportedly feared that the price tag of $185,000 and four players in exchange for Dean would "jack up prices" of players that other teams would offer the Cubs in the future.

"We're adding $50,000 to every deal we make from now on," Weber objected, according to the younger Bill Veeck, who was his assistant at the time, "because everybody is going to figure that if we're this easy a mark, they're going to get their share."

Wrigley merely commented later that Weber had done "his job" as watchdog of the treasury by objecting to spending so much money for Dean, who was damaged goods. Dean turned out to be briefly a bargain, helping the Cubs with a 7–1 record in 1938 before fading away totally.

Weber's last two years on the job were another mixed bag. His best trade came early in 1939 for young pitcher Claude Passeau, who was to be the mainstay of the staff for a decade. His worst was a multiplayer deal with the New York Giants in which the Cubs gave up star shortstop Billy Jurges. In 1940 the Cubs finished in the second division for the first time in 15 years.

Weber's final contribution was to concur with Wrigley in the hiring of Jimmie Wilson as manager for 1941 to replace Gabby Hartnett, who had relieved Grimm in mid-1938 and sparked the Cubs to the pennant.

Wrigley decided it was time for a change, saying, "When a team doesn't click, the manager benches the players and tries some others. Now we'll bench a few executives." Weber was "benched" into retirement in late 1940.

1940–49

Jim Gallagher

Philip K. Wrigley's new general manager was James T. Gallagher, a sportswriter for the *Chicago Herald-American*, whose thoughtful criticism had attracted his attention. As his father had done in 1918 in hiring William Veeck, Sr., Wrigley challenged Gallagher to demonstrate what he could do to improve the Cubs.

One of Gallagher's early moves was to integrate the previously autonomous Los Angeles Angels into a Cub farm system, belatedly following the lead of other teams and home-growing promising players. Pants Rowland was packed off to

James Gallagher

the Angels as general manager. Gallagher also accepted the choice of Jimmie Wilson, a former Phillies manager, to lead the Cubs in 1941.

Gallagher came in with a "five-year plan," which led to much media mockery along the way, but surprisingly made good when the Cubs did win the pennant in 1945, though the manpower situation of World War II contributed to the team's success.

Gallagher made several misguided trades. His most disastrous was that of second baseman Billy Herman to the Brooklyn Dodgers in 1941. The Cubs got nothing of value in return. The Cubs continued to stagnate under manager Wilson, who was replaced by Grimm in midseason 1944.

But holdovers from the previous regime, such as first baseman Phil Cavarretta, slugging outfielder Bill Nicholson, and pitcher Claude Passeau, as well as youngsters such as outfielders Andy Pafko and Peanuts Lowrey and pitcher Hank Wyse, lifted the team into contention in 1945. And Gallagher came up with the deal that won the pennant, the midseason purchase of pitcher Hank Borowy from the New York Yankees. Borowy was 11–2 for the Cubs to push them across the top.

After that, it was all downhill for Gallagher as the Cubs declined into a second-rate team for more than two decades. The farm system Gallagher had strengthened began to produce promising youngsters, but those who were kept seldom lived up to expectations, and those who were traded away often blossomed into stars.

One of his better transactions was to acquire slugging outfielder Hank Sauer from the Cincinnati Reds in 1949. Sauer became a crowd favorite at Wrigley Field and the NL's MVP in 1952 when he led the league with 37 home runs and 121 RBIs.

By 1948, Gallagher and Grimm were at odds. Gallagher wanted to bring along young players for the future; Grimm wanted to acquire veterans for quick results. In 1949, Wrigley intervened by replacing Grimm as manager with the aggressive Frankie Frisch. He named Grimm director of player personnel, but Grimm soon left to manage again, this time in the minor leagues.

To replace Grimm as player personnel director, Wrigley in 1950 hired Wid Mathews, who had held the same position with the highly successful Brooklyn Dodgers, who were in the middle of the golden era later chronicled by Roger Kahn in *The Boys of Summer*.

The advent of Mathews signaled the fading of Gallagher's influence, though he remained on the "council" and with the Cubs until 1956. He rounded out his career as an official in the baseball commissioner's office.

1950–56

Wid Mathews

The development of young talent had been Wid Mathews' assignment for the Dodgers, and P. K. Wrigley counted on him to do the same for the Cubs. Mathews was an optimistic "take-charge guy" who readily won the owner's confidence and relegated the more reserved Jim Gallagher to the background.

Wid Mathews (left) and Branch Rickey of the Pirates, after the 10-player Ralph Kiner deal on June 4, 1953

General manager John Holland (right) with field manager Leo Durocher

Mathews quickly established himself as the de facto general manger of the Cubs and, while pumping up the farm system, also generaled most of the trades during his regime. The most notable of these was the ill-advised multiplayer deal in 1951 that sent start center fielder Andy Pafko to the Dodgers, the Cubs getting mediocrities in return.

Another clinker was the acquisition in June 1953 of lead-footed outfielder Ralph Kiner, who had led the NL in home runs the previous seven seasons. Mathews thought to team him up with Sauer as a tremendous one-two home-run punch. And though Sauer hit 41 home runs in 1954 and Kiner contributed 22, the Cubs finished seventh, as they had the previous year, done in by lack of speed, poor defense, and mediocre pitching.

Mathews had little input in the choosing of managers. Wrigley fired Frankie Frisch on the way to last place in 1951, then dumped Phil Cavarretta in spring training 1954 because he was "pessimistic" after two seventh-place finishes. Cavaretta's successor, Stan Hack, was also Wrigley's choice.

Mathews did, however, convince Wrigley that it was essential for the Cubs to join other teams in turning to black players. He brought up the double-play combination of shortstop Ernie Banks and second baseman Gene Baker in 1953, with memorable results, especially in Banks' case.

After the 1956 season, as the Cubs continued to wallow in futility, finishing last, Mathews had worn out his credit with Wrigley. He was swept out, along with Gallagher and manger Hack. Wrigley brought in John Holland as general manager, along with his Angels manager, Bob Scheffing, and the ever-resilient Pants Rowland, in his customary role as vice president and consultant.

1956–75

John Holland

A career front-office man, John Holland had won P. K. Wrigley's regard by his successful operation of the Los Angeles Angels, who were sold in 1956 for $2 million to the Brooklyn Dodgers in preparation for the latter's move west in 1958.

Holland was slow, methodical, cautious, and lacking in flamboyance, but had shown a gift for developing young talent at Los Angeles and at Des Moines, Iowa. Though not entirely a yes-man, he was easily governed by Wrigley and was to endure a great many blows from his unpredictable boss to his conservative beliefs about how baseball should be conducted.

His directive from Wrigley was to reduce expenditures for player development and acquisition, which had cost the Cubs more than $3 million in the previous five years without tangible results, as well as to lift the team. To help Holland achieve these goals, Wrigley gave him two trusted advisers, vice presidents Pants Rowland and Charlie Grimm, who recently had been fired as manager by Milwaukee. The triumvirate was to run the team, with Wrigley looking over their shoulders as usual.

Improvement the next three seasons, 1957–59, was imperceptible, the Cubs finishing seventh, then fifth twice. Holland proved a whirlwind in the trade market, in one instance making a 10-player deal with St. Louis, but such new Cubs as pitcher Sam Jones, infielder Eddie Miksis, outfielders Lee Walls and Walt Moryn, first baseman Dale Long, and many others proved of limited long-term value.

Holland's farm system produced two promising pitchers, Dick Drott and Moe Drabowsky, and an exceptional second baseman, Tony Taylor, to replace Gene Baker. Taylor teamed with shortstop Ernie Banks, who was at his peak.

Banks won the NL Most Valuable Player award in consecutive years (1958–59).

Almost in desperation, on September 28, 1959, Wrigley bypassed Holland and personally fired Scheffing to resort to an old formula—he gave Grimm a third term as manager, remarking, "Every time we call on Charlie, we win a pennant," recalling the successes of 1932 and 1945.

The third term was no charm. Early in the 1960 season, with the Cubs at 6–11, Grimm admitted that at 63 he was no longer up to the demands of managing. Wrigley transferred him to the radio broadcast booth to replace Lou Boudreau, a veteran major league manager, who was brought onto the field and guided the Cubs to seventh place.

During the winter of 1960–61, Holland sat in on a series of "brainstorming" sessions in which Wrigley and his council developed a revolutionary scheme to run the team on the field—"The College of Coaches." (For details, turn to Chapter 4, "The Skippers," 1961–62.) The discreet Holland never revealed what he thought of Wrigley's multiple-coach plan in which temporary "head coaches" carried out the functions of a manager.

When a reporter asked Wrigley whether Holland, Rowland, and Grimm were receptive to the scheme, P. K. replied, "Merry Christmas to you, son," and hung up the phone.

At the conclusion of the 1962 season, after the Cubs had finished ninth in the now 10-team NL, having crawled into sixth place in 1961, the multiple-coach plan was covertly abandoned. Wrigley's choice as field boss for 1963, Bob Kennedy, became manager in all but title.

Meanwhile, Holland's diligent work with the minor league system was beginning to pay off, producing such future stars as third baseman Ron Santo, second baseman Ken Hubbs, outfielders Billy Williams and Lou Brock, and pitcher Dick Ellsworth. Williams was NL Rookie of the Year in 1961 and Hubbs (who was killed in an air accident before the 1964 season) won the award in 1962. Ellsworth won 22 games in 1963.

Holland also swung one of his better trades after the 1962 debacle, getting starting pitcher Larry Jackson and relief pitcher Lindy McDaniel, both of whom produced well for the Cubs. Jackson was the NL's winningest pitcher in 1964 with a 24–11 record. Other deals brought veteran pitchers Lew Burdette and Bob Buhl, who were temporarily helpful.

The ever-inventive Wrigley, however, continued to test Holland's endurance. Early in 1963 he hired Colonel Robert Whitlow, former athletic director of the Air Force Academy, as "athletic director" of the Cubs. Even Holland and Kennedy were placed under supreme command of the colonel, whose ill-defined duties were not clear even to him. He quit after two years of being ignored by Holland and Kennedy and wondering what he was supposed to do. Again, Holland never revealed what he thought of Whitlow.

The Cubs continued to stagger, finishing seventh under Kennedy in 1963, though they won more games than they lost (82–80) for the first time since 1946. They dropped to eighth in 1964 and stayed there in 1965 when Kennedy was replaced in midseason by Lou Klein.

The most memorable event of these turbulent and unproductive seasons, and the one that was to virtually immortalize Holland to Cubs history, was a celebrated trade. On June 15, 1964, Holland sent Lou Brock and pitchers Jack Spring and Paul Toth to the Cardinals for pitchers Ernie Broglio and outfielder Doug Clemens. Brock went on to help the Cardinals to a pennant that year, as well as others later, as he pursued a career that landed him in the Hall of Fame. The Cubs got very little out of the deal, which became notorious as "the worst" in the team's history.

Once more, Wrigley went against the grain after the 1965 season, adding another hair shirt to the long-suffering Holland's torments. Wrigley hired the controversial Leo Durocher, whose tumultuous past totally contradicted both his and Holland's most deeply held views about how baseball and life should be conducted, as the manager for 1966. The object was to "wake up" the players and provide strong leadership.

Holland did have an input into the hiring of Durocher, telling Wrigley that on a list he had drawn up of successful, experienced managers who were available, "Durocher's name came up number one." But Wrigley made the decision to hire him.

The volatile, overbearing Durocher was the dominant figure during the next seven years, calling the shots on major deals, with Holland his go-between. The key transactions came early in Durocher's tenure. On December 2, 1965, the Cubs acquired pitcher Bill Hands and catcher Randy Hundley from the San Francisco Giants. On April 21, 1966, they obtained pitcher Ferguson Jenkins and outfielder Adolfo Phillips from Philadelphia.

Holland added talent from the farm system, such as pitcher Ken Holtzman, second baseman Glenn Beckert, and shortstop Don Kessinger. After a stumbling start in 1966, when the Cubs finished tenth, they began to move up under Durocher. In 1969 they reached the apex of their fortunes under Holland-Durocher, leading the NL East by five games in early September before collapsing beneath the onrush of the New York Mets.

The Cubs remained respectable for the next three years, Holland trying to find a winning combination by acquiring at intervals such solid veterans as outfielders Jim Hickman, Johnny Callison, Jose Cardenal, and Rick Monday, first baseman Joe Pepitone, and pitcher Milt Pappas. Among the promising youngsters were pitchers Burt Hooton, Jim Colborn, and Rick Reuschel, all of whom were to have successful careers.

Holland increasingly had to intervene to calm the increasing tension between the players and the frustrated, abrasive, and irascible Durocher. Matters came to a head with a clubhouse revolt on August 23, 1971, during which Durocher tore off his uniform and barked, "I quit." Holland was called into the clubhouse and successfully persuaded Durocher to stay on. Wrigley backed him with a newspaper advertisement in which he threatened to trade away players who felt they could not play for Durocher. One of those was Holtzman, who was sent to Los Angeles for Monday.

Despite Holland's constant patchwork, the Cubs finished second in 1970 and tied for third in 1971. They were 48–44 at the All-Star Game break in 1972 when Durocher agreed to resign. Wrigley and Holland turned to Whitey Lockman, the team's director of player development, whose more relaxed managerial style briefly revived the team. He spurred them to a second-place finish.

But after a good start in 1973, with the Cubs leading the division on July 4, the wheels began to fall off, the final result being a fifth-place finish. It was clearly time for rebuilding, and Holland began to rebuild the team that had so excited its fans in 1969 and for a couple of years after. He disposed of Santo, Beckert, Hundley, and Jenkins by the 1974 season, the latter bringing a fine hitting third baseman in Bill Madlock, who won NL batting titles in 1975 and 1976 for the Cubs. In return for Santo, Holland got pitcher Steve Stone from the White Sox.

The deals did not help. The Cubs got off to a poor start in 1974, and Lockman quit as manager in midseason to be replaced by Jim Marshall. The final result was last place.

In his last major trade, Holland sent Billy Williams to the Oakland Athletics after the 1974 season, in return getting fine second baseman Manny Trillo and relief pitchers Bob Locker and Darold Knowles. The acquisitions proved of value in 1975, but Marshall's team was tied for fifth (or last) at the end of the season.

Holland had been ailing for some time. After the disappointment of 1975 he decided on semiretirement during a shakeup of front office personnel by Wrigley, who named E. G. "Salty" Saltwell as general manager. Holland remained as an adviser for another year before retiring totally.

1976

E. G. "Salty" Saltwell

A long-time Cubs employee, E. G. "Salty" Saltwell had been in charge of Wrigley Field, concessions, and ancillary operations when P. K. Wrigley tapped him as general manager. Saltwell attacked his job conscientiously, completing the breakup of the 1969 team by trading shortstop Don Kessinger to the Cardinals for journeyman pitcher Mike Garman. He traded for first baseman Andy Thornton, reacquired catcher Randy Hundley, and made several other minor deals. It was all in vain, the Cubs finishing a dull fourth, though Rick Reuschel was 14–12 and Ray Burris 15–13 while Madlock won his second straight batting title, batting .338 after .354 in 1975.

Under Saltwell, attendance remained over one million for the ninth straight year, but the Cubs again lost money. Wrigley seemed at his wit's end, commenting, "I've got to shake up the club. I'm just trying to line up everybody I can think of. I don't know what else to do."

What he did was return Saltwell to his former job as vice president of park operations and secretary and bring back Bob Kennedy, this time as general manager rather than field manager.

1977–81

Bob Kennedy

In the dozen years since Bob Kennedy had been dismissed as manager of the Cubs in 1965, he had acquired a reputation as an astute evaluator and developer of talent, mostly for the St. Louis Cardinals. P. K. Wrigley gave the tough, candid, and earnest Kennedy almost total command of the organization, though with financial constraints in view of recent financial losses. At 83, Wrigley had grown weary of wrestling with the Cubs' problems and wanted someone forceful who could take most of the load off his shoulders.

Kennedy chose the experienced Herman Franks, who had been a coach in 1969 under Leo Durocher, as his manager. His most immediate problems were the salary demands of Rick Monday and Bill Madlock. Wrigley characteristically met two-time batting champion Madlock's request for a hefty raise by commenting, "No ballplayer is worth more than $100,000, and I'm not sure they're worth that much."

Kennedy responded by trading Monday to Los Angeles in a multiplayer deal in exchange for first baseman Bill Buckner and shortstop Ivan DeJesus, both of whom were to play well for several years. Madlock went to San Francisco in another multiplayer deal that brought the Cubs two more regulars, center fielder Bobby Murcer and third baseman Steven Ontiveros. Several minor trades further reshaped the team.

Wrigley was not to see the results. He died on April 12, 1977, control of the Cubs passing to his son, William Wrigley.

Kennedy's deals seemed to be paying off as the Cubs got off to a fast start in 1977 and led the division until August 4. But they faded quickly, with injuries to reliever Bruce Sutter and starter Rick Reuschel, who was 19–3 in early September, taking a toll. Reuschel finished 20–10, and Sutter earned 31 saves, as the Cubs faded to an 81–81 record and fourth place.

Kennedy's chief acquisition for 1978 was much-traveled and troublesome free-agent outfielder Dave Kingman, whose 28 home runs did not brighten the overall picture, the team finishing 79–83, though a notch higher, in third place.

The next year, despite numerous trades by Kennedy and a banner year for Kingman, who hit 48 home runs and drove in 115 runs, was much the same, with an 80–82 record, good for fifth place. Franks resigned with a week to go in the season, denouncing by name players whom he characterized as selfish, coddled, and unmotivated.

Kennedy tried a different tack, hiring gentlemanly Preston Gomez as manager for 1980. He expected Gomez to get along better with the players, whose relations with the irascible Franks had been acrimonious. The Cubs got off to a poor start (38–52) under Gomez, and he was replaced at midseason by coach Joey Amalfitano, who had no better luck. The results in 1980 were 64–98 and last place.

Kennedy retained Amalfitano for 1981, trading away Kingman and Sutter and acquiring outfielder Leon Durham and third baseman Ken Reitz in the latter deal. The strike-splintered 1981 season was a disaster, the Cubs finishing with the worst record in the NL.

By the time the 1981 season ended, however, Kennedy was gone, having resigned on May 22, in preparation for the sale of the Cubs by William Wrigley to the Tribune Company, which was announced on June 16.

1981

Herman Franks

The tenure of Herman Franks, former coach and manager of the Cubs, as general manager was limited to a few weeks. His role was to provide a "caretaker government" to prepare the way for the takeover of the organization by the Tribune Company. His task completed by the end of the disastrous 1981 season, Franks handed over the reins to the Tribune Company's new front-office team.

1981–87

Dallas Green

Dictatorial, heavy-handed, and impatient, onetime major league pitcher Dallas Green had managed the Philadelphia Phillies to a World Series championship in 1980. His ambition, however, lay in the front office, and he jumped at the Tribune Company's offer to run the Cubs. His hiring with a five-year contract was announced on October 15, 1981.

He took over with a bang, promising to build a "New Tradition" at Wrigley Field. Almost immediately he caused a furor in the ballpark neighborhood and among the media by demanding that lights be installed in the ballpark. He quickly backed down on the threat to move the team to a suburban site.

Green named Lee Elia, one of his coaches at Philadelphia, as manager and plunged into rebuilding the Cubs with a flurry of trades and free-agent signings. The most significant among these was a deal with Philadelphia on January 27, 1982, in which the Cubs got veteran shortstop Larry Bowa and rookie infielder Ryne Sandberg in exchange for shortstop Ivan DeJesus. Outfielder Keith Moreland came in another trade with the Phillies. An old Cub favorite, Fergie Jenkins, returned from the White Sox.

The new left side of the infield, with Sandberg sparkling with the glove at third base, didn't make much difference in Green's first year, 1982. The Cubs finished fifth with a 73–89 record.

Green presevered with deals for 1983, signing an expensive free agent, veteran third baseman Ron Cey, and dealing for pitchers Steve Trout and Dick Ruthven, among others. Sandberg moved to second base, where he was to star until his retirement in 1994. Other young players such as catcher Jody Davis and right fielder Leon Durham began to come into their own.

The pitching, however, was weak, and the Cubs finished 1983 in fifth place again. Their record of 71–91 was even worse than that of the previous year. Elia provided the highlight of a dismal season with a notorious tantrum in which he denounced the fans. Green felt obliged to sack him at midseason, letting veteran scout Charlie Fox finish the campaign as manager. He hired Jim Frey, who had managed Kansas City against Green's Phillies in 1980, to manage the Cubs in 1984.

Green moved to shore up the pitching staff in three major trades in which he obtained experienced starters. He dealt for Scott Sanderson in the off-season, added Dennis Eckersley on May 25, then sent highly regarded outfield prospects Joe Carter and Mel Hall to Cleveland for Rick Sutcliffe on June 13 as the Cubs were faltering. Another key trade with the Phillies brought center fielder Bob Dernier and left fielder Gary Matthews to complete an outfield with Moreland in right.

"I didn't have a five-year plan," Green later explained. "If the opportunity to win it all is there, you have to grab it. The key thing is that we had some quality people like [Bill] Buck-

Dallas Green, the first general manager of the Tribune Company era

ner, [relief pitcher] Bill Campbell, Mel Hall, and Joe Carter to trade away for the pitchers we needed."

With Sutcliffe going 16–1 as a Cub, Lee Smith turning into an outstanding reliever, and Sandberg, Cey, Matthews, and Davis providing the punch, the Cubs caught fire. And Chicago caught "Cub Fever" as the team swept to a NL East Division title. Attendance soared to a record 2,107,665. Sandberg won the NL Most Valuable Player award, and Frey was chosen NL Manager of the Year.

A collapse in the NL Championship Series—the Cubs losing the final three games after winning the first two—hardly diminished the fans' expectations for 1985. Green made only minor changes on the roster, but injuries and a falling off in production resulted in disaster, the Cubs returning to their old ways with a 77–84 record as they sagged to fourth place.

Apparently believing that 1985 been just an off year and that if everyone stayed healthy the results would be different, Green made few changes for 1986. A 13-game losing streak early in the season woke him up, and he fired Frey on June 12 with the Cubs at 23–33. His choice as manager was Gene Michael, who had earned a reputation for being unflappable with the New York Yankees.

Michael couldn't right the sinking ship, and the Cubs staggered to the finish line in fifth place with a 70–90 record. Green retained Michael for 1987 and gave him added power by signing free-agent right fielder Andre Dawson, who turned in a tremendous year with 49 home runs (the most since Hack Wilson's 56 in 1930) and 137 RBIs as he won the NL MVP.

Despite Dawson's heroics, the Cubs stumbled through the '87 season, and Green grew increasingly impatient with Michael's "laid-back" style of managing as well as the player's apparent apathy. He barked that they had "quit." Michael resigned with three weeks left in the season, to be replaced by interim manager Frank Lucchesi. The final result was last place with a 76–85 record.

As impatient as Green was with the players, at one point saying he had been "slapped in the face, and so were the Cub fans," the Tribune Company higher-ups had also become impatient with his high-handed conduct, including his ostensible plan to return to the field in a dual role as manager for 1988. Stripped of some of his authority during post-season meetings, he resigned in late 1987 before he could be fired.

In retrospect, despite the 1984 division championship, Dallas Green's six years as general manager were a failure. The Cubs finished below .500 in five of the six seasons.

1987–91

Jim Frey

After Jim Frey was fired as manager by Dallas Green midway in the 1986 season, the Cubs found him a spot in the radio broadcast booth. On Green's departure after the 1987 season, the Tribune Company executives surprisingly lighted on him to be their new general manager, reasoning that he was more familiar than anyone they could have brought from the outside with the personnel and problems of the team. Frey's first move was to install a friend from high school days, Don Zimmer, as manager. Zimmer had a "track record" as a veteran manager at San Diego and Boston.

Among the promising young players Frey inherited from Green were outfielder Rafael Palmeiro, first baseman Mark Grace, shortstop Shawon Dunston, and pitcher Greg Maddux, though a few veterans of the 1984 division title were still on hand.

Frey tried to shore up the starting pitching by trading reliever Lee Smith to Boston for Al Nipper and Calvin Schiraldi; both were disappointments. A better deal brought pitcher Mike Bielecki in exchange for a minor leaguer. The Cubs, despite Maddux' 18–8 record, and good seasons by Grace, Palmeiro, Ryne Sandberg, and Andre Dawson, were not much better in 1988, finishing fourth with a 77–85 record.

Frey gambled with a major trade on December 5, 1988, sending Palmeiro, who was developing into a star, along with two others to Texas, in return getting five players, the key man being reliever Mitch Williams, who was to earn 36 saves in 1989.

Williams solidified the bullpen, and two rookies, center fielder Jerome Walton and left fielder Dwight Smith, rounded out the outfield. Dawson, Grace, and Sandberg had good years, and a starting rotation of Maddux (19–12), Rick Sutcliffe (16–11), Scott Sanderson (11–9), and the surprising Bielecki (18–7) performed above expectations.

The Cubs finished on top of the NL East in a four-team dogfight in 1989, Zimmer's "hunch" managing paying off with 33 come-from-behind victories. The NL Championship Series, however, was won by San Francisco—the Cubs' ninth consecutive failure in postseason play going back to 1910.

Frey tried pretty much the same cast for 1989, though Sutcliffe was released as a cost-cutting measure. Despite Sandberg's 40 home runs and Dawson's 27, the Cubs crumbled

in 1990, Walton and Williams being particular disappointments. The team sank to fourth place with a 77–85 record.

Frey got the green light to plunge into the expensive free-agent market for 1991 and came up with starting pitcher Danny Jackson, relief pitcher Dave Smith, and left fielder George Bell for some $25.5 million in long-term contracts. Jackson (1–5) and Smith (0–6, 17 saves) were busts, though Bell hit 25 home runs as the left fielder.

The Cubs started slowly, and it became evident Frey was losing control when his pal Zimmer quit on May 22 after team president Don Grenesko refused to assure the manager he would be back in 1992. Frey brought in Jim Essian from the Iowa farm team to manage the rest of the way as the Cubs plodded into fourth place with a record of 77–83.

The Tribune Company council running the team decided on a shakeup, and Frey was shunted to the role of consultant. The new general manager was Larry Himes, who had served in a similar capacity with the White Sox from 1986 to 1990.

1992–94

Larry Himes

During his years with the White Sox, Larry Himes had earned a reputation for developing players in the farm system. He was credited with having turned a sub-.500 team into a contender.

A former minor league catcher, Himes had turned to scouting and had risen to player development director for the California Angels before joining the White Sox organization. A personality clash with White Sox majority owner Jerry Reinsdorf cost him his job as general manager after the 1990 season. He returned to scouting until the Cubs hired

Larry Himes

him on November 14, 1991, in the hope that he could repeat his success as a developer of young players for them.

Vigorous, opinionated, and often abrasive, Himes plunged into his new job with zest, hiring as manager Jim Lefebvre, who had been fired by the Seattle Mariners after the 1991 season despite leading the team to the first plus-.500 record in its history.

Himes' major moves for 1992 were the trading of George Bell to the White Sox for promising young right fielder Sammy Sosa and the signing of free-agent starting pitcher Mike Morgan. Midseason deals brought third baseman Steven Buechele and outfielder Kal Daniels.

Though Maddux won 20 games and the NL Cy Young Award, Morgan was 16–8, Sandberg hit 26 home runs, Dawson hit 22, and Grace batted .307, the Cubs again finished fourth, winning just one more game than the previous year. Injuries to shortstop Shawon Dunston and Sosa and the total failure of Daniels contributed to the disappointing performance.

During the winter of 1992–93, Himes was confronted with the pivotal problem of his regime, the demand of Maddux for a five-year contract at about $28.5 million. Maddux' high expectations were partly fueled by the four-year extension of Sandberg's contract with an average compensation of $7.1 million a year.

In the end, Himes and his Tribune Company superiors decided to let Maddux depart, which he did, signing with Atlanta and continuing a spectacular career with Cy Young Awards in 1993 and 1994. Dawson also left as a free agent.

Himes tried to recover for 1993 by signing free-agent starters Jose Guzman and Greg Hibbard and reliever Randy Myers. He also acquired outfielders Candy Maldonado and Willie Wilson to make up for the loss of Dawson. He put the best face he could on the failure to sign Maddux. "We lost Greg Maddux and Andre Dawson, but we finished 18 games out with them," Himes said. "I don't see that happening this year. I think we're a lot better off with the people we've added."

As it turned out, the Cubs did perform better, surpassing .500 for only the third time in 21 years. They finished fourth with a record of 84–78, Hibbard contributing 15–9, Guzman 12–10, and Myers an NL-record 53 saves. Younger players such as Sosa (33 home runs, 93 RBIs), left fielder Derrick May (.295), shortstop Jose Vizcaino, and catcher Rick Wilkins (.303, 30 home runs, 73 RBIs) made an impact with promise for the future.

Himes put increasing pressure on Lefebvre during the season, suggesting that the manager's job was in jeopardy unless the team was in contention by July. Though the Cubs finished strong despite pitching problems compounded by injuries to Guzman and Morgan, Himes fired Lefebvre after the campaign, handing the job to coach Tom Trebelhorn, who previously had managed at Milwaukee.

Himes also continued the cost cutting for 1994, waving goodbye to Hibbard, who expected a big raise after his 15 wins to lead the staff in 1993. He attempted to shore up the starting pitching by trading for Willie Banks from Minnesota and sending Vizcaino to the New York Mets for Anthony Young.

The NL was rearranged into three divisions for 1994, a year after the expansion to 14 teams, with the Cubs in the five-team Central Division. The Cubs were guaranteed to finish no lower than fifth place, which they did, with a record of 49–63 when the season was halted for good by the players' strike on August 12.

The 1994 season was one of the more frustrating in Cub history. They lost their first 12 games at home, and they lost Sandberg when he abruptly announced his retirement on June 13, by inference—and later openly—questioning Himes' and the ownership's dedication to producing a winning team.

Increasingly disenchanged by Himes, his bosses decided to take still another tack in attempting to turn the Cubs from "lovable losers" into a force. Himes was fired, and Andy MacPhail, who had been successful as general manager at Minnesota, was brought in as the club president. His choice as general manager was Ed Lynch, a former Cub pitcher.

1995–

Ed Lynch

Before assuming the job of general manager, Ed Lynch had enjoyed a moderately successful career as a major league pitcher, including a stint with the Cubs in 1987. After his retirement, he moved into front-office work with the San Diego Padres and New York Mets.

Andy MacPhail plucked Lynch from the Mets' front office to serve as his collaborator in a long-term rebuilding program. They agreed to hire Jim Riggleman, who had managed the Padres the previous two seasons, as their manager.

Lynch, like MacPhail, emphasized that the Cubs were to

Ed Lynch

"go slow" and build mostly from the farm system. No radical cure was contemplated. Among his early moves were the signing of free-agent center fielder Brian McRae and starting pitcher Jaime Navarro for the 1995 season and a decision not to re-sign outfielders Derrick May and Glenallen Hill.

Navarro and McRae were vital to the Cubs' recovery from the dismal previous year, lifting them to a 73–71 finish in 1995, the first year of the MacPhail-Lynch regime. Also contributing to the rebound was a late-June trade in which the Cubs acquired outfielder Luis Gonzalez and catcher Scott Servais from the Houston Astros in exchange for catcher Rick Wilkins.

But the maneuvers for 1996 proved less encouraging. Lynch let stopper Randy Myers depart as a free agent, and his replacement, Doug Jones, proved a flop. He got mixed results from two other free-agent signees, infielders Dave Magadan and Leo Gomez. And the Cubs' deplorable 76–86 finish, in which they lost 14 of their 16 last games, served to emphasize major problems both in pitching and offense.

Lynch promised to address the issues for the 1997 campaign with the help of a bigger budget from MacPhail.

They Also Serve

During the 120 years of their history the Cubs have employed hundreds of people in the tasks required to operate a sports franchise. In the early years the staff was tiny, but as baseball's popularity grew and income rose, the front-office and ancillary staffs increased in numbers, exploding in size particularly after World War II.

Most of those employed in secretarial, financial, personnel, public relations, ticket sales, park maintenance, and concessions areas worked in anonymity, often for 30 to 40 years until retirement. Others more closely associated with the players, such as traveling secretaries, trainers, farm directors, and clubhouse men, occasionally popped into the spotlight, sometimes because of their colorful personalities.

Under the Wrigley family's ownership, loyalty was always at a premium, and a Cub employee was assured of security in his job for decades. Bobby Dorr, the groundskeeper from the beginning of the Wrigley era into the 1950s, even had an apartment in an adjunct to Wrigley Field. Some positions were even filled with or created for loyal Wrigley employees from other parts of the family's huge financial empire, or outsiders whom William Wrigley, Jr., or Philip K. Wrigley wished to help by supplementing the pensions they received after they retired from other occupations.

For instance, though P. K. Wrigley had no great use for sportswriters as a group, after they retired he frequently found jobs with the Cubs for those he liked. Among those "taken care of" in this way were Howie Roberts, a longtime *Chicago Daily News* baseball writer, who also had been traveling secretary of the White Sox. He was given a sinecure taking care of press credentials. Another baseball writer who became a Cub employee was Jim Enright, who was the Cub public address announcer after his newspaper, *Chicago's Today*, went out of business in 1976.

Among the longest-serving employees was equipment manager Yosh Kawano, who was still going strong in the clubhouse in the mid-1990s after more than 50 years on the job. Clarence "Pants" Rowland, who had managed the White Sox to a World Series championship in 1917, became a Wrigley employee in the early 1920s and served the Cubs for almost as long as Kawano in a variety of jobs, ranging from scout to vice president and unofficial assistant general manager, until his death in 1969.

Rip Collins, the first baseman of the 1938 NL championship team, was public relations director for a period in the late 1950s and early 1960s. More surprisingly, if not untypically, G. A. "Gus" Settergren, reportedly Wrigley's former chauffeur, held the title of "assistant traveling secretary" for almost two decades after his retirement from behind the wheel in the 1960s, though his duties were indiscernible.

Undoubtedly the most colorful of the Cubs nonplaying personnel were two who flourished from the 1920s on, trainer Andy Lotshaw until his death in 1953, and traveling secretary Bob Lewis, who continued until 1962.

Lotshaw, a former minor league baseball player and early professional football tackle, began patching up and conditioning athletes with George Halas' Decatur Staleys in 1920 and continued in that role when they became the Chicago Bears, switching to the Cubs during the baseball season. He had taken a course in training from a correspondence school.

Lewis, who grew up in the vicinity of Wrigley Field, gravitated from brief stints in burlesque and a theatrical box office to become John Seys' successor as traveling secretary in 1927. He held the job of arranging transportation and lodging for players, as well as shepherding them, for 35 years (1927–62). He became three-time manager Charlie Grimm's favorite accomplice in practical jokes and impromptu theatrical productions at baseball banquets. Lotshaw, in addition to being trainer, also served as baggage master, assisting Lewis in arranging and conducting road trips, as well as being an unofficial valet to some of the Cub stars.

Lotshaw was an inveterate prankster, though a favorite of the players, but he never let them get away with anything. In one classic bit of revenge, after several players had tossed around one of Lotshaw's favorite possessions, he dropped into the toilet the key to the trunk in which they deposited their money, jewelry, and other valuables before each game. A locksmith had to be summoned.

Lotshaw developed and sold a liniment known as Lotshaw's Body Rub. He persuaded the Cubs to buy him an expensive copy of the book *Materia Medica* so that he could enhance sales of his body rub by wrapping the bottles with its prestigious pages.

The rotund Lewis, irascible though fun-loving, teamed up with Grimm in 1945, the last year of World War II, in the most memorable event of the more than 50 annual Diamond Dinners put on by the Chicago Chapter of the Baseball Writers' Association of America. Both Grimm and Lewis, with his burlesque background, had a gift for parody and were a good fit as a double act.

Dressed in hotel doormen's uniforms, Grimm adorned himself with a mustache and played the role of German dictator Adolf Hitler, while the rotund Lewis took the part of his chief henchman, Marshal Herman Goering. "Hitler" addressed the throng in guttural German, from time to time sending off "Goering" to find out how things were going on the front. Each time "Goering" returned with the bad news, his clothes progressively more torn, "Hitler" slapped him and sent him off for a later report.

Before the act ended, "Goering" was down to his underwear and, after a fifth swipe by "Hitler" that he complained was too hard, knocked Grimm to the floor with a punch delivered in earnest.

Chances are that Grimm, Lewis, and Lotshaw were the most colorful employees the Cubs ever have had.

6

WRIGLEY FIELD
HOME OF
CHICAGO CUBS
SCARF DAY
WILL RECEIVE A C

Budweiser THIS BUD'S FOR YOU! Budweiser

NO TURNS

The Ballparks

Wrigley Field has become a legend, a baseball monument celebrated nationally, and a major fan attraction in itself. The availability of almost all scheduled Cub games on cable television in most parts of the United States has spread the old ballpark's fame far beyond the Chicago area and has made it a major tourist attraction for dedicated fans from all over the country.

As one of the few baseball stadiums still in use from the early part of the 20th century, Wrigley Field has accumulated a treasure trove of legendary moments, such as Gabby Hartnett's celebrated "Homer in the Gloamin'," Ernie Banks' 500th career home run, the notorious "two balls in play" game between the Cubs and St. Louis Cardinals, Babe Ruth's alleged "called shot" home run in the 1932 World Series, Lou Gehrig's home run as a high school boy, and many others that crowd the memories of knowledgeable fans.

The ivy-covered brick outfield walls, the huge manually operated scoreboard beyond center field, the "Bleacher Bums," and the memory of such great Cub hitters as Banks, Hack Wilson, Rogers Hornsby, Phil Cavarretta, Ron Santo, Billy Williams, and Bill Madlock, as well as a throng of outstanding pitchers, among them Grover Cleveland Alexander, Charlie Root, Claude Passeau, Ferguson Jenkins, and Greg Maddux, all have contributed to the aura of what often has been called the perfect setting for a baseball game.

Additionally, the history of the Chicago Bears is inextricably tied up with that of Wrigley Field, where they played for almost 50 years after their inception before moving to Soldier Field in 1971. Many of the legendary Bears, among them Red Grange, Bronko Nagurski, Bulldog Turner, George McAfee, Sid Luckman, Johnny Morris, Mike Ditka, Dick Butkus, and Gale Sayers, performed their greatest exploits in home games on the grass of what now is exclusively a baseball park.

In fact, the last team to win a national championship at Wrigley Field was not the Cubs, who haven't won a World Series since 1908, eight years before they took up residence at Wrigley Field. It was the Bears, who won the National Football League title in 1963, in a memorable 17–13 victory over the New York Giants on a near-zero degree day on the ice-hard grass of the venerable ballpark.

Beyond its crowded history and countless legends, Wrigley Field's natural advantages, together with the major structural improvements that have been made from time to time, have kept it as up-to-date as it was when first erected just before the start of World War I. Among the benefits are easy access from public transportation, good sight lines, nearness of the fans to the field, almost perfectly proportioned dimensions, and a picture-book setting for a game, particularly on an ideal summer day.

This combination of advantages has kept Wrigley Field vibrant, viable, and eminently functional into the late 1990s despite the fact it was constructed in 1914, more than half a century before most of the other baseball parks in current use.

So inextricably have the histories of the Cubs and Wrigley Field been intertwined that it is almost a shock to consider that it is the sixth home of the team from its birth in 1876 as one of the charter members of the National League. The Cubs, of course, are the oldest team in all professional sports, being the only one in continuous existence for more than 120 years—as well as being the only original member of the NL to compete in every season since 1876 in the same city without interruption.

Fans streaming into Wrigley Field, 1984

The Team and Its Parks

The origins of the Cubs and their first ballpark can be traced to baseball's first professional league, the National Association of Professional Base Ball Players (NA), which was formed on March 17, 1871. It started play as a loose confederation of nine teams from cities east of the Mississippi River, including such smaller communities as Rockford, Illinois, Fort Wayne, Indiana, and Troy, New York, as well as the metropolises of Chicago, Boston, Cleveland, New York, Philadelphia, and Washington, D.C.

The new league in part based its hopes for financial success on playing its games in enclosed ballparks, to which admission could be restricted to paying customers. Earlier in the game's history, "crowd control" had been a major difficulty because fields were not enclosed. With the founding of the NA, all nine of its members provided themselves with enclosed ball grounds where a fee could be charged for admission.

Less than a decade had passed since William H. Cammeyer, a farsighted Brooklyn politician, had erected the first enclosed ball grounds in 1862, putting up a fence around what had been an ice-skating rink. A horseshoe-shaped grandstand and benches on three sides provided seating for 1,500 in what was named the Union Base Ball and Cricket Grounds.

Among the innovations were seating specifically designated for "ladies" and the confining of gamblers to a separate area known as the "bettor's ring." A clubhouse was provided for the accommodation of the players, a feature that was not always present in many of the ballparks built subsequently.

The outfield fences of this first enclosed park were more than 500 feet from home plate. They were made of six- or seven-foot-high boards, not tall enough to totally obstruct the view of the playing field from embankments outside the enclosure.

As a result, when the park was inaugurated on May 15, 1862, many of the more than 8,000 spectators on hand remained in carriages or on foot outside the fence to view the ceremony, which included the playing of "The Star-Spangled Banner." It was no doubt a patriotic gesture during the Civil War. It also was a foreshadowing of a practice that was to become universal during subsequent wars.

Most significantly, after allowing all comers free entry on opening day, Cammeyer decided to charge admission from then on. The admission charge started at 10 cents and soon became 25 cents; before long the players of such clubs as the Mutuals, Atlantics, Eckfords, Putnams, and Constellations began demanding a cut.

Professional baseball was on its way, and it burst into early bloom in 1871 with the new NA and its nine enclosed wooden ballparks, including that of the White Stockings in Chicago. As much as anyone, Cammeyer could have laid claim to being the founder of professional baseball, which he had made practical with the first enclosed ballpark.

A frantic building program was needed for each of the NA's nine teams to provide itself with a ballpark, most of them located where land was cheap. The White Stockings built theirs on a city dump between Lake Michigan and Michigan Avenue, within walking distance of the downtown business district.

The first-base side of the park was along Michigan Avenue, with the grandstand placed at the northwest corner, along Randolph Street. The tracks and switchyards of the Illinois Central Railroad were between the ballpark and Lake Michigan to the east.

This first enclosed Chicago baseball stadium had a capacity of 7,000 and provided separate seating for men and women (for protection from hooligans and bad language). Season tickets (for a haphazard schedule) went for $15. A six-foot board fence some 375 feet from the plate at the foul lines, enclosed the park.

The ballpark apparently was officially called Union Base-Ball Grounds, but became variously known as Lake Street Dumping Ground, White Stocking Park, and Lake Park, the last sticking as the favored label.

Lake Park is significant not only because it was the first enclosed ballpark in Chicago, but also because the site eventually became the home of the early Cubs—not, however without a disaster and a period playing at another site where they made their debut.

The NA White Stockings were born under an unlucky star. They started out well, battling for the league's championship into late season, when disaster struck. On October 9, 1871, the Great Chicago Fire began, not only devastating the city for three days, leaving 100,000 homeless and causing an estimated $196 million in damage, but also burning Lake Park down to the ground.

The White Stockings were able to finish their first season on the road, but the loss of their ballpark may have contributed to their falling just short of a pennant. They were eliminated from contention on October 30, the last day of the season.

By the start of the 1872 season they had built a new home, at 23rd Street and State Street. It was appropriately, if unimaginatively, called the 23rd Street Grounds. Within a few years it was to become the first home of the team later to be named the Cubs.

After a promising start, the NA began to stagger under a load of problems, including charges of throwing games, too many players for whom alcoholism and gambling were a way of life, the frequent collapse of underfinanced teams, the jumping of franchises from city to city, no set schedules, and a lack of central authority.

The White Stockings went downhill the next two seasons, sinking to semipro status while the Boston Red Stockings dominated the NA, winning four consecutive pennants. Boston was led by pitcher Albert G. Spalding, who was to play a major role in Cub history. In 1874 the White Stockings reentered the NA, but continued to flounder.

In 1875, William Hulbert, an energetic Chicago businessman, became president of the White Stockings. Determined to make the team a powerhouse, he raided the top two NA teams, Boston and Philadelphia, for their stars. Before the end of the '75 season, he had signed pitchers Spalding and Jim "Deacon" White, infielder Ross Barnes, and catcher-outfielder Cal McVey of Boston and first baseman Adrian "Cap" Anson and third baseman Ezra Sutton of Philadelphia.

Such raids being forbidden under the NA rules, Hulbert was in danger of losing his new players or having the White Stockings expelled from the league. Convinced that the NA, despite isolated successes, was doomed by its ramshackle structure and inability to police its owners and players, Hulbert decided to start a new league.

On February 2, 1876, Hulbert, assisted by Spalding, who had been named manager and captain of the White Stockings and was to receive 25 percent of gate receipts, accomplished his goal at a meeting of prospective owners at New York's Central Hotel. The National League of Professional Base Ball Clubs was born with a charter membership of eight teams, one of them being Hulbert's reconstituted White Stockings, the team we now call the Cubs. The gutted NA went out of business.

As part of the new National League's strategy, and to cut expenses, the eight new teams decided to use the old ballparks of the defunct NA. The White Stockings moved into their predecessor's 23rd Street Grounds, where they stayed for their first two seasons. It was their first of five stops on the way to Wrigley Field.

Just two years later the White Stockings, who won the NL's first pennant in 1876, were able to afford a new venue, Lakefront Park, which was built on the Michigan Avenue site of the NA team's original ballpark that had burned down in 1871.

The next shift came in 1885, after the team had won three more pennants in succession from 1880 to 1882. A posher stadium, West Side Park, was erected at Congress and Throop streets and served the team well as, after a three-year hiatus, the White Stockings again won pennants in 1885 and 1886.

In 1891 the White Stockings used two fields, West Side Park and another at 35th and Wentworth streets, a site adjacent to what later was to become Comiskey Park. It was the second of three that were known as South Side Park and had been the home of the short-lived Chicago Pirates of the upstart Players League for just one year, 1890. In 1891 the White Stockings played there on Tuesdays, Thursdays, and Saturdays and at West Side Park on Mondays, Wednesdays, and Fridays. No Sunday games were permitted by the National League until 1893.

In 1892 the team, now also nicknamed the Colts, played its entire home schedule in South Side Park, but the next year again used two parks, playing Sunday games exclusively at a new, larger facility, the West Side Grounds.

The West Side Grounds, with a capacity of 16,000, was a major innovation, the first double-decked stadium in Chicago. The park, located at Polk Street and Lincoln (now Wolcott) Street, was to be the team's exclusive home from 1894 until the move in 1916 to the former Federal League park now known as Wrigley Field.

Since that time, the Cubs have called Wrigley Field home, with the exception of a brief jaunt to the White Sox's Comiskey Park for the 1918 World Series.

23rd Street Grounds

The newly born White Stockings of the NL marked their home debut on May 10, 1876, in what formerly had been the NA ballpark at 23rd and State streets by defeating Cincinnati 6–0 before a crowd of 5,000 or 6,000, according to an estimate, which might have been stretching it.

Their home was typical of its era: a ramshackle little ballpark with a wooden grandstand that could seat perhaps 1,500 fans and a six- or seven-foot wooden fence surrounding the playing field. Apparently most of the overflow crowd on that first opening day stood around the diamond and in the outfield, which was customary at the time and for long after.

The outfield measurements of the 23rd Street Grounds are unknown, but almost without exception the early parks were asymmetrical, with short foul lines of less than 300 feet and deep center fields. The shape of the outfield was usually determined by the configuration of the real estate (as can be seen in Boston's Fenway Park). The fences were not conceived as barriers to hit the ball over but merely as a means of ensuring that fans would have to pay to enter and see the games.

The White Stockings coasted to the first NL pennant, winning 52 of 66 games for a .788 percentage, still a major league record. Spalding led the way with a 47–13 pitching record. He played first base when he wasn't pitching. The next year the team faded to fifth place, but attendance apparently held up because the White Stockings moved to a new, larger park in '78.

Lakefront Park

The site chosen for the new home of the White Stockings was virtually the same on which had stood the NA park that had burned down in 1871. It had natural advantages, being in the commercial and fashionable heart of the renascent city, with burgeoning State Street just a few blocks away. It was later to become part of Grant Park.

The grandstand was placed at the southeast corner of Michigan Avenue and Randolph Street. Right field extended southward along Michigan Avenue to a point midway between Washington and Madison streets. The left-field fence paralleled Randolph Street. To the east, toward Lake Michigan, lay the yards of the Illinois Central Railroad.

The new park began with a seating capacity of about 3,000, but it was something short of a baseball heaven, particularly for the players. The infield made it evident that the location had long served as a city dump. It was bumpy and littered with rocks, boulders, ashes, glass, and even bottles.

The White Stockings started out slowly in the new park, finishing fourth in '78 and '79, but surged to three consecutive pennants, 1880–82. Cap Anson took over as manager in '79, and when Hulbert died in '82, Spalding became the principal owner. Success on the field translated to increased attendance, an average of almost 3,000 per game, a very respectable figure for the period.

Spalding decided the park needed enlargement and improvement, and allocated the almost unheard of sum of $10,000, including $1,800 for paint, to construct a "palace" of baseball. *Harper's* magazine commented, "The fact that so large can outlay can be safely made tells its own story of the popularity of base-ball."

Although the White Stockings' domination of the NL paused in '83, the team slipping to fourth place, the renovated park was ready for the start of the '84 season. According to Michael Gershman in his book *Green Diamonds*, the new Lakefront Park was "the first ballpark marketed as an attraction in its own right," foreshadowing the continuing lure of Wrigley Field a century later. A Chicago newspaper was enthusiastic, commenting, "Everything is entirely new. The seats, fences, etc. are wholly built of new lumber, rendering them perfectly safe for large crowds." The story detailed that the average spectator was guaranteed an unobstructed view, free scorecards, and the opportunity to rent seat cushions.

Lakefront now was the biggest ballpark in baseball, holding 10,000, including standees. The grandstand seated 2,000 ("on elevated seats so as to command the best view of the play"); the bleachers could hold 6,000; a pagoda built as a bandstand overlooked the main entrance and provided more room; and baseball's first "skyboxes" sat above the grandstand on the third base side.

The 18 luxury boxes featured armchairs and curtains to keep out the sun, wind, and hoi polloi for the "accommodation of reporters, club officials and parties of ladies and gentlemen." Occupying the most luxurious box was White Stockings owner Spalding, retired from pitching and well on his way to becoming a sporting goods magnate. He was furnished with a telephone, patented just six years earlier, "to enable him to conduct the details of the game without leaving his seat" and a Chinese gong with which to summon his employees.

The always innovative Spalding also had another idea: night baseball. In 1883 he asked the NL for permission to play an exhibition game against a "picked nine," chosen from other league teams, "in the evening under electric lights." The NL denied permission, but had it approved the experiment, Lakefront Park would have been the site of the first Cub night game at home, more than a century before one finally was played at Wrigley Field. It is ironical in view of Spalding's early proposal that the Cubs became the last major league team to install lights when they might have been the first.

Spalding had a big payroll, in addition to the players. Lakefront Park was staffed by a then-unheard-of magnitude, a total of 41 people. There were seven ushers, six policemen, four ticket sellers, four gatekeepers, three field men, three cushion renters, six refreshment boys, and eight musicians, who made use of the pagoda when the First Cavalry Band was absent.

Despite all this creature comfort, Lakefront Park was hardly the ideal place to play baseball because of its absurd outfield configuration. The six-foot high left field fence was just 180 feet away down the line, center field was 300 feet, and right field was only 196 (though there was a 20-foot fence topped by 17.5 feet of tarpaulin). The "power alleys" were 280 feet to left-center and 252 feet to right-center.

The result was a potential "home run heaven" even in that dead-ball period. The danger was averted in 1883 because a ball hit over the left field fence was only a double. But in '84 it became a home run.

The result: In '83 the White Stockings hit 13 homers; the next year they totaled 142, all but 11 of them at home. The major beneficiary of the change in ground rules was third baseman Ned Williamson, who went from three home runs in '83 to a record 27 (25 of them at home, the other two at Buffalo) in '84, while his doubles output dropped from 49 to 18. Williamson's major league home run record stood until it was broken by Babe Ruth with 29 in 1919, and the White Stockings' team total record held up even longer, until the "Murderers' Row" New York Yankees surpassed it in 1927. The NL decreed a halt to the Chicago home run farce by setting the minimum distance for an outfield fence at 210 feet for 1885.

As far as Lakefront Park was concerned, the new rule was academic because Spalding decided to move the team again, evidently because he was unable to buy the site on which the stadium was located. The Illinois Central had made an offer of $800,000 to the city for the land, not near its value, and the railroad's bid opened a can of worms. The U.S. government obtained a federal court injunction that resulted in the White Stockings leaving Lakefront Park. It was disclosed that Chicago was prohibited from selling the property. It had been given to the city by the federal government with the stipulation the site not be used for a commercial venture. The railroad couldn't have it, but neither could Spalding, so the White Stockings had to move again in 1885, abandoning their grandiose and ideal site.

West Side Park

Spalding was undeterred. He secured a long-term lease on a square block of land on the West Side, at Congress and Throop streets, and named his new venue Congress Street Grounds, but it soon became popularly known as West Side Park.

Spalding also had obtained an option to buy the site for $400,000, though it was reportedly worth $750,000. The transaction was an indication of how profitable the high-flying White Stockings had become. Incomplete records suggest the team made an annual profit of between $23,000 and $32,000 from 1878 to 1881 and went up from there.

This satisfying cash flow explains Spalding's willingness to spend heavily on the Congress Street Grounds. The new stadium was even more lavish than Lakefront Park, with the woodwork painted a terra-cotta shade. Spalding expended $30,000 on the ballpark, surrounding it with a 12-foot-high brick wall. It had seating for 10,000, private roof boxes, and facilities for track, cycling, and lawn tennis. It also offered a "neatly furnished toilet room with a private entrance for ladies."

As another convenience, gentlemen driving by carriage to the park could reach the grandstand through a covered entrance inside the grounds. Spectators entered the grandstand by a stairway 16 feet wide.

The configuration of the new field was somewhat of an improvement over that of Lakefront Park, the foul lines being 216 feet. It was a bathtub-shaped ballpark with a deep center field, much like the New York Giants' Polo Grounds during the first half of the 20th century.

The White Stockings played their first game at West Side Park on June 6, 1885, and things couldn't have gone better at the gate or on the field. A hot pennant race with the New York Giants stirred fan frenzy, and crowds of more than 10,000, including Chicago Mayor Carter Harrison, jammed the park for four consecutive games in October. The White Stockings won three to clinch the pennant.

Manager Anson led the White Stockings to another pennant the next season. It was the fifth flag for the team in seven seasons; attendance and profits soared. Among the major attractions in addition to Anson were such standouts as pitcher John Clarkson, a 53-game winner in '85, and catcher-outfielder Mike "King" Kelly, later hailed as the Babe Ruth of his day. The song "Slide, Kelly, Slide" added to his fame, and the whole ballpark frequently would sing it whenever he reached first base.

West Side Park became the site of the first "World Series" game played in Chicago. After the '85 season, the White Stockings were challenged to a postseason series by the St. Louis Browns of the American Association (AA), a rival major league that began play in 1882. The Browns were managed by first baseman Charles Comiskey, who was to become the founding father of the Chicago White Sox when the American League assumed major league status in 1901.

A 12-game championship series was agreed on, with the first game to be played at West Side Park, the next three in St. Louis, and the rest at other AA sites. The opener in Chicago ended in a 3–3 tie called because of darkness. The series ended abruptly after six games, either in a three-games-to-two victory for the Browns, according to their partisans, or in a tie at three games apiece, according to the Chicago rooters. The discrepancy was caused by a game that the Browns considered a Chicago forfeit and the White Stockings claimed as a victory. An indication of the playing conditions of the time is that the two teams committed 107 errors in the seven games, 27 of them in the final contest.

The White Stockings and Browns met again after the '86 season, this time in a best-of-seven-games home-and-home series. The Browns won it in the 10th inning of the seventh game, at St. Louis. The series was no contest as to fan interest, the White Stockings drawing 13,106 to four games at West Side Grounds while the Browns drew a near-capacity turnout of 29,460 to three games at Sportsman's Park.

The "World Series" defeat signaled the beginning of the end of the glory years for the White Stockings of Spalding and Anson, with storm clouds gathering in the form of hostility between players and owners and the advent of new leagues, such as the AA and Union Association, to challenge the NL's primacy. The White Stockings were not to win another pennant until 1906, by which time they were known as the Cubs.

For a time, however, the White Stockings continued to prosper at West Side Park, Spalding and the minority stockholders sharing in 20 percent dividends out of a $100,000 surplus after the '87 season. The team reportedly also made profits of $60,000 in '88, and Spalding, looking to the future, purchased a site for another new ballpark.

In 1890 the player's dissastisfaction with the owners' attempts to curb salaries led them to form their own league. And the White Stockings, like the rest of the NL teams, were crippled by a mass exodus of their stars to the new Players League, which lasted only for the 1890 season but caused financial havoc for the established leagues.

Spalding turned to "replacement" players, as they would be called today, and the influx of youngsters earned the White Stockings a new nickname, Anson's Colts, or just Colts. The fans, however, preferred established stars, and early in the 1890 season attendance at White Stockings games dropped to an average of 828 per game at West Side Park while the rival Players League Chicago Pirates were drawing 1,654 per game at the new South Side Grounds.

But Spalding's well-heeled Colts had financial staying power, and after the collapse of the Players League in late 1890 many of the star players returned to the NL and AA, and prosperity again was just around the corner. The Colts were poised to take advantage of the renewed prospects.

Spalding's plans included a new, larger ballpark. In fact, they temporarily included three ballparks. In one of the odder twists of baseball history, the Colts turned into a "moveable feast" for a brief time.

South Side Park

The Players League Chicago Pirates had sputtered out their brief existence at South Side Park, at 35th and Wentworth streets, almost directly across the street from the site that would later be occupied by the original Comiskey Park. Actually, the two playing fields overlapped each other. The left-field corner of South Side Park (for convenience sometimes referred to as South Side Park II because the Chicago Unions of the Union Association had used the name for a facility at 39th Street during their short life span in 1884) corresponded to Comiskey Park I's center field, and foul territory near third base corresponded to the later park's right field. A 10-foot wooden fence surrounded the ballpark, but its outfield dimensions and precise seating capacity aren't known, though it was something over 10,000.

As part of the Colts' effort to recapture the trust and money of their fans, and to appeal to a new section of the city, they split their home schedule in 1891 between South Side Park and West Side Park. Games on Tuesdays, Thursdays, and Saturdays were played at South Side Park, with the team moving to West Side Park on Mondays, Wednesdays, and Fridays.

In 1892 the Cubs played all of their home games at South Side Park, abandoning West Side Park to other uses and awaiting the construction of a new "baseball palace of the world," the West Side Grounds.

Although Al Spalding stepped down as team president in 1891, handing the reins to James Hart, plans were well under way for the new ballpark, one that was to serve the Cubs well until the move to Wrigley Field in 1916.

West Side Grounds

In 1892 the new home of the Colts began to take shape at Polk and Lincoln (now Wolcott) streets on the rising West Side of Chicago. The new park was planned to seat 16,000, with the first double-decked wooden grandstand built in Chicago, somewhat archaic because steel and concrete ballparks were on their way. A small balcony of boxes was built above the grandstand between the bases to accommodate the well-to-do. Among the distinguishing features of the park were unusual round areas bare of grass at first base, third base, and home plate. The outfield dimensions of the park were more gener-

West Side Grounds, where the Cubs played for nearly a quarter of a century before the move to Wrigley Field

ous than those of its predecessors. The left field fence was 340 feet away down the foul line, the distance to center field was an awesome 560 feet, and right field extended 316 feet.

Of course, standees in the outfield, a common practice with overflow crowds in those days, considerably reduced the dimensions, as well as adding to the number of ground-rule doubles. And by 1895 big crowds were frequent, with the Colts often drawing more than 20,000 to their games.

West Side Grounds began its 23-year run as the home of the Cubs on a part-time basis on May 14, 1893, with games there only on Sundays. The rest of the games were played at South Side Park.

The Sunday games were an innovation in the NL, which had banned them from its inception in 1876, though other leagues permitted them where they were not prohibited by "blue laws." The NL lifted the ban in 1892. (Sunday games were prohibited for another 40 years in Pennsylvania, the first being played in Philadelphia on April 8, 1934.) Religious feeling against Sunday games persisted for a time in Chicago. In 1896 a jury acquitted Colts outfielder Walter Wilmot of violating Sunday blue laws by playing baseball.

The reason for the split schedule in 1893 was twofold. First, Sunday games proved a great crowd lure, most working people having only that day off from their six-day-a-week jobs. The second factor was the 1893 Columbian Exposition on the South Side, a world's fair that brought hundreds of thousands of tourists to Chicago. South Side Park was conveniently situated for visitors from around the world if they chose to take in a baseball game.

South Side Park was abandoned in 1894, and the Cubs made themselves at home at West Side Grounds until their final game there on October 3, 1915. It was the location for four pennant-winning Cubs teams, in 1906, 1907, 1908, and

1910. They even won a pair of World Series, in 1907 and 1908, something they were unable to do at Wrigley Field in numerous opportunities before 1946. In a sense, the West Side Grounds period was the Cubs' Golden Era, the time of the famous Tinkers-to-Evers-to-Chance double-play combination.

But the most exciting, and frightening, event at West Side Grounds in its inaugural year was a conflagration that stampeded a large crowd, with about 500 injuries reported, but not because of burns. To keep fans off the field and to protect the umpires and players from rowdies, the bleachers had been cordoned off with barbed wire. In the seventh inning of the game with Cincinnati on Sunday, August 5, 1894, a lit cigar tossed into some rubbish touched off a fire on the field near the bleachers, which held 1,600 fans.

The grass caught fire, and the blaze started to creep under the pavilion. The crowd began to panic and sought to escape from the bleachers onto the field, but the barbed wire fence was a formidable obstruction. Cub players Walt Wilmot, Jimmy Ryan, and George Decker tried to force the barbed wire loose from its staples with their bats.

An eyewitness reported: "The crowd was between the growing fire and the . . . barbed fence. Men began to clamber up these wires like rats in a cage. . . . The first got through easily. Others tried to slip between the wires and hung there, entangled fast in the barbs."

The efforts of the Cub players and the pressure of the crowd finally tore the fence down. But many fans suffered cuts and bruises in the frenzied stampede. There were no fatalities.

Repairs of damage to the stands cost the Cubs $20,000, but they were fortunate their loss was limited because 1894 was a year of fires in NL, touching off allegations of arson by anti-Sunday-game activists. Major fires destroyed ballparks in

Philadelphia and Boston, and severely damaged the park in Baltimore.

The West Side Grounds' earliest seasons were undistinguished as Anson's Colts struggled, the glory years of the '80s fading into a succession of disappointing finishes during the '90s. The player-manager's team finished in eighth place in the now 12-team NL in '94, rose to fourth in '95, dropped to fifth in '96, and sank to ninth in '97, Anson's final season both as manager and player.

Yet the new ballpark provided a few memorable occasions for the patrons, who were swarming out in record numbers as baseball fever rose to a new high toward the end of the 19th century.

Among the highlights was Cap Anson Day, the home opener against St. Louis on May 4, 1897. Anson had announced that it would be his last season as a player, and the fans took the occasion to pay tribute to the man who had managed the team since 1879 and was in his 22nd season as a player.

A near-capacity crowd of 14,960 turned out on a warm, sunny day. Among those in attendance were such celebrities of the day as comedian Eddie Foy and actor Maurice Barrymore with his daughter Ethel, who was to gain fame as a stage and movie actress.

Before the game, the players of both teams stood at attention along the baselines as a band played John Philip Sousa's "El Capitan" march in Anson's honor. Anson was presented with a silver service and many testimonials. In a brief speech, he thanked the fans, calling the occasion "the proudest moment of my life."

Before the season ended, he had collected the 3,000th hit of his career, becoming the first major league player to do so, and officially finished with 3,081. (Note: One current record book lists him with a final total of 3,081, another with 3,041, and a third with 2,995, reflecting a modern tendency to revise figures. His final batting average also varies, from .329 to .333.)

Anson's managerial tenure also was drawing to a close. His relations with James Hart, now the majority owner of the team, were tense from the beginning because Anson had been disappointed in his own efforts to buy the club from Albert G. Spalding in 1892. After the Colts sank to ninth place in 1897, Hart fired him on February 1, 1898, and a new period in the team's history and that of West Side Grounds was under way.

The team also acquired a new nickname, the Orphans, bestowed by sports reporters because the players were bereft of Anson's guidance. This monicker lasted only a couple of seasons until, according to legend, a *Chicago Daily News* sportswriter coined the nickname Cubs in reference to the youth of the new players, and this one stuck. In 1907 it was officially adopted as the nickname of the team.

At the turn of the century, baseball was increasing its hold on the public, with attendance growing, but it was hardly the big business it since has become. Crowds at West Side Grounds ranged from 2,000 to 4,000, sometimes doubling on Sundays. One day a week was set aside as Ladies Day, an innovation of the 1870s, to help increase interest among women.

In West Side Grounds' first season, 1894, the Colts drew 239,000 fans. The next year they attracted 382,300, and in 1898 they reached a 19th-century peak of 424,352. But the advent of the Chicago White Stockings (later White Sox) of the new American League (AL) as a major league in 1901 split the fan base, and the Cubs attendance sank to 205,728 before beginning to surge again with the success of the team from 1906 to 1910.

In 1909, oddly enough the only year the Cubs failed to win the NL pennant from 1906 through 1910, West Side Grounds entertained the peak attendance of its 23-year history with a turnout of 633,480 for 76 home games.

There were few indications immediately after Anson's departure that the West Side Grounds was about to become the home of one of the great dynasties of baseball history. The new manager, Tom Burns, had a tenure distinguished perhaps only by his decision to put a rookie catcher, Frank Chance, not yet 21 years old, behind the plate on April 29, 1898. Chance was to become the "Peerless Leader" of the most successful Cub teams, both as manager and first baseman.

Burns lasted one year and Tom Loftus, his successor, two years, and the team was staggered by player defections to the AL in 1900 and 1901. In 1902, Hart appointed Frank Selee, who had led Boston to five NL pennants in 12 seasons from 1890 to 1901. Selee laid the base for the future Cub triumphs by bringing in such players as shortstop Joe Tinker, second baseman Johnny Evers, and pitcher Ed Reulbach, and by moving Chance to first base.

The Cubs perked up, and attendance began to recover from the shock of the arrival of the White Sox on the South Side. Selee's teams finished fifth in 1902, third in 1903, second in 1904, and fourth in 1905 as they moved to the verge of success.

But neither Selee nor owner Hart was destined to enjoy the fruits of his labors. Hart, in 1905, after operating the team 15 years, sold out his interest to Cincinnati businessman Charles W. Murphy, who was bankrolled by Charles Taft, a brother of future President William Howard Taft. Selee was stricken by tuberculosis during the 1905 season and resigned on August 1, with Chance taking over as manager.

The glory days of West Side Grounds had arrived, with the Cubs winning a record 116 games in 1906 (while losing only 36) as they rolled to a pennant. They won 107 games and another pennant in 1907, repeated in 1908 with 99 victories, and fell to second despite winning 104 games in 1909. But in 1910 the same number of wins gave them their fourth flag in five seasons. Over the five seasons they averaged 106 wins.

There were some setbacks, however, the most annoying being an upset in the 1906 World Series by the White Sox, who were not thought to have a chance against the powerhouse Cubs.

West Side Grounds became the site of the first modern World Series game played in Chicago on October 9, 1906. Baseball's championship event was born in 1903 as the AL and NL had settled differences and, after an interruption in 1904, resumed in 1905. The turnout for the game was surprisingly light considering the burgeoning rivalry between the Cubs and White Sox as only 12,693 showed up. Cold weather and expectations of an easy conquest by the Cubs might have been to blame. The White Sox won the opener 2–1 behind the pitching of Nick Altrock.

A *Chicago Daily News* headline of the day stated in part: "Partisan Feeling Runs High in Vast Throng of Exultant Fans, Whose Heated Arguments Counter Icy Blasts at West Side Park."

A paragraph of the story below the headline painted a word picture of the scene on the field after the game: "The demonstration by White Sox rooters at the close of the game was wildly exciting. The players of the South Side team were carried around on shoulders. Altrock especially had great difficulty in escaping the jubilant throng of fans."

Attendance improved as fan interest and the weather

warmed up, and Game 5 brought out the largest turnout of the Series, 23,257 at West Side Grounds, creating an overflow crowd and necessitating a two-base rule on balls batted among the spectators in the outfield. But the White Sox captured the Series four games to two to put a damper on a great year for the Cubs.

The next two seasons, however, the Cubs were able to hoist the World Series Championship flag over West Side Grounds, defeating the Detroit Tigers four games out of five in both 1907 and 1908. It was a ceremony they were unable to repeat during their remaining seven years in the old ballpark or the next 81 at Wrigley Field.

After the near miss with 104 wins in 1909, the Cubs returned to the World Series in 1910 against the Philadelphia Athletics, but fell in five games. The most notable aspect of this Series for the Cubs was that the final World Series game in West Side Grounds (October 23) drew a record crowd of 27,374.

The park was beginning to show the wear and tear of the years despite haphazard improvements, and so were the Cubs, though Chance kept them in second place in 1911 and 1912, to round out seven consecutive years in which they never finished as low as third. But Chance was deposed as manager in 1913 in favor of Johnny Evers after a contract dispute with Charles Murphy.

In the meantime, wealthy Chicago businessman Charles Weeghman, who had purchased a minor league team in the "outlaw" Federal League in 1912, yearned for a major league team in Chicago. Accordingly, the Federal League branded itself a major league in 1913, and construction began in 1914 on a new ballpark for Weeghman's Chicago Whales at Clark and Addison streets. The new park on the North Side of Chicago eventually was to become known as Wrigley Field, the legendary home of the Cubs.

Wrigley Field

"Lucky Charlie" Weeghman had built a chain of lunchrooms in Chicago into an $8 million fortune before venturing into baseball by purchasing a franchise in the minor Federal League for $25,000 in 1912. The Chifeds, as Weeghman's team was awkwardly named, played their home games at De Paul University on the North Side, the first time a professional team had ventured into that area of Chicago. In the beginning Chicago had grown to the south, then to the west, and the earlier major league parks were located in those areas. Expansion to the north came last. Weeghman sought to capitalize on the boom on the North Side when the Federal League decided to challenge the established NL and AL by declaring itself a major league for 1914.

The site he chose for his new ballpark previously had been occupied by the Chicago Lutheran Theological Seminary, so even then it was "hallowed ground," though not yet in a baseball sense. One reason for the choice of the location was that fans could easily reach the park on the Milwaukee Road train and the elevated train from the Loop.

Putting a ballpark on the underdeveloped North Side was a novel idea, as reflected in an opening day column by Ring Lardner of the Chicago Tribune. Lardner provided tips to the fans on how to get to the new park and commented, "Many of our citizens will today visit the North Side for the first time. . . . The North Side lacks the odor[s] [from the stockyards] that have made the South Side so popular."

Architect Zachary Taylor Davis, who had designed Comiskey Park a few years earlier for the White Sox, was commissioned to plan what at first was to be named North Side Ball Park. It was to be built at a cost of $250,000 and was to seat 14,000. Ground was broken on March 4, 1914, with completion planned for the Chicago Whales' home opener just seven weeks later.

To expedite construction, at one time 490 men worked on the project: 350 on the structure itself and 140 from the George Witthold Florist Company, who hauled in more than 4,000 cubic yards of soil and laid down four acres of bluegrass to create the outfield and the infield.

By April 4 the right-field bleachers had been completed, and Weeghman took newspaper reporters on an inspection tour of the new park. Its dimensions were 345 feet to left field, 440 feet to center field, and 356 feet down the right-field line, but these were to vary considerably almost year by year for more than a decade.

The ballpark was ready on schedule for opening day, April 23, 1914, with the Whales playing host to Kansas City. In pregame ceremonies, Weeghman called his project a "great park" and asked Chicago fans to "Be a Fed Fan." A group from the Ladies' Auxiliary of the Grand Army of the Republic raised the flag, a politician threw out the first ball, and manager-shortstop Joe Tinker (the ex-Cub) was presented with dozens of roses shaped into a huge horseshoe. Capping off the day of celebration, the Whales defeated Kansas City, 9–1.

The future Wrigley Field was much different in appearance from what it would be 80 years later. It was a single-decked structure, with two grades of seating, a press box on the roof behind home plate, a screen to protect fans behind the batter, and partial brick walls, complemented by screens and plywood, surrounding the outfield.

The location and configuration of the stands, the outfield dimensions, the material of the fences and walls, the location of the scoreboard, and even the level of the playing field have changed frequently in the various projects that have kept the park viable for use into the 1990s.

Among the constants, however, are the influence of wind and the site's altitude on the outcome of games. From the beginning, on a warm day, with the wind blowing from the southwest toward Lake Michigan, baseballs flew out of the place, and it was a pitcher's nightmare. In contrast, on a cool day, with the wind blowing in off the lake from the northeast, the park is a paradise for pitchers, with fly balls tending to die long before reaching the fences. The 600-foot elevation above sea level and the warmer air of the mostly day games (before 1988 there were no night games) also contribute to the frustration of pitchers on days when the wind is blowing out.

The park's home run quirk became apparent quickly. The left-field fence started out at 345 feet, but after a month, in May 1914, was reduced to 310 feet. After nine home runs were hit in three games (in a dead-ball era), Weeghman decided in June that the new distance was too short for comfort. He had workmen remove the front porch of a house so the

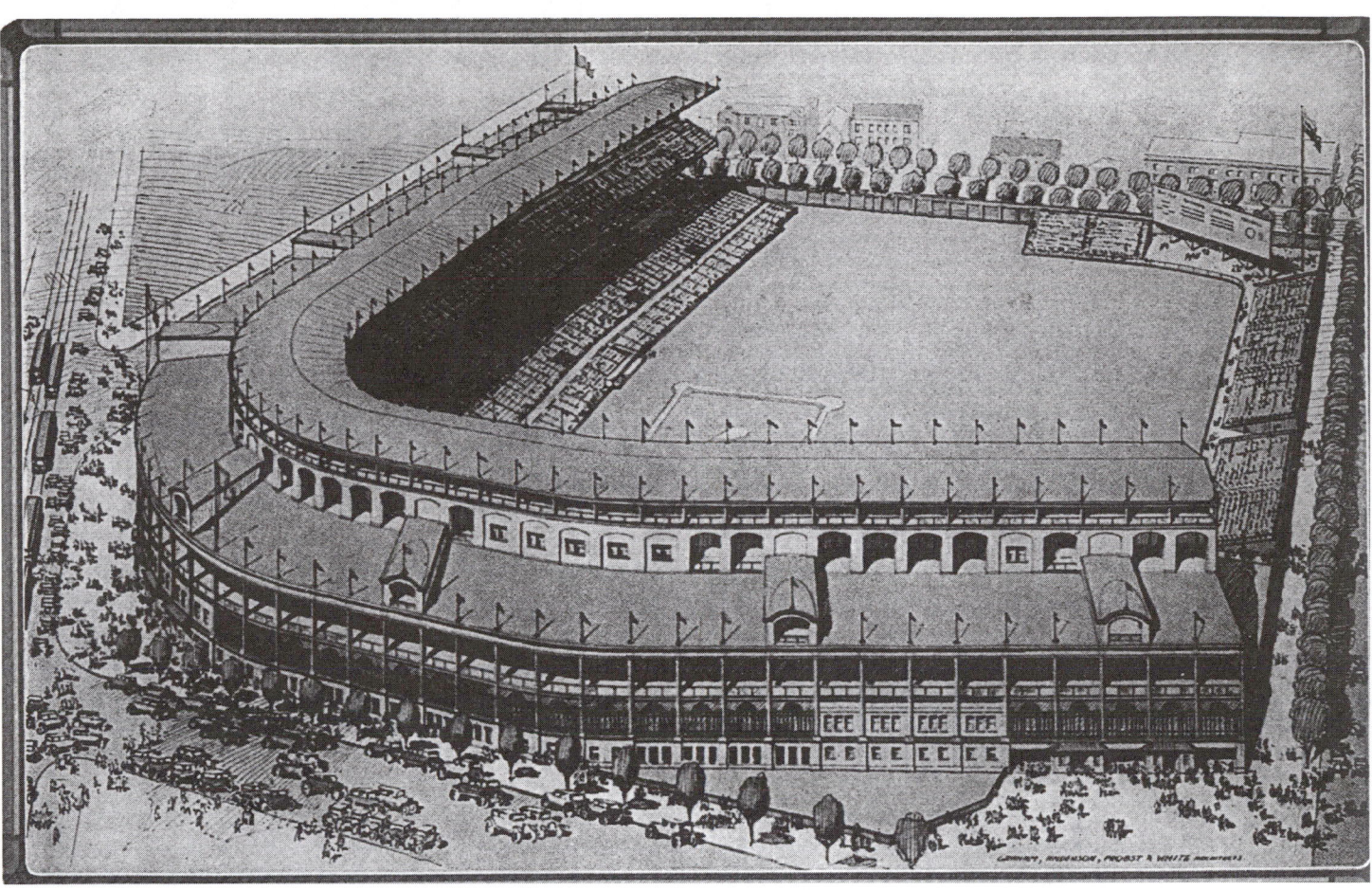

Wrigley Field, 1932

left field wall could again be moved out, this time to 327 feet. Nevertheless, the ballpark continued to be a home run hitter's dream. The Whales led the Federal League in home runs in both 1914 and 1915. The power output helped them to the pennant in 1915.

As an owner, Weeghman was the Bill Veeck or Charlie Finley of his day, catering to the fans' needs and whims. He was the first owner to let fans keep balls hit into the stands. He installed the first permanent concession stand in any park after patrons complained that strolling vendors spoiled their view of action on the field.

Outwardly, it seemed as if the Whales were a commercial and artistic success in their first season. They just missed winning the Federal League pennant, and on the final Sunday of the season drew a crowd of 34,361 to Weeghman Park (the name had changed during the season from North Side Ball Park) while the Cubs attracted fewer than 2,000 to West Side Grounds and the White Sox fewer than 3,500 to Comiskey Park.

Weeghman expanded capacity to 18,000 for 1915, and the ballpark again was renamed, this time Whales Park. But the efforts of the Federal League to gain recognition of major league status from the AL and NL were costly and proved a failure in the courts. As part of a settlement, the Federal League was dissolved and two of its owners, Weeghman one of them, were permitted to buy franchises in the older leagues.

Weeghman formed a 10-man syndicate to buy the Cubs for $500,000 on January 20, 1916, from principal owner Charles Taft. (Charles Murphy had faded out of the picture in 1914, when he was replaced as team president by Charles H. Thomas.) Among the investors was William Wrigley, Jr., a Chicagoan who had made a fortune in chewing gum. Wrigley bought two shares at $50,000 each. Weeghman took over as club president.

On April 20, 1916, the Cubs played their first game in what now was called Cubs Park, defeating Cincinnati 7–6 in 11 innings. Showman Weeghman pulled out all the stops, inaugurating the new era with an automobile parade of city officials, music on the field and in the stands, speeches at home plate, and a fireworks display. The crowning touch was a Cub mascot—a baby bear donated by J. Ogden Armour, one of the team owners. Joa the Cubbie Bear for a time was housed in a cage outside the park on Addison Street.

Attendance at Cubs Park in 1916 was double what it had been at West Side Grounds in 1915, rising from 217,058 to 454,609 despite a fifth-place finish. But in 1917, with the entry of the United States into World War I, attendance sank, not to rise until after the end of the war in 1918. The Cubs finished fifth again in 1917, but played one of the most memorable games in baseball history on May 2 before 3,500 fans. It was baseball's only double, nine-inning, no-hit, no-run game. Jim "Hippo" Vaughn of the Cubs and Cincinnati's Fred Toney held the batters hitless until the Reds broke through in the 10th inning and won 1–0 on two hits.

The Cubs won the pennant in 1918 to give Weeghman a brief taste of glory, but Cubs Park was not to see its first World Series game until 11 years later. The 1918 World Series between the Cubs and Boston Red Sox was transferred to Comiskey Park to take advantage of its much greater capacity of 28,800.

Shortly after the World Series, Weeghman's luck ran out. A financial crisis forced him to sell his controlling interest in the Cubs to Wrigley, who also purchased the shares of other stockholders. After a brief period in which Fred Mitchell, who had managed the Cubs to the pennant in 1918, held office as president of the team, Wrigley named William L. Veeck, a newspaperman, to the job.

In the next few years, Cubs Park was completely reshaped. When Wrigley took control, the park had a single deck of concrete stands from right to left behind the plate and a wooden bleacher in right field. Home plate was where the pitchers mound is located in the 1990s. The postwar boom in baseball interest demanded enlargement and improvement of the park.

Wrigley commissioned the original architect, Zachary Davis, to plan the renovation in the fall of 1922, with a budget of about $300,000, to be completed for the 1923 season. The grandstand was cut into three parts. The right- and left field wings were separated from the section behind home plate, which was moved back about 60 feet into the Clark and Addison streets corner of the field. The right-field wing was retained in its original position. The left-field wing was moved northward toward Waveland Avenue. The playing field was lowered about three feet, and new rows of box seats were installed in front of the existing rows. Additionally, temporary bleachers were installed in left field to benefit slugging outfielder Lawrence "Hack" Miller, a right-handed batter. Miller's home run total rose from 12 in 1922 to 20 in 1923, but he next year he tailed off. The improvements increased the capacity of the park to 20,000 and resulted in new outfield dimensions of 325 feet to left field, 447 feet to center field, and 299 feet to right field.

While the Cubs continued to languish on the playing field for most of the 1920s, the highlight at Wrigley Field probably being a wild 26–23 victory over the Philadelphia Phillies on August 25, 1922, attendance began to rise and Wrigley decided to enlarge and improve the park once more. On November 16, 1926, he announced plans to double-deck the park, which had been renamed Wrigley Field earlier in that season.

The grandstand was double-decked from the right-field corner to the left, and its capacity nearly doubled to 38,396, though the left-field bleachers were removed, replaced by a planting of trees. The scoreboard in the left-field corner was improved. The renovation, which cost $300,000, was complete by the beginning of the 1928 season, though much of the added seating capacity was available during 1927. During the 1930s, Bobby Dorr, the head groundskeeper, lived in a six-room apartment at the ballpark, adjacent to the left-field corner gate.

The expansion of the ballpark coincided with a revival in the Cubs' fortunes on the field. After winning the pennant in 1918 they fell on hard times, then began to assemble a strong cast of players under manager Joe McCarthy, who took over in 1926. Among the new stars were catcher Gabby Hartnett, center fielder Hack Wilson, first baseman Charlie Grimm, second baseman Rogers Hornsby, and pitcher Charlie Root.

Fan interest began to soar. In 1927 the Cubs became the first Chicago team to surpass a million in attendance, drawing 1,163,347. For five consecutive seasons they surpassed a million, reaching a peak of 1,485,166 in 1929, when they won the pennant for the first time since 1918. The attendance record stood for 40 years, until 1969.

The home opener in 1928 drew a crowd estimated at 46,000, and 48,000 reportedly turned out for the second game. The custom of accommodating overflow crowds by permitting the fans to stand on the playing field had not yet been scrapped, and an estimated 10,000 watched each game from behind ropes in the outfield.

In 1929, 1932, and 1935 (all pennant-winning years) extra bleachers were built over the streets in left field and right on Waveland and Sheffield for World Series games. The temporary seats made it possible for 50,740 to attend the first World Series game played at Wrigley Field, on October 8, 1929. The crowd was treated to one of the most celebrated Series games as manager Connie Mack of the Philadelphia Athletics surpassed all expectations by starting a seldom-used veteran pitcher, Howard Ehmke, who struck out 13 for a Series record and held the Cubs to eight hits in a 3–1 victory. The A's won the Series in five games.

Although the Cubs finished second in 1930, attendance held firm, almost matching the 1929 total with 1,467,881 as Wilson boosted interest by setting a still-standing NL record for home runs with 56 and drove in a major-league-record 190 runs. And the biggest crowd in Wrigley Field's history turned out on June 27, 1930, as 51,556 showed up on Ladies' Day. (But since only 19,748 were paid admissions, the regular season attendance record is 46,965, for a game against Pittsburgh on May 31, 1948.)

The 1929 pennant touched off one of the Cubs' brightest periods. They won again in 1932, 1935, and 1938, then were dormant until 1945, when they rounded out the era with a final flag during the waning days of World War II before sliding into a half century of frustration. There was anguish even in the pennant-winning years because the Cubs lost all five of the World Series they played in from 1929 through 1945.

The 1932 World Series, however, provided another memorable, though disputed, highlight of history at Wrigley Field—Babe Ruth's celebrated "called shot" home run for the New York Yankees before a crowd of 49,986. In the third game (October 1) Ruth, badgered by Cub players in the dugout, either gestured at them or pointed to the center field bleachers and then hit a home run into right-center off pitcher Charlie Root.

The early 1930s marked the passing of the "Ruthian era" of baseball, began the dark days of the Great Depression, and brought new men to the top for the Cubs when William Wrigley, Jr., died in 1932 and William Veeck the year after. Philip K. Wrigley became the new majority owner of the team and steered it for almost half a century, with a succession of team presidents and general managers, stating with Boots Weber, the successor to William Veeck.

Baseball attendance collapsed all around the United States. Even in the pennant year of 1935 the Cubs drew on 690,576, less than half the totals of 1929 and 1930. Neither the Cubs' success on the field nor a succession of outstanding new players, among them third baseman Stan Hack, second baseman Billy Herman, first baseman Phil Cavarretta, and pitchers Bill Lee and Lon Warneke could offset economic hardship for a great number of Chicagoans. But the World Series against the Detroit Tigers, another losing effort for the Cubs, drew close to 50,000 for each of the three games at Wrigley Field.

Nevertheless, the development of Wrigley Field toward its present configuration continued, with major changes coming in 1937. Direction of the renovation was largely entrusted to young Bill Veeck, to gain fame later as baseball's "greatest showman," who after his father's death had been hired as an office boy at $18 a week by P. K. Wrigley.

One of the earliest sports bars, in the early 1930s, honored Hack Wilson's slugging prowess. (George Brace photo)

Wrigley spent lavishly on improvements because he was convinced that it was beneficial to emphasize the ambiance of the ballpark, to make it an attractive place for fans to bring their families regardless of the Cubs' won-lost record, which for most teams largely determined attendance levels. His solution was to advertise "Beautiful Wrigley Field," a theme that has continued into the 1990s. Even in the 1930s the announcers of Cub games on radio were instructed to use the phrase "Beautiful Wrigley Field" as often as possible.

Wrigley stationed ushers to guide fans (eventually the blue-uniformed Andy Frain corps) to their sections. He banned sidewalk vendors, panhandlers, and newspaper boys from the vicinity of the ballpark. Ticket vendors were ordered to be friendly and courteous. Concession stands were well-lighted and easily accessible. The park was kept clean and freshly painted.

And Veeck, only 23, who had quickly become Weber's assistant and protégé in running the team, was assigned to oversee a major redevelopment of Wrigley Field, which was begun after the 1937 season. It was no facelift, but almost a reconstruction. New outfield stands, enlarged bleachers, were built, changing the dimensions to the current 355 to left, 400 to center, and 353 to right. Six gates were built into the walls. The boxes and grandstand seats in the lower left-field stands were rebuilt, raised, and turned at a 30-degree angle so that the spectators faced home plate rather than center field, and the same was done in the lower right-field stands. The press box was renovated.

The capacity of the park dropped by a few hundred and was reduced even more in 1941 to 38,396 after batters complained of the distracting background of white shirts directly to center in the bleachers. The empty seats were painted seal brown (to be repainted green later), and the section was closed to fans until 1948, closed again in 1952, and opened since for major league baseball only for the All-Star Game of 1962. Ironically, on the second day after the area was closed off, the Cubs drew an overflow crowd, and there was much grumbling from fans who had to stand while looking at the empty seats.

In the concourse, the concession stands were refurbished and lighted with the new, brighter fluorescent lights. Wrigley erected a memorial to his father, the William Wrigley, Jr., Water Fountain, in the lobby under the first base stands, which was dedicated in 1938 by Joe Tinker and Johnny Evers, who shook hands to end the feud that went back to the early 1900s.

Among Veeck's pet projects were a new, improved scoreboard (which was moved from the left-field corner to the top of the center-field bleachers), the legendary ivy on the brick walls, and potted plants on the bleacher stair steps with eight huge Chinese elm trees complementing them. Additionally, he placed lights on top of the flagpole that allowed homebound passengers on the nearby el to know whether the Cubs had won or lost that day. The flagpole was on top of the new scoreboard, and it had a crossbar with a red light mounted on one side and a green light on the other. Green indicated a Cub victory, red a defeat.

The signal lights were eventually replaced along the left-field line by signal flags with a W or L and pennants of each NL team strung on yardarms in order of the standings on the morning of each game. The potted plants and elm trees, though obtained full-blown at enormous cost, quickly were destroyed by the wind off Lake Michigan. However, the scoreboard and the ivy have remained and flourished as Bill Veeck's legacy.

When the trees and plants failed shortly after being planted in 1937, Veeck decided to immediately put up the ivy, which he had intended to plant after the season, before the final home stand of the season. He and groundskeeper Dorr strung light bulbs all along the fence to enable them to work all night. They planted 350 Japanese bittersweet plants and 200 pots of Boston ivy. By morning the bleacher wall was entirely covered with bittersweet. In time, the ivy took over, and it has been a celebrated ornament of Wrigley Field ever since. In 1979 the Cubs even sold 2,500 pots of ivy cuttings for $1.50 apiece to their fans.

Pride of place among Veeck's projects was the great scoreboard, 27 feet high and 75 feet wide, with its top 85 feet above the field at installation. The crowning touch, a 10-foot-diameter clock, was added in 1941. The scoreboard design was based on a new concept. Instead of having lights that could be switched on and off, like other scoreboards, this one featured brightly painted eyelids that were pulled up and down magnetically. The inventor's concept appealed to Veeck, who ordered its construction. The day before the scoreboard was to be delivered, it was discovered that the inventor had lost heart during the task of assembling it and had disappeared. Veeck summoned a staff of electricians, as well as the ground crew from Wrigley Field, to the factory where the unfinished scoreboard was housed.

Veeck even drilled the frames himself as the crew worked through the night to put the scoreboard together, carting it to the park unit by unit. By game time, the scoreboard was in place atop the center-field bleachers and worked perfectly, as it has continued to do with modifications until now.

It may be an inviting target, but no batted ball has ever hit the scoreboard, only two players coming close. A drive by the Cubs' Bill Nicholson sailed just to the right of it in the early years, and in the 1960s Roberto Clemente of Pittsburgh hit a home run just to the left. Golfer Sam Snead hit the only ball ever to reach the scoreboard. It was a golf ball, teed off from the plate.

In 1938, manager-catcher Hartnett provided the ballpark with another great moment to rank with Ruth's "called shot" home run six years earlier. Hartnett hit the "Homer in the Gloamin'" on September 28, 1938, against the Pittsburgh Pirates that virtually clinched the pennant for the Cubs. The World Series against the Yankees was no bargain, the Cubs going down in four games. With outfield standees a thing of the past and the capacity of the park reduced, attendance for the World Series fell by about 6,000 to a maximum of 43,642 for the first game at Wrigley Field.

By this time almost all major league parks had installed lights for night games, and Veeck urged that Wrigley Field follow suit. But it continued to be without them, as would be the case for another 50 years, because of the veto of the owner. P. K. Wrigley insisted his opposition was dictated not so much by a distaste for night baseball as by respect for his neighbors. He explained, "In deference to people living around our ballpark, we will install lights—only if the standards can be disguised as trees."

Weber retired as team president in 1940, to be replaced by sportswriter Jimmy Gallagher, and Veeck also departed to launch his long career as a baseball owner and showman with the minor league Milwaukee Brewers. With an ever-changing cast of managers and players, including a few standouts, such as slugging outfielder Bill Nicholson, outfielder Andy Pafko, and star pitcher Claude Passeau, the Cubs performed indifferently in 1939 and into the mid-1940s, attendance slipping to just over 500,000 during the early years of World War II, which the United States had entered after the Japanese attack on Pearl Harbor on December 7, 1941.

Among the minor effects of the war was the further postponement of lights for Wrigley Field. Apparently weakening, Wrigley had ordered the installation of lights, and the necessary equipment had been delivered. He decided to contribute it to the war effort on December 8, 1941. Nevertheless, the first night game at Wrigley Field was played before 7,000 under temporary lights in July 1943. It was the All-Star game of the American Girls Professional Baseball League (a league largely financed by Wrigley).

Though Cubs fans didn't have lights, they did have music in 1941. Wrigley ordered Gallagher to install a pipe organ in the ballpark, and on April 26, 1941, the fans were startled by the first notes when Roy Nelson at the console played a program of "classical and soulful" compositions before the game. It was the first organ permanently installed in a major league park, and the innovation drew compliments from the press.

"We feel that Mr. Gallagher has something here," *The Sporting News* rhapsodized. "What a joy! A cushioned seat in a beautiful ballpark, delicious hamburgers with onions, a can of beer, victory, and the restful, dulcet tones of a pipe organ. Baseball, indeed, has moved upward and onward since Abner Doubleday was a resident of Cooperstown."

In 1945 the Cubs broke through for their 16th and final (up to now) NL pennant, a wartime cast of overage and militarily unfit players led by Grimm, manager for the second time (he was to have a brief third term in 1960), prevailing over similarly decimated rivals. With the war ending on September 2, 1945, and the resultant prosperity, attendance soared to 1,036,386 and was to stay over a million for the next five years. The World Series was the same old story, the Cubs losing to the Tigers in seven games, with attendance in Chicago peaking at 43,346 for Game 5. The ivy on the walls, as it was to do so often, provided one of the odder plays of Series history, Cub left fielder Pafko losing Roy Cullenbine's hit in the vegetation. It was ruled a single.

During the next two decades the Cubs were generally futile. Yet they drew large crowds to Wrigley Field until 1953 when total annual attendance dipped under a million and stayed below until 1968. Many, including *The Sporting News,* attributed their drawing power to the ballpark itself. In a typical comment, *The Sporting News* provided its answer to the puzzle of why the generally mediocre and worse Cubs often played before large crowds, such as the 40,222 who turned out on a June day in 1944.

"There is overwhelming evidence that Mr. Wrigley's foresight in demanding neatness, comfort and beauty as an essential (and profitable) adjunct of baseball entertainment has proved a grand success," *The Sporting News* editorialized. ". . . Perhaps there have been those who have scoffed at Mr. Wrigley's vine-covered ivy outfield wall, his terraced bleachers with the Chinese elms. Perhaps some have wondered that the largest prewar buyer of advertising signboards has no signboards in his ballpark.

"Perhaps others have thought him foolish for throwing out hundreds of chairs to install wider and more comfortable seats. Mr. Wrigley is not in the paint business, but he uses hundreds of gallons for his ballparks. Help is scarce [during the war], but the Cub prexy manages to find enough employees to maintain the Wrigley Field rest rooms at a sanitary peak."

Despite encomiums like this, even "Beautiful Wrigley Field" couldn't maintain high attendance levels as the Cubs won more games than they lost in only one season (1963) from 1947 through 1967. With the team losing money, Wrigley tightened the purse strings, and by 1959 the ballpark was badly in need of a coat of paint, and the neighborhood was deteriorating.

A parade of general managers, managers, and players failed to lift the team's fortunes. Among the more notable players of late 1940s and early '50s were sluggers Hank Sauer and Ralph Kiner and pitchers Bob Rush and Moe Drabowsky. And in 1953 the Cubs added their first Afro-American players, second baseman Gene Baker and shortstop Ernie Banks, the latter to become the most popular of all Cubs during the next two decades. By the end of the decade, two other stars had emerged, third baseman Ron Santo and left fielder Billy Williams. After the 1956 season, Gallagher was replaced as Wrigley's lieutenant by

John Holland, who was to direct the team's renascence, though it took more than a decade to achieve.

One of the weirdest incidents in baseball history contributed to the Wrigley Field legend on June 30, 1959, as the Cubs played the St. Louis Cardinals. Two baseballs were in play simultaneously because of mixups and confusion among the umpires and players.

As Wrigley rejected numerous offers to buy the team and continued to resist night baseball, he embarked on novel experiments to put a winning team into Wrigley Field. One of them was to use a staff of eight coaches to direct the team on the field on a revolving basis rather than a single manager. The "College of Coaches" eventually expanded to 12 men, but was quietly abandoned after two seasons. Another innovation was to name an athletic director after the 1962 season, the job going to Colonel Robert V. Whitlow. He had been the first athletic director at the U.S. Air Force Academy. He was put in charge of the whole organization but resigned after two years, stating that he "wasn't earning" his salary.

Whitlow's only noticeable move was to install a batter's background wire fence (8 feet high and 64 feet wide) atop the center-field wall on June 18, 1963. The Whitlow Fence was intended to provide batters with a good hitting background. Its effect was to prevent 10 home runs, four for the Cubs and six for visitors, before it departed along with Whitlow by the start of the 1965 season. Home run hitters, of course, didn't need much encouragement in Wrigley Field. Starting with 1950, the Cubs hit 100 or more home runs for 25 consecutive seasons.

One bright spot in two dismal decades was provided by the tenant Chicago Bears, who won the National Football League championship game at Wrigley Field on December 29, 1963, defeating the New York Giants. The ballpark was the Bears' home and the site of several championship games from 1921 through 1970 when they moved permanently to Soldier Field. The gridiron was shoehorned into the available space, and temporary bleachers were placed on the left-field grass in front of the brick wall. The north end zone ended 18 feet in front of those bleachers. The southeast corner of the south end zone was suspended in air over the top step of the first base dugout.

In 1965, Wrigley startled the baseball world by hiring controversial manager Leo Durocher at the urging of Holland. Along with Banks, Williams, and Santo, such outstanding players as shortstop Don Kessinger, second baseman Glenn Beckert, catcher Randy Hundley, and pitchers Ferguson Jenkins, Bill Hands, and Ken Holtzman enabled Durocher to revive the Cubs, though the end result was more frustration, reaching its peak in 1969. The Cubs seemed on their way to a NL East title in early September but were overtaken by the "Miracle Mets" of New York in the stretch.

Renewed fan interest, which included the formation of the Bleacher Bums in 1966, impelled Wrigley to order another major renovation of Wrigley Field at a cost of almost $3 million, the work getting under way in 1967 and being completed in 1971. A green Astroturf cover was placed on the empty seats in the center-field bleachers to improve the batters' background. It made its debut on May 18, 1967. The upper deck was completely rebuilt during 1968–71; plastic, self-rising, wider contour seats replaced folding chairs in the lower-deck reserved seating area; and the brickwork in the entire park was renovated. The renovations cut the capacity of the ballpark to 37,741. Nevertheless, attendance started to soar with Durocher's competitive teams, reaching a peak of 1,674,993 in 1969, a record that was not to be surpassed for 15 years.

As the 1967–72 Cubs, sometimes labeled "the best team never to win a pennant," kept coming close to winning without going across the top, they continued to provide their fans with memorable moments. One of the most enduring was Banks' 500th career home run on May 12, 1970 before 5,264 at Wrigley Field. His final home run, to bring his total to 512, came in the same park on August 24, 1971.

After the resignation of Durocher in midseason 1972, the death of Holland, and the fading of the Banks-Santo-Williams-Jenkins teams, the Cubs stagnated again, manager following manager in weary succession. The crowds kept coming, though, attracted by "Beautiful Wrigley Field" as much as by the feats of hard-hitting third baseman Bill Madlock, slugging left fielder Dave Kingman, and the pitching of Rick Reuschel and relief ace Bruce Sutter. Kingman, then with the New York Mets, was credited with having hit the longest home run in Wrigley Field history on April 14, 1976. The drive carried 550 feet, over Waveland Avenue and against a house three doors down on the east side of Kenmore Avenue. Kingman joined the Cubs in 1978 and hit 48 home runs in 1979, surpassing Banks' high of 47 in 1958.

Despite the stagnation in the standings, attendance held up remarkably well, reaching 1,439,484 in 1977, the highest figure since 1971. Kingman's debut as a Cub on April 14, 1978, spurred interest even further, Wrigley Field being host to a record opening day crowd of 45,777.

Among the minor modifications to the ballpark during this period were the attachment of a three-foot-wide wire "basket" to the top of the outfield walls—the brainchild of general manager Bob Kennedy. The purpose of the basket was to prevent objects thrown by fans in the bleachers from reaching the field and endangering the outfielders. In the late '40s and early '50s, fans had shown their affection for Cub left fielder Hank Sauer by throwing packets of chewing tobacco at him. Now, however, unruly fans threw dangerous objects such as flashlight batteries at visiting players. The basket also had the effect of cutting the home run distance by three feet. An innovation of 1978 was a new indicator to inform night travelers of how the Cubs had fared that day. A blue light atop the scoreboard signaled victory, and a white one reported defeat.

More significantly, Wrigley Field had embarked on a new era of its history. Philip K. Wrigley died in 1977 and four years later his family's association with the Cubs, which had begun in 1916, came to an end. On June 16, 1981, William Wrigley, Philip's son, sold the Cubs to the Tribune Company, parent firm of the *Chicago Tribune* and numerous other media operations. The Tribune Company paid $20.5 million for Wrigley's 81 percent holdings and all remaining 1,900 shares. Wrigley Field was purchased in a later transaction. The Tribune Company's radio and television outlets in Chicago, WGN and WGN-TV, long had aired the Cubs' games.

William Wrigley explained that estate tax problems resulting from the death of his parents and attempts to find solutions to the Cubs' long-term financial problems had necessitated the sale. The Cubs, the only publicly owned major league franchise, with 600 stockholders, lost $1.7 million in 1980.

Speculation began immediately that the Tribune Company would quickly install lights in Wrigley Field. In September 1981, however, the team announced it had no plans for lights. Despite the denial, night games in the major leagues' last home of all day games were only seven years away.

The Tribune Company moved quickly to make the most of its investment, though the results on the field weren't immediately apparent, the Cubs continuing to stagnate until 1984. Andrew J. McKenna, a well-known Chicago business executive, was placed in charge of the team, and on October 15, 1981, he named Dallas Green as general manager. Green had managed the Philadelphia Phillies to a World Series victory in 1980 and was known for his hard-driving methods. He promised to "Build a New Tradition" at Wrigley Field and appointed Lee Elia, a former Cubs utility player, as manager.

While McKenna supervised the enlargement and refurbishment of the Cubs' offices at Wrigley Field, Green began the arduous task of rebuilding a team that had finished last in the NL East under manager Joey Amalfitano in the strike-curtailed season of 1981. His most significant deal was the acquisition in trade on January 27, 1982, of veteran shortstop Larry Bowa and minor league shortstop Ryne Sandberg from the Phillies in exchange for shortstop Ivan DeJesus. Bowa was a standout fielder, a key ingredient in the mix that produced an NL East championship in 1984, but Sandberg, who played third base as a rookie in 1982, was to move to second base and become one of the greatest of all Cub players both as a hitter and fielder.

The Cubs floundered in '82 and '83 despite the constant influx of new players, among them slugging veteran third baseman Ron Cey, catcher Jody Davis, and relief pitcher Lee Smith. By 1984, Elia was gone, Jim Frey taking over as manager. He had led the Kansas City Royals to an AL pennant in 1980. And four major acquisitions by Green put the Cubs across the top. He got left fielder Gary Matthews and center fielder Bob Dernier from the Phillies before the season, acquired pitcher Dennis Eckersley in May, then in June traded for pitcher Rick Sutcliffe of the Cleveland Indians. Sutcliffe proved the keystone in the Cubs' arch of triumph, with a 16–1 record for the rest of the season.

Cub fever took over Chicago and much of the rest of the nation, with games available on cable television in most of the United States. Sandberg, Matthews, and Cey provided many of the hitting heroics and Sutcliffe and Smith the pitching feats as the team swept to a NL East championship, its first title of any sort since 1945. Wrigley Field became a madhouse, with attendance for the first time soaring over 2 million to reach 2,107,655.

The fever carried on into the NL Championship Series against the San Diego Padres, with a 13–0 Cub victory before 36,282 on October 2, 1984, and continued with a 4–2 triumph the next afternoon. With the Cubs up 2–0 in the best-of-five series, the vision of the first World Series at Wrigley Field in almost 40 years was in sight. But the Padres won the next three games in San Diego.

Despite the stunning setback, the Cubs had established themselves as one of the most entertaining teams in baseball, and Wrigley Field had reinforced its image as the ideal place to view a game, attracting fans from all over the nation. The ballpark had become a cult icon. Despite the renewed floundering of the team, attendance continued at a high level during the next decade, dropping under 2 million only in 1986 and the strike-curtailed 1994 season, while setting a record with 2,491,942 in 1989 when the Cubs again won an NL East championship.

Renovation of the ballpark continued. In 1983 a new ticket office was built. A new home-team clubhouse was built behind the third base dugout under the stands, replacing the old one at the extremity of the left-field line. In July 1985 seats were added to the catwalks near each foul pole in fair territory.

Meanwhile, the lure of Wrigley Field extended even to players as the signing of free-agent outfielder Andre Dawson proved in 1987. Dawson's knees had been battered by 10 years on the artificial turf in Montreal. He urged Green to sign him so that he could extend his career on the grass at Wrigley

Wrigley Field, 1977

Field, and accepted what for a star of his status was a minimal contract. It was a bargain. Dawson hit 49 home runs (the most by a Cub next to Wilson's 56) and drove in 137 runs, a record for a Cub right fielder. He won the NL Most Valuable Player award for 1987, though his team finished last.

By 1988, Green was gone, with Frey taking over as general manager and naming Don Zimmer, a former Cub infielder, as manager. And the battle over the installation of lights at Wrigley Field had been resolved. There had been threats from Major League Baseball that if lights were not installed at Wrigley Field, any future playoff games would be played at Comiskey Park or in St. Louis' Busch Stadium. Green had spearheaded the campaign for the installation of lights even to the extent of suggesting that unless they went up the Tribune Company would abandon Wrigley Field in favor of a new ballpark to be built in a suburb.

Despite the vehement opposition of neighborhood activists, who feared the disruption of the area around Wrigley Field by the noise and other problems associated with evening crowds, the Tribune Company won the battle. The six-year controversy ended on February 25, 1988, when the Chicago city council voted 29–19 to repeal a 1983 ordinance that barred night games at Wrigley Field and to approve a compromise ordinance. Mayor Eugene Sawyer signed a new ordinance upon receipt of a letter from John Madigan, who had replaced McKenna as chairman of the Cubs, agreeing to keep the team at Wrigley Field through the year 2002 "as long as . . . events and circumstances beyond the Cubs' control do not make this . . . either not practicable or financially feasible." The Cubs also agreed to a limit of eight night games in 1988 (though only seven were played) and no more than 18 a year in the future. Coincidentally, just before the city council voted on February 25, the major league owners had awarded the 1990 All-Star Game to the Cubs, contingent upon the availability of lights.

On April 7 installation of the lights began when a helicopter lifted the first steel girders to workmen on the roof of the upper deck. Six 33-foot towers were erected, three down the left field line, three down the right field line. The latticework of the towers blended in with the architecture of the old ballpark, and no towers were placed in the outfield from the left-field foul pole to the right-field foul pole. Care was taken to preserve the customary look of Wrigley Field. The total cost was $5 million.

On July 25, 1988, some 3,000 fans who had paid $100 apiece were given a preview of night baseball at Wrigley Field. An autograph session began at 7 P.M., and at 8:45 P.M., shortly before sunset, the field was cleared and the lights went on for a home run contest. Participating were two Cub Hall of Famers, Ernie Banks and Billy Williams, and two current Cubs, Andre Dawson and Ryne Sandberg.

The first official night game was scheduled for August 8, 1988, with the Cubs playing the Phillies. A crowd of 39,008, including Illinois Governor James Thompson, turned out. At 6:09 P.M., Harry Grossman, 91, a fan who had attended his first Cub game in 1906, threw the switch that activated 540 lights and ended the Wrigley Field tradition of daytime baseball. The game began at 7:01 P.M.

The Phillies' leadoff batter, Phil Bradley, hit the third pitch thrown by Rick Sutcliffe over the left-field wall for a home run. In the bottom of the first, Sandberg hit a two-run homer off Kevin Gross. The Cubs boosted their lead to 3–1 before heavy rain halted play in the fourth inning. After a two-hour, 10-minute wait, the umpires called off the game at 10:25.

As a result, the Cubs–New York Mets game the next evening became the first official night game in Wrigley Field history, with 36,399 turning out. The home team won 6–4.

In addition to the lights, the Tribune Company in 1989 went ahead with another major project, which had been contingent upon the first. Like the lights, it was designed to retain the traditional look of Wrigley Field as much as possible. The mezzanine level and the old press box and broadcasting booths were replaced by 67 private luxury boxes as well as new facilities for the press and broadcasting personnel at a cost estimated at $6.5 million. Wrigley Field's capacity changed once again, this time to 38,765.

In 1989 under Zimmer's leadership the Cubs captured their second NL East championship, and Wrigley Field again was host to the NL Championship Series. The team was a blend of old and young stars, Sandberg, Dawson, and first baseman Mark Grace providing the offense and Sutcliffe, Greg Maddux, and Mike Bielecki pacing the pitching staff. As in 1984, the playoffs (now the best of seven games) opened in Wrigley Field, a crowd of 39,195 turning out on October 4, 1989, to watch the Cubs lose 11–3. The next day the Cubs won 9–5, but when the series shifted to San Francisco the Giants swept the next three games to claim the NL championship. Once more the Cubs' bid to bring the World Series to Wrigley Field for the first time since 1945 had failed.

As the 20th century entered its final decade, the Cubs resumed their wandering in the desert. Manager succeeded manager as the team failed season after season. Only the All-Star Game of 1990, the third to be played at Wrigley Field and its first under the lights, provided a brief highlight. The AL defeated the NL, 2–0, on July 10, 1990, before 39,071, the losers getting only two hits, both singles.

Yet the fans kept coming out, Wrigley Field, according to many baseball experts and those who delve in nostalgia, having become more of an attraction than the Cubs, win or lose. Attendance stayed over the 2 million level year after year even when the team made it clear almost from opening day that it would not be a factor in a division title race.

The old ballpark, now well into its eighties, wears its age well, having been spruced up, renovated, and modernized so often since it was only a twinkle in "Lucky Charlie" Weeghman's eye in 1914 that it bears comparison with some of the fine new stadiums erected in the 1990s in Baltimore, Cleveland, and Arlington, Texas. And in fact, none of the sparkling new ballparks can compare to Wrigley Field in terms of legends, nostalgia, and the associations it has accumulated over the more than eight decades of its existence. To many fans around the United States, and not only Cub fans, Wrigley Field is the ultimate ballpark, the best place in the world to see baseball.

Beyond that, Wrigley Field is assured by the accord between the City of Chicago and the Tribune Company of continuing to house the Cubs into the 21st century. It is possible, even likely, that on April 20, 2014, the Cubs will play Wrigley Field's 100th anniversary game before the great-grandchildren of many who attended the opening of Weeghman's new North Side ballpark a century earlier.

There is no reason to think otherwise.

The Hall of Famers

Baseball's ultimate honor, election to the Hall of Fame in Cooperstown, New York, has been accorded to 39 players, managers, and front office people who in one way or another were connected with the Cubs during their careers, even if only briefly. Among them are some of the most illustrious names in the game's history, including William Hulbert, founder of the National League.

The majority of these 39 men performed at their best and established their reputations while employed by other teams. The Cubs are hardly unique in this respect. From the very earliest days of baseball, even before the advent of full-blown free agency in the 1970s, players seldom finished their careers with the teams they started with.

Still, it may be an oddity that, of the many former Cubs who earned baseball's ultimate honor, only two spent their entire careers as players with them (since the founding of the National League in 1876). They are Al Spalding and Ernie Banks. Spalding, however, had played for other teams before the advent of the NL and finished his playing career with just three seasons as a Cub—or White Stocking. Therefore, Banks stands alone as the ultimate "Mr. Cub," since he spent his entire 19-year major league career in one uniform.

Yet of the other Hall of Fame enshrinees many won election primarily because of their records as Cubs. Among these are Cap Anson, Billy Williams, Three-Finger Brown, Frank Chance, John Clarkson, Johnny Evers, Gabby Hartnett, Billy Herman, Ferguson Jenkins, King Kelly, Joe Tinker, and Hack Wilson. And Grover Cleveland Alexander spent more time with the Cubs than with either his first team, the Philadelphia Phillies, or the St. Louis Cardinals.

Among those whose reputations were established elsewhere either after starting with the Cubs, making a midcareer stop with them, or winding up their playing days in Chicago were such great players as Lou Brock, Dizzy Dean, Rogers Hornsby, Jimmie Foxx, Ralph Kiner, Robin Roberts, Hoyt Wilhelm, Chuck Klein, Kiki Cuyler, Hugh Duffy, and Rube Waddell. Few people would associate some of these Hall of Famers with the Cubs.

Other than Hulbert, Joe McCarthy is the only one never to have played a game in the major leagues, and was elected because of his achievements as manager of the Cubs, New York Yankees, and Boston Red Sox. Several other players, such as Clark Griffith, Anson, and Spalding, were equally outstanding as managers. Spalding and Griffith even ascended to the top as team owners.

Sweet-swinging Billy Williams demonstrates the stroke that won him election to the Hall of Fame.

Grover Cleveland Alexander

Pitcher
Cubs: 1918–26
Major leagues: 1911–30
Elected: 1938
Birthplace: Elba, Nebraska
B: February 26, 1887
D: November 4, 1950
Batted right, threw right

	W	L	Pct	ERA	G	CG	IP	H	BB	K	ShO
Cubs	128	83	.607	2.46	242	166	1,884⅓	1,819	268	614	24
Career	373	208	.642	2.56	696	439	5,189⅓	4,868	953	2,199	90

Grover Cleveland Alexander was the first Cub player to be inducted into the Hall of Fame in 1938, eight years after he ended his career tied with Christy Mathewson as the third-winningest pitchers in the major leagues. He ranks second in career shutouts with 90 and holds the NL record for most shutouts in a season with 16 in 1916. During a little over eight seasons with the Cubs, Alexander twice won 20 games. His record as a Cub was 128–83. Known as Ol' Pete in his later days, he was traded to St. Louis in 1926 and the next year again was a 20-game winner at the age of 40. Alexander started and finished his career with the Philadelphia Phillies, winning 30 or more games for them in three consecutive seasons. As a rookie in 1911 he was 28–13 with seven shutouts, four consecutive. He led the Phillies to their first NL pennant in 1915 with a 31–10 record. He distinguished himself for St. Louis in the 1926 World Series with two wins over the New York Yankees and his relief strikeout of Tony Lazzeri with the bases loaded in the seventh inning of the seventh game.

Adrian Constantine Anson

First baseman–manager
White Stockings, Cubs: 1876–97
Major leagues: 1876–97 (player)
Elected: 1939
Birthplace: Marshalltown, Iowa
B: April 11, 1852
D: April 14, 1922
Batted right, threw right

	G	AB	H	AVG	RBI	R	2B	3B	HR	SLG	SB
White Stockings, Cubs	2,276	9,108	3,000	.329	1,715	1,719	528	124	96	.446	247
Career		2,276	9,108	3,000	.329	1,715	1,719	528	124	96	.446	247

	G	W	L	T	ND	Pct
White Stockings, Cubs	2,258	1,283	932	38	5	.579
Career	2,280	1,292	945	38	5	.578

Considered the outstanding hitter among 19th-century players, Adrian "Cap" Anson was the first to reach 3,000 career hits. He batted .300 or over for 19 seasons. He won three National League batting titles, with .317 in 1879, .399 in 1881, and .344 in 1888. He played for the White Stockings–Cubs from 1876 through 1897 and managed the team from 1879 through 1897, leading it to five NL pennants. He also managed the New York Giants briefly in 1898. He was the first player to hit three consecutive home runs and to hit five home runs in two games. As player-manager of the team for 19 seasons, Anson was credited with such innovations as using two pitchers instead of one on a regular basis and taking a team to spring training. However, as a white supremacist, Anson has been blamed for a major role in keeping black players out of major league baseball until Jackie Robinson broke the color barrier in 1947.

Ernest Banks

Shortstop–first baseman
Cubs: 1953–71
Major leagues: 1953–71
Elected: 1977
Birthplace: Dallas, Texas
B: January 31, 1931
Bats right, throws right

	G	AB	H	AVG	RBI	R	2B	3B	HR	SLG	SB
Cubs	2,528	9,421	2,583	.274	1,636	1,305	407	90	512	.500	50
Career	2,528	9,421	2,583	.274	1,636	1,305	407	90	512	.500	50

Ernie Banks' enormous popularity earned him the title "Mr. Cub" during his 19-year major league career, all with the Cubs. The first half of his career he played shortstop, the second half first base. He established major league records for most games played from start of major league career (424) and most home runs by a shortstop in a season, 47 in 1958. He established a National League record for most seasons leading the league in games played with six. He tied a major league record with five home runs with the bases full in a season in 1955. He hit three home runs in a game four times. Banks twice led the NL in home runs with 47 in 1958 and 41 in 1960, twice led in runs batted in, and hit 40 or more home runs five times. He batted in 100 runs or more in eight seasons. He was named the NL Most Valuable Player in 1958 and 1959. Banks finished his career with 512 home runs.

	G	W	L	T	ND	Pct
Cubs	157	73	80	3	1	.477
Career	775	328	432	14	1	.432

Louis Boudreau

Shortstop-manager
Cubs: 1960 (manager)
Major leagues: 1938–52 (player)
Elected: 1970
Birthplace: Harvey, Illinois
B: July 17, 1917
Bats right, throws right

	G	AB	H	AVG	RBI	R	2B	3B	HR	SLG	SB
Career	1,646	6,030	1,779	.295	789	861	385	66	68	.415	51

	G	W	L	T	ND	Pct
Cubs	139	54	83	2	0	.394
Career	2,404	1,162	1,224	18	0	.487

Lou Boudreau became the youngest manager in major league history in 1942 when he took over the Cleveland Indians at the age of 24. A heady shortstop and outstanding hitter, Boudreau starred as a player for the Indians from 1939 to 1950 and led them to a World Series victory as player-manager in 1948. He won the American League batting title in 1944 with .327, and batted .355 with 18 home runs and 106 RBIs in 1948 when he was named the AL's Most Valuable Player. He led AL shortstops in fielding percentage for eight seasons and in double plays five seasons. After leaving the Indians, Boudreau managed the Boston Red Sox and Kansas City Athletics, then became a radio broadcaster for the Cubs. When the Cubs got off to a 6–11 start in the 1960 season under Charlie Grimm, team owner P. K. Wrigley summoned Boudreau from the broadcast booth to manage the team. The Cubs were 54–83 the rest of the season under Boudreau, who retreated to the broadcasting booth and stayed there for another two decades.

Roger Bresnahan

Catcher-manager
Cubs: 1913–15
Major leagues: 1897, 1900–15 (player)
Elected: 1945
Birthplace: Toledo, Ohio
B: June 11, 1879
D: December 4, 1944
Batted right, threw right

	G	AB	H	AVG	RBI	R	2B	3B	HR	SLG	SB
Cubs	233	632	151	.239	64	81	23	7	2	.307	40
Career	1,430	4,480	1,253	.280	540	683	223	71	26	.379	212

Roger Bresnahan was one of the most versatile of players, playing in the major leagues as pitcher, third baseman, outfielder, and catcher, the last being the position that earned him renown as the best of his era. A veteran at 33, he had been player-manager of the St. Louis Cardinals for four seasons before the Cubs signed him as a catcher for the 1913 season. Named Cub manager in 1915, he led them to a sub-.500 record, then was replaced by Joe Tinker. The first catcher to wear shin guards, Bresnahan had an outstanding career in which he was the battery mate of Christy Mathewson and other great pitchers for John McGraw's Giants in the first decade of the 20th century. In his first major league game, August 27, 1897, he pitched for Washington and shut out St. Louis 3–0, but slipped back into the minor leagues until he found his role as a catcher.

Louis Clark Brock

Outfielder
Cubs: 1961–64
Major leagues: 1961–79
Elected: 1985
Birthplace: El Dorado, Arkansas
B: June 18, 1939
Bats right, throws right

	G	AB	H	AVG	RBI	R	2B	3B	HR	SLG	SB
Cubs	327	1,207	310	.257	86	183	52	20	20	.383	50
Career	2,816	10,332	3,023	.293	900	1,610	486	141	149	.410	938

For Cub fans, Lou Brock's name will always be associated with one of the most infamous trades in the team's history. On June 15, 1964, the Cubs traded young outfielder Brock and pitchers Jack Spring and Paul Toth to the St. Louis Cardinals for pitchers Ernie Broglio and Bobby Shantz and outfielder Doug Clemens. The Cubs failed to profit from the deal, but Brock went on to become one of the finest base stealers in the game's history and a Hall of Fame outfielder. Brock established major league records by stealing 50 or more bases in 12 consecutive seasons, stealing 118 bases in a season (since surpassed), and stealing 938 bases lifetime. He led the National League in stolen bases eight seasons. He batted over .300 eight times and finished with a career average of .293 for 19 seasons and 3,023 hits. Brock played in three World Series for the Cardinals, batting .391 in 21 games. In 1968 he set a record for most hits in a World Series with 13 in seven games.

Mordecai Peter Centennial Brown

Pitcher
Cubs: 1904–12, 1916
Major leagues: 1903–16
Elected: 1949
Birthplace: Nyesville, Indiana
B: October 19, 1876
D: February 14, 1948
Batted right, threw right

Cubs	188	85	.689	1.80	396	206	2,329	1,879	445	1,033	50
Career	239	129	.649	2.06	481	271	3,172⅓	2,708	673	1,375	57

Mordecai "Three-Finger" Brown was the kingpin of the Cub pitching staff during their greatest era when they won four National League pennants in five seasons (1906–08, 1910), as well as two World Series (1907–08). Brown won 20 or more games for six consecutive seasons (1906–1911). He reached his peak with 29 victories in 1908 and led the NL in wins with 27 in 1909. His 26–6 record in 1906 included 10 shutouts and 11 consecutive victories to help the Cubs to their major league record of 116 wins in a season. Brown pitched four consecutive shutouts in 1908. Overall, Brown was 5–4 in four World Series, including a record of 2–0 in the 1908 victory over the Detroit Tigers. Brown's duels with Christy Mathewson, the New York Giants ace, were legendary. Brown won 13 of 24 confrontations with Mathewson, nine of them consecutively. Brown finished his career with a 239–129 record and 57 shutouts.

Frank Leroy Chance

First baseman-manager
Cubs: 1898–1912
Major leagues: 1898–1914 (player)
Elected: 1946
Birthplace: Fresno, California
B: September 9, 1877
D: September 15, 1924
Batted right, threw right

	G	AB	H	AVG	RBI	R	2B	3B	HR	SLG	SB
Cubs	1,274	4,269	1,266	.297	590	795	200	79	20	.394	405
Career	1,286	4,293	1,271	.296	596	798	200	79	20	.393	405

	G	W	L	T	ND	Pct
Cubs	1,182	768	389	19	2	.664
Career	1,622	946	648	26	2	.593

No Cub manager has come close to matching the achievements of Frank "Husk" Chance during his almost eight seasons on the job. Chance took over from ailing Frank Selee midway into the 1905 season, then led the Cubs to four pennants in the next five years and World Series titles in 1907 and 1908. Chance's 1906 team set a major league record by winning 116 of 152 games, with a percentage of .763. In Chance's first five full years at the helm, the Cubs averaged 106 victories a season. Overall, during the "Peerless Leader's" tenure, the Cubs were 768–389 for a .664 percentage. Chance was an outstanding first baseman, as aggressive a player as he was a manager. He compiled a career batting average of .296 in 16 seasons, and in his best season, 1903, batted .327 and stole 67 bases. He left the Cubs after the 1912 season then was player-manager of the new York Yankees for two years.

John Gibson Clarkson

Pitcher
White Stockings: 1884–87
Major leagues: 1884–94
Elected: 1963
Birthplace: Cambridge, Massachusetts
B: July 1, 1861
D: February 4, 1909
Batted right, threw right

White Stockings	136	57	.705	2.39	199	186	1,730⅔	1,523	290	960	15
Career	326	177	.648	2.81	531	485	4,536⅓	4,295	1,191	1,978	37

The premier pitcher of his day, John Clarkson almost single-handedly pitched the White Stockings to National League pennants in 1885 and 1886. His 53–16 record in 1885 included a winning streak of 12 consecutive games as well as a 14–1 total during the month of June. He pitched a 4–0 no-hit game against Providence on July 27, 1885. Clarkson won 35 games in 1886 and 38 in 1887, after which he was sold for $10,000 to Boston, for whom he was 49–19 in 1888. Clarkson threw overhand, unlike most pitchers of his era. In 1892 the NL played a split season, and Clarkson pitched Boston to a title in the first half, then helped Cleveland win the championship of the second half.

Hazen Shirley Cuyler

Outfielder
Cubs: 1928–35
Major leagues: 1921–38
Elected: 1968
Birthplace: Harrisville, Michigan
B: August 30, 1899
D: February 11, 1950
Batted right, threw right

	G	AB	H	AVG	RBI	R	2B	3B	HR	SLG	SB
Cubs	949	3,687	1,199	.325	602	674	220	66	79	.490	161
Career	1,879	7,161	2,299	.321	1,065	1,305	394	157	127	.473	328

A career batting average of .321 for 18 seasons attests to Hazen Shirley "Kiki" Cuyler's skill as a batter, but he also was an excellent right fielder with an exceptional arm, as well as a fine base runner who led the NL in stolen bases four times. At 28, Cuyler was at his peak when the Cubs acquired him in trade after the 1927 season, during which he had incurred Pittsburgh Pirates manager Donie Bush's displeasure. He had become a star with the Pirates, batting .354 in 1924 and .357 in 1925. He tied an NL record in 1925 with 10 hits in succession. He batted .360 for the Cubs in 1929 with 102 RBIs as he teamed up with Hack Wilson and Riggs Stephenson in one of the greatest of all outfields. His best year overall was 1930 when he batted .355 with 50 doubles, 17 triples, 13 home runs, and 134 RBIs, scored 155 runs, and stole 37 bases.

Jay Hanna Dean

Pitcher
Cubs: 1938–41
Major leagues: 1930, 1932–41, 1947
Elected: 1953
Birthplace: Lucas, Arkansas
B: January 16, 1911
D: July 17, 1974
Batted right, threw right

	W	L	Pct	ERA	G	CG	IP	H	BB	K	ShO
Cubs	16	8	.667	3.35	43	13	226	232	45	68	3
Career	150	83	.644	3.02	317	154	1,967⅓	1,925	453	1,163	26

By the time he became a Cub before the 1938 season, Jay Hanna "Dizzy" Dean's fastball was a thing of the past. But the Cubs never regretted the deal in which they sent $185,000 and three players to the St. Louis Cardinals for

Dean. He had been a great pitcher, the last to win 30 games in the NL with a record of 30–7 in 1934, and had been a 20-game winner for four consecutive seasons before he suffered an arm injury in 1937. Dean caught the Cubs' attention in 1933 when he struck out 17 of them in a game, and kept the nation's attention as the most colorful player to come along since Babe Ruth. In four years with the Cubs he was 16–8, and his 7–1 record in 1938 helped them to a pennant. Brash and bright, the onetime itinerant cotton picker's brilliant pitching career was cut short by his lame arm, but he was able to make the most of an engaging personality and become a radio and television broadcaster of national reputation.

Hugh Duffy

Outfielder-manager
White Stockings: 1888–89
Major leagues: 1888–1901, 1904–06 (player)
Elected: 1945
Birthplace: River Point, Rhode Island
B: November 26, 1866
D: October 19, 1954
Batted right, threw right

	G	AB	H	AVG	RBI	R	2B	3B	HR	SLG	SB
White Stockings	207	882	256	.290	130	204	31	11	19	.415	62
Career	1,736	7,043	2,283	.324	1,299	1,551	324	116	105	.448	583

	G	W	L	T	ND	Pct
Career	1,221	535	671	15	0	.444

Hugh Duffy spent the first two seasons of his 17-year major league career with the Cubs, but his batting averages of .282 in 1888 and .295 in 1889 failed to suggest that he would become one of the great hitters of all time. He jumped to the Players League in 1890 and batted .320, starting a run of 10 seasons in which he topped .300. In 1894 he not only compiled the all-time highest batting average of .438, but also won the Triple Crown with 18 home runs and 145 RBIs. He again led the NL in home runs with 11 in 1897, and he drove in more than 100 runs eight times. Later in his career, he managed several teams, including the Chicago White Sox, Philadelphia Phillies, and Boston Red Sox.

Leo Ernest Durocher

Shortstop-manager
Cubs: 1966–72 (manager)
Major leagues: 1925, 1928–41, 1943, 1945 (player)
Elected: 1994
Birthplace: West Springfield, Massachusetts
B: July 27, 1905
D: October 7, 1991
Batted right, threw right

	G	AB	H	AVG	RBI	R	2B	3B	HR	SLG	SB
Career	1,637	5,350	1,320	.247	567	575	210	56	24	.320	24

	G	W	L	T	ND	Pct
Cubs	1,065	535	526	4	0	.504
Career	3,739	2,008	1,079	22	0	.540

He was described as the "supreme egotist," and his long career as shortstop and manager was always turbulent and filled with controversy, but there is no doubt that Leo Ernest "The Lip" Durocher was one of the most interesting characters in the game's history. A fine-fielding but light-hitting shortstop, sometimes labeled the All-American Out, Durocher nevertheless was an integral part of several successful teams, including the St. Louis Cardinals' famous Gashouse Gang of the 1930s, the New York Yankees, and the Brooklyn Dodgers. Scrappy and volatile, notorious for baiting umpires and playing hunches, Durocher had a successful 24-year managerial career, winning three NL pennants—with the Dodgers in 1941 and with the New York Giants in 1951 and 1954. He came late to the Cubs, at the age of 60, but quickly transformed a moribund franchise into an exciting team that fell just short of winning a division title in 1969.

John Joseph Evers

Second baseman–manager
Cubs: 1902–13
Major leagues: 1902–17, 1922, 1929 (player)
Elected: 1946
Birthplace: Troy, New York
B: July 21, 1881
D: March 28, 1947
Batted right, threw left

	G	AB	H	AVG	RBI	R	2B	3B	HR	SLG	SB
Cubs	1,408	4,855	1,339	.276	448	742	183	64	9	.344	293
Career	1,783	6,134	1,658	.270	538	919	216	70	12	.334	324

	G	W	L	T	ND	Pct
Cubs	251	129	120	2	0	.518
Career	375	180	192	3	0	.484

An intense player, John Joseph "Crab" Evers was the sparkplug of the great Cub teams of the early 20th century, the pivot of the famed Tinker-to-Evers-to-Chance double-play combination. A fine base runner, Evers stole home 21 times and had a lifetime total of 324 stolen bases. He batted .300 or better twice in his career, including .341 in 1912. Johnny Evers joined the Cubs in 1902 and succeeded Frank Chance as player-manager in 1913, but was fired after finishing in third place. He was signed by the Boston Braves and led them to the pennant in 1914, when he was named the Most Valuable Player in the National League. Evers again managed the Cubs in part of the 1921 season and managed the Chicago White Sox in 1924.

James Emory Foxx

First baseman
Cubs: 1942–44
Major leagues: 1925–45
Elected: 1951
Birthplace: Sudlersville, Maryland
B: October 22, 1907
D: July 21, 1967
Batted right, threw right

	G	AB	H	AVG	RBI	R	2B	3B	HR	SLG	SB
Cubs	85	225	43	.191	21	25	9	0	3	.271	1
Career	2,317	8,134	2,646	.325	1,921	1,751	458	125	534	.609	88

Jimmie Foxx hit 58 home runs in 1932, which ties for the most ever hit in a season by a right-handed batter, hit 50 home runs in another season, and hit 30 more home runs for 12 consecutive seasons. He had 10 seasons of 35 or more home runs, drove in 100 or more runs 13 times, and 11 times hit over .300. Before he came to the Cubs in midseason 1942 at the age of 34, Foxx had won three Most Valuable Player awards, four home run titles, and two batting championships with the Philadelphia Athletics and Boston Red Sox. The Cubs, hit hard by the World War II manpower shortage, gambled that Foxx might recapture some of his faded glory, but he was near the end. He hit only three home runs for the Cubs before moving on to finish his career with the Phillies in 1945. He finished with a lifetime average of .325 and 534 home runs for 20 seasons.

Frank Francis Frisch

Second baseman–manager
Cubs: 1949–51 (manager)
Major leagues: 1919–37 (player)
Elected: 1947
Birthplace: Bronx, New York
B: September 8, 1898
D: March 12, 1973
Batted both, threw right

	G	AB	H	AVG	RBI	R	2B	3B	HR	SLG	SB
Career	2,311	9,112	2,880	.316	1,244	1,532	466	138	105	.432	419

	G	W	L	T	ND	Pct
Cubs	339	141	196	2	0	.418
Career	2,246	1,138	1,078	30	0	.514

Among the finest of all second basemen, both as a hitter and fielder, Frankie Frisch, "The Fordham Flash," was a born leader who managed three major league teams during his colorful career. Frisch batted .316 during a 19-year career with the New York Giants and St. Louis Cardinals, led the NL in stolen bases three times, and was chosen the league's Most Valuable Player in 1931 when he batted .311 and sparked the Cardinals to a pennant. Frisch was player-manager of the Gashouse Gang as the Cardinals again won a pennant in 1934. Frisch also managed the Pittsburgh Pirates from 1940 to 1946, then managed the Cubs from midseason 1949 to midseason 1951 without much success.

Clark Calvin Griffith

Pitcher-manager-owner
Cubs: 1893–1900 (player)
Major leagues: 1891, 1893–1914 (player)
Elected: 1946
Birthplace: Clear Creek, Missouri
B: November 20, 1869
D: October 27, 1955
Batted right, threw right

	W	L	Pct	ERA	G	CG	IP	H	BB	K	ShO
Cubs	152	96	.613	3.36	265	240	2,188⅔	2,445	517	573	9
Career	240	144	.625	3.31	453	337	3,386⅓	3,670	774	955	23

	G	W	L	T	ND	Pct
Career	2,918	1,491	1,367	58	2	.522

His long subsequent career as principal owner of the Washington Senators has tended to overshadow Clark C. "Old Fox" Griffith's earlier days as an outstanding pitcher and manager. Griffith was the ace of the Cub pitching staff during the 1890s, with six consecutive seasons (1894–99) of more than 20 wins, a feat matched only by Three-Finger Brown and Ferguson Jenkins. Griffith jumped to the new American League in 1901 as player-manager of the Chicago White Sox and won the first pennant, leading the pitching staff with a 24–7 record. He later managed the New York Yankees and Cincinnati Reds, and finally took over in Washington, where he became president of the team and held the job until his death in 1955.

Burleigh Arland Grimes

Pitcher-manager
Cubs: 1923–33 (player)
Major leagues: 1916–34 (player)
Elected: 1964
Birthplace: Emerald, Wisconsin
B: August 18, 1893
D: December 6, 1985
Batted right, threw right

	W	L	Pct	ERA	G	CG	IP	H	BB	K	ShO
Cubs	9	17	.346	4.35	47	13	211	245	79	48	2
Career	270	212	.560	3.53	617	314	4,179⅔	4,412	1,295	1,512	35

	G	W	L	T	ND	Pct
Career	306	131	171	2	0	.434

Burleigh Grimes was a much-traveled veteran by the time he got to the Cubs at the age of 38 in 1932. He was 6–11 that season and 3–6 the next year before they released him on August 4, 1933. Grimes was the last of the legal spitball pitchers, continuing to throw the pitch 15 years after it was banned to newcomers in 1920. His prime years came with the Brooklyn Dodgers and Pittsburgh Pirates in the 1920s when he was five times a 20-game winner. He twice led the National League in wins, with a 22–13 record in 1921 and with 25–14 in 1928. He won 13 consecutive games for the New York Giants in 1927 and lost 13 consecutive decisions with the Pirates in 1917. Grimes managed the Dodgers in 1937 and 1938.

Charles Leo Hartnett

	G	W	L	T	ND	Pct
Career	465	189	274	2	0	.408

Catcher-manager
Cubs: 1922–40
Major leagues: 1922–41
Elected: 1955
Birthplace: Woonsocket, Rhode Island
B: December 20, 1900
D: December 20, 1972
Batted right, threw right

	G	AB	H	AVG	RBI	R	2B	3B	HR	SLG	SB
Cubs	1,926	6,282	1,867	.297	1,153	847	391	64	231	.490	28
Career	1,990	6,432	1,912	.297	1,179	867	396	64	236	.489	28

	G	W	L	T	ND	Pct
Cubs	383	203	176	4	0	.536
Career	383	203	176	4	0	.536

An exceptionally durable catcher who caught 100 or more games for 12 consecutive seasons and played 19 seasons for the Cubs, Charles Leo "Gabby" Hartnett was a powerful hitter who reached a career high of 37 home runs in 1930. He hit 236 home runs in his 20-year career. Hartnett's finest all-around performance came in 1930 when he also batted .339 and drove in 122 runs. He won the NL Most Valuable Player award in 1935 when he batted .344 with 13 home runs and 91 RBIs. On July 26, 1938, Hartnett became the Cubs' player-manager and led the team to a pennant, the decisive blow being his celebrated late-season "Homer in the Gloamin'." Hartnett managed the Cubs the following two seasons, but he was fired after a fifth-place finish in 1940. He was signed as player-coach by the New York Giants for the 1941 season and rounded out his major league playing career with them.

William Jennings Herman

Second baseman–manager
Cubs: 1931–41 (player)
Major leagues: 1931–43, 1946–47 (player)
Elected: 1975
Birthplace: New Albany, Indiana
B: July 7, 1909
Bats right, throws right

	G	AB	H	AVG	RBI	R	2B	3B	HR	SLG	SB
Cubs	1,344	5,532	1,710	.309	577	875	346	69	37	.417	53
Career	1,922	7,707	2,345	.304	839	1,163	486	82	47	.407	67

An exceptional fielder and outstanding hitter, second baseman Billy Herman teamed with shortstop Bill Jurges during the 1930s to give the Cubs an outstanding double-play combination. Herman and Jurges formed the middle of the infield on three pennant winners—1932, 1935, and 1938. Herman batted over .300 in seven of his 10 seasons with the Cubs, reaching a high .341 in 1935 when he led the NL in hits with 227 and doubles with 57. He led the league in putouts seven times and in fielding percentage in three seasons. Herman was traded by the Cubs to the Brooklyn Dodgers early in the 1941 season and helped them win the pennant that year. His playing career ended in 1947. He later managed the Pittsburgh Pirates and Boston Red Sox, as well as various minor league teams.

Rogers Hornsby

Second baseman–manager
Cubs: 1929–32
Major leagues: 1915–37 (player)
Elected: 1942
Birthplace: Winters, Texas
B: April 27, 1896
D: January 5, 1963
Batted right, threw right

	G	AB	H	AVG	RBI	R	2B	3B	HR	SLG	SB
Cubs	317	1,121	392	.349	264	245	91	10	58	.604	3
Career	2,259	8,173	2,930	.358	1,584	1,579	541	169	301	.577	135

	G	W	L	T	ND	Pct
Cubs	259	141	116	2	0	.549
Career	1,530	701	812	17	0	.463

Rogers "Rajah" Hornsby's career average of .358 for 23 seasons ranks second only to Ty Cobb's record .367. Considered the most formidable right-handed hitter ever, Hornsby led the National League in batting seven times, including a run of six consecutive championships with the St. Louis Cardinals from 1920 to 1925. In three of those years he batted over .400. His .424 batting average in 1924 is second only to Hugh Duffy's .438 in 1894. Hornsby also hit for power, leading the NL in home runs twice, with 42 in 1922 and 39 in 1925. The Cubs acquired Hornsby from the Boston Braves in a trade, and he lifted them to a pennant in 1929 by batting .380 with 39 home runs and 149 RBIs. Named the Cub manager late in the 1930 season, Hornsby led them to third place in 1931 and was fired midway in the 1932 season.

William Ambrose Hulbert

Owner–president
White Stockings: 1876–82
Elected: 1995
Birthplace: Burlington Flats, New York
B: October 23, 1832
D: April 10, 1882

William Hulbert, a wealthy Chicago businessman, took over as controlling owner of the financially troubled Chicago White Stockings of the National Association of Professional Base Ball Players (NA) in 1875. One of his first actions was to lure to Chicago several star NA players, among them Al Spalding and Cap Anson, for the 1876 season. Scandals and financial problems were plaguing the NA, however, and Hulbert decided that the association was no longer viable, and that professional baseball needed a fresh start. With the help of legal experts, he drew up a plan for the organization of a new league to replace the moribund NA. At a meeting in New York on February 2, 1876, representatives from Chicago and seven other major cities joined Hulbert in founding the National League of Professional Base Ball Cubs (NL). Eight new franchises were awarded, including one to the White Stockings group led by Hulbert. The name White Stockings (later to become Cubs) was retained for the Chicago team. The new league was determined to enforce both financial solvency and fixed schedules on its franchises, and to demand its players abide by a rigid moral code. Hulbert became the second president of the NL in 1877, when the first president, Morgan G. Bulkeley, a prominent banker and politician, resigned after one year in office. Hulbert turned over active direction of the White Stockings to Al Spalding when he took over the league presidency, but he retained his title as president of the team. He crusaded vigorously to clean up professional baseball and to assure its financial success until he died of a heart attack at the age of 49.

Monford Merrill Irvin

Outfielder
Cubs: 1956
Major leagues: 1949–56
Elected: 1973
Birthplace: Columbus, Alabama
B: February 25, 1919
Bats right, throws right

	G	AB	H	AVG	RBI	R	2B	3B	HR	SLG	SB
Cubs	111	339	92	.271	50	44	13	3	15	.460	1
Career	764	2,499	731	.293	443	366	97	31	99	.475	28

Monford Merrill "Monte" Irvin came late to the major leagues at the age of 30 after a brilliant career in the Negro National League and in the winter leagues in the Caribbean. After Jackie Robinson broke the color barrier against black players, Irvin was signed by the New York Giants. He played his first major league game in 1949 and was a regular outfielder for the Giants from 1950 through 1955, contributing to pennant winners in 1951 and 1954. He led the NL with 121 RBIs while batting .324 and hitting 24 home runs in 1951. After seven seasons with the Giants, he was acquired by the Cubs and finished his playing career with them in 1956. He later became an aide to the commissioner of baseball.

Ferguson Arthur Jenkins

Pitcher
Cubs: 1966–73, 1982–83
Major leagues: 1965–83
Elected: 1991
Birthplace: Chatham, Ontario, Canada
B: December 13, 1943
Bats right, throws right

	W	L	Pct	ERA	G	CG	IP	H	BB	K	ShO
Cubs	167	132	.559	3.29	401	154	2,673	2,402	600	2,038	29
Career	284	226	.557	3.34	664	267	4,499⅔	4,142	997	3,192	49

Few trades have turned out as well for the Cubs as the one on April 21, 1966, with the Philadelphia Phillies in which they acquired Ferguson Arthur Jenkins, a tall, slender young right-hander. The Phillies "threw in" Jenkins in a five-man deal because they had little confidence in his potential. Jenkins proved otherwise, winning 20 or more games for six consecutive seasons (1967–72) to match the achievements of Three-Finger Brown and Clark Griffith. In 1971 he led the NL in victories with a 24–13 record, completed 30 of 39 starts, walked only 37 men in 325 innings, and won the Cy Young Award. He led the league in strikeouts with 273 in 1969. Traded to Texas after the 1973 season, Jenkins won a career-high 25 games in his first AL season. Reacquired by the Cubs in 1982, he led the club with a 14–15 record that year, then finished his career in 1983. He is the only pitcher in major league history to strike out more than 3,000 batters while walking less than 1,000.

George Lange Kelly

First baseman
Cubs: 1930
Major leagues: 1915–17, 1919–30, 1932
Elected: 1973
Birthplace: San Francisco, California
B: September 10, 1895
D: October 13, 1984
Batted right, threw right

	G	AB	H	AVG	RBI	R	2B	3B	HR	SLG	SB
Cubs	39	166	55	.331	19	22	6	1	3	.434	0
Career	1,622	5,933	1,778	.297	1,020	819	337	76	148	.452	65

Georage Lange "High Pockets" Kelly's tenure with the Cubs was brief, just 39 games played late in the 1930 season when he was signed to fill in for injured first baseman Charlie Grimm, then released after the campaign. That was part of a 16-year major league career, in most of which he starred for the New York Giants. Kelly's connection with the Cubs was a family affair of sorts, since he was a nephew of Bill Lange, a great Chicago outfielder of the 1890s. Kelly led the NL with 23 home runs in 1921, and on September 23, 1923, he produced 15 total bases in a game with three home runs, a double, and a single. He also hit seven home runs in six consecutive games. He twice led the NL in RBIs, with 94 in 1920 and 136 in 1924.

Michael Joseph Kelly

Outfielder–catcher–manager
White Stockings: 1880–86 (player)
Major leagues: 1878–93
Elected: 1945
Birthplace: Troy, New York
B: December 31, 1857
D: November 8, 1894
Batted right, threw right

	G	AB	H	AVG	RBI	R	2B	3B	HR	SLG	SB
Cubs	681	2,843	899	.316	323	728	193	49	33	.453	—
Career	1,455	5,894	1,813	.308	793	1,357	359	102	69	.438	315

	G	W	L	T	ND	Pct
Career	329	173	148	4	4	.539

Many have called him the Babe Ruth of the 19th century, and Michael Joseph "King" Kelly indeed was a flamboyant, larger-than-life, exceptionally talented, versatile player who excelled at every position, though mostly as a catcher and outfielder. Kelly starred on five pennant winners for Cap Anson's White Stockings in the 1880s and twice led the NL in batting, with .354 in 1884 and .388 in 1886. His daring on the base paths inspired a popular song, "Slide, Kelly, Slide," on which he capitalized by appearing on the vaudeville circuit. The White Stockings sold him to Boston for the unheard-of figure of $10,000 on February 14, 1887. When Boston also purchased pitcher John Clarkson from Chicago in 1888, with Kelly catching, they became known as the $20,000 Battery.

Ralph McPherran Kiner

Outfielder
Cubs: 1953–54
Major leagues: 1946–55
Elected: 1975
Birthplace: Santa Rita, New Mexico
B: October 27, 1922
Bats right, throws right

	G	AB	H	AVG	RBI	R	2B	3B	HR	SA	SB
Cubs	264	971	276	.284	160	161	50	7	50	.505	3
Career	1,472	5,205	1,451	.279	1,015	971	216	30	369	.548	22

Ralph Kiner is the only player to lead his league (or tie for leadership) in home runs in each of his first seven seasons in the major leagues, all with the Pittsburgh Pirates. He was the first National League player to hit more than 50 home runs twice, in 1947 and 1949 (tied by Willie Mays), and the first to hit 40 or more home runs in five successive seasons (1947–51). Kiner hit eight home runs in four consecutive games in 1947, breaking a major league record of seven that he had tied earlier in the season. Kiner set the NL record by hitting 101 home runs in two consecutive years, 1949–50, with 54 and 47. Kiner batted in more than 100 runs in six of his 10 major league seasons. He was acquired by the Cubs in a midseason deal in 1953 and was traded to Cleveland after the 1954 season.

Charles Herbert Klein

Outfielder
Cubs: 1934–36
Major leagues: 1928–44
Elected: 1980
Birthplace: Indianapolis, Indiana
B: October 7, 1904
D: March 28, 1958
Batted left, threw right

	G	AB	H	AVG	RBI	R	2B	3B	HR	SLG	SB
Cubs	263	978	290	.297	171	168	46	6	46	.497	7
Career	1,753	6,846	2,076	.320	1,202	1,168	398	74	300	.543	79

Most of Charles Herbert "Chuck" Klein's 17-year major league career was spent with the Philadelphia Phillies, with whom he led the National League four times in home runs, twice in RBIs, twice in hits, three times in runs scored, twice in doubles, and once in batting average, with .368 in 1933. In his best overall season, 1930, he batted .386 with 59 doubles, eight triples, 40 home runs, 170 RBIs, and 158 runs scored (a modern NL record). He led the NL in stolen bases with 20 in 1932. He won the NL Most Valuable Player award in 1931 and 1932. Klein is among the Phillies' leaders in almost every hitting category. He holds the modern major league one-season record among outfielders with 44 assists. Traded to the Cubs, Klein played in Chicago in 1934, 1935, and part of the 1936 season, then returned to the Phillies. He was traded to Pittsburgh during the 1939 season, returned to the Phillies in 1940, and finished his career as part-time player and coach in 1944.

Anthony Michael Lazzeri

Second baseman
Cubs: 1938
Major leagues: 1926–39
Elected: 1991
Birthplace: San Francisco, California
B: December 6, 1903
D: August 6, 1946
Batted right, threw right

	G	AB	H	AVG	RBI	R	2B	3B	HR	SLG	SB
Cubs	54	120	32	.267	23	21	5	0	5	.433	0
Career	1,739	6,297	1,840	.292	1,191	986	334	115	178	.467	148

An outstanding, power-hitting second baseman from 1926 to 1937 with the New York Yankees, Anthony Michael "Poosh 'Em Up" Lazzeri is chiefly remembered as the victim of a famous strikeout by Grover Cleveland Alexander in the 1926 World Series. Tony Lazzeri played in six World Series with the Yankees, batted over .300 five times, and drove in 100 or more runs in seven seasons. At the age of 34, Lazzeri was signed as a utility player by the Cubs. He played just 54 games for them in 1938 and pinch-hit twice without success in the losing World Series effort that year. He finished his career in 1939 with the Brooklyn Dodgers and New York Giants.

Frederick Charles Lindstrom

Third baseman–outfielder
Cubs: 1935
Major leagues: 1924–36
Elected: 1976
Birthplace: Chicago
B: November 21, 1905
D: October 4, 1981
Batted right, threw right

	G	AB	H	AVG	RBI	R	2B	3B	HR	SLG	SB
Cubs	90	342	94	.275	62	49	22	4	3	.389	1
Career	1,438	5,611	1,747	.311	779	895	301	81	103	.449	84

Like many other Cub Hall of Famers, Freddie Lindstrom spent only a brief stretch near the end of his career with the team, just the 1935 season. A fine fielding, hard-hitting third baseman and outfielder with the New York Giants and Pittsburgh Pirates from 1924 to 1934, Lindstrom was acquired by the Cubs after the 1934 season. He batted .275 in 90 games in 1935 as the Cubs won the pennant. Released after the season, Lindstrom finished his career with Brooklyn in 1936. Lindstrom compiled a .311 lifetime batting average in 13 major season league seasons, batting over .300 seven times, with career highs of .379 in 1930 and .358 in 1928.

Walter James Vincent Maranville

Shortstop–manager
Cubs: 1925 (player-manager)
Major leagues: 1912–33, 1935
Elected: 1954
Birthplace: Springfield, Massachusetts
B: November 11, 1891
D: January 5, 1954
Batted right, threw right

	G	AB	H	AVG	RBI	R	2B	3B	HR	SLG	SB
Cubs	75	266	62	.233	23	37	10	3	0	.293	6
Career	2,670	10,078	2,605	.258	884	1,255	380	177	28	.340	291

	G	W	L	T	ND	Pct
Cubs	53	23	30	0	0	.434
Career	53	23	30	0	0	.434

An impish, colorful player, as well as an exceptional fielding shortstop, Walter James Vincent "Rabbit" Maranville defied the odds when told he was too small to play in the major leagues. Though only 5–5, Maranville not only became a star, but also had one of the longest playing careers in history, 23 seasons in the major leagues. He compiled a career batting average of .258. He allegedly got his nickname when a fan exclaimed, "Why he bounces around like a rabbit." Most of Maranville's career was spent with the Boston Braves, but he played for the Cubs in 1925, batting .233 in 75 games, and even managed the team for 53 games before being fired. He was released after the season.

Joseph Vincent McCarthy

Manager
Cubs: 1926–30 (manager)
Major leagues: 1926–46, 1948–50 (manager)
Elected: 1957
Birthplace: Philadelphia, Pennsylvania
B: April 21, 1887
D: January 3, 1978

	G	W	L	T	ND	Pct
Cubs	770	442	321	7	0	.579
Career	3,487	2,125	1,333	26	3	.615

A career minor league player (1907–21), Joseph Vincent "Marse Joe" McCarthy found his niche as a manager and became one of the greatest of all time. McCarthy was brought up from the minor leagues to manage the Cubs in 1926. He led the Cubs to a pennant in 1929, though they lost the World Series. Fired by the Cubs with four games left in the 1930 campaign, he immediately signed with the New York Yankees. He managed the Yankees to eight pennants and seven World Series championships in the next 14 years. McCarthy was dropped by the Yankees during the 1946 season. He managed the Boston Red Sox in 1948, 1949, and part of the 1950 season before retiring.

Robin Evan Roberts

Pitcher
Cubs: 1966
Major leagues: 1948–66
Elected: 1976
Birthplace: Springfield, Illinois
B: September 30, 1926
Bats both, throws right

	W	L	Pct	ERA	G	CG	IP	H	BB	K	ShO
Cubs	2	3	.400	6.14	11	1	48⅓	62	11	28	0
Career	286	245	.539	3.41	676	305	4,688⅔	4,582	902	2,357	45

The all-time leader in most Philadelphia Phillies pitching categories, Robin Evan Roberts finished his career with the Cubs by pitching for them in the last half of the 1966 season. Roberts won 20 or more games six consecutive seasons (1950–55) for the Phillies, and he was 28–7 in 1952. Robbie led the National League in victories four consecutive seasons (1952–55) and in strikeouts five consecutive seasons (1952–56), with a peak strikeout total of 324 in 1953. He was named Major League Player of the Year in 1952 and three times was honored as the major leagues' outstanding pitcher. Roberts set an NL record for most seasons as opening-game pitcher for his team (13)—1950 through 1961 (Philadelphia), 1966 (Houston).

Albert Goodwill Spalding

Pitcher–manager–owner
White Stockings: 1876–78 (player-manager)
Major leagues: 1876–78
Elected: 1939
Birthplace: Byron, Illinois
B: September 2, 1850
D: September 9, 1915
Batted right, threw right

	W	L	Pct	ERA	G	CG	IP	H	BB	K	ShO
White Stockings	48	13	.787	1.78	65	53	593⅔	559	26	41	8
Career	48	13	.787	1.78	65	53	593⅔	559	26	41	8

	G	W	L	T	ND	Pct
White Stockings	126	78	47	1	0	.624
Career	126	78	47	1	0	.624

No man had a greater influence in establishing the Cubs (White Stockings) and the National League than Albert Goodwill Spalding as pitcher, manager, and eventual principal owner of the team. Al Spalding also was the greatest pitcher of his time, the game's first 20-game winner. He was a star even before the foundation of the NL in 1876, pitching all games played by Boston of the National Association in 1871 and 1874. He won 24 consecutive games in 1875 and pitched the first one-hit game, June 27, 1871. He led the White Stockings to their first pennant in 1876 as manager and pitcher, the latter with a record of 47–13 while batting .312. An arm injury forced Spalding from the mound in 1877, but he managed the team one more season before concentrating on front-office duties. He later acquired controlling interest in the team, at the same time building a major sporting goods business, A. G. Spalding & Bros.

Joseph Bert Tinker

Shortstop–manager
Cubs: 1902–1912, 1916 (player-manager)
Major leagues: 1902–16 (player)
Elected: 1946
Birthplace: Muscotah, Kansas
B: July 27, 1880
D: July 27, 1948
Batted right, threw right

	G	AB	H	AVG	RBI	R	2B	3B	HR	SLG	SB
Cubs	1,538	5,554	1,454	.262	670	669	221	93	28	.350	304
Career	1,805	6,441	1,695	.263	782	773	264	114	31	.354	336

	G	W	L	T	ND	Pct
Cubs	156	67	86	3	0	.438
Career	626	304	308	12	2	.497

Joseph Bert Tinker's fame rests partly on the verse by Franklin P. Adams that immortalized the great Cub infield of the early 1900s: "Tinker to Evers to Chance, trio of bear cubs and fleeter than birds . . ." But he was doubtless a fine shortstop on the great teams that won four NL pennants in five seasons (1906–08, 1910). A thinking man's infielder, Joe Tinker was a modest hitter (.263 for 15 seasons) and fine base stealer (336 career). After 11 seasons with the Cubs, Tinker was traded to Cincinnati, for whom he was player-manager in 1913. He jumped to the Federal League in 1914 to manage the Chicago Whales for two seasons. He returned to the Cubs in 1916, benched himself, and led the team to a fifth-place finish in the conclusion of his major league career.

George Edward Waddell

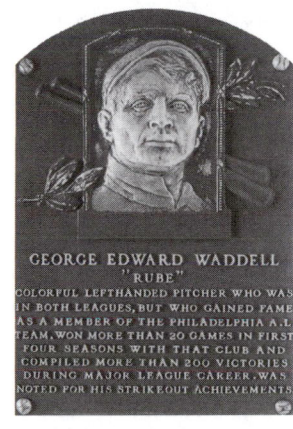

Pitcher
Cubs: 1901
Major leagues: 1897, 1899–1910
Elected: 1946
Birthplace: Bradford, Pennsylvania
B: October 13, 1876
D: April 1, 1914
Batted right, threw left

	W	L	Pct	ERA	G	CG	IP	H	BB	K	ShO
Cubs	13	15	.464	2.81	29	26	243⅔	239	66	168	0
Career	191	145	.568	2.16	407	261	2,961⅓	2,460	803	2,316	50

Rube Waddell's connection with the Cubs was brief, less than one season. He had a 13–15 record for them in 1901 after being acquired by purchase from Pittsburgh, then left the team. George Edward "Rube" Waddell, the prototype of the traditional "flaky" left-hander, joined Philadelphia of the young American League in 1902 with the season half gone, yet compiled a 24–7 record in the first of four consecutive years in which he was a 20-game winner. He struck out 349 batters (then a major league record) in 1904 when he went 25–19, and in 1905 he led AL pitchers in wins with a 26–11 mark and in earned run average with 1.48. Extraordinarily eccentric and undependable, but the possessor of a great fastball and curve, Waddell struck out 10 or more batters in 60 of his 340 starts, with a one-game high of 16. He led the NL in strikeouts once and the AL six times.

James Hoyt Wilhelm

JAMES HOYT WILHELM
NEW YORK N.L., 1952-1956 ST. LOUIS N.L., 1957
CLEVELAND A.L., 1957-1958 BALTIMORE A.L., 1958-1962
CHICAGO A.L., 1963-1968 CALIFORNIA A.L., 1969
ATLANTA N.L., 1969-1970, 1971 CHICAGO N.L., 1970
LOS ANGELES N.L., 1971-1972
BASEBALL'S PREMIER RELIEF PITCHER. USED KNUCKLE
BALL TO WIN 143 GAMES (A RECORD 124 IN RELIEF)
AND AMASSED 227 SAVES OVER 21-YEAR CAREER.
NO-HIT YANKEES ON SEPT. 20, 1958 IN INFREQUENT
START FOR ORIOLES. PITCHED IN RECORD 1070
GAMES WITH LIFETIME ERA OF 2.52.

Pitcher
Cubs: 1970
Major leagues: 1952–72
Elected: 1985
Birthplace: Huntersville, North Carolina
B: July 26, 1923
Bats right, throws right

	W	L	Pct	ERA	G	SV	IP	H	BB	K	ShO
Cubs	0	1	.000	9.82	3	0	3⅔	4	3	1	0
Career	143	122	.540	2.52	1,070	227	2,254	1,757	778	1,610	5

Hoyt Wilhelm spent less than two weeks of his 21-year major league career in a Cub uniform, compiling an 0–1 record in three relief appearances at the end of the 1970 season. One of the greatest of relievers, relying chiefly on a knuckleball, James Hoyt Wilhelm appeared in a total of 1,070 games, more than any pitcher in the game's history. As a rookie with the New York Giants in 1952, he went 15–3 and earned 11 saves in 71 relief appearances. He led the National League in percentage with .833 and in earned run average with 2.43. He was occasionally used as a starter, particularly in 1959 with Baltimore, when he was 15–11 with 27 starts and five relief appearances, and led the American League in earned run average with 2.19. He pitched for nine teams during his career, which ended at the age of 48 in 1972. He finished with a record of 143–122 and 227 saves.

Billy Leo Williams

BILLY LEO WILLIAMS
CHICAGO, N.L., 1959-1974
OAKLAND, A.L., 1975-1976
SOFT-SPOKEN, CLUTCH PERFORMER WAS ONE OF
MOST RESPECTED HITTERS OF HIS DAY. BATTED SOLID
.290 OVER 18 SEASONS SOCKING 426 HOME RUNS. HIT 20
OR MORE HOMERS 13 STRAIGHT SEASONS. 1961 N.L.
ROOKIE OF YEAR. 1972 N.L. BATTING CHAMPION WITH
.333. HELD N.L. RECORD FOR CONSECUTIVE GAMES
PLAYED WITH 1117.

Outfielder
Cubs: 1959–74
Major leagues: 1959–76
Elected: 1987
Birthplace: Whistler, Alabama
B: June 15, 1938
Bats left, throws right

	G	AB	H	AVG	RBI	R	2B	3B	HR	SLG	SB
Cubs	2,213	8,479	2,510	.296	1,354	1,306	402	87	392	.503	86
Career	2,488	9,350	2,711	.290	1,475	1,410	434	88	426	.492	90

Durable and dependable, Billy Williams was a solid fixture in left field for the Cubs from 1960 into the mid-1970s. He set a National League record (since surpassed by Steve Garvey) by playing 1,117 consecutive games from September 22, 1963, to September 3, 1970. A powerful left-handed batter, known for his "sweet swing," Williams hit 20 or more home runs for 13 consecutive seasons, topping 30 five times during that span. His career high was 42 in 1970. He batted over .300 five times, scored 100 or more runs five times, and batted in more than 100 runs in three seasons. In 1970, Williams batted .322 with 42 home runs and 129 RBIs, tied for the league lead in hits with 205, and led in runs scored with 137, the highest NL total in 38 years. In 1972 he led the league in batting with .333, hit 37 home runs, and drove in 122 runs. He was named NL Rookie of the Year in 1961.

Lewis Robert Wilson

LEWIS ROBERT WILSON
"HACK"
NEW YORK N.L., CHICAGO N.L.,
BROOKLYN N.L., PHILADELPHIA N.L.
1923-1934
ESTABLISHED MAJOR LEAGUE RECORD OF 190
RUNS BATTED IN AND NATIONAL LEAGUE HIGH
OF 56 HOMERS IN 1930. LED OR TIED FOR N.L.
HOMER TITLE FOUR TIMES. COMPILED LIFETIME
.307 BATTING AVERAGE AND DROVE IN 100 OR
MORE RUNS SIX YEARS. HIT TWO HOMERS IN
INNING IN 1925 AND THREE IN GAME IN 1930.

Outfielder
Cubs: 1926–31
Major leagues: 1923–34
Elected: 1979
Birthplace: Ellwood City, Pennsylvania
B: April 26, 1900
D: November 23, 1948
Batted right, threw right

	G	AB	H	AVG	RBI	R	2B	3B	HR	SLG	SB
Cubs	850	3,154	1,027	.326	768	652	185	44	190	.593	34
Career	1,348	4,760	1,461	.307	1,062	884	266	67	244	.545	52

A barrel-chested stump of a man at 5–6 and 190 pounds, Lewis Robert "Hack" Wilson for several seasons was the Babe Ruth of the National League. He set two records that haven't been surpassed in almost 70 years: His 190 runs batted in for the Cubs in 1930 still stand as the major league mark, and no NL batter has topped his 56 home runs that season. During his six seasons (1926–31) as a Cub, Wilson led the NL in home runs four times and in RBIs twice. In 1929 he helped the Cubs to a pennant by batting .345 with 39 home runs and 159 RBIs, and in 1930 he batted .356, and led the league in slugging average with .723, along with his 56 home runs and 190 RBIs. Wilson had a strong throwing arm and was a fine outfielder, usually playing center field for the Cubs.

Media in the Hall of Fame

In addition to the players, managers, and owners connected with the Cubs since their birth in 1876, 10 members of the news media have been honored with inclusion in the Hall of Fame. They are Chicago-area sportswriters and radio and television broadcasters who covered the team with distinction for many years.

The recipients of the J. G. Taylor Spink Award and of the Ford C. Frick Award are enshrined in the Hall of Fame at Cooperstown, New York, along with the players, managers, owners, and umpires whose careers and achievements they have chronicled in the print and in the electronic media.

J.G. Taylor Spink Award

Named in honor of the late publisher of *The Sporting News,* the award was established in 1962 by the Baseball Writers' Association of America to recognize meritorious contributions to baseball by members of the BBWAA.

Chicago-area recipients and their year of induction into the Hall of Fame are Ring Lardner (1963), Hugh Fullerton (1964), Charles Dryden (1965), Warren Brown (1973), John Carmichael (1974), Edgar Munzel (1977), and Jerome Holtzman (1990).

Ford C. Frick Award

Named for the late Ford C. Frick, who was a pioneer broadcaster before becoming National League president and then baseball commissioner, this award was established in 1978 by the Hall of Fame to honor broadcasters for meritorious service to baseball and their profession.

The Chicago-area recipients and their year of induction into the Hall of Fame are Bob Elson (1979), Jack Brickhouse (1983), and Harry Caray (1989).

8

The Postseason

No team has suffered through as extended an absence from World Series play as the Cubs, whose last appearance came as the United States celebrated the end of World War II in 1945. Not even the habitually abject St. Louis Browns, who entered the American League in 1902 and made their only World Series appearance 42 years later, in 1944 (then fled to Baltimore in 1954), labored so long in baseball's vineyards without quaffing the champagne of pennant joy.

Paradoxically, few teams have played in as many World Series—though with minimal success—as the Cubs, who dipped into the well 10 times between 1906 and 1945 and came up smiling only twice, in 1907 and 1908. By 1996 only nonagerians could boast of having lived when the Cubs ruled the baseball world, and almost all who merely saw them play in a World Series had begun collecting Social Security benefits.

Five decades of frustration have moderated the expectations, if not the enthusiasm, of Cub fans. Twice since the advent of divisional play in the National League in 1969 they have been brought to the brink of ecstasy as the Cubs approached within one step of a World Series appearance. Each time, in 1984 and 1989, their heroes fell short, losing in the NL Championship Series.

Postseason play may have come early and often to the Cubs, from the birth of the World Series in 1903 until 1945, but it proved a rare treat in the half century that followed.

World Series of 1906 versus Chicago White Sox

In Frank Chance's first full season as manager, the Cubs savaged the NL in 1906, winning 116 of 152 games to set a major league record that still stands. They picked up steam as the season progressed, winning 26 games and losing three in August, then 24 of 29 to close the campaign 20 games ahead of the second-place New York Giants. They seemed unbeatable after a 50–8 stretch drive.

Meanwhile, the White Sox, managed by Fielder Jones, clawed their way to the AL pennant, finishing just three games ahead of the New York Highlanders (later Yankees) with a 93–58 record, largely because of a 19-game winning streak in August. Their woeful team batting average of .230 earned them the label "Hitless Wonders," though a superb pitching staff headed by Frank Owen (22–13), Nick Altrock (20–13), Doc White (18–6), and Ed Walsh (17–13) made the most of the few runs they were able to score.

Baseball fever gripped Chicago for the "dream" World Series between the South Side White Sox and West Side Cubs (who were a decade away from moving to the North Side from the West Side Grounds), though it seemed a mismatch. The gamblers installed the Cubs as 3–1 favorites, with what seemed good reason.

The highest batting average of any White Sox player had been that of second baseman Frank Isbell at .279, while three Cubs (first baseman Chance at .319, third baseman Harry Steinfeldt at .327, and catcher Johnny Kling at .312) had batted over .300. Shortstop Joe Tinker and second baseman Johnny Evers rounded out a legendary double-play combi-

nation with Chance. Mordecai "Three-Finger" Brown (26–6), Jack Pfiester (20–8), Ed Reulbach (19–4), and Carl Lundgren (17–4) headed one of the finest pitching staffs of all time.

Ominously—as it seemed—for the Sox, a late-season injury sidelined veteran shortstop George Davis. Manager–center fielder Jones plugged the hole by moving third baseman Lee Tannehill to short and installing George Rohe, a utility infielder who had batted .258 in 75 games, at third base. The move proved to be a lucky stroke of genius.

Game One

Snow flurries harried a crowd of 12,693 at the Cubs' West Side Grounds on October 9 as Altrock outpitched Brown, each allowing four hits. Rohe tripled in the fifth inning and put the White Sox ahead when Brown picked up an easy roller and threw poorly to Kling for an error. Each team scored a run in the sixth, but that was it. **White Sox 2, Cubs 1.**

Game Two

It was even colder the next day at South Side Park, with a crowd of 12,595, but the Cubs got hot, and Reulbach pitched a one-hitter, yielding a single to Jiggs Donahue in the seventh inning. Steinfeldt went 3-for-3, and Tinker collected two hits and scored three runs. The Cubs scored three runs against Walsh in the second inning and went on from there. **Cubs 7, White Sox 1.**

Gabby Hartnett crosses the plate after hitting his legendary "Homer in the Gloamin'" that propelled the Cubs into the 1938 World Series.

Game Three

A crowd of 13,667 turned out at West Side Grounds on October 11 to witness Walsh stop the Cubs with a two-hit shutout and 12 strikeouts. He yielded a single to Solly Hofman and a double to Frank Schulte in the first inning, then held the Cubs hitless. Rohe struck again, his bases-loaded triple in the sixth inning off Pfiester accounting for all the runs. **White Sox 3, Cubs 0.**

Game Four

Interest surged, and 18,385 turned out at South Side Park the next day for an exceptional pitching duel in which Brown defeated Altrock to even the Series at 2–2. Brown held the Sox to two hits, and the Cubs scored the lone run in the seventh. Chance singled, reached second on Steinfeldt's sacrifice, and scored on a single to left by Evers. **Cubs 1, White Sox 0.**

Game Five

On October 13 the largest crowd of the Series, 23,257 at West Side Grounds, watched the "Hitless Wonders" pummel Reulbach and the Cubs with 12 hits. The crowd overflowed onto the outfield grass, necessitating a two-base rule on balls batted among the spectators. Isbell paced the Sox with four doubles, George Davis batted in three runs, hitting one double left-handed and one double right-handed, and

Rohe went 3-for-4 as the Sox drove Reulbach from the mound in the third inning after the Cubs tagged Walsh for three runs in the first. The Sox took command in the fourth when they scored four runs. **White Sox 8, Cubs 6.**

Game Six

With a crowd estimated at 25,000 in South Side Park, though officially counted at 19,249 (police allegedly tore boards off the fences and let fans in at a dollar a head), the Sox wrapped up the Series four games to two on October 14. They scored three runs off Brown in the first inning, then added four in the second as White contained the Cubs. Davis again drove in three runs, as did Donahue; Rohe contributed two more hits; and leadoff man Eddie Hahn went 4-for-5. **White Sox 8, Cubs 3.**

The White Sox had pulled off what must still be regarded as the greatest upset in World Series history, though they batted only .198 as a team. Mostly instrumental in their victory was the solid pitching of Altrock, Walsh, and White, but the unexpected offensive contribution of the lightly regarded Rohe, who with Donahue led the White Sox batters with .333 average, made the difference.

The Cubs flopped chiefly because they failed to bat up to their season standards, hitting only .196 as a team. Chance did not drive in a run in six games; left fielder Jimmy Sheckard had 21 at bats without a hit; and Tinker, Evers, and Kling had just nine hits in 55 at bats (.164).

World Series of 1907 versus Detroit Tigers

Chastened by their experience of 1906, which may have been partly due to overconfidence, the Cubs were determined to redeem themselves at the expense of the Detroit Tigers in 1907. They had again crushed the NL, winning 107 games and finishing 17 games ahead of the Pittsburgh Pirates, and their roster of 1906 was virtually intact.

Orval Overall had emerged as the ace of the pitching staff with a 23–6 record, Mordecai Brown was 20–6, Carl Lundgren 18–7, Jack Pfiester 15–9, and Ed Reulbach 17–4. Oddly, no batter had reached .300.

The Tigers had 20-year-old sensation Ty Cobb, who had won the first of nine consecutive AL batting championships with .350, and Sam "Wahoo" Crawford, who batted .323, as their offensive spearheads. Ed Killian (23–13), George Mullin (20–20), Eddie Siever (18–11), and Wild Bill Donovan (25–4) led a respectable pitching staff. The Tigers had won 92 games to finish 1½ games ahead of the Philadelphia Athletics.

As in 1906, the Cubs were favored, though some critics recalled how they had trouble with left-handers Nick Altrock and Doc White in 1906, and both Siever and Killian of the Tigers were lefties. As it turned out, there was no cause for concern, the Cubs achieving what in essence was a sweep, though Game 1 was a tie.

Game One

West Side Grounds had been enlarged with bleachers, and 24,377 filled the seats on October 8 as the Tigers took a 3–1 lead into the ninth inning behind Donovan. Detroit had scored three runs off Overall in the eighth, with Crawford driving in a pair. The Cubs finally got to

Donovan, and had runners on third and second with a run in and two out when Del Howard pinch-hit for Joe Tinker. Donovan struck out Howard, but the third strike got away from catcher Charlie Schmidt, and Harry Steinfeldt scored the game-tying run. It was the final run of the game, which was called because of darkness after 12 innings. The Cubs stole seven bases off the hapless Schmidt. **Tigers 3, Cubs 3.**

Game Two

The next day, Pfiester scattered nine hits before 21,901 at West Side Grounds as the Cubs broke a 1–1 tie with two runs in the fourth inning off Mullin. They scored on a single by Jimmy Slagle and a double by Jimmy Sheckard. The Cubs stole five more bases off Schmidt's replacement, Fred Payne. **Cubs 3, Tigers 1.**

Game Three

The West Side Grounds crowd dwindled to 13,114 on October 10 as Reulbach held the Tigers to six hits and a sixth-inning run, batted in by Crawford. The Cubs knocked Siever out after four innings, with Evers contributing three hits. **Cubs 5, Tigers 1.**

Game Four

On October 11, intermittent showers held the crowd to 11,306 in Detroit's Bennett Park, with a rain delay in the fifth inning. Overall pitched a five-hitter to master Donovan again, and the Cubs scored three runs in the seventh without hitting the ball out of the infield. Steinfeldt and Sheckard each had two hits. **Cubs 6, Tigers 1.**

Game Five

Only 7,370 turned out at Bennett Park on October 12, with the Tigers down three games to none in the Series, and Brown applied the finishing touch for the Cubs. He shut out Detroit on seven hits, with Steinfeldt leading the offense with a 3-for-4 day, including an RBI single in the first. **Cubs 2, Tigers 0.**

The sweep of the Tigers demonstrated that despite the upset by the White Sox in 1906 the Cubs were baseball's pre-eminent team. Their pitchers held the Tigers scoreless in 43 of 48 innings in the Series, they stole 18 bases, and their offense hit its stride. Steinfeldt batted .471 and Evers .350 in the five games. Cobb managed only .200, and Crawford was held to .238.

World Series of 1908 versus Detroit Tigers

Unlike the previous two seasons, when the Cubs romped to pennants, they were lucky to make it in 1908, though they won 99 games. They were able to force a postseason one-game playoff victory, 4–2, over New York because of the famous Fred Merkle incident in a September 23 game in which the Giants' first baseman failed to touch second while the apparent winning run was scoring.

All the same, they showed the Tigers they were as formidable as ever, with Frank Chance leading much the same cast to the Cubs' third consecutive NL pennant and second straight World Series victory, almost as easily as in 1907.

Game One

On October 10, the Bennett Field crowd of 10,812 scented victory as the game entered the ninth inning with the Tigers leading 6–5. But the Cubs pounded out six consecutive hits after Ed Summers, in relief, retired the first batter. Solly Hofman drove in two of the Cubs' five runs with a bases-loaded single. Jimmy Sheckard and Johnny Evers each had three hits. **Cubs 10, Tigers 6.**

Game Two

The game originally had been scheduled for Detroit, but because October 11 was a Sunday and the Cubs' park had more than twice the crowd capacity of Bennett Field, it was switched to Chicago. Orval Overall held the Tigers to four hits before a crowd of 17,760. The Cubs broke the game open with six runs in the eighth off Wild Bill Donovan. Joe Tinker had driven in the first two with a home run. **Cubs 6, Tigers 1.**

Game Three

The next day, the Tigers overcame a 3–1 Cub lead with five runs in the sixth off Jack Pfiester. Ty Cobb led the attack with four hits and two runs batted in. George Mullin held the Cubs to seven hits before 14,543 at West Side Grounds. **Tigers 8, Cubs 3.**

Game Four

Three-Finger Brown shut out the Tigers on four hits before 12,907 at Bennett Field as the Cubs took a 3–1 Series lead on October 13. The Cubs had 10 hits, nine off Summers and one off reliever George Winter in a succession of pitchers worthy of a trivia question. Chance, Harry Steinfeldt, and Hofman drove in the runs. **Cubs 3, Tigers 0.**

Game Five

Only 6,210 showed up at Bennett Field on October 14 as the Cubs wrapped up the Series, Overall shutting out the Tigers on three hits and striking out 10. The Cubs scored on Donovan in the first inning. Chance and Evers each had three hits and a run batted in. **Cubs 2, Tigers 0.**

The Cubs had become the first team to enjoy back-to-back Series victories, as well as the first in modern history (since 1900) to win three consecutive pennants.

World Series of 1910 versus Philadelphia Athletics

Despite winning 104 games in 1909, Frank Chance's Cubs finished second by 6½ games behind the Pittsburgh Pirates. But they won 104 again in 1910 and captured their fourth pennant in five years, having averaged 106 victories a season during that stretch. They faced Connie Mack's Philadelphia Athletics in the World Series.

The core of the team was largely unchanged, though age and ailments had slowed some of the players. Johnny Evers was injured and replaced by Heinie Zimmerman. Most altered was the pitching staff, though Mordecai Brown (25–13) was still the kingpin, ably seconded by sensational rookie Leonard "King" Cole (20–4).

The A's boasted a trio of .300 hitters in second baseman Eddie Collins and outfielders Rube Oldring and Danny Murphy. Jack Coombs (31–9) and Chief Bender (23–5) were the aces of a pitching staff that had helped the A's win 102 games.

Coombs and Bender were enough; they pitched every inning of the Series.

The veteran Cubs were slightly favored over the young A's.

Game One

At Philadelphia on October 17, Bender held the Cubs to one hit through eight innings, by which time the A's had a 4–0 lead. They got to Orval Overall for three runs and six hits in the first three innings. Frank "Home Run" Baker went 3-for-4 with two RBIs to support Bender, who gave up a run in the ninth and three hits altogether. **Athletics 4, Cubs 1.**

Game Two

The A's followed up next day by pounding Brown for nine runs and 13 hits in seven innings. Murphy's two-run double was the highlight of a six-run seventh. Coombs staggered to a home-team victory despite yielding eight hits and nine walks. **Athletics 9, Cubs 3.**

Game Three

In Chicago on October 20, the A's hammered Ed Reulbach and the bullpen with 15 hits to take a 3–0 lead in the Series, a five-run third inning breaking a 3–3 tie. Murphy's three-run home run led the assault. Coombs, coming back on one day of rest after winning Game 2, held the Cubs to six hits. **Athletics 12, Cubs 5.**

Game Four

It took them 10 innings, but the Cubs averted a sweep October 22 as Brown picked up the victory in relief of Cole. A double by Jimmy Archer and a single by Jimmy Sheckard broke the tie in the 10th inning. Frank Chance batted in two runs, including one in the ninth when he tripled home Frank Schulte to send the game into extra innings. **Cubs 4, Athletics 3.**

Game Five

On October 23, still in Chicago, Coombs won his third game of the Series as the A's disposed of Brown with a five-run eighth inning to break open a pitching duel and capture the championship. Collins went 3-for-5 with two RBIs. **Athletics 7, Cubs 2.**

The World Series defeat in five games signaled the end of the Cubs' greatest era as the team began to disintegrate. Chance led the team to a second-place finish in 1911, then a third in 1912, before moving on to the New York Yankees.

Infielder Heinie Zimmerman (left) and catcher Jimmy Archer prior to the 1910 World Series

World Series of 1918 versus Boston Red Sox

World War I was in its final months when the 1918 season was curtailed on Labor Day by U.S. government edict. The Cubs were on top of the NL with an 84–45 record, which entitled them to return to the World Series for the first time in eight years.

Although decimated like other teams by the military draft and other wartime restrictions on manpower, the Cubs were more than respectable. Hippo Vaughn won 20 games, and Claude Hendrix and Lefty Tyler each won 19. Manager Fred Mitchell's best hitter was shortstop Charlie Hollocher at .316, and he had able veterans in right fielder Max Flack, catcher Bill Killefer, and first baseman Fred Merkle (of 1908 fame).

But Boston had Babe Ruth, both as ace left-handed pitcher and slugging outfielder, as well as pitchers Carl Mays (21–13), Sad Sam Jones (16–5), and Bullet Joe Bush (15–15). Ruth was 13–7 on the mound and batted .300 with 11 home runs (to tie for the AL lead) in 317 at bats.

Because of its greater capacity, the Cubs switched their home games to Comiskey Park from what was later to be called Wrigley Field, which they had taken over in 1916. Wrigley Field was to wait another 11 years for its first World Series game.

Game One

In one of the great pitching duels in Series history (September 5, at Chicago), Ruth bested Vaughn, giving up just five hits. He extended his shutout streak to 22 innings, having pitched 13 consecutive shutout innings in his only previous Series appearance in 1916. Stuffy McInnis drove in the only run of the game in the fourth inning. Vaughn held the Red Sox to six hits. **Red Sox 1, Cubs 0.**

Game Two

The next day, Tyler not only limited the Red Sox to six hits and one run, but also drove in two of the three Cub runs in the third inning with a single off Bush to even the Series at one victory apiece. **Cubs 3, Red Sox 1.**

Game Three

Continuing the pitching domination in the third game played at Chicago, September 7, Mays held the Cubs to seven hits, beating Vaughn, who gave up the same number. The Cubs' final out came when Charlie Pick was caught in a rundown between third and home while trying to score from second base on a passed ball. **Red Sox 2, Cubs 1.**

Game Four

In Boston on September 9, the Red Sox extended their Series lead to 3–1 and Ruth extended his shutout streak to 29⅔ innings before the Cubs scored twice in the eighth to gain a 2–2 tie. A wild throw on a bunt by pitcher Phil Douglas, who had relieved starter Tyler, allowed Boston to score the eventual winning run in the bottom half of the eighth. Ruth got the win, as well as his first Series hit, a two-run triple in the fourth. **Red Sox 3, Cubs 2.**

Game Five

Vaughn kept the Cubs alive one more day with a five-hit shutout. The Cubs scored a run in the third on a double by Leslie Mann and two in the eighth on a double by Dode Paskert to beat Jones. **Cubs 3, Red Sox 0.**

Game Six

Tyler pitched valiantly, with just one day of rest on September 11, but Mays was even better, holding the Cubs to three hits as the Red Sox won the Series at home. The Red Sox scored their two runs in the third when right fielder Max Flack dropped a line drive by George Whiteman with two men on base. **Red Sox 2, Cubs 1.**

World Series of 1929 versus Philadelphia Athletics

After an 11-year absence from the World Series, the Cubs brought it to a recently renovated and enlarged Wrigley Field in 1929 with one of the hardest-hitting teams of all time, led by center fielder Hack Wilson (.354 with 39 home runs and 159 RBIs) and second baseman Rogers Hornsby (.380, 39 home runs, 149 RBIs).

Other big guns were left fielder Riggs Stephenson (.362, 17 home runs, 110 RBIs), right fielder Kiki Cuyler (.360, 15 home runs, 102 RBIs), and first baseman Charlie Grimm (.298, 10 home runs, 91 RBIs). Rookie manager Joe McCarthy relied for his pitching chiefly on Charlie Root (19–6), Guy Bush (18–7), and Pat Malone (22–10).

Connie Mack's Philadelphia Athletics were similarly loaded, with slugging left fielder Al Simmons (.365, 34 home runs, 157 RBIs), first baseman Jimmie Foxx (.354, 33 home runs, 117 RBIs), and catcher Mickey Cochrane (.331, 7 home runs, and 91 RBIs) leading the offense. Lefty Grove (20–6), Rube Walberg (18–11), and George Earnshaw (24–8) anchored a solid pitching staff.

Yet Mack had a surprise up his sleeve.

Outfielder Riggs Stephenson prior to the 1929 World Series

Game One

With an overflow crowd of 50,740 at Wrigley Field, Mack passed up his ace pitchers on October 8 to start Howard Ehmke, a 35-year-old veteran who had won just seven games all season. Ehmke struck out 13 Cubs for a Series record and scattered eight hits. A home run by Foxx off Root in the seventh inning put the A's ahead to stay, and they added two runs in the ninth. **Athletics 3, Cubs 1.**

Game Two

Earnshaw faced Malone the next day, but it was quickly no contest. Foxx hit a three-run home run in the third inning, and the A's added three runs in the fourth. Simmons also hit a home run. Earnshaw and Grove combined to strike out another 13 Cubs. **Athletics 9, Cubs 3.**

Game Three

In Philadelphia on October 11, Bush outpitched Earnshaw, scattering nine hits, to put the Cubs back into contention. Hornsby and Wilson each had two hits, and Cuyler drove in two runs. **Cubs 3, Athletics 1.**

Game Four

Next day the Cubs appeared en route to tying the Series with an 8–0 lead in the eighth inning behind Root. Grimm hit a two-run homer in the fourth, then a five-run outburst in the sixth drove out A's starter Jack Quinn. A lead-off home run in the eighth by Simmons sparked a 10-run rally by the A's that reached its apogee when center fielder Wilson lost a line drive in the sun. The hit by Mule Haas turned into an inside-the-park homer with two men on to make it 8–7. The decisive blow was a two-run double by Jimmy Dykes. **Athletics 10, Cubs 8.**

Game Five

Ehmke started again, October 14, this time against Malone, but the visiting Cubs got to him for two runs in the fourth inning. Malone held the A's to two hits in eight innings, but the A's rallied for three runs in the ninth, Bing Miller driving in the Series-winning run with a single. **Athletics 3, Cubs 2.**

World Series of 1932 versus New York Yankees

Joe McCarthy, who had managed the Cubs to a pennant in 1929, guided the New York Yankees of Babe Ruth and Lou Gehrig to the World Series confrontation with extra satisfaction three years later, having been fired in 1930 by Chicago.

A late-season push by the Cubs, after manager Rogers Hornsby had been replaced by Charlie Grimm on August 5 with the team in second place, put them across four games ahead of the Pittsburgh Pirates. The Yankees had dominated the AL, winning 107 games to finish 13 games ahead of the Philadelphia Athletics.

Ruth had enjoyed his last big season, hitting .341 with 41 home runs and 137 RBIs. Gehrig had contributed .349, 34 home runs, and 151 RBIs. Lefty Gomez (24–7), Red Ruffing (18–7), George Pipgras (16–9), and Johnny Allen (17–4) were the heart of a superb pitching staff.

The Cubs had lost most of their power with Hornsby and Wilson gone. Center fielder Johnny Moore led the team with 13 home runs while batting .305, and Riggs Stephenson led with 85 RBIs while hitting .324. A new double-play combination of second baseman Billy Herman (.314) and shortstop Billy Jurges (.253) stood out. Young Lon Warneke (22–6) was the ace of the starting rotation, rounded out with veterans Guy Bush (19–11), Charlie Root (15–10), and Pat Malone (15–17).

Whatever the Cubs had, it fell short of Ruth and Gehrig, who dominated the Series—particularly Ruth with the alleged "called shot" home run that made it memorable.

Shortstop Mark Koenig, acquired from the Yankees late in the 1932 season, wasn't given a full World Series share by his teammates.

Game One

At New York on September 28, Bush faced Ruffing on the mound, and the Cubs took a 2–0 lead in the first inning. But Gehrig struck with a two-run homer in the fourth, and the rout was on. The Yankees scored five more in the sixth, and though the Cubs hit Ruffing hard, Stephenson driving in three runs with three hits, he weathered the storm. **Yankees 12, Cubs 6.**

Game Two

Next day, Gomez proved too tough for Warneke and the Cubs, Gehrig contributing three more hits and an RBI. Stephenson and Frank Demaree drove in Cub runs in the first and third. **Yankees 5, Cubs 2.**

Game Three

Almost 50,000 overflowed Wrigley Field on October 1, most of them apparently to taunt Ruth, who had smashed a three-run homer off Root in the first inning. With the game tied at 4 in the fourth, and the crowd and Cub players howling at Ruth, he allegedly pointed toward center field, then hit a home run to put the Yankees ahead 5–4. The Yankees went on to give Pipgras a 7–5 victory, and in the clamor over Ruth's "called shot" it was almost unnoticed that Gehrig also had hit two home runs in the game. **Yankees 7, Cubs 5.**

Game Four

The Yankees knocked out Bush in the first inning on October 2, scoring a run, but the Cubs disposed of Allen in the home half when Demaree hit a three-run homer to cap a four-run burst. The 4–1 Cub lead vanished quickly, with the Yankees storming back on a pair of two-run homers by Tony Lazzeri and a bases-empty homer by Earle Combs. The Yankees rolled to a Series sweep. **Yankees 13, Cubs 6.**

Gehrig stood out, leading the Yankees with .529, eight RBIs, and three homers, but it was Ruth's disputed gesture that made the Series memorable.

World Series of 1935 versus Detroit Tigers

The Cubs rode a 21-game winning streak in September to a four-game edge over the St. Louis Cardinals in the pennant race. Manager Charlie Grimm had replaced himself at first base with 19-year-old Phil Cavarretta (.275, 8 home runs, 82 RBIs), and Stan Hack (.311, 4 home runs, 64 RBIs) was in the early stage of his long run at third base, with Billy Herman (.341) and Billy Jurges (.241) solidifying an exceptional infield.

Outfielders Chuck Klein (.293, 21 home runs, 73 RBIs) and Augie Galan (.314, 12 home runs, 79 RBIs) and veteran catcher Gabby Hartnett (.344, 13 home runs, 91 RBIs) provided much of the power. Veterans Lon Warneke (20–13) and Charlie Root (15–8) and rising stars Bill Lee (20–6) and Larry French (17–10) led the pitchers.

The Detroit Tigers' long suit was the hitting of Hank Green-

Hall of Fame second baseman Billy Herman played on three pennant-winning Cub teams.

Outfielder Chuck Klein's two-run home run won the fifth game of the 1935 World Series.

berg (.328, 36 home runs, 170 RBIs), Charlie Gehringer (.330, 19 home runs, 108 RBIs), and Mickey Cochrane (.319, 5 home runs, 47 RBIs), as well as a fine pitching rotation of Schoolboy Rowe (19–13), Tommy Bridges (21–10), Eldon Auker (18–7), and Alvin Crowder (16–10).

Game One

At Detroit on October 2, it was all Warneke, as he shut out the Tigers on three hits to defeat Rowe. The Cubs scored twice in the first inning, and Hartnett and Frank Demaree each had two hits. **Cubs 3, Tigers 0.**

Game Two

The next day the home team won. A four-run first inning greeted Root, Greenberg capping the burst with a two-run homer. The Tigers coasted behind Bridges, but Greenberg suffered a broken wrist and was out the rest of the Series. **Tigers 8, Cubs 3.**

Game Three

In Chicago on October 4, Rowe beat French in relief in 11 innings, with Jo-Jo White driving in the winning run on a single. Demaree hit a home run for the Cubs, who scored twice in the ninth to extend the game. **Tigers 6, Cubs 5.**

Game Four

Next day, Crowder held the Cubs to five hits to win a pitching duel over Tex Carleton and give the Tigers a 3–1 Series edge. Hartnett's homer in the second comprised the Cub offense. **Tigers 2, Cubs 1.**

Game Five

Warneke and Lee saved the Cubs from elimination at home, curbing the Tigers on seven hits and outpitching Rowe. Klein's two-run homer in the third was decisive. **Cubs 3, Tigers 1.**

Game Six

In Detroit, October 7, Herman drove in three runs for the Cubs, but they were not enough. With the game tied at 3 in the top of the ninth, Hack tripled to lead off the inning, but he was left stranded when Bridges retired the next three batters. Veteran Goose Goslin's single in the bottom of the ninth scored Cochrane from second base to win the Series for the Tigers. **Tigers 4, Cubs 3.**

Herman led the team in hitting with a .333 average in the six games, and Warneke was 2–0, but the Cubs had lost their fifth consecutive World Series.

World Series of 1938 versus New York Yankees

Gabby Hartnett, whose celebrated "Homer in the Gloamin' " had assured the Cubs of the pennant, had replaced Charlie Grimm as manager in late July and saved what had seemed a lost season.

Much of the 1935 cast was still on hand, including Billy Herman, Bill Jurges, Phil Cavarretta, (now in the outfield), Stan Hack, and Augie Galan. What power the Cubs had was provided by veteran first baseman Rip Collins (.267, 13 home runs, 61 RBIs) and Hartnett (.299, 10 home runs, 59 RBIs). Bill Lee (22–9), Larry French (10–19), Clay Bryant (19–11) and Tex Carleton (10–9) were the heart of a pitching staff bolstered by a damaged Dizzy Dean (7–1).

The Yankees had new stars, such as Joe DiMaggio (.324, 32 home runs, 140 RBIs), Joe Gordon (.255, 25 home runs, 97 RBIs), and Tommy Henrich (.270, 22 home runs, 91 RBIs), but veterans Lou Gehrig (.295, 29 home runs, 114 RBIs) and Bill Dickey (.313, 27 home runs, 115 RBIs) were still formidable. So was their pitching, with Red Ruffing (20–12), Monte Pearson (19–7), and Lefty Gomez (13–7) leading the parade.

The Yankees were going after their third consecutive World Series triumph and achieved it with humiliating ease, brushing the Cubs aside in a four-game sweep.

Game One

At Chicago on October 5, Ruffing stopped the Cubs on three hits, and Dickey went 4-for-4 against Lee, scoring one run and driving in another. **Yankees 3, Cubs 1.**

Game Two

Hartnett gambled the next day, starting the lame-armed Dean, and for a time it seemed as if the wager might pay off. He held the Yankees for seven innings, giving up just three hits, and with a 3–2 lead. But a two-run home run by Frank Crosetti in the eighth broke the trance. **Yankees 6, Cubs 3.**

Game Three

Home runs by Dickey and Gordon backed up Pearson's five-hitter, hurled in New York on October 8. The Cubs' stand-

Manager Gabby Hartnett (left) started lame-armed Dizzy Dean in the second game of the 1938 World Series against the Yankees.

out was reserve outfielder Joe Marty, who went 3-for-4 with a home run and drove in both their runs. **Yankees 5, Cubs 2.**

Game Four

Ruffing checked the Cubs for the second time on eight hits to finish the Series on October 9, the Yankees jumping on Lee for three runs in the fourth inning and going on from there. Crosetti drove in four runs with a double and a triple. **Yankees 8, Cubs 3.**

World Series of 1945 versus Detroit Tigers

World War II had just ended as the Cubs and the Tigers met for the fourth time in a World Series. Both clubs had relied largely on players either overage or physically unfit for military service to win pennants, though some ex-servicemen, like Detroit slugger Hank Greenberg, had rejoined their teams.

Hank Borowy, a midseason acquisition from the New York Yankees (11–2 with Cubs, 10–5 with Yankees), Hank Wyse (22–10), Claude Passeau (17–9), and Paul Derringer (16–11) gave recycled manager Charlie Grimm a good pitching rotation.

Still standouts were veterans of the 1930s, Phil Cavarretta, the NL's Most Valuable Player and batting champion (.355, 6 home runs, 97 RBIs), and Stan Hack (.323). Outfielders Andy Pafko (.298, 12 home runs, 110 RBIs), Bill Nicholson

(.243, 13 home runs, 88 RBIs), and Peanuts Lowrey (.283, 7 home runs, 89 RBIs) rounded out a solid offense.

The Tigers similarly relied on veterans, the most formidable being Greenberg, who had returned for the second half of the season and batted .311 with 13 home runs and 60 RBIs. Rudy York (.264, 18 home runs, 87 RBIs) and Roy Cullenbine (.277, 18 home runs, 93 RBIs) also were dangerous. Hal Newhouser (25–9), Dizzy Trout (18–15), and Al Benton (13–8) gave the Tigers three reliable starting pitchers, and Virgil Trucks, who had won 16 games in 1943, had just returned from service in the navy.

Game One

Borowy was superb at Detroit on October 3, pitching a six-hit shutout, as the Cubs made short work of Newhouser,

The 1945 National League champions

Claude Passeau pitched a one-hitter and drove in one of the three Cub
runs in the third game of the '45 World Series.

knocking him out in the third inning. Nicholson drove in three runs with a triple and a single, and Cavarretta and Pafko each went 3-for-4. Cavarretta hit a home run. **Cubs 9, Tigers 0.**

Game Two

The next day Trucks handcuffed the Cubs on seven hits, with Greenberg contributing a decisive three-run homer off Wyse in the fifth inning. **Tigers 4, Cubs 1.**

Game Three

At Detroit on October 5, Passeau turned in one of the finest pitching performances in Series history, a one-hitter (single by York in second inning), and drove in one of the Cubs' three runs. **Cubs 3, Tigers 0.**

Game Four

In Chicago on October 6, Trout yielded just five hits, and the Tigers knocked out Cub starter Ray Prim with four runs in the fourth inning. **Tigers 4, Cubs 1.**

Game Five

Next day, Greenberg led the Tigers with 3-for-5 and an RBI as Newhouser got even for his Series-opening loss. The Tigers pounded Borowy for eight hits in five innings to take a 3–2 edge in the Series. **Tigers 8, Cubs 4.**

Game Six

At Chicago, October 8, neither starting pitcher, Trucks nor Passeau, was around at the finish as the Cubs tied the Series at 3–3 in a 12-inning game won on a double by Hack that bounced over Greenberg's head in left field to score the winning run. Passeau had a 5–3 lead in the seventh inning but had to leave the game after stopping a smash by Jimmy Outlaw with his bare hand. **Cubs 8, Tigers 7.**

Game Seven

The final game, October 9, was the fourth straight played at Wrigley Field. Though Borowy had pitched four innings of relief in the sixth game, Grimm started him for the third time in the Series, against Newhouser, also making his third start. The Tigers scored five runs in the first inning and coasted. **Tigers 9, Cubs 3.**

The Cubs had lost their seventh consecutive World Series after winning in 1907 and 1908. They now were 2–8 in World Series matchups.

NL Championship Series of 1984 versus San Diego Padres

After a 39-year absence from postseason competition, "Cub Fever" took over Chicago as the city's heroes stormed to an unexpected championship in the six-team NL East Division. They were led by pitcher Rick Sutcliffe, a midseason acquisition from the Cleveland Indians, who went 16–1 for his new team.

Manager Jim Frey fused a combination of rising young players such as Ryne Sandberg (.314, 19 home runs, 84 RBIs and NL MVP), Jody Davis (.256, 19 home runs, 94 RBIs), and Leon Durham (.279, 23 home runs, 96 RBIs) with veterans Ron Cey (.240, 25 home runs, 97 RBIs), Gary Matthews (.291, 18 home runs, 82 RBIs), and Larry Bowa (.223), into a winner.

Hard-throwing reliever Lee Smith (9–7, 33 saves) anchored a decent pitching staff led by Sutcliffe with Steve Trout (13–7), Dennis Eckersley (10–8), and Scott Sanderson (8–5) the other principals.

The Padres coasted to the NL West championship behind such standouts as Tony Gwynn (NL batting champion at .351, 5 home runs, 71 RBIs), Steve Garvey (.284, 8 home runs, 86 RBIs), Graig Nettles (.228, 20 home runs, 65 RBIs), and Kevin McReynolds (.278, 20 home runs, 75 RBIs). Veteran reliever Goose Gossage (10–6, 25 saves) picked up for starters such as Eric Show (15–9), Ed Whitson (14–8), Tim Lollar (11–13), and Mark Thurmond (14–8).

The winner of the best-of-five games Championship Series would represent the NL in the World Series.

Game One

At Chicago on October 2, Sutcliffe and reliever Warren Brusstar combined for a six-hit shutout as the Cubs pounded starter Show and two relievers with five home runs

Third baseman Vance Law's late-season performance was critical in the winning of the 1989 East Division championship.

and 16 hits. Sutcliffe hit a home run, as did Cey and Bob Dernier. Matthews hit two. **Cubs 13, Padres 0.**

Game Two

Next day, the Cubs moved to within one victory of their first World Series appearance since 1945 behind strong pitching by Trout and Smith as they hopped on Padres starter Thurmond in the first inning and knocked him out in the fourth. Sandberg and Keith Moreland each had two hits in the home team's second victory. **Cubs 4, Padres 2.**

Game Three

The series moved to San Diego for the last three games. On October 5, a two-run double by Garry Templeton was the key hit in a three-run Padres fifth inning against Eckersley, and San Diego added four runs in the sixth as Whitson and Gossage stymied the Cubs. McReynolds contributed a three-run homer. **Padres 7, Cubs 1.**

Game Four

Neither of the starters, Sanderson or Lollar, was around by the sixth inning. Davis kept the Cubs in the game with three hits, including a homer, and it went into the bottom of the ninth tied at 5. That's when Garvey, who already had a homer, a double, a single, and three RBIs in the game, followed up a Gwynn single with another home run, off Smith, to tie the Series at 2–2. **Padres 7, Cubs 5.**

Game Five

On October 7, the Cubs took a 3–0 lead behind their ace, Sutcliffe, on a two-run homer by Durham in the first inning and a bases-empty homer by Davis in the second, both off Show. The Padres scored two runs in the sixth. An error by first baseman Durham on a grounder by Tim Flannery with one man on and one out opened the gates in the seventh, San Diego scoring four runs. Gossage closed the door on the Cubs in the final two innings. **Padres 6, Cubs 3.**

The Cubs had appeared to be almost assured of ending their 39-year World Series famine after winning the first two games of the NL Championship Series. But the Padres became the first team ever to recover from a 2-0 deficit and win a best-of-five-games playoff test.

NL Championship Series of 1989 versus San Francisco Giants

The Cubs had changed greatly since 1984, but Rick Sutcliffe (16–11) and Ryne Sandberg (.290, 30 home runs, 76 RBIs) were still key elements as they surprised again by winning the NL East Division title under manager Don Zimmer and renewed hopes they would play in the World Series for the first time in 44 years.

Greg Maddux (19–12), Mike Bielecki (18–7), and Scott Sanderson (11–9) joined Sutcliffe as the big four starters, with Mitch Williams (4–4, 36 saves) as the stopper. Andre Dawson (.252, 21 home runs, 77 RBIs), Mark Grace (.314, 13 home runs, 79 RBIs), and Vance Law (.235, seven home runs, 42 RBIs) were joined by two standout rookie outfielders, Jerome Walton (.293, 5 home runs, 40 RBIs) and Dwight Smith (.324, 9 home runs, 52 RBIs) as offensive standouts.

The San Francisco Giants, champions of the West, seemed to have much more firepower, particularly from Kevin Mitchell (.291, 47 home runs, 125 RBIs) and Will Clark (.333, 23 home runs, 111 RBIs). Ex-Cub Rick Reuschel (17–8), Dave Robinson (12–11), and Scott Garrelts (14–5) were the key men on an adequate pitching staff.

As it happened, what now was a best-of-seven-games series turned into a battle of the first basemen, Grace and Clark.

Game One

On October 4, Clark hit two home runs and Mitchell another as the Giants tore into Maddux in the first postseason night game in Wrigley Field history. Clark went 4-for-4 with four runs scored. The only solace for the Cubs was that Grace and Sandberg each had three hits, including a homer. **Giants 11, Cubs 3.**

Game Two

Grace continued his lusty batting with three more hits, including two doubles that drove in a total of four runs, as the Cubs pounded Reuschel and his four successors. Home runs by Mitchell, Robbie Thompson, and Matt Williams couldn't change the outcome. **Cubs 9, Giants 5.**

Game Three

At San Francisco on October 7, the Cubs took a 4–3 lead into the fourth inning, but Thompson connected for a two-run homer off reliever Les Lancaster to finish the scoring. **Giants 5, Cubs 4.**

Game Four

Maddux was hit hard early again on October 8, but the Cubs battled back to a 4–4 tie with two runs in the fifth inning. However, Matt Williams' two-run homer in the Giants' fifth was decisive, and it gave him four RBIs in the game. **Giants 6, Cubs 4.**

Game Five

At San Francisco, October 9, Bielecki came up with a strong effort against Reuschel to keep the Cubs' hopes alive until the eighth inning. The game was tied at 1 when Bielecki lost his control and walked three consecutive batters. Zimmer replaced him with Mitch Williams, whom Clark greeted with a two-run single. The Cubs scored a run in the ninth, but the Giants held on to win the series 4–1. **Giants 3, Cubs 2.**

The Giants went on to their first World Series appearance in 27 years, since 1962, but the Cubs, who last made it in 1945, would have to go without for many more weary years.

Will Clark and Mark Grace were the standouts. Clark had 13 hits in 20 at bats, for a .650 average, and drove in eight runs. Grace virtually matched him with 11 hits in 17 at bats for .647; he also drove in eight runs.

9

It's Fun, Not War

Joe Garagiola, the onetime Cub catcher who became a noted broadcaster and occasional author, titled one of his books *Baseball Is a Funny Game*. He hit it right on the head in every sense of the word "funny." Almost anything can happen and has in baseball, given the long history of the game.

Baseball's achievements, situations, and occurrences are infinite in variety, sometimes humorous and weird, often unparalleled and even almost incredible, occasionally triumphant or tragic. The same can be said of those who play the game, manage the teams, or call the balls and strikes. They come in all sizes, shapes, temperaments, and gradations of character and ability. There are the "geniuses" and the "flakes," the "naturals" and the "blue-collar workers," those to whom the game is fun and those to whom it is a hard way to earn a living.

Frankie Frisch, who once managed the Cubs, enunciated his philosophy of the game in four words: "Make fun, not war." And it is this spirit that we include this chapter—a compilation of remarkable achievements, unusual and odd events, and anecdotes of some of the outlandish and sometimes even bizarre characters who have worn Cub uniforms.

Tinker to Evers to Chance

Baseball may be sheer poetry on the field to intellectuals, but it has yet to find its Keats or Shelley. Nevertheless, it has triggered some immortal if not impeccable verses, among which the most famous are the lines of Franklin P. Adams, who was not a baseball writer but a general columnist for the *New York Mail* in July 1910.

A Cub fan in New York, Adams enjoyed sitting in the press box and rooting for his team against the hated Giants. One day, needing eight lines to fill his column, Adams scribbled the following bit of doggerel, which was to become familiar to fans forever after and keep his name alive:

These are the saddest of possible words,
*   Tinker to Evers to Chance.*
Trio of bear cubs and fleeter than birds,
*   Tinker to Evers to Chance.*
Thoughtlessly pricking our gonfalon bubble,
*   Making a Giant hit into a double,*
Words that are weighty with nothing but trouble—
*   Tinker to Evers to Chance.*

Double plays did not become a part of the game's statistics until 1919, so despite the diligence of latter-day statisticians, it is difficult to determine precisely how many double plays the trio completed. In an era when the game featured sacrifices and the hit-and-run, double plays were far more rare than today. All that's certain is that shortstop Joe Tinker, second baseman Johnny Evers, and first baseman Frank Chance were fine players individually and completed their share of double plays during the decade or so they played together in the early part of the century.

Their total double-play output in four World Series (1906, 1907, 1908, and 1910) was just one in 21 games. In 1907, Chance sat out the fifth and last game of the Series after being hit by a pitch. In 1910, Evers was injured and didn't appear in the five-game Series. So the combination appeared together in only 15 World Series games.

In those 15 games, the Cubs made 13 double plays: four on line drives, two on flies in which the runner was doubled up, one on a strikeout and caught stealing, and six on ground balls to the infield. The only Tinker-to-Evers-to-Chance double play recorded in the 15 games came on October 10, 1907, on a ground ball by Ty Cobb of the Detroit Tigers.

The first Tinker-to-Evers-to-Chance double play was recorded on September 2, 1902. The last a decade later, after which the trio was split up. Tinker led National League shortstops in double plays only once.

April 25, 1976, at Dodger Stadium: outfielder Rick Monday with an admirer after saving the American flag from being burned

Two Balls in Play

The Cardinals were playing the Cubs in Wrigley Field on June 30, 1959, and Stan Musial of St. Louis was at bat with one out in the top of the fourth inning. Baseball writer Jerome Holtzman described the sequence of events.

"The count was 3 and 1. Bob Anderson's next pitch was called a ball by umpire Vic Delmore, entitling Musial to a base on balls.

"But then the confusion began. Cub catcher Sammy Taylor claimed the ball had hit Musial's bat and therefore was foul. Taylor was so convinced of this that the didn't even chase the ball as it rolled back to the screen. Instead, he argued with Delmore.

"Cub manager Bob Scheffing and Anderson joined Taylor in the argument, contending the ball had either grazed Musial's arm or hit his bat. 'It hit something,' Scheffing said.

" 'That's right,' Delmore agreed. 'The ball hit Taylor's glove and then bounced off my arm.'

"Musial, in the meantime, was strolling down to first. When he had almost reached the bag, he heard his Cardinal teammates shout from the dugout and point toward the ball, which had now reached the screen behind home plate.

" 'Run, Stan, run!' they yelled.

"At the same time, Alvin Dark, playing third for the Cubs, realized that if it were ball four as umpire Delmore had ruled, then the ball was still in play, and Musial would be entitled to as many bases as he could get.

"So Dark ran in, full speed, toward the screen. By this time, however, the batboy for visiting clubs, Bob Schoenfeldt, a high school freshman, had picked up the ball and had tossed it to field announcer Pat Peiper.

"Now the stories began to vary. Peiper said he never actually touched the ball and instead let it drop to the ground. Schoenfeldt said first that Peiper caught his toss, but later added: 'Maybe he didn't. I'm not sure.'

"Solly Hemus, Cardinal manager, said later: 'I know damn well Peiper caught the ball. But he dropped it like a hot potato as soon as he saw Dark charging in!

"Peiper, relating what happened, said Dark yelled, 'Gimme the ball.'

" 'There it is, I told him,' Peiper explained.

"Dark reached down, grabbed the ball, and threw to shortstop Ernie Banks. But at this very same moment another ball flew out toward second base.

"Where did this ball come from? Well, while umpire Delmore was listening to the beefs registered by catcher Taylor and pitcher Anderson, he automatically reached into his pocket and gave Taylor a new ball.

"Anderson, seeing Musial run for second, grabbed the new ball out of Taylor's hand and threw it toward second. Anderson's ball—hereafter referred to as Ball No. 2—and the one thrown by Dark were in the air at precisely the same moment.

"Dark's throw was low. Banks came in and fielded it on one hop. Anderson's throw, however, was high and sailed over second baseman Tony Taylor's head into center field. While all this was happening, Musial had slid safely into second.

"But Musial didn't know two balls had been thrown. He said later he saw only the ball that went into center field. (That was Anderson's' ball—Ball No. 2.) He picked himself up and started for third.

"Stan hadn't taken more than two or three steps off the bag when Banks tagged him with the original ball. Ball No. 2 had been retrieved in center field by Bobby Thomson, who then lobbed it toward the Cub dugout.

"One can imagine the confusion that resulted. The umpires appeared to be just as confused as everyone else. They huddled once and ordered Musial back to first. Scheffing continued squawking, and they huddled again and this time ruled that Musial was out, the play going from Dark to Banks.

"Hemus protested immediately, claiming (1) that two balls were simultaneously in play, and (2) that there had been interference on the part of the batboy, who admitted on the spot that he had picked up the ball when it had rolled back to the screen.

"The protest though was never filed because the Cardinals won 4–1."

It's difficult to imagine a weirder play, though this one never should have unfolded as it did. The umpire should have ruled the ball dead the moment the batboy picked it up.

Homer in the Gloamin'

The Cubs had clawed their way back into the pennant race by September 28, 1938, when they played the pace-setting Pittsburgh Pirates in the second game of a three-game series at Wrigley Field. They trailed by just half a game and had managed to hold the Pirates to a 5–5 tie going into the bottom of the ninth.

But it was turning dark at 5:30 P.M., and the umpires after the eighth had agreed to permit just one more inning. If a decision could not be reached in the ninth, the game would be replayed the next day as part of a doubleheader, which the Cubs would have to sweep in order to gain first place.

With two out in the bottom of the ninth, Cubs catcher and manager Gabby Hartnett faced Pirates reliever Mace Brown.

Hartnett swung at and missed the first pitch, then fouled off the second.

"I had just one strike left," he recalled, "and if I didn't connect we'd have to play a doubleheader the next day . . . Brown pumped with everything he had, and I swung with every ounce of strength I possessed. I've heard that some people didn't think the ball would carry into the bleachers. I never had that fear. I felt it was gone the very second I hit it."

Plate umpire George Barr peered through the gloom and saw the ball descend into the left-field bleachers. He signaled home run, and the Cubs had won 6–5 and moved into first place to stay.

"There's a lot of stories to be told," Hartnett said. "The

way the hysterical fans spilled onto the field, and how our bench emptied as the players met me as I was rounding second. They literally carried me the rest of the way, but the picture at the plate is the one I'll never forget. There was old George [umpire Barr] looking and looking like he was doing a double take, making sure I stepped on home plate. He

didn't have to worry because I wasn't going to make that mistake."

A sportswriter immediately labeled Hartnett's blow "The Homer in the Gloamin'," the clutch hit that had won a pennant, though the Cubs didn't actually clinch it until a few days later.

Ruth's "Called Shot"

It is always difficult to disentangle baseball fact from fiction, and no legend of the game has been more disputed than Babe Ruth's alleged called-shot home run for the New York Yankees off Cub pitcher Charlie Root in the 1932 World Series. Ruth himself eventually came to believe the story and often reminisced in later years about how foolish he would have looked had he failed to hit Root's pitch out.

In the third game of the Series, on October 1 at Wrigley Field, the Cubs and Yankees were tied 4–4 when Ruth came to bat in the fifth inning. He had hit a three-run homer off Root in the first inning, and the fans and Cub bench jockeys heckled him as he came to the plate again.

The uproar continued, with Ruth engaging in a shouting match with the Cub bench jockeys. During the sequence of pitches, when the count was 2–2, Ruth happened to point his finger in the general direction of the mound, apparently to indicate that he had still one strike left. He then hit the fifth pitch into the right-center field bleachers.

According to those closest to the scene—pitcher, catcher, and coaches—Ruth did not point toward the stands. Root

and others later claimed that the "called shot" designation was an on-the-spot invention of radio announcer Ted Husing, and was picked up by several sportswriters several days after the incident.

Cub catcher Gabby Hartnett thought that he heard Ruth say, "It takes only one to hit it," that Root hollered something from the mound, and that Ruth shouted back, "I'm going to knock the next pitch right down your goddamned throat."

Root always vehemently denied that Ruth had pointed to the stands, and indignantly declined to re-create the incident for Hollywood. "I got two strikes on him," Root said. "Babe did lift one finger toward the dugout after the first strike and two after the second. The count was two-and-two when I threw him a curve on the outside and he hit it over my head and into the bleachers. But he didn't point. If he had, I'd have knocked him on his fanny. I'd have loosened him up. I took my pitching too seriously to have anybody facing me do that."

So the matter rests, one of baseball's most famous legends, hallowed by the passage of more than six decades.

Merkle's Boner

The three-way pennant race among the Cubs, New York Giants, and Pittsburgh Pirates in 1908 spawned one of the most bizarre of all plays, which hung as a shadow over the otherwise respectable career of Giants first baseman Fred Merkle.

On September 23, 1908, the Giants were playing the Cubs at the Polo Grounds with the score 1–1 in the bottom of the ninth, two out, Moose McCormick on third base, and Merkle on first.

Al Bridwell singled to center, apparently driving in McCormick with the winning run. Merkle, running between first and second, saw McCormick cross the plate and decided to return to the dugout in order to avoid the fans already swarming onto the field. It was nothing unusual. Other players often did the same thing.

But quick-thinking Cub second baseman Johnny Evers stood on the bag and called to his teammates to throw him the ball. When umpire Hank O'Day came over to check, Evers insisted he call out Merkle on a force play.

Evers correctly argued that Bridwell had to get to first to qualify the hit, and if Bridwell had to reach first, then Merkle was forced to second. Since Merkle had never reached sec-

ond, he was out on the play and McCormick's run could not be scored.

Evers' logic prevailed, and O'Day called Merkle out to end the inning without a run having been scored. It was still 1–1 after nine innings.

By this time the crowd on the field made it impossible to resume play. The game was called. When the season finished, the Cubs and Giants were in a tie for first place. In a single-game playoff, the Cubs won 4–2, and won the pennant.

The furious Giants fans hung the nickname "Bonehead" on Merkle, a fine player who is remembered mostly for a legendary freak play rather than for 15 subsequent years as a solid big leaguer, including a stint with the Cubs (1917–20).

Evers and O'Day both were alert to the Merkle situation because a similar event had happened earlier. Evers explained, "It was 19 days earlier at Pittsburgh that we really won the game at New York. The Pirates' Warren Gill . . . didn't touch second in an identical situation in the 10th." Evers complained to O'Day, who was umpiring that game too, and although O'Day let the run stand, he was prepared when the Merkle incident came up.

Star-Spangled Outfielder

Cub left fielder Rick Monday noticed two fans climb out of the stands and run to left-center in the fourth inning of a game on April 25, 1976, at Los Angeles.

"One of them had the American flag tucked under his arm," Monday said. "The next thing I saw was the glint of the can. They were sprinkling its contents on the flag. I figured it wasn't holy water. I said to myself, 'My God, they're trying to burn the sucker.'

"That's when I took off. They couldn't see me coming from behind, but I could see one had a match. The wind blew it out, and just as they lit another and were about to touch it to the flag, I grabbed it. They threw the can of lighter fluid at me, just missing my head."

Monday carried the flag to the bullpen. The culprits, arrested for trespassing, were William Thomas and his 11-year-old son, who were protesting the treatment of Indians during the bicentennial year.

Monday got an ovation from the crowd and was honored around the nation for his feat in rescuing the Star-Spangled Banner.

The Williams Shift

Most fans would credit Lou Boudreau, while manager of the Cleveland Indians in the 1940s, with having devised the exaggerated "Williams shift" against Ted Williams of the Boston Red Sox. But this overshift of the infield actually was first employed by Cub manager Fred Mitchell against Philadelphia Phillies slugger Fred "Cy" Williams in the 1920s.

Cy Williams (ironically, a former Cub), like Ted, was a powerful, left-handed hitter who refused to "give in" to the shift and lay down a bunt toward the unguarded third base area. Both Williamses chose to defy the shift and continue to drive the ball to right field, which they did with some success. They were both powerful pull hitters to right field, and seldom hit to left field.

Coincidentally, they both led their respective leagues in home runs four times and in home-run percentage five times. Ted, of course, is the last man to bat over .400, with .406 in 1941. Cy's best average came in 1926 when he batted .345.

Chuck Connors had a brief and undistinguished career with the Cubs as a first baseman. He later gained considerable fame in the "Rifleman" television series.

The King of Baseball

Often described as the Babe Ruth of the 19th century, White Stockings star Mike "King" Kelly may have surpassed his successor as a larger-than-life character, off the field as well as on it.

A newspaper reporter described Kelly going out for a stroll, "his cane a-twirling as though he were the entire population, his ascot held by a giant jewel, his patent leather shoes as sharply pointed as Italian dirks." At times, he was accompanied by his Japanese valet and a monkey.

Among the many anecdotes relating Kelly's cunning and trickery on the field, there's the one of the uncaught fly ball that resulted in an out. As twilight gathered in the 12th inning of a game against Boston, right fielder Kelly leaped high to apparently catch a ball with two hands, then ran into the dugout.

The game was called on account of darkness with the score tied. Teammates asked Kelly how deep the ball was hit. He replied, "How the hell should I know? It went a mile over my head."

Deadliest of the Species . . .

Fans, particularly female, can be dangerous, as became only too apparent to two players associated with the Cubs during their careers, shortstop Billy Jurges and first baseman Eddie Waitkus.

On July 7, 1932, Jurges received a telephone call in his room at the Carlos Hotel, near Wrigley Field. The caller was Violet Popovich Valli, a showgirl whom Jurges had dated. She said, "Come down to my room. I've got something for you."

"If you have anything to tell me, come up to my room," Jurges said.

On entering Jurges' room, Valli attempted to shoot him with a small handgun. (Her intention apparently, was to kill him and then herself.) While Jurges tried to stop her, three shots were fired. Jurges was wounded in the chest and his left hand, Valli in the right wrist. None of the wounds were serious. Jurges recovered quickly and contributed to the Cubs' pennant drive. He got four hits in the four-game World Series sweep of the Cubs by the New York Yankees.

Valli was arrested, then freed on bail, and the case was dismissed when Jurges declined to prosecute. Valli signed a 22-week contract to sing and dance at various night spots, billed as "Violet (I Did It for Love) Valli—The Most Talked Of Girl in Chicago."

Almost 17 years later, on June 14, 1949, Waitkus was with the Philadelphia Phillies after being traded by the Cubs. He received a note in his room at the Edgewater Beach Hotel in Chicago from Ruth Steinhagen, a fan he did not know.

She insisted on seeing him in her room "as soon as possible" because of "something extremely important" she wanted to tell him. When Waitkus entered Steinhagen's room, she shouted, "Now you're going to die," and shot him in the chest with a rifle.

The psychiatrist's report to the felony court detailed that Steinhagen had developed a crush on Waitkus to the extent of memorizing his every move, making his uniform number (36) her favorite number, and collecting photographs of him, and she had stated that everyone reminded her of Waitkus. She was adjudged to be "schizophrenic" and committed to a mental institution.

Waitkus was in critical condition for several days, but recovered. He came back in 1950 and batted .284, the highest average in the "Whiz Kids" infield, contributing to the Phillies winning the National League pennant.

Fastball to the Devil

A journeyman White Stockings outfielder in the 1880s, Billy Sunday became one of the most notable evangelists of his time after starting to preach in 1896.

His dramatic style in the pulpit was enhanced by his experience as a baseball player. While preaching he would sometimes wind up like a pitcher and slam a fist into the other hand to demonstrate a "fastball to the devil."

To illustrate a sinner coming home for salvation, Sunday would slide headfirst across the stage and grope with his hands for home plate.

The Final Encounter

Few pitching rivalries have ever been as intense or so memorable as those between Mordecai "Three-Finger" Brown and Christy Mathewson in the early years of the 20th century. They confronted one another 24 times from 1904 to 1916, with Brown the winner in 13 games, nine of them consecutively.

One of Brown's victories was the replay of the controversial game at the Polo Grounds in which New York Giants rookie Fred Merkle failed to touch second base, costing his team a clear pennant. When the game was ruled a tie and the NL ordered it to be played over at season's end on October 8, 1908, Brown relieved starter Jack Pfiester in the first inning and earned a 4–2 victory to give the Cubs the pennant.

Their final duel came on September 4, 1916, with Mathewson pitching his first game as pitcher-manager of the Cincinnati Reds and Brown pitching for the Cubs, to whom he had returned that season from the Federal League. Mathewson was the winner, and it was the last time either future Hall of Famer appeared on a big-league mound.

Monumental Catch

The Washington Monument was opened to the public in 1886, and eight years later it inspired an argument between White Stockings manager Cap Anson and the chief clerk of the Arlington Hotel in Washington, D.C., where the team was staying. The clerk doubted that any "baseballist on earth ever had or ever could catch a ball dropped from the Washington Monument." Anson took up the challenge.

Anson assigned catcher William F. "Pop" Schriver to position himself at the base of the monument and sent star pitcher Clark Griffith (later owner of the Washington Senators) to go up to the observation deck 504 feet above the ground and lob the ball down. Schriver was able to make a catch on the first try, settling the debate to Anson's satisfaction.

180 Days Around the World

Ever the innovator, owner Al Spalding transported his White Stockings and an "All-American Team" around the world after the 1888 season on an exhibition tour that took almost six months. Henry Chadwick, a pioneer historian of the game, described the tour as "the greatest event in the modern history of athletic sports."

The trip started November 17, and the first major stop was Australia, where baseball got an enthusiastic reception during three weeks of exhibition games. Ceylon, however, hot as it was, proved cold to baseball.

The next major stop was Egypt, where the players mounted the Sphinx near Cairo "to the horror of the native worshippers of Cheops and the dead Pharaohs," according to Spalding.

Spalding's attempts to get an audience with the pope and to play a game in the Colosseum in Rome were thwarted.

Spalding had to settle for a game in the Borghese gardens. After games in Florence, Italy, and in Paris, the entourage arrived in England, which Spalding had visited in 1874 during a tour by the Boston Red Stockings. The English once again proved cool to baseball, one commentator remarking that it was as out of place in his country as "a nursery frolic in the House of Commons."

After the players rounded out their arduous trip with a two-week series of "welcome-home" exhibition games in the United States, they were feted at a magnificent banquet—served in "nine innings"—at Demonico's in New York, with Mark Twain as toastmaster and Theodore Roosevelt also on hand.

Twain called baseball "the very symbol, the outward and visible expression of the drive and push and rush and struggle of the raging, tearing, booming 19th century."

Tick-Tock

Among the more eccentric personalities who have strutted across the Cubs stage was pitcher Bill Faul, who spent two seasons (1965–66) annoying Cub managers with his peculiarities.

As well as being a lay minister and a pioneer "bodybuilder," Faul believed he was at his most effective under self-hypnosis, which was part of his preparation each time he started a game. His method seemed to work for a time as

he pitched three shutouts in 1965 with a 6–6 record for a mediocre team.

One opposing player tried to bring Faul out of his self-induced hypnosis by pulling out a pocket watch and letting it swing while chanting, "Tick-tock, tick-tock." The chant was soon taken up by others every time Faul pitched.

When Faul became less effective (1–4) in 1966, manager Leo Durocher told him his time had run out.

By Any Other Name

The origins of team names, and their dates of acceptance, are somewhat vague, but the consensus is that the Chicago National League franchise got its various appellations because of changing circumstances.

The Cubs in 1876 were known as the White Stockings. They were labeled the Colts after player-manager Cap Anson appeared in a play called the *Runaway Colts* in the mid-1890s or because he had only young players left after many veterans deserted to the Players League in 1890.

When Anson left after being denied a financial stake in the franchise in 1897, people began calling the team the Orphans. For several years, they also were called the Cowboys and the Broncos.

In 1901, after several veterans jumped to the new American League, sportswriters George Rice and Fred Haynes began referring to them as the Cubs because they had so many young players. The name became official in 1907, though occasionally they also were called the Bruins.

Infielder Davey Lopes celebrates his 500th career stolen base at Wrigley Field, June 5, 1985.

They Said It

Countless sprightly, witty, and sometimes even mean things have been said by those connected with the Cubs, by fans, by sportswriters, and by people in all walks of life fascinated by their history, triumphs, and travails.

Here are a few of the more memorable quotes:

Cub owner P. K. Wrigley on the advent of night baseball, 1935: "Just a fad, a passing fancy."

P. K. Wrigley: "Baseball is too much a sport to be a business and too much a business to be a sport."

Warren Brown, sportswriter, on the quality of the teams in the 1945 World Series won by the Detroit Tigers over the Cubs: "I don't think either team is capable of winning."

Dizzy Dean, Cub pitcher with a "dead" arm: "I ain't what I used to be, but who the hell is?"

Leo Durocher, Cub manager, before the 1966 season: "The Cubs aren't an eighth-place club, and I'm here to find out why they are where they are." Durocher after the season: "I was right, too. It wasn't an eighth-place club. It was a 10th-place club."

Outfielder Hack Wilson, after manager Joe McCarthy dropped a worm into a whiskey bottle as a demonstration of the dangers of alcohol: "Yeah, I learned something. If you drink whiskey, you won't get worms."

King Kelly, when asked if he drank during a game: "It depends on the length of the game."

Manager Frank Chance: "You do things my way, or you meet me after the game."

Ernie Banks, on retirement in 1971 after 19 seasons as Cub player: "I always wanted to bring a pennant to Wrigley Field. It's the one big disappointment in my life."

Outfielder Jose Cardenal, on what he did during the 22–0 loss to Pittsburgh in 1975: "I was watching a spider crawl through the ivy. What else was there to do out there in a game like that?"

First baseman Bill Buckner: "There's nothing wrong with this team that more pitching, more fielding, and more hitting wouldn't help."

The Grab Bag

No book on the Cubs would be complete without a selection from among the countless major and minor accomplishments and incidents that have occurred over more than a century. Some of the more noteworthy and memorable follow, in no particular chronological or other order:

- Thirty-nine pitchers have posted two complete game victories on the same day, but none can match the feat of the Cubs' Ed Reulbach. On September 26, 1908, Reulbach pitched two shutouts over the Dodgers in Brooklyn. He won the opener 5–0 and the second game 3–0.

- Hank Sauer twice hit three home runs in a game in his career with the Cubs. This may not seem unusual for a slugger with Sauer's power, but in both games all the home runs came off Philadelphia Phillies ace Curt Simmons.

- Don Cardwell, making his first start for the Cubs on May 15, 1960, pitched a 4–0 no-hit, no-run victory over the St. Louis Cardinals in the second game of a doubleheader at Wrigley Field. A circus catch by Moose Moryn, not known for his fielding, of Joe Cunningham's sinking liner provided the final out of the game.

- Ordinarily, 57 doubles in a season would be enough to lead the league by a wide margin. And they did for Billy Herman in 1935. But when Herman matched that with 57 more in 1936, he finished second to Joe Medwick of the St. Louis Cardinals, who had 64.

- An unassisted triple play is one of the rarest feats in baseball. The last Cub to turn one was shortstop Jimmy Cooney on May 30, 1927. In the fourth inning of a game against the Pittsburgh Pirates, Cooney speared a line drive hit by Paul Waner and stepped on second to double Lloyd Waner. Clyde Barnhart, the runner on first when the play started, slid into the third out as Cooney tagged him before he could reach second.

- In 1967, Ken Holtzman was limited to pitching just 12 weekend games while on leave from the army and turned in a 9–0 record. An oddity was that he received credit for a victory in the second half of the season for a game which he had started in the first half but which had been suspended.

- En route to winning a major league record 116 games in 1906, the Cubs had a 37–2 record from August 6 to September 18. During the 39-game stretch, they won 11 games in a row, lost a game, won 14 in a row, lost a game, then won 12 in a row.

- The most lopsided Cub victory since 1900 took place on July 3, 1945, when the Cubs defeated Brooklyn 24–2. (The White Stockings defeated Boson 24–0 on July 1, 1885.) The most lopsided loss in club history (and lopsided shutout since 1900) occurred on September 16, 1975, when Pittsburgh won 22–0, with Rennie Stennett getting a record seven hits in seven at bats for the Pirates.

- On September 6, 1883, Cap Anson's White Stockings scored 18 runs in the bottom of the seventh, the biggest one-inning outburst in the game's history, as they walloped Detroit 26–6. Shortstop Tommy Burns set six records, including most extra-base hits in an inning with two doubles and a home run.

- The Cubs provided baseball with its greatest scoring outburst by one team in a game on June 29, 1897, when they thrashed Louisville 36–7. Winning pitcher Jimmy Callahan contributed five hits in seven at bats, including two doubles, and scored four times. The Cubs also are second in most runs scored in a game by one team, beating Cleveland 35–4 on July 22, 1882.

- The Cubs won baseball's greatest shootout ever, a 26–23 victory over the Philadelphia Phillies on August 15, 1922, at Wrigley Field. The record total 49 runs were scored in the regulation nine innings, with the Phillies almost coming back from a 25–6 deficit after four innings. The Phillies outhit the Cubs 26 to 25.

- Tradition was upheld on May 17, 1979, at Wrigley Field when the Cubs and Phillies again engaged in a wild scramble, Philadelphia finally winning 23–22 on Mike Schmidt's home run. At one point the Phillies led 21–9, but the Cubs battled back, with three home runs by Dave Kingman and seven runs batted in by Bill Buckner, four of them on a grand-slam homer.

- The only Cub to lead off two straight games with home runs was Sam Mertes, who homered June 8 and June 9, 1900, against Boston.

- The White Stockings won their first game ever 4–0 on April 25, 1876, at Louisville, with Al Spalding pitching the first shutout in National League history. Center fielder Paul Hines scored the first run on a throwing error in the second inning.

- The first home run in National League history was hit by Ross Barnes of the White Stockings on May 2, 1876, in a 15–9 victory at Cincinnati. The inside-the-park homer was one of only 39 homers hit in the NL's first season.

- The most successful politician to wear a Cub uniform was John K. Tener, who was elected governor of Pennsylvania in 1910. He had pitched for the Cubs in 1888 and 1889 with 7–5 and 15–15 records, and served briefly as an umpire. He was president of the National League from 1913 to 1918.

- Outfielders Max Flack and Cliff Heathcote each played both for the Cubs and St. Louis Cardinals on the same day, May 30, 1922. The Cubs traded Flack to the Cardinals for Heathcote between games of a morning-afternoon doubleheader. Flack, who lived in Chicago, walked home for lunch between games, and didn't discover that he had been traded until 15 minutes before the second game. Both Heathcote and Flack had hit safely in the morning game, but went hitless for their new teams in the second game.

- Milt Pappas, who pitched for the Cubs from 1970 to 1973, is the only pitcher to win 200 games and never have a 20-game season. Pappas won 244 games in his 17-year major league career and never won more than 17 games in any one season.

Slugger Bill Nicholson was one of the few players to receive an intentional walk with the bases loaded.

- The only left-handed catcher since 1900 was Dale Long, who caught two games for the 1958 Cubs. Three other left-handed catchers, Fergy Malone, Jack Clements, and Pop Tate, played in the National League before the turn of the century.

- Cub catcher Clyde McCullough was the only player to play in a World Series game without having played in a regular season contest that year. McCullough returned from military service in 1945 too late to participate in regular season play but was made eligible for the Series against the Detroit Tigers. McCullough came to bat once as a pinch hitter in the Series.

- Frank "Wildfire" Schulte of the Cubs in 1911 was the first player to produce 20 or more doubles, triples, home runs, and stolen bases in a season, a feat that wasn't matched until Willie Mays of the San Francisco Giants did it in 1957.

- Bill Nicholson of the Cubs was one of the few players to be walked with the bases loaded. Nicholson had hit four home runs in the weekend series when New York Giants manager Mel Ott gave him a pass with the bases loaded in the seventh inning of the second game on July 23, 1944.

- The Cubs are the only team to have had two winning streaks of 20 games or more. Cap Anson's 1880 team won 21 consecutive games, and Charlie Grimm's 1935 team matched that figure. The Cubs won the pennant both years.

- When Ernie Banks retired as a player in 1971, he finished with 512 home runs, all for the Cubs. Number 500 came off Pat Jarvis of the Atlanta Braves on May 12, 1970. On the all-time Cub list, at his retirement he was first in games played (2,528), home runs (512), extra-base hits (1,009), and total bases (4,706); second in hits (2,583), RBIs (1,636), and doubles (407); fourth in runs scored (1,305) and slugging average (.500); and seventh in triples (90).

- The Cubs took to radio on a regular basis in 1926 with WGN's Quin Ryan at the microphone, though the first broadcasts were of the City Series with the White Sox starting October 1, 1924. At one time, five different Chicago stations carried the Cubs on the air from Wrigley Field. The first game to be televised was by WBKB-TV on April 20, 1946, with Joe Wilson as the announcer. WGN-TV began regular telecasts of Cubs games on April 5, 1948, with Jack Brickhouse as the announcer.

- Shortstop Bill Dahlen put together the Cubs' longest hitting streak and the fourth longest in the game's history when he hit in 42 consecutive games from June 20 to September 14, 1894. After going hitless on September 15, Dahlen hit safely in another 28 consecutive games. Only Joe DiMaggio, Wee Willie Keeler, and Pete Rose have topped Dahlen's feat. Dahlen batted .362 that year, though his career average for 21 seasons was just .272.

- Stan Musial, one of the greatest of all hitters, pitched to just one batter during his major league career. In the last game of the 1952 season at Sportsman's Park in St. Louis, Musial went out to pitch to Cub outfielder Frankie Baumholtz. Because Musial was a lefty, Baumholtz switched to the right side though he was usually a left-handed hitter. Baumholtz grounded to third baseman Billy Johnson, who fumbled the ball for an error. Musial left the game, having completed his big-league pitching career with no hits or runs allowed and one pitch thrown.

- The records show that Hack Wilson hit 56 home runs for the Cubs in 1930 but Clyde Sukeforth, who was with Cincinnati that year, insisted that it should have been 57. Sukeforth said, "He hit one up in the Crosley Field stands so hard that it bounced right back. The umpires figured it must have hit the screen. I was in the Reds' bullpen, and we didn't say a word."

- In 1942, Cub owner P. K. Wrigley wearied of watching slugging outfielder Lou Novikoff take too many pitches for strikes. He decided to pay Novikoff $5 for every time he struck out swinging. The reward backfired in one game with the bases loaded, two outs, and two strikes on Novikoff. The next pitch was over his head, but he swung and missed. "You must be awfully short of dough," coach Charlie Grimm remarked to Novikoff.

10

Trades, Acquisitions, and Sales

Cub fans generally have a cheerful outlook and forgiving nature but they have never pardoned the club for the Lou Brock–for–Ernie Broglio trade with the St. Louis Cardinals on June 15, 1964, the day of what was then the trading deadline. It was a six-player deal, three-for-three, but only Brock and Broglio are remembered; the others are no more than a footnote in Cub history.

Brock, a 25-year-old outfielder, had had an undistinguished two-and-a-half-year career with the Cubs. His most outstanding achievement, in 1,200 at bats, was a blockbuster home run two years earlier, June 17, 1962, into the right–center field bleachers at the old Polo Grounds, estimated at 485 feet. Only Babe Ruth had ever homered into the same sector—40 years before—but the bleachers were then closer to the plate.

Broglio was a veteran right-handed pitcher and had been a 20-game winner in 1960. General manager John Holland was convinced that another established starting pitcher was all that was needed to win the pennant. But the Cardinals, led by Brock, won the flag. Brock went on to a Hall of Fame career. Broglio was 4–7 with the Cubs in '64 and retired after the '66 season. He won only three more games with the Cubs.

Two of the best deals were the acquisition of Hall of Fame pitchers Three-Finger Brown from the St. Louis Cardinals in 1903 and Ferguson Jenkins from the Phillies in 1966. Brown was a six-time 20-game winner with the Cubs, an accomplishment since equaled only by Jenkins. Another excellent trade for a pitcher was the midseason acquisition for Hank Borowy from the Yankees. Borowy was instrumental in the winning of the 1945 pennant.

Slugger Hank Sauer, who was to become the "Mayor of Wrigley Field," came from Cincinnati in a 1940 deal; second baseman Ryne Sandberg came from Philadelphia in 1982, also at little cost. Other outstanding deals were the acquisition of Hall of Famers Kiki Cuyler from Pittsburgh in 1927, Billy Herman from the Dodgers in 1941, and the battery of catcher Randy Hundley and pitcher Bill Hands from the San Francisco Giants in 1965 for pitchers Lindy McDaniel and Jim Rittwage and outfielder Don Landrum.

Pitcher Hank Borowy (right) is welcomed by batterymate Bob Scheffing after a midseason deal with the Yankees. Borowy was a major force in the winning of the 1945 pennant.

1887, February 14
Outfielder-catcher King Kelly to Boston Beaneaters for $10,000.

1887, April
Pitcher Jim McCormick to Pittsburgh Alleghenys for cash.

1888, April 3
Pitcher John Clarkson to Boston Beaneaters for $10,000.

1889, April 26
Cash to Philadelphia Quakers for second baseman Charlie Bastian.

1892, April 4
Second baseman Fred Pfeffer to Louisville Colonels for shortstop Jimmy Canavan and $2,000.

1898, April 19
Outfielder George Decker to St. Louis Browns for cash.

1899, January 11
Pitcher Walt Woods to Louisville Colonels for Louisville's option on pitcher Jack Taylor.

1899, January 25
Shortstop Bill Dahlen to Baltimore Orioles for second baseman Gene DeMontreville.

1899, August 2
Shortstop Gene DeMontreville to Baltimore Orioles for shortstop George Magoon.

1900
Cash to Boston Beaneaters for pitcher Frank Killen.

1900, January
Cash to St. Louis Cardinals for second baseman Cupid Childs.

1900, January
Cash to Washington Senators (NL) for shortstop Billy Clingman.

1900, January
Cash to Pittsburgh Pirates for pitcher Bert Cunningham.

1900, January
Cash to Louisville Colonels (NL) for outfielder Charlie Dexter.

1900, February 10
$2,000 to Pittsburgh Pirates for outfielder Jack McCarthy.

1900, April 28
Third baseman Harry Wolverton to Philadelphia Phillies for cash.

1901, February
Third baseman Sammy Strang to New York Giants for first baseman Jack Doyle.

1901, February
First baseman John Ganzel to New York Giants for cash.

1901, April
Cash to Cincinnati Reds for outfielder Topsy Hartsel and catcher Mike Kahoe.

1901, May
Cash to Pittsburgh Pirates for pitcher Rube Waddell.

1901, June
Outfielder Cozy Dolan to Brooklyn Superbas for cash.

1902, February
Third baseman Jim Delahanty and first baseman Jack Doyle to New York Giants for cash.

1902, April
Pitcher Mal Eason to Boston Beaneaters for cash.

1902, July
Outfielder Charlie Dexter to Boston Beaneaters for third baseman Bobby Lowe.

1902, July
Cash to Cincinnati Reds for outfielder John Dobbs.

1902, July
First baseman Hal O'Hagen to New York Giants for outfielder Jack Hendricks.

1903, March
Third baseman Sammy Strang to Brooklyn Superbas for cash.

1903, April
Pitcher Bob Rhoads to St. Louis Cardinals for pitcher Bob Wicker.

1903, April
Pitcher Pop Williams to Philadelphia Phillies for cash.

1903, May
Outfielder John Dobbs to Brooklyn Superbas for cash.

1903, June
Pitcher Jack Doscher to Brooklyn Superbas for cash.

1903, July
Cash to St. Louis Cardinals for pitcher Clarence Currie.

1903, July
Cash to St. Louis Cardinals for shortstop Otto Williams.

1903, December 12
Pitcher Jack Taylor and catcher Larry McLean to St. Louis Cardinals for

pitcher Mordecai "Three-Finger" Brown and catcher Jack O'Neill.

1904, January
Cash to Pittsburgh Pirates for outfielder Solly Hofman.

1904, April 20
Second baseman Bobby Lowe to Pittsburgh Pirates for cash.

1904, July 20
Pitchers Frank Corridon and Jack Sutthoff to Philadelphia Phillies for outfielder Shad Barry.

1905, May 20
Outfielder Shad Barry to Cincinnati Reds for cash.

1905, December 30
Pitcher Buttons Briggs, outfielders Billy Maloney and Jack McCarthy, third baseman Doc Casey, and $2,000 to Brooklyn Superbas for outfielder Jimmy Sheckard.

1906, January
Catcher Jack O'Neill to Boston Beaneaters for waiver price.

1906, January
Pitcher Big Jeff Pfeffer to Boston Beaneaters for cash.

1906, February
Cash to Boston Beaneaters for catcher Pat Moran.

1906, March
Third baseman Hans Lobert and pitcher Jake Weimer to Cincinnati Reds for third baseman Harry Steinfeldt.

1906, May 8
Cash to Brooklyn Superbas for first baseman Doc Gessler.

1906, June 2
Pitcher Bob Wicker and $2,000 to Cincinnati Reds for pitcher Orval Overall.

1906, July 1
Pitcher Fred Beebe, catcher Pete Noonan, and cash to St. Louis Cardinals for pitcher Jack Taylor.

1906, October
Pitcher Chick Fraser to Cincinnati Reds for pitcher Jack Harper.

1907, June 24
Outfielder Newt Randall and shortstop Bill Sweeney to Boston Doves (NL) for outfielder Del Howard.

1907, June 27
Catcher Mike Kahoe to Washington Senators for cash.

1908, June
Cash to St. Louis Cardinals for catcher Doc Marshall.

1908, September
Cash to Boston Doves (NL) for outfielder George Browne.

1908, September
Cash to Cincinnati Reds for pitcher Andy Coakley.

1908, November
Catcher Doc Marshall to Brooklyn Superbas for waiver price.

1908, December
Cash to New York Giants for catcher Tom Needham.

1909, January 18
Shortstop Tom Downey and outfielder Kid Durbin to Cincinnati Reds for outfielder John Kane.

1909, May 20
Cash to Cincinnati Reds for pitcher Pat Ragan.

1909, May 21
Outfielder George Browne to Washington Senators for waiver price.

1910, January
Outfielder Vin Campbell to Pittsburgh Pirates for cash.

1910, February
Pinch hitter Fred Liese to Boston Doves (NL) for outfielder Ginger Beaumont.

1910, April
Outfielder Doc Miller to Boston Doves (NL) for pitcher Lew Richie.

1910, July
First baseman Fred Luderus to Philadelphia Phillies for pitcher Bill Foxen.

1911, January
Third baseman Scotty Ingerton and pitcher Big Jeff Pfeffer to Boston Rustlers (NL) for second baseman Dave Shean.

1911, March
Third baseman Harry Steinfeldt to Boston Rustlers (NL) for cash.

1911, April
Cash to Boston Red Sox for pitcher Charlie Smith.

1911, June 10
Pitchers Hank Griffin and Orlie Weaver, catcher Johnny Kling, and outfielder Al Kaiser to Boston Rustlers (NL) for pitcher Cliff Curtis, catcher Peaches Graham, and outfielders Bill Collins and Wilbur Good.

1911, August
Pitcher Cliff Curtis to Philadelphia Phillies for pitcher Jack Rowan.

1911, August 9
Cash to Philadelphia Phillies for first baseman Kitty Bransfield.

1911, October
Catcher Peaches Graham to Philadelphia Phillies for catcher Dick Cotter.

1911, October
Infielder Dave Shean to Boston Braves for cash.

1912, January
Cash to Pittsburgh Pirates for pitcher Ensign Cottrell.

1912, May
Cash to Brooklyn Dodgers for second baseman Red Downs.

1912, June 22
Pitcher King Cole and outfielder Solly Hofman to Pittsburgh Pirates for pitcher Lefty Leifield and outfielder Tommy Leach.

1912, August
Cash to Philadelphia Phillies for third baseman Tom Downey.

1912, November
Cash to Boston Braves for shortstop Al Bridwell.

1912, December 15
Pitcher Grover Lowdermilk, shortstop Joe Tinker, and catcher Harry Chapman to Cincinnati Reds for outfielders Mike Mitchell and Pete Knisely, pitcher Bert Humphries, third baseman Art Phelan, and infielder Red Corriden.

1913, April
Outfielder Jimmy Sheckard to St. Louis Cardinals for cash.

1913, May
Catcher Mike Hechinger to Brooklyn Dodgers for waiver price.

1913, June 8
Cash to St. Louis Cardinals for catcher Roger Bresnahan.

1913, July
Outfielder Otis Clymer to Boston Braves for cash.

1913, July
Cash to Philadelphia Phillies for pitcher Earl Moore.

1913, July
Pitcher Ed Reulbach to Brooklyn Dodgers for pitcher Eddie Stack and cash.

1913, July 29
Outfielder Mike Mitchell to Pittsburgh Pirates for waiver price.

1913, September 23
Cash to New York Yankees for pitcher George McConnell.

1914, February
Second baseman Johnny Evers to Boston Braves for second baseman Bill Sweeney and cash.

1914, June
Cash to Brooklyn Robins for pitcher Casey Hageman.

1914, July 20
First baseman Fritz Mollwitz to Cincinnati Reds for shortstop Claud Derrick.

1914, August
Pitcher Elmer Koestner to Cincinnati Reds for outfielder Johnny Bates.

1915, August
Pitcher Larry Cheney to Brooklyn Robins for third baseman Joe Schultz and $3,000.

1915, August 8
Pitcher Bert Humphries to Philadelphia Phillies for cash.

1915, September 5
Cash to Pittsburgh Pirates for infielder Alex McCarthy.

1915, September 8
Cash to Brooklyn Robins for pitcher Phil Douglas.

1916, January
Shortstop Bob Fisher to Cincinnati Reds for cash.

1916, January
Second baseman Joe Schultz to Pittsburgh Pirates for cash.

1916, February 3
Outfielder Wilbur Good to Philadelphia Phillies for cash.

1916, February 10
Cash to Buffalo Blues (Federal League) for catcher Nick Allen.

1916, February 10
Cash to Chicago Whales (Federal League) for pitchers Three-Finger Brown, Claude Hendrix, and

George McConnell, catchers Clem Clemens and Bill Fischer, shortstops Mickey Doolan and Joe Tinker, infielder Rollie Zeider, outfielders Max Flack and Les Mann, and Dykes Potter.

1916, February 10
Cash to Kansas City Packers (Federal League) for pitcher Gene Packard and third baseman Charlie Pechous.

1916, February 10
Cash to Newark Peppers (Federal League) for pitcher Tom Seaton.

1916, February 10
Cash to Pittsburgh Rebels (Federal League) for second baseman Steve Yerkes.

1916, June 2
Cash to St. Louis Browns for third baseman Charlie Deal.

1916, July
Second baseman Alex McCarthy to Pittsburgh Pirates for cash.

1916, July 22
Cash to Cincinnati Reds for first baseman Fritz Mollwitz.

1916, July 29
Catcher Bill Fischer and outfielder Wildfire Schulte to Pittsburgh Pirates for catcher Art Wilson and second baseman Otto Knabe.

1916, August 28
Shortstop Mickey Doolan and third baseman Heinie Zimmerman to New York Giants for second baseman Larry Doyle, third baseman Herb Hunter, and outfielder Merwin Jacobson.

1916, December 14
Outfielder Joe Kelly to Boston Braves for pinch hitter Fred Mitchell.

1917, January 16
Pitcher Jimmy Lavender and $5,000 to Philadelphia Phillies for pitcher Al Demaree.

1917, February 4
First baseman Fritz Mollwitz to Pittsburgh Pirates for cash.

1917, April
Pitcher Gene Packard to St. Louis Cardinals for cash.

1917, April 26
Pitcher Scott Perry to Cincinnati Reds for waiver price.

1917, July 17
Pitcher Dutch Ruether to Cincinnati Reds for waiver price.

1917, July 31
Pitcher Al Demaree to New York Giants for second baseman Pete Kilduff.

1917, August
Outfielder-infielder Harry Wolfe to Pittsburgh Pirates for cash.

1917, August 16
$3,500 to Brooklyn Robins for first baseman Fred Merkle.

1917, November 11
Pitcher Mike Prendergast, catcher Pickles Dillhoefer, and $55,000 to Philadelphia Phillies for pitcher Grover Alexander and catcher Bill Killefer.

1917, December
Catcher Jimmy Archer to Pittsburgh Pirates for cash.

1917, December 26
Outfielder Cy Williams to Philadelphia Phillies for outfielder Dode Paskert.

1918, January 4
Second baseman Larry Doyle, catcher Art Wilson, and $15,000 to Boston Braves for pitcher Lefty Tyler.

1919, June 2
Third baseman Pete Kilduff to Brooklyn Robins for second baseman Lee Magee.

1919, July 25
Pitcher Phil Douglas to New York Giants for outfielder Dave Robertston.

1919, August
Second baseman Charlie Pick and outfielder Les Mann to Boston

Grover Cleveland Alexander

Buck Herzog

Braves for second baseman Buck Herzog.

1920, January
Cash to Pittsburgh Pirates for shortstop Zeb Terry.

1920, February
Infielder Fred Lear to New York Giants for cash.

1920, May
Pinch hitter Bill McCabe to Brooklyn Robins for cash.

1920, December
Outfielder Dode Paskert to Cincinnati Reds for waiver price.

1921, May
Pitcher Sweetbreads Bailey to Brooklyn Robins for cash.

1921, May 11
Cash to Boston Braves for outfielder John Sullivan.

1921, July 1
Outfielder Dave Robertson to Pittsburgh Pirates for pitcher Elmer Ponder.

1922, May 30
Outfielder Max Flack to St. Louis Cardinals for outfielder Cliff Heathcote.

1923, January 2
Outfielder Turner Barber to Brooklyn Robins for cash.

1923, December 13
Infielder John Kelleher to Boston Braves for cash.

1924, May 16
Pitcher Tiny Osborne to Brooklyn Robins for cash.

1924, October 27
Pitcher Vic Aldridge, second baseman George Grantham, and first baseman Al Niehaus to Pittsburgh Pirates for first baseman Charlie Grimm, second baseman Rabbit Maranville, and pitcher Wilbur Cooper.

1925, May 10
Second baseman Bob Barrett to Brooklyn Robins for outfielder Tommy Griffith.

1925, May 23
Catcher Bob O'Farrell to St. Louis Cardinals for catcher Mike Gonzalez and third baseman Howard Freigau.

1925, June 15
Third baseman Barney Friberg to Philadelphia Phillies for waiver price.

1925, November 9
Shortstop Rabbit Maranville to Brooklyn Robins for waiver price.

1925, December 11
Pitcher Vic Keen to St. Louis Cardinals for shortstop Jimmy Cooney.

1926, June 7
Pitcher Wilbur Cooper to Detroit Tigers for waiver price.

1926, June 21
Waiver price to St. Louis Cardinals for pitcher Walter Huntzinger.

1926, June 22
Pitcher Grover Alexander to St. Louis Cardinals for waiver price.

1927, June 7
Shortstop Jimmy Cooney and pitcher

Rabbit Maranville

Hack Wilson came to the Cubs for $5,000 in the minor league draft following the 1925 season.

Tony Kaufmann to Philadelphia Phillies for pitcher Hal Carlson.

1927, June 14
Cash to Philadelphia Phillies for pitcher Wayland Dean.

1927, July 12
Cash to Boston Red Sox for third baseman Fred Haney.

1927, September 4
Cash to Cincinnati Reds for pitcher Art Nehf.

1927, November 28
Infielder Sparky Adams and outfielder Pete Scott to Pittsburgh Pirates for outfielder Kiki Cuyler.

1927, December
Third baseman Howard Freigau to Brooklyn Robins for shortstop Johnny Butler.

1927, December
Pitcher Fred Fussell to Pittsburgh Pirates for pitcher Mike Cvengros.

1928, November 7
Pitchers Bruce Cunningham, Percy Jones, and Socks Seibold, catcher Lou Legett, second baseman Freddie Maguire, and $200,000 to Boston Braves for second baseman Rogers Hornsby.

1929, April
Cash to Philadelphia Phillies for catcher Johnny Schulte.

1929, July 6
Waiver price to Boston Braves for catcher Zack Taylor.

1929, October 29
Waiver price to Boston Braves for third baseman Les Bell.

1930, June 29
Waiver price to St. Louis Cardinals for shortstop Doc Farrell.

1930, August 24
Cash to Pittsburgh Pirates for pitcher Jesse Petty.

1930, October 13
Cash to Philadelphia Phillies for pitcher Leo Sweetland.

1930, October 14
Cash to Cincinnati Reds for pitcher Jakie May.

1930, October 14
Pitcher Bill McAfee and outfielder Wes Schulmerich to Boston Braves for pitcher Bob Smith and outfielder Jimmy Welsh.

1931, January
Infielder Clyde Beck to Cincinnati Reds for waiver price.

1931, January
Pitcher Bob Osborn to Pittsburgh Pirates for cash.

1931, May
Outfielder Cliff Heathcote to Cincinnati Reds for waiver price.

1931, June 13
Catcher Earl Grace to Pittsburgh Pirates for catcher Rollie Hemsley.

1931, July 27
Pitcher Sheriff Blake to Philadelphia Phillies for waiver price.

1931, December
Pitcher Bud Teachout and outfielder Hack Wilson to St. Louis Cardinals for pitcher Burleigh Grimes.

1931, December 17
Waiver price to Boston Braves for outfielder Lance Richbourg.

1932, May 7
Outfielder Danny Taylor to Brooklyn Dodgers for cash.

1932, November 30
Outfielders Johnny Moore and Lance Richbourg, catcher Rollie Hemsley, and pitcher Bob Smith to Cincinnati Reds for outfielder Babe Herman.

1933, April 29
Waiver price to Cincinnati Reds for outfielder Taylor Douthit.

1933, August 4
Pitcher Burleigh Grimes to St. Louis Cardinals for waiver price.

Gabby Hartnett (center) at the helm with pitchers Charlie Root (left) and Dizzy Dean

1933, November 21
First baseman Harvey Hendrick, infielder Mark Koenig, pitcher Ted Kleinhans, and $65,000 to Philadelphia Phillies for outfielder Chuck Klein.

1934, May 15
Waiver price to St. Louis Browns for pitcher Jim Weaver.

1934, June 11
First baseman Dolph Camilli to Philadelphia Phillies for first baseman Don Hurst.

1934, October 26
Pitcher Pat Malone to St. Louis Cardinals for catcher Ken O'Dea.

1934, November 21
Pitchers Bud Tinning and Dick Ward and cash to St. Louis Cardinals for pitcher Tex Carleton.

1934, November 22
Pitchers Guy Bush and Jim Weaver and outfielder Babe Herman to Pittsburgh Pirates for pitcher Larry French and outfielder Freddie Lindstrom.

1934, December 31
Catcher Babe Phelps to Brooklyn Dodgers for waiver price.

1936, May 21
Outfielder Chuck Klein and pitcher Fabian Kowalik to Philadelphia Phillies for outfielder Ethan Allen and pitcher Curt Davis.

1936, October 8
Pitcher Lon Warneke to St. Louis Cardinals for pitcher Roy Parmelee and first baseman Ripper Collins.

1936, December 2
Outfielder Ethan Allen to St. Louis Browns for cash.

1936, December 5
Shortstop Woody English and pitcher Roy Henshaw to Brooklyn Dodgers for shortstop Lonny Frey.

1938, February 4
Shortstop Lonny Frey to Cincinnati Reds for cash.

1938, April 16
Pitchers Curt Davis and Clyde Shoun, outfielder Tuck Stainback, and $185,000 to St. Louis Cardinals for pitcher Dizzy Dean.

1938, December 6
Outfielder Frank Demaree, shortstop Billy Jurges, and catcher Ken O'Dea to New York Giants for outfielder Hank Leiber, shortstop Dick Bartell, and catcher Gus Mancuso.

1938, December 8
Cash to St. Louis Cardinals for pitcher Ray Harrell.

1939, January 24
$25,000 to New York Yankees for outfielder Jim Gleeson.

1939, May 29
Pitchers Ray Harrell and Kirby Higbe and outfielder Joe Marty to Philadelphia Phillies for pitcher Claude Passeau.

1939, December 6
Shortstop Dick Bartell to Detroit Tigers for shortstop Billy Rogell.

1939, December 8
Catcher Gus Mancuso and pitcher

Billy Jurges

Newt Kimball to Brooklyn Dodgers for catcher Al Todd.

1939, December 27
Pitcher Gene Lillard, shortstop Steve Mesner, and cash to St. Louis Cardinals for pitcher Ken Raffensberger.

1940, July 22
Cash to Washington Senators for first baseman Zeke Bonura.

1940, July 24
Waiver price to Boston Bees for infielder Rabbit Warstler.

1940, December 4
Shortstop Bobby Mattick and outfielder Jim Gleeson to Cincinnati Reds for shortstop Billy Myers.

1941, February 4
Cash to Cincinnati Reds for pitcher Tot Pressnell.

1941, May 6
Second baseman Billy Herman to Brooklyn Dodgers for outfielder Charlie Gilbert, shortstop Johnny Hudson, and $65,000.

1941, June 15
Cash to Boston Braves for first baseman Babe Dahlgren.

1941, August 20
Pitcher Larry French to Brooklyn Dodgers for waiver price.

1941, September 2
Cash to St. Louis Cardinals for pitcher Hank Gornicki. (Gornicki was returned to St. Louis after season.)

1941, December 4
Outfielder Hank Leiber to New York Giants for pitcher Bob Bowman.

1942, May 13
First baseman Babe Dahlgren to St. Louis Browns for cash. (Ten-day conditional sale; Dahlgren was returned to Cubs May 19, 1942.)

1942, May 19
First baseman Babe Dahlgren to Brooklyn Dodgers for cash.

1942, June 1
Waiver price to Boston Red Sox for first baseman Jimmie Foxx.

1942, July 8
$75,000 to St. Louis Cardinals for pitcher Lon Warneke.

1942, November 14
Cash to Cincinnati Reds for outfielder Ival Goodman.

Hank Leiber

1942, November 17
Cash to Pittsburgh Pirates for catcher Bennie Warren.

1943, January 27
Cash to Cincinnati Reds for pitcher Paul Derringer.

1943, April 16
Pitcher George Washburn to Philadelphia Phillies for cash.

1943, May 15
Cash to Brooklyn Dodgers for outfielder Hal Peck.

1943, July
Pitcher Dick Barrett to Philadelphia Phillies for cash.

1943, August 5
Pitcher Bill Lee to Philadelphia Phillies for catcher Mickey Livingston.

1943, September 28
Cash to Brooklyn Dodgers for infielder Al Glossop.

1944, June 6
Second baseman Eddie Stanky to Brooklyn Dodgers for pitcher Bob Chipman.

1944, December
Catcher Billy Holm to Boston Red Sox for cash.

1945, June 23
Waiver price to Pittsburgh Pirates for pitcher Ray Starr.

1945, July 27
$97,000 to New York Yankees for pitcher Hank Borowy.

1946, January 21
Infielder Roy Hughes to Philadelphia Phillies for cash.

1946, April 4
Catcher Bennie Warren to New York Giants for waiver price.

1946, April 20
Outfielder Whitey Platt to Chicago White Sox for waiver price.

1946, May
First baseman Heinz Becker to Cleveland Indians for first baseman Mickey Rocco.

1946, June 15
Outfielder Charlie Gilbert to Philadelphia Phillies for cash.

1947, January 25
Pitcher Hi Bithorn to Pittsburgh Pirates for cash.

1947, April 16
Cash to Cincinnati Reds for second baseman Lonny Frey.

1947, June 25
Second baseman Lonny Frey to New York Yankees for cash.

1947, July 7
Catcher Mickey Livingston to New York Giants for waiver price.

1947, October 8
Outfielder Marv Rickert to Cincinnati Reds for cash.

1948, March 1
Shortstop Bobby Sturgeon to Boston Braves for shortstop Dick Culler.

1948, May 2
Cash to St. Louis Cardinals for infielder Jeff Cross.

1948, May 20
Pitcher Paul Erickson to Philadelphia Phillies for waiver price.

1948, June 17
Waiver price to Brooklyn Dodgers for infielder Gene Mauch.

1948, August 3
Waiver price to Philadelphia Phillies for second baseman Emil Verban.

1948, October 4
Outfielder Bill Nicholson to Philadelphia Phillies for outfielder Harry Walker.

1948, October 11
Pitcher Russ Meyer to Philadelphia Phillies for cash.

1948, December 8
Pitcher Cliff Chambers and catcher Clyde McCullough to Pittsburgh Pirates for pitcher Cal McLish and third baseman Frankie Gustine.

1948, December 14
Pitcher Hank Borowy and first baseman Eddie Waitkus to

Gene Mauch

Philadelphia Phillies for pitchers Monk Dubiel and Dutch Leonard.

1949, May 7
Waiver price to Cleveland Indians for outfielder Hank Edwards.

1949, May 16
Third baseman Hank Schenz to Brooklyn Dodgers for third baseman Bob Ramazzotti.

1949, May 18
Waiver price to Cleveland Indians for first baseman Herm Reich.

1949, June 6
Waiver price to Pittsburgh Pirates for pitcher Bob Muncrief.

1949, June 15
Outfielders Peanuts Lowrey and Harry Walker to Cincinnati Reds for outfielders Frankie Baumholtz and Hank Sauer.

1949, September 14
Third baseman Frankie Gustine to Philadelphia A's for waiver price.

1949, October 14
$100,000 to Brooklyn Dodgers for pitcher Paul Minner and first baseman Preston Ward.

1949, December 14
Infielder Gene Mauch and cash to Boston Braves for pitcher Bill Voiselle.

1950, February 2
First baseman Herm Reich to Chicago White Sox for cash.

1950, February 10
Cash to Cincinnati Reds for pitcher Johnny Vander Meer.

1950, April 18
Pitcher Bob Chipman to Boston Braves for cash.

1950, June 7
Catcher Bob Scheffing to Cincinnati Reds for outfielder Ron Northey.

1950, October 10
Outfielder Hank Edwards and cash to Brooklyn Dodgers for first baseman Chuck Connors and Dee Fondy.

1951, June 15
Outfielder Andy Pafko, pitcher Johnny Schmitz, catcher Rube Walker, and second baseman Wayne Terwilliger to Brooklyn Dodgers for outfielder Gene Hermanski, pitcher Joe Hatten, catcher Bruce Edwards, and infielder Eddie Miksis.

1951, October 4
Outfielder Bob Borkowski and catcher Smoky Burgess to Cincinnati Reds for outfielder Bob Usher and catcher Johnny Pramesa.

1951, October 11
Shortstop Jack Cusick to Boston Braves for outfielder Bob Addis.

1952, January 3
Pitcher Frank Hiller to Cincinnati Reds for pitcher Willie Ramsdell.

1952, June 15
Cash to Philadelphia Phillies for infielder-outfielder Tommy Brown.

1952, December 3
Pitcher Dick Manville and $25,000 to Pittsburgh Pirates for catcher Clyde McCullough.

1952, December 20
Pitcher Monk Dubiel to Boston Braves for pitcher Sheldon Jones.

1953, June 4
Catcher Toby Atwell, pitcher Bob Schultz, first baseman Preston Ward, third baseman George Freese, outfielders Bob Addis and Gene Hermanski, and $150,000 to Pittsburgh Pirates for outfielders Ralph Kiner and Catfish Metkovich, catcher Joe Garagiola, and pitcher Howie Pollet.

Manager Stan Hack (center) with sluggers Ralph Kiner (left) and Hank Sauer

1953, June 12
Pitchers Fred Baczewski and Bob Kelly to Cincinnati Redlegs for pitcher Bubba Church.

1953, November 30
Catcher Carl Sawatski to Chicago White Sox for waiver price.

1953, December 7
Outfielder Catfish Metkovich to Milwaukee Braves for cash.

1954, March 20
Shortstop Roy Smalley to Milwaukee Braves for pitcher Dave Cole and cash.

1954, April 30
$12,500 to St. Louis Cardinals for first baseman Steve Bilko.

1954, May 19
Waiver price to Pittsburgh Pirates for catcher Walker Cooper.

1954, June 14
Outfielder Luis Marquez to Pittsburgh Pirates for outfielder Hal Rice.

1954, September 8
Catcher Joe Garagiola to New York Giants for waiver price.

1954, September 30
Third baseman Bill Serena to Chicago White Sox for waiver price.

1954, October 1
Pitchers Johnny Klippstein and Jim Willis to Cincinnati Reds for outfielders Jim Bolger and Ted Tappe and pitcher Harry Perkowski.

Joe Garagiola, who later gained national renown as a television broadcaster, was acquired from the Pirates in 1953. A weak-hitting catcher, Garagiola got into 137 games in two seasons with the Cubs.

1954, November 16
Outfielder Ralph Kiner to Cleveland Indians for pitcher Sam Jones, outfielder Gale Wade, and $60,000.

1955, March 19
Pitcher Dave Cole to Philadelphia Phillies for cash.

1955, April 16
Cash to Chicago White Sox for outfielder Lloyd Merriman.

1955, October 11
Waiver price to Brooklyn Dodgers for first baseman Frank Kellert.

1955, November 28
Pitcher Hal Jeffcoat to Cincinnati Reds for catcher Hobie Landrith.

1955, December 9
Outfielder Frankie Baumholtz to Philadelphia Phillies for cash.

1955, December 9
Pitcher Don Elston and third baseman Randy Jackson to Brooklyn Dodgers for pitcher Russ Meyer, third baseman Don Hoak, and outfielder Walt Moryn.

1956, March 30
Outfielder Hank Sauer to St. Louis Cardinals for outfielder Pete Whisenant.

1956, May 15
Cash to Brooklyn Dodgers for pitcher Jim Hughes.

1956, September 1
Pitcher Russ Meyer to Cincinnati Reds for waiver price.

Don Hoak

1956, November 13
Pitcher Warren Hacker, third baseman Don Hoak, and outfielder Pete Whisenant to Cincinnati Reds for pitcher Elmer Singleton and third baseman Ray Jablonski.

1956, December 11
Pitchers Jim Davis and Sam Jones, catcher Hobie Landrith, and infielder-outfielder Eddie Miksis to St. Louis Cardinals for pitchers Jackie Collum and Tom Poholsky, catcher Ray Katt, and minor league pitcher Wally Lammers.

1956, December 11
Cash to New York Yankees for catcher Charlie Silvera.

1957, April 16
Third baseman Ray Jablonski and catcher Ray Katt to New York Giants for outfielder Bob Lennon and pitcher Dick Littlefield.

1957, April 20
Outfielder Jim King to St. Louis Cardinals for outfielder Bobby Del Greco and pitcher Ed Mayer.

1957, May 1
Second baseman Gene Baker and first baseman Dee Fondy to Pittsburgh Pirates for first baseman Dale Long and outfielder Lee Walls.

1957, May 13
Cash to Philadelphia Phillies for second baseman Bobby Morgan.

1957, May 23
Pitcher Don Elston to Brooklyn Dodgers for pitchers Jackie Collum and Vito Valentinetti.

1957, June 8
Waiver price to Milwaukee Braves for outfielder Chuck Tanner.

1957, August 24
Pitcher Vito Valentinetti to Cleveland Indians for cash.

1957, September 10
Outfielder Bobby Del Greco to New York Yankees for cash.

1957, November 10
Second baseman Casey Wise to Milwaukee Braves for pitcher Ben Johnson, outfielder Charlie King, minor league outfielder Len Williams, and cash.

1957, December 5
Pitchers Don Kaiser and Bob Rush and outfielder Eddie Haas to Milwaukee Braves for pitcher

Taylor Phillips and catcher Sammy Taylor.

1957, December 10
Pitcher Tom Poholsky to New York Giants for pitcher Freddy Rodriguez.

1958, March 30
Pitcher Dick Littlefield to Milwaukee Braves for cash.

1958, April 3
Outfielder Bob Speake and cash to San Francisco Giants for outfielder Bobby Thomson.

1958, May 6
Cash to Pittsburgh Pirates for first baseman Paul Smith.

1958, May 8
Pitcher Turk Lown to Cincinnati Reds for pitcher Hersh Freeman.

1958, May 20
Pitcher Jim Brosnan to St. Louis Cardinals for third baseman Alvin Dark.

1958, August 23
Waiver price to Baltimore Orioles for first baseman Jim Marshall.

1959, January 23
Pitcher Johnny Briggs and outfielder Jim Bolger to Cleveland Indians for catcher Earl Averill.

1959, March 9
Outfielder Chuck Tanner to Boston Red Sox for pitcher Riverboat Smith.

1959, May 4
Pitcher Riverboat Smith to Cleveland Indians for third baseman Randy Jackson.

1959, May 12
Pitcher Taylor Phillips to Philadelphia Phillies for pitcher Seth Morehead.

1959, May 19
Outfielder Charlie King to St. Louis Cardinals for outfielder Irv Noren.

1959, June 13
Waiver price to Pittsburgh Pirates for pitcher Bob Porterfield.

1959, November 21
First baseman Jim Marshall and pitcher Dave Hillman to Boston Red Sox for first baseman Dick Gernert.

1959, December 1
Outfielder Bobby Thomson to Boston Red Sox for pitcher Al Schroll.

1959, December 6
Pitcher Bill Henry and outfielders Lou Jackson and Lee Walls to Cincinnati Reds for third baseman Frank Thomas.

1960, January 11
Pitcher John Buzhardt and third basemen Alvin Dark and Jim Woods to Philadelphia Phillies for outfielder Richie Ashburn.

1960, April 5
First baseman Dale Long to San Francisco Giants for cash.

1960, April 8
Infielder John Goryl, pitcher Ron Perranoski, minor league outfielder Lee Handley, and $25,000 to Los Angeles Dodgers for shortstop Don Zimmer.

1960, May 13
Second baseman Tony Taylor and catcher Cal Neeman to Philadelphia Phillies for first baseman Ed Bouchee and pitcher Don Cardwell.

1960, May 19
Pitcher Art Ceccarelli, minor league infielder Ray Bellino, and $20,000 to New York Yankees for pitcher Mark Freeman.

1960, June 15
Outfielder Walt Moryn to St. Louis Cardinals for infielder-outfielder Jim McKnight.

1960, August 13
Catcher Earl Averill to Chicago White Sox for minor league catcher Don Prohovich and cash.

1960, August 31
First baseman Dick Gernert to Detroit Tigers for cash.

1961, March 31
Pitchers Moe Drabowsky and Seth Morehead to Milwaukee Braves for shortstops Andre Rodgers and Daryl Robertson.

1961, April 1
Outfielder Lou Johnson to Los Angeles Angels for outfielder Jim McAnany.

1961, May 9
Outfielder Frank Thomas to Milwaukee Braves for outfielder Mel Roach.

1961, July 7
Pitcher Joe Schaffernoth to Cleveland Indians for cash.

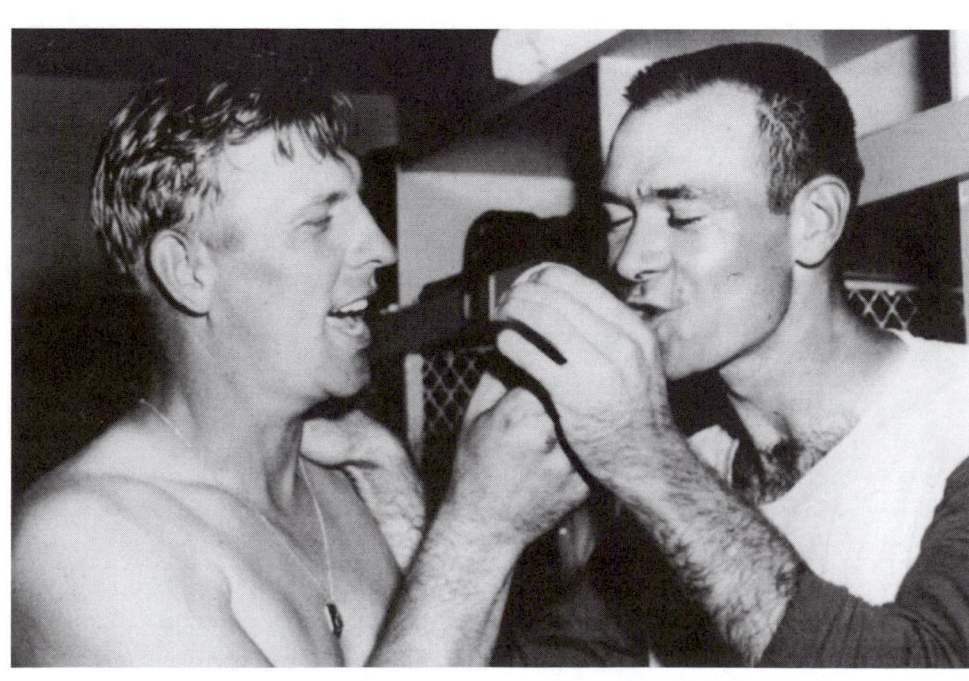

Don Cardwell (right) pitched a no-hitter in his first appearance after being acquired from the Phillies in 1960. Outfielder Walt Moryn (left) saved the no-hitter with a shoestring catch for the final out.

1961, November 27
Infielder Jerry Kindall to Cleveland Indians for pitcher Bobby Locke.

1961, December 8
Outfielder Richie Ashburn to New York Mets for cash.

1962, April 26
Catcher Sammy Taylor to New York Mets for outfielder Bobby Gene Smith.

1962, April 30
Pitcher Jack Curtis to Milwaukee Braves for pitcher Bob Buhl.

1962, June 5
Outfielder Bobby Gene Smith and shortstop Daryl Robertson to St. Louis Cardinals for outfielder Don Landrum and shortstop Alex Grammas.

1962, September 1
Pitcher Harvey Branch to St. Louis Cardinals for pitcher Paul Toth.

1962, October 17
Outfielder George Altman, pitcher Don Cardwell, and catcher Moe Thacker to St. Louis Cardinals for pitchers Larry Jackson and Lindy McDaniel and catcher Jimmie Schaffer.

1962, November 28
Pitcher Bob Anderson to Detroit Tigers for third baseman Steve Boros.

1962, December 3
Third baseman Jim McKnight to Milwaukee Braves for second baseman Ken Aspromonte.

1963, March 28
Pitcher Dave Gerard and outfielder Danny Murphy to Houston Colt .45s for pitchers Hal Haydel and Dick LeMay and catcher Merritt Ranew.

1963, June 24
Pitcher Barney Schultz to St. Louis Cardinals for outfielder Leo Burke.

1963, December 13
Catcher Cuno Barragan and pitcher Jim Brewer to Los Angeles Dodgers for pitcher Dick Scott.

1963, December 15
Outfielder Nelson Mathews to Kansas City A's for pitcher Fred Norman.

1964, May 15
Cash to Los Angeles Angels for pitcher Jack Spring.

Lou Brock

1964, June 2
Pitcher Glen Hobbie to St. Louis Cardinals for pitcher Lew Burdette.

1964, June 3
Catcher Merritt Ranew and $40,000 to Milwaukee Braves for first baseman Len Gabrielson.

1964, June 15
Outfielder Lou Brock and pitchers Jack Spring and Paul Toth to St. Louis Cardinals for outfielder Doug Clemens and pitchers Ernie Broglio and Bobby Shantz.

1964, August 15
Pitcher Bobby Shantz to Philadelphia Phillies for cash.

1964, December 1
Catcher Jimmie Schaffer to Chicago

Ernie Broglio

White Sox for pitcher Frank Baumann.

1964, December 9
Shortstop Andre Rodgers to Pittsburgh Pirates for shortstop Roberto Pena and cash.

1965, January 15
Outfielder Billy Cowan to New York Mets for outfielder George Altman.

1965, March 27
Cash to Detroit Tigers for pitcher Bill Faul.

1965, April 10
Third baseman Bobby Pfeil and minor league pitcher Hal Gibson to St. Louis Cardinals for pitcher Bob Humphreys.

1965, April 14
Cash to Cleveland Indians for pitcher Ted Abernathy.

1965, May 11
Waiver price to St. Louis Cardinals for pitcher Dave Dowling.

1965, May 29
Catcher Dick Bertell and outfielder Len Gabrielson to San Francisco Giants for catcher Ed Bailey, outfielder Harvey Kuenn, and pitcher Bob Hendley.

1965, May 30
Pitcher Lew Burdette to Philadelphia Phillies for cash.

1965, December 2
Pitchers Lindy McDaniel and Jim Rittwage and outfielder Don Landrum to San Francisco Giants for pitcher Bill Hands and catcher Randy Hundley.

1966, January 10
Outfielder Doug Clemens to Philadelphia Phillies for outfielder Wes Covington.

1966, February 15
Catcher Ed Bailey to California Angels for cash.

1966, March 30
Catcher Vic Roznovsky to Baltimore Orioles for outfielder Carl Warwick.

1966, April 2
Pitcher Bob Humphreys to Washington Senators for outfielder Ken Hunt and cash.

1966, April 21
Pitchers Bob Buhl and Larry Jackson

to Philadelphia Phillies for pitcher Ferguson Jenkins, first baseman John Herrnstein, and outfielder Adolfo Phillips.

1966, April 23
Outfielder Harvey Kuenn to Philadelphia Phillies for cash.

1966, April 28
Cash to Atlanta Braves for outfielder Billy Cowan.

1966, May 28
Pitcher Ted Abernathy to Atlanta Braves for first baseman Lee Thomas.

1966, May 29
First baseman John Herrnstein to Atlanta Braves for first baseman Marty Keough.

1966, June 22
Cash to St. Louis Cardinals for pitcher Curt Simmons.

1966, December 7
Pitcher Dick Ellsworth to Philadelphia Phillies for pitcher Ray Culp and cash.

1967, April 3
Catcher Don Bryant to San Francisco Giants for cash.

1967, April 25
Outfielder Bob Raudman and cash to Cleveland Indians for pitcher Dick Radatz.

1967, May 14
Cash to St. Louis Cardinals for outfielder Ted Savage.

1967, May 14
Outfielder Don Young to St. Louis Cardinals for cash.

1967, May 22
Outfielder Jimmy Stewart to Chicago White Sox for cash.

1967, June 12
Pitcher Bob Hendley to New York Mets for pitcher Rob Gardner and catcher Johnny Stephenson.

1967, July 24
Cash to New York Mets for pitcher Bob Shaw.

1967, August 1
Cash to St. Louis Cardinals for outfielder Don Young.

1967, August 2
Pitcher Cal Koonce to New York Mets for cash.

1967, August 2
Pitcher Curt Simmons to California Angels for cash.

1967, August 4
Waiver price to Pittsburgh Pirates for pitcher Pete Mikkelsen.

1967, August 20
Pitcher Bill Connors to New York Mets for cash.

1967, October 13
Outfielder Jim Hicks to St. Louis Cardinals for cash.

1967, November 30
Pitcher Ray Culp to Boston Red Sox for pinch hitter Rudy Schlesinger and cash.

1967, November 30
Outfielder Jim Williams and infielder Paul Popovich to Los Angeles Dodgers for outfielder Lou Johnson.

1968, February 9
Outfielder Lee Thomas to Houston Astros for minor league outfielders Tom Murray and Levi Brown.

1968, March 30
Pitcher Rob Gardner to Cleveland Indians for pitcher Bobby Tiefenauer.

1968, April 3
Cash to Washington Senators for first baseman Dick Nen.

1968, April 22
Pitchers Dave Dowling and Pete Mikkelsen to St. Louis Cardinals for pitchers Jack Lamabe and Ron Piche.

1968, April 23
Pitcher Jim Ellis and outfielder Ted Savage to Los Angeles Dodgers for pitcher Phil Regan and outfielder Jim Hickman.

1968, May 4
Outfielder Byron Browne to Houston Astros for outfielder Aaron Pointer.

1968, June 27
Cash to Boston Red Sox for catcher Gene Oliver.

1968, June 28
Outfielder Lou Johnson to Cleveland Indians for first baseman Willie Smith.

1968, October 1
First baseman Dick Nen to Washington Senators for cash.

1969, January 9
Catcher Bill Plummer, outfielder Clarence Jones, and minor league pitcher Ken Myette to Cincinnati Reds for pitcher Ted Abernathy.

1969, January 15
Infielder Ron Campbell and pitcher Chuck Hartenstein to Pittsburgh Pirates for outfielder Manny Jimenez.

1969, March 28
Cash to San Francisco Giants for third baseman Charley Smith.

1969, April 19
Shortstop Lee Elia to New York Yankees for second baseman Nate Oliver.

1969, April 25
Pitchers Joe Niekro and Gary Ross and shortstop Francisco Libran to San Diego Padres for pitcher Dick Selma.

1969, April 27
Minor league infielder Jim Armstrong and cash to Cincinnati Reds for pitcher Don Nottebart.

1969, June 11
Pitcher Jack Lamabe and outfielder Adolfo Phillips to Montreal Expos for second baseman Paul Popovich.

1969, August 11
Cash to New York Yankees for pitcher Ken Johnson.

1969, September 11
Minor league pitcher Terry Bongiovanni and cash to New York Yankees for outfielder Jimmie Hall.

1969, November 17
Pitcher Dick Selma and outfielder Oscar Gamble to Philadelphia Phillies for outfielder Johnny Callison.

1969, December 4
Pitcher Rich Nye to St. Louis Cardinals for outfielder Boots Day.

1970, March 29
Catcher Randy Bobb to New York Mets for catcher J. C. Martin.

1970, April 22
Outfielder Jimmy Qualls to Montreal Expos for cash.

1970, May 12
Outfielder Boots Day to Montreal Expos for catcher Jack Hiatt.

1970, May 29
Pitcher Ted Abernathy to St. Louis Cardinals for infielder Phil Gagliano.

Joe Pepitone

1970, June 23
Cash to Atlanta Braves for pitcher Milt Pappas.

1970, June 23
Cash to San Diego Padres for pitcher Roberto Rodriguez.

1970, June 29
Outfielder Jimmie Hall to Atlanta Braves for cash.

1970, July 9
Pitcher Archie Reynolds to California Angels for pitcher Juan Pizarro.

1970, July 29
Cash to Houston Astros for first baseman Joe Pepitone.

1970, September 1
Cash to Chicago White Sox for pitcher Bob Miller.

1970, September 16
Cash to Oakland A's for outfielder Tommy Davis.

1970, September 21
Cash to Atlanta Braves for pitcher Hoyt Wilhelm.

1970, October 12
Shortstop Roger Metzger to Houston Astros for shortstop Hector Torres.

1970, November 30
First baseman Willie Smith to Cincinnati Reds for catcher Danny Breeden.

1970, November 30
Pitcher Hoyt Wilhelm to Atlanta Braves for first baseman Hal Breeden.

1970, November 30
Pitchers Pat Jacquez and Dave Lemonds and pinch hitter Roe Skidmore to Chicago White Sox for first baseman Ossie Blanco and outfielder Jose Ortiz.

1970, December 1
Catcher Jack Hiatt to Houston Astros for cash.

1970, December 3
Second baseman Phil Gagliano to Boston Red Sox for third baseman Carmen Fanzone.

1971, May 19
Third baseman Garry Jestadt to San Diego Padres for catcher Chris Cannizzaro.

1971, June 17
Cash to Oakland A's for first baseman Ramon Webster.

1971, August 31
Outfielder Adrian Garrett to Oakland A's for outfielder Bill McNulty and catcher Frank Fernandez.

1971, November 29
Pitcher Ken Holtzman to Oakland A's for outfielder Rick Monday.

1971, December 3
Pitchers Jim Colborn and Earl Stephenson and outfielder Brock Davis to Milwaukee Brewers for outfielder Jose Cardenal.

1971, December 17
Catcher Chris Cannizzaro to Los Angeles Dodgers for cash.

1972, January 20
Outfielder Johnny Callison to New York Yankees for pitcher Jack Aker.

1972, April 7
First baseman Hal Breeden and shortstop Hector Torres to Montreal Expos for pitcher Dan McGinn.

1972, April 20
Cash to San Diego Padres for pitcher Tom Phoebus.

1972, June 2
Pitcher Phil Regan to Chicago White Sox for cash.

1972, June 28
First baseman Art Shamsky to Oakland A's for cash.

1972, August 18
Outfielder Tommy Davis to Baltimore Orioles for catcher Ellie Hendricks.

1972, October 20
Pitcher Tom Phoebus to Atlanta Braves for second baseman Tony LaRussa.

1972, October 27
Catcher Ellie Hendricks to Baltimore Orioles for catcher Francisco Estrada.

1972, November 21
Outfielder Billy North to Oakland A's for pitcher Bob Locker.

1972, November 30
Pitchers Joe Decker and Bill Hands and minor league pitcher Bob Maneely to Minnesota Twins for pitcher Dave LaRoche.

1973, May 19
First baseman Joe Pepitone to Atlanta Braves for first baseman Andre Thornton.

1973, August 13
Cash to Texas Rangers for outfielder Rico Carty.

1973, August 29
First baseman Pat Bourque to Oakland A's for first baseman Gonzalo Marquez.

1973, August 31
Pitcher Larry Gura to Texas Rangers for pitcher Mike Paul.

1973, September 11
Outfielder Rico Carty to Oakland A's for cash.

1973, October 25
Pitcher Ferguson Jenkins to Texas Rangers for third baseman Bill Madlock and outfielder Vic Harris.

1973, November 7
Second basemen Glenn Beckert and Bobby Fenwick to San Diego Padres for outfielder Jerry Morales.

1973, December 3
Pitcher Bob Locker to Oakland A's for pitcher Horacio Pina.

1973, December 6
Catcher Randy Hundley to Minnesota Twins for catcher George Mitterwald.

1973, December 11
Third baseman Ron Santo to Chicago White Sox for pitchers Ken Frailing, Jim Kremmel, and Steve Stone and catcher Steve Swisher.

1974, March 19
Catcher Ken Rudolph to San Francisco Giants for pitcher Willie Prall.

1974, March 23
First baseman Jim Hickman to St.

Louis Cardinals for pitcher Scipio Spinks.

1974, April 1
Second baseman Paul Popovich to Pittsburgh Pirates for pitcher Tom Dettore and cash.

1974, July 10
Cash to Philadelphia Phillies for infielder Billy Grabarkewitz.

1974, July 28
Pitcher Horacio Pina to California Angels for catcher Rick Stelmaszek.

1974, October 23
First baseman Billy Williams to Oakland A's for pitchers Darold Knowles and Bob Locker and second baseman Manny Trillo.

1975, February 25
Pitcher Dave LaRoche and outfielder Brock Davis to Cleveland Indians for pitcher Milt Wilcox.

1975, April 6
Pitcher Jim Todd to Oakland A's for outfielder Champ Summers and cash.

1975, April 28
Third baseman Matt Alexander to Oakland A's for minor league pitcher Howell Copeland.

1975, May 2
Pitcher Burt Hooton to Los Angeles Dodgers for pitchers Eddie Solomon and Geoff Zahn.

1975, July 31
First baseman Adrian Garrett to California Angels for cash.

1975, October 28
Shortstop Don Kessinger to St. Louis Cardinals for pitcher Mike Garman and minor league infielder Bobby Hrapmann.

1975, December 22
Outfielder Vic Harris to St. Louis Cardinals for shortstop Mick Kelleher.

1976, April 13
Cash to San Diego Padres for catcher Randy Hundley.

1976, April 19
Catcher Tim Hosley to Oakland A's for cash.

1976, May 17
First baseman Andre Thornton to Montreal Expos for outfielder Larry Biittner and pitcher Steve Renko.

1976, June 8
Cash to Detroit Tigers for pitcher Joe Coleman.

1976, September 8
Cash to Pittsburgh Pirates for pitcher Ramon Hernandez.

1976, November 24
Pitcher Steve Stone to Chicago White Sox as free-agent signing.

1976, December 8
First baseman Pete LaCock to Kansas City Royals for outfielder Sheldon Mallory.

1976, December 8
Outfielder Sheldon Mallory to New York Mets for outfielder Jim Dwyer.

1976, December 8
Infielder Julio Gonzalez to Houston Astros for outfielder Greg Gross.

1977, January 11
Outfielder Rick Monday and pitcher Mike Garman to Los Angeles Dodgers for outfielder Bill Buckner, shortstop Ivan DeJesus, and minor league pitcher Jeff Albert.

1977, February 5
Pitcher Darold Knowles to Texas Rangers for outfielder Gene Clines and cash.

1977, February 11
Third baseman Bill Madlock and infielder Rob Sperring to San Francisco Giants for third baseman Steve Ontiveros, outfielder Bobby Murcer, and minor league pitcher Andy Muhlstock.

1977, February 16
Outfielder Champ Summers to Cincinnati Reds for outfielder Dave Schneck.

1977, February 28
Pitcher Buddy Schultz to St. Louis Cardinals for minor league pitcher Mark Covert.

1977, March 15
Pitcher Joe Coleman to Oakland A's for pitcher Jim Todd.

1977, March 15
First baseman Jerry Tabb to Oakland A's for cash.

1977, April 20
Pitcher Jim Todd to Seattle Mariners for pitcher Pete Broberg.

1977, May 28
Pitcher Ramon Hernandez to Boston Red Sox for outfielder Bobby Darwin.

1977, July 30
Cash to Detroit Tigers for pitcher Dave Roberts.

1977, August 5
Cash to Oakland A's for pitcher Dave Giusti.

1977, August 18
Pitcher Steve Renko to Chicago White Sox for minor league pitcher Larry Anderson and cash.

1977, October 25
Outfielder Jose Cardenal to Philadelphia Phillies for minor league pitcher Manny Seoane.

1977, October 25
Minor league pitcher Steve Hamrick to Seattle Mariners for catcher Larry Cox.

1977, October 31
Pitcher Bill Bonham to Cincinnati Reds for pitchers Bill Caudill and Woodie Fryman.

1977, November 30
Outfielder Dave Kingman from New York Yankees as free-agent signing.

1977, December 5
Infielder Dave Rosello to Cleveland Indians for minor league pitcher Norm Churchill and minor league outfielder Bruce Compton.

1977, December 8
Outfielder Jerry Morales, catcher Steve Swisher, and cash to St. Louis Cardinals for outfielder Hector Cruz and catcher Dave Rader.

Dave Kingman

1978, March 29
Pitcher Pete Broberg to Oakland A's for second baseman Rodney Scott and cash.

1978, April 1
Outfielder Mike Adams to Oakland A's for cash.

1978, June 9
Pitcher Woodie Fryman to Montreal Expos for outfielder Jerry White.

1978, June 10
Pitcher Ron Davis to New York Yankees for pitcher Ken Holtzman.

1978, June 15
Outfielder Hector Cruz to San Francisco Giants for pitcher Lynn McGlothen.

1978, June 15
Outfielder Joe Wallis to Cleveland Indians for outfielder Mike Vail.

1978, June 26
Pitcher Paul Reuschel to Cleveland Indians for pitcher Denny DeBarr.

1978, August 6
Pitcher Larry Anderson to Philadelphia Phillies for first baseman Davey Johnson.

1978, December 14
Outfielder Jerry White and third baseman Rodney Scott to Montreal Expos for outfielder Sam Mejias.

1979, February 23
Second baseman Manny Trillo, catcher Dave Rader, and outfielder Greg Gross to Philadelphia Phillies for pitcher Derek Botelho, minor league pitcher Henry Mack, second baseman Ted Sizemore, catcher Barry Foote, and outfielder Jerry Martin.

1979, March 20
Catcher Larry Cox to Seattle Mariners for outfielder Luis Delgado.

1979, March 20
Third baseman Ed Putman to Detroit Tigers for second baseman Steve Dillard.

1979, May 3
Minor league pitcher Mark Gilbert to Cincinnati Reds for pitcher Doug Capilla.

1979, May 23
Pitcher Ray Burris to New York Yankees for pitcher Dick Tidrow.

1979, June 26
Outfielder Bobby Murcer to New York Yankees for minor league pitcher Paul Semall and cash.

1979, June 28
Cash to Cincinnati Reds for outfielder Ken Henderson.

1979, July 4
Cash to Oakland A's for outfielder Miguel Dilone.

1979, July 4
Outfielder Sam Mejias to Cincinnati Reds for cash.

1979, August 17
Second baseman Ted Sizemore to Boston Red Sox for catcher Mike O'Berry and cash.

1979, August 30
Cash to Detroit Tigers for catcher Bruce Kimm.

1979, October 17
Pitcher Donnie Moore to St. Louis Cardinals for second baseman Mike Tyson.

1980, April 2
Cash to Seattle Mariners for outfielder Lenny Randle.

1980, April 7
Cash to Toronto Blue Jays for pitcher Mark Lemongello.

1980, May 7
Outfielder Miguel Dilone to Cleveland Indians for cash.

1980, June 23
First baseman Karl Pagel and cash to Cleveland Indians for designated hitter Cliff Johnson.

1980, October 17
Catcher Mike O'Berry to Cincinnati Reds for pitcher Jay Howell.

1980, December 9
Pitcher Bruce Sutter to St. Louis Cardinals for outfielder Leon Durham and third basemen Ken Reitz and Tye Waller.

1980, December 11
Second baseman Keith Drumright and first baseman Cliff Johnson to Oakland A's for minor league pitcher Mike King.

1980, December 12
Outfielder Mike Vail to Cincinnati Reds for outfielder Hector Cruz.

1980, December 12
Outfielders Jesus Figueroa and Jerry

Martin and minor league infielder Mike Turgeon to San Francisco Giants for second baseman Joe Strain and pitcher Phil Nastu.

1981, January 8
First baseman Larry Biittner to Cincinnati Reds as free-agent signing.

1981, February 28
Outfielder Dave Kingman to New York Mets for outfielder Steve Henderson and cash.

1981, March 28
Pitcher Dennis Lamp to Chicago White Sox for pitcher Ken Kravec.

1981, April 1
Infielder Mick Kelleher to Detroit Tigers for cash.

1981, April 6
Cash to New York Mets for catcher Butch Benton.

1981, April 6
Third baseman Lenny Randle to Seattle Mariners as free-agent signing.

1981, April 27
Catcher Barry Foote to New York Yankees for pitcher Tom Filer and cash.

1981, June 4
Cash to Texas Rangers for outfielder Bobby Bonds.

1981, June 12
Pitcher Rick Reuschel to New York Yankees for pitchers Doug Bird and Mike Griffin and $400,000.

1981, August 15
Pitcher Lynn McGlothen to Chicago White Sox for pinch hitter Bob Molinaro.

1981, August 19
Pitchers Bill Caudill and Jay Howell to New York Yankees for second baseman Pat Tabler.

1981, October 23
$50,000 to Cincinnati Reds for second baseman Junior Kennedy.

1981, December 7
Pitcher Doug Capilla to San Francisco Giants for pitcher Allen Ripley.

1981, December 8
Pitcher Bill Campbell from Boston Red Sox as free-agent signing.

1981, December 8
Pitcher Ferguson Jenkins from Texas Rangers as free-agent signing.

1981, December 8
Pitcher Mike Krukow and cash to Philadelphia Phillies for pitchers Dickie Noles and Dan Larson and catcher Keith Moreland.

1981, December 9
Outfielder Jim Tracy to Houston Astros for outfielder Gary Woods.

1981, December 28
Pitcher Dave Geisel to Toronto Blue Jays for pitcher Paul Mirabella.

1982, January 14
Catcher Tim Blackwell to Montreal Expos as free-agent signing.

1982, January 27
Shortstop Ivan DeJesus to Philadelphia Phillies for shortstops Larry Bowa and Ryne Sandberg.

1982, March 16
Pitcher Mike Griffin to Montreal Expos for outfielder Dan Briggs.

1982, March 26
Pitcher Paul Mirabella, minor league pitcher Paul Semall, and cash to Texas Rangers for second baseman Bump Wills.

1982, September 1
Pinch hitter Bob Molinaro to Philadelphia Phillies for cash.

Ryne Sandberg, acquired from the Phillies on January 27, 1982, was a throw-in in the Larry Bowa deal.

1982, October 15
Pitcher Herman Segelke to San Francisco Giants for pitcher Alan Hargesheimer.

1982, November 29
Cash to Chicago White Sox for second baseman Jay Loviglio.

1982, December 9
Outfielder Steve Henderson to Seattle Mariners for pitcher Rich Bordi.

1982, December 10
Pitcher Doug Bird to Boston Red Sox for pitcher Chuck Rainey.

1982, December 10
Designated hitter Wayne Nordhagen from Toronto Blue Jays as free-agent signing.

1982, December 10
Outfielder Tye Waller to Chicago White Sox for pitcher Reggie Patterson.

1983, January 20
Pitcher Vance Lovelace and minor league outfielder Dan Cataline to Los Angeles Dodgers for third baseman Ron Cey.

1983, January 25
Shortstop Scott Fletcher, third baseman Pat Tabler and pitchers Randy Martz and Dick Tidrow to Chicago White Sox for pitchers Warren Brusstar and Steve Trout.

1983, March 30
Cash to Oakland A's for outfielder Thad Bosley.

1983, April 1
Minor league pitcher Rich Bounantony and cash to Milwaukee Brewers for catcher Steve Lake.

1983, April 2
Minor league pitchers Bob Schilling and Craig Weissman to New York Mets for infielder Tom Veryzer.

1983, May 22
Pitcher Guillermo Hernandez to Philadelphia Phillies for pitchers Dick Ruthven and Bill Johnson.

1983, September 26
Minor league pitchers Mitch Cook and Jim Adamczak to New York Mets for pitcher Terry Leach and minor league first baseman Mike Anicich.

1983, September 30
Cash to San Francisco Giants for pitcher Mike Chris.

Rich Hebner

1983, December 7
Pitcher Craig Lefferts, first baseman Carmelo Martinez, and third baseman Fritz Connally to San Diego Padres for pitcher Scott Sanderson.

1984, January 5
Third baseman Richie Hebner from Pittsburgh Pirates as free-agent signing.

1984, March 26
Pitcher Bill Campbell and catcher Mike Diaz to Philadelphia Phillies for outfielders Bob Dernier and Gary Matthews and pitcher Porfi Altamirano.

1984, March 26
Minor league pitcher Stan Kyles and minor league outfielder Stan Boderick to Oakland A's for pitcher Tim Stoddard.

1984, March 30
Pitcher Alan Hargesheimer to Kansas City Royals for pitcher Derek Botelho.

1984, April 9
Pitcher Terry Leach to Atlanta Braves for pitcher Ron Meridith.

1984, April 10
Second baseman Jerry Manuel to Chicago White Sox for minor league infielder Tim Gourley.

1984, May 25
First baseman Bill Buckner to Boston Red Sox for pitcher Dennis Eckersley and shortstop Mike Brumley.

1984, June 13
Outfielders Joe Carter and Mel Hall, pitcher Don Schulze, and minor league pitcher Darryl Banks to Cleveland Indians for pitchers Rick Sutcliffe and George Frazier and catcher Ron Hassey.

1984, July 1
Pitcher Dickie Noles to Texas Rangers for pitcher Dwayne Henry and minor league infielder Jorge Gomez.

1984, July 15
Pitcher Chuck Rainey to Oakland A's for infielder Davey Lopes.

1984, December 4
Pitchers Porfi Altamirano and Rich Bordi, outfielder Henry Cotto, and catcher Ron Hassey to New York Yankees for pitcher Ray Fontenot and outfielder Brian Dayett.

1984, December 7
Cash to Milwaukee Brewers for catcher Jamie Nelson.

1984, December 18
Pitcher Lary Sorensen from Oakland A's as free-agent signing.

1985, January 8
Pitcher Tim Stoddard to San Diego Padres as free-agent signing.

1985, February 28
Pitcher Rick Reuschel to Pittsburgh Pirates as free-agent signing.

1985, April 1
Infielder Dan Rohn to Cleveland Indians for pitcher Jay Baller.

1985, April 8
Shortstop Chris Speier from Minnesota Twins as free-agent signing.

1985, July 26
Minor league outfielder Tom Grant to Cleveland Indians for pitcher Dave Beard.

1985, December 11
Infielder Dave Owen to San Francisco Giants for second baseman Manny Trillo.

1985, December 16
Outfielder Billy Hatcher and pitcher Steve Engel to Houston Astros for outfielder Jerry Mumphrey.

1986, January 17
Minor league pitcher John Cox and minor league infielder Gary Jones to Oakland A's for first baseman Phil Stephenson and minor league infielder Bob Bathe.

1986, February 1
Pitcher Matt Keough from St. Louis Cardinals as free-agent signing.

1986, June 30
Catcher Dave Liddell and minor league pitcher Dave Lenderman to New York Mets for pitcher Ed Lynch.

1986, July 21
Infielder Davey Lopes to Houston Astros for pitcher Frank DiPino.

1986, July 26
Pitcher Ron Meridith to Texas Rangers for pitcher Rich Surhoff and minor league pitcher Bryan Dial.

1986, August 13
Pitchers Ray Fontenot and George Frazier and minor league shortstop Julius McDougal to Minnesota Twins for pitcher Ron Davis and minor league pitcher Dewayne Coleman.

1986, December 10
Third baseman Chris Speier to San Francisco Giants as free-agent signing.

1986, December 17
Minor league outfielder Joe Hicks to Oakland A's for catcher Bill Bathe.

1987, January 30
Third baseman Ron Cey to Oakland A's for infielder Luis Quinones.

1987, February 17
Pitcher Guy Hoffman to Cincinnati Reds for third baseman Wade Rowdon.

1987, March 6
Outfielder Andre Dawson from Montreal Expos as free-agent signing.

1987, March 26
Outfielder Thad Bosley and pitcher Dave Gumpert to Kansas City Royals for catcher Jim Sundberg.

1987, April 3
Pitcher Dennis Eckersley and infielder Dan Rohn to Oakland A's for minor league pitcher Mark Leonette, minor league infielder Brian Guinn, and minor league outfielder David Wilder.

1987, May 16
Pitcher Dave Pavlas to Texas Rangers for pitcher Mike Mason.

1987, July 12
Outfielder Gary Matthews to Seattle Mariners for minor league pitcher David Hartnett.

1987, July 12
Pitcher Steve Trout and cash to New York Yankees for pitchers Rich Scheid, Bob Tewksbury, and Dean Wilkins.

1987, September 22
Pitcher Dickie Noles to Detroit Tigers for player to be named. (Noles was returned October 23, 1987.)

1987, September 22
Outfielder Chico Walker to California Angels for minor league pitcher Todd Fischer.

1987, December 8
Pitcher Lee Smith to Boston Red Sox for pitchers Al Nipper and Calvin Schiraldi.

1987, December 19
Second baseman Vance Law from Montreal Expos as free-agent signing.

1988, February 12
Third baseman Keith Moreland and shortstop Mike Brumley to San Diego Padres for pitchers Goose Gossage and Ray Hayward.

1988, March 17
Pitcher Ray Hayward to Texas Rangers for outfielder Dave Meier and second baseman Greg Tabor.

1988, March 29
Third baseman Wade Rowdon to Baltimore Orioles for minor league shortstop Nick Ramirez and minor league pitcher Tom Michno.

1988, March 31
Minor league pitcher Mike Curtis to Pittsburgh Pirates for pitcher Mike Bielecki.

1988, April 1
Shortstop Luis Quinones to Cincinnati Reds for pitcher Bill Landrum.

1988, May 19
First baseman Leon Durham to Cincinnati Reds for pitcher Pat Perry and cash.

1988, July 14
Outfielder Dave Martinez to Montreal

Expos for outfielder Mitch Webster.

1988, September 29
Catcher Jody Davis to Atlanta Braves for pitchers Kevin Blankenship and Kevin Coffman.

1988, December 5
Outfielder Rafael Palmeiro and pitchers Drew Hall and Jamie Moyer to Texas Rangers for pitchers Mitch Williams, Paul Kilgus, and Steve Wilson, infielder Curtis Wilkerson, minor league infielder Luis Benitez, and minor league outfielder Pablo Delgado.

1988, December 9
Outfielder Rolando Roomes to Cincinnati Reds for catcher-outfielder Lloyd McClendon.

1988, December 21
Pitcher Frank DiPino to St. Louis Cardinals as free-agent signing.

1988, December 21
Infielder Manny Trillo to Cincinnati Reds as free-agent signing.

1989, August 24
Pitchers Pat Gomez and Rick Luecken to Atlanta Braves for pitcher Paul Assenmacher.

1989, August 30
Outfielders Darrin Jackson and Phil Stephenson and pitcher Calvin Schiraldi to San Diego Padres for outfielder Marvell Wynne and third baseman Luis Salazar.

1989, November 20
Outfielder Mitch Webster to Cleveland Indians for designated hitter Dave Clark.

1989, December 7
Pitcher Paul Kilgus to Toronto Blue Jays for pitcher Jose Nunez.

1989, December 13
Pitcher Scott Sanderson to Oakland A's as free-agent signing.

1990, January 3
Minor league infielder Bryan House to Texas Rangers for shortstop Rey Sanchez.

1990, April 30
Minor league pitcher Frank Campos to Chicago White Sox for pitcher Bill Long.

1990, September 3
Minor league pitcher Greg Kallevig to

Danny Jackson

Pittsburgh Pirates for pitcher Randy Kramer.

1990, September 7
Outfielder Lloyd McClendon to Pittsburgh Pirates for minor league pitcher Mike Pomeranz.

1990, November 21
Pitcher Danny Jackson from Cincinnati Reds as free-agent signing.

1990, December 6
Outfielder George Bell from Toronto Blue Jays as free-agent signing.

1990, December 14
Infielder Greg Smith to Los Angeles Dodgers for infielder Jose Vizcaino.

1990, December 17
Pitcher Dave Smith from Houston Astros as free-agent signing.

1991, January 9
Third baseman Curtis Wilkerson to Pittsburgh Pirates as free-agent signing.

1991, March 29
Outfielder Gary Varsho to Pittsburgh Pirates for outfielder Steve Carter.

1991, April 7
Pitcher Mitch Williams to Philadelphia Phillies for pitchers Chuck McElroy and Bob Scanlan.

1991, June 26
Minor league pitcher David Rosario to

New York Yankees for pitcher Steve Adkins.

1991, September 6
Pitcher Steve Wilson to Los Angeles Dodgers for pitcher Jeff Hartsock.

1991, September 29
Catcher Damon Berryhill and pitcher Mike Bielecki to Atlanta Braves for pitchers Yorkis Perez and Turk Wendell.

1991, December 2
Waiver price to Kansas City Royals for catcher Jorge Pedre.

1991, December 3
Pitcher Mike Morgan from Los Angeles Dodgers as free-agent signing.

1991, December 19
Pitcher Rick Sutcliffe to Baltimore Orioles as free-agent signing.

1992, March 30
Outfielder George Bell to Chicago White Sox for outfielder Sammy Sosa and pitcher Ken Patterson.

1992, May 7
Infielder-outfielder Chico Walker to New York Mets for waiver price.

1992, June 27
Minor league pitcher Mike Sodders to Los Angeles Dodgers for outfielder Kal Daniels.

1992, July 7
Outfielder Ced Landrum to Milwaukee Brewers for infielder Jeff Kunkel.

1992, July 11
Pitcher Danny Jackson to Pittsburgh Pirates for third baseman Steve Buechele.

1992, November 17
Shortstop Alex Arias and third baseman Gary Scott to Florida Marlins for pitcher Greg Hibbard.

1992, December 1
Pitcher Jose Guzman from Texas Rangers as free-agent signing.

1992, December 2
Catcher Steve Lake from Philadelphia Phillies as free-agent signing.

1992, December 8
Pitcher Dan Plesac from Milwaukee Brewers as free-agent signing.

1992, December 9
Outfielder Andre Dawson to Boston Red Sox as free-agent signing.

1992, December 9
Pitcher Greg Maddux to Atlanta Braves as free-agent signing.

1992, December 9
Pitcher Randy Myers from San Diego Padres as free-agent signing.

1992, December 11
Outfielder Candy Maldonado from Toronto Blue Jays as free-agent signing.

1992, December 18
Outfielder Willie Wilson from Oakland A's as free-agent signing.

1993, June 1
Pitcher Heathcliff Slocumb to Cleveland Indians for infielder Jose Hernandez.

1993, July 30
Pitcher Paul Assenmacher to New York Yankees for outfielder Karl Rhodes.

1993, August 19
Outfielder Candy Maldonado to Cleveland Indians for outfielder Glenallen Hill.

1993, November 24
Pitcher Dave Stevens and catcher Matt Walbeck to Minnesota Twins for pitcher Willie Banks.

1993, December 10
Pitcher Chuck McElroy to Cincinnati Reds for pitchers Mike Anderson and Larry Luebbers and minor league catcher Darron Cox.

1993, December 19
Pitcher Bob Scanlan to Milwaukee Brewers for pitcher Rafael Novoa and minor league outfielder Mike Carter.

1994, January 14
Pitcher Greg Hibbard to Seattle Mariners as free-agent signing.

1994, February 1
Outfielder Dwight Smith to California Angels as free-agent signing.

1994, March 29
Minor league pitcher Travis Willis to Pittsburgh Pirates for outfielder Scott Bullett.

1994, March 30
Shortstop Jose Vizcaino to New York Mets for pitcher Anthony Young and minor league pitcher Ottis Smith.

1994, April 12
Pitcher Shawn Boskie to Philadelphia Phillies for pitcher Kevin Foster.

1994, October 11
Catcher Mark Parent to Pittsburgh Pirates for waiver price.

1994, November 8
Pitcher Dan Plesac to Pittsburgh Pirates as free-agent signing.

1994, November 18
Pitcher Larry Luebbers to Cincinnati Reds for waiver price.

1994, November 22
Waiver price to San Francisco Giants for pitcher Bryan Hickerson.

1995, April 5
Minor league pitchers Geno Morones and Derek Wallace to Kansas City Royals for outfielder Brian McRae.

1995, April 9
Pitcher Jaime Navarro from Milwaukee Brewers as free-agent signing.

1995, April 12
Pitcher Steve Dixon from Cleveland Indians for waiver price.

1995, May 26
Outfielder Karl Rhodes to Boston Red Sox for waiver price.

1995, June 13
Pitcher Mike Morgan, minor league catcher Francisco Morales, and minor league outfielder Paul Torres to St. Louis Cardinals for first baseman Todd Zeile.

1995, June 19
Pitcher Willie Banks to Los Angeles Dodgers for minor league pitcher Dax Winslett.

1995, June 28
Catcher Rick Wilkins to Houston Astros for catcher Scott Servais and outfielder Luis Gonzalez.

1995, July 7
Outfielder Kevin Roberson to Seattle Mariners for waiver price.

1995, July 31
Pitcher Bryan Hickerson to Colorado Rockies for player to be named.

1995, August 9
Pitcher Rich Garces to Florida Marlins for waiver price.

Brian McRae

1995, August 31
Player to be named to Pittsburgh Pirates for catcher Mark Parent and cash.

1995, December 13
Catcher Mark Parent to Detroit Tigers as free-agent signing.

1995, December 14
Pitcher Randy Myers to Baltimore Orioles as free-agent signing.

1995, December 22
Third baseman Todd Zeile to Philadelphia Phillies as free-agent signing.

1995, December 26
Third baseman Dave Magadan from Houston Astros as free-agent signing.

1995, December 28
Pitcher Doug Jones from Baltimore Orioles as free-agent signing.

1996, January 8
Shortstop Shawon Dunston to San Francisco Giants as free-agent signing.

1996, January 16
Pitcher Bob Patterson from California Angels as free-agent signing.

1996, June 26
Minor league pitcher Ismael Villegas for catcher Tyler Houston.

Milestones, Honors, and Other Facts

Batting-Average Leaders by Year

1876	Ross Barnes	.429	1917	Les Mann	.273	1957	Dale Long	.305
1877	Cal McVey	.368	1918	Charlie Hollocher	.316	1958	Ernie Banks	.313
1878	Joe Start,		1919	Max Flack	.294	1959	Ernie Banks	.304
	Bob Ferguson	.351	1920	Charlie Hollocher	.319	1960	Richie Ashburn	.291
1879	Cap Anson	.396	1921	Ray Grimes	.321	1961	George Altman	.303
1880	George Gore	.360	1922	Ray Grimes	.354	1962	George Altman	.318
1881	Cap Anson	.399	1923	Jigger Statz	.319	1963	Ron Santo	.297
1882	Cap Anson	.362	1924	George Grantham	.316	1964	Ron Santo	.313
1883	George Gore	.334	1925	Howard Freigau	.307	1965	Billy Williams	.315
1884	King Kelly	.354	1926	Riggs Stephenson	.338	1966	Ron Santo	.312
1885	George Gore	.313	1927	Riggs Stephenson	.344	1967	Ron Santo	.300
1886	King Kelly	.388	1928	Riggs Stephenson	.324	1968	Glenn Beckert	.294
1887	Cap Anson	.347	1929	Rogers Hornsby	.380	1969	Billy Williams	.293
1888	Cap Anson	.344	1930	Riggs Stephenson	.367	1970	Billy Williams	.322
1889	Cap Anson	.291	1931	Charlie Grimm,		1971	Glenn Beckert	.342
1890	Cap Anson	.312		Rogers Hornsby	.331	1972	Billy Williams	.333
1891	Cap Anson	.291	1932	Riggs Stephenson	.324	1973	Jose Cardenal	.303
1892	Bill Dahlen	.295	1933	Riggs Stephenson	.329	1974	Bill Madlock	.313
1893	Cap Anson	.314	1934	Kiki Cuyler	.338	1975	Bill Madlock	.354
1894	Cap Anson	.395	1935	Gabby Hartnett	.344	1976	Bill Madlock	.339
1895	Bill Lange	.389	1936	Frank Demaree	.350	1977	Steve Ontiveros	.299
1896	Bill Dahlen	.361	1937	Gabby Hartnett	.354	1978	Bill Buckner	.323
1897	Bill Lange	.340	1938	Stan Hack	.320	1979	Scot Thompson	.289
1898	Jimmy Ryan	.323	1939	Hank Leiber	.310	1980	Bill Buckner	.324
1899	Bill Lange	.325	1940	Stan Hack	.317	1981	Bill Buckner	.311
1900	Danny Green	.298	1941	Stan Hack	.317	1982	Leon Durham	.312
1901	Topsy Hartsel	.335	1942	Stan Hack,		1983	Keith Moreland	.302
1902	Jimmy Slagle	.315		Lou Novikoff	.300	1984	Ryne Sandberg	.314
1903	Frank Chance	.327	1943	Bill Nicholson	.309	1985	Keith Moreland	.307
1904	Frank Chance	.310	1944	Phil Cavarretta	.321	1986	Jerry Mumphrey	.304
1905	Frank Chance	.316	1945	Phil Cavarretta	.355	1987	Jerry Mumphrey	.333
1906	Harry Steinfeldt	.327	1946	Eddie Waitkus	.304	1988	Rafael Palmeiro	.307
1907	Frank Chance	.293	1947	Phil Cavarretta	.314	1989	Dwight Smith	.324
1908	Johnny Evers	.300	1948	Andy Pafko	.312	1990	Andre Dawson	.310
1909	Solly Hofman	.285	1949	Phil Cavarretta	.294	1991	Ryne Sandberg	.291
1910	Solly Hofman	.325	1950	Andy Pafko	.304	1992	Mark Grace	.307
1911	Heinie Zimmerman	.307	1951	Frank Baumholtz	.284	1993	Mark Grace	.325
1912	Heinie Zimmerman	.372	1952	Frank Baumholtz	.325	1994	Sammy Sosa	.300
1913	Heinie Zimmerman	.313	1953	Dee Fondy	.309	1995	Mark Grace	.326
1914	Heinie Zimmerman	.296	1954	Hank Sauer	.288	1996	Mark Grace	.331
1915	Bob Fisher	.287	1955	Ernie Banks	.295			
1916	Heinie Zimmerman	.291	1956	Ernie Banks	.297			

Cal McVey, who led the team in 1877 with a .368 average

Home Run Leaders

Year	Player	HR	Year	Player	HR	Year	Player	HR
1876	Paul Hines	2	1913	Vic Saier	14	1956	Ernie Banks	28
1877	None		1914	Vic Saier	18	1957	Ernie Banks	43
1878	Joe Start, Frank Hankinson, Jack Remsen	1	1915	Cy Williams	13	1958	Ernie Banks	47
			1916	Cy Williams	12	1959	Ernie Banks	45
1879	Johnny Peters, Ned Williamson, Silver Flint	1	1917	Larry Doyle	6	1960	Ernie Banks	41
			1918	Max Flack	4	1961	Ernie Banks	29
1880	George Gore	2	1919	Max Flack	6	1962	Ernie Banks	37
1881	Tom Burns	4	1920	Dave Robertson	10	1963	Ron Santo, Billy Williams	25
1882	Silver Flint	4	1921	Max Flack, Ray Grimes	6			
1883	Ned Williamson	3	1922	Ray Grimes	14	1964	Billy Williams	33
1884	Ned Williamson	27	1923	Hack Miller	20	1965	Billy Williams	34
1885	Abner Dalrymple	11	1924	Gabby Hartnett	16	1966	Ron Santo	30
1886	Cap Anson	10	1925	Gabby Hartnett	24	1967	Ron Santo	31
1887	Fred Pfeffer	16	1926	Hack Wilson	21	1968	Ernie Banks	32
1888	Jimmy Ryan	16	1927	Hack Wilson	30	1969	Ron Santo	29
1889	Walt Wilmot	11	1928	Hack Wilson	31	1970	Billy Williams	42
1890	Walt Wilmot	14	1929	Rogers Hornsby, Hack Wilson	39	1971	Billy Williams	28
1891	Walt Wilmot	11	1930	Hack Wilson	56	1972	Billy Williams	37
1892	Jimmy Ryan	10	1931	Rogers Hornsby	16	1973	Rick Monday	26
1893	Bill Lange	8	1932	Johnny Moore	13	1974	Rick Monday	20
1894	Bill Dahlen	15	1933	Gabby Hartnett, Babe Herman	16	1975	Andre Thornton	18
1895	Bill Lange	10	1934	Gabby Hartnett	22	1976	Rick Monday	32
1896	Bill Dahlen	9	1935	Chuck Klein	21	1977	Bobby Murcer	27
1897	Bill Dahlen	6	1936	Frank Demaree	16	1978	Dave Kingman	28
1898	Bill Lange	6	1937	Augie Galan	18	1979	Dave Kingman	48
1899	Sam Mertes	9	1938	Ripper Collins	13	1980	Jerry Martin	23
1900	Sam Mertes	7	1939	Hank Leiber	24	1981	Bill Buckner, Leon Durham	10
1901	Topsy Hartsel	7	1940	Bill Nicholson	25	1982	Leon Durham	22
1902	Charlie Dexter, Joe Tinker	2	1941	Bill Nicholson	26	1983	Ron Cey, Jody Davis	24
1903	Johnny Kling	3	1942	Bill Nicholson	21	1984	Ron Cey	25
1904	Frank Chance	6	1943	Bill Nicholson	29	1985	Ryne Sandberg	26
1905	Frank Chance, Billy Maloney, Joe Tinker	2	1944	Bill Nicholson	33	1986	Jody Davis, Gary Matthews	21
			1945	Bill Nicholson	13	1987	Andre Dawson	49
1906	Frank Schulte	7	1946	Phil Cavarretta, Bill Nicholson	8	1988	Andre Dawson	24
1907	Johnny Evers, Frank Schulte	2	1947	Bill Nicholson	26	1989	Ryne Sandberg	30
1908	Joe Tinker	6	1948	Andy Pafko	2	1990	Ryne Sandberg	40
1909	Frank Schulte, Joe Tinker	4	1949	Hank Sauer	27	1991	Andre Dawson	31
1910	Frank Schulte	10	1950	Andy Pafko	36	1992	Ryne Sandberg	26
1911	Frank Schulte	21	1951	Hank Sauer	30	1993	Sammy Sosa	33
1912	Heinie Zimmerman	14	1952	Hank Sauer	37	1994	Sammy Sosa	25
			1953	Ralph Kiner	28	1995	Sammy Sosa	36
			1954	Hank Sauer	41	1996	Sammy Sosa	40
			1955	Ernie Banks	44			

RBI Leaders

Year	Player	RBI	Year	Player	RBI	Year	Player	RBI
1876	Deacon White	60	1884	NA		1892	Cap Anson	74
1877	Johnny Peters	41	1885	Cap Anson	114	1893	Cap Anson	91
1878	Cap Anson	40	1886	Cap Anson	147	1894	Walt Wilmot	130
1879	Silver Flint	41	1887	Cap Anson	102	1895	Bill Lange	98
1880	Cap Anson	74	1888	Cap Anson	84	1896	Bill Lange	92
1881	Cap Anson	82	1889	Cap Anson	120	1897	Jimmy Ryan	85
1882	Cap Anson	83	1890	Cap Anson	107	1898	Bill Dahlen, Jimmy Ryan	79
1883	NA		1891	Cap Anson	120			

1899	Sam Mertes	81	1932	Riggs Stephenson	85	1966	Ron Santo	94
1900	Sam Mertes	60	1933	Babe Herman	93	1967	Ron Santo	98
1901	Charlie Dexter	66	1934	Gabby Hartnett	90	1968	Ron Santo,	
1902	Johnny Kling	57	1935	Gabby Hartnett	91		Billy Williams	98
1903	Frank Chance	81	1936	Frank Demaree	96	1969	Ron Santo	123
1904	Jack McCarthy	51	1937	Frank Demaree	115	1970	Billy Williams	129
1905	Frank Chance	70	1938	Augie Galan	69	1971	Billy Williams	93
1906	Harry Steinfeldt	83	1939	Hank Leiber	88	1972	Billy Williams	122
1907	Harry Steinfeldt	70	1940	Bill Nicholson	98	1973	Billy Williams	86
1908	Joe Tinker	68	1941	Bill Nicholson	98	1974	Jerry Morales	82
1909	Frank Schulte	60	1942	Bill Nicholson	78	1975	Jerry Morales	91
1910	Solly Hofman	86	1943	Bill Nicholson	128	1976	Bill Madlock	84
1911	Frank Schulte	107	1944	Bill Nicholson	122	1977	Bobby Murcer	89
1912	Heinie Zimmerman	99	1945	Andy Pafko	110	1978	Dave Kingman	79
1913	Heinie Zimmerman	95	1946	Phil Cavarretta	78	1979	Dave Kingman	115
1914	Heinie Zimmerman	87	1947	Bill Nicholson	75	1980	Jerry Martin	73
1915	Vic Saier, Cy Williams	64	1948	Andy Pafko	101	1981	Bill Buckner	75
1916	Cy Williams	66	1949	Hank Sauer	83	1982	Bill Buckner	105
1917	Larry Doyle	61	1950	Hank Sauer	103	1983	Ron Cey	90
1918	Fred Merkle	65	1951	Hank Sauer	89	1984	Ron Cey	97
1919	Fred Merkle	62	1952	Hank Sauer	121	1985	Keith Moreland	106
1920	Dave Robertston	75	1953	Ralph Kiner	87	1986	Keith Moreland	79
1921	Ray Grimes	79	1954	Hank Sauer	103	1987	Andre Dawson	137
1922	Ray Grimes	99	1955	Ernie Banks	117	1988	Andre Dawson	79
1923	Barney Friberg,		1956	Ernie Banks	85	1989	Mark Grace	79
	Hack Miller	88	1957	Ernie Banks	102	1990	Andre Dawson,	
1924	Barney Friberg	82	1958	Ernie Banks	129		Ryne Sandberg	100
1925	Charlie Grimm	76	1959	Ernie Banks	143	1991	Andre Dawson	104
1926	Hack Wilson	109	1960	Ernie Banks	117	1992	Andre Dawson	90
1927	Hack Wilson	129	1961	George Altman	96	1993	Mark Grace	98
1928	Hack Wilson	120	1962	Ernie Banks	104	1994	Sammy Sosa	70
1929	Hack Wilson	159	1963	Ron Santo	99	1995	Sammy Sosa	119
1930	Hack Wilson	190	1964	Ron Santo	114	1996	Sammy Sosa	100
1931	Rogers Hornsby	90	1965	Billy Williams	108			

200-Hit Club

1912	Heinie Zimmerman	207	1931	Kiki Cuyler	202	1964	Billy Williams	201
1922	Charlie Hollocher	201	1931	Woody English	202	1965	Billy Williams	203
1923	Jigger Statz	209	1932	Billy Herman	206	1970	Billy Williams	205
1929	Rogers Hornsby	229	1935	Augie Galan	203	1982	Bill Buckner	201
1930	Kiki Cuyler	228	1935	Billy Herman	227	1984	Ryne Sandberg	200
1930	Woody English	214	1936	Frank Demaree	212			
1930	Hack Wilson	208	1936	Billy Herman	211			

Hitting for the Cycle

Jimmy Ryan	July 28, 1888, vs. Detroit	Roy Smalley	June 28, 1950, vs. St. Louis
Jimmy Ryan	July 1, 1891, vs. Cleveland	Lee Walls	July 2, 1957, vs. Cincinnati
George Decker	September 16, 1894, vs. Brooklyn	Billy Williams	July 17, 1966, at St. Louis
Frank Chance	June 13, 1904, at New York	Randy Hundley	August 11, 1966, vs. Houston
Frank Schulte	July 20, 1911, at Philadelphia	Ivan DeJesus	April 22, 1980, vs. St. Louis
Hack Wilson	June 23, 1930, vs. Philadelphia	Andre Dawson	April 29, 1987, vs. San Francisco
Babe Herman	September 30, 1933, at St. Louis	Mark Grace	May 9, 1993, vs. San Diego

30-Home Run Club

1927	Hack Wilson	30	1957	Ernie Banks	43	1970	Billy Williams	42
1928	Hack Wilson	31	1958	Ernie Banks	47	1970	Jim Hickman	32
1929	Rogers Hornsby	39	1959	Ernie Banks	45	1972	Billy Williams	37
1929	Hack Wilson	39	1960	Ernie Banks	41	1976	Rick Monday	32
1930	Hack Wilson	56	1962	Ernie Banks	37	1979	Dave Kingman	48
1930	Gabby Hartnett	37	1964	Billy Williams	33	1987	Andre Dawson	49
1944	Bill Nicholson	33	1964	Ron Santo	30	1989	Ryne Sandberg	30
1950	Andy Pafko	36	1965	Billy Williams	34	1990	Ryne Sandberg	40
1950	Hank Sauer	32	1965	Ron Santo	33	1991	Andre Dawson	31
1951	Hank Sauer	30	1966	Ron Santo	30	1993	Sammy Sosa	33
1952	Hank Sauer	37	1967	Ron Santo	31	1993	Rick Wilkins	30
1954	Hank Sauer	41	1968	Ernie Banks	32	1995	Sammy Sosa	36
1955	Ernie Banks	44	1968	Billy Williams	30	1996	Sammy Sosa	40

Three Homers in One Game

Edward Williamson	May 30, 1884	Hank Sauer	June 11, 1952	George Mitterwald	April 17, 1974
Cap Anson*	August 6, 1884	Ernie Banks	August 4, 1955	Dave Kingman	May 14, 1978
Hack Wilson	July 26, 1930	Ernie Banks*	September 14, 1957	Dave Kingman	May 17, 1979
Rogers Hornsby*	April 24, 1931	Lee Walls	April 24, 1958	Dave Kingman*	July 28, 1979
Babe Herman	July 20, 1933	Walt Moryn	May 30, 1958	Andre Dawson*	August 1, 1987
Henry Leiber*	July 4, 1939	Ernie Banks*	May 29, 1962	Tuffy Rhodes*	April 4, 1994
Clyde McCullough*	July 26, 1942	Ernie Banks	June 9, 1963	Sammy Sosa	June 5, 1996
Bill Nicholson*	July 23, 1944	Adolfo Phillips*	June 11, 1967	*Consecutive	
Andy Pafko*	August 2, 1950	Billy Williams	September 10, 1968		
Hank Sauer*	August 28, 1950	Rick Monday*	May 16, 1972		

Double-Figure Seasons

		2B	3B	HR	SB			2B	3B	HR	SB
1886	Cap Anson	35	11	10	29	1912	Heinie Zimmerman	41	14	14	23
1887	Jimmy Ryan	23	10	11	50	1912	Frank Schulte	27	11	12	17
1888	Cap Anson	20	12	12	28	1913	Vic Saier	15	21	14	26
1888	Jimmy Ryan	33	10	16	60	1915	Vic Saier	35	11	11	29
1889	Jimmy Ryan	31	14	17	45	1920	Dave Robertson	29	11	10	17
1890	Walt Wilmot	15	13	13	76	1923	Barney Friberg	27	11	12	13
1891	Walt Wilmot	14	10	11	42	1927	Hack Wilson	30	12	30	13
1892	Jimmy Ryan	21	11	10	27	1930	Kiki Cuyler	50	17	13	37
1894	Bill Dahlen	32	14	15	42	1935	Augie Galan	24	10	18	23
1895	Bill Lange	27	16	10	67	1937	Augie Galan	24	10	18	23
1910	Frank Schulte	29	15	10	22	1953	Dee Fondy	24	11	18	10
1911	Frank Schulte	30	21	21	23	1984	Ryne Sandberg	36	19	19	32

Single-Season Total Bases Leaders

1930	Hack Wilson	423	1965	Billy Williams	356	1930	Kiki Cuyler	351
1929	Rogers Hornsby	409	1929	Hack Wilson	355	1959	Ernie Banks	351
1958	Ernie Banks	379	1955	Ernie Banks	355			
1970	Billy Williams	373	1987	Andre Dawson	353			

Grand-Slam Highlights

Grand-Slam Home Run Leaders

Ernie Banks	12
Bill Nicholson	8
Billy Williams	8
Jody Davis	5
Gabby Hartnett	5
Andy Pafko	5
Ron Santo	5
Ryne Sandberg	5
Andre Dawson	4
Rogers Hornsby	4
Randy Hundley	4
Jimmy Ryan	4
Frank Schulte	4

Inside-the-Park Grand Slams since 1920

Bernard Friberg: July 15, 1923, at New York Giants
Jigger Statz: August 9, 1924, at Boston
Norman McMillan: August 26, 1929, vs. Cincinnati
Eddie Waitkus: August 24, 1947, at New York Giants
John Cusick: May 18, 1951, vs. Philadelphia
Chico Walker: August 28, 1991, at San Francisco

Pinch-Hit Grand Slams

Chick Tolson: May 1, 1927, vs. Pittsburgh (Kremer)
Rogers Hornsby: September 13, 1931, at Boston (Cunningham)
Harvey Hendrick: July 23, 1933, vs. Philadelphia (Collins)
Bob Scheffing: September 20, 1941, at St. Louis (Krist)
Dom Dallesandro: June 21, 1942, at New York Giants (McGee)
Frank Secory: June 6, 1946, vs. New York Giants (Koslo)
Cliff Aberson: September 9, 1947, vs. Brooklyn (Lombardi)
Ron Northey: September 18, 1950, at Brooklyn (Bankhead)
Phil Cavarretta: July 29, 1951, vs. Philadelphia (Roberts)
Bill Serena: August 14, 1953, vs. Milwaukee (Jolly)
Earl Averill: May 12, 1959, vs. Milwaukee (Burdette)
Bill Madlock: September 28, 1974, at Los Angeles (Sutton)
Champ Summers: August 23, 1975, vs. Houston (York)
Pete LaCock: September 3, 1975, at St. Louis (Gibson)
Tim Hosley: September 14, 1975, vs. Philadelphia (Lerch)
Dave Rader: June 26, 1978, vs. New York Mets (Murray)
Mike Vail: June 30, 1979, vs. New York Mets (Murray)
Brian Dayett: May 22, 1985, vs. Cincinnati (Browning)
Jim Sundberg: July 8, 1987, vs. San Diego (McCullers)
Dwight Smith: July 31, 1989, at Philadelphia (Harris)
Andre Dawson: April 19, 1991, at Pittsburgh (Belinda)

All-Time Pinch-Hitting Leaders

Dwight Smith	50	Bob Will	46	George Altman	30
Larry Biittner	46	Dom Dallesandro	45	Gabby Hartnett	29
Thad Bosley	46	Scot Thompson	39	Jerry Morales	29
Phil Cavarretta	46	Mike Vail	31		

All-Time Hitting Leaders

Games

Ernie Banks	2,528
Cap Anson	2,276
Billy Williams	2,213
Ron Santo	2,126
Ryne Sandberg	2,116
Phil Cavarretta	1,953
Stan Hack	1,938
Gabby Hartnett	1,926
Jimmy Ryan	1,660
Don Kessinger	1,648

Batting Average

Riggs Stephenson	.336
Bill Madlock	.336
Cap Anson	.334
Bill Lange	.330
Kiki Cuyler	.325
Bill Everitt	.323
Hack Wilson	.322
Mike Kelly	.316
George Gore	.315
Jimmy Ryan	.310

At Bats

Ernie Banks	9,421
Cap Anson	9,108
Billy Williams	8,479
Ryne Sandberg	7,932
Ron Santo	7,768
Stan Hack	7,278
Jimmy Ryan	6,770
Phil Cavarretta	6,592
Don Kessinger	6,355
Gabby Hartnett	6,282

Runs

Cap Anson	1,719
Jimmy Ryan	1,410
Billy Williams	1,306
Ernie Banks	1,305
Ryne Sandberg	1,262
Stan Hack	1,239
Ron Santo	1,109
Phil Cavarretta	968
Bill Dahlen	918
Billy Herman	875

Hits

Cap Anson	3,041
Ernie Banks	2,583
Billy Williams	2,510
Ryan Sandberg	2,267
Stan Hack	2,193

Ron Santo	2,171			Ryne Sandberg	997
Jimmy Ryan	2,102	**Triples**		Jimmy Ryan	914
Phil Cavarretta	1,927	Jimmy Ryan	142	Phil Cavarretta	896
Gabby Hartnett	1,867	Cap Anson	124	Bill Nicholson	833
Billy Herman	1,710	Frank Schulte	117	Hack Wilson	768

Total Bases

Ernie Banks	4,706
Billy Williams	4,262
Cap Anson	4,109
Ron Santo	3,667
Ryne Sandberg	3,606
Gabby Hartnett	3,079
Jimmy Ryan	3,045
Stan Hack	2,889
Phil Cavarretta	2,742
Frank Schulte	2,351

Triples (cont.)

Bill Dahlen	106
Phil Cavarretta	99
Joe Tinker	93
Ernie Banks	90
Billy Williams	87
Bill Lange	83
Stan Hack	81

Home Runs

Ernie Banks	512
Billy Williams	392
Ron Santo	337
Ryne Sandberg	270
Gabby Hartnett	231
Bill Nicholson	205
Hank Sauer	198
Hack Wilson	190
Andre Dawson	174
Leon Durham	138

Extra-Base Hits

Ernie Banks	1,009
Billy Williams	881
Ron Santo	756
Cap Anson	752
Ryne Sandberg	723
Gabby Hartnett	686
Jimmy Ryan	603
Phil Cavarretta	532
Bill Nicholson	503
Stan Hack	501

Doubles

Cap Anson	532
Ernie Banks	407
Billy Williams	402
Gabby Hartnett	391
Ryne Sandberg	377
Stan Hack	363
Jimmy Ryan	362
Ron Santo	353
Billy Herman	346
Phil Cavarretta	341

Runs Batted In

Cap Anson	1,715
Ernie Banks	1,636
Billy Williams	1,353
Ron Santo	1,290
Gabby Hartnett	1,153

Stolen Bases*

Frank Chance	383
Ryne Sandberg	337
Joe Tinker	304
Johnny Evers	291
Frank Schulte	214
Jimmy Slagle	198
Stan Hack	165
Jimmy Sheckard	163
Kiki Cuyler	161
Solly Hofman	158

*Since 1900

20-Plus-Game Hitting Streaks

Year	Player		Year	Player		Year	Player	
1894	Bill Dahlen	42	1927	Hack Wilson	26	1930	Hack Wilson	22
1989	Jerome Walton	30	1937	Gabby Hartnett	26	1966	Glenn Beckert	21
1894	Bill Dahlen	28	1973	Glenn Beckert	26	1980	Lenny Randle	21
1966	Ron Santo	28	1926	Hack Wilson	25	1934	Billy Herman	20
1929	Hack Wilson	27	1937	Gabby Hartnett	24	1988	Rafael Palmeiro	20
1968	Glenn Beckert	27	1945	Stan Hack	24			
1896	George Decker	26	1912	Heinie Zimmerman	23			

ERA Leaders

For a pitcher two qualify as a leader, the number of innings he pitched must be equivalent to the number of games played by the team during the season.

Year	Player	ERA	Year	Player	ERA	Year	Player	ERA
1876	Albert Spalding	1.75	1887	John Clarkson	3.08	1898	Clark Griffith	1.88
1877	George Bradley	3.31	1888	Gus Krock	2.44	1899	Clark Griffith	2.79
1878	Terry Larkin	2.24	1889	Bill Hutchison	3.54	1900	Ned Garvin	2.41
1879	Terry Larkin	2.44	1890	Bill Hutchison	2.70	1901	Rube Waddell	2.81
1880	Fred Goldsmith	1.75	1891	Bill Hutchison	2.81	1902	Jack Taylor	1.33
1881	Larry Corcoran	2.31	1892	Bill Hutchison	2.74	1903	Jake Weimer	2.30
1882	Larry Corcoran	1.95	1893	Hal Mauck	4.41	1904	Mordecai Brown	1.86
1883	Larry Corcoran	2.49	1894	Clark Griffith	4.92	1905	Ed Reulbach	1.42
1884	Larry Corcoran	2.40	1895	Clark Griffith	3.93	1906	Mordecai Brown	1.04
1885	John Clarkson	1.85	1896	Clark Griffith	3.54	1907	Jack Pfiester	1.15
1886	Jocko Flynn	2.24	1897	Clark Griffith	3.72	1908	Mordecai Brown	1.47

Year	Player	ERA	Year	Player	ERA	Year	Player	ERA
1909	Mordecai Brown	1.31	1939	Claude Passeau	3.05	1969	Bill Hands	2.49
1910	Leonard Cole	1.80	1940	Claude Passeau	2.50	1970	Ken Holtzman	3.38
1911	Lew Richie	2.31	1941	Vern Olsen	3.15	1971	Fergie Jenkins	2.77
1912	Larry Cheney	2.85	1942	Claude Passeau	2.68	1972	Milt Pappas	2.77
1913	George Pearce	2.31	1943	Hi Bithorn	2.60	1973	Rick Reuschel	3.00
1914	Jim Vaughn	2.05	1944	Claude Passeau	2.89	1974	Bill Bonham	3.86
1915	Bert Humphries	2.31	1945	Ray Prim	2.40	1975	Rick Reuschel	3.73
1916	Jim Vaughn	2.20	1946	Johnny Schmitz	2.61	1976	Ray Burris	3.11
1917	Jim Vaughn	2.01	1947	Johnny Schmitz	3.22	1977	Rick Reuschel	2.79
1918	Jim Vaughn	1.74	1948	Johnny Schmitz	2.64	1978	Dennis Lamp	3.30
1919	Grover Alexander	1.72	1949	Bob Rush	4.07	1979	Dennis Lamp	3.50
1920	Grover Alexander	1.91	1950	Bob Rush	3.71	1980	Rick Reuschel	3.40
1921	Grover Alexander	3.39	1951	Paul Minner	3.79	1981	Randy Martz	3.68
1922	Vic Aldridge	3.52	1952	Warren Hacker	2.58	1982	Fergie Jenkins	3.15
1923	Vic Keen	3.00	1953	Paul Minner	4.21	1983	Fergie Jenkins	4.30
1924	Grover Alexander	3.03	1954	Bob Rush	3.77	1984	Steve Trout	3.41
1925	Grover Alexander	3.39	1955	Paul Minner	3.48	1985	Dennis Eckersley	3.08
1926	Charlie Root	2.82	1956	Bob Rush	3.19	1986	Scott Sanderson	4.19
1927	Guy Bush	3.03	1957	Moe Drabowsky	3.53	1987	Rick Sutcliffe	3.68
1928	Sheriff Blake	2.47	1958	Glen Hobbie	3.74	1988	Greg Maddux	3.18
1929	Charlie Root	3.47	1959	Dave Hillman	3.53	1989	Greg Maddux	2.95
1930	Pat Malone	3.94	1960	Dick Ellsworth	3.72	1990	Mike Harkey	3.26
1931	Bob Smith	3.22	1961	Don Cardwell	3.82	1991	Greg Maddux	3.35
1932	Lon Warneke	2.37	1962	Bob Buhl	3.69	1992	Greg Maddux	2.18
1933	Lon Warneke	2.00	1963	Dick Ellsworth	2.11	1993	Greg Hibbard	3.96
1934	Lon Warneke	3.21	1964	Larry Jackson	3.14	1994	Steve Trachsel	3.21
1935	Larry French, Bill Lee	2.96	1965	Cal Koonce	3.69	1995	Frank Castillo	3.21
1936	Bill Lee	3.31	1966	Fergie Jenkins	3.31	1996	Steve Trachsel	3.03
1937	Tex Carleton	3.15	1967	Fergie Jenkins	2.80			
1938	Bill Lee	2.66	1968	Fergie Jenkins	2.63			

Strikeout Leaders

Year	Player	SO	Year	Player	SO	Year	Player	SO
1876	Albert Spalding	39	1904	Jake Weimer	177	1931	Charlie Root	131
1877	George Bradley	59	1905	Ed Reulbach	152	1932	Pat Malone	120
1878	Terry Larkin	163	1906	Jack Pfiester	153	1933	Lon Warneke	133
1879	Terry Larkin	142	1907	Orval Overall	141	1934	Lon Warneke	143
1880	Larry Corcoran	268	1908	Orval Overall	167	1935	Lon Warneke	120
1881	Larry Corcoran	150	1909	Orval Overall	205	1936	Lon Warneke	113
1882	Larry Corcoran	170	1910	Mordecai Brown	143	1937	Bill Lee	108
1883	Larry Corcoran	216	1911	Mordecai Brown	129	1938	Clay Bryant	135
1884	Larry Corcoran	272	1912	Larry Cheney	140	1939	Claude Passeau	108
1885	John Clarkson	318	1913	Larry Cheney	136	1940	Claude Passeau	124
1886	John Clarkson	340	1914	Jim Vaughn	165	1941	Paul Erickson	85
1887	John Clarkson	237	1915	Jim Vaughn	148	1942	Claude Passeau	89
1888	Gus Krock	161	1916	Jim Vaughn	144	1943	Claude Passeau	93
1889	Bill Hutchison	136	1917	Jim Vaughn	195	1944	Claude Passeau	89
1890	Bill Hutchison	289	1918	Jim Vaughn	148	1945	Claude Passeau	98
1891	Bill Hutchison	261	1919	Jim Vaughn	141	1946	Johnny Schmitz	135
1892	Bill Hutchison	316	1920	Grover Alexander	173	1947	Johnny Schmitz	97
1893	Willie McGill	91	1921	Speed Martin	86	1948	Johnny Schmitz	100
1894	Clark Griffith	71	1922	Tiny Osborne	81	1949	Dutch Leonard	83
1895	Adonis Terry	88	1923	Grover Alexander	72	1950	Paul Minner	99
1896	Danny Friend	86		Tony Kaufmann	72	1951	Bob Rush	129
1897	Clark Griffith	102	1924	Tony Kaufmann	79	1952	Bob Rush	157
1898	Clark Griffith	97	1925	Sheriff Blake	93	1953	Johnny Klippstein	113
1899	Nixey Callahan	77	1926	Charlie Root	127	1954	Bob Rush	124
1900	Ned Garvin	107	1927	Charlie Root	145	1955	Sam Jones	198
1901	Tom Hughes	225	1928	Pat Malone	155	1956	Sam Jones	176
1902	Pop Williams	94	1929	Pat Malone	166	1957	Moe Drabowsky	170
1903	Jake Weimer	128	1930	Pat Malone	142		Dick Drott	170

1958	Dick Drott	127	1971	Fergie Jenkins	263	1985	Dennis Eckersley	117
1959	Glen Hobbie	138	1972	Fergie Jenkins	184	1986	Dennis Eckersley	137
1960	Glen Hobbie	134	1973	Fergie Jenkins	170	1987	Rick Sutcliffe	174
1961	Don Cardwell	156	1974	Bill Bonham	191	1988	Rick Sutcliffe	144
1962	Dick Ellsworth	113	1975	Bill Bonham	165	1989	Rick Sutcliffe	153
1963	Dick Ellsworth	185	1976	Rick Reuschel	146	1990	Greg Maddux	144
1964	Dick Ellsworth	148	1977	Rick Reuschel	166	1991	Greg Maddux	198
	Larry Jackson	148	1978	Rick Reuschel	115	1992	Greg Maddux	199
1965	Larry Jackson	131	1979	Lynn McGlothen	147	1993	Jose Guzman	163
1966	Ken Holtzman	171	1980	Rick Reuschel	140	1994	Steve Trachsel	108
1967	Fergie Jenkins	236	1981	Mike Krukow	101	1995	Kevin Foster	146
1968	Fergie Jenkins	260	1982	Fergie Jenkins	134	1996	Jaime Navarro	158
1969	Fergie Jenkins	273	1983	Bill Campbell	97			
1970	Fergie Jenkins	274	1984	Rick Sutcliffe	155			

20-Game Winners

1876	Albert Spalding	47	1898	Nixey Callahan	20	1920	Grover Alexander	27
1878	Terry Larkin	29	1899	Clark Griffith	22	1923	Grover Alexander	22
1879	Terry Larkin	31	1899	Nixey Callahan	21	1927	Charlie Root	26
1880	Larry Corcoran	43	1902	Jack Taylor	23	1929	Pat Malone	22
1880	Fred Goldsmith	21	1903	Jack Taylor	21	1930	Pat Malone	20
1881	Larry Corcoran	31		Jack Weimer	20	1932	Lon Warneke	22
	Fred Goldsmith	24	1904	Jake Weimer	20	1933	Guy Bush	20
1882	Fred Goldsmith	28	1906	Mordecai Brown	26	1934	Lon Warneke	22
1882	Larry Corcoran	27		Jack Pfiester	20	1935	Bill Lee	20
1883	Larry Corcoran	34		Jack Taylor			Lon Warneke	20
1883	Fred Goldsmith	25		(Cardinals-Cubs)	20	1938	Bill Lee	22
1884	Larry Corcoran	35	1907	Orval Overall	23	1940	Claude Passeau	20
1885	John Clarkson	53		Mordecai Brown	20	1945	Hank Wyse	22
1885	Jim McCormick	20	1908	Mordecai Brown	29		Hank Borowy	
1886	John Clarkson	35		Ed Reulbach	24		(Yankees-Cubs)	21
1886	Jim McCormick	31	1909	Mordecai Brown	27	1963	Dick Ellsworth	22
1886	Jocko Flynn	24		Orval Overall	20	1964	Larry Jackson	24
1887	John Clarkson	38	1910	Mordecai Brown	25	1967	Fergie Jenkins	20
1888	Gus Krock	24		Leonard Cole	20	1968	Fergie Jenkins	20
1890	Bill Hutchison	42	1911	Mordecai Brown	21	1969	Fergie Jenkins	21
1890	Pat Luby	20	1912	Larry Cheney	26		Bill Hands	20
1891	Bill Hutchison	43	1913	Larry Cheney	21	1970	Fergie Jenkins	22
1892	Bill Hutchison	37	1914	Jim Vaughn	21	1971	Fergie Jenkins	24
1894	Clark Griffith	21		Larry Cheney	20	1972	Fergie Jenkins	20
1895	Clark Griffith	25	1915	Jim Vaughn	20	1977	Rick Reuschel	20
1895	Adonis Terry	21	1917	Jim Vaughn	23	1984	Rick Sutcliffe	
1896	Clark Griffith	22	1918	Jim Vaughn	22		(Indians-Cubs)	20
1897	Clark Griffith	21		Claude Hendrix	20	1992	Greg Maddux	20
1898	Clark Griffith	26	1919	Jim Vaughn	21			

All-Time Pitching Leaders since 1900

ERA

Mordecai Brown	1.80
Jack Pfiester	1.86
Orval Overall	1.92
Jake Weimer	2.15
Ed Reulbach	2.24
Hippo Vaughn	2.33
Jack Taylor	2.40
Carl Lundgren	2.42
Larry Cheney	2.74
Grover Alexander	2.84

Victories

Charlie Root	201
Mordecai Brown	188
Fergie Jenkins	167
Guy Bush	152
Hippo Vaughn	151
Bill Lee	139
Ed Reulbach	136
Rick Reuschel	135
Grover Alexander	128
Claude Passeau	124

Saves*

Lee Smith	180
Bruce Sutter	133

Randy Myers	112
Phil Regan	60
Mitch Williams	52
Ted Abernathy	39
Lindy McDaniel	39
Paul Assenmacher	33
Don Elston	32
Jack Aker	29

*Since 1960

Strikeouts

Fergie Jenkins	2,038
Charlie Root	1,432
Rick Reuschel	1,367
Hippo Vaughn	1,138
Bob Rush	1,076
Mordecai Brown	1,043
Ken Holtzman	988
Greg Maddux	937
Rick Sutcliffe	909
Dick Ellsworth	905

Games

Charlie Root	605
Lee Smith	458
Don Elston	449
Guy Bush	428

Fergie Jenkins	401
Bill Lee	364
Rick Reuschel	358
Mordecai Brown	346
Bob Rush	339
Willie Hernandez	323

Games Started

Fergie Jenkins	347
Rick Reuschel	343
Charlie Root	339
Bill Lee	296
Bob Rush	292
Hippo Vaughn	270
Guy Bush	252
Mordecai Brown	241
Dick Ellsworth	236
Claude Passeau	234

Complete Games

Mordecai Brown	206
Charlie Root	177
Hippo Vaughn	177
Grover Alexander	159
Fergie Jenkins	154
Bill Lee	153

Ed Reulbach	150
Jack Taylor	144
Claude Passeau	143
Guy Bush	127

Shutouts

Mordecai Brown	48
Hippo Vaughn	35
Ed Reulbach	31
Fergie Jenkins	29
Orval Overall	28
Bill Lee	25
Grover Alexander	24
Claude Passeau	22
Larry French	21
Charlie Root	21

Years

Charlie Root	16
Guy Bush	12
Rick Reuschel	12
Bill Lee	11
Mordecai Brown	10
Fergie Jenkins	10
Bob Rush	10
Lon Warneke	10

Leading Relievers since 1960

		W	SV	ERA
1960	Don Elston	8	11	3.40
1961	Bob Anderson	7	8	4.26
1962	Don Elston	4	8	2.44
1963	Lindy McDaniel	13	22	2.86
1964	Lindy McDaniel	1	15	3.88
1965	Ted Abernathy	4	31	2.57
1966	Bob Hendley	4	7	3.91
1967	Chuck Hartenstein	9	10	3.08
1968	Phil Regan	10	25	2.20
1969	Phil Regan	12	17	3.70
1970	Phil Regan	5	12	4.76
1971	Phil Regan	5	6	3.93
1972	Jack Aker	6	17	2.96
1973	Bob Locker	10	18	2.54
1974	Oscar Zamora	3	10	3.12
1975	Darold Knowles	6	15	5.81
1976	Bruce Sutter	6	10	2.70
1977	Bruce Sutter	7	31	1.34
1978	Bruce Sutter	8	27	3.18

		W	SV	ERA
1979	Bruce Sutter	6	37	2.22
1980	Bruce Sutter	5	28	2.64
1981	Dick Tidrow	3	9	5.06
1982	Lee Smith	2	17	2.69
1983	Lee Smith	4	29	1.65
1984	Lee Smith	9	33	3.65
1985	Lee Smith	7	33	3.04
1986	Lee Smith	9	31	3.09
1987	Lee Smith	4	36	3.12
1988	Goose Gossage	4	13	4.33
1989	Mitch Williams	4	36	2.76
1990	Paul Assenmacher	7	10	2.80
	Mitch Williams	1	16	3.93
1991	Paul Assenmacher	7	15	3.24
1992	Bob Scanlan	3	14	2.89
1993	Randy Myers	2	53	3.11
1994	Randy Myers	1	21	3.79
1995	Randy Myers	1	38	3.88
1996	Turk Wendell	4	18	2.84

No-Hitters since 1900

By Cubs Pitchers

1904 Bob Wicker, June 11, vs. Giants at New York (pitched 9⅓ hitless innings, won 1–0 on one-hitter in 12 innings)

1910 Leonard Cole, July 31, vs. Cardinals at St. Louis, second game of doubleheader, won 4–0 (7 innings)

1915 Jim Lavender, August 31, vs. Giants at New York, first game of doubleheader, won 2–0

1917 Jim Vaughn, May 2, vs. Redlegs at Weeghman Park (pitched 9⅓ hitless innings, lost 1–0 on 2-hitter in 10 innings; Cincinnati's Fred Toney pitched 10-inning no hitter)

1955 Sam Jones, May 12, vs. Pirates at Wrigley Field, won 4–0

1960 Don Cardwell, May 15, vs. Cardinals at Wrigley Field, second game of doubleheader, won 4–0

1969 Ken Holtzman, August 19, vs. Braves at Wrigley Field, won 3–0

1971 Ken Holtzman, June 3, vs. Reds at Cincinnati (N), won 1–0

1972 Burt Hooton, April 16, vs. Phillies at Wrigley Field, won 4–0

1972 Milt Pappas, September 2, vs. Padres at Wrigley Field, won 8–0 (No Cub has pitched a perfect game; Pappas came closest by not allowing a batter to reach base until walking a man with 2 out in the 9th inning.)

Against the Cubs

1903 Philadelphia's Chic Fraser, September 18, at West Side Grounds, second game of doubleheader, won 10–0

1905 New York's Christy Mathewson, June 13, at West Side Grounds, won 1–0

1917 Cincinnati's Fred Toney, May 2, at Weeghman Park, won 1–0 in 10 innings (Cubs' Jim Vaughn pitched 9⅓ hitless innings)

1952 Brooklyn's Carl Erskine, June 19, at Brooklyn, won 5–0

1965 Cincinnati's Jim Maloney, August 19, at Wrigley Field, first game of doubleheader, won 1–0 in 10 innings

1965 Los Angeles' Sandy Koufax, September 9, at Los Angeles, won 1–0 (pitched perfect game)

Top Single-Season Win Streaks

Club			Pitcher		
Games		Year	Games	Pitcher	Year
21		1880, 1935	17	John Luby	1890
18		1885	16	Jim McCormick	1886
15		1936	14	Jim McCormick	1885
14		1906, 1932		John Flynn	1886
13		1892, 1928		Ed Reulbach	1909
				Rick Sutcliffe	1984
			13	Larry Corcoran	1880
				John Clarkson	1885

Most Wins

1876	Albert Spalding	47	1884	Larry Corcoran	35	1892	Bill Hutchison	37
1877	George Bradley	18	1885	John Clarkson	53	1893	Willie McGill	17
1878	Terry Larkin	29	1886	John Clarkson	35	1894	Clark Griffith	21
1879	Terry Larkin	31	1887	John Clarkson	38	1895	Clark Griffith	25
1880	Larry Corcoran	43	1888	Gus Krock	24	1896	Clark Griffith	22
1881	Larry Corcoran	31	1889	Bill Hutchison	16	1897	Clark Griffith	21
1882	Fred Goldsmith	28	1890	Bill Hutchison	42	1898	Clark Griffith	26
1883	Larry Corcoran	34	1891	Bill Hutchison	43	1899	Clark Griffith	22

Year	Pitcher	Wins
1900	Clark Griffith	14
1901	Jack Taylor, Rube Waddell	13
1902	Jack Taylor	22
1903	Jack Taylor, Jake Weimer	21
1904	Jake Weimer	20
1905	Ed Reulbach, Jake Weimer, Three-Finger Brown	18
1906	Three-Finger Brown	26
1907	Orval Overall	23
1908	Three-Finger Brown	28
1909	Three-Finger Brown	27
1910	Three-Finger Brown	25
1911	Three-Finger Brown	21
1912	Larry Cheney	26
1913	Larry Cheney	21
1914	Hippo Vaughn	21
1915	Hippo Vaughn	20
1916	Hippo Vaughn	17
1917	Hippo Vaughn	23
1918	Hippo Vaughn	22
1919	Hippo Vaughn	21
1920	Grover Alexander	27
1921	Grover Alexander	15
1922	Vic Aldridge, Grover Alexander	16
1923	Grover Alexander	22
1924	Tony Kaufmann	16
1925	Grover Alexander	15
1926	Charlie Root	18
1927	Charlie Root	26
1928	Pat Malone	18
1929	Pat Malone	22
1930	Pat Malone	20
1931	Charlie Root	17
1932	Lon Warneke	22
1933	Guy Bush	20
1934	Lon Warneke	22
1935	Bill Lee, Lon Warneke	20
1936	Bill Lee, Larry French	18
1937	Tex Carleton, Larry French	16
1938	Bill Lee	22
1939	Bill Lee	19
1940	Claude Passeau	20
1941	Claude Passeau	14
1942	Claude Passeau	19
1943	Hi Bithorn	18
1944	Hank Wyse	16
1945	Hank Wyse	22
1946	Hank Wyse	14
1947	Johnny Schmitz	13
1948	Johnny Schmitz	18
1949	Johnny Schmitz	11
1950	Bob Rush	13
1951	Bob Rush	11
1952	Bob Rush	17
1953	Warren Hacker, Paul Minner	12
1954	Bob Rush	13
1955	Sam Jones	14
1956	Bob Rush	13
1957	Dick Drott	15
1958	Glen Hobbie	10
1959	Glen Hobbie	16
1960	Glen Hobbie	16
1961	Don Cardwell	15
1962	Bob Buhl	12
1963	Dick Ellsworth	22
1964	Larry Jackson	24
1965	Larry Jackson, Dick Ellsworth	14
1966	Ken Holtzman	11
1967	Ferguson Jenkins	20
1968	Ferguson Jenkins	20
1969	Ferguson Jenkins	21
1970	Ferguson Jenkins	22
1971	Ferguson Jenkins	24
1972	Ferguson Jenkins	20
1973	Ferguson Jenkins, Burt Hooton, Rick Reuschel	14
1974	Rick Reuschel	13
1975	Ray Burris	15
1976	Ray Burris	15
1977	Rick Reuschel	20
1978	Rick Reuschel	14
1979	Rick Reuschel	18
1980	Lynn McGlothen	12
1981	Mike Krukow	9
1982	Ferguson Jenkins	14
1983	Chuck Rainey	14
1984	Rick Sutcliffe	16
1985	Dennis Eckersley	11
1986	Scott Sanderson, Lee Smith	9
1987	Rick Sutcliffe	18
1988	Greg Maddux	18
1989	Greg Maddux	19
1990	Greg Maddux	15
1991	Greg Maddux	15
1992	Greg Maddux	20
1993	Greg Hibbard	15
1994	Steve Trachsel	9
1995	Jaime Navarro	14
1996	Jaime Navarro	15

Managers' Records

Manager	Years	Won	Lost	Pct
Albert Spalding	1876–77	78	47	.624
Bob Ferguson	1878	30	30	.500
Cap Anson	1879, 1880–97	1,283	932	.579
Silver Flint	1879	5	12	.294
Tommy Burns	1898–99	160	138	.537
Tom Loftus	1900–01	118	161	.423
Frank Selee	1902–05	280	223	.557
Frank Chance	1905–12	768	389	.664
Johnny Evers	1913, 1921	129	120	.518
Hank O'Day	1914	78	76	.506
Roger Bresnahan	1915	73	80	.477
Joe Tinker	1916	67	86	.438
Fred Mitchell	1917–20	308	269	.534
Bill Killefer	1921–25	300	293	.506
Rabbit Maranville	1925	23	30	.434
George Gibson	1925	12	14	.462
Joe McCarthy	1926–30	442	321	.579
Rogers Hornsby	1930–32	141	116	.549
Charlie Grimm	1932–38, 1944–49, 1960	946	782	.547
Gabby Hartnett	1938–40	203	176	.536
Jimmie Wilson	1941–44	213	258	.452
Roy Johnson	1944	0	1	.000
Frankie Frisch	1949–51	141	196	.418
Phil Cavarretta	1951–53	169	213	.442
Stan Hack	1954–56	196	265	.425
Bob Scheffing	1957–59	208	254	.450
Lou Boudreau	1960	54	83	.394
Vedie Himsl*	1961	10	21	.323
Harry Craft*	1961	7	9	.438
Elvin Tappe*	1961–62	46	70	.397
Lou Klein*	1961–62, 1965	65	83	.439
Charlie Metro*	1962	43	69	.384
Bob Kennedy	1963–65	182	198	.479

Manager	Years	Won	Lost	Pct
Leo Durocher	1966–72	535	526	.504
Whitey Lockman	1972–74	157	162	.492
Jim Marshall	1974–76	175	218	.445
Herman Franks	1977–79	238	241	.497
Joe Amalfitano	1979, 1980–81	66	116	.363
Preston Gomez	1980	38	52	.422
Lee Elia	1982–83	127	158	.446
Charlie Fox	1983	17	22	.436
Jim Frey	1984–86	196	182	.519

Manager	Years	Won	Lost	Pct
John Vukovich	1986	1	1	.500
Gene Michael	1986–87	114	124	.479
Frank Lucchesi	1987	8	17	.320
Don Zimmer	1988–91	265	258	.507
Joe Altobelli	1991	0	1	.000
Jim Essian	1991	59	63	.484
Jim Lefebvre	1992–93	162	162	.500
Tom Trebelhorn	1994	49	64	.434
Jim Riggleman	1995–96	149	157	.487

*Rotating head coaches

Attendance Records

Single game, home opener	45,777 (vs. Pittsburgh, April 14, 1978)
Single game, home	46,572 (vs. Brooklyn, May 18, 1947)
Single game, home, total attendance	51,556 (vs. Brooklyn, June 27, 1930)
Doubleheader, home	46,965 (vs. Pittsburgh, May 31, 1948)
Single game, road	67,550 (at Los Angeles, April 12, 1960)
Doubleheader, road	61,177 (at Philadelphia, July 15, 1977)
Season at home	2,653,763 in 1993 (80 dates)
Season on road	2,592,790 in 1993 (80 dates)
Season, home and road	5,246,553 in 1993 (160 dates)
Largest crowd, three-date series, home	120,328 (vs. Cincinnati, July 22–July 24, 1994)
Largest crowd, four-date series, home	156,590 (vs. Colorado, July 15–July 18, 1993)
Largest crowd, three-date series, road	194,267 (at Colorado, April 22–April 24, 1994)
Largest crowd, four-date series, road	240,307 (at Colorado, July 2–July 5, 1993)

Year by Year since 1876

Year	W–L	Pct	Pos	GA/GB	Manager	Attendance
1876	52–14	.788	1	+6	Spalding	—
1877	26–33	.441	5	−15½	Spalding	—
1878	30–30	.500	4	−11	Ferguson	—
1879	46–33	.582	4	−10½	Anson/Flint	—
1880	67–17	.798	1	+15	Anson	—
1881	56–28	.667	1	+9	Anson	—
1882	55–29	.655	1	+3	Anson	—
1883	59–39	.602	2	−4	Anson	—
1884	62–50	.554	4t	−22	Anson	—
1885	87–25	.777	1	+2	Anson	—
1886	90–34	.726	1	+2½	Anson	—
1887	71–50	.587	3	−6½	Anson	—
1888	77–58	.570	2	−9	Anson	—
1889	67–65	.508	3	−19	Anson	—
1890	84–53	.613	2	−6	Anson	—
1891	82–53	.607	2	−3½	Anson	—
1892	70–76	.479	7	−30	Anson	—
1893	56–71	.441	9	−29	Anson	—
1894	57–75	.432	7	−34	Anson	—
1895	72–58	.554	4	−15	Anson	—
1896	71–57	.555	5	−18½	Anson	—
1897	59–73	.447	9	−34	Anson	—
1898	85–65	.567	4	−17½	Burns	—
1899	75–73	.507	8	−26	Burns	—
1900	65–75	.464	5t	−19	Loftus	—

Year	W–L	Pct	Pos	GA/GB	Manager	Attendance
1901	53–86	.381	6	−37	Loftus	—
1902	68–69	.496	5	−34	Selee	—
1903	82–56	.594	3	−8	Selee	—
1904	93–60	.608	2	−13	Selee	—
1905	92–61	.601	3	−13	Selee/Chance	—
1906	116–36*	.763*	1	+20	Chance	—
1907	107–45	.704	1†	+17	Chance	—
1908	99–55	.643	1†	+1	Chance	—
1909	104–49	.680	2	−6½	Chance	—
1910	104–50	.675	1	+13	Chance	—
1911	92–62	.597	2	−7½	Chance	—
1912	91–59	.607	3	−11½	Chance	—
1913	88–65	.575	3	−13½	Evers	—
1914	78–76	.506	4	−16½	O'Day	—
1915	73–80	.477	4	−17½	Bresnahan	—
1916**	67–86	.438	5	−26½	Tinker	454,609
1917	74–80	.481	5	−24	Mitchell	363,748
1918	84–45	.651	1	+10½	Mitchell	338,802
1919	75–65	.536	3	−21	Mitchell	421,689
1920	75–79	.487	5t	−18	Mitchell	481,183
1921	64–89	.418	7	−30	Evers/ Killefer	410,110
1922	80–74	.519	5	−13	Killefer	541,993
1923	83–71	.539	4	−12½	Killefer	705,049
1924	81–72	.529	5	−12	Killefer	720,962

Year	W–L	Pct	Pos	GA/GB	Manager	Attendance
1925	68–86	.442	8	−27½	Killefer/ Maranville/ Gibson	623,030
1926	82–72	.532	4	−7	McCarthy	886,925
1927	85–68	.556	4	−8½	McCarthy	1,163,347
1928	91–63	.591	3	−4	McCarthy	1,148,053
1929	98–54	.645	1	+10½	McCarthy	1,485,166
1930	90–64	.584	2	−2	McCarthy/ Hornsby	1,467,881
1931	84–70	.545	3	−17	Hornsby	1,089,449
1932	90–64	.584	1	+4	Hornsby/ Grimm	976,449
1933	86–68	.558	3	−6	Grimm	894,879
1934	86–65	.570	3	−8	Grimm	709,245
1935	100–54	.649	1	+4	Grimm	690,576
1936	87–67	.565	2t	−5	Grimm	701,111
1937	93–61	.604	2	−3	Grimm	897,852
1938	89–63	.586	1	+2	Grimm/ Hartnett	955,401
1939	84–70	.545	4	−13	Hartnett	729,309
1940	75–79	.487	5	−25½	Hartnett	534,878
1941	70–84	.455	6	−30	Wilson	545,159
1942	68–86	.442	6	−38	Wilson	590,972
1943	74–79	.484	5	−30½	Wilson	508,247
1944	75–79	.487	4	−30	Wilson/ Johnson/ Grimm	640,110
1945	98–56	.636	1	+3	Grimm	1,036,386
1946	82–71	.536	3	−14½	Grimm	1,342,970
1947	69–85	.448	6	−25	Grimm	1,364,039
1948	64–90	.416	8	−27½	Grimm	1,237,792
1949	61–93	.396	8	−36	Grimm/ Frisch	1,143,139
1950	64–89	.418	7	−26½	Frisch	1,165,944
1951	62–92	.403	8	−34½	Frisch/ Cavarretta	894,415
1952	77–77	.500	5	−19½	Cavarretta	1,024,826
1953	65–89	.442	7	−40	Cavarretta	763,653
1954	64–90	.416	7	−33	Hack	748,183
1955	72–81	.471	6	−26	Hack	875,800
1956	60–94	.390	8	−33	Hack	720,118
1957	62–92	.403	7t	−33	Scheffing	670,629
1958	72–82	.468	5t	−20	Scheffing	979,904
1959	74–80	.481	5t	−13	Scheffing	858,255
1960	60–94	.390	7	−35	Grimm/ Boudreau	809,770
1961/ cc	64–90	.416	7	−29	Himsl/ Craft/ Klein/ Tappe	673,057
1962/ cc	59–103	.364	9	−42½	Tappe/ Metro/ Klein	609,802
1963/ cc	82–80	.506	7	−17	Kennedy	979,551
1964/ cc	76–86	.469	8	−17	Kennedy	751,647
1965/ cc	72–90	.444	8	−25	Kennedy/ Klein	641,361
1966	59–103	.364	10	−36	Durocher	635,891
1967	87–74	.540	3	−14	Durocher	977,226
1968	84–78	.519	3	−13	Durocher	1,043,409
1969/E	92–70	.568	2	−8	Durocher	1,674,993
1970	84–78	.519	2	−5	Durocher	1,642,705
1971	83–79	.512	3t	−14	Durocher	1,653,007
1972/s	85–70	.548	2	−11	Durocher/ Lockman	1,229,163
1973	77–84	.478	5	−5	Lockman	1,351,705
1974	66–96	.407	6	−22	Lockman/ Marshall	1,015,378
1975	75–87	.463	5t	−17½	Marshall	1,034,819
1976	75–87	.463	4	−26	Marshall	1,026,217
1977	81–81	.500	4	−20	Franks	1,439,834
1978	79–83	.488	3	−11	Franks	1,525,311
1979	80–82	.494	5	−18	Franks/ Amalfitano	1,648,587
1980	64–98	.395	6	−27	Gomez/ Amalfitano	1,206,776
1981/s	38–65	.369	6	−21½	Amalfitano	565,637
1982	73–89	.451	5	−19	Elia	1,249,278
1983	71–91	.438	5	−19	Elia/Fox	1,479,717
1984	96–65	.596	1‡	+6½	Frey	2,107,655
1985	77–84	.478	4	−23½	Frey	2,161,534
1986	70–90	.438	5	−37	Frey/ Vukovich/ Michael	1,859,102
1987	76–85	.472	6	−18½	Michael/ Lucchesi	2,035,130
1988	77–85	.475	4	−24	Zimmer	2,089,034
1989	93–69	.574	1‡	+6	Zimmer	2,491,942
1990	77–85	.475	4t	−18	Zimmer	2,243,791
1991	77–83	.481	4	−20	Zimmer/ Altobelli/ Essian	2,314,250
1992	78–84	.481	4	−18	Lefebvre	2,126,720
1993	84–78	.519	4	−13	Lefebvre	2,653,763
1994/ C/s	49–64	.434	5	−16½	Trebelhorn	1,845,208
1995/s	73–71	.507	3	−12	Riggleman	1,918,265
1996	76–86	.469	4	−12	Riggleman	2,219,110

* Major league record (20th century)
† World champions
‡ Eastern Division champions
** First year in Wrigley Field
t—Tie
E—Eastern Division play begins
C—Central Division play begins
s—Strike-shortened season
cc—College of Coaches

All-Stars

1933 SS Woody English, C Gabby Hartnett, P Lon Warneke

1934 *RF Kiki Cuyler, *C Gabby Hartnett, 2B Billy Herman, LF Chuck Klein, P Lon Warneke

1935 C Gabby Hartnett, *2B Billy Herman

1936 P Curt Davis, *RF Frank Demaree, *CF Augie Galan, *C Gabby Hartnett, *2B Billy Herman, P Lon Warneke

1937 1B Rip Collins, *CF Frank Demaree, *C Gabby Hartnett, *2B Billy Herman, SS Billy Jurges (DNP)

1938 *3B Stan Hack, C Gabby Hartnett (DNP), *2B Billy Herman, P Bill Lee

1939 *3B Stan Hack, 2B Billy Herman, P Bill Lee

1940 P Larry French, *2B Billy Herman, CF Hank Leiber (DNP), RF Bill Nicholson

1941 *3B Stan Hack, CF Hank Leiber (DNP), *RF Bill Nicholson, P Claude Passeau

1942 P Claude Passeau

1943 *3B Stan Hack, *RF Bill Nicholson, P Claude Passeau (DNP)

1944 *1B Phil Cavarretta, 2B Don Johnson (DNP), RF Bill Nicholson

1945 *No Game Was Played*

1946 1B Phil Cavarretta, CF Peanuts Lowrey, *P Claude Passeau, P Johnny Schmitz (DNP)

1947 1B Phil Cavarretta, CF Andy Pafko

1948 C Clyde McCullough (DNP), *3B Andy Pafko, P Johnny Schmitz, 1B Eddie Waitkus

1949 CF Andy Pafko

1950 CF Andy Pafko, P Bob Rush (DNP), *RF Hank Sauer

1951 C Bruce Edwards (DNP), P Dutch Leonard (DNP)

1952 C Toby Atwell (DNP), P Bob Rush, *LF Hank Sauer

1953 LF Ralph Kiner

1954 3B Randy Jackson

1955 2B Gene Baker, *SS Ernie Banks, 3B Randy Jackson, P Sam Jones

1956 SS Ernie Banks (DNP)

1957 SS Ernie Banks

1958 *SS Ernie Banks, LF Walt Moryn (DNP), RF Lee Walls

1959 1st game: *SS Ernie Banks, P Don Elston
      2nd game: *SS Ernie Banks

1960 1st game: *SS Ernie Banks,
      2nd game: *SS Ernie Banks

1961 1st game: RF George Altman, 2B Don Zimmer (DNP)
      2nd game: RF George Altman, SS Ernie Banks, 2B Don Zimmer

1962 1st game: 1B Ernie Banks

2nd game: RF George Altman, 1B Ernie Banks, LF Billy Williams

1963 P Larry Jackson, 3B Ron Santo

1964 P Dick Ellsworth (DNP), 3B Ron Santo (DNP), *LF Billy Williams

1965 *1B Ernie Banks, 3B Ron Santo, RF Billy Williams

1966 *3B Ron Santo

1967 1B Ernie Banks, P Fergie Jenkins

1968 *SS Don Kessinger, *3B Ron Santo, LF Billy Williams

1969 1B Ernie Banks, 2B Glenn Beckert, C Randy Hundley, *SS Don Kessinger, *3B Ron Santo

1970 *2B Glenn Beckert, LF Jim Hickman, *SS Don Kessinger

1971 *2B Glenn Beckert, P Fergie Jenkins, SS Don Kessinger, 3B Ron Santo

1972 2B Glenn Beckert, P Fergie Jenkins (DNP), *SS Don Kessinger, 3B Ron Santo, LF Billy Williams

1973 *3B Ron Santo, *RF Billy Williams

1974 SS Don Kessinger

1975 3B Bill Madlock

1976 C Steve Swisher (DNP)

1977 CF Jerry Morales, P Rick Reuschel, P Bruce Sutter (DNP), 2B Manny Trillo

1978 P Bruce Sutter

1979 LF Dave Kingman (DNP), P Bruce Sutter

1980 *LF Dave Kingman, P Bruce Sutter

1981 1B Bill Buckner

1982 CF Leon Durham (DNP)

1983 RF Leon Durham, P Lee Smith

1984 C Jody Davis, *2B Ryne Sandberg

1985 2B Ryne Sandberg

1986 C Jody Davis, *2B Ryne Sandberg

1987 *RF Andre Dawson, *2B Ryne Sandberg, P Lee Smith, P Rick Sutcliffe

1988 *RF Andre Dawson, SS Shawon Dunston (DNP), 3B Vance Law, P Greg Maddux (DNP), LF Rafael Palmeiro, *2B Ryne Sandberg

1989 RF Andre Dawson, *2B Ryne Sandberg, P Rick Sutcliffe, P Mitch Williams

1990 *RF Andre Dawson, SS Shawon Dunston, *2B Ryne Sandberg

1991 LF George Bell, *RF Andre Dawson, *2B Ryne Sandberg

1992 P Greg Maddux, *2B Ryne Sandberg

1993 *1B Mark Grace, *2B Ryne Sandberg

1994 P Randy Myers

1995 1B Mark Grace, P Randy Myers, OF Sammy Sosa

1996 P Steve Trachsel

*Starter
DNP—did not play in game.

Honored in the Hall of Fame

Grover Cleveland Alexander, 1938
Cap Anson, 1939
Ernie Banks, 1977
Lou Boudreau, 1970
Roger Bresnahan, 1945
Lou Brock, 1985
Mordecai Brown, 1949
Frank Chance, 1946
John Clarkson, 1963
Kiki Cuyler, 1968
Dizzy Dean, 1953
Hugh Duffy, 1945
Leo Durocher, 1994

Johnny Evers, 1946
Jimmie Foxx, 1951
Frankie Frisch, 1947
Clark C. Griffith, 1946
Burleigh Grimes, 1964
Gabby Hartnett, 1955
Billy Herman, 1975
Rogers Hornsby, 1942
William Hulbert, 1995
Monte Irvin, 1973
Ferguson Jenkins, 1991
George Kelly, 1973
King Kelly, 1945

Ralph Kiner, 1975
Chuck Klein, 1980
Tony Lazzeri, 1991
Fred Lindstrom, 1976
Rabbit Maranville, 1954
Joseph McCarthy, 1957
Robin Roberts, 1976
A.G. Spalding, 1939
Joe Tinker, 1946
Rube Waddell, 1946
Hoyt Wilhelm, 1985
Billy Williams, 1987
Hack Wilson, 1979

Award Winners

Most Valuable Player

1911	Frank Schulte
1929	Rogers Hornsby
1935	Gabby Hartnett
1945	Phil Cavarretta
1952	Hank Sauer
1958	Ernie Banks
1959	Ernie Banks
1984	Ryne Sandberg
1987	Andre Dawson

Cy Young

1971	Fergie Jenkins
1979	Bruce Sutter
1984	Rick Sutcliffe
1992	Greg Maddux

Rookie of the Year

1961	Billy Williams
1962	Ken Hubbs
1989	Jerome Walton

Manager of the Year

1984	Jim Frey
1989	Don Zimmer

Rawlings Gold Glove

1960	Ernie Banks, SS
1962	Ken Hubbs, 2B
1964	Ron Santo, 3B
1965	Ron Santo, 3B
1966	Ron Santo, 3B
1967	Randy Hundley, C
	Ron Santo, 3B
1968	Glenn Beckert, 2B
	Ron Santo, 3B
1969	Don Kessinger, SS
1970	Don Kessinger, SS
1983	Ryne Sandberg, 2B
1984	Bob Dernier, CF
	Ryne Sandberg, 2B
1985	Ryne Sandberg, 2B
1986	Jody Davis, C
	Ryne Sandberg, 2B
1987	Andre Dawson, RF
	Ryne Sandberg, 2B
1988	Andre Dawson, RF
	Ryne Sandberg, 2B
1989	Ryne Sandberg, 2B
1990	Greg Maddux, P
	Ryne Sandberg, 2B
1991	Greg Maddux, P
	Ryne Sandberg, 2B
1992	Mark Grace, 1B
	Greg Maddux, P
1993	Mark Grace, 1B
1995	Mark Grace, 1B
1996	Mark Grace, 1B

Sources

America's National Game by A. G. Spalding
Babe by Robert Creamer
The Ballparks by Bill Shannon and George Kalinsky
A Ball Player's Career by Cap Anson
The Baseball Encyclopedia by Macmillan Publishing
Baseball—The Golden Age by Harold Seymour
Baseball Guides, published by *The Sporting News*
Baseball I Love You by Charlie Grimm and Ed Prell
Baseball—An Informal History by Douglas Wallop
Baseball and Mr. Spalding by Arthur Bartlett
Baseball's Greatest Streaks by Allen Lewis
The Chicago Cubs by Warren Brown
Chicago Sun-Times
Chicago Tribune
Cub Media Guides
Diamonds by Marhshall Gershman
Early Innings edited by Dean A. Sullivan
From Cobb to Catfish edited by John Kuenster
The Glory of Their Times by Lawrence Ritter
The Golden Era Cubs by Eddie Gold and Arthur Ahrens
Green Cathedrals by Philip J. Lowry
Hack by Robert Boone and Gerald Grunska
Hank Sauer by John C. Hoffman
Kings of the Diamond by Lee Allen and Tom Meany
Like Nobody Else: The Ferguson Jenkins Story by George Vass
The Man in the Dugout by Leonard Koppett
My Greatest Day in Baseball by John P. Carmichael
My War with Baseball by Rogers Hornsby and Bill Surface
The National Game by Alfred H. Spink
The National League by Lee Allen
The New Era Cubs by Eddie Gold and Arthur Ahrens
One Hundred Years of Baseball by Lee Allen
Phil Regan by Phil Regan and John Hefley
Philip K. Wrigley by Paul M. Angle
Reach Official Guides
Rogers Hornsby by Charles C. Alexander
Spalding Official Guides
The Sporting News
Super Stars of Baseball by Bob Broeg
Total Baseball edited by John Thorn and Pete Palmer
Touching Second by Johnny Evers and Hugh Fullerton
Trade Him! edited by James Enright
Veeck as in Wreck by Bill Veeck and Ed Linn
Who's Who in Baseball (1936–96)

Acknowledgments

The authors are grateful for the assistance of the following: Alex Stern, Elias Sports Bureau; Don Zminda, Stats, Inc.; David Zeman of the Chicago Chapter of SABR; Pat Kelly and Scott Mondore of the National Baseball Hall of Fame and Museum in Cooperstown, New York; Barry Morrill, Temple University Press; Steve Green and Chuck Wasserstrom of the Chicago Cubs; and Eddie Gold and Art Ahrens.

Mark Fletcher photographed the 16-page color section. Materials for the section were provided courtesy of Peter Capolino of Mitchell & Ness, Philadelphia, Tim Benge, Ron Feldman, Mike Kozlowski, Mark Leith, John Mawricz and Walter Onysio, Mike McClellan, and Rich Overmann.

About the Authors

Jerome Holtzman is the baseball columnist and national baseball writer for the *Chicago Tribune*. He is the "dean" of America's baseball Boswells and joined the *Tribune* in 1981 after 38 years at the *Chicago Sun-Times* and the *Daily Times,* its predecessor.

He started as a sports department copyboy in June 1943, at the age of 17, served two years in the Marine Corps during World War II, and upon his return, in September 1946, covered high school sports for the next 11 years. He was assigned to major league baseball in 1957 and traveled with the Cubs and White Sox for 28 years, dividing his time equally between both clubs.

Holtzman has been the patron saint of the bullpen. Aware that earned run averages and won-lost records are not an accurate index of the effectiveness of relief pitchers, he created the formula for "saves." Six years later, in 1966, it was adopted by the Official Rules Committee, the first new major statistic since runs batted in was added in 1920.

The Wall Street Journal, in a 1984 profile, described him as "the quintessential baseball writer." He served eight terms as the chairman of the Chicago chapter of the Baseball Writers' Association of America and in 1996 was elected the national president of the BBWAA. That same year he was appointed to the Hall of Fame Veterans Committee.

In addition to his newspaper work, Holtzman has written scores of magazine stories and the 20,000-word entry on baseball in *Encyclopaedia Britannica,* which he still serves as a consultant. For many years he wrote the summary of each season for the *Official Baseball Guide.* His byline appeared in more than 1,000 consecutive issues of the weekly *Sporting News,* possibly an "iron-man" record.

Holtzman has authored three books, including the classic *No Cheering in the Press Box,* published in 1974 and reissued in 1995 with six new chapters. His other books are *Three and Two,* the biography of Tom Gorman, the late National League umpire, and *Fielder's Choice,* an anthology of baseball fiction.

He has been elected to seven Halls of Fame and was inducted into the writers' wing of baseball's Cooperstown shrine in 1990. He has won four "Stick o' Type" awards from the Chicago Newspaper Guild and in 1996 was chosen Chicago's Press Veteran of the Year.

A native Chicagoan, Holtzman has been married to the former Marilyn Ryan for 48 years and has four children and four grandchildren. He attended Northwestern University and the University of Chicago.

George Vass's career as a sportswriter, columnist, and author has spanned almost 40 years. He covered virtually all sports for the now defunct *Chicago Daily News* from 1958 to 1978, and from 1979 to 1994 served in the sports department of the *Chicago Sun-Times.*

Vass was a baseball beat writer for 13 years, 1965–78. For extended periods he also covered the Blackhawks, the Bulls, the Sting, the Spurs, and many events in other sports, including heavyweight championship bouts and cricket matches.

Since 1965 he has contributed a monthly article—and often two—to *Baseball Digest* magazine, a national publication. Included in his prodigious output have been several hundred interviews on "The Game I'll Never Forget," which has been among the magazine's most popular features for more than two decades.

Vass has authored eight books on sports subjects. They are *Champions of Sports, The Chicago Blackhawks' Story, George Halas and the Chicago Bears, I Play to Win* (ghostwritten for Stan Mikita), *Inside Hockey* (with Mikita), *Like Nobody Else* (Ferguson Jenkins' autobiography), *Steve Garvey,* and *Reggie Jackson.*

Vass has an encyclopedic knowledge of history and literature, is in demand as a speaker, and also has written two unpublished historical works, *King till Night,* a novel about Harold, the last Saxon king of England, and *Tiberius,* a fictional treatment of the tragedy of the second Roman emperor. His current project is a biography of Mark Antony.

The son of a pathologist, Vass was born in Leipzig, Germany, on March 27, 1927, but was a Hungarian citizen and attended his first two years of school in Hungary.

After his family emigrated to the United States in 1935, he attended the public schools in Springfield, Illinois. He served in the U.S. Army from 1945 to 1947, attended Washington University in St. Louis, graduating in 1950, then took a master's degree in journalism at Northwestern University in 1952.

The following year and for three years thereafter he was the managing editor of the *National Jewish Post and Opinion*. He was the news editor and executive sports editor of the *Rockford* (Illinois) *Register-Republic* prior to joining the *Chicago Daily News*. He resigned from the *Sun-Times* in 1994 because of his wife's illness.

Vass lives in Morton Grove, a Chicago suburb, and has four children, two daughters by his first wife, Theresa, who died in 1977, and the two sons of his second wife, Joyce, who died in 1995. He has five grandchildren.